2005

Merry Christmas!
Happy Reading!
Love & hugs
Joe, Linda, Matt, & Allie

CHURCHILL SPEAKS

1897–1963

COLLECTED SPEECHES IN PEACE & WAR

Transworld

Secretary of State for War, 1919

CHURCHILL SPEAKS

1897–1963

COLLECTED SPEECHES IN PEACE & WAR

EDITED BY

ROBERT RHODES JAMES, M.P.

This edition published by Barnes & Noble, Inc., by arrangement with Chelsea House Publishers, a division of Main Line Book Company.

1998 Barnes & Noble Books

ISBN 0-76070-895-9

Printed and bound in the United States of America

98 99 00 01 02 M 9 8 7 6 5 4 3 2 1

MRT

Contents

THE YOUNG TRIBUNE: 1897-1914

Introduction 3

1897 First Political Speech, July 26, Bath 21

1899 Election Address, June 24, Oldham 24

1900 The War in South Africa, July 25, Oldham 27

1901 The Maiden Speech, February 18, House of Commons 29
Army Reform, May 13, House of Commons 34

1903 Free Trade, May 21, Hoxton 44
Preferential Tariffs, May 28, House of Commons 46
Free Speech and Free Trade, November 11, Birmingham 47
Free Trade, November 25, North Chadderton 51

1904 The Parliamentary Situation, February 1, Edinburgh 52
The Free Trade League, February 19, Manchester 54
Government Policy, February 26, Preston 59
Announcement of Candidacy, April 29, Manchester 60
Liberal Policy, June 4, London 63
Administrative Home Rule for Ireland, June 16, Cheetham Hill 65
Free Trade, October 18, Carnavon 68
Protectionism, November 28, North-west Manchester 70

1905 Free Trade, February 6, Gainsborough 72
A Plea for Liberal Unity, March 31, Sheffield 74
South Africa (Chinese Labour), October 6, Manchester 75
The Old Government and the New, December 14, London 77

1906 Election Address, January 4, Ancoats 80
Woman's Suffrage and Irish Reform Policy, January 5, Cheetham 81
"Chinese Slavery," January 9, Manchester 84
The General Election, January 15, Manchester 85

South Africa (Chinese Labour), February 22, House of Commons 87
South Africa (Chinese Labour), March 21, House of Commons 92
The Conciliation of South Africa, April 5, House of Commons 99
South Africa and the Lords, July 7, Bowdon 101
"The Gift of England," July 31, House of Commons 102
Liberalism and Socialism, October 11, Glasgow 105
Transvaal and Orange River Colonies Constitutions, December 17, House of Commons 112

1907 The House of Lords, February 4, Manchester 112
The Colonial Conference, April 16, London 118
Imperial Preference, May 7, London 119
"The Laughing-Stock of Europe," August 24, Cheadle Hulme 121

1908 The East African Tour, January 18, London 124
Socialism, January 22, Cheetham 127
Social Policy, January 23, Birmingham 128
The Joys of Writing, February 17, London 131
Trade and Government, March 18, London 134
Election Address, April 12, Manchester 135
Election Address, April 14, Manchester 137
Licensing Bill, April 18, Manchester 139
Election Address, April 21, Manchester 140
Electoral Defeat and the Liberal Cause, April 24, Manchester 142
The Dundee Election, April 30, Dundee 144
Liberalism and Socialism, May 4, Dundee 146
Coal Mines (Eight Hours) Bill, July 6, House of Commons 151
Government Policy and the Foreign Situation, August 14, Swansea 153
Unemployment, October 9, Dundee 155

1909 Liberalism and the Lords, January 13, Birmingham 157
The Next Election and the Lords, January 29, Nottingham 161
The Budget and Social Reform, May 22, Manchester 162
The Budget, July 17, Edinburgh 166
Liberalism and the German "Menace," July 17, Edinburgh 170
The Budget, August 2, Wimborne 171
The Budget, September 4, Leicester 172
Election Address, December 4, Southport 178
Lord Curzon, December 17, Burnley 179

1910 Dundee Poll Result, January 18, Dundee 183
Treatment of "Political" Prisoners (Women Suffragettes), March 15, House of Commons 184
The Lords and the Budget, March 19, Manchester 185

Parliamentary Franchise (Women) Bill, July 12, House of Commons . . . 189
South Wales Coal Strike, November 15, House of Commons . . . 191
"A House of Swells," November 28, London . . . 193
Election Address, November 30, Sheffield . . . 195

1911 South Wales Coal Strike, February 7, House of Commons . . . 198
Creation of the Peers, August 7, House of Commons . . . 199
Labour Disputes and Employment of the Military, August 22, House of Commons . . . 200
Foreign and Domestic Policy, October 3, Dundee . . . 206
Naval Defence, November 9, London . . . 208

1912 Irish Home Rule, February 8, Belfast . . . 210
Naval Defence, February 9, Glasgow . . . 218
Navy Estimates, March 18, House of Commons . . . 221
Government of Ireland Bill, April 30, House of Commons . . . 229
Defence, May 4, London . . . 239
The German Navy Law, July 22, House of Commons . . . 240
"The Politics of Action," September 11, Dundee . . . 244
Balkan Situation and Defence Preparedness, October 30, Sheffield . . . 249
Naval Preparedness, November 9, London . . . 252

1913 Ulster Problem, February 11, London . . . 253
"A Naval Holiday," March 26, House of Commons . . . 256

1914 The Art of Flying, March 4, London . . . 261
The Ulster Situation, March 14, Bradford . . . 263
Navy Estimates, March 17, House of Commons . . . 274
Vote of Censure, April 28, House of Commons . . . 281
"The Ebb and Flow of Fortune," September 11, London . . . 291
"Rats in a Hole," September 21, Liverpool . . . 299
"Business as Usual," November 9, London . . . 303
Royal Navy, November 27, House of Commons . . . 305

ECLIPSE AND REVIVAL: 1915-1924

Introduction . . . 315

1915 British Command of the Sea, February 15, House of Commons . . . 327
The War, June 5, Dundee . . . 336
Resignation, November 15, House of Commons . . . 343

1916 The Naval War, March 7, House of Commons 350
Military Service Bill (Ireland), May 9, House of Commons 353
The Army, May 23, House of Commons 356

1917 Minister of Munitions, July 21, Dundee 361
The War Situation, December 10, Bedford 362

1918 The War Effort, October 7, Glasgow 367
Constituency Address, November 26, Dundee 368
Germany Must Pay, November 29, Newcastle 369
"A Fair Trial and No Favour," December 4, Dundee 370

1919 "Let Us Face the Future Together," January 28, London 371
The Bolshevik Menace, April 11, London 372
Peace Policy, May 14, Dundee 375
Russia, June 6, House of Commons 376
The Centre Party, July 15, London 378
Allied Policy in Russia, July 17, London 383

1920 The Agony of Russia, January 3, Sunderland 384
"A Policy of Real Peace and Appeasement," February 14, Dundee 388
Punjab Disturbances, July 8, House of Commons 393
Russia and Ireland, October 16, Dundee 398
Bolshevism and Imperial Sedition, November 4, London 401

1921 Justice for Arab and Jew, March 31, Jerusalem (Reply to Moslem Delegation) 403
Justice for Arab and Jew, March 31, Jerusalem (Reply to Jewish Delegation) 404
Irish Free State, December 15, House of Commons 404

1922 Irish Free State Bill, February 16, House of Commons 407
The Socialist Peril, March 4, Loughborough 411
Irish Free State Bill (Third Reading), March 8, House of Commons 412
Plea for National Unity, March 25, Northampton 414
Socialism, April 8, Dundee 417
British Policy in Ireland, June 26, House of Commons 419
Election Address, November 11, Dundee 422
An Attempted Speech, November 13, Dundee 423

1923 Free Trade, November 16, Manchester 424
Mr. Baldwin, December 5, West Leicester 427

1924 Adoption Meeting, March 10, London 428

The Poll Result, March 20, London 430
"Present Dangers of the Socialist Movement," May 7, Liverpool 431
"The Study of English," June 27, London 434
The Socialist Government, September 25, Edinburgh 435
Election Issues, October 3, Waltham Abbey 438
The Zinoviev Letter, October 25, Loughton 441
"Growth of Diseased Opinion," November 1, Chingford 441
The Constitutional Group, November 3, London 442
Conservatism, December 5, Liverpool 444

RECOVERY AND ISOLATION: 1925-1938

Introduction 449

1925 Royal Naval Division War Memorial, April 25, London 464
The Budget, April 28, House of Commons 465
The Economic Situation, July 15, London 470
Coal Mining Industry, August 6, House of Commons 471
"Is England Done?" October 19, Chingford 475

1926 Socialism, January 21, Lancashire 477
The General Strike, May 3, House of Commons 479
Parliamentary Government, May 26, House of Lords 483
Emergency Power, July 2, House of Commons 485
The *British Gazette,* July 7, House of Commons 486
Coal Dispute (Vote of Censure), December 8, House of Commons 487

1927 The Empire, January 3, London 488
Mussolini, January 20, Rome 489
The Financial and Political Situations, February 4, Manchester 490
Socialism and the Trades Dispute Bill, May 6, London 494

1928 The Budget, April 25, Broadcast 496
A Disarmament Fable, October 24, Aldersbrook 498

1929 The Budget, April 15, House of Commons 499
The General Election, April 30, Broadcast, London 502
Egypt (Lord Lloyd's Resignation), July 26, House of Commons 505
Domestic and Imperial Affairs, December 16, London 506
Egypt, December 23, House of Commons 507

1930 Naval Disarmament Treaty, June 2, House of Commons 508
Britain and India, November 5, Loughton 512

India (The Round Table Conference), December 11, London 514

1931 India—"A Frightful Prospect," January 26, House of Commons 518
"The Boneless Wonder"—Trade Disputes and Trade Unions (Amendment) Bill, January 28, House of Commons 521
India and Gandhi, January 30, Manchester 523
"A Seditious Middle Temple Lawyer," February 23, Epping 528
Our Duty in India, March 18, London 533
"The March of Events," March 26, London 538
Disarmament and Europe, June 29, House of Commons 540
The Financial Situation, September 29, Liverpool 543
The New Parliament, October 30, Chingford 545

1932 Disarmament, May 13, House of Commons 546
Reparations Abandoned, July 11, House of Commons 549
European Dangers, November 23, House of Commons 550

1933 Air Estimates, March 14, House of Commons 557
Foreign Policy and German Rearmament, April 13, House of Commons 562
"Europe's Hour of Danger," August 12, Theydon Bois 565
Germany and the League, November 7, House of Commons 567

1934 "Whither Britain?" January 16, Broadcast, London 568
Defence, February 7, House of Commons 570
The Need for Air Parity, March 8, House of Commons 573
Delusion of Disarmament, March 14, House of Commons 579
Air Defence, July 7, Wanstead 580
Germany Approaching Air Parity, July 30, House of Commons 581
"The Causes of War," November 16, Broadcast, London 586
The German Air Menace, November 28, House of Commons 589

1935 Air Parity Lost, May 2, House of Commons 596
"Deepening and Darkening Danger," May 31, House of Commons 598
Government of India Bill, June 5, House of Commons 600
Consequences in Foreign Policy, July 11, House of Commons 606
Foreign Policy and Rearmament, September 26, London 610
International Situation, October 24, House of Commons 612
Election Address, October 28, Epping 617

1936 Foreign Policy, March 26, House of Commons 618
The Abyssinian Crisis, May 8, Chingford 621
Reforming the League of Nations, July 4, Bristol University 623

"Adamant for Drift," November 12, House of Commons 624
Arms and the Covenant, December 3, London 629
The Abdication of King Edward VIII, December 10, House of Commons 632

1937 The Spanish Civil War, April 14, House of Commons 633
Japanese Campaign In China, October 26, Loughton and Waltham Abbey 637

1938 Anthony Eden's Resignation, February 22, House of Commons 638
The Annexation of Austria, March 14, House of Commons 642
Threat to Czechoslovakia, March 24, House of Commons 645
Czechoslovakia, May 23, Chingford 648
"Volcanic Forces Are Moving in Europe," June 2, Birmingham 650
The Threat to Czechoslovakia, August 27, Theydon Bois 651
"Throwing a Small State to the Wolves," September 21, London 652
One Last Peace Effort, September 26, London 653
"A Total and Unmitigated Defeat," October 5, House of Commons 653
The International Situation, November 25, Harlow 662
"A Year of Disaster and Humiliation," December 11, Chingford 663

A TIME OF TRIUMPH: 1939-1963

Introduction 667

1939 The Fruits of Munich, March 14, Waltham Abbey 676
"Do Not Yield Another Yard," April 3, House of Commons 678
National Service (Conscription), April 24, London 681
Russia and Poland, May 19, House of Commons 682
Palestine, May 23, House of Commons 685
"A Hush Over Europe," August 8, Broadcast to the United States, London 689
War, September 3, House of Commons 692
The First Month of War, October 1, Broadcast, London 694

1940 The War Situation: "A House of Many Mansions," January 20, Broadcast, London 697
"Let Us to the Task," January 27, Manchester 700
"A Hideous State of Alarm and Menace," March 30, Broadcast, London 701
"Blood, Toil, Tears, and Sweat," May 13, House of Commons 703
"Arm Yourselves and Be Ye Men of Valour," May 19, Broadcast, London 706

"We Shall Never Surrender," June 4, House of Commons 708
"Their Finest Hour," June 18, House of Commons 714
Destruction of the French Fleet, July 4, House of Commons 721
"The Few," August 20, House of Commons 724
Night Bombing of London: "Every Man to His Post,"
September 11, Broadcast, London 729
The War Situation, October 8, House of Commons 731
"Le Dieu Protége La France," October 21, Broadcast, London 732
Neville Chamberlain, November 12, House of Commons 734

1941 "A Dark and Deadly Valley" (The War Situation), January 22,
House of Commons 736
"Give Us the Tools," February 9, Broadcast, London 737
"A New Magna Carta" (Lend-Lease), March 12, House of
Commons 741
Welcome to Mr. Winant, March 18, London 742
The War Situation, April 9, House of Commons 744
"Westward, Look," April 27, Broadcast, London 748
The War Situation, May 7, House of Commons 753
"Our Solid, Stubborn Strength," June 12, London 757
The German Invasion of Russia, June 22, Broadcast, London 761
The Atlantic Charter, August 24, Broadcast, London 765
The War Situation, September 9, House of Commons 769
The War Situation, September 30, House of Commons 769
"These Are Great Days," October 29, Harrow School 771
The Golden Wedding of Mr. Speaker Fitzroy, November 19,
House of Commons 772
War with Japan, December 8, House of Commons 773
The War Situation, December 11, House of Commons 776
"A Strange Christmas Eve," December 24, Broadcast,
Washington, D.C. 779
"A Long and Hard War," December 26, Washington, D.C. 780
"Some Chicken! Some Neck!" December 30, Ottawa 786

1942 The War Situation, January 27, House of Commons 791
The War Situation, January 29, House of Commons 796
The Fall of Singapore, February 15, Broadcast, London 798
The Conduct of the War, July 2, House of Commons 802
"We Cut the Coal," October 31, Westminster 807
"The End of the Beginning," November 10, London 808

1943 The Fall of Mussolini, July 27, House of Commons 811
The Quebec Conference, August 31, Broadcast, Quebec 813
Anglo-American Unity, September 6, Boston 815

The War Situation, September 21, House of Commons 818
"A Sense of Crowd and Urgency," October 28, House of Commons 820

1944 The Invasion of France, June 6, House of Commons 824
The Flying Bomb, July 6, House of Commons 827
The War Situation, August 2, House of Commons 829
The War Situation, September 28, House of Commons 831
French Unity, November 12, Paris 835
"The Tasks Which Lie Before Us," November 29, House of Commons 837

1945 Review of the War, January 18, House of Commons 839
The Yalta Conference, February 27, House of Commons 847
The Death of Lloyd George, March 28, House of Commons 853
The Death of President Roosevelt, April 17, House of Commons 856
The End of the War in Europe, May 8, Broadcast, London and House of Commons 859
"This Is Your Victory," May 8, London 861
To V-E Day Crowds, May 8, London 862
To the Peoples of the British Empire in the Far East, May 8, Broadcast, London 862
"Good Old London!" May 9, London 863
Party Politics Again, June 4, Broadcast, London 864
A Threat to Freedom, June 21, Political Broadcast, London 868
Resignation Statement, July 26, No. 10 Downing Street 871
"The True Glory" (The Surrender of Japan), August 15, House of Commons 872
The Iron Curtain Begins to Fall, August 16, House of Commons 873

1946 The Sinews of Peace, March 5, Missouri 876
The Darkening International Scene, March 15, New York City 884
Foreign Affairs, June 5, House of Commons 887
"The Tragedy of Europe," September 19, Zurich University 891
"Every Dog His Day," October 5, Blackpool 893
Foreign Affairs, October 23, House of Commons 898
India, December 12, House of Commons 900
Burma, December 20, House of Commons 904

1947 India, March 6, House of Commons 906
National Service, May 7, House of Commons 908
United Europe, May 14, London 909
Burma Independence Bill, November 5, House of Commons 914

1948 The Three Circles—British Foreign Policy, October 9, Wales 915
The North Atlantic Treaty, May 12, House of Commons 918
The Council of Europe, August 12, Strasbourg 919

1949 ''The Short Words Are the Best,'' November 2, London 921

1950 The Moment of Decision, February 17, Political
Broadcast, London 922
Debate on the Address, March 7, House of Commons 925
A Conservative-Liberal Alliance?, May 18, Edinburgh 928
Korea, July 5, House of Commons 931
The Korean War, July 15, Plymouth 932
Housing the People, October 14, Blackpool 933
The International Situation, December 14, House of Commons 935

1951 "Our Race and Destiny," April 27, London 937
"Whose Finger on the Trigger," October 6, Loughton 938
Our Political Future, October 8, London 938
"Abadan, Sudan, and Bevan," October 12, Woodford 942
"A Personal Issue," October 23, Plymouth 943
Debate on the Address, November 6, House of Commons 944
"The Path of Duty," November 9, London 947

1952 Address to the United States Congress, January
17, Washington, D.C. 949
King George VI, February 7, Broadcast, London 951
Sir Stafford Cripps, April 23, House of Commons 953
"The Common Interest of the Whole People,"
November 10, London 954

1953 Westminster Abbey Appeal, January 30, Jerusalem
Chamber 956
Conservative Party Conference, October 10, Kent 957

1954 "A Calmer and Kindlier Age," November 9, London 962
Eightieth Birthday, November 30, Westminster 964

1955 The Deterrent—Nuclear Warfare, March 1, House of Commons 966
Toast to the Queen, April 4, No. 10 Downing Street 971
Election Address, May 16, Woodford 972

1957 Liberty and the Law, July 31, London 972

1958 A Friend of France, November 6, Paris 975

1959 Adoption Meeting, September 29, Woodford 975

1963 Honorary United States Citizenship, April 9, Washington, D.C. 977

INDEX 979

The Young Tribune
1897–1914

The Young Tribune 1897–1914

Winston Leonard Spencer-Churchill was born at Blenheim Palace, the seat of his grandfather the Duke of Marlborough, on November 30, 1874. He was the premature first child of Lord Randolph Churchill and his wife, the former Miss Jennie Jerome.

Lord Randolph, at the time of Winston's birth, was twenty-five years of age, and had just been elected Conservative Member of Parliament for the family constituency of Woodstock. Earlier in 1874, after a whirlwind courtship and in the teeth of fierce parental opposition, he had married Miss Jerome in Paris. She was American, a fact which had at least played some part in the dismay of the Duke and Duchess of Marlborough at this disappointing match for their younger son. These early clouds were never to be fully dispersed, and although the marriage itself survived until Lord Randolph's tragic early death in January 1895, it was often troubled. As a younger son, Lord Randolph had only a relatively modest allowance, and even with a generous contribution from the bride's father, there was a chronic shortage of money. Lord Randolph was restless, mercurial, and subject to intense fits of depression. Few could see in him then the man who, within five years of taking up politics in earnest in 1880, stood as unquestionably the second man in the Conservative Party and one of the most arresting politicians in a decade of political giants.

In his biography of his father, Winston Churchill dwelt at some length upon the disadvantages with which Lord Randolph had had to deal:

> No smooth path of patronage was opened to him. No glittering wheels of royal favour aided and accelerated his journey. Whatever power he acquired was grudgingly conceded and hastily snatched away. Like Disraeli, he had to fight every mile in all his marches.[1]

Sir Winston's son later depicted his father's difficulties in very similar terms.

> He had to fight every inch of his road through life; nothing came easily to him, not even oratory and writing, in which he was later to excel.[2]

It is worth emphasising that the disadvantages under which Lord Randolph and his son laboured were, initially, somewhat minimal. Lord Randolph inherited what was virtually a family constituency, and his subsequent difficulties and successes were of his own making. Sir Winston Churchill did not inherit as much, but he was in no sense a social or political outsider. The story of his early career as a young officer, war correspondent, author and politician is one of skillful and ardent exploitation of his not inconsiderable assets of family, position and name. In this process it was necessary to cut corners with a sharpness that did not universally endear him. Manifestly an adventurer, a soldier of fortune, he was eager for publicity. As his career advanced, he might have complained in Disraeli's words that "when I was a young and struggling man they taunted me with being an adventurer. Now that I have succeeded they still bring the same reproach against me." But, as with Disraeli, the charge would not have been without foundation. Churchill, moreover, made no attempt to conceal his ambition. As A. G. Gardiner wrote in 1908:

> To the insatiable curiosity and the enthusiasm of the child he joins the frankness of the child. He has no reserves and no shams. You are welcome to anything he has, and may pry into any corner you like. He has that scorn of concealment that belongs to a caste which never doubts itself.[3]

Churchill was twenty years of age when Lord Randolph Churchill died at the age of forty-five. All attempts by the son for a close relationship had been brusquely rejected; nevertheless, the influence of Lord Randolph shaped Churchill's character, impelled him towards a political career, and dominated his early attitudes.

The outlines of Lord Randolph's extraordinary career can be swiftly described; the substance is more complex. In 1880, he was an unimportant Conservative back-bencher chiefly known for his involvement in a scandal in 1876 in which he had taken the part of his brother in a somewhat reckless manner, necessitating his tactful withdrawal to Dublin. By 1885, he was indisputably second only to Lord Salisbury in the Conservative Party, and perhaps second only to Gladstone in popular interest. Early in 1886 he became one of the principal architects of the defeat of the First Home Rule Bill and of the foundations of the "Unionist" alliance; by August he was Chancellor of the Exchequer and Leader of the House of Commons. Yet in December, a few days before Christmas, he fell sheer. On a relatively minor matter over the Army Estimates, he threatened resignation. Salisbury, who had been eyeing his young lieutenant with coldness for some time, took advantage of Lord Randolph's first major blunder and made it his last. The professed resignation was gladly accepted. There was no return. All that remained was what Rosebery described as "a public pageant of gloomy years."

In a famous phrase, Lord Randolph described Gladstone as "an old man in a hurry." He himself was a young man in a hurry, driven onwards by some devouring inner demon which none of his biographers has managed to identify. Rosebery wrote of his political career that "while it lasted it eclipsed the fame of almost all who were then engaged in politics," while Max Beerbohm considered that Lord Randolph was "despite his halting speech, foppish mien, and rather coarse fibre of mind . . . the greatest Parliamentarian of his day." Perhaps this was an exaggeration, but he unquestionably stood in the front rank. His rapid rise and startling extinction constitute one of the most astonishing and fascinating political phenomena of modern British politics.

But what, if anything, did Lord Randolph "stand for"? Even at the height of his powers it was difficult to detect any really profound political belief or faith beyond an outrageous opportunism and a somewhat vaguely defined creed of "Tory Democracy." John Morley was struck by Lord Randolph's comment that "Balfour and you are men who believe in the solution of political questions." Morley's response was to the point: "This belief may or may not be a weakness, yet the alternative, that the statesman is a man who does not believe in the solution of political questions, was startling."

Other estimates were less charitable. As Rosebery has written:

> To many persons, both Tory and Liberal, Randolph was little less than an incarnation of evil, a reckless and insolent iconoclast. . . . He was, in their judgment, unscrupulous, violent, unprincipled; an intriguing schemer, a ruthless plotter; one who, to serve the personal ambition which was his sole motive, would stick at nothing.[4]

"His character," Salisbury wrote, "is quite untamed. Both in impulsiveness and variability, and in a tendency which can be described by the scholastic word 'vulgaris,' he presents the characteristics of extreme youth." Lord Ripon described him as "a reckless and unprincipled mountebank." Perhaps Lord Randolph delivered his own epitaph: "No man is so entirely alone and solitary as I am."

I

Lord Randolph was a distant and unsympathetic father, and Sir Winston Churchill's childhood was almost entirely devoid of parental love. The void was filled by his nurse, Mrs. Elizabeth Everest, whom Churchill has described movingly in both *My Early Life* and *Savrola*. It is not easy to assess the full effects of this experience upon his character. He was clearly a sensitive child, although somewhat unprepossessing, as well as unruly and indolent. A contemporary described him as late as 1901 as "a little, square-headed fellow of no very striking appearance," and another, two years later, as "a medium-sized, undistinguished young man, with an unfortunate lisp in his voice." But, by this time, others were seeing different aspects. One wrote:

> It requires two plates to take a fair photograph of him, for the next time you look at him he has sprung to his feet with the eagerness of a boy, his pale blue eyes are sparkling, his lips parted, he is talking a vocal torrent, and his head and arms are driving home his words.

Between his father's death and his entry into Parliament after the 1900 General Election, Churchill's career blossomed dramatically. He underwent a labourious self-education while a soldier in India; he wrote four books, of which *The River War*–his second–immediately was regarded as a contemporary classic; he gained distinction as a war correspondent; he made a dramatic escape from a Boer prisoner of war camp. In short, Churchill was a national figure at the age of twenty-five.

Dr. Anthony Storr has attempted to explain this remarkable development:

> Ambition, when as in Churchill's case it is a compulsive drive, is the direct result of early deprivation. For if a child has but little inner conviction of his own value, he will be drawn to seek the recognition and acclaim which accrue from external achievement.[5]

There are, of course, other possible explanations. Perhaps the most neglected is that of his burning desire to emulate his dead father, a drive so intense that it included imitating Lord Randolph's dress, speaking mannerisms, and political attitudes. Churchill's feeling for his father went beyond filial affection and admiration. In *My Early Life* one finds a particularly poignant and significant phrase: "In fact to me he seemed to own the key to everything or almost everything worth having. But if ever I began to show the slightest idea of comradeship, he was immediately offended." As soon as Churchill entered the House of Commons such resemblances, and particularly those related to Lord Randolph's impetuosity and iconoclasm, became very clear. Within six months of taking his seat on the Conservative benches, Churchill was an admitted and unrepentant rebel, obsessed by politics, "living with Blue Books and sleeping with encyclopedias," as Hugh Massingham wrote.

Between 1901 and 1905 Churchill wrote his father's biography, perhaps his most completely satisfying book. As a biography, it has its deficiencies, and the portrait of Lord Randolph is too tinged with filial devotion. But, as a study of politics it stands in a class by itself.

It would perhaps be too much to say that in writing this book Churchill got his father "out of his system"; no doubt that would have happened in any event. Yet from 1901 to 1903 it seemed that Churchill was hell-bent on recreating his father's career, fighting his enemies, battling for his policies, and repeating his errors. He took an individualistic stance on every issue; he launched a crusade for Economy; he adopted what seemed to be "Little England" attitudes; he fervently advocated Free Trade. Also, by creating a group of Conservative free-lances who called themselves the "Hughligans" in honour of Lord Hugh Cecil, he appeared to revive Lord Randolph's famous "Fourth Party" of 1880-1883. It is not surprising to find Wilfred Blunt writing in 1903 that "in mind and manner he is a strange replica of his father." Yet, much of this faded away between 1903 and 1905, and it is not wholly fanciful to see a connection between this development and the completion of his biography of Lord Randolph.

The biography contains many brilliant insights culminating in his observation that

> there is an England which stretches far beyond the well-drilled masses who are assembled by party machinery to salute with appropriate acclamation the utterances of their recognised fuglemen; an England of wise men who gaze without self-deception at the failings and follies of both political parties; of brave and earnest men who find in neither faction fair scope for

> the effort that is in them; of "poor men" who increasingly doubt the sincerity of party philanthropy. It was to that England that Lord Randolph Churchill appealed; it was that England he so nearly won; it is by that England he will be justly judged.[6]

Here we see one of the first unmistakable signs of his romantic conception of England and its people which became a deeply-held view. Already, Churchill's egocentricity and love of the colourful and dramatic were evident. This trait appeared early, and, although the following comment by Isaiah Berlin was written many years later, it is as relevant to the young Churchill as it is to the old.

> Churchill is preoccupied by his own vivid world, and it is doubtful how far he has ever been aware of what actually goes on in the heads and hearts of others. He does not react, he acts; he does not mirror, he affects others and alters them to his own powerful measure.[7]

His fondness for rhetoric was also becoming apparent, as Charles Masterman observed.

> In nearly every case an *idea* enters his head from outside. It then rolls round the hollow of his brain, collecting strength like a snowball. Then, after whirling winds of *rhetoric,* he becomes convinced that it is *right;* and denounces everyone who criticizes it. He is in the Greek sense a Rhetorician, the slave of the words which his mind forms about ideas. He sets ideas to Rhetoric as musicians set theirs to music. And he can convince himself of almost every truth if it is once allowed to start on its wild career through his rhetorical machinery.[8]

Churchill's attitude to Party closely followed his romanticised conception of England. He regarded the Party as essential in the sense that the horse is essential to the rider. Unhappily, modern political confederations resent such attitudes. "To his imperious spirit," Gardiner wrote in 1911, "a party is only an instrument." And as Churchill's career took shape between 1901 and 1905 it became clear why he had applied Pope's famous lines to his father.

> Sworn to no master, of no sect am I;
> As drives the storm, at any door I knock.

His disillusionment with the Conservative Party developed swiftly, and long before the decisive break over Tariff Reform in 1903 he had become conspicuous as one of the Government's most vigorous and insufferable critics. One contemporary noted that "he seemed to enjoy causing resentment," and Sir Charles Dilke, who in 1880 had written in his diary that "Rosebery is about the most ambitious man I had ever met," added, "I have since known Winston Churchill."

It would be facile to attribute Churchill's break with the Conservatives solely to motives of personal ambition. On this, G. W. Steevens had written in 1899:

> He is ambitious and he is calculating, yet he is not cold—and that saves him. His ambition is sanguine, runs in a torrent, and the calculation is hardly more than the rocks or the stump which the torrent strikes for a second, yet which suffices to direct its course.[9]

Nevertheless, it is significant that many—then and later—considered Churchill's espousal of Tariff Reform as his *casus belli* with the Conservative Party the act of a highly ambitious, frustrated young man who already foresaw the doom that was stalking inexorably upon his Party. No doubt there was some justification in Alfred Lyttleton's jibe that "he trims his sail to every passing wind." We may here note also a passage in *Savrola,* that unique and remarkable self-portrait:

> His nervous temperament could not fail to be excited by the vivid scenes through which he had lately passed, and the repression of his emotion only heated the inward fire. Was it worth it? The struggle, the labour, the constant rush of affairs,—for what? A people's good! That, he could not disguise from himself, was rather the direction than the cause of his efforts. Ambition was the motive force, and he was powerless to resist it.[10]

Again, we may note a significant passage in *Lord Randolph Churchill:*

> Even in a period of political activity there is small scope for the supporter of a Government. The Whips do not want speeches, but votes. The Ministers regard an oration in their praise or defence as only one degree less tiresome than an attack. The earnest party man becomes a silent drudge, tramping at intervals through lobbies to record his vote and wondering why he came to Westminster at all. Ambitious youth diverges into criticism and even hostility, or seeks an outlet for its energies elsewhere.[11]

And, although we should not push this too far, there was some truth in Churchill's statement that the study of his father's career had brought home to him how scurvily Lord Randolph had been treated by his party and his colleagues—and not least by Arthur Balfour, Joseph Chamberlain, and his other nominal leaders. Motives were almost certainly mixed, and the attraction of many of the Liberal notables also had its power. So, in 1904, Churchill changed horses and joined the Liberals. Chamberlain always believed that he could have been held by office, and perhaps the first stroke of real political luck which Churchill enjoyed came when he was passed over when Balfour succeeded Salisbury in 1902.

Thus, by 1904, although only twenty-nine years of age, Churchill aroused emotions similar to those evoked by Lord Randolph. A detached friend, H. W. Lucy, wrote at the time that "Winston Churchill may be safely counted upon to make himself quite as disagreeable on the Liberal side as he did on the Unionist. But he will always be handicapped by the aversion that always pertains to a man who, in whatsoever honourable circumstances, has turned his coat."

Churchill's shift of allegiance won him swift and substantial advantages. From the fall of the Balfour Government in December 1905 until May 1915 Britain was ruled by Liberal Governments. Throughout this period Churchill was in office and, after April 1908, in high office. These were years of high attainment and success. But, even by 1905, he had provoked personal and political animosities and mistrusts that stalked him relentlessly.

Churchill left the Conservatives in 1904. In December 1905 Balfour resigned, and Campbell-Bannerman organised the Liberal Ministry. Churchill became Under-Secretary of State for the Colonies under Lord Elgin. On January 13, 1906, he was elected Liberal M.P. for North-west Manchester. Two weeks before, his biography of his father had been published. It was a significant combination of events. Lord Randolph's shadow was put to rest while his son emerged as a political figure in his own right. As Churchill has written, "Was it wonderful that I should have thought I had arrived? But luckily life is not so easy as all that: otherwise we should get to the end too quickly."

In 1906, he was thirty-one years of age; it was less than nine years since he had made his first political speech. Lord Randolph Churchill was emphatically dead and buried. The triumphant Liberals entered into their inheritance.

II

The period of Churchill's career between January 1906 and May 1915 constitutes perhaps his most dynamic and successful years. He was young and energetic. He devoted enormous attention to everything he undertook. He put his proposals efficiently through the Cabinet and Parliament; he carried his Departments with him; in public his increasing self-confidence was demonstrated almost daily.

One outstanding quality was well discerned by A. G. Gardiner:

> More than any man of his time, he approaches an issue without mental reserves and obscure motives and restraints. You see all the processes of his mind. He does not "hum and ha." He is not paralysed by the fear of consequences, nor afraid to contemplate great changes. He is out for adventure. He follows politics as he would follow the hounds.[12]

This had its perils. To quote Gardiner again: "One man with a conviction will overwhelm a hundred who have only opinions, and Mr. Churchill always bursts into the fray with a conviction so clean, so decisive, so burning, that opposition is stampeded."

Another contemporary portrait comes from Charles Masterman:

> Winston swept me off to his cousin's house and I lay on his bed while he dressed and marched about the room, gesticulating and impetuous, pouring out all his hopes and plans and ambitions. He is full of the poor

> whom he has just discovered. He thinks he is called by Providence—to do something for them. "Why have I always been kept safe within a hair's breadth of death," he asked, "except to do something like this? I'm not going to live long," was also his refrain. He is getting impatient, although he says he can wait. I challenged him once on his exposition of his desire to do something for the people. "You can't deny you enjoy it all immensely—the speeches, and crowds, the sense of increasing power." "Of course I do," he said. "Thou shalt not muzzle the ox when he treadeth out the corn. That shall be my plea at the day of judgment." I always feel an immense age when I am with him—though he's only a year younger than I am. "Sometimes I feel as if I could lift the whole world on my shoulders," he said last night.[13]

His capacities as a public speaker matured remarkably in this period, and his ability to coin memorable phrases almost rivalled that of Lord Randolph at his best. "Terminological inexactitude" was one, as was the description of the House of Lords as "a one-sided, hereditary, unpurged, unrepresentative, irresponsible, absentee." The crudity of some of his early speeches was still evident, as when in 1908 he described the House of Lords as "filled with old doddering peers, cute financial magnates, clever wire-pullers, big brewers with bulbous noses. All the enemies of progress are there—weaklings, sleek, smug, comfortable, self-important individuals."

It was exactly this sort of thing that prompted Balfour's retort in 1905 that "if there is preparation, there should be more finish; and if there is so much violence there should certainly be more obvious veracity of feeling." Churchill's first major Ministerial speech, a condescending defence of Lord Milner, was a disaster, and was justly described by Margot Asquith as "ungenerous, patronising, and tactless." But, thereafter, his speeches were increasingly successful and impressive, in particular that on the granting of independence of the Boer Republics, when he appealed in vain to the Conservatives to make it "the gift of England."

His use of humour also improved, and was applied effectively in his speeches in the General Election campaigns of December 1909-January 1910. For example, his attack on Curzon is reminiscent of Lord Randolph at his most impudent and effective:

> "All civilization," said Lord Curzon, quoting Renan, "all civilization has been the work of aristocracies." They liked that in Oldham. There was not a duke, not an earl, not a marquis, not a viscount in Oldham who did not feel that a compliment had been paid to him. "All civilization has been the work of aristocracies." It would be more true to say: "The upkeep of aristocracies has been the hard work of all civilization."[14]

Churchill was a *bête noire* of the Conservative Party before his defection in 1904; afterwards he was a particular object of their dislike. In the fierce struggles of 1909-1911 over the People's Budget and the constitution of the House of Lords he was second only to Lloyd George as an object of Tory aversion—the "Blenheim Rat." His successes and achievements were but grudgingly acknowledged, and the Opposition eagerly awaited his first major slip which could be ruthlessly exploited. There is no doubt that Churchill enjoyed his notoriety. "The applause of the House," Lloyd George wrote of him at this time, "is the very breath of his nostrils. He is just like an actor. He likes the limelight and the approbation of the pit."

Churchill's marriage in 1908 to Miss Clementine Hozier brought him an ever-loyal—though far from uncritical—ally, and provided him with a private strength which his father had never known. The combination of political success and a happy marriage was a potent one, and played a very definite part in the maturation of his personality, softening the abrasiveness which was so characteristic of his earlier years in politics.

III

In this period Churchill was successively Under-Secretary at the Colonial Office (1905-1908), President of the Board of Trade (1908-1910), Home Secretary (1910-1911), and First Lord of the Admiralty (1911-1915). The years from 1908 to 1911 may fairly be described as his "social reform period." He was—after Lloyd George—by far the most active and successful Minister in the Asquith Government. Some of his most important achievements were the establishment of labour exchanges in 1909, enactment of measures to curb the excesses of "sweated" labour, and passage of the Miners Accidents Act of 1910 and the Coal Mines Act of 1911. Perhaps his most notable achievement was his role in the passage of the National Insurance Act of 1911. This represented, as William Beveridge, the originator of the labour exchanges scheme, has written, "a striking illustration of how much the personality of the Minister in a few critical months may change the course of social legislation." As Home Secretary, his attention to the conditions in prisons and the plight of child labour should also be particularly emphasised. Although this hardly justifies the claim of his son that Churchill was one of the "architects of the Welfare State," it was a solid measure of real achievement, and explains why he rose steadily in the estimation of Asquith and others in the Liberal hierarchy. But, remarkably, this approval was not as evident in the Liberal rank and file, and this requires some analysis.

Churchill had been born into the Conservative Party. He was an aristocrat, and a man who was exceptionally insensitive to the experiences and aspirations of others, though when confronted with poverty and injustice his reactions were warm and vehement. Yet he existed on a different plane from the rest of mankind. His concept of England was romantic and unreal, and he believed in the *status quo*—with suitable amendments. "He desired in England," as Charles Masterman has said, "a state of things where a benign upper class dispensed benefits to an industrious, *bien pensant,* and grateful working class." This is one of the shrewdest comments ever made on Churchill's social attitudes.

Thus, although Churchill was a Liberal, from the outset his Liberalism had a particular stance. As Lady Asquith has remarked, "Lloyd George was saturated with class consciousness. Winston accepted class distinction without thought." Churchill's conception of Liberalism can be examined and explored in those speeches he published as *Liberalism and the Social Problem* in 1909. In October 1906 he declared that "the fortunes and the interests of Liberalism and Labour are inseparably interwoven. They rise by the same forces, they face the same enemies, they are affected by the same dangers." The theme expounded in this speech, and in many subsequent ones, was very close to Lord Randolph's concept of Tory Democracy—in short, that modifications of existing society and government would preserve the fundamental structure, while opposition to a policy of "gradualness" would ensure its downfall. Competition and free enterprise were sacrosanct, but "the consequences of the failure" would be mitigated. "We do not want to pull down the structure of science and civilization, but to spread a net over the abyss."

Churchill's Radicalism during the years 1906-1911 was well displayed. At the Colonial Office his handling of the granting of self-government to the Boer Republics was widely praised—and rightly so—in the Liberal ranks; when he went to the Board of Trade in 1908 and subsequently to the Home Office, he was a notably humane and enlightened Minister. He played a vigorous and well-publicised part in the dispute over the Naval Estimates in 1908-1909. In the battle against the House of Lords, and particularly in the violent controversies that surrounded the Lloyd George People's Budget of 1909, he was ever in the front line of the Liberal army, earning an especial niche in the Tory demonology.

When one looks at this record, one is bound to wonder why it added up to so little politically. There was, of course, the fact that he had defected once, and was viewed warily by his new associates. There was the factor of his almost overpowering ambition and relentless application to his career. His impulsiveness was already causing unease. His theatrics, about which Lloyd George poked good-natured fun, were also not wholly suitable to that sober body, the Liberal Party. Yet, compared with his developing abilities, his capacity in Parliament, and his indefatigable devotion to work, these might have seemed but spots on the sun.

Until 1909 the Liberals had their doubts about Churchill's *bona fides,* but it was the gradual increase in industrial unrest—and Churchill's reactions to it—that brought these doubts to the fore. Initially, Churchill acted with skill and restraint—notably in the South Wales riots of 1910 and in the 1911 London Dock Strike. While the canard of "Tonypandy"—where it was alleged troops sent by Churchill shot down Welsh miners—has proved astonishingly durable, it has no place in serious history. What did the real damage was his conduct in the 1911 Railway Strike. Without waiting for requests from the local authorities, Churchill dispatched fifty thousand troops to strategic points, and—this is the crucial point—gave orders that the military commanders were to ignore the regulation that forbade the use of the military unless specifically requested by the civil authority.

Although his son and biographer hastened somewhat swiftly past this episode, it marked a crucial point in Churchill's relationship with his Party, and particularly with the Labour element. Suddenly, all the latent doubts of Churchill's real attitudes came boiling to the surface. The fact that the episode occurred shortly after the tragic-comic incident known as "the siege of Sidney Street"—in which Churchill personally supervised the deployment of troops and police against an alleged gang of desperadoes—was also not without its significance. It evoked a memorable attack by Gardiner in the *Daily News:*

> He is always unconsciously playing a part—an heroic part. And he is his most astonished spectator. He sees himself moving through the smoke of

> battle—triumphant, terrible, his brow clothed with thunder, his legions looking to him for victory, and not looking in vain. He thinks of Napoleon; he thinks of his great ancestor. Thus did they bear themselves; thus in this awful and rugged crisis will he bear himself. It is not make-believe, it is not insincerity; it is that in this fervid and picturesque imagination there are always great deeds afoot, with himself cast by destiny in the Agamemnon role. Hence that portentous gravity that sits on his youthful shoulders so oddly, those impressive postures and tremendous silences, the body flung wearily in the chair, the head resting gloomily in the hand, the abstracted look, the knitted brow. Hence that tendency to exaggerate a situation which is so characteristic of him—the tendency that sent artillery down to Sidney Street and, during the railway strike, dispatched the military hither and thither as though Armageddon was upon us.

IV

During Churchill's "social reform" period he achieved much of value and importance; politically, however, he won few new friends in the Liberal ranks and made many new enemies among the Conservatives. It all came to an abrupt conclusion in 1911, when he moved to the Admiralty.

Churchill's early opposition to Army reforms and, later, to increased naval expenditure, had ended abruptly even before the Agadir Crisis of 1911. It was then that he became totally absorbed in the political national danger. As he has written:

> Once I got drawn in, it dominated all other interests in my mind. For seven years I was to think of little else. Liberal politics, the People's Budget, Free Trade, Peace, Retrenchment and Reform—all the war cries of our election struggles began to seem unreal in the presence of this new preoccupation. Only Ireland held her place among the grim realities which came one after another into view.[15]

Churchill's work at the Admiralty has been exhaustively, and very fairly, described by Professor Marder.[16] Although a close analysis proves that mistakes were made and his flamboyance was disliked by many, there was much to praise. He had foresight and imagination; he worked indefatigably; and his dedication to the Navy was total. A final assessment is emphatically to Churchill's credit.

The greatest criticism was levelled at his manner and style. Youth and ambition are viewed askance in England; activity and energy are hardly less suspect. Thus, as Churchill charged on, he left in his wake an ever-growing multitude of critics who were repelled less by his actions than by their originator and his methods; they constituted a growing, silent army, that awaited the moment when this mercurial and reckless young man would commit an irretrievable blunder. Churchill, whose egocentricity became more and more evident, was quite unaware of the resentment and hostility he was arousing. As Lady Asquith has commented, "He tended to ignore the need to feel his way about other minds." One of his colleagues remarked that "he does not exactly walk around with an oil-can."

V

In spite of his preoccupation with the Navy, which in itself aroused further doubts about the depth and sincerity of his Radical convictions on the Liberal benches, Churchill could not hold himself entirely aloof from domestic politics which were peculiarly bitter in the years 1912-1914. His good intentions did little to arrest the decline of his position in the Liberal Party, and further heightened the dismay of the Conservatives.

The Irish Crisis of 1912-1914 must be seen against the background not only of Anglo-Irish relations after the advent of Parnell, but also of British domestic politics in the years 1906-1911. Particularly after the General Elections of 1910, relations between the two parties were as bad as anyone in public life could remember. The resignation of Balfour and his replacement by Bonar Law as Conservative leader in 1911 was a significant portent. Bonar Law was profoundly committed to Ulster's cause, in many respects even more than Sir Edward Carson, the new Ulster leader at Westminster. Although Conservatives "played the Orange card" principally for domestic party ends as Lord Randolph had in 1886, Bonar Law was in deep earnest on this issue.

The division between the Unionists on the one hand and the Liberals or Irish Nationalists on the other, concerned the future of the nine counties of Ulster, on whose behalf Lord Randolph in 1886 coined the ringing phrase "Ulster will fight, Ulster will be right." The fact that the Irish again–as in 1886 and 1892–held the balance of power at Westminster further inflamed Unionist feeling. From the outset it was a bitter, exhausting and dangerous dispute which became progressively more bitter, exhausting and dangerous. It brought the United Kingdom to the verge of civil war in 1914. It further poisoned the relations between the two English parties. As so often in the past, it also cast down reputations, and warped and distorted the course of British political history.

As Lord Randolph's son, Churchill was in a difficult position. In his father's biography he had compared the Irish Question to a visit to a long-deserted battlefield. In 1904 he had described the proposal for a separate Irish Parliament as "dangerous and impracticable," and in his 1906 election campaign he had attacked "the harsh and senseless reiteration of the cry of Home Rule." Thus, it was not a cause for which he felt any natural ardour. Nor, it should be emphasised, was it one that greatly stirred the passions of Asquith, Grey or Lloyd George. Miss Mary C. Bromage made a sound point in *Churchill and Ireland* when she wrote:

> Churchill's policy was, in essence, an English policy and not an Irish policy, either Unionist or Nationalist. In his childhood he had grown up on the assumption that the independence of a hostile Ireland menaced Britain. . . . By means of compromise he hoped for a friendly Ireland.

In private Churchill accepted the force of the Ulster case and his actions were designed to produce an accepted solution. In public, however, his stand was more partisan.

A courageous visit to Belfast in February 1912 was his first intervention. It did not greatly contribute to the abatement of passions in that fevered and bigoted city. But it was not until the beginning of 1914 that his intervention aroused real fury. At this time, Churchill was engaged in a prolonged–and very well publicised–struggle in which the sympathies of the Liberal Party were emphatically with the Chancellor of the Exchequer, Lloyd George. It was evident that the Ulster situation was virtually out of control. Urged on by Carson and Bonar Law, the Ulstermen were arming and training; the Home Rule Bill had been twice rejected by the Lords and would accordingly become law in the autumn of 1914.

Two factors impelled Churchill forward. The first was the urgent necessity, in his own words, to ingratiate himself with his Party. The second was his mounting impatience with the drifting nature of Asquith's policies. Churchill's mind always tended towards simplistic solutions. In his view of mankind and of its problems there was a very strong element of Right and Wrong. This can be a source of great strength since it very often happens that political problems are not as complex as they appear, and that a bold, clear analysis is priceless. Nevertheless, there was truth in Haldane's comment that Churchill was "too apt to act first and think afterwards," and even more in Lord Esher's comment that "he handles great subjects in rhythmical language, and becomes quickly enslaved by his own phrases. He deceives himself into the belief that he takes broad views, when his mind is fixed upon one comparatively small aspect of the question."

There is another point of crucial importance in any comprehension of Churchill's political character. Churchill was always prepared to negotiate–but not under duress. Capitulation had to precede negotiation. If an opponent was truculent, he must first be defeated. Magnanimity could then be extended. Duff Cooper noted after a discussion with Churchill in 1920 that "his great line was that you could only make concessions to people you had beaten. He instanced the success of this in South Africa." Churchill himself described this method in *My Early Life:*

> I have always urged fighting wars and other contentions with might and main till overwhelming victory, and then offering the hand of friendship to the vanquished. Thus, I have always been against the Pacifists during the quarrel, and against the Jingoes at its close. . . . I thought we ought to have conquered the Irish and then given them Home Rule: that we ought to have starved out the Germans, and then revictualled their country: and that after smashing the General Strike, we should have met the grievances of the miners.

All these elements combined to make Churchill determined to seize the initiative. The first public indication was a speech of great truculence at Bradford on March 14.

> This is the issue–whether civil and Parliamentary government in these realms is to be beaten down by the menace of armed force. . . . If the civil and Parliamentary systems under which we have dwelt so long, and our fathers before us, are to be brought to the crude challenge of force, if the Government and Parliament of this great country and greater Empire are

to be exposed to menace and brutality; if all the loose, wanton and reckless chatter we have been forced to listen to, these many months, is in the end to disclose a sinister and revolutionary purpose, then I can only say to you: "Let us go forward together and put these grave matters to the proof!"

There is no need to embroil ourselves in the dramas and mysteries of the so-called Curragh Mutiny. To the Conservatives it appeared that Churchill, acting in close cooperation with the Secretary for War, Seely, had attempted to threaten Ulster with massive force. Churchill's movement of warships to Lamlash, cancelled by Asquith on March 21, was the most controversial and most violently denounced of the Government's actions. Asquith's explanation to the Commons that he had no foreknowledge of this act has been proven false, but the evidence—although incomplete—does point strongly in the direction of deliberate action by Churchill and Seely to force the pace and apply direct pressure on Ulster.

There was something to be said for this policy, and it hardly lay in the mouths of the Opposition to condemn Churchill for advocating violent solutions to the Ulster crisis. Churchill justly described the attacks against him as "a vote of censure by the criminal classes upon the police." But the enterprise ended in a complete fiasco. Seely was removed, the warships withdrawn, and the Government humiliated. The Southern Irish, realising that Ulster's position was immensely stronger, moved towards direct action; the Larne gun-running in July was the inevitable response.

The bitterness of the Conservatives toward Churchill personally reached new heights in the summer of 1914, although the eruption of the European crisis at the end of July pushed the Irish Question into abeyance. But political memories are long. When the war opened, no Act of Oblivion could be passed. Churchill joined the long list of English politicians whose fortunes had been grievously harmed by intervention in the unhappy and tangled affairs of Ireland.

VI

The Irish Intervention Crisis of July 24-August 3, 1914, still awaits its historian. It is clear that Churchill at least had no doubts about what action should be taken and, with "his best daemonic energy," in Morley's words, persistently advocated intervention. On his own initiative, the Home Fleet was not dispersed after maneuvres, but was sent to its battle stations. The long Cabinet debates were ended by Germany's ultimatum to Belgium. Churchill wrote:

> Everything tends towards catastrophe and collapse. I am interested, geared up and happy. Is it not horrible to be built like this? The preparations have a hideous fascination for me. I pray to God to forgive me for such fearful moods of levity. Yet I would do my best for peace, and nothing would induce me wrongfully to strike the blow. I cannot feel that we in this island are to any serious degree responsible for the wave of madness which has swept the mind of Christendom.[17]

VII

By August 1914 Winston Churchill had far outstripped his father in speed of elevation to, and solid achievements of, office. At age thirty-nine he held perhaps the most crucial post in the Government. He was a major political figure, nationally and internationally.

Although his closest friends and admirers accepted that he was a prodigy, even they wondered whether he did not, after all, share his father's instability. Lloyd George, Morley and Asquith all expressed reservation about him, and Asquith's comments in particular are worth noting:

> It is a pity that Winston hasn't a better sense of proportion. I am really fond of him, but I regard his future with many misgivings. . . . He will never get to the top in English politics, with all his wonderful gifts; to speak with the tongue of men and angels, and to spend laborious days and nights in administration, is no good if a man does not inspire trust.

Among Conservatives he was regarded with even greater hatred than in the past; Liberals continued to eye him with marked unease; and Labour was already deeply disenchanted. Churchill's political support was shallow, and in peril. Gardiner wrote prophetically in 1912:

> You may cast the horoscope of anyone else; his you cannot cast. You cannot cast it because his orbit is not governed by any known laws, but by attractions that deflect his path hither and thither. It may be the attraction of war and peace, of social reform or of a social order—whatever it is he will plunge into it with all the schoolboy intensity of his nature. His loves may be many, but they will always have the passion of a first love. Whatever shrine he worships at, he will be the most fervid in his prayers. . . .
>
> "Keep your eye on Churchill" should be the watchword of these days. Remember, he is a soldier first, last, and always. He will write his name big on our future. Let us take care he does not write it in blood.

VIII

It is perhaps the principal fascination of politics that nothing ever turns out as anticipated. It could be said there was a general feeling in August 1914 that the war would provide Churchill with the political opportunities which he craved and that he, almost alone among Liberal Ministers, would thrive in the new environment. John Morley wrote in his *Memorandum on Resignation* that "if there is a war, Winston will beat Lloyd George hollow, in spite of ingenious computation," and Sir Maurice

Hankey subsequently wrote of Churchill's "real zest for war." Yet the war brought Churchill's career to an abrupt check, and seemed at one point to have finished it as completely as the War Office Estimates had ended that of his father in December 1886.

The first blows fell quickly. The British were shaken by events of the land war and even more disconcerted by a series of debacles at sea. The German ships *Goeben* and *Breslau* escaped to Constantinople; the cruiser *Emden* for a time paralysed transport in the Indian Ocean; Admiral von Spee's squadron eliminated an inferior British force off Coronel; and three British cruisers were sunk in broad daylight in the North Sea by one U-boat. None of these setbacks were grievous, but they checked public confidence severely and the Cabinet resolved to suppress news of the sinking of the battleship *Audacious.* Asquith reported to the King on November 4 that "the Cabinet were of opinion that this incident [Coronel] like the escape of the *Goeben,* the loss of the *Cressy* and her two sister-cruisers, and that of the *Hermes* last week, is not creditable to the officers of the Navy."

From criticism of the Navy to the censure of the First Lord was but a short step. Churchill drew much unnecessary fire upon himself when he declared in an injudicious speech at Liverpool on September 21 that if the German Navy did not come out to fight, "it would be dug out like rats from a hole." The following day the three British cruisers were sunk, and the King remarked to Asquith that "the rats came out of their own accord and to our cost." The criticism that fell on Churchill for this incident was unmerited, but its fierceness was an indication of the popular temper.

In the Admiralty, as Professor Marder has commented, Churchill "had too inflated a conception of his functions. . . . Churchill's large view of his office—'his business everything and his intent everywhere'—worked badly, and it tended to diminish the authority of the First Sea Lord and the Chief of the War Staff, and to cramp their freedom of action." The summary removal of Admiral Sir George Callaghan from command of the Home Fleet on July 30 upset the Navy; the acceptance of the resignation of the First Sea Lord, Prince Louis of Battenberg, after a vicious Press campaign against his alleged "Germanism," was also widely attacked. Thus, within a few weeks, Churchill's position crumbled in the face of severe criticism from the Conservative Press and Opposition M.P.s. In both the Admiralty and the Navy ominous grumblings were heard.

Churchill's decision to replace Battenberg with Lord Fisher was, at first glance, a master-stroke, but its dangers were discerned by some. "The situation is curious," Admiral Wemyss wrote. "Two very strong and clever men, one old, wily and of vast experience, one young, self-assertive, with great self-satisfaction but unstable. They cannot work together, they cannot both run the show." Beaverbrook later wrote: "Churchill co-opted Fisher to relieve the pressure against himself, but he had no intention of letting anyone else rule the roost. Here, then, were two strong men of incompatible tempers both bent on an autocracy."

Churchill's restlessness and excitability caused serious concern. Admiral Richmond wrote on October 24:

> He was in low spirits . . . and oppressed with the impossibility of *doing* anything. The attitude of waiting . . . and the inability of the Staff to

> make any suggestions seemed to bother him. I have not seen him so despondent before. . . . He wanted to send battleships–old ones–up the Elbe, but for what purpose except to be sunk I did not understand.

There was sound evidence for these apprehensions. In September the almost forgotten episode of the "Dunkirk Circus" occurred in which Churchill organised a diversion with a mixed force of marines and yeomanry. More serious was his attempt to save Antwerp in October, when Churchill took command and even offered to resign his post in the Government. When Antwerp fell, over 2,500 men of the newly formed and largely untrained Royal Naval Division were interned or lost as battle casualties. It is now clear that this action delayed the fall of Antwerp for a week, and that Churchill's handling of the defence was very much to his credit. But he was vulnerable on two counts. First, his theatrical arrival reminded one observer "of a scene in a melodrama where the hero dashes up bare-headed on a foam-flecked horse, and saves the heroine, or the old homestead, or the family fortune, as the case may be." Secondly, the Naval Division was Churchill's creation, and was a source of friction between the War Office and the Admiralty. The episode was, however, better than Richmond's description–"Winston's tuppenny untrained rabble"–would suggest.

In later describing the storm of abuse that fell on his head Churchill acknowledged the strength of the criticisms: "Those who are charged with the direction of supreme affairs must sit on the mountain-tops of control; they must never descend into the valleys of direct physical and personal action."

IX

By the end of 1914, Churchill's insecure position at the Admiralty was further threatened by the loss of Asquith's confidence. The "honeymoon" with Lord Fisher was waning, and the old Admiral was venting his impatience in a series of private letters. Churchill himself was wholly unaware of the tides moving silently but inexorably against him. Beaverbrook has written:

> His attitude from August 1914 was a noble one, too noble to be wise. He cared for the success of the British arms, especially in so far as they could be achieved by the Admiralty, and for nothing else. His passion for this aim was pure, self-devoted, and all-devouring. He failed to remember that he was a politician and as such treading a slippery path; he forgot his political tactics. . . . As he worked devotedly at his own job, the currents of political opinion slipped by him unnoticed.

Churchill's impatience with the conduct of the war was fully justified. Already he, Lloyd George and Hankey had independently seen the appalling prospects opening up on the Western Front, where the competing trench-lines writhed from the Swiss border to the Channel, and where the casualties had already reached a scale undreamed-of by any of the belligerents. To the East, the Russians were sent reeling backwards after Tannenberg; the entry of Turkey into the war at the end of October blocked the warm-water route to Russia and imperilled the Suez Canal. Faced with these utterly unexpected events, the Asquith Government was divided and leaderless, and the creation in November of a War Council did nothing to correct these fundamental deficiencies. The war was making its own rules, and imposing its own demands. The Liberal Government was quite incapable of comprehending the new situation or of meeting the challenge.

Churchill's mounting obsession was with the use of British strength in a more effective manner than sending troops, in his words, "to chew barbed wire in Flanders." He wrote to Asquith on December 29:

> We ought not to drift. We ought now to consider while time remains the scope and character we wish to impart to the war in the early summer. We ought to concert our action with our allies, and particularly with Russia. We ought to form a scheme for a continuous and progressive offensive, and be ready with this new alternative when and if the direct frontal attacks in France on the German lines and Belgium have failed, and fail I fear they will. Without your direct guidance and initiation, none of these things will be done; and a succession of bloody checks in the West and East will leave the Allies dashed in spirit and bankrupt in policy.

Churchill was unquestionably right in his general analysis, but the governmental structure–and Asquith's personality–effectively prevented the kind of planning and coordination that was necessary. Moreover, it was the absence of such machinery that contributed greatly to the Dardanelles disaster in 1915, and which initially assisted Churchill in the formulation of that tragic venture.

NOTES

[1] Winston S. Churchill, *Lord Randolph Churchill* (London, 1951), 11.
[2] Winston S. Churchill, *Lord Randolph Churchill,* 185.
[3] A. G. Gardiner, *Prophets, Priests and Kings* (London, 1908), 108.
[4] Lord Rosebery, *Lord Randolph Churchill* (London, 1906), 27.
[5] Anthony Storr, "Winston Churchill: The Man," in *Churchill, Four Faces and the Man* (London, 1969), 250.
[6] Winston S. Churchill, *Lord Randolph Churchill,* 764.
[7] Isaiah Berlin, *Mr. Churchill in 1940* (London, 1965), 102.
[8] Lucy Masterman, *C. F. G. Masterman* (London, 1939), 97.
[9] G. W. Steevens, "The Youngest Man in Europe," *Daily Mail,* November, 1899.
[10] Winston S. Churchill, *Savrola* (London, 1900), 174.
[11] Winston S. Churchill, *Lord Randolph Churchill,* 66.
[12] A. G. Gardiner, *Prophets, Priests and Kings,* 74.
[13] Lucy Masterman, *C. F. G. Masterman,* 97-98.
[14] Speech of December 17, 1909 in Volume II of this collection.
[15] Winston S. Churchill, *The World Crisis* (London, 1927), 52.
[16] See A. J. Marder, *From the Dreadnought to Scapa Flow,* vols. I and II.
[17] Randolph S. Churchill, *Winston S. Churchill* (Boston, 1966), II, 70-71.

FIRST POLITICAL SPEECH

July 26, 1897

Habitation of the Primrose League,
Claverton Down, Bath

*Churchill's first prepared speech was never delivered. At the age of 20, while an officer cadet at Sandhurst, he was indignant at the endeavours of a Mrs. Ormiston Chant to purify the music halls. She was particularly revolted by conditions in the promenade adjoining the Empire Theatre, Leicester Square, a favourite haunt of Churchill and his friends. Churchill was invited to address the Executive Committee of the Entertainment Protection League, only to discover that it was a non-existent body. In his own account, "I walked out into the street with a magnificent oration surging within my bosom and only half a crown in my pocket" (*My Early Life, *54).*

*Mrs. Chant succeeded in having canvas screens placed between "the offending bars" and the promenade, which were torn down by an angry crowd. Churchill was present. "In these somewhat unvirginal surroundings," he has written, "I now made my maiden speech. Mounting on the debris and indeed partially emerging from it, I addressed the tumultuous crowd. No very accurate report of my words has been preserved. They did not, however, fall unheeded and I have heard about them several times since. . . . The barricades were rebuilt in brick and plaster, and all our efforts went for nothing. Still, no one can say we did not do our best" (*My Early Life, *57-59).*

I have been unable to find any report of this first speech. Its general purport is described in My Early Life, *59.*

*Churchill's real debut as a public speaker was in July 1897, when he made what he called "my (official) maiden effort" at a Primrose League gathering near Bath. It was meticulously prepared. "We repaired to our tent, and mounted the platform, which consisted of about four boards laid across some small barrels. There was neither table nor chair; but as soon as about a hundred persons had rather reluctantly, I thought, quitted their childish amusements in the park, the Chairman rose and in a brief speech introduced me to the audience. . . ." (*My Early Life, *206).*

If it were pardonable in any speaker to begin with the well worn and time honoured apology, "unaccustomed as I am to public speaking," it would be pardonable in my case, for the honour I am enjoying at this moment of addressing an audience of my fellow-countrymen and women is the first honour of the kind I have ever received. (Cheers.) I can assure you that it was a very great pleasure to me to be able to accept Mr. Skrine's invitation to come down to the ancient city of Bath and do what little I can to forward the great work of the Primrose League. (Cheers.)

But every pleasure has its corresponding drawback, just as every rose has its thorn and the corresponding drawback in my case is that at the present time it is exceedingly difficult to find anything to talk about. Everyone has been feeling so loyal and patriotic during the last few weeks that now all is over and the Jubilee is dead and done, a sort of reaction has set in, and people do not want to get enthusiastic about anything for quite a long time to come. (Laughter.) Even Parliament is affected by a general dullness, for the truth is politics are extremely dull, no exciting debates, no close divisions, no violent scenes ruffle the serenity of the House of Commons, no violent agitation disturbs the tranquility of the country—all is rest and sleepy, comfortable peace. (Laughter.) In fact in the words of the popular song you might have heard:

Every eyelid closes,
All the world reposes,
Lazily, lazily, drowsily, drowsily,
In the noonday sun.

(Laughter.) But sleepy, comfortable peace, I must remind you, involves sleepy, comfortable progress, and leads eventually to comfortable prosperity. So that, although bad for the speaker, this rest is good for the people. And though Parliament is dull, it is by no means idle. (Hear, hear.) A measure is before them of the greatest importance to the working men of this country. (Cheers.) I venture to hope that, if you think it presumptuous in one so young to speak on such a subject, you will put it down to the headstrong enthusiasm of youth. (Hear, hear and laughter.) This measure is designed to protect workingmen in dangerous trades from poverty if they become injured in the service of their employers. (Hear, hear.) When the Radicals brought in their Bill and failed, they called it an Employers' Liability Bill. Observe how much better the Tories do these things. (Hear, hear.) We call the Bill the Workmen's Compensation Bill, and that is a much nicer name. (Laughter and hear, hear.) This Bill is a great measure of reform. It grapples with evils that are so great that only those who are intimately connected with them are able to form any idea of them. (Cheers.) Every year it is calculated that 6,000 people are killed and 250,000 injured in trades in this country. That is a terrible total, larger than the greatest battle ever fought can show. (Hear, hear.) I do not say that workmen have not been treated well in the past by the kindness and consideration of their employers, but this measure removes the question from the shifting sands of charity and places it on the firm bedrock of law. (Cheers.) So far it is only applied to dangerous trades. Radicals, who are never satisfied with Liberals, always liberal with other people's money (laughter), ask why it is not applied to all. That is like a Radical—just the slap-dash, wholesale, harum-scarum policy of the Radical. It reminds me of the man who, on being told that ventilation is an excellent thing, went and smashed every window in his house, and died of rheumatic fever. (Laughter and cheers.) That is not Conservative policy. Conservative policy is essentially a tentative policy—a look-before-you-leap policy; and it is a policy of don't leap at all if there is a ladder. (Laughter.) It is because our progress is slow that it is sure and constant. (Hear, hear.) But this Bill might be taken as indicating the forward tendency of Tory legislation, and as showing to thousands of our countrymen engaged in industrial pursuits that the Tories are willing to help them, and besides having the inclination, that they also have the power (hear, hear), and that the British workman has more to hope for from the rising tide of Tory democracy than from the dried-up drain-pipe of Radicalism. (Laughter and cheers.)

I am sorry to say that what is being done in one direction is being undone in another. I allude, of course, to the great strike of engineers. (Hear, hear.) A great war between capital and labour has broken out, and it can not fail to leave a most dreadful desolation behind it (hear, hear), and must bring misery on thousands. Whoever is right, masters or men—both are wrong, whoever might win, both must lose. (Hear, hear.) In the great economic struggles of nations no quarter is ever shown to the vanquished. Every individual and every community has, no doubt, a right to buy the best goods in the cheapest market, and if the British manufacturer can not produce goods for export at the lowest price in the market of our trade—the pride of England and the envy of the foreigner—would simply go to the German Emperor or some other equally unattractive individual. (Laughter and applause.) One of the questions which politicians have to face is how to avoid disputes between capital and labour. (Hear, hear.) Ultimately I hope that the labourer will become (as it were) a shareholder in the business in which he works, and would not be unwilling to stand the pressure of a bad year because he shares some of the profits of a good one. But this is a solution which can be only reached in the distant future, and in the meantime it is the duty of everyone who has influence and opportunity to do what he can to bring these continual disputes to an end, it is still more the duty of any political organisation to do this, and it is no more the duty of any such organisation than it is the duty of the Primrose League.

The League has indeed set itself many hard tasks in the past fifteen years. It has been teaching the people of Great Britain the splendour of their Empire, the nature of their Constitution, and the importance of their fleet. But more remains to be done. (Cheers.) We must carry out the work of popularising those institutions which have made this country what it is, and by which we can alone maintain our proud position. (Cheers.) It is a heavy task, but we are not without encouragement. All this Imperial sentiment, this desire for unity, this realisation of Empire which has characterised and glorified the sixtieth year of the Queen's reign (cheers), is in entire harmony with the principles and sentiments of the Primrose League. (Cheers.) I do not go so far as to say it is entirely the outcome of it, because that would be an exaggeration, and when you have a good cause there is no need for exaggeration. (Hear, hear.) But we might fairly claim to have afforded the rallying point for all who sympathise with the Imperial movement, a sphere of action for all who are enthusiastic about it; we have, as it were, collected public opinion throughout the country and concentrated it for a definite end. And as we have borne our share of work, we might claim our share of the credit. (Hear, hear.)

Those reflections are not unpleasant to many of those who like Mr. Skrine and Colonel Wright, our Ruling Councillor, have watched the Primrose League from its early humble commencement. At first regarded merely as a trick of the Fourth Party, viewed with contempt by the Radicals and with suspicion by the Tories, the League had a narrow shave of existence at all. But it grew, in the face of ridicule and opposition, and extended its ramifications into almost every town and village in the land (cheers); and its influence pervaded all classes, until we see it in one of the most complicated arrangements of political machinery, and one of the most tremendous monuments of Constitutional power that the world has ever seen. (Cheers.)

In 1880 the Tory party was crushed, broken, dispirited. Its great leader, Lord Beaconsfield, was already touched by the finger of Death. Its principles were unpopular; its numbers were few; and it appeared on the verge of extinction. Observe it now.

(Cheers.) That struggling menant of Toryism has swollen into the strongest Government of modern times. (Cheers.) And the great Liberal party which in 1889 was vigorous, united, supreme, was shrunk to a few discordant factions of discredited faddists, without numbers, without policy, without concord, without cohesion, around whose neck is bound the millstone of Home Rule. (Cheers.) In all this revolution of public opinion the Primrose League has borne its share. (Cheers.) It has kept pegging away, driving the principles of the Tory party into the heads of the people of this country, and, though the task has been heavy and labour long, we have had in the end a glorious reward. (Cheers.) The Radical party has been knocked out of time. It is flat upon the ground, and it is the business of the League to see that it never gets up again. (Laughter.) The Primrose League has stood the test of ridicule, it has borne defeat, it remains now to see whether it can stand the higher test of victory. We must not rest. We have three years before the next election. Let us select our quarry–some stalwart Radical–run him down, hold him until the moment comes to take him in triumph to the poll, and then the election of 1901 will be as glorious for the Empire as the election of 1895. (Cheers.)

There are not wanting those who say that in this Jubilee year our Empire has reached the height of its glory and power, and that now we shall begin to decline, as Babylon, Carthage, Rome declined. Do not believe these croakers but give the lie to their dismal croaking by showing by our actions that the vigour and vitality of our race is unimpaired and that our determination is to uphold the Empire that we have inherited from our fathers as Englishmen (cheers), that our flag shall fly high upon the sea, our voice be heard in the councils of Europe, our Sovereign supported by the love of her subjects, then shall we continue to pursue that course marked out for us by an all-wise hand and carry out our mission of bearing peace, civilisation and good government to the uttermost ends of the earth. (Loud cheers.)

ELECTION ADDRESS

June 24, 1899

Conservative Club, Oldham

On June 9, 1899, Mr. Robert Ascroft, one of the Conservative Members of Parliament for Oldham–a two-member constituency–died suddenly. The other Member, Mr. James Oswald, who had been in poor health, took this opportunity to resign his seat. The Oldham Conservative Association had already tentatively approached Churchill to stand as Conservative candidate in Oswald's place at the next General Election with Ascroft. Churchill and Mr. James Mawdsley, the Secretary of the Operative Cotton Spinners' Association, were adopted as the candidates for the unexpected by-election. The Liberal candidates were Mr. Alfred Emmott and Mr. Walter Runciman–both became colleagues of Churchill in the 1905-1915 Liberal Government.

Churchill conducted his by-election campaign with immense enthusiasm and energy. "He was always thinking of the impression which his speeches would make, not in his immediate audience, but in London—as if London were hanging on his lips," Sir Edward Hamilton commented with some asperity.

It was thought at the time that the selection of Mr. Mawdsley was a master-stroke—Tory Democracy in action! Mr. Mawdsley declared himself proud to stand with "a scion of the aristocracy," and it was felt that the combination of "the Scion and the Socialist" would be unbeatable. In the event, as Churchill later recorded, Mr. Mawdsley did not bring the Conservatives many working-class votes, and his presence alarmed several Conservative supporters.

One of the burning issues of the election campaign was the Clerical Tithes Bill, just introduced by the Government. Its purpose was to benefit the Church of England and particularly the Church Schools. This measure aroused vehement opposition from nonconformists, particularly from the Lancashire Methodists. Churchill eventually decided not to support the Government, which provoked the tart comment from Arthur Balfour, "I thought he was a young man of promise; it appears he is a young man of promises."

The result was declared on July 6; Emmott and Runciman were elected. The figures were: Emmott (L), 12,976; Runciman (L), 12,770; Churchill (U), 11,477; Mawdsley (U), 11,449.

Churchill was temporarily chastened by this reverse, but Balfour wrote him a charming letter of commiseration and encouragement. Shortly afterwards the menacing news from South Africa offered him a new opportunity to capture public interest and attention.

It is very pleasant for me to come down here a stranger and to find around me on the eve of the battle so many good comrades who will be prepared to support the Tory candidate, whoever he might be. (Hear, hear.) We are told that public opinion in the country is at this moment running rather against Her Majesty's Government. We have had several by-elections lately, which Mr. Croston will tell you are not quite of the class which satisfies the party organization. There has been an unfortunate change of opinion in Southport, they have had a reverse in South Edinburgh, and the Radicals have secured a victory with an increased majority in East Edinburgh—in fact, there is what Lord Rosebery, who is an acute observer of public opinion, has called a swell of Liberalism. That might be, but the swell is not a very large one. It might be large enough to make the fishing boats and the cockle boats move about, but it will not move the great ironclad of Oldham. (Cheers.) I have no doubt that whatever might be the flux and reflux of opinion in the country at this moment, Oldham will be uninfluenced by it. The people of this city will form their own opinion now, as they have done before. If I have the good fortune to be invited to fight for Oldham, I am going to fight on broad issues. I will not be led into any of the pettifogging questions which the Radical party has lately adopted with such affection and delight. But we will find it very difficult to keep the questions before the constituency on broad lines. The Radicals will want to raise all sorts of questions—they will want to ask the electors whether Mr. Balfour is right or wrong in considering the Clerical Tithes Bill presumably non-contentious; they will want to know whether Lord Salisbury was right or wrong in speaking somewhat facetiously about the British housemaid–(laughter);– they will want to know whether Mr. Chamberlain is right or wrong in publishing Sir A. Milner's despatch, and they will want to know whether Mr. Long was right or wrong in keeping the muzzles on the dogs. (Laughter.) Those are the questions which the Radicals will seek to make the tests–the questions which belong to the verminous persons and undersized fish party. (Laughter.) To such a dismal condition has a once great party come, to such miserable dodges and makeshifts will they have recourse. Trying to keep to the main issues, what is the great claim that the Tory party, the Unionists administration, have to their continued confidence? It is one that can not be disputed. It is a position which has not been paralleled in English history within the memory of anyone in this room. It is a position of such magnificent prosperity that we have to go back to the days of the Ministry of the Earl of Chatham to find its equal. (Hear, hear.) We are tranquil at home; there is no great faction tearing the country in two at this moment. The only complaint about home politics indeed is that they are rather dull. And if you look abroad you will find an equally satisfactory state of affairs. Never were our relations with foreign Powers more excellent; never were we on better terms with the great country across the sea which speaks our language– (cheers);–never was the revenue better collected; never were the trade returns more prosperous; never did the people rally more loyally round the throne than on the occasion of the eightieth birthday of the Queen. (Hear, hear.) I say–and I challenge any Radical to dispute it–that never before were there so many people in the United Kingdom and never before had they so much to eat. (Hear, hear.) Well, how has all this prosperity been obtained? It has been obtained as a result of ten years, nearly eleven years, of Unionist administration, as a result of the Tory party having been supreme or nearly supreme ever since the year 1886. Of course the Radicals would like to claim a good deal of this prosperity because of the way in which they have comported themselves when in Opposition. (Laughter.) The character of the work done by the Tory party is strikingly shown, I contend, by the difference in the condition of Ireland, of India, of the Soudan and Egypt now and in 1885. Coming nearer home a study of the speeches which were made about the year 1885 shows in a still more striking way the difference between the two periods. In 1885 the speeches that were delivered were marked by bitterness and animosity, and there was a great feeling of hostility to all existing institutions. In those days it was said that you could not find a Tory working man. All that has been changed. A great multitude of Tories exists now, and the backbone of the party is in the Tory democracy. (Hear, hear.) I need not say how much of the work of building up this party devolved upon my father. (Cheers.) If you look abroad you will find that in 1885 all the foreign nations looked upon England as a great Power that was going to fall as Rome fell long ago and as we have within the last two years seen Spain fall. That was the attitude in 1885. This year the attitude is somewhat changed. We have seen our ancient enemy, or I would rather say our ancient antagonist, France, lower her sword and decline an unequal contest. We have seen the nations of Europe not afraid that we are going to fall, but afraid that we are going to fall upon them. (Laughter.) All the great change has been accomplished under Unionist administration, and we can not put that fact too clearly or too often before the electorate. When we hear the Radicals say that we are not too considerate in our treatment of verminous persons and undersized fish, let us point out in reply that during the past fifteen years this country has been raised to a position of unequalled prosperity and almost unequalled power. (Hear, hear.) Another great contrast which I would like to point out is that which exists between the Unionist party and the Radical party. It is a contrast between an army and a mob. On the one hand we have a great party, strong in numbers, strong in its organisation, obeying its leaders, working in one direction for ideas which are practicable; and, on the other hand, you have an agglomeration of squabbling factions, fighting each other desperately, agreeing in nothing except their greed for gain, their longing for office, and their thirst for power. Such are the two parties and such are the two policies between which the electors of Oldham have to decide. For myself, if I have the honour to stand as a candidate for the constituency, I confess that I will enter into the contest with mixed feelings. I would come to Oldham with a great feeling of trepidation, because I know how many are my failings and my imperfections, but I would also feel a certain pride that I had been invited to fight the battle of the Unionist party in that famous Lancashire city, and I would cherish the high hope that although there might lie before us a period of tremendous effort, I almost said of exhausting effort, yet in the end, just as the dark shadows of a stormy night are dispersed by the warm clear flush of the morning, we will come out of our fight and our struggle to victory and I think, to peace. (Loud cheers.)

[Editor's Note: At the conclusion of his speech, a resolution was passed inviting Churchill to stand for election. He then said] : I need not say that I will do whatever is in my power to win the seat. But I think that it is very essential that both seats should be won. (Cheers.) We have a great contest before us. Here we are all friends, but I do not doubt that in another place there is a collection of people not less enthusiastic, although perhaps not quite so intelligent–(laughter),–not less determined to win the seat. Our opponents have the impulse of the attack, they have the opportunity of pulling down the Tory majority, and, as you know, pulling down is a congenial task for Radicals. We will have to hold our ground firmly, and we will not do it without a most tremendous effort on the part of everyone. As far as I am concerned I will use every ounce of strength I possess, and if only you support me with energy and enthusiasm I can not doubt that we will have a splendid reward. (Cheers.)

THE WAR IN SOUTH AFRICA

July 25, 1900

Empire Theatre, Oldham

At the end of July 1899, war with the Boer Republics was imminent. Churchill was eager to be involved and sailed to South Africa as a correspondent for The Morning Post *on October 14–three days after the start of the war.*

At this point in his career, Churchill also published The River War, *a brilliant study of the Sudan campaign, which played a major role in furthering his reputation.*

Churchill returned from South Africa on July 20, 1900. His exploits there, particularly his escape from a Boer prisoner of war camp, made him a national figure. With Pretoria captured and the Boer forces in disarray, it appeared that the war was over. In fact, its most serious and frustrating stage was only beginning.

Capitalising on this general jubilation and exploiting the acute controversy on the South African war within the Liberal Party, the Unionist Government dissolved Parliament and initiated what its opponents called "the Khaki Election."

Churchill was adopted as Unionist candidate for Oldham on July 25. His fellow Unionist candidate from the previous election, Mr. Mawdsley, had died while Churchill was in South Africa and was replaced by Mr. C. B. Crisp. The results of the election were declared on October 1. The figures were: Emmott (L), 12,947; Churchill (U), 12,931; Runciman (L), 12,709; and Crisp (U), 12,522. The Unionist majority in the General Election was 134 seats.

[Extract] . . . I noticed this evening a flaring newspaper placard announcing another British military disaster in South Africa. I do not like the exaggerated use of words. (Hear, hear.) These incidents of war are the inevitable accompaniment of military operations. What is a war? It is not a long line of continuous successes. At least it is not usually that. It is an out and fight with rough and tumble in which both sides must give and bear good blows. If we are going to call every insignificant operation on the line of communications a British disaster we should soon run a great danger of losing the calm and self-possession which has hitherto distinguished the demeanour of the country. (Cheers.) But what is really the situation? We have put our arms where we intended to put them–in the enemy's capital. We have captured his railway lines and the great gold mines of the Rand, whereby the Boers get the money to pay their patriotic mercenaries. (Hear, hear and laughter.) We have also got possession of their arsenal at Johannesburg, where they make shot and shell, and, so far as is known to the British authorities in South Africa, the Boers are unprovided with any means of making ammunition. They have no more money with the exception of the two millions which President Kruger captured and managed to save by not paying the salaries of his own Government officials. (Laughter.) I remember how angry the officials were. They were all paid in cheques–excellent cheques every one of them–but when they came to be presented at the bank the officials found that the head of the Government had extracted the money privately from the bank before the cheques arrived. (Laughter.) Two millions is a lot of money, and it will make President Kruger able to hold out for some time yet. How long I will not venture to prophesy. What I mean is this–there is no cause for alarm now. The end is bound to be a matter of months. I do not wish to be sanguine, but I would like to say of weeks. (Laughter.) I do not think that that would be a foolish statement at all, but I would rather keep within the limits of absolute certainty, and President Kruger can not maintain his resistance indefinitely. Ammunition, money, and, what is of more importance, food will give out, and the want of them will tell their tale on the Boers. Although we might expect unsatisfactory incidents to arise from time to time owing to our forces being scattered over an enormous extent of country and having to hold great lines of communication up which the food must pass to armies at the front, although the scattered situation in which they are placed will probably result in the picking up of small posts and convoys, and although these incidents might offer Radical newspapers every opportunity for publishing flaring and alarmist placards, they will not alter and will not in the slightest delay the inevitable conclusion of the war. (Loud cheers.) But what have we got to do in the meanwhile? We have got to see, so far as our constitutional functions allow us, that the War Office is not allowed to relax any effort, and I am convinced, after what I have seen, that there shall be no shred of independence given to the two States, but that they must come entirely under British government. (Cheers.)

THE MAIDEN SPEECH

February 18, 1901

House of Commons

After his Oldham victory, Churchill went on an extended lecture tour in Britain, the United States and Canada. Queen Victoria had died while Churchill was in Canada, and the new Parliament was opened by King Edward VII on February 14. Contrary to usual custom, Churchill resolved to make his maiden speech on February 18, immediately after an inflammatory speech by David Lloyd George. "He had a moderately phrased amendment on the [Order] paper," Churchill wrote in My Early Life, *"but whether he would move it was not certain." As Lloyd George continued, Churchill related that "a sense of alarm and even despair crept across me. Then Mr. [Thomas Gibson] Bowles whispered to me, 'You might say instead of making his violent speech without moving his moderate amendment, he had better have moved his moderate amendment without making his violent speech.' Manna in the wilderness was not more welcome! It fell only just in time" (*My Early Life, *364).*

In the course of the speech, when Churchill said, "If I were a Boer, I hope I should be fighting in the field," Chamberlain muttered, "That's the way to throw away seats." The phrase was warmly cheered by the Irish members.

The speech was very successful; immediately afterwards, Churchill met Lloyd George for the first time.

I understood that the hon. Member to whose speech the House has just listened, had intended to move an Amendment to the Address. The text of the Amendment, which had appeared in the papers, was singularly mild and moderate in tone; but mild and moderate as it was, neither the hon. Member nor his political friends had cared to expose it to criticism or to challenge a division upon it, and, indeed, when we compare the moderation of the Amendment with the very bitter speech which the hon. Member has just delivered, it is difficult to avoid the conclusion that the moderation of the Amendment was the moderation of the hon. Member's political friends and leaders, and that the bitterness of his speech is all his own. It has been suggested to me that it might perhaps have been better, upon the whole, if the hon. Member, instead of making his speech without moving his Amendment, had moved his Amendment without making his speech. I would not complain of any remarks of the hon. Member were I called upon to do so. In my opinion, based upon the experience of the most famous men whose names have adorned the records of the House, no national emergency short, let us say, of the actual invasion of this country itself ought in any way to restrict or prevent the entire freedom of Parliamentary discussion. Moreover, I do not believe that the Boers would attach particular importance to the utterances of the hon. Member. No people in the world received so much verbal sympathy and so little practical support as the Boers. If I were a Boer fighting in the field—and if I were a Boer I hope I should be fighting in the field—I would not allow myself to be taken in by any message of sympathy, not even if it were signed by a hundred hon. Members. The hon. Member dwelt at great length upon the question of farm burning. I do not propose to discuss the ethics of farm burning now; but hon. Members should, I think, cast their eyes back to the fact that no considerations of humanity prevented the German army from throwing its shells into dwelling houses in Paris, and starving the inhabitants of that great city to the extent that they had to live upon rats and like atrocious foods in order to compel the garrison to surrender. I venture to think His Majesty's Government would not have been justified in restricting their commanders in the field from any methods of warfare which are justified by precedents set by European and American generals during the last fifty or sixty years. I do not agree very fully with the charges of treachery on the one side and barbarity on the other. From what I saw of the war—and I sometimes saw something of it—I believe that as compared with other wars, especially those in which a civil population took part, this war in South Africa has been on the whole carried on with unusual humanity and generosity. The hon. Member for Carnarvon Boroughs has drawn attention to the case of one general officer, and although I deprecate debates upon the characters of individual general officers who are serving the country at this moment, because I know personally General Bruce Hamilton, whom the hon. Member with admirable feeling described as General Brute Hamilton, I feel unable to address the House without offering my humble testimony to the fact that in all His Majesty's Army there are few men with better feeling, more kindness of heart, or with higher courage than General Bruce Hamilton.

There is a point of difference which has been raised by the right hon. Gentleman the Leader of the Opposition upon the question of the policy to be pursued in South Africa after this war has been brought to a conclusion. So far as I have been able to make out the difference between the Government and the Opposition on this question is that whereas His Majesty's Government propose that when hostilities are brought to a conclusion there shall be an interval of civil government before full representative rights are extended to the peoples of these countries, on the other hand the right hon. Gentleman the Leader of the Opposition believes that these representative institutions will be more quickly obtained if the military government be prolonged as a temporary measure and no interval of civil government be interposed. I hope I am not misinterpreting the right hon. Gentleman in any way. If I am, I trust he will not hesitate to correct me, because I should be very sorry in any way to misstate his views. If that is the situation, I will respectfully ask the House to allow me to examine these alternative propositions. I do not wish myself to lay down the law, or thrust my views upon hon. Members. I have travelled a good deal about South Africa during the last ten months under varying circumstances, and I should like to lay before the House some of the considerations which have been very forcibly borne in upon me during that period.

In the first place I would like to look back to the original cause for which we went to war. We went to war–I mean of course we were gone to war with–in connection with the extension of the franchise. We began negotiations with the Boers in order to extend the franchise to the people of the Transvaal. When I say the people of the Transvaal, I mean the whole people of the Transvaal, and not necessarily those who arrived there first. At that time there were nearly two and a half times as many British and non-Dutch as there were Boers, but during the few weeks before the outbreak of the war every train was crowded with British subjects who were endeavouring to escape from the approaching conflict, and so it was that the Uitlanders were scattered all over the world. It seems to me that when the war is over we ought not to forget the original object with which we undertook the negotiations which led to the war. If I may lay down anything I would ask the House to establish the principle that they ought not to extend any representative institutions to the people of the Transvaal until such time as the population has regained its ordinary level. What could be more dangerous, ridiculous or futile, than to throw the responsible government of a ruined country on that remnant of the population, that particular section of the population, which is actively hostile to the fundamental institutions of the State? I think there ought to be no doubt and no difference of opinion on the point that between the firing of the last shot and the casting of the first vote there must be an appreciable interval that must be filled by a government of some kind or another.

I invite the House to consider which form of government–civil government or military government–is most likely to be conducive to the restoration of the banished prosperity of the country and most likely to encourage the return of the population now scattered far and wide. I understand that there are hon. Members who are in hopes that representative institutions may directly follow military government, but I think they cannot realise thoroughly how very irksome such military government is. I have the greatest respect for British officers, and when I hear them attacked, as some hon. Members have done in their speeches, it makes me very sorry, and very angry too. Although I regard British officers in the field of war, and in dealing with native races, as the best officers in the world, I do not believe that either their training or their habits of thought qualify them to exercise arbitrary authority over civil populations of European race. I have often myself been very much ashamed to see respectable old Boer farmers–the Boer is a curious combination of the squire and the peasant, and under the rough coat of the farmer there are very often to be found the instincts of the squire–I have been ashamed to see such men ordered about peremptorily by young subaltern officers, as if they were private soldiers. I do not hesitate to say that as long as you have anything like direct military government there will be no revival of trade, no return of the Uitlander population, no influx of immigrants from other parts of the world–nothing but despair and discontent on the part of the Boer population, and growing resentment on the part of our own British settlers. If there was a system of civil government on the other hand, which I think we have an absolute moral right to establish if only from the fact that this country through the Imperial Exchequer will have to provide the money–if you had a civil government under such an administrator as Sir Alfred Milner–[Cries of "Hear, hear," and "Oh"]–it is not for me to eulogise that distinguished administrator, I am sure he enjoys the confidence of the whole of the Conservative party, and there are a great many Members on the other side of the House who do not find it convenient in their own minds to disregard Sir Alfred Milner's deliberate opinion on South African affairs. As soon as it is known that there is in the Transvaal a government under which property and liberty are secure, so soon as it is known that in these countries one can live freely and safely, there would be a rush of immigrants from all parts of the world to develop the country and to profit by the great revival of trade which usually follows war of all kinds. If I may judge by my own experience there are many Members of this House who have received letters from their constituents asking whether it was advisable to go out to South Africa. When this policy of immigration is well advanced we shall again have the great majority of the people of the Transvaal firmly attached and devoted to the Imperial connection, and when you can extend representative institutions to them you will find them reposing securely upon the broad basis of the consent of the governed, while the rights of the minority will be effectively protected and preserved by the tactful and judicious intervention of the Imperial authority. May I say that it was this prospect of a loyal and Anglicised Transvaal turning of the scale in our favour in South Africa, which must have been the original "good hope" from which the Cape has taken its name.

It is not for me to criticise the proposals which come from such a distinguished authority as the Leader of the Opposition, but I find it impossible not to say that in comparing these two alternative plans one with the other I must proclaim my strong preference for the course His Majesty's Government propose to adopt. I pass now from the question of the ultimate settlement of the two late Republics to the immediate necessities of the situation. What ought to be the present policy of the Government? I take it that there is a pretty general consensus of opinion in this House that it ought to be to make it easy and honourable for the Boers to surrender, and painful and perilous for them to continue in the field. Let the Government proceed on both those lines concurrently and at full speed. I sympathise very heartily with my hon. friend the senior Member for Oldham, who, in a speech delivered last year, showed great anxiety that everything should be done to make the Boers understand exactly what terms were offered to them, and I earnestly hope that the right hon. Gentleman the Colonial Secretary will leave nothing undone to bring home to those brave and unhappy men who are fighting in the field that whenever they are prepared to recognise that their small independence must be merged in the larger liberties of the British Empire, there will be a full guarantee for the security of their property and religion, an assurance of equal rights, a promise of representative institutions, and last of all, but not least of all, what the British Army would most readily accord to a brave and enduring foe–all the honours of war. I hope the right hon. Gentleman will not allow himself to be discouraged by any rebuffs which his envoys may meet with, but will persevere in endeavouring to bring before these people the conditions on which at any moment they may obtain peace and the friendship of Great Britain. Of course, we can only promise, and it rests with the Boers whether they will accept our conditions. They may refuse the generous terms offered them, and stand or fall by their old cry, "Death or independence!" [Nationalist cheers.] I do not see anything to rejoice at in that prospect, because if it be so, the war will enter upon a very sad and gloomy phase. If the Boers remain deaf to the voice of reason, and blind to the hand of friendship, if they refuse all overtures and disdain all terms, then, while we cannot help admiring their determination and endurance, we can only hope that our own race, in the pursuit of what they feel to be a righteous cause, will show determination as strong and endurance as lasting. It is wonderful that hon. Members who form the Irish party should find it in their hearts to speak and act as they do in regard to a war in which so much has been accomplished by the courage, the sacrifices, and, above all, by the military capacity of Irishmen. There is a practical reason, which I trust hon. Members will not think it presumptuous in me to bring to their notice, is that they would be well advised cordially to co-operate with His Majesty's Government in bringing the war to a speedy conclusion, because they must know that no Irish question or agitation can possibly take any hold on the imagination of the people of Great Britain so long as all our thoughts are with the soldiers who are fighting in South Africa.

What are the military measures we ought to take? I have no doubt that other opportunities will be presented to the House to discuss them, but so far as I have been able to understand the whispers I have heard in the air there are, on the whole, considerable signs of possible improvement in the South African situation. There are appearances that the Boers are weakening, and that the desperate and feverish efforts they have made so long cannot be indefinitely sustained. If that be so, now is the time for the Government and the Army to redouble their efforts. It is incumbent on Members like myself, who represent large working class constituencies, to bring home to the Government the fact that the country does not want to count the cost of the war until it is won. I think we all rejoiced to see the announcement in the papers that 30,000 more mounted men were being despatched to South Africa. I cannot help noticing with intense satisfaction that, not content with sending large numbers of men, the Secretary of State for War has found some excellent Indian officers, prominent among whom is Sir Bindon Blood, who will go out to South Africa and bring their knowledge of guerilla warfare on the Indian frontier to bear on the peculiar kind of warfare–I will not call it guerilla warfare–now going on in South Africa. I shall always indulge the hope that, great as these preparations are, they will not be all, and that some fine afternoon the Secretary of State for War will come down to the House with a brand-new scheme, not only for sending all the reinforcements necessary for keeping the Army up to a fixed standard of 250,000 men, in spite of the losses by battle and disease, but also for increasing it by a regular monthly quota of 2,000 or 3,000 men, so that the Boers will be compelled, with ever-diminishing resources, to make head against ever increasing difficulties, and will not only be exposed to the beating of the waves, but to the force of the rising tide.

Some hon. Members have seen fit, either in this place or elsewhere, to stigmatise this war as a war of greed. I regret that I feel bound to repudiate that pleasant suggestion. If there were persons who rejoiced in this war, and went out with hopes of excitement or the lust of conflict, they have had enough and more than enough to-day. If, as the hon. Member for Northampton has several times suggested, certain capitalists spent money in bringing on this war in the hope that it would increase the value of their mining properties, they know now that they made an uncommonly bad bargain. With the mass of the nation, with the whole people of the country, this war from beginning to end has only been a war of duty. They believe, and they have shown in the most remarkable manner that they believe, that His Majesty's Government and the Colonial Secretary have throughout been actuated by the same high and patriotic motives. They know that no other inspiration could sustain and animate the Regulars and Volunteers, who through all these hard months have had to bear the brunt of the public contention. They may indeed have to regret, as I myself have, the loss of a great many good friends in the war. We cannot help feeling sorry for many of the incidents of the war, but for all that I do not find it possible on reflection to accuse the general policy which led to the war, we have no cause to be ashamed of anything that has passed during the war, nor have we any right to be doleful or lugubrious. I think if any hon. Members are feeling unhappy about the state of affairs in South Africa I would recommend them a receipt from which I myself derived much exhilaration. Let them look to the other great dependencies and colonies of the British Empire and see what the effect of the war has been there. Whatever we may have lost in doubtful friends in Cape Colony we have gained ten times, or perhaps twenty times, over in Canada and Australia, where the people–down to the humblest farmer in the most distant provinces–have by their effective participation in the conflict been able to realise, as they never could realise before, that they belong to the Empire, and that the Empire belongs to them. I cannot sit down without saying how very grateful I am for the kindness and patience with which the House has heard me, and which have been extended to me, I well know, not on my own account, but because of a certain splendid memory which many hon. Members still preserve.

ARMY REFORM

May 13, 1901

House of Commons

The Secretary of State for War, William St. George Brodrick, had introduced a scheme for Army Reform which involved the creation of six army corps–three regular and three composed of militia and volunteers. The additional expenditure would have been £3 million, bringing the Army Estimates to just under £30 million.

Churchill was already demonstrating signs of restlessness with the Government. "There is a good deal of dissatisfaction in the Party, and a shocking lack of cohesion," he wrote to his mother on March 23 (a month after he had taken his seat in Parliament). "The Government is not very strong . . . the whole Treasury Bench appear to me to be sleepy and exhausted and played out" (Randolph S. Churchill, Winston S. Churchill, *Companion Volume II, Part I, 48-49).*

On April 23 Churchill gave notice of an amendment to a motion proposed by Brodrick which was, in effect, a censure of the Army scheme. On the same day he spoke at Liverpool, in which he declared that "any danger that comes to Britain would not be on land; it would come on the sea."

Churchill reiterated his Liverpool speech in Oxford on April 25, and in letters to The Times *on April 30 and May 2. On May 13, in a crowded House of Commons, he delivered an assault on Brodrick which, as he later wrote, "marked a definitive divergence of thought and sympathy from all those who thronged the benches around me." The speech had been meticulously prepared and learned by heart, and Churchill had sent the text in advance to* The Morning Post. *It was a dangerous move, as there was no guarantee that he would be called by the Speaker. The speech was a devastating indictment of the Government and an astonishing performance for a man of twenty-seven years.*

[Extract] . . . I wish to complain very respectfully, but most urgently, that the Army Estimates involved by the scheme lately explained by the Secretary of State for War are much too high, and ought to be reduced, if not this year, certainly at the conclusion of the South African campaign. I regard it as a grave mistake in Imperial policy to spend thirty millions a year on the Army. I hold that the continued increase in Army expenditure cannot be viewed by supporters of the Government without the greatest alarm and apprehension, and by Members who represent working class constituencies without extreme dislike.

I desire to urge considerations of economy on His Majesty's Government, and as a practical step that the number of soldiers which they propose to keep ready for expeditionary purposes should be substantially reduced. First of all I exclude altogether from this discussion the cost of the South African War. Once you are so unfortunate as to be drawn into a war, no price is too great to pay for an early and victorious peace. All economy of soldiers or supplies is the worst extravagance in war. I am concerned only with the Estimates for the ordinary service of the year, which are increasing at such a rate that it is impossible to view them without alarm. Does the House realise what British expenditure on armaments amounts to? See how our Army Estimates have grown–seventeen millions in 1894, eighteen in 1897, nineteen in 1899, twenty-four in 1900, and finally in the present year no less than twenty-nine millions eight hundred thousand. Indeed we are moving rapidly, but in what direction? Sir, I see in this accelerating increase the momentum of a falling body and a downward course. I do not wish to reproach the Secretary of State for War for the enormous Estimates now presented. He is not to blame. The Secretary of State for War does not usually direct, or even powerfully influence, the policy of a Government. He is concerned with his own Department, and it is his business to get all he can for that Department. I must say the right hon. Gentleman appears to have done his work remarkably well. Indeed, if the capacity of a War Minister may be measured in any way by the amount of money he can obtain from his colleagues for military purposes, the right hon. Gentleman will most certainly go down to history as the greatest War Minister this country has ever had. I think this House ought to take a wider view of our Imperial responsibilities than is perhaps possible from the windows of the War Office.

If I might be allowed to revive a half-forgotten episode–it is half-forgotten because it has passed into that period of twilight which intervenes between the bright glare of newspaper controversy and the calm rays of the lamp of history–I would recall that once on a time a Conservative and Unionist Administration came into power supported by a large majority, nearly as powerful, and much more cohesive, than that which now supports His Majesty's Government, and when the time came round to consider the Estimates the usual struggle took place between the great spending Departments and the Treasury. I say "usual"; at least it used to be so, I do not know whether it is so now. The Government of the day threw their weight on the side of the great spending Departments, and the Chancellor of the Exchequer resigned. The controversy was bitter, the struggle uncertain, but in the end the Government triumphed, and the Chancellor of the Exchequer went down for ever, and with him, as it now seems, there fell also the cause of retrenchment and economy, so that the very memory thereof seems to have perished, and the words themselves have a curiously old-fashioned ring about them. I suppose that was a lesson which Chancellors of the Exchequer were not likely to forget in a hurry. I should like, if I might be permitted, to read the passage, which appears extremely relevant to the question now before the House. Writing from the Carlton Club on the 22nd of December, 1886, the Chancellor of the Exchequer, in resigning his office, wrote to Lord Salisbury, who had pointed out the desperate state of Europe and the possibilities of immediate war, very much in the same way as he has done recently. The Chancellor of the Exchequer replied as follows–

> The great question of public expenditure is not so technical or departmental as might be supposed by a superficial critic. Foreign policy and free expenditure upon armaments act and react upon one another.

That has been said before in this debate, and it is what the Chief Secretary for Ireland called a hackneyed tag. I think, with as much reason, you might also call the Ten Commandments a hackneyed tag.

> A wise foreign policy will extricate England from Continental struggles and keep her outside of German, Russian, French, or Austrian disputes. I have for some time observed a tendency in the Government attitude to pursue a different line of action, which I have not been able to modify or check. This tendency is certain to be accentuated if large Estimates are presented to and voted by Parliament. The possession of a very sharp sword offers a temptation which becomes irresistible to demonstrate the efficiency of the weapon in a practical manner. I remember the vulnerable and scattered character of the Empire, the universality of our commerce, the peaceful tendencies of our democratic electorate, the hard times, the pressure of competition, and the high taxation now imposed: and with these facts vividly before me I decline to be a party to encouraging the military and militant circle of the War Office and Admiralty to join in the high and desperate stakes which other nations seem to be forced to risk.

Wise words, Sir, stand the test of time, and I am very glad the House has allowed me, after an interval of fifteen years, to lift again the tattered flag of retrenchment and economy. But what was the amount of the annual Estimates on which this desperate battle was fought? It may be difficult for the House to realise it, though it is within the memory of so many hon. Members. "The Estimates for the year," said the Chancellor of the Exchequer, in resigning, "for the two services amount to no less than £31,000,000, and I cannot consent to that." What are the Estimates we are asked to vote now? We are now asked to vote, quite irrespective of the drain of a costly war still in progress, something more than fifty-nine millions for the ordinary service of the year.

This incident which I have been bringing to the mind of the House did not happen a century ago. It is quite recent history. The Leader of the House was already a famous Minister, the present Chancellor had already been Leader of the House, Lord Salisbury was already Prime Minister, when thirty-one millions was considered by the Treasury a demand which ought to be resisted tooth and nail. What has happened in the meanwhile to explain this astonishing increase? Has the wealth of the country doubled? Has the population of the Empire doubled? Have the armies of Europe doubled? Is the commercial competition of foreign nations so much reduced? Are we become the undisputed master in the markets of the world? Is there no poverty at home? Has the English Channel dried up, and are we no longer an island? Is the revenue so easily raised that we do not know how to spend it? Are the Treasury buildings pulled down, and all our financiers fled? What has happened to explain this extraordinary change? During the few weeks I have been a Member of this House I have heard hon. Members advocate many causes, but no voice is raised in the cause of economy. The Financial Secretary to the War Office, who above all should keep some eye on the purse strings, speaking the other night at some dinner, boasted that he was not animated by any niggardly spirit of economy. Not one voice is raised for reduced expenditure and lightening the public burden, if I may except, in order to be quite correct, the protests raised and the cries for economy from the Irish benches—economy of money, not economy of time—and even through the Irish protests for economy, I am sorry to say, there ran the melancholy dirge, "and how much is Ireland going to get out of it?" How can this tendency to extravagant expenditure be checked? The Opposition can do nothing. Of course, we shall outvote them. The House has no control whatever over Supply. The Treasury can do nothing against the great spending Departments, and in view of the fate that befell the last Chancellor of the Exchequer, who was obdurate, can we wonder that the present distinguished occupant of that office has been compelled to bow before the storm? The Chancellor of the Exchequer gave an extraordinary reason for not objecting to, but supporting, this military expenditure. He said it had been demanded, that it was popular. Expenditure always is popular; the only unpopular part about it is the raising of the money to pay the expenditure. But if that is an extraordinary reason, it is nothing to that put forward by my right hon. friend to-night, who asked pathetically, "What are we to do with our generals?" When they come home from South Africa with no more worlds to conquer they must keep their hands in, and they must be provided with an army, even if it does cost thirty millions a year, to enable them to keep their hands in, and to save them from getting out of practice. I am, I know, a very young man, but I confess I never heard anything like that before. I had always been led to believe that the generals existed for the Army, and not the Army for the generals. The phrase "happy-go-lucky self-indulgence," which was used by my hon. friend, seems to me to come in very appropriately somewhere about here. My right hon. friend is content to arm me with a blunderbuss. Well, a blunderbuss is a traditional weapon with which the British householder defends himself from those who seek to plunder him. Though it is a very antiquated and obsolete weapon, yet at close quarters, at about the range at which my right hon. friend is sitting now, it has been found very effective. I stand here to plead the cause of economy. I think it is about time that a voice was heard from this side of the House pleading that unpopular cause; that someone not on the bench opposite, but a Conservative by tradition, whose fortunes are linked indissolubly to the Tory party, who knows something of the majesty and power of Britain beyond the seas, upon whom rests no taint of cosmopolitanism, should stand forward and say what he can to protest against the policy of daily increasing the public burden. If such a one is to stand forward in such a cause, then, I say it humbly, but with I hope becoming pride, no one has a better right than I have, for this is a cause I have inherited, and a cause for which the late Lord Randolph Churchill made the greatest sacrifice of any Minister of modern times. Now, bearing all that in mind, I come to the scheme of the Secretary of State. I do not propose to consider that scheme in detail, that would be an interminable labour. When the right hon. Gentleman introduced the scheme–in a speech of surpassing clearness–it looked genuine, but in the weeks that have passed since he disclosed it to the House it has been sadly knocked about, crushed in the press, and exploded in the magazines, and has excited nothing but doubt in the country. The number of Amendments on the Paper shows the feeling of the House, and I know what some of the soldiers say about it. I do not feel equal to repeating their expressions here–but I shall be delighted to inform any hon. Member desiring information privately. It is no good mincing matters. This is not the best scheme that could be devised. I do not say that it does not contain any wise and ingenious provisions, nor that it will not give strength to the Army. Material strength is expected even in this country to follow great expenditure of money. But if the truth must be told, although this scheme involves an expenditure of nearly £30,000,000 a year, with further increases in prospect, it nevertheless leaves most of the great questions connected with Army reform almost entirely untouched. But what could be expected? The ordinary duties of a Minister are, I have always understood, sufficiently arduous. The War Office is a particularly hard job even in peace time. But we are at war. Not only has the Secretary of State to defend in this House every act of military policy big or little, but he has also to see–I hope it will not escape his attention–that an Army of more than two hundred thousand men actively engaged with the enemy lacks nothing that wealth or science can produce. Now that ought to be enough for the energy even of the right hon. Gentleman. Why, Sir, the labours of Hercules are nothing to it. But all this is not enough for the insatiable industry of the right hon. Gentleman. He must, forsooth, rearrange the internal mechanism of the War Office. He must take his engines to pieces while the ship is beating up under full steam against the gale. That is not all. No; in the few moments of leisure that fall to a public man in this country he must thoroughly reorganise and reform the whole system of the Army. Who can wonder that he has increased the quantity of his output only to the detriment of the quality, as happens to literary men? I had put down an Amendment, which it will not be in order now to move, which to my mind possesses advantages over that we are now discussing. In the first place, it removed the question from the party sphere in which it now lies, and in which it must now be decided. In the second place, it provided the Government with a means of retreat from the very uncomfortable position in which they have managed to get themselves. I do not expect hon. members on this side will agree with me, and I recognise that I am putting considerable strain upon their forbearance by the view I take of this matter, but I ask them for their indulgence while I state my view. My view is that we should have gone on with ordinary reforms which do not involve a large increase of expenditure, either of money or men, the better selection and promotion of officers, a question which the Secretary of State has shown himself willing to carry out with unflinching courage, the provision of better arms and the gradual adoption of new military material and weapons. What is called in *The Times* this morning the "grandiose"–that is the word for which I have been looking–the grandiose portion of the scheme should be postponed until such time as the South African war has assumed its true proportions in our eyes, and the men now in South Africa best qualified to do so have come home to give their attention to the reorganisation of the Army, and until those managing the War Office are relieved from the high pressure at which they are now working. That is a tale that has not been unfolded, and this question is now before the House on party lines. I confess I am unable to support the resolution of the Government; but the Amendment of the Leader of the Opposition does not attract me any more. His differences are differences of detail, not of principle. My objections are objections of principle. I hold it is unwise to have no regard to the fact that in this reform we are diverting national resources from their proper channels of development. It may be argued that if other nations increase their armed force so must we. If you look into the tangled mass of figures on this subject you will find that while other nations during the last fifteen years have been increasing their navies we have been increasing our expenditure on our Army, which is not after all our most important weapon. I am pleading the cause of economy first of all. But I have got two strings to my bow, or perhaps I should say two barrels to my blunderbuss. Failing economy, let us have wise expenditure. My contention is that we are spending too much money on armaments, and so may impair our industries; but that if the money has to be spent, then it would be better to spend it on the Fleet than on the Army. Of course we must have an Army, not only as a training school for our garrisons abroad, but because it would be unhealthy, and even immoral, for the people of Great Britain to live sleek, timid, and secure, protected by a circle of ironclad ships. It would have been a pleasant task to examine some of the wise and ingenious provisions which the scheme of the Secretary of State for War contains. But I have assumed a more melancholy duty to-night, one, perhaps, which would be more fittingly discharged by some hon. Member on the other side of the House. I contend that to spend thirty millions a year on the British Army is an unwise policy, against which the House must protest. Sir, at the last election I placarded "Army Reform" as large as anyone. I am pledged to the hilt to Army reform. But what is Army reform? I take it to be one of two things. Either it means the same efficiency at a reduced cost, or increased efficiency for the same cost. Perhaps it might mean greatly increased efficiency for a slightly increased cost. But the one thing it certainly does not mean is a larger number of Regular soldiers. That is not Army reform, but Army increase. In the last four years the present Ministers have added no fewer than fifty-seven thousand men to the Regular standing Army. A further increase–disguised in various ways–is contemplated in the present scheme. Sir, it is against this Army increase that I protest, first in the interests of economy, secondly in the interests of the Fleet. I complain of the increase in Regular soldiers, and particularly of the provision of the three army corps which are to be kept ready for expeditionary purposes. I contend that they ought to be reduced by two army corps, on the ground that one is quite enough to fight savages, and three are not enough even to begin to fight Europeans. I hope the House will let me elaborate this. The enormous and varied frontiers of the Empire, and our many points of contact with barbarous peoples, will surely in the future, as in the past, draw us into frequent little wars. Our military system must therefore be adapted for dealing with these minor emergencies smoothly and conveniently. But we must not expect to meet the great civilised Powers in this easy fashion. We must not regard war with a modern Power as a kind of game in which we may take a hand, and with good luck and good management may play adroitly for an evening and come safe home with our winnings. It is not that, and I rejoice that it cannot be that. A European war cannot be anything but a cruel, heartrending struggle, which, if we are ever to enjoy the bitter fruits of victory, must demand, perhaps for several years, the whole manhood of the nation, the entire suspension of peaceful industries, and the concentrating to one end of every vital energy in the community. I have frequently been astonished since I have been in this House to hear with what composure and how glibly Members, and even Ministers, talk of a European war. I will not expatiate on the horrors of war, but there has been a great change which the House should not omit to notice. In former days, when wars arose from individual causes, from the policy of a Minister or the passion of a King, when they were fought by small regular armies of professional soldiers, and when their course was retarded by the difficulties of communication and supply, and often suspended by the winter season, it was possible to limit the liabilities of the combatants. But now, when mighty populations are impelled on each other, each individual severally embittered and inflamed–when the resources of science and civilisation sweep away everything that might mitigate their fury, a European war can only end in the ruin of the vanquished and the scarcely less fatal commercial dislocation and exhaustion of the conquerors. Democracy is more vindictive than Cabinets. The wars of peoples will be more terrible than those of kings. "Why, then," it may be said, "surely we must neglect nothing to make ourselves secure. Let us vote this thirty millions without more ado." If this vast expenditure on the Army were going to make us absolutely secure–much though I hate unproductive expenditure–I would not complain. But it will do no such thing. The Secretary for War knows–none better than he–that it will not make us secure, and that if we went to war with any great Power his three army corps would scarcely serve as a vanguard. If we are hated, they will not make us loved. They are a broken reed to trust to. If we are in danger, they will not make us safe. They are enough to irritate; they are not enough to overawe. They cannot make us invulnerable, but they may very likely make us venturesome. A prudent man insures his house against fire. We are often told this military expenditure is an insurance premium. Well, there is no doubt about the premium; we are paying that all right. But I would respectfully remind the House that the premium has been put up during the last five years, and is in fact so high now that, so far as I can calculate, in order to make our insurance policy a good bargain we should have to have a war equal to the Boer war every fifteen years. But do we get the insurance? In putting our trust in an army are we not investing in a shaky concern—in a firm that could not meet its obligations when called on? It may be said that it is not a mere question of pounds, shillings, and pence, but that it is a question of the honour and security of the Empire. I do not agree. The honour and security of the British Empire do not depend, and can never depend, on the British Army. The Admiralty is the only Office strong enough to insure the British Empire; and it can only be strong enough to do so because it has hitherto enjoyed the preferential monopoly of the sea. Moreover, the provision of these three army corps, ready to embark and attack anybody anywhere, is undoubtedly most provocative to the other Powers. No other nation makes, or has ever made, such a provision. And what of its effect on us? It is quite true that foreign nations possess gigantic armies and have lived at peace for thirty years. Foreign nations know what war is. There is scarcely a capital in Europe which has not been taken in the last one hundred years, and it is the lively realisation of the awful consequences of war which maintains the peace of Europe. We do not know what war is. We have had a glimpse of it in South Africa. Even in miniature it is hideous and appalling; but, for all our experience, war to us does not mean what it means to the Frenchman, or the German, or the Austrian. Are we not arming ourselves with their weapons without being under their restraints? What I fear is that these three costly and beautiful army corps, which are to be kept ready—almost at a moment's notice—for foreign war will develop in the country, if they need developing, feelings of pride and power, which will not only be founded in actual military superiority, but only on the appearance of it. And in these days, when popular newspapers, appealing with authority to countless readers, are prepared almost every morning to urge us into war against one or other—and sometimes several—of the Great Powers of the earth, surely we ought not to make it seem so easy, and even attractive, to embark on such terrible enterprises, or to think that with the land forces at our disposal we may safely intermeddle in the European game? What is our weapon, then? The only weapon with which we can expect to cope with great nations is the Navy. This is what the Chief Secretary to the Lord Lieutenant calls "trust to luck and the Navy" policy. I confess I do trust the Navy. This new distrust of the Navy, a kind of shrinking from our natural element, the blue water on which we have ruled so long, is the most painful symptom of the military hydrophobia with which we are afflicted. Without a supreme Navy, whatever military arrangements we may make, whether for foreign expeditions or home defence, must be utterly vain and futile. With such a Navy we may hold any antagonist at arm's length and feed ourselves in the meantime, until, if we find it necessary, we can turn every city in the country into an arsenal, and the whole male population into an army. Sir, the superiority of the Navy is vital to our national existence. That has been said before. No one will deny that or thank me for repeating the obvious. Yet this tremendous Army expenditure directly challenges the principle, and those who advocate it are false to the principle they so loudly proclaim. For the main reason that enables us to maintain the finest Navy in the world is that whereas every European Power has to support a vast Army first of all, we in this fortunate, happy island, relieved by our insular position of a double burden, may turn our undivided efforts and attention to the Fleet. Why should we sacrifice a game in which we are sure to win to play a game in which we are bound to lose? For the same rule most certainly has a converse application, and just as foreign Powers by reason of their pressing land responsibilities must be inferior to us at sea, so we, whatever our effort, whatever our expenditure, by reason of our paramount sea responsibilities must be inferior to them on land. And surely to adopt the double policy of equal effort both on Army and Navy, spending thirty millions on each, is to combine the disadvantages and dangers of all courses without the advantages or security of any, and to run the risk of crashing to the ground between two stools, with a Navy uselessly weak and an Army uselessly strong. We are told we have "commitments"–not a very cheerful expression–in three continents, and that it is in consequence of these "commitments" that we must keep three army corps ready for immediate expeditionary purposes. On what principle are there to be three rather than two or eight? I had hoped that the formulation of some definite principle governing our military needs would be a prominent feature of any scheme of Army reform submitted to the nation. I suppose the principle on which the army corps have been selected is, one continent one army corps. Well, Sir, I should like to look into that. In the first place there is Asia. What is our danger there? Of course, it is an Anglo-Russian war on the frontier of India. But if anyone takes Lord Salisbury's advice–and sometimes he gives very good advice–to use large scale maps of Central Asia, they will see that any Russian enterprise against India would either have to be made with a small force, in which case our Indian Army would be sufficient to resist it, or else railways would have to be built, just as Lord Kitchener had to build a railway to Khartoum, to feed the great invading forces in the barren lands through which they must march, in which case we should have plenty of time to levy and train as many British troops as we might think fit. Then we have a "commitment" in North America–a "commitment" which is growing more able to take care of itself every day–not a "commitment" about which we need feel much anxiety. Sir, we must not, however, shrink from the responsibility. Of course, the danger which might assail us in this quarter of the globe would only be a war with the great friendly commercial nation to the southward. Evil would be the counsellors, dark would be the day when we embarked on that most foolish, futile, and fatal of all wars–a war with the United States. But if such a fit of madness should attack the Anglo-Saxon family, then I say both nations, having long enjoyed a glorious immunity from the curse of militarism, would be similarly placed, and no decisive events could be looked for until the war had been in progress for a year or two and enormous armies had been raised by both sides, and in this war, as in any other war of this kind, your three army corps would be merely the first few drops of the thunder shower. We shall be told "the lesson of the South African War must not be forgotten." "We must profit by our experience in South Africa, and be prepared next time for all eventualities." The present scheme of Army increase is justified mainly on the ground of our experience in South Africa. "We must be ready next time," says "the man in the street." Not for worlds would I speak disrespectfully of "the man in the street"; but, Sir, in the first place, I cannot help hoping "next time" may be a long way off. I trust the Government do not contemplate fighting these wars in South Africa septennially. I trust they will finish this one in such a style that future recurrence will be utterly impossible, and that an end will be made once and for all of dangers from within that continent. Dangers from without can never exist in that quarter so long as we preserve our naval supremacy. Once that is lost, such dangers would be dwarfed by greater catastrophes at home. But I will not look only to the future. I have no hesitation in asserting that even if this scheme had been carried into effect five years ago, and we had had our three expeditionary army corps ready for foreign service in October, 1899, even then the course of the South African War would not have been materially different. You would have had your three army corps ready, but would the possession of those three army corps have told the Intelligence officers and the general staff, and the Committee of National Defence that more than one army corps was needed? And even if they had advised that three army corps should be sent forthwith, that would not have been enough, for, as we know to our cost, not three army corps were needed, but six. See what inadequate security this scheme provides—if we are to embark on land enterprises against civilised peoples. The Boers were the smallest of all civilised nations. Yet this precious Army scheme, in spite of the thirty millions a year it is to cost, does not provide half the troops needed to conquer them; and if the scheme were carried into effect—as many people think it cannot be carried into effect—and the South African War were to begin over again, you would again have to call on Volunteers, Yeomanry, and Militia to alter their original contract with the State and serve beyond the seas. Yes, against this, the smallest of all civilised nations, we should have to fall back in these emergencies on the power of unrestricted sea communication, the wealth of a commercial country, and the patriotic and warlike impulses of a people not wearied of the military yoke.

The armies of Europe are bigger than those of the Boers, and cheaper than our own. France, in this present year, for an expenditure of twenty-eight millions, can mobilise twenty army corps. Germany, for twenty-six millions, gets twenty-two army corps. Russia, for thirty-two millions, can set on foot, including twenty-three regular army corps, a total force estimated at over three millions of men. And what can Great Britain do? Taught by the experience of the South African War, rich in her commerce and the generosity of her people, guided by the unfailing instinct of the War Office, Great Britain would be defended, after this scheme has been carried into effect, by no fewer than three trained army corps and three partly trained army corps; and for this she must pay two millions a year more than France, four millions a year more than Germany, and within two millions of the total cost of the whole great Russian army. But in spite of every explanatory circumstance, after every allowance has been made, one great truth glows and glares in our faces, veil it how we may: standing armies, which abound on the European continent, are not indigenous to the British soil; they do not flourish in our climate, they are not suited to our national character, and though with artificial care and at a huge and disproportionate cost we may cultivate and preserve them, they will after all only be poor, stunted, sickly plants of foreign origin. The Empire which has grown up around these islands is essentially commercial and marine. The whole course of our history, the geography of the country, all the evidences of the present situation, proclaim beyond a doubt that our power and prosperity alike and together depend on the economic command of markets and the naval command of the sea; and from the highest sentimental reasons, not less than from the most ordinary practical considerations, we must avoid a servile imitation of the clanking military empires of the European continent, by which we cannot obtain the military predominance and security which is desired, but only impair and vitiate the natural sources of our strength and vigour. There is a higher reason still. There is a moral force—the Divine foundation of earthly power—which, as the human race advances, will more and more strengthen and protect those who enjoy it; which would have protected the Boers better than all their cannon and brave commandos if instead of being ignorant, aggressive, and corrupt, they had enjoyed that high moral reputation which protected us in the dark days of the war from European interference—for, in spite of every calumny and lie uttered or printed, the truth comes to the top, and it is known alike by peoples and by rulers that on the whole British influence is healthy and kindly, and makes for the general happiness and welfare of mankind. And we shall make a fatal bargain if we allow the moral force which this country has so long exerted to become diminished, or perhaps even destroyed for the sake of the costly, trumpery, dangerous military playthings on which the Secretary of State for War has set his heart.

FREE TRADE

May 21, 1903

Hoxton

Since his election, Churchill had been a very articulate and active critic of the Government, and it was evident that if he followed this course there was bound to be a rupture between himself and his Party. In May 1903 the decisive moment came.

In the 1902 Budget, the Chancellor of the Exchequer, Sir Michael Hicks-Beach, introduced a registration duty on imported corn, grain, flour and meal. Ministers emphasised that this was not the first stage of a Protectionist policy, but the apprehensions of Free Traders in both Parties were not wholly quieted. At the London Colonial Conference in July 1902, the subject of Imperial Preference was raised by the Prime Minister of Canada, Sir Wilfred Laurier. Following the end of the war in South Africa, Joseph Chamberlain became obsessed with the preferential tariffs issue. In November 1902, the Cabinet apparently resolved that the corn tax would be maintained, but that preferential remission should be increased for the Empire.

Since the practice of keeping Cabinet minutes was not instituted until December 1916, Ministers had to rely on their memories and on the Prime Minister's private letters to the Sovereign. It was an arrangement which was bound to lead to misunderstandings, a classic example of which occurred in May 1903. Chamberlain asserted that Imperial

Preference had been agreed to in principle; the new Chancellor, C. T. Ritchie, did not accept that view, and the corn taxes were repealed in the 1903 Budget. Thus the stage was set for a vehement clash between the factions of the Conservative Party, and Chamberlain publicly opened the battle on May 15 at Birmingham.

The Government split asunder, despite a series of over-ingenious attempts by Balfour–who had succeeded Salisbury as Prime Minister in July 1902–and the divided Liberals joined ranks.

Churchill, describing himself as "a sober admirer of Free Trade principles," flung himself into the battle. He was advised by his father's old friend and former Treasury official, Sir Francis Mowatt, who also was an ardent Free Trader and one of the founders of the Free Food League to combat the Tariff Reform League. On May 21, at Hoxton, Churchill launched his first counter-attack on Chamberlain.

There are some very important members of the party who have quarrelled with the Government for repealing the corn tax. They are wrong, wrong in economics, wrong in their political conceptions, wrong most of all in their estimate of public opinion. And they will fail in their attempt to force the Government to reimpose upon the people the bread tax which they have wisely taken off. I am one of those who thought last year that the Government were right to put the tax on and who now think they were right to take it off.

The most important and interesting of all questions before the public now is the great issue raised by Mr. Chamberlain's speech in favour of preferential tariffs, which might produce results of a revolutionary character in politics and finance. Any definite proposal which comes from a statesman of such undoubted patriotism, whose services have been so eminent, and whose political views are usually so clear and sound, however impracticable or even destructive it might appear at first sight, is a proposal which the Conservative party must consider with respect and the House of Commons must examine with closest attention. Mr. Chamberlain is hardly the man to make such a declaration unless he has a positive plan which he has worked out in principle and in detail, and which he can support by figures and by arguments, and it will need all his most weighty arguments, his most precise calculations, all his courage, and all his oratory to persuade the English people to abandon that system of free trade and cheap food upon which we have thrived so long and under which we have advanced from the depths of poverty and distress to the first position among the nations of the world. The policy which the Unionist party should pursue must be a policy of Imperialism, but not of one-sided Imperialism. It must not only look abroad or only look at home. While we cherish the loyalty and friendship of our colonies, we must not disregard or think of small consequence the very urgent needs of our immense working-class population and the real sources of our national wealth. The far-seeing eye of Lord Beaconsfield, whose memory is still so fresh and vivid, ranges far across the waters to the most distant colonies and possessions of the Crown, but at the same time he does not neglect the great questions of social reform, and first and foremost in his mind he sets the virtue and prosperity of the English people. It would be by following as closely as we might the example of his statecraft, that we should best serve the interests of the party and of the State.

PREFERENTIAL TARIFFS

May 28, 1903

House of Commons

On May 28 the crisis occasioned by Chamberlain's Birmingham speech broke openly in the House of Commons. Churchill spoke immediately after Chamberlain.

The statement of the Colonial Secretary [Mr. Chamberlain] is one of momentous importance and absorbing interest; and I hope the House will not think me presumptuous if I take the earliest opportunity of saying that I heard it with profound regret. I have read attentively the history of the great Home Rule crisis of 1886; and it seems to me that much injury might have been saved the Liberal Party, if all those who viewed the Home Rule policy of Mr. Gladstone with distrust and suspicion had taken the very earliest opportunity after its inception, of protesting against it in the most emphatic manner. Instead of that, they allowed themselves to slip from point to point; and then, when there was no means of retreat, the Party found itself committed to a policy which for twenty years has hung round its neck like a millstone. But I cannot say the system of preferential tariffs which the Colonial Secretary has advocated this afternoon does or ought to inspire the Conservative Party with enthusiasm and still less the measures which are to carry it to success. It is obvious that we cannot discuss this matter now at great length. These are matters which must be dealt with in the prolonged course of what will be the greatest controversy in the history of our country. But apart altogether from the merits of the question there are two considerations which I would most earnestly submit to the Government and the House of Commons. The first is this: you cannot stop, and the Colonial Secretary will not be able to stop if he desires to, at the simple system of preferential tariffs. He will have to fight a fierce battle in which the manufacturers, fair traders, and agricultural protectionists will be his supporters, and it is perfectly evident that their interests will have to be consulted at every stage. The idea of giving a preference to the colonies in matters which we must in any case tax for revenue, has now been extended to a definite proposal for the taxation of foodstuffs, and although it is perfectly clear that this proposal of protective duties on food will please agriculturists, or, at any rate, will please the bulk of them, what about the working man? And thus you are compelled to take a step forward and include old-age pensions in this scheme. The colonies will be pleased, no doubt, and the working classes may be placated by the promise of old-age pensions. The cost must, therefore, principally fall on the manufacturing fair traders, who will have to pay more for labour, and who will, therefore, lose in neutral markets. They will insist on some tangible return, and the only one possible will be an elaborate system of bounties and duties. This move means a change, not only in historic English Parties, but in the conditions of our public life. The old Conservative Party, with its religious convictions and constitutional principles, will disappear, and a new Party will arise like perhaps the Republican Party of the United States of America–rich, materialist, and secular–whose opinions will turn on tariffs, and who will cause the lobbies to be crowded with the touts of protected industries. What is the cause of this change? Never was the wealth of the country greater, or the trade returns higher, or the loyalty of the colonies more pronounced. Is it that we are tired of these good days? There is no popular demand for this departure. I do not know what popular demand or popular movement the Colonial Secretary with his great popularity and persuasive manners may not be able to excite, but at the present moment there is no demand whatever, and not for the last 100 years has a more surprising departure been suggested.

FREE SPEECH AND FREE TRADE

November 11, 1903

Town Hall, Birmingham

Balfour's precarious balancing act in the Cabinet ended in disaster. On September 14 Ritchie and Lord Balfour of Burleigh (Secretary of State for Scotland) were virtually forced to resign; Lord George Hamilton resigned in sympathy on the following day. On September 16 Balfour accepted Chamberlain's resignation, and the announcement of all four resignations was made on September 18. On October 6 the Duke of Devonshire, who still retained extraordinary public confidence, also resigned.

It is still not clear what Balfour's strategy was. In the event, he rid himself of the leading advocates of Free Trade and Protection and also of the two dominant Unionists of the day. If he had anticipated that this would strengthen his position, his calculations were proved wrong. Chamberlain embarked upon a massive national campaign for Imperial Preference, and the Unionist Free Traders eagerly took up the challenge. To the joy of the Liberals, the Unionists disintegrated into two bitterly warring factions, with the young Churchill vehemently arguing the Free Trade course. In Chamberlain-dominated Birmingham, an anti-Chamberlain speech required real courage, as there was the danger of physical assault. During the Boer War Lloyd George had been lucky to escape unharmed from Birmingham Town Hall after such a speech. When the Free Food League insisted on holding a meeting on November 11 at the same site, the municipal authorities were profoundly alarmed. Appeals for public order and the rights of free speech were issued and buttressed by barricades around the Town Hall and the presence of every available policeman. The crowds, although large, were friendly and greeted Churchill and Lord Hugh Cecil without rancor.

I submit the following resolution:–

> That this meeting, while recognising the right of a British Government to propose to Parliament retaliatory duties in special cases, believes that the establishment of a general protective tariff, including the protective

taxation of foodstuffs, would be disintegrating to the Empire, burdensome to the poor, and harmful to the welfare and prosperity of the nation.

Three years have passed since I last had the honour to address a Birmingham audience in this celebrated hall. Three years have gone, and many things have changed in those three years. Sharp divisions have opened between those who were formerly in the closest political agreement. New questions have arisen, and old friends have gone, and some of those who were the loudest in their welcome when I was at Birmingham three years ago are not at all pleased to see me back again tonight. (Laughter.) I regret most deeply and most sincerely all those changes. Whatever might happen, I will always look back with pleasure and affection to my association with the Midland Conservative Club. (Hear, hear.) I remember how proud I was to be elected its president before I had gone into politics at all. I remember how I was re-elected its president for the third time while out in South Africa, on the eve of the advance to the relief of Ladysmith. I do not see all my old friends of the Midland Conservative Club here tonight. Their absence is part of the price which a politician has to pay if he refuses to jump with the jumping cat. (Cheers.)

But I have not come here tonight to say anything bitter or unkind about anybody. (Cheers and cries of "Oh," and a voice: "What about the cat?") On the contrary, I have come to uphold, as far as I can, two great causes, in both of which Birmingham is most profoundly interested, the cause of Free Trade –(cheers),–and a greater cause than that, the cause of free speech. (Cheers.) I desire to submit to the meeting a reasoned argument against the proposed changes. (Interruption and cries of "Chuck him out.") I ask this great assemblage of Englishmen, in a great city in the van of progress and enlightenment, to give me and Lord Hugh Cecil a fair hearing. (Cheers.)

Perhaps you may have heard that the Lord Hugh and myself belong to that notorious body, the Unionist Free Food League. Do you blame us for it?–("No, no," and "Yes.") We are not ashamed of it. We are proud of it. Perhaps it is not quite the best name, I myself would have liked something a little wider, but at any rate anyone can understand what we are aiming at, anyone can understand what is our principle of action. We say–we may be wrong, but this is what we say–that the staple food of the people shall be sold to the merchants of this country as cheaply as the competition of the world can make it, and we say that no private interests shall intervene by twisting the grain of the land so as to replace food artificially and to get immediate profits in their pockets. That is the ground on which we stand; that is the ground on which we are going to fight. (Cheers.) Our opponents, the advocates of change, are perfectly honest about it. Without the food taxes, this great bribe and bait to the landed interest, the whole glittering fabric of Protection comes clattering in ruins to the ground. (Cheers.)

I am not in the least disconcerted when people say that they have had enough of the "clap-trap" about cheap food for the people, and that they are tired of this parrot-cry. It might be clap-trap to the millionaire proprietor of a dozen newspapers–(laughter),–but to the workman's wife who has to make a week's wages balance the week's bills a half-penny up here or a penny up there is not clap-trap at all, but one of the most grim and grinding necessities of life. (Cheers.) Another class of people who have to take this food question seriously are, I notice, the candidates for Parliamentary honours. They speak of cheap food with becoming respect. (Laughter.) It is not clap-trap in Argyllshire or at Rochester–(cheers),–and if cheap food is a parrot-cry at Leamington, then Mr. Alfred Lyttelton is the loudest parrot of them all. (Cheers.)

I ask you to face the question of free imports generally. The Free Trade plan is quite simple. It is that every Englishman has a right to purchase what he lacks whenever and wherever he chooses, without let or hindrance or discouragement by the State. This is the plan which has been followed in this country for sixty years, and whatever might be said, we are not quite ruined yet. (Cheers.) After quoting the returns of exports from and imports to this country, Free-traders, if there are any left–(laughter)–can declare that both these operations of buying and selling are profitable to us. What we sell we sell at a profit for a sufficient return. What we buy we buy because we think that it serves our interest to buy. (Cheers.) I can speak with satisfaction of the increase of imports in the last 15 years, in the period when England has been mainly under the guidance of Lord Salisbury. (Cheers.) It is especially comforting to notice the great increase when we reflect that in the same period our local agricultural production has actually increased, so that the increased importation was all clear again. (Cries of dissent.) I have got all the figures here. I will quote some instances of these increases since 1888 from this Blue-book. We ate in 1901 three million hundred-weight more of bacon and ham than in 1888, three times as much butter, nearly double as much cheese, six times as much cocoa, a thousand million more eggs than in 1888, and double as many potatoes. If the home supply has not diminished and the foreign importation has not increased, what does that prove? (Cries of "Population" and other interruptions.) The population has not gone up in anything like this proportion. (Hear, hear.) It proves that the masses of this country have been able to enjoy year by year a growing wealth of the country, a larger and more generous fare. It proves that the growing wealth of the country, as attested by the income tax return, has not gone merely into the pockets of wealthy investors, but has been broadly shared among the masses of the people, and if the population has had more food they also had more to buy with. (Cheers.)

When this controversy was first opened it was generally admitted by those who brought it forward that the burden of proof rested with them. They had to prove three things–(1) that we were not a prosperous country, (2) that they had a remedy which would make us a prosperous country, (3) that their remedy was a remedy which would be effectively applied.–(And it will.) They had to prove all these things severally and collectively. Failure to prove one of them vitiated their cases. Were they proved? (No) I submit that, on the contrary, they were altogether disproved. (Hear, hear" and cheers.) We are a very prosperous country, but even if we were not, even if Protection were a remedy, then the corruption of our public life, the restriction of our trade, the meddlesomeness of Governments with the course of business, and the disturbance of our existing state of affairs would more than destroy all the advantage which might be gained.

Let us look back a year. Nearly a year ago we finished the war. Only a year ago we were congratulating ourselves on how we had borne its strain, which would have bent the back of any other nation. Do not underrate that strain, consider it well. The war took 250 millions–gone! (Shame.) I supported the war, and will not go back on that. Three hundred thousand men kept at work destroying instead of producing for three years, and many others employed in making khaki and cannon balls and things like those which were not wanted in times of peace, all these thrown with the reservists back on the labour market of the country, the stream of gold from the South African mines absolutely cut off, and never since revived at its full strength–you must not overlook these factors in our commercial position. Have they no influence on the condition of British trade?

Only a year ago Mr. Chamberlain–(cheers and hisses),–speaking in this hall with all the authority which properly belongs to a Minister of the Crown, thought it right to say that such was the wealth of the country that we could, if necessary, fight such another war just as long over again. The organ is playing a very different tune tonight. The triumphal swell of the majestic march has died away, and we have a most lugubrious dirge. The wealth of Britain, which only a year ago was inexhaustible, is now draining away. Those gossamer threads of Empire, pliant as elastic, tense as steel, of which we used to hear, those kindred States that came to help us in our need, those brave Australians and Canadians who marched and fought with us on veldt and kopje in South Africa–all these, we are told, would fall away for ever–(No)–unless Canadian loyalty is purchased at 2s. a quarter. (Cheers.)

I direct your attention not only to the suddenness with which this issue has been raised but to the amazing disparity between the alleged dangerous nature of the disease and the almost petty nature of the remedy. I think we ought to feel more assurance in the foundations of British dominion than to believe that they will be disturbed by a passing gust of wind, or that if they were so disturbed they could be supported by such a puny prop as was proposed. A more rigid examination has been made during the last few months into the state of trade, into the material progress of the country. Neither trouble nor expense has been spared, and the results of the great inquiry are now before us. We take our stand upon those results. We are prepared as Free-traders to be judged by them. I would ask any unprejudiced man to go through the pages and the tables of the Departmental publications for himself. I would ask him, looking at the state of the country, to consider the increase in the income tax, to consider the rise of wages and the fall in prices, the great increase in railway traffic, in the postal service, in the merchant navy, and, above all, in the value and variety and tonnage of our trade which has taken place in the last thirty years. (A voice: Rainfall.)

I have not got a loaf of bread here tonight, but–[Editor's Note: Cries of "Hold it up," and Churchill responded by waving over his head a copy of the Government's Blue-book, saying]: This impartial account of a scientific inquiry which it was fondly hoped would prove a damning indictment of our commercial system is, indeed, its most supreme and overwhelming vindication. (Cheers.) I deny any truth to the allegation that trade in England is bad. On the contrary, the returns of the current year indicate a considerable improvement, particularly in exports. I note Mr. Chamberlain's illustration about the great emporium underselling the little shops. I have the greatest respect for Mr. Chamberlain–(cheers and booing),–but I deny that England is a little shop. (Cheers.) The scale of business in this country exceeds many scores of times the values of the commodities sold here by foreign countries at unremunerative prices. (Cheers.)

I believe Mr. Chamberlain is doing what he is doing because he thinks it best for the Empire and the country. (Cheers.) But what about the motives of some of his supporters? What about those wealthy landowners who jostled one another on his platform? What about those manufacturers and company promoters who are pouring their cheques–in strict secrecy, of course–into Mr. Vince's office? What is their little game? Is it all for the unity of the Empire? (Cries of "No" and interruption.) Is it all for the good of the working man? (Cries of "No.") I notice that [the Chambers of Agriculture] have come to the conclusion that the time has now arrived when something must be done–to raise prices? Oh, no, that would be letting the cat out of the bag, but to strengthen the bonds of Empire. (Laughter.)

The English working classes are better off in every respect than their fellows in protected countries. If, as Mr. Chamberlain said, we are not so happy as other nations which are poorer, it is to social reform rather than Protection, to temperance rather than to tariffs, it is to the sanitary inspector, the schoolmaster, and the minister rather than to the Custom-house official and the tax-gatherer that we must look for a remedy. (Cheers.) To say that Protection means a greater development of wealth is an economic delusion, and to say that Protection means a fairer distribution of wealth is unspeakable humbug. The Democratic party of the United States is composed of the poorest and least fortunate of the people, who have learned by bitter experience that high protective tariffs, although they might increase the profits of capital, are to the poor and the poorest of the poor a cursed engine of robbery and oppression.

Little Englander, I suppose I shall be called. I have seen enough in peace and war of the frontiers of our Empire to know that the British dominion all over the world could not endure for a year, perhaps not for a month, if it was founded upon a material basis. The strength and splendour of our authority is derived not from physical forces, but from moral ascendency, liberty, justice, English tolerance, and English honesty. These are the qualities which have raised in comfort and in character the homely life of our island far above the standards of surrounding nations. It is by these alone that the future, as in the past, we shall remain, under an inviolable circle, the proud possessions of the King. (Cheers.)

FREE TRADE

November 25, 1903

Conservative Club, North Chadderton

For the loyal Unionists of Oldham, Churchill's assaults on the Balfour Government over the Free Trade issue were the last straw. Churchill's case was that he was consistent; he had been elected as a Free Trader and a Free Trader he remained.

One portent of the mounting Unionist irritation with Churchill was the decision of the

Bell Street Conservative Club to refuse Churchill use of their premises for an advertised constituency meeting.
On November 25, Churchill was denied admission to the North Chadderton Conservative Club. The meeting had been advertised, but the hall was locked and in darkness. Churchill addressed the large crowd assembled outside.

I take this opportunity of saying three or four words to you. We are invited to make the most momentous departure in the policy of this country that any nation has ever been asked to make. If it turns out badly it means ruin to our greatest industries, and poverty and distress in the homes of the working classes; it means vast fortunes for millionaires; it means the corruption of the representative institutions–the Parliamentary institutions–of this country. We are asked to make this great departure, and after the most inadequate inquiry fair and free discussion is refused.–(Cries of "Shame.") I do not intend to accept the decisions of any caucus. I was elected as member for Oldham–(cheers),–and I am not going to depart from those principles of Free Trade on which I was elected. There are plenty of halls in Oldham where meetings can be held, and meetings shall be held.–(Cheers.) Mr. Hilton is not Oldham, though he may think so. Do not imagine for one moment that I have embarked upon this fight without intending to see it through.–(Cheers.) If my conduct is seriously challenged I shall not hesitate to appeal to the working classes of Oldham, and I am perfectly certain that the vast majority of the electors are absolutely true to the great cause of Free Trade.–(Cheers.)

THE PARLIAMENTARY SITUATION

February 1, 1904

Unionist Free Trade Demonstration,
Edinburgh

On December 23, 1903, following several speeches by Churchill attacking the Balfour Government, the General Purposes Committee of the Oldham Unionist Registration Association passed a resolution to the effect that Churchill had forfeited their confidence in him. This was submitted to a meeting of the General Executive on January 8, 1904. In a long public letter Churchill argued his position, but in the vote he had only one supporter.

Parliament is about to meet, and we are about to begin a session which is shrouded in unusual uncertainty. I do not expect the Government to be destroyed unless and until Mr. Chamberlain desires it, and there are indications that a period of grace will be accorded while that potentate takes a holiday. (Laughter.) Meanwhile, the position of the Unionist Free-traders is one of unusual difficulty. The question of Free Trade is of such supreme importance that unless Mr. Balfour definitely repudiates complicity with Mr. Chamberlain we will be bound in consistency and honour to vote for any amendment to the Address which deliberately challenges Mr. Chamberlain's policy. (Cheers.) No doubt the pressure which will be brought to bear on individual members will be in many cases effective. (Hear, hear.) The Government will treat the question as one of confidence, and some very respectable gentlemen, with whom I deeply sympathise, will shield themselves behind that. (Laughter.) But I do not believe that the country at large sets very great store, when matters of such grave importance are at stake, upon the technicalities of Parliamentary procedure. A plain, blunt issue will be raised, and we will have to answer "Aye" or "No." (Cheers.)

At least two hundred Conservative members are conscientiously opposed to Mr. Chamberlain's proposals–(cheers),–and a very large number have publicly declared against them. How many will back their convictions with their votes? (Laughter.) I speak for no one but myself, and can only say that as I have spoken so I will vote. (Loud cheers.) What does it matter what others do? If our cause is right, the fewer men the greater our share of honour. If all those who are opposed to Protection had spoken out at the beginning the Conservative party would have been saved from its present trouble. I have not the slightest intention of voting either for Protection or Home Rule, and if there is no room in the House of Commons for a member who will not swallow one or the other I will have to stop outside. (Laughter.) But that is a matter which has yet to be proved to the satisfaction of an English constituency. (Cheers.) I think that on the whole the Free-traders have had much the best of the autumn campaign. We are at a great disadvantage in the matter of money and an organised press. But somehow or other the paid orators of the Tariff Reform League do not seem to impress the working men either in England or in Scotland–(laughter),–while the magnitude of the injury which Mr. Chamberlain and his headstrong friends have done to the Unionist party, which has nourished him and his headstrong friends so long, is every day more apparent. (Cheers.) In Parliament we will meet on more even terms, and I sincerely hope every opportunity will be seized for debating the tariff question, not only on the Address but on other occasions, so that the false figures of the Protectionists can be discredited and their fallacies exposed. The Protectionists have to prove that we are not a prosperous country, that they have a remedy which will make us more prosperous, and that their remedy is one which will not break down in the details of its application. Have they made those propositions good? ("No" and cheers.) Every one has not only not been made good but it has been specially disproved. Mr. Bonar Law has made an interesting speech in Edinburgh which seemed to prove that the best way to enrich a country is to encourage and enable its traders to export at a loss. Mr. Bonar Law took a very gloomy view of the existing conditions and the future prospects of trade in Great Britain, and it is consoling to know that the opinions he expressed were not supported by the great department of which he was Parliamentary Secretary, and were absolutely traversed by the figures which he had collected. (Cheers.) He ought to spare time to study his own Blue-books. (Laughter and cheers.) But if his pessimistic statements are true it is wonderful that he can remain a member of a Government which in five years has added forty millions to the annual expenditure of a country in such a tottering and impoverished condition. (Cheers.)

[Editor's Note: Speaking of the effect of shutting foreign competition out of the home market, Churchill said]: You can see very plainly how the manufacturer would gain. I see it too–(laughter),–but what the manufacturer did not see is where he would lose. Free-traders are often told to consider the producer, but the manufacturer is a great consumer as well as a producer. (Cheers.) The greater the scale of his production the greater the scale of his consumption. If all his extra cost had to be recovered the manufacturer would have to charge the public a pretty figure even to recoup himself, quite apart from higher profits. (Cheers.) Protection might bring enormous gains to a few great speculators, who would be able to effect corners and establish syndicates, but the ordinary workaday manufacturer might easily lose his independence, be absorbed in some gigantic concern, and become the salaried servant of a great combine. (Cheers.)

THE FREE TRADE LEAGUE

February 19, 1904

Free Trade Hall, Manchester

This speech, which lasted for more than one and a half hours, was described by The Times *as "one of the most powerful and brilliant he has made."*

[Extract] We are met to consider a very momentous question–whether the name of the great Free Trade Hall is to be altered, and whether the statue of Sir Robert Peel is to be pulled down and replaced by the statue of Sir Howard Vincent.–(Laughter.) All last week the House of Commons was engaged in discussing this matter, and although our debate was robbed of some of its animation through the regrettable absence of the two principal protagonists of Protection, I do not think any Free-trader can feel much dissatisfaction either with the course of the debate or with its result.–(Cheers.) Only a month ago the Chancellor of the Exchequer–(laughter),–I think it more complimentary if I allude to him by his title than by his name–(laughter),–told the electors of Stalybridge that although the Unionist Free-traders might make a great splash in the autumn campaign in the country they would be put in their proper places as soon as Parliament met. But what happened! We went to Parliament to find the great Protectionist party–the party that was sweeping the country, only the country did not know it–(laughter),–and what did we find! We found that Tariff Reformers whose eloquence had been so much praised, whose rhetoric was so convincing, were such powerful orators that when they rose to address the House of Commons the members hurried out of the Chamber by the nearest way.–(Laughter.)

We found a number of very respectable gentlemen, with unsettled convictions–(laughter)–and still more unsettled constituencies–(great laughter and cheers),–looking extremely foolish, and extremely ashamed of themselves and of the Government–(laughter),–but perfectly prepared to back the Government up through thick and thin. We found Ministers alternately prostrating themselves before the opposing deities of Free Trade and Protection, at one moment proudly and even arrogantly demanding a mandate for tariff reform in the name of the Empire, and the next moment trying to wheedle a few Unionist Free-traders into their lobby by explaining, after all, that all they wanted to do was to resume our liberty of negotiation subject to the consent of the House of Commons in each particular case.

Well, Mr. Chairman, it would not be at all surprising if there were a good many people who, having read those debates last week, came to the conclusion that the battle was already won–(hear, hear),–and I dare say there are some here to-night who will wonder whether it is really worth while for us to call into being the formidable political machinery of the Free Trade League. I confess that I am myself not able to share in this optimism.–(Hear, hear.) It is quite true that so far as verbal assurances are concerned the Government have pitched Mr. Chamberlain and his policy overboard. But I am bound to say I find it difficult to believe in the honesty of His Majesty's Government.–(Cheers.) I think we have got to look at the signs of the weather for ourselves. I observe that the Chamberlainite press–that powerful press, that well-organised, well-drilled organisation of newspapers–appears perfectly content with the Government attitude. I notice that Mr. Chaplin gives the Government his vote. I notice that the tariff reformers walk about the House of Commons trying to look like the accomplished whist players the "Times" says they are, and I don't forget–I don't think any of us can forget–the manoeuvres, not to use a harsher word, by which the Free Trade Ministers were ejected from the Government. We cannot forget that Mr. Austen Chamberlain is still at the Exchequer, and that Mr. Walter Long is still at the Local Government Board.

Although we are told that the Government is opposed to Protection, to preferential tariffs, to food taxes, to a 10 per cent duty, and to retaliation except with the consent of Parliament–although we are told all this, I notice that this same Government is using the whole force of its organisation to procure the return for South Birmingham of Lord Morpeth, who has declared himself in favour of all these things to which the Government say that they are opposed.–(Cheers.) Our duty as Free-traders is plain. We are not concerned with the shifts and manoeuvres of an embarrassed Administration. We do not believe that our principles are safe in the hands of the present Administration–(hear, hear),–and we feel that the time has come when we have got to make our own arrangements for defending those principles.–(Cheers.) The Free Trade League, which is inaugurating its campaign to-night, is the lineal successor of the famous Anti-Corn Law League.–(Hear, hear.)

It is outside party; it is above party. We mean to make it worth while for both political parties to be true to Free Trade–(cheers),–and we mean to make it distinctly not worth while if we can for any candidate who wants to go to the House of Commons, whether Labour or Liberal or Conservative, to go in for Protection.–(Cheers.) In directing the operations of the League it will be found that the Unionist party is divided into three parts. First, there are the "whole-hoggers," so-called, I suppose, because they wish to tax everything except bacon.–(Loud laughter.) Secondly, there are the Unionist Free-traders, who wish to tax nothing except for revenue. Both these groups are perfectly easy to understand; you know in a moment whether you agree with them or not.–(Hear, hear.) And then there is the third part of the party–a much larger part than either of those two I have mentioned,–consisting of gentlemen who say, from various reasons, that they are loyal to the great policy of

Sheffield, whatever that may be.

I think we may call these people the "Sheffield Shufflers"–(loud laughter)–because it is quite clear that they are ready to support any policy, and to fight and shout for any formula, however meaningless, however dishonest, which they think will put off a general election.–(Laughter.) You ought to make it impossible if you can for any candidate within your sphere of influence to be returned to the next House of Commons who is not perfectly clear in his determination to do his best to resist Protection and Protectionist tendencies.–(Cheers.) I think you ought to do your best to succour and give cordial support to all those who in their different ways have made exertions and sacrifices for the cause of Free Trade.–(Hear, hear.) It is a very remarkable thing that no less than 27 Unionist members, in spite of the confusion into which our politics have been thrown and the uncertainty of the issue, have taken their political existence and fortunes in both hands and given a straight vote on Monday last.–(Cheers.) The Liberal party will, I think, make an error in statecraft and in foresight if it compels those gentlemen definitely to change their political character and individuality.–(Hear, hear.) I think that the Liberal party should whole heartedly support those who–I am not speaking for myself–(laughter),–I dare say I shall be all right–(renewed laughter and cheers)–have made great sacrifices for a principle vital to Liberalism–(cheers),–just as the Conservative party were ready to take the Liberal Unionists in 1886, and if that course be followed, other difficulties and differences will in the course of time, by the irresistible pressure of circumstances, be smoothed away, and the cause of Free Trade be greatly strengthened.–(Cheers.)

This controversy comes home with particular force to a Lancashire representative.–(Hear, hear.) We have only to travel about in a train through the County Palatine and look out at the window to be impressed with the artificial position which it occupies. You see all these crowded cities and townships containing many hundreds and thousands of people, a great multitude crowded together upon a soil not sufficiently fertile to maintain one-tenth of their number. We know that these people are absolutely dependent for the food they eat and the raw material of their industry upon over-sea trade–(cheers)–the like of which the world has never seen in this or any other country, in this or any other age, and I confess I feel the gravest anxiety when I see the reckless hands of politicians struggling for political mastery, laid upon all that delicate and stupendous structure, of such vast consequences to as many thousands of very poor people.–(Cheers.) . . .

If the small manufacturer is likely to be disturbed how about the working man? At the present when a man has a quarrel with his employer he may go elsewhere. But once your great universal combination is made, like the great steel trust in the United States–when that combination was made any man who quarrelled with Charley Schwabe, or whoever was the ruffian in charge–(loud laughter),–found every steelworks in the country shut against him.–(Hear, hear.) I have often heard it said that the old economists did not foresee modern conditions. Quite true; they did not know how strong their case was, and I say that this danger of great combinations is alone sufficient to make the case for Free Trade to-day stronger than it ever was.

How are we going to find out the point beyond which combination becomes unhealthy? I do not attempt to speak with certainty. I will only tell you my belief. My belief is that no combination or hardly any combination which can grow up in a Free Trade country under natural conditions can be seriously injurious to the public welfare. But the combinations which grow up in great protected countries, where they have bribed the Legislature, obtain the right to fleece the public, to charge their own people what they like. The monopolies and combinations which grow up on an illicit tariff advantage–these are the combinations which are injurious–(Cheers.) We have experienced in Lancashire in the last two years the dangers and the vexations of a limited and a localised supply of cotton. We have to get nearly all our cotton from the United States, and when there is a shortage, a bad crop there, all kinds of gamblers and speculators are able to come in and deprive thousands of hard-working people of the legitimate fruits of their industry. . . .

It is the theory of the Protectionist that imports are an evil. He thinks that if you shut out the foreign imported manufactured goods you will make these goods yourselves, in addition to the goods which you make now, including those goods which we make to exchange for the foreign goods that come in. If a man can believe that he can believe anything.–(Laughter.) We Free-traders say it is not true. To think you can make a man richer by putting on a tax is like a man thinking that he can stand in a bucket and lift himself up by the handle.–(Laughter and cheers.)

But supposing it were true; what a curious position we should be in. What a mistake it would have been to have built the Manchester Ship Canal. Here is this great work, built what for? To facilitate dumping–(cheers),–to pour a stream of foreign imports into the heart of industrial Britain. But that is not the only curious reflection that would occur to one if the Protectionists were right in their theory. If it be true that imports are an evil, and that by shutting them out you could acquire great wealth, then I say that is just as true for Ireland as it is for England, for India as it is for Australia. Now, Mr. Chamberlain said at Greenock–I have abbreviated the passage a little, but I have not altered the sense–that since 1882 the imports of foreign manufactures had increased on the balance by 52 millions, and he calculated that if these had been shut out, and made at home instead, we should have gained 26 million in wages alone, provided constant employment at 30s a week for 330,000 people with their families–that is, for more than one and a half million persons altogether. If seems easy, doesn't it?–(Laughter.) And Mr. Bonar Law–(laughter),–the Parliamentary Secretary to the Board of Trade in this Free Trade Administration–(laughter),–went even further, and, as often happens to people who go further, he fared worse.–(Laughter.) He said, speaking at the Constitutional Club, that there was an import of 150 millions of manufactured goods, representing a loss in wages of 70 or 80 millions, and he thought "that a large part of that sum could, by a stroke of the pen, be secured to the British workman without any loss at all corresponding to the advantages that the country would gain by the change."

All this is very interesting. Suppose these gentlemen–and they are very distinguished persons, and the whole of this great agitation depends on what they say–(laughter),–suppose they are right (I admit it is a great effort of imagination), suppose that by a stroke of the pen all this vast wealth can really be secured for Britain, then I say the plan holds good everywhere else too. I say it is just as true for India as for Canada, if it be true that foreign goods displace British labour, it is not less true that

British goods displace Indian labour.—(Hear, hear.) If it be economically wise for England to shut out foreign imported manufactures, it must be economically wise for India to shut out British imported manufactures.—(Cheers.)

The condition of India is of vast importance in Lancashire.—(Hear, hear.) It is important to us that her markets should be free, and that her people should be prosperous and contented.—(Hear, hear.) But that is not all. India, as your chairman has reminded you, is a great trust. We owe a duty to the land and the people of Hindustan.—(Hear, hear.) The lives, the liberties, the progress towards civilisation—towards a better and a happier state of life of 300,000,000 of human souls, is confided to our care; and the priceless possession of India, with its traditions of immemorial antiquity and its unmeasured possibilities for the future—the possession of India raises the authority of these small islands, more than all our colonies and dependencies, above the level of the greatest empires of the present or the past.—(Cheers.) . . .

Here we are, in the dawn of the twentieth century, in spite of the drain of a costly war, in spite of our easy-going methods, in spite of the profuse and profligate expenditure, in spite of the luxury of our wealthy classes—(hear, hear),—here we are in the dawn of the twentieth century not inferior in wealth, power, contentment, and in fame to any nation on the face of the globe.—(Cheers.) But what is the conclusion to which these reflections lead us? Surely it is full of encouragement and inspiration. Large views always triumph over small ideas. Broad economic principles always in the end defeat the sharp devices of expediency; science is better than sleight of hand; justice outwits intrigues; free imports can contend with hostile tariffs; honesty is, in fact, the policy that pays the best.—(Cheers.) It is the fashion nowadays to sneer at the Manchester school; and no abuse, however ribald, is considered bad enough for Mr. Cobden. But I dare say there are some people to-night who will think that it is about time that the philanthropic, peaceful, progressive, socialising doctrines which were prescribed by Mr. Cobden and Mr. Bright—(cheers)—were a little more considered by the statesmen who govern our land.—("Hear, hear" and cheers.) No one will pretend that these doctrines were a complete revelation of human policy; but it was Mr. Cobden's work to lay a great and valuable stone in the long stairway of human achievement.—(Cheers.) We may differ widely—we probably do—in this great hall to-night as to how far, how fast, or in what direction our next advance is to be made, but on one point we are all united—we are not going back one inch.—(Cheers.)

I move "That this meeting affirms its unshaken belief in the principles of Free Trade adopted more than fifty years ago, and expresses its conviction that Free Trade is now more than ever necessary for the well-being of the United Kingdom."

GOVERNMENT POLICY

February 26, 1904

Public Hall, Preston

The violence of Churchill's disillusionment with the Unionist Government–of which he remained a nominal member–can be seen from this characteristic speech.

[Extract] . . . Parliament has now been sitting a little more than three weeks. We have had a very interesting fiscal debate, which has proved unmistakably that, whatever success the Protectionists might meet with in the country, they are quite unable to sustain their case, either by argument or authority, in the arena of the House of Commons. There is another thing which the session has made plain. I could almost regret to inform you of it. If you have tears, prepare to shed them now. The first Parliament of His Majesty King Edward VII is about to die. (Laughter.) The very air of Westminster smells of dissolution. (Laughter.) The triumphant majority which three years ago was returned to support a Free Trade Unionist party–a majority of 134–has dwindled down to a beggarly 14. (Applause.)

[Editor's Note: Speaking further on the position of the Government, Churchill said]: There is no public policy before the country except the proposed introduction of Chinese labour into the Transvaal and the weary progress of the Somaliland muddle, and over all hangs the shadow of the Budget. Many things operate to bring home to a people their evil deeds, but, in my opinion, nothing is to be trusted so much as a want of money. That is the great constable. Mr. Balfour and his party have spent–I almost said squandered–as much money as the Government could lay their hands on. In five years the cost of governing this country has mounted up by forty millions a year. The Government has found in the expenditure of money an easy solution for every difficulty and a convenient palliative for every administrative muddle. Chancellor after Chancellor of the Exchequer have fought against this in vain. The war is over, but the war taxation goes on. Now, in a time of peace, with income tax at 11d.; with all the special war taxation on coal, sugar, beer and spirits; with the whole new yield of the death duties in full operation, the new Chancellor of the Exchequer–new in more senses than one–(laughter)–is going to be confronted with a huge and hideous deficit. Bad finance might be written on the indictment of the Government, and it will be written on their tombstone. (Laughter.) I will not pretend any longer to regret the inevitable change of party authority in the House of Commons. The spectacle presented by the Government during the last three weeks has been unusual and demoralising. What valuable legislation do they desire to propose; what useful public object do they serve; upon what principle of policy are they agreed–unless it is the policy of putting off a general election? The Government represents nothing, unless it is the desperate efforts of a weak man to clutch at the shreds of power. For my part, I say the sooner they are put out of their misery the better for all concerned. (Applause.)

ANNOUNCEMENT OF CANDIDACY

April 29, 1904

Liberal Association Meeting,
Memorial Hall, Manchester

When Churchill rose to speak in the House of Commons on March 29 in the Debate on the Motion for the Adjournment for the Easter Recess, Balfour walked out of the Chamber. When Churchill protested at his "lack of deference and respect" to the House, all Ministers present walked out, followed by the majority of Unionist M.P.s. Some remained at the door to jeer at Churchill, who was supported only by a small group of Unionist Free Traders.

On April 3 Churchill had drawn the attention of the Oldham Unionist Association to the statement in his Commons speech of March 29 announcing his willingness to resign and stand in a by-election. The decision would be in the hands of the Association. The Association declined to accept the offer, and Churchill remained M.P. for Oldham.

Churchill's confidential negotiations with the Liberals–conducted principally through his uncle, Edward Marjoribanks (Lord Tweedmouth)–resulted in his adoption as Free Trade candidate for North-west Manchester at the next General Election. This was Churchill's first speech to a Liberal meeting. Churchill's responses to the Irish Question are of significance in the light of later events.

[Extract] I come before you in response to the invitation which was tendered to me on Friday week by the officers of your Association, and which was, as you know, strongly endorsed by the Committee of that powerful non-party body the Free Trade League. That invitation called upon me to come forward as the Free Trade candidate for North-west Manchester, and it offered me (subject, of course, to your approval) the full and effective support of the Liberal organisation in that division. I have lately found myself in rather an enviable position. I have been in the position of a young lady with several suitors.–(Laughter.) It is not an unpleasant position, though it is perhaps rather an agitating position. Various electoral proposals have been made to me in this country and also from Scotland. Some of these proposals have offered almost the certainty of victory. Others, like the invitation which was conveyed to me from your Association, offered the certainty of a hard fight.–(Hear, hear.) Some time ago I decided that if I took any part in the approaching general election I would fight where my services would be of the greatest use to the Free Trade cause, and I felt, and still feel, most strongly that if Lancashire–where any political work I have hitherto been able to perform has chiefly lain–that if Lancashire and Lancashire Free-traders considered I should be of any use to them, and that it would be advantageous to the cause of Free Trade that I should fight for them in this city, I ought not to refuse any invitation which they extended to me merely because I should have a better chance of getting into Parliament elsewhere.–(Cheers.) . . .

I think the British public understands the difficulties with which Unionist Free-traders have been confronted, and understanding them does not desire to deal ungenerously with those who, at a time when there is so much subtlety, intrigue, and manoeuvre about, have done their best to speak their minds plainly and faithfully with the masses of the people. Trusting in the goodwill which I have found I was never at all worried about results personal to myself. I would be sorry to be out of Parliament, but I can find plenty of other things to do. Indeed, under ordinary circumstances, I would have been quite willing to stand aside at the next election. Profoundly as I dislike and distrust the present Government, it is painful, very painful–more painful than I imagined it would be–to quarrel irreparably with the Conservative party, but I am convinced that, unless the greedy gospel of materialism and expediency–(hear, hear),–which emanates from Birmingham, and the policy of extravagance at home and aggression abroad–(hear, hear),–which is its logical and inevitable outcome–(hear, hear),–are decisively repudiated by the country on an early occasion they will work a permanent and enduring mischief to the British Empire, and impose severe privations upon those millions of people on whose progressive well-being the very existence and value of the Empire depends.–(Cheers.)

Therefore, in respect to the invitation which has been extended to me from North-west Manchester, what I have to say is this: that if the Free-traders of Manchester desire me to fight their battle, and if the Liberal Association in the division will give me their powerful support I will accept the candidature irrespective of the odds, and I will do my very best to win.–(Loud cheers.) Such an alliance presents difficulties from which the ordinary party candidature is free. In the first place the Unionist Free-traders are marked men. We are suspected–and I am not concerned to defend myself from the charge–of having had a good deal to do with spoiling Mr. Chamberlain's game, and you have seen yourselves that the four or five Unionists who have stood out against him from the beginning have been singled out as special objects of attack, and I think you should consider most carefully whether you care to identify yourselves with a candidate who has aroused such antagonism, and whether a better result might not be obtained by someone who was less obnoxious to the enemy.–(Laughter) . . .

I am against a separate Parliament for Ireland. No such proposal could be made except by a Government elected above all with an overwhelming majority for that purpose –(hear, hear),–and it would be to court destruction for a Government elected–as the next Government will be–mainly upon the Free Trade issue to embark upon such a policy. Let us not labour this point. Let us rather consider that aspect of the Irish question in which we can all agree–the continued application to the Irish problem of Liberal principles, and the continued if gradual extension of wider powers of local self-government, and perhaps the creation of provincial councils, or at any rate local bodies, so that purely domestic Irish questions, whether they be secular or whether they be religious, may be settled in a greater measure, in a greater degree in harmony with Irish ideas and Irish sympathies. (Cheers.) . . .

In North-west Manchester the issue will be perfectly plain and definite. You will not be confronted with any "retaliation rubbish"–insincere rubbish for the most part.–(Hear, hear.) You are face to face with Mr. Chamberlain's policy, and it is Mr.

Chamberlain's policy which Sir William Houldsworth—who was never suspected of such opinions—has put forward. I am prepared, if you desire it, to prove to the best of my ability to the satisfaction of the working classes in Manchester that that policy, quite apart from the evil it would work upon the solidarity of our Empire, quite apart from its effect upon the morality of public life, the general trade of the country, and the best progress of the world, is a policy injurious in a special degree to the interests of Lancashire and injurious to an extreme degree to the interests of this great commercial city and the surrounding towns.—(Hear, hear.) I deprecate the suggestion of engaging with Sir William Houldsworth in a contest of personalities. This will be a conflict not of personalities but of principle.—(Hear, hear.) We have reached a critical period in the history of our country. It is a climacteric in our national life. If I correctly interpret the signs of the times we shall be asked at the next election a momentous question, and that question will be whether we are to model ourselves upon the clanking military empires of the Continent of Europe, with their gorgeous Imperial hierarchy fed by enormous tariffs, defended by mighty armies, and propped by every influence of caste privilege and commercial monopoly, or whether our development is to proceed by well-tried English methods towards the ancient and lofty ideals of English citizenship.—(Cheers.) We shall have to choose between an imitation German Empire founded in force and a real British Empire founded on freedom. —(Cheers.) We shall have to choose between our peaceful league of progressive peoples under the Union Jack and a greedy Jingo profit-sharing domination. My choice is already made.—(Hear, hear.) Here in the constituency of the Free-trade Hall I suggest to you that we might try over again the cause for which Bright and Cobden and Sir Robert Peel fought for so valiantly.—(Cheers.) Here in the city historically associated with their labours and their triumph, here in this famous battle-ground, before the eyes of all Lancashire, we might establish once again upon an unshakable foundation, beyond the breath of partisan controversy or political intrigue, those great economic truths which are at the foundation of British justice and human liberty.—(Cheers.)

In coming to a decision upon the resolution which will be submitted to you directly do not consider me in any way. Consider your principles, consider your cause. If you think that either your principles or your cause will suffer from my advocacy do not have the slightest hesitation in voting against the resolution. But if you think there is between us a sufficient measure of agreement, a substantial bond of sympathy strong enough to undertake so great a contest on so great a stage, then let us go forward together boldly, leaving behind us the shades of night, marching steadily towards the dawn.—(Loud cheers.)

[Editor's Note: Churchill then left the room, and the meeting proceeded to adopt a resolution requesting that "he will become the Free-trade candidate in the North-west Division of the city when a vacancy will occur, and assures him in that event of the full and effective support of the Liberal party." Churchill then re-entered the room and said] : I come to you as a Unionist Free-trader in distress. You show that you are willing to throw over me the large and generous aegis of the Liberal party in the Central Division. Perhaps you believe that the contest which we may embark upon together will have its effect not alone in this division, and whatever its results, it may animate and inspire the cause of Free Trade throughout the great district of which this city is the center. If that be so, I confess I feel myself unequal in many ways to undertake that work, but if I have the loyal and earnest co-operation of every Liberal in the Central Division, I am not at all sure whether we may not produce at the general election results which will surprise other people besides ourselves. I think you have acted very wisely as an association in taking me on my own terms.–(Laughter.) I value and appreciate the confidence you have shown me, and I will endeavour to the best of my ability to be worthy of it.

LIBERAL POLICY

June 4, 1904

Cobden's Centenary,
Alexandra Palace, London

On May 31 Churchill "crossed the Floor" and sat on the Opposition benches in the House of Commons, placing himself beside Lloyd George. He was now, in fact as well as in sympathy, a member of the Liberal Party. On June 4, he shared the platform with the Liberal leader, Sir Henry Campbell-Bannerman, and Lloyd George.

[Extract] I beg to move,

> That this meeting, assembled to do honour to the memory of Richard Cobden on the one hundredth anniversary of his birth, declares its enthusiastic adherence to the principles of Free Trade, peace, retrenchment, and reform for which Cobden laboured, and its belief that only through the fuller application of those principles can the industry and commerce of our country be firmly established and the well-being of the people secured.

About a year ago, after half a century of almost unprecedented triumph, the system which Mr. Cobden established was subjected to the attack of a responsible statesman. Up to that time that system had been criticised only by persons like Sir Howard Vincent, to whom no serious politician, I almost said no sane person, would think of paying the smallest attention. (Laughter.) But when the most powerful political leader in the country–(No),–the then most powerful political leader–enlisted the whole force of his personality in the cause of Protection, when he found himself supported by a well-organised press, when his efforts were aided and abetted by the Prime Minister–(cheers),–and he received the support of one of the greatest political organisations in the country, it was clear that the time had come when Free-traders of every description should band themselves together and do what they could to defend the faith that is in them. (Cheers.) Since then we have had some very curious experiences. We have heard a great many curious things. We have been told of the state of the manufacture of pearl buttons–(laughter),–we have heard of the importations of jewellery from Morocco–(laughter),–and we have listened to the mysteries of "scientific taxation"–there seems to be a good deal more taxation than science about it. (Laughter and cheers.) We have also heard of "the offer of the colonies," though what that offer is no one has ever been able to find out, and we have heard of the dark and treacherous designs of the foreign members of the Cobden Club. (Laughter.) All this valuable material has been placed before us by Mr. Chamberlain and his colleague, Mr. Chaplin–(laughter)–I hope they will both appreciate my coupling them together. It has been emphasised by the megaphones and the magic lanterns of the Tariff Reform League, and expounded and illuminated by the exertions of 400 newspapers addicted to the cause of Protection, and it has also been celebrated in upwards of 215 pantomimes and music halls. (Much laughter.) Is it not wonderful after all these months of storm and turmoil that there should still be found, huddled away in an obscure corner of the Alexandra Palace, a handful of undaunted Free-traders–(laughter),–prepared confidently to assert that under ordinary circumstances two and two will continue to make four? A year has come and a year has gone and it might not be unprofitable to see for a moment where we stand as a result of our exertions. I do not think that the battle is over yet. This is going to be a prolonged engagement, and our cause is too valuable for us to endanger it by over-confidence. But it is an evident fact which we might safely notice that by the exertions of the Liberal party and its leaders, by the massive authority of the Duke of Devonshire, and most of all, I think by the sacrifices of the Free-trade Ministers, the Protectionists have been hurled back, and that the old banner still waves over a victorious fighting line. (Cheers.) . . .

We are here this afternoon to celebrate the centenary of Mr. Cobden, and I am proud of the high and honourable duty which has been entrusted to me in moving this resolution. It is the fashion nowadays to speak with a great deal of contempt of the Manchester School, and no abuse seems to be bad enough for Mr. Cobden. But I venture to think there will be some of you here who will believe it is very nearly time that the peaceful, philanthropic, socialising doctrines of Mr. Bright and Mr. Cobden were a little more considered by the statesmen who rule our land. (Cheers.) We do not pretend that everything Mr. Cobden said was right, or that the political system of thought which he established was a complete and final revelation of worldly wisdom. But in the long stairway of human progress and achievement which the toil and sacrifice of generations are building it was Cobden's work to lay a mighty stone. (Cheers.) Other stones had been laid upon that stone, stones of social standards and social reform, stones of Imperial responsibility, and you have only got to walk about the streets of London to see that there is plenty more work waiting to be done by a master mason. (Cheers.) But we believe that the work which Cobden did was done for ever; that the stone he laid shall never be transplanted, that the heights he gained shall never be abandoned. (Cheers.) We may differ among ourselves, we probably do, as to how far, how fast, or in what direction we shall move forward, but on one point we are all agreed–we are not going back one inch. (Loud and prolonged cheers.) We are not going back because the principles we defend are principles which endure from one generation to another. Men change, manners change, customs change, Governments and Prime Ministers change, even Colonial Secretaries change–(laughter),–sometimes they change their offices, sometimes they change their opinions. (Laughter.) But principles do not change. Whatever was scientifically true in the economic proportions which were established 60 years ago in the controversy of a far greater generation than our own is just as true in 1904 as it was in 1846, and it will still be true as long as men remain trading animals on the surface of the habitable globe.

ADMINISTRATIVE HOME RULE FOR IRELAND

June 16, 1904

Public Hall, Cheetham Hill

We are gathered here and I stand here with Liberal support as the Free Trade candidate for North-west Manchester because a distinguished politician has changed his mind. Many people change their minds in politics. Some people change their minds to avoid changing their party.–(Laughter.) Some people change their party to avoid changing their mind.–(Renewed laughter.) There have been all sorts of changes in English politics, but I think that Mr. Chamberlain's change is much the most remarkable of any that history records.–(Hear, hear.) When you think that the man who broke up or was breaking up the Liberal Government of 1885 by being more Radical than Mr. Gladstone, and was driving the Duke of Devonshire out of the Liberal party and Liberal Government in 1885, is the man who is now breaking up the Conservative Government in 1904 by being more Tory and more reactionary than any Conservative in that Government, I think you will agree with me that it is a world's record–(laughter and cheers),–that it is less like an ordinary political manoeuvre than like one of those acrobatic feats which are so popular in circuses and hippodromes. There is one particular feat of which I am forcibly reminded to-night–the novel and exciting spectacle of "looping the loop."–(Laughter.) It is a very dangerous and a very difficult performance. I don't know whether you have ever seen it. Sometimes it succeeds and sometimes it fails. When it succeeds great applause is accorded to the performer. When it fails he is usually carried away on a shutter.–(Laughter.) But whether it succeeds or whether it fails the performance always commands the attention and the interest of the audience.

In 1885 Mr. Chamberlain made a brilliant series of speeches in support of Free Trade and against Fair Trade, and he ridiculed the idea of once again bringing forward the old Protectionist doctrines and prophecies which had been so greatly falsified by events during the past 18 years. I think Mr. Chamberlain's personal position to-day compared with what it was two years ago in the eyes of the great majority of his countrymen is a measure of the injury he has inflicted on himself by his reckless crusade.–(Cheers.) I read to-day a pathetic and interesting note in the columns of the "Times" newspaper. Mr. Chamberlain is going to have a birthday, and he proposes to celebrate it by a dinner.–(Laughter.) He will recruit his exhausted strength with cheap and untaxed food.–(Much laughter.) I learn that upwards of 150 Unionist members have applied for tickets. Among them I notice the respected name of Sir William Houldsworth. There are, I suppose, 400 Unionists in the House of Commons. One hundred and fifty propose to come to his birthday to dine. Two years ago, I suppose, there would have been no difficulty in at least twice that number attending, and he would have received the cheers and support of a united party.–(Hear, hear.) But I read further that the occupants of the Treasury bench are not invited to attend. Their exclusion from the movement is the result of careful deliberation on the part of the Committee. Most of them would have liked to be present, but some have made prior engagements.–(Laughter.) In another paper I learn that in consequence of this decision Mr. Austen Chamberlain will not be present. Really I think this is going too far.–(Laughter.) We ought not to part a father from his son. I think I may say in the name of the Free-traders of Manchester–no inconsiderable unit–I think I may assure Mr. Chamberlain that he might with perfect safety allow his son to go to his birthday banquet, and that we will not draw any sinister or ill-natured deductions from his presence at the dinner.–(Cheers.)

I call attention to the recent utterance of Lord Rosebery on the subject of Home Rule, to the effect that it would not be possible to introduce a new Home Rule measure on the lines of Mr. Gladstone's bills. I have a great respect and friendship for Lord Rosebery. I believe that Lord Rosebery of all the men on the Liberal side has a greater gift of eloquence and a greater command on the imagination of the English people, and I think it would be a great disaster if Lord Rosebery's influence and service were withdrawn from the effective championship of the Free Trade cause.–(Hear, hear.) I do most earnestly hope–I speak as an outsider–that the distinguished leaders of the Liberal party will try to get along with one another peacefully and patiently.–(Cheers.) I do hope they will not take to proscribing each other and ruling each other off the course and out of the rules altogether, for what we are mainly anxious about is the preservation of great principles, and we require the men who wield great power in the country to do their best to champion these principles and not worry too much about the personal aspect of the things.–(Cheers.) But still more remarkable than Lord Rosebery's pronouncement is that of Mr. Birrell, the chairman of the National Liberal Federation. Mr. Birrell has to a great extent, if not entirely, endorsed the statement which Lord Rosebery has made. I welcome these statements. I don't pretend for one moment that I do not. It would put me, and others like me, who wish to work with the Liberal party, to help it to win a great victory, in a position of hideous difficulty, in a most hateful and monstrous dilemma, if we were suddenly confronted with a definite proposal to create a separate Parliament in Ireland.–(Hear, hear.)

But I don't pretend–I would not suggest to you for a moment–that the Irish question, which, as Mr. Morley rightly says in his book, never blows over, has ceased to be a real and practical factor in English politics. It may be quite true, as Lord Rosebery says, that an alliance between the Irish party and the Liberal party is difficult because of the divergence of their views on temperance and education. It may be quite true that Free-traders may not find that agreement on Free Trade as against Protection in the Irish party which we should like. But whatever our relations with the Irish Nationalists, the responsibilities and difficulties of the position remain. Our duty towards Ireland is undiminished. I would much rather deal with the Irish question on its merits, according to the conscience and conviction of the English people, than have to deal with it according to some bargain or pact which had been made in some lobby or some corner as the price by which a particular member received a particular number of votes, or a particular Government assumed the reins of office.–(Cheers.)

I say the policy we must pursue towards Ireland is a policy of administrative Home Rule.–(Hear, hear.) I say, as my father said in 1890–(cheers),–I do not look forward to the day when there shall be created a separate Parliament in Ireland to be a rival of, and perhaps an enemy of, the central Parliament here at home, but I do most earnestly look forward to the day–I hope I may do something to accelerate it–when Irishmen shall feel themselves free, as they are not free now, when a wise and liberal and sympathetic policy applied to Ireland shall have made Ireland free, as England, Scotland, and Wales are free, when we young men who have to look far out into the future will in the years that are to come turn to each other and ask how it was that through so many years of anxiety and trouble Ireland was a source of danger and weakness to the Empire.–(Cheers.)

Both Free-traders and Liberals must have a definite, practical, reasonable, and substantial policy of reform in regard to the great questions connected with the liquor law–(loud cheers),–in regard to the new problems and difficulties which recent judicial decisions have created in the labour world–(cheers),–and a practical solution of some of the most marked and monstrous anomalies which exist in the rating of land.–(Loud cheers.) I hope in the autumn to lay before the electors a statement upon these subjects at greater length. When the election comes, it is on these points that I will ask for your support, and I will put on my bills–

Vote for Churchill, Cheap Food, Peace, Retrenchment, and Reform.

The Protectionists have failed to prove that this country is not prosperous; they have failed to prove that they have a remedy which will make us prosperous; and they have failed to prove that their remedy can be effectively applied. As the world goes, we are undoubtedly a prosperous nation, and, man for man, the most prosperous nation. But even if we were not prosperous, Protection would only accelerate our decline and exacerbate our misfortunes. Is it a strange thing that there has been some disorganisation of our commerce after the close of a great and costly war? Mr. Chamberlain told a Birmingham audience two years ago that England was rich enough to fight just such another war. Ah! the Birmingham barrel-organ is playing a different tune today.–(Laughter.) England is now bleeding to death, and we are told that the colonies will leave us unless Canadian loyalty is purchased at 2s. a quarter and Australian allegiance at a penny a pound.–(Laughter.)

Mr. Chamberlain's motives no doubt are pure enough, but what about some of those who were supporting him–those rich landlords and wealthy manufacturers who jostled one another on his platforms? Was it all for the unity of the Empire; was it all for the good of the Empire?–(Laughter.) I will show by quotations that the working men of Spain, France, and Germany are more discontented than the English working men, and that a Free Trade movement is in progress both in Germany and America. I do not look upon foreign peoples as if they are our enemies.–(Loud cheers.) The King has gone from one European capital to another endeavoring to spread goodwill among the nations. What is the good of that if we have another lot of people with a distinguished man at their head going about appealing to every narrow, bigoted, insular prejudice, representing every foreigner as an enemy, spreading ill-will and dissention among the nations of the earth?–(Cheers.) The union of the Anglo-Saxon race is a great ideal, and if ever it is to be achieved it will be by increasing and not diminishing the friendly intercourse of trade between this country and the United States. Against such wanton folly as a tariff war with the United States, Free-traders appeal with confidence to Lancashire, and we hope that, as in years gone by, Lancashire will point the path of honour and wisdom to the people of the British islands.–(Loud cheers.)

FREE TRADE

October 18, 1904

Carnarvon

[Extract] I will preface my speech by stating that, like the member for Carnarvon Boroughs [Mr. Lloyd George], I have acquired the habit of thinking of myself and forming my own opinion. (Laughter and cheers.) No constitutional actions should be left untried from the very beginning of the Parliamentary Session to harass, to embarrass, and ultimately to drive from power an Administration which has forfeited the confidence of the country, and whose continuance in power is a danger and scandal to the nation. (Cheers.) We must, however, not be content with impeding the proceedings, but must take advantage on every occasion which the procedure of Parliament permits, to bring before the House of Commons and before the country certain definite and important reforms too long delayed and upon all sides urgently demanded.

I am convinced that the energy and courage of Mr. Lloyd George are absolutely essential to the accomplishment of those objects, whether constructive or destructive. (Loud laughter and cheers.) The fact remains that Mr. Lloyd George is the best fighting general in the Liberal ranks. (Loud cheers.) Free-traders must be urged, whatever their opinions might have been in the past, to stand together in one long line of battle. (Cheers.) What the relations might be between Mr. Balfour and Mr. Chamberlain, or what their mental conditions or their conflicting public statements might be, or what mental reservations or equivocations they might nourish in their hearts (laughter), are probably matters of great interest to those who are dependent upon those gentlemen. But now I am free and no longer dependent upon Mr. Balfour's caprice. (Loud cheers.) I decline, and advise my audience also to decline, to wade any further into that dirty labyrinth of subtlety and sham which does not take in the very stupid people and disgusts and perplexes all whom it does not deceive. (Laughter and cheers.) I am content to adopt the opinion of *The Times,* that great Tory organ.

Mr. Balfour and Mr. Chamberlain are pursuing the same course, and the victory of either or both will mean the establishment of a complicated tariff and the erection of that self-same system of protection which hampers the industry and corrupts the Governments of America, Germany, and France. (Cheers.) Free Trade is unifying its forces at present, and the support given in every constituency by those who are transferring their allegiance to the Liberal flag will exert an influence upon the whole course of public policy. It is a question which does not stand alone. It is a touchstone, and people who can agree upon that are capable necessarily of agreeing upon a great many other things as well. (Cheers.) But we must be opposed to the policy which the present Government has pursued in endeavouring to purchase political support from particular interests in the country (cheers) by handing over to those classes property and privileges which really belong to the public. (Cheers.)

Lord Rosebery has called for a clean slate, but the slate has engraved upon it certain things which cannot and must not be swept away. The next Government party will have to provide some solution of the distressing sectarian bitterness and educational confusion which recent legislation has brought into the country. (Cheers.) It will also have to deal with the licensing question, and so undo the damage done to temperance and the insult which was offered to equity by the passing of a Bill which, though called an Act of Parliament, was really an act of private bribery and public plunder. (Cheers.) Another question is that of restoring trade unionism to its rightful position (cheers); and it will be also necessary to give effect to an almost unanimous demand for the equitable rating of urban land. (Cheers.) There is also a question of electoral reform with one man one vote. (A voice—"Good old Radical," and cheers.)

Dealing with the question of devolution, the new Government must introduce the provision of provincial or national councils, and will have to transfer to those bodies a large quantity of the business now inadequately performed by Westminster. The settlement of this question must be left to Liberal politicians. It was withheld from the Conservative party because the interests of the party were necessarily hostile to such a scheme. We are not asked to commit ourselves to the exact form of Lord Dunraven's scheme, which, however, constitutes a real step forward and indicates the direction in which advance might be safely and prudently made. Why can we not achieve for Ireland and Wales what has been achieved for Scotland, and give them the same educational liberties as Scotland possesses? Why should they not be compelled to mind their own business and manage their own affairs? Such matters as licensing and education should be left to local government, while in all that concerns Customs and Excise, the defence of the country, and the fundamental rights of property the British islands must be one country. (Cheers.)

The Irish demand and the Welsh demand for devolution ought not to go forward separately, but together hand in hand. (Cheers.) The Liberal party must not enter into competition with the opposite party on the main lines of Imperial politics. We have to do our duty after our own likes and according to our own principles. The only way in which an Opposition can and ought to win is by presenting a policy radically different from the policy of the party in power. Liberals are prepared to carry forward their ideas with regard to devolution in the teeth of all opposition; and if we only all join together, without any of the jealousies which disfigure great causes, I see no reason why in the near future this country should not have a new policy—a policy which will have at heart the interests of the nation as a whole. (Cheers.)

PROTECTIONISM

November 28, 1904

Cheetham Town Hall,
North-west Manchester

Churchill's opponent at North-west Manchester was William Joynson-Hicks (generally known as "Jix"), a future Home Secretary and colleague of Churchill's in the 1924-1929 Conservative Government.

As you can see, the weather has caused me to be late this evening. I have never known such a fog since I listened to Mr. Balfour making one of those perfectly plain pronouncements on the fiscal question. (Laughter.) I have, as you might have noticed, been to Wales and to Scotland, where I have met great and earnest audiences of intelligent and determined people. But it is not much use my going to Wales or to Scotland unless everything is all right in North-west Manchester. If in the future I can be of any use to the cause in which we believe it can only be because here, in the central division of this famous city, I am given a platform and a position from which on a larger scale I can defend the great principles of Free Trade. (Cheers.)

Mr. Joynson-Hicks has been making a number of speeches, and has been describing himself as a fighting man. (Laughter.) That is the kind of thing which is usually left to other people to say–(laughter),–but I am inclined to ask Mr. Joynson-Hicks what it is he is fighting for? Is he fighting, for instance, for Imperial unity? That is a great and splendid object, and Mr. Chamberlain, who has been eight years at the Colonial Office, tells us that it is only to be achieved in one way, by preferences based on the taxation of food. Mr. Joynson-Hicks wants to sit on the same side of the House with Mr. Chamberlain, and should certainly pay great attention to what Mr. Chamberlain says. (Hear, hear.) But what in fact did he say? He [Mr. Joynson-Hicks] said that he agreed with Mr. Balfour, and that the time was not ripe for the taxation of food. (Laughter.) But if Mr. Joynson-Hicks believes that Mr. Chamberlain's object is desirable and his method right what nonsense it is to say that the time is not ripe. The man who said that classed himself as an Imperialist. (Laughter.) What would have been said of the Manchester Regiment or the Lancashire Fusiliers if when they were ordered to make an attack upon a position they replied, "We have unabated sympathy with the object but we think that the time is not ripe." (Loud laughter.) They would not with such conduct as that have got the reputation of being fighting men. (Renewed laughter.) . . .

My opponent shows, when he is trying to get at the truth, a grasp of economic principles which I am glad to recognise, but he has a tendency to cease thinking of what is best for the country, and to try to invent some formula which will support a platform on which the real Chamberlainites of the division can stand with him side by side. With this object Mr. Joynson-Hicks repeats the old and stale observations about Retaliation, a policy which nobody has been able to explain and which cannot be understood. (Hear, hear.) It is impossible to base the commercial system of this gigantic country upon the word "Retaliation," like the blessed word "Mesopotamia," which comforted the old lady so much. (Laughter.) We must find out what Retaliation means, what definite acts it involves, and what differences there would be under that state of things from what we know under the present state of things. The Government today has perfect liberty to negotiate a commercial treaty if they choose. If it is a good one they will get the credit; if it is a bad one, like the Sugar Bounties Convention, they will get the discredit. (Hear, hear.) It is trifling with the electors of a great commercial centre to say, "We ask you to support us because of our declaration that if we can make a good bargain we will make it." (Laughter.) . . .

There are two or three serious things to which I would like to allude without wishing it to be understood that they comprise the whole indictment against the Government on that positive social programme which I desire to see in the battle-front of the advancing Liberal and Free Trade army. One is the grave decline of Parliamentary influence. The power of the House of Commons is decaying, and with this power there is a growth of the power of the Executive which is dangerous to the civil liberties of the people. (Hear, hear.) The Cabinet is becoming so arrogant that a young minister, Mr. Arnold-Forster, has said that he thought it too much trouble to sit and listen to the debates of the House, and that he thought he ought to have his vote recorded by proxy. (Laughter.) But side by side with this arrogance of the Executive there is a growing subservience on the part of the same Government to great vested interests and to the power of organised capital. Let us not under-rate the importance of this. Money, money, money is more and more a powerful agent. (Hear, hear.) I do not suggest that members or Ministers are corrupt, but all the great vested interests are organising themselves for political action, and the present Government has shown themselves increasingly contemptuous of the House of Commons and increasingly respectful to the proprietors of capital. (Hear, hear.) The last Liberal Government, though they were a body of men not rich in worldly goods, made it a rule that nobody should be a member of the Government and a company director at the same time. (Cheers.) I have nothing to say against company directors, but the large number of directorships which are held by members of the present Government show a deterioration in the standard of public duty. (Hear, hear.)

In North-west Manchester we will be prepared for the fight when it comes. I appeal to you for unity, for comradeship–(cheers),–and for great and continuous exertion. The power of money is vast, but the power of active and energetic men is greater. The power of syndicate organisations is very great, but the power of the people is greater still. (Cheers.) Selfishness is always a force in the world, and is always strong, but the generous forces are strong enough to overcome it, and if we stand together we might look forward to the day when there will be established in England a Government which, instead of trying to make friends with every interest with a strong voting power, will stand for the cause of social reform and administer the trust of the nation in the interests of the nation as a whole. (Loud cheers.)

FREE TRADE

February 6, 1905

Kings Theatre, Gainsborough

Churchill remained one of the most active speakers on the fiscal question throughout 1904 and 1905, and was a welcome speaker at by-elections, including an appearance at Gainsborough in support of the Liberal candidate, Major Leslie Renton.

[Extract] . . . Protection is the art of doing business at a loss. The more we carry out the principle of Protection the greater and the deeper will be the loss. None can complain that Mr. Chamberlain has not laid his proposals fairly and fully before the country. I only wish that the Prime Minister would imitate him. (Laughter and cheers.) Mr. Chamberlain's programme at Glasgow was taxes on food and taxes on manufactured goods. Taxes on food are to be the basis of his colonial preference scheme. The Prime Minister has agreed to summon a conference which, if it arrives at any conclusion, must arrive at the conclusion that food taxes are to be the basis of Imperial preference.

I have never based my main argument against food taxes on the increased cost in living which will follow therefrom. I think that taxes on food will raise the cost of living, but if you put only a small tax on it will only raise the cost of living a little. The objection which I have urged is that a tax on food restricts our free rights to purchase our food in any part of the world where we may think it fit to buy. In Lancashire this comes home to us, because we have a gigantic population there, more people than the soil can possibly support under natural conditions. In spite of our disadvantages, we have built up there a great fabric of industry. In the last two years we have suffered greatly by a shortage in the cotton supply and the high prices of cotton. What is the remedy suggested for that? To vary and multiply the sources of cotton supply, so that when there is a bad harvest in one part of the world there may be a good one somewhere else to make up for it. (Cheers.) We have had our experience of a corner in cotton, and we do not mean to have a corner in corn. I may say incidentally that we are having our experience now of a sort of corner in sugar. (Cheers.)

After examining the proposal to impose a duty on manufactured articles, I must insist that the duty will be paid not by the foreigner but by the home consumer, and as surely as thunder follows after the lightning so surely the development of trusts and syndicates follows in the wake of protective tariffs. As for the fears of the tariff reformers with regard to the home market, I submit that they are groundless. But although the foreign competition in the home market is not large, yet it exercises a powerful effect in keeping prices down over the whole area. It is only the people who want to sell goods dear who do not like this. The people who want to buy things as cheaply as possible do like it. Without this "small pinch" of foreign competition which ensures to the consumer a cheap supply, prices would assuredly rise. (Cheers.) I admit that Mr. Chamberlain's motives are fair and above-board, but I must say that when I see these rich landowners and wealthy manufacturers crowding and jostling each other on his platform I cannot help asking myself what their little game is. Is it all for the good of the working man, for the consolidation of the British Empire? (Cheers.) These gentlemen see very well where they will gain, but what they do not see is where they will lose.

But Free-traders are not hostile to the idea of Imperial unity. We rejoice in the natural growth of inter-Imperial trade. We look forward to the abolition of all fiscal barriers within the Empire. But what is it that hampers and delays the advent of that time, that delays the growth of trade within the Empire and prevents us from arriving at a system of free exchange within the Empire? Is it the Free-trade system of this country or the protective tariffs of the colonies? Imperial unity is impeded by fiscal divergence, and Imperial uniformity can be reached only in one of two ways. The colonists must change or we must. I submit, as a Free-trader, that there is no reason why we, being right, should depart from our system and adopt their system, which we believe to be wrong, or why they should not leave their system, which we believe to be wrong, and adopt ours. (Cheers.) Nothing could be more commendable than the attitude which colonial statesmen have adopted in this unhappy brawl. As for the colonial preferences which we have received, I refuse to believe that they were offered as a bribe to secure a bargain. (Cheers.) They were a frank recognition of the benefits which the colonies receive from the motherland, and a token of unity and good-will between men living under different skies and different circumstances.

We have lost a great opportunity. With Mr. Chamberlain's popularity and prestige, and with the conditions which were excited by the long reign of Queen Victoria, it would have been very easy to have raised colonial sentiment to a higher level than it has yet reached. If Mr. Chamberlain had exerted his matchless power of exposition, his glittering talents and abilities in trying to persuade the colonies to lower their tariffs in our favour, he might indeed have earned himself a niche in history and won the applause of all parties in the land. He might have united States instead of dividing friends, he might have sought to lower tariffs, instead of seeking to raise them. But he has chosen otherwise, and with disastrous results. His track is marked with footprints of ruin. Wherever I go I find a great setback in Imperial sentiment, electoral ruin to the friends who followed him, political ruin to the great party he has broken up, ruin, plainest of all, most irreparable of all, to himself. (A voice: "He's played out," and laughter.) Is it not melancholy and a tragic spectacle to see this famous man, capable of so much good to the State and to the working classes, compelled by his own impulsive acts to mumble for the rest of his life the old woman's jargon of Protectionist superstitions and the stale rhetoric of a Mafeking debauch? (Cheers.)

I have no doubt whatever of the result of the coming appeal to the electors. The power of the syndicated press is very strong, but the power of the people is stronger still. (Cheers.) The power of the selfish forces of this world is very great, but the generous forces always in the end prevail.

A PLEA FOR LIBERAL UNITY

March 31, 1905

Albert Hall, Sheffield

Despite the misfortunes of the Balfour Government, now limping miserably towards a catastrophic election, the Liberals still nursed the animosities which had rendered it impotent in the 1890s and early 1900s. The Liberal League was the organ of those Liberal Imperialists whose distaste for Campbell-Bannerman still remained, these divisions providing the only gleam of hope for the Government's position.

[Extract] We have travelled a good way since the National Union of Conservative Associations met in Sheffield eighteen months ago. Free-traders have nothing to regret. What has happened? At immense cost, through the sacrifices of Free Trade Ministers who resigned their offices and terminated their political careers for the sake of their consciences, and through the labours of the Liberal party all over the country, the Protectionist assault has been hurried back and the great economic truths which are associated with the names of Cobden and Bright are more firmly established today than at any time within the memory of man. The arrogant folk who started out two years ago, confident that they were going to change the settled opinion of this great nation by cheap electioneering propaganda, are very meek and humble now. They are unable to defend their principles in the House of Commons. They have to be content with spitting out their spite upon individual Free-traders in the country, whose activity, they think, has been the main cause of their undoing. . . .

The next Liberal Government has great problems to face and dangerous enemies to confront, and I hope it may represent the whole strength of the Liberal party, its whole talent and authority; and that it may not represent the triumph of a single section. I have always urged a Free Trade concentration–that we should stand together in one long line of battle without any of the little jealousies and bickerings which too often disfigure great public causes. It is fortunate that at this time the party contains two men who are honoured and admired wherever the English language is studied and spoken–Mr. Morley and Lord Rosebery. We are told that it is impossible for these two leaders to work together–that the question of Ireland interposes between their co-operation. I think that is all nonsense. There is no question of a Home Rule bill being introduced into the next Parliament, so that there is no reason why these men should not agree upon the policy which is then to be pursued. The next Government will have to undertake the reform of Dublin Castle and some measure of devolution, but they can do this without impairing the effective integrity of the United Kingdom. These two men have attracted me to Liberalism. I decline to choose between them, and I repudiate the suggestion that to be loyal to one is to be disloyal to another. If this unity can be obtained we can succeed in erecting once again in England a great governing instrument, the prop of liberty, and the lever of reform, which will revive the strength and vigour of Gladstone's famous Administration of 1868.

A Liberal victory will be shorn of half its usefulness and all its splendour unless it carries with it a message of comfort to the most unfortunate of our fellow subjects; unless it is shown that power has once again passed into the hands of men who will labour long and valiantly in the cause of the poor.

SOUTH AFRICA (CHINESE LABOUR)

October 6, 1905

'95 Club Dinner,
Grand Hotel, Manchester

The introduction of Chinese labour into the Transvaal, as well as their working and living conditions, created an immense outcry against the Government and much Liberal outrage. Churchill did not share these emotions, but it was clearly an issue on which a Liberal candidate had to make a pronouncement. His policy was to fight the Manchester election on Free Trade. Nonetheless, the fervour of his remarks on this subject in this speech demonstrates that he went rather further than what one biographer dismisses as "nominal oblations on the issue" (Randolph Churchill: Winston S. Churchill, *II, 115).*

In this speech Churchill also made capital out of the August resignation of Lord Curzon, the Viceroy of India, after a prolonged and bitter dispute with Lord Kitchener, the Commander-in-Chief.

[Extract] . . . I don't know when the general election is coming. Some people tell me it will be in March, and some say it will be in October–next. I am not going to attempt to prophesy. I am quite sure Mr. Balfour will never leave the Treasury bench until he is compelled–(hear, hear),–and that nothing but a good stout rope and two strong horses will ever move him from the dignified position which he occupies. (Cheers.) But one thing I predict–that the longer the present Government go on ruling the nation in flat defiance of its will, in the face of the plainest indications of its displeasure, the greater their fall, the more irrevocable the disaster, and the more enduring the discredit with which their names are associated. (Cheers.) The differences that divide parties in the country have never been more plain than they are to-night, in India, in Ireland, and in this country. On every side arise questions which occasion in all our minds feelings of profound anxiety and of fierce disagreement. But those differences, numerous and serious as they are, they are internal and not external. They are limited to the confines of the British Empire. They do not extend to our relations with foreign States. In the Anglo-French agreement and in the Japanese alliance the Government have acted with the concurrence of the nation as a whole and not merely of the factions which adhere to them whatever they are. (Hear, hear.) . . .

When we look at South Africa the differences which divide English parties are more unbridgeable and more acute than any I have mentioned to you to-night. I have never been one of those who have used unrestrained language about the importation of Chinese labour in South Africa. I have been astonished at the vehemence of my friends. I thought when it was first proposed it was a cold-blooded and a rather sordid experiment, which certainly ought not to be attempted unless supported by a plebiscite from the colony concerned, and I voted against it on all occasions on that ground, and on that ground alone. I have never applied the word "slavery" to the Chinese ordinance. But I think experience has shown that the instinct which prompted the working men of this country and of the great colonies of Australia and New Zealand to protest so passionately, so vehemently, against the introduction of Chinese labour was a true instinct, founded on real reason and a great perception of the underlying causes and forces which were at work.—(Hear, hear.) Dangers which were utterly unforeseen, even by those who were the most implacable opponents of this labour, have arisen. Ugly and vicious consequences which they had never predicted have actually come upon us.

A situation has been created in South Africa which I venture to say is full of peril to British honour—aye, and to British authority.—(Cheers.) Here we are, gathered together to-night at the Grand Hotel, Manchester, in the year of grace 1905, and what is going on in certain parts of South Africa under the shadow and shelter of the British flag? If we could penetrate these walls and carry our vision to South Africa what should we see? First of all we may discern a cordon of police, armed with rifles, loaded, in pickets every few hundred yards, supported by an imposing column of mounted men who can gallop instantly to any threatened spot. Inside this cordon are herded unnaturally together a number of men, burrowing for gold, ill-used by the white miners with whom they work, flogged by their overseers, in flat defiance of the law, when they do not burrow fast enough. Outside the cordon of police are the deserters, the men whom even the luxuries of a Johannesburg compound could not keep in content, roaming about over those vast plains, crouching among the rocks, hunted like wild beasts, shot at sight, living by murder and rapine, the terror of the world, half the world between them and their own sunny China. Surely the grimmest spectacle of moral havoc for which this Christian and civilised nation has been made responsible within the lifetime of living men!—(Cheers.)

What consolation is it to us who are offended by these things that they make for the prosperity of a certain class, that the exchanges of London, Paris, and Berlin are able to calculate accurately in sixteenths, thirty-seconds, and even sixty-fourths, the market value of the mining shares? I say this experiment of Chinese labour has proved a disastrous failure. It has proved a greater failure than even those who hated it most were able to anticipate or to describe.—(Hear, hear.) The status of manual labour all over the world has been parodied and discredited. South Africa is convulsed by a new racial problem. The fair fame of the British Empire has been soiled by greed, and all those sacrifices of moral and material advantage have not prevented an enormous depression in the very share market to support which at all hazards they were made.

I feel that this question of Chinese labour must be the great moral issue at the general election. I feel that we must draw a hard and sharp line between those people who wish to see the experiment continued and those who wish to see it brought to an end. I have no doubt on which side of the line I find myself, and I have no doubt on which side those electors whose support I am seeking will be. Here within the confines of these islands we find cause of quarrel more widespread and deep-seated, more hotly contested even than the labour issue in South Africa. It is here, in England, that a Liberal victory will mean the greatest change and reversal of policy.

Surely it is about time there was a change and reversal of policy.—(Cheers.) Our finances are disorganised, expenditure rampant, armaments have been multiplied, efficiency has not been obtained, security has not been notably increased. The British army, in attempted reforms to put it right once for all, has been reduced to chaos; the volunteers have been snubbed, starved, bullied, and abused; and the most necessary reforms have been neglected. The most sacred pledges—and I think no Conservative member who stood at the last election but one is prepared to say that old-age pensions was not a sacred pledge—sacred pledges have been violated. Session after session has been barren except in so far as it has been disfigured by reactionary or sham legislation.

I am very glad to find by the manner in which I have been treated here to-night that the harsh and fierce language which I have used in Parliament in the last session, and for which I have been so much rebuked, condemned, and censured, is not altogether without some measure of support.—(Hear, hear.) You may be sure that I shall make it my business to say all I have to say in the future without the smallest restraint.—(Cheers.)

THE OLD GOVERNMENT AND THE NEW

December 14, 1905

City Liberal Club, London

On December 4, the Balfour Government suddenly resigned, hoping to exploit continuing divisions within the Liberal ranks. The King sent for Sir Henry Campbell-Bannerman, who, after brief difficulties with Asquith, Grey, and Haldane (who had agreed only to serve under him if he went to the Lords), formed a new Government. Grey became Foreign Secretary; Asquith, Chancellor of the Exchequer; and Haldane, Secretary of State for War. Lord Elgin became the new Colonial Secretary, and Churchill asked for—and was given—the post of Under-Secretary. The appointment was announced on December 13. Parliament was formally dissolved on January 8 but the General Election campaign began when the Balfour Government resigned.

How has the Liberal Government come into existence? Mr. Balfour resigned because, as he said himself, his party was so hopelessly divided that even he could go on no longer with the Government. His supporters with the utmost candour supplied the reason why he did not dissolve. Dissolution, they said, is a weapon which should only be advised by a Minister who believes that he will secure a majority in the new Parliament. Mr. Balfour is not such a Minister; therefore, unable to go on with this

Parliament and despairing of any better fortune in the next, he has no choice but to tender his resignation to the King. That is the explanation. It is not often in history that a great party has through its recognised leader publicly proclaimed its own impotence and incompetence to form or maintain a Government. (Hear, hear.) Whatever might be the future fortunes or action of the new Government, at any rate at its beginning it is admitted to be necessarily indispensable even by its most obvious opponents. Such a Government deserves some consideration from those whose conduct and tactics have rendered it a necessity; and a Government admittedly necessary should have been at least allowed to get into the saddle before it is condemned. Not at all. Before the Government had been even formed Mr. Balfour had already described it as a Government of Imperial disintegration, and Mr. Chamberlain declared that Sir Henry Campbell-Bannerman took his orders from the enemies of his country, and is using his position to undermine the Constitution that it is his duty to support. Really, that sort of thing is rather thin. It might be good enough for some newspapers, but statesmen, men of light and leading, long honoured in the service of the public, about to appeal for the independent judgment of their fellow-countrymen upon a record which, at any rate, gave rise to legitimate differences of opinion, to put it mildly, should surely provide us with more sober and reasonable arguments. Mr. Balfour at Manchester said that his resignation was received ungratefully by those who had so long demanded it. Sir Henry Campbell-Bannerman had no reason to be grateful to Mr. Balfour. It was not out of any consideration for him that Mr. Balfour resigned. Nothing but the bluntest compulsion procured his retirement. (Cheers.)

In what condition has he left the public estate? The property is heavily mortgaged, the banking account overdrawn, the annual charges are vastly increased, and national credit has been gravely impaired. The philanthropy of the late Government made Consols cheap enough to be within the range of the comparatively poor people. (Laughter.) Sir Henry Campbell-Bannerman came to the counsels of a Sovereign who was deserted at an awkward moment in the interests of a party manoeuvre. He will find nothing in the condition of the public business, legislative, administrative, Parliamentary, or financial, to make him indebted to his predecessor. (Cheers.) Indeed the change of Government that has just taken place is less like an ordinary transfer of power from one great party to another than the winding up of an insolvent concern which had been conducted by questionable and even shady methods to a ruinous conclusion. (Cheers.) The firm Balfour, Balfour, and Co. has stopped payment. The managing director, a Birmingham man of large views and unusual versatility, absconded two years ago, leaving heavy outstanding liabilities, and he is believed to have since devoted himself mainly to missionary work. (Loud laughter.) Ever since, the business has been going downhill; it is now in liquidation. (Cheers.) Its paper is no longer accepted in the City and it has been "hammered" on Change. (Cheers and laughter.) No more sinecures for guinea pigs, no more garters for dukes, no more peerages for the faithful press—(laughter);—the crash has come at last. Sir Henry Campbell-Bannerman presented himself in the capacity of the official receiver to secure the rights of the creditors and safeguard the interests of the shareholders, according to the regular law of the land. (Cheers.) Look where you will throughout the spheres of the Government's action, you will see on every hand the same evidences of disorder. There is one thing on which I as the Under Secretary for the Colonies must say. It is a small, humble post, but it has one powerful attraction for me. It will enable me to keep in touch with Mr. Chamberlain in the special subject of his later activities. (Cheers and laughter.) Mr. Chamberlain might have been the great Colonial Minister his friends declared, but against the services he rendered there must be set one great disservice which has gone far to undo his good work and to injure his reputation—he has never hesitated to drag the colonial empire into the vortex of British politics. He has sought to associate the British Empire not with the whole nation, but with that section of the nation which happened to support the Government of which he was a member. Nothing could be more detrimental to the cause he had at heart. If the colonies were not much too sensible to be misled by such talk, if colonial statesmen had not always been most careful to keep themselves clear of the party politics of this country, some real injury might have very easily been done.

But do not let us get into a jumpy, nervous state about the colonies. The bonds which unite the various portions of our widespread empire have stood strains prolonged, sudden, direct, transverse, and oblique during the generations through which they have endured and strengthened. (Cheers.) It is only the platform Imperialist who imagines, in his conceit, that the mighty structure raised by so much valour, wisdom, and sacrifice is about to collapse, and that only his meddlesome finger can avert the ruins. We should not sink to the level of a fifth-rate power as easily as Mr. Chamberlain supposes. (Cheers.) The British Empire will not enter upon a period of crisis because a Birmingham election campaign is now somewhat overdue; the British Empire will not break into pieces because Mr. Chamberlain broke out into poetry—and such poetry. (Loud cheers and laughter.) There is no doubt at the present time an unnatural number of difficult questions of colonial policy which await treatment or settlement. Lord Elgin finds himself confronted with questions of strategy and commerce, of transit and education, with racial questions not less vast and scarcely less varied than those which he faced with so much composure ten years ago in India. An under secretary is, as Lord Hugh Cecil once caustically remarked, only a stipendiary echo; well, there is no such thing as an anticipatory echo. (Laughter.) We must wait upon these matters definite declarations of policy from those whose duty it is to make it. But at any rate there is no secret about the principles that will govern the Liberal colonial policy. They are known to all the world and have long been esteemed in England. They are, I believe, to be affirmed again at the approaching election. (Cheers.) Free Trade, self-government, and, above all, peace—(renewed cheers)—they are the only methods by which it has been found possible to reconcile the interests of democracy with the responsibility of overseas dominion. In proportion as we have faithfully observed them our affairs have prospered until, in the dawn of the twentieth century, we are at the head of what is on the whole the most considerable of states and dependencies ever witnessed in the modern world. The nation which gave with an open hand and an open heart to the colonies all that it has a right to give—its protection, its credit, its great, free market—gave them all freely and fully, asking no price, driving no bargain, asking for no repayment, is the only nation which has been able to preserve through all the years loyal, powerful, prosperous, and profitable colonies. (Cheers.) "Cast your bread upon the waters and it will return to you after many days." It returns in that perfect loyalty which springs from perfect freedom, in that deepening sympathy which comes with widening knowledge, in that true commercial independence which is the child of free exchange and peace. (Loud cheers.)

ELECTION ADDRESS

January 4, 1906

Heywood Street School, Ancoats

An unexpected development in the election was the activity of the woman suffragettes, who made Churchill a particular target of their disruptive tactics.

It is clear by the size of this meeting that politics attracts the attention of the whole of the electorate. This is a very important fact for the Liberal party, because our chance of success depends upon the vote of the masses of the people. And I come of a stock that has always found some recognition in the hearts of the working classes—(cheers),—and I should not care to go to Parliament except with the assent and agreement of a democratic electorate.

[Editor's Note: At this point he was interrupted by a young woman in the gallery, who unfolded a banner with the words "Votes for women," and spoke in an excited but rather incoherent manner. For some minutes confusion reigned. When Churchill was again able to make himself heard he said he was willing to give the interrupter five minutes at the end of his speech and also to answer any questions in regard to women's suffrage. In spite of this offer the young woman in the gallery continued to speak, and it became clear that if the meeting was to go on she must be removed. Churchill, while expressing regret that the incident had occurred, said he did not understand why it was that these ladies always select Liberal and Radical meetings for their demonstrations. He also pointed out that the right of public meeting is one of the most valuable privileges the people possess, and that it would be absurd to admit the right of a single individual to bring it to nought.]

As I was saying when I was interrupted half an hour ago, how often have we thought that the Balfourian Administration was at the end of its course of profligacy and devastation. The new Government is not like the last. We are not contented with office; we want power. Mr. Balfour resigned because his party was so hopelessly divided that he could not go on any longer. It is not often in our history that a great party has made such a confession of impotence and powerlessness to carry on the government of the country either in this Parliament or the next. Shall Mr. Balfour come back to power? ("No.") But I assure you he is quite ready to do so. Regardless of expense, he is perfectly willing to undertake the duty of manipulating a party majority, what with his wirepullers and whips, his gagging and guillotining closures. If he gets a majority he will be able to get it terrorised and organised together to carry anything, however flagrant, to vote any Estimates however extravagant, to carry any legislation, however reactionary, which the vested interests which support his party may demand.

Mr. Gerald Balfour is quite ready to turn out of the Local Government Board Mr. John Burns, who ought to have a fair chance of dealing with the social problems, which no one knows better than he and no one is more able to handle. Mr. Lyttelton is perfectly willing to come back and to send to South Africa any number of Chinamen. The new Government declines to accept the smallest responsibility for the experiment, which was the outcome of sordid motives and has been attended by lamentable consequences. We ask the working classes to support us in the action we have taken. When we get to the House of Commons we do not anticipate any difficulty in making our case good. . . .

I am astonished to see that Mr. Joynson-Hicks described me as a supporter of Mr. Balfour. From the beginning of the controversy my whole object has been to maintain intact and unimpaired the existing Free Trade system. Has Retaliation ever succeeded? (A voice, "It has never been tried.") Oh, yes, it has been tried in every country in the world, and the only result has been that tariff walls have grown higher and higher. I have no doubt of the result of the election if it is made clear that the great issue is between fiscal reform and "as you were." (Cheers.)

[Editor's Note: In accordance with Mr. Churchill's promise, at the end of his speech a spokeswoman of the Women's Suffrage Association was invited on the platform in order to lay their case before the meeting. . . .

I have fully explained my views on women's suffrage to a deputation, and I voted in favour of the enfranchisement of women in the session before last. Although I think this a question of great difficulty, I was steadily moving forward to the position of a whole-hearted supporter of their case. But I have been much put off by what has happened in the last few months. I have seen five or six great meetings thrown into disorder by people getting up and shouting till they were turned out. I will not go one inch beyond my declaration to the deputation. I should in that way be giving way to the violent interruptions which have happened at my meetings. With regard to what my future action may be, having regard to the pressure put upon me, I utterly decline to state. . . .

WOMAN'S SUFFRAGE AND IRISH REFORM POLICY

January 5, 1906

Public Hall, Cheetham

Nothing is so encouraging as the numbers of the people who want to attend these meetings. If the enthusiasm which we already see generated continues till the end of next week we will have won a memorable electoral victory in the history of the country. We will have our chance on Saturday week–

[Editor's Note: At this point a young woman rose from the very centre of the densely packed audience and, standing on her chair, waved the now familiar black and white flag bearing the words "Votes for women." There was immediately a storm of hooting, and the flag was snatched away and flung from hand to hand. Mr. Churchill resumed his seat. The uproar became louder and louder, and the Chairman appealed in vain for order. Rising after a few minutes, during which the meeting continued to show the greatest indignation against those who had made the disturbance, Churchill said]: I am perfectly willing to answer any question.–(Loud cheers.) I have to go to another meeting, and if I am to speak here first I must ask you to hear me. (Loud cries of "Hear, hear.") May I say to the lady in the centre of the hall–(cries of "She's not a lady.")–that if she wishes to ask a question we will extend to her a courteous hearing? I will answer the question now–(renewed interruption)–if I am listened to. If not I won't answer it at all.–(Loud cheers.)

[Editor's Note: There was a renewed uproar at the back of the hall. When it had partially subsided Mr. Churchill, who was again loudly cheered, rose and said]: The lady who has interrupted has, I understand, asked a definite question–whether or not I am in favour of votes for women."–(Prolonged cries of "No," and continued disorder.) I suggest that the woman who is at the center of the disturbance come upon the platform and ask her question from this advantageous position. If she declines to take such an offer as that we are not going to allow hundreds of people gathered here to be upset in this way. (Loud and prolonged cheers.)

[Editor's Note: The woman, who was quite youthful, and who was stated to be a sister of Miss Christabel Pankhurst, then came up the centre of the hall to the platform. Her appearance on the platform was greeted with loud and continued hissing. She faced the audience with a smiling face, which appeared to provoke still more indignation. When silence was partially restored she said, "The question I have asked is this. Will the Liberal Government–(cries of "Rot")–give women the vote?–(Loud cries of "Never.") I ask this question on behalf of thousands of working women–(cries of "No")–and thousands of women of all classes. The reason we have resorted to these means of asking the question–"(Renewed interruption.) Continuing, the young woman said: "The reason we have had to resort to these probably unfair and unconstitutional methods–(hear, hear)–of asking the question is that if we wait till the end of the meeting we get no reply. We have not the same opportunities as men."]

I have been asked a question, and for that question I have done my best to secure a hearing. That question is–Will I use what influence I possess to secure votes for women. This is the answer. On the only occasion when I have voted I have voted for giving votes to women. Now, having regard to the treatment I have received, and to the destruction of great public meetings which I have witnessed time after time, nothing will induce me to vote for giving votes to women. (Loud and prolonged cheers.)

I am sorry such an incident has occurred.–(Hear, hear.) One of our greatest privileges is the power of holding large public meetings. If a single person is to be able to prevent a whole meeting being conducted in an orderly fashion we may as well give up representative and democratic government, and develop a system of government by shouting.–(Cheers.) I am especially sorry that this should have happened, for the young lady bears a name which is greatly and deservedly respected in Manchester. I recognise the conscientious zeal which makes her do these things, but they are wholly undemocratic and for anyone who desires to show how fit women are to receive the franchise I cannot imagine a more foolish course to pursue. (Loud cheers.) I am not so hostile to the proposal as I thought it right to say just now–(laughter),–but I am not going to be hen-pecked–(much laughter)–on a question of such grave public importance.–(Hear, hear.)

The attention of Parliament has been directed to Irish matters for upwards of twenty-five years, and the attention of Parliament is rarely fruitless in the long run. Time has largely vindicated the policy which Mr. Gladstone declared for in 1886. We have seen a great measure of local government passed by a Conservative Ministry, and it is working extremely well. We have seen a Land Bill very similar to the one which wrecked the Home Rule Bill of 1886 passed into law by the party which opposed the bill of 1886. We cannot be blind to the fact that these are great events, and their consequences should encourage us to go further. I consider that these great acts of legislation are a credit to the Conservative party, but I think it also true to say that if it had not been for the impulse given by the espousal of the Irish cause by the Liberal party it is probable these great measures would never have been carried into law. These measures have produced a new situation. There never was a time when there was a greater mass of opinion in this country arrayed against any extreme departure in Irish Government, when the declarations of leading politicians, the speeches of candidates, and the conjunction of political parties was so unfavourable to anything in the nature of a startling plunge in Irish legislation.

But there never was a time when a greater number of sensible and patriotic people were prepared to give a fair and unprejudiced consideration to the Irish question, prepared to admit that a wrong system of government prevailed in that country, and prepared to approach without passion or prejudice what is, after all, one of the most difficult, as it is one of the most attractive, problems with which statecraft can have to deal. . . .

I am myself not prepared to support any legislation which, in my opinion, will affect or injury the integrity of the United Kingdom–(cheers),–or which would lead to a separation between England and Ireland, or to the setting up by the side of England of any foreign or hostile power.–(Renewed cheers.) You could not have two more conscientious or disinterested Unionists than Lord James of Hereford–(cheers)–and the Duke of Devonshire–(renewed cheers),–and they see no reason why people should be deterred from voting for Free Trade because the Conservative party has raised this old cry. You have in the Liberal Government several of the most prominent Ministers–Sir Edward Grey, Mr. Asquith, and Mr. Birrell,–without whom the Cabinet would not have impressed itself upon the country so strongly as it has as a Cabinet of strong and able men, and who have all said that it would not be fair at the present time to use a majority created on the Free Trade issue for the purpose of slipping through a measure of Home Rule for Ireland. Then you have got the House of Lords.–(A voice: Down with them.) If you want to down the House of Lords you had better pick your ground and your quarrel. To run full tilt at the House of Lords on a question on which they have a majority of the people behind them is to establish them much more strongly than before.–(Cheers.)

Lastly, you have this, that whatever anybody says it is Free Trade and not Home

Rule that is the great issue at this election. Even if a Home Rule bill were introduced and passed in the House of Commons, the House of Lords would throw it out, and there would have to be another election fought on Home Rule.–(Hear, hear.) The Home Rule bogey ought not to frighten any Free-trader or to prevent him from doing his duty at this election and giving effect to his honest economic convictions. –(Cheers.)

"CHINESE SLAVERY"

January 9, 1906

Lever Street Schools, Manchester

Particular note should be taken of Churchill's words where his position on the wave of "Chinese slavery" was markedly more moderate than that of most of his fellow Liberal candidates. As Under-Secretary for the Colonies, Churchill was now in a better position than he had been in October to realize how difficult the question was.

[Extract] . . . I have read Mr. Balfour's speech of last night. He seems very fond of Chinese labour; he talks about nothing else; it has become the apple of his eye. He regards it as the one great and splendid achievement of his Government. I do not so regard it. I think that Mr. Lyttelton and Mr. Balfour had no right to introduce Chinese labour into South Africa while they were responsible for the government of the Transvaal. The Transvaal was not a self-governing colony, but a Crown colony, and it is so now. I do not believe that the people of the Transvaal were favourable to the introduction of Chinese labour. I have been told on the highest authority that it would have been quite impossible to get a plebiscite in its favour. It is true a petition was signed by a large number of persons in favour of the importation, but it was got up by the mineowners. There was no reason or right for making this grisly experiment. At the same time, if it had not been made, I believe it is true to say that the revival in South Africa would not have been so rapid.

If the mineowners had been made to realise that they could not have Chinese labour, they would have fallen back on something else. What else? To a greater measure on white labour, which would have been employed with very much improved machinery; and although the revival of the gold industry would have been slower, it would have been surer and better, and more calculated to maintain the true interests of the white man in South Africa.–(Cheers.) . . .

The experiment of Chinese labour was made in defiance of the wishes of the Liberal party, and 45,000 Chinamen were set to work upon the mines in South Africa. Now that they are there the whole of the industries of the country have adapted themselves to this labour, and if you suddenly repatriated these Chinese it would undoubtedly cause a great relapse in South Africa and many thousands of English workmen would be thrown out of employment. We do not approve of this system, but we think that if the serious step of repatriating the Chinese at once is to be taken that step must be taken upon the authority of a representative South African Government, because it is a matter which affects South Africa much more than our own interests in this country. Only six days before the late Government went out of office they issued 12,000 more licences to import Chinese. These licences are, however, lawful documents, carrying with them the weight and authority of the British Government. The moment Lord Elgin obtained power his first act was to say "No more."–(Cheers.)

I have to say this. The new Government is a Government of law and order. It has to obey as well as administer the law, and where people have definite legal claims against the Government to which we have been committed by our predecessors we cannot get away from them. It would mean that heavy compensation claims would be sustained in the courts. We decline to allow the system of Chinese labour to be extended; we intend to submit the whole matter to a really representative South African Assembly.

Mr. Balfour has contended that we have termed this labour slavery, and that we ought to use force of arms to end it. I have never called it slavery, because I think there are conditions which do not constitute slavery. For instance a labourer cannot be bought or sold. On the other hand it is certainly servile and improper labour.–(Hear, hear.) Mr. Balfour has also said that the conditions of the Chinese labour ordinance are identical with those of the British Guiana ordinance sanctioned by the Liberals.

A Voice: They are better.

Mr. Churchill: Better, you say. That shows the study you have given to this question. In the first place, under the Chinese ordinance a man contracts himself out of the right to hold real property–a house or land. That is an improper provision. He contracts himself out of the right to reside in the country on the completion of the engagement. He contracts himself out of the right to an open trial, out of the right to be the master of his own actions in so far as he is not needed for employment; he contracts himself into the liability of being arrested at sight without a warrant. All these five points may be urged against the Chinese ordinance and make it worse than the Guiana ordinance passed before.–(Hear, hear.)

THE GENERAL ELECTION

January 15, 1906

Reform Club, Manchester

The North-west Manchester result was declared on January 13. The figures were:

Churchill (Liberal)	*5,639*
Joynson-Hicks (Conservative)	*4,398*
Majority	*1,241*

The reader may be startled by these small figures, but it should be remembered that the vote was strictly limited to adult males–and a limited number of adult males at that. It is an indication of the excitement of the election that 89 percent of the registered voters voted. In Manchester and Salford the Unionists were routed, not a single candidate surviving the Liberal-Labour onslaught. In 1900 the nine constituencies had been held by eight Unionists and one Liberal. In 1906 the Liberals won seven seats, Labour two. Arthur Balfour was among the vanquished.

We are met in the hour of victory. And what a victory! (Cheers.) I do not speak only of my own victory in North-west Manchester, but of the victories of the Liberal party throughout this great city. Believe me, these victories were never more needed than now. After all, it is Protection that is ruined, and nothing could more signally mark its defeat than the repudiation, utter, flat, and total, by the great city of Manchester on the first opportunity it had of expressing its opinion. Did they think that after sixty years we could not tell truth from falsehood? (Cheers.) Did they think that after sixty years we had forgotten the work of John Bright and Richard Cobden? (Cheers.) Did they think that after sixty years Lancashire was asleep and would be false to its traditions? (Cheers.)

[Editor's Note: After acknowledging the self-sacrificing labours of his committee, Churchill said]: I must remind you at this moment of success that I came to Manchester in rather a dark hour for my own fortunes, and at an hour when it seemed as if Free Trade itself ran some risk of being swept away as if it were an obsolete dogma. Well, we have put all that right now.–(Cheers.) Now that I am member for the central division I hope I shall be able to serve the interests of this great city with effect and usefulness in the House of Commons, and I trust that the victory which has been won here will light the Liberal cause and light the Liberal army on its upward march. We have had opposed to us in this fight some of the most courteous and honourable gentlemen. Let us make no recrimination upon them. It is their cause that has destroyed them, not their character. I gladly recognise at this moment the courtesy I have received throughout the contest from my opponent. I think you will do well to treat him with respect when you are brought into contact with him as Manchester men.–(Cheers.) But, believe me, much more than a personal issue has been decided. What we have done to-night has been to stop the reaction which had begun, and which for the last four or five years had been active and aggressive in our English life. You have given the new Government a splendid start. You have given it the fair chance for which I have appealed. If the future course of the election should bear out its beginning the Government will have an ample majority. Let us hope that we shall use that majority with wisdom and moderation, and let us hope that five years hence, when perhaps we shall not be so full of enthusiasm as we are now, we may be able to look back upon solid achievements in the interests of the people and upon an added glory to the lustre of the British Empire.–(Cheers.)

SOUTH AFRICA (CHINESE LABOUR)

February 22, 1906

House of Commons

The Unionists had gone down to shattering defeat. In the new House of Commons, the Liberals had 377 seats, Labour 53, and the Irish Nationalists 83; the Unionists numbered only 157, of whom 11 were Free Traders, and the rest either Tariff Reformers or supporters of Balfour's indeterminate middle-of-the-road position. In Balfour's absence–he returned to the Commons shortly after the General Election in a by-election for the City of London–Chamberlain led the Opposition.

Churchill's reputation had been further enhanced by the publication, during the election campaign, of his two-volume biography of his father, which was widely acclaimed.

The new Parliament met on February 19, and it was clear that the Liberal majority was in a truculent mood. A great number were new to the House of Commons, and their behavior in the first weeks was somewhat raucous. The new Government, furthermore, had little in the way of a constructive programme beyond an Education Bill, proposals for reversing the Taff Vale judgment of 1901 (which had ruled that unions could be sued for the actions of their members), and the granting of responsible government to the Transvaal. Churchill was deeply involved in this last matter, and the successful completion of this task was his first major achievement as a Minister.

On February 22, in the Debate on the Address, the Opposition moved an amendment condemning the Liberals for their use of "Chinese slavery" during the election. Churchill's speech contained the famous phrase, "terminological inexactitude." This, Churchill's first ministerial speech, was disappointing to the Liberals, and laid the way open for an effective counter-attack by Chamberlain later in the Debate.

[Extract] . . . The Party opposite, or rather the Party who sit in that corner of the House opposite, have taken up a clear position on the subject of Chinese labour. They are its authors, its admirers and its champions, they believe with all the sincerity of the hon. Gentleman who has just sat down that it is necessary for the welfare of South Africa, and that without it the British Empire would collapse. Yet I think the tendency of their Amendment and speeches, and certainly the tendency of some remarks made by the right hon. Gentleman the Member for West Birmingham the other day is to urge His Majesty's Government on to courses more extreme than those upon which they are resolved and to precipitate the very catastrophe which the right hon. Gentleman professes himself so anxious to avoid. Do not let us judge this too harshly. We have been in Opposition ourselves and we know very well that the Opposition is always seeking for opportunities to embarrass the Government, not always successfully seeking, and we know very well that an Opposition is bound in regular custom to oppose and to criticise the Government, and has no real measure of responsibility for anything it may say or do. I will only venture to congratulate the great Imperial Statesmen who sit upon that bench upon the ease and celerity with which they have exchanged the responsibilities of office for the irresponsibilities of Opposition. I must confess that I listened with very great pleasure the other day to the speech of the right hon. Member for West Birmingham in which he so strongly condemned anything in the nature of electioneering misrepresentation. I am sure we all agree that every effort should be made to raise the standard of our electioneering contests and to keep out of them any aspersions upon the humanity, the loyalty, or the patriotism of the candidates who may be engaged in them. The Prime Minister will welcome the co-operation of the right hon. Gentleman in anything that may tend to raise the standard of our Party life, and I can assure him that his departure upon so praiseworthy and new a course will be watched with sympathy and respect in all quarters of the House. I took occasion during the elections to say, and I repeat it now, that the conditions of the Transvaal Ordinance under which Chinese labour is now being carried on do not, in my opinion, constitute a state of slavery. A labour contract into which men enter voluntarily for a limited and for a brief period, under which they are paid wages which they consider adequate, under which they are not bought or sold and from which they can obtain relief—I shall have to say a word about that later—on payment of £17 10s., the cost of their passage, may not be a desirable contract, may not be a healthy or proper contract, but it cannot in the opinion of His Majesty's Government be classified as slavery in the extreme acceptance of the word without some risk of terminological inexactitude. . . .

Let me say at the outset that no responsibility for this system rests upon His Majesty's Government. We are not concerned to defend it, or to justify it. It was passed in spite of our votes and in spite of our protests. We have nothing to conceal, nothing to palliate, nothing to deny. The whole burden of this subject, whether it be a cause of glory, or of discredit, rests, and can only rest, upon the Conservative and Protectionist Party. We, the present Government, are the heirs to their evil inheritance; but we are doing the very best we can to undo the harm which has been done. We ask the support and confidence of the House, not in reference to matters which we could not deal with from the beginning, but in regard to measures that are projected. We ask for confidence and approbation for what we do ourselves, upon our own responsibility, and upon our own initiative. . . .

Once an improper or unjust contract has received the sanction of law it becomes the basis on which all manner of perfectly healthy and unobjectionable agreements are founded. Bargain is added to bargain, plan is built on plan, and a whole economic structure rises, tier above tier, upon the faulty foundation. If in erecting some great building it is found that a girder in the lowest story is defective, the building becomes a cause of peril and danger to the public, but it is not possible immediately to withdraw it. To wrench it away would be to involve the certainty of ruin; but to whom? The jerry-builder might have decamped. The contractor might have made a fortune from the job and retired. It is upon the humble occupants that the miseries of the downfall would descend. It is my duty to lay before the House all the facts and materials of this grave matter, and I cannot but doubt that the sudden and arbitrary deportation of a third of the labour supply of South Africa would produce an utter economic collapse. We need not waste our sympathy upon the Rand magnates. Whatever we may do or whatever may take place in South Africa, many of them will still retain as many millions as the hon. Member for Merthyr Tydvil would consider it desirable that any individual should enjoy. But to thousands of small people, to honest investors, to shopkeepers and tradespeople in Johannesburg, to British miners and Boer farmers, to railway servants on South African railways, to hard-working colonists and others, there might come, if any violent or immediate action were taken and 60,000 coolies were deported, the harsh and unexpected pinch of poverty and suffering. The progress of Colonies struggling feebly forward out of the agony of the war would be rudely thrown back; the finances of every State in South Africa would be embarrassed, the whole course of South African trade would be dislocated, and something very like famine on a considerable scale might ensue in Johannesburg, and the great mining district connected with it. If such a catastrophe resulted from our action, however benevolent our intention was, however benevolently right in principle that action might be, we could not escape the most grievous responsibility; and let me remind the House that when this country incurs a grievous responsibility the discharge of that responsibility takes the form of a serious financial payment. It is not beyond the resources of engineering to remove the defective girder by means of levers and other mechanical appliances. The lever which His Majesty's Government desire to use to carry out their policy and to bring to an end the present system of indentured labour in the Transvaal, is, first of all, the opinion of the people of the Transvaal. We have good hopes of that opinion. I do not think for a moment that any Parliament in the Transvaal would violently and immediately expel the Chinese, but I most firmly believe that a Parliament fairly elected and representative of all classes and both races in the country will decide against the continuance of this experiment in a permanent form, and will certainly reject the impudent demands—I can call them nothing else—now being put forward vastly to extend its scope. I read in the interesting letters which Mr. Massingham has contributed to the *Daily News*—hon. Members on the other side are perfectly entitled to laugh at that authority, but it is nevertheless an authority which on this side of the House will carry weight—Mr. Massingham shares very closely the views which we hold; and I observe that in those letters he states that if the opinion of the Transvaal is fairly consulted, and a really representative assembly is brought into life, the opinion of that assembly will be, as I have indicated, against the perpetuation of the system. I believe that the maxim: "Trust the people" ought to follow the flag, and a very considerable body of evidence which we have been able to collect, shows that a representative assembly which has never yet been consulted will probably effect a termination of this experiment. I would say also in the second place that the mineowners themselves are beginning to realise that Chinese labour is economically a failure, that it is expensive and uncertain, and exposes them to an amount of criticism and vexation which greatly unsettles their business, and that it is likely to be more expensive, more uncertain, and more liable to expose them to criticism in the future. There is no greater delusion than that low wages mean high profits. No labour is so dear as cheap labour, and the labour which costs nothing is the dearest of all. I am fortified in that paradoxical reflection by the enormous depreciation which I observe to have taken place in the prices of South African stock since this policy was initiated. If only the late Government had had the courage to stand firm and refuse their sanction to this Ordinance, hard and increasing pressure would have enforced the employment of more machinery and more skilled white labour. . . .

I respectfully submit to the House that the question whether Chinese are cheaper than Kaffirs, whether white men and machinery can work the mines at a profit, whether the Chinese are on the whole a law-abiding people or a terror to the countryside, whether the importation of Chinese was in the true interests of the white people in South Africa, whether the product per stamp was less or more and why, whether the big houses discouraged Kaffir labour when they wished to establish a case for Chinese, whether it would really make a difference to South Africa if the mines are worked out in ninety years instead of in forty-five—all these questions are, no doubt, very interesting and important, but they are not the business of the House of Commons. This is not the place to thrash them out with advantage. They are questions that can be fought out in the Transvaal Assembly, and it is there that the material and political issues should be fought out. It is in a Parliament of their own that the people of the Transvaal must make up their minds on social, technical, and economical grounds whether Chinese labour is a good foundation on which to build the permanent welfare of the land in which they live. But there is another set of considerations which, without exciting the derision of the Party opposite, I might perhaps call humanitarian and moral considerations. On those this House is fully competent to pronounce, and is entitled and even bound to pronounce. On these great matters of principle the opinion of the House of Commons must always be expressed as a guide to the practice of other Legislatures all over the Empire. . . .

The steps which the Government have taken remove all danger of cruelty, of impropriety, or of gross infringement of liberty. I believe they remove the practical objections which have been urged against the Ordinance, but they do not, of course, remove our fundamental objections in principle to this system of labour. In these days, with every important nation of the globe in communication, and brought closer together, with Asiatic labour fluid as it never was fluid before, I think it is necessary to state the clear principle by which we should be guided so far as possible in the future. What is the cause of the innate and instinctive aversion which is maintained by this Parliament and the country to the system of Chinese indentured labour? It is that underlying that system there is the idea that men are to be treated as if they were implements. Are the Chinese necessary to Africa, to the development of the gold mines, to the fertilisation of its fields? Is it really true, as those who sit opposite say, that their co-operation is necessary for the prosperity of the country? Is it true that without their co-operation, collapse, stagnation, and bankruptcy must ensue? Does your great business really depend upon the laborious industry of these strangers? Is your empire to be maintained, are your fortunes to be amassed by the day to day consumption of their vital energies? Then, at least, receive them with that gratitude and respect which you owe to persons having it in their power to render such indispensable and inestimable services. Is it not an unworthy thing to accept wealth and security at their hands, and at the same time to shrink from the contamination of their touch? I lay down this principle in this democratic Parliament, that no man should be imported into a country as a labourer unless you also accept him as a human being. A great matter of principle like this affects not only the particular colony chiefly concerned, but it affects the working of our whole colonial system. That system can only rest upon the basis of self-government—or Home Rule, whichever name you prefer. Home Rule implies within broad limits the right to govern or misgovern, manage or mismanage, for good or for ill, the community upon which it is conferred. No one can watch the unceasing flow of business transacted through the Colonial Office without seeing that many things are being done, by persons to whom the Government has been forced to give wide discretionary powers, of which the people at home would not approve. Laws which are hard and narrow are being applied in certain British dominions. There are instances of the treatment of native races and the infliction of punishments and penalties which do not commend themselves to the sense of this House or the people of England. We have got in some cases to put up with those things, but there is no reason why we should cease to keep over South Africa the same regulating control that we do over other great self-governing colonies like Canada, New Zealand, and Australia. I believe that, generally speaking, given free institutions on a fair basis, the best side of men's nature will in the end surely come uppermost.

But this doctrine has its limits. Honestly, I do not believe that the Transvaal Parliament, fairly elected on a reasonable basis, will decide in favour of the retention of the Chinese. I think they will bring the experiment gradually, but surely, to an end. But while believing that, it would be unreasonable not to face the other alternative, however remote the contingency of it may be. What if the colony should decide to continue the importation of Chinese? I must point out that while the responsibility of the Imperial Government would be lessened, our objections to the present conditions under which Chinese labour is carried on will not be removed by any vote of the Transvaal Assembly, however unanimous, however representative. Nor should we be altogether without our remedy, quite apart from the power always reserved to the Crown. Anyone who knows the Acts and Conventions under which this system of Chinese labour is obtained and maintained will see how vital Imperial co-operation is and how fatal Imperial opposition would be. In Lord Elgin's original telegram he expressly says:—

> While reserving their opinion and form of action in the whole matter His Majesty's Government, . . .

Those are words to which a real and serious significance should be attached. It should not be taken for granted for one moment that while the conditions of Chinese labour continue to be repugnant to the opinions and feelings of the people of this country, Imperial sanction for the extension and maintenance of such a system would be forthcoming. This is the policy of the Government. For this policy I invite and claim the confidence and support of the House of Commons. It is a policy of integrity, a policy earnest, yet not violent, a policy which, without being impatient in its beginnings, will in the end prove very sure.

SOUTH AFRICA (CHINESE LABOUR)

March 21, 1906

House of Commons

On February 26, in the House of Lords, the former High Commissioner and Governor of the Transvaal, Lord Milner, made a lengthy defence of the conduct of his office. Milner was a particular target of Liberal hostility but was warmly supported by his friend Chamberlain and the Unionist Opposition. In reply to a direct question, Milner admitted on Feburary 27 that he had authorised the flogging of Chinese coolies. The Liberals fell upon this admission with cries of triumph and vengeance. A motion of censure on Milner was tabled by a group of Liberal M.P.'s headed by Mr. Byles, and was debated on March 21.

The mood on both sides was belligerent. Churchill took the offensive against Balfour–who had just returned to the House–and Chamberlain. Chamberlain called for an official inquiry into Chinese labour. In his first speech, Churchill rejected this proposal.

The main debate on Byles' motion and the Government's amendment began after dinner on March 21. Chamberlain opened with a fierce attack on the motion and on the Government's "cowardice," and had some sharp comments to make on Churchill's own position. Churchill followed his oration with this speech. The Unionists regarded it as condescending towards Milner. It was a long time before this speech was forgotten–indeed, by Milner's friends, admirers, and family it was never really forgotten or forgiven. The passage beginning, "Lord Milner has gone from South Africa, probably for ever . . ." was the one which gave the greatest offence. The references to the Parnell Commission and the Bradlaugh case were also calculated as being ungratifying to the Unionists–and least of all to Chamberlain and Balfour. The "defence" of Milner did not please the Liberals.

Churchill's words were clearly injudicious, but there must have been something in his manner and delivery which made the situation worse, and which so dismayed friends as well as opponents.

[Extract] Mr. Speaker, I rise to-day for the second time to follow the right hon. Member for West Birmingham, but I hope I shall not be drawn by that association into imitating or attempting to imitate the protracted, superlative, and, I think, rather laboured exhibition of contempt with which he has occupied the attention of the House. Sir, the right hon. Gentleman has heaped contempt and contumely upon my hon. friend the Member for North Salford [Mr. William Byles], and upon the Motion which he has placed upon the Paper. The right hon. Gentleman has used even stronger, or, if it had been in his power, he would have used even stronger, expressions against the Amendment which I have placed on the Paper by the direction of the Prime Minister, and which enjoys the support of those who give him their sympathy and act with him. He described that Amendment as base, cowardly, and dishonest. Then, at least, I hope I may ask for a special measure of the indulgence of the House in order to say anything that may be said in support of a course which has been subjected to such very severe condemnation. I would ask the House to clear their minds of the fierce and bitter elements which the right hon. Gentleman has been the first to introduce into this discussion. I hope the House will try to give a fair consideration to the view which His Majesty's Government desire to submit for their consideration. . . .

The Motion which the hon. Member for North Salford has placed on the Paper embodies a proposition, the truth of which I venture to think very few on this side of the House would care to dispute. It has been moved with sincerity and good feeling in speeches of much ability, delivered under great restraint. But I observe that other Amendments have been placed on the Paper during the period that the Motion of the hon. Member has been set forth, and I think that, when divergent views are expressed by Members of the same Party, it would be unbecoming in the Government—and I said something like this last session—to sit silent and refuse to give any clear or direct guidance to the House. Even on a private Members' night, when a Motion of so unusual a character is brought forward, it is the duty of the Government to offer its counsel to the House.

We need not lose any time in disputing about the main facts of this case. They have been forcibly repeated to us to-night. We have the admission of Lord Milner that he permitted his subordinate to authorise the illegal flogging of Chinese labourers. We know that, in consequence, flogging was inflicted on a large scale and during several months; we know that that permission was abused, as all permission to administer flogging without the restrictive regulation of the law will infallibly be abused; and we know that actual cruelty and outrage resulted. We know that this was a distinct breach of the treaty obligations which this country had contracted with a Foreign Power, and we know that all the while the Secretary of State in this House, and the Under-Secretary in the other House, were occupied in giving Parliament assurances that nothing of the sort was going on or could possibly go on. Any one who reads the Blue-book will see the facts put forward on the authority of Lord Selborne. I have never been one of those who used the exact term of slavery in characterising the Chinese Labour Ordinance. But I say that, in face of the abuses that grew up from this wicked permission, there has arisen a state of things which makes it impossible to wonder that persons should have been carried away by honest indignation to use the strongest language of condemnation about such a system. If Gentlemen on the other side of the House have suffered from such controversial attacks, all I can say is that the responsibility which they have accepted throughout, and which even to-night they are anxious to assume, convinces me that they have received no more than they deserved.

When I was asked in the course of a conversation a week ago to express an opinion on Lord Milner's share in the transaction, I said that I believed his action constituted a grave dereliction of public duty and an undoubted infringement of the law; and that, I had thought, was the opinion of all of us. Can anyone dispute the fact that for a public officer to authorise illegal flogging is to infringe the law? Can any one deny that an infringement of the law by an officer especially charged to maintain and administer the law is a direct dereliction of public duty? Such an expression of opinion on behalf of the Minister who is for the time being charged with the duty of representing a public department was not merely legitimate but necessary. Most of all is it necessary in the case of the Colonial Office. Under the Secretary of State for the Colonies there are thirty or forty officers of high rank administering under different forms and varying conditions as many separate and distinct provinces, comprising a population of something like 30,000,000 of human beings of many races, creeds, and of almost every colour. To the Secretary of State all these important officers are responsible; and it is from the expressions which the Secretary of State, as the servant of this House, may use that these officers all over the world must be guided in the character of their administration and in the manner in which they discharge their responsibilities to all these many races over whom our authority is exercised. So far from withdrawing or minimising in any way the words which I then used on behalf of and with the assent of the Secretary of State and His Majesty's Government, I can only say that in spite of any difference of opinion entertained on the opposite side of the House, I believe these words amounted to a very fair and very reasonable and proper judgment on the transaction that has taken place.

But now we are invited to take a much graver step. We are invited to place a formal censure on the journals of the House. Many hard things have been said rightly or wrongly and in different times about many persons through the mouths of Ministers of the Crown. Very few Motions of this character have ever been placed on the journals of the House. While I do not disagree in any way with the terms of the Motion as stated by my hon. friend, while I admit its truth and admire its moderation, while the Government have no intention whatever of disparaging the motives which induced the hon. Member to place it on the Paper, yet we do dispute the wisdom and the convenience of procedure which he has adopted, and we do most gravely doubt the practical utility of the step which the House is now asked to take. There are certain objections to passing this Motion in its present form which will readily occur to any one who considers the subject. In the first place the offence was committed under another Government and a different House of Commons. It is, I think, clear from what we have heard to-night that had it been brought to the notice of the other House of Commons it would have received a much more lenient consideration than it does at the hands of the new House of Commons. I admit that there is something of the flavour of retrospective retribution in a new House of Commons going back upon events which have happened under the auspices and the authority of its predecessor.

Secondly, it is I think contrary to usage and to right feeling to censure a man unheard. It is true that as Lord Milner is a peer of Parliament we have no authority to bring him to our bar unless he desires to come; but this Motion does not give him the chance or the option of coming. We have, of course, Lord Milner's admissions contained in the Blue-book. We have moreover his statement and expression of regret which he made in another place; but although these statements and admissions establish Lord Milner's acceptance of responsibility for a breach of the law, through which disastrous consequences resulted, I cannot help thinking that just-minded men, and I am sure my hon. friend, would say that before taking the serious step of placing this Resolution on the journals of the House we should examine much more closely the circumstances attending the giving of this permission, not indeed for the purposes of clearing the noble Lord concerned from the charge of having condoned wrong, or from the charge of having accepted the responsibility of wrong–for that is beyond dispute, and the right hon. Gentleman himself did not attempt to dispute it–but for the purpose of ascertaining how far really he was cognisant of what was taking place, and how far he realised to what excesses and improprieties his subordinate was committing him. I do not wish to try and put some measure of blame on Mr. Evans; but I am bound to say that after a severe examination of Mr. Evans on the subject at the Colonial Office by Mr. Lyttelton his memory appeared to be singularly unretentive on several important points. He could not remember how, where, when, and in what terms this all-important permission had been given, or how he had conveyed it to those in charge of Chinese coolies. In so far as he referred to memoranda and records his statements, so far from being confirmed, were upset. So doubtful and vague were his statements on the subject that Mr. Lyttelton thought it to be his duty to write to Lord Milner and ask whether, in view of the vagueness of Mr. Evans's statements, he could persist in his acceptance of responsibility for these transactions. Lord Milner, after careful consideration, proceeded to accept the responsibility of the statements made; and he gave an account to the House of Lords which not merely took the form of the statement that he accepted responsibility, but which purported to be almost a summary, or, at all events, a report of the conversation he had had with Mr. Evans–an account which is so far conclusive that, as the right hon. Gentleman himself has said, we cannot for a moment attempt to go behind it.

I do not attempt to go behind Lord Milner's acceptance of responsibility. It is quite impossible for us in this House to attempt to do so; and yet I say there is just that element of doubt as to his real moral responsibility for the grave circumstances of this case which I think must tend somewhat to mitigate and also somewhat to suspend the severity of our judgment. But, whether or not, I say without hesitation that it would be peculiar and unprecedented if we were, after only three hours debate, without hearing the person principally concerned, unfortified by the report of a Committee, to record our censure on the noble Lord in terms so solemn and unusual that they have only been employed, I think, twice in the last 100 years.

And what about Lord Milner himself? Lord Milner's career has comprised three distinct spheres of activity–Egypt, the Treasury during the famous Death Duties Budget, and South Africa during these last eight lamentable years. With regard to the first of these fields, I suppose there would be no disposition to pass censure in any quarter of the House. With regard to the last two, various opinions are and will be held as between the great political Parties. But I do not think it can fairly be denied in any part of the House that in all these three important sets of public affairs, Lord Milner has worked, according to his lights, strenuously, faithfully, and disinterestedly. Still less can it be denied that during the long period covered by these events, he has played a part which must leave its imprint, for good or for ill, extensively upon the pages of history. I have carefully refrained from passing either censure or eulogy on all or any of these events, not because I am without opinions which at other times I may think or have thought it proper to express–I trust with sufficient clearness–but because I think it would be impossible for us to do justice to his conduct either in the one direction or the other within the compass of a three hours debate, and because I am quite certain it is impossible for the House within such a period to make even a superficial examination of such matters. I mention them for one purpose, and for one purpose alone—to submit to the House that they are very grave matters, which will be talked of for a very long time, and that they lie wholly in the past.

Lord Milner has gone from South Africa, probably for ever. The public service knows him no more. Having exercised great authority he now exerts no authority. Having held high employment he now has no employment. Having disposed of events which have shaped the course of history, he is now unable to deflect in the smallest degree the policy of the day. Having been for many years, or at all events for many months, the arbiter of the fortunes of men who are "rich beyond the dreams of avarice," he is to-day poor, and I will add, honourably poor. After twenty years of exhausting service under the Crown he is to-day a retired Civil servant, without pension or gratuity of any kind whatever. [Opposition cries of "Shame."] If it is a shame, there [pointing to the Front Opposition Bench] is where the responsibility lies for any neglect. But I do seriously say to my hon. friend, "Is it worth while to pursue him any further?" There is— [Interruption which was unheard in the gallery] —Really, I must ask the right hon. Member for Croydon to practice a little more courtesy in his demeanour—There is another consideration to which I desire to draw the attention of the House. This new House of Commons is full of earnest, purposeful and vehement men. Let them not overlook or underrate the vexation and mortification which must be experienced by any vehement and earnest man who sees the ideals, the principles, the policies for which he has toiled utterly discredited—[Opposition cries of "By whom?"] —by the people of Great Britain—and who knows that many of the arrangements in which he has consumed all the energies of his life are about to be reversed or dissolved.

Lord Milner has ceased to be a factor in public events. Let my hon. friends beware that with the ever ready aid of the right hon. Gentleman the Member for West Birmingham he may not be recreated. Mr. Speaker, I think that great Parties should endeavour to avoid conflicts with private persons. My hon. and learned friend the Member for South Donegal, who asked me the other day whether we proposed to strike the name of Lord Milner from the Privy Council, no doubt is prepared to support that course with instances from that accurate constitutional knowledge for which he is noted. About twenty years ago there came into power a Government not indeed supported by a majority so large as that upon which we rely, but still a Government not inferior in elements of strength and stability to any other of modern times. That Government was carried away by its exultation of victory and its pride of strength to embark upon what I must call the persecution of a political opponent. The House knows well, the Irish Members particularly know well, how this mood of intolerance led that powerful Government to the Parnell Commission, to the infamous Parnell Commission, as I shall call it. And what was the result? What was the advantage which that Government reaped in the end? That great Party was covered with confusion and shame as the result of the course which they followed, and the man against whom all their power was directed was raised high in public esteem and popularity. Great cities conferred their freedom upon Mr. Parnell. He received on every side manifestations of public respect. The cause for which he was fighting was greatly advanced. [An Hon. Member on the Ministerial Benches: But he was innocent.] I do not for one moment want to institute any exact comparison between the circumstances of that case and the case with which we are now called upon to deal. I do say that in the one case upon the specific fact alleged, Lord Milner is clearly guilty, and in the other case upon the specific fact alleged that Mr. Parnell was proved to be unjustly accused. But the moral which I draw from the Parnell affair—a moral which, I think, may be drawn also from the conflict of the House of Commons with Mr. Bradlaugh in 1880—is that it is never worth while for a great Party to pursue a private person, and least of all when that private person happens also to be a political opponent.

If we were a political Party clutching precariously at power it might be worth while to strike a blow at a prominent political opponent. But we have won so completely that the very ideas and forces to which we were opposed seem to have melted away as if they had never been. As we have triumphed, so we may be merciful; as we are strong, so we can afford to be generous. There are transactions in the government of States about which people may hold strong opinions, but which it may be much wiser, in the tolerance of overwhelming victory, deliberately to consign to silence and oblivion. I frankly own that I should not press these considerations on the House if the range of the Motion and the Amendment we are discussing was confined to this House, or even to this country. The Colonial Office deals with many questions which are almost as critical and almost as perilous as any questions with which the Foreign Office is concerned. But whereas the Foreign Office is increasingly regarded as outside the scope of Party politics, the Colonial Office lies in the heart and centre of the fiercest partisanship and controversy. It is inevitable, in view of what has occurred in South Africa, that the people should follow with the keenest attention events that take place in a land for which they have sacrificed and suffered so much. I do not complain. On the contrary, the Government are prepared to assert the right of the House of Commons to be consulted on all matters affecting the Colonies which may be said to involve in their largest and truest sense Imperial interests. But the situation in South Africa is difficult and complex. For its difficulty and complexity we are not responsible. We have succeeded to a legacy of financial, social, and racial confusion. There, on that bench, are the testators of evil. And, sir, what an inheritance! A country struggling back to civilization after being laid waste by fire and sword, with all the after consequences of rebellion and civil war, a great army from over the seas mobilised for immediate war, a ponderous constabulary, a costly and not too efficient nominated and imported bureaucracy, the great industries on which the development of the country depends all resting on an essentially unnatural, unhealthy, and unstable basis—in all this vicious tangle no circumstance of first importance can be discerned for which we on this side of the House are responsible. But we have got to face them all, and surely we have got difficulties enough without going out of the way to find them. [Opposition ironical cheers.] Do not let hon. Gentlemen on this side be misled by those derisive cries, which, let me say, do very little honour to the Party, the Imperial Party, which, on every occasion for the last ten years, has been swift to impute want of patriotism to those who might not wholly share their views.

When we have so many real things to do which must be done in the present and in the future, why cannot we leave the past alone? I feel it my duty to say to the House to-night that we believe, having some access to information of authority, that this Motion, if accepted, would undoubtedly aggravate social and racial animosity in South Africa, and that it would have the effect of increasing any tension which may unhappily exist there without any really effective purpose, or without securing in return any substantial advantage to Parliament or to this country. For 100 years South Africa has been divided by the quarrels of two white races, who are equally intolerant of each other, in a land where they are almost equally balanced. The noble Lord who is the subject of this Motion has played the chief part in the climax of that long and bitter duel; he has left behind him in South Africa many friends and partisans, and many foes. If the House of Commons takes the extreme step of passing a formal vote of censure upon that officer, one party in South Africa will be affronted, the other party in South Africa will be exultant. Every demonstration of hostility against Lord Milner on the one hand will be followed by a counter demonstration in his favour on the other—not because of any violent opinion which is entertained on account of the treatment of these Chinese labourers, but because Lord Milner has been the central figure in the tremendous events of the last eight years in South Africa. And I do say that we, who have the real difficulties of this problem thrust upon us day after day, should be incurring a grave responsibility if we lent ourselves to any circumstances or manifestation, however desirable, which had the effect of inflaming anew the bitter passions by which South Africa is racked. . . .

The Government nourish large designs for the establishment of Parliaments and the reconciliation of races, and there is no room in those designs for any exact or pedantic meting out of proper doses of justice to individuals concerned in the tragic events of the past. This Parliament has rightly aspired and has rightly claimed to exert an influence upon the course of politics which shall be intimate, immediate, and direct. No other Parliament in modern times has put forward that claim. Often the House of Commons can only speak words; to-night it is enabled to take substantial and definite action; to-night, by carrying the Amendment which we have placed on the Paper, by showing that we at any rate are prepared to set an example in saying, "Let bygones be bygones," the House of Commons can send a message to South Africa which cannot be perverted, misrepresented, or misunderstood—a message of comfort to a troubled people, a message of tolerance and conciliation to warring races, a message, indeed, of Good Hope to the Cape. . . .

THE CONCILIATION OF SOUTH AFRICA

April 5, 1906

House of Commons

The Lyttelton Constitution–proposed by Alfred Lyttelton, the Colonial Secretary in the Balfour Government–was put forward in 1905. Under it, the Transvaal would receive representative government as a first step towards full self-government. This completely failed to meet the wishes of the Boers, and Churchill took a significant part in persuading the new government to renounce this proposal, and to move towards granting full responsible self-government for both the Boer colonies. The generosity, vision and eloquence of Churchill's speech on April 5 did much to raise his position in the House of Commons beyond that of a vehemently partisan speaker. He was not yet thirty-two years of age.

[Extract] . . . The right hon. Gentleman the Member for Dover asked me to state, first of all, the general position of the Government with regard to the constitutional issue in the Transvaal and Orange River Colonies. In doing so the right hon. Gentleman referred in almost slighting terms to the Committee which was appointed to inquire into that matter, and which so far as I have been informed, has been received with almost universal approval even in quarters beyond the range of His Majesty's Government. Let me ask the Committee to realise what a long way we have travelled in the discussion of the Transvaal and Orange River Colony constitution. When the change of Government took place there was Mr. Lyttelton's constitution before us. That proposed representative and not responsible government. . . . His Majesty's Government came to the conclusion that it would be right to omit the stage of representative government altogether and to go directly to the stage of responsible government. It is the same in politics as it is in war. When one crest line has been left it is necessary to go to the next. It is quite idle to halt half way in the valley between. That is to court imminent and certain destruction and the moment you have abandoned the safe position of a Crown Colony Government, or Government with a nominated majority, there is no stopping place whatever on which you may rest the sole of your foot until you come to a responsible Legislative Assembly with an executive obeying that Assembly. [An Irish Member: Why not in Ireland too?] I do not attempt to localise the logic of these arguments. If there be any logic in them, they convinced his Majesty's Government that it would be necessary to annul the letters patent issued on 31st March, 1905, and make an end of the Lyttelton Constitution. That constitution now passes away into the never never land, into a sort of chilly limbo that is reserved for the discarded and abortive political progeny of many distinguished men. I think I may congratulate the Government and those who support them on the fact that we have been able to take this first most important step in our South African policy with such a very general measure of agreement, with, indeed, a consensus of opinion which almost amounts to unanimity. Both races, every Party, every class, every section in South Africa has agreed in the course which His Majesty's Government have adopted in abandoning representative government and going at once to responsible government. That is already a very great thing, but it was not always so. Hon. Gentlemen who sat in the last Parliament will remember that it was not always so. We remember that Lord Milner was entirely opposed to granting responsible government. We know that Mr. Lyttelton wrote pages and pages in the Blue-book of last year proving how futile and dangerous responsible government would be . . .

Now I do most respectfully say to the Committee that, in dealing with nationalities, nothing is more fatal than anything like a dodge. Wrongs will be forgotten, sufferings and losses will be forgiven, battles will be remembered only as they recall the memory of the martial virtues of the combatants, but anything like chicane, anything like a trick, will always rankle. The Government are concerned in South Africa not only to do what is fair, but to do what South Africa will accept as fair. They are concerned not merely to choose a balance which will deal evenly between the races, but which will secure the acceptance of both races.

Whatever the amount of good-will the Government may have, we cannot take all these things for granted from our predecessors; we are Philistines rather in regard to their handiwork. We know what money our predecessors have spent, and what a poor result they have produced. We are not inclined to take all that they tell us so glibly on trust. That is the reason why the Government have sent out this Committee of Inquiry to assure us of information on controverted and disputed points, so that the decision we take should not only be the decision of fresh minds, but a decision based on freshly ascertained facts. I recognise the injury which is caused by protracted uncertainty. I recognise the fact and deplore it, and it will be the effort of the Government to curtail by every reasonable means in our power the period of uncertainty and delay. We desire nothing more than that this question shall be settled, and we hope that it will be settled within the course of three or four months. . . .

There is a profound difference . . . between the schools of thought which exist upon South African politics in this House. We think that British authority in South Africa has got to stand on two legs. Hon. Gentlemen opposite have laboured for ten years to make it stand on one. We on this side know that if British dominion is to endure in South Africa it must endure with the assent of the Dutch as well as of the British. We think that the position of the Crown in South Africa, and let me add the position of Agents and Ministers of the Crown in South Africa, should be just as much above and remote from racial feuds as the position of the Crown in this country is above our Party politics. We do not seek to pit one race against the other in the hope of profiting from the quarrel. We hope to build upon the reconciliation and not upon the rivalry of races. We hope that it may be our fortune so to dispose of affairs that these two valiant, strong races may dwell together side by side in peace and amity under the shelter of an equal flag.

SOUTH AFRICA AND THE LORDS

July 7, 1906

North-west Manchester Liberal Association Event,
Bowdon

Immediately after the Unionist debacle, Balfour made the ominous statement that the Unionist Party would still control, "whether in power or opposition, the destinies of this great Empire." What this implied was soon revealed. The Government's Education Bill, designed to soothe the nonconformist hostility to the 1902 Act, was rejected by the House of Lords. A Plural Voting Bill and a Licensing Bill met the same fate. The Unionists were carefully selective in their use of the Lords, but within a few months of the Liberal triumph it was evident that Balfour had meant what he said. The first shadows of the bitter conflicts of 1909-1911 had fallen.

[Extract] . . . Mr. Lamb has spoken of the native troubles and misfortunes which are occupying our attention in South Africa. I am quite sure we all agree with him that it is a very sad and terrible thing that so many persons should be losing their lives in the course of these tumults, and the measures which are taken to preserve them. I am not going to pretend that I quite admire in every detail the previous policy which in recent years has been pursued towards the native population by the Government of Natal. But whatever opinion we may have as to the wisdom of their native policy, this, I think, is not the time for us to criticise closely or to make adverse comments upon their action. The people of Natal are going through a time of great trouble and crisis. They are exposed to very serious danger, and they are meeting that danger with their own resources, out of their own money, with the employment of their own soldiers. I hope that this trouble, this dark cloud, will soon pass away, and that the loss of life which we all deplore will soon come to an end. After it has passed away I am quite sure that the lessons which it has brought home to the mind of every white man in South Africa will have the effect of producing considerable reforms in the general treatment of the native races.–(Hear, hear.) That would be our earnest hope, but in the meantime I think it is a message of sympathy that you should send to the white community of men, women, and children, who are, after all, a little more than a drop in the great ocean of coloured people by whom they are surrounded, and whose lives and whose fortunes may at any moment be swept into the abyss by some sudden uprising of millions of natives.

There is also in South Africa another problem of even greater importance than that to which I have referred. I mean the question of granting free parliaments to the two colonies which passed into our possession as a result of the late war. It has always been the intention of this country that free democratic representative institutions should be given to the people of those territories. Both parties have equally assented to that, but it has fallen to the Liberal party–and it has fallen, I venture to think, with great appropriateness to the Liberal party–to make that great grant of self-government, that great boon which it has always been our policy to extend, and to make that grant in the early months of the new House of Commons. I will not attempt myself to prophesy about the future until I know–(laughter),–but I do say that you have every reason to hope that the solution which we shall be able to arrive at of the difficulties and disputes which now surround South African affairs will be satisfactory, will be sound in principle, and will be durable in its results.–(Hear, hear.) We have seen a growing desire on the part of the two white races, whose long quarrel has so much disturbed the prosperity of their own country, to come together and join hands, to accept a recognised Parliamentary institution, and to work it in the same sort of way, in the same sort of rough and tumble manner, that we in this country work our Parliamentary institution. And if we can, by the grant of liberal institutions, enable those two races to lay aside their animosities and to devote their energies and their virtues–for they are great–to the advancement of their country, then I say that will be a great achievement which we shall be justly entitled to be proud of, and which others who come after us will be grateful to us for.–(Cheers.) . . .

. . . I ask Liberals not to suppose because the election has been won and lies behind us that the need for political exertion is at an end.–(Hear, hear.) It is not so. It is not enough to win a battle. The energy which was necessary to achieve victory will be utterly wasted unless every means is taken to secure a permanent and lasting conquest.

Those who desire to see our principles prevail ought, I think, to work all the harder after a great victory is won, or at any rate allow no abatement in the earnestness of their personal effort in order that if at any time we are brought into collision with the forces of reaction and with an unsound, irresponsible assembly–(hear, hear)–that has ceased to fulfil the regular and normal function in the State of a chamber of review, and has become the partisan weapon of one particular faction in the State–if at any time we are forced into collision with such an assembly we must be able to feel that we have behind us the people and the Liberal party–our supporters, who turned out in such thousands at the last election at the call of duty. And supported by that force, be sure of it, a collision will be avoided, or if it comes it will be very bad for those who run up against us.–(Cheers.)

"THE GIFT OF ENGLAND"

July 31, 1906

House of Commons

Shortly after Balfour's return to the House of Commons, Chamberlain suffered a serious stroke. It was at first hoped that he would recover, but it gradually became evident that his long political career was at an end, and although he lived until 1914 he took no further part in public life. His elder son, Austen, who was Chancellor of the Exchequer from 1903 to 1905, now attempted to take his father's place as the dominant protagonist of Tariff Reform.

Churchill had an exceptional amount of Parliamentary business in the 1906 session, and was constantly making speeches and answering questions on African affairs. The Chinese issue, a Zulu uprising in Natal, the opium trade in Malaya and a number of other Colonial matters also interested M.P.s greatly. Above all else, the reconciliation of the Boer Republics was the dominant problem. In this remarkable speech Churchill endeavored–unsuccessfully–to persuade the Opposition to support the Government in making the grant of self-government to the Transvaal "the gift of England." The speech is very long, and only some of the salient points are given here.

[Extract] It is my duty this afternoon, on behalf of the Government, to lay before the Committee the outline and character of the constitutional settlement which we have in contemplation in regard to the lately annexed colonies in South Africa. This is, I suppose, upon the whole, the most considerable business with which this new Parliament has had to deal. But although no one will deny its importance, or undervalue the keen emotions and anxieties which it excites on both sides of the House, and the solemn memories which it revives, yet I am persuaded that there is no reason why we should be hotly, sharply, or bitterly divided on the subject; on the contrary, I think its very importance makes it incumbent on all who participate in the discussion–and I will certainly be bound by my own precepts–to cultivate and observe a studious avoidance of anything likely to excite the ordinary recriminations and rejoinders of Party politics and partisanship. After all, there is no real difference of principle between the two great historic Parties on this question. The late Government have repeatedly declared that it was their intention at the earliest possible moment–laying great stress upon that phrase–to extend representative and responsible institutions to the new Colonies; and before His Majesty's present advisers took office the only question in dispute was, When? On the debate on the Address, the right hon. Member for West Birmingham [Mr. Joseph Chamberlain]–whose absence to-day and its cause I am quite sure are regretted in all parts of the House–spoke on this question with his customary breadth of view and courage of thought. He said–

> The responsibility for this decision lies with the Government now in power. They have more knowledge than we have; and if they consider it safe to give this large grant, and if they turn out to be right no one will be better pleased than we. I do not think that, although important, this change should be described as a change in colonial policy, but as continuity of colonial policy.

If, then, we are agreed upon the principle, I do not think that serious or vital differences can arise upon the method. Because, after all, no one can contend that it is right to extend responsible government, but not to extend it fairly. No one can contend that it is right to grant the forms of free institutions and yet to preserve by some device the means of control. And so I should hope that we may proceed in this debate without any acute divergences becoming revealed. I am in a position to-day only to announce the decision to which the Government have come with respect to the Transvaal. The case of the Transvaal is urgent, for it is the nerve-centre of South Africa. It is the arena in which all questions of South African politics–social, moral, racial, and economic–are fought out; and this new country, so lately reclaimed from the wilderness, with a white population of less than 300,000 souls, already reproduces in perfect miniature all those dark, tangled, and conflicting problems usually to be found in populous and old-established European States. The case of the Transvaal differs fundamentally from the case of the Orange River Colony. The latter has been in the past, and will be again in the future, a tranquil agricultural State, pursuing under a wise and tolerant Government a happy destiny of its own. All I have to say about the Orange River Colony this afternoon is this—that there will be no unnecessary delay in the granting to the Orange River Colony of a Constitution; and that in the granting of that Constitution we shall be animated only by a desire to secure a fair representation of all classes of inhabitants in the country, and to give effective expression to the will of the majority....

One guiding principle has animated His Majesty's Government in their policy—to make no difference in this grant of responsible government between Boer and Briton in South Africa. We propose to extend to both races the fullest privileges and rights of British citizenship; and we intend to make no discrimination in the grant of that great boon between the men who have fought most loyally for us and those who have resisted the British arms with the most desperate courage. By the Treaty of Vereeniging, in which the peace between the Dutch and British races was declared for ever, by Article 1 of that treaty the flower of the Boer nation and its most renowned leaders recognised the lawful authority of His Majesty, King Edward VII, and henceforth, from that moment, British supremacy in South Africa stood on the sure foundations of military honour and warlike achievement, far beyond the reach of any transference of one or two seats, this way or that way, in a local Parliament. This decision in favour of even-handed dealing arises from no ingratitude on our part towards those who have nobly sustained the British cause in years gone by. It involves no injustice to the British population of the Transvaal. As will be seen from the statement I am about to make, we have been careful at every point of this constitutional settlement to secure for the British every advantage that they may justly claim. But the future of South Africa, and, I will add, its permanent inclusion in the British Empire, demand that the King should be equally Sovereign of both races, and that both races should learn to look upon this country as their friend....

I come now to the question of Chinese labour.... On November 30, 1906, the arrangement for recruiting Chinese in China will cease and determine, and our consuls will withdraw the powers they have delegated, and I earnestly trust that no British Government will ever renew them. A clause in the Constitution will provide, in accordance with the pledge given by the Chancellor of the Exchequer, for the abrogation of the existing Chinese Labour Ordinance after a reasonable interval. I am not yet in a position to say what will be a reasonable interval, but time must be given to the new assembly to take stock of the position and to consider the labour question as a whole. I said just now there would be a clause with regard to differential legislation as between white persons and other, and to this clause will be added the words—

> No law will be assented to which sanctions any condition of service or residence of a servile character.

We have been invited to use the word "slavery" or the words "semblance of slavery," but such expressions would be needlessly wounding, and the words we have chosen are much more effective, because much more precise and much more restrained, and they point an accurate forefinger at the very evil we desire to prevent. . . .

I have now finished laying before the House the constitutional settlement, and I should like to say that our proposals are interdependent. They must be considered as a whole; they must be accepted or rejected as a whole. I say this in no spirit of disrespect to the Committee, because evidently it is a matter which the Executive Government should decide on its own responsibility, and if the policy which we declare were changed new instruments would have to be found to carry out another plan. We are prepared to make this settlement in the name of the Liberal Party. That is sufficient authority for us; but there is a higher authority which we should earnestly desire to obtain.

I make no appeal, but I address myself particularly to the right hon. Gentlemen who sit opposite, who are long versed in public affairs, and not able to escape all their lives from a heavy South African responsibility. They are the accepted guides of a Party which, though in a minority in this House, nevertheless embodies nearly half the nation. I will ask them seriously whether they will not pause before they commit themselves to violent or rash denunciations of this great arrangement. I will ask them, further, whether they will not consider if they cannot join with us to invest the grant of a free Constitution to the Transvaal with something of a national sanction. With all our majority we can only make it the gift of a Party; they can make it the gift of England. And if that were so, I am quite sure that all those inestimable blessings which we confidently hope will flow from this decision will be gained more surely and much more speedily; and the first real step taken to withdraw South African affairs from the arena of British Party politics, in which they have inflicted injury on both political parties and in which they have suffered grievous injury themselves. I ask that that may be considered; but in any case we are prepared to go forward alone, and Letters Patent will be issued in strict conformity with the settlement I have explained this afternoon if we should continue to enjoy the support of a Parliamentary majority.

LIBERALISM AND SOCIALISM

October 11, 1906

St. Andrew's Hall, Glasgow

Mr. Randolph Churchill incorrectly states that this speech was delivered "during the General Election campaign" (Winston S. Churchill, *II, 267). In this speech–one of the most thoughtful and interesting Churchill had made up to this point of his career–he boldly dealt with a situation which was causing considerable unease in the Liberal Party.*

The agreement between Ramsay MacDonald and Herbert Gladstone in 1902 had in effect created the Labour Party as a Parliamentary factor, but it remained–and con-

tinued to remain until 1918–an appendage of the Liberals. Yet the presence of "socialists" in the "Lib-Lab" confederation disturbed many Liberals, and not only Lord Rosebery. Churchill had, therefore, to walk a very delicate path between offending the traditional Liberal supporters and alienating the substantial number of working-class voters who had helped to give the Government its large majority.

Despite its assault on Socialism, this speech contains some of the most radical proposals which Churchill had yet made–including the implicit advocacy of the nationalisation of the railways. The phrase "the cause of the Liberal Party is the cause of the left-out millions" demonstrates the impact on Churchill of the poverty and lack of opportunity in Britain of which he had become aware after reading Seebohm Rowntree's classic study of poverty in York.

Few of Churchill's other early speeches so repay careful study as this one.

The first indispensable condition of democratic progress must be the maintenance of European peace. War is fatal to Liberalism. Liberalism is the world-wide antagonist of war. We have every reason to congratulate ourselves upon the general aspect of the European situation. The friendship which has grown up between Great Britain and France is a source of profound satisfaction to every serious and thinking man. The first duty of a nation is to make friends with its nearest neighbour. Six years ago France was agitated in the throes of the Dreyfus case, and Great Britain was plunged in the worst and most painful period of the South African war; and both nations–conscious as we are of one another's infirmities–were inclined to express their opinion about the conduct of the other in unmeasured terms, and keen antagonism resulted. What a contrast to-day! Ever since the King, whose services in the cause of international peace are regarded with affection in every quarter of his dominions, ever since by an act of prescience and of courage his Majesty went to Paris, the relations between Great Britain and France have steadily and progressively improved, and to-day we witness the inspiring spectacle of these two great peoples, the two most genuinely Liberal nations in the whole world, locked together in a league of friendship under standards of dispassionate justice and international goodwill. But it is absurd to suppose that the friendship which we have established with France should be in any degree a menace to any other European Power, or the great Power of Germany.

If the prospects on the European continent are bright and tranquil, I think we have reason to feel also contentment at the course of Colonial affairs. We have had unusual difficulties in the Colonies; but in spite of every effort to excite Colonial apprehension for Party purposes against a Liberal Ministry through the instrumentality of a powerful press, the great States of the Empire have felt, and with more assurance every day, that a Liberal Administration in Downing Street will respect their rights and cherish their interests.

But I am drawn to South Africa by the memory that to-night, the 11th of October, is the anniversary of the declaration of war; and I think it is in South Africa that we have especial reason to be satisfied with the course which events have taken, since we have been in any degree responsible for their direction. One great advantage we have had–a good foundation to build on. We have had the Treaty of Vereeniging, by which peace was established between the Dutch and British races in South Africa upon terms honourable to both. We have had that treaty as our foundation–and what a mercy it is, looking back on the past, to think that the nation followed Lord Rosebery's advice at Chesterfield to terminate the war by a regular peace and a regular settlement, and were not lured away, as Lord Milner would have advised them, when he said that the war in a certain sense would never be over, into a harsh policy of unconditional surrender and pitiless subjugation.

The work of giving these free Constitutions to the two Colonies in South Africa, so lately independent Republics, is in harmony with the most sagacious instincts, and the most honoured traditions of the Liberal Party. But I notice that Lord Milner, who, as we remember, was once a Liberal candidate,–and who now appears before us sometimes in the guise of a silent and suffering public servant, sometimes in the aspect of an active, and even an acrid, political partisan, haranguing his supporters and attacking his Majesty's Ministers,–Lord Milner describes all this improving outlook as "the dreary days of reaction." Progress and reaction are no doubt relative terms. What one man calls progress another will call reaction. If you have been rapidly descending the road to ruin and you suddenly check yourself, stop, turn back, and retrace your steps, that is reaction, and no doubt your former guide will have every reason to reproach you with inconsistency. And it seems to me not at all unnatural that to one who regards three years' desolating civil war as a period of healthy and inspiring progress, a good deal of what his Majesty's Government have lately done in South Africa must appear very dreary and reactionary indeed.

But I would recommend you to leave this disconsolate proconsul alone. I do not agree with him when he says that South Africa is passing through a time of trial. South Africa is emerging from her time of trial. The darkest period is behind her. Brighter prospects lie before her. The improvement upon which we are counting is not the hectic flush of a market boom, but the steady revival and accumulation of agricultural and industrial productiveness. Soberly and solemnly men of all parties and of both races in South Africa are joining together to revive and to develop the prosperity of their own country. Grave difficulties, many dangers, long exertions lie before them; but the star of South Africa is already in the ascendant, and I look confidently forward to the time when it will take its place, united, federated, free, beside Canada and Australia, in the shining constellation of the British Empire.

When we have dealt with subjects which lie outside our own island, let us concentrate our attention on what lies within it, because the gravest problems lie at home. I shall venture to-night to make a few general observations upon those larger trendings of events which govern the incidents and the accidents of the hour. The fortunes and the interests of Liberalism and Labour are inseparably interwoven; they rise by the same forces, and in spite of similar obstacles, they face the same enemies, they are affected by the same dangers, and the history of the last thirty years shows quite clearly that their power of influencing public affairs and of commanding national attention fluctuate together. Together they are elevated, together they are depressed, and any Tory reaction which swept the Liberal Party out of power would assuredly work at least proportionate havoc in the ranks of Labour. That may not be a very palatable truth, but it is a truth none the less.

Labour! It is a great word. It moves the world, it comprises the millions, it combines many men in many lands in the sympathy of a common burden. Who has the right to speak for Labour? A good many people arrogate to themselves the right to speak for Labour. How many political Flibbertigibbets are there not running up and down the land calling themselves the people of Great Britain, and the social democracy, and the masses of the nation! But I am inclined to think, so far as any body of organised opinion can claim the right to speak for this immense portion of the human race, it is the trade unions that more than any other organisation must be considered the responsible and deputed representatives of Labour. They are the most highly organised part of Labour; they are the most responsible part; they are from day to day in contact with reality. They are not mere visionaries or dreamers weaving airy Utopias out of tobacco smoke. They are not political adventurers who are eager to remodel the world by rule-of-thumb, who are proposing to make the infinite complexities of scientific civilisation and the multitudinous phenomena of great cities conform to a few barbarous formulas which any moderately intelligent parrot could repeat in a fortnight.

The fortunes of the trade unions are interwoven with the industries they serve. The more highly organised trade unions are, the more clearly they recognise their responsibilities; the larger their membership, the greater their knowledge, the wider their outlook. Of course, trade unions will make mistakes, like everybody else, will do foolish things, and wrong things, and want more than they are likely to get, just like everybody else. But the fact remains that for thirty years trade unions have had a charter from Parliament which up to within a few years ago protected their funds, and gave them effective power to conduct a strike; and no one can say that these thirty years were bad years of British industry, that during these thirty years it was impossible to develop great businesses and carry on large manufacturing operations, because, as everybody knows perfectly well, those were good and expanding years of British trade and national enrichment.

A few years ago a series of judicial decisions utterly changed the whole character of the law regarding trade unions. It became difficult and obscure. The most skilful lawyers were unable to define it. No counsel knew what advice to tender to those who sought his guidance. Meanwhile if, in the conduct of a strike, any act of an agent, however unauthorised, transgressed the shadowy and uncertain border-line between what was legal and what was not, an action for damages might be instituted against the trade union, and if the action was successful, trade union funds, accumulated penny by penny, year by year, with which were inseparably intermingled friendly and benefit moneys, might in a moment have been swept away. That was the state of the law when his Majesty's present advisers were returned to power. We have determined to give back that charter to the trade unions. The Bill is even now passing through the House of Commons.

We are often told that there can be no progress for democracy until the Liberal Party has been destroyed. Let us examine that. Labour in this country exercises a great influence upon the Government. That is not so everywhere. It is not so, for instance, in Germany, and yet in Germany there is no Liberal Party worth speaking of. Labour there is very highly organised, and the Liberal Party there has been destroyed. In Germany there exists exactly the condition of affairs, in a Party sense, that Mr. Keir

Hardie and his friends are so anxious to introduce here. A great social democratic party on the one hand, are bluntly and squarely face to face with a capitalist and military confederation on the other. That is the issue, as it presents itself in Germany; that is the issue, as I devoutly hope it may never present itself here. And what is the result? In spite of the great numbers of the Socialist Party in Germany, in spite of the high ability of its leaders, it has hardly any influence whatever upon the course of public affairs. It has to submit to food taxes and to conscription; and I observe that Herr Bebel, the distinguished leader of that Party, at Mannheim the other day was forced to admit, and admitted with great candour, that there was no other country in Europe so effectively organised as Germany to put down anything in the nature of a violent Socialist movement. That is rather a disquieting result to working men of having destroyed the Liberal Party.

But we are told to wait a bit; the Socialist Party in Germany is only three millions. How many will there be in ten years' time? That is a fair argument. I should like to say this. A great many men can jump four feet, but very few can jump six feet. After a certain distance the difficulty increases progressively. It is so with the horse-power required to drive great ships across the ocean; it is so with the lifting power required to raise balloons in the air. A balloon goes up quite easily for a certain distance, but after a certain distance it refuses to go up any farther, because the air is too rarefied to float it and sustain it. And, therefore, I would say let us examine the concrete facts.

In France, before the Revolution, property was divided among a very few people. A few thousand nobles and priests and merchants had all the wealth in the country; twenty-five million peasants had nothing. But in modern States, such as we see around us in the world to-day, property is very widely divided. I do not say it is evenly divided. I do not say it is fairly divided, but it is very widely divided. Especially is that true in Great Britain. Nowhere else in the world, except, perhaps, in France and the United States, are there such vast numbers of persons who are holders of interest-bearing, profit-bearing, rent-earning property, and the whole tendency of civilisation and of free institutions is to an ever-increasing volume of production and an increasingly wide diffusion of profit. And therein lies the essential stability of modern States. There are millions of persons who would certainly lose by anything like a general overturn, and they are everywhere the strongest and best organised millions. And I have no hesitation in saying that any violent movement would infallibly encounter an overwhelming resistance, and that any movement which was inspired by mere class prejudice, or by a desire to gain a selfish advantage, would encounter from the selfish power of the "haves" an effective resistance which would bring it to sterility and to destruction.

And here is the conclusion to which I lead you. Something more is needed if we are to get forward. There lies the function of the Liberal Party. Liberalism supplies at once the higher impulse and the practicable path; it appeals to persons by sentiments of generosity and humanity; it proceeds by courses of moderation. By gradual steps, by steady effort from day to day, from year to year, Liberalism enlists hundreds of thousands upon the side of progress and popular democratic reform whom militant Socialism would drive into violent Tory reaction. That is why the Tory Party hate us. That is why they, too, direct their attacks upon the great organisation of the Liberal

Party, because they know it is through the agency of Liberalism that society will be able in the course of time to slide forward, almost painlessly—for the world is changing very fast—on to a more even and a more equal foundation. That is the mission that lies before Liberalism. The cause of the Liberal Party is the cause of the left-out millions; and because we believe that there is in all the world no other instrument of equal potency and efficacy available at the present time for the purposes of social amelioration, we are bound in duty and in honour to guard it from all attacks, whether they arise from violence or from reaction.

There is no necessity to-night to plunge into a discussion of the philosophical divergencies between Socialism and Liberalism. It is not possible to draw a hard-and-fast line between individualism and collectivism. You cannot draw it either in theory or in practice. That is where the Socialist makes a mistake. Let us not imitate that mistake. No man can be a collectivist alone or an individualist alone. He must be both an individualist and a collectivist. The nature of man is a dual nature. The character of the organisation of human society is dual. Man is at once a unique being and a gregarious animal. For some purposes he must be collectivist, for others he is, and he will for all time remain, an individualist. Collectively we have an Army and a Navy and a Civil Service; collectively we have a Post Office, and a police, and a Government; collectively we light our streets and supply ourselves with water; collectively we indulge increasingly in all the necessities of communication. But we do not make love collectively, and the ladies do not marry us collectively, and we do not eat collectively, and we do not die collectively, and it is not collectively that we face the sorrows and the hopes, the winnings and the losings of this world of accident and storm.

No view of society can possibly be complete which does not comprise within its scope both collective organisation and individual incentive. The whole tendency of civilisation is, however, towards the multiplication of the collective functions of society. The evergrowing complications of civilisation create for us new services which have to be undertaken by the State, and create for us an expansion of the existing services. There is a growing feeling, which I entirely share, against allowing those services which are in the nature of monopolies to pass into private hands. There is a pretty steady determination, which I am convinced will become effective in the present Parliament, to intercept all future unearned increment which may arise from the increase in the speculative value of the land. There will be an ever-widening area of municipal enterprise. I go farther; I should like to see the State embark on various novel and adventurous experiments. I am delighted to see that Mr. Burns is now interesting himself in afforestation. I am of opinion that the State should increasingly assume the position of the reserve employer of labour. I am very sorry we have not got the railways of this country in our hands. We may do something better with the canals, and we are all agreed, every one in this hall who belongs to the Progressive Party, that the State must increasingly and earnestly concern itself with the care of the sick and the aged, and, above all, of the children.

I look forward to the universal establishment of minimum standards of life and labour, and their progressive elevation as the increasing energies of production may permit. I do not think that Liberalism in any circumstances can cut itself off from this fertile field of social effort, and I would recommend you not to be scared in discussing any of these proposals, just because some old woman comes along and tells you they are Socialistic. If you take my advice, you will judge each case on its merits. Where you find that State enterprise is likely to be ineffective, then utilise private enterprises, and do not grudge them their profits.

The existing organisation of society is driven by one mainspring–competitive selection. It may be a very imperfect organisation of society, but it is all we have got between us and barbarism. It is all we have been able to create through unnumbered centuries of effort and sacrifice. It is the whole treasure which past generations have been able to secure, and which they have been able to bequeath; and great and numerous as are the evils of the existing condition of society in this country, the advantages and achievements of the social system are greater still. Moreover, that system is one which offers an almost indefinite capacity for improvement. We may progressively eliminate the evils; we may progressively augment the goods which it contains. I do not want to see impaired the vigour of competition, but we can do much to mitigate the consequences of failure. We want to draw a line below which we will not allow persons to live and labour, yet above which they may compete with all the strength of their manhood. We want to have free competition upwards; we decline to allow free competition to run downwards. We do not want to pull down the structures of science and civilisation: but to spread a net over the abyss; and I am sure that if the vision of a fair Utopia which cheers the hearts and lights the imagination of the toiling multitudes, should ever break into reality, it will be by developments through, and modifications in, and by improvements out of, the existing competitive organisation of society; and I believe that Liberalism mobilised, and active as it is to-day, will be a principal and indispensable factor in that noble evolution.

I have been for nearly six years, in rather a short life, trained as a soldier, and I will use a military metaphor. There is no operation in war more dangerous or more important than the conduct of a rear-guard action and the extrication of a rear-guard from difficult and broken ground. In the long war which humanity wages with the elements of nature the main body of the army has won its victory. It has moved out into the open plain, into a pleasant camping ground by the water springs and in the sunshine, amid fair cities and fertile fields. But the rear-guard is entangled in the defiles, the rear-guard is still struggling in mountainous country, attacked and assailed on every side by the onslaughts of a pitiless enemy. The rear-guard is encumbered with wounded, obstructed by all the broken vehicles that have fallen back from the main line of the march, with all the stragglers and weaklings that have fallen by the way and can struggle forward no farther. It is to the rear-guard of the army that attention should be directed. There is the place for the bravest soldiers and the most trusted generals. It is there that all the resources of military science and its heaviest artillery should be employed to extricate the rear-guard–not to bring the main army back from good positions which it occupies, not to throw away the victory which it has won over the brute forces of nature–but to bring the rear-guard in, to bring them into the level plain, so that they too may dwell in a land of peace and plenty.

That is the aim of the Liberal Party, and if we work together we will do something for its definite accomplishment.

TRANSVAAL AND ORANGE RIVER COLONIES CONSTITUTIONS

December 17, 1906

House of Commons

[Extract] . . . The responsibilities of the Government are heavy. They now pass in a large measure to the members of the new Parliaments. Other liberties besides their own will be enshrined in those Parliaments. The people of these Colonies, and, in a special measure, the Boers, will become the trustees of freedom all over the world. We have tried to act with fairness and good feeling. If by any chance our counsels of reconciliation should come to nothing, if our policy should end in mocking disaster, then the resulting evil would not be confined to South Africa. Our unfortunate experience would be trumpeted forth all over the world wherever despotism wanted a good argument for bayonets, whenever an arbitrary Government wished to deny or curtail the liberties of imprisoned nationalities. But if, on the other hand, as we hope and profoundly believe, better days are in store for South Africa, if the long lane which it has been travelling has reached its turning at last, if the words of President Brand, "All shall come right," are at length to be fulfilled, and if the near future should unfold to our eyes a tranquil, prosperous, consolidated Afrikander nation under the protecting ægis of the British crown, then, I say, the good as well as the evil will not be confined to South Africa; then, I say, the cause of the poor and the weak all over the world will have been sustained; and everywhere small peoples will get more room to breathe, and everywhere great empires will be encouraged by our example to step forward–and it only needs a step–into the sunshine of a more gentle and a more generous age.

THE HOUSE OF LORDS

February 4, 1907

Free Trade Hall, Manchester

Balfour's cynical use of the House of Lords had startled and confused the Liberal Government in its first year of office, and Ministers had no agreed policy on how to meet this unexpected antagonist. Some urged immediate abolition of the Lords' veto power on legislation; others favoured even more radical measures; and there were those who argued that the Government should proceed with its legislation, daring the Lords to defeat it or emasculate it. In this speech, Churchill went into the attack against the Lords with a vigor which was not wholly opposed in the Government. But he did not appreciate at this stage that the Lords were likely to deny to the Commons "the power of the purse."

[Extract] . . . In one respect the legislation of last session was brought to nothing. The Education Bill has been destroyed. (Cries of "Hurrah" and "Shame.") A couple of hundred bishops and peers have taken it upon themselves without hesitation–(a voice: "What you didn't do")–to throw out the principal measure of the year, which was sent up to them by the votes of an overwhelming majority of the House of Commons newly elected. (Cheers and counter-cheers.) Now let us discuss this matter without heat and interruption. Before we examine the motives and the pretensions of these noble lords to rule over us, let me say a word about the bill itself. I am one who has always laboured for compromise upon the education question, and as such a one I profoundly regret the loss of the late bill. (Hear, hear.) In its final form–and it is in its final form that it must be judged, because when you are fighting a battle you do not put all your forces in the front line at the beginning of the day–it was, I unhesitatingly assert, a workable and fair arrangement. (Cries of "No" and cheers.) . . .

Well, the harm is done. The bill is dead. ("Hear, hear," and laughter.) The future–and it is no matter to laugh about, because, whatever views we may take on this question, it concerns the education of all the children of the country, their spiritual education and their secular education at the same time, and this is a most grave and terrible matter, because I often feel that if we are to do anything to advance the social condition of our land we must build our hopes upon the children who are growing up (cheers), whose control and education we have so exclusively in our hands. The future, I say, in education is overclouded, and I cannot pretend to-night to lift the veil and say precisely what is going to happen. Speaking for myself, but pronouncing the doctrine to which every Liberal is ready to give his adherence, I am bound to say I consider that the definite separation of Church and State, of religious and secular teaching, would be good both for the Church and for the State. (Loud and prolonged cheering.) I believe that faith would become stronger and that education would be more efficient; I believe that spiritual and religious forces would be vitalised and stimulated; and I believe that the State itself would gain dignity and power from placing itself on the broad, symmetrical foundations of truth. (Cheers.) . . .

Our quarrel we will carry to another court. We will carry our quarrel to the House of Lords. (Loud cheers.) We will fight our battle not in the schools, which are the fountains of progress and knowledge; we will fight it in the House of Lords, which is the fortress of negation and reaction. (Hear, hear.) I want to speak to you about the House of Lords. (Cheers.) Since the general election I think there are a good many people who have been rather surprised. I think that the great majority of people in this country were under the impression till quite recently that we were a self-governing country. They thought we had an elaborate arrangement of elections, of voting for members of Parliament, and so forth, by which we decided what laws we were to be ruled by and what we were not to be ruled by. It is all a mistake; it is all a delusion. ("Hear, hear," and laughter.) We have no right apparently to any such liberties as we thought we were possessed of. We are asked to believe that the government we should receive is a government which the Lords, spiritual and temporal, choose to give us. Do not let us speak disrespectfully of them. (Laughter.) I have no time to deal to-night with the plain absurdities in the composition of our hereditary Chamber (hear, hear), where a man acquires legislative functions simply through his virtue in being born (laughter), where the great majority of the members never come near the place from year's end to year's end, where if they go mad (laughter) or are convicted of a crime or become mentally incompetent to manage their estates (laughter), acquire an unwholesome acquaintance with intoxicating beverages, nevertheless they are still considered perfectly fit to exercise the highest legislative functions. (Shame.) I pass that over, and say nothing about it. (Laughter.) I might be betrayed into using disrespectful language if I did, and I am sure you would all be very sorry for that. ("Hear hear," and laughter.)

I pass that over altogether—all the great political tumults that they have given rise to, all the great measures of reform that we now accept as commonplaces of the political life of both parties which they have resisted, which they have kept back often for generations, all the hard, oppressive laws which they have kept in force until a whole age and whole generation of men who might have otherwise been happy have passed suffering and oppressed from the world. I will deal with only two aspects, with only two functions, of the House of Lords—their function as the spoke in the wheel and their function as a dog in the manger. (Laughter.) I only use those expressions metaphorically; there is not intended to be any disrespect in the use of them. The action of the House of Lords deserves to be watched with very close attention, not only in the bills which they rejected last session but in the bills which they passed. (Hear, hear.) We see that they rejected the Plural Voting Bill, of which they disapproved, and they passed the Land Tenure Bill, of which they disapproved still more strongly. They rejected the Radical Education Bill, and they passed the still more Radical Trade Disputes Bill. (A voice: They had to do.)

But what I want to know is upon what principle do they proceed in dealing with new laws that are put before them? Clearly they don't deal with them on their merits; clearly they don't deal with them according to their honest conviction of what is right and what is wrong in the law, of whether it is good for the country or bad for the country. Because if that were so, how could they ever have passed the Trade Disputes Bill, which according to them—not according to us; we know perfectly well that it is a bill which will make for industrial peace—is a tyrannical bill, an immoral bill, a wicked bill, and an unjust bill? And yet they passed it. Well, what is their motive? If it is not on the merits that they deal with legislation, if they do not deal with it according to the degree of Radicalism which it contains, or according to the amount of support which it receives in the House of Commons, what is the motive power? Surely it is very important for us to know. We are the Commons of England and their elected representatives; we are the 44 million people who live in this country. Surely then it is very important for us to know what is the principle on which the 200 mitred clergy and coroneted landlords who govern us proceed. (Loud cheers.) And what is the principle which regulates the action of these noblemen who claim authority over all our legislation and affairs, and in the exercise of that authority are quite prepared to disdain and to defy, to override and to overrule every other body in the State? Surely we ought to know what is the rule they follow. (Hear, hear.)

I am going to tell you what is the principle the House of Lords go upon. This is the principle—party tactics, pure and simple. ("Hear, hear" and loud cheers.) Only one motive—the interest of the Conservative party ("Hear, hear" and cheers); only one question is asked by them of any bill—not is it a good or a bad bill but will it serve the Conservative party most if we chuck it out or let it through? (Hear, hear.)

Only one object is held in view—openly admitted, frankly avowed,—and that object is to strike down at the earliest possible moment the Liberal Government and to replace the Conservative Government in the position from which the people of the country have just ejected them. (Hear, hear.) In this delicate operation they have their guides. Mr. Balfour is no longer Prime Minister of the country. He sits in Opposition, in a lonely, solitary place on the left of the Speaker's chair. But he has power. He has the power to write a note—on a half sheet of notepaper (laughter), and to give it to a messenger and send it 200 yards down the corridor to the House of Lords. And by writing that note he can mutilate or reject or pass into law any clause or any bill which the House of Commons may have spent weeks in discussing. (Shame.) Yes, it is a shame. (Cheers.) I think it is a shame that a man who does not occupy a position of responsibility to the Crown, who is not in possession of a majority drawn from the people, should sit there with his hand on the throttle-valve of obstruction and should regulate, in defiance of the will of the Chamber to which he belongs, the fortunes of the legislation which it has passed. (Cheers.)

There is Mr. Wyndham; he is a great man for Home Rule and water. (Laughter.) Home Rule and hot water it was for him. (Cheers and laughter.) Mr. Wyndham did a good many wise things when he was in Ireland, and has been trying to get forgiven for the wise things he did in Ireland by the silly things which he says in England. (Laughter.) Mr. Wyndham describes the acts of the House of Lords which I have just explained to you as being the attitude of umpire. Umpire, forsooth! (Cheers and laughter.) It looks to me more like the attitude of the footpad who waits for the dark night to stab his enemy than the act of an impartial chamber of review. That is the first cardinal fault in the position and character of the Second Chamber of the present time which I submit to you; and it is not fair that it does not attempt to deal with questions on merits, but it is actuated by party motives—that it strikes as an instrument for party purposes, and for party purposes alone. (Cheers.) That is what I mean when I refer to the function of the spoke in the wheel—an irresponsible body which is ready at any moment to thrust a spoke in the wheels of the ever-complicated machine of social and public government and life.

Yes, but now there is another aspect, and it is one you should not overlook. I observe that Lord Ridley—he is the chairman of the Tariff Reform League (laughter) the numbers of that body have got rather few lately, but they have still got a chairman. (Laughter.) Lord Ridley—he used to be a member for Stalybridge till he got into difficulties over Free Trade, and luckily escaped from the rage of his constituents into an asylum in the House of Lords,—speaking somewhere a few days ago, said that the House of Lords ought to be consulted on legislation, because, after all, they owned one-third of the land of the whole country. (Shame.) Think of that. Is not that a very significant fact: One-third of the land of the whole country owned by the House of Lords. I am sure we are very much obliged to Lord Ridley for reminding us of it. These famous islands, which have been preserved by the sacrifices and the valour of the British people, which have been preserved inviolate from the invader through all the shocks and dangers of a thousand years—this land of England in which we live does not belong to the people at all. Oh, no, it does not even belong to any large proportion of them. It belongs—one-third of it—to the 600 gentlemen—noblemen, I beg their pardon—who sit in the House of Lords. You would think they were very lucky and very happy. You would not think they were downhearted. You would think that those who own these great possessions, who occupy such an immense geographical area of the earth's surface, would have had no great cause to complain.

But believe me they are not in the least contented with their great landed possessions. They complain every day that there is no profit in them; that their landed possessions are a burden and an encumbrance. Yes, in this land of England, in this British country of ours, the only country of any note in the whole civilised world where you have the awful spectacle of a landless peasantry, you have also the spectacle of a withered and blighted agriculture, and you find that even those few persons to whom the whole advantage and richness of the soil has been accorded are themselves but little better for the great possessions with which they have been endowed, and like the dog in the manger, they only stand in the way of those who would seek to put them to a better use. (Loud cheers.)

I am no Socialist, as I have said before, if by Socialism is meant those wild voices and predatory appetites in which some people allow themselves to indulge. But I hold most strongly that our present social organization is imperfect and incomplete (loud cheers), that it contains great and gross injustices and anomalies which are wasteful and foolish and diminish the total sum of good which might be enjoyed by all. And I think it is our duty as a Liberal and Radical party to march forward boldly not only to the constructive extension of our social machinery but the rooting out of those evils and injustices to which I have referred. (Cheers.)

And which of them, I should like to know, are more obvious than these two, these twin evils, the lords and the land–the 300 titled gentlemen who claim to overrule the authority of the representatives who are elected all over the country, and the 600 titled gentlemen who condescend to own one-third of the land in which we live. (Hear, hear.) I think that the proper battle-ground for the lords of England is the land of England (hear, hear) and that is the issue which I trust I shall be able to put before some of you when the general election comes round again. (Cheers.) If the House of Lords–because it is that body I am considering–are the agents of one party they are also the champions of one interest, and that the landed interest.

I see on the platform many commercial men of this great commercial division. What security do you find in a Second Chamber constituted as is the present Second Chamber for the protection of your commercial interests? Personally I entirely approve of the Trade Disputes Bill–and I would not have used this argument while it was in passage through the House of Lords, because I desired to see it passed,–but it is not quite clear that the House of Lords were quite prepared to sacrifice what they considered to be the interests of the manufacturers in order to strengthen their position and to preserve the interests of the landed proprietors. Second Chambers have a purpose of some sort; but judged even by the lowest possible standard, of being an instrument to protect the rights of property, I mean, against the rights of human beings–judged even by that standard the House of Lords is a defective instrument because it protects only the property of one particular interest, and in protecting that is ready to sacrifice the property of every other class.

What are we to do? I said the situation was intolerable. There are two plans which have been put forward lately. I don't agree with either. One has been called filling up the cup, and the other is an immediate dissolution. The one seems to me to be a very weak and humble plan, and the other seems to me a very foolish and unwise plan. (Cheers.) There are more ways of killing a cat than drowning it in cream (laughter), and I am certainly not in favour of a Liberal Government going on sending up bills to the House of Lords for them to throw out until the country gets exasperated—the policy of bowling lobs for the House of Lords to sky in the hope (laughter) that the spectators will take pity on the bowler. I am quite sure of this—that the present House of Commons would never stand such a policy for a month. (Cheers.) We have not provoked the fight. I take you to witness in North-west Manchester who have heard my speeches for the last two years. I have never in this constituency indulged in attacks upon the House of Lords. I have always hoped they would give us fair-play. They have denied us fair-play (cheers), they have deliberately thrown down the challenge to us; they have refused in the most insulting manner every effort of compromise and solution; and I think that this new democratic Parliament in the next day of its youth and strength, should take that challenge up. (Loud and prolonged cheering.)

Now is the time. There is nothing like coming to an understanding with your antagonist at the very beginning. (Hear, hear.) It saves a lot of trouble afterwards, and I am quite sure that if we were to pass by what happened last year and to proceed upon the ordinary legislative and financial business of the year as if nothing had occurred we should have before us only discredit and vexation, ending in hopeless disaster. (Cheers.) No, now is the time for us to let it be clearly proved that it is the House of Commons and not the House of Lords that will be master in the second Parliament of His Majesty King Edward the Seventh. (Loud cheers.) You will say, Are we going to have another general election? (A voice: "Not yet, I hope.") It will come soon enough. No doubt the end of any constitutional struggle such as this must be an appeal to the people, but there are a good many things to do first. (Hear, hear.)

We have got to pass one or two good Radical Budgets first. (Cheers.) We have got to formulate and develop our policy upon the land first; we have got to educate the country on the constitutional issue involved in the present position of the Second Chamber. The battle between Lords and Commons has to be fought out in Parliament first; then it will be fought out afterwards in the country. (Cheers.) A great constitutional issue has been raised. Let us face it soberly, patiently, firmly; let us face it without haste but also without hesitation. The electors have given us an immense majority; they can do no more. They expect to see us use that majority (loud cheers); they have done their duty, they expect us to do ours. (Cheers.) And I think the House of Commons is not so destitute of means of making its will effective as is commonly supposed by some of our opponents. I look back on history and I see that the House of Commons has always in the past succeeded in bringing its will to bear upon the course of events. In the many struggles we have fought in the old, old days against the autocratic power of the Crown and in the battles for Catholic Emancipation, for Reform, for the Repeal of the Corn Laws, for the extension of the franchise—in all these struggles the House of Commons has found means to make its will effective when it has been supported by a loyal majority and by the masses of the people outside. (Loud cheers.)

I am not going into all the methods which can be employed—the method of tacking bills to money bills, for which there are many respectable precedents; the method of new creations of peers, perhaps even of temporary peers; and all the resources of legislation and of Parliamentary resolution; but I will single out only one great power of the House of Commons before I sit down—the greatest and the finest weapon of all—the power of the purse ("Hear, hear," and cheers.) That was the power which was effective against the Monarchy in the past and which will be effective against this effete oligarchy at the present time. The whole great business of finance is entirely in the control of the House of Commons—not only the selection of what taxes shall be imposed but also the expenditure of every penny of money. It is the House of Commons which alone is addressed by the Sovereign—"Gentlemen of the House of Commons the estimates of the year will be laid before you"—and it is in our power to control the expenditure of every penny of the vast sums of money which are raised for the public service, to issue it where we will and to whom we will from the public Exchequer, to direct it to whatever objects we may select and under whatever conditions or provisions the House of Commons may choose to decree and affirm.

And I must say that with that great weapon, the first of the weapons which we assess for making our will effective over the whole area of government and legislation, we should be simple-minded people if we were at the first difficulty which confronts us to throw up our commission and to come hurrying back to the country asking for a fresh mandate without having even attempted to use those noble and formidable weapons which under the Constitution of a free country have been so abundantly placed at our disposal. (Loud cheers.)

THE COLONIAL CONFERENCE

April 16, 1907

Eighty Club Dinner, London

Churchill had played a considerable part in the organization of the 1907 Colonial Conference, which was attended by General Botha. On May 1, in recognition of his work at the Colonial Office, he became a Privy Counsellor.

I earnestly hope that the Colonial Conference now meeting in London will remove one or two misunderstandings. I hope that our colonial guests will return to their colonies and their Governments convinced, if they need convincing, that there is not such a thing in the whole surface and compass of our island as an anticolonial party. (Cheers.) The Liberal party is now in power, and it has fallen to their lot, for the first time, to conduct one of these great Imperial gatherings; but, if the Liberal party were out of power and the Labour party were called upon to form a Government in this country, then I can assure the representatives from the Colonies that their welcome would not be less spontaneous and genuine—that they would find under any Government which ruled here true comradeship and open hospitality. (Cheers.) The other misunderstanding which I trust will be removed is that there is any idea or intention on the part of the Government or the Liberal party to infringe in any degree upon the self-governing authority of the various Colonies and dependencies of the Crown. What could be more absurd? You all know perfectly well that the principle of self-government is the only one on which this Empire has been bound together, and that without its strict observance that great union could not long continue; and we not only intend to guard the independence of the self-governing colonies with the utmost strictness and scrupulous propriety, but we are in this island, fortunately, in a position to protect their independence, if ever it should be challenged, with the resources which are at the disposal of the supreme naval Power. (Cheers.) There is no need to get into a nervous or "jumpy" state about the British Empire. It is said in various quarters that we have now arrived at another crisis, and that we are at the parting of the ways. I do not believe a word of it. The British Empire has got past the parting of the ways; it has got a clear run home. I am an optimist and I believe that our affairs will proceed better and better and better. They are good already, but they are going steadily to improve. The speech which we have had from General Botha is a memorable and stirring one. The words which he spoke will be telegraphed all over the world and will give satisfaction and pleasure in thousands of homes in the most distant portions of his Majesty's dominions. (Cheers.) Those at the Colonial Office know better than any one else something of the difficulties which General Botha will have to face in South Africa, and the Government will give him their whole-hearted support. (Cheers.)

Don't let us be in too much of hurry in that in which we set our hands to do. Let us remember that it is a great and solemn business we undertake. Cologne Cathedral took 600 years to build. Successive generations of architects died during its erection. Some built what had to be unbuilt afterwards; some were occupied in rectifying what had previously been erected ill—but all laboured reverently and faithfully, in caring for the cause. The work went on until it was finished, as now stands forth the great monument to excite and evoke the inspiration and imagination of all who behold it. That is the kind of work upon which we are engaged. Let us remember that the British Empire is a far larger fabric than any that was ever planned by a man; and that the materials we have to use in its construction and its consolidation are materials at once more intangible and more intractable than that into which masons and ordinary architects of the world are concerned with.

IMPERIAL PREFERENCE

May 7, 1907

Colonial Conference Meeting,
Colonial Office, London

The most critical subject before the Colonial Conference was imperial preference, put forward by the Prime Minister of Australia, Mr. Deakin, and supported by the New Zealand representatives. Asquith, Lloyd George and Churchill resisted the proposal. The result was a somewhat vague formula which resolved nothing.

The financial and trade aspects of preference have been fully examined by the Chancellor of the Exchequer [Mr. Asquith] and Mr. Lloyd George [President of the Board of Trade], but I desire to draw attention to considerations less of an economic than of a political and Parliamentary, and almost of a diplomatic character. I feel that enormous Parliamentary difficulties would be involved in the adoption of a system of preferences. Colonial affairs always suffer from being brought into the arena of party politics, and a system of preference would involve them in its very midst. Many attractive things can be said about preference in the abstract, but discussion on the subject is valueless without precise details, and many of those who might favour preference as an evidence of good will and good feeling would recoil from the schedule of taxation such as it would involve. It is clear that existing duties cannot form a complete and satisfactory basis for the grant of preference. Dr. Smartt [Cape Colony Commissioner of Work] has proposed beginning merely upon tobacco; but he explained with much frankness that this was to ensure that his Majesty's Government should concede the general principle. The representatives of the self-governing Colonies should state bluntly and abruptly what taxes preference would impose upon the Mother Country. Mr. Deakin [Prime Minister of Australia] has said that each of the parties should select the duties as they might think best. That answer is no doubt correct, but inadequate. It avoids the unpleasant fact that any logical, uniform, or even fair system of preference must involve taxation of six or seven staple articles of food and raw materials. These taxes, to us new taxes, would have to be included in our Budget each year. Those interests which were benefited would support the taxes. Those that were injured would oppose them. Severe Parliamentary criticism will be directed against the taxes year after year: and the value of the colonial preference will be examined with severity and exactitude. Their military contributions will also be examined rigidly, and there will be an annual casting up of accounts. I think the debate which took place recently in the House of Commons ought to be satisfactory to the representatives of the Colonies. It was argued by myself and generally accepted that the relations of the Mother Country and the Colonies are those of a family and not of a syndicate. One can scarcely conceive any process better calculated to manufacture what does not now exist—an anti-colonial party. A system of preference must further, it seems to me, affect the principle of self-government, the root principle by which the Empire is maintained. In the House of Commons the maxim is that grievances must be dealt with before Supply is granted, and whenever the preferential duties were under discussion they would afford opportunities and provoke occasions for criticizing internal matters in the different Colonies. Perhaps the House would be asked to refuse to vote them until some particular colony had met their view upon native policy or some other matter. It is now open to the Government to point out that the matter is one directly within the proper competence of the colonial Government and Legislature, but it will be hardly possible to secure recognition for this attitude when the members are called upon to vote the money of their constituents to whom they are responsible. From that would flow a frequent and almost inexhaustible source of vexation. The preferences hitherto accorded have been free preferences; as soon as reciprocity was established the preferences would become locked preferences, and could not be removed except by consent. Preference can only operate through the agency of price. It means better prices; that is to say, higher prices. If it does not mean that it means nothing, and can effect none of the purposes for which it is intended. Every tax, however small, must be a factor in price. Its effect might be obscured by all manner of other more powerful forces, such as the acts of nature and speculative operations. Great fluctuations occur in the price of all commodities subject to climatic conditions. It is highly dangerous to associate the idea of the Empire in the minds of the masses of the people with enhanced food prices. Many causes of the fluctuations of prices are beyond our control, but the taxes, however small, being the only factor absolutely within our control, will bear all the unpopularity in times of scarcity, and there may easily arise an irresistible demand for their adoption. At present any unpopular tax can be reduced or removed, but these preferential food taxes, these crucial links of Empire, will be irremovable. They will be fixed as if by treaty with the self-governing dominions, and in return for them advantages will have been accorded, upon the basis of which the whole industry of the Colonies affected will have grown up tier upon tier. If ever the day came when the electors demanded in overwhelming majority the removal of a food tax, which could not be removed without consultation and agreements with Governments and Parliaments scattered all over the globe, a shock and a wrench would be administered to the structure of the British Empire such as it had never before sustained. Even if the economic case against preference were waived, the political objections to such a system were insuperable. Even at this Conference, where all has been discussed with so much good will and good feeling, it has been an apple of discord. I agree with the Chancellor of the Exchequer that any proposal involving the principle of preferential tariffs will be rejected in the present House of Commons by three to one. But his Majesty's Government feels bound to decline to join in a preferential system, not because we are not willing to take electoral risks, or still less to make sacrifices for the Empire, but because we believe it to be a system vicious in itself and dangerous for the concord of the British Empire. Some day when Imperial unification has reached a higher development than is now possible I believe that men will look back to the Conference of 1907 as a date when one grand wrong turn was successfully avoided.

"THE LAUGHING-STOCK OF EUROPE"

August 24, 1907

Garden Party, Cheadle Hulme

[Extract] We have now completed the second Parliamentary session of the new Parliament elected in 1906. We have been in office practically now for two whole years. During that time we have passed a great quantity of legislation. Last year, when I spoke in the Free-trade Hall, I was able to congratulate you on having had the finest summer any of us had ever known. I am sorry to say that this year I cannot pass the same eulogy upon the clerk of the weather, but although the weather has not been so propitious as it was last year we have succeeded in reaping very nearly as large a harvest of legislative enactments. When Sir Henry Campbell-Bannerman made his speech about a month ago and said that he intended to pass more than forty bills into law before the end of the session there was a good deal of irreverent and, as it afterwards turned out, uninstructed laughter in the camp of the Hittites. (Laughter.) The month has gone, and forty bills have been successfully passed through the House of Commons. (Cheers.) Now the financial situation of our country has notably improved. . . .

The great Liberal majority which you returned to power in January, 1906, has shown that it is ready to sit up all night, and every night if need be, to carry on public business–has shown that it is ready to sit far into the summer holiday months of the year, to sacrifice the comfort, and even the health, I fear, of some of the members, in their desire to deal as effectively as we can deal with the social problems which our ever-extending civilisation thrusts upon us year by year. No, the fault does not lie with the House of Commons or with its members.

If some of our legislation has not attained its fruition the fault lies at the other end of the passage, in the "Gilded Chamber," separated from us only by 200 yards of corridor, but separated from us by what a vast gulf of principle and of policy!–(Hear, hear.) Liberal legislation affecting the largest questions may easily be wrecked and ruined, not, mind you, with a healthy regard to the merits of that legislation, but in the interests of a particular class and a particular party. (Hear, hear.)

Now, you could not very well have a second chamber more unsuited to a great modern commercial and industrial community like we have in Lancashire than is the present House of Lords. It is the laughing-stock of Europe. (Hear, hear.) There is no such unreformed second chamber claiming absolute equal authority with the representative chamber in any of the democratic Constitutions of Europe. I do not deny for a moment that the House of Lords contains in its ranks men of the highest character and ability, men who have rendered splendid service to the State, but in spite of the greatest private and public virtues, I do say, as a body and as an institution, it is wholly unsuited to the needs and requirements of a community which is now coming into its own, and it is wholly out of harmony and out of accord with the democratic principles which we profess, which we have pursued for so many years, and which, pursuing, we have found yielded us a great and increasing measure of satisfaction and tranquillity. (Hear, hear.)

But if there is one set of questions with which the House of Lords is more unfitted to deal than with any other it is that of the tenure and transfer of land. (Hear, hear.) It is not that they do not know a good deal about the tenure and transfer of the land of this country. (Laughter.) I think they have managed to get hold and keep hold of most of it. (Laughter.) But they cannot even wish to deal with large problems of land in a national and impartial spirit. They are all personally and directly interested themselves. When I went to the House of Lords the other day and saw them listening to a debate on the English Land Bill with such rapt attention I thought to myself "We must make 60 per cent discount from their attention on account of the immense personal interests in which all these gentlemen are involved in the passage of such measures."

The Scottish Land Bill has been destroyed in the House of Lords. (Shame.) That was a measure which claimed the support of the vast majority of the Scottish representatives. They were enthusiastic in its support. Hardly any representatives from Scotland were found to oppose it in its passage through the House of Commons, and yet when it got to the House of Lords this measure, supported by all those who had a right to speak in the name of Scotland—a representative's right, I mean, to speak in the name of Scotland,—was rejected and destroyed incontinently by a Chamber which has absolutely no representative authority. Well, I do not know whether the Scottish people fought the Battle of Bannockburn in order to have their national will, as expressed by their elected representatives, flouted and perverted by a few nobles and landlords in the British House of Lords. I should think if Robert Bruce were alive to-day he would find something to say which Lord Lansdowne and his friends would scarcely like to hear. Mr. Elverston has told you that because our bills are mutilated in the House of Lords we shall none the less persist in forcing them forward. (Hear, hear.) If we are compelled to withdraw or sacrifice a bill in this particular session it will be reintroduced and passed through the House of Commons with the greatest rapidity in the new session, and the fight will go steadily on until, at the proper moment, the people of this country will be asked to pronounce definitely and decisively in favour of democratic government against class government. (Cheers.) . . .

Well, if the strength of the Government, its solidity and its vitality, is quite undiminished and unexhausted by the two years' severe Parliamentary battles in which we have been engaged, what are we to say about the strength of the Opposition? (Laughter.) I really do not think in the whole history of Parliament there has ever been such an incompetent and weak Opposition in the House of Commons. (Hear, hear.) Whether they deal with large matters or with small, they have always shown themselves perfectly irresponsible, perfectly sterile in ideas. They have nothing to offer the country but the old, played-out heresy of Protection. They have nothing to offer to South Africa but a severe and repressive form of government, accompanied by the limitless importation of Chinese. They have nothing to offer the temperance party in this country, to Ireland, to that large section of our fellow-countrymen who believe that England would be much stronger and much better if a larger number of persons could be associated with the ownership of the soil. To all these questions, whenever and wherever they arise, the official opposition is one of dull, sterile negation—"No," "No," "No," "No"; and even that they do not say well. (Laughter.) The great divisions which racked the Conservative party before the general election are quite unhealed. The disputes between Free-trades and Protectionists in the party continue with unabated ferocity, although I am bound to say the cause of Protection is making steady headway within the ranks of the Conservative party. (Laughter.) The Free Trade minority are still unreconciled. If the Conservative party were to come into power I am certain they would be compelled by the force which their own followers would exert to introduce tariff reform in some form or under some pretext or another, and their party would be split and broken in the process of trying to carry that tariff through the House of Commons. As long as the Conservative party has Protection tied round its neck you may be quite sure, if we manage our affairs with dignity and prudence, we shall retain an increasing measure of confidence and support of all classes in the country. (Cheers.) . . .

THE EAST AFRICAN TOUR

January 18, 1908

National Liberal Club, London

In September Churchill attended French maneuvers before starting on a lengthy tour of East Africa. The journey began in Malta and was continued via Cyprus to British East Africa, Uganda, the Sudan, and Egypt. Churchill's own account is to be found in My African Journey, *which first appeared in article form in the* Strand *magazine.*

Churchill returned to England on January 17, 1908. On the following evening he was the guest of honour at a special dinner at the National Liberal Club.

Churchill's comments upon South African hostility to immigrants from India, and the opportunities which existed for them in East Africa, are of particular interest in the light of the difficulties created for Asians after these nations received independence–and particularly in Uganda, which fell into evil hands.

[Extract] . . . You have welcomed me back tonight from my African tour. It is, I dare say, more to the subjects connected with my journey you would wish me to speak than on political matters. It was rather a doubtful attempt of an Under-Secretary to visit these countries beyond the seas. There were precedents, but they were not numerous. There was criticism, which was not always friendly. But I venture to think that it is a matter of importance, particularly in the administration of the Colonial Office, that those who are responsible for taking a share, however small, in large decisions of policy should have first-hand information in regard to some of the countries, and a realisation of the values and proportions of the issues with which they have to deal. There is another reason. Parties come and parties go, but we are all working for great ends. It is important that those who in distant countries are called upon to work hard and lead lives in bad climates and under conditions of great difficulties, and even dullness and monotony, should feel that the great revolutionary change which occurred in January, 1906, did not mean that there was any lack of sympathy or interest or zeal or any indisposition to study the problems and needs of the large possessions of the Crown beyond the seas. (Cheers.)

If you ask what is my prevailing impression–my preponderating impression–in the journey I have taken, I would say frankly it is one of astonishment. It is not the first time I have travelled abroad. I have had the opportunity of examining Africa from both ends–from the Sudan and from the South–and I have travelled very widely over India. But I confess I have never seen countries so fertile and so beautiful outside Europe as those to which I have travelled on the journey from which you welcome me back tonight. There are parts of the East African Protectorate which in their beauty, in the coolness of the air, in the richness of the soil, in their verdure, in the abundance of running water, in their fertility–parts which absolutely surpass any of the countries which I have mentioned, and challenge comparison with the fairest regions of England,

France, or Italy. (Cheers.) I have seen in Uganda a country which from end to end is a garden–inexhaustible, irrepressible, and exuberant fertility upon every side,–and I cannot doubt that the great system of lakes and waterways, which you cannot fail to observe if you look at the large map of Africa, must one day become the great centre of tropical production, and play a most important part in the economic development of the whole world. . . .

But the real argument I would urge upon the Liberal party, as a cause for our not relaxing our efforts to develop these countries is the interest of the native races who dwell there. (Cheers.) Of course from time to time in the administration of large affairs detached incidents occur which everybody regrets, and which scarcely anybody defends. But I must say that I was most pleasantly surprised–no, I won't say surprised; I was pleasantly impressed with the manner in which a great number of our civil and military officers whom I met construed their duty towards the native populations among whom they lived. I found them resolved to protect these populations against the mere exploiter and the speculator, and those who merely wished to use them for some financial advantage. (Cheers.) I am sure it would be an evil day for the very large populations of East Africa and of Uganda if they were handed over from the careful, the disinterested control of British officials to the mere self-interest of some small local community. (Cheers.) . . .

There is one other point in connection with East Africa which I will touch upon before I sit down. It is a matter of gravity and delicacy. We have all been concerned at the position and the situation of the British Indians in South Africa. No doubt we shall have a debate on the subject when Parliament assembles, and I think it would only be respectful for me to reserve the full argument which I wish to use if I am called upon in the House of Commons. All I will say on that particular point tonight is that, while I yield to no one in my admiration for the Indian Empire and in my respect for the people of Hindustan, I cannot dispute the right of General Botha's Government in the Transvaal to make what arrangements they may think necessary for the welfare of their own people in respect to immigration from Asia. (Hear, hear.) I cannot dispute their right any more than I can dispute the right of the people of Australia. It is entirely within the authority deliberately conceded to them by this House of Commons, and from which such very great advantages have flowed in other ways which we all recognise, and for which we are all grateful. . . .

I hope that in the discussions which will take place before Parliament assembles, or in the House of Commons on a subject on which the white populations of South Africa are absolutely united, and which affects their most vital and intimate interests, there will be an honest attempt to grasp their point of view, to understand their difficulties, and above all, to avoid the use of harsh and intemperate language, which will only have the effect of weakening the moderating and conciliatory influences which the Colonial Office will not cease to exercise by the various channels which are open to us. (Cheers.)

The approach of this difficulty has not been unexpected. I told my right hon. friend Sir Charles Dilke when he brought a deputation to me before I started on my travels that I would make it a matter to be particularly considered whether the equatorial Protectorates of Africa could not in some manner or degree be made to supply a compensating field for the colonising enterprise of our British subjects in India. After all, the East Africa Protectorates and Uganda are the countries nearest to India. The Uganda Railway was built by Indian labour. Sikh soldiers at the present moment maintain the authority of the Crown throughout Uganda. Indian traders have been for generations intimately associated with the development of the East African territories, and are at this moment indispensible to the cheap and convenient development of trade and of communications throughout large areas. The Government welcome their entry into the country. Their rights are fully safeguarded, and official employment, in many cases of a responsible character, is open, and will continue to be open, to our Indian subjects of intelligence and trustworthy character.

I should say, however, that it will be our duty, in view of this fact, which every one must recognise, that the two races, Asiatic and European, do not mix well on even terms in trade competition and social life, and in view of the very strong feeling which was expressed vehemently to me by the white settlers in the country–it will be our duty to reserve certain areas, where the coolness of the air and the elevation of the land make life particularly easy for the Europeans, for the settlers of British origin who have already arrived in the country. I think we shall also be forced and are bound to consider the rights of the aboriginal natives, who are the real possessors, the moral possessors, of as much of the country as they require for their natural comfort and development, and who have sometimes been injuriously affected by influences which have reached them from the outside. But when all that has been said and disposed of there is room enough in these splendid lands for all. There are enormous areas of fertile and beautiful country in which Asiatics can live and thrive and multiply, and which in a very short time can be opened, if they are not opened already, to the enterprise of colonists from India. . . .

I have been dealing exclusively with colonial questions, but I trust you will not think that I wish to divert the attention of the British public from the grave problems of social reform which confront us in our own country. A just sense of proportion will easily convince anyone who thinks that the fame and the prosperity of our people can only be won, and having been won can only be preserved, by maintaining the spirit and the quality of those who dwell here in our own island. (Hear, hear.) The only foundation for the British Empire is a healthy, contented, prosperous, generous-hearted democracy, dwelling together with uplifted hearts and seeking, under just laws, high and lofty ideals. Territorial possessions, the wide control of subject races, the accumulation of material forces, however imposing, the organisation of Governments however elaborate or perfected–all kinds of magnificence abroad can never repair and can only for a short time conceal the effects of misery, squalor, vice, and social injustice at home. (Cheers.) If the British people will have a great Empire, if any ray of true glory is to fall upon it, they will need an Imperial race to support the burden. They will never erect that great fabric upon the shoulders of stinted millions crowded together in the slums of cities, trampled in the slush of dismal streets. Not that way lies the future of the British race, and any neglect of these considerations will lead to the destruction not merely of our material dominion but of the moral forces upon which that material dominion is based. Yet, I think that all legitimate interests are in harmony. I believe that the strength of this Liberal Government, as of others, will be increased and not diminished by efficient action in all useful directions to grapple with the social evils that confront us. . . .

SOCIALISM

January 22, 1908

Cheetham

Mr. Victor Grayson had created a great sensation by winning the Colne Valley by-election in July 1907 as virtually an independent Socialist. His political career was brief indeed, and he disappeared permanently from politics after the 1910 election.

[Extract] . . . The Socialists–the extreme and revolutionary party of Socialists–are very fond of telling us they are reviving in modern days the best principles of the Christian era. They consider they are the political embodiment of Christianity, though, to judge by the language which some of them use and the spirit of envy, hatred, and malice with which they go about their work, you would hardly imagine they had studied the teaching of the Founder of Christianity with the attention they profess to have given to the subject.–(Hear, hear.)

But there is one great difference between Socialists of the Christian era and those of which Mr. Victor Grayson is the apostle. The Socialism of the Christian era was based on the idea that "all mine is yours," but the Socialism of Mr. Grayson is based on the idea that "all yours is mine."–(Cheers.) And I go so far as to say that no movement will ever achieve any real advantage for the mass of the people that is based upon so much spite and jealousy as is the present Socialist movement in the hands of its extreme men. We are all of us prepared to recognise that in a great many ways the community must come more together. I am prepared to go a very long way in the direction of trying to build up and fortify a minimum standard of life, but if that is to be done, if you are to have greater combinations and greater harmonies in society you can only have it by becoming better men and women.–(Hear, hear.) Any attempt to replace the existing organisation of society by an official hierarchy, for that is what it means–to replace the men who now manage mills by officials who are elected in some way will end in failure.

It is very easy to make promises of pensions and the like when you have no prospect of being called to make them good. An extreme Socialist policy would plunge the country into a violent social struggle, and there would be no pensions for anybody at all. No, the future lies with us. We tread the middle path between the party of reaction on the one side and the party of revolution on the other. Move forward. Don't let us be content with the existing state of society, with all its anomalies and injustices. Round them off, rub the edges off, and reconstruct on a sound basis. I am most earnestly desirous of seeing the condition of our people improved. It is not right that men should be forced to work for wages which will not keep them in comfort and physical health. You cannot expect the children to do justice to their country and their race as long as they are not properly fed when they have to attend school and are allowed at the age of 14 to pick up odd jobs when they should be learning a trade and fitting themselves to carry on the industries of the country. You cannot say that we are making the best of our opportunities while half the land is in the hands of seven or eight hundred persons, mostly members of the House of Lords. You cannot say that we are doing our duty, that we have a fair and just social system when you see millions of money accumulated without effort and service rendered to society by the persons who enjoy all that advantage. So we have a great field in which we can work. Our work is practical, and must lead to a substantial amelioration of the people. Let us go on and steadily build up, stage by stage, and tier by tier, the assured and comfortable happiness of English homes.

I hope that the coming session of Parliament will see a substantial scheme which will sensibly mitigate the lot of a portion, at any rate, of the aged poor.

SOCIAL POLICY

January 23, 1908

Town Hall, Birmingham

Churchill's speeches on non-colonial questions during this time demonstrated his awakened interest in social reform, which preceded his movement to the Board of Trade.

[Extract] . . . All Parliaments become exhausted, all Governments become unpopular. I do not think a general election will come for three years, but the unexpected might occur. It is open to the House of Lords at any moment to render the word of the Government intolerable. They only require to be assured of a fair chance of getting off scot free to stab the Government in the back. On the other hand, the House of Lords might make a mistake; it might be the Government's turn to strike; it might be the arm of the House of Commons which would bring the Lords unexpectedly before the judgment of the constituencies. If after another election has been fought Liberals are found possessed of a working majority in the House of Commons, we ought not to undertake the responsibility of national administration unless the very moderate constitutional reform which the Prime Minister has proposed have finally secured the effective supremacy of the House of Commons.–(Loud and prolonged cheers.)

The way to make Parliament memorable, the way to secure, or at any rate to deserve the confidence of the people, is to let each year be signalised by some one large solid achievement. In 1906 the charter to trade unions; in 1907 the South African settlement. What are we to do this year? There are to be bills on two great domestic questions–upon the question of temperance and on that of education. We propose to submit bills which will be simple and bold assertions of principles to which many of you have long given your faith. These principles will be applied in each case with every desire not to cause needless irritation to those who do not agree with us, and in a sincere attempt to injure no legitimate interest. It is possible, nay it is certain, that we shall lose as well as gain from these legislative proposals. Never mind, let us work according to our lights for what we think is right, and trust to that to pull us through and carry us on through good or evil fortune.–(Cheers.)

Important, however, as these two subjects are, they will not be the centrepiece of Parliamentary labours in the coming session. The time has now come when we must pay a debt. It was not the Liberal party who first raised the cry of old-age pensions, or promised to the aged poor that measure of relief from their distresses which statecraft indicates and which compassion demands. Thirteen years ago a great election was won in England in which nearly every member of the Conservative party proclaimed the grant of old-age pensions as one of the principal planks in the programme of Lord Salisbury's Government. Thirteen years are gone–dark years many of them for Liberalism, years of war and wild expenditure, years of reaction, years of change, years of struggle, years of victory–and we are now here to take up this dishonoured pledge by which so many hopes have so long been mocked, and in some measure at any rate to make it good. But I hope you will allow me to speak to you quite frankly upon this subject, for I do not want to imitate the vague and reckless assurances of others, and to create that disappointment which waits on over-expectation. I see it stated by politicians on the extremes of both great parties, and by that third new party who have permanently taken their place in our political life, that any scheme of old-age pensions must be immediate and universal in its application. I do not think there is a chance of that. It is very easy for persons having no public responsibilities, with hardly any chance of ever being called upon to give effect to what they urge, to declare themselves in favour of an immediate system of universal old-age pensions at a cost of thirty millions, or even at a much larger figure. When one is dealing only with promises it costs no more to make them large and fine, but I hope we have at least got out of the region of mere words and phrases upon this question.–(Hear, hear.)

What I am concerned to see in any scheme of old-age pensions to which His Majesty's Government may become a party is that so far as it goes it should be a real scheme and not a sham scheme–(hear, hear),–that it should involve a solid and substantial sum of money, that it shall operate without injury to the immense fabric of provident machinery already in existence–(hear, hear),–that it shall be proposed by practical methods and within the limits of prudent finance. These conditions, I believe, Mr. Asquith will succeed in satisfying–(cheers),–and I trust his declarations upon the subject will be awaited with a spirit of sober and business-like interest, and not in moods of unmeasured and extravagant hope.–("Hear, hear," and cheers.) I have been for some time of opinion, from such study as I have been able to give to the public finances and the general social conditions prevailing in this country, that the amount and proportion of direct taxation are capable of being considerably increased. I think it is about twenty-five years ago since Mr. Chamberlain expressed a similar opinion. In making any increases of direct taxation which are really to be productive it is necessary for a Minister to proceed with prudence as well as determination, for, as our Socialist friends are often inclined to forget, if the burden placed on wealth in any one country notably exceeds the burdens which exist in others capital in the present imperfect organisation of the world will take to its wings and fly away, and actual loss will result to the revenue and suffering to the people. Yet, bearing this in mind, I remain of opinion that there is room year by year for a steady augmentation of direct taxation; and if to that augmentation we are able to add the normal growth of existing taxes, and if at the same time we are able to keep in reasonable check the unproductive military expenditure of the State, it is evident that very considerable funds will gradually and continually be at the disposal of a Free Trade Government for the purposes of social reform. But if these funds amounted in the present year to thirty millions—which we are told will be the cost of a universal scheme of old-age pensions at sixty-five—I should certainly not recommend you to devote the whole of that sum to that single purpose.—(Hear, hear.)

For, after all, there are other not less important and more productive branches of social reform for which public money is indispensable. I mention only one which, to my mind, is not a whit less necessary than provision for old age. It operates at the other end of the line. I mean the proper education and training of the young. Is it really worth while to feed hungry children on lesson-books? Is there any better investment that the State can make, any more reproductive and profitable employment of its capital, than putting good, simple food into the stomachs of young children? But, further, is it not a terrible thing that the whole of our educational system, upon which so many millions are lavished, stops short at the age of fourteen, and that boys and girls, just at the age when they ought to receive training and discipline to make them good craftsmen and careful housekeepers, are allowed to slip away from all guidance and control and fritter away priceless years on odd jobs and idleness, and be awakened at twenty or twenty-one by the stern realities and harsh revenges of life? The German, Frenchman, Austrian, and Italian has a year or two years taken from the whole of his life for the military service of his country. In our happy island, protected by an all-powerful fleet, we are relieved from that oppressive burden. Every Englishman starts in the competition of the world with an extra two years to the good, but his two years if properly employed would give him a lead in all kinds of skilled employment far greater than any we have ever enjoyed in any period of our history, and I say that the organisation by the State of the proper training and apprenticeship of any persons, even though it involves a very large new expenditure, would do more than any other proposal now before the public to relieve the unskilled labour market, to diminish casual labour, and to increase the productivity and healthy energy of British labour.—(Cheers.) Where is there the general and compulsory system of technical and secondary instruction which alone can sift the clever from the skilled and the skilled from the simply industrious? Where are there those broad ladders which ought to stretch from the exit of the board school to the entrance of the university and learned professions? Where are those roadways and stairways by which the trampled-down natural talent of our people may raise itself to eminence and fame? All this could be provided by money, all this could be organised by thought, all this could be executed by power, and much though I desire to see every person in England rescued from the bitter affliction of aged poverty, I am not prepared to recommend to you an expenditure of indefinite character and of extravagant scale upon any one branch of social reform which will suck up automatically like a sponge whatever funds we may from time to time require to the exclusion of all other projects.—(Hear, hear.)

Even in regard to old-age pensions themselves it is, in my opinion, actually desirable that the effects of so striking a departure should be carefully observed before it is universally applied. We do not know, we cannot know except by experiment, exactly what the effects of old-age pensions will be upon existing friendly and provident societies, upon private thrift, upon the general rate of wages in the labour market, and particularly upon the rate of wages paid to persons approaching the pensionable limit; and I therefore regard a gradual and partial application as actually advantageous at the present moment, and not merely forced upon us by lack of funds. I have spoken frankly on this grave subject.–(Hear, hear.) Three distinct political parties make their appeal to the conscience and intellect of England. Two of those parties, the Socialist party and the party of Tariff Reform, do not hesitate to assure you that they possess a secret by which, after merely passing a number of bills through Parliament, the masses of the people will immediately become rich and happy and secure. We put forward no such pretensions. We have no panacea for human sorrows and complexities. We march along that fruitful temperate zone which stretches between the elevated latitudes of Tory reaction and the heat of the Socialist equator. We believe that reform must be patient, that progress must be steady, and that improvement must operate as much in the social and economic qualities of the people as in any reconstruction of political machinery. Yet I think that the Liberal party has a wide field of activity before it, and that its mission will carry far more real advantages to the people than all the clap-trap and conjuring tricks of irresponsible bodies desperately competing for the public favour. In promoting the cause of temperance, in nationalising and extending our system of education, in developing proper methods of technical instruction, in mitigating the sorrows of old age, in opening the land more freely to the millions, in adjusting more fairly the burden of taxation upon earned and unearned increment, we shall find the means, session after session, Parliament after Parliament, of widening the circle of comfort and of culture. In that way only we shall win something for ourselves and more for the children who will follow us along the road.–(Loud cheers.)

THE JOYS OF WRITING

February 17, 1908

Author's Club, London

The fortunate people in the world–the only really fortunate people in the world, in my mind,–are those whose work is also their pleasure. The class is not a large one, not nearly so large as it is often represented to be; and authors are perhaps one of the most important elements in its composition. They enjoy in this respect at least a real harmony of life. To my mind, to be able to make your work your pleasure is the one class distinction in the world worth striving for; and I do not wonder that others are inclined to envy those happy human beings who find their livelihood in the gay effusions of their fancy, to whom every hour of labour is an hour of enjoyment, to whom repose–however necessary–is a tiresome interlude, and even a holiday is almost deprivation. Whether a man writes well or ill, has much to say or little, if he cares about writing at all, he will appreciate the pleasures of composition. To sit at one's table on a sunny morning, with four clear hours of uninterruptible security, plenty of nice white paper, and a Squeezer pen–(laughter)–that is true happiness. The complete absorption of the mind upon an agreeable occupation–what more is there than that to desire? What does it matter what happens outside? The House of Commons may do what it likes, and so may the House of Lords.–(Laughter.) The heathen may rage furiously in every part of the globe. The bottom may be knocked clean out of the American market. Consols may fall and suffragettes may rise.–(Laughter.) Never mind, for four hours, at any rate, we will withdraw ourselves from a common, ill-governed, and disorderly world, and with the key of fancy unlock that cupboard where all the good things of the infinite are put away.–(Cheers.)

And speaking of freedom, is not the author free, as few men are free? Is he not secure, as few men are secure? The tools of his industry are so common and so cheap that they have almost ceased to have commercial value. He needs no bulky pile of raw material, no elaborate apparatus, no service of men or animals. He is dependent for his occupation upon no one but himself, and nothing outside him that matters. He is the sovereign of an empire, self-supporting, self-contained. No one can sequestrate his estates. No one can deprive him of his stock in trade; no one can force him to exercise his faculty against his will; no one can prevent him exercising it as he chooses. The pen is the great liberator of men and nations.–(Cheers.) No chains can bind, no poverty can choke, no tariff can restrict–(laughter)–the free play of his mind, and even the "Times" Book Club–(laughter)–can only exert a moderately depressing influence upon his rewards. Whether his work is good or bad, so long as he does his best he is happy. I often fortify myself amid the uncertainties and vexations of political life by believing that I possess a line of retreat into a peaceful and fertile country where no rascal can pursue and where one need never be dull or idle or even wholly without power. It is then, indeed, that I feel devoutly thankful to have been born fond of writing. It is then, indeed, that I feel grateful to all the brave and generous spirits who, in every age and in every land, have fought to establish the now unquestioned freedom of the pen.–(Cheers.)

And what a noble medium the English language is. It is not possible to write a page without experiencing positive pleasure at the richness and variety, the flexibility and the profoundness of our mother-tongue. If an English writer cannot say what he has to say in English, and in simple English, depend upon it it is probably not worth saying. What a pity it is that English is not more generally studied.–(Hear, hear.) I am not going to attack classical education. No one who has the slightest pretension to literary tastes can be insensible to the attraction of Greece and Rome. But I confess our present educational system excites in my mind grave misgivings. I cannot believe that a system is good, or even reasonable, which thrusts upon reluctant and uncomprehending multitudes treasures which can only be appreciated by the privileged and gifted few. To the vast majority of boys who attend our public schools a classical education is from beginning to end one long useless, meaningless rigmarole. If I am told that classics are the best preparation for the study of English, I reply that by far the greater number of students finish their education while this preparatory stage is still incomplete and without deriving any of the benefits which are promised as its result.

And even of those who, without being great scholars, attain a certain general acquaintance with the ancient writers, can it really be said that they have also obtained the mastery of English? How many young gentlemen there are from the universities and public schools who can turn a Latin verse with a facility which would make the old Romans squirm in their tombs.–(Laughter.) How few there are who can construct a few good sentences, or still less a few good paragraphs of plain, correct, and straightforward English. Now, I am a great admirer of the Greeks, although, of course, I have to depend upon what others tell me about them–(laughter),–and I would like to see our educationists imitate in one respect, at least, the Greek example. How is it that the Greeks made their language the most graceful and compendious mode of expression ever known among men? Did they spend all their time studying the languages which had preceded theirs? Did they explore with tireless persistency the ancient root dialects of the vanished world? Not at all. They studied Greek.–(Cheers.) They studied their own language. They loved it, they cherished it, they adorned it, they expanded it, and that is why it survives a model and delight to all posterity. Surely we, whose mother-tongue has already won for itself such an unequalled empire over the modern world, can learn this lesson at least from the ancient Greeks and bestow a little care and some proportion of the years of education to the study of a language which is perhaps to play a predominant part in the future progress of mankind.

Let us remember the author can always do his best. There is no excuse for him. The great cricketer may be out of form. The general may on the day of decisive battle have a bad toothache or a bad army.–(Laughter.) The admiral may be seasick–as a sufferer I reflect with satisfaction upon that contingency.–(Laughter.) Caruso may be afflicted with catarrh, or Hackenschmidt with influenza. As for an orator, it is not enough for him to be able to think well and truly. He must think quickly. Speed is vital to him. Spontaneity is more than ever the hall-mark of good speaking. All these varied forces of activity require from the performer the command of the best that is in him at a particular moment which may be fixed by circumstances utterly beyond his control. It is not so with the author. He need never appear in public until he is ready. He can always realise the best that is in him. He is not dependent upon his best moment in any one day. He may group together the best moments of twenty days. There is no excuse for him if he does not do his best.–(Hear, hear.) Great is his opportunity; great also his responsibility. Someone–I forget who–has said: "Words are the only things which last for ever." That is, to my mind, always a wonderful thought. The most durable structures raised in stone by the strength of man, the mightiest monuments of his power, crumble into dust, while the words spoken with fleeting breath, the passing expression of the unstable fancies of his mind, endure not as echoes of the past, not as mere archæological curiosities or venerable relics, but with a force and life as new and strong, and sometimes far stronger than when they were first spoken, and leaping across the gulf of three thousand years, they light the world for us to-day.–(Cheers.)

TRADE AND GOVERNMENT

March 18, 1908

Chambers of Commerce Association, London

[Extract] . . . I distrust profoundly the positive intervention of Government—particularly party Government—in the delicate and intricate world-wide operations of trade. They do not understand it. I reject as impracticable the insane Socialist idea that we could have a system whereby the whole national production of the country, with all its infinite ramifications, should be organised and directed by a permanent official, however able, from some central office. The idea is not only impossible, but unthinkable. (Cheers.) If it was even attempted it would produce a most terrible shrinkage and destruction of productive energy. I am drawn to the conclusion that the intervention of Government in regard to trade must be mainly of a liberating character, of a negative character in that sense.—(Applause.) But even so there are very considerable spheres into which they might advance without risk of peril. They might try to set the taxpayer free from the burden of debt which presses upon him, they might set the canals free—(applause),—and they might attempt to set railways free from internecine competition, which though it might have been all right in the early days has for a long time ceased to be economical and has lately become wasteful and injurious. Best of all, governments could try to set nations free from the hideous terrors of war which hang over us. It is a melancholy reflection upon Christendom that at this time of day nations should have to arm and be on their guard lest a civilised neighbour should suddenly spring upon them with butchery and rapine.—(Hear, hear.) To my mind it is this grim and shocking state of affairs that governments ought to devote themselves to, in the interests of trade and commerce.—(Applause.) Kings and Presidents might do much, diplomats might do a great deal, newspapers might do a great deal more than they always did, but after all it is to the blessed intercourse of trade and commerce that I will look more than to anything else to weld the nations of the world together, without their knowledge and even without their will.—(Applause.)

ELECTION ADDRESS

April 12, 1908

Manchester

By February, 1908, it was evident that the health of Sir Henry Campbell-Bannerman was deteriorating rapidly, and that Asquith would succeed him in the premiership. Churchill's achievements at the Colonial Office had marked him out for promotion to the Cabinet. He would have preferred to become Colonial Secretary, and he was very unenthusiastic about the Local Government Board. On April 3, Campbell-Bannerman resigned, and Asquith kissed hands as Prime Minister on April 8. On the same day, the new Prime Minister offered Churchill the Cabinet post of President of the Board of Trade, which Churchill accepted. He was thirty-three years of age.

Under the then electoral law, all Cabinet members were obliged to seek re-election, and a by-election at North-west Manchester was inevitable when the Unionists announced their intention of opposing his candidacy, Joynson-Hicks again being their candidate. It was clear that it would be a hard and close contest.

Meanwhile, an event of profound importance in Churchill's life had occurred when he became acquainted with Miss Clementine Hozier.

Two years ago you returned me to the House of Commons by an impressive majority on behalf of Liberalism and free trade. Since then I have endeavoured to serve your interests and your cause. I have lost no opportunity in or out of Parliament of disputing the path of those who seek to reverse the free trade basis of our commercial system and to erect in one form or another, under one pretext or another, a preferential, retaliatory, or protective tariff. Believing as I do that taxation should be levied for revenue only, and that other fiscal objectives are illusory, wasteful, and vicious, it is my intention to resist all attempts to establish in this country a general tariff against foreign manufactured articles—that policy of chronic tariff wars called retaliation—and, above all, the preferential and protective taxation of bread and meat for the profit of private interests here or in the Colonies.

The two years that have passed have been the best two years of trade that Manchester has ever known. It is one of Nature's revenges upon those who seek to violate economic harmonies that the very period which had been predicted for our downfall and disaster should have witnessed the most surprising manifestation of our industrial productivity.

To me these have been years of exacting labour. The state of South Africa at the change of Government was such as to cause grave anxiety to all involved by any tie of responsibility. To-day the sky is much brighter. Governments have been called into being in the two new colonies which command the confidence of the people, and render faithful service to the Crown. South Africa is now moving forward smoothly yet irresistibly to a strong Afrikander federation under the Union Jack.

The development of the tropical possessions of the British Empire has also proceeded apace. A railway 600 miles long is being constructed with the utmost rapidity in Nigeria to secure the expansion of cotton-growing, with its consequent advantages. Soon a similar railway will be begun on the other side of Africa to unite without undue expense the Victoria and the Albert Lakes and open the cotton potentialities of Uganda to British enterprise. Whatever your action may be now or at any future election, I shall always be sincerely grateful to the electors of this division for having enabled me to take even a subordinate share in these considerable affairs, and I invite specifically your unprejudiced verdict upon them.

The melancholy illness of Sir Henry Campbell-Bannerman has required the formation of a new Government at home. I have accepted the office of the President of the Board of Trade. This office, however superior to any personal merit of my own, cannot be deemed wholly unsuited to the representative of the Exchange Division of Manchester. It is by the Board of Trade that, within the limits of prudent State intervention, the commercial interests of our country must be fostered. It is thence that the gravest trade disputes are sometimes reconciled or adjusted. It is by the Minister responsible for that Department that free trade must be most directly defended. The Patents Act, already productive of substantial advantages to British industry, has now to be administered fairly, but thoroughly. The tragic question of unemployment, considered in relation to the decasualization of labour, also falls–in its economic aspect–upon the Board of Trade. In attempting to deal with such intricate business I count upon your generous consideration.

Two important questions–licensing and education–are immediately before us. The Licensing Bill is a great forward heave in the temperance movement. All social reform, all commercial efficiency wait on its success. The health of English manhood, the happiness of English homes, the virtues and ascendency of our race and age are involved in this tremendous effort. We have been informed by the liquor trade that their organization is so perfect, and their power so formidable, that any Government who touches their privileges and monopoly will be beaten to the ground. That is one of the things we want to find out now.

I come forward to defend the Licensing Bill in its integrity. We assert the right of the State to resume possession of the monopoly value of all licenses at the earliest moment compatible with fair treatment to the ordinary prudent trader or investor. To argument we will listen with attention; but we are not going to be bullied. In this country private interests should be respected, but the public interest must have right of way.

The dispute which has arisen over the Licensing Bill has tended to smooth the education controversy. The brave part played by many leaders of the Church of England for the sake of temperance reform has moved men in every political party. Cannot distressing and distracting differences, harmful alike to religion and to education, be generously adjusted? The principles of the Liberal party are clear. Schools maintained by public funds must be amenable to public control. State paid teachers as Civil servants cannot be subjected to religious tests. But his Majesty's Government is perfectly ready to meet in a cordial spirit any proposal, not discordant with those two principles, which responsible authority may advance on behalf of the Church of England for an amicable and a lasting settlement. Provision must, of course, be made for the case of the Catholics, whose religious faith diverges so widely from that of the great majority of the people of these islands that a special type of school may well be demanded; and for the same reasons similar provisions must be made for the Jews.

Upon these issues, as upon the whole policy and record of the Government, I shall be prepared to make good the Liberal case in the fight which has now begun. To oppose the re-election of a Minister, already once elected as a member of Government, is, to say the least, unusual. To delay and hamper the work of a great Department charged with important and complicated legislation of a purely non-party character betokens a keener zest for faction than for the public interest. Yet antiquated and anomalous as is the technicality which renders a contest possible, mischievous as is the opposition which makes it necessary, I welcome this opportunity of dealing with the taunts and challenges so cheaply uttered during 18 months by politicians still smarting from their last defeat. I have nothing to regret or to excuse in the conduct of his Majesty's Government or its results at home or abroad. The machine-made calumnies of partisanship will dissolve under the honest examination of the people. The constituency, which gave the signal for the free trade triumph of 1906, will not now consent to obey the dismal trumpet of retreat. And with European peace preserved, international friendships cemented, Africa conciliated, India tranquillized, taxation reduced by five millions, unproductive expenditure reduced by eight millions, debt reduced by nearly 30 millions, and many important Acts of Parliament already placed, in spite of every difficulty, upon the Statute-book—all in two short years—I appeal with sober confidence to the loyalty and fair play of Lancashire electors.

ELECTION ADDRESS

April 14, 1908

Grand Theatre, Manchester

[Extract] . . . "But," they say, "the Government is too Radical." They say "property is not secure," and that "business will suffer through the injury to credit," and that "Radical legislation and Radical principles are disturbing influences." They say: "We don't like these continued class fights, we don't like this social legislation. What does the Government want to bring in this Trades Disputes Bill and the Workmen's Compensation Act for, and above all what do they bring in this wicked temperance bill for? Why can't they let well alone? We want to remain quiet; we are content with things as they are." That is the argument often put to me. Let us look into that and handle it, not as partisans, but as Englishmen.—(Hear, hear.)

Let us look into it again by the light of history and philosophy. Why is it that life and property are so much more secure in England than in any other country? Why is it that wealthy men from many other countries come to England, come to reside here and spend their closing years? Why is it our credit is so high and our commerce stretches so far? Is it because we have repressive laws which are harshly enforced? Why, other countries have laws for more savage and harsh than anything which has existed in England for a long time. Yet in these countries, in spite of all these laws, there is not security to life and property. Is it because we have in England the House of Lords?–(Laughter.) No doubt they have a great and legitimate power. It is very often wrongly used, very often used, as history shows, against the light. After all, in other countries aristocracies far more powerful and closely organised, far more unscrupulous and violent in their class action, have been swept away and shattered till not a vestige of them remains. Is it because of the British Constitution, then? You know the British Constitution is mainly British common sense. No country in the world has such a flexible Constitution as ours. The Constitutions of France, Germany, and the United States are far more rigid, far more fortified against popular movements than the Constitution under whose gradual evolution this peaceful, law-abiding country has dwelt secure for so many centuries. I will tell you the secret why life and property are so much more secure in England than America or the Continent. Our security of property–I put this to the business men of Manchester–arises from that very class struggle which you see ceaselessly going on here in this country, and of which this election is only the incidental manifestation.

That is the cause of the security of property. We are always changing in England. Like nature, we are always changing–changing vastly but changing gradually. We are never standing still, and we have never for many years, thank God, moved distinctly backwards. We are always endeavouring in our country to broaden the basis–not of taxation–(laughter)–but of society; to admit new classes to larger, a happier and a brighter life. We are always occupied in trying to raise the level–not of tariffs–but of the standard of life and wages. We are always occupied in attempting, and with an increasing measure of success, to widen the circles of comfort and culture among the masses of the people. Lord Beaconsfield once wrote of the earlier years of this century that in those days England was for the few and the very few. England is now for the million. What we have got to do in the future is to work for an England for all.–(Cheers.)

The Government of a State is like a pyramid, and I have told you before that the function of Liberalism is to broaden the base of the pyramid and so increase the stability of the whole. There lies the true evolution of democracy; that is the true method whereby reform is always made to step in to block the path of revolution. It is because that has been our fortune in the past that we have preserved in England what scarcely any other State in the world can show, a long historical continuity of national life and the only way–I say it with profound conviction–in which you will preserve your English life as you know it and as you love it; the only way in which you can preserve it with its freedom and its reverence, in which you can expand it, elevate it, and illuminate it for those who will come after us and be the heirs of our exertions, is by a continuance of this social battle, which never degenerates into violence and never sinks into lethargy.–(Cheers.) And I appeal to the rich men of Manchester, to the citizens, the prominent citizens, of this great centre of fortune and the happy and the powerful to range themselves decidedly upon the generous side of things, to take a broad view of policy, to range themselves definitely on the side of vigilantly seeking for the welfare of the whole mass of the people, of sternly refusing to profit by anything which can be shown to be to the detriment of the people. Believe me, it is in that way, and that only, we shall succeed in raising the conditions, social and political, which prevail in our country. It is by doing that we shall succeed in gaining not only moral satisfaction, but material prosperity. And whether you look to our great empire abroad, or to the fortunes of this island home in which we dwell, we shall be forced to have built our house on the rock.–(Cheers.)

LICENSING BILL

April 18, 1908

Crumpsall View, Manchester

Churchill mounted a waggonette and asked his audience what they wanted him to speak about. In reply, a man held up a cartoon directed against the Licensing Bill, and Churchill decided to speak on that subject.

What do you think is the object of this cartoon and others like it? The object is to defend the interests of a great monopoly which too long has ruled and bullied England. The Government wish to do no injustice to anyone. We do not want to hurt a child or a fly. But we want to make sure that the public interests in regard to the traffic in drink should prevail over the special monopoly interests of a class. A man might have a house worth £300 or £400. He gets a license, and at once it becomes worth £3,000 or £4,000. Where does the extra money come from? It comes from the State. The State when it gives a license gives a monopoly, an exemption from competition. Our contention is that the monopoly value which the State creates really belongs to the public and ought to come back to the public. The law says that a license is an annual privilege. But the Government wish to be compassionate, and to take into account the fact that the State has not strictly exercised its rights and has allowed private interests to grow up. Therefore a time limit of fourteen years is given. At the end of that time the public houses are not closed, the publican is not turned out, the brewer is not prevented from brewing beer or the public from buying it. But a tax will be imposed equal to the monopoly value of the house and for the rest, the owner will trade on even terms with his neighbours in other trades around him. Can that be called robbery? Nobody proposes to shut up all the public houses at the end of fourteen years. It is not possible to make England sober by Act of Parliament. But we can by Act of Parliament give England power to make itself sober by giving to the people in any district power to control the sale of strong drink. Mr. Joynson-Hicks knows all about this. He has been a temperance reformer all his life. There is nothing in the bill half so strong as what he has said himself.–(Laughter.) You will always find people willing to defend private interests. That is a soft billet enough. But I say to you, range yourself behind the Liberal party, and make sure that those interests shall conform to the general interests of the whole community. The publican, who must by his vocation be a most respectable man, is better treated under this bill than under the Act of 1904.

Your industry in Lancashire depends upon power to buy and sell in the markets of the whole world. Don't give that away.–(Cheers.)

ELECTION ADDRESS

April 21, 1908

Gaiety Theatre, Manchester

You have listened this afternoon to some of the best speakers alive to-day, and in particular to a moving address from my right hon. friend the Chancellor of the Exchequer. That is his first great speech in public since he has assumed his important office. I think it added a special appropriateness to the occasion that he should come down here at this important juncture and make his first speech as Chancellor of the Exchequer to an audience drawn from the city where his youth was spent, and I think that the matter of that speech, its close arguments, and its moving conclusion, are worthy of one who is called to play a leading and perhaps the leading part in the immediate destinies of our country.–(Cheers.) The forces which are arranged against us are very strong. Do not underrate them.

There are immense forces embattled against us now. Thirteen separate organisations whose expenses would not be included in the candidate's return have already embarked on the work of wresting Manchester from her Free Trade allegiance. And there are other forces more sinister even than those organisations–forces which are blatant, which glare from every wall, and which address themselves to the public in every issue of a million multiplied publications.–(Cheers.) The practice which that newspaper has introduced in this contest will certainly require the attention of those who are engaged in amending and extending the Corrupt Practices Act.–(Cheers.) We have against us all these powerful forces.

Well, what have we on our side to put against them? We have, in the first place, ourselves.–(Cheers and laughter.) A good, strong army, well organised, in high spirits, marching forward over ground which they know, already memorable and glorious by former victories, and we have guiding that army many speakers to whom you have listened and who are devoting themselves with energy to the work. I confess I feel in this great combat almost unworthy to play the part which has been assigned to me.–(No.) I have been called to occupy a very high and responsible office in the State at an age far younger than that when almost anyone is asked to encounter such responsibilities and lift such burdens. But if I have been honoured by the confidence of my colleagues and friends, and have been placed in a high position, it is very largely to you of Manchester that I owe my debt. You came forward to help me at a time when I had very few friends and very many enemies. At a time when I was detached from political parties and contemplated my withdrawal from public life for a time, this great constituency offered me a foothold and a vintage ground. And it is to you that my gratitude, whatever the issue now may be, will permanently be due.

But, as to this conflict, if we had only to depend on ourselves, I should have no doubt.–(Cheers.) But we depend, not on ourselves only; we depend also upon our cause. It is, I think, the cause of civilisation.–(Hear, hear.) You know, you who consult the history of the past, the successive stages by which Liberalism has rendered services and benefits to the mass of the English people. No one would pretend that a mere adherence to the knowledge of our ancestors, or of the last generation, would enable us to deal with the ever more and more perplexing problem of the present day.—(Hear, hear.) But as Mr. Hammerde has said, the new Liberal party—heir to the traditions of the old, whilst faithful to its own—with new energies and forces behind it, is advancing to grapple with new social problems; and it is a sign of the times that the Government, which is soon to meet in conclave, is one of the youngest and most vigorous (as far as the health and strength of its different members are concerned), of which we have any record in our history.—(Hear, hear.) The cause of Liberalism is well worthy of your support. Free Trade is only one branch of that great liberating process, the liberating of trade from those tariffs which hinder alike the enterprise of the manufacturer and the energies of the workman. Liberalism, which implies the freedom of conscience—an earnest attempt to win and sustain freedom in foreign lands—Liberalism, which implies a lively respect for the rights of nationalities; Liberalism, which seeks to set people free from intemperance and from the bad conditions of our congested cities—all these are the liberating functions of the party for which we stand.—(Cheers.)

And you know well—you have only to look around this place where you live, to see—how earnest is the need for effort and exertion in order that continued advance may be made. At the last election you were asked the same great questions as you will be asked on Friday—you will be asked to speak upon the most vital political issues that ever a Lancashire constituency was confronted with.—(Cheers.) Your decision greatly influenced your fellow-countrymen. If on this occasion you are able, as I firmly believe you are, to show a convinced attachment to the Liberal cause, and to our Free Trade system, all England will be strengthened and fortified by your decision.—(Cheers.)

And I would ask you whom you are going to trust to direct your public affairs.—(Cries of "You.") What creed of men, what school of political thought, is going to claim your allegiance? At the last election you dismissed from power a great party. No city in the country was more decisive in its repudiation of the late Government. As I said all the time, they were scourged out of Manchester and Salford with a cat-o'-nine-tails—(laughter),—and the whole of this great city was found upon the side of Liberalism and progress. Two years and a half are gone by and a powerful body of citizens, headed by a candidate of ability and character, invite you now to dismiss from power to the best of your ability a Government which succeeded that Conservative Administration. And suppose you were to do so, what are the alternatives, the further alternatives, that you would consider? You would have dismissed the Conservatives from power. You surely would not propose, after an interval so short to reverse your solemn verdict of January, 1908, and replace them in their old position, to continue, unimproved by any period of reflection, untaught by any prolonged measure of repentances or adversity, but precisely the same in all their ambitions and aspirations. Save this, the added venom and poison of a Protectionist campaign. You cannot propose, you Lancashire men, with all your interests and history, to replace them in power and to surrender yourselves to Protection.—(Cheers.)

If they are not to come back, if it is to be said that we are to go, what remains if it be not the wild abstractions of daring and fantastic thoughts and remains of those who belong to the revolutionary parties in this country? I say that between the Liberal party in the centre, marching along on the road of progress, and the Conservative party, pointing to the deserts of Protection from which we have emerged, on the one hand, and those who urge social revolution, on the other, there is only one sure and safe path, and that is that patient, struggling, forward of Liberal and Radical policy, which although it is subject to attacks from this and that, nevertheless has within itself the best hope for the future of the greatest number.

From these alternatives I believe the good sense of this great city will recoil. From these alternatives I believe I shall draw the support not only of those staunch adherents of the Liberal cause whose faith has been so abundantly shown in years of misfortune, but I trust I shall also gain the support of sober, moderate-minded men who stand a little aloof from the general drift and current of political contention, but who will welcome an opportunity of throwing in their help upon a movement of progress which, while it is earnest and constant, contains in it no element of violence or of impropriety. And so I urge upon you to give me your help and your aid. I think I shall have them.–(Cheers.) I think you will not desert me, your cause, or His Majesty's Government at this critical and important juncture.

You will send me back as your representative to speak with authority on the great questions of Free Trade, to do what I can for the cause of which Mr. Lloyd-George has spoken. We will show you a Government which, whether at home or abroad, is animated by the spirit of earnest reform–a Government which cares more for the health of the miner at the bottom of the mine than it does for the health of the mine-owner at the top. We will show you a Government which, while it respects the legitimate claims of private interests and asserts the right of private freedom and exertion, will at the same time register the trust of the nation in the interests of the nation as a whole.–(Cheers.)

ELECTORAL DEFEAT AND THE LIBERAL CAUSE

April 24, 1908

Reform Club, Manchester

Churchill was defeated by Joynson-Hicks by 429 votes. His disappointment was quite apparent; however, he accepted the offer of the Dundee Liberal Association to contest the by-election.

Dundee was a primarily working-class constituency, and at one point Churchill seemed to be threatened by the appearance of a Labour candidate. Churchill's speeches were, accordingly, considerably more radical in tone and content than they had been in Manchester.

It would be useless to deny the fact that we have had a heavy blow. It is a heavy blow; its consequences will be grave and serious. It is a heavy blow to all who care about the Liberal cause.–(Hear, hear.) It is a heavy blow to all whose interests or whose principles are interwoven with the maintenance of Free Trade.–(Hear, hear.) We have discussed these issues so much during the last ten days that I do not need to labour them now. I prefer rather to dwell upon those circumstances which, I think, we should not overlook in considering the results of this election, and which are of a more encouraging nature.

First, it has been a fierce election, a fierce, hard-fought election from beginning to end. And I am here to say that there has never been a contest conducted in England with more decorum, with more propriety, and with more genuine good humour than this hard fight.–(Hear, hear.) I think the result of the election is disastrous to the interests of Lancashire; I think the conduct of the election was honourable to the people of Manchester. I think it shows, at any rate, that we know how to fight our great political battles. I have now fought four elections in Lancashire, and I say that I have not seen an election which has been conducted with so much seriousness and at the same time with so much good-will as this election.

It is far from my intention to deal with controversial matters to-night. Yet one exception I must note in this general survey. There has been one exception, one blemish, upon the conduct of this election. I allude to the influence of the Harmsworth press.–(Hear, hear.) That throughout has been a low and blatant influence. I do not think it fair or right that Lancashire should be saddled with any share of responsibility for, or sympathy with, that influence.

But when I turn from these ephemeral topics of the contest now over, I think it is only right to say that after the great issues of principle have been decided, so far as persons are concerned, the central division of Manchester will have a worthy representative. I have known my friend Mr. Joynson-Hicks for a long time, and I think he is very competent to represent your views in Parliament with dignity and with credit.–("No," and "Hear, hear.") I am certain he has fought this fight very fairly and decently so far as I am concerned. Political attacks no doubt he has made; political attacks politicians *will* make; and after the many defeats he has had in the past, I cannot find it in my heart to say that, apart from the great issue in which he is engaged, I grudge him from a personal point of view the triumph–and it is a triumph–that he has gained.

Now I proceed to look at the larger questions which always lie behind and beyond the issues of a fight. Men may come, men may go, causes go on for ever. The Liberal cause doesn't depend upon the individuals who are selected to represent it. They may fail. It doesn't depend upon the fortunes of any single by-election, but upon certain deep principles and impulses which are found in the heart of man, which have in themselves so strong a regenerative power that year after year new harvests are reaped to replace the deficiencies time and accident create. You will find that there is a recuperative force in Liberal principles–that the great truths of economics will not be altered by any vote, however capricious. They will continue, and men will have to conform to them, however much they may wish to diverge, however loudly they may cheer when these principles are contradicted. The cause goes on. When I look round this crowded room, and think of the good friends who have helped me in this fight–no man ever had better friends–when I think of the efforts they have made, knowing as I do the forces there are on our side, I cannot but exhort you to be of good courage, and not allow such a blow as this–heavy, bitter, crushing though it is–to depress you, or alter your stern resolution to make your principles triumph. I am satisfied we have done our best. I am satisfied that nothing has been neglected to achieve success, and, that being so, I think we may feel good and clear consciences to-night, even in this hour of despondency. I, at all events, have a clear conscience.–(Cheers.) I have done my best to uphold your cause. When I leave this city, I leave it with a heart devoid of hate. Remember that the future will be influenced by your exertions. You have in Manchester a great school of political thought; you have a vast number of persons earnest and determined to support of those principles. You will not let an accident like this weaken your efforts.–(No.) Let it rather spur you, nerve you till your determination is such that you yourselves will enjoy again the triumph of two short years ago, and then our opponents, to-day so exultant, will once more feel the overwhelming force and power of great Liberal and democratic principles. Win or lose, sink or swim, in good days or bad days, have faith in the cause.–(Cheers.) Remember the fine verses which Carlyle has rendered:–

Heard are the voices,
Heard are the sages,
The world and the ages,
Choose, and your choice is
Brief, and yet endless.
Here eyes do regard you
In Eternity's stillness;
Here is all fulness,
Ye brave, to reward you.
Work, and despair not.

THE DUNDEE ELECTION

April 30, 1908

Message to Dundee

The Manchester Reform Club is scarcely 300 yards from the Town Hall, yet as I entered it immediately after the declaration of last Friday's poll I was handed a telegram from Dundee. This spontaneous act of kindness and succour will ever be gratefully remembered by me, and, without the slightest disparagement of other proposals by which I have been honoured, I accepted the unanimous invitation of your Executive to contest the city of Dundee at the impending by-election for the Liberal and Free Trade cause. I do not mean in this letter to enter upon a catalogue of measures and issues. The policy of His Majesty's Government is plain and published. My own personal views upon the great controverted questions of the day have been set forth abundantly during the strenuous election which has just been decided. I shall come among you to justify them, and I only claim the fullest opportunity. Upon the maintenance of our Free Trade system, upon the temperance cause and its conflict with the organised forces of the liquor trade, upon the hope of a concordat in education which shall give in England that freedom of conscience and secular efficiency you in Scotland have so long enjoyed, upon land reform in town and country, upon South Africa, upon Ireland, I avow myself entirely unrepentant.

You will be asked to endorse the appeal of the coalminers for a little larger share of life and sunlight, and thereby to take another practical step in the long movement which seeks to make all processes of economic production conform to the laws of health and science.

You will be urged to fortify the Government against the arbitrary and irresponsible partisanship of the House of Lords, to approve an orthodox and thrifty administration of the public finances, and to bang, bar, and bolt the door against protective and preferential taxes upon bread and meat, no matter under what pretext they may be imposed.

It would be foolish for us not to recognise that British democracy is now confronted by a vigorous Tory reaction. The social battle swings to and fro in uncertain decision. The fate of important legislation conceived in the highest interests of the labouring classes of Britain hangs in the balance. An electoral blow which should sweep the Liberals from power would fall with aggravated force upon labour representation in all its degrees. Let us be united. By inviting me to be your candidate in the place which ill-health has caused our respected friend Mr. Edmund Robertson to relinquish, you have chosen, as you are well aware, to fight in a situation of exceptional dispute.

In order to sustain the cause of progress the Liberals of Dundee have set aside all personal considerations. Citizens whom a life-long knowledge of your industries and particular interests had equipped and whose position in public esteem had entitled them to represent you have sacrificed, unasked and unhesitatingly, their honourable aspirations. It has been your choice to play a direct part in national affairs rather than to seek the gratification of local needs, and to strike a blow in the cause of the common good rather than to gain a special advantage for Dundee.

Believe me, I am deeply sensible of this. If I were to press my personal claims upon you I should feel indeed that my case was weak, but I, too, have come gradually and with widening knowledge to serve great causes, and, upborne by them, I feel an ample confidence and authority. The levers of social progression are still in the grasp of the Liberal party. We have but to set them forward to govern the destinies of Britain and guide the onward march of the peoples. Shall we be given the strength? That is the question I come to ask Dundee.

LIBERALISM AND SOCIALISM

May 4, 1908

Kinnaird Hall, Dundee

This speech deserves particular attention for it was made during an important period of Churchill's career and reflects his transition from concentration on foreign affairs to social problems.

[Extract] . . . It is not the enemy in front that I fear, but the division which too often makes itself manifest in progressive ranks–it is that division, that dispersion of forces, that internecine struggle in the moments of great emergency, in the moments when the issue hangs in the balance–it is that division which, I fear, may weaken our efforts and may perhaps deprive us of success otherwise within our grasp.

There are cross-currents in this election. You cannot be unconscious of that. They flow this way and that way, and they disturb the clear issue which we should like to establish between the general bodies of those whose desire it is to move forward on the lines of modern civilisation and those who wish to revert to the old and barbarous prejudices and contentions of the past–to their fiscal systems and to their methods of government and administration, and to their Jingo foreign policies across the seas, from which we hoped we had shaken ourselves clear. (Cheers.)

I want to-night to speak about three cross-currents, and let me first say a word about Socialism. There are a great many Socialists whose opinions and whose views I have the greatest respect for–(hear, hear)–men some of whom I know well, and whose friendship I have the honour to enjoy. A good many of those gentlemen who have these delightful, rosy views of a great and brilliant future to the world are so remote from hard facts of daily life and of ordinary politics that I am not very sure that they will bring any useful or effective influence to bear upon the immediate course of events. I am dealing rather with those of violent and extreme views who call themselves Socialists in the next few observations I shall venture with your indulgence to address to you. To the revolutionary Socialist I do not appeal as the Liberal candidate for Dundee. I recognise that they are perfectly right in voting against me and voting against the Liberals, because Liberalism is not Socialism, and never will be. (Cheers.) There is a great gulf fixed. It is not only a gulf of method, it is a gulf of principle. There are many steps we have to take which our Socialist opponents or friends, whichever they like to call themselves, will have to take with us; but there are immense differences of principle and of political philosophy between the views we put forward and the views they put forward.

Liberalism has its own history and its own tradition. Socialism has its own formulas and its own aims. Socialism seeks to pull down wealth; Liberalism seeks to raise up poverty. (Loud cheers.) Socialism would destroy private interests; Liberalism would preserve private interests in the only way in which they can be safely and justly preserved, namely, by reconciling them with public right. (Cheers.) Socialism would kill enterprise; Liberalism would rescue enterprise from the trammels of privilege and preference. (Cheers.) Socialism assails the pre-eminence of the individual; Liberalism seeks, and shall seek more in the future, to build up a minimum standard for the mass. (Cheers.) Socialism exalts the rule; Liberalism exalts the man. Socialism attacks capital; Liberalism attacks monopoly. (Cheers.) These are the great distinctions which I draw, and which, I think, you will think I am right in drawing at this election between our philosophies and our ideals. Don't think that Liberalism is a faith that is played out; that it is a philosophy to which there is no expanding future. As long as the world rolls round Liberalism will have its part to play—a grand, beneficent, and ameliorating part to play—in relation to men and States. (Cheers.)

Ah, gentlemen, I don't want to embark on bitter or harsh controversy, but I think the exalted ideal of the Socialists—a universal brotherhood, owning all things in common—is not always supported by the evidence of their practice. (Laughter.) They put before us a creed of universal self-sacrifice. They preach it in the language of spite and envy, of hatred, and all uncharitableness. (Cheers.) They tell us that we should dwell together in unity and comradeship. They are themselves split into twenty obscure factions, who hate and abuse each other more than they hate and abuse us. (Hear, hear, and laughter.) They wish to reconstruct the world. They begin by leaving out human nature. (Laughter.) Consider how barren a philosophy is the creed of absolute Collectivism. Equality of reward, irrespective of service rendered! It is expressed in other ways. You know the phrase—"From each according to his ability, to each according to his need." (Laughter.) How nice that sounds. Let me put it another way—"You shall work according to your fancy; you shall be paid according to your appetite." (Cheers.) Although I have tried my very best to understand these propositions, I have never been able to imagine the mechanical heart in the Socialist world which is to replace the ordinary human heart the palpitates in our breasts. What motive is to induce the men, not for a day, or an hour, or a year, but for all their lives, to make a supreme sacrifice of their individuality? What motive is to induce the Scotsmen who spread all over the world and make their way by various paths to eminence and power in every land and climate to make the great and supreme sacrifice of their individuality? I have heard of loyalty to a Sovereign. We have heard of love of country. Ah, but it is to be a great cosmopolitan, republic. We have heard of love of family and wives and children. These are the mere weaknesses of the bad era in which we live. We have heard of faith in a world beyond this when all its transitory pleasures and perils shall have passed away, a hope that carries serene consolation to the heart of men. Ah, but they deny its existence. (Laughter.) And what then are we to make this sacrifice for? It is for the sake of society.

And what is society? I will tell you what society is. Translated into concrete terms, Socialistic "society" is a set of disagreeable individuals who obtained a majority for their caucus at some recent election, and whose officials in consequence would look on humanity through innumerable grills and pigeon-holes and across innumerable counters, and say to them, "Tickets, please." (Laughter.) Truly this grey old world has never seen so grim a joke. (Applause.) Now, ladies and gentlemen, no man can be either a collectivist or an individualist. He must be both; everybody must be both a collectivist and an individualist. For certain of our affairs we must have our arrangements in common. Others we must have sacredly individual and to ourselves. (Cheers.) We have many good things in common. You have the police, the army, the navy, and officials–why, a President of the Board of Trade you have in common. (Applause.) But we don't eat in common; we eat individually. (Laughter.) And we don't ask the ladies to marry us in common. (Laughter.) And you will find the truth lies in these matters, as it always lies in difficult matters, midway between extreme formulae. It is in the nice adjustment of the respective ideas of collectivism and individualism that the problem of the world and the solution of that problem lie in the years to come. (Applause.) But I have no hesitation in saying that I am on the side of those who think that a greater collective element should be introduced into the State and municipalities. I should like to see the State undertaking new functions, particularly stepping forward into those spheres of activity which are governed by an element of monopoly. (Applause.) Your tramways and so on; your great public works, which are of a monopolistic and privileged character–there I see a wide field for State enterprise to embark upon. But when we are told to exalt and admire a philosophy which destroys individualism and seeks to replace it by collectivism, I say that is a monstrous and imbecile conception which can find no real foothold in the brains and hearts–and the hearts are as trustworthy as the brains–in the hearts of sensible people. (Loud cheers.)

I make my respectful acknowledgement to those here who are strong supporters of the Socialistic creed for the courtesy and patience with which they have listened to some observations to which they may not possibly agree. But I pass over the convinced Socialists, who, I admit, if they feel inclined, are justified in throwing away their votes on Saturday next–(laughter)–and I come to the Labour influence–the Labour element–the Trades Union element in our midst. There I have one or two words to say of a rather straight character, if you don't object, and which, I hope, will be taken in good part, and will be studied and examined seriously. (Applause.) Now, Labour in Britain is not Socialism. It is quite true that the Socialistic element has imposed a complexion on Labour, rather against its will, and has been largely supported in its actions by funds almost entirely supplied by Trade Unions. But Trade Unions are not Socialistic. They are the antithesis of Socialism. They are undoubtedly individualistic organisations, more in the character of the old Guilds, and much more in the direction of the culture of the individual, than they are in that of the smooth and bloodless uniformity of the masses.

Now, the Trade Unions are the most respectable and the most powerful element in the labour world. They are the bulwarks of our industrial system. They are the necessary guard-rails and bulwarks of a highly-competitive industrial system, and I have the right, as a member of His Majesty's Government, to speak with good confidence to Trade Unionists, because we have done more for Trade Unionists than any other Government that has ever been. (Cheers.) We have given them a charter.

By the judicial decisions of 10 years Trade Unions had been displaced from the position which they had been intended to occupy by a Liberal Administration in 1870, and under a Conservative Administration in 1874 and 1876. We have given them back that position in the Trades Disputes Bill, and I do not doubt we have been attacked and penalised in the country by those who disapprove of that measure in consequence of what we have done. And I say to the Trade Unionists, many of whom support the Government on all occasions–all of whom support the Government on 99 occasions out of 100, according to Mr. Shackleton, one of the most respected leaders of the Labour party–it is to the Trade Union element in Labour that I now venture to address myself. How stands the case of the Trades Unionists? Do they really believe–I put this question to them fairly–do they really believe that there is no difference whatever between a Tory and a Liberal Government? (A Voice–"None.") One gentlemen in this great gathering believes that there is no difference between a Tory and a Liberal Government. (Laughter.) Now, his cure is simple. He has only to listen to Sir George Baxter. (Laughter.) The Unionist candidate is quite capable of telling him of the difference between a Tory and a Liberal Government. Do Trade Unionists really desire the downfall of the existing Liberal Government? Would they really like to send a message of encouragement to the House of Lords–for that is what it comes to–to reject and mutilate Liberal and Radical legislation–and Labour legislation now before Parliament? Would they really send such a message of encouragement to the House of Lords as this–"House of Lords, you were right in your estimate of public opinion when you denied the extension of the Provision of Meals to School Children Bill to Scotland, when you threw out the Scottish Land Valuation Bill, when you threw out the Scottish Small Holders Bill–when you did all this you were right." Do you wish to send that message to the House of Lords? (Cries of "No.") But that will be the consequence of every vote subtracted from the Liberal majority. (Hear, hear.)

Well, it may be said, what we think about is not so much politics as Labour representation. Let me look at that? Is their claim really a just one at the present moment? ("No," and cheers.) After all, 9000 Radical and Liberal votes were cast for my esteemed and respected friend, your late member, Mr. Edmund Robertson. It is no longer a question of whether the Labourist element in this city should find effective representation in the House of Commons. They have representation in the very capable and well qualified member, Mr. Wilkie. (Cheers.) It is no longer a question whether they should have representation, but it is a question of whether they will deny to the great majority of the citizens of this important city of Dundee the right to return a representative of their own. (Great cheering.) When I am told that the campaign on which they are now embarked is destined to further the cause of Labour representation I should like to say–Ask Labour representatives who sit for double-barrelled constituencies in England or Scotland whether they really think the cause of Labour representation is advanced or retarded by so wanton and so reckless an escapade as what we are now witnessing. . . .

Liberalism will not be killed. (Cheers.) Liberalism is a quickening spirit–it is immortal. (Loud cheers.) It will live on through all the days, be they good days or be they evil days. No, I believe it will even burn stronger and brighter and more helpful in evil days than in good–(cheers)–just like your harbour lights which shine out across the waters, and which on a calm night gleam with soft refulgence, but through the storm flash a message of life to those who toil on the rough waters. (Cheers.) But it takes a great party to govern Great Britain–no clique, no faction, no cabal, can govern the 40 millions of people who live in this island. It takes a great concentration of forces to make a governing instrument. You have now got a Radical and democratic governing instrument, and if this Administration is broken that instrument will be shattered. It has been re-created painfully and laboriously after 20 years of courage and fidelity. It has come into being–it is there. It is now at work in legislation and in the influence which it can exercise throughout the whole world, making even our opponents talk our language–(laughter)–making all parties in the State think of social reform, and concern themselves with social and domestic affairs. I say, beware of how you injure that instrument–that great instrument as Mr. Gladstone called it–or weaken it at a moment when I think the masses of this country have great need of it. Why, what would happen if this present Government were to perish? On its tomb would be written–"Beware of social reform. (Laughter.) The working classes–the labour forces will not support a Government engaged in social reform. Every social reform will cost you votes. Beware of social reform. Learn to think Imperially." (Great laughter and tremendous cheering.)

An inconclusive verdict from Dundee, the home of Scottish Radicalism–(hear, hear)–an inconclusive or, still more, a disastrous verdict–(loud cries of "No" and "Never")–would carry a message of despair to every one in all parts of our island and in our sister island who is working for the essential influences and truths of Liberalism and progress. Down, down, down would fall the high hopes and elevated aspirations of the social reformer. The constructive plans now forming in so many nimble brains would melt into air–the light which had begun to gleam over the mountains would fade and die. The old regime would be reinstated, reinstalled; the Balfours and the Chamberlains, the Arnold-Forsters and the Lansdownes, and the Cecils will return. Like the Bourbons they will have learned nothing and will have forgotten nothing. (Loud cheers.) We shall step out of the period of adventurous hope in which we have lived for a brief spell–we shall step back to the period of obstinate and prejudiced negations. (Cheers.) For Ireland–ten years of resolute government; for England–dear food and cheaper gin–(great laughter)–and for Scotland–the superior wisdom of the House of Lords. (Laughter.) Is that the work you want to do, men of Dundee? (Loud cries of "No, no.") Is that the work to which you will put your precious franchises–your votes which have been won for you by so much exertion and struggle in the past? Is that the work you want to do on Saturday? No, I think not. I have a great confidence that the message you will send will be to encourage different work to that. (Hear, hear, and cheers.) I am confident that this city which has of its own free will plunged into the very centre of national politics will grasp the opportunity now presented–that its command will not be back but forward–(loud cheers)–that its counsel will be not timidity but courage, and that it will aim not at dividing but at rallying the progressive forces, not at dissipating but at combining the energies of reform. That will be the message which you will send in tones which no man can make–(cheers)–so that a keen, strong northern air shall sweep across our land to nerve and brace the hearts of men, to encourage the weak, to fortify the strong, to uplift the generous, to correct the proud. When an action has been joined for a long time, and the lines are locked in fierce conflict, and stragglers are coming in and the wounded drifting away, when the reserves begin to waver here and there, it is on such an occasion that Scottish regiments have so often won distinction; it is on these occasions that you have seen some valiant brigade march straight forward into the battle smoke, into the confusion of the battlefield, right into the heart of the fight. That is what you have to do at this moment. "Scotland to the front." . . .

COAL MINES (EIGHT HOURS) BILL

July 6, 1908

House of Commons

Churchill's majority at Dundee was 2,709 over the Unionist candidate. The Labour candidate polled third. Mr. Scrymgeour, a Prohibitionist candidate, secured only 655 votes.

The campaign for the Eight Hours Bill for miners had lasted for over twenty years before action was taken by the Liberal Government. The Bill had been introduced by the Home Secretary, Herbert Gladstone. Churchill's speech on winding up the Second Reading debate was his first major speech as President of the Board of Trade, and gave indications of his approach to his new office.

[Extract] . . . The hon. Member for Windsor, who moved the rejection of the Bill, described it as a reckless and foolhardy experiment. I see the miner emerging from the pit after eight hours' work with the assertion on his lips that he, at any rate, has paid his daily debt to his fellow men. Is the House of Commons now going to say to him, "You have no right to be here. You have only worked eight hours. Your appearance on the surface of the earth after eight hours' work is, to quote the hon. Member, a dangerous and foolhardy experiment"? Two hours more are demanded in the interest of economics. I do not wonder a bit at the miners' demand. I cannot find it in my heart to feel the slightest surprise, or indignation, or mental disturbance. My capacity for wonder is entirely absorbed, not by the miners' demand, but by the gentleman in the silk hat and white waistcoat who has the coolness, the calmness, the composure, and the complacency to deny that demand and dispute it with him. The hon. Member for Dulwich—himself a convinced protectionist, with a tariff with 1,200 articles in its schedules in his coat-tail pocket—has given us a delightful lecture on the importance of cheapness of production. Think of the poor consumer. Think of the importance to our industries of cheapness of production. We on this side are great admirers of cheapness of production. We have reminded the hon. Gentleman of it often; but why should cheapness of production always be achieved at the expense of the human factor? The hon. Gentleman spoke with anxiety of the possibility of a rise in miners' wages as a consequence of this Bill. Has he considered the relation of miners' wages to the selling prices of coal? At the pit's mouth the underground-workers' wages are only 60 per cent. of the selling price of coal. Free on board on the Tyne the proportion is only 38 per cent. As coal is sold here in the south of England the proportion is less than one-fifth of the whole price. Is it not clear that there are other factors at least which require consideration before you decide to deal with the human factors which first attracts the right hon. Gentleman? What about mining royalties? In all this talk about the importance of cheap coal to our industries and to the poor consumer we have had no mention of mining royalties. No. We never mention that. That is never heard. Yet, will the House believe it, it is estimated that mining royalties impose a toll of 6 per cent., calculated on the price of coal at the pit's mouth, or considerably more than half the total diminished production which could result from this humane Act of labour legislation. The hon. Gentleman went further, and said: "Why stop here? Why don't your arguments apply elsewhere?" The Member for Cambridgeshire mentioned people whose conditions of life he thought worse than some of those of coalminers. Why stop here, we are asked. Who ever said we would stop here? I welcome and support this measure, not only for its own sake, but much more because it is, I believe, simply the precursor of the general movement which is in progress all over the world, and in other industries besides this, towards a reconciling of the conditions of labour with the well-ascertained laws of science and health. When we are told that because we support this measure we shall be inflicting an injury or injustice on other classes of the population, I say there is a great solidarity among all classes. I believe that when they consider this matter they will see that all legitimate interests are in harmony, that no one class can obtain permanent advantage by undue strain on another, and that in the end their turn will come for shorter hours, and will come the sooner because they have aided others to obtain that which they desire themselves. When the House is asked to contemplate gloomy pictures let them recur to the example of Parliaments gone by. When the Ten Hours Bill was introduced in 1847, a Bill which affected the hours of adult males inferentially, the same lugubrious prophecies were indulged in from both sides of the House. Distinguished economists came forward to prove that the whole profit of the textile industry was reaped after the eleventh hour. Famous statesmen on both sides spoke strongly against the measure. That Parliament, in 1847, was in the same sort of position as we are to-day in this respect, but how differently circumstanced in other respects. That Parliament did not enjoy the wide and accurate statistical information in every branch of labour which enables us to-day to move forward with discretion and prudence. They were not able to look to the general evidences of commercial security and expansion on which modern politicians can rely. They could not show as we can show, overwhelming examples of owlish prophecies directly disproved; they could not point as we can point to scores of cases where not only increased efficiency, but a positive increase in output has followed the reduction of the hours of labour. The principle was new, the future was vague. But Parliament in those days did not quail. They trusted the broad generous instincts of common sense; they drew a good, bold line; and we to-day enjoy in a more gentle, more humane, more skilful, more sober, and more civilised population the blessings which have followed their acts. Now it is our turn. Let us vote for the Second Reading of this Bill, and in so doing establish a claim for respect from Parliaments to come such as we owe to Parliaments of the past.

GOVERNMENT POLICY AND THE FOREIGN SITUATION

August 14, 1908

Albert Hall, Swansea

This speech, with its dismissal of the German menace, drew a strong protest from the Foreign Secretary, Sir Edward Guy. It was delivered at a time when Churchill and Lloyd George were attacking the naval estimates.

[Extract] I can assure you I am very glad indeed to come here to-day. I am glad to come to Swansea. I am glad to come to the miners' demonstration. (Cheers.) This is the third time in the course of the summer months that I have had the honour to address a Welsh audience. I have come to the conclusion that I must be considered to be making myself a favourite down here. (Laughter and cheers.) I shall always be glad to come back to hear you sing (cheers)–to hear you sing those beautiful hymns and songs with so much harmony and so much unison, because one feels in listening to your singing the strength and the virtue of the Welsh race. (Cheers.) . . .

There is another matter connected with foreign affairs on which I am going to ask your patience while I say a word–our relations with Germany.–(Applause.) I have been astonished and grieved to read much of the wild language which has been used lately by people who ought to know better–(hear, hear),–by Lord Cromer in the House of Lords and by Mr. Blatchford in the "Clarion."–(Laughter and applause.) I think it is greatly to be deprecated that persons should try to spread the belief that war between Great Britain and Germany is inevitable. It is all nonsense.–(Hear, hear.) In the first place the alarmists have no ground whatever for their panic or fear. This country is an island, and no Government which is in power in this country, or which is likely to be in the future, will depart in any degree whatever from a naval policy which shall secure us effectively against attack from invasions. All parties are pledged to those reasonable measures of naval defence which shall secure our peaceful development in this island, which will free us from the curse of Continental militarism, and which will never be a member to any other great Power in the world.–(Hear, hear.) I say in the second place there is no collision of primary interests, big or important interests, between Great Britain and Germany in any quarter of the globe. Why, they are amongst our very best customers–(hear, hear),–and if anything happened to them I don't know what we should do in this country for markets. And while there is no danger of collision of material interests there is no result which could be expected from any struggle between the two countries except a disaster of a most appalling and idiotic character.–(Applause.) People say, "Oh, it would be worth our while to fight for the sake of the trade." Gentlemen, it is not worth fighting for the sake of trade. One month of fighting would destroy more wealth than successful trading of five years could produce, even if everybody worked twelve hours a day.–(Loud cheers.) We are told that there are colonies which could be seized. Why, gentlemen, nothing will alter the destiny of great communities like Canada, Australia, South Africa, and India. They will pursue their own paths and destiny, and their destiny will not be altered, in my opinion, as a result of any struggle between European Powers. What then remains for a prize to be fought for between the two countries? In fact nothing, except perhaps a few tropical plantations and small coaling stations scattered about the world. Look at it from an independent view, or from any view you like, I say you will come to this conclusion–there is no real reason for any quarrel between England and Germany.–(Hear, hear.) There is no cause to create differences between them, although there might be snappings and snarlings in the newspaper and in the London clubs.–(Laughter and applause.) No; these two great peoples have nothing to fight about, no prize to fight for, and no place to fight in.–(Loud laughter and applause.)

And what does all this snapping and snarling amount to after all? How many people do you suppose there are in Germany who really want to make a marauding attack on this country? I do not suppose that in the whole of that great country, with its 50,000,000 or 60,000,000 of population, there would be found more than 10,000 who would seriously contemplate such a hellish, and wicked crime.–(Hear, hear.) And how many do you think there are in this country? I don't believe there are even that number–that is if we exclude the inmates of Bedlam and the writers in the "National Review."–(Loud laughter and applause.) But we are told that these mischief-makers, these snappers and snarlers, may be few, yet they are very influential.–(Oh.) I am not so sure of that, for they are not more influential than the people on the side of peace. Of one thing I am certain–that the King is making for peace.–(Hear, hear.) The King is working nobly, it is clear, for peace, and doing everything against the fears and troubles and trials of war. I think it is clear now that there are laurels to be gained by European sovereigns by working for peace which are much more glorious, which win more applause and from a far wider circle, which enable them to write a much fitter page in the history of their own times than were ever gained by barbarous and purposeless battles. But even if the 15,000 persons who, we will say, in Germany and England desire to make war on one another–(a voice: "Not one would fight," laughter, and "Hear, hear")–I quite agree; they are not the people to fight as soldiers and sailors–(cheers);–those others like to stay at home and read about it–(laughter and applause),–even if these persons were as influential as one would think from all the noise they make and the clatter they keep up, what about the rest of us? What about the hundred millions of people who dwell in these islands and Germany? Are we all such sheep? Is democracy in the twentieth century so powerless to effect no will? Are we all become such puppets and marionettes to be wire-pulled against our interests into such hideous convulsions?

I have a high and prevailing faith in the essential goodness of great peoples. I believe the working classes all over the world are recognising that they have common interests and not divergent interests. I believe that what is called the international solidarity of labour has an immense boon to confer on all people. I have come here this afternoon to ask you to join with me in saying that far and wide throughout the masses of the British democracy there is no feeling of ill-will whatever towards

Germany.–(Hear, hear.) I say we honour that strong, patient, industrious German people, who have been for so many centuries divided, a prey to European intrigue, and who now in the fulness of time at last, after many tribulations, have, by their virtues and by their fame, won themselves a foremost place in the van of civilisation.–(Cheers.) I say we don't envy them their good fortune, their power, and prosperity. We are not jealous of them. We rejoice in everything which brings them good. We wish them well from the bottom of our hearts, and we believe most firmly that the victories they will win for science, for learning, against barbarism will be victories in which we shall share, and which if continued will also benefit all the children of men.–(Cheers.) . . .

UNEMPLOYMENT

October 9, 1908

Kinnaird Hall, Dundee

On August 11 Churchill became engaged to Miss Clementine Hozier at Blenheim. The marriage took place at St. Margaret's Church, Westminster, on September 12, and the best man was Lord Hugh Cecil. It would be impossible to improve upon the words written by the Churchills' son, Randolph: "This marriage, which was to survive until Churchill's death at the age of ninety in 1965, proved the sheet anchor of his career. The young couple were to move into an age of broken marriages and of divorce followed by remarriage, often several times over. Throughout the convulsions of political life and the waging of the two greatest wars in history, their love remained constant and abiding. As Churchill often remarked in other contexts: 'Here firm, though all be drifting.' " (Randolph S. Churchill, Winston S. Churchill, *II, 22.)*

[Extract] . . . Let it be remembered that aged poverty is not the only evil with which, so far as our means allow, we have to grapple. What is the problem of the hour? It can be comprised in one word, unemployment. (Hear, hear.) After two years of unexampled trade expansion, we have entered upon a period of decline. We are not alone in this. (Hear, hear.) A reaction from overtrading is general all over the world. Both Germany and the United States are suffering from a similar commercial contraction, and in both countries, in spite of their high and elaborate protective tariffs, a trade set-back has been accompanied by severe industrial dislocation and unemployment. In the United States of America, particularly, I am informed that unemployment has recently been more general than in this country. Indeed, the financial collapse in the United States last autumn has been the most clearly marked of all the causes to which the present trade depression may be assigned. It is not yet possible to say that the end of that period of depression is in sight; but there are some signficiant indications which I think justify the hope that it will be less severe and less prolonged than has been known in other trade cycles, or than some people were at first inclined to believe. But the problem of unemployment is not confined to periods of trade depression, and will not be dissolved by trade revival; and it is to that problem in its larger and more permanent aspects that I desire to draw your attention for a short time to-night. There is no evidence that the population of Great Britain has increased beyond the means of subsistence. On the contrary our wealth is increasing faster than our numbers. Production is active; industry grows, and grows with astonishing vigour and rapidity. Enterprise in this country requires no artificial stimulant; if it errs at all, it is from time to time upon the side of overtrading and of overproduction. There is no ground for believing that this country is not capable of supporting an increasing population in a condition of expanding prosperity. It must, however, be remembered that the British people are more than any other people in the world a manufacturing people. It is certain that our population could never have attained its present vast numbers, nor our country have achieved its position in the world, without an altogether unusual reliance upon manufacture as opposed to simple agriculture. The ordinary changes and transitions inseparable from the active life and growth of modern industry, therefore, operate here with greater relative intensity than in other countries. An industrial disturbance is more serious in Great Britain than in other countries, for it affects a far larger proportion of the people, and in their distresses the urban democracy are not sustained by the same solid backing of country-folk and peasant cultivators that we see in other lands. (Hear, hear.) It has, therefore, become a paramount necessity for us to make scientific provision against the fluctuations and set-backs which are inevitable in world commerce and in national industry; and we have lately seen how the back-wash of an American monetary disturbance or a crisis in the Near East or in the Far East, or some other cause influencing world trade and as independent of our control as are the phases of the moon, may easily have the effect of letting loose upon thousands of humble families and households all the horrors of a state of siege or a warlike blockade. Then there are strikes and trade disputes of all kinds which affect vast numbers of people altogether unconcerned in the quarrel. (Hear, hear.)

Now, I am not going to-night to proclaim the principle of the "right to work." There is not much use in proclaiming a right apart from its enforcement; and when it is enforced there is no need to proclaim it. But what I am here to assert, and to assert most emphatically, is the responsibility of Government towards honest and law-abiding citizens (cheers); and I am surprised that that responsibility should ever be challenged or denied. When there is a famine in India, when owing to some unusual course of nature the sky refused its rain and the earth its fruits, relief works are provided in the provinces affected, trains of provisions are poured in from all parts of that great Empire, aid and assistance is given to the population involved, not merely to enable them to survive the period of famine, but to resume their occupations at its close. (Hear, hear.) Now, an industrial disturbance in the manufacturing districts and the great cities of this country presents itself to the ordinary artisan in exactly the same way as the failure of crops in a large province in India presents itself to the Hindu cultivator. (Hear, hear.) The means by which he lives are suddenly removed, and ruin in a form more or less swift and terrible stares him instantly in the face. That is a contingency which seems to fall within the most primary and fundamental obligation of any organization of Government. I do not know whether in all countries or in all ages that responsibility could be maintained, but I do say that here and now in this wealthy country and in this scientific age it does in my opinion exist, is not discharged, ought to be discharged, and will have to be discharged. (Cheers.) The social machinery at the basis of our industrial life is deficient, ill-organized, and incomplete. (Hear, hear.) While large numbers of persons enjoy great wealth, while the mass of the artisan classes are abreast of and in advance of their fellows in other lands, there is a minority, considerable in numbers, whose condition is a disgrace to a scientific and professedly Christian civilization, and constitutes a grave and increasing peril to the State. Yes, in this famous land of ours, so often envied by foreigners, where the grace and ease of life have been carried to such perfection, where there is so little class hatred and jealousy, where there is such a wide store of political experience and knowledge, where there are such enormous moral forces available, so much wisdom, so much virtue, so much power, we have not yet succeeded in providing that necessary apparatus of insurance and security, without which our industrial system is not merely incomplete, but actually inhuman. (Cheers.) . . .

LIBERALISM AND THE LORDS

January 13, 1909

Liberal Club Dinner, Birmingham

In this belligerent speech Churchill in effect dared the Lords to reject the forthcoming Budget.

[Extract] I am very glad to come here to-night to wish good luck in the new year to the Liberals of Birmingham. Good luck is founded on good pluck, and that is what I think you will not fail in. Steadfast is a faithful friend; but something more is needed to win battles. You will want a touch of moral exaltation–or dare-devilry–(laughter)–which you please–one or the other–both for preference, if you are to batter down the frowning fortifications that have so long confronted you. Birmingham Liberals have for twenty years been over-weighted by the influence of a remarkable man, and by the peculiar turn of events. This great city, which used to be the home of militant Radicalism, which in former days supplied with driving power the cause of national representation against hereditary privilege, has been captured by the foe. The banner of the House of Lords has been flung out over the sons and grandsons of the men who shook all England into the Great Reform Bill; and while old injustice has but been replaced by new, while the miseries and the privation of the poor continue in your streets, while the differences between class and class have been even aggravated in the passage of years, Birmingham is held by the enemy and bound to retrogression in its crudest form. . . .

The circumstances of the period are peculiar. The powers of the House of Lords to impede, and by impeding to discredit, the House of Commons, are strangely bestowed, strangely limited, and still more strangely exercised. There are little things which they can maul; there are big things they cannot touch; there are bills which they pass although they believe them to be wrong; there are bills which they reject although they know them to be right. The House of Lords can prevent the trams running over Westminster Bridge; but it cannot prevent a declaration of war. It can reject a bill prohibiting foreign workmen being brought in to break a British strike; it cannot amend a bill to give old-age pensions to 600,000 people. It can thwart a Government in the minute details of its legislation; it cannot touch the whole vast business of finance. (Hear, hear.) It can prevent the abolition of the plural voter; but it could not prevent the abolition of the police. (Laughter.) It can refuse a constitution to Ireland; but not, luckily, to Africa. (Laughter and cheers.) Lord Lansdowne, in his leadership of the House of Lords during the present Parliament, has put forward claims on its behalf far more important and crude than ever were made by the late Lord Salisbury. No Tory leader in modern times has ever taken so high a view of its rights, and at the same time no one has shown a more modest conception of its duties. (Laughter.) In destroying the Education Bill of 1906 the House of Lords asserted its right to resist the opinion of a majority of 309 members of the House of Commons fresh from election upon a subject which had been one of the most prominent issues of the election. In rejecting the Licensing Bill of 1908 they have paraded their utter unconcern for the moral welfare–(hear, hear)–of the mass of their fellow-countrymen. There is one feature in the guidance of the House of Lords by Lord Lansdowne which should specially be noticed, and that is the air of solemn humbug with which this ex-Whig–(laughter)–is always at pains to invest its proceedings. The Nonconformist child is forced into the Church school in single-school areas in the name of parents' rights and religious equality. The Licensing Bill is rejected in the highest interests of temperance. (Laughter.) Professing to be a bulwark of the commercial classes against Radical and Socialistic legislation, the House of Lords passes an Old-age Pension Bill, which it asserts will be fatal alike to public finance and public thrift; a Miners' Eight Hours Bill, which it is convinced will cripple British industry; and a Trades Disputes Bill, which it loudly declared tyrannous and immoral. Posing as a chamber of review, remote from popular passion, far from the swaying influences of the electorate, it nevertheless exhibits a taste for cheap electioneering, a subserviency to caucus direction and a party spirit upon a level with many of the least reputed elective Chambers in the world; and beneath the imposing mask of an assembly of notables backed by the prescription and traditions of centuries we discern the leer of the artful dodger who has got the straight tip from the party agent. (Laughter and cheers.) It is not possible for reasonable men to defend such a system or such an institution. Counter-checks upon a democratic Assembly there may be, perhaps there should be. But those counter-checks should be in the nature of delay and not in the nature of arrest; they should operate evenly and equally against both political parties and not against only one of them; and, above all, they should be counter-checks conceived and employed in the national interest and not in a partisan interest. These abuses and absurdities have now reached a point when it is certain that reform, effective and far-reaching, must be the necessary issue at a general election–(cheers); and whatever may be the result of that election, be sure of this, that no Liberal Government will at any future time assume office without securing guarantees that that reform shall be carried out. (Cheers.) . . .

But, if we have been powerful in the past, shall we then be powerless in the future? Let the year that has now opened make its answer to that. We shall see before many months are passed whether His Majesty's Government and the House of Commons by which it is supported, do not still possess effective means–(cheers)–to secure substantial results, not only upon those important political issues in which we have been for the time being thwarted, but also in that still wider and, in my opinion, more important field of social organisation into which under the leadership of the Prime Minister–(cheers),–we shall now proceed to advance. I do not, of course, ignore the fact that the House of Lords has the power, though not, I think, the constitutional right, to bring the Government of the country to a standstill by rejecting the provision which the Commons make for the financial service of the year. That is a matter which does not rest with us; it rests with them. If they want a speedy dissolution, they know where to find one. (Cheers.) If they really believe, as they so loudly proclaim, that the country will hail them as its saviours, they can put it to the proof. If they are ambitious to play for stakes as high as any Second Chamber has ever risked, we shall not be wanting. And, for my part, I should be quite content to see the battle joined as speedily as possible–(cheers),–upon the plain, simple issue of aristocratic rule against representative government–(cheers),–between the reversion to Protection and the maintenance of Free Trade–(cheers),–between a tax on bread and a tax on–well, wait a bit. (Cheers and laughter.) And if they do not choose, or do not dare to use the powers they most injuriously possess, if fear, I say, or tactics, or prudence, or some lingering sense of constitutional decency restrains them, then for heaven's sake, let us hear no more of these taunts, that we, the Liberal party, are afraid to go to the country, that we do not possess its confidence, and that we are impotent to give effect to the essential purposes of our policy. (Cheers.)

Subject to such a constitutional outrage as I have indicated, His Majesty's Government will claim their right and use their power to present the Liberal case as a whole to the judgment of the whole body of electors. That case is already largely developed. How utterly have all those predictions been falsified that a Liberal Government would be incapable of the successful conduct of Imperial affairs! Whether you look at our position in Europe or at the difficult conduct of Indian administration, or the relations which have been preserved, and in some cases restored, with our self-governing colonies, the policy of the Government has been attended with so much success that it has not only commanded the approval of impartial persons, but has silenced political criticism itself. It was in South Africa that we were most of all opposed and most of all distrusted, and by a singular inversion it is in South Africa that the most brilliant and memorable results have been achieved. Indeed, I think that the gift of the Transvaal and Orange River Constitutions and the great settlement resulting therefrom will be by itself as a single event sufficient to vindicate in the eyes of future generations the administration of Sir Henry Campbell-Bannerman–(cheers),–and to dignify his memory in Parliaments and periods which we shall not see. But our work abroad is not yet completed, has not yet come to its full fruition. If we should continue, as I expect we shall, to direct public affairs for the full five years which are the normal and the healthy period of British Administrations–(cheers),–we may look for a further advance and improvement in all the great external spheres of Imperial policy. We may look in India for a greater sense of confidence and solidarity between the people and the Government. We shall salute the sunrise of South Africa united under the British Crown. (Cheers.) And in Europe I trust that Sir Edward Grey will have crowned his work at the Foreign Office by establishing a better and kindlier feeling between the British and the German peoples. (Cheers.) That will be the record of policy beyond the seas on which we shall appeal for judgment and for justice.

If it be said that, contrary to general expectation, our policy has prospered better abroad than at home, you have not far to look for the reason. Abroad we have enjoyed full responsibility, a free hand, and fair play–(hear, hear);–at home we have had a divided authority, a fettered hand, and the reverse of fair play. We have been hampered, and we have been harassed. We have done much; we could have done much more. Our policy at home is less complete and less matured than it is abroad. But it so happens that many of the most important steps which we should now take are of such a character that the House of Lords will either not be able or will not be anxious to obstruct them–and could not do so except by courting altogether novel dangers. The social field lies open. There is no great country where the organisation of industrial conditions more urgently demands attention. Wherever the reformer casts his eyes he is confronted with a mass of largely preventable and even curable suffering. The fortunate people in Britain are more happy than any other equally numerous class have been in the whole history of the world. I believe the left out millions are more miserable. Our vanguard enjoys all the delights of all the ages. Our rearguard straggles out into conditions which are crueller than barbarism. The unemployed artisan, the casual labourer, and the casual labourer's wife and children, the sweated worker, the infirm worker, the worker's widow, the underfed child, the untrained, undisciplined, and exploited boy labourer, it is upon these subjects that our minds should dwell in the early days of 1909. The Liberal party has always known the joy which comes from serving great causes. It must also cherish the joy which comes from making good arrangements. (Cheers.) We shall be all the stronger in the day of battle if we can show that we have neglected no practicable measure by which these evils can be diminished, and can prove by fact and not by words that, while we strive for civil and religious equality, we also labour to build up–so far as social machinery can avail–tolerable basic conditions for our fellow-countrymen. (Cheers.) There lies the march, and those who valiantly pursue it need never fear to lose their hold upon the heart of Britain. (Cheers.) . . .

THE NEXT ELECTION AND THE LORDS

January 29, 1909

Liberal Meeting, Victoria Hall, Nottingham

[Extract] We are met together at a time when great exertions and a high constancy are required from all who cherish and sustain the Liberal cause. Difficulties surround us, and dangers threaten from this side and from that. Exultant enemies are gathering; weak friends are nervous or disheartened. Voices are raised in counsels, both equally unwise, of impatience or of lassitude. From such a situation you may emerge triumphant, but to do that there will have to be, in leaders and in followers, shrewd, clear plans of action, true stout-hearted comradeship, and unwearying determination. (Cheers.) You know the position which has been created by the action of the House of Lords. Two great political parties divide all England between them in their conflicts. Each commands a powerful organisation; each is backed by numbers; each has its functions, its aspirations, and its sources of strength; and to and fro they swing in their struggles with varying fortunes from year to year, and from election to election; and from their struggles, strange as it may appear, over a long period of years, a steady stream of progress is born. Now, it is discovered that one of these parties possesses an unfair weapon, that one of these parties, after it is beaten at an election, after it is deprived of the support and confidence of the country, after it is destitute of a majority in the representative Assembly, when it sits in the shades of Opposition without responsibility, or representative authority, under the frown, so to speak, of the Constitution, nevertheless possesses a weapon with which it can harass, vex, impede, affront, humiliate, and finally destroy the most serious labours of the other. When it is realised that the party which possesses this prodigious and unfair advantage is, in the main, the party of the rich against the poor, of the classes and their dependents against the masses, of the lucky, the wealthy, the happy, and the strong against the left-out and the shut-out millions of the weak and poor, you will see how serious the constitutional situation has become. (Cheers.) . . .

In moving forward in this great struggle which is approaching, we are going to carry our social policy along with us. We are not going to fight alone upon the political and constitutional issue, nor alone upon the defence of Free Trade. We are going, fearless of the consequences, confident of our faith, to place before the nation a wide, comprehensive, interdependent scheme of social organisation; to place it before the people not merely in the speeches or placards of a party programme, but, by a massive series of legislative proposals and administrative acts. (Cheers.) If we are interrupted or impeded in our march, the nation will know how to deal with those who stand in the path of vital and necessary reforms. (Cheers.) And I am confident that in the day of battle the victory will be to the earnest and to the persevering, and then again will be heard the doleful wail of Tory rout and ruin, and the loud and resounding acclamations with which the triumphant armies of democracy will march once again into the central place of power. (Loud cheers.)

THE BUDGET AND SOCIAL REFORM

May 22, 1909

Free Trade Hall, Manchester

The conditions in the "sweated labour" industries–principally in the clothing trade–were scandalous. Under the Trade Boards Bill a Trade Board was established to fix minimum rates of pay and conditions. It was a major piece of legislation and together with the introduction of Labour Exchanges, assisted in improving Churchill's growing reputation as a social reformer. All matters, however, were dominated by the Budget and the approaching issue with the Lords.

Lloyd George's "People's Budget" of 1909 sought to raise additional income principally by increased taxation on property and income. Part of the increased expenditure was on the Navy, which Churchill and Lloyd George had vigorously opposed almost to the point of resignation in the Cabinet in 1908, but now accepted. The "land taxes" in particular aroused the fury of the Opposition, and paved the way for the rejection of the Finance Bill by the Lords in November after seventy Parliamentary days in the Commons and 554 divisions.

[Extract] Considering that you have all been ruined by the Budget–(laughter),–I think it very kind of you to receive me so well. When I remember all the injuries you have suffered–how South Africa has been lost–(laughter);–how the gold mines have been thrown away; how all the splendid army which Mr. Brodrick got together–(laughter)–has been reduced to a sham; and how, of course, we have got no navy of any kind whatever–(laughter),–not even a fishing smack, for all the 35 millions a year we give the Admiralty; and when I remember that in spite of all these evils the taxes are so oppressive and so cruel that any self-respecting Conservative will tell you he cannot afford either to live or die–(laughter),–when I remember all this, Mr. Chairman, I think it remarkable that you should be willing to give me such a hearty welcome back to Manchester. Yes, gentlemen, when I think of the colonies we have lost, of the Empire we have alienated, of the food we have left untaxed–(laughter),–and the foreigners we have left unmolested–(laughter),–and the ladies we have left outside–(laughter)–I confess I am astonished you are glad to see me here again.

It is commonly said that people are becoming hysterical, and that Britain is losing her old deep-seated sagacity for judging men and events. That is not my view. I have been taught that the dock always grows near the nettle. I am inclined to think that in every free community every evil carries with it its own corrective, and so I believe that sensationalism of all kinds is playing itself out and, "overdoing, is himself undone." (Cheers.) And the more our scaremongers cry havoc, and panic, and airships–(laughter),–and sea-serpents, and all the other things they see floating around–(laughter),–the greater is the composure and the greater is the contempt with which the mass of the nation receives these revelations and the more ready they are to devote their mind to the great and serious problems of national and social organisation which pray for solution and for action at the present time, and upon which His Majesty's Government have notable proposals to make. (Cheers.)

I have come to you this afternoon to speak about the political situation and the Budget–(cheers),–or rather I have come to speak to you about the Budget, because the Budget is the political situation; and I have come to ask you, as if it were at an election, whether you will support the policy of the Budget or not. (Cries of "Yes.") Let us look into it. What is the position in which we find ourselves? After reducing the taxes on coal, on tea, on sugar, and on the smaller class of incomes by nearly £7,000,000 a year, and after paying back £40,000,000 of debt in three years–(cheers),–we find that new circumstances and new needs made it necessary that we should ask fresh revenue for the service of the State. (Cheers.)

What are the reasons for this demand? There are three reasons–and only three. Old age pensions–(cheers),–the navy, and the decrease in the revenue derived from alcoholic liquor. (Cheers.) From those three causes we require 16 millions more money this year than we did last year. Now who has a right–this is my first question–to reproach us for that? Certainly the Conservative party have no right.

Take first the case of old-age pensions. I do not think their record is a very good one on that. They promised old-age pensions to win the general election of 1896. They were in power for ten years and they made no effort to redeem their pledge. (Hear, hear.) Again, Mr. Chamberlain, in 1903, promised old-age pensions as a part of his Tariff Reform proposal, but the Conservative party refused to agree to the inclusion of old-age pensions in that programme and forced that great man in the height of his power and his career to throw over old-age pensions from the Tariff Reform programme and to write a letter to the newspapers to say that he had done so.

We, the Liberal party, did not promise old-age pensions at that election of 1906. I do not think the subject was mentioned; it was scarcely mentioned by any of the candidates who are now your members. (Hear, hear.) Certainly it did not occupy at all a prominent position. We did not promise old-age pensions; we gave old-age pensions. (Loud cheers.) When the Old-age Pensions Bill was before the House of Commons what was the attitude of the Conservative party? Did they do anything to try to reduce or control the expenditure of that great departure? On the contrary. As my right honorable friend the Chancellor of the Exchequer–[Mr. David Lloyd George]–(long continued cheers)–has told the House of Commons, amendments to the Old-age Pensions Bill were moved or received the official support of the Whips of the Conservative party which would have raised the cost of that scheme to 14 millions a year. (Shame.) And the Liberal Government, which was making this great effort, which was doing the work, which was keeping its promise, was reproached and was derided for not accepting the proposals which these irresponsible philanthropists, these social reformers on the cheap, these limited liability politicians–(laughter)–were so ready to move. And Lord Halsbury, the late Lord Chancellor, one of the leaders of the Conservative party, a man with a powerful influence in their councils, said in a public speech that the old-age pensions as proposed by the Government were so paltry as to be almost mockery. . . .

I come to the navy. The Naval Estimates have risen by three millions this year. I regret it. (Hear, hear.) But I am prepared to justify it. (Hear, hear.) There will be a further increase next year. I regret it, but within proper limits necessary to secure national safety I shall be prepared to justify it. I hope you will believe–having known me for very nearly ten years in this neighbourhood here and at Oldham–that I am not one of those who admire politicians who think it worth while to win cheap cheers by advocating a braggart and sensational policy of expenditure upon armaments. (Hear, hear.) I have always been against that, as my father was before me. (Cheers.)

In my judgment a Liberal is a man who ought to stand as a restraining force against an extravagant policy. He is a man who ought to keep cool in the presence of Jingo clamour. He is a man who believes that confidence between nations begets confidence, and that the spirit of peace and good-will makes the safety it desires to see. And, above all, I think a Liberal is a man who should keep a sour look for scaremongers of every kind and of every size, however distinguished, however ridiculous–and sometimes the most distinguished are the most ridiculous,–a cold, chilling, acidulated, sour, verjuice flavoured look for all of them whether their panic comes from the sea or from the air or from the earth or from the waters under the earth. (Cheers and laughter.)

His Majesty's Government are resolved that the defensive measures of this country shall be prescribed by the policy of Ministers responsible to Parliament and by the calculation of the experts on whom those Ministers rely and shall not be prescribed by the folly and the clamour of party politicians or sensational journalists. (Cheers.) . . .

I have spoken to you of the causes which in the past have led up to this Budget. I have spoken to you of its present justification. What of the future? If I had to sum up the immediate future of democratic politics in a single word I should say "insurance." That is the future–insurance against dangers from abroad, insurance against dangers scarcely less grave and much more near and constant which threaten us here at home in our own island. I had the honour and opportunity a few days ago of explaining to the House of Commons the proposal for unemployment insurance. (Loud cheers.) That is a considerable matter. It stands by itself. It is a much simpler question than invalidity insurance; but it is a great matter by itself. (Hear, hear.) Indeed, I thought while I was explaining it to the House of Commons that I had not made such an important speech since I had the honour of explaining the details of the Transvaal Constitution. (Cheers.)

Well, what is the proposal? The proposal is that you should make a beginning. We have stood still too long. (Hear, hear.) The proposal is that we should begin forthwith–(hear, hear),–that we should take some of the greatest trades of the country in which unemployment is most serious, in which fluctuations are most severe, in which there are no short-time arrangements to mitigate the severity to the individual; and that a system of compulsory contributory insurance, with a large subvention from the State, should be introduced into those great industries.

But our proposals go further than that. The State assistance to unemployment insurance will not be limited to those trades in which it is compulsory. Side by side with the compulsory system we shall offer facilities to voluntary systems–we shall offer facilities to voluntary insurance schemes in other trades, managed by trade unions or other societies or groups of workmen. Moreover, we contemplate that the State insurance office should undertake, if desired, the insurance against unemployment of any individual workman in any trade outside of those for which compulsory powers are required, and should afford to these individuals an equivalent support to that which is given in the trades which are subject to the compulsory system.

Of course you will understand that the terms that can be offered under a voluntary or partial system are not so good as those which can be obtained in a universal system or a great trade. Where all stand together it is much better for each. (Hear, hear.) But still it is certain that individuals who take advantage of the insurance policy which will be introduced and I trust carried through Parliament next year will be able to secure terms which will match more favourably than any which are open to them by their unaided contributions at the present time, because their contributions will be reinforced by the contributions of the State. Further, if our beginning proves a success the attempt and the system will not stop there. It will be extended, and in proportion as experience and experiment justify its extension, in proportion as the people of this country desire its extension, it must eventually cover, in course of years, the whole of our great industrial community. (Cheers.) . . .

The decisive question is this–will the British working classes embrace the opportunities which will shortly be offered to them? They are a new departure; they involve an element of compulsion and of regulation which is unusual in our happy-go-lucky English life. The opportunity may never return. For my own part I confess to you, my friends in Manchester, that I would work for such a policy and would try to carry it through even if it were a little unpopular at first, and would be willing to put the forfeit of a period of exclusion from power in order to have carried such a policy through (loud cheers) because I know that there is no other way within the reach of this generation of men and women by which the stream of preventable misery can be cut off.

If I had my way I could write the word "insure" over the door of every cottage and upon the blotting-book of every public man, because I am convinced that by sacrifices which are inconceivably small, which are all within the reach of the very poorest man in regular work, families can be secured against catastrophes which otherwise would split them up forever. I think it is our duty to use the power and the resources of the State to arrest the ghastly waste not merely of human happiness but of national health and strength which follows when a working man's house which has taken him years to get together is broken up and scattered through a long spell of unemployment or when through the death, the illness, or the invalidity of the bread winner the frail boat in which the fortunes of the family are embarked founders, and the women and children are left to struggle helplessly in the dark waters of a friendless world. (Cheers.) I believe it is well within our power now, before this Parliament is over, to establish, vast and broad throughout the land, a mighty system of national insurance which will nourish in its bosom all worthy existing agencies and will embrace in its scope all sorts and conditions of men. (Cheers.)

I think it is not untrue to say that in these years we are passing through a decisive point in the history of our country. The wonderful century which followed the Battle of Waterloo and the downfall of Napoleon, which secured to this small island so long and so resplendent a period, has come to an end. We have arrived at a new time. Let us realise it. And with this new time strange methods, huge forces and combinations—a Titanic world—have spread all around us. The foundations of our power are changing. To stand still would be to fall; to fall would be to perish. We must go forward. (Cheers.) We will go forward. (Loud cheers.) We will go forward into a way of life more earnestly viewed, more scientifically organised, more consciously national than any we have known. Thus alone shall we be able to sustain and to renew through the generations which are to come the fame and the power of the British race. (Loud and long cheering.)

THE BUDGET

July 17, 1909

King's Theatre, Edinburgh

As the controversy over the Budget mounted, Churchill increasingly became one of the most articulate and vigorous defenders of the Lloyd George proposals.

[Extract] We are often assured by sagacious persons that the civilisation of modern States is largely based upon respect for the rights of private property. If that be true, it is also true to say that respect cannot be secured and ought not indeed to be expected unless property is associated in the minds of the great mass of the people with ideas of justice and of reason.—(Cheers.) It is therefore of first importance to the country, to any country, that there should be vigilant and persistent efforts to prevent abuses, to distribute the public burdens fairly among all classes, and to establish good laws governing the methods by which wealth may be acquired. The best way to make private property secure and respected is to bring the process by which it is gained into harmony with the general interest of the public. When and where property is associated with the idea of reward for services rendered, with the idea of reward for high gifts and special aptitudes displayed or for faithful labour done, then property will be honoured. When it is associated with processes which are beneficial or which at the worst are not actually injurious to the common wealth, then property will be unmolested. But when it is associated with ideas of wrong and of unfairness, with the processes of restriction and monopoly, and other forms of injury to the community, then I think that you will find that property will be assailed and will be endangered....

Some years ago in London there was a toll bar on a bridge across the Thames, and all the working people who lived on the south side of the river had to pay a daily toll of one penny for going and returning from their work. The spectacle of these poor people thus mulcted on so large a proportion of their earnings appealed to the public conscience. An agitation was set on foot, municipal authorities were roused, at the cost of the ratepayers the bridge was freed and the toll removed. All those people who used the bridge were saved sixpence a week. Within a very short period from that time the rents on the south side of the river were found to have advanced by about sixpence a week–(laughter and cheers),–or the amount of the toll which had been remitted. A friend of mine was telling me the other day that in the parish of Southwark about £350 a year, roughly speaking, was given away in doles of bread by charitable people in connection with one of the churches, and as a consequence of this the competition for small houses, but more particularly for single-roomed tenements, is so great that rents are considerably higher than in the neighbouring district. All goes back to the land, and the landowner, who in many cases, in most cases, is a worthy person, utterly unconscious of the character of the methods by which he is enriched, is enabled with resistless strength to absorb to himself a share of almost every public and every private benefit, however important or however pitiful those benefits may be.

I hope you will understand that when I speak of the land monopolist I am dealing more with the process than with the individual landowner. I have no wish to hold any class up to public disapprobation. I do not think that the man who makes money by unearned increment of the land is morally a worse man than anyone else who gathers his profit in this hard age under the law, and according to common usage. It is not the individual I attack; it is the system.–(Cheers.) It is not the man who is bad, it is the law which is bad. It is not the man who is blameworthy for doing what the law allows and what other men may do; it is the State which would be blameworthy were it not to endeavour to reform the law and correct the practice. We do not want to punish the landlord; we want to alter the law. We do not go back on the past as to the increment tax. Look at our actual proposal. We do not go back on the past. We accept as our basis the value of the land as it stands to-day. The tax on the increment of land begins by recognising and franking the past increment. We look only to the future, and for the future we say only this–that the community shall be the partner in any further increment above the present value after all the owner's improvements have been deducted. We say that the State and the municipality should jointly levy a toll upon the future unearned increment of the land. The toll of what? Of the whole? No. Of a half? No. Of a quarter? No. Of a fifth; that is the proposal of the Budget–(cheers),–and that is robbery–(laughter),–that is plunder, that is communism and spoliation, that is the social revolution at last–(laughter),–that is the overturn of civilised society; that is the end of the world foretold in the Apocalypse.–(Loud laughter.) Let us get on with the argument.–(Renewed laughter.) Such is the increment tax about which so much chatter and outcry is raised at the present time, and upon which I will say that no more fair, considerate, or salutary proposal for taxation has ever been made in the House of Commons.–(Cheers.) . . .

Sixty years ago our system of national taxation was effectively reformed and immense and undisputed advantages accrued therefrom to all classes, the richest as well as the poorest. The system of local taxation to-day is just as vicious and wasteful, just as great an impediment to enterprise and progress, just as harsh a burden upon the poor as the thousand taxes and Corn Law sliding scales of the "hungry forties." We are met in an hour of tremendous opportunity. "You who shall liberate the land," said Mr. Cobden, "will do more for your country than we have done in the liberation of its commerce."–(Cheers.) You can follow the same general principle of distinguishing between earned and unearned increment through the Government's treatment of the income tax. There is all the difference in the world between the income tax upon what a man makes from month to month or from year to year by his continued exertion and which may stop at any moment, but will certainly stop if he is incapacitated, and the income which is derived from the profits of accumulated capital, which is a continuing income irrespective of the exertion of its owner. Nobody wants to penalise or to stigmatise income derived from dividend, rent, or interest where the element of monopoly is excluded; for accumulated capital, apart from monopoly, represents exertions and thrift and prudence, qualities which are only less valuable to the community than the actual energies of industry.

But the great difference between the two classes of income remains, and we are sensible of it, and we think that that great difference should be recognised and that the necessary burdens of the State should be divided and shared between the two classes. The application of this principle of differentiation of the income tax has enabled the present Government sensibly to lighten the burden of the great majority of income tax payers. Under the late Conservative Government about 1,100,000 income tax payers paid income tax at the statutory rate of a shilling in the pound. Mr. Asquith, the present Prime Minister–(cheers),–when Chancellor of the Exchequer reduced the income tax in respect of earned incomes under £2,000 a year from a shilling to ninepence, and it is calculated that 750,000 income tax payers–that is to say, very nearly three-quarters of the whole number of income tax payers,–who formerly paid at the shilling rate, have obtained an actual relief from taxation to the extent of nearly twelve hundred thousand pounds a year in the aggregate. The present Chancellor of the Exchequer in the present Budget has added to this abatement a further relief, a very sensible relief, I venture to think you will consider it, on account of each child–(laughter and cheers)–to parents who possess under £500 a year, and that concession involves a further abatement and relief equal to £600,000 a year. It is founded on the highest principle and authority, for it figures in one of the Budget proposals of Mr. Pitt and it is to-day recognised by the law of Prussia. Taking together the income tax reform of Mr. Asquith and Mr. Lloyd George–taking the two together, because they are all part of same policy and they are all part of our treatment as a Government of this great subject–it is true to say that very nearly three out of every four persons who pay income tax will be taxed after this Budget–this penal Budget, this wicked, monstrous, despoilatory Budget–(laughter)–three out of every four persons will be taxed for income tax at a lower rate than they were by the late Conservative Government.–(Cheers.)

You will perhaps say to me, "That may be all very well; but are you sure that the rich and the very rich are not being burdened too heavily?–(Laughter.) Are you sure that you are not laying on the backs of people who are struggling to support existence–(laughter)–with incomes of upwards of £3,000 a year–(laughter)–burdens which are too heavy to be borne? Will they not sink crushed by the load of material cares into early graves–(laughter),–followed there even by the unrelenting hand of the death duties collector?–(Laughter.) Will they not take refuge in wholesale fraud and evasion, as some of their leaders ingenuously suggest, or will there be a general flight of all rich people from their native shores to the protection of the hospitable foreigner?" Let me reassure you on these points. The taxes which we now seek to impose to meet the need of the State will not appreciably affect, have not appreciably affected, the comfort, the status, or even the style of living of any class in the United Kingdom. There has been no invidious singling out of a few rich men for special taxation. The increased burden which is placed upon wealth is evenly and broadly distributed over the whole of that wealthy class which are more numerous in Great Britain than in any other country in the world, and who when this Budget is passed will still find Great Britain the best country in the world to live in.—(Laughter.) When I reflect upon the power and influence that class possesses, upon the general good-will with which they are regarded by their poorer neighbours, upon the infinite opportunities for pleasure and for culture which are open to them in this full, prosperous, and orderly commonwealth, I cannot doubt that they ought to contribute, and I believe that great numbers of them are willing to contribute, in a greater degree than heretofore towards the needs of the navy for which they are always clamouring and for those social reforms upon which the health and wealth of the whole population depend. And, after all, when we are upon the sorrows of the rich and the heavy blows that have been struck by this wicked Budget, let us not forget that this Budget itself—denounced by all the vested interests in the country and in all the abodes of wealth and power—after all draws nearly as much from the taxation of tobacco and spirits, which are the luxuries of the working classes, who pay their share with silence and dignity.—(Laughter and cheers.) It draws nearly as much from them—(cheers)—as it does from those wealthy classes upon whose behalf such heartrending outcries are made. . . .

We want the Budget not merely to be the work of the Cabinet and of the Chancellor of the Exchequer—we want it to be the shaped and moulded plan deliberately considered by the House of Commons. That will be a long and painful process to those who are bound from day to day to take part in it, but we shall not shrink from it.—(Cheers.) But, gentlemen, when that process is over, when the Finance Bill leaves the House of Commons, I think you will agree with me that it ought to leave the House of Commons in its final form.—(Loud and prolonged cheers.) No amendments, excision, modifying, or mutilating will be agreed to by us.—(Cheers.) We will stand no mincing—(renewed cheers),—and unless Lord Lansdowne and his landlordly friends choose to eat their own mince up again—(laughter),—Parliament will be dissolved—(great cheering),—and we shall come to you in a moment of high consequence for every cause for which Liberalism has ever fought. See that you do not fail us at that hour. (Loud cheering.) . . .

LIBERALISM AND THE GERMAN "MENACE"

July 17, 1909

Scottish Liberal Club Dinner,
Edinburgh

In this speech, Churchill reiterated his view that the forecasts of an inevitable conflict with Germany were unjustified. It was an opinion which he was to change in altered circumstances, but one never forgotten by his Conservative critics.

[Extract] . . . We live in a period of superficial alarms.–(Cheers.) We live in a period when it is thought to be patriotic and statesmanlike and far-seeing and clever and Bismarckian–(laughter)–to predict hideous and direful wars as imminent and approaching. I do not believe all this nightmare nonsense at all.–(Cheers.) In the last ten or twelve years I have heard men–not light-headed people, but men of gravity and piety, supposed to be very responsible, who certainly have had access to the best information which the machinery of government can supply,–I have heard such men say, with a wag of their heads, first, that a war with Russia was inevitable and only a question of time that the steady advance of Russia upon India or China, or some other place, was bound to culminate in a measureable period in a hideous struggle between Great Britain and Russia. I have then heard similar important persons inform us that a war with France was only a question of time, that the ambitions of France or the diplomatic methods of France, were bound in the end to bring us into a catastrophe and a collision with France, which was, after all, only a question of time. And now I live in a period when I hear similar people say that a great collision and struggle with Germany is only a question of time. I have seen the inevitable war with Russia change smoothly in the passage of time into a very smooth working arrangement with Russia, which has greatly consolidated and strengthened the cause of peace. I have seen the hostility we were told was bound to culminate in war with France turn into a close bond of friendship and unity of sentiment such as has never existed between the two peoples.–(Cheers.) And, looking at facts as they are, and not as foolish or mischievous people try to make them out to be, I say there are now far fewer grounds of friction between England and Germany than there were fifteen years ago between Great Britain and Russia, or seven or eight years ago between Great Britain and France.

There is no real antagonism of interest between Great Britain and Germany. Don't allow yourselves, I implore you, to be led away by those foolish guides who try to make out that there is great and fundamental collision between those two peoples. They have nothing whatever to fight about, and nowhere whatever to fight in, and, in my judgment, you will find that in the course of a few years, if people keep their heads, the good relations which exist to-day between Great Britain and Germany will steadily increase, and will develop, and we shall talk of the friction which was represented to exist in the year 1908-9 as if it were as much a back-number as the stories of the Russian danger and the French peril, which we have successively outlived. I think if you look at the situation in Europe and the world generally you will see that, in spite of the mischief-making done by individuals, and in spite of the power which the evil forces, the restless forces, and the half-civilised forces in each country continually exert, there is a growing sense of interdependence between the great modern States of the world. Their commercial relations lead them to have their interests more and more closely interwoven. There is a more frequent movement between prominent individuals of every class from one country to another. There is a great sense of community of interest between labouring peoples of all countries which is growing stronger, and which we should certainly foster by every means in our power; and, finally, it has become well worth the while of Sovereigns to seek the applause of nations, not leading them into the hateful paths of war, but by guiding them, as His Majesty has done so strenuously and so well, into those smoother, brighter, and more delectable regions of peace. For all those reasons I think that Liberalism, which perishes in time of war, has bright prospects before it, because we shall find that the new facts and the new circumstances which are every day becoming more powerful in the world, will clear the path of the statesman of those distracting the perturbing external influences which arrest development at home, and that in the work of development at home Liberalism is a policy creative and constructive, permanent and far-reaching, which we have only to work at with courage and with decision to carry to a glorious and triumphant conclusion.–(Cheers.)

THE BUDGET

August 2, 1909

Budget League Meeting,
Canford Park, Wimborne

On July 30, Lloyd George delivered one of his most celebrated attacks upon the Lords, his "Limehouse Speech." His language and imagery provoked a fierce response from the Unionists and the Unionist Press.

[Extract] Nothing amuses me more about the Conservative party than their infinite capacity for being shocked. (Laughter.) One never knows that the day will not come when they might be shocked at something that I might happen to say. (Great laughter.) But the thing which seems to have shocked them more than anything else was Mr. Lloyd George's last speech at Limehouse. (Cheers.) They are never shocked at anything they say themselves. That is a very lucky thing, because there is hardly a single word in Mr. Lloyd George's Limehouse speech which is not directly taken from Conservative speeches and newspapers engaged in the attack on the Budget. (Hear, hear.) The Conservative party does not mind in the least using such words as fraud and folly and robbery and plunder and spoilation and treachery when these are applied to Liberal Ministers of the Crown. But if any of these harsh terms should by chance be made to apply, not to individuals–Liberals do not seek to attack individuals–but to the system which the Conservative party supports, then they hold up their heads in holy horror. Why, *The Times* blushed as pink as the *Sporting Times* (laughter)–that other great organ of Tory refinement (more laughter)–and the *Daily Telegraph* became purple with purple patches, all over, of repressed emotion (laughter), and as for the *Daily Mail,* it assumed the sort of air of sorrow and deportment that one would associate with the headmistress of a seminary for young ladies (more laughter), and they set the office boy to work to write a leading article on how to elevate the tone of public controversy. (Cheers.) I notice, however, that, while the Conservative party was occupied in being shocked at Mr. Lloyd George's speech they did not give themselves the trouble to answer any of it by argument. (Cheers and a voice, "They can't.") . . .

Political office under the Crown is a great and splendid duty for a man, but office without power is a degradation. If Liberal Governments are not to have the power given them by the country, if they are to be baulked and thwarted in their legislation, if financial proposals they make–which are solely within the province of the House of Commons–are to be mutilated, amended, or destroyed by the House of Lords, then the position of a Liberal Government will be one of responsibility without power, and the retention of office by us will not conduce to the dignity of public affairs or to the advantage of the country. (Cheers.) But, quite apart from our own personal feelings upon such a subject, it would be a crime against the British democracy if we were to acquiesce in the slightest mutilation of the Budget by the House of Lords. (Cheers.) We are quite willing to discuss in the House of Commons the provisions of this Bill, but when the process is completed there the matter must stop. As the Budget leaves the House of Commons so it must stand or fall. (Cheers.) The Government are ready to fight for public rights. The armies are marshalling forward. Unless one or other retreats a great battle is inevitable. The Government are not going to retreat. (Cheers.) We are going on, and all who are with us will share the honour and the glory of victory. (Loud cheers.)

THE BUDGET

September 4, 1909

Palace Theatre, Leicester

This speech deeply shocked many of Churchill's former friends and provoked a letter of protest to the Times *from the King's secretary. The central point of controversy was the threat to abolish the veto of the Lords–for which Churchill was also rebuked by the Prime Minister.*

[Extract] You have very rightly said that the Budget League has very successful meetings. We have a great many of them, and, as you have said, there are a good many meetings of the Budget Protest League which are, in fact, little less than demonstrations in favour of the Budget.–(Laughter and "Hear, hear.") But there is one great difficulty which confronts a speaker at Budget League meetings–he has nobody to reply to.–(Laughter.) It is quite true that the small fry of the Tory party have been splashing actively about in their proper puddles. It is true that Mr. Balfour, however, the great leader who means to lead–(laughter)–he has been meaning to lead for the last six years if he could only find out where on earth to lead to;–it is quite true that Mr. Balfour from time to time emits four or five columns of insipid equivocation which the newspapers whose proprietors he has taken the precaution to make into barons hasten to claim as "another epoch-making pronouncement."–(Laughter.) It is quite true that from time to time Mr. Walter Long lets off his small cannon in various parts of the country, and sometimes hits the wrong man and sometimes hits himself.–(Laughter.) And at intervals we have a laboured attempt at impudence from Mr. F. E. Smith. I can assure you that the last thing in the world that I want to do is to disparage the efforts of those over-weighted and harassed patriots. They are doing their best, and all I will say about them is that I only hope their performances will give more satisfaction to their employers the brewers and the ground landlords–(laughter and cheers)–than they have hitherto given to the audiences they have addressed, if I may judge from the reports in the daily newspapers.

But what I want to draw your attention to is the appalling lack of anything like a leader or a spokesman on the Tory side who is capable of commanding public attention, of conducting adequately this great controversy and debate upon which we are now engaged. The millionaire newspapers–do not forget that, although they are sold very cheap and sometimes play rather low, nevertheless they are the organs of rich gentlemen and are used in the interests of wealth as such,–the millionaire newspapers are painfully conscious of the absence of any popular and effective figure on their side. (A voice: "No, no.") The "Times" for some time made an effort to bring out Lord Rothschild as a "great" Tory democratic leader–(laughter),–but he retired hurt–(laughter and cheers)–after one round with Mr. Lloyd George. (Laughter and cheers.) The "Daily Mail"–("Oh, oh")–was rather inclined to take up Lord Rosebery–(a voice: "They can have him")–if they only knew what he was going to say.–(Laughter.) The "Daily Telegraph" holds up its hands in pious lamentation and says, "Oh, if we only had Mr. Chamberlain in his prime, how he would have answered that wicked Limehouse speech."–(Laughter.) I am sure we are all very sorry that Mr. Chamberlain cannot take part in this controversy, and we all deplore the perverse misfortune which keeps him at once so near and so far from the fighting line. When the "Daily Telegraph" talks about Mr. Chamberlain in his prime, we are forced to remember that that would be the Mr. Chamberlain of 1885.–(Cheers.) If we had the Mr. Chamberlain of 1885 to-day he would not have answered the Limehouse speech. He would have made it.–(Cheers.)

And so in the absence of anything popular and effective, in the absence of any commanding voice, the Tory party have had to put up their "dooks."–(Great laughter and a voice: "What about your grandfather?") That is how these unfortunate individuals who ought to lead quiet, delicate, sheltered lives, "far from the madding crowd's ignoble strife"–(laughter)–are being dragged into the centre of the football scrimmage–(laughter),–and have, I am sorry to say, got rather roughly mauled in the process. All this may be very sad and may be very true, but it is no good to me. I do not come down here to-day to bandy words with dukes. Let us beware that we do not start a reaction in our favour–petitions for reprieve awaiting signature in all the public-houses–deputations to the Home Secretary to have them treated as first-class demeanants. Do not let us be too hard upon them. It is poor sport almost like catching goldfish. These ornamental creatures blunder on every hook they see, and there is no sport whatever in trying to catch them.–(Laughter.) It would be barbarous to leave them gasping on the bank of public ridicule upon which they have landed themselves. Let us put them back gently and tenderly into their fountains, and if a few bright golden scales have been rubbed off in what the Prime Minister calls the variegated handling they have received they will soon get over it. They have got plenty more. . . .

We are strong in the consciousness of a persistent effort to sweep away anomalies and inequalities, to redress injustice, and to open more widely to the masses of the people a good chance of life.–(Cheers.) I think we may also say that we are strong in the support and enthusiasm of the great majority of our fellow-countrymen. We are strong in the triumph of our policy in South Africa.–(Cheers.) But most of all we are strong in the hopes and plans which we are forming for the future. It is about this future that I will speak to you this afternoon, and let me tell you that I do not feel at all inclined to plead exhaustion in consequence of the exertions we have made in the past, or to dwell upon the successes which we have had in the past, or to survey with complacency the record of the Government, or to ask you to praise us for the work which we have done. No; when I think of the work that lies before us, upon which we have already entered, of the long avenue of social reconstruction and reorganisation which opens out in so many directions and ever more broadly before us, of the hideous squalor and misery which darkens and poisons the life of Britain, of the need of earnest action, of the prospects of effective and immediate action–when I dwell upon this it is not with a feeling of lassitude or exhaustion over the work done in the past, but only a vehement impulse to press onward that we all of us ought to feel.–(Loud cheers.)

The social conditions of the British people at the dawn of the twentieth century cannot be contemplated without deep anxiety. The anxiety is keen because it arises out of uncertainty. It is the gnawing anxiety of suspense. What is the destiny of our country to be? Nothing is settled for or against us. We have no reason to despair. Still less have we any reason to be self-satisfied. All is still in our hands. For good or for ill, we have the power to-day to choose our future, and I believe there is no nation in the world, perhaps there never has been in history any nation which at one and the same moment was confronted with such opposite possibilities. We are threatened on the one hand by more melancholy disaster, and cheered on the other by more bright, yet not unreasonable, hopes. The two roads are open. We stand at the crossways. If we stand on in the old happy-go-lucky way–the richer classes ever growing in wealth and in number, and the very poor remaining plunged or plunging ever deeper in helpless, hopeless misery–then I think there is nothing before us but savage strife between class and class, with the increasing disorganisation, with increasing waste of human strength and human virtue, nothing but that dual degeneration which comes from the simultaneous waste of extreme wealth and of extreme want.–(Hear, hear.)

We have had over here lately Colonial editors from all the colonies of the British Empire. What is the opinion which they expressed as to the worst thing they saw in the old country? From every colony they have expressed the opinion that the worst feature they saw was the extremes of poverty side by side with the extremes of luxury.–(Hear, hear, and some interruptions.) I am sure the gentleman will be quiet. Don't you think it is very impressive to find a statement like that made in all friendship and sincerity by men of our own race who have come from lands which are so widely scattered over the surface of the earth, and are the product of such varied conditions? Is it not impressive to find that they are all agreed–coming as they did from Australia or Canada or South Africa–that the greatest danger to the British Empire and to the British people is not to be found among the enormous fleets and armies of the European Continent or in the solemn problems of Hindustan? It is not in the Yellow Peril, or the Black Peril, or any danger in the wide circuit of colonial and foreign affairs. It is here in our midst, close at home, close at hand, in the vast growing cities of England and Scotland, and in the dwindling and cramped villages of our denuded countryside. It is there you will find the seeds of Imperial ruin and national decay. The awful gap between rich and poor, the divorce of the people from the land–(cheers),–the want of proper discipline and training in our young people–(hear, hear),–the exploitation of boy labour–(hear, hear),–the physical degeneration which seems to follow so swiftly on civilised poverty, the awful jumble of an obsolete Poor Law–(hear, hear),–the horrid havoc of the liquor traffic–(loud and prolonged cheers),–the constant insecurity in the means of subsistence and employment which breaks the heart of many a sober, hard-working man–(hear, hear),–the absence of any established minimum standard of life and comfort among the workers, and the other end, the swift increase of vulgar, joyless luxury–(hear, hear),–here are the enemies of Britain. Beware lest they shatter the foundations of her power.–(Loud cheers.)

Then look at the other side. Look at the forces for good–the moral forces, the spiritual forces, the civic, the scientific, the patriotic forces which make for order and harmony and health and life,–are they not tremendous? Do we not see them everywhere, in every town, in every class, in every creed–strong forces worthy of old England, coming to her rescue, fighting for her soul? That is the situation in our country as I see it this afternoon. Two great armies, evenly matched, looked in fierce conflict with each other all along the line, swaying backwards and forwards in strife, and, for my part, I am confident that the right will win.–(Cheers.) That the generous influences will triumph over the selfish influences, that the organising forces will devour the forces of degeneration, and that the British people will emerge triumphant from their struggles to clear the road and lead the march amongst the foremost nations of the world. I want to ask you a question. I dare say there are some of you who do not like this or that particular point in the Budget, who do not like some particular argument or phrase which some of us may have used in advocating or defending it. But it is not of these details that I speak. The question I want each of you to ask himself is this–On which side of this great battle which I have described to you does the Budget count?–(Loud cheers.) Can any of you, looking at it broadly and as a whole, looking on the policy which surrounds it, which depends upon it, looking at the arguments by which it is defended as well as the arguments by which it is opposed–can anyone doubt that the Budget, in its essential character and meaning, in its spirit, and in its practical effect, will be a tremendous reinforcement, almost like a new army coming up at the end of a day, upon the side of all those forces and influences which are fighting for the life and health and progress of our race? (Cheers.) . . .

I have tried to show you that the Budget and the policy of the Budget is the first conscious attempt on the part of the State to build up a better and a more scientific organisation of society for the workers of the country, and it is for you to say at no very distant date–(a voice: "We'll say it," and cheers)–whether all this effort for a great coherent scheme of social reconstruction is to be swept away into the region of lost endeavours.–(Cries of "Never," and a voice–"What are you going to do with the Lords?" and cheers.) That is the main aspect of the Budget to which I wish to draw your attention. But there is another significance of the highest importance which attaches to the Budget. I mean the new attitude of the State towards wealth. Formerly the only question of the taxgatherer was: "How much have you got?" We ask that question still–(laughter and cheers),–and there is a general feeling recognised as just by all parties that the rate of taxation should be greater for large incomes than for small. As to how much greater, parties are no doubt in dispute.–(Laughter.) But now a new question has arisen. We do not only ask to-day: "How much have you got?" We also ask: "How did you get it?–(Cheers.) Did you earn it by yourself, or has it just been left you by others? Was it gained by processes which are in themselves beneficial to the community in general, or was it gained by processes which have done no good to anyone, only harm? Was it gained by the enterprise and capacity necessary to found a business, or merely by squeezing and bleeding the owner and founder of the business? Was it gained by supplying the capital which industry needs, or by denying, except at an extortionate price, the land which industry requires? Was it derived from active reproductive processes, or merely by squatting on some piece of necessary land till enterprise and labour and natural interests and municipal interests had to buy you out at fifty times the agricultural value? Was it gained from opening new minerals to the service of man, or by sucking a mining royalty from the toil of others? Was it gained by the curious process of using political influence and converting an annual licence into a practical freehold, and thereby pocketing a monopoly value which properly belongs to the State? How did you get it?

That is the new question which has been postulated, and which is vibrating in penetrating repetition through the land–a tremendous question, never previously in this country asked so plainly, a new idea, pregnant, formidable, full of life, that taxation should not only have regard to the volume of wealth, but so far as possible to the circumstances of its origin. I don't wonder it has raised a great stir. I don't wonder there are heart-searchings and angry words, because that simple question, that modest proposal which we see embodied in the new income tax provisions, in the land taxes, in the licence duties, and in the tax on mining royalties–that modest proposal means, and can only mean, the refusal of the modern State to bow down unquestioning worth before the authority of wealth.–(Cheers.) This refusal to treat all forms of wealth with equal deference, no matter what may have been the process by which it was acquired, is a strenuous assertion in a practical form that there ought to be a constant relation between acquired wealth and useful service previously rendered. Where there has been no service, but rather disservice, then whenever possible the State shall make a sensible difference in the taxes it is bound to impose.

It is just as well that you should keep these issues clearly before you during the weeks in which we seem to be marching towards a grave constitutional crisis. But I should like to tell you that a general election consequent upon the rejection of the Budget by the Lords would not, ought not, and could not be fought upon the Budget alone.–(Cheers.) Budgets come, as the late Lord Salisbury said in 1894, and Budgets go. Every Government has its own expenditure for each year. Every Government has hitherto been entitled to make its own provision to meet that expenditure. There is a Budget every year. Memorable as the Budget of my right hon. friend may be, far-reaching as is the policy dependent upon it, the Finance Bill, after all, is only in its character an annual affair. But the rejection of the Budget by the House of Lords would not be an annual affair.–(Loud and prolonged cheering.) It will be a violent rupture of constitutional custom and usage extending over 300 years, and recognised during all that time by the leaders of every party in the State. It would involve a sharp and sensible breach with the traditions of the past. And what does the House of Lords depend upon if not upon the traditions of the past?–(Cheers.) It would amount to an attempt at revolution, not by the poor but by the rich, not by the masses but by the privileged few, not in the name of progress but in that of reaction, not for the purpose of broadening the framework of the State, but greatly narrowing it. Such an attempt, whatever you may think of it, would be historic in its character, and the results of the battle fought upon it, whoever won, must inevitably be not of an annual but of a permanent and final character.–(Cheers.) The result of such an election must mean, an alteration of the veto of the House of Lords.–(More cheers.) If they win–(Voices: "They won't" and "Never")–they will have asserted their right not merely to reject the legislation of the House of Commons but to control the finances of the country. And if they lose we will smash to pieces their veto.–(Loud and prolonged cheers.)

I say to you that we do not seek the struggle. We have our work to do. But if it is to come it could never come better than now.–(Loud cheers.) Never again, perhaps not for many years in any case, will such an opportunity be presented to the British democracy. Never will the ground be more favourable. Never will the issues be more clearly or more vividly defined.–(Cheers.) Those issues will be whether taxation which is admitted on all sides to be necessary shall be imposed upon luxuries, superfluities, and monopolies, or upon the prime necessaries of life, whether you shall put your tax upon the unearned increment in land or upon the daily bread of labour, whether the policy of constructive social reform on which we are embarked and which expands and deepens as we advance, shall be carried through and given a fair chance, or whether it shall be brought to a dead stop, and all the energies and attention of the State devoted to Jingo armaments and senseless foreign adventure. And lastly, the issue will be whether the British people in the year of grace 1909 are going to be ruled through a representative Assembly elected by six or seven millions of voters and about which everyone in the country has a chance of being consulted, or whether they are going to allow themselves to be dictated to and domineered over by a miserable minority of titled persons–(laughter),–who represent nobody, who are responsible to nobody, and who only scurry up to London to vote in their party interests, in their class interests, and in their own interests. These will be the issues of the struggle, and I am glad that the responsibility for such a struggle, if it should come, will rest with the House of Lords themselves.–(Hear, hear.) But if it is to come we do not need to complain. We will not draw back from it.–(Hear, hear.) We will engage in it with all our hearts, it being always clearly understood that the fight will be a fight to the finish–(loud cheers),–and that the fullest forfeits which are in accordance with the national interests shall be exacted from the defeated foe.–(Loud cheers.)

ELECTION ADDRESS

December 4, 1909

Empire House, Southport

The Finance Bill was rejected by the Lords by 350 votes to 75, and Asquith immediately advised the dissolution of Parliament and a general election.

[Extract] . . . We are met together in times of acute constitutional crisis. (Hear, hear.) The quarrel between a tremendous democratic electorate and a one-sided hereditary Chamber of wealthy men has often been threatened, has often been averted, has been long debated, has been long delayed, but has always been inevitable, and it has come at last. (Cheers.) It is now open, it is now flagrant, and it must now be carried to a conclusion. (Cheers.). . .

What is the nature of this Assembly which claims to use these tremendous powers? Who are these men who assert that they possess that right to superior jurisdiction over their fellows? What is the Assembly which claims to exercise these astonishing powers, and which claims to exercise them over all elective processes and over all representative persons? What qualifications have they got? What are their characteristics? What special knowledge do they possess? How are they chosen? Whom do they represent? To whom are they responsible? By whom can their action be called in question? (Hear, hear.) These are the questions which immediately arise, and these are the questions to which they have forced the mind of every thinking man in England to turn. (Cheers.) Why should five or six hundred titled persons govern us, and why should their children govern our children for ever? (Hear, hear.) I invite a reply from the apologists and the admirers of the House of Lords. I invite them to show any ground of reason, or of logic, or of expediency, or of practical common sense in defence of the institution which has taken the predominant part during the last few days in the politics of our country. There is no defence, there is no answer, except that the House of Lords, the unreformed House of Lords, has survived out of the past. It is a lingering relic of the feudal order. (Laughter and cheers.) It is the remains–a solitary remainder–of a state of things and of a balance of forces which has wholly passed away. (Hear, hear.) I challenge the defenders and the backers and the instigators of the House of Lords (cheers)–I challenge them to justify and defend in the next six weeks before the electors of this country the character and composition of this hereditary Assembly. (Hear, hear.) Of course, as long as the House of Lords accepted a secondary and subordinate position these questions slumbered. There were other matters of great importance on which the minds of reformers were centred, and the question of altering the character of the Second Chamber, and of restricting its veto, though always recognised as one of great importance, did not receive that priority of consideration which in the future it absolutely requires. But now that it usurps the main power in the State, now that it has invaded at one moment the prerogative of the Crown and the rights of the House of Commons (hear, hear), these questions which I have put, these brutally fundamental questions, simple and plain, that any man can understand, that few can refuse to answer in one sense, must be asked all over the country, and, being asked, they must be answered. The answers to these questions will, I think, be fatal to the veto and to the character of an hereditary House of Lords. (Cheers.) . . .

I want to ask, On what principle does the House of Lords deal with the legislation they receive from the House of Commons? Do they act impartially? ("No.") Are they a Chamber of review and of restraint? ("No.") Do they, for instance, reject Bills which are extreme and pass Bills which are moderate in their character? ("No.") Is that the standard by which they are judged? Do they act according to their judgment and conscience? ("They have none," and laughter.) Not one of these questions can be answered in the affirmative by any men who honestly and quietly ask them for themselves. (Cheers.) I say without hesitation that the attitude of the House of Lords towards all measures which reach them from the House of Commons is entirely partisan. (Hear, hear, and cheers.) I say they pass Bills which they believe to be wrong when they think it will pay the Tory party to have a question settled. (Hear, hear.) They reject Bills, however moderate these Bills may be, whenever they think they will injure the Liberal party by keeping the question open. That is the sole canon by which the House of Lords–this Second Chamber which is said to have a supreme monopoly of political wisdom–judge of the legislation they receive. (Cheers.) . . .

LORD CURZON

December 17, 1909

Victoria Opera House, Burnley

On December 16 Lord Curzon passionately defended the hereditary principle in a speech at Oldham. Churchill's retort was one of the most effective of his many speeches during the election campaign.

[Extract] . . . When I began my campaign in Lancashire I challenged any Conservative speaker to come down and say why the House of Lords, composed as the present House of Lords is, should have the right to rule over us, and why the children of that House of

Lords should have the right to rule over our children.–(Cheers.) My challenge has been taken up with great courage–(laughter)–by Lord Curzon.–(Groans.) No, the House of Lords could not have found any more able and, I will add, any more arrogant defender, and at Oldham on Wednesday–you have heard of Oldham–(laughter),–so have I.–(Laughter.) Well, at Oldham Lord Curzon treated a great public meeting to what I can only call a prize essay on the Middle Ages.–(Laughter.) I do not say it was not a very eloquent speech. It was a beautiful speech. I read it with the most intense pleasure, with feelings of artistic pleasure, and also a sense of satisfaction, because I would like Lord Curzon to make that speech in every town and city throughout our country. I would ask nothing better than that he should have an opportunity of putting these views forward with all his ability and address to great audiences throughout the country. I am sure it would save some of us a lot of trouble.–(Laughter.)

Let us look at one or two of the arguments on which Lord Curzon relied. He began with a defence of hereditary legislators. That is a very plucky thing to do.–(Laughter.) He said, "Look at the Monarchy!" But the Sovereign is not a hereditary legislator. In this country the Sovereign reigns but he does not govern. The King acts on the advice of Ministers. The Crown in England has not had for hundreds of years the power of making laws, and for two or three centuries has not had the power of stopping laws when they have been passed. It is a very wise thing in every State that the supreme office should be removed beyond the reach of private ambition and should be above the shock and change of party warfare. It is as a constitutional Monarchy that we reverence and honour the British Crown. I do not think the people of England would be prepared for one moment to agree to the Sovereign of these realms exercising the power which the Tsar of Russia exercises.–(Hear, hear.) Lord Curzon could scarcely have chosen a more inaccurate "fact" upon which to rely.

Then he told us that Mr. Pitt, Mr. Fox, and Grenville in days gone by exercised great dominance in the House of Commons, and that forty years after all their sons were also in great offices and playing a very important part. He went on to say that something like that had reproduced itself to-day, though on a smaller scale. Whereas some years ago you had Mr. Gladstone, Mr. Chamberlain, and Lord Robert Cecil (afterwards Lord Salisbury) in the House of Commons, so now you saw their sons distinguished. Then he turned to me.–(Laughter.) Did I owe anything to my father? Why, of course, I owe everything to my father.–(Laughter and cheers.) But what defence is all this of a House of hereditary legislators? Because my father was member for Woodstock, I do not suggest that I should be permanently member for Woodstock, irrespective of what the people of Woodstock may think of me. It is quite true that some instances can be cited of men who have succeeded distinguished fathers and have attained equal and even greater distinction themselves. But how many cases can be shown of the contrary?–(Laughter, and a voice: "Rub it in.") You can almost count the hereditary instances on your fingers. In fact Lord Curzon did not cite as many instances as there are fingers on his hands. But only consider the enormous number of contrary instances which have been veiled in a decent and merciful obscurity.–(Laughter.) If the electors of a particular constituency like to let old associations count–if they choose to say "We will voice for this young man because we knew his father"–what derogation is it from their free right of choice; in what way is their full power to choose their own representative affected in any degree? If that argument of Lord Curzon proves anything, it proves that if there is anything in the doctrine of heredity that doctrine will receive consideration under the representative system wherever it deserves.

But the claim of the House of Lords is not that if the electors like the sons of distinguished men may have legislative functions entrusted to them; it is that, whether they like it or not, the sons and the grandsons and the great-grandsons, and so on till the end of time, of distinguished men shall have legislative functions entrusted to them. That claim resolves itself into this, that we should maintain in our country a superior class, with law-giving functions inherent in their blood, transmissible by them to their remotest posterity, and that these functions should be exercised irrespective of the character, the intelligence, or the experience of the tenant for the time being–(laughter),–and utterly independent of the public need and the public will. That is a proposition which only needs to be stated before any average British jury to be rejected with instantaneous contempt.–(Cheers.) Why has it never been rejected before? In my opinion it has never been rejected, because the House of Lords has never before been taken seriously by the democratic electorate, which has been in existence since 1885. They have never been taken seriously because they were believed to be in a comatose and declining condition, upon which death would gradually supervene. Now we see the House of Lords stepping into the front rank of politics; not merely using their veto over any legislation sent up by any majority, however large, from any House of Commons, however newly elected, but also claiming new powers over the whole of the finances–powers which would make them the main governing centre in the State. (Cheers.) That is why we are forced to examine their pretensions very closely; and when we have examined them, I venture to think there will not be much left of them.–(Cheers.)

"Oh, but," says Lord Curzon, going on with his defence of this hereditary Chamber, "we don't have to trim our sails to catch passing gusts of popular passion." Well, what are they doing now. Their whole contention is that they consider the Budget is a bad Budget, that it is wrong and vicious, and that it will do all manner of evil to the country. But they say if at the election the nation, the electors, upon a gust of popular passion, return a majority favourable to the Budget they will immediately pass the Budget.–(Laughter and cheers.) That may be very prudent of them, and it may be very proper of them, but it certainly is not standing against the gusts of popular passion.–(Laughter and cheers.) And what about the Trades Disputes Act? Why, I don't hesitate to say that the House of Lords, or a great majority of that House, regarded that as a thoroughly wicked bill. Lord Halsbury, the ex-Lord Chancellor, described it as pernicious and wicked, as a bill which contained a section more disgraceful than had appeared in any other statute. But it had what the House of Lords thought was "a gust of popular passion" behind it; they stepped aside, and it passed.–(Laughter and cheers.) . . .

Now I come to the third great argument of Lord Curzon. "All civilisation," he said–he was quoting a great French writer, an Agnostic, Renan–"all civilisation has been the work of aristocracies."–(Laughter.) They liked that in Oldham.–(Laughter.)

There was not a duke, not an earl, not a marquis, not a viscount in Oldham who did not feel that a compliment had been paid to him.–(Loud laughter.) What does Lord Curzon mean by aristocracy? It is quite clear from the argument of his speech that he did not mean Nature's aristocracy, by which I mean the best and most gifted beings in each generation in each country, the wisest, the bravest, the most generous, the most skilful, the most beautiful, the strongest, and the most active. If he had meant that I think we should probably agree with him. Democracy properly understood means the association of all through the leadership of the best, but the context of Lord Curzon's quotation and the argument of his speech, which was designed entirely to prove that the House of Lords was a very desirable institution for us to maintain in its present form, clearly shows that by aristocracy he meant the hereditary legislator, the barons, earls, dukes, etc.–I do not mean anything disrespectful by the etc.–(laughter),–and their equivalents in other countries. That is what he meant by aristocracy in the argument he employed at Oldham. Well, again I say this has only to be dismissed as absurd.–(Cheers.)

"All civilisation has been the work of aristocracies." Why, it would be much more true to say the upkeep of the aristocracy has been the hard work of all civilisations.–(Loud cheers and "Say it again.") Nearly all great ideas and the energy by which all the great services by which mankind has been benefited have come from the mass of the people. Take the great agent of civilisation–religion. The religions of the world have come from the people, the religions of the world have come from the poor, and most of all is that true of Christianity. Christianity was preached by poor men, humble men in the smallest employments, and preached to the poor, the outcast, the despised and rejected of those hard times–Christianity which to-day rules the world, and has contributed to civilisation all those precious ideas which keep our modern life clean and healthy. What great picture was ever painted by a duke?–(Laughter.) I have heard of a lord who wrote good poetry–Lord Byron,–but he did not write the sort of poetry that the House of Lords liked. In science all the great discoveries have been made by men outside this charmed circle which Lord Curzon conceives to embrace all the talents. And is mechanical invention–another great agent of civilisation–there again you come right down to the working people of Lancashire, in many cases, for some of the most notable inventions upon which the prosperity of our civilised life has been erected.–(Cheers.) Even when you come to war–though you can hardly call war one of the causes of civilisation; it certainly has been a very potent agent in the destinies and development of humanity–well, there have been many great generals who have become peers, but there have been much fewer peers who have become great generals. Lord Curzon reminded us that many Lords have filled high offices in the State. He described how they had 41 Prime Ministers in the House of Lords and only 16 in the poor, miserable House of Commons; what Secretaries of State, First Lords of the Admiralty, and a long succession of offices they had had in the House of Lords, whilst so very few had been held in the House of Commons. I can quite believe that. It only shows the undue political authority which has been engrossed all these years by a small, limited, and unrepresentative class.–(Cheers.) Lord Curzon proceeds to tell us that many distinguished men were proud to join the House of Lords in former times. I think it was only natural that they were eager to put their feet upon such an easy and at times absolutely indispensable road to almost any great employment in the services of the country. "All civilisation," Lord Curzon tells us, "is the work of aristocracies." He has his quotation; I will have mine. Mine is not nearly such an elegant or recondite extract as his. You have all heard mine before. Let us say, in the words of Robbie Burns, "A man's a man for a' that."–(Cheers.) I back my horse against his over any course in Lancashire. I will back it over any course in Scotland.–(Laughter.)

All these questions might have been allowed to slumber. But they have been raised by the action of the House of Lords; and, as they are raised, you are bound to give your answer to them. Mr. Chamberlain, I notice, in his letter to the papers, sorrowfully laments that Tariff "Reform" is not going to be the only issue at the election. No, it is not going to be the only issue. I think the Conservative party would have been beaten on either of the issues, but on the two together they will be overwhelmed.–(Loud cheers.)

DUNDEE POLL RESULT

January 18, 1910

Street Crowd, Dundee

The General Election result was a profound disappointment to the Liberals. The Unionists won 273; the Liberals, 275; Labour, 41; and the Irish Nationalists, 71. The independence of the Liberals from Labour and the Irish had gone, and this fact was to have a considerable influence on subsequent events.

In Dundee, Churchill's majority over the leading Unionist candidate was above 6,000; the persistent Mr. Scrymgeour was again bottom of the poll with 1,512 votes. The other elected candidate with Churchill was Mr. A. Wilkie (Labour). In the course of the election campaign Churchill had made twenty-eight major speeches to large audiences. After the Dundee result he spoke in a dozen constituencies which had not yet voted.

Dundee has pronounced its opinion. It has given a vote, the biggest vote ever recorded in the history of the city, for the two great causes of Free Trade and popular government. The course of the electoral battle cannot yet be determined; but we are going to win. But a great struggle lies before us. This is not the end of the battle. It is only the first blood in the war. A great struggle lies before us. We have got to smash the veto of the Lords.–(Great cheering.) We have worked together very harmoniously in this election. Let us go on that way. Mr. Wilkie and I will have to pull together till this struggle is decided. I thank you all most sincerely for all your kindness to me and my wife. You have answered nobly to the call I made upon you. You have given your decision here in so emphatic a manner that it must ring through all Scotland. So far as

I am concerned I will do my best to serve the interests of the city, and I will consume every sap of life and strength in my body to carry forward those great causes for which you have so generously given your votes. In this struggle we have had the support of all parts of the Progressive army. I do not overlook the support I have received from the Irish electors of Dundee. They were with us in the battle, and when the victory is won Ireland shall be there too. Let us hold together now. A great battle lies before us, but united, concentrated, combined, working together in true comradeship, there is no foe who can bar our path. Good night, good luck, let us win in the whole country a victory which shall be worthy of the exertions of Dundee.

TREATMENT OF "POLITICAL" PRISONERS (WOMEN SUFFRAGETTES)

March 15, 1910

House of Commons

The new Parliament assembled in a confused political situation. Many Liberals–including, it appears from his election speeches, Churchill–were under the impression that Asquith had received a commitment from the King to create sufficient new Peers to eliminate the Unionist majority in the Lords. On February 21 Asquith informed the House of Commons that this was not the case; he did not mention that he had sought such a guarantee, but that the King had refused. For a few days it appeared that the Government might resign. Churchill was strongly opposed to such an action, and after several days hesitation, the Government continued.

The vehemence of Churchill's speeches before and during the election, although they had evoked enthusiasm in his audiences, had aroused considerable criticism within the Liberal Party. In his speeches in the new House of Commons, Churchill struck a more moderate note.

Following the election, Asquith made changes in the Government and Churchill was appointed Home Secretary. The question of women's suffrage was a particular concern of Churchill's in this office, and it had personal aspects as well. His meetings had been interrupted by suffragettes in the Manchester elections of 1906 and 1908, at Dundee in the same year, and at the end of 1909 he had been attacked by Miss Theresa Garnett with a whip at Bristol. Churchill's enthusiasm for their cause had not been augmented by this incident. The hunger strikes and forcible feedings in the prisons were now becoming a matter of real public concern, and in the spring of 1910 a Conciliation Committee under Lord Lytton was established to promote legislation on women's suffrage.

I have given my best consideration to this subject with reference not solely to the treatment of women suffragist prisoners, but generally to the regulations which govern the treatment of those whom the hon. Member [Mr. John O'Connor] calls "political" prisoners. I do not feel that any differences of prison treatment should be based upon a consideration of the motives which actuated the offender. Motives are for the Courts to appraise, and it must be presumed that all due consideration has been given to them in any sentence which is imposed. It is, however, my duty, in carrying out the various Acts of Parliament, and the regulations made under them, to secure that the treatment of prisoners should not be inappropriate or harmful. I feel, as did my predecessor, that prison rules which are suitable to criminals guilty of dishonesty or cruelty, or other crimes implying moral turpitude, should not be applied inflexibly to those whose general character is good and whose offences, however reprehensible, do not involve personal dishonour.

I propose, therefore, to give power to the Prison Commissioners, under the direction of the Secretary of State, to mitigate in such cases the conditions of prison treatment which are generally regarded as of a degrading character; and, in order to effect this, I propose to lay upon the Table the following Rule which will acquire statutory force in the ordinary manner:

> In the case of any offender of the second or third division whose previous character is good, and who has been convicted of, or committed to prison for, an offence not involving dishonesty, cruelty, indecency, or serious violence, the Prison Commissioners may allow such amelioration of the conditions prescribed in the foregoing rules as the Secretary of State may approve in respect of the wearing of prison clothing, bathing, hair-cutting, cleaning of cells, employment, exercise, books, and otherwise. Provided that no such amelioration shall be greater than that granted under the rules for offenders of the first division.

THE LORDS AND THE BUDGET

March 19, 1910

Free Trade Hall, Manchester

The Government's policy with regard to the Lords was now determined. Legislation would be introduced whereby the Lords were to be prohibited from rejecting or amending any legislation involving taxation; they could delay other legislation only for two years; and the maximum duration of a Parliament would be reduced from seven to five years.

Lord Rosebery, who had proposed Lords reform on several occasions in the past, now produced an alternative in the House of Lords on March 14. This would have reduced the size of the upper House, and improved its procedures, but would not have limited the absolute veto rights.

Churchill's speech at Manchester, with its references to the Crown, provoked a protest from the King.

[Extract] . . . The power of Parliament cannot be increased. It is supreme; it is complete. What is gained by one House must be taken from the other. What is gained by the House of Lords must be taken from the House of Commons and from those who elect the House of Commons. All schemes of reform, without a limitation of the Veto, are useless and dangerous. (Cheers.) What is the evil of the present situation? It is the divergence between the two Houses of Parliament and the absence of any means of relieving the deadlock. The two Houses, if there are to be two Houses, must work together in general harmony unless the whole Constitution is to go awry. But for the last four years the House of Lords has been in open warfare with the majority in the House of Commons. For the last four years it has been playing a bitter and partisan game in the interests of their own political friends. (A voice: "Why does the Liberal Government create more?") For the last four years they have been engaged in mutilating bill after bill and in rejecting our most important legislative acts. If they have passed any measures, it is only with a view to Conservative electioneering interests. Finally they have thrown out the Budget and plunged the whole finances of the country into confusion. There is the evil. There is the urgent need of remedy. But the House of Lords, and those who are now advising them, in their proposals for the so-called reform of their constitution make no provision, so far as I can see, to meet this question of a deadlock owing to a difference of opinion between the two Houses. On the contrary, the proposals that Lord Rosebery has put forward would have the effect, as I read them, of destroying the prerogative of the Crown to create peers, which is the last resource of the Crown and the people against this oligarchy, and which every great constitutional authority has always indicated as the last resource by which the deadlock can be removed. . . .

They think in their hearts that it was a great mistake to give the vote at all to those enormous multitudes of weekly wage-earners. They would argue, if they spoke their true minds to you, that the great mass of the population has little time to study politics, that by its small worldly wealth and constant needs it is readily inclined to change, and that it is easily led away by this cry and that. They know they cannot take back the votes now, but what they will try to do, and what they are trying to do, both by what was done in the last Parliament and by what is being attempted in this, is to diminish, if not to destroy, the value of those votes by weakening, curbing, and overruling the House of Commons elected by those votes. (Cheers.) All their plans—even Lord Rosebery's, and certainly the plans which Lord Curzon, Lord Lansdowne, and Mr. Balfour are maturing,—all their plans for what is called "reform" of the House of Lords, however vague they may be, however varied, however well intentioned, however specious, however fair-seeming, however fanciful, all these plans lead straight on to one conclusion, viz. the establishment in an unshakable position beyond the reach of Crown or people of a large permanent Tory majority of wealthy persons, having full powers to veto not merely legislation but finance, so that when they have achieved that they will for the future, unless there were a violent overturn, succeed in shutting out the working classes from their present share in the government of this country. (Cheers.) . . .

I will tell you quite frankly what my position is and also what the position of the Government is. We stand for the supremacy of the House of Commons. (Loud and prolonged cheers.) That supremacy can only be secured by the abolition of the absolute veto of the House of Lords. (Renewed cheers.) Everything else in this great controversy, however important, I regard as essentially secondary, as essentially subsidiary and of less practical urgency. The supremacy of the House of Commons is and must remain the only position on which the Liberal party can fight this contest. (Cheers.) But I have also come to the conclusion that we cannot any longer agree to leave untouched the principle of hereditary legislators. We have derided it on every platform, we have denounced it in all our newspapers, we have exposed its absurdity and injustice with an unpitying zeal. At Southport, in my Lancashire pilgrimage (laughter), which I hope left some seed behind which sprang up into a harvest for the reaping (cheers), I remember asking this question—"Why should the heads of 500 or 600 families govern us, and why should their children govern our children?" I also took the pains to show that the position of an hereditary Sovereign is entirely different from that now claimed by an hereditary House of Lords. The Monarch is not a legislator. His Majesty reigns, but does not govern. He exercises no veto. He acts upon the advice of responsible Ministers. For these good reasons and their long observance British Sovereigns have come to occupy the strongest Throne in Europe. (Cheers.) But the hereditary peer legislates and vetoes with the utmost vigour. He acts upon no advice except what reaches him from the leaders of the Tory Party. A system whereby important and peculiar political privileges are to be transmitted from father to son, generation after generation, to the remote end of time, are to be enjoyed and exercised irrespective of the merits, the intelligence, or the character of the descendants, and utterly regardless of the wishes of their fellow-subjects, is in my judgment not a system which can be left untouched in any scheme of democratic policy. (Cheers.) I feel very strongly that while we continue to denounce it, and yet to leave it unaltered, we expose ourselves to taunts and suspicions which are injurious to the Liberal cause and are a stumbling block to many. (Cheers.) Further, the Conservative Party are now eagerly pretending that they have themselves abandoned the hereditary principle. Lord Lansdowne will lead his followers into the lobby of the House of Lords next week, nominally—let me say that again, "nominally" (laughter)—to vote against the hereditary principle. Scarcely a voice is raised on its behalf. Powerful sections of the Conservative Party are now engaged in, or pretending to be engaged in, cutting the House of Lords to ribbons. We cannot as a party stand outside the repudiation of hereditary and aristocratic privilege, which is the feature of the age and of the hour. (Cheers.) Still less can we stand by and watch inertly the attempt to replace hereditary privilege by other and more objectionable forms of securing Conservative predominance. We must proclaim true principles, we must make our policy conform to those principles, and we must back our words with our actions. (Cheers.) Let me use an argument which you will think it strange of me to use. I think the peers themselves would be benefited by being relieved of their political functions. If they have individual merit, be sure it will obtain a generous recognition. There is no hostility to the peers as peers. It is as hereditary legislators that they cannot be supported. Once they have taken their place on equal terms with the general life of their fellow-countrymen, once they have ceased to be employed to do the squalid work of the great vested interests, I believe they will become a respected and, on the whole, a deservedly popular class; and having, like the Crown, abandoned their Veto, they will repose with dignity and honour upon the good will and esteem of the nation. (Cheers.) . . .

All I will say is that it seems to me there will be three conditions which must attach to any Second Chamber that we could recognize. First, it would have to be democratic. It would have to be based upon the votes or associated with the voting strength of the great mass of the wage-earning population. (Cheers.) Secondly, it would have to be fair, by which I mean that all parties and all shades of opinion would have to have an equal chance. And thirdly, and most important of all, it must be subordinate to the House of Commons. (Cheers.) The undivided authority of the House of Commons over finance and its predominance in legislation must be established. They must be established not by convention, not by usage. You see how that has broken down. You saw it last year. You can see it this year if you follow what has happened on the London County Council, where, by an act of incredible violence and meanness, the Moderate party, which had gained a majority of a single vote, and thus a majority of a single seat, has grasped the whole of the aldermanic vacancies in defiance of precedent and custom, and in violation of the example set them in similar circumstances by their Liberal opponents. I say we cannot in these matters trust to usage and custom, we must have a law upon the Statute-book (cheers); and it is with that that I come back to the immediate question of the hour–the abolition of the absolute Veto of the House of Lords. (Cheers.) On Tuesday or Wednesday next we shall lay upon the table of the House of Commons our resolutions for dealing with the Veto. (Loud cheers.) They will, as the Prime Minister has said, be few and simple. They will deal with the financial Veto of the House of Lords, and they will deal with the legislative Veto. I do not think I can better describe or better commend these resolutions to you than by saying that they are the Campbell-Bannerman resolutions (loud cheers); they are the Campbell-Bannerman resolutions strengthened in one or two particulars by Mr. Asquith. (Cheers.) On the 29th of March, that is to say in ten days from now, the debate upon these resolutions will begin, and it will be carried uninterruptedly forward to its conclusion. If the resolutions pass the House of Commons, as I believe they will by a majority of considerably over a hundred (cheers)–either these resolutions or a Bill founded upon them–I purposely keep both alternatives open–will be introduced into the House of Lords without delay, and upon the treatment of those resolutions by the House of Lords the action of the Government and the fate of the Parliament will be immediately decided. (Cheers.) . . .

Now I have explained to you fully, and I hope you will say frankly (cheers), the situation as we see it. You made a splendid effort at the last election. Had others done as well the decision of that election would have been final on the great question in dispute. I deeply regret that a further struggle may be necessary. When we have exerted ourselves so much every one must feel a consciousness of exhaustion. When in war time that feeling of weariness comes upon the soldiers who are fighting, they ought always to remember that if they are wearied themselves, their enemy is more wearied still. At the moment when you are weak and strained and brought low, your foeman, if you only knew it, lies fainting on the ground. One step more, one effort more, and all the prizes you have fought for from dawn to dusk may be gained. In peace or in war victory consists in the last hour and in the last inch. (Cheers.) Let us, then, in true comradeship go forward together. Advance with courage, and the cause of the people shall prevail. (Loud cheers.) . . .

PARLIAMENTARY FRANCHISE (WOMEN) BILL

July 12, 1910

House of Commons

The Budget was passed by the Commons on April 27, and was accepted by the Lords without a vote. The fate of the Resolutions relating to the Lords' powers was still in the balance when, on May 6, King Edward VII died.

This unexpected event had immediate political consequences. King George V found himself confronted with a major constitutional crisis, and there was a general desire to honour what J. L. Garvin called "the truce of God." Throughout the summer there was an attempt to negotiate a settlement at a Constitutional Conference which opened on June 17. Churchill was not a member, but at this time he was briefly enamored of a proposal by Lloyd George for a national coalition. The Conference ended without agreement in November, and Asquith received a secret guarantee from the unhappy King for the creation of sufficient peers to pass the Resolutions if the Liberals won another election. The scene was accordingly set for the second General Election within a year, and in a mood of intense bitterness between the parties.

Meanwhile, the work of government continued.

In July, the Home Secretary incurred additional hostility. The Conciliation Committee on women's suffrage had produced the Parliamentary Franchise (Women) Bill which gave the vote to women who possessed a property qualification. Churchill's attitude was a deep disappointment to its sponsors. The Bill was put to a free vote, and was passed by a majority of over 100, but made no progress thereafter. The advocates of women's suffrage were even more venomous towards Churchill after this speech and subsequent events.

[Extract] I ask the indulgence of the House to allow me for a very short time, and in as few sentences as I can, to declare my own personal opinion upon the measure now before the House. It is, of course, a personal opinion. We are all talking here upon this matter as individuals and not for any Government or party. Sir, I cannot support this Bill. I do not want to roam into the abstract question of the relations between the sexes, their relative capacities and capabilities. I shall not go into that further than to say that I believe that there is a proportion of women capable of exercising the Parliamentary franchise, not merely for their own satisfaction, but to the public advantage, and I believe that that proportion of women is found in every class throughout the community. I believe the State would be the gainer if they had the vote, and if, in consequence of the vote, they had what I think myself follows from that—access in the fullest sense to all positions in our public life. I feel that the line of sex disqualification is not in accordance with obvious facts. I do not think it is necessary for the security of society. On the other hand, I think the grievance is greatly exaggerated. I think the great mass of women are not in any sensible degree losers by the disability under which they lie. It cannot be proved that they suffer any disadvantage in legislation. The Statute Book in fact leaves them a privileged class. The greatest measure of social reform and social benefaction which has ever passed from the point of view of expense to the State is the Old Age Pensions Act, passed by a man-made Parliament, who at the very least considered the cause of woman as fully as that of man. [Mr. Snowden at this point interjected a loud laugh.] There is much more of bitterness than of hilarity in that laughter. That is the only comment I will make upon it. The hon. and learned Gentleman the Member for the Walton Division (Mr. F. E. Smith) in a part of his speech dealt with the question as to whether the franchise would have any effect in helping women to raise their wages. I fully agree with him that the standard of wages for women would not be raised by the possession of the Parliamentary franchise. It would be raised by making economic conditions better, and I think by further trade unionism amongst women. I do not believe that the great mass of women want a vote. I think they have made singularly little use of the immense opportunities of local and municipal government which have been thrown open to them. Although there are numerous brilliant exceptions, these exceptions do not alter the actual fact. I confess I am not in the least convinced that the male electorate of the country is in favour of making a change, and I also see a grave danger in creating without great consideration a vast body of privileged and dependent voters, who might be manipulated and manoeuvred in this direction or that. . . .

May I say quite coolly what I think the grievance actually is. It is a twofold grievance. First of all, there are a number of women who take a very keen interest in politics. They belong, as my right hon. Friend the Secretary of State for War told us, to the different political organisations. They work with the utmost keenness and enthusiasm for the success of their various parties, and they are bitterly disappointed when they find that at the conclusion of all their labours those who have invoked their aid, as my right hon. Friend pointed out, suddenly turn round and say, "Your assistance is not now required; you are unfitted to exercise the franchise, although you are fitted to exercise every other function leading up to it." I think that is a grievance. It is a serious grievance. But there is a second grievance which is a more serious one, though it is purely sentimental. It is a grievance which deserves attention and respect. I mean that the denial of a recognised political status for the whole sex implies, and women think it implies, the slur of inferiority—a slur of inferiority, not to individuals, but to the entire race of women. I frankly say I should like to see that grievance redressed and that slur effectively removed. I believe that there are—I speak only for myself—only two ways in which the House will be able to redress that grievance. They can give the vote to some of the best women of all classes. That is the first way. Or they can give the vote to all women. I believe these are the only two ways in which that grievance can be redressed. First of all, you may give a vote to a comparatively small number of women of all classes by means of a series of special franchises—which, no doubt, will be disrespectfully called "fancy franchises"—franchises, that is to say, arising from considerations of property, arising from considerations of wage-earning capacity, or arising from considerations of education. You could give a vote to a comparatively small number of women on a series of special franchises which would be fairly balanced one against the other, so as not, on the whole, to give an undue advantage to the property vote against the wage-earning vote. That, I believe, could be done, and could only be done by agreement among all parties. I had always hoped that the conciliation committee would move forward on that road. That would not be giving votes to women on the same terms as men; neither does this Bill. That would not be a democratic proposal, but, at any rate, it would not be anti-democratic as this Bill is. It would not provide protection for the weakest and feeblest among women. It would provide for the representation of the sex through the strongest, most capable, and most responsible women of every class, and that would meet the main grievance in my humble judgment. I have urged the friends of this movement in the House not to close their minds altogether to some attempt to advance along that path. Apart from that method, which I quite recognise is not likely to excite any enthusiasm, there is only one other, in my judgment, that is worthy of consideration, and that is a broad measure of adult suffrage, or practically adult suffrage, by which every person should have a vote over the age of twenty-five years. . . .

I thank the House very much for the great kindness with which they have listened to me. I have said nothing but what I absolutely think and feel on the subject. In my judgment the Member who can honestly say, "I want this Bill passed into law this Session, regardless of all other consequences. I want it as it is, and I want it now. I want it sent to the House of Lords. I am prepared to fight the House of Lords if they reject it, as they very likely would"—the man who is prepared to say all that, who can think it honestly and sincerely, is fully justified in voting for the Second Reading of this Bill. I am not such a Member, and as it would be cowardly of me to seek immunity by abstaining from the Second Reading of this Bill, as it would be cowardly to allow burdens to be borne by others, I shall, after long reflection, and without any doubt whatever, give my vote this evening for the rejection of this measure on the Second Reading.

SOUTH WALES COAL STRIKE

November 15, 1910

House of Commons

Serious industrial tensions arose in 1910 and 1911 while Churchill was at the Home Office and in which, as the Minister responsible for the maintenance of public order, he was directly involved. The first was the strike at Newport Docks, which stemmed from a loading dispute. When the employers brought in other workers they were resisted by the dockers, and there were reports of violence and looting. At the urgent request of the local authorities, police reinforcements were authorised by Churchill, and at one stage a request for troops was sent to the Home Office. Fortunately the dispute ended before this was necessary, but it was an ominous episode.

Early in November a major industrial crisis arose in the Rhondda coal mines. Some 30,000 men were involved, and there were reports of looting and violence. The local authorities appealed for troops, but Churchill decided to send police, with troops held in reserve. Order was restored, but the canard *that Churchill had sent soldiers to shoot down the miners of Tonypandy–one of the towns involved–although totally untrue, became part of the folklore of the trade union movement. It was significant, as Mr. Randolph Churchill has pointed out (*Winston S. Churchill, *II, 362-4), that Churchill was attacked in the* Times *for not sending troops to South Wales, and applauded by the* Manchester Guardian *for his decision. Mr. Randolph Churchill failed to mention that soldiers, under the command of General Macready, were subsequently sent into the area. They were few in number, but their presence certainly exacerbated the situation. Churchill's speech of November 24 dealt with the accusations against the police and the soldiers and himself.*

[Extract] . . . It is quite true that the Central Government has intervened in this matter more prominently and more directly than is usual in these disputes, and than I think would as a general rule be desirable. But what has been the nature of my intervention? The hon. Gentleman has told us there was no need for the military. The justices upon the spot summoned the military, and they were sent from the Southern Command in response to the summons of the justices on the spot, without any reference being made to the Home Office at all. When this was brought to my notice I, in consultation with my right hon. Friend the Secretary of State for War (Mr. Haldane), and in full concurrence with his wishes, took the responsibility–I am here to accept it to the full–of arresting the movement of the troops and of going out of the ordinary practice to such a point that I prepared with the utmost rapidity a powerful contingent of Metropolitan Police to set off to the scene of the disorders, and they arrived on the evening of the day when notice was first given of serious disturbances. The policy which I have pursued in this matter has been to avoid, at considerable risk, the danger of a collision between the military and an excited mob. My desire has been that the police should handle the crowds.

In the police you have a force which should be involved in the maintenance of order, while as to the military, in so far as they are brought on the scene at all, they should be in reserve, and they should not be brought into contact with the strikers until or unless the situation had become so serious that it was quite clear police methods could no longer be of any avail. That is the policy which I have ventured to follow, and it is a policy which I should hope it may be possible often to follow in the future. It no doubt has involved a certain departure from the usual course in these matters. It has involved the quite unusual though not in any way illegal step of sending as many as 850 constables from the large police force of the Metropolis down to South Wales. You have that policy, and if that policy, with all its unusual aspect, should be the means of carrying us through this period of severe and dangerous tension without any collision between the troops and the people it will be a policy which will, I venture to say, well repay any extra expense it may have entailed, and any risks which may have been run by those responsible for it. That policy will have to continue while the present state of tension is maintained. The police will be there to maintain order. They will secure for the strikers all their rights under the legislation which Parliament has passed. They will be impartial in all questions as between capital and labour, and they will guard property, especially property precious to the livelihood of the people in those valleys. They will maintain order effectively where order is disturbed. It is only in the most improbable event of this strong force of police not being able to cope with these disturbances, which I fully admit have been grossly exaggerated by the sensational Press, it is only in that most improbable event that the Military will be called upon to take any direct part in dealing with the disturbances. I look forward, with my hon. Friend, the Member for the Rhondda Valley to the cessation, on fair and honourable terms, of that labour warfare which has distracted this beatufiul valley. I look forward earnestly to the re-establishment of order, not only by the consent but at the wish and by the agency and co-operation of the mining population as a whole. In that way, more effectively than by any inquiry, it will be possible to clear and maintain the honour of the Welsh mining population, whose virtues, on both sides of the House, are the subject of admiration.

"A HOUSE OF SWELLS"

November 28, 1910

Lambeth Baths, London

The "Truce of God," having failed to reach a solution to the constitutional crisis, Parliament was dissolved on November 28, and the nation faced its second General Election of the year. In his election address Churchill had struck an aggressive note, describing the Unionists as regarding themselves "as the ruling caste, exercising by right a Divine superior authority over the whole nation," and claiming on November 14 that they had frustrated the Constitutional Conference.

Although he did not speak as often as in the first campaign, his speeches demonstrated that he had not taken the criticisms of his speeches during the first 1910 General Election too seriously.

[Extract] It is always a sad thing when an old institution which has done business for a long time is putting its shutters up. (Laughter.) When we see a long string of people with demand notes in their hands blocking the pavement, and when we know that inside the building there is very little that is going to satisfy anybody—[A voice: "Certainly not the women, Sir." He was ejected after much confusion and shouting.] I regret that we should be forced to take violent measures against any person who comes to this hall, but we have the right to fair play. (Cheers.) We have a most valuable right, that democracy should be able to conduct its public gatherings with decency and order. If those persons who have come treacherously among us to disturb our meeting with deliberate intent—probably paid for their services—choose to interrupt large public gatherings, that is an insult not to the speaker, but to the audience. These systematic, deliberate, cold, calculated, money-fed attempts to break up meeting after meeting are to rob the masses of the people of the essential safeguards of free government. I am told that individuals are to be singled out for villainous assaults. If that is so there is only one word for it, and that is "come on." (Loud cheers.) If a public man were to allow his course to be altered by mere threats of personal violence he would be unworthy of the slightest respect or confidence.

It is a melancholy thing when an old institution goes bankrupt, and what could be more patent at the present moment than the bankruptcy of the Tory Party? They have got no leaders. I do not mean that they have not got any people who stand up and call themselves leaders (laughter), but they have nobody who can show them the way. Mr. Balfour is an amiable dilettante philosopher who is content to brood serenely, sedately, over the perversity of a world which he longer attempts to influence. Mr. Austen Chamberlain is a very admirable and honourable young gentleman, but, after all, with all his faults, I would rather have old Joe. (Laughter and cheers.) I would rather always have the principal than the understudy. (Cheers.) I would always rather have the man himself than the wooden effigy, or a doll, even though he is made up to look the part and has learnt by heart to speak the same patter. (Laughter.) Then there is Mr. F. E. Smith. Mr. Smith is a man of excessive sensibility. (Laughter, and a voice: "Expert on offal.") He would have played a very effective part in this election but for one fact. At the outset he was terribly shocked by the wicked language of Mr. Lloyd George, because it revealed to him heights to which he was confident he could never attain. And he has been running about ever since endeavouring to say things which he believes will be as effective for his party as the things Mr. Lloyd George says are undoubtedly effective for the Radical Party (cheers)–but with this difference–that whereas Mr. Lloyd George is invariably witty, Mr. F. E. Smith is invariably vulgar. So much for their leaders. I do not think these will work out at more than about six and a half pence in the pound.

What of their policy? The Tory Party has no policy on any of the great contested questions of the day. The Tory Party talks prettily about temperance, but they do not want to do anything to reduce the turnover and the output of their brewery friends. They have called the land taxes "robbery," "Socialism," and every other epithet which their extremely limited vocabulary allows. (Laughter.) Yet there is not a Tory candidate standing for any democratic seat who dares say that if returned to power he will repeal the land taxes. The Tory policy in regard to Ireland can be expressed in the words "insult and coercion." Into their dark minds no idea of social organisation has ever penetrated. I defy any Tory to mention a single original idea which that party has put forward for the solution of our social evils. Oh, I have forgotten Tariff Reform. (A voice: "Leave the poor old corpse alone.") At the last election the Tory Party had one policy, and, it being the only one, they made it go a long way. Like Homocea, it touched the spot. There was nothing that they could not achieve for the working classes through the agency of Tariff Reform. They said that work will do itself. (Laughter.) Every man in moderate circumstances would become a millionaire just like the Germans. All the German workmen are millionaires. It is a great mistake to think that they eat black bread and horse flesh and that they do not like it. No, it is their taste. If they liked they could live entirely on truffles and quails, but they like horse flesh. Tariff Reform would mean work for all. Mr. Balfour did not say that, but left it to Mr. F. E. Smith and the lower class of Tariff Reform orators. (Laughter.)

I wish to say a word about the Labour Exchanges. They have only just begun; they have only been working nine months. (A voice: "Nine months too long.") In that time they have found situations for nearly two hundred thousand people. There are nine thousand people a week now placed in situations by the exchanges. The Labour Exchanges will survive the diseases of infancy and here, as in Germany, they will become an essential element in the effective social organization of labour.

. . . Why should we not do for Ireland what we have done for South Africa? It is the greatest prize within the reach of the British people, a good settlement and understanding with the Irish people, carrying with it, as it does, a far greater chance of imperial unity and international peace. There can be no peace, there can be no progress, until the veto of the House of Lords is smashed to pieces. We can do it if we try now, but we may never be able to do it again. Our opponents hope to construct a new house on the ruins of the old House of Lords, on a narrow franchise, which will be a house quite removed from popular influence—a house whose members will not have to present themselves before the constituencies, a house of superior persons, a house of Lord Curzons and Lord Milners, a house of swells, who are removed from ordinary methods of control. That is the very real danger, and the chance is in our hands to save the situation. (Cheers.)

ELECTION ADDRESS

November 30, 1910

Drill Hall, Sheffield

We have got them on the run. (Laughter and cheers, and a voice, "We must keep them running.") Nothing is more astonishing in this wonderful election than the panic fear which has overtaken the once proud and powerful Tory party. They have found themselves unable at any point to make headway in argument against the Liberal or Radical attack. Not a day passes but some new dodge or double, some new twist or turn or subterfuge is presented to us in order that the Conservative leaders may escape from the extremely simple issues of this election. Not a day passes but some ancient principle to which the Tory party has long been attached is cast aside or refuted by one or other of their many leaders. (Laughter.) Only a year ago today the House of Lords rejected the Budget. Only a year ago tonight the patriotic, fearless, impartial backwoodsmen—(laughter)—were summoned from their sylvan retreats—(laughter)—at the imperious call of the Tory Whip to stand between the nation and a Socialist scheme that would ruin our trade and shock our Empire, and go far to destroy the fabric of British society. (A voice: "And you will ruin the women if you don't give them votes.") [Editor's Note: The interruption was met with loud cries of "Out him," and the interrupter was promptly ejected.]

In all the long centuries during which the House of Lords has endured and been endured–(laughter)–never have they aspired to so predominant and overriding a position as they took up only a year ago tonight. That was their culminating point twelve months ago–twelve short months ago. Ah! but a year has gone, and with it a more or less silent irresistible revolution has been in progress. (A voice: "That is votes for women.") I say that during the year public opinion, all pervading, formidable, remorseless, has been at work, and now what a continued amount of tergiversation we witness on every hand. The Budget which was to be the end of family, faith, monarchy, Empire, the Budget rejected so haughtily last year, has been swallowed, and it is on the Statute-book. (Cheers.) No evil consequences have followed therefrom. On the contrary, we have had improved trade–(cheers),–reviving employment, and overflowing revenue–(cheers),–while every other nation in Europe has been forced to borrow. The Budget, I say, which they rejected last year has now been definitely placed upon the Statute-book of our country. (Loud cheers.) The hereditary principle, on which Lord Curzon stumped Lancashire–(laughter)–with such disastrous results–(cheers),–the hereditary principle has been cast bodily away. The faithful Backwoodsmen–hard, indeed, is their fate! These faithful heroes–(laughter)–who obeyed the call of duty one short year ago, who were told by the Conservative party that they were saving the country, are now to be calmly excluded by their own Conservative friends from any share in the government of their own country. (Laughter.)

Where now is Tariff "Reform"? (Hear, hear.) Only a year ago it was going to unite the Empire, to cure unemployment, to make all work done automatically, and to enable all our taxation to be paid by the happy and obliging intervention of the foreigner. (Laughter.) Only a year ago! But what now do we find but dismal and disingenuous apologetics in the mouths of the advocates of Tariff "Reform"? (Applause.) Their faith is weak, their leaders are doubting in their allegiance. The march of events all over the world and, I think I may say also, the march of the human intellect–(applause)–have robbed the Tariff Reform League of its old glamour, and its principle representatives can only gibber. (Laughter.) As for Mr. Bonar Law–(loud laughter),–the great champion of Tariff "Reform," who went to Manchester to convert Lancashire to food taxes, what shall we say of him? I will tell you one result of his campaign, it will entitle him to a very high reward. (Laughter.) It will entitle him to the £10,000 prize offered by the "Daily Mail"–(laughter)–for the man who makes the record flight. (Loud laughter.)

Are these not good times for those who are Free-traders and for those who stand for the abolition of the veto of the House of Lords? What do all these ignominious retreats, surrenders, and evacuations mean. They mean one thing. Our opponents know well in their hearts what all these manoeuvres portend. They are wrong, they know they are wrong and they know that you know they are wrong. (Cheers.) The inconsistencies of their action betray the uncertainty of their mind. Last year they told us that the wild peers were right to reject the Budget. Why, then, do they propose to punish them now? (Laughter.) Last year they told us that the power of the House of Lords over finance was essential to good government. Why, then, do they now profess–I say profess–to abandon that idea throughout? In February of the present year they told us that the election had proved that the nation was against the Budget. In March they proclaimed that the Budget had only passed the House of Commons as a result of an intrigue with the Irish. Why, then, if the Budget was not passed without an intrigue with the Irish did not the Lords reject it a second time? Only a year ago they were telling us that the land taxes would sap the commercial prosperity of the country; yet today, only a year afterwards, there are very few candidates–none of any consequence or importance–who aspire to a democratic constituency, who will stand up and dare to say they are in favour of the repeal of those taxes. (Cheers.) For seventeen out of the last twenty-five years the Tory party has enjoyed power, and in all that long period they have never shown any inclination to reform or remodel the House of Lords. During the last five years, when they have been in Opposition they have shown even less desire. They have taken no step in that direction. On the contrary we have seen them push their claims higher year by year. Why then are we to pay any serious attention to these frantic efforts to retain or to reform at the last moment? Why then are we to allow our steady and sustained policy to be deflected by one hair's-breadth from its course by those futile efforts to evade the issue? Only a month ago the young bloods in the Conservative party–(laughter)–were clamouring for an election. They told us they must have an election in order that the Tory Government should be in power when the next Imperial Conference is held in May, in order that our colonies may be told that the Conservative party is ready to purchase their loyalty by taxing the food of the poor. Well, now they have got their general election, now the armies are in battle, now the Ironsides of Sheffield are on the march, now the powerful forces of a united democracy are advanced upon them. And what do we say? They try to make us believe that Tariff "Reform" is not an issue at this election. They try to make us believe that Imperial Preference would not be offered to the colonies next May if a Tory Government were returned to power. Why, gentlemen, do these shifts deceive anyone? What a ridiculous and pitiful spectacle is the rout of a great political party! General Scuttle is in command–(laughter),–frantic appeals for quarter and for mercy rend the air, the white flag is hung out over the Tory clubs, over many noble residences and many a public-house.–(Laughter.) Arms, colours, baggage, and ammunition are all scattered behind a long line of flight.

England has never witnessed such a spectacle since the days of Naseby and Marston Moor. And in the complex confusion at the head of the rout what do we discern? In the very forefront of the retreat gleams the white feather of their leader, the leader who, as I heard him say in this very building some seven years ago, "means to lead."–(Laughter.) The leader who means to lead the flight.–(Laughter.) Mr. Balfour, like Charley's Aunt–(laughter),–is still running.–(Laughter.) Indeed, this is the first really strong and decided guidance he has ever given about anything–(laughter)–since that memorable night when on this platform seven years ago he executed what I have always presumed to call the Sheffield shuffle.–(Laughter.) Well, we have got them on the run, and what we have to do is to keep them on it.–(Cheers.) We are not going to have them coming forward and saying, "We are wrong. We admit it. Vote for us." We are not going to allow their attempt to abandon every position on which they have fought, or their pretences to abandon those positions, to avert for one moment the fruition, the long fruition of the solid and sober aims which the Liberal and Radical party set before themselves and the country.–(Cheers.) We will give no quarter to the food-taxers or veto-mongers. Out with the lot.–(Cheers.) End them, not Referendum.–(Loud cheers.)

SOUTH WALES COAL STRIKE

February 7, 1911

House of Commons

Destruction of property and continued violence in the South Wales minefields exposed Churchill to Opposition criticism for not bringing in troops quickly enough and attacks from the Labour Party for excessive use of force by the police. Balfour, opening the Debate on the Address when the new Parliament met on February 6, was particularly scathing. Churchill defended his actions ably but intense bitterness against him in Wales proved enduring.

[Extract] . . . I have only two more observations to make. First of all, I entirely agree with what was said by the right hon. Member for Rhondda that the rioters of Tonypandy did not represent the mining population of South Wales. The mining population of South Wales are, as the House knows, a well-educated, peaceable, intelligent and law-abiding class of men, and have often, I may express the personal opinion here, been very hardly tried in more ways than one during these troubles, for which, in my judgment, they are not the only people to blame. In my opinion the riots were largely caused by rowdy youth and roughs from outside, foreign to the district, and I think it only just to place that on record in fairness to the miners of South Wales, who have been attacked in a general way by people who know nothing at all about the matter. Local authorities and private employers are very ready sometimes, and from insufficient cause, to call for troops. Troops cost them nothing, police cost money to the local authorities; and there is a very general disposition in some quarters to suppose that the whole British Army is always to be available, irrespective of the circumstances, upon the demand of any local authority. The local authority sends for troops, and they think that troops should always be sent, very often not thinking of the effect of military weapons or the difficulty which surrounds military action. Law and order must be preserved, but I am confident that the House will agree with me that it is a great object of public policy to avoid a collision between soldiers and crowds of persons engaged in industrial disputes. All such collisions attended, as they must be, by loss of life and by the use of firearms, do great harm to the Army, which is a volunteer Army, and whose relation with the civil forces of the country must be carefully safeguarded, and they also cause feuds and resentments which last for a generation. For soldiers to fire on the people would be a catastrophe in our national life. Alone among the nations, or almost alone, we have avoided for a great many years that melancholy and unnatural experience.

CREATION OF THE PEERS

August 7, 1911

House of Commons

The Parliament Bill, which abolished the Lords' veto and replaced it with a delaying power of three years, occupied much of Churchill's attention in the summer of 1911, in addition to his work as an exceptionally active Home Secretary. In an atmosphere of acute political bitterness, the battle was joined in the House of Lords. The Unionist Peers divided sharply between those who were prepared to "die in the last ditch" to save the old House of Lords, and those who–fearful of the creation of some 500 new Liberal Peers–were prepared to accept the Parliament Bill as the lesser evil. The bitterness between the "Ditchers" and the "Hedgers" became intense, and was used in the Commons to undermine Balfour's already precarious leadership.

[Extract] . . . Why should we shrink from the creation of 400 or 500 Peers? At any rate, that is one way of arriving at an impartial Second Chamber evenly balanced in which Liberal legislation will have some chance. At any rate, it is one way of putting the House of Lords in touch with the real feelings and forces of all classes and all parties in the country. And although an assembly of 1200 Peers may seem somewhat unwieldy it might form a very convenient panel from which a smaller body might be chosen to carry on the business of the country. In fact, all we want is the smooth working of the Parliament Bill. The Noble Lord whose excitement is always pleasurable to witness will admit–[Hon. Members: "Redmond."] The decision rests with the House of Lords. [Hon. Members: "Redmond."] How can the decision of the House of Lords next Wednesday rest with Redmond? Has the hon. and learned Member for Waterford been tampering with the Die-hards? The decision does not rest with us. I have here a letter written by the right hon. Gentleman the senior Member for Oxford University a few days ago to "The Times." In it he says:–

> And in all this talk of the ignominy of surrender what has become of the doctrine that the House of Lords has never failed to acquiesce in the decision of the electorate clearly expressed. We may say that the last general election was a snap vote, taken before the people had time to understand the issue; but I doubt if there are many Unionists who think that a general election this month or next would appreciably alter the position of the House of Commons, and if we believe that the electors would now return a majority in favour of the Bill the Lords will only follow the course adopted by the Duke of Wellington, by Lord Cairns, and by Lord Salisbury, if they accept, however reluctantly, the verdict of the nation as it is now represented.

But why were those words not spoken before? That is a question which we have a right to ask. Why were they not spoken by those higher in the party councils than the right hon. Gentleman (Sir W. Anson)? Why were they not spoken by the leader of the party, who is more versed in Parliamentary public business than any other man in the House of Commons, and who yet tells us that he thinks that the announcements of the last few days have fallen on him with a shock of surprise? Leaders who lead their party from day to day by doing the popular thing, by staving off difficulties, and by withholding their true counsel until it is too late, cannot complain if, when disaster culminating in catastrophe is reached, some of their followers are reluctant to share in the odium of capitulation, however necessary, however inevitable. There are no grounds for this Vote of Censure. The object we have in view, the measure which we put forward, is one of moderation. We have tried to the best of our ability to be guided by constitutional interests. The remedy which we apply is one approved by precedent and by every constitutional authority. We have not invoked it except upon absolute justification. It is a remedy which we think is not only efficacious for its purpose in any case, but actually beneficial in itself. You censure us because you say we are going to pass Home Rule in this Parliament. So we are. Let the Opposition search the British Empire, let them go to any Parliament in any Dominion, any Province, or State. Let them go to any Parliament in the whole world where the English language is spoken, and they will find that the grant of Home Rule to Ireland will be applauded as a wise measure. Censure us then if you will, by all means, for that. Censure us for that if you have the power. You have not the power. We repel your censures to-night, and we are sure that this censure will be even more decisively repudiated before these matters have passed from action into history.

LABOUR DISPUTES AND EMPLOYMENT OF THE MILITARY

August 22, 1911

House of Commons

The long struggle over the Parliament Bill now reached its climax. The Government refused to accept the majority of the amendments proposed by the Lords, and stuck firmly to their position. After intense negotiations and compelling pressures, the Lords accepted the situation by 131 votes to 114.

The passage of the Parliament Bill was not the only dramatic event of the summer of 1911. The combination of strikes by dockers and railwaymen created a crisis situation by August; as the problems increased the Home Secretary was inevitably involved.

By this time nerves were so strained that the King telegraphed Churchill that "accounts from Liverpool show that the situation there [is] more like revolution than a strike." The Lord Mayor of Liverpool and Mayor of Birkenhead joined to ask that a warship be sent to the Mersey. Initially, Churchill opposed the use of troops, as he had previously in the South Wales dispute, but by the middle of August the situation was so threatening that he changed this policy.

On August 18, the railwaymen refused Asquith's offer of a Royal Commission and a national railway strike was ordered. Appeals for troops continued to reach the Home Office, and Churchill authorised their deployment at the discretion of the commanders of the military areas.

The use of troops to settle the labour unrest aroused intense bitterness in the Liberal and Labour ranks, and Churchill was vigorously attacked for his actions. In particular, he was accused of over-reacting to an industrial conflict–an accusation which is given some justification by the tone of this speech.

The railway strike was called off after the intervention of Lloyd George, and the matter would have passed into political limbo but for the intervention of the troops. The only actual fatalities caused by the firing were at Llanelly where four people were killed, and this incident further increased the resentment in the Labour movement against Churchill which was to be enduring. It also revived doubts about his judgment in this crisis among his colleagues.

[Extract] . . . Let me point out to the House at the very outset that no illegal or extra constitutional action of any kind has been taken. The law has been absolutely observed in all the measures for which the Government is responsible. All we have done is to make exceptional use of obvious and well-known legal powers, and that exceptional use we submit the emergency fully justified. Let the House consider what that emergency was. We were confronted with the National Railway Strike. That is a thing which has never occurred before in this country. At twenty-four hours' notice the railways of the country were to be brought to complete paralysis and rest. I am not going to animadvert on the conduct of either side in this dispute, I am only concerned with the actual fact, which was that we were threatened with a stoppage of all railway transit on twenty-four hours' notice. England, I think it is true to say, more than any other country in the world is dependent upon railways and open ports. It is true that all parts of England are not equally dependent upon railways and ports. In the Home counties, in the south and in the east, where agriculture has not fallen so far behind manufacture, the dependence upon railways and oversea importations is not so pronounced; but in the great manufacturing areas of England, in South Wales, on the North-East coast, and, above all, in Lancashire, Yorkshire and the North Midlands, there is an absolute dependence on railways and open ports for the whole means of industry and daily food. It was in these areas that the strike developed most effectively. Just in those very parts of the country which literally cannot exist without railways, there it was that the largest proportion of the skilled, indispensable railway servants came out on strike and the difficulty of maintaining the railway service was greatest. In fact, the danger was at its worst where the consequences would have been the most fatal.

It is not in the agricultural regions to the south, where so many of the wealthy people live, that the pressure was brought to bear. The southern lines worked smoothly; the Continental services were scarcely interrupted. Motor cars rendered the well-to-do citizens practically independent of the railways. The agriculture of the southern counties and of the county districts can easily sustain their own population, at any rate for a time. There is no special need there for the daily importation of raw material to keep the industries going. Food prices would not have risen over large parts of the country, even if the railway strike had been protracted; and even if they had risen they would only have risen to a point which would have injured the poor, and of which the rich would scarcely have been conscious. No, it was in those very parts where immense populations of working people are concentrated together, who have come into existence as communities entirely by reason of the railways and overseas transport, that the pressure of a national railway strike would be, and had actually begun to be, powerfully exerted. And what a pressure! Had the strike proceeded for a week on the lines which its authors apparently intended–that is to say, had it succeeded for a week in producing an entire stoppage of trains in those parts–there must have been practically a total cessation of industry. Everyone would have been thrown out of work. Every mill, every mine, every factory must have been closed. The wages for the household would have ceased. Had the stoppage continued for a fortnight, it is, I think, almost certain that in a great many places to a total lack of employment would have been added absolute starvation.

I have a right to ask the House to look at the emergency with which we were faced, and which alone would justify the strong and unusual measures which we thought it necessary to take. Let the House realise it. In that great quadrilateral of industrialism, from Liverpool and Manchester on the West to Hull and Grimsby on the East, from Newcastle down to Birmingham and Coventry in the south–in that great quadrilateral which, I suppose, must contain anything between 15 to 20 millions of persons, intelligent, hard-working people, who have raised our industry to the forefront of the world's affairs–it is practically certain that a continuance of the railway strike would have produced a swift and certain degeneration of all the means, of all the structure, social and economic, on which the life of the people depends. If it had not been interrupted it would have hurled the whole of that great community into an abyss of horror which no man can dare to contemplate. Let me remind the House that at this time, before the railway strike began, we had had a prolonged interruption of the entry of food supplies from Liverpool and Manchester; the ports on the other side were closed by the railway dispute, and the lines from north to south were being cut off. I am sure the House will see that no blockade by a foreign enemy could have been anything like so effecting in producing terrible pressure on these vast populations as the effective closing of those great ports, coupled with the paralysis of the railway service. Meanwhile the populations of the south, the east, and the west, of this island would have remained comparatively unaffected by what was going on–not suffering themselves, and yet almost helpless to come to the aid of their fellow countrymen.

The hon. Member (Mr. Ramsay MacDonald) spoke of mediaeval methods. This is a new peril. I do not know whether in the history of the world a similar catastrophe can be shown to have menaced an equally great community. I remember a gentleman who had returned from the East telling me of the breaking of the great Nimrod Dam of the Euphrates in the fifteenth century. It had been built in times of antiquity, but had been neglected by the ignorant conquerors of the country. In the fifteenth century it broke, and there were no means of repairing it. Above the Dam there was a great canal running 300 or 400 miles, and along the banks of that canal four or five million persons lived in a fertile province. Immediately the Dam broke the water flowed out of the canal, and, though history gives no details, it is certain that that enormous population who lived by that artificial means, except for a few thousands who lived on pools by the canal or found their way across the desert, were absolutely wiped from the book of human life. These are the considerations which it is no exaggeration to say have to be borne in mind at this present juncture. Peace is restored. Thank God for it. The danger is removed. But last Friday and Saturday this sort of consideration began to stare in the face the people who were responsible. Of course, hon. Gentlemen below the Gangway will say that it could never have happened. I agree. But why could it never have happened? What was it that could have prevented it? Not, assuredly, the people who were picketing the stations.

Mr. Wardle: Nor the soldiers either.

Mr. Churchill: Not, assuredly, the people who threw stones at the trains and cut signal wires. No, it would have been prevented because it was obvious and certain that any Government must, with the whole forces of the State, exert itself to prevent such a catastrophe, and because it was certain that in taking such action they would be supported by the good sense and resolution of the whole mass of the people. That was the emergency, and to avert such an emergency all useful and lawful measures must, if necessary, be employed by the Government. The railway must be kept running at all costs for the food supply. All other considerations, however important, fade into insignificance beside this paramount necessity. No Government could possibly sit still with folded hands and say, "A trade dispute is going on. We must remain absolutely impartial. We cannot possibly take any action which will have the effect of helping one side or the other." Both sides, employers and railway men, possessed the means to continue the dispute for a period far greater than the rest of the country could have lasted out without this frightful disaster to which I have referred. I say that no Minister, even the hon. Member for Leicester himself, if he sat on this Bench, would have hesitated to use the whole power of the State and direct the whole forces of the community to maintaining the vital service of the food supply and the scarcely less vital service of transport of the goods indispensable to the industrial production. The steps we took were, I admit, exceptional and of great extent. But they were nothing to the measures which would have had to be adopted promptly and without hesitation had the dispute continued and the scale of events become more tremendous. Employment, wages, food and the lives of many millions of people were threatened and at stake. Personal, political, and party considerations could not count for a moment. It was not a question of taking sides with capital against labour, or with the companies against their employés. We took sides only with the public. We could not look on impartially and allow their vital interests to be affected. We became, and must always become in such circumstances, active partisans of the food supply.

I was criticised very severely at the beginning of the year for trying to deal with the difficulties and troubles on the South Wales coal field without using the military forces. I think the House will admit that on that occasion, at any rate, I strained every effort in my power, ran considerable risk, and put the country to considerable expense, to try to substitute other means of maintaining order for the employment of the military forces. I can assure the House that the feelings with which I acted then have never departed from my mind. But Tonypandy was a small affair and produced no great national reaction, and when that took place we had other resources available. I had it within my power—by a very unusual step, I admit—to send a thousand, or, if necessary, two thousand Metropolitan Police to South Wales to stand between the people and the troops, and to put off the employment of the military to the last minute. But on this occasion, with the whole country in a state of disturbance, with disorder actually breaking out in scores of places, the Metropolitan Police would have been totally inadequate to render any assistance to the local forces. Even if they had been adequate, not one single man could be spared from his duty in the Metropolis. I recognise and wish to recognise, because my reports from many quarters confirm it, that the railway men throughout the country did not share in the discredit and disgrace of some persons for the riotous and disorderly scenes which have lately been enacted. Military officers and police constables alike send in their reports, and state in a great many of them that the railway men, while continuing their dispute, have been all for peace and order throughout. It is my duty in having to say some things which are not pleasant to put that also on record, in order that a self-respecting and respectable class may not be branded with the discredit in which the action of rowdies and roughs, and also of perfectly thoughtless and foolish people, might easily have involved them.

But when I have said that, it is quite idle for anyone to pretend that the strike was conducted peacefully and without violence. Even in the forty-eight hours which it lasted serious riots occurred in four or five places, and minor riots in twenty or more places. There were six or more attacks on railway stations, and a very great many on signal-boxes all along the line. I need not enlarge on the peril of driving people out of the signal-boxes at a time when even a few trains were running. There were nine attempts to damage the permanent way, of which we have a record at present, or to wreck trains, or to tamper with points. There were a great number of cases, almost innumerable in fact, of attempts to stop trains, and to stone them. I do not suppose the people of this country realise that these are a class of offences that the law says are punishable with penal servitude, up to penal servitude for life. There were many cases of telegraph and signal wires being cut. There were in several places gross instances of incendiarism, and in two cases in South Wales, at any rate, of wholesale loot by persons previously of good record. That is an amazing feature in the recent disturbances. I was told that at Tredegar there had been a case of anti-Semitism; and, quite peculiar and quite unknown in this country before, persons hitherto respectable were seen going home with bundles of clothes which they had taken from shops and which they were taking away as if they were not in the least ashamed of what they had done.

I say that with that sort of disturbance going on all over the country, accompanied as it was by dangerous violence in many places, it is certain that if the local police only had been available, as the hon. Gentleman the Member for Leicester suggests ought to have been the case—the local police, sometimes not more than thirty or forty men in a large town with a great population of many thousands and crowds in the streets—then there would have been an immediate and absolute stoppage of the railways, accompanied in many centres by bloody riots, loss of life, and wholesale destruction of property. Not only would this have been the railway companies' property, but the property of small persons, in many cases quite unconnected with the quarrel between the railway men and their employers. To prevent this it was necessary to use the military forces of the Crown with the utmost promptitude. Let me say that when a task is entrusted to bodies of soldiers they must be left to carry that task out under their officers in accordance with the instructions given to them by the civil power. The task which was entrusted to the military forces was to keep the railways running, to safeguard the railways, to protect the railway men who were at work, to keep the railways running for the transport of food supplies and raw material. And it was necessary, if they were to discharge that task, that the general commanding each area into which the country is divided, the general responsible for each of the different strike areas, should have full liberty to send troops to any point on the line so that communication should not be interrupted. That is how it arose, of course, that on Saturday the soldiers arrived at places to protect railway stations, signal-boxes, goods yards, and other points on the line without their having been requisitioned by the local authorities. There is nothing against the law in that. Let no man imagine that there is. . . .

The policy which we have pursued throughout was wherever soldiers were sent to send plenty, so that there could be no mistake about the obvious ability of the authorities to maintain order, and so that the soldiers themselves could be in sufficient force to do what was necessary without taking advantage of the terrible weapons which modern science had placed in their hands. That decision has been taken with a view to the prevention of loss of life. I believe that it has achieved the results which we had in view. Some loss of life has, unhappily, occurred. In what the hon. Gentleman the Member for Leicester calls "the reckless employment of force," about twenty shots, carefully counted, have been fired with serious intent. Four or five persons have been killed by the military. The House sees these instances chronicled everywhere to-day. Their painful effect is fresh in our minds. What is not seen, what cannot be measured, is how many lives were saved and how many tragedies and sufferings were averted—that can never be known! But there are some things which indicate how great are the benefits which have been derived from the maintenance of order by the military forces. We know that people die from many causes. The death-rate in Liverpool has doubled during the course of these troubles. It is a death-rate which has not fallen upon those who live in the Toxteth district. It is contributed by the working-class children, who have suffered in the course of these disputes, and who would have suffered if the evils of the cessation of industry and of the stoppage of food supplies had been added to those of anarchy and riot.

The House should remember that the Llanelly rioters, left to themselves, with no intrusion of the police, and no assistance from the military for some hours, in a few streets of the town during the evening wrought in their drunken frenzy more havoc to life and limb, shed more blood, produced more serious injury among themselves, than all the 50,000 soldiers who have been employed on strike duty all over the country during the last few days. That is the answer which I make to the criticisms and the attacks of the hon. Gentleman the Member for Leicester. I say on behalf of the Government that we will cheerfully, confidently, face any reproaches, attacks or calumniations which anger may create, or malice may keep alive, because, as trustees for the people, responsible for their welfare and for their safety, thinking only of that and of their vital needs, we tried to do our duty.

FOREIGN AND DOMESTIC POLICY

October 3, 1911

Constituency Meeting,
Kinnaird Hall, Dundee

The second Moroccan Crisis in July 1911 marked another ominous movement towards heightened tension in Europe. It also brought over Lloyd George from the pacifist ranks in the Liberal Party, and revealed the inadequacy of British naval preparations. This discovery led immediately to Churchill's appointment as First Lord of the Admiralty on October 25.

[Extract] ... We have emerged from the Constitutional struggle in full command of the political situation, with a victorious and united party at our backs, and with the prospect of several years of power and progressive action before us. (Cheers.) It is well that it should be so. It is well, not only for Liberals, but, if I may say it without undue presumption, it is well for the nation at large, that at the present important juncture in the world's affairs there should be in power a Government composed of men who have worked together–very often in the face of great difficulties–in the spirit of comradeship, who have a chief whom they follow with loyal confidence, who have gathered the threads of national and Imperial policy into hands which are no longer without some considerable experience, a Government who can count upon the steadfast support of solid, organized masses of democratic opinion; a Government which could command, if need be, for any serious emergency, either in external or internal affairs, the main strength of the State and of the people. (Cheers.) God forbid that we should arrogate to ourselves the assumption that, on our own individual merits, we are the only people who could govern the country. On the contrary, the more one learns about political business the more one feels how inadequate one's best efforts are, and how pitifully disproportionate are the abilities of individuals to the vast scale and intricacy of modern politics. Let us also be guarded against forgetting how quickly the political ties can change their hue and how easily one mistake may squander the work and accumulation of years. Still, when all these reflections have worked their sobering influence upon our minds, the facts remain as I have stated them to you, and it is well, I say, that the King's Government in these days should be so composed and circumstanced that it should be capable of firm and consistent action, for the aspect of European affairs has became more harsh and troubled than any which has been seen for many years.

A strong tremor of unrest has passed through the gigantic structure of fleets and armies which impress and oppress the civilization of our time. The ponderous machines seem to press and grind against each other, and force certainly does not play a less predominant part, either in the policy of nations or in the equipoise between them. We must perceive, however, that the nations of the 20th century, when these moods take them or their rulers, awake to find themselves in a very different position from that of the States and Governments of even 50 years ago. They find themselves bound together, interlaced and interwoven one with each other, by a tenacious network of trade interests, of commercial transactions, of inter-communication, of reciprocal insurance, and of friendly connexion. They find themselves also standing upon a dizzy and precarious platform of International credit and complex artificial industry—a platform which, were it to collapse or to be violently overturned, would produce consequences which no man and no Monarch can foretell.

The day will surely come when the restraining forces will be found strong enough and widespread enough to guarantee to themselves the security of the world's peace. Some there are who hope that it has dawned already. It is at any rate satisfactory that the forces of restraint are strongest with the strongest nations, and that Great Britain, Germany, and France, leading Powers, dwelling as they do in the full sun-blaze and glory of the modern world, are the very Powers who would find the greatest difficulty in breaking the peace with one another, and who would have most to lose and farthest to fall if a rupture occurred.—(Cheers.) Meanwhile we are passing through an anxious and a critical time, and it would have been far more anxious and far more critical were it not for the fact that the British navy, thanks to the ample provision made in recent years by the House of Commons, is strong enough to secure us beyond all doubt and question the effective command of the seas.—(Cheers.) The dispute between Italy and Turkey has unhappily passed into a stage where for the moment words are useless; but in regard to the difficulty in Morocco the policy of this country can be easily stated. It is the policy declared by the Prime Minister and the Chancellor of the Exchequer.—(Cheers.) It is a perfectly straightforward and honest policy.—(Hear, hear.) We earnestly desire to see France and Germany reach an agreement about Morocco satisfactory to both of them and not injurious to us.—(Cheers.) We rejoice at every step by which the negotiations advance towards that conclusion. We have never uttered and we have not written a single word, a single syllable, publicly or secretly, which could retard or obstruct such a happy conclusion. We want to see a settlement effected which shall close the Morocco question once and for all, and which—far more important than anything that could happen to Morocco—will make, will enable these two great nations, each of whom has rendered and is still to render inestimable service to mankind, to dwell side by side together on terms of mutual respect.—(Cheers.) That is the only sure and permanent foundation upon which to base the peace of Europe. It is that foundation which constitutes the whole policy of Sir Edward Grey and the British Government, and which is also the earnest desire of the British people.—(Cheers.) . . .

NAVAL DEFENCE

November 9, 1911

The Lord Mayor's Banquet,
The Guildhall, London

Churchill's career now reached one of its most significant turning-points. He had vigorously supported Lloyd George in the battle against increased naval expenditure in 1908, and he had on several occasions publicly derided the possibility of war with Germany. But the deterioration of relations between Germany and France, and the evident expansion of the German fleet, had become a matter of concern to him even before the Agadir incident of July 1911, when the German gunboat Panther *made an unexpected appearance off the Moroccan port. The Prime Minister and Grey were sufficiently concerned to summon a special meeting of the Committee of Imperial Defence on August 23. Churchill had written a remarkable memorandum entitled "Military Aspects of the Continental Problem," which he described as "an attempt to pierce the veil of the future; to conjure up in the mind a vast imaginary situation; to balance the incalculable; to weigh the imponderable." The performance of the Admiralty at this meeting was so lamentable that it was evident that a major change was required. After a flurry of activity and a certain amount of Ministerial intrigue, Churchill replaced Reginald McKenna at the Admiralty, while McKenna–who was disturbed by the move–went to the Home Office in his stead. Henceforth, until May 1915, the Navy was Churchill's life.*

This is the first time that I have enjoyed the great honour of replying on such an occasion as this to the toast so happily and so kindly proposed, and I am very glad to be associated in that duty with my old friend and former commander Sir William Nicholson, whom I first knew and served under when he was Chief of the Staff on the North-west Frontier, and when I was Sir William Lockhart's orderly officer. I can assure you that I have assumed the duties of the office to which I have been called with a deep sense of reverence for the great traditions of the navy and with a simple and sincere desire to discharge without failure what must ever be regarded as a national trust.–(Cheers.) I begin under circumstances which are unusually favorable. I would like to express my obligation to men of all parties, and particularly to my political opponents, for the fairness and good feeling with which I have been treated at this juncture. I succeed also to a situation of great advantage. The navy is strong. It is strong actually, it is strong relatively, it is highly efficient.–(Cheers.) The officers and men whom you have complimented to-night are the best that our manhood can produce.–(Cheers.) The more closely the ships of every type are scrutinised, the more accurately they are compared with the corresponding vessels in other fleets, the more certain and unmistakable will the superiority and preponderance of the British navy become. I owe much to the courage and foresight of my predecessor, Mr. McKenna.–(Cheers.) I recognise, and ask you here to recognise, the liberal provision which

Parliament in recent years has made for the maintenance of its first line of defence. The services and the country owe besides a deep and lasting debt to Lord Fisher—(cheers),—the ablest naval administrator which this country has known.—(Cheers.) And now that the controversies which real reforms and the animosities which a forcible personality often creates are passing away, we are beginning to enjoy the results of his great work without the friction which perhaps inevitably was attendant upon this question; and I can to-night reply to the toast on behalf of a service united in sentiment, free within the proper limits of professional opinion, and animated in all ranks by a single hearted desire to serve the State.—(Hear, hear.) My voyage, therefore, begins in bright and favourable weather, if I may be allowed thus early to adopt metaphors which are proper to the office I hold.

The navy is strong—we have got to keep it strong—(loud and prolonged cheers),—strong enough, that is, to use for all that it may have to do. And not only strong but ready, instantly ready, to put forth its greatest strength to the best possible advantage.—(Cheers.) I speak, of course, with the reserves which are necessary to a Minister who has newly entered upon his duties; but, as far as I know, there is no reason at present why this double task of maintaining its immediate readiness for service should not be achieved without a failure to fulfill the expectations of my right hon. friend who is now Home Secretary when he said that the Estimates for the forthcoming year will show some reduction from the abnormal level on which they now stand.—(Hear, hear.) On every ground, provided that national security is not in the slightest degree compromised, such a reduction is to be desired.—(Hear, hear.)

But here let me say a few words of the utmost plainness. Our naval preparations are necessarily based upon the naval preparations of other Powers. It would be affection—and quite a futile kind of affection—to pretend that the sudden and rapid growth of the German navy is not the main factor in our determination whether in regard to expenditure or new construction. To disguise this would be to do less than justice to the extraordinary and prodigious developments which have resulted from German energy and German science in recent years. It would further be foolish to deny the plain truth that naval competition between these two mighty Empires—who all the time have such enormous common interests, who all the time have no natural cause for quarrel—it would be foolish to deny that naval competition between them lies at the root and in the background of almost every difficulty which has baffled the earnest efforts which are repeatedly made—and in which the city of London has taken a noble part—to arrive at really friendly feelings between the two countries. While that competition continues every element of distrust and unrest is warm and active, and one evil leads to another in a long and ugly concatenation. We are not so arrogant as to suppose that the blame and the error which follows so often on human footsteps lies wholly on one side. But the maintenance of naval supremacy is our whole foundation. Upon it stands not the Empire only, not merely the great commercial prosperity of our people, not merely a fine place in the world's affairs. Upon our naval supremacy stands our lives and the freedom we have guarded for nearly a thousand years.

Next year the Navy Law—which when completed will give Germany a magnificent and formidable fleet, second only to our own—next year the law prescribes that the limit of expansion has been reached and that the annual quota of new ships added to the German navy will fall to a half the quota of recent years. Hitherto that law, as fixed by Parliament, has not been in any way exceeded, and I gladly bear witness to the fact that the statements of the German Ministers about it have been strictly borne out by events. Such is the state of affairs in the world that the mere observance of that law without an increase would come to Europe as a great and sensible relief. We should feel that heavy as naval expenditure will undoubtedly be, the high-water mark at any rate has been reached, and all over the world men would breathe more freely and the nations would enter upon a more trustful and more genial climate of opinion. In this we should readily associate ourselves; and if, on the other hand, my Lord Mayor, the already vast programmes of other Powers for war upon the sea should be swollen by the new and added expansions, that would be a matter of extreme regret to us and other States. But I am bound to say on behalf of His Majesty's Government that of all the states and nations of the world Britain will be found the best able to bear the strain and the last to fail at the call of duty.–(Cheers.)

IRISH HOME RULE

February 8, 1912

Celtic Park Football Ground,
Belfast

The bitterness of the constitutional crisis claimed one conspicuous victim. Arthur Balfour resigned the Conservative leadership in November 1911, and was replaced, rather surprisingly, by Bonar Law.

As his speeches on the subject have demonstrated, Churchill's devotion to the cause of Irish Home Rule–against which his father had battled with such brilliant, if unscrupulous, skill and success–was not very profound. Nor was that of Asquith or Lloyd George. In the 1908 Manchester by-election, Churchill had declared that "I have become convinced that a national settlement of the Irish difficulty . . . is indispensible to any harmonious conception of Liberalism," but the matter did not really occupy his attention until the two 1910 General Elections made the Liberals dependent upon the Irish votes for their majority in the House of Commons. Confronted with this situation, and with the great struggle against the Lords pending, Ministers were reluctantly obliged to take interest in the subject which had been the ruin of their party in the 1880s and 1890s.

The Ulster M.P.s also acquired a new leader, Sir Edward Carson. The tone of the Home Rule debate assumed a markedly ugly character. Until the outbreak of the war in August 1914, this issue dominated British politics.

It was characteristic of Churchill to take the offensive; he did so by announcing his intention to speak in Belfast. That the son of Lord Randolph should do this aroused passions to further heights, and there were well-founded fears for his personal safety.

In the Roman Catholic area, where Churchill spoke to a crowd of over five thousand, the mood was different.

[Extract] I am glad to be with you today. Contact with Ireland is contact with history. And how can we tell that this great meeting which is assembled here under circumstances of such peculiar significance this afternoon may not in future years be looked back to as a beneficent landmark in Irish and in British history? (Cheers.) I come before you as the representative of a Government which for more than six years has directed the affairs of the State, which has presided over six years of peaceful progress and the six best years in trade which these islands have ever known, and a Government which has passed great legislation, which has had to deal with powerful antagonists, and which has usually succeeded in its undertakings. And I come to you on the eve of a Home Rule Bill. (Loud and prolonged cheers.) We intend to place before Parliament our plan for the better government of Ireland. It will be a plan harmonious with Imperial interests–(hear, hear),–and we are resolved that it shall be a plan creditable to its authors. (Cheers.) We do not desire to be responsible for the fortunes of a measure not seriously intended to become the law of the land. (Hear, hear.) We have consulted, and we shall consult fully, with the leaders of Irish public opinion, but the decision rests with us. The bill which we shall introduce, and I believe carry into law–(cheers),–will be a bill of a British Government designed to smooth the path of the British Empire, and liberate new forces for its services. (Hear, hear.) In making this clear we put no strain upon the confidence of our Irish friends. For more than twenty-five years Home Rule has been the adopted child of the Liberal party–(cheers),–and during a whole generation, in office and in Opposition, in good luck or in bad, Liberals have been taught by Mr. Gladstone–(cheers)–to believe that the best solution of Irish difficulties lies in the establishment of an Irish Parliament with an Executive responsible to it–(hear, hear),–and every year the reasons upon which they have relied have been strengthened by new facts and by new experiences, and have marched forward with the general march of events.

The case for Home Rule as it stands today, after the controversies of so many years, rests upon three main sets of arguments–the Imperial argument, the House of Commons argument, and the Irish argument. (Hear, hear.) Let me survey these very briefly. I take the largest and the widest first, and I leave that which is nearest home to the end. I take the Imperial argument. A settlement of the long quarrel between the British Government and the Irish people would be to the British Empire a boon and a blessing, a treasure-ship, a wonderful reinforcement, precious beyond compare. (Cheers, and a voice: "And to America.") In their own island the Irish race have dwindled. While the populations of Europe have overflowed, that of Ireland has ebbed away. But elsewhere, all over the world, they have held their own, and in every country where the English language is spoken the Irish are a power for good or a power for ill, a power to harm us or a power to help us, a power to unite us, a power to keep us asunder. What can we say of these Irishmen who, we are assured, are in their own island incapable of managing their own affairs, but who in every other part of the English-speaking world have won their way, out of all proportion to their numbers, to positions of trust, affluence, and authority–(hear, hear)–particularly political authority–what shall we say of them? Speaking as an English Minister, I must say that on the whole in varying degrees, no doubt with notable exceptions, they have been our enemies. They have been filled with feelings of resentment and anger against the British power and name–(a voice: "But no longer"),–and they have counter-worked our interests. As the years have passed by, and especially since Mr. Gladstone rallied half the British nation to the Home Rule cause, things have got better, a gentler feeling has supervened. But still the Irishmen overseas have done us much harm in the past. They have been an adverse force in our colonies. They have on more than one occasion unfavourably deflected the policy of the United States. They are now the most serious obstacle to Anglo-American friendship.

We have got along in spite of all that. We have got along in spite of a great many things. But–and I speak not only to you but to the great audience in all parts of our Empire, all those who follow the Home Rule cause, either on the one side or on the other side–only think if we had had their aid instead of their enmity, their help instead of their opposition, how much smoother our path, how much quicker our progress, how much brighter our fortunes–(cheers),–what new possibilities would be opened, what old dangers would vanish away. And there is no final reason for this antagonism between the races or the countries. The Irish people are by character and tradition attached to monarchial institutions. The idea of a King, a King not only of Great Britain but a King of Ireland, is familiar and grateful to Irish minds. No natural barriers stand between the Irish people and the Throne. Here, as elsewhere throughout the British Empire, the Crown may become the supreme and central link of unity and acceptance.–(Hear, hear.) Since his accession King George has travelled widely. He has reviewed his fleet and his armies. He has been to Scotland. He has been to Wales. He has journeyed through the vast provinces of the Indian Empire. Many great and famous cities have rendered him their allegiance. But it was Dublin–Catholic and Nationalist Dublin–(cheers),–that gave him the warmest welcome of them all, and it is this that makes me put my first question to earnest and generous-minded Unionists in Ulster.

This is my question–Is it really necessary to your safety and welfare that this natural sentiment of Irish loyalty should be repulsed? Must the British Empire be made for all time to stand out of all advantages therefrom? Are British Governments to be condemned to maintain a perpetual quarrel with the Irish nation?–for it is a nation.–(Cheers.) Are British Governments to be compelled to govern them only by force as a subjugated race? Are we to be forbidden on both sides to achieve a friendship so full of hope and benefit for all? Surely at the very least it is incumbent upon Ulster Unionists, if they take that view, to offer very grave and substantial reasons, to make it clear to the British public–and to the colonies who are also inquiring–to make it clear to them that they are not swayed by obstinacy or partisanship, and to justify, if they can justify, with patience and with heart-searchings, the attitude which attempts to bar the path at once to Irish hope and Imperial needs. For our part we look forward to a time, which has been long retarded and which we believe is now near, when this island, instead of being a disruptive force in the British Empire, shall be transformed into a new centre of union, when the harsh and lamentable cry of reproach which has so long jarred upon the concert of the Empire will die away, when the accursed machinery by which hatred is manufactured and preserved will be broken for ever–(cheers),–and when from every country where our language and institutions are established hands will be joined across the seas in peace and cordiality.

Why then, then indeed, there will be a victory worthy to stand for ever with Trafalgar and with Waterloo.–(Cheers.) Every part of the British Empire would join in our rejoicings. Every Parliament in its bounds and in the United States would approve and would applaud our decision. The self-governing dominions would draw more trustfully towards the motherland.–(A Female Voice: "Will you give self-government to the women of Ireland?" The interrupter was ejected.) I think we had better leave that question for the Irish Parliament to decide.–(Cheers.) If, I say, this good result can be achieved, every part of the Empire would share in our rejoicings and approve our action.–(Hear, hear.) Great as are the difficulties which, as we all know, stand in the way of a federation of the Empire, those difficulties would be sensibly diminished by a reconciliation between Great Britain and Ireland, and, far wider even than the unity of the British Empire, the great dream could be dreamed of good relations and ultimate unity with the English-speaking peoples all over the world.–(Cheers.) Why should it not come true? Why cannot this great settlement be made? Why cannot we all make friends? We have done it in Canada.–(Hear, hear.) We have done it in South Africa.–(Cheers.) Something perhaps has been accomplished–much perhaps has been accomplished–in the last few months in Bengal.–(Hear, hear.) Meet the grievance, heal the quarrel, bury the hatred, link the interests, conciliate, consolidate, and unify–thus, and thus alone, shall we be able to surmount the toils and the perils which the future may have in store.–(Cheers.)

They tell me that you have long memories in Ireland.–(Hear, hear, and laughter.) I hope they will be evenly balanced memories. I am not quite sure that always they dwell with equal attention on both sides of the story. How often have we been reminded of the handful of Irishmen–(here another suffrage interruption took place, and a woman was evicted). How often have we been reminded of the handful of Irishmen who voted against us in the Boer War? Have we forgotten the brave Irishmen that never failed in their duty to the Queen and to the army? Why in these days, when Irish Catholics are assailed with so much ill-nature, are they never to be remembered, too? I cannot help thinking of the scenes of which I was a witness when the heights of the Tugela were stormed, and when Ladysmith was at last relieved.–(Cheers.) On the crest of the hill facing the fire of sixty guns, in a veritable whirlwind of exploding shells, stood the valiant Boers. Up the slopes marched unflinchingly the Dublins and the Inniskilling Fusiliers.–(Cheers.) That was a struggle of heroes, of heroes ranged by fate and duty on opposite sides. What a tragedy, what a cruel pity, that such noble breeds of men should be locked together in hateful carnage!–(Hear, hear.) And now we have got them both.–(Cheers.) We have made friends with our enemies. Can we not make friends with our comrades, too?–(Cheers, and further interruption from a suffragist, whose words failed to reach the platform.) Can we not win and keep them both?–(cheers)–both and all within the shelter of the great mother-empire, which, for all the disparagement of modern times, still raises her broad shield against every foe that threatens, and still keeps open what is perhaps upon the whole the surest road to human progress.–(Cheers.) There is the Imperial argument, and to those whose minds are darkened by bigotry, or those, less excusable, whose hearts are rank with faction, these sentiments will not appeal. But we believe that there are thousands of Protestants in Ulster, as there are tens of thousands of Unionists in England, to whom the Imperial aspect of the Irish question–(further interruption from a woman in the grand stand, who, however, was at once quieted). But we believe that there are thousands of Protestants in Ulster, as there are tens of thousands of Unionists in England, to whom the Imperial aspect of the Irish question will be at least as important as discussions about "Ne Temere" or "Proprio Motu." (Laughter and cheers.) . . .

Now I come home–(laughter and cheers)–to Ireland and to Ulster.–(Cheers.) I must say you have made me feel quite at home here.–(Cheers.) We are told, perhaps with truth, that a deep fear is with the Protestants of Ulster, or a number of them, that Home Rule will bring great evils upon them, that their property and their liberty will be assailed, and that their faith will be persecuted and oppressed. We are sure those fears are groundless.–(Loud cheers.) They have been proved groundless at other times.–(A Voice: "And will again," and cheers.) Exactly the same fears were expressed in Ulster in 1829 about Catholic Emancipation, in 1885 about the extension of the franchise, and, above all, in 1869 about the disestablishment of the Irish Church. Each of those changes, the wisdom of which no one now disputes, was declared in Ulster by these same gentlemen who are so positive to-day to be a fatal disaster which would ruin the prosperity of Belfast, which would destroy the last bulwark against Rome, and which would compass the downfall of the Protestant religion. We now hear the same violent language, the same threats of armed rebellion, so recklessly and lightly made. Not a word has been used on the present occasion that cannot be exactly matched by what was said about all these three events. But the world has moved on.–(Laughter and cheers.) The Protestant faith holds its own high place unshaken in the hearts of men, and the prosperity of Belfast has grown from generation to generation. The gloomy prophecies have failed. The threats of fire and slaughter have cooled off into shrewd and sensible behaviour, and we believe history will repeat itself again. (Cheers.) The genuine alarms of an industrious population deserve, and will receive, the earnest and respectful attention of His Majesty's Government.–(Cheers.) We shall labour to reassure them–it is the duty of all who care about the cause of Ireland,–labour to reassure the Protestants of Ulster, and make it clear to them that what they fear may happen cannot possibly come to pass.–(Cheers.)

But there are two counsels of warning which I would like to offer very respectfully to the Protestants of Ulster and Belfast–first, when they are insisting on their own rights and interests they are in a very strong and a very respectable position, but when, or if, they become agents, the tool, or the cat's-paw of the Tory party in England, who are very anxious to get into office, and let their own honest alarm be exploited for British party purposes, then they might find themselves in a much less strong and less respectable position; secondly, the working men of Belfast ought not to quarrel with the democratic forces in Great Britain from whose progressive movement, as my honourable friend Mr. Devlin has no doubt pointed out to you, they have derived great social benefits, with whom on every question except Home Rule–on

Free Trade, the temperance question, and Radicalism—they are in substantial agreement, and on whom they may always count for aid in any truly democratic cause.—(Cheers.) I utter these two counsels of warning by the way.

What, then, are the guarantees of the safeguards which will be provided for the Protestants of Ulster and of Ireland against oppressive laws affecting their religion or their prosperity? The first of all safeguards will be the Irish Parliament—the Irish Parliament which will be so constituted, both in its House of Commons and in its Senate, as to be fully and fairly representative of the Irish nation, and of Protestants as well as of Catholics, of urban interests as well as of agricultural interests, of minorities even more than majorities. We Liberals believe in Parliamentary government carried on under the full glare and pressure of public opinion, and we believe that any Parliament which may be set up in Ireland will be found, in Ireland as in every other part of the modern world, to be the natural and inveterate enemy of religious intolerance in every form.—(Cheers.) That is our conviction. But for the assurance of those Protestants who are genuinely disquieted the following additional rampart will be maintained:—First, the Crown will be able to refuse assent to an unjust bill. Secondly, the Imperial Parliament will be able to repeal such a bill or enact another law. Thirdly, the Home Rule Bill will contain provisions safeguarding religious freedom and fair play for both Protestants and Roman Catholics. Fourthly, if any law passed in Ireland transgresses the limit laid down by the Home Rule Act, then the Privy Council would be able to declare it void. Fifthly, the Home Rule system will be worked in the face of Great Britain as well as of Ireland. The Imperial Parliament is overwhelmingly Protestant, and would certainly resent any attempt to act in a spirit of religious intolerance or unfairness. Sixthly, the power of the Imperial Parliament to interfere is unquestioned in law and equally unquestioned in fact, for all military forces will be under the Imperial control. . . .

The Home Rule Bill will give to the Irish Parliament a real responsibility in finance.—(Hear, hear.) That Parliament will be able to grip and to control large areas of taxation, and it will have the power, within reasonable and wise limits, to supplement its income by new taxation.—(Hear, hear.) Ulster will, however, be in no danger of invidious or unfair taxation. The taxable capacity of Ulster is scarcely greater than that of Leinster or of Munster. The conditions of the farmers of Ulster are sufficiently like those of other Irish farmers, and the interests of the citizens of Waterford and Cork so closely resemble those of the citizens of Belfast, that it would not be possible for an Irish Parliament, even if it wished to do so, to impose taxation that would fall upon Ulster and would not at the same time fall upon the rest of Ireland too—(cheers);—unless, that is to say, an unfair and exceptional discrimination were made, and such a discrimination, as I am sure Mr. Redmond would agree, would be one of those matters in which the Imperial Parliament would be rightly entitled to have a say.—(Cheers.) But why should we anticipate such insane action by an Irish Parliament?—(Laughter and cheers.) The interests of Ireland are the interests of Ulster, and the interests of Ulster are the interests of Ireland. There is an absolute interdependence. A Parliament in Dublin would be one of the chief glories of the island, and I should not be surprised to learn that the banking or credit arrangements by which the splendid industries of Belfast are nourished were at this moment largely dependent upon the savings of

Catholics and Nationalists in all parts of the country.–(Cheers.) . . .

The main argument which all these years has sustained the Home Rule cause has been the continuous and unalterable demand of the Irish people, in an overwhelming majority, through every recognised channel of the national will, for the establishment of an Irish Legislature. The Irish claim has never been fairly treated by the statesmen of Great Britain. They have never tried to deal with Ireland in the spirit in which both great parties face the large problems of the British Empire. And yet, why should not Ireland have her chance? Why should not her venerable nationhood enjoy a recognised and respected existence? Why should not her own distinctive point of view obtain a complete expression? Why should the Empire, why should the world at large, be deprived of a new contribution to the sum of human effort? History and poetry, justice and good sense, alike demand that this race, gifted, virtuous, and brave, which has lived so long and has endured so much, should not, in view of her passionate desire, be left out of the family of nations, and should not be lost for ever among the indiscriminated multitudes of men.–(Cheers.) What harm could Irish ideas and Irish sentiments and Irish dreams, if given their free play in the Irish Parliament, do to the strong structure of the British power? Would not the arrival of an Irish Parliament upon the brilliantly lighted stage of the modern world be an enrichment and an added glory to the treasures of the British Empire?–(Cheers.)

And what of all this vain and foolish chatter about separation? The separation of Ireland from Great Britain is absolutely impossible.–(Cheers.) The interests and affairs of the two islands are eternally interwoven. Ireland, separated by thousands of miles by ocean from any Western country, finds at her door across the Channel the great English market on which she depends for the welfare of her agriculture, as well as the materials for her trades and industries. It is not impossible that Ireland may in the future wholly displace Denmark in the supply of agricultural products to the great cities and populous districts of England and Scotland.–(Hear, hear.) The whole tendency of things, the whole irresistible drift of things, is towards a more intimate association. The economic dependence of Ireland on England is absolute. And quite apart from naval, military, and constitutional arguments, and quite apart from all considerations of the Imperial Parliament, of the flag, and of the Crown, none of which ties will be in any respect impaired, the two nations are bound together till the end of time by the natural force of circumstances. Is it not worth while for English statesmen to try to make their lifelong partner happy and content and free?–(Cheers.) Of course there are difficulties. No one underrates the difficulties of a Home Rule Bill. But I can tell you here this afternoon that there are no difficulties which good will cannot solve easily.–(Cheers.) The problem would present no difficulty if the statesmanship of both the great British parties were enlisted, and if it were approached in the same spirit which under a Conservative Government had dealt with Irish land–(hear, hear),–and under a Liberal Government with the King's Declaration and the Irish University.–(Hear, hear.) All those three great questions had long been regarded as among the most thorny and perilous which any Ministry could touch. They had split Governments and shaken parties. Everyone was afraid of them. And yet a little courage, a little enlightenment, a little fair play, a resolve to adapt national institutions to modern conditions and sentiments, a sincere desire to heal the wounds of the State, to make us a more united people–and all the difficulties vanished, and we have seen the House of Commons carrying these bills by vast majorities, and problems deemed insoluble for generations being settled promptly and in the public interest amid general approval and assent.

Only 18 months ago, at the time of the Constitutional Conferences, this mood prevailed in England about Home Rule.–(Hear, hear.) Then there was a widespread disposition in the Unionist party in Great Britain to consider in loyalty and good faith a settlement, at any rate on federal lines, of the Irish national claims. All their great organs in the press, like a squadron of battleships, made their turrets revolve together and turned their powerful guns in a new direction. All of them, the "Times," the "Morning Post," the "Daily Mail," Mr. Garvin himself–(laughter),–I am not going to afflict you with quotations–all, I say, all said then and all know now that Ireland could be freed and Britain could be strengthened and the Empire brought into a closer unity by some great act of reconciliating statecraft.–(Hear, hear.) We are prepared to fight this matter through–(hear, hear),–but I ask in the first instance most earnestly for a fair consideration of the Irish case. I ask it from the Unionist party. I ask it without diffidence, because it is a fact that it would cost them no party advantage. It would not delay their return to power by a single day. The electoral arrangements necessarily contingent upon Home Rule cannot be otherwise than advantageous to Tory party interests. In the reduction of the Irish representation which will accompany Home Rule lies the only chance the Conservative party have of obtaining some offset to the abolition of the plural voter and the reform of the franchise. It would cost them nothing to act with simplicity and sincerity. That is all we ask, and I am sure the good Fairy Fortune whom they have so clumsily driven away time and again–(laughter)–would owe them no grudge for dealing fairly with the Emerald Isle. Ah! gentlemen, let us contemplate for one moment the consequences to Ireland of another failure, the depression, the despair, the awful hiatus in the mind and spirit and intellect of the nation. Ulster, we should be told, had triumphed. Triumphed over what? Triumphed over the dearest aspirations of their own fellow-countrymen. And what is to happen then? The Unionist party, by the manner in which they have approved and preached the doctrines of violence and lawlessness in the last few weeks–(cries of "Name"),–have disqualified themselves for ever from governing Ireland.–(Loud cheers.) The flame of Irish nationality is inextinguishable.–(Cheers.) The quarrel will go on here and all over the world.

Ah! I appeal, I say, to the Unionist party and to Imperialists in our colonies, and I appeal to Ulster Protestants in Ulster itself, and though my words may be scorned by many, they can be judged by all. I appeal to Ulster to step forward with noble courage, and by a supreme act of generosity and public spirit to win the great prize of Irish peace for themselves and the world. I have been reminded often and again in the last few weeks of the words Lord Randolph Churchill used more than a quarter of a century ago. The reverence which I feel for his memory and the care with which I have studied his public life make me quite content to leave it to others to judge how far there is continuity between his work and any I have tried to do. I am sure the Liberal party will never become an instrument of injustice and of oppression to the Protestants of Ulster. I know this is a duty in which the people of Ulster must not fail. It is a task and a trust placed upon them in the name of Ireland, in the name of the British Empire, in the name of justice and good-will to help us all to settle the Irish question wisely and well for ever now. There is the task which history has assigned to them, and it is in a different sense that I accept and repeat Lord Randolph Churchill's words, "Ulster will fight and Ulster will be right." Let Ulster fight for the dignity and honour of Ireland. Let her fight for the reconciliation of races and for the forgiveness of ancient wrongs. Let her fight for the unity and consolidation of the British Empire. Let her fight for the spread of charity, tolerance, and enlightenment among men. Then, indeed, "Ulster will fight and Ulster will be right."–(Loud cheers.)

NAVAL DEFENCE

February 9, 1912

Clyde Navigation Trustees Luncheon,
Glasgow

The German Navy Law of 1912 aroused renewed apprehensions in the Government about German intentions and ambitions. This, Churchill's first major speech as First Lord of the Admiralty, was ill received in Germany, but it gave public evidence of British concern.

[Extract] . . . You all realize, but it is still our duty to affirm, that the purposes of British naval power are essentially defensive. (Cheers.) We have no thoughts, and we have never had any thoughts, of aggression–and we attribute no such thoughts to other Great Powers. There is, however, this difference between the British naval power and the naval power of the great and friendly Empire–and I trust it may long remain the great and friendly Power–of Germany. The British Navy is to us a necessity and, from some points of view, the German Navy is to them more in the nature of a luxury. Our naval power involves British existence. It is existence to us; it is expansion to them. We cannot menace the peace of a single Continental hamlet, nor do we wish to do so no matter how great and supreme our Navy may become. But, on the other hand, the whole fortunes of our race and Empire, the whole treasure accumulated during so many centuries of sacrifice and achievement would perish and be swept utterly away if our naval supremacy were to be impaired. It is the British Navy which makes Great Britain a Great Power. But Germany was a Great Power, respected and honoured all over the world, before she had a single ship.

Those facts ought clearly to be stated because there is no doubt that there is a disposition in some quarters to suppose that Great Britain and Germany are on terms of equality so far as naval risks are concerned. Such a supposition is utterly untrue. (Cheers.) The Government is resolved to maintain the naval supremacy which this country enjoys. (Cheers.) The Prime Minister and his colleagues, without exception, are resolved to maintain it, and they would none of them tolerate my presence at the Admiralty for a single hour unless they were satisfied that all steps would be taken and were being taken to assure the safety of the country. (Cheers.) In fact, I am not sure if

I should tolerate it myself. (Laughter and cheers.)

We now see, so far as the public prints inform us, that there are prospects of further naval increases among the Powers of the European Continent, and that is a very serious matter, because, not only are navies increasing in size, but everything connected with navies is increasing in cost. Ships are getting larger and longer and broader. Appliances with which they are provided are becoming every day more complicated and more expensive. The means of repairing these ships require every day more elaborate and more costly machinery. The accommodation for docking these vessels involves every year a provision of docks on a scale and of dimensions not hitherto foreseen. The size of the guns increases the size of the ammunition and the expense both of armament and ammunition. The increasing horsepower of the new vessels now being added to the fleets means a greater consumption of coal and oil. Altogether there is no doubt whatever that the nations of Europe are at the present time pressing forward, and pressing each other forward, into an avenue of almost indefinite naval expansion and expense. (Hear, hear.) We may have our own opinion as to how far future generations will compliment the present age upon the wisdom, the Christianity, and the civilization which have made that sterile and dangerous competition so large a feature of our lives.

But there it is, and we shall have to meet it, and I am glad to be able to tell you that there is no need whatever for alarm, there is no need for the raising of any excited panic, and there is no need for disparaging the resources of our country. (Cheers.) We may face the situation with great composure, because it is just and true to say that on every point and in every detail we have it well in hand. (Cheers.) We were never in a better position, and the country was never more united in its resolve to see the supremacy of the British Navy maintained. (Cheers.)

The first of all our resources is money. The race and nation to which we belong have a remarkable habit of self-depreciation, and from time to time yields itself with an air almost of enjoyment to moods of the blackest pessimism. We are told on the one hand that the burden of armaments is crushing and, on the other hand, that Radical finance is ruinous. (Laughter.) Generally, it might be supposed from reading accounts which may be gathered from the organs of both great parties that Great Britain was financially in a very tottering, weak, and parlous condition. But, of course, as you know—as I hope our foreign friends fully recognize—that is all our talk. (Laughter.) The resources which a British Chancellor of the Exchequer can command are amply equal to all requirements of the State. The revenues of the country—I must not attempt to forecast the conclusions which will be reached at the end of the financial year—the revenues of the country give us at the present time every expectation of being at least equal to the expenses which they were designed nearly a year ago to meet, and our credit has been sustained during the last five or six years by repayments of debt and reduction of the capital liabilities of the State on a scale unexampled in the history of this or any other country. We have also—though I do not think we are likely to have to draw upon them—the resources of additional taxation, and we know that in any question where the Navy is concerned we can count upon the ready and spontaneous patriotism of all classes of the population—even the most wealthy. (Laughter and cheers.)

But now let me enter a caveat. I notice in the newspapers—which after all are great guides–(laughter)–and which must guide us right as they guide us in all directions–I learn from the newspapers that there is a considerable body of opinion in this country which favours the flotation of a great naval loan. I cannot help thinking that that suggestion is put forward by persons who have not had an opportunity of properly comprehending the problem of British naval supremacy as it now presents itself. It would no doubt be perfectly easy for the British Government at the present time to float a loan of fifty or a hundred millions for naval purposes. They might be assured that they could float it upon terms better than those of any other European State, and the money would be subscribed and over-subscribed many times within a few hours of the issue and the stock would stand at a high premium. (Cheers.) But what would be the use to the Navy of such a step? We have to build for the Navy enough ships to secure us the effective mastery of the seas. It is sheer waste to build more ships than are necessary for that purpose in any one year. We are now deciding upon the programme of construction which will give us the Navy of two years hence, and we are now enjoying the Navy which was settled in the programme of construction two years ago. If to-day our position is eminently satisfactory, we owe much to the foresight and resolution of Mr. McKenna. (Cheers.) But naval finances and naval construction must proceed upon a system of our sowing each year a crop which we harvest two years later, or two and a half years later, and there would be no sense and no use in sowing in any one year a larger crop than we have reasonable need for two years later.

What is wanted is steady building on a regular plan. No sensational or violent departure from our existing methods is required, or will be required. (Cheers.) Navies cannot be created or expanded in a year, and a steady and regular development of naval power can best be achieved on the basis of large annual supplies of money, either by taxation or credits, and not by the capricious adoption of great loans. . . .

I say, Sir Thomas, we are under no anxiety about money. Whatever is needed for the safety of the country will be asked for by the Government and granted by the representatives of the nation with universal assent. (Cheers.) Neither is there any need for anxiety in regard to our shipbuilding capacity. You are building a great fleet of war vessels at the present time upon the Clyde–you are building nearly 30 war vessels of different classes on the Clyde–the fleet of a second-class Power–(cheers)–and that is part of your ordinary business. And yet I have no doubt, if it were necessary to increase the scale and accelerate the pace of naval construction, there are men in this room–plenty of them–who could here and now assure the Admiralty of their ability to make substantial contributions to any policy of that kind. (Cheers.) There is no chance whatever of our being overtaken in naval strength unless we want to be. We think that we can build as well and as good ships as any other constructors in the world. I could put it higher, but, as Dr. Pangloss observes, "on their own merits modest men are dumb." (Laughter and cheers.) But we know, whatever may be said about quality, that we can build as fast, and faster, cheaper, and on a far larger scale than any other Power in the world. (Cheers.) So that if the money is all right the shipbuilding plant is all right.

But what of the men? We have to-day 135,000 men in the active service ratings of the Navy. The great bulk of them are long-service men–long-service men who have begun as boys and have been trained as a life-long profession to the naval service. We have no difficulty in recruiting for the Navy, because the Navy offers practically a life-long career to those who render good service (cheers), and there is no doubt whatever of our ability to make any increases which may be necessary, and which I think will be necessary, in the personnel of the Navy. Then we have great reserves of seamen in this country of men; and I am inclined to think that there are measures which may be taken to make a greater use of our reserves than has hitherto been found possible, and I have given directions for that part of the subject to be carefully studied by the naval experts upon whom I rely. (Cheers.) Our reserves, both from the Royal Navy and from the Mercantile Marine, are a great resource, and this island has never been, and never will be lacking in trained and hardy mariners bred from their boyhood up to the service of the sea. (Cheers.)

Whatever may happen abroad there will be no whining here, no signals of distress will be hoisted, no cries for help or succour will go up. (Cheers.) We will face the future as our ancestors would have faced it, without disquiet, without arrogance, but in stolid and inflexible determination. (Cheers.) We should be the first Power to welcome any retardation or slackening of naval rivalry. We should meet any such slackening, not by words, but by deeds. But, if there is to be an increase, if there are to be increases upon the Continent of Europe, we shall have no difficulty in meeting them to the satisfaction of the country. (Cheers.) As naval competition becomes more acute we shall have, not only to increase the number of the ships we build, but the ratio which our naval strength will have to bear to other great naval Powers, so that our margin of superiority will become larger, and not smaller, as the strain grows greater. (Cheers.) Thus we shall make it clear that other naval Powers, instead of overtaking us by additional efforts, will only be more outdistanced in consequence of the measures which we ourselves shall take. (Cheers.)

Now, I tell our friend, Sir Thomas, who has entertained me and my wife in your name here to-day so handsomely, build your great dock (cheers), build it long and build it deep, and, above all, build it wide. (Loud cheers.) We will provide you with no lack of great vessels to fill it, and you will know that your citizens of this famous shipbuilding centre are aiding and supporting the British Navy, which enables us to pursue our path through the world, seeking no quarrel and fearing none. (Loud cheers.)

NAVY ESTIMATES

March 18, 1912

House of Commons

In this brilliant speech–too long and detailed to give in its entirety–Churchill clarified the situation concerning Germany with almost brutal lucidity, while at the same time proposing a "naval holiday" in shipbuilding to avert a naval arms race. The speech also dealt with oil supplies, naval aviation, the reorganization of the fleet, and the creation of an immediate Reserve.

[Extract] The foundation of naval policy is finance, and the only credit that can be claimed by a Board of Admiralty is for keeping the requirements of the Navy at a minimum consistent with public safety, and for securing the utmost possible development of war power from the funds entrusted to them. If the country is of opinion that the needs of the Navy have been well and amply provided for, it is to the House of Commons and not to the Board of Admiralty—to the Chancellor of the Exchequer and not to the First Lord—that their thanks and gratitude are due. It is necessary that this should be recognised, and it is right for me to say at this point that the great scale which our naval armaments have been forced to assume has only been rendered possible (without additional taxation or recourse to borrowing) by the wonderful fertility of the great Budget of 1909, for which my right hon. Friend, the Chancellor of the Exchequer, will be long and variously remembered and increasingly respected. The financial aspect of the Naval Estimates is not cheerful. All the world is building navies, and everything connected with every navy is constantly increasing in size, complexity, and cost. Naval finance cannot be conveniently studied on the basis of a single year. Annual Estimates, however useful they may be for certain purposes of Parliamentary control, do not give the House of Commons a fair chance of understanding or of measuring naval expenditure. Capital ships affect the Estimates of three successive years. The Estimates I present to-day are almost entirely governed by what was settled last year and two years before, and the Estimates and war strength of two years hence will be mainly decided by what is determined this year by the House of Commons. So far as possible, I have tried to look ahead, and the effect of every measure which I shall propose to-day has been and is being worked out on the various Votes for three, four, and five years ahead. It may be, though of course I do not make any pledge on the point, that during the course of the present year we shall find ourselves able so far to forecast future naval finance as to be able to present in the House of Commons next year the Estimates not of one but of a series of years. For the present, however, my study of this immense business does not enable me to go beyond certain general indications in regard to prospective finance which are given, and will, I trust, be taken strictly without prejudice. . . .

I propose, with the permission of the House, to lay bare to them this afternoon, with perfect openness, the naval situation. It is necessary to do so mainly with reference to one Power. I regret that necessity, but nothing is to be gained by using indirect modes of expression. On the contrary, the Germans are a people of robust minds, whose strong and masculine sense and high courage does not recoil from, and is not offended by, plain and blunt statements of fact, if expressed with courtesy and sincerity. Anyhow, I must discharge my duty to the House and the country. The time has come when both nations ought to understand, without ill-temper or disguise, what will be the conditions under which naval competition will be carried on during the next few years. The cost and strength of a navy depend upon two main things: first of all, there is the establishment of ships and men maintained in the various scales of commission; secondly, the rate and amount of new construction by which the existing fleets are renewed or augmented. An increase in the establishment of great Navies like the British and the German Navies does not involve such heavy additions to the annual expenditure as an increase in the new construction. On the other hand, the cost of increases in new construction is confined to the years in which it takes place and comes to an end with the completion of the ships, while increases in the number of men, although comparatively small so far as the cost is concerned in one year, involve charges in pay and pensions which recur year after year for a whole generation. Increases in new construction mean increased strength for fighting, through having better military plant. Increases in establishment mean increased readiness for fighting, through being better organised and better trained. It will be convenient for the House to bear these distinctions in mind.

Before I discuss the actual standards of new construction which we should take as our guides in the next few years, there are three general observations which I shall venture to make. The first is, that in times of peace we measure the relative naval construction of two navies by percentages, and that is perhaps as good a way as any other. In naval war, and especially in modern naval war, another system of calculation becomes dominant. Battles are not decided by ratios or percentages. They yield definite and absolute results, and the strength of conflicting navies ought to be measured, and is measured, not as in peace by comparison, but by subtraction. We must expect that in a fleet battle between good and efficient navies equally matched, tremendous damage will be reciprocally inflicted. Many ships on both sides will be sunk or blown up. Many more will sustain injuries which will take months to repair. Others, again, will not come out again during the whole of the war. Indeed, the more we force ourselves to picture the hideous course of a modern naval engagement, the more one is inclined to believe that it will resemble the contest between Mamilius and Herminius at the Battle of Lake Regillus, or the still more homely conflict of the Kilkenny cats. That is a very satisfactory reflection for the stronger naval Power. It will always pay the stronger naval Power to lose ship for ship in every class. The process of cancelling would conduct us, albeit by a ghastly road, to certain victory, and to a condition, not of relative, but of absolute superiority. Further, with a reciprocal destruction of the newer ships, the older vessels will rise swiftly in value. When the Ace is out, the King is the best card, and so on. We possess more "Dreadnoughts" than any other two Powers in the world to-day, and if all the "Dreadnoughts" in the world were sunk to-night, our naval superiority would be greater than it is at the present time. We cannot imagine the course of a naval war which would not tend steadily to increase the relative fighting value of the large resources we possess in pre-"Dreadnoughts," until, as time went on, quite old vessels would come out and play an important part. We are, therefore, keeping such vessels carefully in a material reserve, and arrangements are being perfected by the War Staff to bring them into commission at the sixth, ninth, or twelfth month of any war. All this must be considered in judging the standards of new construction which are appropriate to our needs.

The second observation which I would wish to make is this: It is very easy to make rapid increases in new construction, so long as you are not burdened by the expense of maintaining a great establishment. Our German neighbours have not yet begun to feel the weight of maintaining year after year a gigantic naval service. These charges mature slowly, but remorselessly. The expense of maintenance, apart from the new construction, must grow irresistibly with every year, and therefore it may be found that, as time passes, the very rapid rate of new construction which we have seen elsewhere may, to some extent, be abated by the deadweight drag of increasing maintenance charges. We have a very wide and long experience in the Admiralty. We know the forces that are operative upon the finance of a great Navy, and we are not yet convinced that they will not be found, sooner or later, to operate elsewhere. My third observation is this: It is wrong and wasteful to build a single ship for the Navy before it is wanted. Up to the moment when the contract for a battleship has been definitely signed, the vessel is the heir to all the expanding naval science of the world, but from the day when the design has been finally fixed, she becomes obsolescent, and she has become a wasting security. Nearly three years of her brief life have been lived before she is born. Before she is even launched, the vessels which are capable of destroying her have been projected. It is an ill service to the Navy and to the State to build a single ship before its time. We have to sow each year for the harvest we require two years later—as much as we require and no more. What I might venture to call "the more the merrier" argument is detrimental to efficiency as to economy. The only safe rule which the British Admiralty can follow is to maintain the minimum consistent with full security.

Having reviewed our existing naval resources in the light of the foregoing observations, we are not prepared to recommend at the present time the two-keels-to-one standard in new construction against Germany. The time may come when that will be necessary, but it is not necessary now. I will, however, state precisely the standards which we regard as appropriate to the present situation. Before doing so, I should like to make it clear that, as a result of the measures taken by my right hon. Friend the Home-Secretary, there is no cause whatever for alarm or despondency. The Admiralty are prepared to guarantee absolutely the main security of the country and of the Empire, day by day for the next few years, and if the House will grant us what we ask for the future, that prospect may be indefinitely extended.

I propose first of all to deal with new construction, and to leave the establishment of the Navy to the last. Standards of naval strength must vary with circumstances and situations. Adequate naval superiority is the object, and the standards which we adopt are necessary, though arbitrary guides for securing it. When the next two strongest naval Powers were France and Russia, and when those two Powers were also what one might call the most probable adverse diplomatic combination, the two-Power standard was a convenient rule, based upon reality, for us to follow as a guide. The passage of time and the rise of the Navy of a single Power to the first place upon the Continent has changed this. We have no longer to contemplate as our greatest potential danger, the alliance, junction, and co-operation of two naval Powers of approximately equal strength, with all the weakness and uncertainty inherent in such combinations, but we have had for some time to consider the growth and development of a very powerful homogeneous Navy, manned and trained by the greatest organising people of the world, obeying the authority of a single Government, and concentrated within easy distance of our shores. In consequence the two-Power standard, if applied to Europe alone, would be quite inapplicable, because wholly inadequate. On the facts of to-day, the Navy that we should require to secure us against the most probable adverse combination would not be very much greater than the Navy we should require to secure us against the next strongest naval Power. In order, therefore, to provide a reason for the necessary measures which have been taken during the last few years, it has become customary to extend the two-Power standard so as to include the United States of America, and thereby, I think, the two-Power standard has lost much of its good sense and its reality. The time has come to readjust our standards in closer accord with the actual facts and probable contingencies. The actual standard in new construction–I am not speaking of men or establishment–which the Admiralty has, in fact, followed during recent years, has been to develop a 60 per cent. superiority in vessels of the "Dreadnought" type over the German navy on the basis of the existing Fleet Law. There are other and higher standards for the smaller vessels, with which I will not complicate the argument, as they do not greatly affect finance.

If Germany were to adhere to her existing law we believe that standard would, in the absence of any unexpected development in other countries, continue to be a financial guide for the next four or five years so far, that is to say, as this capital class of vessel is concerned. Further than that it is idle to speculate. This, however, I must say. I must not be taken as agreeing that the ratio of sixteen to ten could be regarded as sufficient preponderance for British naval strength as a whole above that of the next strongest naval Power. Even if we possessed an Army two-thirds as strong as that of the strongest military Power, we could not agree to that. We are able for the present to adhere to so moderate a standard because of our great superiority in vessels of the pre-"Dreadnought" era, among which the eight King Edwards and at least eight of the armoured cruisers are quite unmatched among contemporary ships. As these vessels gradually decline in relative fighting value, our ratio of new construction will have to rise above the 60 per cent. standard. Every addition which Germany makes, or may make, to the new ships she lays down each year must accelerate the decline in the relative fighting value of our pre-"Dreadnoughts," and, therefore, requires special measures on our part. Applying the standard which I have outlined to the existing German navy law without any addition, that is to say, two ships a year for the next six years, for that is what the law prescribes, and guarding ourselves very carefully against developments in other countries which cannot now be foreseen, it would appear to be necessary to construct for the next six years four ships, and three ships in alternate years, beginning this year with four. That is a little above the 60 per cent. standard, it is over seventeen to ten, but that is the least which will maintain a 60 per cent. standard, and that is what we have had in our minds when we framed the Estimates which are now presented to the House of Commons. If we are now, as it would seem, and as I fear it is certain to be, confronted with an addition of two ships to German construction in the next six years–two "Dreadnoughts–[Hon. Members: "Annually?"] No, two ships spread over the six years, we should propose to meet that addition upon a higher ratio of superiority by laying down four ships in the same period, spreading them, however, conveniently over the six years so as to secure the greatest convenience in our finance. If, of course, we were confronted with three ships additional we should lay down six, and the forecast of new construction, which I now make under all reserve, would become four, beginning with this year, five, four, four, four, four, as against the German construction of two, three, two, two, three, two. So alternatively, if three were laid down by Germany in the six years, our construction would become five, four, five, four, five, four, as against the German alternation of three's and two's. It is clear that this number could be varied to suit the circumstances.

Let me make clear, however, that any retardation or reduction in German construction will, within certain limits, be promptly followed here, as soon as it is apparent, by large and fully proportioned reductions. For instance, if Germany elected to drop out any one, or even any two, of these annual quotas and to put her money into her pocket for the enjoyment of her people and the development of her own prosperity, we will at once, in the absence of any dangerous development elsewhere not now foreseen, blot out our corresponding quota, and the slowing down by Germany will be accompanied naturally on our larger scale by us. Of course both Great Britain and Germany have to consider, among other things, the building of other Powers, though the lead of both these countries is at present very considerable over any other Power besides each other. Take, as an instance of this proposition which I am putting forward for general consideration, the year 1913. In that year, as I apprehend, Germany will build three capital ships, and it will be necessary for us to build five in consequence. Supposing we were both to take a holiday for that year. Supposing we both introduced a blank page in the book of misunderstanding; supposing that Germany were to build no ships in that year, she would save herself between £6,000,000 and £7,000,000 sterling. But that is not all. We should not in ordinary circumstances begin our ships until she has started hers. The three ships that she did not build would therefore automatically wipe out no fewer than five British potential super-"Dreadnoughts," and that is more than I expect them to hope to do in a brilliant naval action. As to the indirect results, even from a single year, they simply cannot be measured, not only between our two great brother nations, but to all the world. They are results immeasurable in their hope and brightness. This, then, is the position which we take up, that the Germans will be no gainers, so far as naval power is concerned, over us by any increases they may make, and no losers for the basis I have laid down by any diminution. Here, then, is a perfectly plain and simple plan of arrangement whereby without diplomatic negotiation, without any bargaining, without the slightest restriction upon the sovereign freedom of either Power, this keen and costly naval rivalry can be at any time abated. It is better, I am sure, to put it quite frankly, for the Parliaments and peoples to judge for themselves. . . .

The House is entitled to be relieved of any anxiety which they feel in regard to the expansive power of the shipbuilding resources of the country. It is not possible to say whether our most prominent competitors can build as fast as we do. What is certain, is that they do not in practice do so, and it is also true, I am pleased to say, that we can build, arm, and equip great ships each year—and continue the process year after year—upon a scale largely in advance of any other single Power in the world, according to its present resources. The House may take it for certain, therefore, that there is absolutely no danger of our being overtaken unless we decide as a matter of policy to be so. I leave new construction and now turn to our establishment. Upon the establishment of ships maintained in full commission, and upon the number of active service ratings permanently available, depends our immediate readiness for war. The growing strength in the establishment of foreign navies, and the increases, actual and prospective, on which we must reckon in their personnel, makes it now necessary somewhat to strengthen the force which we keep constantly ready for immediate service in home waters. I do not think it would be particularly useful at this juncture for me to enter into detailed comparisons between the force which we keep immediately available and the forces which are at the disposal of various foreign Powers, and I hope I shall not be pressed to do so. I would prefer to pursue a general argument. We ask Parliament to assent to large margins of safety. That is not because we do not believe our Fleet man for man, ship for ship, would not acquit itself with credit and to the satisfaction of King and country. There is, however, a very practical reason which any layman can understand. We stand as a nation upon the defensive. It is inconceivable that we should make a surprise attack upon Germany or any other European Power. But apart altogether from the moral aspect, which I am not now discussing, what would be the use of it. We have no means of following up such an attack, even if it were successful, and no means of bringing the war to a speedy conclusion. Therefore, I say we are relegated to the defensive.

This entails certain obvious consequences. There is a considerable difference between the number of ships which are available any day taken at random throughout the year by chance, and the number which could be got ready for a particular date or period marked out in advance. For instance, if the House of Commons sent a Committee to Portsmouth to-night, and orders were given to mobilise all the ships in the harbour, we could produce a certain number, but if we were told privately that the Committee were going down to see how many ships we could turn out on short notice on 1st April or 1st May, we could produce from twenty-five to thirty per cent. more. That is a very important fact which anyone can appreciate. It is a fact which makes it necessary for us to have a sufficient margin to be able to meet at our average moment the naval force of an attacking Power at their selected moment. The second reason why we should have an ample margin is that the consequences of defeat at sea are so much greater to us than they would be to Germany or France. There is no similarity between our naval needs and those of the two countries I have mentioned. There is no parity of risk. Our position is highly artificial. We are fed from the sea; we are an unarmed people; we possess a very small Army; we are the only Power in Europe which does not possess a large army. We cannot menace the independence or the vital interest of any great continental State; we cannot invade any continental State. We do not wish to do so, but even if we had the wish we have not got the power.

These are facts which justify British naval supremacy in the face of the world. If ever any single nation were able to back the strongest fleet with an overwhelming army, the whole world would be in jeopardy, and a catastrophe would swiftly occur. People talk of the proportion which the navies of different countries should bear to the commercial interests of the different nations—the proportion of France, the proportion of Italy, the proportion of Germany—to their respective mercantile marines; but when we consider our naval strength we are not thinking of our commerce, but of our freedom. We are not thinking of our trade, but our lives. Nothing, of course, can make us absolutely safe against combinations which the imagination can summon up. We have faced combinations again and again in the past, and sometimes at heavy odds, but we must never conduct our affairs so that the navy of any single Power would be able to engage us at any single moment, even our least favourable moment, with any reasonable prospect of success. If this is insular arrogance, it is also the first condition of our existence. I am glad to be able to assure the House that no difficulty will be experienced in making arrangements to maintain our relative positions in the near future, and to secure as quickly as we need them adequate margins of safety. I am glad also that these measures will not involve any excessive or disproportionate expense. We do not, of course, require to build any more ships other than those I have referred to under the head of "new construction." All we should need to do is to bring, as we require it, and no sooner, a larger proportion of our existing Fleet into a higher status of commission, and consequently of greater readiness. We propose also at the present time, in view of the increases which are in progress, to re-cast completely the organisation of the Fleet. Under the new organisation the ships available for home defence will be divided into first, second, and third Fleets, the whole three Fleets, comprising eight battle squadrons of eight ships each, together with their attendant cruiser squadrons, flotillas, and all auxiliaries. Each of these three Fleets will represent a distinct administrative status and standard of commission. The First Fleet will comprise four battle squadrons of fully commissioned ships, together with one Fleet flagship. . . .

I hope the House will discern from the account I have given the general principle of naval administration to which we adhere–homogeneity of squadrons; simplicity of types and classes; modernity of material; concentration in the decisive theatres; constant and instant readiness for war; reliance upon gun power; reliance upon speed; and above all, reliance upon 136,000 officers and seamen, the pride of our race, and bred from their boyhood up to the permanent service of the sea. These are the principles which we ask the House of Commons to approve. For the rest I have only a word to say.

The spectacle which the naval armaments of Christendom afford at the present time will no doubt excite the curiosity and the wonder of future generations. Here are seen all the polite peoples of the world, as if moved by spontaneous impulse, devoting every year an immense and ever-growing proportion of their wealth, their manhood, and their scientific knowledge, to the construction of gigantic military machinery, which is obsolescent as soon as it is created; which falls to pieces almost as soon as it is put together; which has to be continually renewed and replenished on a larger scale; which drains the coffers of every Government; which denies and stints the needs of every people; and which is intended to be a means of protection against dangers which have perhaps no other origin than in the mutual fears and suspicions of men. The most hopeful interpretation which can be placed upon this strange phenomenon is that naval and military rivalries are the modern substitute for what in earlier ages would have been actual wars; and just as credit transactions have in the present day so largely superceded cash payments, so the jealousies and disputes of nations are more and more decided by the mere possession of war power without the necessity for its actual employment. If that were true the grand folly of the twentieth century might be found to wear a less unamiable aspect. Still we cannot conceal from ourselves the fact that we live in an age of incipient violence and strong and deep-seated unrest. The utility of war even to the victor may in most cases be an illusion. Certainly all wars of every kind will be destitute of any positive advantage to the British Empire, but war itself, if ever it comes, will not be an illusion—even a single bullet will be found real enough. The Admiralty must leave to others the task of mending the times in which we live, and confine themselves to the more limited and more simple duty of making quite sure that whatever the times may be our Island and its people will come safely through them.

GOVERNMENT OF IRELAND BILL

April 30, 1912

House of Commons

In this magnificent speech, Churchill attempted to cool the passions which Home Rule aroused, but unhappily without success. The proponents of all-out Ulster resistance—to the point of war—steadily gained influence in the Opposition.

[Extract] The precedents of former years, following the example of Mr. Gladstone, would seem to require that the Second Reading of a Home Rule Bill should not be moved without some general observations from a Minister of the Crown, and I would ask the House to accord me the good will and indulgence usually shown to a Member who has a difficult task to discharge and to accord me also that full liberty of Debate which we, for our part, shall gladly give to our opponents on this subject. I desire, not at undue length, I hope, to address my argument to the House conceived from the point of view of one of the many of its younger Members to whom the controversies of the 'eighties and even the controversies of the 'nineties have never made their appeal, and one of those many Members of the House whose active political life lies wholly or almost wholly in the new century into which we have now begun to make some headway. There are many of us here, and in the Debates on this Bill no doubt we cannot contribute to the discussions the experience which those who have been over this extensive battlefield before are endowed with. We cannot have the experience or the knowledge of those who fought in 1893, and still less of the veterans of 1886. All that we can hope to bring to the lengthy discussions in which the House is now to embark is the modern eye. That we can contribute. We have seen a century begin in war and we have all the nations of the world embarking on military preparations and naval preparations on a scale altogether without example for many generations. We have witnessed a vast expansion in the scale and business and functions of government. We have seen an enormous expansion of science and wealth, the fruit of science. We have seen the most striking development of internationalism both as affecting capital and labour; we have seen the growing consolidation of the British Empire under a system of many Parliaments. We have seen a South African settlement and its consequence, and we now perceive that the two most formidable and powerful and progressive Powers of the modern world, the United States of America and the Empire of Germany, conduct their business and carry on their development through a gigantic system of federated States and subordinate legislatures. These are the features of the landscape such as open to the modern eye, and it is in relation to them and in proportion to them that we are led to look at this question of Home Rule about which our fathers used to get so angry and about which they used to fight such invigorating party battles in the good old days.

The first impression which I venture to think this class of Members to whom I refer will sustain as they approach this question, is that Irish Home Rule is no longer as big a question for Great Britain as it used to be. The seriousness of a grant of autonomy or a division of the powers of self-government in a State is necessarily affected by the relative size and population of the two countries concerned. Norway and Sweden, Holland and Belgium, and Austria and Hungary were, I believe I am correct in saying, though I have not got the statistics at hand, equal or almost equal bodies. [Hon. Members: "No."] At any rate, they were both great and important bodies, but even at the time of the Union the population of Great Britain was twice as big as the population of Ireland, so that the question of the relations between the two countries was never such a great question to us as it has been to these other States whose names I have mentioned. But a change has taken place since the Union–it has been continually in progress, and there is no evidence that the change is not still in progress–in the relative power and wealth and population of the two countries. The population of Great Britain is no longer twice as great as that of Ireland; it is now ten times as great. That has made a very great difference in the scale and importance of the problem to British eyes. There is no arguing against a change like that; it obviously alters the proportion all through. I do not say that it alters the merits of the controversy, but it alters the proportion of things. We are told that Home Rule involves the disruption of our country. If a hundred years ago Home Rule for Ireland would have disrupted the United Kingdom to the extent of one-third, and if in 1886 it would have disrupted the United Kingdom to the extent of one-sixth, it is at any rate open to those who urge this argument of disruption to console themselves in our discussion with the reflection that at the present time it can only disrupt the United Kingdom to the extent of one-tenth. [Hon. Members: "No."] I am anxious so long as possible to avoid controversy. Therefore I begin with a proposition which, of course, is absolutely indisputable. It is undoubted that the complete change in the proportion of the two countries has made all Irish questions less vital to the security and safety of this country. If you work out the ratio of the wealth of the two countries, which is, I suppose, some measure of their relative power–wealth can be easily converted into armed force–far greater changes will be seen to have taken place in the relative proportion in the period which I have mentioned. There is another reason why the importance of the Irish question to English eyes has diminished with the passage of time. The violence of the Irish movement has been steadily reduced as time has passed. The fierce revolutionary agitation for the repeal of the Union, which was led by O'Connell in the forties, and the serious disturbance of 1848, were far less horrible and dangerous in their character and course than the rebellion of 1798. The Fenian movement of the sixties was less dangerous in its manifestation than the agitation of O'Connell, and the land movement of the eighties, though marked by many shocking incidents, was less violent than its precursor in the sixties, and since Mr. Gladstone in 1886 identified one of the great English parties with the Home Rule cause no scenes or incidents of violence have been witnessed in Ireland more serious than those which have attended labour disputes in Great Britain. . . .

What is remarkable is that through all these years of struggle, uncheered by fortune, and even abandoned by hope, the great mass of Irish Nationalist opinion should have assented at every important juncture to the formal and deliberate statement and restatement of their claims in a form absolutely antagonistic to the separation of the two Kingdoms. I say that the Irish demand now put forward, and now met by this measure, which has been accepted as a full settlement by almost every important element in Irish life, is an essentially moderate and reasonable demand. It is no demand for a divorce of the two Kingdoms; it is no demand for separation from the United Kingdom or for separation from the British Empire; it is not even a demand for the termination of the Parliamentary Union; it is not even a demand for Colonial autonomy; it is, as the hon. Member for Cork (Mr. W. O'Brien), in his brilliant speech the other day, contended with perfect truth, the acceptance of a measure which implements, amplifies, and carries out the union of the two countries under forms which for the first time will receive the assent of the Irish people. All the time that this modified process has been in progress, let me remind the House, the diminution both in the violence of method and in the extravagance of demand which has been taking place has not been accompanied by any diminution in the volume of opinion in Ireland in favour of the restoration of their Parliament. On the contrary, it is perfectly true to say that never before has so little been asked; and never before have so many people asked for it. The character of our Bill is displeasing to the Opposition, and why is it displeasing? They do not give us at present quite a clear indication as to the main direction in which their dislike of it lies. Is it displeasing because it is so moderate, or is it displeasing because it is so extreme? . . .

I was saying, at the outset of my remarks, that we ought not to exaggerate the importance of the Irish question. It is a great, difficult, and historic problem, but it is not so important as it was one hundred years ago from the British point of view. Its importance has been altered by the great increase in the scale of other things. The whole scale of our business and affairs has multiplied and expanded vastly, perhaps beyond our power to realise. The great questions of the Victorian era which convulsed the politics of the 'eighties, which seemed then to absorb the whole mind of the nation, are as much outclassed by the questions of the present time as the battleships and liners of 1880 are dwarfed by vessels we are launching now, and the dangers which Mr. Pitt apprehended, and properly apprehended, are as obsolete as now are the three-deckers with which he surmounted them. Everyone in this House, wherever he may sit, knows perfectly well, even the representatives of Ulster know it, that events might happen on the frontiers of India or in the North Sea—nay, they might happen here at home, on our railways, in our colliery districts, on our great markets and exchanges—incomparably more important to the welfare of the whole masses of the people of this country, incomparably more important to the structure and form of our society, and to the general welfare of the Realm, than anything which could happen in Ireland. We are confronted in this Parliament, in these times in which we live, and upon which we are entering with two tremendous groups of questions, one internal the other external, both of such profound gravity and import that party strife is hushed in their presence. We have to face the growing discontent of the immense labouring population of this country with the social economic conditions under which they dwell. We have somehow or other to create for them decent and fair conditions of living and of labour. We have also, at the same time, to guard and maintain our interests and position in the world, filled with mighty nations and empires, whose minds and energies are turned more and more each year to the science and preparation of war. We have got to succeed in solving both those great sets of questions, both those great sets of problems, if we are to maintain our station in the world as it has been handed to us by those who have gone before.

Everyone knows, whatever opinion he may hold upon Irish policy, that it raises no issue comparable to either of those two questions I have mentioned. I am going to subject this statement to one very crude test. I am going to test the statement that the Home Rule question, important and vital as it is to Irishmen, does not touch vitally British issues. [Hon. Members: "Oh!"] That is my contention. I may be wrong. I am going to subject it to the crude test of bringing it before the tribunal of absolute force, and by asking, as I asked last year in a few sentences, whether our military security is in any way affected by such a measure as this. This matter was referred to by the right hon. Gentleman the Member for the City of London (Mr. Balfour) in his powerful and suggestive speech the other day, to which we all listened with such deep attention. And I take it that this question, Will Home Rule weaken our power or security in war? is one which we are bound to discuss quite early in the Debate upon this measure. Could anything be done by a Parliament in Dublin, as constituted by the Bill, to add to the military risks or impair the effectiveness or integrity of our military measures? To examine this question fairly one ought to assume—what I believe to be impossible, as I shall presently endeavour to show is extremely unlikely—namely, that there will be a violent divergence of opinion and sentiment between the British and Irish Parliament during the course of a war of first magnitude. Let us assume for the purpose of argument that such a divergence takes place. Is there anything that an Irish Government or Parliament could do if they were unfriendly that would sensibly affect the efficiency of our defences, particularly of our naval defences? The answer to that question is, I submit to the House, that there is absolutely nothing. Even putting it at its very worst, and even assuming the impossible, the action of an Irish Parliament upon our naval defences would be practically negligible. The fact that such an answer can be given now shows the enormous change that has come over the Irish question as time has passed. . . .

There is no statement more devoid of deep truth, whatever superficial plausibilities may attach to it, than the common statement, "England's difficulty is Ireland's opportunity." But I believe it has never been true, and when this Bill has passed and when every ground of quarrel has been obliterated between the two peoples, when Ireland is not only economically but financially dependent upon Great Britain, and when no bar of national sentiment divides, and when every prompting of self-interest unites and every tie of custom and convenience welds them together, then I say the identity of interest between Ireland and England will be absolute, and I defy respectfully, and I dialectically defy you by the utmost exercise of your imagination to conjure up or picture even any set of circumstances in which the ruin of England would not mean the ruin of Ireland also.

It is the same identity of interests on which we rely to make this Bill work smoothly, to make its safeguards thoroughly effective, and to prevent friction and divergence between the two Governments and the two Parliaments. Why should we not rely with confidence upon the identity of interests? What conceivable reason would any Irish Government have to put itself on bad terms with the Government of Great Britain. To maintain good relations with each successive British Administration will be the first interest of Ireland, unless we are to assume what our daily experience shows us is absurd and untrue, that Irishmen are absolutely blind to their own interests, that no sooner have they obtained a Constitution than they would endeavour to wreck it, it seems to me that those dangers are illusory. There is hardly any step which a British Government could take even on matters unconnected with Ireland that would not in many ways affect Irish interests, and to be considered to stand well with the Imperial Government, and to have good and cordial relations with the Ministry of the day will be the pride and constant care of Irish statesmen called upon to direct the affairs of the smaller island. [Hon. Members: "How do you know?"] I am not prophesying, I am drawing a conclusion from an argument. My premise is that there is an identity of interests and that there is continuity in the relations of mutual interest between the two countries. From that I argue as a fair deduction that it is unlikely that persons not blind to their own interests and who have managed their own affairs whenever they had the chance with great grit and discretion, will be anxious to quarrel with those with whom they have so many intricate and important relations. That is my proposition.

I say we see these forces at work every day and year and with our Colonies increasingly at work every day, in bringing about closer union with all parts of the British Empire. But the Dominions are far off, they are at the end of the world, they are self-supporting; they are not represented in our body; they have no great and continual volume of business with us–[Hon. Members: "Oh, oh!"]–such as undoubtedly would occur between the two sister Islands. Ireland is close by. I am putting a proposition which, of course, like every other proposition in connection with Ireland, there would be two opinions about. I say Ireland is close by, and I say Ireland will be thrown into continual, serious, and close intimate business and political relations with this country to the end of the world. Our affairs are interwoven; our interests are the same; they can help us often, and we can help them always. Remove the cause of quarrel, restore their national self-respect, give them a fair Constitution, and you will find, swiftly and surely, results beyond your utmost dreams. That is prophecy, I admit; but I will run the risk of it. But suppose we are wrong, suppose there is one island in the world and one race upon the surface of the earth so curiously disposed, so strangely fashioned, that self-interest does not stir them, that the desire of prosperity does not dwell in their hearts; suppose there were a race whose two fiercest passions were, first of all, to quarrel with their own bread-and-butter, and, secondly, to cut off their noses to spite their faces; suppose there were such a people, suppose that the Irish were that people, suppose they deliberately set themselves—all this concatenation of absurd suppositions must be made—to wreck and ruin the Constitution they had so painfully acquired, to bring about a deadlock, to infuriate or to irritate their all-powerful neighbour, to quarrel with the great protecting, credit-giving, revenue-paying, and produce-purchasing Power—what then? Why then, even for this inverted pyramid of absurd and unnatural assumptions, there is full provision in the Bill. The Imperial Parliament, in which the Irish will be represented, will have not only the legal but the moral right to legislate. The Imperial Parliament can resume its delegated powers in whole or in part. It can legislate as it chooses for Ireland. It can justify force by law, and, if necessary, vindicate law by force.

We believe that immense benefits will be derived by the British Empire, particularly in its Colonial and foreign relations, from a thorough good feeling between the British and the Irish people. We are sensibly hampered at the present time in the progress of our Colonial policy by hostility and distrust in every one of the great English-speaking dominions, which, traced home to its source, arises from the presence of unreconciled Irish in positions of prosperity and honour in their midst. Everyone knows that this influence has worked much evil in our relations with the great English-speaking Republic on the other side of the Atlantic, but though there are great advantages to be gained, though Ireland has great gifts to give us, which we have never enjoyed so far, I believe it to be true, and I have been trying to submit the argument to the House, that no serious injury worse than we suffer now can come to us from Ireland. The gain to the Empire by a settlement would be very great. The risk to Britain even from failure is small. We have much to hope for; we have nothing to fear. . . .

Although in the British Isles there are greater questions, Home Rule is the greatest and the most agitating question of all to every Orangeman and Nationalist in Ireland. On those benches sit the representatives of the two opposing Irish parties, differing one from another so sharply, severed from each other by all the sorrowful events of the long quarrel into which, through no fault of either party, they have been plunged. This question to them is one of life or death, as they believe it to be. It is in view of these two parties sitting side by side in this House that I, speaking as a British Member to other British Members, would ask what ought to be our duty as British Members? It is an Irish quarrel in the first instance. Ought we to make it a British quarrel too? Ought the two great parties to draw out their lines of battle and their standards of Orange and Green, which are not their standards, and to fall to? Ought we to set these two cocks to fight, and stake our party fortunes on the upshot? As good and faithful citizens, with dangers to face in common, with treasures to enjoy in common, with work to do in common, are we not bound to do our best to appease and not to foment Irish hatred, and to effect an honourable and lasting settlement if we can? There is one form of argument which I myself do not like very much to employ, and that is for a Government to appeal to an Opposition with whom they have been fighting hammer and tongs at party politics, and to say to them, "Be generous, be conciliatory, be statesmanlike, be patriotic—and keep us in office *ad infinitum.*" I much prefer another style of political controversy. But this Irish question and its solution matters as much to the Conservative party as to the Liberal party. It is your interest as much as ours, perhaps more, to have it settled. It is your duty as much as ours to try to settle it.

Can you say that you are satisfied with the existing condition of things? Is not your whole political argument at the present time, one long complaint that the Irish Members hold the balance in the House of Commons, that Bills are passed, that Budgets are passed, that ministries are maintained in power largely by the Irish vote? That is what you tell us night and day. You reproach us harshly for the consequences and conditions which you yourselves have decreed, and which you declare you are resolved to maintain unaltered. You say that Ireland is to be represented at Westminster, and only there. What position and what status do you accord to four-fifths of her representatives? They are to remain here, but they are to be regarded as political pariahs. [Several Hon. Members: "Why?"] Anyone who co-operates with them or accepts their co-operation in the ordinary working of Parliamentary business–[Several Hon. Members: "Oh!"]–we are told is guilty of dishonourable and contemptible conduct, of paltering with the unclean thing. That is your contention. [Several Hon. Members: "No."] What other contention than that could justify the stream of strong, harsh, and insulting words which we heard from the hon. Member for Warrington (Mr. H. Smith) this afternoon? Anyone who has political relations with the Irish Nationalist party is guilty of something like treachery to the country. According to the language that is held–I am honestly doing my very best to meet the charges which are made, and the very generally accepted opinion in Conservative circles–there ought to be a tacit understanding that whatever differences may sunder British parties, neither is to be influenced by nor to profit from the Irish vote. I remember, when my right hon. and gallant Friend the Under-Secretary of State for War (Colonel Seely) and I were followers of the right hon. Member for the City of London (Mr. A. J. Balfour), and, I am bound to admit, we had the misfortune to differ from him on one or two occasions, the right hon. Gentleman made a speech in which he referred to the Members who were attacking the Government–I am not sure that the Noble Lord (Lord H. Cecil) was not included–and said that there were certain Members of the party who were in it but not of it. That is the kind of position which, according to much of the language that we hear and in harmony with the charges that are made, is to be assigned to the Irish Members in the House of Commons. They are to be in it but not of it. That voting strength, given to them for their express use and protection, which is the one substitute that you offer them in exchange for a Parliament of their own, is to be nullified and neutralised and made ineffective by the superior voting strength of the two great English parties. As for the Irishmen in their own country, they are, to put it bluntly, to be held down and kept in order by a great system of constabulary directed from across the sea.

This is the situation in our Parliament and in their own Island which is offered to an ancient people, famous in history, influential all over the English-speaking world, whose blood has been shed on our battlefields, whose martial qualities have adorned our ensigns, whose humour has cheered our spirits, whose poetry has touched our hearts, whose private virtues may serve as no unworthy example to our homes. They are to be content with that. They are even to be enthusiastic about that. They are to sing "Rule, Britannia," and rejoice that, whatever may happen to Irishmen, Britons, at any rate, never will be slaves. Young English Members of Parliament will rise in their places and let off little speeches proving that the Irish are naturally, intellectually, and temperamentally incompetent and incapable of managing their own affairs, that they are a very agreeable people when taken the right way, but that there is something about their nature which makes it necessary for them to be treated like children, like aborigines, and kept in a state of tutelage and subjection. An argument like that will be used by Members of this House, when all the time the hon. Member for Waterford (Mr. J. Redmond), or the hon. Member for Cork (Mr. T. Healy), the hon. Member for West Belfast (Mr. Devlin), and others, who, in the broad and just judgment of the House of Commons, stand in the very first rank of the Parliamentary debaters of the day, are sitting silently and critically behind them. All I can say is, when I contemplate the real meaning of the status and position which you offer to the Irish Members of this House, and to the Irish people in their own land, that I do not envy the nation that tried to put such treatment upon John Bull. Of this I am sure, that until we have comforted the soul of Ireland, until we have given to her national honour the solace of mutual forgiveness–of which we both stand in need–until we have made her a freely consenting party to an act of reconciliation, we shall never secure integrity in national action or unity in Imperial structure.

I have never believed in the nonsense which crops up from time to time in the Press about there being no alternative Government. The personnel of several good Administrations can always be found in the House of Commons. But I would ask it amicably and earnestly of the Opposition, "Have you not a real interest with us in making a settlement, and in getting this question cleared out of the way?" What are your own remedies for it? Can you feel any great confidence in them? Will you really–I ask the right hon. Gentleman (Mr. Austen Chamberlain)–give to Ireland a preferential tariff as against Canada? Do you think that that would be a good plan? Do you really think that would be a consolidating measure for the Empire? If you do, do you suppose for one moment that will buy off the Irish national movement? What shall a nation have in exchange for its soul–a tax on imported butter? Despair attendant on the failure of this Bill would produce disastrous consequences. [An Hon. Member: "No."] Yes. Can anyone–for others are in earnest besides the hon. Member –others feel deeply and strongly, and are prepared, perhaps, to risk their lives–can anyone look forward to being a Minister in a Government committed from the outset to a policy of coercion? Can anyone who has used the language and the doctrine of civil war–I have no doubt under great stress of strong, sincere personal feeling–violence always arises from very strong and sincere feelings–and promulgated on that Bench, look forward with pleasure or without, an anxious conscience to having to discharge his duty in such a situation, and having to mete out to others that measure which has not been meted out to him? What about Irish representation here? Do you mean to keep the Irish Members as an extraneous body under the insulting conditions of inferiority to which I have referred, and just vote them down, or do you propose without their agreement to cut down their representation from the numbers fixed in the Treaty of Union without giving them any compensating increase in their own control over their own domestic affairs? Is that your remedy, your reconciliation? Is that to be the final word which the governing genius of Britain, successful in so many lands, has to speak upon the melancholy relations between the two Kingdoms? Even this relief, if such you regard it, is distant, and cannot be attained until another Parliament beyond this one has run its appointed course. The march of history may in that period bring us to many grave events at home and abroad, whoever is in power, and we shall all of us be glad to have by our side a reconciled Ireland, and a friendly Irish party to share our hopes and fears; not a hostile band in our very citadel to raise their cry of unappeased resentment at the position in which they are placed. That is my argument to the Conservative party as a great power in the country.

I know well the answer that we shall receive to this. The answer will be that Ulster bars the way; that the Unionist party is bound in honour to Ulster. I am not going to indulge in recrimination. These are, so far as I can see them, the facts as they lie before us. It is because Ulster, or, rather, because North-East Ulster, objects that the whole settlement by agreement is to be prevented for ever. The right hon. Gentleman the Leader of the Opposition indeed thinks so seriously of the Ulster case that he seems to apprehend that the limit of conflict will not be confined to this world, but will trench upon celestial regions. Did he not in a powerful sentence say, "If Home Rule was passed Heaven help Ulster, but God help the Government"? Apparently we are threatened with a renewal of those divine incidents which form the subject of "Paradise Lost." I had always hoped that they had happily ceased in the concluding canto of "Paradise Regained." But I admit that the perfectly genuine apprehensions of the majority of the people of North-East Ulster constitute the most serious, and in my humble judgment, the only serious obstacle to a thoroughly satisfactory settlement of this question. It is impossible for a Liberal Government to treat cavalierly or contemptuously, for any British Government to ignore, the sincere sentiments of a numerous and well defined community like the Protestants of the North of Ireland. We may think them wrong; we may think them unreasonable; but there they are! We may think that their opinions are prejudiced, but their opinions are facts of a most stubborn kind. We are not likely to under-rate the forces and the influences which they can exercise upon the party opposite. We are not likely to under-rate forces that drove Mr. Gerald Balfour from the Irish Office–[An Hon. Member: "Wyndham"]–and, though we all hope only for the time being, has interrupted the career of the right hon. Gentleman the Member for Dover.

We are not likely to under-rate these forces. We know perfectly well how firm is the grip which Ulster politicians have upon the mainsprings of the Unionist party. For reminder–if reminder were needed–there sits opposite the right hon. and learned Gentleman, a horseman armed with whip and spur, resolved at all costs to drive Orange colours to the fore! What are the legitimate rights of Ulster? No one on this side of the House, no Liberal, will deny that it is the right of every citizen, nay a duty, provided the circumstances are sufficient, to resist oppression. That is a great and far-reaching principle. But it can be only applied with great moderation if societies and States into which men have formed themselves are to retain coherent structure. Let me ask another question? Have citizens the right even, if there is no oppression, to resist an Act of Parliament which they dislike? Not only by the men of Ulster, but in various parts of the country, in different circumstances, we feel the growth of this disposition to offer unconstitutional resistance, passive resistance, to the acts of the Legislature. I do most seriously ask the House to consider the great dangers which the continued development and exaggeration of this new feature will undoubtedly cause to our national life. . . .

Whatever Ulster's rights may be she cannot stand in the way of the whole of the rest of Ireland. Half a province cannot impose a permanent veto on the nation. Half a province cannot obstruct for ever the reconciliation between the British and the Irish democracies, and deny all satisfaction to the united wishes of the British Empire. The utmost they can claim is for themselves. I ask, do they claim separate treatment for themselves? Do the counties of Down and Antrim and Londonderry, for instance, ask to be excepted from the scope of the Bill? Do they ask for a Parliament of their own, or do they wish to remain here? Is that their demand? We ought to know.

I listened with profound interest to the colloquy which took place in the Debate on the introduction of this measure between the hon. and learned Member for Waterford (Mr. John Redmond) and the right hon. Gentleman the Member for Trinity College (Sir Edward Carson), and I think I am stating the views of the House as a whole when I say we should have liked to hear that colloquy carried further. It would be a great disaster to Ireland if the Protestant population in the North stood aloof from a national Parliament. It would be deeply injurious to the balance, interest, power, and distinction of the new Assembly. It would sensibly diminish the hopes which we attach to the establishment of self-government. We seek no quarrel with Ulster. We contemplate no violence, we seek to make friends not foes, to make peace not war, to redress grievances and not to create them, to appease not to offend, to enfranchise and not to enthral. But Ulster has duties as well as rights. There is a plain duty upon the Protestants of Ulster, though I am afraid hon. Gentlemen opposite will not agree as to what that duty is, but perhaps they will permit me to say what I believe it to be—there is a plain duty laid upon the Protestants, on the Loyalists of Ulster, as Mr. Gladstone used to call them, a duty which they owe first of all to the land of their birth, and in the second place to their friends and co-religionists all over Ireland, and, thirdly, to the self-governing Dominions of the Empire of which they are proud, and that duty is to stand by the ship and bring it safely into port. It is no doubt a great sacrifice that is asked of them, but a great opportunity is also offered to them.

No man can measure in words, or can tell, the blessing that Ulster men have it in their power to bestow upon their fellow-countrymen or the benefits which they would confer upon the State, or the fame and honour they would reap themselves, if they would lead a united Ireland home. At one stroke of the wand they could sweep the Irish question out of life into history and free the British realm from the canker which has poisoned its heart for generations. If they refuse, if they take to the boats, all we say is they shall not obstruct the work of salvage, and that shall go forward at any rate to the end. We present this Bill with good faith and good will to the House of Commons. We think the Irish have too much power in this country and not enough in their own. We feel that the growth of business requires a complete recasting of the Parliamentary machine. We intend this Bill to be the forerunner of a general system of devolution in the United Kingdom, and we are sure it is an indispensable preliminary to any such reform or any large improvement in Imperial organisation. We believe it will reconcile the two Kingdoms and bring the Irish race closely and truly into the British Empire, and make them loyal to the monarchy and good friends and comrades of the British people. We are convinced that there are no inconveniences and dangers in this policy which are not smaller than those under which we now lie, and we ask most earnestly for a fair and faithful consideration for that policy, and we believe, should this Bill pass into law and ultimately receive the full embodiment which we expect and ask for it, that men will look back across the gulf of years to that great statesman, first of all British Parliamentarians, who had the wisdom and the courage to point with unerring finger the true path along which the States and peoples of the British Empire might march to power and peace.

DEFENCE

May 4, 1912

Royal Academy Banquet,
Burlington House, London

On behalf of the British Navy, it is my duty to return you thanks for the manner in which you have drunk the health of the senior Service. The business of the Admiralty differs from the business of many great public departments in one important aspect. In many offices of State there is a great succession of interesting and important questions which are detached from one another, but at the Admiralty everything contributes and converges on one single object, namely, the development of the maximum war power at a given moment and at a particular point.–(Applause.) Upon that precise object are directed all the science our age can boast, all the wealth of our country, all the resources of our civilisation, all the patience, study, devotion to duty, and the sacrifice of personal interests which our naval officers and men supply–(hear, hear),–all the glories of our history in the past–everything is directed upon this one particular point and object, namely, the manifestation at some special place during the compass of a few minutes of shattering, blasting, overpowering, force. This may not, perhaps, seem a very amiable topic to which civilised men should devote many hours of their lives, but yet I venture to think that in the world in which we live and in the circumstances amid which we find ourselves, the study of absolute force for its own sake is not perhaps altogether unworthy of those who are called upon to take a share in the counsels of a free people. For what lies on the other side? What lies behind this development of the force of war power? Why, Mr. President and gentlemen, behind it lie all our right and claims for our great position in the world.–(Cheers.) Behind it lies all our power to put our own distinctive and characteristic mark upon the unfolding civilisation of mankind; for under the shelter of this manifestation we may agree or quarrel as we please, we may carry on our own party politics in perfect security.–(Cheers.) So long as that quality of our civilisation, so long as the patriotism and organisation of our country are sufficiently high to enable us to produce the maximum of force at a particular point, there is no reason why we should not hand on undiminished to those who come after us the great estate we have received from those who have gone before. I would not dwell even for a few moments upon wicked topics–(laughter)–without saying that there is a great danger that the study of force and the development of force may lead men into the temptation of using the force they have themselves developed. There is a danger of men and of nations becoming fascinated with the terrible machinery they have themselves called into being, and I think when we refer to it, it is also right for us to remember that if ever we do get engaged in war, or if any of the great civilised and scientific nations of the world become engaged in war, they will all be heartily sick of it long before they have got to the end.–(Applause.) For the rest, the best way to make war impossible is to make victory certain–(cheers),–and I am glad to be able to assure you that we see no difficulty in maintaining the main securities of the country and in providing an effective margin for our security at all the decisive points without adding very greatly to the generous provisions which Parliament has made in the past year and which it will doubtless renew in the years that are to come.

I thank you most sincerely, on behalf of the great Service it is my privilege to represent this evening, and for the gracious courtesy which has led you to bear it in mind. (Cheers.)

THE GERMAN NAVY LAW

July 22, 1912

House of Commons

Churchill's speeches on the promulgation of the German Navy Law had aroused public concern. Churchill realised that the Estimates he had inherited from McKenna were inadequate, and he sought an additional £5 million. The proposal met with no resistance in the Cabinet or in the House of Commons, and it enabled Churchill to spell out another warning to Germany about the perilous implications of her policy.

[Extract] . . . I think it will be for the convenience of the Committee if first of all this afternoon I proceed to examine in detail the scope and character of the new German Navy Law. The main feature of that law is not the increase in the new construction of capital ships, though that is an important feature. The main feature is the increase in the striking force of ships of all classes which will be available, immediately available, at all seasons of the year. A Third Squadron of eight battleships will be created and maintained in full commission as part of the active battle fleet. Whereas, according to the unamended law, the active battle fleet consisted of seventeen battleships, four battle or large armoured cruisers, and twelve small cruisers, in the near future that active fleet will consist of twenty-five battleships, eight battle or large armoured cruisers, and eighteen small cruisers; and whereas at present, owing to the system of recruitment which prevails in Germany, the German fleet is less fully mobile during the winter than during the summer months, it will, through the operation of this law, not only be increased in strength, but rendered much more readily available. Ninety-nine destroyers, torpedo-boat destroyers—or torpedo-boats, as they are called in Germany—instead of sixty-six, will be maintained in full commission out of the total of 144. Three-quarters of a million pounds had already been taken in the general estimate for the year for the building of submarines. The new law adds a quarter of a million to this, and that is a provision which, so far as we can judge from a study of the finances, would appear to be repeated in subsequent years. Seventy-two new submarines will be built within the currency of the law, and of those it is apparently proposed to maintain fifty-four with full permanent crews.

Taking a general view, the effect of the law will be that nearly four-fifths of the entire German navy will be maintained in full permanent commission—that is to say, instantly and constantly ready for war. Such a proportion is remarkable, and, so far as I am aware, finds no example in the previous practice of modern naval Powers. So great a change and development in the German fleet involves, of course, important additions to their personnel. In 1898 the officers and men of the German navy amounted to 25,000. To-day that figure has reached 66,000. Under the previous Navy Laws, and various amendments which have preceded this one, the Germans have been working up to a total in 1920, according to our calculations, of 86,500 officers and men, and they have been approaching that total by increments of, approximately, an addition of 3,500 a year. The new law adds a total of 15,000 officers and men, and makes the total in 1920 of 101,500. The new average annual addition is calculated to be 1,680 of all ranks, but for the next three years by special provision 500 extra are to be added. From 1912 to 1914, 500 are to be added, and in the last three years of the currency of the law 500 less will be taken. This makes a total rate of increase of the German Navy personnel about 5,700 men a year. The new construction under the law prescribes for the building of three additional battleships—one to be begun next year, one in 1916, and two small cruisers of which the date has not yet been fixed. The date of the third battleship has not been fixed. It has been presumed to be later than the six years which we have in view. The cost of these increases in men and in material during the next six years is estimated as £10,500,000 above the previous estimates spread over that period. I should like to point out to the Committee that this is a cumulative increase which follows upon other increases of a very important character. The law of 1898 was practically doubled by the law of 1900, and if the expenditure contemplated by the law of 1900 had been followed the German estimates of to-day would be about £11,000,000. But owing to the amendments of 1906 and 1908, and now of 1912, that expenditure is very nearly £23,000,000. The actual figures of the expenditure have been given by my right hon. Friend the Chancellor of the Exchequer on a recent occasion in Committee of Supply. But the fact that personnel plays such a large part in this new amendment and that personnel is more cheaply obtained in Germany than in this country makes the money go further there than it would do over here.

The ultimate scale of the new German fleet, as contemplated by the latest Navy Law, will be forty-one battleships, twenty battle or large armoured cruisers, and forty small cruisers, besides a proper proportion—an ample proportion—of flotillas of torpedo-boat destroyers and submarines. [An Hon. Member: "By what year?"] By 1920. That is not on paper a great advance on the figures prescribed by the previous law, which gave thirty-eight battleships, twenty battle or large armoured cruisers, and thirty-eight small cruisers. That is not a great advance on the total scale. In fact, however, there is a remarkable expansion of strength and efficiency, and particularly of strength and efficiency as they contribute to striking power. The number of battleships and large armoured cruisers alone which will be kept constantly ready and in full commission will be raised by the law from twenty-one, the present figure, to thirty-three—that is to say, an addition of twelve, or an increase of about 57 per cent. The new fleet will in the beginning include about twenty battleships and large cruisers of the older type, but, gradually as new vessels are built, the fighting power of the fleet will rise until in the end it will consist completely of modern vessels. This new scale of the German fleet—organised in five battle squadrons, each attended by a battle or armoured cruiser squadron, complete with small cruisers and auxiliaries of all kinds, and accompanied by numerous flotillas of destroyers and submarines, more than three-fourths, nearly four-fifths, maintained in full permanent commission—the aspect and scale of this fleet is, I say, extremely formidable. Such a fleet will be about as numerous to look at as the fleet which was gathered at Spithead for the recent Parliamentary visit, but, of course, when completed it will be far superior in actual strength. This full development will only be realised step by step. But already in 1914 two squadrons will, so far as we can ascertain, be entirely composed of "Dreadnoughts," or what are called "Dreadnoughts," and the third will be made up of good ships like the "Deutschlands" and the "Braunschweigs," together with five "Dreadnought" battle-cruisers. It remains to be noted that this new law is the fifth in fourteen years of the large successive increases made in German naval strength, that it encountered no effective opposition in its passage through the Reichstag, and that, though it has been severely criticised in Germany since its passage, the criticisms have been directed towards its inadequacy.

Before I come to the measures which will be necessary on our part, perhaps the Committee will permit me to make a general observation. There are two points with regard to navies and naval war which differentiate them from armies and land war. The first is the awful suddenness with which naval warfare can reach its decisive phase. We see on the continent of Europe immense military establishments possessed by nations dwelling on opposite sides of political frontier lines; yet they dwell and have dwelt for a whole generation in peace and tranquillity. But between those armies and any decisive collision there intervenes an inevitable period of delay that acts as a great buffer, a cushion of security. I mean the vast process of mobilisation, the very first signs of which must be noticed, and which, once it begins, lays idle the industry of both countries and dominates the whole course of national life. So it is that through all these years nations are able to dwell side by side with their tremendous military establishments without being a prey to undue anxiety as to immediate attack. But none of these considerations apply to fleets. The Fleet which was assembled for the manœuvres the other day was fully capable of going into action as soon as the ammunition could be brought up and put by the side of the guns. And that is true of all the great highly efficient navies of the world.

I am bound to say, looking far ahead, and farther than the purpose of this Vote, at the aspect which Europe and the world will present when the power of States, which has been hitherto estimated in terms of armies, will be estimated very largely in naval strength, and when we have a number of Great Powers all possessed of very powerful navies, the state of Europe and of the world would seem to contain many more germs of danger than the period through which we have been passing in our lifetime.

The second general point to which I would direct the attention of the Committee is the extreme slowness with which naval preparations can be made. Small ships take eighteen to twenty months to build; large ships take from two to three years, sometimes four years. Docks take more than four years to build. Seamen take from two to three years to train; artificers take much longer; officers take between six and seven years. The efficiency which comes from the harmonious combination of these elements is a plant of very slow growth indeed. Cool, steady, methodical preparation, prolonged over a succession of years, can alone raise the margin of naval power. It is no use flinging millions of money about on the impulse of the moment, by a gesture of impatience, or in a mood of panic. Such a course only reveals your weakness and impotence. Those who clamour for sensational expenditure, who think that the kind of danger with which we are faced needs to be warded off or can be warded off in that way, are either ignorant themselves of naval conditions or take advantage of the ignorance of others. The strain we have to bear will be long and slow, and no relief will be obtained by impulsive or erratic action. We ought to learn from our German neighbours, whose policy marches unswervingly towards its goal across the lifetime of a whole generation. The two general principles which I would deduce from these observations, and which will guide my remarks this afternoon, are, first, that we must have an ample margin of strength instantly ready; and, secondly, that there must be a steady and systematic development of our naval forces untiringly pursued over a number of years. . . .

I have one thing more to say before I sit down. I have endeavoured to place, as frankly and as fully as I can, the naval situation before the Committee, and it has been, I can assure the Committee, a source of comfort and of encouragement during these last weeks to have had by our side the Prime Minister and other Ministers of the Dominion of Canada. It has been like the touch of the hand of a strong friend when serious business has to be done. The task of maintaining the naval power of the Empire under existing conditions is a heavy one. All the world is arming as it has never armed before. We have to face the simultaneous building by many nations of great modern ships of war. We have to protect from all danger or alarms Dominions and territories scattered over every Continent and across every ocean. Well do we understand the truth of Mr. Borden's [Prime Minister of Canada] words—"The day of peril is too late for preparation." There is an earnest disposition on the part of the self-governing Dominions to assist in the common defence of the Empire. The time has now come to make that disposition effective. Apart altogether from material aid, the moral effect of the arrival upon blue water of these new nations of the British Empire cannot be measured. The unity of the British Empire carries with it the safety of its component parts, and the safety of the British Empire probably carries with it the peace of the world. If we are told that the beginnings of co-operation in defence must carry with them the beginnings of association in policy, then I say that both in measures of defence and in the direction of policy the co-operation of the Dominions with the United Kingdom will be of estimable benefit to the strength of the Empire and to the general cause of peace. . . .

I have now finished–I am afraid I have trespassed a great deal upon the indulgence of the Committee–the statement with which I desire to commend this Supplementary Estimate to their attention. It always happens that these occasions of naval discussions are preceded by a crop of lively rumours and contradictory forecasts, and some of those who appear to have specially close and detailed information of Cabinet and Admiralty secrets delight to depict from day to day the varying fortunes of the Imperialist and economist sections of the Cabinet, who are represented as waging a savage and perpetual warfare, only suspended from time to time by unsatisfactory and unnatural compromises. These ingenious speculations indeed, if I may say so with respect, betray a great lack of understanding, The kind of questions with which we have been dealing this afternoon are not matters into which compromise can easily enter. They are not suitable subjects for hagglings and bargainings. The Minister who for the time being is responsible for Admiralty business to the House is brought directly face to face with very serious and very definite facts. It is quite easy for the House to change a Minister; it is quite easy for a party to change a spokesman; but changing a Minister or changing a spokesman does not change the facts. There they are, and they march towards you, and some one or other, somehow or other, has got to deal with them, however unpleasant they may be and however unpleasant their consequences may be. The policy which I have submitted to the Committee this afternoon is the policy of the Admiralty, which we ourselves have steadily developed and pursued, and in which we have confidence. On behalf of the Admiralty I shall ask for nothing that is not necessary, and I have asked for nothing that I have not got.

"THE POLITICS OF ACTION"

September 11, 1912

Constituency Meeting,
Kinnaird Hall, Dundee

The bitterness of political acrimony became greater during the summer of 1912. At Blenheim, on July 27, Bonar Law described the Government as "a revolutionary committee which has seized upon despotic power by force," and warned that on the question of Ulster "there are things stronger than Parliamentary majorities" at work.

[Extract] I thank you very warmly for the kindness with which you have received me.–(Cheers.) I am told that one of the signs of advancing age is that the time begins to pass more quickly the less there is of it.–(Laughter.) If so, I must be beginning to get old–(laughter),–for the year since I last addressed a Dundee audience from the board platform of the Kinnaird Hall has certainly slipped away very rapidly indeed, and I can hardly believe that the earth has had time to get all round the sun and back again while I have been working away at the Admiralty in London.–(Laughter and cheers.) But so it is. Whatever faults the Liberal Government have committed, they have not yet succeeded in interrupting the revolutions of the heavenly bodies.–(Laughter and cheers.)

A year has gone, not, indeed, a year of unmingled sunshine–it would be too much to expect two sunshiny years in succession under a Liberal Government–(laughter),–but still a year of prosperity to our country, and a year, indeed, akin to peace, a year of active and expanding trade and employment, a year which bids fair to establish a new record in British trade, and a year which also, I am glad to say, has been a good year for the trade of Dundee.–(Cheers.) Yes, Sir George Ritchie–"My dear Sir George Ritchie"–(laughter and cheers),–in spite of our blind adherence to the shibboleth of an outworn fiscal system, in spite of the wilful neglect of the Government to put any tax, even the smallest, upon bread or upon meat, in spite of the fact that our markets have been invaded by goods which foreigners send us because we want to buy them–(laughter),–British trade and British industry have been buoyant and booming as they have never been before, and upon a greater scale than ever hitherto witnessed. In spite of that wicked Chancellor of the Exchequer, who, as every good Tory knows, has ruined our credit and shattered our finances and driven all the money out of the country, we have as a nation never made so much of it in twelve months before, we have never done so great a trade, we have never sent such valuable cargoes across the seas, we have never received back so good a return from those in other lands with whom we trade.–(Cheers.) . . .

Mr. Bonar Law–(hisses)–at the beginning of the session Mr. Bonar Law–(Some cheers and laughter.) He is the successor of Mr. Balfour, a man who, in Opposition or out of it, leader of the Opposition or private member, is among the first men in the country. He took the place of Lord Salisbury, a wise leader of our people, and Lord Salisbury was the successor of Mr. Disraeli, whose services have not gone unregarded by later generations, irrespective of party, as Mr. Disraeli was the successor of Sir Robert Peel, who swept away the Corn Laws for ever from the land.–(Cheers.) And it is after that long hierarchy of remarkable men that I come back to my point. Mr. Bonar Law. (Laughter.) Mr. Bonar Law was a digression. I don't mean Mr. Bonar Law is a digression.–(Laughter.) No; I have every desire to see him reign long and prosperously over the fortunes of the Conservative party.–(Laughter and cheers.) Mr. Bonar Law blurted out at the beginning of the session a threat to repeal the Insurance Act, just as Lord Selborne the other day threatened to repeal the Parliament Act. But Mr. Bonar Law was forced within a day to explain himself away. It was a very simple point, but he had to make it clear. It is quite plain that when he said "Certainly," what he meant to say was "Certainly not."–(Laughter and cheers.) Now he contents himself with declaring that he will drastically amend it. But how he will drastically amend it he does not say. He cannot tell us, because he does not know.–(Laughter.) He has no ideas. All he knows is that it will be drastic, but what form the amendment will take he does not know. But he does not understand, perhaps, enough about social problems to enable him to commit himself to an articulate idea upon the subject. (Laughter and cheers.)

I said that the Act was irrevocable. But it is not irrevocable, because Parliament and the electors have not the full power to revoke it if they choose. It is because they could never use that power. The Act is irrevocable because the Act is indispensable.—(Cheers.) It was necessary. It was a duty which had to be done, and that had to be done quickly by some one or by some party unless great and crying evils were to go unremedied, and unless greater evils were to be added to them.—(Cheers.) . . .

[Editor's Note: Churchill spoke at length of the Government's social programmes.] These are the politics of action, not of faction. (Cheers.) They are what Prince Bismarck once called, in a memorable phrase, the politics of practical Christianity.—(Cheers.) They are the politics of construction, not of confusion; or organisation, not of drift; of a nation, and not of a party. I have not hesitated to speak at length upon those social measures to-night, and you will observe that I speak of them in absolute and entire confidence. I am glad to speak of them to you to-night at my annual meeting of my constituents here, because I am so much bound and locked in the special practical work of the office I now have the honour to hold that I am not able to take so active a part as I was able to do in former years in regard to general matters of political concern.

I think that we have a right as Liberals to dwell on this great measure of social organisation and to vindicate our action in these matters against all the ignoramuses and ne'er-do-wells and fly-by-nights who are vapouring on social topics to-day. We have studied the interests of the millions. We have marched, like Napoleon, with the opinions of millions of men. We have faith in our work and we are proud of it. We know that it will last longer than our lives; we are sure it was necessary; we are sure it is good; we know that we have done our best; that we have done our duty. Confident of that we may be careless of the rest, and we may leave to the Tory obstructors or the Socialist wreckers the barren task of picking holes, of finding fault, snarling and sneering and jeering and gibing, deriding and exploiting the difficulties of the great enterprise which they would never have had the wit to conceive.—(Prolonged cheers.) If the conditions of British politics were such that there was no party in the State and no Government strong enough to carry necessary legislation of this character, irrespective of its temporary popularity or unpopularity—if that condition were ever reached then I say it would prove the bankruptcy of our Parliamentary constitution. But I speak to-night to you in a mood of optimism—(cheers),—and I am confident that good work, done not for a class but for the whole people, will win its way and will win the regard and respect of the masses of the people, and will enable the party which has been responsible for such work to retain its hold upon their support and their confidence. I am sure that those who are merely opportunists, looking for this little wind and that slight breeze, and seeking for a small opportunity to cavil, and with obvious prejudice, and trying to make up out of those little bits of dissatisfaction a policy to which a great Government could stand, will be found to be among those who have built their castles on the sand, and who when the storm, the rising storm and renewing storm, of Liberal enterprise and enthusiasm breaks again on the land, as it has done three times running, will be swept once again into the contempt and discredit that they deserve.–(Cheers.)

I turn to another cause to which the Liberal party was pledged and bound a quarter of a century ago by Mr. Gladstone–(cheers),–a cause which is now nearing its full fruition. There is no more valuable prize that could be secured for the British Empire than the reconciliation of the Irish people.–(Cheers.) There is no other Imperial work so important, so urgent, so safe, and so hopeful as the creation of an Irish Parliament, subordinate to the Imperial Parliament, for the settlement of purely Irish affairs.–(Cheers.) I do not believe that the Unionist party are in their hearts opposed to this. I do not believe it whatever their leaders may say.

The old fear–you know it in your daily life and among the men you meet; those good friends you no doubt have on the other side of politics,–you know that the old fear and prejudice in Great Britain against Home Rule is dying out with the generation that brought it in 1886. You men who are in touch with the great self-governing colonies know the marvellous results which have crowned the gift of self-government in South Africa. The only thing that the anti-Home Ruler holds to now is the opposition of the three or four Orange counties in North-east Ulster. If that obstacle were removed or avoided the whole structure of resistance would tumble to the ground and nothing but ordinary party feeling and the hugger-mugger business–(laughter)–of the ins and outs would remain. But still it is a serious obstacle, and it is an obstacle I have never underrated.

I think the time is coming when the leaders of the Opposition should be required to state frankly and honourably and sincerely where they stand in relation to North-east Ulster.–(Cheers.) I won't dwell to-night on the language of violence and rebellion which some of their leaders have so recklessly used, and of which the party as a whole, as if perfectly clear, is silently ashamed, and about which it is extremely embarrassed. I ask seriously all men who profess to be patriotic men, who profess to care for the welfare of the country and the concord of the Empire, what is it that they claim on behalf of the Orange counties of Ulster. Do they claim for them the right to remain as they are in the British Parliament, or do they claim that these few counties are to have the right to bar the way for all time to all the rest of Ireland? That is a question the leaders of the Opposition ought to answer simply and sincerely. The answer would greatly simplify the forward movement of events. Their interest in the settlement of the Irish question is not less than ours.

They tell us it is their opinion that they are coming into power. They have been coming into power long before this.–(Laughter.) They thought it was four years ago, then three years ago, then two years ago, and they think so still.–(Laughter.) But they believe they are coming into power.–(Laughter.) On their hypothesis you may ask them this question: Have they no contribution to make to the settlement of this great difficulty with Ireland? Do they want an ungovernable Ireland on their hands? Do they want to begin a new era of coercion of Nationalist Ireland? I am aware that in the eighties a Tory Government were able to keep themselves going on a basis of coercion, and that it even proved popular with certain elements of their party, but times have changed, opinions have changed, the proportion of things has changed. The British Government cannot afford to remain indifferent to the feelings of the colonies. The coercion of Ireland, after the hopes that have been raised, the coercion of Ireland by men who have uttered these doctrines and have given their approval to them would be a cruel and hateful business. It would be deeply wounding to all our colonial fellow-subjects all over the world.

Why, even from a Unionist standpoint the failure of Home Rule would be a great disaster. It would be a setback to the movement of Imperial unity. Much of the good of the last ten years would be destroyed, and the harsh cry of Ireland, once again repulsed from the very circle of the Empire which she sought to join, would find an echo in every land where the British flag is flying over the self-governing dominions of the Crown.–(Cheers.) I have heard five thousand Nationalists in Belfast sing the National Anthem; I have seen the King's health drunk in "rebel Cork"; I know that in Australia and in Canada large sections of Irishmen, large numbers of Irishmen of influence and power in the Governments of these countries and in the political system which prevails there are on the verge of throwing in their lot whole-heartedly with the British Empire and with our united trade. Are these things of no consequence to Tory Imperialists? Is the loyalty of Orangemen, even when that loyalty takes the form of rebellion–(laughter),–is that the only loyalty which they are prepared to accept from Ireland? Is the British Empire to be cut off for ever from being friendly because of the bigotry and bitter hatred of a small and highly localised minority? A little fair play, a little goodwill, a little of that sense of responsibility which I fully admit the Conservative party show in dealing with foreign affairs, or with the navy or with colonial matters–a little of that sense of responsibility and the Irish question can be settled so easily, and can be settled so well. Already the light of a better day is beginning to shine in the sky, and those dullards would quench it if they could. But they cannot quench it, and they shall not quench it.–(Loud cheers.)

It may be that the leaders of the Opposition will say, "We are not going to answer your question. We want to turn the Government out, and to get into their place ourselves. We have in the enthusiasm and vigour of the Irish population of North-east Ulster a weapon which we shall use without regard to the public interest or the law of the land. The worse things go in Ireland the better we shall be pleased. We hope there will be bloodshed. We hope there will be civil war, and we hope that the Government will get discredited to-day, so that we (the Opposition) can go into office." If that is the attitude which the Conservative party is going to take up during a period not free from other anxieties than those to which I have referred to-night, I say with confidence that we have nothing to hope for from them, and neither have we anything to fear.–(Cheers.) We shall proceed through our course with firmness and patience. If we show ourselves ready to reason it is not that we are not prepared to act. We have every intention of using to the full the power given us by the electors at the last general election–(cheers)–and to use that power to carry out the purpose for which it was bestowed. No split votes at by-elections–(laughter),–no snatch divisions in the House of Commons, no abuse of Tory platforms or Tory newspapers, no rowdyism at Westminster will deter us as long as we are supported by an adequate Parliamentary majority from executing our commission to the full and carrying into law and into effect, in the lifetime of the present Parliament, the Home Rule Bill and other great measures for which the Liberal party has laboured valiantly and long.

BALKAN SITUATION AND DEFENCE PREPAREDNESS

October 30, 1912

Cutlers' Feast, Sheffield

The Balkan War, which broke out on October 8, caused early disaster for the Turkish forces and virtually drove the Ottoman Empire out of Europe. This situation created a serious crisis between Austria-Hungary and Russia, which was resolved at the London Conference of May 1913.

I am proud to be invited to your board at one of these Cutlers' Feasts about which I have read so often, and of course it is especially interesting to one charged with the duties I at present endeavour to fulfil to come to Sheffield, which, though a considerable distance from the sea, nevertheless contributes an essential part to the naval security of our country.–(Hear, hear.) But although the speeches to-night have largely dealt with domestic affairs, I suspect that many of your minds have strayed from this festive and auspicious scene in safe and comfortable England to the tremendous events which are marching forward in rapid succession in the East of Europe. For the drama or the tragedy which is moving to its climax in the Balkans we all have our responsibility, and none of us can escape our share of it by blaming others or by blaming the Turks. If there is any man here who, looking back over the last 35 years, thinks he knows where to fix the responsibility for all the procrastination, all the provocation, for all the jealousies and rivalries, for all the religious and racial animosities which have been working together for this result, I do not envy him his complacency. But whether we blame the belligerents or criticise the Powers or sit in sackcloth and ashes ourselves is absolutely of no consequence at the present moment. Historians may some day occupy themselves in unravelling the sequence of events, but here and now we can only hope and so far as lies in our power work for a peace which when it comes will for ever banish the spectre of war from these broad and once fertile provinces now distracted by tumult, and which will give tranquillity and security to those who live their lives in those regions. It is the third great war which men now living have seen waged over the quite measurable problem presented by the Balkan peoples of the Balkan peninsula. Let us hope and pray that when it is over all the nations will be united in a resolve that about these affairs at any rate there shall never be another war.–(Cheers.) Let us hope that they will insist that the long and dismal chapter in human history which has been unfolded in that quarter of the world shall in one way or another be closed once and for all. There are happily many signs which may encourage us in this expectation, but here we are face to face with events which, if Europe were really animated with the passion of hatred and ambition which pessimists occasionally ascribed to it, might easily have brought us within reach of the long-predicted Armageddon. So far we see all the Governments, without exception, honestly striving to adjust their differences, to preserve their amity, and to bring their combined influence to bear to make an end of a long and fierce and disastrous quarrel and to secure a settlement which shall be just to the belligerents and for the benefit of the populations concerned. So long as a loyal and honest spirit continues to govern the Great Powers no problem will arise from the Balkan struggle which cannot be settled to their common advantage and to the lasting good of the Balkan people without any extension of the area now devastated.

These are not satisfactory considerations, but there is another aspect of this war which awakens graver reflections. We have sometimes been assured by the persons who profess to know that the danger of war has become an illusion, and that in the modern days the danger would not exist at all but for the machinations of statesmen and diplomatists, but for the intrigues of financiers aided by the groundless suspicions of generals and admirals–(laughter),–fomented by the sensationalism of the press–(laughter),–and all directed upon the ignorance and credulity of the people. Well, here is a war which has arisen from none of these causes, and here is a war which has broken out in spite of all that rulers and diplomatists could do to prevent it, and a war in which the press had no part, a war in which the whole force of the money power has been subtly and steadfastly directed to prevent it, directed to prevent a war which has come upon us not through the ignorance or credulity of people, but, on the contrary, from their knowledge of their history and of their destiny and from their intense realisation of their wrongs and of their duty, as they conceived them. A war which from all these causes has burst upon us with all the forces of a spontaneous explosion, and which within the limits in which it is operating has carried all before it in destruction and in strife–face to face with such a manifestation, who is the man who is bold enough to say, for instance, that force is never a remedy? Who is the man who is foolish enough to say that martial virtues do not play a vital part in the health and honour of every people?–("Hear, hear" and cheers.) Who is the man who is vain enough to suppose that the long antagonisms of history and of time can in all circumstances be adjusted and compacted by the smooth and superficial conventions of politicians and ambassadors?

When I consider what is passing elsewhere and the position of our country I cannot help feeling–and I think you will share my mood–that we are fortunate indeed among the nations of the world. We are fortunate; we are born under a lucky star, born in a good age for ourselves. We have no old scores to pay off, we have no modern enmities to prosecute, we can survey our past without a pang, we can survey our future without a grudge. (Hear, hear.) But we must be prepared. (Loud cheers.) We must be ready for all eventualities. It is good to be patient, it is good to be circumspect, it is good to be peace-loving; but it is not enough. We must be strong–(hear, hear),–we must be self-reliant, and in the end, for all our party politics, we must be united. (Cheers.) If our hearts are British hearts, are devoid of hate, if our skies are clear, we owe it to those valiant generations who by their prowess and manly wisdom have slowly raised the fortunes of this small island to the summit of a glorious Empire, an Empire which draws each year into a closer unity under the influences of freedom and of peace. I am entitled to remind you that we owe it also in a special sense to that hardy breed of sailors, to that unfailing succession of skillful sea captains who in every kind of vessel against every kind of vessel, against every kind of enemy on all oceans and through all the centuries have maintained unbroken that naval power and–why should we not say it?–naval supremacy–(cheers)–on which the greatness and the safety of our country depend.

We live in a world of unceasing change, The spirit of decay pervades all human arrangements. No race, no empire, no institution can repose for any length of time on past virtues or past achievements. Unless we renew our strength continually, unless we revive and exalt without ceasing those impulses of comradeship and of duty which are the true source of national strength, we cannot hope to preserve indefinitely our happy and prosperous situation. (Hear, hear.) We must so manage our affairs, we must so organise our corporate life, that those who come after us shall have an easier and not a harder burden to bear, and they shall have fewer dangers to face and greater resources to meet those dangers with. When we compare our fortunate position in the world with that of those other peoples now desperately struggling we cannot but feel how much we have to be thankful for. (Hear, hear.) It would indeed be shameful if we, who have inherited so much, if we who had so much done for us before we came into the world at all, if we who started so fair on the path of life, were to leave our children nothing but bitter memories to avenge and vast misfortunes to retrieve. (Cheers.)

There are no doubt many features in the organisation of British politics and of British society in all its grades which are anxious and perplexing. There are military and industrial and constitutional problems which rightly exercise and divide the minds of thoughtful men. The tasks that have devolved upon us are serious, the times in which we live are critical; we have to hold what we have, to unite and to consolidate the Empire. We have to reconcile where reconciliation is needed in its various spheres, we have to create conditions of life and labour which are worthy of an Imperial democracy. Of course there are those out of this country and even in it who say that we shall fail; but standing here to-night I believe I shall express our true convictions when I say that although perfect solutions of our difficulties are not to be looked for in an imperfect world, and although persistent disagreement as to methods is inevitable and not necessarily unblessed, yet in our own British fashion, which no one else understands–(laughter)–we shall in our lifetime make a notable advance in most of the directions I have mentioned and hold our ground.–(Hear, hear.) To that work all parties in their turn can and ought to contribute.–(Hear, hear.) If they do simply and sincerely according to their lights then the nation, which is far greater than all the parties put together, will have no reason to doubt itself or fear for its future.–(Loud cheers.)

NAVAL PREPAREDNESS

November 9, 1912

The Lord Mayor's Banquet,
The Guildhall, London

It is a year since I had the honour to respond to the toast of "The Navy" in this famous hall. I had at that time too little official information upon the wide range of Admiralty business. Since then I have endeavoured to see things as much as possible for myself–(cheers),–and I have had the advice and guidance of some of the ablest officers in the Service, and the resources of a great Department have been placed at my disposal. It is therefore with a greater measure of authority that this year I invite you to place your full confidence in the solid efficiency of our naval organization. (Cheers.) No harm has been done during the year by plain speech on naval questions. On the contrary, the effect has been extremely good. The Germans are a nation with robust minds. They are a nation with a high sense of honour and fair play, and they look on affairs in a practical military spirit. They like to have the facts put plainly and squarely before them. They do not want them wrapped up for fear they should be shocked by them, and the relations between the two countries have steadily improved during the year–(cheers),–and they have steadily improved side by side with every evidence of our determination to maintain our naval supremacy. And the best way to make those relations thoroughly healthy and comfortable is to go right on and put an end to this naval rivalry by proving that we cannot be overtaken. (Loud and prolonged cheers.)

The year has witnessed various important naval developments. The fleet has been reorganized upon a complete and symmetrical plan. An entire new squadron of very powerful ships has been placed in full commission. We have recruited the largest number of sailors and stokers of any year in modern times. Nearly three times as many men have been recruited in each month upon the average of the present year as was the case in the last year which preceded it. Before the end of the Session I shall submit to Parliament proposals, which the Government have sanctioned, for improving the pay of the officers and men of the Royal Navy (cheers), and this, it may be hoped, will still further stimulate our already buoyant recruiting. We had not proposed last year to create the Sixth Battle Squadron until 1915, but by various administrative arrangements which have been very carefully studied, and which are too complex for me to refer to here, it will be possible to bring that squadron into existence next year. (Cheers.) When I say bring it into existence, I mean bring it into existence fully manned on mobilization with active service ratings. This will increase the margin of security to which I have on several occasions referred in the House of Commons.

At the present time a strong British fleet is cruising in the Eastern basin of the Mediterranean. More than 20 British battleships and cruisers are found where they are wanted, and when they are wanted, in those classic waters, now the theatre of such tremendous events. The absence of those powerful forces at a time of crisis in Europe requires special vigilance from the Admiralty, and certain precautions, designed to increase our immediate preparedness, have been taken. We have no reason to apprehend trouble of any kind. But my advisers at the Admiralty are satisfied that the number of fleets and flotillas in home waters is by no means unequal to any task that might devolve upon them. It would be a poor thing to belittle or depreciate the undoubted resources of British naval power in serious times like these, and there is no reason whatever to do so, for that power has not often stood upon a firmer basis than it does to-night. (Cheers.)

But, after all, what has made this year memorable in the history of the navy has been the spontaneous and simultaneous movement of the great Dominions of the Crown towards an effective participation in Imperial naval-defence. (Loud cheers.) Mr. Alderman and Sheriff Cooper, in proposing this toast, referred to the hope I have cherished of a union between the English-speaking peoples for the purpose of mutual defence. My lords and gentlemen, that is already on the high road to consummation. The year began by the Government of the Dominion of New Zealand placing their splendid battle cruiser at our disposition. (Cheers.) The year has witnessed the steady development of the Australian fleet unit and the consequent relief to British naval resources from this strong and useful naval organization. At this very moment, at the other side of the globe, the Prime Minister of the Commonwealth, at such a banquet as this at Melbourne, is explaining the arrangements under which the Royal Australian Navy will pass under the general control of the Imperial Admiralty in times of war (loud cheers); and in a few days, when the Canadian Parliament meets, we may expect the announcement of a naval policy worthy of the power and loyalty of the great Dominion and of momentous consequences to the needs of the Empire as a whole.

The future will require renewed exertions from us all. No one can tell what its difficulties or its dangers may be, but no one who does justice either to the virility of the British Empire or to the efficiency of the British Navy will doubt our resolve, or will doubt our ability to come safely through them. (Loud and prolonged cheers.)

ULSTER PROBLEM

February 11, 1913

Home Rule Council Luncheon,
Hotel Cecil, London

The passage of the Government of Ireland Bill was marked by scenes of uproar, heated exchanges, and even occasional disorder in the House of Commons. On November 13, 1912, Mr. Ronald McNeill threw a copy of the Standing Orders at Churchill. Meanwhile, confidential conversations about the possibility of a compromise, in which Churchill took an active part, continued to reveal the gulf between the two sides.

We are gathered here together to-day in great numbers to congratulate and to welcome our friend the victor of Derry.—(Cheers.) I do assure him on your behalf of the keen feelings of personal satisfaction, apart altogether from political emotions, with which we receive him among us. Mr. Hogg's victory was a timely, and it may well prove a famous, event. One can hardly imagine any electoral episode which could at that particular moment have more fully embodied all the features of a triumph—a triumph, a battle-flag, a trophy bringing with it encouragement all along the fighting-line—than did the victory of Derry. But the victory of Derry was much more than any mere triumph of partisanship, much more even than valuable encouragement given to the Parliamentary forces who are sustaining this long contest. It was a victory less of partisanship than of conciliation and goodwill. It was a victory which represents much that we hope for in the new Ireland which is coming every day into being—(cheers),—and which has, we confidently hope, a fine part to play on the stage of the world's affairs. To that Ireland, prosperous and contented, loyal and free, the accession of a man like Mr. Hogg, coming into public life for the first time, bringing new forces and new resources to the aid of Irish administration, is a noteworthy and a hopeful event. May I be permitted to make one reference to the candidate who did not stand for Derry, my friend and kinsman Mr. Shane Leslie? He cheerfully made and would cheerfully make any sacrifice which could in the least advance the cause of his country. "They also serve who only stand and wait," and while a sincere spirit of self-suppression and loyalty to the general interests of Ireland continues to animate all sections and classes of that country, the great difficulties which still lie before us cannot seem formidable or at any rate insuperable.—(Cheers.)

We are reminded to-day by the presence of our friend Mr. Hogg that the Ulster minority—(cheers)—must and will also be considered. The Prime Minister said, speaking earlier in the year, that there was no case which would better have repaid good and reasonable presentation than the case of the minority of the Ulster representatives.—(Cheers.) But what have we had? During the whole of these long discussions have we had one word of sober reason or of genuine goodwill from those who have constituted themselves in the House of Commons the spokesmen of the Ulster minority?—("No.") We have had during all these months nothing but hothouse hatred and incubated bigotry.—(Cheers.) We have been confronted with a dreary succession of violent and extravagant threats, and at no time or period in our debates have we seen in Parliament, at any rate, any desire to face the real facts of the situation or meet the real needs which Ireland demands, and which this time she shall have.—(Cheers.) The wildest threats, the most absurd statements have come from the leader of the Unionist party himself. No one should, I think, be more careful and circumspect in the language he uses than the leader of a great English party possessed with the idea, as he so frequently tells us, that he is shortly to be summoned to undertake the august responsibilities of the first Minister of the Crown. But Mr. Bonar Law prepares himself for the duties of an English Prime Minister by adopting, eagerly and recklessly, every statement, threat, or assertion, however extreme, that the most rabid partisans in his own faction are able to utter. We have heard from him language applied to violence which I venture to say would make his due execution of the law practically impossible if ever he were himself called upon to undertake those responsibilities.—(Cheers.) We have heard the absurd threat, which I understand has been circulated in some quarters of Belfast, that the Ulster minority would secede to Germany. We have heard this absurd threat—so ridiculous that no man in his senses would have cared to notice it—actually repeated with gusto in the House of Commons by the leader of the Unionist party, and it is only on a par with such extravagances that Mr. Bonar Law should in a recent speech have endeavoured most improperly to draw the person of the Sovereign into a great and fierce political controversy of this character. Anyone who could be so minded as for party purposes to give criminal advice of that character—(cheers)—to the constitutional ruler of this country—to step down into the arena of party politics and take a violent action against a great portion of his fellow-subjects and the overwhelming majority of one of the kingdoms over which he rules—anyone who could give such criminal and foolish advice as that has shown himself indeed to be unfitted for a responsible position in the Government or Parliament.

When the history of these events comes to be written, and all these hotly contested matters are reviewed in the cold light of another age, how very different will the attitudes of the English Unionist leader and the Irish Nationalist leader appear! On the one hand folly, spite, and venom in defeat; on the other statecraft, generosity, and goodwill marching to victory. Mr. Redmond has again and again, in Parliament and in the country, made it clear that he realises that the greatest triumph of the Home Rule cause will be a triumph which does not leave a minority of his fellow-countrymen smarting bitterly from the sense of defeat, and everything that it is in his power to do to promote a reasonable settlement and the dismissal of unfounded fears will be done in the months of reflection which lie before us. But we cannot be turned from our path by threats. Half a province cannot claim to stand for all time in the way not only of the demands of a nation but of the needs of an Empire. We must ask our friends who differ on this question sometimes to believe that we are in earnest too, and although we may not use their violent language, that is not because we do not feel as resolved to see a good settlement reached in this matter as some of their most extreme men are who oppose the Home Rule solution. We meet at this moment under conditions which entitle us to be confident and hopeful as to the future of the Home Rule Bill. It has just been rejected by the House of Lords.—(Laughter.) But that is not the end of the story. In the next session of Parliament, which is shortly to begin, the Home Rule Bill will be promptly sent back to the House of Lords, I trust without an undue waste of Parliamentary time, and we are satisfied that the great majority which through all its passage through the House of Commons have sustained it will not fail in the Parliamentary support which is necessary to carry this measure through the various stages before it passes into law. No, I say, we ask our friends or enemies, if they choose to call themselves so, who use such violent language to believe that we also have our purpose to carry out, and that mere violence will not turn the State from its course nor destroy upon the path a measure of long-needed justice and reform; and it is because when we are moving forward on that path such an event as the Derry election is particularly gratifying that we welcome here to-day Mr. Hogg, and I ask you in drinking his health, which you will with whole-hearted enthusiasm, to drink to the arrival of another grand old man bringing new hope to the old cause.—(Cheers.)

"A NAVAL HOLIDAY"

March 26, 1913

House of Commons

The Naval Estimates for 1913-1914 aroused considerably more opposition in the Liberal Party than those of 1912-1913, but were eventually agreed at £49 million. Churchill's speech introducing the Estimates was, therefore, deliberately pacific in tone. One of the major elements in the larger Estimates was an increase in naval pay, a subject about which Churchill felt strongly.

[Extract] I do not at all complain of any delay which may have occurred this afternoon, because what has happened illustrates a very important naval and strategic truth which I have several times endeavoured to impress upon the House—I mean the difficulty under which the strongest naval Power always lies of being ready to meet at its average moment the attack of the next strongest naval Power at its selected moment. If our proceedings this afternoon have inculcated that valuable principle to the minds of the Members on both sides of the House, the Admiralty, at any rate, will have no reason to complain of any inconvenience. . . .

There is no prospect in the future of avoiding increases of the Navy Estimates unless the period of acute naval rivalries and rapid scientific expansion through which we are passing comes to an end. Of all nations we are perhaps the best able to bear the strain, if it should be continued. There are greater accumulations of capital in this country than anywhere else. We are freed from the necessity of maintaining an Army on the Continental scale. Our fiscal and financial system enables us to make large expansions of taxation without directly, at any rate, raising the cost of the living of the masses of the people. [An Hon. Member: "Question."] But although we are not likely to be in any difficulty in regard to men or money, and although the upkeep of our Navy will always be regarded as the first charge on the resources of the British Empire, the folly, the pitiful folly, of what is taking place here and all over the world is so patent to the meanest intelligence that a concerted effort to arrest or to modify it should surely rank amongst the first of international objects! There is, happily, a way which is open which would give almost instantaneous mitigation to the nations of the world from the absurd thraldom in which they are involving themselves at the present time. We are all in very much the same case. A good deal of what I am going to say could, I think, be repeated by the Minister of every other Great Power, or almost every other Great Power, without the slightest prejudice to his own national interests. In the sphere of naval competition everything is relative. The strength of one navy is its strength compared to another. The value of a ship depends almost entirely upon the contemporary ship which it may have to meet. The usefulness of a naval invention ceases when it is enjoyed by everybody else. A 30-knot ship has no greater advantage over a 27-knot ship than has a

20-knot ship over a 17-knot ship. The results are the same. The conditions of their competing are exactly the same. The cost alone is perhaps double. The same may be said of guns and armour. Their value is purely relative. There is no practical naval advantage to be gained by improvements in *matériel,* except where one nation possesses over others the monopoly for the time being of a secret, or where it has been able to make some advance which the others have not been able to share.

As the science of the great nations advances, broadly speaking, together, it is probable that special conditions on the one hand or the other are soon averaged out, and that the general advance is uniform and equal for all. I believe that to be true in the main, though there are no doubt exceptions of a partial character. Yet we see the ship types of every naval Power superseding those of the previous year with remorseless persistency, scores of millions being absolutely squandered without any result, and the pace and scale continually increasing without any real gain in the relative position of any of the competing Powers. Every year the great nations of Christendom not only make obsolete the fleets of their rivals, but they make obsolete their own fleets. They do that without adding in the least either to their actual security or relative strength. We are in the position of half a dozen competing manufacturers who are each year perpetually scrapping and renewing their plant without adding either to the volume or the profits of their business. Could anything be more stupid? Could anything be more wasteful? There is no practical result so long as all are advancing equally. On the other hand, no one Power can stand still whilst the others are advancing without in a very short time being hopelessly outclassed. This is a question which I would ask, if I may presume to do so, and which ought to be asked, not only of the Great Powers, but of the great peoples. It is a practical question; I am not putting any sentiment into my examination of this subject. This is the question: If, for the space of a year, for twelve calendar months, no new ships were built by any nation, in what conceivable manner would the interests of any nation be affected or prejudiced? You have good ships to-day. They are the best in the world—till better ones are built. Can they not have at least one year's reign before they are dethroned? Why should we not take a naval holiday for one year, so far, at any rate, as new construction of capital ships is concerned?

That is the question that I foreshadowed last year. That is the proposal I repeat this year. It is a proposal, I should like to point out, which involves no alteration in the relative strength of the navies. It implies no abandonment of any scheme of naval organisation or of naval increase. It is contrary to the system of no Navy Law. It imposes no check upon the development of true naval efficiency. It is so simple that it could lead to no misunderstanding. The finances of every country would obtain relief. No navy would sustain the slightest injury. We in Great Britain can speak with simplicity and directness upon such a subject. Our naval science is not inferior to that of any other country. Our resources are greater. Our experience is far greater. Our designs at every stage in the world's competition have maintained their old primacy, and, judged by the custom which we receive from other countries, our prices and the quality of our workmanship lie under no reproach. Each year, so long as new ships are built, we shall build the best that science can project or money can buy. We shall do the utmost to preserve that leadership in design which is no less necessary to naval supremacy than is preponderance in numbers. Sir, it is no appeal of weakness, panting or lagging behind, that we make, but rather an appeal of strength striding on in front. It is an appeal which we address to all nations, and to no nation with more profound sincerity than to our great neighbour over the North Sea. Let me say at once how much we welcome the calm and friendly tone and temper which has characterised recent German naval discussions. After a period of active naval preparation and direct comparison of naval strength, it is very satisfactory to observe that the relations between the two countries have sensibly improved, and that from the perils and anxieties under which Europe has dwelt these many months Great Britain and Germany have known how to draw the conviction that both of them are earnest to preserve the peace unbroken. Sentiments of goodwill, the growth of mutual confidence and respect, do much to rob the naval rivalries of their alarms and dangers, and permit us to approach the iron facts of the situation with composure and with a certain sense of detachment. Consciousness of our strength and the resolution of all parties in the House to do what is necessary to maintain it, ought to banish from our discussions anything in the nature of scaremongering or bluster which when applied in distortion of military facts are a certain means of producing errors in one's own policy and illwill in the policy of others. There is another mistake which we ought to be able to avoid. We must not try to read into recent German naval declarations a meaning which we should like, but which they do not possess; nor ought we to seek to tie German naval policy down to our wishes by too precise interpretations of friendly language used in the German Reichstag with a good and reassuring purpose. If, for instance, I were to say that Admiral Von Tirpitz had recognised that a British preponderance of sixteen to ten in "Dreadnoughts" was satisfactory to Germany, that such a preponderance exists almost exactly in the present period, and that in consequence Germany ought not to begin any more capital ships until we did, that might be a logical argument, but it would, I am sure, do a great deal of harm, and if my right hon. Friend the Secretary of State for Foreign Affairs were to press this point upon the German Government and to urge them through diplomatic channels to build no new ships this year, it would only lead to a direct refusal and subsequent recrimination, which would be very injurious. As a matter of fact the increased German programme of three vessels for the year 1913 has already passed the Reichstag, and there is good reason to believe that they will be begun without delay, and no remonstrance or appeal on our part would have any effect that would not be regrettable.

The naval policy towards Germany which I have been permitted to lay before the House and which has so far received very general acceptance in the country and produced no evil consequences in any quarter, is based on strength, candour, and simplicity. It excludes all ideas of entangling bargains which would only break down in disputes and irritations. Both nations must be perfectly free to take whatever course in naval armaments may seem to them at any time wise and right, and to modify and extend their programmes and elevate or vary their standards as they may see fit. It has long been the policy of Germany to announce beforehand for a series of years what their naval programme will be. It has lately been our policy to forecast, as far as we can, and subject to all necessary reservations against what cannot be foreseen, what consequences these German programmes will produce in our own construction over more or less the same series of years; and to state, as I now state, that if in any particular year, not as a matter of bargain, but as a matter of fact, the programme of causation is reduced or cancelled, the programme of consequence will, subject to all necessary reservations against what cannot now be foreseen, be reduced or cancelled, too. Thus a framework and structure for events is established by which dangerous ambitions and apprehensions alike are effectively excluded and under the shelter of which good will all the forces of good will may work without misconception or interference.

All our forecasts in this swiftly changing human scene are liable to revision by unexpected events, but I am glad to say that nothing which has happened in the year that has passed has led us to alter the numerical programmes I submitted to the House in March and July of 1912 or the guiding standards on which they were based. Had new construction under the German Naval Law remained at the augmented rate of two capital ships a year for six years, British programmes of four ships and three ships alternately would, in the Admiralty view, have sufficed to maintain the 60 per cent. "Dreadnought" standard. As the German new construction has been increased by two capital ships in the six years' period under review, the British programmes will be increased by four capital ships, two of which require to be laid down in the present year, making, as I stated last July, our total construction in capital ships for the year five, as against three of the next strongest naval Power. The British programmes as revised of the six years under review will thus, as I explained to the House in July last, aggregate a total of twenty-five ships against fourteen. Two ships will be added to this total for every extra vessel laid down by Germany. Additional to this total will be any ships which we may have to build in consequence of new naval developments in the Mediterranean. I am glad to say that no such developments are to be observed at the present time. Thirdly, the ship presented by the Federated Malay Straits and the three ships now under discussion in Canada will also be additional to the total I have mentioned, that being the specific condition on which they were given and accepted.

These are the bases of a naval policy which, coolly and inflexibly pursued during the next few years, will, we believe, place our country and the British Empire beyond the reach of purely naval pressure, and which need not at any stage of its execution be fomented into a cause of quarrel with our German neighbours. . . .

I have now finished, and I thank the House for the indulgence they have extended to me. Our expanding organisation, no doubt, taxes our manning resources to the full, particularly in regard to the specialist lieutenants and the highly-skilled ratings which are so necessary. But no one should go away with the impression that we could not to-morrow, upon a general mobilisation, man fully, with trained men, every ship in the Navy fit to be put to sea. In the whole of the First and Second Fleets, comprising 90 per cent. of our naval strength, there would not be employed one single reservist, and even after the Third Fleet had been fully manned, there would be a substantial reserve on shore, numbering several thousand, for whom no room could be found in any vessel of the war fleets. It is not for us to boast the quality of our race, but we are justified in putting our confidence in that thorough sea training and disciplined initiative which can be the product only of long years of service on the sea.

In the 700 war vessels, which apart from auxiliaries, we could mobilise to-morrow, the service and training of every man would average at least twice, and probably three times, as great as that of the personnel of any other Navy in the world. That is a factor which cannot be measured, and it is a factor which ought not to be overlooked.

I must, before I sit down, explicitly repudiate the suggestion that Great Britain can ever afford to allow another Naval Power to approach her so nearly as to deflect or to restrict her political action by purely naval pressure. Such a situation would unquestionably lead to war. Small margins of safety would mean in the present state of the world a vigilance at the naval ports little removed from a state of war. It would involve a strain on officers and men intolerable if it were prolonged. It would mean a continued atmosphere of suspicion and alarm, with all the national antagonisms consequent upon such a state of affairs. It would mean that instead of intervening, as we do now in European affairs, free and independent to do the best we can for all, we should be forced into a series of questionable entanglements and committed to action of gravest character, not because we thought it right, but as a result of bargains necessitated by our naval weakness. Margins of naval strength which are sufficient when the time comes to compel a victory, are insufficient to maintain a peace. We believe that the margins to which we are working are sufficient in the full sense of the word. If at any time we should revise our judgment, we should not hesitate to come at once to Parliament for further authority. His Majesty's Government in making these extensive preparations have to ask the House of Commons, and to ask our fellow country-men all over the Empire not represented here, to trust them not to abuse the great powers placed in their hands.

For more than 300 years we alone amongst the nations have wielded that mysterious and decisive force which is called sea-power. What have we done with it? We have suppressed the slaver. We have charted the seas. We have made them a safe highway for all. Was there any State which during the last hundred years could, more easily than Great Britain, have closed her unequalled foreign possessions to the trade of other countries? Is there any other State in the world which leaves them open freely as we do? Is there any part of the world where the White Ensign does not revive associations of good feeling and fair play? Is there any part of your national life more healthy and more admirable than this great service of sacrifice and daring? Is there any small nation in Europe, any young people struggling to acquire or maintain its independence, which would not hear with rejoicing of a reinforcement of the British Fleet? Is there any Great Power which during these months of tension and anxiety has not been thankful that the influence of Britain in the European concert is a reality and not a shadow, and that she has been free and strong to work for that general peace, precious to all, and precious most of all to us? Sir, it is because these things are true that we may justly claim that that naval supremacy which is vital to Britain is also a part of the common treasure of mankind, and that in maintaining it effectually against any challenge we pursue no selfish or unworthy end.

THE ART OF FLYING

March 4, 1914

Royal Aero Club Dinner,
Savoy Hotel, London

Churchill took a keen interest in aviation, and the establishment of the Royal Naval Air Service was the direct result of his enthusiasm. He also learned to fly–to the alarm of many of his friends.

[Extract] ... I share with those who are present a keen interest in the development of the art of flying by the people of these islands. (Cheers.) Whether you deal with airships or aeroplanes all must recognize that we have come very late into the field. Other countries on the Continent, both in regard to lighter-than-air and heavier-than-air machines, have made the pioneer advances, and we are, not for the first time, engaged in the process of overhauling and catching up.

Some people think it is a melancholy thing that this new art of flying should have been appropriated so markedly, should have been almost monopolized by war and war requirements. Many of the people who are prepared to admire the scientific aspect of aviation are sorry when they realize that, at the present time, the great moving power is derived from its military aspect and utility. But, after all, the two great services, the Navy and the Army, working together in flying as they have never worked together on any other great common operation, with a greater cordiality and greater comradeship than they have ever worked together before–must be the main propulsive force to aviation, at any rate in this country. (Cheers.) We recognize absolutely the brilliant work and solid achievement of the civilian flyers in every sphere and in every branch of aviation. But I think it is true to say that in the present circumstances nothing but the supreme stimulus of war consideration and nothing but the large and generous floods of money which the taxpayer can provide will carry British aviation forward as it has to be carried forward to the foremost place among the nations of the world. (Cheers.) This is a particularly difficult country to fly in. Its winds and its enclosed nature make it incomparably a more severe test of aviation than do the conditions which present themselves on the Continent, and until British engineers are able to devise an arrangement of engine or a combination of engines which will assure that the pilot is not forced to make an unexpected and possibly a very inconvenient landing, I am not very hopeful that flying for the million will reach a point at which it can be a sure foundation or a strong propulsive power for our aviation service. (Cheers.) The risk of flying is very greatly exaggerated by the newspapers. The man-in-the-street only reads in the headlines in the evening papers that some airman has been killed or injured, and he assumes that those conditions are the ordinary concomitants of an adventure in the air. But since I have been at the Admiralty many more lives have been lost in the submarine service than in the air service. It is very important that these facts should not be exaggerated, that the public should realize that, though there is an element of risk in flying, it is not undue or excessive, or one which should prevent the active development of the service.

The provision of landing facilities is the most important feature in the development of aviation in this enclosed country, and I think the Aero Club might guide the public on the path of providing satisfactory landing facilities; if not over the whole country, at least along certain well-marked aerial routes. It ought to be quite easy; and not very expensive, to make two or three fields into one at intervals and to arrange a small compensation fund for the farmers or landowners concerned. Such a scheme will enable flying to be conducted much more safely and surely than is possible at the present time. All this is the subject of naval and military investigation; but it is a question in which the public may fairly be asked to help. Then there is the question of insurance; the British aviator may reasonably ask his fellow-countrymen to enable him to enjoy the ordinary insurance rates. That again is a matter in regard to which the Aero Club might use its influence upon the public.

The progress which has been made in this country in the last few years, and especially in the last year, has been very great. Though we started last we have profited to the full by all that has been discovered in other lands, and we have contributed ourselves, in some important particulars, to the sum of knowledge. Not only with aeroplanes but with airships things are done today which nobody would have thought right or prudent to do twelve months or even nine or six months ago. The neophyte today flies in a wind which the expert would have thought dangerous two years ago; and we are talking today as hopefully of crossing the Atlantic as people talked four years ago of flying the Channel. In my view talk of flying the Atlantic is in present circumstances premature, and an undue element of risk would appear to be attached to any such enterprise. Still, the progress has been enormous, and we cannot doubt that in the near future we shall see heavy aeroplanes and airships making as a matter of common experience voyages which nowadays we should look upon as most extraordinary events. (Cheers.) This new art and science of flying is surely one in which Great Britain ought to be able to show herself–I do not say supreme in numbers, but supreme in quality. Perhaps flying is one of the best tests of nationality which exists. It is a combination of science and skill, of organization and enterprise. The forces in our country are unconquerable and incomparable if they are only properly directed. It has been reserved for us to see flying a commonplace and ordinary event. That is a great fact, because no one can doubt that the development and discovery of the flying art definitely and indefinitely enlarges the boundaries of human activity. One cannot doubt that flying, to judge from the position which it has reached even today, must in the future exercise a potent influence, not only upon the habits of men, but upon the military destinies of states. (Cheers.)

THE ULSTER SITUATION

March 14, 1914

St. George's Hall, Bradford

The attempts to reach a negotiated settlement in Ireland had foundered by the beginning of 1914, and the tone of the Ulster resistance was highly belligerent. In these circumstances Churchill delivered a strong warning at Bradford on March 14 which aroused the expectation that the Government was prepared, if necessary, to impose Home Rule upon Ulster by force.

It is difficult to give a brief description of the fierce and complex crisis which followed Churchill's speech. The Unionists were convinced that the Government–and particularly Churchill and the Secretary for War, Seely–were determined to coerce Ulster. Concern was expressed in the Army, and particularly in the Third Cavalry Brigade, based at the Curragh. Brigadier-General Gough and fifty-seven officers resigned their commissions, and Seely felt obliged to give written assurances that they would not be ordered to undertake military operations against Ulstermen. This ended Seely's career, and plunged the Government into a deep humiliation. Irish opinion, which had welcomed Churchill's speech, became suspicious of the Government's real intentions. Ulster and Unionist feeling was enflamed. Until this moment, Churchill had enjoyed good relations with the Opposition, who applauded his determination to improve the Navy, but the Bradford speech and its aftermath destroyed that relationship permanently. In a negative sense it was one of the most important speeches of his career.

It was above all the movement of the Third Battle Squadron to Lamlash (on the western coast of Scotland, with a short passage to Belfast) which particularly incensed the Opposition, and heightened their belief in Churchill's personal involvement in the policy of coercing Ulster. The order, issued by Churchill on March 19, was rescinded on March 21, but the damage had been done. What was called the "Ulster Pogrom" haunted Churchill's career, and was a major factor in his downfall in May 1915.

I have come here this afternoon to speak to you about Ireland–(hear, hear),–and about the situation which has developed there and here in Great Britain. This great meeting was fixed without any special reference to other affairs. It was not arranged in connection with events at Westminster, but I consider myself very fortunate at a moment when some plain words have to be spoken, and when it is the duty of a Minister of the Crown to speak them–I think myself lucky to be face to face with this great audience representative of the Liberalism of England, and here in the heart of unshakable Liberal and Radical Yorkshire. (Cheers.)

The counsels which I wish to offer to you to-day are serious, and they are rightly addressed to earnest men who know their own minds, who are thoughtful men, who are law-abiding men, who, having considered well what course they would pursue, are prepared to carry it through to the end. (Cheers.)

It is six months or more, I think, since I last had the opportunity of speaking on the Irish question. It was at a place to which I cannot help being partial–Dundee. (Cheers.) It was the first speech which any of us had made since Parliament rose, and in consequence it was a speech of particular difficulty. We had had a demonstration which had taken place in Ulster in September. We had had–we still have–the restless agitations of the Conservative press. We had Lord Loreburn's letter, and following upon that letter we had for the first time language used by the Orange leaders and by those who were associated with them–and in particular by Sir Edward Carson and Mr. Smith–language to the effect–I am not quoting their actual words–to the effect that North-east Ulser would not bar the way to the rest of Ireland, that Orange resistance would not be used as a pawn in the Tory party game, and that agreement in some form or other might prove the means not merely of avoiding a collision, but of a lasting agreement.

In common with Sir Edward Grey and with the Chancellor of the Exchequer and with Mr. Birrell and other of my colleagues, and in full harmony with the views and leadership of the Prime Minister, I have always held that, within proper limits, the Ulster Protestant counties had a strong case for special treatment. There is no case, said the Prime Minister more than two years ago in the House of Commons–there is no case which would better repay temperate and reasonable statements. On the second reading of the Home Rule Bill which I had the honour of moving–a memorable honour which I shall long treasure–on that occasion and during the passage of that measure through the House of Commons I was always very careful to keep the door open for a friendly settlement, even if that settlement should require, as I had long foreseen it would require, the temporary exclusion in one form or another of what may be called the Orange counties.

And so when I came to speak at Dundee in the autumn I thought it right to use the following words, and as they were spoken six months ago perhaps you will let me read them to you. I said:

> Our Home Rule Bill holds the field. In the circumstances which have hitherto prevailed it is the best solution open to us of a question which must be settled now. Our bill is not unalterable, and the procedure of the Parliament Act renders far-reaching alterations possible, but only upon one condition–there must be an agreement. Only one thing could make it worth while, or even possible, to recast or alter a measure upon which so much depends. It is a very simple thing–good-will. Only one thing can compensate an Irish Parliament for the grievous loss to its efficiency and strength which would result from even a temporary absence of the representation of North-east Ulster–I mean the binding in honour of both political parties in this country to carry the settlement through, and bring it in the course of years to final and complete success.

That was going a very long way. (A Voice: "Too far.") I fully recognised at the time that it was going further than many of my Liberal friends were then prepared to go. Perhaps it was going further than some here to-day thought it wise to go, and I knew before I made that speech that it would be looked at by some whose opinion I value, and that I should be blamed by others, and I was quite right. But I feel, and I think many of you will feel, in a question of this kind, where one may easily proceed to extremes–in a question of this peculiar character it is of importance not merely to be legally right, but to be absolutely fair, and not only to be fair but to be considerate, and not only to be considerate but to be generous. It would never do for you or me or any of us who pursue a question like this to its final stage to get-drawn into the crisis of it without being quite sure that everything possible had been done to reach an agreement.

Strictly speaking, no doubt, the Constitutional remedy of the Ulster Protestants and of the Unionist party is clear and plain. They should obey the law. (Loud cheers.) If they dislike the law–it is a free country–(hear, hear)–let them agitate for a majority when an election comes, and then, if they choose, they can amend or at the very worst repeal a law against which the country would then have pronounced. That is a full remedy. It is the only remedy which is open to Liberals when we are in a minority. And when Liberals are invaded, as they have been and may be again, by reactionary or one-sided legislation, in temperance–(hear, hear),–in education–(hear, hear),–on tariffs–(hear, hear),–on land, on ratings, or on other grave political issues, we have no remedy but that. (Hear, hear.) It is the only remedy which the Conservative party would ever offer to Labour or to labouring men engaged in a dispute, no matter how keen and fierce opinion might be, and however bitter the pinch of suffering and poverty might have become. Obey the law, agitate, and, having persuaded the country, amend or repeal the law. Repeal itself is a step so drastic and so extreme that there are scarcely any precedents in modern times for its employment.

But I repeat what I said in Dundee that the most extreme course in which the Opposition would be justified would be to obtain a majority, and then to amend or repeal the Home Rule Bill. That is their right. It is their extreme right. And it is their only right. This right is no empty form, because we know, as we have always known, that an election, which cannot be very far distant–(hear, hear),–was bound to take place in this country before any administrative or legislative action of an Irish Parliament in Dublin could possibly have affected prejudicially the interests of the Orange counties of Ulster. Still, in dealing with a larger community and in dealing with a question which raises in acute form racial and religious passion, and around which so much melancholy history gathers, I felt, and I think you feel, that you must not always stand on the strict and hard interpretation of your rights–that you must sometimes go further than that.

It is enough for Liberals to remember that the Ulstermen are anxious and unhappy and alarmed and resentful, that in Ireland we are seeking to allay old hatreds, not to kindle new ones, that we are seeking to unite, not divide, to conciliate, not to offend, that we want to give them what they wish, and not to force upon them what they dislike. (Cheers.)

And therefore I have always hoped and always urged that a fair and full offer should be made to North-east Ulster in all friendship and goodwill, an offer going beyond anything which on a strict interpretation of our rights was required of us, but which should be made as an earnest effort to produce agreement and lasting peace. I hoped that offer would be in such a form as to remove altogether not merely reasonable fears, which perhaps are few, but unreasonable fears, which no doubt are many, and, more than that, to cut away altogether the ground and foothold of fear and apprehension, and to deprive the Ulster movement of the slightest excuse for unconstitutional action. That was the offer I have always hoped would be made. (Cheers.)

That offer has been made. (Cheers.) It was made last Monday by the Prime Minister. (Cheers.) It was made with the assent of the Irish National leader. It is made in all sincerity. It is made in earnestness. It is a real offer. It is a straightforward offer. It is an offer which as a safeguard is thoroughly effective.

God forbid that I should ever stand in the path of conciliation, but it seems to me, and I daresay it will seem to you, that in principle–I do not speak of detail–in principle this is the last offer–(great and prolonged cheers)–which his Majesty's Government can make or ought to make. (More cheering.) Consider what the offer is. Any Ulster county upon the requisition of a tenth of the electors can by a simple vote stand out for six years of the whole operation of the Home Rule Bill, and remain exactly as they are. That is to say that two general elections in this country must take place before any county exercising its option would be compelled to change the system of government under which it has hitherto been administered. Consider what that offer must have cost to the Irish Nationalist leader. (Cheers.) When I think of the patience, the wisdom, and the eloquence with which Mr. Redmond–(cheers)–has conducted this great historic controversy, and when I think how dearly he and those who are working with him cherish the dream, the hope of a united and self-governing Ireland, I can measure the cruel pang with which this temporary but none the less serious change has been accepted by him–(hear, hear)–and by the great mass of the Irish nation. It is their hope–and I think they are right and wise in hoping–that the day will come, perhaps before that period is passed, when of their own free will the Ulster counties that have exercised the option will seek to be incorporated in the ancient Parliament of their mother-land, when the brilliant and courageous Mr. Devlin will lead the democracy of Belfast to take their true position in the council of a united and progressive Ireland. (Cheers.)

But that offer, which represented the hardest sacrifice ever asked of Irish Nationalism, has been made. How has it been received? Before the offer was made the Unionist party demanded exclusion or a general election. We have now given them both. (Laughter.) Unless they had exclusion or a general election they said there would be civil war. They have got both, but they still say there is going to be civil war. Before the Prime Minister's speech the Tory cry was for a general election on Home Rule. How often have we pointed out in the last few months that it is practically impossible to have an election fought in this country exclusively on Home Rule? Witness the by-elections, about which we have nothing to be sick or sorry. (Cheers.) We have pointed out again and again that a general election now would not in any special degree or in any particular way help the solution of either the Ulster or the larger Irish question. But still the Tories have gone on demanding one. Again and again they have droned this demand for one into our ears. But now there are to be two before any Orange Ulster county can be brought within the scope of the Home Rule Bill.

But are they satisfied, are they pleased, are they gratified? Oh, dear, no. Within a few hours of the Prime Minister's statement Lord Robert Cecil was writing to the "Times" newspaper pointing out that two general elections would be no protection to Ulster, because the country might vote Liberal on other matters. (Laughter.) What! Two general elections are no protection for Ulster! Where, then, are the Tory hopes of victory? (Laughter and cheers.) Don't they think they can even win one out of these two elections–not even the second one, six years hence? (Laughter.) We knew that in their hearts they were very disappointed, but we never had such an open and such an abject confession of their sorrows. (Laughter.) What, then, becomes of all this clamour that we do not represent the electors, and we have not got the electorate behind us, and that the constituencies are only waiting to instal the Conservatives in power, when, in the next breath, they tell us that even two elections would be so little safeguard to Ulster, that the Tory chance of victory is so desperate throughout the whole of the next six years, that rebellion must raise her grisly head at once–they cannot even afford to trust their case to the repeated verdict and consideration of the British electorate? (Cheers.)

Why, gentlemen, to satisfy these gentry–(laughter)–you would have not only to promise them an election, but you would have to guarantee that it will go the way they want. (Laughter.) You will have to promise that they are to have a majority at the election, or else, of course, there will be civil war. (Laughter.) To satisfy their friends in Ulster you must not only arrange that the counties where there is an Orange majority should be excluded, but those counties where they are in a minority must be excluded too. Of course–what did you expect? (Laughter.) Majority or minority, they must have their own way–or else it will be civil war. (Laughter.) But what is the last unmeasured infamy of Radical power of which they complain? (Laughter.) It has all been put off for six years. "Here," they say, "we had our rebellion all ready. (Much laughter.) It is costing us a lot of money to pay our volunteers–(laughter),–and we can't keep it up indefinitely. (More laughter.) And now the Government has had the incredible meanness to postpone all possible provocation for six long years." (Laughter.) And they say "For all we know now it may never come off at all." (Renewed laughter.) No, it may never come off. (More laughter.)

No Liberal will ever deny that there may be circumstances and that there have been circumstances in many periods and in many States which have justified and which, if repeated, would justify again rebellion. But there are two supreme conditions–by no means the only conditions, but two supreme and indispensable conditions which must be satisfied. First, there must in the first instance be real and unbearable oppression, and, in the second place, it must be clear that there is no other remedy except a resort to arms. Now apply those tests, which are moderate and reasonable tests, to the Ulster position at the present. There is no oppression. (Laughter.) Even if there was going to be, it has not begun yet. (Laughter.) Nor can it begin, even if it ever would begin, for six long years. (Laughter.) As for the remedy, they have it in their hands. If they reject the offer we have made, it can only be because they prefer shooting to voting–(cheers),–because they would rather use the bullet than the ballot. (Cheers.) We live in a strange world. (Hear, hear.) Many extraordinary things have happened. But what are we to say of persons, professing to be serious, who are ready to raise an impious hand against the laws of their country, who are ready, so they tell us, to shed the blood of their fellow men, all because they won't take the trouble to walk into the polling-booth and mark a voting paper?

Is it not strange that they should be so eager to begin the horrid work–which at the very best must be a tragic adventure–that they cannot even wait for the result of the general election which cannot now be long delayed, and which, according to what they say of their prospects, may quite easily remove all need for revolution? (Hear, hear.) Why, in European affairs it has for some years past been considered wicked and immoral to use the argument of an inevitable war. No European statesman would be acquitted in the comity of nations who brought a war on in a hurry because he believed that sooner or later it was bound to come. The conscience of the modern world revolts–the wisdom of the modern world revolts, against such a doctrine. We have learned, however paradoxical it may seem, that inevitable wars can be postponed. (Laughter and cheers.)

But in Ulster a six years' interval of peace is apparently an added insult. Although they can secure this period by the simple exercise of their voting power, they tell us that they will have nothing of it, that nothing will satisfy them but to begin killing and shooting us almost immediately. (Laughter and cheers.) They might, at any rate at least, allow their intended victims to pass the six years' interval with their wives and families. (Laughter.) And gentlemen, after this offer has been made any unconstitutional action by Ulster can only wear–in a phrase which Mr. Gladstone once used on another occasion–can only wear the aspect of unprovoked aggression, and I am sure and certain that the first British soldier or coastguard, bluejacket, or Royal Irish Constabulary man who is attacked and killed by an Orangeman will raise an explosion in this country–(cheers)–of a kind they little appreciate or understand, and will shake to its very foundations the basis and structure of society. (Cheers.)

A fair offer has been made, and up to the present–it is only up to the present we can view it–it has been not only spurned, but taken advantage of. I wish to speak with all respect of Sir Edward Carson. He is bitter in his feelings. He is unfair in his controversial methods. He is wrong on their merits. And he will be proved wrong by history and by time. No doubt he is moved by passion the depth of which no one can doubt. But let me point out this. Passion in itself, however intense, is not necessarily proof that one is right. Nor is it necessarily exclusive as regards other people. What does Sir Edward Carson say in reply to the offer of the Prime Minister? I was reading coming down in the train a report of a letter which he has written to some organisation in Ulster since the Prime Minister's offer was made, in which the following passage occurs:–"So far as our preparations are concerned, it (that is, the Prime Minister's offer) necessitates, if anything, a still more forward movement." What did he say in the House of Commons? This was his reply:–"If you will agree to the permanent exclusion of Ulster, then and then only, will I consent." To what? To accept? "Then and then only will I lay your proposal before the Ulster Convention." (Laughter.)

Observe what that means. If His Majesty's Government, supported by a great Parliamentary majority, go much further than they have gone up to the present, if concessions even greater than those which have been made were put forward, then, and only then, would Sir Edward Carson bring their offer to the notice of the Ulster Convention–a self-elected body composed of persons who, to put it plainly, are engaged in a treasonable conspiracy, and this Convention is graciously to consider the matter while the Imperial Parliament stands on tiptoe outside the door waiting for the verdict. (Cheers and laughter.)

And then this Convention is to dictate its further terms, and communicate them to His Majesty's Government. Then, if these terms were accepted, what is to happen? Agreement, peace, reconciliation? Oh, no; we are to let off civil war. (Laughter.) That is the best we are to hope for. The fullest constitutional opposition to the general policy of Home Rule is to be maintained. Even if an agreement were to be reached over Ulster, even if we met the full and extreme demands of the Ulster Convention, still there is to be no settlement, no fair chance for an Irish Parliament, no cooperation between parties for the future government of Ireland, no pledge against repeal of the measure. But the threat of violence, having served its purpose, would be laid aside. That is all. That is the sole result that would be offered for concessions far beyond those which we are prepared to offer. The sole result would be that they would graciously consent not to commit acts of rebellion and levy war against the State. (Hear, hear.) Well, I go as far as any in my desire to see a conciliatory treatment, and an agreed settlement of this question. But I think when we look at the position which has now unfolded itself before us a good many of you will feel, as I certainly feel, that we have had just about enough of this sort of thing. (Loud cheers.) Many years ago, in the darker periods of the Irish controversy, there was a great attempt made to bring about a common policy of action between the physical force party in Ireland and the anti-physical force party. These two parties met together in Dublin, and had prolonged conferences, in hopes of reaching an agreement. In the end these conferences were terminated brutally by the anti-physical force party throwing the physical force party downstairs. (Great laughter.) Well, I am on the side of the anti-physical force party. (Renewed laughter.)

What treatment do you suppose these Orangemen would mete out to their Nationalist fellow-countrymen who are in a minority in their midst if language like that was held over them? What treatment do you think we should receive from a Tory Government if we were to adopt such a tone? Why, they scarcely take the trouble to veil their intentions now. An incident occurred in the House of Commons in the debate on the Address. The Prime Minister asked in one of his great speeches–"If Home Rule were to fail now, how could you govern the West of Ireland?" Captain Craig, an Ulster member, a man quite representative of those for whom he speaks–(laughter),–interjected blithely, "We have done it before." Ah! now, observe that here is a man claiming to rebel himself, and asking for special consideration, asking that he shall not be ridden rough-shod over, and in the very midst of this agitation, of this act of his, he shows the kind of measure he would mete out to others.

There you get the true insight into the Tory mind. Coercion for four-fifths of Ireland is a healthful, exhilarating, salutary exercise, but lay a finger upon the Tory fifth–sacrilege, tyranny, murder. (Laughter.) "We have done it before, and we will do it again." There is the ascendancy spirit. There is the spirit with which we are confronted. There is the obstacle to the peace and unity of Ireland. There stands the barrier which, when all just claims have been met and all the fears, reasonable and unreasonable, have been prevented, still blocks the path of Irish freedom and British progress. There stands the barrier, and it is a barrier before which Liberalism cannot recoil. (Loud cheers.)

But at any rate when you are dealing with Orange Ulster you are dealing with real passions and with real anxieties of real people. No such excuse is open to Mr. Bonar Law. Behind every strident sentence which he rasps out–(laughter)–you can always hear the whisper of the party manager–"We must have an election–(laughter)–before the Plural Voting Bill passes into law. (Ah!) Ulster is our best card. It is our only card. This is our one chance to smash the Parliament Act. This is our one chance to restore the veto of the House of Lords and carry a protective tariff on to the Statute-book." (Cheers.) Oh, it is this grave complication which adds so seriously to the difficulty of the Irish problem to-day. And let me say this. We must be careful that the honest necessities of the Ulster case do not suffer from their entanglement with Tory party interests and intrigue.

I daresay your experiences in thinking of this question have not been dissimilar from my own. I have found in my mind two different trains of thought and feeling. First, I have greatly desired that we should not do an unliberal or hard thing to the Ulster community, mistaken though I think they are; and, secondly, and not less strongly, I have felt that we cannot let ourselves be bullied by threats of force or, let me add, by force itself–(cheers)–from doing justice to the rest of Ireland, and from making good arrangements for the future of the whole of Ireland and maintaining the authority of the State.

Mr. Bonar Law is really in some respects a public danger. (Laughter.) He believes apparently–I suppose he measures others by what he finds in himself–he believes apparently that these threats of force are the only means by which a settlement will be achieved. He quite sincerely thinks, if I may judge from his speeches, that he has only to continue to terrorise the Government to wreck the Home Rule Bill and force his way into the councils of the Sovereign. Why, gentlemen, that is a disastrous and a fatal delusion. (Cheers.) Those who think that these events can be adjusted by the use of threats of violence against the Government do not know the British democracy; they do not know England; they do not know Yorkshire–(loud cheers);–and they do not know Asquith. (Renewed cheers.)

Mr. Bonar Law says in effect if there is civil war in Ulster it will spread to England too. (Laughter.) I agree with him. (Cheers and laughter.) I go further. Once resort is had to violence by the leaders of a great British party Ulster and Ulster's affairs will dwindle to comparative insignificance. They will become a matter mainly of local concern. It will not be an Ulster question, with all its intricate and perplexing tangles, which we shall have to face, but a much larger and a much simpler issue. This will be the issue–whether civil and Parliamentary government in these realms is to be beaten down by the menace of armed force. Whatever sympathies we have for Ulster we need have no compunction here. It is the old battle-ground of English history. It is the issue fought out 250 years ago on the field of Marston Moor. (Cheers.) From the language which is employed it would almost seem that we are face to face with a disposition on the part of some sections of the proprietary classes to subvert Parliamentary government, and to challenge all the civil and constitutional foundations of society. Against such a mood, wherever it manifests itself in action, there is no lawful measure from which the Government should shrink, and there is no lawful measure from which this Government will shrink. (Loud cheers.)

Bloodshed, gentlemen, no doubt is lamentable. I have seen some of it—more perhaps than many of those who talk about it with such levity. (Hear, hear.) But there are worse things than bloodshed, even on an extreme scale. An eclipse of the central Government of the British Empire would be worse. The abandonment by our public men of the righteous aims to which they are pledged in honour would be worse. The cowardly abdication of responsibility by the Executive would be worse. The trampling down of law and order which, under the conditions of a civilised state, assure life, liberty, and the pursuit of happiness—all this would be worse than bloodshed. (Cheers.) Three years ago there was a great railway strike, a most momentous and anxious event. I was Home Secretary at the time, and the Government felt that they were bound to make sure that great cities were not starved through a breakdown of the vital supplies. (Interruption.) We had to act. The railwaymen were our good friends. We laboured—and we shall labour—to secure fair conditions for them in their employment. But many who were not strikers had joined in. There was widespread disorder and interruption of traffic. It became my duty, from which, however reluctant, I did not shrink, to send 50,000 soldiers—(cries of "Shame," "Hear, hear," and cheers)—on to the railways of England. Order was kept, and then, thank God, Lloyd George made peace. (Cheers.)

But why do I refer to this now? I do so because I do not remember on this occasion that we have had any letter from Lord Roberts advising the Territorials that there was nothing contrary to their duty if they joined the strikers or that he made a speech in the House of Lords saying that this employment of troops would ruin the army, or that the Conservative newspapers invited soldiers to make up their minds whether they would go or not, or that a lot of Tory old women of both sexes—(laughter)—hurried off to sign a covenant declaring that any means, fair or foul, lawful or unlawful, innocent or sanguinary, might be employed to drive the Government from power. Not at all. These were the very people who were first clamouring for the use of the military.

I well remember how on one occasion I was abused for sending police instead of soldiers to the South Wales coalfield. We know well how the Conservative party governed Ireland in the eighties and in the nineties. We know the treatment that they considered quite appropriate to mete out to Nationalists to-morrow if they obtained a majority. We cannot help watching with amusement the transports of unaffected enthusiasm with which they have applauded the exercise of martial law in South Africa. When Generals Botha and Smuts were fighting in the field in defence of their own people no word of abuse was too harsh for them from Tory lips. But the moment—(interruption)—they take violent action—(more interruption and "Hear, hear")—the action that they have taken in the last few months, which I am not discussing one way or the other—at that moment they become heroes and the idols of the Tory party. From that very moment we are told what a pity it is they are not brought over here to govern us. (Laughter.)

Ah! so long as it is working men in England or Nationalist peasants in Ireland there is no measure of military force which the Tory party will not readily employ. They denounce all violence except their own. They uphold all law except the law they choose to break. They always welcome the application of force to others. (Hear, hear.) But they themselves are to remain immune. They are to select from the Statute-book the laws they will obey and the laws they will resist. They claim to be the party in the State free to use force in all directions, but never to have it applied to themselves. Whether in office or Opposition, as they have very often told us, they are to govern the country. If they cannot do it by the veto of privilege, they will do it by the veto of violence. If constitutional methods serve their ends they will be constitutionalists. If law suits their ends they will be law-abiding, aye, and law-enforcing. When social order means the order of the Tory party, when social order means the order of the propertied classes against the wage-earners, when social order means the master against the man, or the landlord against the tenant, order is sacred, holy, and it is dear to the heart of the Tory party, and order must be maintained by force. But if it should happen that the Constitution or the law or the maintenance of order stand in the path of some Tory project, stand in the path of the realisation of some appetite or ambition which they have conceived, then they vie with the wildest Anarchists in the language which they use against the Constitution, against the law, and against all order and all means of maintaining order. And that is the political doctrine with which they salute the twentieth century. (Cheers.)

We do not like threats ourselves, and so we will not use them to others. So far the violence has been all on one side. They confront us with the menace of civil war, or what they are proud to say will be civil war. We meet them with fairness. We meet them with a Parliamentary majority. (Cheers.) And in due course we meet them in an appeal to the people. But we also must meet them with firmness. (Cheers.) We must not forget we are the supreme executive authority of this great State and Empire, and we are responsible to the Crown, whose Ministers we are, and to the House of Commons, on whose confidence we depend, for the peace and order of the British dominions and for the strict and punctual discipline of the armed forces charged with their protection by land and sea. (Cheers.)

Around the fabric of the Imperial Government stir and heave the uneasy movements of the world. The tremendous armies and fleets of Europe ever grow and ever gather. The anxious shifting combination of diplomacy, the girding of great States one against the other, the unrest and ferment of unhappy millions of labouring men, all sway around the structure of the Imperial Government; and beneath that Government shelter not only the nation which dwells in these islands, but the vast native populations across the sea, guided and ruled by handfuls of soldiers. The administrators of ancient kingdoms and warlike races and noble provinces and principalities dwell in prosperous progress and security in the long sunshine of British peace. (Cheers.)

Who will dare to break up that British peace? Let us see who will dare with lethal weapons and of deliberate purpose–(interruption),–let us see who will dare to break up that peace. For them, whoever they are, there must be had recourse to law. (Cheers.) There must be only one law. (Cheers.) It must be the same for the rich as for the poor. (Cheers.) It must be the same for the Tory as for the Liberal or the Labour man. (Cheers.) It must be the same for Orange as for Green. (Cheers.) It must be even-handed in its enforcement. It must not be swayed by fear or favour. (Cheers.) Law and order must prevail in this country at all risks. (Cheers.) We are not going to have the realm of Britain sunk to the condition of the Republic of Mexico. (Cheers.) Those who for the time being–I say for the time being, because Ministers come and go. We are servants of the State and of the House of Commons, and at any time when the constituencies have decided it on election those who are now responsible will disappear into private stations, and others will assume the heavy burdens and responsibilities. We do not exercise any authority we have not received from its true and proper source, and while we are charged with the high duties of government we must act on such an issue as if we were the trustees not only for the present but for the past and for the future, and we are bound in honour not to flinch and not to fail.

I thank you most earnestly for the way in which you have listened to my words. I recognise that I cannot be in all respects a complete exponent of Liberal thought and opinion. I hope I have a firm grip of democratic principles. In know I earnestly desire the social betterment of the masses of the people. But still there are many others in this hall, on this platform, in the Government, or among our colleagues in the House of Commons who have a far better right than I have, who are much more capable of interpreting the instinctive promptings and the inner thoughts of Liberals and of Liberalism. ("No, no.")

It is, however, possible that at particular moments I may be able to be of some use. (Cheers.) There are times and there are occasions when I have a message to give which is of vital consequence, and here I am this afternoon, and here is the message which I bring you. (Cheers.) If Ulster seeks peace and fair-play, she can find it. She knows where to find it. If Ulstermen extend the hand of friendship it will be clasped by Liberals and by their Nationalist countrymen in all good faith and in all goodwill. But if there is no wish for peace, if every concession that is made is spurned and exploited, if every effort to meet their views is only to be used as a means of breaking down Home Rule and of barring the way to the rest of Ireland, if Ulster is to become a tool in party calculations, if the civil and Parliamentary systems under which we have dwelt and our fathers before us for so many years are to be brought to the crude challenge of force, if the Government and the Parliament of this great country and greater Empire is to be exposed to menace and brutality, if all the loose, wanton, and reckless chatter we have been forced to listen to all these many months is in the end to disclose a sinister and revolutionary purpose–then, gentlemen, I can only say to you let us go forward together and put these grave matters to the proof. (Loud cheers.)

NAVY ESTIMATES

March 17, 1914

House of Commons

The Naval Estimates for 1914-1915 caused a brief but intense crisis in the Liberal Government. Churchill's proposal was for Estimates of nearly £53 million–an increase of £4 million–and his colleagues were hostile. The Liberal Press and a number of influential back benchers had reacted strongly to Churchill's Guildhall speech the previous November in which he had spoken of "the measured and unbroken development of the German Navy" and the need for greater naval expenditure. They accused him of deliberate belligerence. Lloyd George made his opposition public, and there was widespread speculation that Churchill might be forced to resign. "The increase is unexampled at a time of international calm," Lord Beauchamp wrote to the Prime Minister in a letter of protest signed by four other Cabinet Ministers. In the event, Lloyd George and Churchill compromised; the Estimates would be for £51,580,000 and Churchill promised a reduction of £2 million in the 1915-1916 Estimates. When the time came, he was not asked to honour his pledge.

This speech, made three days after the Bradford speech, and at the height of the Curragh crisis, may be regarded as one of the finest he made during his tenure of the Admiralty. It lasted over two hours, and was described by the Daily Telegraph*–not a friendly source–as "the longest and perhaps also the most weighty and eloquent speech to which the House of Commons have listened during the present generation."*

The speech is very detailed and only brief extracts are given here.

[Extract] These are the largest Estimates for naval expense ever presented to the House, but I hope the House will not think it necessary on that account that I should introduce them in the longest speech ever delivered. On the contrary, I think I might almost say that those who delight in great naval expenditure should take deeds for words, and that those who deplore it should be glad that as little as possible should be said about it. It has also to be borne in mind that, except in one respect to which I shall refer later, there is no change in the policy adopted two years ago. That policy and the standards and programmes which give effect to it have been repeatedly explained in the utmost detail to the House. I myself made long speeches on the subject in March and July, 1912, and in March and July, 1913, and only recently upon the Supplementary Estimates I entered very fully into some of the financial aspects. I do not wish to cover the whole ground again; therefore I will do my best not to make an undue strain upon the patience of the House. I propose, first of all, to explain to what the increases are due, and to deal primarily with the financial aspects of naval policy. Secondly, I shall proceed to examine some of the principal causes which are at work, and to show how the increases either arise out of past decisions or are consequential upon standards which Parliament has approved. In this connection I shall deal with three principal causes of increase, namely, oil, air, and personnel. In the third place, I will come to matériel, the new programme, and a few miscellaneous questions either connected therewith or disconnected with any other large topic or head into which my subject is divided. In the next place I will examine the standards of new construction which we are pursuing. This will lead me to the position in the Mediterranean and also to the position in the Pacific, and to the Imperial aspects of naval policy. Finally, I will deal with the general question in so far as it affects this country and our interests as a whole. That is a considerable programme. . . .

There cannot be much argument about the automatic increases, but it is a fair question to ask: Why is it necessary to have this larger and more costly Fleet? The scale of our Fleet, and the cost of its maintenance depend first, on the number, and secondly, on the character of the ships maintained in the various grades of commission. The number of ships maintained in commission is proportionate to what other Powers do. I have frequently explained the new Fleet organisation to the House. We are seeking to complete eight battle squadrons by the time the next strongest naval Power has completed five. Battle cruisers would be additional in both cases, and there would be the proper proportion of cruisers and flotillas. Ships on foreign stations do not, of course, come into this calculation, which affects only the Home Fleet of this country, and the next strongest naval Power. The standards of establishment are reasonable and moderate, and I was very glad to see that the Grand Admiral Von Tirpitz has taken occasion to say that they are. Quite recently in the debates of this year in the Reichstag he also said:—

> Neither nation has completed the naval organisation at which it is aiming. Germany needs forty-one battleships for her five squadrons; England needs sixty-five battleships for her eight squadrons.

It is quite true that neither nation has yet completed its organisation. It would have been possible for us to complete our developments at a somewhat earlier period than we now propose to do, but the development of the German fleet organisation has not been so rapid as I anticipated two years ago to this extent: the new third German squadron will be completed at the end of this financial year, but apparently because of manning difficulties the second squadron is to be reduced temporarily by three ships, so that there are three less ships in the organisation of the German fleet than we expected. We have therefore postponed the completion of the fourth squadron—the Gibraltar Squadron—which remains during the year at four ships.

Mr. Lee: Might I put a question to the right hon. Gentleman? He said "at the end of the financial year." Does he mean to say the year we are now in or the year 1914-15?

Mr. Churchill: The year 1914-15. I am obliged to the hon. Gentleman for his interruption. When I talk of this financial year, I am looking forward to the year on which we are now entering, and which is the subject of our debate to-day. Every delay, accidental or deliberate, on the part of the next strongest naval Power in the development of its enormous fleet organisation will be matched by us. We shall only complete our organisation as it is needed, and in proportion as it is needed. When completed, apart from the battle cruisers on both sides and ancillary vessels of the fleet—which I do not refer to because, though it would be quite easy to do so, it would add much to the complexity of the argument—apart from the battle cruisers our organisation when completed will yield thirty-three battleships in full commission to twenty-five, and sixteen battleships in reserve to an equal number. Then, as a make-weight, we have the Second Fleet of sixteen battleships all manned on mobilisation with the regular active service ratings, against which there is no corresponding organisation in the German Navy. No one can say that this is an extreme or excessive provision on our part. On the other hand, we consider it adequate. So much for numbers. I am dealing with the scale of the Fleet, and why it is necessary that the scale of the Fleet should be increased. . . .

The present Board of Admiralty associate themselves fully with the decisions of their predecessors which we regard in every respect as wise and foreseeing and vitally necessary to the Naval Services. All these decisions have been approved by the House of Commons, and we are bound to meet the cost involved in the maintenance of ships which Parliament has ordered to be built. I should be quite ready myself to accept responsibility for past decisions if it were open to me to do so. I do not shelter myself in the slightest degree; but if I am personally criticised for the great increase which has taken place in the cost of maintenance, and if it is represented that it is all due to my reckless extravagance and megalomania, then I should point out that, except for one flotilla of a few small cruisers, no ships for whose design I have been responsible come under the Estimates of the coming year. . . .

I have one consoling observation to make for those who eye the monster ship with disfavour. The offensive power of modern battleships is out of all proportion to their defensive power. Never was the disproportion so marked. If you want to make a true picture in your mind of a battle between great modern ironclad ships you must not think of it as if it were two men in armour striking at each other with heavy swords. It is more like a battle between two egg-shells striking each other with hammers. In the light of that illustration, the awful importance of good gunnery must come home to us. The importance of hitting first, and hitting hardest and keeping on hitting, and the necessity of spending money on arriving at the highest possible efficiency in that respect, really needs no clearer proof. But the fact also, I think, suggests doubts as to whether this form of warfare between these enormous ships is not now approaching its culminating phase. The cruiser design of the year is still under consideration, and a further statement will be made by me in July on Vote 8 in general terms.

Lord C. Beresford: Small cruisers?

Mr. Churchill: The cruiser design. I am not talking of battleships. The destroyer problem is very interesting at the present time. The destroyer has two functions. Its first function is to destroy the enemy's torpedo craft by gunfire in its own waters. Its second function is the attack by the torpedo on the heavy ships of the enemy. Last year I explained how light cruisers were cutting in on one province of the destroyer, namely, its function in gunnery, and how submarines were cutting in on its torpedo functions. All these tendencies continue, and the North Sea, on account of its size, is less favourable than the Channel was to the effective operations of destroyers. The light cruiser is the true destroyer of torpedo craft in the North Sea. She goes out and stays out in all weathers, and her battery is such that it is instantly decisive against a destroyer. A reduced destroyer programme must be viewed in relation to the abnormal light cruiser programmes of the last two years, when, I may remind the House, we built sixteen cruisers to the German four; but then, of course, the Germans build heavier cruisers than we have been building lately. But then, again, our cruisers must be considered in relation to our armoured cruisers, in which we have a great superiority. So much for cruisers.

The submarine programme of the year is large enough in view of our effective lead in this type of vessel, but further effort will be required in the near future on account of what is going on elsewhere. £1,150,000 is taken for submarines, and the House very properly does not desire to know how many craft will be built for that money. That would unduly reveal the design. We are increasingly convinced of the power of the submarine and the decisive part which this weapon, aided perhaps in some respects by the seaplane, may play in the naval warfare of the future. It is sufficient at the moment to say that the whole system of naval architecture, and the methods of computing naval strength, are brought under review by the ever-growing power, radius, and seaworthiness of the submarine, and by the increasing range and accuracy of its fatal torpedoes. The personal element counts for much in this service, and we are lucky. Frequently in all weathers, in deep water, far out at sea, with no attendant vessel, submarine flotillas exercise with audacity against a swiftly moving fleet or squadron. A certain amount of risk is unavoidable if the captains are to acquire the necessary practical experience. Since I have been in office nine officers and thirty-seven men have perished in submarines. The peace risks of the submarine service approximate more nearly to war risks than in any other branch. It is the most dangerous service in time of peace, and I am bound to say I should not be surprised if it turned out to be the safest service in time of war. Such are the conditions under which this formidable engine is developed. We have at present 268 officers and 3,000 men, all thoroughly trained in the submarine service. The destroyer flotillas are at present maintained upon an establishment of eighty destroyers in the First Fleet, which will be reached before the end of the year, and an equal number in the patrol flotilla. I may remind the House that patrol flotillas are all manned with active service ratings in time of war. They have no Reservists at present, and the complements which they have on board are sufficient to enable them to put to sea at once. They could not keep the sea for a long time with their reduced complements, but they can perfectly well discharge their functions for a few days before taking on their balance crews—they are therefore counted as instantly ready for sea. The steady influx of new boats makes it necessary to degrade older vessels continually, and we are now considering a scheme of establishing reserve flotillas to correspond with the Third Fleet, which will be filled in part with Reservists who have recently served in the flotillas, when mobilised. We are using every effort to reduce to the narrowest limits compatible with efficiency the oil consumption of the flotilla while we are building up a reserve, and an intricate system has been devised by the flotilla officers, with the approval of the Board, which has effected a considerable saving. All use of oil-burning destroyers for tenders during torpedo practice, and other ancillary purposes connected with the Battle Fleet, has been stopped, and eight coal-burning destroyers are attached to the Battle Fleet for the subsidiary duties. The flotillas are for the present in the highest state of efficiency, and a remarkable advance in their gunnery and torpedo practice has marked the last two years. . . .

I come now to the central problem of our standard. Formerly we have followed the two-Power standard—that is to say, 10 per cent. over the two next strongest Powers. Now that standard has become quite meaningless. The two next strongest Powers, if you take the whole world, would be Germany and the United States, and if you left out the United States, as common sense would dictate, the two next strongest Powers would be Germany and France, which is not a very helpful or reasonable standard to adopt. As a matter of fact, in 1914-15 we shall be conforming to both these tests, absurd and unreasonable though they be. It would not be in the naval interest to base our strength on foundations from which common sense recoils. The 60 per cent. standard was adopted by the Admiralty in 1908 or 1909, and it was announced publicly by me two years ago. That is a building standard of new construction only, and it refers to capital ships only. For cruisers we follow a 100 per cent. standard, and have been for many years. There are other standards for other classes. The 60 per cent. standard was described by me as follows:

> To develop a 60 per cent. superiority in vessels of the "Dreadnought" type over the German Navy on the basis of the Fleet law before its latest amendment, and to build at the rate of two keels to one for every ship added under that law, either by the last amendment or by subsequent amendments.

That is the standard we are following, and for which we claim full Parliamentary assent. That standard, of course, is not eternal; still less could it be made a binding international instrument. It is capable of revision in either one direction or the other. I have always carefully guarded myself against any inference that it could be made an absolute standard. Let me read to the House what I said on 18th March 1912:

> If Germany were to adhere to her existing law we believe that standard would, in the absence of any unexpected development in other countries, continue to be a financial guide for the next four or five years, so far, that is to say, as this capital class of vessel is concerned. Further than that it is idle to speculate. This, however, I must say, I must not be taken as agreeing that the ratio of sixteen to ten could be regarded as sufficient preponderance for British Naval strength as a whole above that of the next strongest naval Power. Even if we possessed an Army two-thirds as strong as that of the strongest military Power, we could not agree to that.

That was what I said originally on the first occasion this was announced to the public. There have been various disputes as to what ships should or should not come into the 60 per cent. standard, and I have no doubt the hon. Gentleman opposite has a well filled arsenal of artillery on the subject. Some contend that the "Lord Nelsons," the "New Zealand," and the "Malaya" should be counted, and others contend that none of these should count at all, and a flood of sterile controversy and partisan statistics, which sensible people would avoid, has been poured out on both sides on this subject. The editor of the "Economist" arrives at the conclusion that no ships should be built at all this year, while the editor of the "National Review," in a comparatively lucid interval, announces that nothing less than sixteen "Dreadnoughts" will save the Board of Admiralty from the traitor's doom. All this should be taken for what it is worth. The Admiralty have no need and no intention to enter into such a controversy. We have not merely stated our standard, but we have declared our programme. Programmes supersede standards, and actual figures are better than percentages. Two years ago I gave the whole series of programmes to the House which we considered necessary. They were 4, 5, 4, 4, 4, 4, as against German construction 2, 3, 2, 2, 3, 2. Parliament approved of the principle of that request. That is what we ask for now–no more, no less. That is the Admiralty interpretation of the 60 per cent standard. It takes into consideration all the disputable factors and makes all the necessary allowance for older ships declining in value. It has been carefully safeguarded so as not to tie the hands of this country in future, and to provide for the unforeseen. Since then we have had the "New Zealand" made available for Home service, the "Malaya" presented to us without conditions, and we have had the talk about the Canadian ships, but our programmes have remained unaltered in spite of these additions.

We have now reached the third of these programmes, and when we consider that British shipbuilding is necessarily dependent on what other people do, it will be seen that three years is a long way to look ahead, and certainly a long way to look ahead successfully. I should not hesitate to admit that we were wrong if we had changed our minds, or to say that new steps must be taken if new circumstances had arisen, but after a full survey of the whole situation at home and abroad we consider that four ships are enough for the programme of this year, and we ask the House to affirm the proposals I submitted in my first year of responsibility for this Department. In March, 1912, speaking in the name of the Government and the Admiralty, I said:

> The Admiralty are prepared to guarantee absolutely the main security of the country and the Empire day by day for the next two years, and if the House will grant what we ask for the future that prospect may be indefinitely extended.

. . . I thank the House for the patience with which they have listened to me. No survey, let me say in conclusion, of British Naval expenditure, and no controversy arising out of it, can be confined to our naval strength. It must also have regard to our military resources compared with the resources of all other European States that are building navies. In 1913, when the five great Powers of Europe have increased their naval expenditure by more than £50,000,000 a year, and greater increases are still being made, the British Army, owing to causes which have been fully explained, has actually diminished in numbers. We must take that into consideration when we judge the size of the Naval Estimates. Our naval standards, and the programmes which give effect to them, must also be examined in relation not only to Germany but to the rest of the world. We must begin by recognising how different is the part played by our Navy from that of the navies of every other country. Alone among the great modern

States, we can neither defend the soil upon which we live nor subsist upon its produce. Our whole Regular Army is liable to be ordered abroad for the defence of India. The food of our people, the raw material of our industries, the commerce which constitutes our wealth, have to be protected as they traverse thousands of miles of sea and ocean from every quarter of the globe. Here we must consider the disparity of risks and stakes between us and other naval Powers. Defeat to Germany at sea means nothing but loss of the ships sunk or damaged in battle. Behind the German "Dreadnoughts" stand four and a half million soldiers, and a narrow sea-front bristling with fortresses and batteries. Nothing we could do, after a naval victory, could affect the safety or freedom of a single German hamlet.

Behind the British line of battle are the long, light-defended stretches of the East Coast, our endless trade routes and food routes, our small Army and our vast peaceful population, with their immense possessions. The burden of responsibility laid upon the British Navy is heavy, and its weight increases year by year. All the world is building ships of the greatest power, training officers and men, creating arsenals, and laying broad and deep the foundations of future permanent naval development and expansion. In every country powerful interests and huge industries are growing up, which will render any check or cessation in the growth of navies increasingly difficult as time goes by. Besides the Great Powers, there are many small States who are buying or building great ships of war, and whose vessels may, by purchase, by some diplomatic combination or by duress, be brought into the line against us. None of these Powers need, like us, navies to defend their actual independence or safety. They build them so as to play a part in the world's affairs. It is sport to them. It is life and death to us. These possibilities were described by Lord Crewe in the House of Lords last year. It is not suggested that the whole world will turn upon us, or that our preparations should contemplate such a monstrous contingency. By a sober and modest conduct, by a skilful diplomacy, we can in part disarm and in part divide the elements of potential danger. But two things have to be considered: First, that our diplomacy depends in great part for its effectiveness upon our naval position, and that our naval strength is the one great balancing force which we can contribute to our own safety and to the peace of the world. Secondly, we are not a young people with a blank record and a scanty inheritance. We have won for ourselves, in times when other powerful nations were paralysed by barbarism or internal war, an exceptional share of the wealth and traffic of the world.

We have got all we want in territory, but our claim to be left in undisputed enjoyment of vast and splendid possessions, largely acquired by war and largely maintained by force, is one which often seems less reasonable to others than to us. Further, we have intervened regularly, as it was our duty to do, and as we could not help doing, in the affairs of Europe and of the world, and great advantage to European peace has resulted, even in this last year, from our interference. We have responsibilities in many quarters to-day. We are far from being detached from the problems of Europe. We have passed through a year of continuous anxiety, and, although His Majesty's Government believe the foundations of peace among the Great Powers have been strengthened, yet the causes which might lead to a general war have not been removed and often remind us of their presence. There has not been the slightest abatement of naval and military preparation. On the contrary, we are witnessing this year increases of expenditure by Continental Powers in armaments beyond all previous experience. The world is armed as it was never armed before. Every suggestion or arrest or limitation has so far been ineffectual. From time to time awkward things happen, and situations occur which make it necessary that the naval force at our immediate disposal, now in this quarter, now in that, should be rapidly counted up. On such occasions the responsibilities which rest on the Admiralty come home with brutal reality to those who are responsible, and unless our naval strength were solidly, amply, and unswervingly maintained, the Government could not feel that they were doing their duty to the country.

VOTE OF CENSURE

April 28, 1914

House of Commons

Ireland was now aflame, and passions in the House of Commons were intense. On the night of April 24/25 the Ulster Volunteers landed a substantial quantity of rifles and ammunition, and the tangled Ulster situation took an even more grave turn. The Unionists had tabled a Vote of Censure on the Government, and Churchill's counter-attack was considerably helped by the blatant gun-running episode. Nonetheless, he attempted–unsuccessfully–to recover lost ground by making conciliatory gestures towards Carson, to the fury of the Irish Nationalists and many Liberals.

[Extract] This is a Vote of Censure and a demand for a judicial inquiry. In all the circumstances, I venture to say it is the most audacious Vote and most impudent demand for a judicial inquiry of which our records can provide a parallel. The first maxim of English jurisprudence is that complainers should come into Court with clean hands. Here we get the right hon. Gentleman the Member for Dublin University (Sir E. Carson), and the hon. Member who sits behind him, fresh from their gun-running exploits–

Sir E. Carson *made an observation which was inaudible in the Reporters' Gallery.*

Hon. Members: Behave like a king!

Sir E. Carson: You behave like a cad!

Mr. MacCallum Scott: On a Point of Order. I desire to call your attention to the conduct of the right hon. Gentleman the Member for Dublin University (Sir E. Carson), who has been shouting across the floor of the House to Members on this side that they are cads.

Mr. Speaker: It is a most improper expression to use. I do not know whether the hon. Member was one of those who used the taunting and offensive expression, but he cannot deny that there are several of his colleagues who did so. I hope the right hon.

Gentleman will not repeat the observation, and under the circumstances I do not propose to call on him to withdraw it.

Sir E. Carson: May I say I listened patiently through all these discussions–I always do–and it is only when I am taunted across from the other side that I used that expression. If I have said anything disorderly, I regret it, but certainly I shall not be taunted from the other side without asserting myself.

Mr. Churchill: I am pointing out, as I am quite entitled to do, the curious position occupied by the right hon. and learned Gentleman and his colleague behind him coming here fresh from their exploits in Ireland to demand a judicial inquiry into the conduct of those responsible for the maintenance of law and order. The right hon. Gentleman who has just sat down (Mr. A. Chamberlain) made to us a very long speech which was altogether out of date. He began by admitting that his speech was out of date. He said, "I have not to deal with subsequent facts." How very convenient! Subsequent facts, he clearly sees, are fatal to the Motion. Are we quite sure they are "subsequent facts"? It is very convenient, no doubt, to represent that after the revelations of the fiendish plot it was necessary for the law-abiding people of Ulster to obtain weapons to protect themselves from such horrible machinations, and that what took place at Larne and other places on Friday night last was the answer to the events which are now under discussion before the House. I do not think that is the case at all. On the 18th of February, a month before we had made these preparations to protect our depots, the right hon. and learned Gentleman (Sir E. Carson), speaking at the Cannon Street Hotel, said:

> They were daily entering into commitments of thousands of pounds, and he himself in the last few days, it was not any harm to confess–

I agree. I think he has always been perfectly frank.

An Hon. Member: He always tells the truth.

Mr. Churchill: I would point out to the hon. Member that he has not the power to insult me.

> had authorised the expenditure of at least £60,000 to £80,000 towards their defence that became immediately necessary.

So I think it is quite clear that the large consignments of arms which have lately been landed in such lawless fashion were part of the policy which the right hon. Gentleman was carrying out before the Government even embarked upon the military precautions. A great many hard words are used about us, and the right hon. Gentleman who has just sat down used the expression "criminals" with regard to us, and his supporters in the Press use extraordinary language. But we can meet those accusations with composure. We have not broken the law, and we are not engaged in breaking the law. Anyone who is familiar with the law knows perfectly well that there are half a dozen Statutes, some of the gravest character, which are being openly flouted and defied at the present time by Members who sit opposite to us, and by their followers in Ireland, and that they are being flouted and defied with the full connivance and approval of those hon. Members. So what we are now witnessing in the House is uncommonly like a vote of censure by the criminal classes on the police. [An Hon. Member: "You have not arrested them!"] Is that the complaint—that we have not arrested the criminals? Is it the complaint, that we have been too lenient? That is the only accusation I am not prepared to answer. Language is used of us—let me read to the House language of the laws of this country: 12 Victoria, cap. 12 (Treason Felony Act, 1848):

> Be it enacted that if any person whatsoever after the passing of this Act shall within the United Kingdom or without compass, imagine, invent, devise, or intend to deprive, or depose Our Most Gracious Lady the Queen, her heirs or successors, from the style honour or Royal name of the Imperial Crown of the United Kingdom, or of any other of Her Majesty's Dominions and countries, or to levy war against Her Majesty, her heirs or successors, within any part of the United Kingdom, in order by force or constraint to compel her or them to change her or their measures or counsels, or in order to put any force or constraint upon or in order to intimidate or overawe both Houses or either House of Parliament, or to move or stir any foreigner or stranger with force to invade the United Kingdom or any other of Her Majesty's Dominions . . . every person so offending shall be guilty of felony. . . .

I should like the House to note that the offence of using force to induce the King to change his counsel or of trying to intimidate and overawe either or both Houses of Parliament, is placed on a level with two of the foulest crimes, namely, endeavouring to subvert the throne of this country, or to bring in the foreign enemy. We have to face every day the revilings of your ferocious Press, but your condemnation is contained in the Statute, in the laws of the British realm, in Acts of Parliament, which have for generations and centuries been respected and enforced by the people of these islands, and which are indeed the necessary foundation, the indispensable foundation, of orderly government and civilised society. Language far stronger, far crueller than any which you have it in your wit to use against us, than any which your most partisan speaker, your most patriotic editor is capable of introducing into speech or leading article, is found in the grave and sober pages of the English Statute Book. Under those circumstances we can afford to retain our composure. But what is the position of the Conservative party in regard to the events which have taken place in Ireland? The Conservative party, the party of the comfortable, the wealthy—[Hon. Members: "No, no!"]—the party of those who have most to gain by the continuance of the existing social order, here they are committed to naked revolution, committed to a policy of armed violence, and utter defiance of lawfully constituted authority, committed to tampering with the discipline of the Army and the Navy, committed to obstructing highways and telegraphs, to overpowering police, coastguards and Customs officials, committed to smuggling in arms by moonlight, committed to the piratical seizure of ships and to the unlawful imprisonment of the King's servants—the Conservative party as a whole committed to that. The right hon. and learned Gentleman the Member for the Walton Division of Liverpool (Mr. F. E. Smith) has left us in no doubt about that.

He said, speaking at the annual dinner of the Junior Imperial League:

> Sir Edward Carson has taken no step, and he will take no step, however extreme it may be, for which we shall not make ourselves responsible here, representing a majority of the English constituencies.

That is their position, and all the time while their newspapers are chuckling with nervous glee at each sorry event which is recorded, and while they are hurriedly collecting information as if it was news from Mexico, or some other disturbed area, and bringing out special editions with the utmost satisfaction, all the time that that is going on, let me point out to the Conservative party, and those who are associated with them, that there is in this country a great democracy, millions of whom are forced to live their lives under conditions which leave them stripped of all but the barest necessities, who are repeatedly urged to be patient under their misfortunes, repeatedly urged to wait year after year, and Parliament after Parliament, until, in the due workings of the Constitution, some satisfaction is given to their clamant needs, all the time this great audience is watching and is learning from you, from those who have hitherto called themselves "the party of law and order" how much they care for law, how much they value order when it stands in the way of anything they like! If that great audience is watching here at home, what of the great audiences that watch in India. Think of the devastating doctrines of the Leader of the Opposition. The right hon. Gentleman may laugh in a brief leadership of the Conservative party, but he has shattered treasure which greater men than he have guarded for generations. Think what the effect of his doctrines would be applied, let us say, to the people of India or of Egypt. Take his doctrine in regard to the Army–his doctrine of what the officers are entitled to choose or not to choose. He was obliged to carry that further, and to say that the men might choose also. I am not going to push this matter too far, but consider the application of that doctrine to the native officers of the Indian Army, or to the native soldiers of the Indian or Egyptian Army, and you will see that, in his insatiable hunger to get into office he is subverting principles which are absolutely vital to the continued organised government of the British Empire.

I say that we can remain calm under all the abuse to which we are subjected, and even in the face of all the difficulties of the situation. We are proceeding strictly along constitutional lines. We are not breaking the law; we are upholding it. We are striving to defend the State from anarchy and affronts. But you–I do not wonder that there are two views, very apparent to us, in the party opposite. There are the old Conservatives. I do not wonder that they are uncomfortable. My nerves are, I hope, as good as those of most Members of this House, but I thank God, that I have not to play for the stakes to which they are committed. Then there is another section, I think a minority, who take a much bolder line, and to whose initiative it is no doubt due that this Vote has been moved to-day. There are those who say, "We are Tories. No laws apply to us. Laws are made for the working people, to keep them in their proper places. We are the dominant class. We are the ruling forces of the State. When laws suit us, we will obey them. If they do not suit us, so much the worse for the laws. We will not bow down to the rules appropriate to the common herd of British subjects. It will be time enough for us to talk about law and order when we have got into office, and have to deal with

Irish Nationalists and British labour men." May I ask–[Interruption.]

Earl Winterton: Oh, let him go on.

Mr. Churchill: It is an infinite encouragement to me that my words can produce a salutary impression, however superficial or transient, upon the Noble Lord. But I would ask the party opposite to consider very seriously for a moment before I come to the point, how the present situation strikes Liberals and Irish Nationalists. Irish Nationalists have always been urged by both great parties in the State to abandon unconstitutional agitation. They have not only been urged to do so, but great violence has been used against them. For a very long time they have staked their fortunes upon constitutional and Parliamentary agitation–[Hon. Members: "Cattle driving," "Moonlighting"]–and now they have brought their cause to the very threshold of success. If by an act of violence and under threats of violence the cause of Home Rule were to be shattered now, I say that the Conservative party would themselves have taught the Nationalists of Ireland the truth that there was in John Bright's famous saying that Ireland never gained anything but by force. You would have discredited utterly and for ever, in regard to every class in this country which is discontented, and in regard to every nationality within the British Empire that is not satisfied with existing conditions, all hope of redress by constitutional means. You, the Conservative party, would have pointed out to them that the surest and most effective method of obtaining redress of grievances is violent, lawless, and armed agitation and rebellion. How does it strike us? We have been nine years in power. [An Hon. Member: "Nine years too long."] We have in that period fought three General Elections, so that the country does not agree with the hon. Gentleman. In the whole of that time we have disposed of great affairs at home and abroad. When we came into office–I must put this point if I may–there were five great questions upon which Liberals desired to legislate: Education, Temperance, Welsh Disestablishment, Plural Voting, and Home Rule. Not one single one of those have we yet succeeded in carrying into law. . . .

I say that the use which is now being made of the Orange Army is a use far outside any question connected with Ulster. Its purpose and intent is to rupture and destroy the whole movement of Liberal and Radical reform. Its object is to show that, if the veto of the Lords is gone, there still remains the veto of force, and, by the use of that veto, to deny to at least one-half of the nation that fair share of political rights and political activities to which they are undoubtedly entitled. . . . If I may go back to that controversy, I would like to begin at what I must consider the turning point in the Home Rule discussion–I mean the rejection of the Prime Minister's offer on the 9th March. The right hon. Gentleman tried to make out–it was necessary for his argument that he should make out–that there had been no rejection. But he quoted, with approval, the expression "hypocritical sham," which had been applied to those proposals of the Prime Minister. He said, "The Government had made an advance, and we recognised it." How did they recognise it? On the 10th March, the day after the offer, the right hon. and learned Member for Dublin University wrote:

> It is clear to my mind, so far as our preparations are concerned, that the pronouncement of the Government, if anything, necessitates a still more forward movement.

That is what the right hon. Gentleman (Mr. A. Chamberlain) describes as the Government making an advance and the Conservative party recognising it. I cannot understand why, when that pronouncement was made by the Prime Minister, the spokesman of the party opposite could not have said, "Although this is not what we need, or what we require, it constitutes the greatest step forward towards settlement that has ever been made." Had that language been used, I venture to think that threads would never have been severed which have now been interrupted. That is the point from which I start in considering the situation in Ireland. We made the greatest offer in our power, and it was summarily and incontinently rejected. What were the results of that act? It was perfectly clear that there was no possibility of settlement so long as one party in the House believed that it had only to go on bullying the other, and in the end the other would be incapable of taking any effective steps to maintain its authority. While one party in a dispute is prepared to go to extremes—and it is firmly believed that under no circumstances will the other party even take the necessary action to defend its right and to discharge its duties—there is no possibility of any effective parley between them. From the moment the declaration of the Prime Minister was made there was no more question of coercing Ulster by this Government. Six years and two elections must intervene before the question of the inclusion of Ulster arose again. It was no longer the question of our coercing Ulster; it was a question of our preventing Ulster coercing us. The smallness of the outstanding differences as far as Ulster was concerned only made the situation more grave and more awkward. In the differences which remain on the subject of Ulster, taking it by itself, there was no foothold and no foundation for civil war—none whatever. It is clear that those who were preparing for civil war had other purposes in their mind besides Ulster. They were preparing to defeat the general policy of Home Rule. They were preparing to subvert the regular system of Parliamentary government in this country. I say that whatever compunction and sympathy we have for Ulster, there is no room for concession or weakness in face of a challenge of that kind. If Parliamentary government is exposed to a challenge in this country, we are bound to take up that challenge and fight it out to the very end. Nothing could be more disastrous than that hon. Members opposite should suppose that they and their Ulster friends are the only people in this country prepared to risk their lives for great issues. The supreme issue lies here; the actual events are taking place on the Irish stage. After the utter repulse and breakdown of our efforts at conciliation, it was to the military situation in Ireland that we were forced to look.

What was that situation in the second week in March? There was the Orange Army, strong and efficient no doubt—no one can do more justice to it than has been done to it by its own friends. Scattered about Ulster were the scanty police and military forces of the Crown, and depots of arms and ammunition of great consequence to this growing, illegal military force. We had, of course, police and military reports which had been accumulated for a long period of time. We had the information and the advice of the General Officers, and we had many other sources of information as to what was proceeding. We had the statement of the right hon. and learned Gentleman, which I have read to the House, about his expenditure of large sums of money upon arms and ammunition. We had the statement of 10th March about the forward movement, and we were, I say, in view of all these matters, and when we had reached the breakdown of our hopes and efforts at conciliation, absolutely bound to review and survey the whole military scene in Ireland in all its possibilities, actual and contingent. That survey comprised three perfectly separate spheres. First of all, there was the question of a large naval force, in principle a Battle Squadron with its attendant ships, which it was decided in the Cabinet of 11th March, should be stationed upon the West Coast of Scotland with a view to being at hand should intervention in Irish disorders become necessary or desirable. [An Hon. Member: "Hear, hear!"] I have never attempted to conceal the fact. It was the details of that force, the date when it should be moved, and as to its actual composition in units which were, of course, left to the Admiralty.

Can anyone say, after what has occurred, that it was an improper or improvident proceeding on the part of the Government to have a naval force available for necessary service in Irish waters in the circumstances which then existed. [An Hon. Member: "Why countermand, then?"] The force is now on the spot. That was the first step which was taken in the Cabinet on 11th March. That was entirely separate and having regard to the general situation of the Irish question. It is entirely separate from the particular moves relating to the defence of the depots, which was the second sphere of our inquiry, to which I now come. I have dealt at length before in the House with the protection of the ammunition depots. I have gone *seriatim* through the various points. The right hon. Gentleman has expended a great deal of time in trying to make mysteries, difficulties and obscurities out of what is perfectly plain and clear. These large depots of arms and ammunition, ranging from thirty tons to eighty-five tons of small-arms ammunition—the right hon. Gentleman knows exactly how many rounds there are in eighty-five tons!—were scattered about in an entirely unprotected condition, with very small bodies of Infantry, largely recruits, or old soldiers watching them, and these men were in some cases almost equally divided between Protestants and Catholics. There was either the possibility of their being under temptation, either by a serious movement by responsible people or of their being a prey to some spontaneous and irresponsible movement of mischievous hotheads. We were absolutely bound to safeguard these depots once we were clear that our efforts to meet hon. Gentlemen opposite on the Irish question had for the time being failed, and once it became so clearly apparent that perhaps no effort we could make on the Irish question would ever be accepted by them. . . .

If British troops, marching on the King's highway, were shot down and slain by rebel rifles, if the guns at Dundalk had been attacked before they could be covered by Infantry, if we saw that the eighty-five tons of ammunition at Carrickfergus had been assailed, it would be the duty, the absolute duty, of the Executive Government, to strike back with every man or gun they could command, and it would be the duty of the Military Departments to be fully prepared to execute any orders they might receive from the Government. As far as I am concerned, I wish to make it perfectly plain that if British troops were attacked and fired on, and loss of life occurs to them, I will take every measure that is in my power and that I have authority for, to secure that the persons making that attack will receive most condign chastisement at the time, and are afterwards proceeded against with the full rigour of the law.

But hon. Members opposite may say, and I think from their cheers they are inclined to say, these things could never have happened, that they did not happen, and that they never could have happened. Then, in that case, nothing would happen on our part either. In that case, none of these purely hypothetical contingencies which we are considering could have existed; none of the measures which we considered would be appropriate to such a state of affairs could be taken or would have been taken. What I am anxious to impress upon hon. Members is that the use of force rests with them, and does not rest with us. It rests with them. They are the masters of the situation in that respect. We shall not use force till force is first used against the representatives of law and order. We shall in no circumstances use more legal force than is necessary to maintain or restore order. Unless they take life first, their own lives will not in any sense of the word be in danger; but if they do, we are bound to use all the force at our disposal, and to take all necessary measures to secure the vindication of the law and repression of disorder. From that there is absolutely no escape. Whatever mistakes hon. Members opposite may make, do not let them imagine that they are dealing with a Government or individuals who will flinch from doing their duty in this respect. Let me make it quite clear, however, that though the movements we were making in Ulster were these limited movements–and none were approved, authorised, or ordered in any way, beyond them–the Government have absolute right, if they choose, at any time to make movements far in excess of these.

We have a perfect right, for instance, if we at any time think fit, to put 40,000 or 50,000 men into Ulster, to begin the arrest of leaders, the seizure of arms, and the general prevention of drilling. We have always rejected the idea of such measures, and we do not consider, and have not at any time considered, that they would be wise or proper in the circumstances with which we have so far had to deal. But I am very anxious indeed that no word should come from me or any Member of the Government which would seem to admit for a moment that we limit at all our rights to dispose of His Majesty's forces within the King's Dominions in any way we may choose to maintain law and order. The right hon. Gentleman who has just sat down treated us to an illuminating insight into his mental position on this subject when he accused us of having wished to seize strategic points. To what a pretty pass we are come when we are told that British troops may not march about the United Kingdom in any way they choose! I did not believe at the time, when these definite precautionary moves were authorised, that they would provoke an outbreak, nor did they, but we took every care so to carry them out that there would be the smallest possible chance of an interference or outbreak. Speed and secrecy were essential. Nothing was to begin before Friday night. Everything was to be complete on Saturday morning. Nothing began before Friday night, and everything was complete on Saturday morning. Naval officers in plain clothes, troops taken by sea to avoid going through Belfast, were only a part of the careful measures which we took to prevent it being possible to bring armed opposition to bear upon these small bodies or small movements while they were actually in process of completion. I think it was a good thing we did so; for what did the right hon. and learned Gentleman the Member for the Walton Division of Liverpool (Mr. F. E. Smith) say when speaking upon this subject three weeks ago? I really must ask the House to give their attention to that. I wonder whether the right hon. Gentleman the Member for the City of London fully appreciated the position to which he is committed by the right hon. and learned Member. This is what he said:

> If an attempt was made in force to seize the decisive strategical positions in Ulster, I say, though I know it will be received with extreme dissatisfaction on the other side, that my right hon. Friend (Sir E. Carson) would have justified everything that has been said on the other side of the House in disparagement of himself and of the Ulster Volunteers, if he had allowed that movement to be carried through.

Here is the right hon. Gentleman who has just spoken who says, "If you wish to seize strategical points, why not do it openly? Who would ever complain of your doing it openly?" The other right hon. Gentleman who sits further along the bench says, "If we had known that you were going to seize these strategic points openly, we should certainly have used force to prevent you occupying them." What more does the House or the country want, I should like to know, to justify the precautions we took than the statement made here in the name of the Conservative party by the right hon. and learned Gentleman the Member for the Walton Division of Liverpool (Mr. F. E. Smith), a clear statement that if he and his Friends, rightly or wrongly, interpreted the movements of His Majesty's troops in the United Kingdom as being of a nature to occupy strategic positions they would, without delay, have attacked those troops, and prevented their arriving at the stations to which they had been ordered. No, Sir, nothing more is needed to justify the care and pain with which we considered all the contingencies and possibilities that might arise from the limited and restricted precautionary movements we were making. All this talk of civil war has not come from us; it has come from you, from the party opposite. For the last two years we have been forced to listen to a drone of threats of civil war with the most blood-curdling accompaniments and consequences. What did they mean by civil war? Did they really think that if a civil war came it was to be a war in which only one side was to take action? Did they really believe it was all going to be dashing exploits and brilliant, dramatic, gun-running coups on the side of rebellion, and nothing but fiendish plots on the part of the Government?

These two right hon. Gentlemen and hon. Members who have come up here and honoured us by their presence to-day, do they really suppose that they will be able to be conducting a campaign against the Government and the Crown in the field on the one hand, and at the same time asking the Government, the Prime Minister, and the Minister for War all the awkward questions they can think of about their military operations on the other hand? A sense of humour ought, at least, to have saved them from that. I do not believe myself, even at the present time, that rebellion or civil war will come, but I wish to make it perfectly clear that if rebellion comes, we shall put it down, and if it comes to civil war, we shall do our best to conquer in the civil war. But there will be neither rebellion nor civil war unless it is of your making.

I have only a few more remarks to make, and then I will conclude, because I have already addressed the House at length on these points. References have been made repeatedly to my Bradford speech, and especially to the concluding words of that speech. I would like, if the House will permit me—and I am very sorry to have to read my own words again—in fairness to myself, to read the actual context in which those words are bound, because I believed it then, and I adhere to it most strongly now, that it is part of all I have said on this subject during the whole period it has been under discussion. I said:

> If Ulster seeks peace and fair play she can find it. She knows where to find it. If Ulstermen extend the hand of friendship it will be clasped by Liberal and by their Nationalist countrymen in all good faith and in all good will; but if there is no wish for peace, if every concession that is made is spurned and exploited, if every effort to meet their views is only to be used as a means of breaking down Home Rule and of barring the way to the rest of Ireland: if Ulster is to become a tool in party calculations, if the civil and Parliamentary systems under which we have dwelt so long and our fathers before us are to be brought to the crude challenge of force, if the Government and the Parliament of this great country and greater Empire are to be exposed to menace and brutality, if all the loose, wanton, and reckless chatter we have been forced to listen to these many months is in the end to disclose a sinister and revolutionary purpose, then I can only say to you: Let us go forward together and put these grave matters to the proof.

I say so still, but I will venture to ask the House once more at this moment in our differences and quarrels to consider whither it is we may find ourselves going, and I will ask them to consider whether we ought not to try even at this period, and even so far as this Debate may be a vehicle of such matters, to make some final effort to reach a better solution? Apart from the dangers which this controversy and this Debate clearly shows exists at home, apart from those dangers, look at the consequences abroad.

Mr. Hunt: Who brought it about? [Hon. Members: "You did!"]

Mr. Churchill: Anxiety is caused in every friendly country by the belief that for the time being Great Britain cannot act. The high mission of this country is thought to be in abeyance, and the balance of Europe appears in many quarters for the time to be deranged. Of course, foreign countries never really understand us in these islands. They do not know what we know, that at a touch of external difficulties or menace all these fierce internal controversies would disappear for the time being, and we should be brought into line and into tune. But why is it that men are so constituted that they can only lay aside their own domestic quarrels under the impulse of what I will call a higher principle of hatred? Why cannot we find in our own virtues and our own wisdom, without the pressure of external danger, some higher principle of amity and some new basis of co-operation in regard to vital things? The right hon. Gentleman the Member for the City of London (Mr. Balfour) said in the course of a speech the other day—which was not very helpful, and less helpful to the cause of peace than my most vehement utterances—that the House was not agreed, but frightened. That is an inadequate view, because on both sides of the House some of those who are least frightened are most anxious to agree. The right hon. Gentleman the Member for the

University of Dublin (Sir E. Carson) is running great risks—and no one can deny it—in strife. Why will he not run some risk for peace? The key is in his hands now. Any day some event may happen which will condemn us all to a continuance of this struggle on the hateful lines on to which it has now got, and shatter perhaps irretrievably the greatness of our country. Let the right hon. and learned Gentleman consider whether he will not run some risk for peace.

To-day I believe most firmly, in spite of all the antagonism and partisanship of our politics and our conflicting party interests, that peace with honour is not beyond the reach of all. To-morrow it may be gone for ever. I am going to run some little risk on my own account by what I will now say. Why cannot the right hon. and learned Gentleman say boldly, "Give me the Amendments to this Home Rule Bill which I ask for, to safeguard the dignity and the interests of Protestant Ulster, and I in return will use all my influence and good will to make Ireland an integral unit in a federal system." If the right hon. Gentleman used language of that kind in the spirit of sincerity with which everybody will instantly credit him, it would go far to transform the political situation, and every man would be bound to reconsider his position in relation to these great controversies. If such language were used, I firmly believe that all that procession of hideous and hateful moves and counter-moves that we have been discussing and are now forced to discuss, and that hateful avenue down which we have looked too long, would give place to a clear and bright prospect, which would bring honour and not discredit to all concerned, and would save these islands from evils for which our children will certainly otherwise hold us accountable.

"THE EBB AND FLOW OF FORTUNE"

September 11, 1914

National Liberal Club, London

It appeared in July 1914 that Britain was on the verge of civil war over Ulster. A conference summoned by the King at Buckingham Palace in a desperate attempt to find a last-minute solution to the Irish crisis ended in failure on July 25. At this precise moment the British Cabinet learned of the ultimatum of Austria to Serbia, and, in Churchill's words, "the parishes of Fermanagh and Tyrone faded back into the mists and squalls of Ireland, and a strange light began immediately, but by perceptible gradations, to fall and grow upon the map of Europe."

On July 26 Prince Louis of Battenberg ordered the fleet not to disperse after its test mobilisation, an action immediately endorsed by Churchill, and approved by the Cabinet on July 28.

The Cabinet, suddenly confronted by this unexpected crisis, was deeply divided. Churchill, convinced that it was a grave situation, made all preparations for war, including the somewhat abrupt dismissal of Admiral Sir George Callaghan as Commander-in-Chief of the Home fleet and his replacement by Admiral Sir John

Jellicoe on July 30. Two Turkish warships under construction in British shipyards were commandeered, and a complete mobilisation was ordered on July 31. By the beginning of August the Navy was established in its war positions.

In the Cabinet, Churchill was unwavering in his opinion that German aggression must be met with a united front of Britain, France and Russia. The decisive event was the German invasion of France and Belgium on August 3, and only three members of the Cabinet (Morley, Burns and Trevelyan) resigned. The Government issued an ultimatum to Germany to maintain Belgian neutrality. This expired at midnight on August 4 (11 p.m. British time) and at that moment all His Majesty's ships were instructed to commence hostilities against Germany. The First World War had begun.

To the surprise and dismay of the British public, it did not open with a series of British naval triumphs. The loss of H.M.S. Amphion *was only the first of a number of unexpected losses.*

The plans of the principal belligerents were swiftly compromised. The much-vaunted "Russian steamroller" was shattered at Tannenberg; the rapid German advance was abruptly checked at the Marne; the small but superb British Expeditionary Force (the "contemptible little army" as the Kaiser derided it) played a major role in the failure of the German strategy. After less than a month of violent movement and terrible casualties, the trench-lines were beginning to writhe across Europe.

Meanwhile, a serious criticism was being levelled at the performance of the Royal Navy. The German warships Goeben *and* Breslau *had evaded the Mediterranean fleet and arrived safely at Constantinople–a major factor in the decision of the Turkish Government to enter the war on the German side. For a time the German cruiser* Emden *paralysed the movement of British ships in the Indian Ocean. In the Southern Hemisphere the squadron under the command of Admiral von Spee eliminated an inferior British force off Coronel. A vicious Press campaign forced the resignation of Prince Louis of Battenberg–a resignation which Churchill accepted too readily for the satisfaction of the Navy–and his replacement was the former First Sea Lord, Lord Fisher, with whom Churchill had been in close contact from the time he went to the Admiralty. "Churchill co-opted Fisher to relieve the pressure against himself, but he had no intention of letting anyone else rule the roost," Lord Beaverbrook has commented. "Here, then, were two strong men of incompatible temper, both bent on an autocracy."*

I beg to move,

That this meeting of the citizens of London, profoundly believing that we are fighting in a just cause, for the vindication of the rights of small states and the public law of Europe, pledges itself unswervingly to support the Prime Minister's appeal to the nation, and all measures necessary for the prosecution of the war to a victorious conclusion, whereby alone the lasting peace of Europe can be assured.

These are serious times, and though we meet here in an abode of diversion and of pleasure in times of peace [London Opera House], and although we wish and mean to encourage each other in every way, yet we are not here for purposes of merriment or jollification. I am quite sure I associate my two friends who are here to-night and who are to speak after me when I say that we regard the cheers with which you have received us as being offered to us only because they are meant for our soldiers in the field and our sailors upon the sea (cheers), and it is in that sense that we accept them and thank you for them.

We meet here together in serious times, but I come to you to-night in good heart (cheers), and with good confidence for the future and for the task upon which we are engaged. It is too soon to speculate upon the results of the great battle which is waging in France. Everything that we have heard during four long days of anxiety seems to point to a marked and substantial turning of the tide.

We have seen the forces of the French and British Armies strong enough not only to contain and check the devastating avalanche which had swept across the French frontier, but now at last, not for an hour or for a day, but for four long days in succession, it has been rolled steadily back. (Cheers.) With battles taking place over a front of 100 or 150 miles one must be very careful not to build high hopes on results which are achieved even in a great area of the field of war. We are not children looking for light and vain encouragement, but men engaged upon a task which has got to be put through. Still, when every allowance has been made for the uncertainty with which these great operations are always enshrouded, I think it only fair and right to say that the situation to-night is better, far better, than cold calculation of the forces available on both sides before the war should have led us to expect at this early stage. (Cheers.)

It is quite clear that what is happening now is not what the Germans planned (laughter), and they have yet to show that they can adapt themselves to the force of circumstances created by the military power of their enemies with the same efficiency that they have undoubtedly shown in regard to plans long preferred, methodically worked out, and executed with the precision of deliberation.

The battle, I say, gives us every reason to meet together to-night in good heart. But let me tell you frankly that if this battle had been as disastrous as, thank God, it appears to be triumphant, I should come before you with unabated confidence and with the certainty that we have only to continue in our efforts to bring this war to the conclusion which we wish and intend. (Cheers.)

We did not enter upon the war with the hope of easy victory; we did not enter upon it in any desire to extend our territory, or to advance and increase our position in the world; or in any romantic desire to shed our blood and spend our money in Continental quarrels. We entered upon this war reluctantly after we had made every effort compatible with honour to avoid being drawn in, and we entered upon it with a full realization of the sufferings, losses, disappointments, vexations, and anxieties, and of the appalling and sustaining exertions which would be entailed upon us by our action. The war will be long and sombre. It will have many reverses of fortune and many hopes falsified by subsequent events, and we must derive from our cause and from the strength that is in us, and from the traditions and history of our race, and from the support and aid of our Empire all over the world the means to make this country overcome obstacles of all kinds and continue to the end of the furrow, whatever the toil and suffering may be.

But though we entered this war with no illusions as to the incidents which will mark the progress, as to the ebb and flow of fortune in this and that part of the gigantic field over which it is waged, we entered it, and entered it rightly, with the sure and strong hope and expectation of bringing it to a victorious conclusion. (Cheers.) I am quite certain that if we, the people of the British Empire, choose, whatever may happen in the interval, we can in the end make this war finish in accordance with our interests and the interests of civilization. (Cheers.) Let us build on a sure foundation. Let us not be the sport of fortune, looking for victories here and happy chances there; let us take measures, which are well within our power, which are practical measures, measures which we can begin upon at once and carry through from day to day with surety and effect. Let us enter upon measures which in the long run, whatever the accidents and incidents of the intervening period may be, will secure us that victory upon which our life and existence as a nation not less than the fortune of our Allies and of Europe absolutely depends. (Cheers.)

I think we are building on a sure foundation. (Cheers.) Let us look first at the Navy. (Cheers.) The war has now been in progress between five and six weeks. In that time we have swept German commerce from the seas. (Cheers.) We have either blocked in neutral harbours or blockaded in their own harbours (laughter) or hunted down the commerce destroyers of which we used to hear so much and from which we anticipated such serious loss and damage. All our ships, with inconsiderable exceptions, are arriving safely and punctually at their destinations, carrying on the commerce upon which the wealth and industry and the power of making war for this country depends. We are transporting easily, not without an element of danger, but hitherto safely and successfully, great numbers of soldiers across the seas from all quarters of the world to be directed upon the decisive theatre of the land struggle. (A voice, "Russians," and laughter.) And we have searched the so-called German Ocean without discovering the German flag. (Cheers.) Our enemies, in their carefully worked out calculations, which they have been toiling over during a great many years, when the people of this country, as a whole, credited them with quite different motives (hear, hear), have always counted upon a process of attrition and the waste of shipping by mines and torpedoes and other methods of warfare of the weaker Power, by which the numbers and the strength of our Fleet would be reduced to such a point that they would be able to steel their hearts and come out and fight. (Cheers.) We have been at war for five or six weeks, and so far—though I would certainly not underrate the risks and hazards attending upon warlike operations and the vanity of all over-confidence—but so far the attrition has been on their side and not on ours (cheers), while the losses which they have suffered greatly exceed any that we have at present sustained.

I have made careful inquiries as to the condition of our sailors in the Fleet under the strain put upon them, and this continued watching and constant attention to their duty under war conditions, and I am glad to say that it is reported to me that the health of the Fleet has been much better since the declaration of war than it was in time of peace (loud cheers and laughter), both as to the percentage of sickness and the character of the sickness (laughter), and that there is no reason why "we should not keep up the same process of naval control and have the same exercises of sea power, on which we have lived and are living, for what is almost an indefinite period.

By one of those dispensations of Providence, which appeals so strongly to the German Emperor (laughter) the nose of the bulldog has been slanted backwards so that he can breathe with comfort without letting go. (Laughter and cheers.) We have been successful in maintaining naval control thus far in the struggle, and there are also sound reasons for believing that as it progresses the chances in our favour will not diminish but increase. In the next 12 months the number of great ships that will be completed for this country is more than double the number which will be completed for Germany (cheers), and the number of cruisers three or four times as great. (Cheers.) Therefore I think I am on solid ground when I come here to-night and say that you may count upon the naval supremacy of this country being effectively maintained as against the German Power for as long as you wish. (Cheers.)

Now we must look at the Army. (Loud cheers.) The Navy has been, under every Government and during all periods of modern history the darling of the British nation. On it have been lavished whatever public funds were necessary, and to its efficiency has been devoted the unceasing care and thought of successive Administrations. The result is that when the need came the Navy was absolutely ready (cheers), and, as far as we can see from what has happened, thoroughly adequate to the tasks which were required from it. But we have not been in times of peace a military nation. The Army has not had the facilities of obtaining the lavish supplies of men and money for its needs which have in times of peace and in the past to our good fortune at the moment been so freely given to the Navy. And what you have to do now is to make a great Army. (Cheers.) You have to make an Army under the cover and shield of the Navy strong enough to enable our country to play its full part in the decision of this terrible struggle. (Cheers.)

The sure way—the only sure way—to bring this war to an end is for the British Empire to put on the Continent and keep on the Continent an army of at least one million men. (Cheers.) I take that figure because it is one well within the compass of the arrangements which are now on foot and because it is one which is well within the scope of the measures which Lord Kitchener—(Loud cheers drowned the rest of the sentence).

I was reading in the newspapers the other day that the German Emperor made a speech to some of his regiments in which he urged them to concentrate their attention upon what he was pleased to call "French's contemptible little Army." (Laughter.) Well, they are concentrating their attention upon it (laughter and cheers) and that Army, which has been fighting with such extraordinary prowess, which has revived in a fortnight of adverse actions the ancient fame and glory of our arms upon the Continent (cheers), and which to-night, after a long, protracted, harassed, unbroken, and undaunted rearguard action—the hardest trial to which troops can be exposed—is advancing in spite of the loss of one-fifth of its numbers, and driving its enemies before it—that Army must be reinforced and backed and supported and increased and enlarged in numbers and in power by every means and every method that every one of us can employ.

There is no reason why, if you set yourselves to it—I have not come here to make a speech of words, but to point out to you necessary and obvious things which you can do–there is no doubt that, if you set yourselves to it, the Army which is now fighting so valiantly on your behalf and our Allies can be raised from its present position to 250,000 of the finest professional soldiers in the world, and that in the new year something like 500,000 men, and from that again when the early summer begins in 1915 to the full figure of 25 Army Corps fighting in line together. The vast population of these islands and all the Empire is pressing forward to serve, its wealth is placed at your disposal, the Navy opens the way for the passage of men and everything necessary for the equipment of our forces. Why should we hesitate when here is the sure and certain path to ending this war in the way we mean it to end? (Cheers.)

There is little doubt that an Army so formed will in quality and character, in native energy, in the comprehension which each individual has of the cause for which he is fighting, exceed in merit any army in the world. We have only to have a chance of even numbers or anything approaching even numbers to demonstrate the superiority of free-thinking active citizens over the docile sheep who serve the ferocious ambitions of drastic kings. (Cheers.) Our enemies are now at the point which we have reached fully extended. On every front of the enormous field of conflict the pressure upon them is such that all their resources are deployed. With every addition to the growing weight of the Russian Army (cheers), with every addition to the forces at the disposal of Sir John French (cheers), the balance must sag down increasingly against them.

You have only to create steadily week by week and month by month the great military instrument of which I have been speaking to throw into the scales a weight which must be decisive. There will be no corresponding reserve of manhood upon which Germany can draw. There will be no corresponding force of soldiers and of equipment and of war material which can be brought into the line to face the forces which we in this island and in this Empire can undoubtedly create. That will turn the scale. That will certainly decide the issue. Of course, if victory comes sooner so much the better. (Cheers.) But let us not count on fortune and good luck. (Cheers.) Let us assume at every point that things will go much less well than we hope and wish. Let us make arrangements which will override that. (Cheers.) We have it in our power to make such arrangements, and it is only common prudence, aye, and common humanity, to take steps which at any rate will fix some certain term to this devastating struggle throughout the whole of the European Continent.

Let me also say this. Let us concentrate all our warlike feeling upon fighting the enemy in the field and creating a great military weapon to carry out the purposes of the war. There is a certain class of person who likes to work his warlike feelings off upon the unfortunate alien enemy within our gates.

Of course all necessary measures must be taken for the security of the country and for the proper carrying out of military needs; but let us always have this feeling in our hearts that after the war is over people shall not only admire our victory but they shall say they fought like gentlemen. (Cheers.) The Romans had a motto–

Parcere subjectis et debellare superbos.

Let that be the spirit in which we conduct this war. Let all those who feel under the horrible provocations of the struggle their hearts suffused with anger and with wrath–let them turn it into a practical channel–going to the front or if circumstances prevent them, helping others to go, keeping them maintained in the highest state of efficiency, giving them the supplies and weapons which they require, and looking after those they have left behind.

I have not spoken to you much about the justice of our cause, because it has been most eloquently set out by the Prime Minister (cheers) and Sir Edward Grey (cheers) and by Mr. Bonar Law (cheers), and other leaders of the Opposition; and much more eloquently than by any speakers in this or any other country the justice of our cause has been set out by the brutal facts which have occurred and which have marched upon us from day to day. (Cheers.) Some thought there would be a German war, some did not; but no one supposed that a great military action would exhibit all the vices of military organization without those redeeming virtues which, God knows, are needed to redeem warlike operations from the taint of shame. We have been confronted with an exhibition of ruthlessness and outrage enforced upon the weak, enforced upon women and children. We have been confronted with repeated breaches of the law of enlightened warfare, practices analogous to those which in the private life are regarded as cheating, and which deprive persons or country adopting them, or condoning them, of the credit and respect due to honourable soldiers.

We have been confronted with all this. Let us not imitate it. (Cheers.) Let us not try to make small retaliations and reprisals here and there. Let us concentrate upon the simple, obvious task of creating a military force so powerful that the war, even in default of any good fortune, can certainly be ended and brought to a satisfactory conclusion. However the war began, now that it is started it is a war of self-preservation for us. Our civilization, our way of doing things, our political and Parliamentary life, with its voting and its thinking, our party system, our party warfare, the free and easy tolerance of British life, our method of doing things and of keeping ourselves alive and self-respecting in the world—all these are brought into contrast, into collision, with the organized force of bureaucratic Prussian militarism.

That is the struggle which is opened now and which must go forward without pause or abatement until it is settled decisively and finally one way or the other. On that there can be no compromise or truce. It is our life or it is theirs. We are bound, having gone so far, to go forward without flinching to the very end. (Cheers.)

This is the same great European war that would have been fought in the year 1909 if Russia had not humbled herself and given way to German threats. It is the same war that Sir Edward Grey stopped last year. (Loud cheers.) Now it has come upon us. If you look back across the long period of European history to the original cause, you will, I am sure, find it in the cruel terms enforced upon France in the year 1870 (hear, hear), and in the repeated bullyings and attempts to terrorize France which have been the characteristic of German policy ever since. (Cheers.) The more you study this question the more you will see that the use the Germans made of their three aggressive and victorious wars against Denmark, against Austria, and against France has been such as to make them the terror and the bully of Europe, the enemy and the menace of every small State upon their borders, and a perpetual source of unrest and disquietude to their powerful neighbours. (Cheers.)

Now the war has come, and when it is over let us be careful not to make the same mistake or the same sort of mistake as Germany made when she had France prostrate at her feet in 1870. (Cheers.) Let us, whatever we do, fight for and work towards great and sound principles for the European system. And the first of those principles which we should keep before us is the principle of nationality (cheers)—that is to say, not the conquest or subjugation of any great community or of any strong race of men, but the setting free of those races which have been subjugated and conquered (cheers); and if doubt arises about disputed areas of country we should try to settle their ultimate destination in the reconstruction of Europe which must follow from this war with a fair regard to the wishes and feelings of the people who live in them.

That is the aim which, if it is achieved, will justify the exertions of the war and will make some amends to the world for the loss and suffering, the agony of suffering, which it has wrought and entailed, and which will give to those who come after us not only the pride which we hope they will feel in remembering the martial achievements of the present age of Britain, but which will give them also a better and fairer world to live in and a Europe free from the causes of hatred and unrest which have poisoned the country of nations and ruptured the peace of Christendom.

I use these words because this is a war in which we are all together (cheers)—all classes, all races, all States, Principalities, Dominions, and Powers throughout the British Empire—we are all together. (Cheers.) Years ago the elder Pitt urged upon his countrymen the compulsive invocation, "Be one people." It has taken us till now to obey his appeal, but now we are together, and while we remain one people there are no forces in the world strong enough to beat us down or break us up.—(Cheers.)

I hope, even in this dark hour of strife and struggle, that the unity which has been established in our country under the pressure of war will not cease when the great military effort upon which we are engaged and the great moral causes which we are pursuing have been achieved. I hope, and I do not think my hope is a vain one, that the forces which have come together in our islands and throughout our Empire may continue to work together, not only in a military struggle, but to try to make our country more quickly a more happy and more prosperous land, where social justice and free institutions are more firmly established than they have been in the past. (Cheers.) If that is so we shall not have fought in vain at home as well as abroad.

With these hopes and in this belief I would urge you, laying aside all hindrance, thrusting away all private aims, to devote yourselves unswervingly and unflinchingly to the vigorous and successful prosecution of the war. (Loud cheers.)

"RATS IN A HOLE"

September 21, 1914

Tournament Hall, Liverpool

Churchill's capacity for phrase-making could sometimes have a counter-productive effect, as in Belfast in March. This speech, with its arrogant reference to the German Navy, was immediately followed by the sinking of three British cruisers in the North Sea in broad daylight. The event caused the King to remark that "the rats came out of their own accord and to our cost."

This speech marked a further decline in Churchill's position. In September he had been involved in a demonstration at Dunkirk designed to alarm the Germans on their right flank; the so-called "Dunkirk Circus" irritated his colleagues, and increased the number of his critics in the Navy and in the House of Commons. His activity, flamboyance, and ardour to be involved in all aspects of the war were arousing a dangerous admixture of amusement and hostility, not least in the Admiralty itself and in the Navy. "The fundamental fault of his system," Lord Selborne subsequently wrote, "is his restlessness." By September 1914 the comments of his contemporaries and colleagues were becoming sharper.

I have not come here to-night to ask for your cheers. I have come here to ask you for a million men. (Cheers.) I do not mean a million men with the colours and under arms. We have got that already. I mean a million men on the Continent of Europe in line with the gallant army of Sir John French–a million men, the flower of our manhood, nothing but the best, every man a volunteer–(cheers);–a million men maintained in the field, equipped with everything that science can invent or money can buy, maintained and supported by the resources which, while we maintain the command of the seas, we can draw from every quarter of the globe, made up steadily, whatever the losses, whatever the slaughter, until this war is settled in the only way. (Cheers.)

I ask it with confidence because it can be done easily so long as we continue all of one mind, and because I know Lancashire well from both sides. (Laughter.) We all know it now from both sides, marching good and true on the path of duty. (Cheers.)

These are days of action rather than of speech, and I think you have no need to be anxious about the result. (Cheers.) God has blessed our arms with unexpected good fortune. I had certainly expected that the great battles in France would have been fought much further south, and that a greater measure of privation and oppression and outrage would have been inflicted upon the gallant people of France. Still, we must not build on the fleeting changes of the field, but I am sure that if the present battle and others are sinister in their consequences for the Allies, the British people and the British Empire can, if its resolution does not fail, finally settle this matter as it chooses. (Cheers.)

The navy cannot fight while the enemy remains in port–(laughter),–but despite this we are enjoying the command of the sea as fully as if the German navy had been destroyed. Although we hope that a decision at sea will be a feature of this war, although we hope that our men will have a chance of settling the question with the German fleet, yet if they do not come out and fight in time of war they will be dug out like rats in a hole. (Loud cheers.)

Under the shield of the navy you can raise an army in this country which will settle the war. Our ally Russia has immense reserves upon which she can draw, but upon the side of your enemies everything they have got has already been expended. They are all out. In six or seven months we can without difficulty put into the field 25 army corps, comprising a million men, who for their personal qualities, their understanding of the quarrel, their spontaneous and voluntary energy and initiative will not find their match or counterpart in the armies of Europe. There is no reserve of manhood or vitality on the side of our enemies which can prevent that million men from turning the scale in our favour. (Cheers.) The end may come sooner, the victory may come to us more easily; then let us rejoice, but let us not count on an easy solution. Let us make our resolutions calmly and soberly that in a reasonable time we shall compel our antagonists to come to our conclusion of this fight. (Cheers.)

To find the cause of this war we must look back to the period between 1860 and 1870, when Germany was raised to the first position in Europe in the three wars deliberately organised by Bismarck. Those were the three carefully planned acts of violence upon which the greatness and power of the German Empire was founded. Some people who use rough methods to get power afterwards improve. That has not been the case with the German Empire. They had not even been content with their wonderful victory. They had not even enjoyed their reign at the summit of the European position. They had sought to humiliate and terrorise France. On at least three occasions Europe had been brought to the verge of war, and war had only been averted by the patience and self-restraint of France. During all these forty-four years Germany has not induced any of the provinces she gained to look with feelings even of toleration upon her rule. Wherever she has conquered an alien people, those people to-day only await the hand of the deliverer. (Cheers.)

What has been her attitude towards Russia? When Russia was weak and crushed in military power after the Japanese War Germany made use of brutal power to humiliate and affront the great Russian people. What has been the attitude of Germany towards international law and the abatement of armaments? Could anyone point to a single word spoken by any responsible leader of German thought or any ruler of German policy during the whole of her great reign over European affairs in favour of the right of small nations, or the higher sanction of international law, or some abatement of the wasteful struggle and competition of armaments?

During all that time she preached the gospel of force–not the force that comes from virtue and consenting minds and ardent spirits, not the force that comes from moral courage, but the crude, brutal force of adding regiment to regiment, bureaucrat to bureaucrat, and ramming it down the throat of everyone to the tune of "Germany over all." Force in its highest expression is a manifestation not of material, but of spiritual things. That is what Germany has yet to learn. "Blood and Iron" is their motto. Let "Soul and Fire" be ours. (Cheers.)

What has been Germany's attitude towards this country? We had no wish to be thrust into a position of antagonism with her. We had no evil feeling against her. Every effort had been made in this country to avoid saying things which might lead to antagonism. Although Lord Salisbury tried hard to work in amity with Germany, he finally came to the conclusion that it was impossible to maintain a foreign policy in association with Germany, because she expected us to buy her over again every year. By intrigue she endeavoured to create trouble between us and France or Russia, and then asked what we were prepared to do to keep her friendship. The British Foreign Office, which only changes its policy once in a quarter of a century–and quite rightly too–is absolutely worn out and disgusted with the impossible attempts to keep the peace of Europe on the basis of a close Anglo-German co-operation.

Then, with the consent of all parties in the State, we adjusted our differences with France direct. King Edward went to Paris and made that friendship which is now being tried in the fire of War, and will ultimately shine forth in the glow of victory. (Cheers.) Then Germany began, while we were still on terms of amity with her, to construct a great navy, which had no other object–I am so glad to be able to tell you what I think about it now–(loud cheers)–and never had any other object but our own undoing; every detail of the construction of the German fleet–a long conceived plan, slowly unfolding year by year, programme by programme, on which such extraordinary efforts were directed, and to which so much foresight and skill were devoted,–every detail of it showed and proved that it was meant for us, for our exclusive benefit. (Laughter.)

I came into office at the Admiralty after the Agadir crisis. I thought this war would have taken place then if the Chancellor of the Exchequer had not gone to the Mansion House and made a speech. They just thought they would wait a little longer. After that I became responsible for this great department, and I have had to see every day evidences of the espionage system which Germany has maintained in this country. (Cries of "Shame.") I have had the evidence put under my eye month by month of the agents they have maintained here year after year in great numbers to report to them all the details of our naval organisation which they could get by bribery and subornation. That, you may say, was a protective measure because we had the stronger fleet. But every dirty little German lieutenant–(laughter and cheers)–coming on his knees to England, thought he would curry favour with his superior by writing home the details of where water could be got, where there was a blacksmith's forge, how much provisions there were for a battalion or a brigade in this little village or township of our peaceful island. We have been made the subject in the last eight or nine years, just in the same way as France was before 1870 and Austria was before 1866, and Denmark was before 1864, of careful, deliberate, scientific, military reconnaissance. Well, we knew all about it. (Cheers.) If they like to come they know the way. We are not asking any favours. (Cheers.)

Germany was not content with the victory over France, but made it a starting-point for fresh usurption and domination over European powers. She preached the gospel of force, and backed it by the greatest development of military organisation and efficiency yet seen in the world. But if we look beyond these deep causes of the war to its immediate fountain stream, I say without hesitation that so far as I am concerned I went into it to prevent France from being crushed. Three years ago I gave some attention to the military aspect of the problem, and I was quite sure that Germany would violate the neutrality of Belgium. All her plans were made in cold blood to do that. She broke the treaty and poured the tremendous avalanche of fire and steel through Belgium. But the unexpected happened. Always in commission of a crime something is forgotten by the criminal. Some quite unforeseen and wonderful occurrence undoes all the calculations of fraud and violence. A small valiant people sprang suddenly into heroic life, and will live down the centuries for the part it played in the history of the world. We cannot undo the harm that has been done, but we can with our strong right arm make Belgium a prosperous and happy country again.

This is a worthy task upon which we may all unite. Is it not an exhilarating thing to feel that we are all together? I rejoice to feel that in this crisis we have the whole Irish people with us. Party politics are put aside. But when we go to the cupboard after the war is over to take them out again they will never be quite the same. The Orangemen of Belfast have given their rifles to the Belgians. (Cheers.) No British Liberal or Irish Nationalist would allow them to be any the worse for that. (Cheers.)

We do not seek in this war the subjugation of the German and Austrian peoples. Nothing is farther from our intention. However complete our victory may be, however shattering their defeat may be, they need never fear that the measure which they meted out to Alsace or to Denmark, to Italy or to Transylvania or to Poland will be meted out to them. Their independence, their customs, their language, all that they care about in their own Government, their rights as citizens and freemen will never be assailed by us.

We shall hold these rights inviolate and inviolable even if the last Prussian soldier has been forced to capitulate and the last German ship has been sunk. Those rights stand not on the basis of the struggles of nations but on the necessary vital foundations of human society. We are fighting for the elementary rights of civilised men and States. We are not going to give them up, no matter how bitter our defeats may be, and we are going to maintain them however complete our victory. The ultimate exactions which the victorious Allies will inflict upon the peoples of Germany and Austria is the liberation of the imprisoned nationalities within their grip. (Cheers.)

We have heard from the German Ambassador in the United States some vague talk of peace as insincere as the information of which he is the sower. (Laughter.) Peace ought not to be on the lips of those who are invading the territories of their neighbours, who are carrying fire and the sword through the peaceful villages of France and Belgium. And while that spectacle continues, while the smoke of their abominable cruelties goes up to heaven, that is no time for talk of peace upon the lips of the German Ambassador in the United States. Peace? Why we are only just beginning. Peace with the German people might be arranged in good time, but peace with Prussian militarism? No peace short of the grave with that vile tyranny. (Cheers.)

The results of this war will not be unworthy even of the prodigious sacrifice demanded. Across the smoke and storm of the battlefields one can see great dim structures of a new and better Europe, of a new and better Christendom than we have ever known before. We see emerging from the conflict so far as it has gone, first, the great principle of the rights of nationalities; second, the great principle of the integrity of States and nations; and we see also the sanctions of international law so established that the most audacious Power will not be anxious to challenge them. We may see a Poland united and in loyal and harmonious relations with the Crown of Russia. We may live to see a federation of the Christian States of the Balkans restored to their proper racial limits. We may see an Italy whose territory corresponds with the Italian population. We may see France restored to her proper station in Europe, and we may see that old England had something to do with it all. (Cheers.)

"BUSINESS AS USUAL"

November 9, 1914

The Lord Mayor's Banquet,
The Guildhall, London

The doctrine of "business as usual" was regarded by the Government's critics as its basic failing at a time when the belligerents were fully engaged. As the war progressed, these criticisms became more intense, particularly over the issues of conscription and the war economy.

Eighty miles away the greatest battle in the world is going on. Our countrymen and their Allies are striving from minute to minute to breast and stem the cruel tides of German devastation. And here we sit in this old hall, as we have so often sat before in bygone years, and, as we hope, future generations will sit when the sorrows of this time are forgotten and only the glories remain. (Cheers.) Here we sit, and to the outward eye, to the material sense, nothing is altered. An unthinking stranger coming here to-night would scarcely distinguish any characteristic which marks our gathering from those which have so often taken place before, when each year we celebrate this important civic festival. That is the Navy. (Loud cheers.) It is due to the Navy that we are able to sit here to-night and while we do not shirk or shrink from the full rigours of war, we are, through the Navy, so far happily guarded from most of them.

Some few weeks ago I had a talk with Sir John Jellicoe and his principal Admiral. They spoke to me of the distress with which all the great Fleet watched the heroic struggles of our Army in France and in Belgium and saw the fearful sacrifices demanded of them and given by them. They spoke also of their keen desire to bring more direct and immediate aid to bear with the mighty weapon which they wield, and of their natural desire to share more immediately in the sufferings and losses of the Army in the field. "But," they said, "Cornwallis was nearly three years off Brest and Admiral Nelson was more than two years off Toulon. We are only just beginning. We must not be impatient. Our turn will come." (Loud cheers.) It is not always easy to be patient, and I express to-night, on behalf of the Navy and Admiralty, our gratitude for the generous confidence you have so abundantly and unswervingly bestowed upon us.

The conditions of naval warfare are curious and novel. We have a great preponderance in force and numbers, but we have also a task to discharge infinitely greater and more difficult than that which our enemies are called upon to undertake. (Hear, hear.) We are endeavouring to maintain all the seas; we are endeavouring to secure all the highways across the seas; we are endeavouring to secure the most peaceful commerce of the world against a multitude of new dangers, against methods never before practised in the warfare of civilized nations. (Hear, hear.) We also transport great armies to the decisive theatre of the war. We are endeavouring to preserve the whole trade of this country on an enormous scale in all quarters of the globe. We have conveyed and convoyed expeditions to attack and take every German colony which exists. And this great task forces us to expose a target to the enterprise of the enemy incomparably greater than any target exposed to our own daring and vigilant sailors.

The British people have taken for themselves this motto—"Business carried on as usual during alterations on the map of Europe." (Laughter and cheers.) They expect the Navy, on which they have lavished so much care and expense, to make that good, and that is what, upon the whole, we are actually achieving at the present time. (Cheers.) It is very difficult to measure the full effects of naval pressure in the early stages of the war. The punishment we receive is clear and definite. The punishment we inflict is very often not seen, and even when seen cannot be measured. The economic stringency resulting from a naval blockade requires time, if it is to reach its full effectiveness. We are only looking at it in the third month. But wait a bit. Examine it in the sixth month, in the ninth month, in the twelfth month, and you will begin to see results, results which will be gradually achieved, silently achieved, but which spell the doom of Germany—(loud and prolonged cheers)—doom of Germany as surely as the approach of winter strikes the leaves from the trees. (Cheers.) There is another way in which the Navy contributes to the vast decision of this war. It gives to Britain and to the British Empire the time necessary to realize their vast military power. It gives to my noble friend Lord Kitchener the time to organize, equip, discipline, arm, and place in the field a million men of a quality and power such as have never been employed yet in this struggle on the Continent. (Cheers.)

At the end of very nearly 100 days the Navy, whose memory and work you have paid your tribute to to-night—in spite of losses of ships of no great consequence, of officers and men irreparable—the Navy, in spite of losses, is actually and relatively stronger than it was on the day war was declared, and it is stronger most particularly in those branches of the Naval Service which all the circumstances of modern war prove exercise most powerful influence upon the struggle.

I shall not stand between you further and the other speakers who present themselves on this memorable occasion, but I will say just one last word. In this famous hall, where we have so often gathered, we must to-night feel ourselves in the company of the great men of the great war. We see the monuments of the men who fought Napoleon. We may feel to-night almost as if we have their counsel and their aid, and we may derive inspiration and encouragement from their memory. The scale of events to-day is greater—vastly greater—than those with which they had to deal, but the problems they had to face were more desperate, more full of anxiety and peril, than those with which we are confronted, and the resources with which they faced them were infinitely less ample and less wide. They were often alone against the whole of Europe. They never counted, as we can count, upon an absolutely united nation. (Cheers.) They only spoke for a little island; we exert and wield the power of world-wide Empire. Yet with all their difficulties and dangers they came safely through the conflicts, and we, by imitating their example and redoubling our exertions, will surely come safely through them too. (Loud cheers.)

ROYAL NAVY

November 27, 1914

House of Commons

Deadlock now gripped the Western and Eastern Fronts. Everywhere, the belligerents were engaged in a stunned re-evaluation of the conflict. The general belief in a brief war had required new thought.

In Britain, dissatisfaction with the performance of the Navy, however unfair, had reached the point that the Cabinet had formally resolved on November 4 that the series of reverses at sea "is not creditable to the officers of the Navy." In October, Churchill had taken personal charge of the defence of Antwerp; when the city fell, over 2,500 men of the newly created Royal Naval Division—a Churchill creation—were lost or interned, and the brunt of public hostility fell upon Churchill. This was unfair, but, as he subsequently admitted, "those who are charged with the direction of supreme affairs must sit on the mountain-tops of control; they must never descend into the valleys of direct physical and personal action." This episode, coming so quickly after the reverses at sea and the "Dunkirk Circus," perceptibly damaged his position. All but he realized this. "As he worked devotedly at his own job," Beaverbrook subsequently wrote, "the currents of political opinion slipped by him unnoticed." It was significant that when the battleship Audacious *was sunk the Government decided to suppress all news of the loss.*

Meanwhile, Turkey had entered the war on the side of the Central Powers, and Russia had lost her warm-water link with her allies. Churchill had already proposed naval and military action to clear the Dardanelles, but had been rebuffed.

[Extract] I certainly have no cause to complain of the tone of the Noble Lord's brief remarks, and I must say that I think the principle on which he goes, that everything that goes right is to be attributed to the Navy and everything that goes wrong is to be attributed elsewhere is an exceedingly sound principle, one with which I am quite content, and one which cannot be too widely adopted. The Noble Lord sees, as most Members of the House know, that the time has not yet arrived when we can discuss with any profit some and probably most of the particular incidents to which he has referred. It is no use attempting to discuss the rights and wrongs, if rights and wrongs there be, of particular actions unless all the facts can be disclosed. If I take the incidents to which he has referred—the action in the Pacific, the loss of the cruisers off the Dutch coast, or the expedition to Antwerp—as good examples of his principle I would say that before it is possible to form a judgment it is necessary that the orders should be disclosed, that the telegrams which have been passed should be disclosed, and that the dispositions which prevail, not only at the particular point, but generally throughout the theatre of war, should also in their broad outline and even in considerable detail be made known. That is clearly impossible at the present time. It would be very dangerous for the Minister representing the Admiralty to be drawn into what would necessarily become a controversial, and what might easily become an acrimonious discussion of these matters. And, above all, to disclose partially what has taken place would only lead to demands for fuller and further publication, which would be very prejudicial, not only to the actual conduct of the War, but to the general interests of the Naval Service, during the course of the War.

It is not possible, however desirable it may be, at present for the public or the House to form any judgment on these matters. The only rule which should guide us in regard to information is that nothing must be published which is against the public interest, or hampers naval or military operations. It is the only rule, and it is a rule which must be capable of wide interpretation. Of course, it would be entirely wrong for a Department or a Minister to use the term "public interest" on naval and military matters in order to shield the Department or himself from blame or censure. This is a war so serious and formidable in its character that persons ought not to be spared. If an improvement can be made in any command the officer ought to give way for others who can better discharge the public duty. That is a rule and principle that should not be confined to naval and military officers, but equally to heads of Departments. The Prime Minister is especially charged by the country at this time, and it is his duty, if he considers any improvement can be made in the conduct of a public Department, not to allow any considerations of party association or personal friendship to stand in the way of making any change that is necessary in the public interests.

The Prime Minister in times like these is the servant of the Crown directly and personally responsible that the withholding of information in the public interest shall not be abused by the Departments of State and Ministers specially affected. It is also the desire of the Admiralty to give as much information as is possible on all these matters without prejudice to the interests to which I have referred, and I think we have done so. I think we have done it, and we shall continue to do so whenever the opportunity offers and the season presents itself. Once information has been given about any action or incident I am of opinion that comment upon it should be perfectly free. Criticism is always advantageous. I have derived continued benefit from criticism at all periods of my life, and I do not remember any time when I was ever short of it. But there is a salutary rule about criticism which applies in time of peace as well as in time of war, in private as well as in public things, and that is that criticism should be very restrained when the party criticised is not able to reply, and it is especially so when he is not able to reply without disclosing facts which would do harm to the critic as well as the party criticised if they were disclosed.

But I recognise the great difficulties of the Press during the present War, and I sympathise very keenly with them in the prohibitions and limitations which fence them about on every side, and which from day to day deny them the opportunity of publishing quantities of information which reach them—information which is most interesting and which may have been collected in many cases with great trouble and expense. There is often a tendency to underrate the acute discomfort under which our great newspapers are living at the present time, and speaking as one of the heads of one of the combatant Departments I feel bound to say that we owe the Press a very great debt, so far as this War has proceeded, for the way in which it has helped, with inconsiderable exceptions and with only momentary lapses, the course of the military operations, and has upheld the interests of the country. I would like to say that I greatly appreciate the kindness and confidence with which the House during this Session has treated the Admiralty and its representatives in not pressing for information on many matters in which the keenest interest is taken, and upon which there is a natural desire to arrive at conclusions and to pronounce judgment.

Ultimately, and as soon as possible, all the facts connected with past operations, and with the administration of the Navy, now and immediately before the War, will be made public in a form in which they can be studied and weighed by the nation. For my part I look forward hopefully to that day. There is, however, one other reason why I think it is not desirable to dwell too much on particular incidents at the present time. The incidents which are seen are a very small proportion of the work which is going forward all over the world, and it would be a great pity if the mind of the public were disproportionately concerned with particular incidents, and if the departments concerned were occupied in defending themselves or in justifying themselves in regard to these incidents. We are waging this War, on which from day to day our vital safety depends, and no one who is concerned with military departments ought to have his attention drawn away from the immediate needs of the military and naval operations for the purpose of going at undue length into matters which lie in the past. I am going in a few words, if the House will permit me, to draw the attention of the House, and through the House the attention of the country, to some of the larger aspects of the naval situation at the present time.

The British Navy was confronted with four main perils. There was first the peril of being surprised at the outbreak of War before we were ready and in our war stations. That was the greatest peril of all. Once the Fleet was mobilised and in its war station the greatest danger by which it could be assailed had been surmounted. Then there was the danger, which we had apprehended, from the escape on to the High Seas of very large numbers of fast liners of the enemy, equipped with guns for the purpose of commerce destruction. During the last two years the sittings of the Committee of Imperial Defence have been almost unbroken, and we have been concerned almost exclusively with the study of the problems of a great European War, and I have always, on behalf of the Admiralty, pointed out the great danger which we should run if, at the outset of the War, before our cruisers were on their stations, before our means of dealing with such a menace had been fully developed, we had been confronted with a great excursion on to our trade routes of large numbers of armed liners for the purpose of commerce destruction.

That danger has for the present been successfully surmounted. Our estimate before the War of losses in the first two or three months was at least 5 per cent. of our mercantile marine. I am glad to say that the percentage is only 1.9, and the risks have been fully covered under a system of insurance which was brought into force, the premiums on which it has been found possible to steadily and regularly reduce. The third great danger was due to mines. Our enemy have allowed themselves to pursue methods in regard to the scattering of mines on the highways of peaceful commerce that, until the outbreak of this War, we should not have thought would be practised by any civilised Power. And the risks and difficulties which we have had to face from that cause cannot be underrated. But I am glad to tell the House that, although we have suffered losses, and may, no doubt will, suffer more losses, yet I think the danger from mining, even the unscrupulous and indiscriminate mining of the open seas, is one the limits of which can now be discerned and which can be and is being further restricted and controlled by the measures, the very extensive measures, which have been taken, and are being taken.

Fourthly, there is the danger from submarines. The submarine introduces entirely novel conditions into naval warfare. The old freedom of movement which belongs to the stronger power is affected and restricted in narrow waters by the development of this new and formidable arm. There is a difference between military and naval anxiety, which the House will appreciate. A division of soldiers cannot be annihilated by a Cavalry patrol. But at any moment a great ship, equal in war power, and a war unit, to a division or an army, may be destroyed without a single opportunity of its fighting strength being realised, or a man on board having a chance to strike a blow in self-defence. Yet it is necessary for the safety of this country, it is necessary for the supply of its vital materials, that our ships should move with freedom and with hardihood through the seas on their duties, and no one can pretend that anxiety must not always be present to the minds of those who have the responsibility for their direction. It is satisfactory, however, to reflect that our power in submarines is much greater than that of our enemies, and that the only reason why we are not able to produce results on a large scale in regard to them, is that we so seldom are afforded any target to attack.

Those are the four dangers. I do not include among them what some people would perhaps wish to include as a fifth, the danger of an oversea invasion, although that is an enterprise full of danger for those who might attempt it. The economic pressure upon Germany continues to develop in a healthy and satisfactory manner. My right hon. Friend the President of the Board of Trade published some remarkable figures yesterday upon the relative condition of British and German trade since the War. Out of 20,500,000 tons of British shipping, 20,122,000 tons are plying, or 97 per cent. of the whole, whereas out of five millions of German tonnage only 549,000 tons remain plying or unaccounted for, and of those plying it is estimated that only ten ships are at present carrying on German commerce on the sea. On the average very nearly 100 ships per day of over 300 tons burden arrive and leave the ports of the United Kingdom, and we are not only carrying on our own business effectively but we are applying special restrictions to certain vital commodities required for military purposes by the German and Austro-Hungarian Empire. The German Army depends primarily on its military materiel. The enormous supplies of all kinds of explosives and of all kinds of scientific apparatus directed to warlike purposes which they have prepared in times of peace gave them then, and gives them to-day, an advantage most marked in both theatres of War. But that advantage will no longer, as time passes, be wholly theirs. Gradually that advantage will change sides. We are able to draw, in virtue of sea-power from all over the world, for the cause of the Allies everything that is needed to procure the most abundant flow of munitions of war which can possibly be required, and, on the other hand, the deficiencies in essential commodities necessary for the waging of war is already beginning to show itself clearly marked as far as we can discern, in our enemy's military organisation.

I see no reason at all for any discontent in regard to the protection of British commerce or the restriction which is being placed on the enemy's supplies. Risks, of course, have to be run. The great number of troops which we have had to move to and fro freely across the world and their convoying, have involved serious risks; and although one's eye is fixed on the mischances which have occurred in this War, knowing as I do all the circumstances and all the incidents which have occurred, I am bound to say that I think we have had a very fair share of the luck. If our enemies did not attack on the high seas on the outbreak of war or just before it, we must presume that it was because they did not consider themselves strong enough to do so; because then would have been the moment of greatest advantage, when the dispatch of an Army to the Continent might have been prevented or delayed. If that moment was not used, it could only be because they were counting upon reducing the British Fleet, by a process of attrition, to a condition of greater equality with their own. We have been at war for four months. I should like to consider how that process of attrition is working. The losses of submarines have been equal, as far as we know; but, of course, the proportion of loss has been much greater to the Germans than to ourselves, because we have more than double the number of submarines in constant employment. With regard to torpedo-boat destroyers, our boats have shown their enormous superiority in gun power, which, of course, was not unknown before the war. No loss has been experienced by us, while eight or ten of the enemy's vessels have been destroyed. Of the older armoured cruisers we have lost, I think, six, and Germany has lost two. But there again the number of vessels of this class which we have disposed was three or four times as great as that of our opponents, and, of course, we have of necessity to expose them more frequently and more openly to possible attacks. . . .

It is a matter of great importance to keep secret the number of vessels which at any one moment are available with the Flag of the Commander-in-Chief, and it is the duty of every Englishman, every British subject, and every friend of our country, to do his utmost to wrap that fact in secrecy and mystery. Although, however, I cannot tell the number of ships which have joined the flag since the declaration of War, I can say, firstly, that the relative strength of the Fleet is substantially greater now than it was at the outbreak of the War; and, secondly, I can indicate the reinforcement which both countries will receive between now and the end of 1915. The maximum reinforcement which Germany can receive–it is not possible by any human agency to add to these numbers in the period–is three ships on the figures I have given–the "Lützow," the "Kronprinz," the "Salamis," which is a Greek ship which has presumably been taken over.

Two years ago I set up a Committee of the Admiralty to go into the whole question of the acceleration of new construction immediately after the outbreak of war so that the greatest possible number of deliveries could be made in the shortest possible time and very elaborate reports were furnished, and a complete system was worked out in every detail. In carrying out this system we have been aided by the patriotism and energy of the workmen in all the yards, who have strained their physical strength to the utmost, and have, by so doing, made themselves, in fact, the comrades of their fellow citizens who are fighting in the trenches at the front. During this period–between the beginning of the War and the end of 1915–while the Germans will be receiving an accession of three ships we shall receive the following ships: the "Agincourt" and the "Erin," acquired from Turkey, the "Tiger," the "Benbow," the "Emperor of India," the "Queen Elizabeth," the "Warspite," the "Valiant," the "Barham," the "Resolution," the "Ramilies," the "Revenge," the "Royal Sovereign," and the "Malaya" and the "Ammirente Latorre," renamed the "Canada," that we acquired from Chile–fifteen ships in all. All these ships are, of course, of the greatest power of any vessels that have ever been constructed in naval history, and it is no exaggeration to say that we could afford to lose a super-"Dreadnought" every month for twelve months without any loss occurring to the enemy and yet be in approximately as good a position of superiority as we were at the declaration of the War.

I hope that these facts will be of comfort to nervous people during the months that lie before us. They prove that so far as any policy of attrition is concerned the results so far, and the forecast so far as we may judge it, are not unsatisfactory to us: nor is there any attrition by wear and tear. The refits of the Fleet and flotillas are being regularly conducted. The health of the sailors is nearly twice as good as in time of peace. Six hundred thousand pounds has been spent by the Admiralty on warm clothing, and I have every reason to believe that the arrangements are thoroughly satisfactory, though, of course, if friends like to send additional comforts, arrangements are made for their reception and distribution. The sailors have received with warm gratitude the separation allowance which the Navy had, always hitherto, been completely denied. The conduct of the Fleet is exemplary, and any crime there is arises mainly among men who have been a long time in civil life, and who have not fully remembered the excellent precepts of their naval training. In the Grand Fleet the conduct of the men is almost perfect. The whole personnel of the Navy consists of a most intelligent class of skilled workmen and mechanicians. They have studied fully the conditions of the War, and they follow with the closest interest the heroic struggles of our soldiers in the field, and the zeal and enthusiasm with which they are discharging their duties inspires those who lead them with the utmost confidence.

I have thought it right to offer these few remarks of a general character to the House because despondent views are prejudicial to the public interest, and ought not to be tolerated by persons in the responsible position of Members of Parliament while they are in any public situation. There is absolutely no reason whatever for nervousness, anxiety, or alarm. We are now separating for an adjournment of some weeks, which will probably be very important weeks in the history of this War. There is every reason for complete confidence in the power of the Navy to give effect to the wishes and the purposes of the State and the Empire. We have powerful Allies on the seas.

The Russian Navy is developing in strength; the French Navy has complete command of the Mediterranean, and the Japanese Navy has effective command of the Pacific, and the utmost cordiality characterises the working of the Admiralties of the four countries. But even if we were single-handed, as we were in the days of the Napoleonic wars, we should have no reason to despair of our capacity—no doubt we should suffer discomfort and privation and loss—but we should have no reason to despair of our capacity to go on indefinitely, drawing our supplies from wherever we needed them, and transporting our troops wherever we required them, and to continue this process with a strength which would grow stronger with each month the War continued until, in the end, and perhaps not at any very distant date, the purposes for which we are fighting are achieved.

Eclipse and Revival
1915–1924

Eclipse and Revival 1915–1924

The idea of forcing the Dardanelles by a naval force was carefully examined and rejected in 1906 at the request of the Committee of Imperial Defence. In 1911 Churchill himself wrote that "it should be remembered that it is no longer possible to force the Dardanelles, and nobody would expose a modern fleet to such peril." But since that time he had been deeply impressed by the effects of the German bombardment of the Belgian forts in the early days of World War I; as First Lord of the Admiralty he was very anxious to eliminate the German battleships *Goeben* and *Breslau* and this area seemed to provide the best opportunity for a quick and easy victory. Gradually, the advantages of bombardment became so alluring to Churchill that he discounted the dangers. As early as September 1, 1914, he was exploring the possibilities; on November 25 he tried it on the War Council. Lloyd George subsequently wrote that "when Mr. Churchill has a scheme agitating in his powerful mind . . . he is indefatigable in pressing it upon the acceptance of everyone who matters in the decision."

Under these circumstances, the appeal by the Russians to a diversion at the beginning of 1915 provided the occasion, rather than the cause, of the plan which had been maturing since the first month of the war. The Director of Military Operations, General Callwell, later told the Dardanelles Commission: "Mr. Churchill was very keen on attacking the Dardanelles from a very early stage. . . . He was very keen to get to Constantinople somehow."

The first stage in Churchill's scheme was to obtain the acquiescence of Admiral Carden, the British commander of the squadron lying off the Dardanelles. Carden's response to Churchill was cautious. As he later explained to the Dardanelles Commission: "I did not mean distinctly that [the Dardanelles] could be forced. . . . I thought it *might* be done." But Churchill treated his response as agreement to the project, and began his reply with "high authorities here concur in your opinion," a phrase which led Carden to believe that Admiralty approval was much stronger than in fact it was. The "high authorities" subsequently turned out to be the Chief of Staff and Sir Henry Jackson, whose views–conveyed orally–were very guarded. Neither First Sea Lord Fisher nor the War Staff Group were consulted. Carden's detailed plans arrived on

January 11, and envisaged a careful step-by-step advance through the Dardanelles to the Marmara.

By the time of the arrival of Carden's plans, it was possible to discern the first signs of concern in the Admiralty. Fisher was startled by Carden's optimism. Sir Percy Scott, the leading gunnery authority, considered the task "impossible." The Third Sea Lord tried to raise it with Churchill, but was curtly rebuffed; Jackson was highly sceptical. Basically, Admiralty hostility to the plan was founded on two elements. The first was the nature of the task itself, long accepted as an impossibility for a purely naval operation. The second lay in concern that the resources–particularly of man-power–would denude other operations, notably Fisher's cherished plans for a Baltic landing and the margin of reserve required in the North Sea.

Carden's apparent confidence gave Churchill his strength at this moment. In addition, Churchill's personal influence over Fisher was a major factor. The aged First Sea Lord found himself incapable of matching Churchill's powers of persuasion–"He out-argues me," was a frequent lament–and he refused to criticise Churchill at the War Council. "I made it a rule that I would not at the War Council kick Winston Churchill's shins. He was my chief, and it was silence or resignation."

Two days after he received Carden's report (January 13, 1915), Churchill swept the plan through an enchanted War Council. "He was beautiful!" Fisher later said. "He has got the brain of Moses and the voice of Aaron. He would talk a bird out of a tree, and they were all carried away with him. I was not, myself." Churchill took the decision of the War Council as definite, and pressed forward with the operation. The Admiralty, even with ever-mounting doubts and apprehensions, went along reluctantly.

The possibility of using troops in the scheme arose towards the end of January, largely as a result of the pressures applied by Fisher and Jackson. Over a month of animated argument and discussion followed, in which the Secretary of State for War, Lord Kitchener first authorised the dispatch of his last Regular Division, the 29th, to the Middle East, then withdrew it. Finally he agreed to the dispatch. Most military historians have echoed Churchill's criticisms of this dilatoriness. What they did not appreciate–and Churchill did not stress in *The World Crisis*–was that Churchill repeatedly emphasised that the troops were not required for the passage of the Dardanelles, but for the subsequent occupation of Constantinople. Churchill made this vital statement to the War Council on February 26, 1915: "The actual and definite object of the army would be to *reap the rewards of the naval success*" (my italics). Not until March 10, and as a result of a confidential report by Lt. Gen. W. R. Birdwood, did Kitchener definitely make up his mind to dispatch the 29th Division to the Dardanelles. Two days later, Gen. Sir Ian Hamilton was instructed to take command of the new Mediterranean Expeditionary Force. He arrived at the Dardanelles on March 18.

Meanwhile, Carden's squadron was experiencing increasing difficulties. The ships, with the exception of the new battleship *Queen Elizabeth,* were obsolete, and the crews were inexperienced. The mine-sweeping unit consisted of East Coast trawlers commanded by civilians who had considerable difficulty in making any progress whatever against the fierce Dardanelles current. Therefore, the ships were forced to operate almost at point-blank range. The weather was bad–a factor that should have been taken into consideration beforehand–and the Turkish resistance was more tenacious than had been expected. The Outer Forts quickly succumbed, but the Intermediate and Inner Defences were more obdurate. Carden collapsed from exhaustion on March 17, and his post was taken by Rear Admiral John de Robeck. On March 18 the Allied fleet attempted once more to silence the forts and mobile batteries, so that the minesweepers could deal with the minefields. By the end of the day three battleships had been sunk and three crippled; only three battleships remained.

Churchill was undismayed at this reverse, and was eager for the naval attack to be resumed. But other factors intruded. Hamilton, who had witnessed the failure, was anxious to join in a combined operation; de Robeck, appalled and baffled by his losses, was ready to accept the offer; the Board of Admiralty was itself very willing to proceed on the lines which it had considered the only possible ones from the outset. The Board of Admiralty overruled the First Lord at an angry meeting, and the stage was set for landings on the Gallipoli Peninsula on April 25. It was the first step in the long agony of a campaign which cost the Allies a quarter of a million casualties before it was abandoned at the end of 1915.

The failure of the naval attack, and the subsequent limited success of the military landings, brought Admiralty discontent with Churchill to a head. The operation had been approved by the War Council without any realistic assessment of the available resources, and its members could reasonably complain that they had not been sufficiently informed of Admiralty objections. Churchill's confidence in the naval operation and the military capture of the Peninsula had both been shown to be overly optimistic. The Gallipoli landings took place on April 25, and by the middle of May 1915, some 20,000 casualties were suffered in establishing two tenuous beach-heads on the Gallipoli Peninsula and three more battleships were sunk. No progress was made in France, and the Second Battle of Ypres in April, during which the Germans used gas for the first time, nearly broke the British lines. It was against this sombre background that the Ministerial Crisis of May 1915 occurred.

I

No single event occasioned the crisis; Fisher's resignation on May 15 was its catalyst but not its cause. Nevertheless, to Churchill it was highly important that it was Fisher who started the process whereby the Liberal Government fell. All the resentment against Churchill personally was suddenly and dramatically manifest. In spite of his desperate efforts, he could not preserve his position. When the crisis was over, and the first Coalition was formed, Churchill was in a relative backwater as Chancellor of the Duchy of Lancaster. He was fortunate to have any office at all, in face of the virulent feeling against him in the Conservative Party and in the Navy.

Despised by the Conservatives, he had no reservoir of Liberal support to fall back on. He had lost the confidence of his Service advisers. He had been closely involved in what were regarded as two major disasters–Antwerp and the Dardanelles. He could count on no territorial loyalty such as had maintained the Chamberlains and

Lloyd George in their darkest moments. He was utterly and completely alone, as had been Lord Randolph Churchill when he resigned from the Treasury in 1886. He never forgave Asquith for his weakness and alleged disloyalty to him, yet it was only because of Asquith that he was still in the Government at all.

This was the first reverse Churchill suffered in his political career. Lloyd George had written that for a time "the brutality of the fall stunned Mr. Churchill," and Churchill himself wrote: "Like a sea-beast fished up from the depths, or a diver too suddenly hoisted, my veins threatened to burst from the fall in pressure. . . . At a moment when every fibre of my being was inflamed to action, I was forced to remain a spectator of the tragedy, placed cruelly in a front seat."

Yet Churchill possessed compensations denied to Lord Randolph in December 1886. His family was a core of devotion, loyalty and calm. For the first time in his life a world other than that of politics opened before him. He discovered painting. His obsession with his career did not lessen, but other distractions made his downfall bearable.

Nonetheless, he had his defenders. J. L. Garvin wrote in the *Observer*: "He is young. He has lion-hearted courage. No number of enemies can fight down his ability and force. His hour of triumph will come." And F. S. Oliver wrote to his brother: "The only two men who really seem to understand that we are at war are Winston and Lloyd George. Both have faults which disgust one peculiarly at the present time, but there is a reality about them, and they are in earnest, which the others aren't."

But even so, such supporters were few indeed. As Churchill once wrote in another context: "Thus the beaver builds his dam, and when his fishing is about to begin, comes the flood and sweeps his work and luck and fish away together. So he has to begin again."

II

The two years following Churchill's summary removal from the Admiralty were the most dismal of his life. Although successful in his attempts to reinforce the Gallipoli forces, he watched as the August campaign turned into a tragic failure. He fought the consequent movement towards evacuation strenuously, unsuccessfully, and probably wrongly. His status in the Coalition fell, and he found his new colleagues uncongenial and even hostile. In November 1915 the Dardanelles Committee was reconstituted into a new War Committee, and Churchill was excluded. For the first and only time in his career, he resigned. After delivering a defiant speech to the House of Commons, he left to serve on the Western Front.

The shadow of the disastrous campaign hung over him for many years. In 1925 an American historian wrote that "it is doubtful if even Great Britain could survive another world war and another Churchill." As late as 1931 a hostile biographer could be found observing: "The ghosts of the Gallipoli dead will always rise up to damn him anew in time of national emergency. Neither official historians, nor military hack writers, will explain away or wipe out the memories of the Dardanelles."

In his resignation speech on November 15, defending his record at the Admiralty, Churchill described the campaign as "a legitimate war gamble." This description might have been justified. Fundamentally, the project was viable under certain circumstances, but not under those in which it was carried out. There is no evidence of a cool prior estimate of the difficulties and advantages of the operation. Entranced by Churchill's glowing portrait, the War Council embarked upon the enterprise with no clear idea of how it could be accomplished or what rewards it might bring. It was ill-planned, rushed and essentially amateurish. As Lloyd George wrote before the operation began, "Expeditions which are decided upon and organised with insufficient care generally end disastrously." In short, it was an instructive example of both the advantages and dangers of Churchill's fertile imagination and his impatience with criticism.

Later comment was less condemnatory. Perhaps the revisionists went too far. Historians with a knowledge of what happened in Flanders from 1915 to 1918 tend to be dazzled by Gallipoli. As Major John North observed, "No battlefield so lends itself to retrospective sentimentality." Yet contemporary criticism was not wholly unmerited. Churchill himself over thirty years later wrote: "I was ruined for the time being over the Dardanelles, and a supreme enterprise was cast away, through my trying to carry out a major and combined operation of war from a subordinate position. Men are ill-advised to try such ventures." The comment of his friend F. E. Smith may be appended: "His able, restless, ambitious temperament was hardly content with its own legitimate ambit. He saw too much, and he tried to do too much. No one department, hardly one war, was enough for him in that sublime and meteoric moment."

III

Thus began a deeply unhappy period of Churchill's political career. He participated in Western Front operations for barely six months, making a brief return in March 1916 to urge—to the astonishment of everyone—the recall of Lord Fisher. This hapless undertaking occasioned a vicious attack in the *Spectator*, which fired Pope's savage lines at him:

> See the same man, in vigour, in the gout
> Alone, in company, in place or out,
> Early at business and at hazard late,
> Mad at a fox chase, wise at a debate,
> Drunk at a borough, civil at a ball,
> Friendly at Hackney, faithless at Whitehall.

In the summer of 1916 he returned to the political arena, principally to give evidence to the Dardanelles Commission. He wrote a series of articles on naval affairs in the *London Magazine* which were replete with inconsistencies and shallow thinking, and did his reputation much harm. Balfour called upon him to write an account of the Battle of Jutland in order to portray it in terms of a great naval victory.

In the complicated intrigues which dislodged Asquith in December 1916, Churchill played a very minor role. His position was even more difficult in the aftermath of Lloyd George's triumph. He had no real contact with the Conservatives who now emphatically dominated the Government. Yet he loathed being out of office and found the company of the Asquithites highly uncongenial. His chance finally came on May 10, 1917, when he eclipsed Lloyd George in secret session debate. Lloyd George decided to brave the Conservative fury and bring him back to the Government, more in recognition of Churchill's potential danger than in memory of past alliances. And indeed a violent storm did ensue over his appointment as Minister of Munitions. It is best to look to the words of Lloyd George to explain the hostility to Churchill at this time:

> Here was their explanation. His mind was a powerful machine, but there lay hidden in its material or make-up some obscure defect which prevented it from always running true. They could not tell what it was. When the mechanism went wrong, its very power made the action disastrous, not only to himself but to the causes in which he was engaged and the men with whom he was co-operating. . . . He had in their opinion revealed some tragic flaw in the metal.

The decision to align himself with Lloyd George was as momentous as that to desert the Conservatives in 1904. The old Liberal Party was split in twain after the events of December 1916. Henceforth, those Liberals who followed Lloyd George were dependent upon Conservative goodwill for their political survival. So long as his star was in the ascendant, all was well; as soon as it began to decline, they would become men without a party. Between 1917 and 1922 Churchill survived politically because Lloyd George did. Yet for the moment he could congratulate himself for having weathered the storm of 1915 and, after all, in politics to survive disaster is itself a victory of sorts. In 1918 he was forty-five, the age at which his father had died. Unlike his father, he had successfully met a shattering check to his political career. He had now to build on the new foundations which he, and good fortune, had provided.

IV

Save for the 1931-1935 National Government no Administration in modern British politics had been treated more severely than the 1919-1922 Lloyd George Coalition. Harold Laski observed in 1919 that Lloyd George "seems determined to sacrifice upon the altar of his private ambition the whole spirit of our public life," and Edward Grey commented that the Coalition moved him "to indignation and despair such as I have never felt about any other British Government."

Such emotions were more the consequence of the Coalition's character than its policies. There was something about its leading members which did not arouse sympathy. Collectively, they seemed to personify Lord Birkenhead's men "with stout hearts and sharp swords" who won the "glittering prizes." There was about them the undefinable but real atmosphere of the *parvenu.* Arnold Bennett, after spending a weekend at Cherkley with Austen Chamberlain, Lloyd George and Birkenhead noted that he "never heard the principle or the welfare of the country mentioned."

The irony of the situation lay in the fact that the "Coupon" Election of 1918[1] demonstrated that, politically, the Conservative Party had won the war. Of the Coalition leaders, Austen Chamberlain commanded affection; Lord Curzon commanded a rather grudging respect; but Bonar Law alone commanded both. Lloyd George's position remained reasonably secure so long as Bonar Law stayed; when Bonar Law retired in 1921 he took the rock on which the Coalition stood with him. When he finally turned against it in October 1922 it collapsed utterly. Yet for a time it seemed impregnable, the great Centre Party itself, and the extreme self-confidence of its leaders was not so misplaced as it subsequently appeared.

V

Churchill was one of the most controversial of the Coalition members. The period of relative quiescence at the Ministry of Munitions passed, and by the spring of 1919 his actions were again arousing hostility. It is not possible here to fully describe the tangled events connected with the intervention in the Russian Revolution, the attempted suppression of the Irish Revolution, and the Chanak Crisis of September 1922, the three major episodes in which Churchill was deeply involved. He cannot, of course, hold sole responsibility for Government policy in these areas, although his active prosecution of intervention in Russia was so intense, and his role as Secretary of State for War so pivotal that the public justifiably identified him personally with that policy. The important point is that all three policies totally failed, and it was this association with failure that so harmed the Coalition generally and Churchill personally.

Churchill became officially involved in the Russian intervention at the beginning of 1919, after the Cabinet had resolved not to withdraw British troops. As he frequently pointed out, technically he was the executor of Cabinet decisions. In fact the records clearly show he quickly became the most ardent Ministerial supporter of active intervention; when that became impossible, he fought as long as he could for direct assistance in arms and equipment. Unlike Lloyd George's position, which was highly equivocal until the failure of the White Russians became manifest, Churchill's was wholly consistent. It is also fair to point out that the advice given to the War Office was not of high quality. One example will suffice. In his comments to the Cabinet, General Poole said on February 13:

> In his opinion General Denikin was not a great soldier nor a good administrator, but he was thoroughly patriotic and enjoyed the respect of everybody . . . the Bolsheviks had never been very serious fighters. The element of surprise was everything in a campaign against them. The impression the Bolshevik gave him was that he was a man who wanted to live a long time . . . if we supplied the guns we had promised, that would be quite enough.[2]

Partly because Lloyd George was involved with the negotiations in Paris during this period, and partly because he was equivocating, the Prime Minister gave no clear leadership. Ministers wanted the Bolsheviks to fall, but were increasingly uneasy about the extent of British commitment needed to secure it. Throughout the first half of 1919, until the series of defeats that sent the forces of Admiral Koltchak reeling backwards and destroyed Denikin's ambitious northward advance to Moscow, the Government drifted. "There was no British policy," Robert Bruce Lockhart wrote, "unless seven different policies at once could be called a policy." A striking instance of this fact occurred in the Cabinet on July 4. The Deputy Chief of the Naval Staff raised a crucial question: "Both the Admiralty and the Naval Officers on the spot were really in ignorance as to exact position: were we, or were we not, at war with the Bolsheviks?" Lloyd George replied that "actually we were at war with the Bolsheviks, but we had decided not to make war. In other words, we did not intend to put great armies into Russia to fight the Bolshevik forces."

Churchill's sense of obligation to the White commanders was a real one, but his hatred of the "foul baboonery" of Bolshevism was the stronger element in his attitudes as can be seen in both *The World Crisis* and *The Aftermath*, as well as in his public speeches at the time. He wrote to Lloyd George in March 1920: "Since the Armistice my policy would have been 'Peace with the German people, war on the Bolshevik tyranny.' Willingly or unavoidably, you have followed something very near the reverse."

Labour and Liberal unease with the Government's Russian policy quickly ripened into hostility. At the T.U.C. conference in September 1919 Churchill was described, *inter alia*, as an "insistent, persistent, and consistent liar," and the National Hands Off Russia Committee launched personal attacks against him of very remarkable virulence, to which Churchill vigorously responded. "The theories of Lenin and Trotsky," he said in January 1920, "have driven man from the civilisation of the twentieth century into a condition of barbarism worse than the Stone Age, and left him the most awful and pitiable spectacle in human experience, devoured by vermin, racked by pestilence, and deprived of hope." There was some justice in Ramsay MacDonald's retort:

> Churchill pursues his mad adventure as though he were Emperor of these Isles, pacifying us with a pledge, and delighting his militarists and capitalists with a campaign. Again, we have been told one day that we are withdrawing our troops from Russia, and the next we read of new offensives, new bogus governments, new military captains as allies.[3]

On January 27, 1920, the Cabinet resolved that "we have neither the men, the money, nor the credit, and public opinion is altogether opposed" to further involvement in the Russian tragedy. Henry Wilson, Chief of the Imperial General Staff, wrote: "So ends in practical disaster another of Winston's military attempts–Antwerp, Dardanelles, Denikin."

Although this was not a wholly fair judgment, it had some merit. In effect, Churchill had repeated the error he had made in the Dardanelles: he had attempted to run a major operation from a relatively junior position. Politically, the uproar from the

Left was of less significance than the deterioration of Churchill's relations with Lloyd George. In 1921 Churchill wrote that Lloyd George's thinking "stopped short of reaching any conclusion of a definite character on which a policy, or even a provisional policy, could be based." Lloyd George's comments on Churchill were even more scathing.

Hard on the heels of the Russian fiasco came Ireland, once again. Throughout 1919 the situation had deteriorated while the self-styled Irish Government proceeded to usurp the functions of Dublin Castle. In retrospect, it was a quiet year, with only 18 murders and 77 armed attacks including an attempt to assassinate the Viceroy. By the beginning of 1920, however, more sinister possibilities were in the air, as the Irish Republican Army moved towards more direct and violent methods.

Irish crises have consistently taken British Governments by surprise, as the events of 1880-1881, 1916 and 1919 demonstrate. Churchill was not untypical when he proposed in Cabinet on August 5, 1919, that "the present was not a good time to look for an Irish solution. In a few months the position would probably be easier. It had already improved, and the people were not only very prosperous, but they were beginning to lose faith in the protagonists of Sinn Fein. . . . His own opinion was that if we allowed matters to remain as they were for the next five months, the Irish people would be more ready to accept a settlement than they had ever been."

It is important to emphasise that other Ministers shared this confidence, but by March 1920 it was evident that it had been grimly misplaced. The harassed and demoralised Royal Irish Constabulary appealed for reinforcements, and on May 11, Churchill undertook to raise what he called the "Special Emergency Gendarmerie," to be paid for by the War Office. He subsequently claimed they were recruited "from a great press of applicants on account of their intelligence, their characters, and their record in the War." Other estimates of the "Black and Tans" are less favourable. Unquestionably, they soon had much to be revengeful about, and their record has been excessively besmirched. After every allowance had been made, however, the record of the Black and Tans is not one over which English historians care to linger. Churchill vigorously defended them, then and subsequently; in private, he urged even more Draconian measures, including a policy of deliberate reprisals and summary executions of suspects, throughout 1920 and well into 1921.

Churchill's fundamental approach was exactly the same one he had used in 1914. He was prepared to negotiate, but not under duress. The defeat of the rebels had to precede negotiations. But, as the burning months passed, opinion in England and abroad was increasingly appalled by the Irish situation, to the point that even ardent Unionists such as Birkenhead conceded that the situation was becoming untenable. A combination of pressures propelled Ministers towards a truce in July 1921, and to the subsequent negotiations which produced the Irish Treaty of December 1921.

This controversial agreement was perhaps the one tangible achievement of the Coalition. Yet it immediately imperilled the Coalition's relationship with the bulk of the Conservative Party, which might have been reduced if the Treaty had been promptly ratified by the Dail. Southern Ireland plunged swiftly into a civil war more costly and terrible than the fight against the British. Henry Wilson was assassinated in broad daylight in London. Bonar Law delivered dark warnings. Having been led to believe that the Treaty was a genuine and realistic solution, Conservatives now viewed with dismay and aversion the spread of an even graver state of anarchy.

Thus by the summer of 1922 the Conservative Party was in a condition of simmering revolt. The Government had ingloriously blundered into Russia and out of it again. They had failed to put down insurrection in Ireland. They had manifestly not built a land fit for heroes, and unemployment, particularly in the North, Scotland and Wales, was reaching dreadful proportions. Lloyd George's personal glitter had faded badly, further tarnished by the failure of the grandiloquently heralded Genoa Conference in April and the first revelations of squalid trafficking in Honours. In Leo Amery's words: "Unionists felt that they no longer had any policy of their own, but were being dragged along in the wake of an erratic Prime Minister whom they once again profoundly distrusted, by a little group of their own leaders who had lost, not only their principles, but their heads."

In these circumstances, it only required one catalytic event to destroy the Coalition, and this was supplied by the Chanak Crisis.

VI

Churchill had been a consistent critic of Lloyd George's pro-Greek policies until the condition of the Greek forces in Turkey-in-Asia became desperate in the summer of 1922. With the triumphant Kemalist forces advancing upon the neutral zone at the Dardanelles he vehemently advocated firmness, and involved himself deeply in one of the most unnecessary crises imaginable. Indeed, a kind of collective irrationality seemed to afflict Ministers, with some notable exceptions, and the "Chanak affair" soon assumed a quite disproportionate significance in their minds. In the event, the actions of the British commander, Sir Charles Harington, averted actual conflict at Chanak, and paved the way for negotiations with the Kemalists.

The political impact of the crisis was particularly strong because of its total unexpectedness. In the Cabinet itself, Curzon and Baldwin were particularly outraged by the precipitateness of the Government action, and on October 7 Bonar Law publicly condemned it.

As the Conservative revolt against the Coalition gathered momentum, the Coalition leaders decided upon a bold counter-stroke by proposing a General Election before the Conservatives' annual meeting in November. The famous Carlton Club meeting of October 19 was provoked by the Coalition leaders to ensure Conservative support, but the tactic boomeranged spectacularly. The Conservatives voted overwhelmingly against continuing the Coalition. That afternoon Lloyd George resigned, and the King sent for Bonar Law. The ensuing General Election provided a Conservative majority. The best comment made on it was that of Philip Guedalla: "Mr Bonar Law . . . became Prime Minister of England for the simple and satisfying reason that he was not Mr Lloyd George. At an open competition in the somewhat negative exercise of not being Mr Lloyd George that was held in November 1922, Mr Law was found to be more indubitably not Mr Lloyd George than any of the other competitors; and, in consequence, by the mysterious operation of the British Constitution, he reigned in his stead."

VII

The fall of the Coalition, swiftly followed by Churchill's electoral defeat at Dundee, marks the third crucial point in his career, comparable with the movements to the Liberals in 1903-1904 and to Lloyd George in 1917. The Conservative supporters of the Coalition could look forward to returning to the fold in due course; Churchill had no fold to return to. His links with the official Liberals were tenuous, and those with the Conservatives non-existent. His relations with Lloyd George were cool. Prostrated at the crucial moment by an emergency appendectomy, he has wryly recorded that "in the twinkling of an eye I found myself without an office, without a seat, without a party, and even without an appendix."

A brief period of political turmoil followed the fall of the Coalition. Baldwin succeeded the dying Bonar Law in May 1923; in December he unexpectedly called a General Election. Churchill stood at West Leicester as a Liberal Free Trader but was defeated by over four thousand votes. Offered other Liberal seats, he declined.

By now it was quite apparent he was moving to the Right. It was his natural political habitat, only rendered unattractive by the actual composition and memories of the Conservative Party. The opportunity to signify this movement came in January 1924, when Asquith decided to put in Labour. "The enthronement in office of a Socialist Government," Churchill warned in a public letter, "will be a national misfortune such as has usually befallen great states only on the morrow of defeat in war. It will delay the return of prosperity, it will open a period of increasing political confusion and disturbance, it will place both the Liberal and Labour parties in a thoroughly false position. . . . Strife and tumults, deepening and darkening, will be the only consequence of minority Socialist rule."

In February he supported a Conservative candidate in a by-election at Burnley, and early in March he narrowly lost a by-election in the Abbey Division of Westminster as an "Independent and Anti-Socialist." In May he stepped on a Conservative platform, in Liverpool, for the first time in twenty years to speak darkly of the "Present Dangers of the Socialist Movement," and warned that the Labour Government was "driven forward by obscure, sinister, and in part extraneous forces." Shortly afterwards he was adopted as the "Constitutionalist" candidate for Epping by its Conservative Association. Although the movement from Lloyd George Coalitionist to Liberal Free Trader to virtual Conservative was somewhat rapid, it reflected what was in reality already a fact of Churchill's attitudes. In the 1924 General Election hardly any candidate was more assiduous in warning his hearers of the "Red Menace." When the Conservatives returned to power, the former Coalition Conservatives, Austen Chamberlain and Birkenhead received Cabinet office; more surprisingly, so did Churchill as Chancellor of the Exchequer. Baldwin did not share Bonar Law's conviction that he would rather have Churchill against him than with him. As Churchill remarked at a celebratory dinner organised in Liverpool, "I realise the truth of the remark of Disraeli that 'the vicissitudes of politics are inexhaustible.' "

NOTES

[1] So-called because supporters of the Coalition received a letter of endorsement signed by Lloyd George and Bonar Law. The document, derided by those who did not receive it as "the coupon letter," was usually decisive at the poll. Only a few survived its withdrawal, and Asquith was among those who lost their seats.

[2] Cabinet Minutes for January 24, 1919.

[3] *The Socialist Review,* October 1919.

BRITISH COMMAND OF THE SEA

February 15, 1915

House of Commons

At the end of December 1914, Churchill, Lloyd George and Maurice Hankey (Secretary to the recently created War Council) decided that serious thought should be given to using British strength–and particularly sea power–in a more rewarding manner. In August 1914, when it was evident that Turkey would enter the war on the German side, Churchill had advocated a joint Anglo-Greek attack on the Gallipoli Peninsula in order to close the Dardanelles. This proved impossible, but on November 25, 1914, after the declaration of war was made, Churchill again proposed a naval attack on the Dardanelles. No decision was made, but the idea was planted in the minds of the members of the Council.

Early in January 1915, the hard-pressed Russians asked the British "to arrange for a demonstration of some kind" against the Turks. This appeal marked the beginning of the British naval attack on the Dardanelles, which was sanctioned by the War Council on January 18, 1915.

In this speech, Churchill was able to refer to two British naval victories–at the Falklands (December 8, 1914) and Dogger Bank (January 24, 1915).

[Extract] After the outbreak of war my Noble Friend Lord Kitchener, the Secretary of State for War, had to create an Army eight or ten times as large as any previously maintained or even contemplated in this country, and the War Office has been engaged in vast processes of expansion, improvisation and development entirely without parallel in military experience. Thanks, however, to the generous provision made so readily for the last five years by the House of Commons for the Royal Navy, no such difficulties or labours have confronted the Admiralty. On the declaration of war we were able to count upon a Fleet of sufficient superiority for all our needs, with a good margin for safety in vital matters, fully mobilised, placed in its war stations, supplied and equipped with every requirement down to the smallest detail that could be foreseen, with reserves of ammunition and torpedoes up to and above the regular standard, with ample supplies of fuel and oil, with adequate reserves of stores of all kinds, with complete systems of transport and supply, with full numbers of trained officers and men of all ratings, with a large surplus of reserved and trained men, with adequate establishments for training new men, with an immense programme of new construction rapidly maturing to reinforce the Fleet and replace casualties, and with a prearranged system for accelerating that new construction which has been found to yield satisfactory and even surprising results.

I would draw the attention of the House in illustration to only three particular points. First of all, ammunition. If hon. Members will run their eye along the series of figures for Vote 9, in the last five or six years, and particularly during the latter years, they will see an enormous increase in the Vote. In time of peace one gets little credit for such expenditure, but in time of war we thank God it has been made. Then, Sir, oil. Most pessimistic prophesies were made as to the supply of oil, but no difficulty has been found in practice in that regard. The estimates which we had formed of the quantity of oil to be consumed by the Fleet in war proved to be much larger than our actual consumption. On the other hand, there has been no difficulty whatever in buying practically any quantity of oil. No single oil ship has been interfered with on passage to this country. The price of oil today is substantially below what it was when I last addressed the House on this topic. Indeed we have found it possible to do what we all along wished to do, but hesitated to decide upon, on account of all the gloomy prophecies and views which were entertained–we have found it possible to convert the "Royal Sovereigns" to a completely oil fuel basis, so that this equally with the "Queen Elizabeth" class will enjoy the great advantages of liquid fuel for war purposes.

Then as to manning. No more widespread delusion existed than that although we might build ships we could never find men to man them. In some quarters of this country the idea was fostered that when mobilisation took place ships could not be sent fully manned to sea; but when mobilisation did take place we were able to man, as I told the House we should be able, every ship in the Navy fit to send to sea. We were able to man a number of old ships which we did not intend to send to sea, but which, after being repaired and refitted, were found to have the possibility of usefulness in them. We were able to man in addition powerful new vessels building for foreign nations for which no provision had been made. We were able to man an enormous number–several score–of armed merchantmen which have played an important part in our arrangements for the control of traffic and trade. We were able to provide all the men that were necessary for the Royal Naval Air Service which did not exist three years ago, which is already making a name for itself, and which has become a considerable and formidable body. We were able to keep our training schools full to the very brim so as to prepare a continual supply of drafts for the new vessels which are coming on in such great numbers, and over and above that we are able, without injury to any of these important interests, to supply the nucleus of instructors and trained men to form the cadres of the battalions of the Royal Naval Division which have now reached a respectable total and which have developed an efficiency which enables them to be counted on immediately as a factor in the defence of this country, and very soon as an element in the forces which we can use overseas.

We have never been a military nation, though now we are going to take a hand in that. We have always relied for our safety on naval power, and in that respect it is not true to say we entered on this War unprepared. On the contrary, the German Army was not more ready for an offensive war on a gigantic scale than was the British Fleet for national defence. The credit for this is due to the House, which, irrespective of party interests, has always by overwhelming, and in later years by unchallengeable majorities, supported the Government and the Minister in every demand made for naval defence. Indeed, such disputes as we have had from time to time have only been concerned with the margins of superiority, and have turned on comparatively small points respecting them. For instance, we have discussed at enormous length what percentages of "Dreadnought" superiority would be available in particular months in future years, and we have argued whether the "Lord Nelsons" should be counted as "Dreadnoughts" or not. The House of Commons as a whole has a right to claim the Navy as its child and as the unchanging object of its care and solicitude; and now after six months of war, with new dangers and new difficulties coming into view, we have every right to feel content with the results of our labours.

Since November, when I last had an opportunity of speaking to the House on naval matters, two considerable events have happened–the victory off the Falkland Islands, and the recent successful cruiser action near the Dogger Bank. Both of these events are satisfactory in themselves, but still more are they satisfactory in their consequences and significance, and I shall venture to enlarge upon them and hang the thread of my argument upon them.

The victory off the Falklands terminated the first phase of the Naval War by effecting a decisive clearance of the German flag from the oceans of the world. The blocking in of the enemy's merchantmen at the very outset, and the consequent frustration of his whole plans for the destruction of our commerce, the reduction of his base at Tsing-tau, the expulsion of his ships from the China Sea by Japan, the hunting down of the "Könisberg" and the "Emden," the latter by an Australian cruiser, were steps along the path to the goal finally reached when Admiral von Spee's powerful squadron, having been unsuccessfully though gallantly engaged off Coronel, was brought to action and destroyed on 8th December by Sir Doveton Sturdee. Only two small German cruisers and two armed merchantmen remain at large of all their formidable preparations for the attack on our trade routes, and these vessels are at present in hiding. During the last three months–that is to say, since Parliament rose–on the average about 8,000 British vessels have been continuously on the sea, passing to and fro on their lawful occasions. There have been 4,465 arrivals at and 3,600 sailings from the ports of the United Kingdom. Only nineteen vessels have been sunk by the enemy, and only four of these vessels have been sunk by above-water craft. That is a very remarkable result to have been achieved after only a few months of war. I am sure, if we had been told before the War that such a result would be so soon achieved, and that our losses would be so small, we should not have believed it for a moment. I am quite sure, if the Noble Lord whom I see in his place (Lord Charles Beresford), who has always felt, and quite legitimately, anxiety for the trade routes and the great difficulty of defending them–if he had been offered six months ago such a prospect, he would have said it was too good to be true.

Lord Charles Beresford: Hear, hear.

Mr. Churchill: Certainly the great sailors of the past, the men of the Revolutionary and Napoleonic Wars, would have been astounded. During those two great wars, which began in 1793 and ended, after a brief interval, in 1814, 10,871 British merchant ships were captured or sunk by the enemy. Even after the decisive battle of Trafalgar, when we had the undisputed command of the sea so far as it can be tactically and strategically attained, the loss of British ships went on at a rate of over 500 ships a year. In 1806, 519 ships were sunk or captured–that is, the year after Trafalgar; in 1807, 559; in 1808, 469; in 1809, 571; and in 1810, 619. Our total losses on the high seas in the first six months of the present War, including all ships other than trawlers engaged in mine-sweeping–including losses by mines and vessels scuttled by submarines—our losses in the whole of that period are only sixty-three. Of course, we must always be on the look-out for another attempt by the enemy to harass the trade routes. Although the oceans offer rather a bleak prospect to the German cruisers, and the experience of their consorts is not encouraging, the Admiralty must be fully prepared for that possibility, and we shall be able to meet any new efforts with advantages and resources incomparably superior to those which were at our disposal at the beginning of the War. The truth is that steam and the telegraph have enormously increased, as compared with sailing days, the thoroughness and efficiency of superior sea power. Coaling, communications, and supplies are vital and constant needs, and once the upper hand has been lost they become operations of almost insuperable difficulty to the weaker navy. Credit is due to our outlying squadrons and to the Admiralty organisation by which they have been directed. It must never be forgotten that the situation on every sea, even the most remote, is dominated and decided by the influence of Sir John Jellicoe's Fleet—lost to view amid the northern mists, preserved by patience and seamanship in all its strength and efficiency, silent, unsleeping, and, as yet, unchallenged.

The command of the sea which we have thus enjoyed has not only enabled our trade to be carried on practically without interruption or serious disturbance, but we have been able to move freely about the world very large numbers of troops. The Leader of the Opposition in a speech which he made the other night—I do not at all quarrel with the moderate and temperate tone of his criticism—quoted a letter of a shipowner as applied to the Admiralty Transport Department, in which the word "incapacity" occurred. Of all the words which could be applied to the Admiralty Transport Department no word could be more unsuitable than the word "incapacity." . . .

We are at war with the second Naval Power in the world. When complaints are made that we have taken too many transports or armed too many auxiliary cruisers, or made use of too many colliers or supply ships, I must mention that fact. The statement that the Admiralty have on charter, approximately, about one-fifth of the British Mercantile Marine tonnage is correct. With that we discharge two duties, both of importance at the present time; first, the supply, fuelling, and replenishing with ammunition of the Fleets; second, the transport of reinforcements and supply for the Army in the Field, including the return of wounded. It must be remembered in regard to the Fleet that we have no dockyard or naval port at our backs, and that the bases we are using during the War have no facilities for coaling from the shore. We are not like the Germans, living in a great naval port at Wilhelmshaven, on which £15,000,000 or £16,000,000 has been spent. Rosyth is not finished, and will not be available for some time. Everything, therefore, required to keep the Fleet in being—supplies, stores, and, above all, fuel—has to be not only carried but kept afloat in ships. What are called the "afloat reserves"—the great mobile reserves of fuel and stores maintained at the various bases used by the Fleet—are those which are fixed by the War Staff and approved by the Board of Admiralty after consultation with the Commander-in-Chief. When those amounts have been fixed the Transport Department have no choice but to supply them. It is necessary that there should be sufficient colliers to enable all the Fleet units at a particular base to coal simultaneously with a maximum rapidity twice over within a short interval, and extensive naval movements at high speed may at any moment necessitate this being put to the test. After two such coalings there must still be sufficient coal available for unforeseen contingencies, including delays in bringing further supplies through storm or foggy weather, or hostile operations leading to the closing of particular areas of water, or through the temporary suspension of coaling in South Wales, through damage to docks, railways, bridges, pits or other local causes.

We cannot possibly run any risk of having the Fleet rendered immobile. We must make assurance doubly sure. The life of the State depends upon it and it follows, having always to be ready for a great emergency, with all the Fleet steaming at once continuously for days together–having always to be ready for that, it follows that during periods of normal Fleet movements the reserves of coal are often and necessarily turned over slowly, and colliers may in consequence remain at the bases for considerable periods. That is our system. The fact, therefore, that particular vessels are noticed by shipowners to be kept waiting about for long periods is no sign of mismanagement or incapacity on the part of the Admiralty, but it is an indispensable precaution and method without which the Fleet could not act in a time of emergency. The position at every home coaling base and of every ship is telegraphed to the Admiralty nightly, and a tabulated statement is issued the same night. This statement is issued as the basis for comprehensive daily criticism, with a view to securing the highest possible economy compatible with and subject to the vital exigencies of war. So much for the Fleet and its supply and its coaling.

With regard to the Army, it should be remembered that we are supplying across the sea, in the teeth of the enemy's opposition, an Army almost as large as the Grand Army of Napoleon, only vastly more complex in organisation and equipment. We are also preparing other Armies still larger in number. I do not know on what day or at what hour the Secretary of State for War will ask the Admiralty to move 20,000 or it may be 40,000 men. It may be at very short notice. He does not know, until we tell him, how we shall move them, by what route or to what ports. Plans are frequently changed on purpose at the very last moment; it is imperative for the safety of our soldiers and the reinforcement of our Armies and the conduct of the War. We have at the present moment a powerful and flexible machinery which can move whole Armies with celerity wherever it is desired in a manner never before contemplated or dreamt of, and I warn the House most solemnly against allowing grounds of commercial advantage or financial economy to place any hampering restriction or impediment upon these most difficult and momentous operations. Careful and prudent administration does not stop at the outbreak of war. Everything in our power will be done to enforce it and avoid extravagance. We shall therefore welcome the advice of business men on points where they can help us. Gradually, as we get more and more control of the situation, higher economy in some respects may be possible, but military and naval requirements must be paramount, rough and ready although their demands often are, and they must be served fully at the cost of all other considerations. I am afraid that I cannot hold out any hope of any immediate reduction in the tonnage required by the Admiralty. . . .

I have said that the strain in the early months of the War has been greatly diminished now by the abatement of distant convoy work and by the clearance of the enemy's flag from the seas and oceans. There were times when, for instance, the great

Australian convoy of sixty ships was crossing the Indian Ocean, or the great Canadian convoy of forty ships, with its protecting squadrons, was crossing the Atlantic, or when the regular flow of large Indian convoys of forty or fifty ships sailing in company was at its height both ways, when there were half a dozen minor expeditions being carried by the Navy, guarded and landed at different points and supplied after landing; when there was a powerful German cruiser squadron still at large in the Pacific or the Atlantic, which had to be watched for and waited for in superior force in six or seven different parts of the world at once, and when, all the time, within a few hours' steam of our shores there was concentrated a hostile fleet which many have argued in former times was little inferior to our own; and when there was hardly a Regular soldier left at home, and before the Territorial Force and the New Armies had attained their present high efficiency and power—there were times when our naval resources, considerable as they are, were drawn out to their utmost limit, and when we had to use old battleships to give strength to cruiser squadrons, even at the cost of their speed, and when we had to face and to accept risks with which we did not trouble the public, and which no one would willingly seek an opportunity to share. But the victory at the Falkland Islands swept all these difficulties out of existence. It set free a large force of cruisers and battleships for all purposes; it opened the way to other operations of great interest; it enabled a much stricter control and more constant outlook to be maintained in Home waters, and it almost entirely freed the outer seas of danger. That was a memorable event, the relief an advantage of which will only be fully appreciated by those who have full knowledge of all that has taken place by those who not only knew, but felt, what was going forward.

I now come to the battle cruiser action on the Dogger Bank. That action was not fought out, because the enemy, after abandoning their wounded consort, the "Blücher," made good their escape into waters infested by their submarines and mines. But this combat between the finest ships in both navies is of immense significance and value in the light which it throws upon rival systems of design and armament, and upon relative gunnery efficiency. It is the first test we have ever had, and, without depending too much upon it, I think it is at once important and encouraging. First of all it vindicates, so far as it goes, the theories of design, and particularly of big gun armament, always identified with Lord Fisher. The range of the British guns was found to exceed that of the German. Although the German shell is a most formidable instrument of destruction, the bursting, smashing power of the heavier British projectile is decidedly greater, and—this is the great thing—our shooting is at least as good as theirs. The Navy, while always working very hard—no one except themselves knows how hard they have worked in these years—have credited the Germans with a sort of super-efficiency in gunnery, and we have always been prepared for some surprises in their system of control and accuracy of fire. But there is a feeling, after the combat of 24th January, that perhaps our naval officers were too diffident in regard to their own professional skill in gunnery. Then the guns. While the Germans were building 11-inch guns we built 12-inch and 13½-inch guns. Before they advanced to the 12-inch gun we had large numbers of ships armed with the 13-5. It was said by the opposite school of naval force that a smaller gun fires faster and has a higher velocity, and therefore the greater destructive power—and Krupp is the master gunmaker of the world—and it was very right and proper to take such a possibility into consideration. Everything that we have learnt, however, so far shows that we need not at all doubt the wisdom of our policy or the excellence of our material. The 13-5-inch gun is unequalled by any weapon yet brought on the scene. Now we have the 15-inch gun, with which the five "Queen Elizabeths" and the five "Royal Sovereigns" are all armed, coming into line, and this gun in quality equals the 13-5-inch gun, and is vastly more powerful and destructive.

There is another remarkable feature of this action to which I should like to draw the attention of the House. I mean the steaming of our ships. All the vessels engaged in this action exceeded all their previous records without exception. I wonder if the House and the public appreciate what that means. Here is a squadron of the Fleet which does not live in harbour, but is far away from its dockyards and which during six months of war has been constantly at sea. All of a sudden the greatest trial is demanded of their engines, and they all excel all previous peace-time records. Can you conceive a more remarkable proof of the excellence of British machinery, of the glorious industry of the engine-room branch, or of the admirable system of repairs and refits by which the Grand Fleet is maintained from month to month and can, if need be, be maintained from year to year in a state of ceaseless vigilance without exhaustion? Take the case of the "Kent" at the Falklands. The "Kent" is an old vessel. She was launched thirteen years ago and has been running ever since. The "Kent" was designed to go 23½ knots. The "Kent" had to catch a ship which went considerably over 24½ knots. They put a pressure and a strain on the engines much greater than is allowed in time of peace, and they drove the "Kent" 25 knots and caught the "Nürnberg" and sank her.

It is my duty in this House to speak for the Navy, and the truth is that it is sound as a bell all through. I do not care where or how it may be tested; it will be found good and fit and keen and honest. It will be found to be the product of good management and organisation, of sound principle in design and strategy, of sterling workmen and faithful workmanship, and careful clerks and accountants, and skilful engineers, and painstaking officers, and hardy tars. The great merit of Admiral Sir David Beatty's action is that it shows us and the world that there is at present no reason to assume that, ship for ship, gun for gun, and man for man, we cannot give a very good account of ourselves. It shows that at five to four in representative ships—because the quality of the ships on either side is a very fair representation of the relative qualities of the lines of battle—the Germans did not think it prudent to engage, that they accepted without doubt or hesitation their inferiority, that they thought only of flight just as our men thought only of pursuit, that they were wise in the view they took, and that if they had taken any other view they would, unquestionably, have been destroyed. That is the cruel fact, which no falsehood—and many have been issued—no endeavour to sink by official communiqués vessels they could not stay to sink in war, can obscure.

When, if ever, the great Fleets draw out for general battle we shall hope to bring into the line a preponderance, not only in quality, but in numbers, which will not be five to four, but will be something considerably greater than that. Therefore, we may consider this extra margin as an additional insurance against unexpected losses by mine and submarine, such as may at any moment occur in the preliminaries of a great sea battle. It is for these important reasons of test and trial that we must regard this action of the Dogger Bank as an important and, I think I may say, satisfactory event. The losses of the Navy, although small compared with the sacrifices of the Army, have been heavy. We have lost, mainly by submarine, the lives of about 5,500 officers and men, and we have killed, mainly by gun fire, an equal number, which is, of course, a much larger proportion of the German forces engaged. We have also taken, in sea fighting, 82 officers and 934 men prisoners of war. No British naval prisoners of war have been taken in fighting at sea by the Germans. When they had the inclination they had not the opportunity, and when they had the opportunity they had not the inclination. For the loss of these precious British lives we have lived through six months of this War safely and even prosperously. We have established for the time being a command of the sea such as we had never expected, such as we had never known, and our ancestors had never known, at any other period of our history. There are those who, shutting their eyes to all that has been gained, look only at that which has been lost, and seek–they are not a very numerous class–to dwell unduly upon it. . . .

Losses have to be incurred in war, and mistakes will certainly be made from time to time. Our Navy keeps the sea; our ships are in constant movement; valuable ships run risks every day. The enemy is continually endeavouring to strike, and from time to time accidents are inevitable. How do you suppose the battle-cruiser squadron of Sir David Beatty was where it was when the action of 24th January took place? How many times is it supposed that the squadrons of the Grand Fleet, the cruiser and battle squadrons, have been patrolling and steaming through the North Sea, always exposed to risk by mine and torpedo, before at last they reaped their reward? If any mood or tendency of public opinion arises, or is fostered by the newspapers, or given countenance in this House, which too much of our losses, even if they are cruel losses, and even if it may be said that they are in some respects avoidable losses, then I say you will have started on a path which, pressed to its logical conclusion would leave our Navy cowering in its harbours, instead of ruling the seas. When I think of the great scale of our operations, the enormous target we expose, the number of ships whose movements have to be arranged for, the novel conditions to which I have referred, it is marvellous how few have been our losses, and how great the care and vigilance exercised by the admirals afloat and by the Admiralty Staff, and it appears to me, and it will certainly be regarded by those who study this War in history, as praiseworthy in the highest degree.

The tasks which lie before us are anxious and grave. We are, it now appears, to be the object of a kind of warfare which has never before been practised by a civilised State. The scuttling and sinking at sight, without search or parley, of merchant ships by submarine agency is a wholly novel and unprecedented departure. It is a state of things which no one had ever contemplated, and which would have been universally reprobated, and repudiated, before this War. But it must not be supposed because the attack is extraordinary that a good defence and a good reply cannot be made. The statutes of ancient Rome contained no provision for the punishment of parricide, but when the first offender appeared it was found that satisfactory arrangements could be made to deal with him. Losses no doubt will be incurred–of that I give full warning–

but we believe that no vital injury can be done. If our traders put to sea regularly and act in the spirit of the gallant captain of the merchant ship "Laertes," whose well merited honour has been made public this morning, and if they take the precautions which are proper and legitimate, we expect that the losses will be confined within manageable limits, even at the outset, when the enemy must be expected to make his greatest effort to produce an impression.

All losses can of course be covered by resort on the part of shipowners to the Government insurance scheme, the rates of which are now one-fifth of what they were at the outbreak of War. On the other hand, the reply which we shall make will not perhaps be wholly ineffective. Germany cannot be allowed to adopt a system of open piracy and murder, or what has always hitherto been called open piracy and murder, on the high seas, while remaining herself protected by the bulwark of international instruments which she has utterly repudiated and defied, and which we, much to our detriment, have respected. There are good reasons for believing that the economic pressure which the Navy exerts is beginning to be felt in Germany. We have to some extent restricted their imports of useful commodities like copper, petrol, rubber, nickel, manganese, antimony, which are needed for the efficient production of war materials, and for carrying on modern war on a great scale. The tone of the German Chancellor's recent remarks, and the evidences of hatred and anger against this country which are so apparent in the German Press, encourage us to believe that this restriction is proving inconvenient. We shall, of course, redouble our efforts to make it so. So far, however, we have not attempted to stop imports of food. We have not prevented neutral ships from trading direct with German ports. We have allowed German exports in neutral ships to pass unchallenged. The time has come when the enjoyment of these immunities by a State which has, as a matter of deliberate policy, placed herself outside all international obligations, must be reconsidered. A further declaration on the part of the allied Governments will promptly be made which will have the effect for the first time of applying the full force of naval pressure to the enemy.

I thank the House for the attention with which they have listened to me. The stresses and strains of this War are not imperceptible to those who are called on to bear a part in the responsibility for the direction of the tremendous and terrible events which are now taking place. They have a right to the generous and indulgent judgment and support of their fellow countrymen, and to the goodwill of the House of Commons. We cannot tell what lies before us, or how soon or in what way the next great developments of the struggle will declare themselves, or what the state of Europe and the world will be at its close. But this, I think, we can already say, as far as the British Navy is concerned, that although no doubt new dangers and perplexities will come upon us continuously, and anxiety will make its abode in our brain, yet the dangers and anxieties which now are advancing upon us will not be more serious or more embarrassing than those through which we have already successfully made our way. For during the months that are to come the British Navy and the sea power which it exerts will increasingly dominate the general situation, will be the main and unfailing reserve of the allied nations, will progressively paralyse the fighting energies of our antagonists, and will, if need be, even in default of all other favourable forces, ultimately by itself decide the issue of the War.

THE WAR

June 5, 1915

Dundee

The naval assault on the Dardanelles reached its climax on March 18, when the British suffered a severe reverse. The two senior officers at the Dardanelles, Adm. John de Robeck and Gen. Sir Ian Hamilton, decided that a joint operation was essential. Churchill's desire to press forward with the naval attack was not endorsed by his advisors, whose uneasiness had been increasing rapidly over the previous weeks.

On April 25, the British landed on the Gallipoli Peninsula; they met heavy resistance and were clinging precariously to two small bridgeheads.

Lord Fisher's attitude on the Dardanelles venture was ambivalent at the outset; by the beginning of May it hardened into opposition. The turbulence of his relationship with Churchill was now public knowledge. The Opposition was well informed of the movement within the Admiralty, and a concerted drive to remove Churchill developed. The battleship Queen Elizabeth *was withdrawn from the Dardanelles, and the Navy experienced serious losses. Meanwhile, the troops were also suffering severe difficulty against strong Turkish resistance, and it soon became apparent that reinforcements were necessary. The Gallipoli Campaign thus developed into a major war operation.*

The movement against Churchill had many causes, and his break with Fisher was not wholly the result of their disagreement and misunderstandings over the Dardanelles. Rather, a combination of factors was making Churchill's position at the Admiralty increasingly precarious.

The Ministerial Crisis of May 1915 is a highly complex episode in British political history. The immediate cause was Lord Fisher's resignation on May 14, but other elements–notably a sensational attack in the Times *the previous day, alleging a severe shell shortage in France–played their part. A reconstruction of the Government was inevitable, and after days of complex negotiations the first Coalition Government of the war was formed. Churchill's removal from the Admiralty was a* sine qua non *for the Opposition. He struggled desperately to remain, but the pressures upon Asquith–and not only from the Opposition–were too great. He became Chancellor of the Duchy of Lancaster, with a seat in the Cabinet. It was a shattering demotion. "At a moment when every fibre of my being was inflamed to action" he subsequently wrote, "I was forced to remain a spectator of the tragedy." During this period he was not able to defend his position publicly but did so on June 5 in his constituency.*

I thought it right to take an opportunity of coming here to my constituency in view of all the events which have recently taken place, and also of the fact that considerably more than a year has passed since I have had the opportunity of speaking in Dundee. I have not come here to trouble you with personal matters, or to embark on explanations or to indulge in reproaches or recriminations. In war time a man must do his duty as he sees it, and take his luck as it comes or goes. I will not say a word here or in Parliament which I cannot truly feel will have a useful bearing upon the only thing that matters, upon the only thing I care about, and the only thing I want you to think about–namely, the waging of victorious war upon the enemy. (Cheers)

I was sent to the Admiralty in 1911, after the Agadir crisis had nearly brought us into war, and I was sent with the express duty laid upon me by the Prime Minister to put the Fleet in a state of instant and constant readiness for war in case we were attacked by Germany. (Cheers.) Since then, for nearly four years, I have borne the heavy burden of being, according to the time-honoured language of my patent, "responsible to Crown and Parliament for all the business of the Admiralty," and when I say responsible, I have been responsible in the real sense, that I have had the blame for everything that has gone wrong. (Laughter and cheers.) These years have comprised the most important period in our naval history–a period of preparation for war, a period of vigilance and mobilization, and a period of actual war under conditions of which no man has any experience. I have done my best, (cheers), and the archives of the Admiralty will show in the utmost detail the part I have played in all the great transactions that have taken place. It is to them I look for my defense.

I look also to the general naval situation. The terrible dangers of the beginning of the war are over. The seas have been swept clear: the submarine menace has been fixed within definite limits; the personal ascendency of our men, the superior quality of our ships on the high seas, has been established beyond doubt or question. (Cheers.) Our strength has greatly increased, actually and relatively from what it was in the beginning of the war, and it grows continually every day by leaps and bounds in all the classes of vessels needed for the special purpose of the war. Between now and the end of the year, the British Navy will receive reinforcements which would be incredible if they were not actual facts. Everything is in perfect order. Nearly everything has been foreseen, all our supplies, stores, ammunition, and appliances of every kind, our supplies and drafts of officers and men–all are there. Nowhere will you be hindered. You have taken the measure of your foe, you have only to go forward with confidence. (Cheers.) On the whole surface of the seas of the world no hostile flag is flown. (Loud cheers.)

In that achievement I shall always be proud to have had a share. My charge now passes to another hand, and it is my duty to do everything in my power to give to my successor loyal support in act, in word, and in thought. (Cheers.) I am very glad indeed that Mr. Balfour (cheers) has been able to undertake this great task. (Cheers.) The operations which are now proceeding at the Dardanelles will give him the opportunity of using that quality of cool, calm courage and inflexibility which 15 years ago prevented Ladysmith from being left to its fate and surrendered to the enemy.

I have two things to say to you about the Dardanelles. First, you must expect losses both by land and sea; but the Fleet you are employing there is your surplus Fleet, after all other needs have been provided for. Had it not been used in this great enterprise, it would have been lying idle in your southern ports. A large number of the old vessels of which it is composed have to be laid up, in any case, before the end of the year, because their crews are wanted for the enormous reinforcements of new ships which the industry of your workshops is hurrying into the water. Losses of ships, therefore, as long as the precious lives of the officers and men are saved, as in nearly every case they have been—losses of that kind, I say, may easily be exaggerated in the minds both of friend and foe.

And military operations will also be costly, but those who suppose that Lord Kitchener (loud cheers) has embarked upon them without narrowly and carefully considering their requirements in relation to all other needs and in relation to the paramount need of our Army in France and Flanders—such people are mistaken and, not only mistaken, they are presumptuous.

My second point is this—in looking at your losses squarely and soberly, you must not forget, at the same time, the prize for which you are contending. The Army of Sir Ian Hamilton, the Fleet of Admiral de Robeck, are separated only by a few miles from a victory such as this war has not yet seen. When I speak of victory, I am not referring to those victories which crowd the daily placards of any newspapers. I am speaking of victory in the sense of a brilliant and formidable fact, shaping the destinies of nations and shortening the duration of the war. Beyond those few miles of ridge and scrub on which our soldiers, our French comrades, our gallant Australians, and our New Zealand fellow-subjects are now battling, lie the downfall of a hostile empire, the destruction of an enemy's fleet and army, the fall of a world-famous capital, and probably the accession of powerful Allies. The struggle will be heavy, the risks numerous, the losses cruel; but victory when it comes will make amends for all. There never was a great subsidiary operation of war in which a more complete harmony of strategic, political, and economic advantages has combined, or which stood in truer relation to the main decision which is in the central theatre. Through the narrows of the Dardanelles and across the ridges of the Gallipoli Peninsula lie some of the shortest paths to a triumphant peace. That is all I say upon that subject this afternoon; but later on, perhaps, when the concluding chapters in this famous story have been written, I may be allowed to return again to the subject.

I am not with the croakers. (Cheers.) I see some of our newspaper friends are reproaching themselves and reproaching others for having been too optimistic. Let them lay their consciences to rest. It is the general duty of the Press, for the most part faithfully discharged, to sustain the public confidence and spirit in time of war. All the great commanders of the past, the rulers of States in time of crises, have always laboured to discourage pessimism by every means in their power. (Cheers.) Our Allies the French have a recent saying that pessimism in the civilian is the counterpart of cowardice in the soldier. That does not mean you must not face facts. You should face facts, but surely from the facts of our situation you will find the means of deriving much encouragement. Why, when we look back and remember that we entered this conflict of military nations, of great States prepared mainly for war, that we entered this conflict ten months ago a powerful civilian nation, that no part of our national life, excepting always the Navy (cheers)—the British Navy was as ready as the German Army (loud cheers) and has proved itself more equal to its task (cheers)—but when we remember that no part of our national life, except the Navy, was adapted to war on a great scale, have we not in all that has happened since much to be proud of and much to be thankful for? (Cheers.) Is it not wonderful, for instance, that after so many years of peace we should have found ready to hand a Kitchener to recruit and organize our armies (cheers), a dauntless leader like Sir John French to command them (cheers), skilful generals like Sir Douglas Haig, Sir Ian Hamilton, a naval Commander-in-Chief like Sir John Jellicoe. Admirals like Beatty and Sturdee and De Robeck, and the gallant commodore who flies his broad pennant in the saucy Arethusa? And depend upon it behind them there are many more only waiting for the golden gleam of opportunity to perform surprising deeds of men in our cause. It is the duty of all in times like these to give loyalty and confidence to their leaders, be they the soldiers in the active sphere or the statesmen who sit in anxious council here at home, to give them loyalty and confidence, not only when all goes smoothly, for that is easy, but to make them feel that they will not be blamed for necessary losses incurred in valiant enterprise or rounded on in reproach at the first check or twist of fortune. Then you will get from your leaders, be they military or civilian, you will get from them the courage, the energy, the audacity, and readiness to run all risks and shoulder the responsibilities without which no great result in war can ever be achieved. (Cheers.)

Now I would like to say something which will get me into trouble. (Laughter.) I do not think that the newspapers ought to be allowed to attack the responsible leaders of the nation (loud cheers), whether in the field or at home, or to write in a manner which is calculated to spread doubts and want of confidence in them or in particular operations, or to write anything which is calculated to make bad blood between them. I apply this not only to the Admirals and Generals, but to the principal Ministers at home, and especially the heads of the great fighting departments. No other nation now at war would allow the newspapers such a license in the present time, and if there is to be criticism, if there must be criticism, first, it should be only the loyal criticism of earnest intention. But if there is to be criticism, let it be in Parliament. If the speeches are such that we cannot allow the enemy to be a party to our discussions, then let Parliament, as is its right, sit for the time being with closed doors. But it seems imperative, in the interests of the country for the future, and for the safety and success of our arms, that irresponsible or malicious carping should not continue.

We in this country are the firm supporters of a free Press. A free Press is a natural and healthy feature in national life, so long as you have also a free Parliament and a free platform; but when, owing to war conditions, Parliament observes a voluntary but severe restraint, and when many of the subjects cannot be freely discussed without giving information to the enemy, then the balance of society is no longer true and grave injury results from the unrestricted action of the newspapers.

I have very much regretted that the Liberal Government which is now no more had no opportunity of stating its case in Parliament. It would, I think, have been found that Lord Kitchener had a very strong case to unfold on behalf of the War Office, and even I might have had something to say on behalf of the Admiralty; but the Government has perished, its long career, so memorable in our home affairs, is ended, its work whether in South Africa or Ireland has passed for good or for ill into history. I know that there are gathered here this afternoon many of those who were its opponents, and that we are going to work together on a different basis now; but before I come to the new Government and its prospects, I must ask your leave and your courtesy to say a few words in justice to the old. (Cheers.) There was a

Government which sought peace long and faithfully and to the end, but which, nevertheless, maintained our naval defence so that all the needs and dangers were provided against; there was a Government who placed in the field six times as many divisions of soldiers as had ever been contemplated by any party in the State at any time in our history; there was a Government which fulfilled in your name, in the name of the nation, every obligation of duty and of honour to France and to Belgium (cheers); there was a Government which brought us into the war a united people and with such a record that in future times, when the wounded world looks back with its searching scrutiny upon all the events which have led up to this great catastrophe–will leave us such a record as will show to all time that Britain was absolutely guiltless of the slightest stain. (Cheers.) I thought you would permit me to say these few words about the Liberal Administration of which I have had the honour to remain for so many years a member, and that I might say them in justice to those who compose it and to the Chief who led it, and to the great party which so faithfully sustained it.

And before I leave it I would ask your leave to say a word about a great friend of mine, well-known to you in Scotland and passed now out of public life–Lord Haldane. (Cheers.) I deeply regret that he has ceased to fill the great office which he adorned. No more sincere patriot has served the Crown. There never has been an occasion in the Cabinets of the last seven years in which I have sat, that, as the need arose, Lord Haldane has not from his great knowledge of the German governmental system, warned us to be on our guard against the dangerous side of their nature. (Cheers.) There never has been a time when he has not supported every provision for the defence of this country, military or naval. He it was who entered into those intricate arrangements with France which enabled our Army to be so swiftly brought to the scene of action, just in the nick of time. He it was who prepared that Expeditionary Army in the face of much opposition and in days when every penny was hard to get. He it was who organized the Territorial Force (cheers), which has so-splendidly vindicated itself and its founder, and upon whose gallantry, discipline, and numbers the weight and even the success of our military operations hitherto have notably if not mainly depended. (Cheers.) Till a few months ago all the land forces which we employed in this war, which we put in the field, were the products of Lord Haldane's organization, and in the fateful and convulsive days before Great Britain drew the sword of honour, when the chill of doubt struck into many hearts, whether we should act as we were bound–in those days no man stood closer to Sir Edward Grey and no man saw more clearly where our duty led us. (Cheers.)

With that I leave the past. A new Government has been formed, old opponents have laid aside their differences, personal interests and party interests have been adjusted or suppressed, and the Administration may now claim to represent the political energies and abilities and to command the loyalties of a united nation. (Cheers.) To support that Government, to make it a success, to make it an efficient instrument for waging war, to be loyal to it, to treat it fairly, and judge it with consideration and respect is not a matter of likes and dislikes, not a matter of ordinary political choice or option. It is for all of us a matter of self-preservation. (Cheers.) For nearly three weeks the country has had its attention diverted from the war by the business of Cabinet making and the dividing of offices and honours, and all those commonplace but necessary details of our political system which are so entertaining in time of peace. (Laughter.)

Now that is all over. It has taken long enough, but it is over, and I ask myself this question–What does the nation expect of the new National Government? I can answer my question. I am going to answer it in one word–action. (Loud cheers.) That is the need, that is the only justification, that there should be a stronger national sentiment, a more powerful driving force, a greater measure of consent in the people, a greater element of leadership and design in the rulers–that is what all parties expect and require in return for the many sacrifices which all parties have after due consideration made from their particular interests and ideals. Action–action, not hesitation; action, not words; action, not agitation. The nation waits its orders. The duty lies upon the Government to declare what should be done, to propose it to Parliament, and to stand or fall by the result. That is the message which you wish me to take back to London–Act; act now; act with faith and courage. Trust the people. They have never failed you yet.

Long speeches are not suited to the times in which we live, and, therefore, I shall detain you only a very few minutes more. As to the rights of the State in the hour of supreme need over all its subjects there can be no dispute. They are absolute. Nothing matters but that the nation lives and preserves that freedom without which life would be odious. The only question which arises is as to the degree to which it is necessary to exercise these indisputable rights. Now, I say frankly to you that if it were not possible to win this war without taking men by compulsion and sending them into the field, I should support such a measure; but I do not believe that it will be found necessary (cheers), and I am sure it is not necessary now. On the contrary, such is the character of our people that the only places which will never lack volunteers are the bloody trenches of France and Flanders. (Cheers.)

No nation has never at any time in history found such a spirit of daring and sacrifice widespread, almost universal, in the masses of its people. The French Revolution could not defend the soil of France without compulsion. The American Commonwealth could not maintain the integrity of its State without compulsion, but modern Britain has found millions of citizens who all of their own free will have eagerly or soberly resolved to fight and die for the principles at stake and to fight and die in the hardest, the cruellest, and the least rewarded of all the wars that men have fought. Why, that is one of the most wonderful and inspiring facts in the whole history of this wonderful island, and in afterdays, depend upon it, it will be taken as a splendid signal of the manhood of our race and of the soundness of our institutions. (Cheers.) And having got so far, being now on the high road to three millions of men in the service of the Crown as Volunteers–having gone so far, to cast away this great moral advantage which adds to the honour of our Armies and to the dignity of our State, simply for the purpose of hustling into the firing line a comparatively small proportion of persons, themselves not, perhaps, the best suited to the job, who, even when taken, could not be for many months equipped to do that after all that happened would, it seems to me, be unwise in the extreme. (Cheers.)

But service at home, service for home defence and to keep our fighting men abroad properly supplied and maintained, that seems to me to stand on a different footing. Remember, we are confronted with a foe who would without the slightest scruple extirpate us, man, woman, and child, by any method open to him if he had the opportunity. We are fighting a foe who would not hesitate one moment to obliterate every single soul in this great country this afternoon if it could be done by pressing a button. We are fighting a foe who would think as little of that as a gardener would think of smoking out a wasps' nest. Let us recognize that this is a new fact in the history of the world–(cheers)–or, rather, it is an old fact, sprung up out of the horrible abysses of the past. We are fighting with a foe of that kind, and we are locked in mortal struggle. To fail is to be enslaved, or, at the very best, to be destroyed. Not to win decisively is to have all this misery over again after an uneasy truce, and to fight it over again, probably under less favourable circumstances and, perhaps, alone. Why, after what has happened, there could never be peace in Europe until the German military system has been so shattered and torn and trampled that it is unable to resist by any means the will and decision of the conquering Power. (Loud cheers.) For this purpose our whole nation must be organized–(cheers)–must be socialized, if you like the word, must be organized and mobilized, and I think there must be asserted in some form or other–I do not attempt to prejudge that–but I think there must be asserted in some form or other by the Government, a reserve power to give the necessary control and organizing authority and to make sure that every one of every rank and condition, men and women as well, do, in their own way, their fair share. (Cheers.) Democratic principles enjoin it, social justice requires, national safety demands it, and I shall take back to London, with your authority, the message "Let the Government act according to its faith." (Cheers.)

Above all, let us be of good cheer. (Cheers, and a voice, "Shame the devil and to hell with the Huns.") Let us be of good cheer. I have told you how the Navy's business has been discharged. You see for yourselves how your economic life and energy have been maintained without the slightest check, so that it is certain you can realize the full strength of this vast community. The valour of our soldiers has won general respect in all the Armies of Europe. (Cheers.) The word of Britain is now taken as the symbol and the hall mark of international good faith. The loyalty of our Dominions and Colonies vindicates our civilization, and the hate of our enemies proves the effectiveness of our warfare. (Cheers.) Yet I would advise you from time to time, when you are anxious or depressed, to dwell a little on the colour and light of the terrible war pictures now presented to the eye. See Australia and New Zealand smiting down in the last and finest crusade the combined barbarism of Prussia and of Turkey. (Cheers.) General Louis Botha holding South Africa for the King. (Cheers.) See Canada defending to the death the last few miles of shattered Belgium. Look further, and, across the smoke and carnage of the immense battlefield, look forward to the vision of a united British Empire on the calm background of a liberated Europe.

Then turn again to your task. Look forward, do not look backward. Gather afresh in heart and spirit all the energies of your being, bend anew together for a supreme effort. The times are harsh, need is dire, the agony of Europe is infinite, but the might of Britain hurled united into the conflict will be irresistible. We are the grand reserve of the Allied cause, and that grand reserve must now march forward as one man. (Loud and prolonged cheers.)

RESIGNATION

November 15, 1915

House of Commons

Throughout the summer Churchill did his utmost to arrange further reinforcements to Sir Ian Hamilton and to make the Dardanelles a major preoccupation of the War Council. At the beginning of August, Hamilton made his decisive move with new landings at Suvla Bay and an attempt to break out of the Anzac (Australian and New Zealand Army Corps) area to the south. The venture failed, with heavy losses, and the Gallipoli fronts relapsed into bitter stalemate. Voices now urged evacuation.

On October 14, the War Council (now called the Dardanelles Committee) decided to recall Sir Ian Hamilton and replace him with General Sir Charles Monro. His advised evacuation of the Suvla-Anzac positions precipitated a vehement dispute in the Cabinet. The Dardanelles Committee was replaced by a War Committee on November 11, of which Churchill was not a member. It was by now evident that the tide was running strongly in favour of evacuation from Gallipoli. Churchill resigned from the Government and announced his determination to serve with the Army in France.

Churchill gave a detailed defence of his actions at the Admiralty. It should be read with caution, and recognized as a personal defence– not as an historical record. Although Churchill was listened to with sympathy, the reference to Gallipoli as "a legitimate war gamble" was not well received. At the time it seemed that his career had been irretrievably ruined.

[Extract] My letter to the Prime Minister gives fully and truthfully the reasons which led me to ask for release from His Majesty's Government, and I do not need to add anything, so far as I am concerned, to it this afternoon. But I think it important to point out that those reasons do not apply to any other Member of the Cabinet. No other Minister who does not hold a laborious office, and is not on the War Council, has been so closely connected as I have been with the conduct of the War for its first ten months. In the second place, I alone have open to me an alternative form of service to which no exception can be taken, and with which I am perfectly content. Neither does the fact that I do not take my place on the Front Opposition Bench imply any criticism of those who do. In particular I earnestly hope that the right hon. Member for Dublin University (Sir E. Carson) will find it possible to be constantly in attendance in the House.

It is a high public interest that someone with complete secret information of the whole position as it is to-day, someone unimpeachably devoted to the public cause and altogether independent of the Government, should be available. That bench is the right hon. Gentleman's war station, and I hope that he will continue to occupy it for the good of the House, for the good of the country, and for the good of the Government. I had great doubts as to whether I should trouble the House at all this afternoon, but I feel that I ought not to leave this country without dealing to some extent, so far as the public interests permit, with certain episodes and incidents in the Admiralty war direction which occurred during my tenure of office. These have been the subject of much comment in the country, and I have lain under serious reproach in regard to them. These incidents are, first, the destruction of Admiral von Spee's squadron in the series of operations which included the actions at Coronel and the Falkland Islands; second, the loss of the three "Bacchante" cruisers; third, the attempt to relieve Antwerp; and fourth, the initiation of the naval attack at the Dardanelles.

With the first two points I can deal very shortly. It is for the First Lord of the Admiralty to decide when the story of Coronel and the Falklands can be told. I see no reason why it should not be told now. More than a year has passed. The seas have been swept clear of the enemy's flag. For more than six months the entire naval situation has altered, and I cannot conceive of any military or naval reason which should prevent the story being told. If it were thought undesirable to lay a Paper containing paraphrases of the authentic telegrams, I would suggest to my right hon. Friend that a full account should be prepared from the authentic documents by some good naval writer–Julian Corbett or someone like that–with Admiralty authority, in which it would be shown that the political head of the Admiralty was in full agreement with his expert advisers, at that time Prince Louis of Battenberg and Admiral Sturdee. It would be shown that the Admiralty's dispositions were sound, probably the best that could have been made in all the circumstances, and I think that this can be proved without detracting from the gallant devotion of Admiral Craddock. It would also tell a fine story of blue-water operations, of which, owing to our preparedness and our strength, we have only had too few in the case of the present War. All my directions and comments had been made in writing. All my business at the Admiralty was conducted in writing, and my right hon. Friend has my full authority to quote or publish any minute of mine on this subject which may be considered relevant or of interest. More than that I cannot say. It would be impossible to give an idea of that operation without maps, charts, and an intrusion on the time of the House which I certainly cannot think of making, and I will leave the matter entirely in the hands of my right hon. Friend. . . .

I now come to the Dardanelles. What am I going to prove or try to prove about the Dardanelles? I am not going to prove that we forced the Dardanelles. No amount of argument, however excellent, will do that. Nor am I going to try to prove that the plan we adopted was the best plan that could have been adopted. No amount of argument will do that. Nor, least of all, am I going to try to prove that my responsibility in the matter is not a great one. I am concerned to make it clear to the House, and not only to the House but to the Navy, that this enterprise was profoundly, maturely, and elaborately considered, that there was a great volume of expert opinion behind it, that it was framed entirely by expert and technical minds, and that in no circumstances could it be regarded as having been undertaken with carelessness or levity. That, I am concerned to prove. It is important to me to do so, and it is also important in the general interest. . . .

The House is fully acquainted with what followed [on March 18]. I should like to point out that the total British casualties in this formidable adventure scarcely exceeded

100. The French, it is true, had the misfortune to be unable to save the crew of the "Bouvet," who perished. We lost two old vessels, of a class of which we had about thirty, and which, if they had not been employed at the Dardanelles, would have been rusting uselessly in our southern ports. Therefore I do not think in making this attack–on which so much depended, and the results of which, if successful, would have been so far-reaching–we risked or lost any vital stake. Meanwhile, time was passing. The Army, which earlier in the year we had been told would not be available, was gradually assembling, and Sir Ian Hamilton had arrived with the leading Divisions of his Force. The Admiral, on coming out of the attack on the 18th, determined to renew it at the first opportunity, and telegraphed accordingly. After, however, consultation with the General, it was decided to substitute, for the purely naval operation, a joint naval and military attack. I regretted this at the time, and I endeavoured to persuade the First Sea Lord to send a telegram ordering a resumption of the naval attack. But we could not reach an agreement, and, in view of the consensus of opinion of the naval and military authorities on the spot, I submitted to the alternative, but I submitted with great anxiety.

Every day the danger of the German submarines arriving–a danger which we greatly exaggerated in our minds–seemed to become more imminent. Every day the possibility of a renewed German attack on Serbia–I think already it has almost succeeded–seemed to draw nearer. Every day I knew the Turks were digging. I knew they were drawing reinforcements from all parts of the Empire; and I can assure the House that the month which apparently had to be consumed between the cessation of the naval attack on 18th March and the commencement of the military attack on 20th April was one of the least pleasant I ever experienced. I have gone through this story in detail in order to show and to convince the House that the naval attack on the Dardanelles was a naval plan, made by naval authorities on the spot, approved by naval experts in the Admiralty, assented to by the First Sea Lord, and executed on the spot by Admirals who at every stage believed in the operations. I am bound–not only in justice to myself, but in justice to the Fleet, who require to know that the orders sent to them from the Admiralty are those which always carry the highest responsible professional authority–I am bound to make that clear. I will not have it said that this was a civilian plan, foisted by a political amateur upon reluctant officers and experts.

I am not going to embark upon any reproaches this afternoon, but I must say I did not receive from the First Sea Lord either the clear guidance before the event or the firm support after which I was entitled to expect. If he did not approve the operation, he should have spoken out in the War Council. War is a hard and brutal job, and there is no place in it for misgivings or reserves. Nobody ever launched an attack without having misgivings beforehand. You ought to have misgivings before; but when the moment of action is come, the hour of misgivings is passed. It is often not possible to go backward from a course which has been adopted in war. A man must answer "Aye" or "No" to the great questions which are put, and by that decision he must be bound. If the First Sea Lord had not approved the operations, if he believed they were unlikely to take the course that was expected of them, if he thought they would lead to undue losses, it was his duty to refuse consent. No one could have prevailed against such a refusal. The opeations would never have been begun. That was the time for resignation. He did not take that course. He hoped, as I did, as the French Admiralty did, as the War Council did, that a speedy success would result. Had it resulted, I think he would have had some of the credit.

On the other hand, I wish to say that I do not at all regret having insisted on Lord Fisher's return, in the face of great opposition, to the Admiralty in November, 1914. No man has ever been able to put war purpose into the design of a ship like Lord Fisher. At the beginning of this War megalomania was the only form of sanity. Prince Louis and I had ordered large war programmes on the outbreak of war, and, perhaps, from some points of view, they may have been considered sufficient for the moment. But Lord Fisher came along with a new wave of impulse and enthusiasm. He was able to produce vast schemes of ship construction of every kind, with new designs and improvements on old designs. Hardly a day passed without his bringing new projects to me which I was delighted to encourage, and which, without Treasury control, I was happily able to finance, and if my right hon. Friend the First Lord of the Admiralty to-day finds himself, as he does, week by week upborne upon an ever-swelling tide of deliveries of craft of all kinds, and of the best kind suited to the purposes of this War, that is the consequence of Lord Fisher's return to the Admiralty in November, 1914. I am quite prepared to console myself with that for any difficulties which arose at a later stage.

For the naval operations, subject to what I have said, I take the fullest personal responsibility. I did not make the plan. Not a line, not a word, not a syllable that was produced by naval and expert brains of high competency, without the slightest non-expert interference, but I approved of the plan; I backed the plan; I was satisfied that in all the circumstances that were known to me–military, economic, and diplomatic–it was a plan that ought to be tried, and tried then. After weighing and sifting all the expert evidence with the personal knowledge I had of all the officers concerned, I recommended it to the Prime Minister and the War Council in the presence of my principal naval advisers, believing, as did everyone there, that I carried them with me, and I pressed it with all the resources at my disposal. I recommended it to the War Council, and to the French Government, not as a certainty, but as a legitimate war gamble, with stakes that we could afford to lose for a prize of inestimable value–a prize which, in the opinion of the highest experts there was a fair reasonable chance of our winning, a prize which at that time could be won by no other means. On that basis clearly understood it was accepted by all concerned.

On that basis I accept the fullest responsibility. I require no shield. I do not desire to reduce or to divide my burden in the slightest degree. For the military operations at the time they were embarked upon, for the methods by which they were executed, for the numbers of troops estimated to be necessary, for their quality and for their commanders I take no responsibility, except by what is implied by my having remained a member of the Government. That general Ministerial responsibility, of course, I accept; but I accept it only subject to my written and recorded opinions, expressed in every case before, and not after the event. Luckily there is no dispute about this. In the early days of March, when it became clear that military operations might be required, and that military support would be forthcoming, I sought, in view of my experience at Antwerp, an interview with the Prime Minister, at which I asked

Lord Kitchener directly whether it was understood that he assumed the responsibility for the military operations, by which I meant, and said I meant, the measuring of the forces required to achieve success; and, after he had replied in the affirmative, I transferred the Naval Division on the 12th March to military command. My right hon. Friend the Prime Minister told me the other day that he recollected this interview vividly, and, therefore, it is not necessary for me at this time to enter upon an analysis of the military movements. I am glad that is so.

But I must examine this question. Did the fact that the naval operations had been begun necessarily and inevitably compel the beginning of, and persistence in, the military operations? I have shown how, at the beginning of the naval attack, we kept open an alternative operation of an amphibious character on which we could at any time, if necessary, ride off. But would it have been possible, after the naval attack of 18th March had been broken off, to sail away and cut the loss? A careful survey of the facts as we know them to-day shows that undoubtedly it would. The naval attack finished on the evening of 18th March. The military attack did not begin until the 25th of April. If in that period we had known what we now know of the course of the military operations, I cannot conceive that anyone would have hesitated to face the loss of prestige in breaking off the attack on the Dardanelles. I do not consider the naval operations, begun as they were, necessarily involved the military operations begun as they were. That was a separate decision, which did not rest with me or the Admiralty either in principle or in method; but I wish to make it quite clear that I was very glad that the War Office authorities were willing to prosecute the enterprise by military means, and I certainly did my best to induce them to do so, and to support them in doing so.

There are, however, two observations which I wish to make of a general character upon the military operations. First, the essence of an attack upon the Gallipoli Peninsula was speed and vigour. We could reinforce from the sea more quickly than the Turks could reinforce by land, and we could, therefore, afford to renew our attacks until a decision was obtained. To go slow, on the other hand—to leave long intervals between the attacks, so as to enable the Turks to draw reinforcements from their whole Empire, and to refresh and replace their troops again and again—was a great danger. Secondly, on the Gallipoli Peninsula, our Army has stood all the summer within a few miles of a decisive victory. There was no other point on any of the war fronts, extending over hundreds of miles, where an equal advance would have produced an equal, or even a comparable, strategic result. It has been proved in this War that good troops, properly supported by Artillery, can make a direct advance of two or three miles in the face of any defence. The advance, for instance, which took Neuve Chapelle, or Loos, or Souchez, if it had been made on the Gallipoli Peninsula would have settled the fate of the Turkish Army on the promontory, would probably have decided the whole operations, might have determined the attitude of the Balkans, might have cut Germany from the East, and might have saved Serbia.

All through this year I have offered the same counsel to the Government—undertake no operation in the West which is more costly to us in life than to the enemy; in the East, take Constantinople; take it by ships if you can; take it by soldiers if you must; take it by whichever plan, military or naval, commends itself to your military experts, but take it, and take it soon, and take it while time remains. The situation is now entirely changed, and I am not called upon to offer any advice upon its new aspects. But it seems to me that if there were any operations in the history of the world which, having been begun, it was worth while to carry through with the utmost vigour and fury, with a consistent flow of reinforcements, and an utter disregard of life, it was the operations so daringly and brilliantly begun by Sir Ian Hamilton in the immortal landing of the 25th April.

That is all I have to say about the Dardanelles. I do not intend to be drawn into any further controversy on this subject, whatever is said by way of reply to my speech. I leave all the Papers and documentary evidence, which justifies everything I have said, with my right hon. learned and gallant Friend the Attorney-General. I do not leave them to him in his capacity as a Cabinet Minister, nor in his capacity as Attorney-General, but as an old friend, to look after my interests in the matter, and I am quite sure that his tact will be found fully equal to the task of adjusting these different obligations.

I do not propose to occupy the House by discussing such matters as the resignation of Lord Fisher, which occurred on the 14th May, or the circumstances immediately preceding the formation of the Coalition Government. This will, no doubt, afford a fine "theme for the Crokers and the Creeveys of our time." But it has no bearing on the military questions, on which I have ventured to address the House, and with which alone I am concerned. When Lord Fisher's resignation occurred, I told the Prime Minister to consider my office at his disposal if his convenience required it. On the next day, being acquainted with all the facts, he told me he wished me to continue. Sir Arthur Wilson undertook to be the First Sea Lord, and the other members of the Board remained at their posts. The next day (Monday) great political events of consequence supervened, arising principally out of matters connected with the War Office and the attitude of important Ministers, and the old Liberal Government passed away. The fact that I knew I had retained the confidence of the Prime Minister, and that his decision had been on the merits that I should remain at the Admiralty, enabled me to comply with his request to join the new Government in the office from which I have this morning retired. That, Sir, is all I have to say to the House by way of personal explanation, and I am extremely grateful to hon. Members for the patience and indulgence they have shown me. But before I sit down, if I may, with the special indulgence of the House–I have not addressed the House for a long time, and I do not expect to address hon. Members again for some time–I think it is necessary and right that I should say a word on the general situation. There is no reason to be discouraged about the progress of the War. We are passing through a bad time now, and it will probably be worse before it is better, but that it will be better, if we only endure and persevere, I have no doubt whatever. Sir, the old wars were decided by their episodes rather than by their tendencies. In this War the tendencies are far more important than the episodes. Without winning any sensational victories, we may win this War. We may win it even during a continuance of extremely disappointing and vexatious events. It is not necessary for us to win the War to push the German lines back over all the territory they have absorbed, or to pierce them. While the German lines extend far beyond their frontiers, while their flag flies over conquered capitals and subjugated provinces, while all the appearances of military successes attend their arms, Germany may be defeated more fatally in the second or third year of the War than if the Allied Armies had entered Berlin in the first.

Our well-established command of the seas, and the rapid and enormous destruction of German military manhood, are factors upon which we many confidently rely. At the outset of the War the number of males capable of bearing arms in Germany, as compared with England, was three or two; but to-day our numbers are probably superior, and at the end of the second year the original proportions will be reversed. We are becoming, therefore, a continually stronger Power, actually and relatively, as far as military manhood is concerned. We owe this fact of profound significance to the valiant sacrifices of the French and Russian peoples, who have so far borne the brunt of the struggle. We are the Reserve of the Allied cause, and the time has come when that Reserve must be thrown fully into the scale. The campaign of 1915 has been governed mainly by a shortage of munitions. The campaign of 1916 may be settled against Germany by a shortage of men. It is, therefore, vital to us, as a matter of honour and sacred duty, to increase and maintain the numbers of our Armies in the Field, and to render this possible the best economic organisation and the most unsparing thrift must be applied at home. It is no doubt disconcerting for us to observe the Government of a State like Bulgaria convinced, on an impartial survey of the chances, that victory will rest with the Central Powers. Some of these small States are hypnotised by German military pomp and precision. They see the glitter, they see the episode; but what they do not see or realise is the capacity of the ancient and mighty nations against whom Germany is warring to endure adversity, to put up with disappointment and mismanagement, to recreate and renew their strength, to toil on with boundless obstinacy through boundless suffering to the achievement of the greatest cause for which men have ever fought.

THE NAVAL WAR

March 7, 1916

House of Commons

Churchill's career now reached its nadir. His decision to serve on the Western Front–where his courage won him many new admirers–removed him from the critical political arena. He kept in touch with politics at home, but ached to return to office. Balfour's conduct of the Admiralty was regarded as lacking in vitality, and criticism of Asquith was mounting rapidly. Churchill was on leave in London in February when the movement to bring him together with Fisher again at the Admiralty gathered momentum. Churchill decided to accept the proposal and to ask for Fisher's reinstatement. The speech was perhaps the most measured indictment of the Government made up to that time, and was particularly directed against the Admiralty and Balfour. The House of Commons was impressed with the oration–until the end, when he launched his incredible proposal for the return of Fisher.

[Extract] . . . We have not only reached a period in the War when all the capital ships begun before the War can certainly be completed, but we are just entering upon a period when new capital ships begun since the War may be ready on either side. Here, again, I know of course what we have done, and that secret is jealously guarded; but we cannot tell what Germany has done. We have left the region of the known, of the declared or defined; we have left the region of naval annuals and almanacks; and we have entered the sphere of the uncertain. We have entered a sphere which is within certain limits not merely uncertain but incalculable. For this reason we cannot afford to allow any delay to creep into the execution of our programme, because we must from now on provide, not only against the known and against the declared ships, but against what will be a continually increasing element of the unknown. I must also just point out another argument which shows that, great as were the anxieties with which we were faced in the first four months of the War, they have not by any means been removed, or, indeed, sensibly diminished by the course of events. The House will remember the old argument I used to feed them with, that of the average moment and the selected moment.

On the outbreak of War we were fortunate in being able to place every single ship ready in its proper war station, so it was not our average moment at all. For a certain time that position held. Then came the need for refits, making a steady reduction from every squadron and every flotilla. But by that time new ships purchased, and others, had come in, and so the general progress was maintained. The principle of the average moment as against the selected moment still operates, because when the German fleet comes to sea, if comes it ever does, it will come with its maximum strength, and it will be faced by a cruising Fleet always at sea, which will always have a portion deducted from it. The War is full of surprises to all of us; but so far the Admiralty has kept ahead. But that has not been done—I am very anxious to couch my argument in language which will not be offensive or vexing to my right hon. Friend, whose courtesy I have always experienced, but I must say that it has not been done by easy methods. It was done by rough and harsh and even violent methods, and by a tireless daily struggle. Remember, everything else is in movement too. We see our own great expansion, but remember, everything else around us is expanding and developing at the same time. You cannot afford to indulge even for the shortest period of time in resting on your oars. You must continually drive the vast machine forward at its utmost speed. To lose momentum is not merely to stop, but to fall. We have survived, and we are recovering from a shortage of munitions for the Army. At a hideous cost in life and treasure we have regained control, and ascendency lies before us at no great distance. A shortage in naval material, if it were to occur from any cause, would give no chance of future recovery. Blood and money, however lavishly poured out, would never repair the consequences of what might be even an unconscious relaxation of effort.

I have come down here this afternoon to say these things with the deepest sense of responsibility. I say them because I am sure there is time to avoid all these dangers, because I am sure that it is not too late. If it were too late, silence would be vital. It is not; there is time; and I am anxious that the words of warning and exhortation which I am going to use, and am using, which may possibly excite resentment, but which must, nevertheless, be said, should be spoken while it is quite certain they may produce a useful effect. But I say advisedly that, though there is time, the Admiralty must not think the battle over. They must forthwith hurl themselves with renewed energy into their task, and press it forward without the loss of a day. What I have said of the great vessels applies with undiminished force to the flotillas of every description, but most especially to destroyers. . . .

If they have been allowed to fall into arrears, if their delivery has been allowed to slide back from month to month, then I say the Navy and the Grand Fleet might find themselves deprived of securities and advantages which we had prepared for them, and which we deemed it indispensable they should receive. I am very sorry I have to trouble the House after they have listened to a most comprehensive statement from the responsible Minister, but the matter is of supreme importance. It is no use saying, "We are doing our best." You have got to succeed in doing what is necessary. The right hon. Gentleman spoke about the limit of labour. There is no limit of labour where the British Navy is concerned. The vital units of the Fleet and of the flotillas which are being constructed must be a first charge on all our naval resources. There are no competing needs with paramount needs. . . .

I pass from the programmes of material for which the Board were responsible, to the possibility of novel dangers, requiring novel expedients. In a naval war particularly, you must always be asking about the enemy—what now, what next? You must always be seeking to penetrate, and your measures must always be governed and framed on the basis that he would do what you would least like him to do. My right hon. Friend (Mr. Balfour) showed that the late Board had surmounted some of the very serious and difficult dangers at the beginning of the War, but one he did not mention, the menace of the submarine attack on merchantmen was overcome by measures taken this time last year of an extraordinary scale and complexity. But although the German submarine campaign has up to date been a great failure, and although it will probably continue to be a failure—here again you cannot afford to assume that it will not present itself in new and more difficult forms, and that new exertions and new inventions will not be demanded, and you must be ready with your new devices before the enemy is ready with his, and your resourcefulness and developments must continually proceed upon a scale which exceeds the maximum you expect from him. I find it necessary to utter this word of warning, which for obvious reasons I should not proceed to elaborate.

There is another matter which I cannot avoid mentioning, though I shall do so in language of the utmost precaution. A strategic policy for the Navy, purely negative in character, by no means necessarily implies that the path of greatest prudence is being followed. I wish to place on record that the late Board would certainly not have been content with an attitude of pure passivity during the whole of the year 1916. That is all I say upon a matter of that kind. But there is one smaller matter which illustrates what I mean. We hear a great deal about air raids. A great remedy against Zeppelin raids is to destroy the Zeppelins in their sheds. I cannot understand myself why all these many months, with resources far greater than those which Lord Fisher and I ever possessed, it has not been found possible to carry on the policy of raiding which, in the early days even, carried a handful of naval pilots to Cologne, Dusseldorf, and Friedrichshafen, and even to Cuxhaven itself. But I have not spoken to-day without intending to lead up to a conclusion. I have not used words of warning without being sure first that they are spoken in time to be fruitful, and secondly, without having a definite and practical proposal to make. When in November, 1914, Prince Louis of Battenberg told me he felt it his duty to retire and lay down the charge he had executed so faithfully, I was certain that there was only one man who could succeed him. I knew personally all the high officers of the Navy, and I was sure that there was no one who possessed the power, the insight, and energy of Lord Fisher. I therefore made it plain that I would work with no other Sea Lord. In this way the oppositions, naval and otherwise, which have always, perhaps not unnaturally, obstructed Lord Fisher's faithful footsteps, were overcome. He returned to his old place, and the six months of war administration which followed will, I believe, rank as one of the remarkable periods in the history of the Royal Navy.

I did not believe it possible that our very cordial and intimate association would be ruptured, but the stress and shocks of this War are tremendous, and the situations into which men are plunged expose them to strain beyond any that this generation have had experience of. We parted on a great enterprise upon which the Government had decided and to which they were committed and in which the fortunes of a struggling and ill-supported Army were already involved; it stood between us as a barrier. I therefore should have resisted, on public grounds, the return of Lord Fisher to the Admiralty—and I have on several occasions expressed this opinion in the strongest terms to the Prime Minister and the First Lord of the Admiralty. We have now reached an entirely different situation, and I have no doubt whatever what it is my duty to say now. There was a time when I did not think that I could have brought myself to say it, but I have been away for some months, and my mind is now clear.

The times are crucial. The issues are momentous. The great War deepens and widens and expands around us. The existence of our country and of our cause depend upon the Fleet. We cannot afford to deprive ourselves or the Navy of the strongest and most vigorous forces that are available. No personal consideration must stand between the country and those who can serve her best. I feel that there is in the present Admiralty administration, for all their competence, loyalty, and zeal, a lack of driving force and mental energy which cannot be allowed to continue, which must be rectified while time remains and before evil results, and can only be rectified in one way. I am sure the nation and the Navy expect that the necessary step will be taken. I agree with my right hon. Friend here (Mr. G. Lambert) in the proposals which he made to the Navy when he last spoke, and I urge the First Lord of the Admiralty without delay to fortify himself, to vitalise and animate his Board of Admiralty by recalling Lord Fisher to his post as First Sea Lord.

MILITARY SERVICE BILL (IRELAND)

May 9, 1916

House of Commons

After his total humiliation over the March 7 speech, Churchill returned to France, principally at the urging of his wife and against the advice of those who wanted him to lead an insurrection against the Government. "But I am sure my true war station is in the H[ouse] of C[ommons]," he wrote to his wife.

On May 3 the long dispute over military conscription was resolved and all males between the ages of 18 and 41 became eligible for compulsory conscription–with the exception of those in Ireland. On May 6 Churchill formally applied to return to his Parliamentary duties, and the application was accepted.

Meanwhile, an event of major significance had occurred in Ireland. The Easter Rising of April had been crushed and its effect would have been negligible had it not been for the subsequent executions of the principal leaders by the British commander, Gen. Sir John Maxwell. The truce declared at the beginning of the uprising had now disintegrated, and Ireland was moving once again towards civil war. Churchill, obsessed by the need for more troops and unsympathetic towards the Easter Rising, spoke out against the Government's exclusion of Ireland from compulsory military conscription.

I do not suppose that much practical good may come of our Debate this afternoon. But surely this is a great problem which is before us, and it ought not to be left finally after the very inadequate discussion and examination which it has so far received in this Debate. It is a tremendous question, vital in its consequences to Ireland and of the highest possible importance to our military needs. It is a time when men are urgently needed, and from the British and Imperial point of view the desirability of obtaining fresh and extended supplies from Ireland is clear and patent to the minds of everyone. But from an Irish point of view the considerations which were put forward by my right hon. and learned Friend (Sir E. Carson) and many others which could be added from the point of view of Irish Home Rulers, the omission of Ireland altogether from this Bill must be a serious and lamentable fact which adds to the difficulties that have obstructed the settlement of that question. Do not let us be content with taking very readily "No" for an answer in these difficult matters. There is much, too much, inclination to say, "Oh! there is a difficulty, therefore we must avoid it." This is a time for trying to overcome difficulties and not for being discouraged or too readily deterred by them. I agree–I imagine everyone has got the feeling in their minds–that in spite of these serious losses to Ireland–

Mr. Ginnell: What about the Dardanelles?

Colonel Churchill: I am afraid I should be out of order if I were to deal with that matter. In spite of the serious losses to Ireland and the serious losses to Great Britain by the omission of Ireland by this Bill, I agree with the Government that it is not worth while at the present time to court a serious Irish row, with great embarrassment in the House of Commons, if such a thing were possible, and with difficulties in the Government of Ireland. But I agree fully that this is not a question of mere logic or of fairness. It cannot be settled on those lines. I repeat, in the few words I venture to address to the Committee, that we must not be content with the present position in which this question rests. The right hon. Baronet the Member for Mid-Armagh (Sir J. Lonsdale) made an appeal to the hon. and learned Member for Waterford (Mr. J. Redmond), couched in the most courteous language, and an appeal to Nationalist Ireland generally. I could not help feeling that, courteous and considerate as the hon. Baronet was, he did not show in his speech a full appreciation of the difficulties of the hon. and learned Member for Waterford, nor an appreciation of other points of view in regard to Irish affairs except those with which he has for so long been associated. Is it not clear that if the Nationalists of Ireland were to be appealed to, to come forward and to make themselves the agents and supporters of making this great, this tremendous further contribution to the Allied cause, and to the common cause, that that effort on their part could only be a part of some more general settlement, founded on the basis of mutual concessions?

After all, I am one of those who think that the hon. and learned Member for Waterford has rendered immense services to the British Empire and to our country in this time of need. The Prime Minister said that the spirit of Ireland is as keen on the War as it is in any other part of the British Empire. I am not quite sure that this is altogether a true statement of the case. There are many different problems in different parts of the British Empire in regard to this War, and the spirit is not the same in every part. There are different ways and different degrees in which help has been given, and with an Empire so variously composed as ours is, it is necessary to recognise that. But we owe a very deep debt of gratitude to the Irish party for the exertions they have made in the present struggle. It is the first of all our struggles in which Ireland has been a friend, a powerful and valiant friend, and not a foe and a source of weakness to the British Empire. I have always looked upon the position of the hon. and learned Member for Waterford, in regard to Ireland, as being very similar to that occupied by General Botha in regard to South Africa. There you have the same tri-partite division of opinion, and I should certainly feel the same sort of difficulty in pressing a question like this against the opinion of the hon. and learned Member for Waterford, as one would think, for instance, of pressing a South African question against the opinion of General Botha. I am only sorry–I agree with what fell from the hon. and learned Member–that the comparison between Ireland and South Africa cannot be carried further, and that the hon. and learned Gentleman should not have associated with him the power and responsibility necessary for an effective solution of Irish questions. I know there are great dangers in definite statements on this subject, not only dangers from the point of view of order, but of a much wider character, and I am not going to make them, but I heard with the very greatest interest, and I think the Committee was curiously attentive at that moment, the tone of some of the remarks of my right hon. and learned Friend who spoke from this bench (Sir E. Carson). The Committee appreciated the significance of those sentiments as to the association of power and responsibility. Can we doubt that the responsibility should be borne by those who have the power. That is true not of this question only, but that observation will not bear useful or practical fruit as long as it is confined to only one question in regard to the government of Ireland.

I feel very strongly that the immediate future of Ireland depends upon two men–the two leaders of Irish parties in this House. Together, there is hardly any difficulty which they cannot surmount. When we are face to face with the imminent perils and vast labours of our situation, it is the supreme duty incumbent upon them to make every effort to face those difficulties together. I know there are those who say that it is not good widening these questions and raising other matters not directly concerned in the prosecution of the War at the present time. I do not agree at all. I believe this is a time when we are much nearer the solution of other questions than is commonly supposed. I believe this is a time when metals are molten and could easily be cast into new shapes and new moulds. The tragic episodes of Dublin have at any rate shown Nationalists and Orangemen that they have opponents whom they can recognise as opponents at home in common, as well as the foes whom they have recognised since the War began as their enemies abroad. I offer these few words to the Committee because I do not want to see this question–the question of the inclusion of Ireland in a Bill of National Service–put aside, as it were, as one out of the range of practical politics, and one for which it is not worth our while to make further efforts. I earnestly hope that some of the language which was used by the hon. and the learned Member for Waterford in his speech to-day, and which, I think, was not out of harmony with the expressions used by the Member for Cork City (Mr. W. O'Brien), may be taken into further consideration, and that efforts will continue to be made on the basis of mutual concessions–mutual concessions means concessions, not merely by Nationalists, but by Unionists–to arrive at a really national policy for Ireland, which shall enable her to take that share in the prosecution of the general War which is of the utmost consequence to us, and will be found to be of permanent advantage to her.

THE ARMY

May 23, 1916

House of Commons

Churchill was by now politically isolated. He sat on the Opposition benches, facing the Liberal-Conservative Coalition, without position or influence. This speech, like several previous ones, was almost totally ignored. Yet it was strangely prophetic. Six weeks later the terrible and futile Battle of the Somme began.

[Extract] This is the first time in my Parliamentary experience that I have been called upon to follow in Debate my right hon. Friend [the Prime Minister] , and I am glad that I am not led to do so in any hostile sense. Certainly it is not my purpose to resist or oppose in any way the financial demand that he has made upon the House. The House is rightly resolute, and the country is resolute, that the Government shall have in the most convenient manner and with the least possible delay all the sums that may be required, the great sum now asked for, and any others which may subsequently become necessary, to the utmost limits of our resources. The occasions of these Votes of Credit afford to Parliament an opportunity of reviewing various aspects of the general position in the progress and conduct of the War, and we should fail in our duty if we did not take proper advantage of them as they arise. The right hon. Gentleman has not entered upon any discussion of the main situation, and from some points of view that is to be regretted because his statements on these occasions have always the advantage of concentrating the minds of the nation upon the supreme issue, too often obscured by passing episodes, and also they have on many occasions rendered encouragement to the Allied Powers with whom we are co-operating. But the right hon. Gentleman has made no reference to these matters, and I shall only make a very brief and general observation on the main strategic situation. It is this.

It is unreasonable for people to expect that the War will turn decisively and suddenly in our favour at the present time. The contending Armies are far too evenly matched at the present time for that. We believe ourselves the strongest. We know we have a certain substantial preponderance in numbers, but against this must be set the advantage which our adversaries have in their central position, the great advantage they have in the unity, the superior unity, of their war direction, now concentrated in two or three minds, and, finally, the advantage which cannot accurately be measured, though it is certainly very great, of having been able throughout the course of the conflict to retain the initiative. There is very little in it if you survey the forces on each side at the moment. We have, however, Reserves actual and potential, behind our lines far greater than those which we believe to be at the disposal of the enemy, and it is upon the use and development of those Reserves as they become available that our confidence in our final victory may justly be reposed. The great energy and even frenzy with which the Germans and Austrians are now attacking at so many points of the line is a sign and a measure of their enormous strength, but it may also be some measure of their profound anxiety. But for the present numbers of men and formations actually engaged do not show those great differences which are necessary nowadays to give decisive results on the fortune of the general war. . . .

The first thing that strikes a visitor to our Armies in France or in Flanders—and I make no doubt that our armies in the East exhibit a similar condition—is the very large number of officers and men in the prime of their military manhood who never, or only very rarely, go under the fire of the enemy. In fact, you perceive one of the clearest and grimmest class distinctions ever drawn in this world—the distinction between the trench and the non-trench population. All our soldiers, all our officers, are brave and honest men. All are doing their duty, a necessary duty, and are ready to do any other duty which they may be asked to perform. But the fact remains that the trench population lives almost continuously under the fire of the enemy. It returns again and again, after being wounded twice and sometimes three times, to the front and to the trenches, and it is continually subject, without respite, to the hardest of tests that men have ever been called upon to bear, while all the time the non-trench population scarcely suffers at all, and has good food and good wages, higher wages in a great many cases than are drawn by the men under fire every day, and their share of the decorations and rewards is so disproportionate that it has passed into a byword. I wish to point out to the House this afternoon that the part of the Army that really counts for ending the War is this killing, fighting, suffering part.

This War proceeds along its terrible path by the slaughter of Infantry. It is this Infantry which it is most difficult to replenish, which is continually worn away on both sides, and though all the other services of the Army are necessary to its life, and to its maintenance—and I am not in the least disparaging their importance and their value—it is this fighting part that is the true measure of your military power, and the only true measure. All generals in the field make their calculations in rifles, but my right hon. Friend knows well how immense is the disparity between rifle strength and rations strength. We have suffered together disappointment in hearing that Armies, so imposing on paper, so large in numbers when they left our shores, were whittled down by calculations of rifle strength by the generals on the spot to two-thirds or even a lesser fraction of their total number. Like him, I have rebelled against that calculation in the past, but, nevertheless, I have become convinced that it is really the true and proper method of computing your war effort at a given moment. Every measure which you can take to increase the proportion of rifle strength to rations strength will be a direct addition to your war power, and will be just as direct an addition to your war power as if you ordered new classes of recruits to join the Colours. Nay, more, it will be a net addition and not a gross addition to your war power. If I may use the language of business—and after all this War is becoming in many aspects to resemble a vast though hideous business—I would say that the rifle strength actually under the fire of the enemy is the dividend. Everything else of the whole vast military effort may be classed as working expenditure, the result of which is the production of war power. The object of the Army is to produce war power. Everything else that takes place leading to the lining up of men in battle is the preliminary steps by which the final result is achieved. . . .

My right hon. Friend the Prime Minister, some time ago, put the military effort of the British Empire at 5,000,000 men. That, I think, was the total military effort, and, of course, he included not only casualties but the Navy and the garrisons in India and elsewhere. But the fact remains that he did place before the House, for its contemplation, the broad figure of 5,000,000 men, representing the war effort of the country.

The simple calculation which I have laid before the House raises the impression in our minds that this general figure may not be a very representative way of estimating the war effort of the country. Where are these 5,000,000 men? Certainly they are not, and never have been, in contact with the enemy. What has been done, what is being done, with these vast numbers, equalling, certainly, the whole military effort at the present moment of Germany? . . .

Let us take another consideration. I find, again giving rough figures, that there are in the Army at the present time something like 200,000 officers. Every officer has his servant, making 200,000 servants, and probably there are 50,000 grooms in addition, bringing the number up to 250,000 servants and grooms. That is an Army in itself. These are points which are really worthy the care and attention of the House to study and to reflect upon. How many of these are in their prime of life? How many of them should be replaced with substitutes? How many should be replaced by natives? Remember that every man saved counts. It may be said that they are included in the fighting strength. They are, but they do not count in it. Then there is the question of the great mass of Cavalry, which have been kept all these months, now years, behind the lines in France and Flanders. Although the whole front, from the mountains to the sea, is wired and entrenched, this great mass of Cavalry have never struck a blow, and for at least eighteen months they have served in the trenches as Infantry. Is not that a matter which the military advisers should carefully reconsider, having regard to the enormous cost of the War and the immense strength of this force and its great value if employed in other directions? In these Cavalry regiments you have the cadres of three divisions, equal to the finest battalions that could be named, equal to the finest battalions of the Guards; you have all the Regular non-commissioned officers, warrant officers, and trained professional troops, with the full complement of officers, when officers are so scarce, with which you could fill up the regiments that now go into the trenches and add to our strength. You would be able to obtain recruits or men from other formations to add to those battalions, so that you would be able to raise a force of the highest possible quality at the very time of the process of degeneration of the Infantry strength which must ensue in both the contending armies. Although in the early stages young troops can storm the trenches, yet in the confusion which arises in the second or third stage of the fight, you want supplies of men with officers and warrant officers, and everything which is absolutely necessary, if you are to reap the result achieved by the gallantry of the first assault. I think that is a matter which ought to be carefully considered.

There is one other aspect of this question as to the use of the men at the front to which I venture to refer very guardedly. I think the question arises whether, in a war which is so very largely one of attrition, we should continue to hold indefinitely for months those posts which are of no vital consequence, where our men are at a disadvantage, and where, owing to the superior position and artillery of the enemy, the proportion of our daily loss is very much higher–sometimes calculated to be three or four times as great as that of the enemy. There is one part of the line where, it is said, the Germans have orders not to try to push our men out, in order that they may be able to reap the daily toll which has been so profitable to them. I suggest that this is a matter which requires very careful attention on the part of those here and elsewhere who are responsible; and I presume that the military authorities have been made aware by the Government that no reproach would be made against them if they chose for good reasons in any particular case to redress and readjust their lines at particular parts where our men are suffering undue loss, owing to their inferior position. All these matters are of very great consequence. The nation has given itself to the Government and to the War Office, and we are bound to follow with the utmost attention their fortunes at the front. How do the Germans find the men to keep up their forces in the field? All the military calculations and the calculation of unofficial writers, have been vitiated by the continuing force and power which the enemy supplies. That may be because the Germans have studied in this time and pressure of circumstances, with the utmost refinement, all these problems of using men where they could develop the greatest possible proportion of fighting strength to the number of men fed and employed. I was told the other day of a circumstance which sounded very extraordinary, that the Germans were now forming several battalions of men with heart disease, and at first sight your optimist will say they must be at their last gasp; but the very sinister reflection may be that if they were at their last gasp they would know how to utilise it to the full. At any rate, the use which you should make of this power of compulsion, this absolute power which has now been given, is to have every fit man in his place, so as to secure the maximum development of war power. . . .

No man should be retained who is not going to be of use. There is no need to try to swell mere numbers now for paper purposes. No man need be taken until he is required, and no man should be taken who can do more to beat the Germans by staying at home than by serving as a soldier. I have never looked on compulsion as a means to sweep a vast mass into the military net, though it is perhaps the only way in which large aggregate numbers can be obtained. I have regarded compulsion not as the gathering together of men as if they were heaps of shingle, but the fitting of them into their places like the pieces in the pattern of a mosaic. The great principle of equality of sacrifice requires in practice to be applied in accordance with the maxim, "A place for every man and every man in his place. . . .

The total military effort of 5,000,000, or 4,500,000, or 3,500,000–I do not care how much you put it–at one end, and the actual war resultant of 500,000 enemies engaged actually in contact in the field, is a fact so striking, and the disparity is so large, that the continued attention of all who think about the means of securing victory in this War should be directed to it. It is very hard for civilians to believe that so small a result of all the great numbers we dispose of is really the last word in military organisation. I am sure I am expressing a widespread and well-founded opinion, not only in this House but outside, when I say that there is a very large margin at home of men, not now allocated to general service abroad, who should and could be made available for raising the strength of the units in actual contact with the enemy. I do not think we ought to rest content with general assurances that all that is available is being done. I have not the slightest doubt that it will be stated that all these points have been carefully considered, and action has proceeded upon them. I do not think we ought to rest content with general assurances of that kind. The case of every man, the employment of every man now in uniform, should be subjected to at least as severe a scrutiny as the case of every man not yet joined.

I have now finished my survey of the resources of men—a survey which, I think, deserves the careful attention of those who are responsible. There is only one more point about the man-power to which I wish to refer before I sit down. Many of our difficulties in the West at the present time spring from the unfortunate offensive to which we committed ourselves last autumn. My right hon. Friend knows that this is no new view of mine taken after the event. Let us look back now. Only think if we had kept that tremendous effort ever accumulating for the true tactical moment. Think if we had kept that rammer compressed ready to release when the time came—if we had held in reserve the energies which were expended at Loos, Arras, and in Champagne—kept them to discharge at some moment during the protracted and ill-starred German attack on Verdun! Might we not then have recovered at a stroke the strategic initiative without which victory lags long on the road? Let us not repeat that error. Do not let us be drawn into any course of action not justified by purely military considerations. The argument which is used that "it is our turn now" has no place in military thought. Whatever is done must be done in the cold light of science. We must not be deflected by any sentimental argument from whatever is thought to be the right course on military grounds. We mean to spend all we have in this quarrel, and we have only to consider how it may be best employed. In this connection let us never forget that the development of the full war-power of Russia is necessarily slow, and that it has not yet reached its culminating point. For one man Russia had in her line at her worst period last year she has now certainly two, and possibly three. For one man she can put into the line to-day she may perhaps be able to put two into the line next year. The whole world is available for the equipment of the manhood of Russia. When you are able to gather round the frontiers of Germany and Austria armies which show a real, substantial preponderance of strength, then the advantage of their interior situation will be swamped and overweighed, and then the hour of decisive victory will be at hand. This hour is bound to come if patience is combined with energy, and if all the resources at the disposal of the Allies are remorselessly developed to their extreme capacity.

MINISTER OF MUNITIONS

July 21, 1917

Election Meeting,
Kinnaird Hall, Dundee

The contrived disputes over conscription, the inconclusive Battle of Jutland, the prolonged agony of the Battle of the Somme, all increased public dissatisfaction with the Asquith Government.

The creation of the Unionist War Committee under Carson's leadership was an ominous portent of the general dissatisfaction with the conduct of the war. On November 8, Carson led a vigourous attack on the Government over its handling of the disposal of enemy property in Nigeria. Sixty-five Conservatives and eleven Liberals voted with Carson–including Churchill.

During this period, Churchill expressed his views in the Press, particularly in the Sunday Pictorial, *more frequently than in speeches, which were seldom reported. During the complicated intrigues which resulted in Lloyd George replacing Asquith in December, Churchill played only a very minor role. His principal preoccupation was with his case to the Dardanelles Commission.*

When Lloyd George formed his Government on December 6, Churchill was not involved. The Conservatives were implacably opposed to reinstating him in office, and he was compelled to watch, with intense personal bitterness, mighty events unfolding from afar.

But, Churchill was appointed Minister of Munitions by Lloyd George on July 18, against vehement Conservative opposition. His acceptance of this post necessitated a by-election at Dundee. His only opponent was Mr. Scrymgeour, who polled 2,036 votes to Churchill's 7,302.

Churchill's prognosis of an overwhelming victory in this speech was to prove very accurate.

[Extract] . . . Before the war, when we talked together here, as we often did, about affairs in those far-off days of peace, you will remember that I often used to draw your attention to the great difference between countries where the people owned the Government and the countries where the Government owned the people. I believe that is the true and final dividing line. But never did I, and never did you or any of us, expect to see the nations of the world ranged up in deadly battle along that dividing line. Yet it has come to pass. Now that Russia has freed herself–(cheers),–there is not a single exception on either side. All the countries whose Governments owned the people, as if they were a kind of cattle, are on one side, and the countries where the people owned the Governments, which are controlled by free citizens acting through Parliamentary institutions, and based on popular election, are on the other. Is that not a tremendous fact when stated in the simplest terms?

The broad principles for which the Allies are fighting are comprehended by the humblest and simplest soldier in every Army, and they are fortified in their struggle by this comradeship of great ideas. And this is the great idea–that Governments must never again own the people in any part of the world–(loud cheers),–but that the people, on the contrary, shall everywhere dispose of their own fortunes and their own fate.

There are all sorts of people–I have great respect for them–whose minds are full of glorious schemes of what they are going to do after the war is over. All those noble and by no means visionary hopes depend on one thing–victory. (Cheers.) Without victory all will wither. If this war does not end in victory, or if it ends in what is called an inconclusive peace, which leaves Germany stronger than she was before, and quite impenitent under her autocratic rulers–if this war comes to such a conclusion, then good-bye to all your hopes of a brighter and better prospect for the world and our country at its close.

Then you will enter upon a period of unrest, suspicion, and further preparation. You will enter upon a period when the national life of every country will be torn by duality. On the one hand there will be those who will say "Never go into such a war again." On the other hand, you will have others saying "They are making ready to attack us; be prepared," and the conflict of these two perfectly natural groupings of opinion must inevitably produce faction, disturbance, alarms, disorders, vast expenditure of money, and probably ineffective preparation for security as the result.

No, without victory we have nothing before us but ruin and strife. Therefore I say to you what I have always said, in office or out of it–concentrate all your energies upon the war. Allow nothing to distract your attention from the war. Lay aside every impediment, every emotion, which weakens your power to bring the war as speedily as possible to a successful conclusion. (Cheers.) We are fighting for our lives. We are fighting to redeem the precious lives which have been given so freely in the public cause, to redeem them in the only way in which they can be redeemed–by making their sacrifice fruitful in victory, so that the words "Not in vain" may be written above the battlefield graves of our gallant dead. . . .

THE WAR SITUATION

December 10, 1917

Corn Exchange, Bedford

The year 1917 was the bleakest for the Allied cause. The collapse of the Nivelle offensive severely harmed the spirit of the French Army. The British offensive at Paschendaele became a bogged-down nightmare. Russia collapsed. Only the entry of the United States into the war provided any light in this grim situation.

[Extract] Two months ago I stated in London that the war was entering upon its sternest phase, but I must admit that the situation at this moment is more serious than it was reasonable two months ago to expect. The country is in danger. It is in danger as it has not been since the Battle of the Marne saved Paris and the Battle of Ypres and of the Yser saved the Channel ports. The cause of the Allies is now in danger. The future of the British Empire and of democracy and of civilisation hangs and will continue to hang for a considerable period in a balance and an anxious suspense.

It is impossible, even if it were desirable, to conceal these facts from our enemies. It would be folly not to face them boldly ourselves. Indeed, I am inclined to think that most people in this country, in this wonderful island, are already facing squarely and resolutely the facts of the situation. We read in the newspapers and in some speeches which are delivered of appeals to the Government to tell the truth about the war, to tell the truth about our war aims, but as a matter of fact the great bulk of the British people have got a very clear idea of how we stand and a still clearer idea of what we are aiming at. (Hear, hear.)

Anyone can see for himself what has happened in Russia. Russia has been thoroughly beaten by the Germans. Her great heart has been broken not only by German might but by German intrigue, not only by German steel but by German gold. Russia has fallen on the ground prostrate, in exhaustion and in agony. No one can tell what fearful vicissitudes will come to Russia or how or when she will arise, but arise she will. (Cheers.)

It is this melancholy event which has prolonged the war, that has robbed the French and the British and the Italian armies of the prize that was perhaps almost within their reach this summer. It is this event, and this event alone, that has exposed us to the perils and sorrows and sufferings which we have not deserved, which we cannot avoid, but under which we shall not bend. (Loud cheers.)

There never was a moment in this war when the choice presented to us was so brutally clear as it is to-night, or when there was less excuse for patriotic man to make the mistake of being misled by sophistries and dangerous counsels. Are not our war aims clear? Can we not discern what our war aims are? Do we not know in our hearts what our war aims are? Why, they are exactly what they were on that breathless night in August, 1914–(Cheers),–when we knew that the Belgian frontier had been crossed by the German armies in flat repudiation of their solemn covenant and of all law that had existed in the world: when that small weak people, who trusted to the plighted word of the German rulers, were brutally and mercilessly trampled in the mire.

The same spirit exists in us to-day, and the satisfaction of that feeling is just as vital, as just, and as necessary as it was three years ago. Our war aims are the same as they were in 1914. We have not increased them, we have not diminished them . We shall not diminish them by one jot or tittle. (Cheers.)

Our sole war aim is this, that those who have committed crimes too numerous for one to recount shall not profit by them, and shall not emerge from the struggle stronger than when they began it; that Germany shall not be able when this is over to retire and plan another hideous catastrophe to let loose upon her unsuspecting neighbours; that Prussian militarism shall go out of the conflict abased, not exalted; condemned, not fortified; stultified, not vindicated; and that the German people who have allowed themselves to become the instrument of the miseries of mankind shall realise that the rulers whom they have trusted have not, after all, led them to a comfortable place in the sun, but only through wrong-doing and infinite misfortune to vast disaster to themselves, and to shame unending in the book of history. (Cheers.)

That is our war aim; that is Mr. Asquith's–(cheers),–Mr. Lloyd George's–(cheers),–and President Wilson's meaning–(cheers)–when they say our war aims are reparation, restoration, and security. (Cheers.) More than that we do not ask; less than that we cannot take.

The rights and interests of native populations must be respected. Still I can't conceive a situation arising where this war would be prolonged for one unnecessary day solely on account of any question of territorial gain. We did not enter this war with any idea of territorial gain. We have never fought and we are not fighting for booty or revenge. The sacred call of honour alone drew the citizens of this country into the field, and when that call has been satisfied fully and unequivocably, Great Britain will be satisfied. (Cheers.) . . .

No peace, however fair-seeming, which is based upon weakness and war weariness on the part of the Allies can be honourable or lasting. There are no substitutes for victory, and no League of Nations would be worth a scrap of paper if it were based upon the triumph of Hindenburg and Tirpitz. A League of Nations at whose council board an impenitent Prussian militarism sat, would be the most hollow and dangerous of mockeries and shams that have ever deluded man. Let us concentrate upon the vital fact. We mean to win this war, however long it takes, however cruel the passage of the road may be. To make peace now would be simply to rivet for ever upon our children the temporary consequences of the Russian collapse.

The military situation is an anxious one; still I do not fear military misfortune. I am confident that there are no means by which this country can be overcome on land or sea if everyone does his and her duty.

It is not military danger which is most prominent in our minds; it is the danger that the people of this country might be tempted by some specious peace terms that would leave Germany stronger than before. I am afraid there are some people who go about saying, "Restate your war aims," when what they really mean is "Make friends with the victorious Huns." They ask, "What are we fighting for?" when they really mean "Let us leave off fighting." Be on your guard in your homes, in your streets, in your workshops, in your public places, against this deadly danger. Peace with Prussian militarism now means that we should have to put up with defeat, and defeat to-day would mean ruin to-morrow.

We hear a lot of the pacifist tendencies said to be so rife in the country. I represent myself a great democratic electorate, and a few months ago we heard of this talk being indulged in vehemently and even violently in the streets; but when the electorate came to deal with the matter they swept it away as it deserved. (Cheers.) The British people do not mean to put up with anything but the legitimate and righteous aims with which they entered upon the war, and if such an issue as this were seriously raised it could only be decided by the nation as a whole. (Cheers.) I cannot see that there would be the slighest risk or danger in submitting that question for the free decision of the nation as a whole. (Renewed cheers.)

We have a clear line marked out for us, which will certainly bring us to victory if we pursue it to the end. (Cheers.) We have all the means of continuing the war successfully. The heart of our people is sound as a bell. Our output of munitions is steadily increasing–growing every week in spite of shortened hours and in spite of our making a continual contribution of men to the military needs of the country. Why, for one day's work that is lost in the munition works of the country through strikes there are a thousand days of work done; for one day that a man is on strike there are nearly three years that men are working–that is the proportion between striking and working in the month of October throughout the great area of the munition factories of this country. (Cheers.) You hear about the strikes; the Germans hear about the rest. (Laughter and cheers.)

I have absolute confidence in the loyalty and the resolve of the people of this island. Our reserves of manhood are still large. We have not by any means reached the end of the reserves which can be made available to sustain our Armies in the field. Our Navy is grappling with the submarines. It is a dangerous and deadly struggle, but not only are we striking under the seas at this menace, but side by side with the sinking of submarines there is a large and broadening flow of newly-built ships coming into the water. Do not relax for one moment your efforts. We may to-night feel a solid assurance that if all do their best, if every scrap of food and material is saved, the submarines will not prevent us from doing all that we have to do. (Cheers.)

Our people are war hardened and not war-weary. We have all the means of doing our part in bringing about victory. (Cheers.) But there is something much greater than all this. If Russia has, for the time being, fallen out of our ranks, the United States of America have entered them. (Cheers.) The great Republic of the West, more than a hundred millions, of the most educated and scientific democracy in the world are coming to our aid, marching along all the roads of America, steering across the ocean, organizing their industries for war, spending their wealth like water, developing slowly but irresistibly and unceasingly the most gigantic, elemental forces ever yet owned and applied to the triumph of a righteous cause. The appearance of this mighty champion at the other end of the world has restored to us the fortunes of the war, and has repaired and more than repaired all that we have suffered in the loss of Russia. (Cheers.)

The intervention of America means the uniting of practically the whole world, and the whole of its resources against the German Power. It cannot fail in the end to be decisive. (Cheers.) It will secure us victory, and–if there were any danger of it–it will prevent that victory from being abused. It offers deliverance to the nations of Europe. Deliverance, sure, merciful, lasting and complete. (Cheers.) But it imposes on the British people a duty so plain, and yet so formidable, a task so glorious and yet so heavy, that we cannot undertake it without the deepest feelings of gravity and awe. For unless the British race, unless we inhabitants of this small island, can bear during the greater part of next year the main weight and burden of the war on land upon our shoulders, and unless at the same time we can keep the submarine choked down under the sea, there can be no American aid; there can be no deliverance, no victory. Is not this, I ask you, the greatest responsibility ever laid upon any nation of men? Is it not the most splendid opportunity ever offered to any nation of men? Is it not the climax to which all English history has led us, in which all the work of all our heroes and worthies of the past and present time finds its consummation?

The longer Britain and America are fighting side by side, the fiercer the struggle, the greater the effort they make together, the more closely that these two branches of the English-speaking family of the Anglo-Saxon world are drawn together, the truer will be their comradeship and the struggle will be a bond between them. That is a tremendous fact making amends for all that we are suffering now. (Cheers.) It is to this that we must look, and may rightly look, as the true reward for our exertions and sacrifices in the war, and it is to this comradeship and reconciliation of the great Anglo-Saxon world here, in the United States, in Canada, in Australia, and in New Zealand, that we may rightfully look on the mainstay of the future of the world when the war is over.

But this would be cast over irretrievably if we were to fail to do our part at this juncture. If we were to allow ourselves to be led astray by weak and cowardly counsels, owing to the discouragement of the Russian collapse, and if we were to commit the fatal crime of registering a peace based upon the temporary German advantage, we should commit the folly of casting the glowing metal of our fortunes into a narrow misshapen mould and we should hand down to our children, generation after generation, a condition of circumscribed and oppressed existence, from which it is in our power, easily at this moment to free them for ever.

To talk of peace now, to make a peace based upon military weakness and war weariness, would be to reject the proffered comradeship of the United States. It would be to cut ourselves off from the bright prospects of the future, it would be to squander the solid assets of victory which are at our disposal, it would be to repudiate all that our brave men have won for us by their intense suffering, it would be to disperse the world-wide league of nations of which we are proud to be the centre.

What is the one great practical step we take without a day's delay? We must raise the strength of our Army to its highest point. A heavier strain will be thrown upon that Army than it has ever had to bear before. We must see that it is stronger than it has ever been before. Do not put too heavy a burden on those heroic men by whose valiant efforts we exist from day to day. (Cheers.) Husband their lives, conserve and accumulate their force. Every division of our Army must be raised to full strength; every service–the most scientific, the most complex–must be thoroughly provided; we must make sure that in the months to come a large proportion of our Army is resting, refreshing, and training behind the front line ready to spring like leopards upon the German hordes. (Cheers.) Masses of guns, mountains of shells, clouds of aeroplanes–all must be ready, all must be there; we have only to act together and we have only to act at once.

[Editor's Note: Replying to a vote of thanks, Churchill announced the capture of Jerusalem.] What Richard Cœur de Lion was not able to achieve, British troops have accomplished. (Cheers.)

THE WAR EFFORT

October 7, 1918

Luncheon on Tour of Munitions Factories, Glasgow

The German offensive in March and April had eventually been checked, but it was some time before it was realised that the turning-point in the war had occurred. Most military authorities expected the war to last at least another year, when the new American armies would be a decisive element. But the collapse of Turkey and Bulgaria, combined with the substantial Allied advances on the Western Front, persuaded the German Government to approach President Wilson on October 4 for an armistice. But as this speech emphasises, Ministers were doubtful that the war was almost at an end.

[Extract] . . . There is not a man, looking back on the extraordinary cycle of events through which we have been passing, who will not say that he utterly underrated the majestic, the limitless, power of the land of his birth and the glorious virtue of the race to which he belonged.

I cannot say that I am over-sanguine at the present time of the speedy termination of the conflict. I cannot feel any degree of assurance that our righteous and indispensable war aims will at the present time receive that recognition which they require, nor can I feel that, having regard to the time that must elapse before the winter weather comes in France and Flanders, we have any right to count upon an immediate decision of a final character there. It may be that events will be better than we have any right to hope for now, but we must not count or build upon too favourable a development of events. We have started out to put this business through, and we must continue to develop to the utmost every resource that can make certain that whatever may be the course of the war in 1918, the year 1919 will see our foe unable to resist our legitimate and rightful claims. Therefore I urge upon you all, as representatives not only of the great manufacturing firms in Glasgow and along the Clyde, but as officers of the various organizations of the Ministry of Munitions from Glasgow and Edinburgh, after all these months of struggle and of effort, to grip your strength and your courage for the supreme effort of all; to brace yourselves for a period of exertion, of energy, mental and physical, of daring enterprise, of assiduity in work, of excellence in execution–brace yourselves in such an effort as shall in the next few months place us in a position to obtain that peace without which we shall have sent many scores of thousands of our bravest and best to their final end in vain. . . .

CONSTITUENCY ADDRESS

November 26, 1918

Dundee

On November 9 the Kaiser went to Holland and announced his abdication. A republic was proclaimed in Berlin, and at 11 a.m. on November 11 the Armistice went into effect.

In the General Election, which took place immediately after the armistice, Churchill stood as a Coalition Liberal with endorsements from Bonar Law and Lloyd George–the celebrated or notorious "coupon" which was only granted to candidates approved by the party leaders. Few Asquithian Liberals were thus favoured. At the onset of this speech–the first in his Dundee campaign–he was greeted with considerable tumult.

[Extract] . . . This tremendous victory, staggering, astounding, in its completeness, is not only a triumph of our fleets and armies; it is a triumph of our political ideals. We have beaten the Germans not only out of their trenches. We have beaten them out of their political system. Our institutions have been proved to be better than theirs not only for peace, but for war. Our British way of doing things is nowhere more admired than among the nations we have overthrown. It is the wonder of the world. Let us be very careful not to catch the infection of German ideas at the moment when we have defeated the German armies. If the other nations of the world are content to allow us to keep the supremacy of the seas without demur, it will be because we hold it as a trust for all. Let us preserve our great and old renown as the first of the free and liberal nations of the world, as the birthplace of Parliaments, as the pioneer of popular government, and as an unfailing fountain of enlightened thought and humanitarian sentiment.

That does not mean we should give up the fruits of victory. Practically the whole German nation was guilty of the crime of aggressive war conducted by brutal and bestial means. It is no use their pretending that their late Government is solely to blame. They were all in it, and they must all suffer for it. In particular, individuals against whom definite breaches of the laws of war on land and sea can be proved, or who can be proved to have treated prisoners with cruelty, should be brought to trial and punished as criminals, however highly placed. Alsace-Lorraine must be completely restored to France. Poland must be reconstituted a nation with access to the sea, and Germany must give up her Polish provinces. None of the German colonies will ever be restored to Germany, and none of the conquered parts of Turkey will ever be restored to Turkey. Whoever has them, they will not. Reparation must be made by Germany to the utmost limit possible for the damage she has done. I cordially sympathize with those who say, "Make them pay the expenses of the war." If the Allies have not claimed this it is for one reason only. It is not physically possible for them to do so.

Reparation for damage will alone run into thousands of millions.

Why should not all the splendid qualities displayed by our people in war be devoted to the peaceful work of reconstruction? Surely if the sense of self-preservation enabled us to combine to conquer, the same sense of self-preservation should enable us to restore and revive our prosperity? See how serious is the position. We have an enormous load of debt, far more than we shall ever get out of the Germans; capital is scarce and credit strained. The cost of living has risen to an unusual pitch, not only food, but boots and clothing, every necessity is scarce and costly. Our industries have all been distorted to war. They have to be turned back to peace. Railways, factories, housing–all have been neglected. Hundreds of thousands of men and women have got to change their employment and find a new job. On top of all this, we have to bring our soldiers home, and make homes worthy for them and worthy of the deeds they have done.

Five years of concerted effort by all classes, like what we have given in the war, but without its tragedies, would create an abundance and prosperity in this land, aye, throughout the world, such as has never yet been known or dreamt of. Five years of faction, of bickering, of class jealousies and party froth, will not merely not give us prosperity; it will land us in utter and universal privation. The choice is in our own hands. Like the Israelites of old, blessing and cursing is set before us. To-day we can have the greatest failures or the greatest triumph, as we choose. There is enough for all. The earth is a generous mother. Never did science offer such fairy gifts to man. Never did their knowledge and organization stand so high. Repair the waste. Rebuild the ruins. Heal the wounds. Crown the victors. Comfort the broken and broken-hearted. There is the battle we have now to fight. There is the victory we have now to win. Let us go forward together. (Cheers.)

GERMANY MUST PAY

November 29, 1918

Pavilion Theatre, Newcastle

The 1918 General Election–the first in which Labour stood as an independent party–was not the most edifying of modern contests. There was an almost universal call to exact punitive reparations from Germany and to try the leading Germans–particularly the Kaiser–for war crimes. Cries of "squeeze Germany until the pips squeak" and "hang the Kaiser" were the dominant themes of the election, with Lloyd George's pledge to build "a fit country for heroes to live in" providing a more positive rhetorical flourish. As this extract demonstrates, Churchill's oft-quoted maxim, "In victory, magnanimity," was sacrificed to electoral considerations. The Coalition (339 Conservatives and 136 Coalition Liberals) won an overwhelming victory. Labour won 59 seats, although Ramsay MacDonald, Arthur Henderson, and Philip Snowden were defeated–at least partly because of the hostility of MacDonald and Snowden to the war. The Asquithian Liberals were reduced to 26, Asquith being among those defeated.

[Extract] . . . It would not be in the interests of the future of the world if the guilty nations, and those who instigated its criminal actions, were to escape from the consequences of their crimes unpunished and unchallenged, with their deeds alone to haunt their consciences. (Cheers.) To the utmost limit of their ability they must be made to pay for the damage they have done. We must make it perfectly clear that mere whining will not enable them to escape. (Loud cheers.) What about reparation for the vile outrages to our mercantile marine? In one form or another we must have ton for ton, and individuals against whom definite breaches of the laws of war and humanity can be brought, particularly those who have been guilty of cruelty to helpless prisoners, must be brought to trial, and if convicted must be punished as they deserve, no matter how highly placed. (Cheers.) . . .

"A FAIR TRIAL AND NO FAVOUR"

December 4, 1918

Lochee District, Dundee

It will be seen that in response to questions, Churchill advocated the nationalisation of the railways. This theme was not pursued subsequently in office; nor was that of trying the Kaiser with "a fair trial and no favour."

[Extract] . . . Stern justice must be meted out to the Kaiser and his accomplices. (Cheers.) A fair trial and no favour. (Renewed cheers.) We have, as far as Great Britain is concerned, decided that so far as our influence goes we shall demand his surrender, and we shall do our utmost to have his share in the responsibility for the unequalled catastrophe tested to the full before a tribunal of justice. (Cheers.)

We shall also insist that those German subjects in this country, or others of German origin, who have abused our hospitality, and who are interned, shall go back to their country when the peace is signed, and, in my opinion, it would not be right until the country has again been consulted, in three, four, or five years' time, that we should reconsider the whole situation of allowing other Germans to come into this country from outside. (Cheers.)

We intend to make the Germans pay for the harm they have done to the uttermost farthing they are capable of paying. Ton for ton, or gold, or other securities, or any other liquid assets of which they might dispose we intend to exact from them, subject to the condition that in exacting them we must not do anything which will injure our own trade. I should not myself agree to enforce a policy which would produce labour conditions in Germany of a sweated or servile character, because I believe that would react on the wage conditions in our own country.

"LET US FACE THE FUTURE TOGETHER"
January 28, 1919

Dinner of the Aircraft Production Department,
Claridge's Hotel, London

The euphoria of victory was short-lived, and the Coalition had little time in which to savour its overwhelming election triumph. While the peace negotiations began in Paris, severe domestic unrest in Britain–starting in the Army over the method and pace of demobilisation–became sharp and uncomfortable. The miners, railwaymen, and transport workers formed a "Triple Alliance," and there were serious disturbances in Luton and Glasgow. The reaction of Ministers was one of alarm–perhaps excessive, but understandable–and the mood of the overwhelmingly Conservative Parliament was mercurial. In these circumstances, and given Lloyd George's own temperament, the Coalition Government proceeded in a somewhat haphazard and disorganized manner towards its hazily defined objectives.

In January Churchill became Secretary of State for War and Air, but was not included in the Cabinet until November 1919, when the small War Cabinet was replaced by the normal arrangements. He held this post until February 1921.

In this period two issues dominated Churchill's attention–the Allied involvement in the Russian Revolution and the Irish Question.

By the end of the war there were substantial Allied forces in Russia, including some 20,000 British troops at Murmansk and Archangel. Their presence was justified so long as the war lasted, but became more equivocal after the Armistice. The British Government drifted into support of the more prominent anti-Bolshevik elements. Although not directly responsible for this movement, Churchill warmly supported it, and identified himself eagerly with the principle of active support. The Cabinet was uneasy, Lloyd George indecisive, and the result was a policy of half-hearted intervention.

It is the first time I have been called upon to respond to the toast of "The Army." We have lived to see the "Contemptible Little Army" of Great Britain expanded into the best-equipped force in Europe of two millions of men, marching forward steadily day after day, making a mock of all that has been written in the text-books and of all our misgivings of our own greatness and power. We must look to the future, which seems to me full of anxiety. We run a great risk, in the moment of inertia, of temporary relaxation, which necessarily follows supreme exertion, of falling a prey to the weak and subversive forces, which at every stage in the war would have led us wrong, which at every moment in that great struggle would have put our names to a base and dishonourable peace, and which now, in other forms, while we are resting after the exertions we have made, are coming forward with counsels of cowardice, weakness, and faction, to divide and to weaken the great onward movement by so many heroic achievements, it has gained into its strong hands.

Let us face the future together. We have come to this table by many different roads, but with one purpose—the true greatness of our country, its long, enduring prowess and honour among the nations of the earth, not in the vulgar domination which the Germans sought to achieve, but in being on the merits the leading nation of the world, leading other nations forward to a better arrangement for all mankind. Let us join hands whenever opportunity serves. Let there be a Freemasonry for the future with a common bond, amid the play of interests and parties and classes and creeds. When I think of the nervous mood which sometimes sweeps across people, which is so quickly reflected in the Press, and which suggests that the majesty of Britain, which has lasted all these hundreds of years, and which has never stood higher than it does this night, is going to collapse before vague eddies of unrest or before Bolshevist impatience, I am certain that these strong forces have only to stand together, to work together, to carry us through all these difficulties and to secure permanently for the generations of the future the triumphs which the British Army has achieved by its struggles in the war.

THE BOLSHEVIK MENACE

April 11, 1919

Aldwych Club Luncheon,
Connaught Rooms, London

The "White Book" (White Paper) issued by the Foreign Office on "Bolshevik atrocities" in Russia has not been very respectfully treated by historians. Churchill's speeches on this subject at this time were not inaccurate, but his one-sidedness aroused intense antipathy within the Labour movement toward him personally and the increasing British involvement in Russia's civil war.

[Extract] . . . I only wish that the march of events on the Continent had been as favourable as in our own island. On the contrary, the process of degeneration has been steady and even rapid over large parts of Europe. The British Government has issued a White Book giving a vivid picture, based on authentic evidence, of Bolshevist atrocities. Tyranny presents itself in many forms. The British nation is the foe of tyranny in every form. That is why we fought Kaiserism and that is why we would fight it again. That is why we are opposing Bolshevism. Of all tyrannies in history the Bolshevist tyranny is the worst, the most destructive, and the most degrading. It is sheer humbug to pretend that it is not far worse than German militarism. The miseries of the Russian people under the Bolshevists far surpass anything they suffered even under the Tsar. The atrocities by Lenin and Trotsky are incomparably more hideous, on a larger scale, and more numerous than any for which the Kaiser himself is responsible. There is this also to be remembered–whatever crimes the Germans have committed, and we have not spared them in framing our indictment, at any rate they stuck to their Allies. They misled them, they exploited them, but they did not desert, or betray them. It may have been honour among thieves, but that is better than dishonour among murderers.

Lenin and Trotsky had no sooner seized on power than they dragged the noble Russian nation out of the path of honour and let loose on us and our Allies a whole deluge of German reinforcements, which burst on us in March and April of last year. Every British and French soldier killed last year was really done to death by Lenin and Trotsky, not in fair war, but by the treacherous desertion of an ally without parallel in the history of the world. There are still Russian Armies in the field, under Admiral Koltchak and General Deniken, who have never wavered in their faith and loyalty to the Allied cause, and who are fighting valiantly and by no means unsuccessfully against that foul combination of criminality and animalism which constitutes the Bolshevist *régime.* We are helping these men, within the limits which are assigned to us, to the very best of our ability. We are helping them with arms and munitions, with instructions and technical experts, who volunteered for service. It would not be right for us to send our armies raised on a compulsory basis to Russia. If Russia is to be saved it must be by Russian manhood. But all our hearts are with these men who are true to the Allied cause in their splendid struggle to restore the honour of united Russia, and to rebuild on a modern and democratic basis the freedom, prosperity, and happiness of its trustful and good-hearted people.

There is a class of misguided or degenerate people in this country and some others, who profess to take so lofty a view that they cannot see any difference between what they call rival Russian factions. They would have you believe that it is "six of one and half-a-dozen of the other." Their idea of a League of Nations is something which would be impartial as between Bolshevism on the one hand, and civilization on the other. We are still forced to distinguish between right and wrong, loyalty and treachery, health and disease, progress and anarchy. There is one part of the world in which these distinctions which we are bound to draw can translate itself into action. In the North of Russia the Bolshevists are continually attacking the British troops we sent there during the course of the war against Germany in order to draw off the pressure from the West, and who are now cut off by the ice from the resources of their fellow countrymen. Here we are in actual warfare with the representatives of a Bolshevist Government and with its Army, and, whatever views may be held by any section in the country on Russian affairs, we must all agree that our men who were sent there by the Government have to be properly supported and relieved from their dangerous situation. (Cheers.) We have no intention whatever of deserting our lads and of leaving them on this icy shore to the mercy of a cruel foe. The Prime Minister has given me the fullest authority to take whatever measures the General Staff of the Army think necessary to see that our men are relieved, and brought safely through the perils with which they are confronted, and so far as is physically possible we shall take whatever measures are required. (Cheers.)

A second White Book issued by the Government deals with the interior situation in Germany. When the Aldwych Club last entertained me, I remember saying to you that in war there are no substitutes for victory. You must either win or lose. And in victory there are no substitutes for peace. (Cheers.) I am in favour of making peace with Germany. After the war is over, after the enemy is beaten, after he has sued for mercy, I am in favour of making peace with him. Just as in August, 1914, our duty was to make war on Germany, so now our duty is to make peace with Germany.

Making peace with Germany does not mean making friends with Germany. (Cheers.) Peace means–I do not say forgiveness, for after all that has happened this generation can never forgive–but peace, put at its very lowest, means a state of affairs where certain common interests are recognized, where the beaten side, having taken their beating and having paid their forfeit–that is a matter which must be attended to, and will be attended to–(cheers)–may have still a chance of life, and have a chance for the future and some means of atonement. I do not think we can afford to carry on this quarrel, with all its apparatus of hatred, indefinitely. I do not think the structure of the civilized world is strong enough to stand the strain. With Russia on our hands in a state of utter ruin, with a greater part of Europe on the brink of famine, with bankruptcy, anarchy, and revolution threatening the victorious as well as the vanquished, we cannot afford to drive over to the Bolshevist camp the orderly and stable forces which now exist in the German democracy. All the information I receive from military sources indicates that Germany is very near collapse. All my military advisers, without exception, have warned me that the most vital step we ought to take immediately to secure victory is to feed Germany, to supply Germany with food and the raw materials necessary to them to resume their economic life. . . .

The Russian Bolshevist revolution is changing in its character. It has completed the Anarchist destruction of the social order in Russia itself. The political, economic, social, and moral life of the people of Russia has for the time being been utterly smashed. Famine and terror are the order of the day. Only the military structure is growing out of the ruin. That is still weak, but it is growing steadily stronger, and it is assuming an aggressive and predatory form, which French Jacobinism assumed after the fall of Robespierre, and before the rise of Napoleon. Bolshevist armies are marching on towards food and plunder, and in their path stand only the little weak States, exhausted and shattered by the war.

If Germany succumbs either from internal weakness, or from actual invasion, to this Bolshevist pestilence, Germany no doubt will be torn to pieces, but where shall we be? Where will be that peace for which we are all longing; where will be that revival of prosperity without which our domestic contentment is impossible. Where will be that League of Nations on which so many hopes are founded? If that should come to pass there will be two Leagues, not one. There will be the League of defeated nations and the League of victorious nations, and the League of defeated nations may easily be rearming while the League of victorious nations is laying aside the sword and shield. Once again there will have been created that terrible balance of antagonism which was the prelude to the explosion of the Great War five years ago. (Cheers.)

We must not allow our attention to be diverted from the truth by our wishes or our inclinations. Those present have great influence on the formation of public opinion and I say to you, keep a strong Army loyal, compact, contented, adequate for the work which it has to do; make peace with the German people; resist by every means at your disposal the advances of Bolshevist tyranny in every country in the world.

PEACE POLICY

May 14, 1919

Constituency Meeting, Dundee

[Extract] . . . I come before you in Dundee for the first time as Secretary of State for War and the Air. I have had very difficult work to do since you last returned me to the House of Commons. The demobilization of the Army has been rendered very difficult by the adoption of a system of pivotalism, which, to the ordinary soldier, looked like favouritism. We have substituted a new plan, and though there are still an enormous number of cases of great hardship under it, broadly speaking it has been accepted. I have had the greatest difficulty in carrying it out in practice. It is extremely difficult to get men home from the distant theatres. (A voice.–"What about Russia?") There are very few there. The gentleman apparently thinks our troops have no business in Russia.

Why did they go to Russia? (A voice, "Because they were sent.") They went to Russia in the days when we were trying to keep the Germans from coming over from Russia to attack our boys on the Western front (cheers), and the ones in the north of Russia were cut off by ice and they had to defend themselves, and we are going to bring them away safely, honourably, and victoriously. (Cheers.) When asked for volunteers to help those men and to extricate them, I got more volunteers in three weeks to go to the north of Russia than came forward to fill the whole of the rest of the Army. Our soldiers are not nearly so much in love with the Bolshevists as some people think. There is great difficulty with regard to Egypt and India. The soldiers were in process of coming home, and then a wave of trouble and disorder swept across Egypt. There is no doubt that the downfall of Turkey has caused an immense perturbation throughout the East. A feeling of unrest and revolt has passed over these great populations. It is not because they have not prospered under our rule; it is certainly not because our institutions do not admit of their taking from year to year a larger part and increasing share of the government of their own affairs as they become fitted for it.

The difficulty I have is that these Armies are largely composed of men who went out at the beginning of the war and are the men beyond all others whom we want to bring home. (Cheers.) Therefore what we are engaged in doing now is to recreate as quickly as we possibly can the old voluntary Army. We are not going to be a conscript nation. We are going to be a nation based on the old voluntary system. We are going to make the Germans give up conscription and we are going to give it up ourselves, but we are not going to throw away all the fruits of the war for the matter of 12 months. We have already got 150,000 men. The young lads are coming voluntarily, nearly double as quickly as they ever came in before the war. (A voice: "They do not know any better.") The gentleman does not want any young men to volunteer to go into the voluntary Army. Does he mean to leave those men who went out in 1914 indefinitely in India and Egypt? He means to sacrifice and give up India and Egypt. (A voice: "Self-determination.")

What has self-determination done for Russia? (Cheers.) Self-determination does not mean the right of every half-wit to order great communities about. (Loud cheers.) Self-determination is one of those ridiculous expressions which were coined by the Bolshevists in the early days of the attack upon the prosperity and freedom of the Russian people. (Oh, oh.) I know they have got a few friends here, but it is very lucky for those people that the great mass of the British nation is sensible, solid, and sound, because when it comes to revolutions the revolutionaries are the first to suffer, and when the revolution has come to an end all the most excitable people have been put out of the way, and you have got a great period of reaction, with probably a military dictator at the head of the State. . . .

Our policy must be directed to prevent a union between German militarism and Russian Bolshevism, for if that occurred these tyrants and tyrannical masses would swiftly crush the little weak States which lie between, and they would then form a combination which would stretch from China to the Rhine, which would be unspeakably unfriendly to Britain and to the United States and France, and to all that those free democracies stand for. There are three great lines of policy which we can pursue by which these dangers can be warded off—the first is to make peace with the German people after they have paid their forfeit for their offences (cheers), the second is to aid those forces in Russia which are making war successfully upon the Bolshevist tyranny, and the third is to keep firm friends with France and the United States of America. Only in this way can we shield the homes of Britain from a renewal of those horrors and tolls and sorrows from which we have, with great exertion, successfully emerged. (Cheers.)

RUSSIA

June 6, 1919

House of Commons

British policy concerning Russia remained highly confused, and aroused increasingly intense opposition, directed primarily against Churchill. On May 26 a British volunteer relief force reached Archangel and Admiral Koltchak's forces advanced to within 400 miles of Moscow. The British recognized Koltchak's Government and approved the plans of General Ironside to advance from Archangel "to strike a heavy blow against the Bolsheviks."

Five days after Churchill made this speech, Koltchak suffered a major defeat, and the British advance from Archangel was postponed, and eventually cancelled on July 7 after a mutiny in Ironside's army. On July 23 the Government finally decided to abandon the Northern positions. By this stage the Labour Party and the trade union movement had vehemently taken up the cause of the Bolsheviks and vigorously opposed the British intervention. Churchill continued to advocate support for General Denikin, operating in the South, until it was evident that the White Russian cause was hopeless.

[Extract] . . . With regard to what fell from the Leader of the Opposition with reference to Russia, I would strongly deprecate making more of what we are doing in Russia than the facts warrant. One would think, to hear his remarks and to read certain very influential organs of opinion in this country, that we were engaged in large formidable operations in Russia which were absorbing a great portion of our military strength. I have given on several occasions a very clear account of what we are doing. We are endeavouring to wind up our affairs in North Russia, and it is our hope that North Russia will become self-supporting before the end of the summer, and that then we shall be able to come away, having honourably discharged our duty to those people to whom we committed ourselves during the time of the War. That is really not challenged in any part of the House. In the Caucasus our troops are not in contact with the enemy; they are hundreds of miles away from the enemy. They are occupying that country until it has been decided what its future is to be as part of the general Peace settlement. It has, however, already been decided that they are to be withdrawn. Plans for the evacuation have been perfected, and it is expected that before long the actual recall of our troops will begin. So far as Siberia is concerned, we have no troops in Siberia except the two battalions who remain hundreds of miles away from the fighting at the centre of government, where they act as a symbol of British sympathy and support, and as a support and a prop to the Omsk Government. None of our troops have been engaged in any of this fighting which has taken place on the Siberian front. I warned the House the other day against exaggerated hopes being based on Admiral Koltchak's advance. I pointed out that a considerable set-back had taken place in the southern sector of his advance. That set-back the hon. and gallant Gentleman (Colonel Wedgwood) will rejoice to hear has become more pronounced in the interval; but, broadly speaking, of the ground gained since the advance began in March, between one-quarter and one-third had been lost again.

Sir D. Maclean: One hundred and twenty miles.

Mr. Churchill: The advance was 250 miles on a front of 750 miles, and there has been a withdrawal of 120 miles on a front of about 200 or 250 miles. The House will realise that this is an extremely attenuated form of warfare. A few thousand men are spread over twenty miles of front. The railways are few and far between. The rolling stock is limited and defective on both sides. Occasionally local concentrations are arranged which produce these changes. This line sways backwards and forwards. It is often a case of easy come and easy go with accessions of land in this kind of warfare. But, as I say, I have not at all attempted to encourage extravagant hopes being based upon the advance of Admiral Koltchak, and I very much deprecate the kind of suggestion that I see in some of the newspapers that he is likely to be at the gates of Moscow within a short time. He is hundreds of miles from the gates of Moscow, and no such expectation would be at all reasonable. Our share in these operations, as I say, is nil so far as men are concerned. We have no troops there at all. Our contribution to

Admiral Koltchak's operations is limited to the supply of the munitions which we have sent for the equipment of his armies. I would like to ask my right hon. Friend: Were we right in continuing to supply the Omsk Government with munitions? Consider how they came into being. They were called into being by the Allies at the time of the German War, when there was every desire and every need to build up in Russia elements which would tend to prevent the whole country falling into the hands of the Germans as well as the Bolsheviks and all our intervention was based solely with the object of preventing a substantial transference of troops from the Eastern front to fall upon our men in the West. We called this Government into existence, and I am quite sure that my right hon. Friend, or anyone with the slightest sense of responsibility, would repudiate the idea, the War having been won and Germany having been defeated, that we should immediately disinterest ourselves in the fortunes of those who had been called into the field to aid us and who have compromised themselves on our behalf. The hon. and gallant Member (Lieut.-Commander Kenworthy) said that we had had enough bloodshed. Does he suppose, if the Allies cut off the supply of munitions to the anti-Bolshevik forces and left them to their fate, that the end of bloodshed would have been reached?

Lieut.-Commander Kenworthy: The Bolshevik Government offered peace.

Mr. Churchill: The hon. and gallant Gentleman puts more confidence than I do in the promises of the Bolshevik Government. It is very remarkable that a naval officer should be so very trustful of them when we think that, in defiance of every law and of the sanctity of diplomatic agreements, Captain Cromie was foully murdered at the Legation in Petrograd by these very men on whose tender mercies the hon. and gallant Gentleman is now urging that we should rely. I am surprised that the hon. and gallant Gentleman does not express his opinions more circumspectly in matters of this kind. . . .

THE CENTRE PARTY

July 15, 1919

Criterion Restaurant, London

Churchill wrote the following explanation of the publication of this speech: "This speech was intended to form part of a private discussion with a number of fellow-members who are supporters of the Coalition Government, and as such it stood protected by all the usages of the House of Commons. As, however, fragmentary versions and summaries have been made public, and as many speculations have arisen on the subject, I have thought it better to publish it, subject only to one omission which does not in any way affect the substance of the argument.

"It is not true that the speech was typewritten or written out beforehand, though even if it had been this would not have implied any special significance. A shorthand writer was, however, present, and it is from this text that the present report has been taken.

"It is not true that the Prime Minister or anyone else imposed or attempted to impose any ban or veto on the publication. I take the fullest responsibility for the speech, and,

although on general grounds the publication of discussions of this kind is to be deprecated, as hampering the freedom of Parliamentary intercourse, there is no reason why an exception should not be made in this case."

This speech elaborates upon a theme frequently advanced by Churchill and his father, and always brought instant success or a positive response.

[Extract] . . . I thank you very much for the compliment which you have paid me and the honour you have done me in asking me to come here this evening and join in one of these interesting dinners which I understand you hold at irregular intervals, and at which you discuss with the freedom of private intercourse the political issues and situations of the day. When I received your invitation, and as the time got nearer to the day when I should have the opportunity and duty of meeting you here, I naturally possessed myself of the details of your constitution. I have here the resolutions which, I understand, govern your political activities, and on reading them through, in order to ascertain entirely what you wish to stand for, I was very much struck by the close adherence which you have paid to the maxims of Napoleon.

"A constitution," said Napoleon, "must be short and obscure," and it seems to me that you have followed very closely this maxim of the great master of the military art. But if a constitution may be cryptic, the spirit which animates a group of men, or a body–a great body of human beings–may be perfectly clear. The great thing is to have the union of consenting minds, to have the union of people who are aiming at the same objective, and feel that, however they may be divided by political origin or antecedents, however they may be divided by what they happened to say in the past, or anything else like that, they still feel that the greatness and the glory of Britain and the happiness of her people have always been, and are still, the objective on which they are marching. Party spirit, party interests, party organization, must necessarily play a great part in British political life. Do not let us underrate that.

I understand that your idea is not to break with existing political parties, but to prevent existing political parties from breaking with each other. I understand that you do not challenge the importance of party in British political life, and that you even vindicate it, but that you hold in addition that party spirit, party interests, party organization, must, in these very serious times, be definitely subordinated to national spirit, national interests, and national organization. If these are your main views, I am whole-heartedly in sympathy with them. I cannot think of anything more wrong and more foolish than that those who have come together in the great war, and who, working and fighting together in comradeship, in true comradeship, grudging nothing, keeping nothing back, have won the great victory, should at some date in the near future divide themselves again into two factions, hating each other, despising each other, abusing each other, without any real moral or mental cleavage, and go off into their opposite camps and unfurl their party standards, and by artificial faction, by sham antagonisms, by personal or group rivalries and ambitions, by fomented passions, set to work to fill the world with words to blacken each other's character, to traduce each other's motives, to hamper each other's policies, and so to darken the counsels of the nation and paralyse the action of the State.

I cannot conceive any course of action less proportioned to the times, the great times, the great and formidable times, in which we live. That, indeed, would be a crazy game to play, It would be a dreary game to play, and it would be, if I may say so, a squalid game to play. And what a time to play such a game in! Now that our country has arrived at the supreme pinnacle of splendour and of power, when the fame of this little island is resounding through every nation and every village in the world, when the British way of doing things, the British political and social conceptions are accepted in the most remote districts, the most obscure places, as being on the whole the best solution of the problem of practical government; when all over the world men admire the achievement of our arms and the permanence of our institutions, at such a time as this to indulge in faction for the sake of faction would, indeed, be a criminal enterprise. We should be unworthy of the land which bore us and of the men who have in this great war and in other great wars, which we have forgotten now, carried our country forward, if we were to lend ourselves to such counsels.

We occupy an extraordinary position. Indeed, foreign lands overrate us; they do not see the many weaknesses and anomalies from which we suffer. The name of our country never stood higher, nor perhaps did the name of any country ever stand so high, and it is not only our splendid position but, also, it is our dangerous position which should make us consider. We are at this moment exposed not only to the duty of bearing enormous responsibilities, but to very grave difficulties and to dangers which, if neglected, might easily rob us of all that we have so painfully and so brilliantly achieved. And when we feel ourselves, as every one of us does, called upon to make new efforts despite all the exertions of this great struggle, when we feel ourselves called upon to lash ourselves up to new efforts to hold the position which has been gained, to meet the problems which are hurrying upon us in uninterrupted succession, this is not the time when we should go off into opposite camps, to disperse in opposite directions, for the mere purpose of having a party fight. It is a time of all others when men should not think of reverting to the ordinary party basis. What folly, what crime! And those who urge that we should do so should be asked a question.

What is your object, what is your reason? Why are we to plunge into faction and set our batteries firing at each other with poison-gas shells? Is it because there is some deep division of principle in the ranks of those who now support the Coalition Government? Is it because there is some class interest at stake? Is it because party politics are more exciting than national politics, because a dog fight draws a crowd, because those who have no other wares to sell than party cries find their market closed or occupied by graver men? Well, I am going to examine, if you will permit me, all these things.

Where is division of principle? Events have been moving in the direction of united action between the two historic political parties for a very long time. The democratic forces in the Conservative Party, and the patriotic forces in the Liberal Party and in the Labour Party, have made repeated instinctive efforts to come together for common purposes during the last 30 or 40 years. I have in my possession (I was looking over some old letters the other day) a letter of the late Mr. W. H. Smith to my father, written during the interval between the election of 1885-6, proposing to change the name of the Conservative Party. Now, Mr. W. H. Smith was the most staid, unimpeachable, blameless Tory who ever lived, and what do you think he proposed as the new name for the Conservative Party? He proposed to call it the "Liberal Party." Then, in the later eighties, came the attempt to form a National Party by Mr. Chamberlain and Lord Randolph Churchill. That was a movement which did not come to fruition, but it excited hopes from a very large class of thinking men. Those were the days of Tory Democracy.

Lord Randolph Churchill used to be asked "What is Tory Democracy?" He replied on a well-known occasion: "Tory Democracy is democracy which supports the Tory Party; but I will add," he said, "that Tory Democracy implies a Government animated by lofty and by liberal ideas." Or we may go back farther, to the days of Disraeli and of Lord Shaftesbury, when they mitigated the severities of a *laissez-faire* policy carried to its ruthless logical conclusion by the Factory Acts and Trade Union Acts, which regained for the Tory Party a share in the appreciation of the toiling people of the country. There is nothing new in this, but never before have these ideas taken a more concrete, definite, and real form than now, never before have they been expressed by a powerful Government, and an immense Parliamentary majority, armed with a victory such as the world has never seen, and armed with the prestige necessary for the guidance of the people. There is nothing new in these ideas, and, coming to much more recent and necessarily more delicate times, I come to the year 1910.

There was an attempt made in that year to arrive at a working compromise between parties in view of the dangerous situation that was developing at home and abroad.

My object in discussing these matters is to show that the kind of movement which you are stimulating and supporting in your group is a movement which has repeatedly occurred in the last 40 years to the leading men of both political parties. Well, in 1910 it failed, and we went into the second election of that year, and from that we slid headlong into the most bitter, dangerous political period which has ever happened in this country in modern times. Each British party, girded and goaded on by its Press and its caucus, each spurred on by its own Irish Party animated by hatreds which, thank God, in this country we do not equal, was driven forward with unmeasured violence, until at last we came to the very verge of civil war. And from that horrible situation we were rescued by Armageddon! With all the tragedy of the war, we must never forget that it shook us out of our old machine-made quarrellings and showed us how small these were compared with all we had in common. The great war, with all its horrors, at any rate rescued us from the disasters of that epoch. We must not get back to it again.

I take it that your intention is to be a kind of bond of union which will prevent this rancour and extravagance of party politics from breaking out in these critical times through which we are passing, when you will form a powerful body of opinion, and of fighting opinion, which will make it not good business for people to indulge in violent partisan extravagances either on the side of Bolshevism or on the side of reaction, but rather which will tend to cement and gather together the great forces in this country which have a right to share in the enjoyment of the triumphs of the victory. Such an organization, such a movement, may render the very greatest service to the country at the present time. It may become a bulwark against a renewal of barbarous and unnecessary controversy; but it must be united, formed upon sincere conviction, and with a strong realization of definite objectives towards which we are advancing within a reasonable period of time.

Now, I say, where is the deep division of principle between us? I hope you will not think the worse of me if I say that what is needed now is not so much principle as the application of principle. Volumes have been written about political principle, and it is a very old world. It is full of principles, but the application of principle is at least as important as the selection of principle. Look at the Bolshevists. They have proclaimed the most wonderful Utopian ideals, but they have coupled them with the most cruel and the most wicked behaviour that has ever been seen among men, and with action which would disgrace the Stone Age or the Hottentots of Central Africa. We must recognize that good citizenship must be the foundation of a good, well-organized State. With good men in decent homes, working hard, doing their duty, being anxious to give something to their country, or town, or village, or their fellow-men, it is on a basis of citizenship of that kind and of that order rather than in the mere formulation of fantastic idealism that the safety, the health and the glory of nations reside, and so I say it is more in the application of principle than in the propounding of principle that our task consists. . . .

We are here to-night because we recognize the immense impression which the great war has made upon our country and upon ourselves. There is only one other reason why we should not work together, and that is we are told that politics are not exciting enough if they are pursued on a non-party basis. Well, we cannot afford this. We really cannot afford such indulgences. The times are too solemn, the margin is too small, our risks are too high, our hopes are too bright for us to involve ourselves in strife for mere sport. Those who mean the same thing have got to act together, and have got to take all the necessary steps to render their common action effective.

Not only have we got a common inheritance and a common purpose, but we have a common danger. We cannot afford at this juncture to throw away the prestige of victory and to go off quarrelling in opposite directions, when we are face to face with the Bolshevist peril which follows upon the general disorganization of the war and upon the perturbation of men's minds. We must be united. We must act together in the years that are to come as we did in the sternest days of the war, and there I see the advantage of this body of members of Parliament holding great constituencies by enormous majorities coming together and declaring the time is too grave for party fireworks.

We must advance together, hand in hand. We have not only got a common cause and a common danger, but we have also got leaders who by their action and the risks they have run for their opinions have proved themselves in full harmony with modern requirements. I have told you about my friend, Mr. Lloyd George, who really is the most necessary man this country has had for many years. There is no man that you can think of in your lifetime in this country who, if he were to withdraw or disappear, would leave a greater blank behind. He is seconded by Mr. Bonar Law, who has never had a thought for himself, and who has played a brilliant part as Leader of the House of Commons, and who works in devoted comradeship with a political chief whom he has learned to trust and like. And I think that with all these circumstances that I have mentioned, general and personal, in this long disquisition which I have ventured to make, we look forward to a future, you look forward and I look forward with you to a future of bright and useful political work and of real action. We are not only the representatives of constituencies, we are the trustees for the whole people of this island. We have the most enormous responsibility and the most splendid opportunities because of our great power.

It is a sacred trust to us to use that power and those opportunities in the interests of the people as a whole, not in the interests of any class in them, however much we may be associated with it, but to try to solve the problems of the British Nation, to think for Britain and to solve her problems as a whole, finding our way through all the puzzles of politics, keeping steadily that central point in view. We have, many of us, seen men and officers in the trenches throw away their lives as though they were nothing for the sake of taking some obscure village or holding some trench line, and we members of Parliament ought to be ready to work and labour and put forward any amount of fighting power that our abilities and our energies supply in order to safeguard and carry forward the splendid and dear-won glory of the country which we have the honour to serve.

ALLIED POLICY IN RUSSIA

July 17, 1919

Dinner of the British Russia Club,
Connaught Rooms, London

[Extract] . . . All Europe is sheltering behind the frail defence of a chain of new and feeble Powers to prevent the union of the Bolshevist army with the discontent of the mighty German region. The efforts of the Bolshevists to invade these States has been weak, because two-thirds of the whole Bolshevist army is taken up in fighting the forces of Koltchak and Denikin. If the whole of Russia and its resources falls into the unchallenged power of Lenin and Trotsky the whole weight of the Bolshevist military power will be thrown against those foundering little States. All those States have been promised protection by the League of Nations so far as it is in existence. If they are attacked and cry out for help, either serious efforts would have to be made by the Allies, or else the League of Nations would be shown to be utterly impotent, and the control of Central Europe, and very likely of Russia would pass into the hands of Germany.

When our pacifists or Bolshevist featherheads in this country raise their shrill voices in hysterical glee at every Bolshevist victory, let them remember that but for the Armies of Koltchak and Denikin the whole weight of Bolshevist aggression would be thrust upon these little States, for whose future the League of Nations have accepted a solemn and binding responsibility. It is no good living in an atmosphere of peroration. The fact must be faced that we, the victorious nations, are disarming, but the Bolshevists are arming, and with every suggestion of negotiation they have increased their armaments and are doing the utmost which their fantastic organization of society allowed to develop large conscript armies under the most brutal discipline.

If that is true of Lenin and Trotsky it is also true of Bela Kun or Bela Cohen—another fungus sprung up in the night amid the ruins, stately if obsolete, of the Austro-Hungarian Empire. This adventurer is becoming rapidly possessed of a strong Hungarian Army determined to resist the imposition of the Peace terms in Bolshevist livery, and preparing to attack Rumania. We are told that the Bolshevists have thrown away three-quarters of the Utopian principles with which they embarked upon the struggle, but the only possible palliation we can offer is that they are fanatics. Bolshevism is developing into a military power which would be able to work with Germany. Supposing that from China to the Rhine there is one one vast mass of armed human beings animated by hatred for all the Allied Powers, spurred on by hopes of plunder and vengeance, I am bound to deliver my warning, so that in future years it would be on record that the facts have not been withheld from the British people. The League of Nations is on its trial with regard to Russia, and if the League can not save Russia, Russia in her agony will destroy the League.

THE AGONY OF RUSSIA

January 3, 1920

Victoria Hall, Sunderland

This, among the most virulent of Churchill's assaults upon the Bolshevik leaders, followed the withdrawal of British forces from Russia and the collapse of the White forces. It was a speech which was long remembered.

[Extract] . . . National unity does not mean national unanimity. (Hear, hear.) You cannot expect to conciliate everybody. It is no use whittling away our own strong position in the hope of satisfying, for instance, those thin-blooded defeatists, who at every period in the war, whenever they saw the slightest chance, obstructed the measures necessary for victory and eagerly urged upon us a patched-up peace. We shall never succeed in satisfying them, nor ought we to compromise our own position by running after them. Our ideas are fundamentally opposed. The power and the splendour of the British Army make no appeal to these gentry. Their ideas are essentially cosmopolitan. They consider that one race of men is as good as another—unless it be their own race. ("No," and laughter.) I don't mean to misrepresent my friend there (laughter)—I say, unless it be their own race, which they are always ready to believe is in the wrong, and which they are always ready to chasten and to humble on every occasion. What is the use of breaking our hearts because we cannot have their help at this critical time? We can do without them. We have done without them before. We have got through the war without their aid, and we will get through this period of reconstruction in spite of their naggings and carpings.

There is another class which, in my judgment, it is no use our trying to conciliate. I mean those Bolshevists, fanatics who are the avowed enemies of the existing civilization of the world–(A voice: "It's a lie.")–,who if they had their way would destroy the democratic parliaments on which the liberties of free peoples depend, and would also shatter the economic and scientific apparatus by which alone the great millions of modern populations can be maintained alive. So far from conciliating these people and trying to make them believe that we are going in the same direction as they are, only not quite so fast and not quite so far, we ought to take every opportunity of going for them–(laughter and cheers)–of discrediting them of exposing them to the nation, of showing how enormous and unbridgable is the gulf which separates them from us. We believe in Parliamentary Government exercised in accordance with the will of the majority of the electors constitutionally and freely ascertained. They seek to overthrow Parliament by direct action or other violent means. (Voices: "Good old Smillie" and "Damn Smillie.") Well, I have not been mentioning names (laughter); and then to rule the mass of the nation in accordance with their theories, which have never yet been applied successfully, and through the agency of self-elected or sham-elected caucuses of their own.

They seek to destroy capital. We seek to control monopolies. They seek to eradicate the idea of individual possession. We seek to use the great mainspring of human endeavour as a means of increasing the volume of production on every side, and of sharing the fruits far more broadly and evenly among millions of individual homes. We defend freedom of conscience and religious equality. They seek to exterminate every form of religious belief that has given comfort and inspiration to the soul of man. They believe in the international Soviet of the Russian and Polish Jew. We are still putting our confidence in the British Empire. (Cheers.) We believe that patriotism, a sense of national honour, backed up by love of home and pride of race, must still, for many hundreds of years, be an essential element in the maintenance of a noble and progressive State. (Cheers.) And I would point out to you that these extremists are themselves aiming at the worst abuses of bygone generations of mankind. They seek to establish a class of government–and a class of government by no means the best instructed–to deal with the difficult problems of our community–they seek to establish a class of government of particular sections of organized manual labour.

We are opposed to class government in every form, whether it be a government of aristocracy or of plutocracy, or of the military classes, or of the priest class, or of the trade unions. We are against the predominance–the undue predominance–in the State of any single class. There is room for all, and we are going to make sure that all have room. Against all conspiracies to establish class government we unfold the stately conception of the British Commonwealth in which every class has its rights and every class has its place; in which there is room for all sorts and conditions of men and where everyone by merit may rise from the humblest to the highest station in public or in private life. And are we really in these islands, where we have been able to build up a system of free government step by step for over a thousand years–are we really to take lessons in constitutionalism from the crazy fanatics of Central Europe? A nice mess they have made of their own affairs–first allowing themselves to be trampled down and held down by autocratic governments, then bursting out like a gang of mutinous slaves, wrecking everything upon which their own livelihood depended.

Was there ever a more awful spectacle in the whole history of the world than is unfolded by the agony of Russia? This vast country, this mighty branch of the human family, not only produced enough food for itself, but, before the war, it was one of the great granaries of the world, from which food was exported to every country. It is now reduced to famine of the most terrible kind, not because there is no food—there is plenty of food—but because the theories of Lenin and Trotsky have fatally, and it may be finally, ruptured the means of intercourse between man and man, between workman and peasant, between town and country; because they have shattered the systems of scientific communication by rail and river on which the life of great cities depends; because they have raised class against class and race against race in fratricidal war; because they have given vast regions where a little while ago were smiling villages or prosperous townships back to the wolves and the bears; because they have driven man from the civilization of the 20th century into a condition of barbarism worse than the Stone Age, and have left him the most awful and pitiable spectacle in human experience, devoured by vermin, racked by pestilence, and deprived of hope.

And this is progress, this is liberty, this is Utopia! This is what my friend in the gallery would call an interesting experiment in social regeneration. (Laughter.) What a monstrous absurdity and perversion of the truth it is to represent the communistic theory as a form of progress when, at every step and at every stage, it is simply marching back into the dark ages. That gallant soldier and stalwart Labour man, Colonel John Ward, who has seen these things with his own eyes—(A voice—"He has not.")—who, I say, has seen these things for many months with his own eyes, and has played an honourable part on every occasion, has summed all up in one biting, blasting phrase—"Back to the jungle." "Ah! but," say the Bolshevists and the sympathisers of the Bolshevists, and the panderers of the Bolshevists, and the would-be imitators in this country of the Bolshevists, "they have not had a fair chance—there has been so much disorder that Comrade Lenin and Comrade Trotsky have not had an opportunity of carrying their theories smoothly and peaceably into effect." They can never have such a chance, and for this grave and vital reason, that the theories that have held are fundamentally opposed to the needs and dictates of the human heart, and of human nature itself. (A voice—"What about self-determination?) They are fatally opposed to self-determination. (Cheers.) My friend has not been studying this with sufficient attention. He probably thinks that the Bolshevists overthrew the Tsar. That is absolutely untrue. They overthrew the Russian Republic. What was the first step they took? It was to destroy the Russian Parliament, to put the greater number of its members to death. What did Litvinoff say when he met Mr. O'Grady at Copenhagen? He said, "We admit we have not got a majority of our country. We are not prepared to hold a constituent assembly, we are not prepared to allow any interference in the internal affairs of Russia."

Very well, what about self-determination? I am quite content with self-determination in this or in any other country, but we must be sure that the great mass of the nation have a fair, a full, a free, and an instructed chance to record their opinion, and I have absolute trust in the doctrine of the will of the people. (Cheers.)

What we have got to guard against is minority rule, rule which takes no regard of the will or wishes of the nation, is not influenced by public opinion–the rule of men who in their insane vanity and conceit believe they are entitled to give a government to a people which the people loathe and detest, and in regard to which they are never consulted. Self-determination, indeed! No, the fact is that the attempt to carry into practice those wild theories can only be attended with universal confusion, corruption, disorder, and civil war. That has happened in Russia and every other country where the attempt has been made, and will happen, and out of the bloodshed and foment of this struggle there emerges not the ideal, visionary, communistic republic of my interrupting friend, but something quite different. The ferocious military leaders and artful political wirepullers are the people who emerge in their own interest and the interest of their belongings. That is the universal experience in the history of mankind in these matters.

But, you say to me, "You surely do not think that this sort of thing could possibly happen in our country?" No, I do not, and I will tell you why I do not. It is not going to happen in this country because we are not going to let it happen. First of all, we are going to see that the mass of the British people are warned against this evil beforehand, that there is a widespread diffusion of political knowledge, that there is a strong and vigorous public opinion in every village and every street capable of exposing the sophistries and delusions which were good enough for the ignorant Russian peasant, but which British common sense, once it is on its guard, will decisively reject. (Cheers.) There is another reason why it is not going to happen. Because we are going to take care that our country and its institutions are organized upon a proper basis, and so organized as to give every one a share in the show, and to prevent any one class from taking too much out of it. (Cheers.) That is the work which lies before us. That is the work which lies right to our hands at the present time, and why I think I am entitled to say to you, "Do not let us waste our time in trying to conciliate these defeatists and Bolshevists, but let us resist at every point their insane encroachments, and expose their fallacies before the broad tribunal of the British nation." . . .

But it is no use dealing with illusions and make-believes. We must look at the facts. The world in which we are living is too dangerous for anyone to be able to afford to nurse illusions. We must look at the realities. Russia is in anarchy, Austria is in fragments, Germany is at present excluded, the United States of America, the author of the whole scheme, is happy to now decline to bind herself in any effective way. Well, after all is said and done, there is little left at present but England and France, with Italy and Japan and a cluster of smaller States or doubting neutrals. Certainly there is nothing sufficiently solid at the present time to justify us in laying aside those reasonable and moderate precautions of our Army, of our Air Force, and, above all the British Navy, which, whatever may happen elsewhere, will keep us safe and sound in our island home as they have kept us safe and sound before. It would be the greatest possible mistake for us to cast away those reasonable and prudent measures of defence to which we owe our present existence and to put our trust instead in an International Council from which the most powerful nations of the world are absent and in which there will still be working, whatever they may say, all those national and racial ambitious and animosities which have already inflicted such immense injury upon mankind. (Cheers.)

I think I have now reached a point where I may sum up for you in a definite form the advice I respectfully and sincerely offer to Sunderland and the North country. First, let us work together in comradeship and unity, as we did in the war, to rebuild the strength and prosperity of the British Empire. Secondly, let us resist by every means at our disposal, and at all times and so far as is possible, in all countries, the advance and propagation of the subversive and morbid doctrines of Bolshevism and Communism. Thirdly, let those who find themselves in general political agreement upon practical measures of the immediate future policy, and on the real and living issues of the day, let them bind themselves together by such organizations for any action as will best enable them to secure the permanent ascendency of their political principles and beliefs. Fourthly, let our influence in Europe be used to mitigate and not aggravate the misery and ruin which prevails. Fifthly, while helping forward in every way the establishment of a genuine League of Nations, let us not strip our country of reasonable measures of defence amid the perils of this tumultuous world. (Cheers.)

"A POLICY OF REAL PEACE AND APPEASEMENT"

February 14, 1920

King's Theatre, Dundee

[Extract] . . . I should like to . . . deal with the general European situation, and I will give you my view of it, based on what is now becoming a considerable experience. I daresay it is not a very popular view, but I want you, notwithstanding, to consider it very carefully, because these events affect your peace and safety, and the safety and future of your children. (Cheers.) The only thing that enabled France to stand up to Germany before the war was the might of Russia, to which France was allied. But for Russia's being on her side, France would never have been able to defend herself against Germany. (Cheers.) Even with Russia and Britain fighting in all their strength for three years on the side of France, the struggle still hung, as you all know, in the balance, and the United States were needed. (Cheers.) Russia had been betrayed–and do not let us forget how sorely the United States were needed to turn the scale in our favour. Now Russia is no longer available. She is no longer the great counterpoise to Germany. On the contrary, she is very likely to go over to the other side, very likely to fall into the hands of the Germans and make a common policy with them. Our interest has been to try to secure a Government in Russia which will not throw itself into the hands of Germany. That is what we have been trying to do. (A voice–"Economic purpose, and don't stand telling so many lies.") It is also in our interest not to drive Germany into the arms of Russia.

The present Government in Germany is a Government of moderate views, which is trying to keep the country's head above water and to find work and food for the people. That Government may be overthrown at any time, either by a Bolshevist—or, as they call it in Germany, a Spartacist—uprising, or by a militarist conspiracy. Either one or the other of these Governments would make a close partnership with Bolshevist Russia to avoid this danger. This is a very great and imminent danger. We ought to do all we can to help the present German Government, provided, of course, they make genuine efforts to carry out their obligations.

When you are fighting a man fight him with all your might. When you have beaten him, when he has acknowledged defeat, stop fighting him. Take another view. It is not British to trample on a prostrate foe. Still more is that true when that foe is not a man, but a nation, and a nation which we have got somehow or other to live with in the world; a nation with whose well-being and prosperity, however little we like it, our own prosperity is involved; and a nation which, if driven to despair and into collapse, may easily let loose again in the world the horrors of anarchy or the horrors of war. (Cheers.)

I am in favour of a League of Nations. But what is wanted to make the League of Nations a success is a League of Nations' spirit. The world would have no use for a League of revengeful nations, or a League of jealous and callous nations, or a League of selfish and greedy nations. What is wanted is a League of brave, strong, merciful nations, seeking unitedly the peace and the glory of mankind. (Cheers.) But, quite apart from all those lofty visions, Britain has got to walk warily and soberly in her own interests and for her own sake.

We cannot afford to indulge in ill-will towards so many great nations at the same time. We have never ventured to do so in the past. When Germany was our enemy, Russia was our friend. When Russia was our enemy, Turkey was our friend. The delay of making peace with Turkey has thrown a special burden on Great Britain, through the disturbance of India and throughout the Middle East. We must make peace with Turkey. We must make peace with Turkey soon—(interruption)—and must make a peace which does not unite against us the feelings of the whole Mahomedan world. Again, I say, "When you have beaten a man, don't go on trampling on him, but see whether, in his chastened frame of mind, he may not somehow or other be made to help to repair the damage and be made of some use to you after all." These are my views. In short, I am, and have always been since the firing stopped on November 11, 1918, for a policy of peace, of real peace and appeasement. Everything I have said, and everything I have done, has had that sole object in view. I could use most sentimental arguments to you, but have confined myself this afternoon to those of common sense.

You will say to me, "Are you for peace with Russia?" My regret is we have not got a Russia with whom we can make a real peace. I do not believe that the despotism of Lenin and Trotsky, although it has some admirers in this country (laughter), is fit company for a democratic Government like ours. (Cheers.) I fear that, while they rule their own subjects, or slaves, or "comrades," or whatever they call them—(laughter)—with what Lenin has described as "iron revolutionary discipline," they will do their utmost to stir up rebellion and sedition and fan the flames of class hatred in every other land, and especially in the Eastern world, where we in Britain have such great interests. (Cheers.) I fear also that they will become a partner in any revengeful intrigues, which German militarism may attempt to set on foot under a thin camouflage of Communism.

At the same time I recognize that the character of the Bolshevist Government has changed in many ways. They began by being a gang of mad anarchists, tearing to pieces every civilized institution, and beating down all law and authority. They have now swung to the other extreme. They are now a despotic oligarchy, ruling the Russian masses with a tyranny no Tsar ever equalled. Not only do they enforce a rigorous conscription, not only do they maintain discipline in their army by terrible executions and flogging–(Voices:–"It is a lie.")–but they have now instituted–and I would like some of my friends in the gallery to address their minds to it–they have now instituted industrial conscription (cheers), what they call a Labour Army. (Interruption.) I am sorry the truth is so painful. (Loud laughter.) They have instituted this Labour Army, and thousands of men are compelled, under pain of death, to work as State slaves in the mills, in the mines, in the forests, on the railways. They are liable to be sent hither and thither, to any part of the country, at the orders of their master. (A voice:–"What have we here?") All independent newspapers, all free speech, all representative institutions, all public meetings except their own–(laughter)–are ruthlessly suppressed. (A voice:–"Here.") Strikers are punished with death (laughter), the hours of toil have been lengthened, in many cases reaching 12 in a day–(A voice:–"The same as here")–with extra voluntary labour on Saturdays and Sundays. (Laughter.) Every worker has become a mere chattel of the Government. (A voice:–"You will never be a chattel.") No, nor will the people of this country. (Cheers.) If those gentlemen are afraid of the arguments they will show it by interrupting. If they are not afraid of it they will listen to it, and then they will know how to answer it.

I say that every worker has become a mere chattel of the Government–(A voice:–"We are that here")–ground down not only by the tyranny of brute force, but by a reinforcing tyranny of doctrinaire, of opinion. In fact, and this is the point to which I desire your attention, instead of being a Government of wild anarchy, they have become a Government of iron discipline. I tell you quite plainly that I abhor them in this form just as much as I did under the other. I hope we shall keep our country free from both these hateful extremes–(hear, hear, and cheers)–free from the licence of anarchy and free from the slavery of despotism. (Interruption, and a voice:–"Conscription.") I hope we shall keep this country a free land–(A voice:–"What about Egypt?")–a law-abiding land, and a liberal land. (Cheers and interruption.)

But what surprises me is that the Labour Party should still be in love with these Bolshevist autocrats, and let themselves be sucked in with a lot of foolish formulas of "The Dictatorship of the Proletariat," "The Union of Workmen, Peasants, and Soldiers," &c. Why, the Russian proletariat has been reduced to slavery. (A voice, "By the Tsar.") Not at all by the Tsar. (A voice, "Yes.") No, they have been reduced to slavery by Lenin and Trotsky. (Cheers.) After they had freed themselves from the Tsar and set up a democratic Government, after a Parliament of their own, they overturned that Parliament, dissolved that Parliament, scattered it to the four winds, and established themselves as autocrats on the Throne from which they ejected the Tsar. As for being a Government of "workmen, soldiers, and peasants," there is not a single workman, soldier, or peasant in this gang of miscreants and criminals who have acted upon this unfortunate Empire.

Still, as you see, those simpletons of the Socialist Party go and bow down and chant hymns and burn incense before the Russian idol, and what their own ill-informed imaginations led them to believe was the Russian idol. All the time they show themselves, as I have already once before said this year in the country, more than ever unfitted in their present stage of development for the tasks of responsible Government. (Cheers.) Therefore, I do not think that we ought to enter into friendly relations with, or extend our recognition to, a tyrannical or anti-democratic Government of the kind, while they are actually maintaining themselves by murder and terrorism on an unprecedented scale, and while they refuse the Russian people all chance of expressing their own opinion freely on the form which they wish their Government to take. The most we ought to do is to allow trade to spring up, when its mellowing influences may lead to an easier state of things. But that is doubtful.

No one knows what is coming out of the Russian cauldron, but it will almost certainly be something full of evil, full of menace for Britain, France, and the United States. It seems to me, therefore, that our dangers, particularly the dangers to France and Britain, have not been finally removed by the war, and that, after a few years, they may come back again in a new, but still in a grave, form. In order to prevent this we ought to try to make a real and lasting peace with the German people and the German Republic. We ought to help and protect the sound elements in Turkish national life. We ought to help Central Europe, particularly Poland, so far as this lies in our power, to recover from the shock of the war. . . .

What would happen if all Liberals took Mr. Asquith's advice, broke up the existing Government, and, leaving the problems of the nation to go hang, settled down to a good hearty fight with the Unionists? I will tell you what would happen. The Labour or Socialist Party would come into power. (Labour cheers.) They would come into power at a period in their development when, as we all no doubt have noticed this afternoon, they are quite unfitted to discharge the responsibilities of Government (cheers), and when through their incompetence, when through their erroneous doctrines, they would shatter the reviving prosperity of the country and cast away the Empire which British genius has built up.

Why do I say that the Socialist Party–(interruption and booing)–at this stage in their development are unfit to govern the country? Not, assuredly, because they are not able men, in every class of life. Why, there is no country in the world like Britain, where men can rise by their ability, their brains, their character, from the humblest to the highest rank in every sphere. (Interruptions and cheers.) Indeed, I go so far as to say that there is–(interruption)–hardly any great profession in this country which is not headed by the men who began life without wealth or influence. The Prime Minister is the first example. (Cheers.) Mr. Lloyd George rose from a cottage and a village school to the leading place in Europe. (Cheers.) Sir William Robertson rose, after being eight years a trooper in the cavalry, to be the Chief of the Imperial General Staff at the height of the great war.

Lord Fisher has told you how he entered the Navy, friendless and penniless and forlorn. I could easily multiply these instances. Nearly all the leading positions are held by what is called "self-made men." All the greatest fortunes are held by men who have risen from the ranks. (Cheers and interruption.) I am trying to give some words of encouragement to my friends in the gallery. There may be still an opportunity for them to make up for the lost time–by their character, ability, industry, enterprise, genius, wits–they may still rise–(laughter)–in a free country like ours, to positions of eminence and respect among their fellow-citizens. The ability of our countrymen springs up fresh and perennial from every class and every part of the country, and, I think you in Scotland are entitled to have me say, from no part more than the Northern Kingdom.

The first reason why I say the Socialist Party are unfit, in their present stage, to undertake the government of this great Empire is that by their constitution they have, over a long period of time, cut themselves off from a fair representative share of the ability of the country and made themselves into a class party, led by class leaders, and fighting the battle of class interests in predominance over all other interests. (Cheers.) My second is they have shown no evidence of being provided with any useful or helpful solutions of the difficult problems which are in front of us. . . .

I have said that the second reason is that they have no definite solution, no helpful solution, to offer for the great problems with which we are confronted at the present time. (Cries of "Nonsense.") But there is a third reason why the advent of the Socialist Party to power at the present time would be disastrous. The doctrines which they hold, which constitute the driving power of their movement, and its appeal to large sections of the electorate are doctrines which, if put into practice, would shatter the prosperity of the country or inevitably subvert its peace and order and break up and cast away the Empire we have been so long gathering together. (Cheers.) If the Socialists mean anything by what they say, if they are sincere, they stand for nationalization, not only of mines, but of all the industries of the country. They stand, therefore, for a system of society where the whole business of the country would have to be run by Government officials, under the direction of "political bosses."

If they do not mean that, what do they mean? According to their principle of self-determination, if Ireland chooses to be a Republic, if she chooses to ally herself to Germany, or any other unfriendly nation, and lend her harbours and submarine bases to cut off our food, the Labour Party are logically bound, the Socialist Party are logically bound, to let them do so or be false to their principles. Logically that is what their principles involve. If India or Egypt leave the country, their dogma of self-determination says, "We have got to do it." We are not going to do it, not a bit of it. (A voice–"Why not?") We have not defended our Empire all these years against the strongest enemies in the world, and beaten them at last with a prodigious sacrifice, in order to surrender it piecemeal at the hysterical dictation of the foolish, the feeble-minded, and the flighty. (Cheers.) Nor will we succumb to revolutionary violence in any form or from any quarter, in India, in Egypt, in Ireland. Sure of our rectitude, sure of our enlightened purpose, we are determined to persevere.

At the same time, let me make it perfectly clear to you that the matter is one which rests in the hands of the British electorate. This is a free country, based on an enormous electorate. The people have their own destiny in their hands. As they decide, so shall it be. The Socialist Party have every right, under the Constitution, to work night and day to win the confidence of the electorate and obtain a majority at the poll. That is their right and we do not grudge it them. We do not propose to interrupt their meetings; we do not propose to impede their discussions. (Laughter.) On the contrary, we desire them to have every fair and full opportunity of pursuing their campaign of trying to educate or instruct those of their fellow-men who like their views. We also have our rights. And our rights are to take every legitimate step in fair and hard political controversy to warn the country against their unwise policies, and to defeat what we regard as their premature ambitions. (Cheers.) . . .

PUNJAB DISTURBANCES

July 8, 1920

House of Commons

Throughout the first half of 1920 the political situation in Ireland had become progressively more serious. On January 21, 1919, the seventy-three Sinn Fein M.P.s met in Dublin as the Irish Parliament (Dail Eirann) and issued a declaration of independence. The newly created Irish Republican Army, under the command of Michael Collins, instigated a campaign which in 1919–a relatively quiet year, in retrospect–resulted in eighteen murders and seventy-seven armed attacks, including an attempt to assassinate the Viceroy, Lord French. Sinn Fein was "proclaimed" in August, and the Dail declared an illegal organization. But the authority of the Government continued to decline, and Ireland slithered into anarchy and virtual civil war. The War Office recruited reinforcements for the hard-pressed Royal Irish Constabulary (R.I.C.) in Britain, and their khaki uniforms–with the black belts and dark-green caps of the R.I.C.–earned them the name of the "Black and Tans." The decision to meet terror with terror created a situation of unparalleled bitterness, and did not immediately achieve anything apart from increasing anti-British feeling in Ireland.

As if this were not enough, unrest in India erupted into open violence. In April 1919, under order of General Dyer, troops opened fire on a crowd at Amritsar, killing 379 unarmed civilians and wounding over a thousand. The Commander-in-Chief in India recommended that Dyer should be ordered to retire, and the matter came before the Army Council for review. The Council accepted the recommendation, as did the Cabinet.

There were two distinct groups hostile to this decision. One supported Dyer vehemently, and considered that he had been harshly treated. The other argued that sterner penalties should be imposed upon him. Churchill's speech in defence of the Cabinet's decision–one of his most effective in this Parliament–was often quoted against him in the 1931-1935 debates on the Government of India Act.

[Extract] . . . However we may dwell upon the difficulties of General Dyer during the Amritsar riots, upon the anxious and critical situation in the Punjab, upon the danger to Europeans throughout that province, upon the long delays which have taken place in reaching a decision about this officer, upon the procedure that was at this point or at that point adopted, however we may dwell upon all this, one tremendous fact stands out–I mean the slaughter of nearly 400 persons and the wounding of probably three or four times as many, at the Jallian Wallah Bagh on 13th April. That is an episode which appears to me to be without precedent or parallel in the modern history of the British Empire. It is an event of an entirely different order from any of those tragical occurrences which take place when troops are brought into collision with the civil population. It is an extraordinary event, a monstrous event, an event which stands in singular and sinister isolation.

Collisions between troops and native populations have been painfully frequent in the melancholy aftermath of the Great War. My right hon. Friend has reminded the House that in this particular series of disturbances there were 36 or 37 cases of firing upon the crowd in India at this particular time, and there have been numerous cases in Egypt. In all these cases the officer in command is placed in a most painful and difficult position. I agree absolutely with what my right hon. Friend has said, and the opinions he has quoted of the Adjutant-General in India, of the distasteful, painful, embarrassing, torturing situation, mental and moral, in which the British officer in command of troops is placed when he is called upon to decide whether or not he opens fire, not upon the enemies of his country, but on those who are his countrymen, or who are citizens of our common Empire. No words can be employed which would exaggerate those difficulties. But there are certain broad lines by which, I think, an officer in such cases should be guided. First of all, I think he may ask himself, Is the crowd attacking anything or anybody? Surely that is the first question. Are they trying to force their way forward to the attack of some building, or some cordon of troops or police, or are they attempting to attack some band of persons or some individual who has excited their hostility? Is the crowd attacking? That is the first question which would naturally arise. The second question is this: Is the crowd armed? That is surely another great simple fundamental question. By armed I mean armed with lethal weapons.

Sir W. Joynson-Hicks: How could they be in India?

Mr. Churchill: Men who take up arms against the State must expect at any moment to be fired upon. Men who take up arms unlawfully cannot expect that the troops will wait until they are quite ready to begin the conflict–

Mr. Donald: What about Ireland?

Mr. Churchill: I agree, and it is in regard to Ireland that I am specially making this remark–or until they have actually begun fighting. Armed men are in a category absolutely different from unarmed men. An unarmed crowd stands in a totally different position from an armed crowd. At Amritsar the crowd was neither armed nor attacking. [*Interruption.*] I carefully said that when I used the word "armed" I meant armed with lethal weapons, or with firearms. There is no dispute between us on that point. "I was confronted," says General Dyer, "by a revolutionary army." What is the chief characteristic of an army? Surely it is that it is armed. This crowd was unarmed. These are simple tests which it is not too much to expect officers in these difficult situations to apply. . . . But there is another test which is not quite so simple, but which nevertheless has often served as a good guide. I mean the doctrine that no more force should be used than is necessary to secure compliance with the law. There is also a fourth consideration by which an officer should be guided. He should confine himself to a limited and definite objective, that is to say to preventing a crowd doing something which they ought not to do, or to compelling them to do something which they ought to do. All these are good guides for officers placed in the difficult and painful situation in which General Dyer stood.

My right hon. Friend (Sir E. Carson) will say it is easy enough to talk like this, and to lay down these principles here in safe and comfortable England, in the calm atmosphere of the House of Commons or in your armchairs in Downing Street or Whitehall, but it is quite a different business on the spot, in a great emergency, confronted with a howling mob, with a great city or a whole province quivering all around with excitement. I quite agree. Still these are good guides and sound, simple tests, and I believe it is not too much to ask of our officers to observe and to consider them. After all, they are accustomed to accomplish more difficult tasks than that. Over and over again we have seen British officers and soldiers storm entrenchments under the heaviest fire, with half their number shot down before they entered the position of the enemy, the certainty of a long, bloody day before them, a tremendous bombardment crashing all around—we have seen them in these circumstances taking out their maps and watches, and adjusting their calculations with the most minute detail, and we have seen them show, not merely mercy, but kindness, to prisoners, observing restraint in the treatment of them, punishing those who deserved to be punished by the hard laws of war, and sparing those who might claim to be admitted to the clemency of the conqueror. We have seen them exerting themselves to show pity and to help, even at their own peril, the wounded. They have done it thousands of times, and in requiring them, in moments of crisis, dealing with civil riots, when the danger is incomparably less, to consider these broad, simple guides, really I do not think we are taxing them beyond their proved strength. . . .

I say I do not think it is too much to ask a British officer in this painful, agonising position, to pause and consider these broad, simple guides—I do not even call them rules—before he decides upon his course of conduct. Under circumstances, in my opinion, infinitely more trying, they have shown themselves capable of arriving at right decisions. If we offer these broad guides to our officers in these anxious and dangerous times, if there are guides of a positive character, there is surely one guide which we can offer them of a negative character. There is surely one general prohibition which we can make. I mean a prohibition against what is called "frightfulness." What I mean by frightfulness is the inflicting of great slaughter or massacre upon a particular crowd of people, with the intention of terrorising not merely the rest of the crowd, but the whole district or the whole country. . . .

We cannot admit this doctrine in any form. Frightfulness is not a remedy known to the British pharmacopoeia. I yield to no one in my detestation of Bolshevism, and of the revolutionary violence which precedes it. I share with my right hon. and learned Friend (Sir E. Carson) many of his sentiments as to the world-wide character of the seditious and revolutionary movement with which we are confronted. But my hatred of Bolshevism and Bolsheviks is not founded on their silly system of economics, or their absurd doctrine of an impossible equality. It arises from the bloody and devastating terrorism which they practice in every land into which they have broken, and by which alone their criminal regime can be maintained. I have heard the hon. Member for Hull (Lieut.-Commander Kenworthy) speak on this subject. His doctrine and his policy is to support and palliate every form of terrorism as long as it is the terrorism of revolutionaries against the forces of law, loyalty and order. Governments who have seized upon power by violence and by usurpation have often resorted to terrorism in their desperate efforts to keep what they have stolen, but the august and venerable structure of the British Empire, where lawful authority descends from hand to hand and generation after generation, does not need such aid. Such ideas are absolutely foreign to the British way of doing things.

These observations are mainly of a general character, but their relevance to the case under discussion can be well understood, and they lead me to the specific circumstances of the fusillade at the Jallian Wallah Bagh. Let me marshal the facts. The crowd was unarmed, except with bludgeons. It was not attacking anybody or anything. It was holding a seditious meeting. When fire had been opened upon it to disperse it, it tried to run away. Pinned up in a narrow place considerably smaller than Trafalgar Square, with hardly any exits, and packed together so that one bullet would drive through three or four bodies, the people ran madly this way and the other. When the fire was directed upon the centre, they ran to the sides. The fire was then directed upon the sides. Many threw themselves down on the ground, and the fire was then directed on the ground. This was continued for 8 or 10 minutes, and it stopped only when the ammunition had reached the point of exhaustion.

Commander Bellairs: That is absolutely denied by General Dyer.

Mr. Churchill: It stopped only when it was on the point of exhaustion, enough ammunition being retained to provide for the safety of the force on its return journey. If more troops had been available, says this officer, the casualties would have been greater in proportion. If the road had not been so narrow, the machine guns and the armoured cars would have joined in. Finally, when the ammunition had reached the point that only enough remained to allow for the safe return of the troops, and after 379 persons, which is about the number gathered together in this Chamber to-day, had been killed, and when most certainly 1,200 or more had been wounded, the troops, at whom not even a stone had been thrown, swung round and marched away. I deeply regret to find myself in a difference of opinion from many of those with whom, in the general drift of the world's affairs at the present time, I feel myself in the strongest sympathy; but I do not think it is in the interests of the British Empire or of the British Army for us to take a load of that sort for all time upon our backs. We have to make it absolutely clear, some way or other, that this is not the British way of doing business.

I shall be told that it "saved India." I do not believe it for a moment. The British power in India does not stand on such foundations. It stands on much stronger foundations. I am going to refer to the material foundations of our power very bluntly. Take the Mutiny as the datum line. In those days, there were normally 40,000 British troops in the country, and the ratio of British troops to native troops was one to five. The native Indian Army had a powerful artillery, of which they made tremendous use. There were no railways, no modern appliances, and yet the Mutiny was effectively suppressed by the use of a military power far inferior to that which we now possess in India. Since then the British troops have been raised to 70,000 and upwards, and the ratio of British to native troops is one to two. There is no native artillery of any kind. The power and the importance of the artillery has increased in the meantime 10 and perhaps 20-fold. Since then a whole series of wonderful and powerful war inventions have come into being, and the whole apparatus of scientific war is at the disposal of the British Government in India—machine guns, the magazine rifle, cordite ammunition, which cannot be manufactured as gunpowder was manufactured except by a scientific power, and which is all stored in the magazines under the control of the white troops. Then there have been the great developments which have followed the conquest of the air and the evolution of the aeroplane. Even if the railways and the telegraphs were cut or rendered useless by a strike, motor lorries and wireless telegraphy would give increasingly the means of concentrating troops, and taking them about the country with an extraordinary and almost undreamed-of facility. When one contemplates these solid, material facts, there is no need for foolish panic, or talk of its being necessary to produce a situation like that at Jallian Wallah Bagh in order to save India. On the contrary, as we contemplate the great physical forces and the power at the disposal of the British Government in their relations with the native population of India, we ought to remember the words of Macaulay—

> and then was seen what we believe to be the most frightful of all spectacles, the strength of civilisation without its mercy.

Our reign in India or anywhere else has never stood on the basis of physical force alone, and it would be fatal to the British Empire if we were to try to base ourselves only upon it. The British way of doing things, as my right hon. Friend the Secretary of State for India, who feels intensely upon this subject, has pointed out, has always meant and implied close and effectual co-operation with the people of the country. In every part of the British Empire that has been our aim, and in no part have we arrived at such success as in India, whose princes spent their treasure in our cause, whose brave soldiers fought side by side with our own men, whose intelligent and gifted people are co-operating at the present moment with us in every sphere of government and of industry. It is quite true that in Egypt last year there was a complete breakdown of the relations between the British and the Egyptian people. Every class and every profession seemed united against us. What are we doing? We are trying to rebuild that relationship. For months, Lord Milner has been in Egypt, and now we are endeavouring laboriously and patiently to rebuild from the bottom that relation between the British administration and the people of Egypt which we have always enjoyed in the past, and which it was so painful for us to feel had been so suddenly ruptured. It is not a question of force. We had plenty of force, if force were all that was needed.

What we want is co-operation and good-will, and I beseech hon. and right hon. Gentleman to look at the whole of this vast question, and not merely at one part of it. If the disastrous breakdown which has occurred in a comparatively small country like Egypt, if this absolute rupture between the British administration and the people of the country had taken place throughout the mighty regions of our Indian Empire, it would have constituted one of the most melancholy events in the history of the world. That it has not taken place up to the present is, I think, largely due to the constructive policy of His Majesty's Government, to which my right hon. Friend the Secretary of State for India has made so great a personal contribution. I was astonished by my right hon. Friend's sense of detachment when, in the supreme crisis of the War, he calmly journeyed to India, and remained for many months absorbed and buried in Indian affairs. It was not until I saw what happened in Egypt, and, if you like, what is going on in Ireland to-day, that I appreciated the enormous utility of such service, from the point of view of the national interests of the British Empire, in helping to keep alive that spirit of comradeship, that sense of unity and of progress in co-operation, which must ever ally and bind together the British and Indian peoples. . . .

RUSSIA AND IRELAND

October 16, 1920

King's Theatre, Dundee

[Extract] Everything which I ventured to say to you on former occasions or have said in Parliament or elsewhere in the country about the Bolsheviks has been abundantly and overwhelmingly proved true. (Cheers.) The cruel tyranny they have inflicted upon the miserable people of Russia is now admitted, even by those who were most favourable to them. We do not need to take the testimony of Conservatives or Liberals. We can take evidence from people like Mrs. Philip Snowden and Mr. Bertrand Russell, both most advanced and extreme politicians, both life-long Socialists.

And what are the results of this prodigious exercise of tyrannical authority? Russia, which was one of the great granaries of the world, is starving. The cities of Russia are dying of Communism.

You may call that the principle of self-determination, or self-extermination if you like it better. (Laughter.) If Russia survives, as survive she will, it will be because Lenin's evil power and the Communist system can't extend to the great bulk of the villages, and nearly three-quarters of the Russian populations live in the villages. But fancy what would happen if this sort of experiment were tried in this country—a country of great cities living on a highly artificial basis, having to get three-quarters of its food from over the sea. Why, if such experiments were tried here it would simply mean the annihilation of two-thirds or three-quarters of those who now draw their breath and gain their living in this island. . . .

Ireland is a country which, like Russia, is deliberately tearing itself to pieces and obstinately destroying its own prosperity. The Nationalist party's power was growing at the moment when the Parliamentary area was abandoned. And now, all is gone and there is nothing but a gang of squalid murderers plotting the doom of unsuspecting men—a brutal business of popping up and down behind hedges and shooting poor policemen in the back—and skirmishing about the highways and byways of Ireland with the troops and the police and the "Black-and-Tans."

It is amazing that a nation so gifted should allow itself to be robbed of its birthright and its dignity by such shameful and paltry methods. It is amazing that Irishmen themselves cannot react against them and throw them off, and rid themselves of a disease which is paralysing them, rotting them, and robbing them of their political power and status. If they cannot, if they succumb before these methods of terrorism, then, I say, we in this stronger island and nation must react for them and must show them there are resources in the United Kingdom capable of rescuing Ireland from this horrible fate and setting them, free and sane and strong, upon the path of their future. . . .

Personally I deplore more than I can say what is taking place in Ireland, but I keep my sympathy in the first instance for those brave and loyal soldiers and policemen who are foully shot down doing their duty for King and country, and whose wives and children are left to mourn their loss. (Cheers.) The Sinn Feiners consider that they are entitled to kill without warning, without uniform or open challenge, any policeman or soldier or British official whom they can waylay, and they have formed an army all over Ireland of over 100,000 who were bound to obey their orders and to attack any one to whom they chose to direct their attention, and they have in fact killed, mostly by treacherous murder, 115 policemen and 22 soldiers during the course of the present year, and grievously wounded a larger number. They have so terrorised the Irish population that not a single one of these murderers has been brought to justice and hanged.

Can you imagine a more agonising ordeal for a policeman or a soldier than to go day by day about his ordinary business with this deadly murder all around him, nudging his elbow, whispering in his ear, having to try to read in the eyes of everyone who approaches him whether that man is an assassin or not and knowing all the time that not a single murderer has been brought to justice, knowing also that if some people had their way, even if they had been arrested, they might get out of prison simply by refusing to take their food? (Laughter.) I am told by those who have gone through it and are going through it that the strain on a man's nerves far exceeds the bombardment of the trenches.

That is the situation in Ireland which all men ought to unite in condemning, but apart from a few perfunctory sentences scarcely a word has been said by the Opposition or the Labour party in its denunciation. It is not until these policemen and soldiers, rendered desperate by their sufferings and their peril, rendered furious by the bloody and cowardly murder of their comrades and finding no redress in the law, broke from the bounds of discipline and execute reprisals upon notorious members of the Sinn Fein army and organisation in the neighbourhood of the murderers–it is not until this has occurred and life has been taken in perhaps a dozen cases that Mr. Asquith and others are roused to passionate fury, pour out their wrath upon the head of the Government and clamour for the condign punishment of these unhappy policemen, who, I suppose, if some people had their way would be the only men hanged for murder in Ireland this year.

If, while the Government is quite unable to bring to justice the murderers of 115 policemen and 22 soldiers, they had fallen upon the police and infuriated military and punished them for reprisals against the persons of perhaps a dozen of the Sinn Feiners, then I say to you the police and military force in Ireland would be dissolved altogether and not a man would have been left to do his duty. That is a fact that must be faced.

The problem is indeed a terrible one and one which must wring the heart of every man, but it is imperative to face the realities which exist and to deal with them as in the end they always have to be dealt with in this hard world.

Assassination, it has been said, has never changed the history of the world, and we are going to take care that it does not change the history of the British Empire. (Cheers.) We are going to break up this murder gang. (Renewed cheers.) That it will be broken up absolutely and utterly is as sure as that the sun will rise to-morrow morning. (Hear, hear.) . . .

We cannot adopt a policy of scuttling in regard to Ireland. It is absurd to suppose that we will escape from the Irish problem and Irish difficulties by mere flight. Those difficulties would pursue us in an aggravated form. My study of British history convinces me that a surrender of that kind would never be accepted by the British people.

If, in a moment of weakness or of exhaustion on the part of those to whom we should look for guidance, a British Parliament was found to agree to the setting up of an independent Republic in Ireland, I am certain that after a few years that independent Republic would be flattened out by open war, and that the British people would never rest till they had rid themselves of so fearful a danger.

Surrender to a miserable gang of cowardly assassins like the human leopards of West Africa would undoubtedly be followed by a passionate repentance and a fearful atonement. (Cheers.) We might abandon our responsibilities in Ireland, but what would happen in Ireland? Out of their secret hiding-places would emerge the triumphant murderers to claim that they had won the independence of Ireland, and that they should now direct its fortunes.

The Protestants in North-east Ulster would certainly, after all that has happened, defend themselves desperately and to the last. The Sinn Feiners on their part with an army already practically in existence would buy arms from abroad and from the United States. They would no doubt avail themselves, as they were even ready to do during the late war, of any German assistance and officers that might be forthcoming.

Meanwhile thousands of volunteers would go over from England and Scotland to help the North, and when you had these organised and marshalled armies on both sides, when you had allowed the furnaces of hell to be stoked up to full blast, then a fierce and furious struggle would begin with the double bitterness of civil war and the triple bitterness of religious war.

Would this struggle remain within the limits of Ireland? Would it not as it developed take the form of the overwhelming sympathies of Britain being with the North and the sympathies of many influential elements in the United States being with the South? Would not the names of the British volunteers filling the casualty lists in the paper day after day excite the passion of this country and would not the arrival of reinforcements and supplies from the United States rouse in an acute form partisanship among that great people, and might not this process and tension and antagonism bring us to the verge of the greatest danger of all to the civilisation of the world, namely, a deep quarrel between us and our kith and kin across the Atlantic?

These are consequences which in my sincere judgment would follow remorselessly and inevitably from the abduction by Great Britain of her responsibilities in Ireland. They are consequences compared to which the present state of affairs in Ireland, lamentable though it be, would seem tolerable and even satisfactory.

Every one who is not prepared to support the Government in taking effective measures to put down the murder campaign in Ireland and to maintain these measures if necessary for several years, all such persons, although they may not do or mean it, are in fact lending themselves to a course of weakness, impotence, and surrender which can only result in the establishment under the worst possible conditions of an Independent Irish Republic (Cheers.)

The measure of autonomy and independence for Ireland ought not to be what the victory of a murder gang in Ireland can extort. (Cheers.) A hundred policemen are murdered, so they are to have Dominion Home Rule, but without an army or navy: 150 are murdered, then we given them control of the army and the navy, but under conditions; shoot another 50, we give up these conditions; go on shooting and we will throw in the control of foreign relations. (Laughter and cheers.) Kill a thousand British policemen or soldiers, kill if you will a few more Cameron Highlanders, shoot more of the Black Watch for a change–(Cries of dissent and booing)–and then for the sake of a quiet life–(laughter)–we will give them sovereign independence. (Cheers and more dissent.) Well, a number of Cameron Highlanders have been shot already. What's wrong with that? I do not see why they should be shot. (Cheers.) Indeed, we shall be very lucky if we get off without paying an indemnity. (Laughter and cheers.) Once you start on the road of flight and of panic no one knows where he will stop.

Woe betide the political party or the public men who yield themselves to the fatal promptings of lethargy or weakness. On them will fall the ban of national displeasure. The strong, loyal, valiant forces that broke the Hindenburg Line will break the Irish murder gang and all who countenance, encourage, or seek to profit by its crimes. (Loud and continued cheers.) Once that has been done then your moment for settlement will come. We made a great settlement in South Africa–(A Voice: Cinder heap)–and I had something to do with that–but in the magnanimity of victory, not in the impotence of defeat. So in Ireland if you are to make, as I trust we may make, a permanent settlement on a Home Rule basis with the Irish people, it can never be on the basis of surrender to treacherous murder, but only on the basis of justice and of generosity freely extended by a British nation which has established its lawful authority beyond challenge or dispute. (Loud cheers.)

BOLSHEVISM AND IMPERIAL SEDITION

November 4, 1920

United Wards Club Luncheon,
Cannon Street Hotel, London

This speech developed Churchill's theme of the "Communist conspiracy," which further alienated Labour from the Coalition and drew him closer–at least in outlook–to the Conservatives.

[Extract] . . . For Russia we can do little. The fearful series of events must run their course. One can only hope that some day in our own time deliverance will come to the Russian people and that they will stand again on their own feet and be masters in their own house.

But if we can do little for Russia, we can do much for Britian. We do not want any of these experiments here. (Cheers.) Any such experiments in this country would be followed by the destruction of the great majority of the persons dwelling in these islands. We can at any rate make sure that in our life and time the deadly disease which has struck down Russia should not be allowed to spring up here and poison us as it is poisoning them.

In every city there are small bands of eager men and women, watching with hungry eyes any chance to make a general overturn in the hopes of profiting themselves in the confusion, and these miscreants are fed by Bolshevist money. (Cheers.) They are ceaselessly endeavouring by propagating the doctrines of communism, by preaching violent revolution, by inflaming discontent, to infect us with their disease. If there is no danger it is only because we have an enlightened, active political life in Britain, because we have a considered, instructed, organized public opinion, and because we have a free Constitution which we are determined to make an instrument of continuous and progressive reform. In order that that condition shall be maintained, ceaseless political exertion must be made in all parts of the country by citizens in every class, each using to the full his political rights.

The danger at the present time does not exist only, or even mainly, in these islands. What of India, Egypt, and Ireland? Do you not think it possible that there is some connection between all the revolutionary and subversive elements by which we are now being assailed? When we see all these movements from so many different quarters springing up simultaneously, does it not look as though there is a dead set being made against the British Empire? Why, for instance, should the Egyptian extremists give money to the *Daily Herald*? (Cheers.) Why does Lenin send them money, too? Why does he also send money to Sinn Fein? We know that intense efforts are being made to disturb India, and that similar efforts are being made to cause a great breakdown of trade and industry at home in the hopes of creating unemployment and consequently suffering and discontent.

It is becoming increasingly clear that all these factions are in touch with one another, and that they are acting in concert. In fact there is developing a world-wide conspiracy against our country, designed to deprive us of our place in the world and to rob us of the fruits of victory. (Cheers.) They will not succeed. They will fail. We must be ready: we must be on our guard to recognize every symptom of danger, and to act with strong conviction against it. Having beaten the most powerful military empire in the world, having emerged triumphantly from the fearful ordeal of Armageddon. We will not allow ourselves to be pulled down and have our Empire disrupted by a malevolent and subversive force, the rascals and rapscallions of mankind who are now on the move against us. (Loud cheers.)

Whether it is the Irish murder gang or the Egyptian vengeance society, or the seditious extremists in India, or the arch-traitors we have at home, they will feel the weight of the British arm. It was strong enough to break the Hindenburg Line, it will be strong enough to defend the main interests of the British people, to carry us through these stormy times into calmer and brighter days. (Cheers.)

JUSTICE FOR ARAB AND JEW

March 31, 1921

*Reply to Moslem Delegation,
Government House, Jerusalem*

The year 1921 opened in a sombre atmosphere. The immediate postwar prosperity had crumbled, and unemployment rose sharply until there were more than two million workers unemployed by the summer. The miners–now back in the tender hands of the owners–struck between April and July, but were completely defeated. Wages almost everywhere fell, and the Government's housing programme was harshly–and, it is now recognized–unfairly criticised.

But even more menacing was the political situation in Ireland, which deteriorated until the summer when serious negotiations between the Nationalists and the British Government opened after a truce was accepted on July 8. Churchill's attitude remained, as he subsequently wrote, "a tremendous onslaught (combined) with the fairest offer," but he was moving in the direction of a negotiated settlement.

In February Churchill became Colonial Secretary but remained actively involved in the Irish situation throughout the remainder of the life of the Coalition Government.

In March Churchill convened a special meeting of senior British officials operating in the Middle East in Cairo, and visited Jerusalem. Already, the dichotomy in British attitudes and statements to the Jews and Arabs was causing concern, and the White Paper of 1922, which attempted to confirm the establishment of a Jewish National Home in line with the Balfour Declaration of 1917, while recognizing Arab rights, predictably enraged both sides. At the time it appeared that Churchill had managed to reconcile the conflicting wartime assurances, but subsequent events were to disprove that hope.

[Extract] I consider your address partly partisan and incorrect. You ask me to repudiate the Balfour declaration and stop immigration. This is not in my power and is not my wish. . . . Moreover it is manifestly right that the scattered Jews should have a national centre and a national home in which they might be reunited, and where else but in Palestine, with which the Jews for 3,000 years have been intimately and profoundly associated? We think it is good for the world, good for the Jews, and good for the British Empire, and it is also good for the Arabs dwelling in Palestine, and we intend it to be so. They shall not be supplanted nor suffer but they shall share in the benefits and the progress of Zionism.

I draw your attention to the second part of the Balfour declaration emphasizing the sacredness of your civil and religious rights. I am sorry you regard it as valueless. It is vital to you, and you should hold and claim it firmly. If one promise stands, so does the other. We shall faithfully fulfil both. . . . Examine Mr. Balfour's careful words, Palestine to be "a national home" not "the national home," a great difference in meaning.

The establishment of a national home does not mean a Jewish Government to dominate the Arabs. Great Britain is the greatest Moslem State in the world, and is well disposed to the Arabs and cherishes their friendship. . . . You need not be alarmed for the future. Great Britain has promised a fair chance for the Zionist movement, but the latter will succeed only on its merits. . . . We cannot tolerate the expropriation of one set of people by another. The present form of Government will continue for many years. Step by step we shall develop representative institutions, leading to full self-government, but our children's children will have passed away before that is completed.

JUSTICE FOR ARAB AND JEW

March 31, 1921

Reply to Jewish Delegation,
Government House, Jerusalem

[Extract] . . . One principle of the Balfour declaration is that the process of the establishment of a national home for the Jews is to be without prejudice or unfairness to the Arab and Christian inhabitants, which together form an overwhelming majority.

I am convinced that the Zionist cause will bring good to the whole world, and will bring welfare and advancement to the Arabs of this country. The success of Zionism will depend upon the good it will bestow upon the whole country. The Arabs have expressed alarm at the Bolshevist character of some of the Jewish immigrants. Whatever we believe of this, your duty is to dispel these fears by a good and friendly attitude, and propagate peace between all. You must use patience and prudence, and allay alarm.

IRISH FREE STATE

December 15, 1921

House of Commons

After months of negotiations and moments of high drama the Irish Treaty was signed on December 6. It proposed that Ireland would become the Irish Free State with Dominion Status, but Ulster would retain the right to withdraw and establish her own Government and Parliament. The treaty was highly unpalatable to many Irish Nationalists and Conservatives, and soon civil war between de Valera's Republican Party and the more moderate Irish led by Michael Collins broke out.

[Extract] . . . Here then is the question which those who take most sincerely the extreme view on either side of the Channel should be asked and should answer. They say the Treaty is not satisfactory. They point to various provisions in which it is unsatisfactory, but are the differences outstanding between what they would wish and the Treaty on their side sufficient to make it imperative to renew the fighting, with all the loss and risk entailed thereby? I cannot believe you will find any body of responsible men here or in Ireland, Liberal or Conservative, North or South, soldier or civilian, who would solemly declare that on the margin of difference remaining between these extreme views and the Treaty it would be justifiable to lay the land of Ireland waste to the scourge of war, or to drag the name of Great Britain through the dirt in every part of the world. For you cannot embark on such a struggle without being prepared to face conditions of public opinion all over the world which undoubtedly would be profoundly detrimental to your interests. You could not do it without being prepared to inflict the most fearful injury on the land and people of Ireland. When we have this Treaty, defective, admittedly, from your point of view, but still a great instrument, I ask: Are the differences between the Treaty and the extreme desire worth the re-embarking on war? You cannot do it. If you tried, you would not get the people to support you. On the contrary, they would complain in both countries of their leaders, and they would complain with violence and indignation that they were dragged from their hearths to maltreat each other on pretexts which had been reduced to such manageable dimensions. It is high time that the main body of Irish and British opinion asserted its determination to put a stop to these fanatical quarrels.

Let me direct the attention of the House to a remarkable phenomenon. Yesterday, at the other end of the passage, I heard Lord Carson, with sonorous accents and with brilliant and corrosive invective, denouncing Lord Curzon as a turncoat and a traitor. I do not think it necessary to deal with such a charge, because everyone in this House knows that Lord Curzon's whole life has been devoted to the patriotic service of this country, and those of us in this country who have served with him know well that his counsel was always robust and vigorous in the time of the greatest difficulty and danger through which we passed. At the very moment when Lord Carson was denouncing the Secretary of Foreign Affairs as a traitor and a turncoat, Mr. de Valera in Dublin was almost simultaneously denouncing Mr. Collins for a similar offence. Both were held up as traitors to their respective countries, and for what? For having supported a treaty of peace which nineteen-twentieths of the people of both countries are determined to carry through. Are we not getting a little tired of all this? These absolutely sincere, consistent, unswerving gentlemen, faithful in all circumstances to their implacable quarrels, seek to mount their respective national war horses, in person or by proxy, and to drive at full tilt at one another, shattering and splintering down the lists, to the indescribable misery of the common people, and to the utter confusion of our Imperial affairs. . . .

But when we have just come out of a world-war with our record such as it is, in which our armies have broken the German line, in which our navies have carried on the whole sea business of the Allies, in which our finances have sustained Europe, when we have come out of all these dangers, and have shown that we are capable of taking a leading part, if not the leading part, in the great struggle which has overthrown the largest and most powerful military Empires of which there is a record—when all these facts are considered, surely we can afford to carry on these Irish negotiations according to a clear, cool judgment of what is best in the country's interest, without being deflected or deterred from any particular course of action by a wholly unjustifiable self-accusation of humiliation. But in truth it is not humiliation. It is not as a humiliation that this event is viewed by the world or by the Empire. It is as a great and peculiar manifestation of British genius, at which the friends of England all over the world have rejoiced. Every foe of England has been dumbfounded. Ever Colonial statesman will feel that if this succeed, his task in his Dominion of bringing people closer and closer into the confederation of the British Empire will be eased and facilitated. There is not a Dominion Parliament throughout the British Empire where this Treaty will not be accepted and endorsed. And these are facts which we are entitled to deal with at a time when undoubtedly there is so much ground for hard and bitter taunts to be directed against our policy.

It is a curious reflection to inquire why Ireland should bulk so largely in our lives. How is it that the great English parties are shaken to their foundations, and even shattered, almost every generation, by contact with Irish affairs? Whence did Ireland derive its power to drive Mr. Pitt from office, to drag down Mr. Gladstone in the summit of his career, and to draw us who sit here almost to the verge of civil war, from which we were only rescued by the outbreak of the Great War. Whence does this mysterious power of Ireland come? It is a small, poor, sparsely populated island, lapped about by British sea power, accessible on every side, without iron or coal. How is it that she sways our councils, shakes our parties, and infects us with her bitterness, convulses our passions, and deranges our action? How is it she has forced generation after generation to stop the whole traffic of the British Empire, in order to debate her domestic affairs? Ireland is not a daughter State. She is a parent nation. The Irish are in ancient race. "We too are," said their plenipotentiaries, "a far-flung nation." They are intermingled with the whole life of the Empire, and have interests in every part of the Empire wherever the English language is spoken, especially in those new countries with whom we have to look forward to the greatest friendship and countenance, and where the Irish canker has been at work. How much have we suffered in all these generations from this continued hostility? If we can free ourselves from it, if we can to some extent reconcile the spirit of the Irish nation to the British Empire in the same way as Scotland and Wales have been reconciled, then indeed we shall have secured advantages which may well repay the trouble and the uncertainties of the present time.

I am told that we are not to refer to South Africa, because the cases are not parallel. Of course they are not, but surely it would be very foolish for us to cut ourselves off from the encouragement and inspiration which we may naturally and legitimately derive from studying the most adventurous and most modern instance of trust and conciliation which the annals of the British Empire records! I remember when I was charged with the duty of commending the Transvaal Constitution in this House. I remember many facts which were known to me, and which certainly would have justified the gravest pessimism, and would have caused the deepest anxiety. I remember the intelligence reports which we got of Boer wagons moving about the veldt in the moonlight, leaving their dumps of rifles and ammunition here and there in lonely farms. They were reports which caused the greatest disquietude in all who were responsible for the policy. But we persevered. We grasped the larger hope, and in the end, when our need was greatest, we gained a reward far beyond our hopes. In those days we had far less satisfactory Parliamentary circumstances than now exist. Party fighting was very bitter in those days. I appealed to the Opposition of that time to join with the Government in this matter. I said:

> With all our great majority we can only make this the gift of a party, but you can make it the gift of Britain as a whole.

The appeal was not acceded to. To-day in this enterprise, which also is full of uncertainty, but full of hope, we can undoubtedly count upon the active and energetic support of all the three great parties in the State, who are resolved to take what steps are necessary to bring, if possible, this Irish peace to its consummation, to carry it out in the spirit and in the letter, and to stand firmly against all efforts to overthrow it, whether they be in Parliament or out of doors.

IRISH FREE STATE BILL

February 16, 1922

House of Commons

The Dail, after a bitter debate, approved the Irish Treaty by sixty-four votes to fifty-seven on January 7. De Valera resigned as President, and a Provisional Government was formed under Arthur Griffith, who had led the negotiating team in London. Ireland began to drift towards civil war.

The bitterness of de Valera against the treaty was paralleled by that of the Ulster Unionists and many Conservatives, who considered that the partition of Ireland was a betrayal by the Coalition of its repeated undertakings. Outrages continued in Northern and Southern Ireland between Protestants and Catholics. The debate on the Irish Free State Bill was, accordingly, fierce.

[Extract] . . . It is my duty to ask the approval of the House for this Bill. It gives effect to the Treaty which both Houses of Parliament have already approved by such large majorities. It clothes the Provisional Government with lawful power and enables them to hold an election under favourable conditions at the earliest moment. The importance and urgency of this Bill are plain. Take, for instance, the object of clothing the Irish Provisional Government with law. Is it not fatal to peace, social order and good Government to have power wielded by men who have no legal authority? Every day it continues is a reproach to the administration of the Empire. Every day tends to bring into contempt those solemn forms of procedure on the observance of which in every country the structure of civilised society depends. Only three days ago I spoke about some criminals, murderous criminals, who had been caught by the Irish Provisional Government in Southern Ireland, accused of murdering and robbing a British officer, and I said that I presumed that they would be handed over to be dealt with with the full rigour of the law. I was interrupted by an hon. Friend on these Benches with the remarks: "There is no law," and "What law?" It is perfectly true, but is it reasonable to make such interruptions and not support the Bill which alone can clothe with law the acts of the Irish Government? A Provisional Government, unsanctified by law, yet recognised by the Crown, by His Majesty's Ministers, is an anomaly, unprecedented in the history of the British Empire. Its continuance one day longer than is necessary is derogatory to Parliament, to the Nation, and to the Crown. We must legalise and regularise our action. Contempt of law is one of the great evils manifesting themselves in many parts of the world at the present time, and it is disastrous for the Imperial Parliament to connive at or countenance such a situation in Ireland for one day longer than is absolutely necessary.

Mr. Ronald McNeill: It is your own creation.

Mr. Churchill: Yes, with the full approval of both Houses of Parliament. Moreover, what chance does such a situation give to the Irish Executive who, at the request of the King's representative in Ireland–made, of course, on the advice of His Majesty's Government–have assumed the very great burden and responsibility of directing Irish affairs? How can you expect such a Government to enforce a respect for its decisions when such decisions are absolutely unsanctioned by law? How can you wonder that such Ministers are set at defiance by the more turbulent elements amongst their followers and that the prisoners captured from the Northern Border have to be released, not by powerful authoritative action, but by processes of expostulation and persuasion? I am asked questions every day about the non-payment of rents in Ireland, about the spread of lawlessness, and even anarchy, in different parts of the country, about crimes of violence against persons and property increasingly committed among a population hitherto singularly free from common crime as opposed to political crime. I am asked these questions every day, and I ask in my turn: "How can you expect these tendencies to be arrested except by a Government entitled to display the insignia of lawful power and to proceed by methods which have the sanction of antiquity and prescription?" I notice that this succession of unanswerable truisms excites no challenge. . . .

There is another suggestion which is made and with which I must deal. There are those who think that the present Irish Government may be overturned by a *coup d'état* and that a red Soviet Republic may be set up. We do not think that is at all likely, but if it were it is quite clear that a Soviet Republic in Ireland would ruin the Irish cause for 100 years, but would not in any respect impair the foundations of the British Empire or the security of Ulster. No people in the world are really less likely to turn Bolshevik than the Irish. Their strong sense of personal possession, their respect for the position of women, their love of country and their religious convictions constitute them in a peculiar sense the most sure and unyielding opponents of the withering and levelling doctrines of Russia. What we know of the characters and personalities at the head of the Provisional Government in Ireland leads us also to believe that they are not the men who would tamely sit still and suffer the fate of a Kerensky. Therefore I do not think this second evil alternative is one which we need allow to embarrass us or obstruct our thoughts and decisions at the present time. But this Irish Government, this Irish Ministry, ought not to be left in the position in which even the most necessary measures which they take for their own defence or for the enforcement of authority, or even for the maintenance of law and the suppression of brigandage or mutiny, are devoid of formal sanction.

If you want to see Ireland degenerate into a meaningless welter of lawless chaos and confusion, delay this Bill. If you wish to see increasingly serious bloodshed all along the borders of Ulster, delay this Bill. If you want this House to have on its hands, as it now has, the responsibility for peace and order in Southern Ireland, without the means of enforcing it, if you want to impose those same evil conditions upon the Irish Provisional Government, delay this Bill. If you want to enable dangerous and extreme men, working out schemes of hatred in subterranean secrecy, to undermine and overturn a Government which is faithfully doing its best to keep its word with us and enabling us to keep our word with it, delay this Bill. If you want to proclaim to all the world, week after week, that the British Empire can get on just as well without law as with it, then you will delay this Bill. But if you wish to give a fair chance to a policy to which Parliament has pledged itself, and to Irish Ministers to whom you are bound in good faith, so long as they act faithfully with you, to give fair play and a fair chance, if you wish to see Ireland brought back from the confusion of tyranny to a reign of law, if you wish to give logical and coherent effect to the policy and experiment to which we are committed, you will not impede, even for a single unnecessary week, the passage of this Bill. . . .

Now I hope my argument will be carefully considered; although I say it myself, it is worthy of consideration. Not only should we defend every inch of Ulster soil under the Treaty as if it were Kent, but we should be bound to take special measures to secure that Ulster was not ruined by her loyalty to us. It is evident that our position, if we only study it and reflect upon it, is one of tremendous strength, and that with patience and with care we may easily succeed in bringing about a result acceptable to all. If I were an Irish Nationalist I should dread more than anything else such a development as I have indicated, against which I could do absolutely nothing, nothing by force against the British Empire, nothing by persuasion against the inflexible will of the Northern Protestants, nothing by appeal to the judgment of the world, for the world, be assured, will always uphold the Treaty and Ulster's right to self-determination under the Treaty. If I were an Irish Nationalist, I would far rather say: Take more Catholics, not less; make a more even balance in your Assembly; agree with us in friendship for common purposes; keep all your own rights, but share ours too, and instead of cutting this partition line deeper and deeper across the soil of Ireland, instead of painting the map on either side of this line in ever more vivid contrasts of orange and green, let us try to blend a little more and modify those contrasts and divisions.

Pursuing that line of thought, if that line of thought is found to have validity, it is clear the boundary line would cease to have the same bitter significance in proportion as North and South are associated for important common purposes in some higher organisation than their existing Parliaments. Nothing in the agreement between Sir James Craig and Mr. Collins was more important than the improved arrangements for a Council of Ireland, on the subject of which I have read a letter to the House.

Since then we have had a bad set-back, but we are, I think, repairing and restoring the situation. We must have time, we must have patience, we must have this Bill. Ulster must have British comfort and protection. Ireland must have her Treaty, her election and her constitution. There will be other and better opportunities of dealing with the difficult boundary question, and if the House will take the advice of the Government, we strongly deprecate any attempt to reach a final conclusion upon that subject now.

Let me, before I sit down, leave Ireland and the Irish point of view and Irish interests, and say to the House what is the function of the Imperial Parliament. That, after all, is our point of view. That is our first and proper care in this House. Our interest is very clear, and it should be everywhere recognised and proclaimed what our interest is. The Imperial interest, taking a long view, seeks both the unity of Ireland and the unity of the British Empire, or if you prefer it, Commonwealth of Nations. We can help Ireland to the one if Ireland helps us to the other, and we may be willing to help Ireland to the one in proportion as she helps us to the other. We ought to use our great power and our great unmeasured strength to that end, and in this method of policy, and we shall be justified in so doing at every step by our interest, by our honour, by our good faith and by fair play. From an Imperial point of view we are bound to endeavour to act in an impartial manner; but though we are impartial we cannot be indifferent. Naturally, our hearts warm towards those in the North who are helping, and have helped so long, to keep the old flag flying, and who share our loyalty and our sentiments, and address us in terms of common kinship and not in those of forced aversion.

Ulster has a great part to play in these next few months, an immense part, and the opportunity perhaps of rendering service to the British Empire of inestimable value, and of long lasting consequences in history, and I am very glad indeed to think that at this juncture there should be a man like Sir James Craig as Premier of the Northern Government and that Ulster will be represented in this House and in the House of Lords by representatives who are fully alive to the Imperial aspect of this great question, and are not likely ever to lose sight of that. I end in the way I began, upon the Treaty to which we now ask the House to give statutory effect, and the Bill which we ask the House to read a second time. For generations we have been wandering and floundering in the Irish bog, but at last we think that in this Treaty we have set our feet upon a pathway, which has already become a causeway–narrow, but firm and far-reaching. Let us march along this causeway with determination and circumspection, without losing heart and without losing faith. If Britain continues to march forward along that path, the day may come–it may be distant, but it may not be so distant as we expect–when, turning round, Britain will find at her side Ireland united, a nation, and a friend.

THE SOCIALIST PERIL

March 4, 1922

Loughborough

After defending the record of the Coalition Government and describing national prospects in glowing terms, Churchill again turned upon the Labour Party.

[Extract] . . . Do not delude yourselves by supposing that we are not confronted with a very serious attack. (A voice: "You are not getting the wind up, are you?") It is better to be alarmed while time remains than when it is too late. One of the most insidious methods of our Socialistic friends is to send out an advance guard of people whose business it is to reassure the electorate, to smooth them down, to lull them to sleep, while the Red Army is marching up behind to deliver the assault.

I will examine why the Socialist Party at present is unfit to govern the country. I said so three years ago, and I have never hesitated to keep my word. But I do it in no spirit of offence. I will give you three reasons why at the present stage in their development–I am not talking about the distant future, I cannot pretend to see beyond more than five or ten years, that is enough for the present–they are unfit to govern.

First, they are a class party with a class policy. We want to avoid class politics. For people to be divided up in this country on purely class lines would I am sure be disastrous, and would not give the nation that confidence which it requires. It takes a great party to govern Great Britain. No clique or faction ought to be allowed to do it. It would be disastrous if at the present time, a purely class view prevailed, either Aristocratic or Communistic.

My second reason is that the Labour or Socialist Party consists of very different and bitterly divided elements. Its leaders have been flouted again and again. They have shown themselves in the last three years on critical occasions to be too timid to lead. They have shown themselves afraid of their followers and when some of them have stood up with manly courage they have been brushed aside and disregarded. Anything more lamentable than the spectacle of impotence and distraction which prevailed at the headquarters of the Labour party at the outbreak of the miners' strike could hardly be imagined.

The third reason is their absurd doctrines, which are contrary to the deepest instinct of the human heart. The great mistake the Socialists make is that they follow a lot of logical and symmetrical theory and forget all about human nature. But I ask myself this question. Can Communism or Socialism give to the mass of the people a better, a fuller, and a freer way of life than the existing social system? That is surely a great question which will be discussed more and more in this country. There is nothing new in Socialism. It is not a great new modern conception. It is one of the oldest and most often expounded delusions and fallacies which this world has ever been afflicted by. It consists not merely in a general levelling of mankind, but in keeping them level once they have been beaten down. (Cheers.)

We should have to submit to iron State regulations in every detail. The hours of labour, the method of our daily life would all require to be regulated in the most rigorous manner and regulated by whom? By a little political band or set of men who happened to have seized upon the machinery of power and who, once they have seized upon it, you may depend would be reluctant to let it go. I think the present social system must steadily aim at the building up of a minimum standard of life and labour which, as the general fortunes of the State advance, shall be broadened, consolidated, and heightened.

There is the answer we are entitled to make to our Socialist opponents. It is perfectly true, we do not pretend that the system of society which exists at present is perfect, but we do say this: it is capable of indefinite improvement, it offers the open career to talent, it provides increasing safeguards against misfortune, and faithfully sustained, there is no reason why you should not realize a decent minimum standard of comfort and of happiness for the great mass of the nation. (Cheers.)

IRISH FREE STATE BILL (THIRD READING)

March 8, 1922

House of Commons

[Extract] . . . This debate is now drawing to a close. No one will pretend it has been a pleasant Debate to conduct. I have felt acutely conscious, during its passage, of the intense and natural feeling of the Ulster Members on the whole of the great issue that is before the House of Commons. I have also felt conscious of the inevitable feelings of self-questioning which must arise in the breasts of those who for so many years have been, in one form or another, the opponents of Home Rule settlement in Ireland. I listened, as others in the House listened, with the greatest attention to the admirable speech of the hon. and gallant Member for North Bradford (Major Boyd-Carpenter), in whose eloquent periods and tones one discerned the gifts which he has inherited from his distinguished father. No one could have listened to that appeal without being affected by it, and I say at once, if I have to address myself to that argument, that there is no one who pretends that this solution is an ideal solution, or that it has been brought about in the way which, if we had had an absolute, plenary, unchallenged direction of events, we should ourselves have chosen. No one pretends that.

I feel intensely some of the incidents which have occurred in Ireland since the truce, where loyal, faithful officials, policemen, soldiers, standing at their posts, not only under the authority of the British Crown but under the safeguard of the Irish nation, as signified in a compacted document and Treaty, have been shot dead, and no penalty has been exacted so far—though I am sure it will be, in the name of the Irish people—from those who have done these criminal and detestable deeds. I feel the wrecking, the squandering, of so many loyalties in Ireland, which have been held firm through all these long years of tension. I feel also the position of my hon. Friend the Member for the Falls Division of Belfast (Mr. Devlin) and of the hon. and gallant Member for Waterford (Captain Redmond), who spoke earlier in the Debate. The hon. and gallant Member for Waterford said he was bitter, and he said some things which I think were a little wounding to the House. But he had a right to be bitter. I do not think we are in a position to ask for compliments from him. After all, he is one whose father devoted the last few years of his life, after a lifetime spent in advocating the Irish cause, to aiding the British Empire, and he himself served with distinction and courage in the Guards Division; and when men like him and like my hon. Friend the Member for the Falls Division, who used all his powerful, human, persuasive eloquence to urge recruits to join the fighting line at the moment when the bayonet was literally at our throats, have suffered so terribly by their adherence to constitutional methods and by their loyalty to the great conception of the British Commonwealth of Nations, it is no use pretending that we, who are for the time being the anxious custodians of the interests of the Imperial Government, are in a position to rejoin upon them with acrimonious severity. But you must not look at this settlement as if it were your ideal. You must look at it in relation to the possible alternatives. What are the possible alternatives? No doubt if we had persevered through these last six months raising military and police forces, developing all our mechanical methods of warfare, pressing on the process of subjection by every means at our disposal—and they are very great—we should be further on our road to-day than we were in June and July, when the Treaty was signed. But we should have paid a very heavy price in the whole security of our social and political structure to-day in this island, we should have paid a heavy price in the opinion held of us all over the world, and I think we should have been forced, in spite of all our efforts, into action which would have inflicted in many forms reproaches upon ourselves, in our own hearts and in our own consciences. It was because we found we were being drawn increasingly into action on a great scale of a kind which Britain cannot effectually carry through, not because of her weakness, but because of her strength, that we were definitely brought in a great atmosphere of national feeling to an attempt to make a solution, even under the most unfavourable circumstances, even when we were exposed to every kind of taunt, by peaceful means and reconciliation.

We are now embarked in the full tide of that experiment and effort and act of faith, for such it is, and I should like to ask the House to be very careful when obviously it is a matter of common interest to us all and common importance—all our fortunes, whatever view we take, are affected by the success or failure of this effort—not to allow itself to despair too soon, not to allow itself to lose heart and faith and hope in the long, weary, disappointing, vexing journey in which we have got to persevere. In the first place do not let us exaggerate the state of Ireland. It is quite natural, when the newspapers collect the information each day and present to us in the morning their budget, that all the things that go wrong should be collected, all the disasters, all the outrages, all the unfortunate episodes and regrettable incidents should figure on the morning page. But there is much more in the life of Ireland than the many unfortunate incidents which are chronicled in the papers. You would get an entirely distorted view of Ireland if you were to take your opinions entirely from the daily budget of incidents. I have been making one or two inquiries into the social, sporting, religious, and industrial life of Ireland, and I have acquired a few facts quite different from those that give one the impression of a general condition of anarchy. For instance, a glance at the sporting columns of the daily newspapers will suffice to show that the social activities of the general public in Ireland have almost reverted to the conditions of normal lives. . . .

If you strip Ireland of her grievance, if you strip Ireland of the weapon she has hitherto used, if you strip her of the accusation against Great Britain of being the oppressor, if you strip her of her means of exciting and commanding the sympathy of almost the whole world, of the support she has received in the United States, in our own Dominions, indeed, throughout the whole English-speaking world, if by acting in strict, inflexible, good faith you place Ireland in the position that if she breaks the Treaty she is in the wrong and you are in the right, that she is absolutely isolated in the whole world–then, I say, the strength of your economic position emerges in its integrity. Is it not an extraordinary thing that Ireland should play such a great part–I hope this argument will not be offensive to my hon. Friend who sits there all alone representing Belfast (Mr. Devlin), but I must express the situation as I see it–and has played for so long such a great part in British Imperial affairs–convulsing parties, disturbing Governments, holding the balance for years, putting the Conservatives out of office in 1885, and the Liberals in office in 1892 and again in 1910–[Hon. Members: "1906!"]–in 1910, holding the balance in all our great affairs? Naturally, when we look back and see what Ireland has done in this matter through the agency of the Parliamentary party, we have a feeling that Ireland is an enormous power, bulking in our affairs as a factor of first magnitude. But when Ireland is stripped of her grievance and stands on her own resources, then, and then alone, will you know how weak she is, how little power she has to do us harm. When the Sinn Fein ideal is realised–"Ourselves Alone"–though they may wish to follow their own way of life in Ireland, as they have a right to wish, the power to stand in the path of the British Empire and to obstruct our world-wide policy will have absolutely departed. Even if she has the will–and I do not think she would have the will–she would not have the power. . . .

PLEA FOR NATIONAL UNITY

March 25, 1922

Coalition Meeting, Northampton

By this stage, the unity of the Coalition was showing clear signs of strain, and there was particular restiveness in the Conservative Party at Lloyd George's erratic leadership.

[Extract] It would be a great disaster to the country if the Conservative Party were broken up, and I urge the importance of a united stand by Liberals and Conservatives against the Bolshevist and Communist menace. There is nothing insincere or inconsistent in such action, and I cannot see why Liberals and Conservatives cannot continue to work together.

During the three weeks there has undoubtedly been a marked revival of unity and comradeship throughout the ranks of those on whom lies the duty of sustaining the Government. I attribute this largely to the statesmanlike speech and wide influence of Sir Arthur Balfour and also to the sense of responsibility which draws together in these critical times those forces that make for national stability. It is greatly to be hoped that no new disturbing issue will be raised to mar the process of consolidation. I have seen it suggested that those who speak, as I often speak, of a National Party have some deep design against the unity of the Conservative Party, that our idea is to drive out of the Conservative Party some of its most valued members and some of its strongest and most virile elements. I have no hesitation in declaring on this Coalition platform that it would be a great disaster to the country if the Conservative Party were broken up, as our great Liberal Party has unhappily, in the convulsion of events, been broken up. Such an event would be a prelude to the institution in our country of a number of jealous, discordant groups, such as we see in foreign Parliaments, united only by intrigues to gain a precarious tenure of power and shifting and changing their relationships with baffling and kaleidoscopic rapidity. Such an event would weaken those resolute forces by which the dangerous and subversive elements in society, now so active and sometimes so threatening, are held in check. . . .

The line of division is not on . . . old quarrels. It is being drawn for us before your eyes in quite a different way. Conservative conviction and Liberal principles and sentiments are both exposed to the new and gathering attack of the Socialist parties, behind which crouches the shadows of Communist folly and Bolshevist crime. It is no good telling me that this is not important and is not a real danger—that we could afford to disregard it. When I see that we are confronted with the attack all over the country of 450 candidates who, although in many cases respectable and patriotic Labour men and women, are all bound hand and foot to some form or other of Socialist doctrines; when I see the steady growth of the Socialist vote in one election after another; when I see all the misery there is for agitation and discontent to feed on—I think we should be mad to go on in supine apathy, not taking any steps to protect the interests in our charge.

In my own constituency of Dundee there is much distress and unemployment. There are industries which are stagnant or slowly reviving. There are many of its thousands undergoing painful privations, many citizens who lost their dearest in the Great War; there are violent Socialist and Communist candidates in the field eager to dismiss their present representative from his duties. They do not hesitate to attack us; and why should we hesitate to attack them? I have no patience with the doctrine that the Labour Party are to be calmly allowed to go about the country attacking 400 seats. They have their rights under the British Constitution. (A voice: "Why lock them up?") When they go beyond the particular opportunities which the English Constitution accords them, then sometimes the law has to intervene. A strong message will go out from Dundee when the time comes—as come it will—that revolutionary action or

Socialistic theories are no remedies for the evils that exist in our country at the present time; that peace at home and abroad, work, enterprise, and thrift, public and private, must make the foundation on which the prosperity of these islands, and indeed of the world, can alone be rebuilt.

Why is it impossible for Liberals to work with a united Conservative Party? Why cannot Liberals who care about the Empire work with Conservatives who care about the social welfare of the people? Is there not really an identity and community of aim? There is nothing insincere and inconsistent in such action. We have been used to the names "Liberal" and "Conservative" standing for opposite parties, but there is nothing absurd in their being blended in one. Why, in Canada there has been for many years a party called by the actual name of Liberal-Conservatives. I am prepared to argue that Liberalism is the truest form of Conservatism. Lord Randolph Churchill said in 1888, "Tory democracy involves the idea of a Government who in all branches of their policy and in all features of their administration are animated by lofty and liberal ideas." I believe that I am justified in bringing these considerations before them at a time when we are working together in common political action against common political opponents and we have a right to assure ourselves that there is no inconsistency in terminating the party disputations of the past.

But a strong unity by itself will not suffice. Surrounded as we are by difficulties, weighted with so many burdens, we must walk wisely and warily and prudently. We must endeavour to secure a breathing space, a period of tranquility, in which the native energy of our country can resume its normal strength and flow. In this mood we should examine the Irish settlement. The government of the whole of Ireland has now been, broadly speaking, entirely confided to Irishmen. What will they do with it? Will they shatter its prosperity with the quarrels of a bygone age, with vile persecutions and counter-persecutions, with corroding hatreds such as we in Great Britain have not known in our island for many generations? Will they sink in a welter of anarchy and strife, or will they rise hopefully and faithfully to the bright future of peace and freedom which is within their grasp? It is for them to choose; their fate is in their own hands. We can hope, we can cheer, but it rests with them. (Cheers.) Even at this not particularly cheering moment I avow my strong faith and hope that things will come right. (Cheers.) . . .

We must not fail to evolve and follow a national policy which can be an Imperial policy. We must be careful in these busy days, when we are so occupied with Austria, Russia, Czecho-Slovakia, Yugo-Slavia, and Poland, and so rightly anxious to set them on their feet again, that we do not forget the existence of the British Empire. If in order to revive our trade we have to make credit investment without the hope of immediate return, do not let us give it all to foreigners. Let us keep something at any rate, for the Colonies which we have planted in so many lands and for the great self-governing Dominions which have risen to splendour at our side. (Cheers.)

SOCIALISM

April 8, 1922

Caird Hall, Dundee

[Extract] . . . One supreme issue is arising in our country, which not only at the next Election, come when it may, but perhaps at many others that will follow in its tram, will array the British people into two opposite camps. It is the great issue of a Socialistic organization of society versus individual enterprise. You know well where I stand over this. My views upon it were stated here when I first stood on a Dundee platform, now 14 years ago.

The Socialist and the Liberal conceptions represent two absolutely opposite ideas of the government of men. I remember drawing some of these distinctions for you 14 years ago. Liberalism attacks monopoly; Socialism attacks capital. The Liberal seeks to level up; the Socialist seeks to level down. Liberalism believes that Government must be based on the goodwill of the masses of the people; Socialism knows that it can only operate through an agency of bureaucracy under the direction of an autocratic sect, can only operate through some forms of minority power. The policy of the Socialist is that the Government should own all the means of production, distribution, and exchange; that there should be no such thing as private enterprise or private property; no private shop or house or cottage; no bank or ship; no private savings, no private business, no buying and selling; no enterprise, no wages, no profits; everything is to be owned by the State; everybody is to be directed by the State; everybody is to be rationed by the State; everyone will be told what they are to do, what their employment is to be, where they are to live, when they are to travel. The whole of our vast community of five and forty millions is to be directed according to this theory of government–and it is of fundamental theories that we are speaking this afternoon–like a great army according to absolutely settled discipline and absolutely unchallengeable authority.

But who is to decide all these important matters? The Socialist Government must decide. The whole nation, in fact, would have to be conscribed into one great army kept everlastingly mobilized, and would have to receive their orders from a sort of gigantic War Office or Government Department or group of Government Departments. Why, I say, once such a Government was set up, everyone would be at the mercy of those controlling the system. No one could stand against it for a moment. Whoever he was, he could be starved in a moment by the simple order of the Government withdrawing his ration tickets. The people would be absolutely prostrate in the hands of the Government. They would be reduced at once to State slaves, moved hither and thither like cattle at the will of their own. We have often drawn in Dundee the distinction between Governments that own the people and peoples that own the Governments. There never was a Government yet erected that would own the people as a Socialist Government would. No Tsar, no Kaiser, no Oriental potentate has ever wielded powers like these. When the only employer in the country is the State, a strike becomes a rebellion. No strikes can therefore be tolerated. Workers who strike would have to be punished, and punished severely; first, no doubt, by reducing their rations, then by imprisonment, and in the last resort by death. Where is the incentive to labour under the Socialist ideal—where is the incentive, in the words of your poet, "to make a happy fireside clime for weans and wife"? It has been destroyed. Where are the prizes of inventiveness and enterprise?—the reward of thrift and self-denial? Where are the rights of genius and ability? They are gone. Individualism offers an infinitely graduated and infinitely varied system of rewards for genius, for enterprise, for exertion, for industry, for faithfulness, for thrift. Socialism destroys all this. Socialism can only substitute for a system of graduated rewards, a system of graduated punishments. Think for a moment of the power which would be in the hands of the men who obtained the control of this terrific governing machine of Socialism. During their term of office they would sit high above the masses, ruling their lives, and appointing their toil as if they were gods in heaven. Is it conceivable that they will be ready to step down from their high places and take up the life of Socialist slaves? Why, gentlemen, they will never give up their power once they have got it. They will form themselves into a sort of priesthood, with a caucus below them for rigging the elections, and if they lasted long enough they would undoubtedly put themselves on an hereditary basis and transmit, or seek to transmit, their tyranny unbroken to their descendants and their relations.

You will say to me, "You are exaggerating; no one would ever think of things like that." But they have done things like that. They are doing them now before your very eyes. As we sit here in this hall this afternoon, free to live our lives in our own way, to express our political views, to criticise or change our Governments, to enjoy under the Union Jack all the varied possibilities which life gives to the free-born Briton—and of which no race has taken more advantages than the free-born Scot—as we sit here, 120 millions of Russians are prostrate under Socialist and Communist tyranny which has proceeded point by point exactly as I have described.

There you see the rule of the few made absolute over the wishes of the many. There you see the complete nationalization of all the means of production, distribution, and exchange. There you see complete the suppression of freedom in every form. There you see compulsion in every form; and, side by side with it—which is inevitable—corruption in every form. And what are the results? The one claim which Socialist thinkers have always made is that their system would secure for the masses a larger portion of this world's goods. Men have been invited to give up their liberty in order to obtain a greater measure of prosperity. But what has happened? What has happened on the only occasion when this terrible experiment has been carried out with ruthless logic to its final conclusion upon the body and carcass of a great nation? Russia, the great granary of Europe, is rapidly being reduced to a desert. Famine and pestilence are ravaging her people and carrying them off literally by tens of millions. No help that we can afford to send will appreciably relieve their sufferings. The deed is done. Things are what they are, and their consequences will be what they will be. Why, then, should we deceive ourselves?

Socialism is the negation of every principle of British Liberalism (cheers), of every sentiment of the British heart. Socialism is barbarism; Socialism is slavery; and now we know that in addition to that, Socialism is starvation (cheers). Is it not a very serious situation that there should be growing so rapidly in this country a gigantic Party pledged in one form or another, some going further than others, no doubt, some wishing to proceed peacefully and others violently, but all pledged in allegiance to the Socialist ideal, all moving forward, consciously or unconsciously, towards that absurd, visionary and perilous Utopia? . . .

BRITISH POLICY IN IRELAND

June 26, 1922

House of Commons

On April 14 opponents of the Provisional Government seized the Four Courts in Dublin, and serious fighting broke out. With considerable difficulty, a truce was arranged until the elections to the new Dial, scheduled for June 16, could be held.

On June 22 Sir Henry Wilson was assassinated in London. This outrage brought bitter criticism on the Government from the Ulster and Conservative opponents of the Irish Treaty, and played a major part in greater British assistance to the Provisional Government in its difficulties with the I.R.A. General Macready was ordered to drive the Irregulars out of the Four Courts, but in the event it was undertaken by forces of the Free State Government with British assistance.

[Extract] . . . I admit to the Committee quite frankly that I recognised a fortnight ago–a week or 10 days ago–increasingly that the defeat of the extremists in the North, by the growing power of the Ulster Government and by the vigorous applications of British military force on the border, and the defeat of the extremists in the South by the clear pronouncement of the Irish people–of which I am going to speak in a few moments –I admit that this situation, and the excitement and tension consequent upon it, impressed themselves upon me as being likely to make it necessary to resume, and extend, the police protection to individuals, and to put in force many of those precautions which we had formerly used, but during the last six months had discontinued. Acting in this sense, we had already begun the protection of various persons, some of whom were Ministers and others–a larger number–of whom were private, unofficial persons, and in some cases humble persons, whose names I shall certainly not disclose. We had also arranged with the Northern Government to be kept fully informed of the movements of certain personages in the North, about whom, when they visited this country, we began to feel anxiety; and we should, of course, have welcomed any additions which the Northern Government themselves might have suggested to our list. These persons were in all cases protected.

No warning came to us from the Northern Government about the position of the late Field-Marshal Sir Henry Wilson. I should have thought myself that, while he was in the greatest danger in Ulster, going about Belfast and about the Border, he would not have been in any more danger in this country than 30 or 40 other persons whose names will readily occur to one's mind. However, we have been confronted with a shocking and abominable crime, and no doubt the resources of the State will be employed in a much fuller measure in the future than they have been during the prolonged immunity of the past, but this I will say, that we must put our main reliance, in the future as in the past, upon securities much broader than those which can be achieved by police protection. We must continue to show that assassination will not change the course of British policy and that in this robust and manly country murderers will be caught and delivered to speedy justice. Nothing could exceed the courage of the police and the spontaneous indignation of the loyal, vigorous population when they were confronted, all unarmed, with the heinous evidences of this crime. That fact is, in itself, a great deterrent upon the development, on this side of the Channel, of the murder schemes which have laid Ireland low; but a still greater deterrent will be the fact that this country pursues unmoved the policies which it has deliberately adopted, being deflected neither in one direction nor another by any considerations other than those which arise from the careful study of general principles and of the main propositions governing the policy which we have adopted. . . .

The Irish people have pronounced, and I beg the House not to under-rate the significance of that pronouncement. Look at their difficulties. A doubtful pact between Mr. Collins and Mr. de Valera, a pact doubtfully made and doubtfully kept, robbed the Irish people of the power to contest a great number of constituencies. In others, the candidates stood, and the electors voted, under the duress of many abominable forms of intimidation. Proportional representation cast its baffling cloak over a defeated minority.

But, in spite of all this, the will of the Irish nation has become abundantly plain. Any candidate of whatever description who stood for the Treaty received strong or overwhelming support. Any candidate of whatever description who opposed it was rejected, or only scraped in through the protection of this complicated system of voting. The Irish people, on this first opportunity they have had of expressing their view, seemed to single out particularly for their reprobation persons like the ferocious Countess Markievicz and the renegade Erskine Childers. Moreover, not only were the first preferences of the electors given in a vast majority for the Treaty candidates, but the second and third preferences were bestowed always from one point of view—the plain and simple point of view of the kindly, good-hearted multitudes of decent, honest Irish men and women who, across all these horrors and difficulties, stretched forth their hands at the only moment open to them, by the only means open to them, in favour of the Treaty of peace, which, within the circle of the British Empire, gives them the power to manage their own affairs. If I were to attempt to interpret the will of the Irish nation as expressed unmistakably at this election, I would sum it up as follows: "You have given us our freedom; we wish to give you our friendship. You will help us towards a united Ireland; we will help you towards a united Empire." That, I believe, is the true reading of the verdict of the Irish nation at the polls, and that indicates the road along which we are marching, and along which we are going to march. Do not let us be drawn from it; do not let us bring to confusion the wishes of the great masses on both sides of the Channel.

I wish I could end here, but I cannot. I should not be dealing honestly and fully with this subject if I left in the minds of the House the impression that all that is required is patience and composure. No, Sir. Firmness is needed. Firmness is needed in the interests of peace as much as patience. The constitution which we have seen, which has been published, satisfactorily conforms to the Treaty. It has now to be passed through the new Irish Parliament. There is no room for the slightest diminution of the Imperial and Constitutional safeguards and stipulations which it contains. That is not all. Mere paper affirmations, however important, unaccompanied by any effective effort to bring them into action, will not be sufficient. Mere denunciation of murder, however heartfelt, unaccompanied by the apprehension of a single murderer, cannot be accepted. The keeping in being within the Irish Free State by an elaborate process of duality, verging upon duplicity, of the whole apparatus of a Republican Government will not be in accordance either with the will of the Irish people, with the stipulations of the Treaty, or with the maintenance of good relations between the two countries. The resources at the disposal of His Majesty's Government are various and powerful. There are military, economic, and financial sanctions–to use a word with which we frequently meet in Continental affairs–there are sanctions of these kinds which are available, and which are formidable. They have been very closely studied, and the more closely they are studied, the more clearly it is seen that those measures will be increasingly effective in proportion as the Irish Government and State become more fully and more solidly organised. His Majesty's Government do not feel that, after this election has clearly shown what are the wishes of the Irish people, we can continue to tolerate many gross lapses from the spirit of the Treaty, and improprieties and irregularities in its execution, with which we have put up, and in which we have acquiesced, during the last six months.

Hitherto we have been dealing with a Government weak because it has formed no contact with the people. Hitherto we have been anxious to do nothing to compromise the clear expression of Irish opinion. But now this Provisional Government is greatly strengthened. It is armed with the declared will of the Irish electorate. It is supported by an effective Parliamentary majority. It is its duty to give effect to the Treaty in the letter and in the spirit, to give full effect to it, and to give full effect to it without delay. A much stricter reckoning must rule henceforward. The ambiguous position of the so-called Irish Republican Army, intermingled as it is with the Free State troops, is an affront to the Treaty, The presence in Dublin, in violent occupation of the Four Courts, of a band of men styling themselves the Headquarters of the Republican Executive, is a gross breach and defiance of the Treaty. From this nest of anarchy and treason, not only to the British Crown, but to the Irish people, murderous outrages are stimulated and encouraged, not only in the 26 Counties, not only in the territory of the Northern Government, but even, it seems most probable, here across the Channel in Great Britain. From this centre, at any rate, an organisation is kept in being which has branches in Ulster, in Scotland, and in England, with the declared purpose of wrecking the Treaty by the vilest processes of which human degradation can conceive. The time has come when it is not unfair, not premature, and not impatient for us to make to this strengthened Irish Government and new Irish Parliament a request, in express terms, that this sort of thing must come to an end. If it does not come to an end, if either from weakness, from want of courage, or for some other even less creditable reasons, if it is not brought to an end and a very speedy end, then it is my duty to say, on behalf of His Majesty's Government, that we shall regard the Treaty as having been formally violated, that we shall take no steps to carry out or to legalise its further stages, and that we shall resume full liberty of action in any direction that may seem proper and to any extent that may be necessary to safeguard the interests and the rights that are entrusted to our care.

ELECTION ADDRESS

November 11, 1922

Caird Hall, Dundee

The simmering discontent of the Conservative rank and file against the Coalition reached its climax in the autumn of 1922. The passage of the Irish Free State Act and the suppression of the capture of the Four Courts had not checked the civil war. Unemployment in Britain was still high. The immediate cause of the fall of the Coalition was a crisis which arose over a confrontation between the triumphant forces of Kemal Ataturk and British troops at the town of Chanak, on the Dardanelles, defending the neutral zone created by the Treaty of Sevres in 1920. The Cabinet decided to refuse to negotiate under duress, and a telegram was sent by Churchill to the Dominion Prime Ministers seeking their support. There had been no preparation of the public for this unexpected major crisis, and Lord Curzon and Stanley Baldwin (the hitherto obscure President of the Board of Trade) were among the most critical Ministers against this belligerent policy. On October 7 Bonar Law (who had retired from the Government in 1921 on grounds of ill-health) publicly criticised the impetuousness of the Cabinet. The Coalition leaders decided that the Conservative Party must resolve whether to remain in the Coalition–having little doubt of the verdict. The plan misfired dramatically and totally. Bonar Law and Baldwin spoke vigorously against Lloyd George and the Coalition and in favour of the Conservatives fighting the next election as a separate party. The "Carlton Club Meeting" on October 19 emphatically endorsed this advice, and Lloyd George resigned that afternoon.

Bonar Law formed a Government from which the leading Conservatives–Austen Chamberlain, Arthur Balfour, and Lord Birkenhead–were notably absent, and immediately called for a General Election. It was one of the most confused elections in modern political history, with Lloyd George Liberals, Asquith Liberals, Coalition Conservatives, and Bonar Law Conservatives hopelessly intermingled. Only Labour presented a united front.

At this critical moment in his fortunes, Churchill was prostrated by an emergency appendectomy. This did not prevent him from issuing vigorous statements attacking the new Conservative Government.

Churchill's opponents at Dundee were the persistent Mr. Scrymgeour (Prohibition); E. D. Morel (Labour); and W. Gallacher (Communist). Because of his illness Churchill did not arrive at Dundee until two days before the poll, and was still very unwell. It was a rowdy, bitter election.

[Extract] . . . My Labour opponents are two anti-British gentlemen and I am surprised that the Labour Party could not find two solid, reputable trade unionists in their place. (A voice: "You have got the wind up.") There are only two sides to the election–there are only two policies–Liberalism and Socialism. If we are successfully to combat the visionary doctrines and wild schemes, the capital levy, and the confiscations of the Socialists, it can be only by an earnest and untiring effort for the social, intellectual, and moral advancement of the people. A policy of mere negation will never be accepted by the electors of this country. I do not believe it is a possible policy in a society in a state of constant development. It would be lamentable if our rulers–I hope they do not mean it–were to take up an attitude or give an impression to the masses that the time has come to call a halt in all the great processes of social betterment or reform. I can not subscribe to such a policy.

We seem to be moving back again towards the days of party strife and tumult. Many people seem most anxious to see them renewed, but I am not among those who think that they were the palmy days of British politics or who wish them to return. I do not think the country is in a fit condition to be torn and harried by savage domestic warfare. What we require now is not a period of turmoil, but a period of stability and recuperation. Let us stand together and tread a sober middle way. (Cheers.)

AN ATTEMPTED SPEECH

November 13, 1922

Drill Hall, Dundee

Amid much uproar Churchill attempted to address some 5,000 constituents on the eve of the poll. The hostile elements soon took control of the meeting, however, and it had to be abandoned. "I was struck by the looks of passionate hatred on the faces of some of the young men and women," he later wrote. "Indeed, but for my helpless condition I am sure they would have attacked me."

Churchill went down to overwhelming defeat. Mr. Scrymgeour was triumphant at last–and by a majority of over 10,000! "In the twinkling of an eye," Churchill wrote, "I found myself without office, without a seat, without a party, and even without an appendix."

[Editor's Note: In an effort to address the crowd Churchill rose but was forced to resume a sitting position when he was met with renewed hostility and hooting. There were cries of "We'll do the same as Manchester this time." Shouting amidst the uproar, he exclaimed] : I have not had time to prosecute my campaign in Dundee.

A Voice: You are beaten. (Cheers, and shouts of "You deserve it.")

Mr. Churchill: Well, whether I deserve it or not, I have a right to make my answer. (Cheers.) No man is condemned unheard in Britain. The poll is on Wednesday. (Howls of "And you'll be at the bottom.") Then if I am to be at the bottom, you might let me have my last dying fling. I won't go any longer than you wish me to. (Chorus of: "Then stop now.")

I am not going to be muzzled, or told I must not attack this man or that!

[Editor's Note: Then he made an attack on the Dundee newspapers, and commented on Conservative and Liberal newspapers in Dundee being run from the same office.] It's all humbug. (Interruption) I am not going to attempt to put arguments before you!

[Editor's Note: Shaking his fist at those leading the disorder, he continued]: If about 100 young men and women in the audience choose to spoil a whole meeting–(interruption)–if about 100 of these young reptiles choose to deny democracy and the masses of the people the right to conduct great assemblies, the blame is on them, and the punishment will be administered to them by the electors. [Editor's Note: At this point Churchill rose and shook a warning fist at the interrupters, and tried to persuade the hecklers to keep silent. His attempts were entirely unsuccessful. He tried again to speak]: Now you see what the Gallacher (his Communist opponent) crowd are worth.

A Voice: Rub it in.

Mr. Churchill: Now you see the liberties you would have if the country was run by them. No voice, no brains; just break up a meeting that they have not the wit to address. The electors will know how to deal with a party whose only weapon is idiotic clamour.

[Editor's Note: Churchill undertook to answer questions before making any further attempts to get on with his speech. One questioner asked him: "Didn't you give a free hand to Blacks and Tans in Ireland, to shoot the women and the children down?" He replied]: I say when our soldiers and our policemen were shot down and murdered we had every right to strike back and defend ourselves.

[Editor's Note: After answering other questions, the interruptions resumed and it became clear that they would not permit Churchill a further hearing. Then he rose and said ironically]: I thank you for the very attentive hearing you have given me, and I think you have vindicated in the most effective manner the devotion of the Socialist party to free speech. It has been shown very clearly that a handful of rowdies can break up a great meeting. We may not be heard to-night, but we will carry out our purpose at the poll. We will not submit to the bullying tyranny of the featherheads. We will not submit to the roar of the mob, the supporters of the Socialist candidate, who, if they had their way, would reduce this great country to the same bear-garden that they have reduced this meeting to.

FREE TRADE

November 16, 1923

Free Trade Hall, Manchester

Churchill's career had reached a major crisis. The other ex-Coalition leaders–Birkenhead, Balfour, Austen Chamberlain, Lloyd George–at least had positions in Parliament, and were members of recognised political parties. Churchill was disen-

chanted with Lloyd George, and it was perfectly evident that his sympathies lay with the Conservatives. Nonetheless, in the General Election called unexpectedly in November 1923 by Baldwin (who had succeeded the fatally ill Bonar Law in May), Churchill stood unsuccessfully as a Liberal Free Trader at West Leicester. For the whole of this year–and, indeed, until the autumn of 1924–Churchill was out of Parliament. Although he did a great deal of writing–notably on The World Crisis *and on newspaper articles–he made relatively few public speeches in the course of the year.*

Early in May it was discovered that Bonar Law had inoperable cancer of the throat, and he was succeeded as Prime Minister by Stanley Baldwin.

On the grounds that he was honouring Bonar Law's pledge not to introduce Protection without seeking the views of the people, Baldwin suddenly and unexpectedly dissolved Parliament in November. For the last time, Churchill stood as a Liberal.

[Extract] Ten years have passed since I last stood on this historic platform, and they have been ten years of unexampled strain for all of us. But I assure you I am very glad to come again to Manchester, and to come again to Manchester in her hour of need. (Hear, hear.)

The futile and inglorious Parliament elected a year ago is about to terminate its brief existence by the attempted assassination of Free Trade. The Government which has accomplished nothing of the slightest consequence or value, whose tenure of office has been accompanied by no improvement in affairs at home and by the virtual extinction of our influence abroad, now rushes out to the electors upon a hurriedly conceived and utterly unexplained scheme to revolutionise the commercial, financial, fiscal system of our country by putting thousands of taxes on imported goods and use the revenue thus obtained for the purpose of encouraging their supporters in the agricultural districts. (Laughter.)

That is the situation which is before us. Free Trade is blamed for all the evils which followed the destruction of the war, and for all the mistakes and shortcomings of new and inexperienced Ministers. We are invited to revert precipitately to a system of Protection, which we are assured is the only remedy for unemployment. No time is given, either to the House of Commons or in the constituencies, for the discussion of this grave matter; no details are presented whereby the facts may be examined. The subject has not been studied and has not been produced in a reasonable or scientific spirit. It is thrust upon us as a crude issue of party politics, and a vague mandate is to be snatched at a snap election, pressed forward with every circumstance of indecent haste. (Cheers.) Free Trade is to be tried by drumhead court-martial and shot at dawn. (Cheers and laughter.) No fair hearing of the case, no judicial examination of the facts, no consideration is to be shown to the trading interests of the country or the needs of the shopkeeping and business communities. A party verdict is to be obtained by party politicians and exploited for party purposes.

The Prime Minister and the Government–a Government which had so many chances of serving the country–blundered into an impossible position, a position of hopeless confusion, and they have decided to brazen it out; like another Government of which we heard, they are to hack their way through in the hope of extricating themselves by violence from difficulties into which they have fallen.

This is no measure of statecraft. It is the act of a faction, and confronted by this it is the duty not only of all Free-traders but of all constitutionalists of all parties–(cheers)–to make common cause to stand in one line, to do their best to avert the threatened catastrophe.

Let us begin by asking ourselves the simple question, Has Free Trade served this country well or ill? Has it been proved a failure in peace or war? Surely nothing has been more remarkable than the gigantic financial, commercial, and economic strength of this island of ours, revealed in the great struggle and tribulation through which we have passed. We are the only nation in the whole world which has borne the burden we had to bear without breaking. From the first day to the last day of the war the iron strength of this old country sustained the whole Allied cause. (Cheers.)

Not only did we maintain armies which eventually exceeded 5,000,000 men in the field, not only did we lend tremendous sums of money to our European allies, but we kept the seas open, we carried their troops and their supplies, we safeguarded ourselves and fed ourselves, and after the victory was won Britain stood forth as the only nation heavily engaged in the war paying its debts and paying its way. (Cheers.) If all the evils of the aftermath, if all the sufferings and privations of hard years and winter months are to be attributed to Free Trade, let it also be remembered that the greatest and most prolonged manifestation of economic power which the history of the whole world can show was produced by Great Britain after 70 years of Free Trade. (Cheers.) Surely before Free Trade is led out to execution, before the firing party of prejudice, interest, and sheer ignorance level their rifles, we are entitled to say a few words on its behalf.

There is a second question which we should ask ourselves–has Free Trade prevented or impeded the unity of the British Empire? Twenty years ago, Mr. Garnett reminds me–our memories go back over the same period–when Mr. Chamberlain, the great Mr. Chamberlain–(loud laughter)–I am sure neither of his two distinguished sons will do other than endorse that epithet–made his attack upon Free Trade, he placed the unity of the British Empire in the forefront of his proposals. It was his prime object. It was the motive power that let him on that course. He uttered the most gloomy predictions of what would happen to the British Empire if a preferential system of taxation were not adopted based upon duties of food. We Free-traders thought his methods wrong, and certainly his prophecies did not come true, but no one could deny that Mr. Joseph Chamberlain's aim was lofty and inspiring.

We beat his food taxes. We defeated his proposals. And what happened? All the component parts of the British Empire continued to enjoy complete fiscal freedom. And in the hour of need the Empire was found united, heart and hand, after 70 years of Free Trade, in a manner far beyond the brightest and most sanguine dreams of any Imperialist–(hear, hear),–far more so than Mr. Chamberlain himself had ever dared to hope. And that union of the Empire, founded as it was on freedom and on justice, stood every shock and strain in that terrible period which has scarred and darkened all our lives.

How, then, can it be said on the morrow of this tremendous event that Free Trade has prevented the unity of the British Empire? . . .

MR. BALDWIN

December 5, 1923

Women's Meeting, Liberal Club,
West Leicester

Churchill was defeated by over 4,000 votes. It was a fortunate escape. The results were: Conservatives, 258 seats; Labour, 191; Liberals, 191. The Lloyd George Liberals were reduced to 26.

After various schemes had failed to avert the disaster of a Labour Government–described by Churchill in a public letter on January 17, 1924, as "a national misfortune such as has usually befallen great states only on the moment of defeat in war"–the Asquithian Liberals supported Labour in a vote of confidence on January 21 in which the Government was defeated by 72 votes. The first Labour Government, headed by J. Ramsay MacDonald, took office.

[Extract] ... The election is destined to be a memorable one, because its circumstances are unparalleled. I consider that Mr. Baldwin is responsible for what I can only describe as a constitutional outrage. The Prime Minister, for party purposes, has broken up Parliament in the endeavour to snatch a verdict at an election rushed forward with indecent haste upon a programme which he has shown himself incapable of explaining or unwilling to explain. Mr. Baldwin has said that, even if there is a great majority of votes against protection, if, by a number of triangular contests and split votes, he is in possession of a Parliamentary majority, he will use that majority to the full to force a scheme of protection–any scheme he can get the great vested interests to agree to. He will force it through the House of Commons and make it the law of the land in defiance of the will of the majority of the people.

I call that a constitutional outrage. It is an act of political travesty, an act which carries us back to days when tyrannical ministers thought to rule this country against its will. Mr. Baldwin complains that his opponents are not honourable. In the whole of my experience I have never known a Prime Minister to treat the country with such gross unfairness, to treat his political opponents with such a total lack of anything in the nature of fair play as has been done by the present Prime Minister in the time and circumstances in which he launched this protectionist campaign.

Mr. Baldwin says he is an honest man. A man might believe himself to be an honest man, and yet might lend himself to very wrong courses. As much mischief has been done in the world by honest men who have been agents of dark and sinister influences as has been done by ordinary persons of comparatively light weight. Who is Mr. Baldwin to acclaim himself such a singularly honest man? He is a man whom we have only known in the last few months, through the eulogies of the newspapers. He has no achievements to his record; he is an unknown man.

Because I have endeavoured to raise the serious aspects of the question, it must not be supposed that I am not broadly hopeful of the main results. I have put my faith in the well-tried common sense of the people. I have put my faith in the inherent instincts of prudence and fairness which women have in their hearts. I have put my faith in the fact that a united Liberal Party, working and fighting as rarely in my experience it has before, will make a great impression upon the doubtful and divided ranks of Toryism, and will succeed in securing in the next House of Commons so commanding a position that it will be impossible for a tariff to go through, whatever happens. I am confident of my success in Leicester.

ADOPTION MEETING, WESTMINSTER

March 10, 1924

Essex Hall, London

In February Churchill had supported the Conservative candidate in the Burnley by-election. In March he accepted an invitation to stand as an "Independent and Anti-Socialist" candidate in the Abbey Division of Westminster by-election, with Conservative support. To his dismay, the local association insisted on putting forward an official Conservative candidate–Mr. O. W. Nicholson, the nephew of the former Member. The other candidates were Fenner Brockway (Labour) and J. S. Duckers (Liberal).

[Extract] . . . I am an Independent Anti-Socialist candidate. I have not altered my position in regard to any of the great questions of the day. I have stood always in a central position, opposing extreme movements whether they come from the Left or Right. I have been fighting Socialist candidates in every election I have fought since 1908. At the last election I acted in entire consistency in my attitude towards Protection, but I chose as the object of my attack not a Conservative candidate in a Conservative seat, but one of the strongest Labour seats in the country–West Leicester. If I had not been opposed most unwisely and improvidently by a Conservative, we would not have had Mr. Pethick Lawrence, the author of the capital levy, in the House, and I would not be troubling the electors of Westminster to-day.

The issue before you is an extremely serious one, and you have a great opportunity. The whole world is looking at this contest. The situation is so critical in this country that people are anxiously waiting for a strong indication from some great constituency. I am not in the least deceived by the moderation of the present Socialist Government. I believe they are well advised from their own point of view to try to gain as much prestige as possible while they are in office without being in power and to try to lull the country into a sense of confidence and security to give the impression that, after all, Socialism does not mean anything except what Liberals and Conservatives would do, that they can keep up the defences of the country and maintain the unity of the Empire just as well as or better than the Conservative or Liberal Party.

But I pay them a greater compliment. I do not believe they have deserted those doctrines of collectivism, the nationalization of all the means of production, distribution and exchange on which their party has flourished and thrived, and on which they have grown to the great position they are in. I am sure that the moment will come, and come soon—certainly within a year, perhaps with a few months—when, whatever the Ministers of the Government may feel about continuing to pose as Liberals or Conservatives while in office or as revolutionaries when they are out, the rank and file of their own party will say, "That is quite enough, you have done very well, but let us resume the fight." I confidently look forward to a struggle in the very near future in which the Socialist Party will arm itself with a programme of bribes and doles, very attractive until one is called upon to find the means of paying, will bring this programme forward and will present that issue to the country. There will ensue an election fraught with the gravest consequences to the prosperity and tranquillity of the country.

You have a chance in Westminster of giving a signal to the whole of Britain. (Cheers.) Your chance is to say that the Socialists are not going to have it all their own way—(cheers)—that society, with all its shortcomings and defects, is after all the only structure of civilization we have painfully reared in centuries of misfortune and toil and progress; that society and its structure of economic civilization, with free enterprise, private property, and the enjoyment of individual liberty, is not going to be overturned without a struggle. There are arguments which can be used in defence of the existing system which no man or woman need feel the slightest misgiving or doubt about. There is no other way except on the existing capitalist basis of society that the exports can be manufactured and sold all over the world, by which the millions who live in this island can get their daily bread. Try to carry on these extraordinary processes of world trade, which keep our population here alive, by public departments, by enormous offices filled with bureaucrats, by compulsion, the conscription of labour, in place of the freedom which now exists, and in place of the incentive of private profit; try to substitute for this incentive this vast Socialist scheme of State slavery—for it is nothing less—and although you might go through the gestures of producing your goods or merchandise you would utterly and totally fail to do that on terms which would enable you to carry the process forward from year to year.

Let us send a message to our administrators in the great Oriental countries—to India and Egypt—to inspire them with confidence in their work and give them the feeling that the old country has not lost heart or faith in its destiny and its mission of right and justice throughout the world and that if they do their duty faithfully they will be supported and sustained. Let us send a message also to our friends in foreign countries and to friendly foreign nations, and also to those who are suffering dreadful oppression and tyranny in Russia, a message to say that from beneath the shadow of Westminster Abbey there is a concourse and a community of human beings who are determined that freedom and justice shall not be trampled down. (Cheers.)

THE POLL RESULT

March 20, 1924

Caxton Hall, London

Despite much unofficial Conservative support, and that of both the Rothermere and Beaverbrook Presses, Churchill was defeated by Nicholson by 43 votes after what he called "incomparably the most exciting, stirring, sensational election I have ever fought."

[Extract] . . . I am too old a campaigner to be disheartened (cheers) by the ups and downs of political life. It was not on personal grounds or for personal reasons that I came forward to make this effort. I have been considering throughout what was the real need of this country and of the stable forces of this country on which it must increasingly rely in future years. Although the dead weight of a strong party machine, aided by the exertions of two other party machines, has proved effective against a single individual, I believe that we have roused the attention of the whole country to an aspect of their political affairs which merited their urgent attention. We have succeeded in setting on foot a movement and in proclaiming a policy which will exercise a material, a potent, and possibly a decision influence upon the immediate future of our political affairs.

I do not believe that the Conservative Party can afford to reject and repulse the forces which are represented in the 8,000 votes for an Independent Anti-Socialist candidate. I do not believe that narrow, bitter, party views or weak, incoherent party action will receive the approval of the mass of patriotic, loyal, progressive British men and women throughout the land, who see very clearly the direction in which the leaders of the historic parties ought to lead their followers. I am content to let this lesson be studied in all parts of the country, and I predict that the course of events in the next few months, and certainly within a year, will show very clearly the foresight, the clarity of judgment, the patriotic resolution, which has animated all those who have fought this contest on my side.

It is to that day to which I look forward, when you will see the great Conservative Party in its senses and still occupying a broad and progressive platform, united with large numbers of Liberals in all parts of the country. You will see these combined forces repulsing the Socialist attack which is levelled at our institutions, and you will see the inauguration of a Government worthy to rank with the Governments of the Unionist Party in the days of the great Lord Salisbury, and capable of affording a stable foundation for the administration and conduct of our affairs at home and abroad.

"PRESENT DANGERS OF THE SOCIALIST MOVEMENT"

May 7, 1924

Working Men's Conservative Association and
Women's Unionist Federation Joint Meeting,
Sun Hall, Liverpool

This meeting–the first Conservative gathering Churchill had addressed for twenty years–was organised by Sir Archibald Salvidge, who had also organised the last Liverpool meeting of Lord Randolph Churchill in 1893. It marked a major turning-point in Churchill's attempt to rehabilitate himself with the Conservative Party.

[Extract] This is the first great Conservative meeting I have addressed for twenty years, but for nearly ten years I have been working in close accord in the Cabinet, or outside, with many of the principal leaders of the Conservative party. I do not feel, therefore, that my presence at this meeting need be taken as marking any exceptional or extraordinary departure either by my audience or myself.

I recall that in February, 1922, Mr. Lloyd George, then Prime Minister, wrote to the official chiefs of the Unionist party offering to resign the Premiership, to withdraw from the Government with his followers, and to give whole-hearted support to a Conservative Administration. I, like other prominent National Liberals, was consulted in the drafting of this letter, and agreed thereto. My only regret is that our sincere and well-meant offer was not at the time accepted by our Unionist colleagues. In that event much of the confusion and weakness which has since come upon us all would have been avoided.

Both the Conservative and Liberal parties in succession have, in my opinion, thrown away great opportunities in the last year or so through a sincere but excessive indulgence in purely party feelings and purely party views. If you want to measure how great is the opportunity which the Conservative party have lost, you have only to read Mr. Snowden's Budget. (Cheers.) Here you find this Socialist Chancellor of the Exchequer distributing a great surplus raised by the Conservative party, a surplus gained by the labours and sacrifices of his opponents, and distributing it in the manner most likely to win votes for the Socialistic party at an approaching general election.

This political cuckoo–(loud laughter)–if I may without disrespect borrow a metaphor from our tardy spring–(laughter)–is strutting about in borrowed plumes. This Socialist, whose life has been one long sneer at the British Empire, is able to appropriate as unearned increment to himself and his friends the whole of the fruits of the toil, the thrift, and the self-denial of his predecessors. Without that constitutional authority which springs from a majority at the polls, and without having had to do a hand's turn of work or make the slightest effort, he has been placed in a situation where he was able to distribute a surplus for which he had neither toiled nor spun. (Cheers.) . . .

But what of the future? What is the great danger to our national trade and prosperity with which we are confronted at the present time? It is purely the rapid growth in numbers, in influence, in prestige, of a great body of our fellow citizens who are being taught to repeat and believe in the false doctrines of Socialism, which, if ever seriously put into practice, would reduce this island to chaos and starvation.

Now it is in the face of this danger that I ask: How long are we going to continue to allow the artificially fomented jealousies and quarrels of Conservatives and Liberals to play into the hands of the Socialists? How long are the interests of the country to suffer from sterile party conflicts in the presence of an advancing peril? How long are the Liberals and Conservatives to paralyse each other so that both may be ruled by a Socialist minority?

The deliberate policy of the Socialists is, of course, to prevent any common action between Liberals and Conservatives in order that Socialism may progress and devour the Liberals at leisure. (Laughter.) All their tactics are conceived with this intention. . . .

The present Government is one vast monument of sham and humbug. It presumes to speak in the name of the people. It represents less than one-third of the electors. It maintains itself in office precariously by playing upon the jealousies and divisions of the two older parties and by giving a sop now and again to the Liberals. Sometimes it offers what you might call an inverted sop, pleasing the Conservatives by offending the Liberals, or pleasing the Liberals by irritating the Conservatives. There never has been such a condition of log-rolling and intrigue.

The Government has no political principles. It is purely an opportunist party living perforce from hand to mouth and from day to day. Mr. Ramsay MacDonald is assiduously courting France and Belgium. (Laughter.) This is the same Mr. Ramsay MacDonald who has solemnly testified–and I am making no imputation upon the sincerity of his convictions, because he certainly was ready to suffer for them–that in his opinion it was France who was wrong in the war and provoked it in the most unscrupulous manner, and that Germany was innocent and guiltless.

Everywhere they let it be understood they had some great remedy or scheme which would improve the position and put an end to this lamentable state of affairs. Yet although the session is half over it is perfectly clear that they have no scheme or plan for dealing with unemployment except to go on in a more or less feeble way with the plans and schemes for unemployment of the Liberal and Tory parties in the past. As for housing, they propose, I understand, to build fewer houses next year–if they are there to build them–(laughter)–than the wicked, reactionary Coalition Government were building three years ago.

I say that these are examples of political inconsistencies beyond compare in modern life. While the Socialist Ministers are priding themselves on doing the same sort of thing that Liberal and Conservative Governments would have done, while they have put themselves off in practice and in office from their wild theories, they tell us in the same breath that they believe in those theories as ardently as ever, and that they are only waiting for an opportunity to put them into force. Somebody is being deceived. (Cheers.) Either it is the public, who are lulled into a sense of false security, or it is the Socialist party, if they allow their creed to be repudiated by their leaders for the sake of office.

It is time this farce should end. (Loud cheers.) The truth is that Socialism in England is permeated from end to end with humbug. The leaders do not believe in the doctrines they preach. They do not weigh with them for one moment in comparison with the prospect of obtaining office or retaining office. They cater for one side of their followers with every argument of Christanity and altruism, while another set receive instruction in the Socialist Sunday school in the vilest garbage of atheism and revolution. (Cheers.)

They are a minority holding office on sufferance, and are always claiming fair play for themselves. What fair play do they show to others? Even the elementary right of free speech has been challenged by the Socialist party in a manner unknown to this country for generations. No word of censure of this rowdyism has been spoken by their leaders. I read a speech delivered by the Solicitor General at Leeds on Sunday. No doubt it would be Sunday. (Laughter.) The Socialist Solicitor General was so shocked at a body called the British Fascisti having intervened to prevent the supporters of his Government from breaking up Sir Donald Maclean's meeting that he said that the proceedings of this body appeared to him and other high authorities to be highly seditious, and might indeed require the intervention of the Law Officers of the Crown. Sir Henry Slesser, if he asked some of his friends and supporters, would find them good judges. But what an illustration of the kind of mentality with which we have to deal!

But my gravest accusation against the Socialist party is that they are deliberately and wantonly corrupting the character of the British nation. If their only object is to carry out practical reforms without revolution or disorder what is the need and what is the sense of teaçhing great masses of great-hearted English people to perform the antics and grimaces of Continental Socialism, to mouth the exploded doctrines of Karl Marx, to sing or drone that dreary dirge the Socialist International instead of the National Anthem–(cheers),–and to be proud of the Red Flag instead of the Union Jack?

The harm that has been done already is very great. Nearly a third of the electorate has been marshalled around these foreign standards and taught to regard the institutions, the history, and the greatness of our country and Empire as if they were odious means of oppression to be repudiated or swept away at the earliest possible moment.

My proposal or policy which you have allowed me to lay before you to-night is simple and plain. I do not seek, as has been suggested, to bring division to the Conservative party. God forbid! It is a reinforcement, not a division. I propose to you that we should return to the arrangement offered to the Conservative party by the National Liberals in the spring of 1922–and it was also the position in 1886 of the Liberal Unionists–that is to say, a strong and active Conservative party united under its own leaders with a Liberal wing co-operating in whatever may be found most useful and helpful for the national and common interest and honourable principles.

Co-operation means that we should make common causes, that we should stand together, and, laying aside every impediment, that we should fight shoulder to shoulder in the endeavour by every means in our power to secure the defeat of Socialism at the polls.

Such co-operation would also involve the adherence by the Conservative party to the broad progressive platform of public policy such as their leaders have now definitely adopted and formally and definitely proclaimed. That is the road to victory; it is the only road to victory of the cause which we have at heart. (Loud cheers.)

"THE STUDY OF ENGLISH"

June 27, 1924

London School of Economics

[Extract] . . . I have chosen as the subject upon which I will venture to make a few disputable, controversial, and, I fear, heterodox observations, the importance of the study of English. I have chosen the subject because I am anxious to offer to a number of young Englishmen and Englishwomen a suggestion which might perhaps be of practical use and service to them. To be able to give exact and lucid expressions to one's thoughts, to be able to write a good clear letter upon a complicated or delicate subject; to be able to explain shortly, precisely, and correctly what you mean, what you have seen, what you have read, what you have been told, or what you want to understand; to appreciate and express the various shades of meaning which attach to words—these are surely among the most important acquirements which young Englishmen and young Englishwomen can possibly seek for to aid them in their life's career.

Such acquirements are equally advantageous to the Cabinet Minister unfolding his bill, or to the youthful applicant for his first position. They can be carried everywhere and employed at every moment. Some of those who have risen to positions of great responsibility have been woefully hampered because they do not possess these simple primary qualifications.

It has become the fashion in Britain to affect to distrust or disdain the arts of speaking and writing so far as they are concerned with ordinary every-day life. There is a good deal of affectation and nonsense mixed up with our national attitude on the subject. Too often the strong, silent man is silent only because he does not know what to say, and he is reputed strong only because he has remained silent. Government by talking has been the message which Britain has taught to so many countries.

I am sorry to say that our great public schools have made themselves a ready agency in this crippling process. I have the greatest respect for classical education, and I never ceased to envy those who have attained the serene delights of scholarship, but I am convinced that to enforce the study of Latin and Greek on the multitude of our youths who in their thousands attend the public schools and universities and to enforce this as the main foundation—as it is in so many cases—of their education is an absurd mistake, a mistake which does injustice to the moderns, and, for all I know, inflicts even crueller injustice upon the ancients.

I would like to see English made the universal study, to form the gateway to our education. We used to be assured that the best way to learn English was to learn Latin. This argument has been somewhat destroyed by the new and if I may say so ridiculous change in pronunciation which in recent years has become general. It used to be a comfort to me to recognize occasionally some of the Latin words which I had learned. (Laughter.) But that comfort has departed. Take the well-known verb *audire*, from which are derived such words as "audience" and "audible." We are now directed to pronounce it as "ow-dearie." (Laughter.) Presumably, therefore, we should say "owdience." This pernicious innovation into which our schoolmen have plunged emphasizes the need of a proper study of English.

With regard to the relations between the French and British Prime Ministers, as affected by the recent meeting between them, I am quite sure the present difference arose–if it arose in any serious form–far more from the difficulty of finding exact words to define the ideas and statements which both have in common than from any real divergence in spirit or on merit.

THE SOCIALIST GOVERNMENT

September 25, 1924

Scottish Unionist Association Meeting,
Usher Hall, Edinburgh

This meeting, presided over by Balfour, marked a further step in Churchill's campaign to return to the Conservative ranks, and was another major event in his career.

[Extract] Certainly in a few months, possibly in a few weeks, a general election will be fought at which all citizens will have to decide whether they wish to see a Socialist Government installed in office with an effective Socialist majority behind them. It is an issue which has never been presented to the electors before, but it is about to be brought before the nation squarely, bluntly, nakedly, and unavoidably. (Cheers.) This is an issue which will not last only for one election. It will probably be the dominant cleavage in British politics for a long period of time. Compared with this paramount issue, the differences which have separated Liberals and Conservatives are secondary. (Cheers.) There is at the present time no gulf of principle between the two historic parties. Nor is there any great practical issue of domestic or foreign policy upon which they are seriously divided. There are real differences of mood, of method, and of degree. There are political rivalries, conflicting party interests, and a number of minor questions on which there is divergence; but the great differences and urgent political questions which before the war divided Great Britain into Liberal and Conservative camps do not now exist, and I challenge the official Liberal leaders to define in terms of principle, or state specifically the large practical measures which separate them fundamentally from their Unionist fellow-countrymen.

Pre-war party questions are settled. They are obsolete, they no longer interest or divide the British nation. They are controversies which have passed out of life into history. Their place is filled by a series of problems which are not controversial in a party sense, but which are nevertheless puzzling and baffling. All the new electors are busy upon a series of problems which every party wishes to solve, which raise no question of party principle, and which require for their solution not controversy but cooperation, not fiery speeches but hard and steady work. What is wanted above all is three or four years of stable government, undisturbed by electioneering and resting upon an adequate and coherent Parliamentary majority. (Cheers.) Cooperation between leading politicians and between political groups or parties for the sake of sharing offices or stopping progress would never command the approval of the nation. But cooperation for a given period for the purpose of solving urgent non-party problems and for securing a revival of the national strength, such honourable and fruitful cooperation would explain and justify itself. (Cheers.) The King's Speech of the late Conservative Government unquestionably afforded a good and fair basis for the cooperation of reasonable men of all parties. There are two questions which survive as fragments of the old controversies, and as fragments of great controversies. One is the question of trade policy, and there are the painful issues connected with the Irish Treaty. The Conservative leaders have definitely announced that a general tariff is excluded from their platform at the next election. They have stated again and again that they will not tax staple foods and necessaries of popular consumption. These are great and sweeping declarations, and it is absurd for Liberals and Free-traders to continue the fiscal controversy as if they had not been made. (Cheers.) . . .

Now let me turn to the conduct of our opponents. A great new party has sprung into being. It has largely devoured the Liberal Party. It is resolved to destroy what remains. In 20 years we have seen it grow from a handful of Socialist freaks—(laughter)—and a band of steady old trade unionist leaders into the foundation of a Government which is at this moment ruling the land. At present they are still in a minority. The Liberals and Conservatives flank them about as a rogue elephant is held by his disciplined and trained companions. (Laughter.) To change the metaphor, the Socialist Government dwells, if not in a state of grace, to a large extent in one of compulsory virtue (laughter); but by every word they speak, by every action they dare to take they reveal and indeed proclaim what their conduct would be should they obtain unbridled power. (Hear, hear.)

By abandoning the naval base at Singapore the Socialist Government has made it impossible for the British Navy to enter the Pacific, and consequently to afford the slightest assistance to Australia and New Zealand, no matter how terrible there need might be. Yet almost at the same time that the British Navy is stripped of its old power of defending the British Empire we know well that they would gladly hawk it round Europe to be the drudge of an international organization and fight in every quarrel but its own. (Cheers.)

Again, since Parliament rose we have learned that the Socialist Government has perverted the administration of justice for political expedience, for personal affairs. The editor of a Communist newspaper published an incitement to sailors, soldiers, and airmen to disobey the orders of their officers, and use their weapons against capitalists and employers in the cause of world revolution. The Secretary of State for War and the First Lord of the Admiralty were scandalized. They brought the matter before the Home Secretary. The Home Secretary referred it to the law officers. The Attorney-General, after examining the whole case, authorized the Director of Public Prosecutions to act. No State prosecution can be instituted or withdrawn except by the decision of the Attorney-General, and that decision the Attorney-General is bound to give, as if he were a Judge, without the slightest interference on political or party grounds. That prosecution was ordered by Sir Patrick Hastings. The man was arrested, brought up before the magistrate, and remanded for a week. What happened in that week? Political pressure was brought to bear. A handful of obscure figures lurking in the background behind every Socialist administration made their power felt. The Government was terrified. The Attorney-General ordered the withdrawal of the prosecution. An apologetic explanation was offered; the case fell to the ground, and the man walked off scot free.

But that was not the end. The Communist editor resolved openly to humiliate the Government. He repudiated the explanation which the Government had invented for him. He proceeded to glory in his offence, and he loudly proclaimed that the Ministers of the Crown had not dared to proceed with the prosecution because of the opposition of his political friends. Not one word has been said in reply to these grave and insulting charges by any Minister who has spoken. The position of the Attorney-General is gravely affected. Parliament is going to reassemble, and Lord Haldane–that stringent stickler for judicial etiquette–will, when he returns from chasing some old Liberal passive resister off the Bench of Magistrates, find in his own sphere and Department of State what seems to be little less than a flagitious perversion of law and justice at the dictates of political expediency. (Cheers.)

If these things are done by a Socialist Government which has no majority, if a scandal like this can arise under the present safeguards, we may judge for ourselves what may happen if a Socialist Government secures an actual majority of the House of Commons.

Others have told you the business aspects [of the Russian treaty]. How because the Bolshevists have stolen all the private property of foreigners in Russia and have repudiated all their debts they cannot borrow any more money by ordinary means; how, in these circumstances, they come to their friends in the British Government and ask them for forty or fifty millions of the taxpayers' money in the form of a guarantee to enable them to carry on their despotic rule; how the Prime Minister said in June that he would never do such a thing, and how in August he was compelled by subterranean pressure to sign a treaty on conditions which, only a few hours before, his Government had publicly repulsed. Others have told you that; but I base my opposition to this treaty on reasons which stand above financial policy or political misdemeanour. I object to subsidizing tyranny. (Cheers.) I object to endowing, if I may use the word, cruelty, wickedness, and persecution. (Cheers.) I believe that the mainspring of the national revolt against this treaty is moral, and not commercial. (Cheers.) I believe that Mr. Gladstone would have made the land ring with arguments which would far transcend material considerations. Judged by every standard which history has applied to Governments, the Soviet Government of Russia is one of the worst tyrannies that has ever existed in the world. (Cheers.) It accords no political rights. It rules by terror. It punishes political opinions. It suppresses free speech. It tolerates no newspapers but its own. It persecutes Christianity with a zeal and a cunning never equalled since the times of the Roman Emperors. It is engaged at this moment in trampling down the peoples of Georgia and executing their leaders by hundreds. It is for this process that Mr. MacDonald, himself acquainted with Georgia, asks us to make ourselves responsible. We are to render these tyrannies possible by lending to their authors money to pay for the ammunition to murder the Georgians, to enable the Soviet sect to keep its stranglehold on the dumb Russian nation, and to poison the world, and so far as they can the British Empire, with their filthy propaganda. (Cheers.) That is what we are asked to take upon ourselves. It is an outrage on the British name. (Cheers.)

But contrast the attitude of the Socialist Government towards their Bolshevist friends and their attitude to the great self-governing Dominions of the Crown. To the enemies of Britain, of civilization, of freedom, to those who deserted us in the crises of the war—smiles, compliments, caresses, cash. But for Canada, Australia, New Zealand, South Africa, who sent their brave men to fight and die by scores of thousands, who never flinched and never wearied, who are bone of our bone and flesh of our flesh—to them nothing but frigid repulsion. Our bread for the Bolshevist serpent; our aid for the foreigner of every country; our favours for the Socialists all over the world who have no country; but for our own daughter States across the oceans, on whom the future of the British island and nation depends, only the cold stones of indifference, aversion, and neglect. (Cheers.) That is the policy with which the Socialist Government confronts us, and against that policy we will strive to marshall the unconquerable might of Britain. (Cheers.)

ELECTION ISSUES

October 3, 1924

Waltham Abbey

Churchill's long search for political sanctuary was over. The chairman of the Epping Conservative Association, James Hawkey, successfully sponsored him as candidate for that safe Conservative constituency. Churchill stood as a "Constitutionalist," but he was a Conservative in all but name.

The history of the decline and fall of the minority Labour Government cannot be fully related here. The proposal to give a loan to Russia was one element in the Liberals' decision to abandon MacDonald, but the immediate cause of the Government's defeat at the end of September was the abandonment under backbench pressure of the proposed prosecution of J. R. Campbell for an allegedly seditious article in the Workers' Weekly. *The nation proceeded to its second General Election within a year.*

When I received your invitation to come forward as a constitutional candidate for this traditionally Conservative seat I was greatly honoured. I felt that the Conservatives of West Essex had come to the conclusion that they wished to make a definite gesture in the public life of this country. They wished to indicate by their action in inviting me to contest this seat that they thought the time had come when there should be a very great rally and concentration of those who care about the greatness of Britain, and advancing the prosperity of her people. (Cheers.) I think that the invitation was conceived in a broad-minded and in a generous spirit, and, this being so, if was my duty to place my services at your disposal. I shall do my best in the fight which is coming upon us to explain and expound to this great populous constituency the views on the political situation which I sincerely hold and which I believe have in them the solution of many of our present difficulties. (Cheers.) I shall endeavour to face all the issues that will be presented.

I feel that when you sent me this invitation you must have been prepared for a somewhat lively election when it comes. (Laughter.) It may be my misfortune, or it may be my fault, but most of the elections I have fought have been distinctly lively. (Laughter.) I thought you would probably have made up your minds to that before your executive took the step of inviting me to come forward. If it is a lively election, then let it not be disfigured in any way by personalities or personal abuse. At any rate, if there is to be personal abuse, let us not be participators in it in any way. Let it not be marked by disorder of any kind. If there is disorder, I am certain it will not be home-grown. It will be imported from various external, extraneous, and foreign inspired areas which may be around us. (Laughter.)

Another political crisis is swiftly approaching, and it may well be that in a short time I shall present myself before you, not as a prospective candidate, but actually as your candidate in the hour of battle. (Cheers.) The crisis in British politics is in my opinion very near, and I do not see how a General Election can be long delayed. I believe it will be in the next few months, or even possibly in the next few weeks. In that election there stand out two special issues–two questions which, because they occupy men's minds at the moment, will be brought directly before the electors for their decision should an election take place. I shall go on to tell you of the larger issues which lie behind this. I am speaking now of the special issues of such an election.

First of all, there is the question of whether we can make a guaranteed loan of 30, 40, or it may be 50 millions sterling to the Russian Bolshevist Government. I am wholly opposed to that. (Cheers.) I have always been opposed to that, and it is only three or four months ago that the Prime Minister, Mr. Ramsay MacDonald, was also opposed to it. He announced in the House of Commons that there was no question of giving a guaranteed loan to Soviet Russia. (Cheers.) By all means let us trade with Russia; by all means let our traders or merchants or business men make what bargains they can at their own risk; by all means let us free their trade and traffic from every obstacle; let no impediment be placed in their way; but do not let us go out of our way to show a special advantage which we do not show to friendly, civilized foreign countries, which we do not extend to our self-governing Dominions in the ordinary course–do not let us go out of our way to show special favour to a Government, a *régime* in Russia, which is unquestionably one of the worst and the meanest tyrannies which have ever existed in the world. (Cheers.)

Every principle that British Conservatives and Liberals alike have long held dear of personal liberty and the ordinary decencies of social life, every principle of religious freedom, has been trampled down by the iron rule of those Russian despots. At the present moment they are engaged in massacring, in circumstances of great brutality, large numbers of the people of the Georgian Republic who only a few years ago were visited by Mr. Ramsay MacDonald, and who had a special claim on his confidence and good will. You might say it is none of our business to interfere with what is done in Russia. I agree that now the war is over, and the situation created by the war is ended, we should not intervene in Russian matters, and that is the reason I oppose the granting of British money on a large scale in order to enable this tyrannical *régime* to continue to enforce its iron heel upon the great broad dumb masses of the Russian people.

That will be one of the issues upon which an election will be fought. We will use all the arguments there are to refute it, and I know of no case where a greater wealth of argument can be marshalled. We can quote the testimony of the Socialist Prime Minister of Britain himself, who in June declared that he would not guarantee this money to the Russian Bolshevists. But he has been forced against his better judgment, by forces and influences that lie behind and beneath him, to go against his ordinary conviction.

I shall say in the course of this campaign that I am speaking a political doctrine and expounding a political view which I hold with the utmost sincerity and which I have held in these very changing times with exceptional consistency. . . .

It seems to me that in this great issue men of the old historic parties are bound to stand together and co-operate. The old questions have largely been settled–Home Rule, the Lloyd George Budget, the Welsh Church, Plural Voting, the extension of the franchise all vanished in the deluge of the war. In their place is another set of questions, difficult and complicated, but not controversial in the party sense. These are problems connected with the reduction of public expenditure, National Insurance, housing, agriculture, the state of our trade, and colonization of our Empire. Those are difficult questions, but not party questions dividing Socialist from Liberal or Liberal from Conservative. They are questions which, if we can unite and solve them, will enormously advance and improve the general social conditions of our age and time. (Cheers.)

The programme outlined by the Leader of the Conservative Party, Mr. Baldwin, offers a broad basis upon which men and women of good will who wish to see these questions solved should be able to co-operate. But we will never solve those questions by a series of weak minority Governments.

A Voice: Labour will go back next time.

Mr. Churchill: That is what we are going to see about. My friend must not count his eggs before they are addled. (Laughter.) One of the greatest needs of this country is political stability and tranquillity. (Cheers.) There is now the opportunity for ending this period of chaos by placing in power an Administration which would have behind it a substantial and effective working majority, which by its character could not be a class Administration or a sectional Administration, but which would represent the wishes of the people. We have the opportunity of placing such an Administration in power, so that for the next three or four years there would not be the disturbing element of repeated elections. The time has come when we must think of British interests, when we must stand together and study how best we can promote the fortunes of Britain and the happiness and welfare of the British people. (Cheers.)

THE ZINOVIEV LETTER

October 25, 1924

Loughton

Shortly before polling day a letter from Zinoviev, President of the Communist International, giving instructions to the British Communists, was published. It was almost certainly a forgery, but it was eagerly seized upon by Conservative candidates as further proof of links between Moscow and the Labour Party.

[Extract] .... Even if the Moscow letter [the Zinoviev letter] is a forgery it in no way alters the facts that Bolshevik propaganda has never ceased during the last four years. They have never ceased to stir up bloody revolution in India and to foster strife in this country.

The Prime Minister said he believes this letter is authentic, but the Communist forces are already on his track, and the moment is coming when this futile Kerensky will make another surrender. The process of conversion has already begun. Mr. MacDonald said he was going to probe the matter to the bottom, and he described the affair as a new Guy Fawkes gunpowder plot. The Guy Fawkes plot was a very real plot, seeing that Parliament only escaped being blown sky-high.

The Prime Minister is preparing already to turn about, and I venture to predict that before the election is over we will find Mr. MacDonald singing in chorus with the rest of his Ministers that the letter he has said he honestly believes is authentic is a gross forgery and a dodge of the Conservative party.

"GROWTH OF DISEASED OPINION"

November 1, 1924

Chingford

The General Election of 1924 gave the Conservatives 419 seats; Labour, 151; and the Liberals, 40. Asquith, defeated again, retired to the Lords. Churchill was returned for Epping by over 10,000 votes.

[Extract] . . . The battle which we have now fought shows us that the political war which has now so clearly opened will be a very long one. It is by no means an ordinary political conflict, such as that which used to be waged between the Whigs and Tories and between Liberals and Conservatives. It is a far graver schism which is opening in the life of the nation.

It seemed to me that this attempt to foist upon our country these German ideas and Russian fashions, and to rule it, not in its own interest, but in the interest of some wide international conception of a very visionary character, was so fraught with peril and so unsuited to the whole character and feelings and interests of the British people, that it would be rejected with the most complete contempt, but although it has been rejected in a manner which is almost unparalleled so far as emphasis is concerned, the extraordinary fact remains that a million more people recorded their votes for the Socialist party than were recorded for it a year ago.

We are in the presence of a growth of diseased opinion, which is steadily and remorselessly corrupting the public mind and steadily drawing good, loyal, decent, English men and women from the old standard of patriotism and national honour to which they have in the past shown themselves so firmly attached. I see no signs that the process has been arrested. What has happened has been that great reserves of good sense and of strength and of patriotism which lie latent in this country and which it takes a great emergency to evoke have been thrown into the electoral battle.

But here in the moment of success, it is only prudent to look forward to a period when once again the country will have to face the same issue. It may well be then that the enemy will not be on the defensive and that the attack will be far more formidable than that which we have just surmounted. It is necessary therefore, that we should crystallise our enthusiasm and prepare for the renewal of the struggle.

A great responsibility rests upon the Unionist party. The Liberal party has ceased for the time being to be an effective Parliamentary factor. The situation therefore requires from the Unionist party the most strenuous endeavour to give the fullest effect to the national mandate with which it has been entrusted—a mandate to keep the honour of our country clean, to preserve the peace and order of the British Dominions, to cement the bonds of unity between us and the great self-governing States of the British Commonwealth, and patiently and soberly and resolutely to remedy the grave evils of the housing shortage, of the scarcity of employment, and to sustain by every sensible and practicable means our agricultural industry and to revive if necessary by bold experiment the prosperity of British trade and commerce. These are the tasks which lie before the new Parliament.

THE CONSTITUTIONAL GROUP

November 3, 1924

Constitutional Club Dinner,
London

To general astonishment—including his own—Churchill was invited to become Chancellor of the Exchequer in the second Baldwin Government. He accepted with alacrity. Birkenhead returned as Secretary for India; Austen Chamberlain became Foreign Minister, and Neville Chamberlain became Minister of Health.

Churchill's denial that he had ever said that "Labour is unfit to govern" should be compared to his statements quoted on pages 391 and 411.

This is an occasion for rejoicing on account of a great deliverance. We have been mercifully guided in the course of the last few months, and events have fallen into a favourable channel in a manner which must make every one of us feel renewed confidence in the luck of Britain. It might so easily have happened that the conflict in the constituencies should have arisen on a far less favourable battlefield and at a far less opportune moment, but thanks to sound and broad views and honest leadership, thanks to prudent and skillful treatment of the Parliamentary emergencies which arose in such swift succession, we have been able to return from the battlefield victorious. . . .

The aim of the Constitutionalists to-day is quite superfluous but we intend to aid the Conservative party at every stage by all our means in the long struggle which has now begun to rescue large sections of our fellow-countrymen from the economic fallacies and un-English and anti-national vices of Socialism. For the first time since the great war we are enjoying a breathing space. We have time to take stock of the position, a chance to look ahead, and the country has once again power to control its own destinies.

In regard to the position of the Labour party, five years ago I made a remark about them which has been misquoted from one end of the country to the other. I was alleged to have said that Labour was unfit to govern. I never said anything of the sort. I would never attempt to bring such an offensive accusation against any class of my fellow-countrymen, because everyone knows that the genius of the British people wells up strongly from the heart of the nation, and that there is no class from which men are not rising every day to high positions and great functions in public and private affairs.

What I said actually at the beginning of 1919 was that the break-up of the national forces would rush the Labour party into power when they were not in a condition to govern. Do we not see to-day the full justification of those words? It is quite true that the Labour party has since advanced in numbers, force, and experience, but they have proved to be an organism too weak to sustain the burden of Government. Any one can go into the great departments of Government and pull over the levers, but the test of a party is how they can withstand subversive pressures, and after the first few months the Labour Ministry showed itself completely unable to stand against the forces which were beneath it and which were operative upon it. That justified the statement that at the present period of its development it was unfit to govern, and that opinion has been endorsed by the great majority of the electorate.

The break-up of the Liberal party was due to causes which have been operative in every country in Europe. The chief cause has been the rise of a Socialist party, but in the case of Britain there is a special cause. It was the great mistake made by the Liberal leaders in January of the present year.

The Liberal leaders chose to adjust themselves to the Socialists. They chose to proclaim what is a profound falsehood—what I have never ceased to denounce as a falsehood—that they had greater sympathy with the Socialist party than they had with the Unionists. Now Socialism is the very antithesis of Liberalism. Moreover, the Socialist party can only progress by destroying and devouring the Liberal party.

The Liberals' attitude resembles a conversation which might take place between a band of hopeful missionaries and a band of cannibals while the cooking pot is being actually heated. This great party has been reduced to a representation so exiguous as not to exceed twenty independent members.

What is going to be the destiny of those three million voters who are now to all intents and purposes disfranchised so far as Parliamentary representation is concerned? It seems to me that the consideration of the future direction of that great mass of voting strength is one of the most important thoughts which will weigh in the minds of those who now have the supreme responsibility for the directing of our affairs. It may be that by a wise, far-seeing policy the whole of those forces may on a future day be found marching with the Unionist forces in defence of the liberties of this country against the Socialist or Communist attack.

I look forward to seeing the new Parliament take up the broken pledges given to the Dominions at the Imperial Conference—pledges which can be fulfilled within the declarations made by the Conservative leaders. I look forward to seeing the spade set to work again on the naval base at Singapore, and with sure confidence I look forward to the necessary action being taken to cope with the poisonous foreign propaganda which is being dispersed in our midst.

CONSERVATISM

December 5, 1924

Conservative Party Banquet,
Midland Adelphi Hotel, Liverpool

This dinner was organised by Sir Archibald Salvidge to celebrate the Conservative triumph and Churchill's success, although Churchill did not formally rejoin the Conservative Party until 1925.

[Extract] . . . When I look upon the course of the present year and remember that it was in March that I was trying to enter the House of Commons and found myself resisted by the entire force and power of each great party organisation, when I remember that in November I was returned to Parliament by a majority of nearly 10,000, and in circumstances which I shall not attempt to explain, have been invited to accept one of the most important offices of the Crown and have seen the facts accepted with tolerable acquiescence—when I reflect on this transformation I recognise the truth of Disraeli's remark that the vicissitudes of politics are inexhaustible. . . .

The conceptions on politics which were principally associated with the life-work of Lord Beaconsfield were not confined to progress in domestic affairs. They always carried with them, side by side with an earnest aspiration towards social betterment, a sober determination to defend our legitimate rights and interests in every quarter of the globe. And that aspect of our political position was not lacking from the speech which Mr. Baldwin delivered last night. His declaration about Egypt expressed very clearly the position which the Government occupies. The murder of Sir Lee Stack was in itself only the culminating point in a long series of acts of an offensive and aggressive character on the part, not of the Egyptian people, but on the part of an organised faction in Egypt, which acts ill-repaid the long services which Britain has rendered to the people of Egypt and the new liberties which for the first time Britain in recent years voluntarily conferred upon them.

Even in this hour of stern decision and action, the policy of the British Government has remained unchanged. While it is our duty to safeguard our own vital interests and rights in Egypt and the Sudan, to safeguard the lives and property of the Europeans of every nation who are in the Sudan, we have never been diverted from the central purpose that has animated the British nation since the earliest occupation of Egypt—namely, to make friends with the Egyptian people, to guard their interests not less earnestly than our own, and, above all, to develop those common interests which we have built up together in Egypt and the Sudan and all along the valley of the Nile.

Recovery and Isolation
1925-1938

Recovery and Isolation 1925-1938

The full details of Churchill's tenure in the Treasury between 1924 and 1929 have not yet been published or analysed, but we know enough to make more balanced judgments than many of those made at the time and immediately afterwards. It was not an office for which he was well suited by training or temperament, but he was assiduous, and his Budget speeches developed into great Parliamentary occasions. His Parliamentary Private Secretary, Robert (now Lord) Boothby has written:

> The essence of genius is vitality, fecundity and versatility. These were the most impressive things about him. His output was colossal. He was basically uninterested in the problems of high finance. But his Budgets were skilfully contrived and superbly presented. And, given the conditions under which he was obliged to work . . . he could hardly have done better, or other, than he did.[1]

The judgements of others–notably Leo Amery, John Maynard Keynes and Hubert Henderson, to say nothing of the Labour Party–were more critical. "It is with regret," Henderson wrote, "that we are disposed to write him down as one of the worst Chancellors of the Exchequer of modern times." But a balanced judgement would be that although Churchill was miscast at the Treasury, his term was far from being the total disaster so often depicted. The decision to return to the Gold Standard in 1925 at the prewar parity was almost certainly wrong, but the weight of official advice was very strong, and would probably have overwhelmed any Chancellor. Although the series of clever balancing acts that characterised Churchill's Budgets were ingenious, they certainly give no indication of any carefully thought-out strategy. Sir James Grigg wrote that "his financial administration as a whole disclosed a great hankering to be considered orthodox." He was not, however, as rigid a Free Trader as his Labour predecessor and successor, Philip Snowden, and his cooperation with the social legislation brought forward by Neville Chamberlain was a very fruitful one. There have been much worse Chancellors, before and since.

The two most serious charges against Churchill arise from his attempts to further curtail defence expenditure–which will be described later–and his actions before and during the General Strike of 1926. What was less appreciated was his genuine effort to meet the worst of the miners' grievances when the General Strike was over, thereby emphasising again this strong feature of his personality–fair negotiation after withdrawal of threat. He was unsuccessful, his efforts were largely unknown, and the unions were left with the bitter memories of his editorship of the vehemently anti-union *British Gazette* during the strike and with the unanswerable fact that although the general national prosperity had risen, the pall of heavy unemployment still hung bleakly over the North of England, Scotland and Wales.

The failure of the 1924-1929 Government and an economic non-system was hardly the personal responsibility of one man alone, but it can be argued that Churchill's negative contribution was not the most appropriate. His unjustified attack on Keynes's elaborate plans for curbing inflation as "camouflaged inflation" was significant, as was the comment of the *Annual Register* that "as a financier his success had been questionable."

I

In spite of these and other criticisms, Churchill's political position in 1929 was immeasurably stronger than it had been six years before. "He is an Ishmael in public life," A. G. Gardiner wrote in 1926, "loathed by the Tories whom he left and has now returned to; distrusted by the Liberals, on whose backs he first mounted to power; hated by Labour, whom he scorns and insults, and who see in him the potential Mussolini of a wave of reaction." It is arguable that this is too severe a portrait. One detects in criticisms of Churchill in this period an absence–or at least a strong diminution–of the venom that had been so evident up to 1923. The publication of *The World Crisis* was a formidable achievement unmatched by any other man in public life. "Winston Churchill is the most interesting man in England," Harold Nicolson wrote in 1931. "He is more than interesting; he is a phenomenon, an enigma. How can a man so versatile and so brilliant avoid being considered volatile and unsound? . . . His dominant qualities are imagination, courage and loyalty; his dominant defect, impatience." And there is little harshness in the criticisms of Arthur Ponsonby:

> He is so far and away the most talented man in political life besides being charming and a "gentleman" (a rarish bird these days). But this does not prevent me from feeling politically that he is a great danger, largely because of his love of crises and faulty judgement. He once said to me years ago, "I like things to happen, and if they don't happen I like to make them happen."[2]

The 1920s were not a particularly distinguished period of Churchill's career. He was still a controversial, major public figure, but there was about him something vaguely old-fashioned, and one realises why Leo Amery described him in his diary at this time as a "mid-Victorian . . . steeped in the politics of his father's period, and unable ever to get the modern point of view." His oratory, even at its best, had a dated air, to be relished and appreciated as a performance, but not enduring in its effect. It was already evident that radio was not his medium, and his thunderous declamations sometimes seemed comical when heard in the calm of a home. His party political broadcast in the 1929 election is a case in point: "We have to march forward steadily and steadfastly, along the highway. It may be dusty, it may be stony, it may be dull; it is certainly uphill all the way, but to leave it is only to flounder in the quagmires of delusion and have your coat torn off your back by the brambles of waste."

His newspaper articles and many of his speeches emphasise the ponderousness and theatrics which were perhaps even slightly dated when his career opened, and at this time certainly *déclassé*. There are dangers in having been around too long, and in having rung the tocsin too often. It is difficult to believe that his dark picture of England in 1931 could have alarmed many:

> An anxious and bewildered nation is waiting for Guidance, and not only for guidance, but for Action. The loyal forces in every street and village do not know what to do. The subversive forces are gaining in confidence and audacity.
>
> No one can doubt the malignity of the appeal to class-hatred and revolutionary promptings for which the Socialist Party is now apparently prepared to be responsible. The disturbances in the Fleet and the signs of disorder in great cities are symptoms which none should ignore. Business is at a standstill; prices are rising; the pressure of life upon all classes must inevitably grow greater. Faction is rampant, and winter is at hand. . . .[3]

What, in short, did he stand for? His career had never been fastened for very long to any particular subject or theme, a fact which undoubtedly ensured its continuance, but which also gave it an unimpressive looseness. In 1929 he was fifty-five years of age, and the career which had opened with such dash and drama was becoming almost humdrum. Gardiner wrote of him in 1908:

> His eye is less on the fixed stars than on the wayward meteors of the night. And when the exhilaration of youth is gone, and the gallop of high spirits has run its course, it may be that this deficiency of abiding and high-compelling purpose will be a heavy handicap. Then it will be seen how far courage and intellectual address, a mind acutely responsive to noble impulses, and a quick and apprehensive political instinct will carry him in the leadership of men.

Partly by good fortune, but mostly because of his own talents, he was still a major political personality in 1929. Although the Conservatives had little cause to love him, they had accepted him. The position was now to be hazarded and then destroyed.

II

For some understanding of Churchill's mood in 1929-1930 we may recall the frustration of Lord Randolph Churchill in the autumn of 1886 when confronted by the calm, massive, and negative obstruction of Lord Salisbury. Churchill's relations with Baldwin had been infinitely better than those with Bonar Law, but there was a substantial gulf of background and attitude between the two men. Churchill was combative on those issues which Baldwin believed required pacification. Churchill's sense of drama and colour in life contrasted sharply with Baldwin's calmness, shrewdness and preference for the deliberate and calculated solution. Baldwin was a far more sensitive man–as Thomas Jones wrote, "He felt things deeply, and his conscience was more active than his intellect"–and he was in his way a romantic, with a strong (and healthy) strain of good-natured sceptisism. Amery has written that "Baldwin was a personality, with a breadth of outlook, a tolerance and a warm humanity which commanded the admiration, as well as the affection, of those who chafed most under the weaknesses of his leadership." And Amery has also emphasised Baldwin's "strong Celtic MacDonald strain–emotional, impulsive, secretive, and intensely personal in its likes, dislikes and moral judgements."

Churchill depicted Baldwin in *The Gathering Storm* as a masterly Party tactician, yet the irony of this description lies in the fact that Baldwin was never really at home in the Conservative Party. As Lord Attlee observed, "He always seemed more at home with our people, particularly the older trade union people, than with his own lot." And it was significant that Ramsay MacDonald said in 1923 that "in all essentials, his outlook is very close to ours."

In the cool shades of Opposition the Conservative Party becomes exceptionally factious and querulous. Disraeli noted in his biography of Lord George Bentinck that

> There are few positions less inspiriting than that of the leader of a discomfited party. . . . He who in the Parliamentary field watches over the fortunes of routed troops must be prepared to sit often alone. Few care to share the labour which is doomed to be fruitless, and none are eager to diminish the responsibility of him whose course, however adroit, must necessarily be ineffectual. . . . Adversity is necessarily not a sanguine season, and in this respect a political party is no exception to all other human combinations.

From the outset, Baldwin was viewed with heavy reservations by a substantial element in the party. Harold Macmillan observed: "The young and progressive wing of his party had a special regard for him. His speeches, particularly on industrial problems, struck just the note which we thought appropriate and illuminating. The fact that the Right Wing and especially the so-called 'industrials' had little love for him, confirmed our feelings."

When Baldwin was successful, the mutterings against his leadership were of little account; the moment he stumbled as in 1923 and again in 1929, the discontent at once came to the surface. On each occasion, he tolerated much abuse until he suddenly turned on his opponents. One contemporary observer remarked in March 1931 that "it is one of Mr. Baldwin's most unfailing characteristics that he never rises to the heights of which he is capable until the causes for which he stands seem almost desperate. His spiritual home is always the last ditch."

III

Conservative discontent with Baldwin after the 1929 election was first demonstrated by a persistent campaign against his close friend J. C. C. Davidson, the chairman of the Party and the author of the "Safety First" campaign theme, who was obliged to resign in June 1931. This was accompanied by the curious phenomenon of the Empire Free Trade "crusade" in which Beaverbrook and Rothermere allied, parted, then allied again, for a cause that aroused immense support in the Conservative Party but whose implications were but dimly realised. This was soon joined by another campaign–which overlapped but was not identical–which arose over the future of India, and first emerged in October 1929.

The situation that finally culminated in the 1935 Government of India Act seems very remote today. It is hard to see why this modest proposal aroused such passions and so occupied and monopolized Parliament for a period of nearly six years, to the point where it seemed to be the only issue of contemporary significance. Yet, it is impossible to understand the politics of the 1930s without comprehending this issue.

As with all major crises, it began stealthily. Under the Montagu-Chelmsford reforms of 1917-1919–themselves the logical heirs of the Morley-Minto reforms of 1908-1909–some degree of nominal self-government had been conceded to India. It was too little and, as the events of the early 1920s demonstrated, too late. Birkenhead, as Secretary of State between 1924 and 1928, was the only member of the Cabinet who opposed the Montagu-Chelmsford reforms, and although his contempt for the new forces of Indian nationalism was even more naked in private than in public, the Government's policy was clear enough. Under the 1919 Act that had put the reforms into effect, a Commission to examine the workings of the new Constitution had to be set up within ten years. Alarmed by the possibility of a Labour-dominated Commission, Birkenhead hastened its establishment, under the Chairmanship of Sir John Simon. Its membership was carefully designed to permit no serious possibility of extreme solutions. Birkenhead was not directly responsible for the appointment of Lord Irwin as Viceroy in 1926, but he commended it by saying, "How much better in life and how much more paying it is to be blameless rather than brilliant." Yet this appointment, combined with the pressure of events in India, effectively wrecked the strategy implicit in the Simon Commission.

To summarise a complex situation, Lord Irwin concluded that a serious Anglo-Indian Conference could be the only basis for a long-term settlement, and that to secure such a Conference the British must concede that a grant of Dominion Status had been implicit in the 1917 Declaration. He had little difficulty in persuading the Labour Government of the merits of his arguments, and suitable announcements were made in the *Indian Gazette* of October 31, 1929. It was the reference to Dominion Status that sparked the tumult in the Conservative Party that raged until 1935.

Churchill suffered from two grievous disabilities in this affair. The first was that he knew virtually nothing about India, beyond his experience as a young subaltern. The second was that he took his attitudes from Birkenhead, whom he admired extravagantly, and whose death in 1930 left him the leader of the movement against granting Dominion Status. There were also tactical considerations, which he touched on in *The Gathering Storm*:

> My idea was that the Conservative Opposition should strongly confront the Labour Government on all great Imperial and national issues, should identify itself with the majesty of Britain as under Lord Beaconsfield and Lord Salisbury, and should not hesitate to face controversy, even though that might not immediately evoke a response from the nation.[4]

Baldwin's reactions to the Irwin Declaration were at first somewhat confused, but soon it was plain that his attitudes were close to those of the Viceroy and the Government. Churchill's were vehemently hostile, and throughout 1930 the rupture between him and his leader steadily grew. By the end of the year, when it seemed that Baldwin's position was almost hopeless, Churchill was the dominant element in the rapidly growing campaign against the grant of Dominion Status to India. In January 1931, after Irwin had released Gandhi from detention, Churchill resigned from the Conservative "business committee" and spoke out in defiant opposition. For the next four years, as the volume of his speeches on the subject indicates, India was a major obsession.

IV

It is perhaps desirable to disentangle ourselves from the complex and wearying history of the 1935 Government of India Act to examine certain salient features of that episode insofar as they concerned Churchill. It has already been noted that his knowledge of the subject was minimal. This remained true throughout the controversy, as was painfully demonstrated when he gave evidence before a Joint Committee of both Houses of Parliament in 1933. Had the violence of his language been compensated for by informed judgement, his reputation with those who were struggling with the issues would have been higher. That he felt passionately about India could not be gainsaid, but his policy really rested on the simple concept that British power in India must be preserved without qualification. The supreme irony of the events from 1929 to 1935 was that the strategy of the Act was to give India the title of Dominion Status without the reality, and that in actual political terms the gulf between Churchill and Ministers was only one of degree.

It is possible to argue that Churchill's motives were dominated by a desire to remove Baldwin. No doubt, this factor played its part, but no observer can contemplate this prolonged campaign without realising that deeper elements were involved.

The first element was Churchill's lifelong lack of serious interest in the Empire. He accepted it, and was dismayed by any possibility of its power or authority being diminished, but he was not greatly interested in it. He opposed Imperial Preference in 1903, greatly disliked the Statute of Westminster of 1931, and had no zest for Empire Free Trade. He made speeches and wrote fine passages in his books about the Empire, but he never visited any part of it except Canada after 1908. The Imperial-Commonwealth aspirations of men like Lionel Curtis, Amery and Brand were incomprehensible to him. He viewed the Empire essentially through English eyes–as an asset of incalculable value in world-power terms. He once described his approach as that of "an optimistic Liberal Imperialism," but what was an enlightened viewpoint in the 1908 settlement with the Boers did not appear in the same light in the 1930s. Mr. Ronald Hyam, in his account of Churchill at the Colonial Office in 1906-1908, described Churchill's memorandum on the Transvaal as "a classic statement of the primary principle of political conduct of the Victorian and Edwardian ruling elite, the principle of timely concession to retain an ultimate control," and has also emphasised the paternal and condescending nature of Churchill's attitude to black Africans. Without putting too much weight on this, it can be said that Churchill's lack of faith in Indians to manage their own affairs was as profound as that of Birkenhead.

This factor was very evident in his speeches. He described Gandhi as "a fanatic and an ascetic of the fakir type well known in the East," as "this malignant and subversive fanatic," and as "this half-naked fakir." He vividly depicted how India would degenerate under Indian rule, "when the British will be no more to them than any other European nation, when white people will be in India only upon sufferance, when debts and obligations of all kinds will be repudiated, and when an army of white janisseries–officered, if necessary, from Germany–will be hired to secure the armed ascendancy of the Hindu."

Churchill's speeches on the India Question do not make agreeable reading. One constantly reiterated theme was that famine in Britain would be an immediate result of a grant of Dominion Status. Another was that a third of the working population would be unemployed. His allegations concerning the incompetence of Indians aroused indignation and not merely in India. The Lothian Report on Indian Franchise was denounced as "nothing but the cheapest chop-logic, crude, raw, semi-obsolete, half-distrusted principles of mid-Victorian Radicalism, dished up to serve the ends of India."

Most depressing of all is the total absence of any constructive suggestions. When he made his last speech on the subject, in June 1935, Leo Amery–who followed him–opened with the words: "Here endeth the last chapter of the book Jeremiah," and described the speech as "like all his speeches on the subject, utterly and entirely negative and devoid of constructive thought."

V

Throughout this struggle, dubbed "Winston's Seven Years' War" by Sir Samuel Hoare, Churchill was supported by some sixty Conservatives in the House of Commons and by a larger proportion of the Party in the country. It is ironic that, as Churchill became more Conservative, the balance in the Party was swinging to the Left; this movement not only made Baldwin's ultimate victory more certain but alienated virtually all of the younger and more progressive Conservatives. Churchill's allies were allies on India alone; those whom he alienated could have formed the basis of a group around him opposing the Government's foreign policy.

The immediate losses from this dismal campaign can be easily categorised. Despite the brilliance of many of his speeches–brilliant at least in style, if not in substance–his Parliamentary reputation definitely declined. His break with Baldwin in January 1931 cut him off from the virtual certainty of Cabinet office when the National Government was formed in August 1931, and denied him even the possibility of office until June 1935, at least. The violence of his language against Baldwin personally did not improve his chances of returning to the Government when the long dispute was over. His basic ignorance of the subject had deeply offended those who were genuinely working for Anglo-Indian cooperation. In the long term, his violent campaign destroyed what chances there were for a realistic and generous solution, and the Act of 1935 has as its monument the loyalty of India in the Second World War, a fact that Churchill never comprehended or appreciated.

But, so far as his own reputation was concerned, the most grievous consequence of all was that he debased the language of alarmism. He applied to the Indian nationalists phrases far more ferocious and condemnatory than those he used against the German leaders up to the outbreak of the Second World War. The theme of "Wake up, England!" became so stereotyped in the India dispute that it had little impact when, in 1933, he began to speak about the German menace. Thus we find him warning in July 1931 that "on we go, moving slowly, in a leisurely manner, jerkily onwards, towards an unworkable conclusion, crawling methodically towards the abyss which we shall reach in due course." When he began to apply such phrases to the real menace arising in Europe, the impact was small. This was the real, and tragic, price of the lengthy controversy over the 1935 Government of India Act.

VI

It is important to realise how the lamentable Indian controversy affected the infinitely more serious problem of Germany. Churchill made his first major speech on Germany in the spring of 1933; in 1934 and 1935 his warnings became more insistent and commanding, yet the audience was liable, within a few days, to be subjected to equally formidable harangues about India. The campaign on improving defence cannot, accordingly, be seen in isolation. It was carried out by a man whose claim to respect had been grievously reduced, and who always seemed to speak as though Doom were about to fall. Constant reiteration of this theme dulled the sensibilities of his audience. Increasingly, Churchill appeared a remote figure from a distant age, much like Sir Austen Chamberlain, that noble but pathetic figure in his top-hat, ancient frock-coat and frayed shirts. Churchill's speeches, replete with fine phrases and dire warnings, came thundering forth; the audience listened with appreciation and interest, much as young audiences must have listened to Caruso in his last months, and carried away an impression of having been present at a great and fascinating historical occasion–but no more.

In 1930, Churchill published *My Early Life*, which may be fairly described as a classic of autobiography. Writing of the resignation of Lord Randolph Churchill, he noted: "It is never possible for a man to recover his lost position. He may recover another position in the fifties, but not the one he lost in the thirties or forties." Churchill was over sixty years of age when the 1935 Government of India Act reached the statute book. The position he had gained in his fifties had been thrown away over India. What remained was lost on the Abdication crisis of 1936, when he foolishly but not ignobly espoused the cause of King Edward VIII. There are few spectacles less deserving of admiration than the aging political adventurer, and it was as such that Churchill appeared to his bored and irritated listeners when the dark and ominous shadows gathered over Europe after 1933.

VII

In politics a man carries on his shoulders his full reputation—private as well as public. The strength of his speeches lies not in their words and phrases but in their total impact, what Lord Rosebery has called "the character breathing through the sentences." When Churchill began to turn his attention to the potential dangers from Germany in 1933, the campaign over India was at its height. That he had once again alienated a substantial element in the Conservative Party won him no adherents among the Opposition. Indeed, as his campaign over defence developed, the gulf between him and the Labour Party sharply increased. His personal following in the House of Commons on this issue consisted of Brendan Bracken, Robert Boothby, and, after 1935, Duncan Sandys. Significantly, when a group of disaffected younger Conservatives emerged in 1938, it grouped itself around Anthony Eden rather than Churchill.

By this time Churchill was in his sixties and his political personality had fully matured. Indeed, in the eyes of some, it seemed that he was past his prime. The ardent professionalism of his earlier years was lacking in the India campaign, and old suspicions that his judgement was faulty in moments of crisis were fortified with new evidence. His Parliamentary style appeared increasingly out-of-date, and there was much wisdom in Clement Attlee's later remark that Churchill was a great Parliamentary figure rather than a great Parliamentarian. His deep Conservatism showed itself more and more clearly in his writings and speeches; he had strongly opposed the granting of equal franchise to women in 1927, and wrote in 1934 that "all experience goes to show that once the vote has been given to everyone, and what is called full democracy has been achieved, the whole [political] system is very speedily broken up and swept away." He complained that universal suffrage "deprives the House of Commons of the respect of the nation," and his solution in effect was a return to the pre-1914 arrangements, before, as he put it, "the liquefaction of the British political system had set in."

Even on the issue of national defence, which increasingly obsessed him from 1934 on, his arguments and his alleged facts sometimes went beyond the point of credibility, and in retrospect appear absurd. He persistently denied the effectiveness of aircraft against warships, declared that the submarine and the tank were obsolete, and predicted that the war of the future would be essentially static. He eagerly took up some of the more preposterous of the ideas of his friend and scientific adviser, Professor F. A. Lindemann (later Lord Cherwell), and at one point in 1938 was writing scathing memoranda about the Hurricane and Spitfire aircraft, on the grounds that "the latest developments increasingly suggest that hostile aircraft can only be engaged with certainty on parallel or nearly parallel courses, hence that the turret type of equipment will become paramount."

Furthermore, in his preoccupation with Germany, he sometimes seemed to validate Lord Esher's 1917 criticism that he deceived himself into believing that he took wide views while in fact he concentrated upon one particular aspect. His comments on Mussolini were not notably critical; we find Churchill writing of him in May 1935 as "a really great man," and in October 1937 he observed: "It would be a dangerous folly for the British people to underrate the enduring position in world-history which Mussolini will hold; or the amazing qualities of courage, comprehension, self-control and perseverence which he exemplifies."

In these circumstances it is not surprising that his reactions to the Abyssinian crisis and the proposed Hoare-Laval Pact seemed somewhat unheroic or that he was a virtually open supporter of Franco up to April 1938. On the merits of each case his course may have been justifiable, but such positions lost him the confidence of some of those who began to see the European crisis in wider and deeper terms than the threat of German nationalism.

Throughout the 1930s it seemed that some perverse fate was stalking Churchill's progress. In spite of his isolated and weak position, the quality and power of his speeches on defence often embarrassed the Government and Churchill's status rose. Yet the harm done to his reputation by his allegations of breach of Parliamentary Privilege by Hoare and Lord Derby in 1934, by his hapless intervention in the Abdication crisis, and by episodes such as the Irish ports and the "Sandys storm" in 1938 was considerable.[5]

His own position vis-a-vis the Government was itself ambivalent until 1935. As soon as the India dispute ended he made no secret of the fact that he wished to return to the Government after the 1935 General Election. This desire probably was at the root of his silence over the Hoare-Laval Pact, and was certainly responsible for the mildness of his speech on the German remilitarisation of the Rhineland in March 1936. When rebuffed, he returned to his charges against Ministers with renewed vigour. In fact, as this campaign developed, the actual gulf between Churchill and the Government narrowed. The pace of British rearmament may have been much too slow, as Churchill argued, but at least it had begun, over the clamorous opposition of the Labour Party. Unhappily, every Churchill speech attacking Ministers was delivered to the Conservative Party exclusively, and therefore to an audience that was, at best, sceptical of the judgement of the speaker.

The ambivalence of Churchill's position was heightened by the fact that from 1935 until the outbreak of the war he was a member of the Air Defence Research Committee (A.D.R.C.) and accordingly, to some extent, *parti pris* to many of the most vital decisions taken in this period. He had no official responsibility, but the manner in which he used the information thus gained caused some to consider withdrawing the privilege from him. Lord Swinton subsequently commented:

> Winston certainly believed in my expansion plans. . . . At the same time he was determined to use anything he could find to attack the Government. So he used any evidence, good or bad, relevant or irrelevant, he could find about German air strength to attack the Government. . . . And the last thing he bothered about was consistency. He knew I should go on with the plans we both believed in; and at the same time he could go for the Government. . . .[6]

It is not necessary to enter into the bitter disputes instigated by Lindemann that racked this small committee of scientists set up under Sir Henry Tizard to appreciate that Churchill's contributions to the A.D.R.C. were not invariably constructive. His faulty grasp of technical detail and his tendency to seize upon wholly impractical and ill-thought-out projects earned him considerable mistrust among professionals, particularly in the Air Ministry. One must also remember that throughout this period Churchill was regarded by many Ministers and officials as the author of the Ten-Year Rule of 1927 which had decreed that Defence Estimates should be based upon the assumption that the Empire would not be involved in a major war for ten years; it had had baleful effects on the British armaments industry. In the words of Sir Warren Fisher, in the 1924-1929 Government "we converted ourselves to impotence," and the build-up from 1933 onwards owed at least part of its slowness to this basic factor.

Nevertheless, Churchill's campaign, for all its inconsistencies, errors of fact, bad timing and fundamental ambivalence had one increasingly and outstandingly demonstrable strength. Alone, and perhaps as a result more of intuition than of knowledge, he had quickly appreciated the desperate shortage of time available for rearming. Even those who believed that war was probably inevitable–and, for a variety of reasons, these were few–could not believe that the German rearmament would proceed as speedily as it did. Hitler was a terrible phenomenon; Churchill's great contribution was that he sensed this fact.

Significantly, Churchill's published judgements up to the end of 1937 were not too severe. In 1935 he wrote a lengthy portrait of Hitler, which was republished in 1937 in *Great Contemporaries*. It did not avert attention from "the darker side of [Hitler's] work and creed," but his account of Hitler's "long, wearying battle for the German heart" was not unsympathetic: "The story of that struggle cannot be read without admiration for the courage, the perseverence, and the vital force which enabled him to challenge, defy, conciliate or overcome, all the authority or resistances which barred his path." In October 1937 we find him writing of Hitler that "if our country were defeated, I hope we should find a champion as indomitable to restore our courage and lead us back to our place among the nations." One doubts these were tactical niceties. One has the feeling, which grows steadily on close examination of Churchill's speeches and writings in this period, that he fully understood Hitler, and conceded him his achievements while warning of the menace he posed.

It has been emphasised that Churchill's personal judgements were uneven, and were often the despair of his friends, admirers and his family. But in the case of Hitler—whom he never met—we may make a significant exception. And it was on this point that his campaign ultimately rested. So long as his evaluation of Hitler appeared erroneous, his campaign made little progress; from the moment—which I date in March 1939 with the collapse of the Munich policy by the occupation of Czechoslovakia—it was shown to be right, the tide turned.

VIII

Throughout the 1930s Churchill was an isolated, solitary figure. It was, quantitatively, the most productive period of his literary life, and it was also in this period that he made Chartwell his real home. It became, as one friend has said, "an extraordinary mixture of Grand Hotel and a Government Department."

As his interest in defence matters grew, Churchill's zest for politics returned. His autobiography, *Marlborough, His Life and Times* and the *History of the English-Speaking Peoples*, to say nothing of a steady output of articles for British and American newspapers and journals, provided him an outlet for his still formidable energies and supplied an income sufficient to maintain himself and his family in the style he deemed appropriate. Although Churchill glossed lightly over the effects of his political ostracism on himself, that he felt it deeply could not be concealed.

Churchill's character was not a simple one. Behind the facade which some described in terms of insensitivity and bluster, there lay a keen and acute mind. By his sixties, it was perhaps less keen and acute than it had been, but still formidable by normal political standards. His egocentricity was, no doubt, a fault, but in this period his faith in himself—despite some dark hours—proved incalculably valuable. His love of colour and drama grew with the years, and often blurred his judgement, but it enabled him to view events with a freshness which was remarkable. His impatience with detail and his reluctance to get to the hearts of matters himself—as evidenced by his dependence on Lindemann and his young research assistants—was new, and unfortunate. Yet along with his tendency to oversimplify complex issues, which had become more marked with age, these qualities enabled him to see certain issues and broad effects during the 1930s that many younger and more subtle minds failed to detect.

Throughout his life, his intense antipathy to negotiating under duress grew always stronger. In many situations this had been a grievous handicap, but his reiterated emphasis on the air arm as a bargaining factor was sound. It is also true that he never appreciated that the real strength of Germany lay in the German Army, with its attendant air arm, and that he seriously overestimated both the French and Polish armies. It is also very arguable whether Hitler was ever really "stoppable"; but Churchill's fundamental policy of building up military strength in order to be able to negotiate on something approximating equal terms had a realistic basis. In short, although he was wrong on many details, he was absolutely right on the main issue.

From his own viewpoint, Churchill's political career was the paramount factor in his life. He was a refreshingly bad intriguer, fiercely loyal to his friends, and his sense of political honour was considerable. But there was in him enough of John, Duke of Marlborough (and perhaps of his grandfather, Leonard Jerome) to enable him to convince himself that the national interest frequently coincided with his own. Lord Beaverbrook has emphasised this capacity for self-deception, and T. E. Lawrence once remarked with feeling that "if Winston's interests were not concerned in a matter he would not be interested." Leo Amery has considered that in working on the life of Marlborough "he discovered that fusion of political and military ideals, as well as the inspiration of family piety, for which he had all his life been groping." It might be more true to say that he had discovered, in his sixties, a cause which had eluded him the whole of his career. Up to 1934 it would have been difficult to say what Churchill "stood for." After that date, although many might recoil from his attitudes, there were no doubts. Indeed, his constant harping on the theme became positively boring. India had seemed, for a time, such a cause. The German menace was the real thing.

The fact remains that Churchill's brilliant campaign on defence, in which he made perhaps the greatest speeches of his career, was, until March 1939, almost wholly unsuccessful in political terms, and even the support of some elements of the national Press in the summer of 1939–which ranged from the *Daily Mirror* to the *Daily Telegraph*–lacked any solid Party or national base. The causes principally lay in his past, in his character, and in the context of the times. The trade union movement, as George Isaacs has emphasised, remembered his attitudes over almost thirty years. The Conservatives, in the main, abhorred him. The "Focus" movement, designed to arouse public awareness of the German menace, never got very far, partly because of the debacle over the Abdication. To the younger members of the Conservative Party who were increasingly discontented with Government policy in 1938, Anthony Eden–dismissed by Neville Chamberlain as Foreign Secretary early in 1938–was a more natural and more hopeful leader. Churchill's attitude of intense loyalty cut him off from many who agreed with him on essentials but were not prepared to become total disciples on the Bracken or Lindemann pattern. His definition of friendship was a severe one. "He demanded," Lady Asquith wrote, "partisanship from a friend, or, at the worst, acquiescence," and Robert Boothby observed that " 'Thou shalt have none other gods but me' has always been the first, and the most significant, of his Commandments." The comment of Sir Desmond Morton is perhaps the most fair:

> The full truth, I believe, is that Winston's "friends" must be persons who were of use to him. The idea of having a friend who was of no practical use to him, but being a friend because he liked him, had no place. . . . [But] he certainly gave all those who knew him at least as much pleasure as they may have given him use or interest. He owes them no debt![7]

Among men who liked and admired him, several serious qualifications remained, which have been well described by Sir Alan Herbert:

> I never liked Mr. Chamberlain (I hardly knew him): but I admired him. For more than twenty years I had adored (that is the right word, I fear)

> Mr. Churchill. . . . I did not think then, as so many thought in those days, that he was brilliant, resourceful, brave, but nearly always wrong. . . . But I did think that he rather enjoyed a war: and, after three years in the infantry, in Gallipoli and France, I did not.[8]

IX

We are now very close to discovering why Churchill failed in the 1930s and succeeded in May 1940. We have seen how Churchill's undisguised relish in the Navy aroused deep apprehensions in the Liberal Party in 1911-1914, and why Fisher, after his break with Churchill, said of him with admiration, "He was a *war* man!" John Maynard Keynes, reviewing *The World Crisis* in 1927, had commented upon that fact that "Mr. Churchill does not dissemble his own delight in the intense experiences of conducting warfare on the grand scale which those can enjoy who make the decisions." Keynes's comments were fair, for he also emphasised Churchill's awareness of the horrors of war, and he did not go nearly as far as H. G. Wells, who wrote that Churchill's "violent imaginations have caused the deaths of thousands of people." One need not accept the grotesque charges that he was a warmonger or, in Herbert Morrison's phrase of 1935, "a fire-eater and a militarist," to appreciate that there is a relish about his military writings–from *The River War* to *Marlborough*–which is of much significance, and which led so moderate a person as Alan Herbert to conclude that Churchill "rather enjoyed a war."

Wells was harsh when he wrote of Churchill that "he believes quite naively that he belongs to a peculiarly gifted and privileged class of beings to whom the lives and affairs of common men are given over, the raw material of brilliant ideas" but it was not the reverse of the truth. Isaiah Berlin, many years later, made substantially the same point:

> As much as any king conceived by a Renaissance dramatist or by a nineteenth century historian moralist he thinks it is a brave thing to ride in triumph through Persepolis; he knows with an unshakeable certainty what he considers to be big, handsome, noble, worthy of pursuit by someone in high station and what on the contrary he abhors as being dim, grey, thin, likely to lower or destroy the play of colours and movement in the universe.[9]

We have also touched upon Churchill's romantic concept of England, first seen in the concluding passage of his father's biography. His daughter compared England in Churchill's eyes to a mistress to be courted; the analogy is relevant. In Churchill's later writings this obsession with a near-mythical Laurania, the nation-state depicted in his novel, *Savrola*, is striking. As Lady Asquith observed, "Armies are just as necessary in politics as war. And they can only be recruited by persuasion."

Many commentators have emphasised the strong consistencies in Churchill's career, and have remarked that Churchill was justified in his observation that it was the world, not he, which had changed. There is much truth in this, as Berlin has emphasised: "When biographers and historians come to describe and analyse his views . . . they will find that his opinions on all these topics are set in fixed patterns, set early in life, and later only reinforced." The man that we beheld in the early 1900s had altered in many respects by the late 1930s, but the consistencies of attitude are more striking than the changes. This lack of significant development between his early forties and his sixties might be considered a failing. This would certainly have been the judgement of 1938, and perhaps even of 1939.

Had the story ended then, we could have concluded with the words employed by Churchill himself in his biography of Lord Randolph:

> His part in national affairs is not to be measured by long years in office. . . . No tangible or enduring records exist of his labours, and the great and decisive force which he exerted might be imperfectly realised by a later generation, unless it were explained, asserted, and confirmed by the evidence of those who came in contact or collision with his imperious and vivifying personality. . . . This account will, I think, be found to explain in almost mechanical detail the steps and the forces by which he rose to the exercise of great personal authority, as well as the converse process by which he declined.

But the story had not yet concluded. Another, and even more startling, chapter was about to open. In 1938 "appeasement" as a policy and as an attitude had widespread public support. The apprehension of war was profound. The policies of Neville Chamberlain, culminating in the Munich Agreement, had few critics. Virtually alone, Churchill spoke with sombre and unreserved censure against this dismal drift towards disaster. To this he devoted some of the most memorable speeches of his entire career, but, at the end of 1938, it appeared that all this had been in vain.

NOTES

[1] Robert Boothby, *I Fight to Live* (London, 1947), 44.
[2] Quoted in Christopher Hassall, *Edward Marsh* (London, 1959), 565.
[3] Winston S. Churchill, *Daily Mail*, October 2, 1931.
[4] Winston S. Churchill, *The Gathering Storm* (London, 1948), 26.
[5] See R. Rhodes James, *Churchill: A Story in Failure, 1900-1939* (London, 1970).
[6] James, *op. cit.*, 276.
[7] Quoted in R. W. Thompson, *The Yankee Marlborough* (London, 1963), 253.
[8] A. P. Herbert, *Independent Member* (London, 1952), 109.
[9] Isaiah Berlin, *Mr. Churchill in 1940* (London, 1965), 17.

ROYAL NAVAL DIVISION WAR MEMORIAL

April 25, 1925

Unveiling Ceremony, Admiralty Building, London

This brief speech may be regarded as one of the most perfect in expression and conception that Churchill ever delivered.

Every one, I think, must admire the grace and simplicity of this fountain, which the genius of Lutyens has designed. The site also is well chosen. Here, under the shadow of the Admiralty building, where, 11 years ago, the Royal Naval Division was called into martial life, this monument now records their fame and preserves their memory. Their memory is thus linked forever with the Royal Navy, whose child they were, of whose traditions they were so proud, and whose long annals, rich with romantic and splendid feats of arms, contain no brighter page than theirs. But if the place is well chosen, so also is the day. This is April 25, and ten years ago the astonishing exploit of landing on the Gallipoli Peninsula was in full battle. And we here, who have so many memories in common, almost seem to hear the long reverberations of the distant cannonade, and certainly we feel again in our souls the awful hopes and awful fears of those tragic hours.

A mellow light seems to the mind's eye to surround this monument. The passers-by who in other days pause to drink of its water or to examine its design will be held by something else. The famous lines of Rupert Brooke inscribed upon its panel will make their own appeal and tell their own story to anyone who loves this island or speaks the English tongue.

These verses, and others given in the order of service, have brought comfort to so many who sought it long and wearily, and whose spirit seemed broken, but who nevertheless found relief in reading and repeating their noble utterance. Their high, calm peace rises confidently above the tumult and the carnage, and beyond all error and confusion; it reigns by right divine over men and over centuries. We meet his verses everywhere. They are quoted again and again. They are printed in newspapers, written in books, blotted by tears, or carved in stone. But they belong to us, to the Royal Naval Division, to the memory of Rupert Brooke and his comrades and companions. They were the inheritance he bequeathed to them, and through them to us all. They are inscribed on this memorial because it is their proper home, and from here, while these stones endure, they will carry to the ears of generations differently attuned from ours the chant of valiant youth entering willing and undaunted into the Valley of the Shadow of Death.

Ten years and more have gone since this parade ground used to be thronged by bands of volunteers marching off to join the Army amid the blare of music and at their country's call. Nearly seven years have gone since victory was won; since all the kings and emperors against whom we warred were driven into exile, and all their mighty armies shattered and dispersed. Those years have not been years of joy or triumph. They have been years of exhaustion, despondency, and bickerings all over the world, and we are often tempted to ask ourselves what have we gained by the enormous sacrifices made by those to whom this memorial is erected. But this was never the issue with those who marched away. No question of advantage presented itself to their minds. They only saw the light shining clear on the path of duty. They only saw their duty to resist oppression, to protect the weak, to vindicate the profound but unwritten law of nations, to testify to truth and justice, and mercy among men. They never asked the question, "What shall we gain?" They asked only the question, "Where lies the right?" It was thus that they marched away for ever, and yet from their uncalculating exaltation and devotion, detached from all consideration of material gain, we may be sure that good will come to their countrymen and to this island they guarded in its reputation and safety so faithfully and well. Bold indeed will be the tyrant who seeks again to overthrow by military force the freedom which they established. After the confusion has passed away and the long period of reconstruction has been closed it will be perceived by all that the freedom, not only of individuals, but also of States, has been established upon a broader and stronger foundation.

Humanity, for all its sufferings and disappointments, has yet moved forward through the Great War at least one long stage towards the realization of its ideals. And this country and Empire, saved by its sons from the worst perils which have confronted it during its long history, remains still able to guide, to encourage, and in a large measure to inspire the peoples of the world. Doubts and disillusions may be answered by the sure assertion that the sacrifice which these men made was not made in vain. And this fountain to the memory of the Royal Naval Divison will give forth not only the waters of honour, but the waters of healing and the waters of hope.

THE BUDGET

April 28, 1925

House of Commons

The most controversial feature of Churchill's first Budget was the announcement of the return to the gold standard at the prewar parity. At the time, the decision was generally applauded–although the restoration of the prewar parity was criticised in some quarters–and the vehement attacks of John Maynard Keynes in a series of withering articles (subsequently published under the title The Economic Consequences of Mr. Churchill*) were isolated ones. Hubert Henderson was another critic, forecasting trade depression and aggravation of unemployment as a consequence of Churchill's action, adding: "It is with regret that we are disposed to write him down as one of the worst Chancellors of the Exchequer of modern times." Historians have almost wholly endorsed Keynes and Henderson, but at the time their voices were not dominant.*

Another item which aroused controversy was the re-imposition of the McKenna Duties of 1915. These modest measures of protection for British industry had been repealed by Snowden in 1924; Churchill restored them on the principal grounds of their revenue capacity, and was careful to make it clear that no abandonment of Free Trade principles was involved.

[Extract] . . . Before I come to the prospects of 1925 I have an important announcement to make to the Committee. It is something in the nature of a digression, and yet it is an essential part of our financial policy. Ever since the Spring of 1919, first under War powers and later under the Gold and Silver (Export Control) Act, 1920, the export of gold coin and bullion from this country, except under license, has been prohibited. By the express decision of the Parliament of 1920 the Act which prohibits the export was of a temporary character. That Act expires on the 31st December of the present year, and Great Britain would automatically revert to the pre-War free market for gold at that date. Now His Majesty's Government have been obliged to decide whether to renew or prolong that Act on the one hand, or to let it lapse on the other. That is the issue which has presented itself to us. We have decided to allow it to lapse. I am quite ready to argue the important currency controversies which are naturally associated with a decision of that kind, but not to-day–not in a Budget speech. To-day I can only announce and explain to the Committee what it is that the Government have decided to do, and I will do that as briefly as I can.

A return to an effective gold standard has long been the settled and declared policy of this country. Every Expert Conference since the War–Brussels, Genoa–every expert Committee in this country, has urged the principle of a return to the gold standard. No responsible authority has advocated any other policy. No British Government–and every party has held office–no political party, no previous holder of the Office of Chancellor of the Exchequer has challenged, or so far as I am aware is now challenging, the principle of a reversion to the gold standard in international affairs at the earliest possible moment. It has always been taken as a matter of course that we should return to it, and the only questions open have been the difficult and the very delicate questions of how and when.

During the late Administration the late Chancellor of the Exchequer (Mr. Snowden) appointed a Committee of experts and high authorities to examine into the question of the amalgamation of the Treasury and the Bank of England Note Issues. The inquiry resolved itself mainly into an examination of whether and in what manner we should return to the gold standard. The Committee was presided over by my right hon. Friend who is now Secretary of State for Foreign Affairs (Mr. A. Chamberlain), and then a private Member, and its other members were Lord Bradbury, Mr. Gaspard Farrer, Professor Pigou, and the Controller of Finance at the Treasury. This Committee heard evidence from a great number of witnesses representing every kind of interest: financial and trading interests, manufacturing interests, the Federation of British Industries and others, were heard. It has presented a unanimous Report in which it expresses a decided opinion upon the question of the gold standard, and it sets forth its recommendations as to the manner in which a return to that standard should be effected.

I have had the Report of this Committee printed, and it will be available in the Vote Office as I finish my remarks this afternoon. It contains a reasoned marshalling of the arguments which have convinced His Majesty's Government, and it sets forth a series of recommendations, in which my right hon. Friend, though he ceased to be Chairman on becoming Foreign Secretary, has formally concurred, and which His Majesty's Government are intending to follow in every respect.

So much for the principle. There remain the questions of time and of method. There is a general agreement, even among those who have taken what I think I am entitled to call the heterodox view–at any rate, it is the view which we on this bench do not accept–that we ought not to prolong the uncertainty, that whatever the policy of the Government, it should be declared, and that, if we are not going to renew the Act which prohibits the export of gold coin and bullion, now is the moment when we ought to say so. It is the moment for which the House of Commons has patiently waited at my request–and I express my obligation because I have not been pressed on this matter before–the moment at which it was, after long consideration, judged expedient that decisions should be made and actions taken. This is the moment most favourable for action. Our exchange with the United States has for some time been stable, and is at the moment buoyant. We have no immediate heavy commitments across the Atlantic. We have entered a period on both sides of the Atlantic when political and economic stability seems to be more assured than it has been for some years. If this opportunity were missed, it might not soon recur, and the whole finance of the country would be overclouded for a considerable interval by an important factor of uncertainty. Now is the appointed time.

We have therefore decided, although the prohibition on the export of gold will continue in form on the Statute Book until the 31st December, that a general licence will be given to the Bank of England for the export of gold bullion from to-day. We thus resume our international position as a gold standard country from the moment of the declaration that I have made to the Committee. That is an important event, but I hasten to add a qualification. Returning to the international gold standard does not mean that we are going to issue gold coinage. That is quite unnecessary for the purpose of the gold standard, and it is out of the question in present circumstances. It would be an unwarrantable extravagance which our present financial stringency by no means allows us to indulge in. Indeed, I must appeal to all classes in the public interest to continue to use notes and to make no change in the habits and practices they have become used to for the last ten years. The practice of the last ten years has protected the Bank of England and other banks against any appreciable demand for sovereigns or half-sovereigns. But now that we are returning publicly to the gold standard in international matters with a free export of gold, I feel that it will be better for us to regularise what has been our practice by legislation. I shall therefore propose to introduce a Bill which, among other things, will provide the following:

> First, That until otherwise provided by Proclamation the Bank of England and Treasury Notes will be convertible into coin only at the option of the Bank of England;
>
> Secondly, That the right to tender bullion to the Mint to be coined shall be confined in the future by law, as it has long been confined in practice to the Bank of England.

Simultaneously with these two provisions, the Bank of England will be put under obligations to sell gold bullion in amounts of not less than 400 fine ounces in exchange for legal tender at the fixed price of £3 17s. 10-1/2d. per standard ounce. If any considerable sum of legal tender is presented to the Bank of England the bank will be under obligation to meet it by bullion at that price. The further steps which are recommended by the Currency Committee, such as the amalgamation of the Bank of England and Treasury Note issues, will be deferred, as the Committee suggest, until we have sufficient experience of working a free international gold market on a gold reserve of, approximately, £150,000,000. It is only in the light of that experience that we shall be able to fix by permanent statute the ultimate limits of the fiduciary issue. All that will be in the Bill.

The Bill also has another purpose. We are convinced that our financial position warrants a return to the gold standard under the conditions that I have described. We have accumulated a gold reserve of £153,000,000. That is the amount considered necessary by the Cunliffe Committee, and that gold reserve we shall use without hesitation, if necessary with the Bank Rate, in order to defend and sustain our new position. To concentrate our reserves of gold in the most effective form, I have arranged to transfer the £27,000,000 of gold which the Treasury hold against the Treasury Note issue to the Bank of England in exchange for bank notes. The increase of the gold reserve of the Bank of England will, of course, figure in their accounts.

Further, the Treasury have succeeded in discreetly accumulating dollars, and we have already accumulated the whole of the 166 million dollars which are required not only for the June payment but also for the December payment of our American debt and for all our other American debt obligations this year. Therefore–and it is important–the Treasury will have no need to go on the market as a competitor for the purchase of dollars. Finally, although we believe that we are strong enough to achieve this important change from our own resources, as a further precaution and to make assurance doubly sure, I have made arrangements to obtain, if required, credits in the United States of not less than 300 million dollars, and of course there is the possibility of expansion if need be. These credits will only be used if, as, and when they are required. We do not expect to have to use them, and we shall freely use other measures in priority. These great credits across the Atlantic Ocean have been obtained and built up as a solemn warning to speculators of every kind and of every hue and in every country of the resistance which they will encounter and of the reserves with which they will be confronted if they attempt to disturb the gold parity which Great Britain has now established. To confirm and regularise these credit arrangements, which I have had to make provisionally in the public interest, and to deal with the other points that I have mentioned, a short three-clause Bill will be required. The text of it will be issued to-morrow, and we shall ask the House to dispose of it as a matter of urgency.

These matters are very technical, and, of course, I have to be very guarded in every word that I use in regard to them. I have only one observation to make on the merits. In our policy of returning to the gold standard we do not move alone. Indeed, I think we could not have afforded to remain stationary while so many others moved. The two greatest manufacturing countries in the world on either side of us, the United States and Germany, are in different ways either on or related to an international gold exchange. Sweden is on the gold exchange. Austria and Hungary are already based on gold, or on sterling, which is now the equivalent of gold. I have reason to know that Holland and the Dutch East Indies—very important factors in world finance—will act simultaneously with us to-day. As far as the British Empire is concerned—the self-governing Dominions—there will be complete unity of action. The Dominion of Canada is already on the gold standard. The Dominion of South Africa has given notice of her intention to revert to the gold standard as from 1st July. I am authorised to inform the Committee that the Commonwealth of Australia, synchronising its action with ours, proposes from to-day to abolish the existing restrictions on the free export of gold, and that the Dominion of New Zealand will from to-day adopt the same course as ourselves in freely licensing the export of gold.

Thus over the wide area of the British Empire and over a very wide and important area of the world there has been established at once one uniform standard of value to which all international transactions are related and can be referred. That standard may, of course, vary in itself from time to time, but the position of all the countries related to it will vary together, like ships in a harbour whose gangways are joined and who rise and fall together with the tide. I believe that the establishment of this great area of common arrangement will facilitate the revival of international trade and of inter-Imperial trade. Such a revival and such a foundation is important to all countries and to no country is it more important than to this island, whose population is larger than its agriculture or its industry can sustain—[Hon. Members: "No!"]—which is the centre of a wide Empire, and which, in spite of all its burdens, has still retained, if not the primacy, at any rate the central position, in the financial systems of the world. . . .

I have thus balanced the Budget in the public ledger in pounds, shillings, and pence, and I have also tried, as I am sure hon. Members opposite will not deny, according to my lights—we all have our own point of view—to balance it fairly in the scales of social justice between one class and another in our varying community. Having limited resources to dispose of, and heavy burdens to carry, I have tried to present, on behalf of this new Parliament and the large Conservative majority, a scheme which has both unity and combination, which is national and not class or party in its conception or intention, which seeks to give to every class the assistance it most requires in the form most acceptable to the individual and most useful to the State—a scheme from which no class of men or women in the country, from the poorest to the richest, is excluded, and in which the proportion of advantage or relief progressively increases as the ladder of wealth is descended. I cherish the hope that by liberating the production of new wealth from some, at least, of the shackles of taxation, the Budget may stimulate enterprise and accelerate industrial revival; and that, by giving a far greater measure of security to the mass of the wage-earners, their wives and children, it may promote contentment and stability, and make our island more truly a home for all its people.

THE ECONOMIC SITUATION

July 15, 1925

Mansion House, London

As the industrial situation deteriorated, particular tension was seen in the coal-mining industry, and the first shadows of the 1926 General Strike fell.

[Extract] I am speaking tonight in that cloud of uncertainty which overhangs all our national life at the present time, but in the observations which I propose to address to you I do not intend to deal at all with the possibility of a general or prolonged stoppage in the coal industry. If such a catastrophe were to occur it would completely derange the whole economic and commercial conditions of the country. It would inflict injuries and wounds from which we would not recover for a very long time. It would falsify all calculations; it would render impossible all assurance, every prediction, and it would unquestionably inflict a measure of injury upon all classes of people and of actual privation upon the masses of the people.

I hope and believe that wise counsels, common feelings of prudence, and national self-preservation will lead the difficult disputes into safe channels, and the remarks which I propose to make to you on various aspects of our financial and economic situation are based upon the assumption which I am bound to make although I cannot claim any especial information—on the assumption that we shall not be subjected to a violent eruption of a great cessation of work in the coal mines of the country. . . .

Sound and honest finance requires as its first essential a resolute reduction of public expenditure. I am doing and I will do my best. The task is very difficult, and I should certainly fail if I were not encouraged and supported by my colleagues in the Cabinet and by the Prime Minister. Even so the task will be very difficult. The vested interests of expenditure are so strongly entrenched that it will take all the efforts of a united Cabinet to achieve even a moderate reduction next year. I should be misleading you if I led you to suppose that such a reduction is now in sight; on the contrary we are endeavouring at present not so much to reduce the total of expenditure, but to prevent that total being seriously increased by the dull tide of upward expansion. It is not until we have stemmed that tide and resisted the automatic growth of expenditure that we shall be free to move forward into the more hopeful sphere of a positive reduction.

I have only one thing more to say. As long as we are in contact with reality, however stern it may be, we may suffer, but we shall live. If we lose contact with reality we might quite swiftly get ourselves into a position where recovery would be impossible. As long as we keep on sound lines we shall have warning of every economic danger. If wages or hours of labour are out of economic relation to our competitors, if employers become slack or unenterprising, if businesses are overlaid with burdens, if the plant of our industries becomes obsolete, if their organisation is antiquated or awkward, if we consume too much or borrow too much or lend too much, as long as we are in contact with reality, all the alarm bells begin to ring immediately. You can hear them now ringing in your ears.

I am glad we can hear the alarm bells ringing. I rejoice that we have not been doped and drugged, and stupefied by reckless inflation, by fabricated credits, by unwholesome stimulants, or lulled by any method into a false security in which we should fail to realise our position. Whatever may be the condition of our affairs we can see where we are, where we are going, what is coming towards us, but we can alter our conduct in so far as it may be necessary before it is too late. Work, thrift, enterprise, effort, co-operation, science—set the teeth, cudgel the brains, cut down expenses, hand in hand, shoulder to shoulder—we have done it before, we can do it again. In that spirit alone shall we prosper and survive.

COAL MINING INDUSTRY

August 6, 1925

House of Commons

By 1925 the coal-mining and cotton industries, which in 1913 had formed over 50 percent of British exports, were in serious decline. Together, they employed over one and a half million workers, and accounted for some 60 percent of abnormal unemployment. As the demand for British coal declined, production fell, and the number of unemployed miners remorselessly rose. The mine-owners sought a solution in reducing wages and closing unprofitable pits, and a major confrontation developed, which reached its climax in 1926. Churchill's tax on artificial silk in his 1925 Budget was a major blow to the textile industry, at the moment when it was seriously turning to the development of man-made fibres, but it was the deteriorating situation in the coal-mining industry which was the most explosive factor in creating a confrontation between organised labour and the Conservative Government. At the beginning of August the Government averted a major crisis by a subsidy to the industry to prevent further reductions of wages and the appointment of a Royal Commission to examine the future of the industry.

[Extract] . . . A number of questions have been asked about the White Paper and about the manner in which this subvention is to be paid. I think I should take up more time than I wish to do if I were to go into those details. If I am to epitomise the White Paper, I would say it is based throughout upon the idea that the mine-owners are to receive the advantages they hoped to obtain from the reduction of wages for which they asked, without those reductions of wages being at present made effective upon the mine-workers. But subject to that, with that additional subvention, made good by the State, everything in the mining industry will move upwards or downwards in accordance with the ordinary conditions of supply and demand, and if, as is inevitable when you proceed, as you must proceed, upon the basis of district rates, the prosperous mine will have advantages over the unprosperous, such advantages exist in the world to-day and this system, which does not in any way interfere with the natural movement of events, obviously perpetuates those differences. You will no doubt have anomalies. That is admitted. You will have districts which are poor, and which get a large subvention. In them there will be prosperous mines which, in spite of their prosperity, will get an additional subvention. You will get districts that are rich and which will rise above the profitable level and will get no subvention. In them there will be several mines that will have to close because they are not entitled under the district rate to a sufficient subvention to enable them to live. Those are obvious and admitted anomalies. We have followed, in the emergency which has arisen, perfectly well known and well understood precedents. We have followed the precedent of 1921. The right hon. Gentleman the Member for Carnarvon Boroughs has been courteous enough to explain that he has had to leave for another engagement. We have followed exactly the machinery and procedure which he, and my right hon. Friend the then Chancellor of the Exchequer, adopted in the arrangements for a subsidy in 1920 and 1921, and that is the only way in which such a temporary measure of assistance could be given to the coalmining industry. The moment you started to pick and choose between individual mines, you would have been involved in immense labour and in inextricable confusion. You can only proceed on the basis of district rates, and on the basis of district rates, though you will have many anomalies, nevertheless upon the whole the industry will proceed on its economic basis plus a temporary Government subvention. . . .

The existing position is plainly intolerable. There is no industry, or there are only a few great industries in which masters and men for a long period of years have done better than in the coal industry. The average employer and the average miner, taking a long period of years, has certainly enjoyed advantages greater than those of the average ordinary workmen or employer throughout the country. Now this industry, which has always held, and rightly held such an exceptional position, has been quartered on the general taxpayer. I hope I may be allowed to say this, speaking for the outside world not connected with the mining industry on the one side or the other, that they have so managed or, if you like, mismanaged their joint affairs that they have confronted the State with the alternative either of seeing the trade of the whole country ruined, perhaps, for two years to come, or else making a subsidy payment in aid of this particular industry out of the income of the struggling business man, out of the beer and tobacco of working men all over the country, and out of the tea and sugar of the poorest people in the land.

This is a humiliating position for a great industry to have reached as the final result of all the immense, complex organisation which they have built up for dividing profits and for adjusting disputes. It is quite impossible that such a system can continue. To bring it to an end in one way or another by the beginning of May next must henceforward be one of the main and predominant objects of public policy. We have decided to pay what may well be £15,000,000, in order to gain nine months of breathing space, but not by resting, to quote the words of my right hon. Friend. Let us see that that time is well spent and that we have not made this sacrifice at the expense of the general taxpayer without achieving some effective advantage. I am not going to make any attempt to deal with the different questions of organisation which have been made in various interesting speeches. The question which the House has to decide to-night is whether the Government is right in paying the high price which it did in order to postpone a wasteful and disastrous conflict, in the hope and on the chance that it may be averted in the interval. . . .

Was the decision which His Majesty's Government took right or wrong in the circumstances? Ought we to have accepted this conflict, or were we justified in making further efforts at a heavy cost, efforts which are open to many objections, to avert it? That is what the Committee must decide to-night, and it is really the only question on which their opinion is asked. May I say one word about public criticism. It is certainly not at all scarce at the present time. People do not like the subsidy, but not many people would have liked the strike. We have chosen the subsidy, and we see and feel its disadvantages. But we have avoided the strike or lock-out, so no-one knows what its disadvantages would have been. It is very easy to minimise in public opinion a stoppage of this kind, and to represent it as a salutary and exhilarating experience, sharp at the time, but really useful for British trade. In such a mood it is very easy to condemn the Government who accepted the grave disadvantages of the subsidy when all the time there was the perfectly simple, straightforward, manly remedy of accepting the strike.

But if we had chosen the other course, does anyone suppose that we should have escaped the criticism to which we have been subjected, or that all parties would have joined together in supporting us in facing the recurring and increasing difficulties which would have come upon us from day to day? Would the Liberal party and the London Press have given the Government support in the immense crisis which would have ensued? Would the public have been encouraged to endure the hard, long ordeal with determination? Why, Sir, I can hear the speeches which would have been delivered. I can see in imagination the leading articles and the headlines which would have been printed. "His Majesty's Government were utterly incapable of inducing the owners and the miners to come together. Were they proposing no solution of their own?" Hon. Members opposite would have said, "We have said all the time it is quite simple. Only let them nationalise the mines." Hon. Members of the Liberal party would have said, "It is quite simple. Only let them follow the guidance which we gave in our 'Coal and Power,' published a whole year ago by the Liberal Publication Department." Those great popular organs which have such a wide circulation and a very great though superficial influence, which have set themselves deliberately for many months past to discredit and undermine the position of the Government—do you think that the hostile criticisms which they are making now would have been lacking then? They would have been different only in form. The "Mail" would have said, "The whole blame for this situation rests with the wasteful Government." The "Express" would have said, "What did we tell you would follow the gold standard?"

That being so, it being clear that we should be criticised whatever course we took, for the best thing is for the House to discount interested and partisan criticisms, and to consider in a practical spirit the extremely disagreeable alternative which the Government had to face on Thursday last, whether in all the circumstances that existed they would plunge the country into this confusion and struggle, or whether they would make what is a most objectionable payment from the Exchequer in the hope that time would promote a better solution. That is the question. I have absolutely no doubt myself that the decision which was taken on Thursday was right and wise. I have no doubt that it will be found the best in the long run, in the interests of the public. I am not usually accused of being specially or unduly deficient in combative energy. I have seen as a Minister, almost continuously during the last 20 years, many repeated occasions of strife. I have never known a case where the arguments for patience, for restraint, for delay, for gaining time, for securing a breathing space, for avoiding an immediate rupture, were so strong; nor have I ever seen a situation in which a plunge into decisive and irrevocable action would have been more wanton and more inexcusable.

I say that without the slightest fear of what the result would have been. I put aside altogether any question of doubt as to the result of such a conflict. I have entire faith in the power of the Government of this country to maintain order, entire faith in the power of this great country to overcome any section or group of sections, however powerful, which may challenge its authority. In the event of a struggle, whatever its character might be, however ugly the episodes which would mark it, I have no doubt that the State, the national State, would emerge victorious, in spite of all the rough and awkward corners it might have to turn. But if you are going to embark on a struggle of this kind, be quite sure that decisive public opinion is behind you; be quite sure that the majority of the nation understand what the quarrel is about; be quite sure that they realise that the Government are only defending fundamental national interests and liberties. . . .

There is another aspect of challenge to which, I know, the Committee would wish me to refer. It is a challenge to our Parliamentary institutions from persons far removed from those to whom I have been referring, but it is none the less a very serious, and, in some ways, in a practical sense, a more dangerous aspect. There is a growing disposition among the great trade union authorities of the country to use the exceptional immunities which trade unions possess under the law, not for the purpose of ordinary trade objects, but in the pursuit of far-reaching political and economic aims. It is, obviously, impossible for a Parliament, elected as we are upon what is virtually a universal suffrage, to allow its authority to be disputed by any section or organisation however respectable or however powerful. We have heard in this Debate of an attempt to hold up the whole community, of the threat of cutting off the vital supply services. The use of such a threat as a political weapon, which has been more and more apparent in recent years, is a grave fact which will require the profound and continuous attention of the House of Commons. [*Interruption.*] I am not going to dwell upon these aspects of the strife beyond saying that it is justifiable to put them forward, because it must not be supposed that, because we are for peace, we are incapable of the defence of the great interests of the country.

What is the main object of all parties in this Parliament? It is to get a little more prosperity–if we can–for our people, and for all classes in our country. I trust that this Parliament may see an advance, moderate yet definite, and appreciable in all parts of the country, towards a better condition of material well-being. The decision which was taken on Thursday was taken because we have not yet abandoned that hope. If we had plunged into a struggle, allowed a stoppage of the mines, had faced a general strike on the railways, had accepted a temporary paralysis of the entire industry of the country, allowed trade to be checked, allowed social reform to be arrested, our finances to be deranged, had postponed pensions, and restored taxation–if we had taken that position, then for us, and so far as this Parliament is concerned, the door would have been closed to an advance to a better state of things. It may yet happen. But that is not a decision that any sane man or Government would take until every other reasonable possibility had been exhausted. Even if it should be our duty, if ever it should be our duty, to take such a position, then the work of this Parliament is absolutely ruined. For the rest of its life it would be simply toiling back to reach the position occupied in 1924 and 1925–a position which to-day we find much to be discontented with. No chance of improvement! No hope of expansion! No alleviation of the burdens! Just a simple struggle to work back to where we are now. We have refused to accept such a melancholy conclusion. It would be good-bye to the sincere and earnest desires which animate Members of this House of Commons. It would be good-bye to the high hopes which are placed by their constituents in the country on their exertions, and on the achievements which may follow from their efforts.

"IS ENGLAND DONE?"

October 19, 1925

Queen's Pavilion, Chingford

[Extract] There is a mood of extravagant pessimism abroad. When I was on the Continent the other day enjoying a holiday I was repeatedly asked in all seriousness, "Is there going to be a revolution in England?" When I reached my hand out for an English newspaper I found the heading, "Is England done?" I will admit that the editor made some attempt to say that perhaps it is not so bad as that. (Laughter.)

I notice that Mr. Cramp told the railwaymen the other day that we are in for the worst winter since the hungry forties, and, needless to say, the politicans belonging to the Opposition party are only anxious to vie with each other in painting the colours of our country's future in black colour. Mr. Lloyd George said only a week ago of this great, solid, enduring, and triumphant country, "We are like a man walking along a constantly narrowing ledge until he comes to a point where he finds the foothold swept away by the landslide and underneath yawning a chasm." (Laughter.) No, there is one thing about Mr. Lloyd George's chasms–they always yawn. (Laughter.) When Mr. Lloyd George is making a speech it is usually not only the chasm that does yawn. My chasm yawns, but my audience never does. (Laughter.)

Mr. Lloyd George said that we are along a path that is crumbling and shelving away from us. Although there are many causes for anxiety, there is absolutely no justification for these panic-stricken and methodically exploited cries of pessimism and alarm. It is my deliberate opinion that things are not getting worse; indeed, I believe that they are getting better and not worse, not only in this country but in the whole world.

Take, for instance, unemployment. Many speakers say unemployment is increasing rapidly, but that is not true. There has been no increase in unemployment for nearly five months. If we take the last 18 weeks for which figures are available we would find that there are 32,000 less unemployed than there were, and it is more remarkable that it should be so, because these 18 weeks were part of the ordinary seasonal period at which one would expect the figures to go up. Last year in the same 18 weeks the figures of unemployment rose by 180,000. The latest returns, which will be published to-morrow, showed a diminution of nearly 40,000 on the week. Somebody will say that there are 30,000 more unemployed than at this time last year, but I remind you that the coal industry, and the special and exceptional depression which has overtaken the coal industry, has caused an enormous increase in our unemployment figures. If we leave out coal mining and look at the general trade of the country there has not been an increase since last year—there has been a decrease of 150,000. A decrease like that, does not justify public men in proclaiming that our affairs are steadily getting worse. They may not be getting better in this respect, but they have certainly not got any worse.

[Editor's Note: Referring to the Locarno peace pact, Churchill said] : I welcome that firstly for two different sets of reasons—first, because it draws a merciful veil across the lurid and tragic past, and, secondly, because it affords great, a sure, and, I believe, the only possible security for the maintenance of peace in the future. (Cheers.)

There are some who say 'Why should we call the Germans into council?' There are others who say 'Why should we commit ourselves in any contingency in safeguarding the frontiers between the nations on the continent of Europe?' And there are, no doubt, arguments of value which can be used on both these points, but I, for my part, rejoice to see Germany taking what can only be her great place in the League of Nations. I take that event as a sign that Europe has definitely begun to look forward and not to look back. When Europe begins to look forward she will move forward, and I feel that this is an event of immense hope and confidence.

Here you have four great nations of Europe joining hands together in a sort of four-sided pyramid of strength and security, firm and solid, joining hands together for mutual protection and for the prevention of war between themselves. I do not know of any other way in which you can take effective precautions against a struggle in which we should very likely be involved, and if it came could only end in the rebarbarisation of the whole world. I believe this great pact of reciprocal insurance is not only the foundation but the symbol and the herald of still wider associations which will be possible among the States of Europe and the world when better days and wiser generations come to the world.

I am very glad to think that this Conservative Government has been able to carry forward work which has been done with the assent of all parties—has been able to carry it one great step forward to an achievement which made the safety of the British home stand upon a surer footing. (Cheers.) . . .

SOCIALISM

January 21, 1926

Grand Theatre, Bolton, Lancashire

The tenor of this speech–which is not untypical–helps to indicate why Churchill continued to be deeply disliked by the Labour Party, in spite of his progressive and humanitarian approach to social legislation.

[Extract] As I travel about the country I come across quite a lot of people, and I have noticed recently that those who are Conservatives have something like a grin on their faces. There is no doubt at all from what I hear that there has been a great sensible improvement in the position of the Government in the last six months. Various causes are assigned for this, and I expect all of these played their part. There was the great Treaty of Locarno, the Irish settlement, and a sensible improvement in trade. From every quarter we hear that things are on the mend. I do not pretend for a moment that any great or violent change in our material circumstances is going to occur, but by other tests which it is possible to apply we are entitled to say that things are not getting worse. On the contrary, they are getting better. (Cheers.) . . .

There is a deeper reason for the gathering feeling of confidence and unity which is noticeable in the country. People had not quite appreciated six months ago the consequences of the national decision of the General Election of 1924. I have served under four Prime Ministers, and no one becomes Prime Minister of this country without possessing high and exceptional qualities. I would not for a moment embark on invidious comparisons, or indulge in flattery of the chief under whom I now serve, but whenever there is anything which is a fine achievement in any department, Mr. Baldwin invariably effaces himself and insists upon the entire credit being taken by the Minister responsible. But when, on the other hand, there is rough weather to be encountered, when there is something unpopular or disputable, and when the House of Commons is very doubtful about it, then you will find it is the Prime Minister who comes forward himself to take the brunt. Such leadership gets the service it deserves. (Cheers.) But the confidence of the country is due to the new House of Commons, even more than a united Cabinet. We have a good Parliament; it may even become a great Parliament. It is the first Parliament for many years in which there has appeared a considerable proportion of young men of first-rate Parliamentary and political ability.

There are in the Conservative party to-day at least a dozen young members of whom one can say with confidence that there are no great offices of State which they will not be able to fill with success and with dignity in the future. The great majority which supports the Government has no grudges to pay off against its opponents. It was returned to power by more than a party mandate, and it has pursued, ever since, a national policy. (Cheers.) The Opposition are divided and broken among themselves.

Both the Liberal and Labour parties are split from end to end by deep rifts. I give credit to the Liberal Party for its great liberation work during the 19th century. Our liberties were gained; they have now to be guarded. We must make sure they are not lost. It might be said that the price of freedom, like the price of safety, is eternal vigilance. The Conservative Party is now the only organized force strong enough to defend the popular liberties of Britain and to defend them against new dangers which everyone can discern quite clearly. I was reading this morning a speech by Mr. Tomsky, who is a very important person in the Government of Russia, and who attended the Scarborough Conference of the trade unionists of this country. [Editor's Note: Churchill read quotations from the speech, and described them as] barbaric nonsense, produced out of ignorance and suffering, and exploited by crime and villainy.

I am of opinion, that in this country we are fully capable of managing our own affairs without any assistance. (Cheers.) We do not want to have this new-laid crocodile's egg from Moscow put upon our breakfast table. (Laughter and cheers.) The day will come–although our Liberal friends may not admit it–when the Liberals will have to render the whole of their aid and strength to the Conservative Party in finally eradicating such foolish and subversive and reactionary doctrines from the minds of a large section of our fellow-countrymen. (Cheers.) These Russian Bolshevists have been having a very expensive education. I do not know how many hundreds of thousands of people they have killed, or how many millions they have let starve in the course of their educational period. But they are getting their education. What they are gradually realizing, not by argument, but by cruel experience, is that the gospel of hatred leads only to the death of a nation.

The Russian Bolshevists are going to undergo an increasing tension of temptation. The country is prostrate at their feet. But they have learnt not only how to gain and hold power; they have also learnt that all those theories in which they formerly believed will not work, and are exploded. They know it; they do not conceal it; and by a score of actions they are marching back to capitalism month by month. They robbed the Russian people of prosperity, or freedom; all for a fanatical dream, all for a shameful delusion; and now they are forced by the inexorable logic of events, by the profound force of Nature and of human nature, to abandon the theme, the doctrine, in the enforcement of which they have not hesitated to shed the blood ruthlessly of any man or woman who stood in their path. Now their temptation is this: They have to be continually asking themselves how long must they keep Russia shut up in the freezing cellar of Communism for the sake of their own consistency to dogmas which they are now convinced have been exploded by practice, when all the time they have only got to unlock the door and let the sunshine and let the spring warm mighty Russia into life and wealth and joy. That is their temptation. That is their dilemma. They must be super-human or subhuman if in the end they are not forced to yield to the ameliorating pressure of events.

I do not fear a Bolshevist revolution in this country. All my criticisms against Socialism are directed to the erroneous doctrines, to the criminal excesses of Socialists when they have obtained power. I do not criticise individuals. I know quite well that in any great body of Englishmen the good forces predominate over the bad, pick them where you will. I am not in the least alarmed of our educated democracy being made sport of, deluded and tormented in the way these poor country Russian *moujiks* have been. But I do say that in this country it would mean a great curtailment of our liberty if it were attempted by a Socialist majority to put Socialism arbitrarily into practice. (Cheers.) Britain is not like Russia. One-tenth of the dose of Socialism which has ruined and injured Russia would kill Britain and Lancashire stone dead. Why should people go about pretending that, in spite of all its injustices yet to be righted, the present State . . . is a foul thing, to be cut down and fettered and torn to pieces and thrown away? The great accusation I make against the Socialist Party is the manner in which they have corrupted and are trying to corrupt the character of the British nation. If their only object is a "square deal," and an improved standard of living for the masses, and a hard hand against monopolies and vested interests, what is the need to go and teach thousands of good-hearted English people to perform these ridiculous antics of Continental Socialism? (Cheers.) What is the good of making them all swallow the dreary doctrines of Karl Marx; to teach them to sing the Internationale out of tune–(laughter); to regard the national anthem as a party tune; to teach them to applaud and cheer and champion the red flag–which has brought nothing but disaster wherever it has been flown; and to look with disdain and dislike on the Union Jack, which has for centuries sheltered the growth of freedom in every quarter of the globe?

That is the condemnation we make of them. Let them quit these gospels of envy, hatred and malice. Let them eliminate them from their politics and programmes. Let them abandon the utter fallacy, the grotesque, erroneous, fatal blunder of believing that by limiting the enterprise of man, by riveting the shackles of a false equality upon the efforts of all the different forms and different classes of human enterprise, they will increase the well-being of the world. Let them abandon these; let them hold firm to the principles of individual liberty, and strike against abuses wherever they may be found, and they will immediately restore in England the situation of two parties which may differ profoundly in the ordinary struggle and ebb and flow of party politics, but which will, nevertheless, be united on certain grave and fundamental issues vital to the welfare and prosperity of the nation as a whole. (Cheers.)

THE GENERAL STRIKE

May 3, 1926

House of Commons

The Royal Commission on the coal-mining industry, under Sir Herbert Samuel's chairmanship, had reported on 11 March. Its principal positive recommendations were for the future; its short-term proposals involved a reduction of wages for the miners. The owners also wanted longer hours. These terms were unacceptable to the unions, and deadlock occurred. On 1 May the miners were locked out, and a special trade union meeting approved plans for a national strike to take place on May 3. Negotiations took place throughout May 2, and were broken off by the Government late at night when it learned that the Daily Mail *compositors had refused to typeset the newspaper in protest against a fiery editorial by the editor. In such confused circumstances Britain lurched towards her first General Strike. The feeling that Churchill had been one of the Ministers most hostile to a negotiated settlement seriously damaged his relations with organised labour until the Second World War, and to some extent even after it.*

[Extract] . . . I have . . . a general view of the position and I have the information of my colleagues here in regard to particular details and I say, without hesitation, that the impression left upon me is that for all practical purposes the miners have not budged one inch since July last. I do not see, and I do not know in what practical way they have at all receded from the position which they then held so strongly and intensely that there must not be one minute's prolongation of the time or one shilling's diminution of the wage. If they will not accept a reduction of wages, and if the owners cannot be forced to carry on the business at a loss, it is perfectly clear the only alternative left is for the State to continue the subsidy for a prolonged period. [Hon. Members: "A fortnight."] Does anybody suppose that the continuance of the subsidy for a fortnight is going to allow this matter to be settled? I cannot believe it for one moment. How can we justify prolonging this subsidy while the coal trade is being reorganised? . . .

Is there anyone who does not believe that my right hon. Friend the Prime Minister has desired to avert this breakdown more than any other man in the whole country? Is there anyone who can dispute the fact that, as Chancellor of the Exchequer, I have as great a political interest in averting this disaster as any other Member of the House. Does anybody seriously hold the idea that the question of a small prolongation would have stood in the way if there had been any practical hope of settlement? We would gladly have made the sacrifice and, even if we had made a statement to the contrary, we would not have allowed that statement to stand in the way provided we were sure there was, not a certain, but a reasonable, hope of getting a permanent solution. Obviously, however, things cannot get into the position where we are committed to an indefinite prolongation of the subsidy while a somewhat vague reorganisation is going on laboriously in the coal trade as preliminary to any readjustment of economic conditions.

It has been said, "What does it mean–it is taxpayers' money." It is money taken from the pockets of the people of the country; it is taken from the necessities and comforts of the working classes. Agriculture, steel, iron, shipbuilding, are all suffering too, and in some cases and in many parts, the conditions both of hours and labour are worse in those industries than they are in the coal industry, or parts of it. How can you justify the whole country being forced to pay this particular levy almost indefinitely, when there is no prospect of any solution? Anyhow, whether it is just or not that there should be a continuance of the coal subsidy to the miners and mineowners in the pressing circumstances, that is a question which Parliament and Parliament alone can competently decide. This Parliament representing 45,000,000 is the only body that can judge of the correlation of all the interests in the country.

If that be so, if I have given a fairly accurate account of the situation, what is the position created by the decision to call a general strike? That decision is the second fact in the situation. The first fact is the demand for a continuance of the subsidy; the second is the terrible, blasting, devastating menace of a general strike throughout the country. The right hon. Gentleman drew distinctions between general strikes. He said there were general strikes to force legislation, and that these were shocking and unconstitutional, but a general strike out of mere sympathy in a wages dispute, apparently, he regarded as legitimate. I see no difference whatever between a general strike to force Parliament to pass some Bill, which the country does not wish for, and a general strike to force Parliament to pay a subsidy. There is a great distinction between a trade dispute, designed to bring about a solution as between masters and men, and a general strike of this character. We all deplore strikes, but the strike has been found almost the only way, when other means have failed, of getting to a conclusion in regard to trade disputes, and organised labour has repeatedly repulsed the idea of compulsory arbitration. We have recognised it for years as a lamentable method of adjusting disputes when everything else has failed.

Suppose we have a miners' strike; as we have seen twice before it is a process of reducing people, by cruel losses on all sides. Government, miners and mine-owners all are reduced to the same position where, after the lapse of time, they come into a more reasonable frame of mind and offer in weakness or in sorrow to make a settlement. That is the process, and it is the process that British labour has always claimed to have the right to exercise. But that is an entirely different thing from the concerted, deliberate, organised menace of a general strike in order to compel Parliament to do something which it otherwise would not do. A general strike in a great number of trades, which have been selected, and of which we have been informed, in the very elaborate and thorough accounts which have been given in the papers, obviously means, if it were continued for any length of time, the ruin of the country. Therefore, the country and Parliament, which represents the nation, are confronted quite simply with the choice either of being ruined or of submitting to pay very large sums of the taxpayers' money to one particular trade, which they do not think justified. It is really not possible. I am not going to use one single provocative word, for, after all, what is the use of provocative words on such an occasion, here in the House of Commons? Probably our words may go no further than the House of Commons, but all the more should they be sincere and unprovocative. It is absolutely impossible to justify the submission by Parliament to such a demand. We know how hard the leaders opposite have tried to get the miners to make some concession, but the miners were unable to. Time and again, my colleagues inform me, they were not able, their leaders, to give any practical acceptance of the Commission's Report. But whether or not the miners are right really does not arise for the purpose of the argument. You may think they are right, and we may think they are not right, but anyhow, right or wrong, the position we are in to-night is that we have either got to face the ruin of the country or submit to a demand which is placed on us under duress. Therefore, it seems that the general strike turns, not upon the decision of the Trade Union Congress even as to whether the claims of the miners are just, it turns on the failure of the Trade Union Committee to persuade the miners to accept some modification. . . .

I am told this is not a strike to starve the nation into submission, and I readily recognise the offer which was made to convey food and necessaries by the Trade Union Committee, but what difference does it really make to the issue whether the country is immediately to be starved into submission or whether ruin is to be brought upon it out of which famine will emerge in a few weeks or months? There is no difference. It may have been a wise thing for the trade unions to have done, but as far as affecting the situation is concerned, it affects it in no way, and what Government in the world could enter into partnership with a rival Government, against which it is endeavouring to defend itself, and society, and allow that rival Government to sit in judgment on every train that runs and on every lorry on the road? Our title deeds in this House—and, after all, we represent a great mass of electors—[An Hon. Member: "Not the majority!"]—We do not represent a majority, but we represent a larger number than hon. Members opposite. Our title deeds do not allow us to contemplate such a situation. We cannot by any means divest ourselves of the responsibility of maintaining the life of the nation in essential services and in public order, and in pursuance of that we are bound to take every measure, and even perhaps, as time goes on, measures which, if they were ventured to-day, would seem very drastic, but which in a few weeks everyone might consider necessary.

In the nature of things that is what is so serious about the situation. It is a conflict which, if it is fought out to a conclusion, can only end in the overthrow of Parliamentary Government or in its decisive victory. There is no middle course open. Either the Parliamentary institutions of the country will emerge triumphant, and the nation, which has not flinched in the past through many ordeals, the nation, which indeed has always shown itself stronger and nobler and more generous in its hours of trouble, will once again maintain itself and be mistress in its own house, or else, on the other hand, the existing constitution will be fatally injured, and, however unwilling hon. Members opposite may be to produce that result, the consequences of their action will inevitably lead to the erection of some Soviet of trade unions on which, whether under Parliamentary forms or without them, the real effective control of the economic and political life of the country will devolve. Such a transference could only mean the effectual subversion of the State, and, therefore, weighing all the consequences, we feel bound to act as circumstances may require. It is hardly to be conceived that any considerations of weakness or fear would prevent Ministers or Members of Parliament from doing their duty to the end. No one can doubt what the end will be, but let me say this one last word before I sit down.

If the executive Government of the country were at this crisis, and face to face with the situation which has now, for the first time, developed in our land, for never before has it emerged in this form, if we were in this crisis to show ourselves incapable and impotent and unable to make head and to carry on the control and authority with which the nation has entrusted us, that would not end the conflict. The Government may be brushed out of the way, but other forces, enemies to the Parliamentary constitutional system of this country, forces which deserve and require the consistent control of democrats in every land, would emerge and carry on the struggle in infinitely more disastrous and tragical forms than that with which we are now threatened. From every point of view, including that of our duty in the long interests of the working classes of this country, we are bound to face this present challenge unflinchingly, rigorously, rigidly, and resolutely to the end. . . .

PARLIAMENTARY GOVERNMENT

May 26, 1926

International Parliamentary Commercial Conference Dinner, Royal Gallery, House of Lords

At the outset of the General Strike, Baldwin entrusted Churchill with the task of publishing a Government newspaper, which appeared as the British Gazette. *It was described by Lloyd George, not unjustly, as "a first-class indiscretion, clothed in the tawdry garb of third-rate journalism." Its fiercely anti-union tone further convinced the Labour Party that Churchill was their most vehement opponent. His defence (July 7) was that he declined "utterly to be impartial as between the fire brigade and the fire." The refusal to publish an appeal for conciliation issued by the Archbishop of Canterbury was a particularly flagrant example of the bias of the* British Gazette. *The strike ended in defeat for the T.U.C. on May 12.*

[Extract] . . . The critics of Parliamentary institutions complain that those institutions do too much talking, but the very name of Parliament implies a certain amount of talking is likely to be done. Personally I am strongly in favour of government by talking; it is better than government by shouting, and it is better than government by shooting. (Cheers.) In the spirit of Parliamentary confraternity I welcome the representatives of 40 Parliaments to the Palace of Westminster, which, without any undue assertion of national pride, we might regard as the birthplace of Parliaments, the home of Parliaments, and the abiding citadel of Parliamentary institutions. In this country we avow our faith in Parliamentary government—we are unshaken by certain developments of the modern world. All wisdom is not new wisdom, and we rest with confidence on the institutions created by the wisdom of our ancestors. We are not blind to the defects of the Parliamentary system, but we are still convinced that, properly worked and properly understood, it is the most flexible and practical form for the government of men that has yet been discovered. (Cheers.)

There is a great deal of truth in the saying that the worst chamber in the world is better than the best ante-chamber. It is said that the age of democracy spells ruin to Parliamentary government, that the Parliamentary system has created political democracy, and now in its train political democracy will destroy the Parliamentary system. Certainly the 20th century has had none of that reverence for Parliaments which distinguished the 19th century. Certainly where Parliaments have failed to be effective, where they have failed to be the real vehicle of the national will, or have failed to be the sure defence of national interests or honours of individual rights and freedom, certainly in the present temper of the world for a time at least another process or system might readily supersede them. It is difficult for the citizens of one country to understand the politics of another—they usually find it extremely hard to understand the politics of their own country (laughter)—the same results are produced by such different methods in different countries.

In Great Britain Parliament—and the House of Commons is the centre of the life of Parliament—has always set the strictest limits on its own functions. In this country Parliament legislates and criticizes, and changes of Government supply the foundation and sanction. It acts as a sort of college for which Ministers are chosen, but it does not attempt to govern. It rigidly abstains from any inroad upon the direct functions of the Executive. We believe that is a wise division of power. There is another function of Parliament which, if successfully discharged, will in every country preserve the power of representative institutions. Parliament, properly viewed and properly guided, is the greatest instrument for associating an ever-widening class of citizens with actual life and policy of the State. There is provision for growth, which is just as necessary in the political world as in the physical world of Nature. . . .

There are present representatives of 40 nations. We are a great company, almost a unique company, and certainly at this moment we cannot be matched in any quarter of the globe. We might almost, if we were in the frame of mind so to do, declare ourselves the Parliament of Man, and proceed forthwith to frame the Federation of the World. But that would, perhaps, be going a little too quickly. We may find it necessary, perhaps, to consult our respective constituents before taking final decisions. Nevertheless, our gathering suggests with great force that one can be a good citizen of the world without ceasing to be a good citizen of his own country. (Cheers.) It suggests that one cannot be a good citizen of the world unless one is a good citizen of one's own country—(cheers)—or, as we in Great Britain would say, a good subject of the Crown, for we are as proud of that term as any nation is proud of the title of citizenship. (Cheers.)

Sane and instructed people should find no difficulty in reconciling national and international duties, just as a good citizen can reconcile his duty to his family and to his town, to his country, and to the State. All men are necessary to one another; all legitimate institutions are in harmony; and it is folly to suggest that there is a limited heap of happiness or prosperity or wealth or trade which is to be divided and scrambled for between the nations, and that what is gained by one can only be taken from another. Such ideas find no sanction either in science or in the practical experience of modern times. The only limits to human progress are those that are made by our own shortcomings. Science is ready to extend the frontiers of every country without injury to the rights of any other, and to increase the well-being of every people at the expense of none. There will be enough for all if the virtues of men keep pace with their growing knowledge, and if all in every land are willing to walk forward together in the majesty of justice and of peace. (Cheers.)

EMERGENCY POWER

July 2, 1926

House of Commons

Despite the collapse of the General Strike, the long dispute in the mining industry continued for several months. All attempts by the Government to reach a solution, in which Churchill was actively involved, were unsuccessful, and eventually the miners were forced to accept the employers' terms.

[Extract] . . . No one desires a settlement more than His Majesty's Government. Obviously it is our interest to desire a settlement. We are responsible for the good government and prosperity of the country, although it is not in our power to control the prosperity of the country any more than it is in our power to control the weather. Yet Governments are judged to a very large extent by the result of their administration, and the result of the administration is measured by a diminution in the national trade, a shrinkage in the consuming power, an increase in unemployment and so forth. After a time, and when the time comes, all that is held in very severe reckoning against the Government. Therefore, on the ordinary grounds of self-interest, if for no higher reason, no one has a stronger desire and a stronger interest than the Government to try to find a way out of these difficulties as speedily as possible, and I am sure no one has a more earnest desire, as every man in the House, wherever he may sit, knows in his heart, than the Prime Minister. Next to the Prime Minister would come the individual who has the duty of occupying the position of Chancellor of the Exchequer, who sees his finances year after year, and now far into the future, compromised and mortgaged by what has already taken place. We have no greater desire than to bring this to a conclusion. Our intentions are obvious, and we have approached the problem throughout in a perfectly sincere and single-minded spirit. If, therefore, we have not succeeded up to the present, it is not because of our intention or our desire. It may, of course, be caused by errors of judgment due to the inferiority of our ability. If that be so, that is our misfortune rather than our fault. There ought to be a Motion, not of censure, but of condolence. . . .

THE *BRITISH GAZETTE*

July 7, 1926

House of Commons

[Extract] . . . When you say to me that this paper ought not to have been partisan, but ought to have been entirely impartial, there I entirely differ. I decline utterly to be impartial as between the fire brigade and the fire. When you are in a great difficulty and in a fight of this kind, however unfortunate it may be, it is absolutely no use people pretending they do not know what side they are on. Here I am sure the hon. Gentleman will agree with me. The ancient Greeks had a very salutary law that in disturbances of this kind, which sometimes in that country took a very serious form, anyone who could not make up his mind which side he was on was put to death.

Hon. Members: You would have died young.

Mr. Churchill: At any rate, I want to make it perfectly clear that it was no part of our duty in producing a newspaper at a time of great crisis to put our very limited staff to work on filling the paper with a lot of defeatist trash. I hope that we got out of that difficulty in such a way that it will not be necessary for either of the parties in the State to conduct their disputes in future on the basis of the whole of the newspaper Press going out of action. It is very much better to let them all bay and blare away together, because in some way or other they correct each other. When you talk of the "British Gazette" and the organising of a newspaper, you have to make up your mind first of all whether you wish to fortify the faithful or to convert the heathen. We thought it essential, in the early days of this dispute, to rally and organise as well as we could those people in the country who were going to help in keeping the vital services going, and from that point of view we undoubtedly disposed of the limited forces which we controlled to the best possible advantage.

I cannot think that this was an unworthy achievement, with all its faults, which I perfectly clearly see. I cannot pretend to have read every word that appeared or to have sifted and garnered all the things that were published, but I am sure that if we had gone on for another week or 10 days a very wide latitude of opinion would have been possible in its pages, so long as it tended to a peaceful solution of the difficulty in which the country had found itself. But that did not arise. In eight or nine days it came to an end. In that time we achieved something. With a handful of experts and a lot of amateurs of all kinds we printed a paper which in its last issue attained 2,500,000 copies, and was delivered next morning at breakfast time from Newcastle to Bristol. I believe that it played an important part in raising the general strike, and some part in upsetting the Liberal party.

One last word. The hon. Member for the Forest of Dean (Mr. Purcell) has indicated that a time may come when another trial of strength will occur–which I devoutly hope may not be the case–and when something like this will be tried again upon the country or the community. I have no wish to make threats or to use language which would disturb the House and cause bad blood. But this I must say: Make your minds perfectly clear that if ever you let loose upon us again a general strike, we will loose upon you—another "British Gazette."

COAL DISPUTE
(VOTE OF CENSURE)

December 8, 1926

House of Commons

[Extract] . . . We are the objects to-night of a Vote of Censure. Let me say at the outset, in order to begin upon a proposition with which I hope everyone may agree, that I should certainly not suggest that this is an occasion or a topic in which there is any great room for mutual congratulation. A seven months' stoppage in the coalfields of Great Britain is not an occasion which should lead to any distribution of bouquets. There is nothing in it for any party or group of Members in this House or for any element concerned in these transactions—there is nothing for them to write home about in what has occurred. In fact, the Prime Minister has said, with complete candour, that the period through which we have been passing has been a period of great humiliation. We all feel, or ought to feel, that it has marked a signal breakdown of that common sense, of that spirit of give-and-take, of that power to adjust difficulties, of which this country has always boasted, for which it has long been renowned, and in regard to which foreign nations have been ready so often to pay us tribute. . . .

I am not trying to fix the whole blame of this upon the Opposition of the Labour party. I think it would be just as absurd for me to do that as it is for them to try to throw the whole blame on the Government. We tried to do our best. We had every incentive to bring this matter to a happier issue. But I will show that the official Opposition have a very great responsibility, and I believe they have a greater responsibility even than the Government. The very constitution of their party and the whole history of its growth are built upon bringing politics into industry and industry into politics. I do not make it as an accusation. I have seen the Labour party grow from a handful of men in this House to the official Opposition of the country. I dare say what has occurred could not have been helped. But I am stating the facts. I say that the association of the trade union movement in the country with ordinary party politics, and its intermingling with the perfectly legitimate work of a Parliamentary Opposition to the Government of the day, has inevitably produced a spirit of faction in British industry, which is not present in the industries of many foreign countries who are our competitors, which would never have been there on ordinary trade grounds and which would never have been there but for the intrusion of party politics.

For my part I am all for party politics in their proper place. I think it is the right of every Opposition to attack the Government of the day, to try to put that Government out and to take its place. That is the way in which the Constitution works, and I think we should endeavour to take it in good part. But it is a very different matter when politics are brought into industry and when the fortunes of a

Parliamentary Opposition, for instance, become involved in the success of a general strike or when its leaders, however unwillingly, find its fortunes associated with the possibility of a breakdown in the means of feeding the country during a prolonged stoppage such as we had. That introduces most dangerous elements into the Constitution and into the ordinary party struggle of Government and Opposition. It is not fair to Parliamentary institutions. It is still more injurious to the industries of the country. If the industries of this small overcrowded, over industrialised and highly artificial island are going to be plunged into the political bear-pit, and if their antagonisms, their inherent antagonisms, already serious, are to be used as pawns in the party fight, then you are not only going to injure Parliament, but you are far more gravely going to strike at those industries upon which the mass of the industrial wage-earners of this country depend for their daily bread. In so far as basic industries are involved in these party politics, those who depend upon them, be they capitalists or wage-earners, will sink increasingly into utter and permanent destitution. . . .

I am one of those who more than or most of all have, as a Minister, to suffer by what has occurred. Our finances have been stricken and wounded by this long stoppage. The means which we might have used for further social development have been sadly crippled. The trade of the country has been held back from the revival which was overdue and perhaps at hand. The unemployment figures, which would have been far below the mean, are now far above it. Out of all this evil there may come some good. At any rate, we have all learned certain things which were unmeasured before. We have learned that neither a general strike nor a prolonged stoppage on the coalfields can break down the life and organisation of our country. These threats hung over us for many years, and we are a stronger country to-day because we know they have no power against the nation. We have learned that, and can we not also learn, from what we have gone through, that higher comprehension of the common interest which we all have in the vital industries of the country, without which in this island we shall not succeed for any lengthy period of time in nourishing our teeming millions?

THE EMPIRE

January 3, 1927

Wolfe Society Bicentenary Dinner,
Savoy Hotel, London

The Imperial Conference in 1926, which Churchill refers to in this speech, laid the foundations for the Statute of Westminster of 1931, which set out the relationship between the self-governing Dominions and Britain for the first time. The British Parliament would no longer have any legislative rights beyond the United Kingdom and the Colonies, and the Imperial link was limited to the symbol of the Crown and voluntary association. This put into formality what had been the case for some time–certainly since the war. Churchill–as will be seen in his later speeches–was not enthusiastic about this development.

[Extract] . . . This last year has witnessed a recognition–for I must not put it at more than a recognition–of a memorable change in the Constitution of the British Empire. It is a change in form rather than in spirit, and like so many of the great changes we make in our country, it is a change gradual and not abrupt. But nevertheless it is a change of first-class importance. And what does it amount to? The age of control in Imperial relationships has ended; it has been formally closed. The Age of Control is gone, the Age of Comprehension has begun. The Constitution of the British Empire depends now and henceforward solely upon good sense, good will, and loyalty to the Imperial Crown. (Cheers.)

We are not unduly sanguine if we believe that the Age of Comprehension will be the most illustrious period in the long history which Britain and Canada will share together. We are not unduly sanguine if we believe that the self-discipline of each part of the British Empire in the Age of Comprehension will yield an even higher comradeship, an even more generous service to the common cause than we ever realized–I do not say in the time of arbitrary control, but even in those more enlightened days which preceded the memorable change which we have just inaugurated. And we will not be stultified in history if we hold firmly to the belief that out of perfect freedom, there will spring a more complete and practical unity than has ever yet been achieved by peoples and by States so numerous, so powerful, or so widely separated by salt water. (Cheers.) . . .

MUSSOLINI

January 20, 1927

Press Statement, Rome

Churchill's visit to Italy, and the warmth of his compliments to Mussolini and the Fascist Regime did not endear him further to his opponents in Britain.

[Extract] . . . Like so many others, I could not but be charmed with the friendly and simple attitude of Signor Mussolini, and by his calm and serene manner despite so many burdens and dangers. It was easy to see that his sole thought is the lasting well-being of the Italian people as he conceives it, and that any other interest of less import has no importance in his eyes. . . .

If I had been an Italian I am sure I should have been entirely with you from the beginning to the end of your victorious struggle against the bestial appetites and passions of Leninism. But in Great Britain we have not yet had to face this danger in the same form. We have our own particular method of doing things. But on one thing I have not even a doubt–namely, that in the struggle with Communism we shall succeed in strangling it.

I will, however, say a few words on the internal aspect of Fascism. Your movement has abroad rendered a service to the whole world. The greatest fear that ever tormented every Democratic or Socialist leader was that of being outbid or surpassed by some other leader more extreme than himself. It has been said that a continual movement to the Left, a kind of fatal landslide towards the abyss, has been the character of all revolutions. Italy has shown that there is a way to combat subversive forces. This way can recall the mass of the people to co-operation that is loyal to the honour and interests of the State. Italy has demonstrated that the great mass of the people when it is well led appreciates and is ready to defend the honour and stability of civil society. It provides the necessary antidote to the Russian virus. Henceforth no nation will be able to imagine that it is deprived of a last measure of protection against malignant tumours, and every Socialist leader in each country ought to feel more confident in resisting rash and levelling doctrines.

THE FINANCIAL AND POLITICAL SITUATIONS

February 4, 1927

Conservative and Unionist Association Meeting, Free Trade Hall, Manchester

This speech foreshadowed the Trade Disputes Act of 1927 which made strikes "designed or calculated to coerce the Government" illegal and compelled Unionists who wished to contribute to the political levy to sign a special form, thus "contracting in" rather than, in the former arrangement, to "contract out." This was deliberate and spiteful attempt to reduce the finances of the Labour Party. It was initially successful, but had no long-term effects beyond further embittering the trade union movement against the Conservatives, and against Churchill in particular. Churchill's language in this speech is a good example of that which made this feeling so profound and so enduring.

[Extract] . . . We are at the beginning of a new year, on the threshold of a new session of Parliament, and we are also very nearly at the point when half the life of that Parliament will certainly have been lived. I must recall your minds, first of all, to the conditions under which that Parliament was elected. We had passed through three years of unexampled political confusion. Governments were formed and Parliaments ascended only to be dispersed. Three general elections in three years, with all their waste and turmoil; three changes or reversals of policy in almost every part of our affairs; Ministries rising and falling like houses of cards; and in a country to which Continental nations had been accustomed to look as a model of political stability there was chaos and total lack of continuity of thought or action detrimental beyond description to our widespread and extremely complicated public interests. ("Hear, hear.") Was it wonderful that the nation with its sure instinct called out amid this confusion for a period of strong and stable administration; for a period of political calm, of peace abroad and of peace at home; or that they should identify their wish for a steady, sincere, and upright Government with the character and personality of Mr. Baldwin? . . .

But across our domestic life in this island there fell last year the blighting shadow of unprecedented industrial strife. We were called upon to face a general strike the effect of which, had it been successful, would have invoked the subversion of constitutional and Parliamentary government in Britain. (Applause.) We had to face a stoppage for nearly seven months in that output of coal on which the whole manufacturing greatness of the nation has been built up. Never before in living memory have such lamentable events occurred inside our island. Never before have we witnessed such a breakdown of British common sense—(applause)—or such a display of irresponsibility on the part of a large section of our fellow-countrymen. The nation has survived these assaults upon its institutions and its prosperity. All that could be done to break down the State and overturn our slowly established system of Parliamentary government was done, make no mistake, with reckless and ruthless malice. But we have survived. We are here to-day. (Applause.) Britain is here today—scarred, weakened, impoverished, disillusioned, somewhat embittered but nevertheless intact, unbroken, mistress in her own house.

Let us look a little at the results of these lamentable events and at the lessons which we should draw from them. What is the first lesson? What is the first great fact which emerges now that the dust of conflict has cleared away? It is surely the extraordinary economic strength of our country and of its national and social life. Personally, I never doubted that the general strike, the assault on the Constitution, the attempt to coerce Parliament and the community into submission to the will of unrepresentative and unelected forces—(hear, hear)—would be smashed to pieces by the strength of the nation. (Cheers.) I think we were most of us always sure of that. But if anyone had told me this time last year that the whole island of Britain could remain almost completely paralysed for seven months without a general collapse of commerce and industry I should have disbelieved him. (Hear, hear.) The truth is we are a good deal tougher than even the boldest knew. Our economic structure, at a time when everybody said it was impossible to carry on a struggle even for a month in this modern world, is stronger, more adaptable, more resilient than even optimists are accustomed to believe. . . .

What is the second great lesson to be learned from the events of last year? The trade unions ought to keep clear of party politics. (Loud applause.) They ought to make it a point, a principle, to keep clear of them, and to keep before them if you will, just as the Lord Mayor or the president of the Chamber of Commerce, the obligation to stand aside from ordinary party politics. The Socialist party has declared in favour of class warfare, and they are at present using the trade union organisation and funds as a weapon of the class war. In this country we have always been a people of party politics and our parliamentary institutions work best on that basis, and perhaps they work best of all on a two-party basis, which basis may well come back again. Now the class war is party politics. It may be party politics in a most degraded form; a lamentable feature in the programme of any party, but still, it is a free country. And if any party chooses to inscribe class war on its party banner the conflict can be fought out in the public arena and in Parliament, according to the usual practice. Our institutions are strong enough and wide enough to enable such a foolish and squalid conflict to blow itself out without serious injury to the State.

But there is one thing we cannot stand. We are a small, over-populated, over-industrialised, highly artificial island. We cannot stand political struggle within the bosom of our own industries. The disputes which must arise between employers and employed are numerous and difficult enough in any case. If to these are to be added the venom and organised malice, the worked-up antagonisms of Socialised politics and their reactions, the basic industries of this country will collapse, and with them will fall the wage earners who depend on them, the shops they use, and the cities and districts in which they dwell. We cannot afford to bring the already burdened, fully taxed basic trades, which also have to meet foreign rivalry, into the bearpit of Socialist and anti-Socialist contention.

If we do, and in so far as we do, the basic industries, capitalists and wage-earners alike, will sink into ruin. Nothing is more striking than the way in which the misfortunes and the suffering of last year fell upon different parts of our island. I do not know whether they have thought of that. Look around you. Look at the state of the country as it is and, still more, as it was a few months ago. I saw a comparison made in the "Nation" newspaper of the conditions prevailing north and south of a line which the writer had drawn across the country from Cardiff to Hull. It was a diagonal line and a most surprising and disquieting picture. North of that line, where the great trade union population resides, where the great industrial districts are, unemployment was double what it was south of that line. North of it everyone was impoverished by what had taken place. The workers were impoverished; some of the greatest firms were in grave difficulty; whereas, to the south, not only agriculture and finance were being maintained but a thousand minor and subsidiary industries were active and lucrative and progressing.

Now that is a state of affairs which I have a right to come up to Manchester and in the Free Trade Hall bring to the notice of such an audience as I see before me to-night. (Cheers.) We must be very careful we do not see a division spring up in this country–a geographical division–where, on the one hand, the country and the people seem to be tearing themselves to pieces as they did last year, and, on the other hand, a steady growth and progress is maintained. We have to help each other. We have to try to bring the resources of one part to the aid of another, and we have to bring the wisdom of the whole to the guidance of our country in this period of stress and difficulty. (Hear, hear.)

Now, the trade unions are not ordinary associations. They are strongly privileged bodies. For many years past Parliament has conferred advantages and immunities upon them such as are accorded to no other organisations. In some respects they have been placed above the law. They can inflict injuries upon people without being called to account before courts of justice. These privileges, for which both the great historic parties have responsibility, were accorded to the trade unions in order that they might conduct disputes on trade matters in their own particular trades. The special privileges accorded to trade unionism could never have been justified, and can never be defended, once the trade unions entered the political sphere. (Cheers.)

Nor can they be justified and defended when we see trade unions used–in some cases, for I am not making a general charge–used as a sort of battering ram, as they were last year, to break down the existing order of society. After the shocking events of last year it is the bounden duty of Parliament, without delay and without hesitation, to review and to revise the laws relating to trade unions. (Cheers).

Now I am not going to-night to discuss in detail the changes which we consider should be made in these laws. The Government have a right to lay their scheme as a whole in due course before Parliament. But this I can say. No legislation for which we shall be responsible will deprive trade unions of the full power of collective bargaining in trade disputes, or of the right to strike, or of practical and reasonable means of conducting a strike. Our legislation will have for its object the protection of the State and of the public from the abuse of that right, (Cheers),—and from its perversion to political or revolutionary objects. Our legislation will also have for its purpose the liberation of trade unionists themselves from petty persecution and intimidation in the exercise of their ordinary rights as citizens—(hear, hear),—and will seek to release them from a thralldom to which no man in a free country should be compelled to submit. (Cheers.)

We are not going to have the old unfair oppressions of the individual worker which used to be charged against landlords and employers, and which have been banished by law from our public life. We are not going to have them renewed in an even more dangerous form by gangs of Communists who happen to have seized upon the machinery of the old trade unions. (Cheers.)

This is not a question of right. It is a question of privileges. Privileges are sometimes allowed to slumber when they do no harm. But when they are abused by any class, then it is necessary to recur to first principles and redefine the laws of the land. (Cheers.) It is my belief that when our legislation has been passed into law, as no doubt it will—(hear, hear)—it will open a new and fruitful path to British trade unionism. The traditional outlook of British trade unionism always used to be practical. While in many Continental countries the thoughts of the industrial population were being absorbed by political theories, British trade unionism was concentrated upon the standard of living, and it did not allow itself to be divorced from the welfare of the community on which its members depended. It did not pursue political aims at the expense of the bread-and-butter interests of the labouring people employed in the great basic trades. It did not try to overturn the State, or build up a new world after going through the preliminary process of destroying the old world, regardless of the well-being of the working masses.

We hope to see, and, indeed, it is vital that we should see, a return to paths of common sense, and I am sure that if British trade union leaders and members consciously and earnestly identify their interests with the interests of the industries with which they are concerned, and banish machine-made formulas and slogans, and leave politics, with their party bickering and their class warfare, to Parliament and party politicians like ourselves—(laughter)—if they do that, that is to say, if they devote themselves to looking after the interests of their own members, there will grow up quite speedily a spirit of co-operation far beyond anything which is possible to-day. I am sure that unless the spirit of co-operation is forthcoming in British industry, a long period of misery is before us, in which a considerable proportion of the inhabitants of this island dwelling together in large areas, and mostly in the northern region, will have great difficulty in earning their daily bread. From that position no distribution of State charity, however lavish, will for any lengthy period be able to rescue them.

The word co-operation is often used. There are two ways of securing co-operation in human action. You can get co-operation by control, or you can get it by comprehension. Those are the two methods. Both involve discipline, and it may well be that the discipline of comprehension will be more searching, more efficacious than the discipline of control. There is discipline in a flock of sheep, but a different discipline in a flock of sheep from what there is in a pack of hounds. The future belongs to the nations which can develop the highest degree of comprehension. In Imperial affairs we have committed ourselves absolutely to comprehension. In the British Empire the age of control is ended. Control has vanished, and there is in its place a wide and ever-growing comprehension. The British Empire is held together only by good sense, by goodwill, and the Imperial Crown. (Applause.)

Can we not extend the principle which sprang into life and formal recognition at the late Imperial Conference to our own domestic industrial affairs? Can we not do it in advance of other nations? If we do we may all of us march forward with confidence into a fuller and fairer social life, and into the sunshine of a better age.

SOCIALISM AND THE TRADES DISPUTES BILL

May 6, 1927

Grand Habitation of the Primrose League,
Albert Hall, London

[Extract] . . . Do not let us boast, but neither let us be ignorant of the causes which have led to the rise of Britain. A natural instinctive hatred of tyranny in any form–aristocratic, theocratic, plutocratic, bureaucratic, democratic, all forms are equally odious–a natural and instinctive hatred of tyranny is the chief characteristic of the British Islander. (Cheers.) It has been the main cause alike in the building of the British Empire and in its preservation. It remains to-day the surest guarantee and proudest hope of its expanding future. (Cheers.) The British Empire has come through the great convulsion, and it stands more sure and more solid in relation to the external world than at any time in its history.

But the freedom which gave it birth and preserved it has had to face a new challenge. It is having every year to face that new challenge in a more menacing form. It is a very serious challenge. The rise of the Socialist movement at home and abroad strikes at the principles of individual and national liberty from a new direction and in a new and peculiarly dangerous manner. The Socialist movement strikes at freedom in two quite different ways. Socialism is the antithesis of freedom. (Cheers.) If the Socialists gain power in any country they trample down by brutal methods or by actual terrorism all other movements but their own. They prohibit the expression of all opinions but their own, they discipline their own followers into the strictest and most rigid obedience, and, armed with the power of their followers, they then proceed to dragoon the general public. (Cheers.) This is what happens if they succeed. What happens if they fail? If they fail, their movement has very often had the effect, which we have seen in so many European countries, of setting up a reaction which is equally damaging to Parliamentary institutions.

Thus we have seen over a very large part of Europe that the Parliaments which were so hopefully erected in the 19th century have been, from one cause or another, overturned and subjugated in the 20th century and replaced by other systems which, whatever their merits or demerits, are entirely different from those which the genius of the English people has evolved, and from which we have grown up from small beginnings to a considerable estate. That is the new danger to which freedom is exposed, and it is a kind of warfare which for a long time past has been set in motion against the British people. In this issue you will find, I think, a struggle in which in one form or another we shall occupy probably the remainder of all our lives. To preserve the rights of citizens and the individual citizens, to preserve the broad interests of the Commonwealth, and to preserve the unity of the British Empire against the Socialist attack must become for all of us, now and henceforward, the main and common purpose of political action and of public life. (Cheers.)

An immense responsibility at this period rests upon the Conservative Party. The Liberal Party, so long the champion of the rights of the individual, has no longer the strength, and only, I regret to say, very partially the will, to defend the rights of citizens against tyranny. The exigencies of their position, the lack of clear and decided guidance from their leaders, have led them into the absurd course of resisting all forms of oppression or alleged oppression which come from the right of the political arena, and prostrating themselves humbly before all forms of oppression which come from the Left. (Laughter.) They will expostulate and deprecate and palliate and equivocate, but they are not at the present time able to form any bulwark against Socialist tyranny, by which they are themselves in the first instance being steadily devoured.

The issue presented by the Bill which the House of Commons debated all this week is essentially a conflict between the rights of the citizen and the privileges of a sect. Now, privileges in this country have always been liable to be called in question. Nevertheless, if they are used with discretion and modesty, they have often been allowed to survive. But when privileges are abused, when privileges indulgently granted to the weak are maliciously exploited by the strong, and when these privileges come into conflict both with the rights of the individual and with the general interests of the State, then it becomes necessary for Parliament to return to first principles and promulgate just laws regulating the relationship of his Majesty's subjects to one another. (Cheers.) You are no doubt acquainted with the principles of the Trade Unions Bill. On those principles we are inflexible—that the general strike must be stigmatized as an illegal conspiracy (cheers): that the intimidation of workers, particularly at their homes, is illegal (cheers); that Conservative and Liberal trade unionists are not to be compelled, directly or indirectly, to pay for Socialist candidates (cheers); and that Civil servants owe an undivided allegiance to the State they serve. (Cheers.) On these principles we are resolved. More than this we do not ask. Less than this we will not take. (Cheers.) . . .

THE BUDGET

April 25, 1928

Broadcast

Churchill introduced his third Budget on April 24, the principal feature of which was special local rates for industry.

I have a set of my own and I know how it feels to get into touch through this marvellous invention with the actual events and the men who are shaping them. So I was very glad when I was invited to talk to-night. I shall not say anything that is partisan or in the nature of party politics; and really I do not need to do so because this Budget is aimed sincerely at national objects in which men of all parties, and even those of no party at all, have an equal interest.

In my position and with all the information I have about income-tax, I can see, probably more clearly than anyone else, what trades are prospering and what industries are suffering most. I have come to the conclusion that we must make a special effort to help the basic and heavy industries. The basic and heavy industries of our country, iron, and coal, and cotton, steel, and shipbuilding, all these are flagging. Great numbers of men are unemployed and numbers of firms making no profit, or indeed an actual loss. I am therefore trying to give them a helping hand, and practically every one is agreed that the first and most useful way of doing this is to relieve them of their burden of rates. I have, therefore, proclaimed a fundamental proposition that the tools and plants of production–the properties, the buildings, the land, the machinery used for actual creative production–should not be taxed.

Let us tax profits, but not the tools. The present system of rating dates from the days of Queen Elizabeth and is quite unfitted for modern life. Rates for each district are dependent on the politics of the district. The rates press more heavily on unsuccessful businesses than on successful ones. Where business is bad the rates press more heavily upon it. Now all this is wrong, there is no sense in it at all. We depend for our existence upon export trades and millions of people get their wages from these basic industries. Railway freights are another burden. These are oppressively high in those industries which depend upon the use of vast masses of heavy material.

The agricultural produce on which we live, the coal on which all industry lives, the mining timber, iron ore, steel, all rating relief going to railways will help these. Now observe the cumulative effects of relief, how they pile up. First, let us take the vicious circle, coal rated, coke rated, iron ore rated, pig iron rated again, and other rated products used to make steel, rated again, and, moreover, all these commodities have to be transported by rail which is rated. In these circumstances you get many districts suffering which, but for this invidious and ill-applied rate burden, might support a happy and healthful industrial population, and which in many cases are well fitted to do so. Let us take the other side of the picture.

Coal, coke, and limestone, relieved of rates, arriving at steel works with all these new advantages to find the steel works relieved of rates. Out of the steel works comes the material for construction of bridges and railways; from these same steel works will come material for cheaper ships, cheaper not by cutting down wages, but by cutting down burdens. Rates or freights by themselves, however reduced, will not be enough to solve the problem. Something more has to be added, something that may arise out of psychological impulse. We are seeking good will and cooperation in industry. This is the chance for employers and workers to take hands and purge out inefficiency in industry. This is the time; relief itself is not sufficient, but, used properly and used to full advantage, the relief may well mean the opening of a new era. The opportunity is here. Do not let us miss an opportunity that may not easily or soon recur.

Such is the problem with which we are grappling, and such is the remedy we are seeking to apply. And how are we going to get the money to pay the local authorities? You cannot take rates away from them without giving them something back. Here, again, there is another very big story which I can do no more than outline. In the 19th century the glory of Great Britain was her coal; on that we built our great industrial system, on that millions of British people came into the world, on that our mighty power was founded. Without that we cannot live.

In the 20th century we have entered the oil age. In the 19th century we were far ahead of our competitors, but in the 20th century we have hardly any oil in the British Empire. It is absolutely necessary for us to obtain this oil at the present time, and to get it we have to buy or import it from foreign lands. Whereas we used to sell great quantities of coal, last year we paid as much for the oil we imported as the value of the coal we exported. We used to be a source of fuel. We are becoming a sink. We need it; we must have it. Can't we make it ourselves? Scientists tell us they can already turn British coal into oil. Germans are doing it in their country. I agree it must be gradual, but it took a long time to build the British Constitution and to found the British Empire; it is a long way to Tipperary!

Our ancestors were not afraid of time. Now I am sure the motoring community, who are not by any means the least fortunate or the least patriotic or the least farsighted of our fellow-citizens, will take a broad and a long view about this tax on foreign imported liquid fuel. I expect them to look at this tax of 4d. a gallon on imported fuel, not as if they were doing a penny-wise sum of what it actually costs them, but as if they were trustees for the future of Great Britain.

I want to make you understand that we are on the move, and that we are marching to the aid of British productive industry in town and country, with every shilling, and every man and every gun we can get together. I must explain that a large policy like this can only be unfolded step by step and stage by stage. If we have relieved three-quarters of the rates of productive industry and relieved agriculture of all its rates, we have got to pay the local authorities back, otherwise how could they carry on? But in this process of paying them back we are going to have a more modernized and better system of local government. Months of labour have been spent on it. All the difficulties which occur to the mind of any intelligent person who examines this subject have been weighed and balanced.

The policy begun in the Budget yesterday deals with two equally great objects:

First, the relief of productive industry, and secondly, the modernization of our local government system. The first part is what we are doing now, and the second part will occupy Parliament all the winter. Do not let us mix them up together; one step at a time, and each step made good. Let us go forward together, let us not be afraid of taking trouble or risks. Britain is not going to be done in this new age. She is going to hold her own and keep her place in this new gigantic world that is going up around us. But she will survive only if her people are more intelligent, her policy is more far-sighted, and her economic system more highly organized, her social standards more just, her people more united, and more consciously self-governed. Let us make sure none of us fail in our zeal and in our duty at this critical time.

A DISARMAMENT FABLE

October 24, 1928

Aldersbrook

[Extract] The newspapers have been pressing during the past two months for the publication of all the papers relating to the Anglo-French Agreement, and when at last they had been made public they were very indignant to find there was nothing that anyone could possibly object to in all that had been done. They then complained that it was not all made public before. When there is nothing of any serious consequence to make public it is very difficult to make it public. When an agreement has been reached between Great Britain and France to leave off criticizing various points in each other's technical armaments as a step forward towards the larger measure of agreement, if possible, for world disarmament, there is no reason why it should be made public until the different Powers to whom we communicated it, including the United States, had replied to the communication which we made, and having preferred to await their replies, we did not think it right to move from that position by the criticism or clamour in certain sections of the Press. Now, however, the whole is laid before them, they are disappointed to find that there is nothing or very little in it.

The discussion of the last two years has tended to bring naval, military, and air matters into a position of international consequence and prominence which is not at all warranted by anything in the present peaceable state of the world. Governments have been forced to examine all sorts of imaginary and immature possibilities which will never be translated into reality if any of the great and free democracies of the world are able to make their opinion prevail.

In order not to give offence to anyone, I will use a parable: Once upon a time all the animals in the Zoo decided that they would disarm, and they arranged to have a conference to arrange the matter. So the Rhinoceros said when he opened the proceedings that the use of teeth was barbarous and horrible and ought to be strictly prohibited by general consent. Horns, which were mainly defensive weapons, would, of course, have to be allowed. The Buffalo, the Stag, the Porcupine, and even the little Hedgehog all said they would vote with the Rhino, but the Lion and the Tiger took a different view. They defended teeth and even claws, which they described as honourable weapons of immemorial antiquity. The Panther, the Leopard, the Puma, and the whole tribe of small cats all supported the Lion and the Tiger. Then the Bear spoke. He proposed that both teeth and horns should be banned and never used again for fighting by any aniaml. I would be quite enough if animals were allowed to give each other a good hug when they quarreled. No one could object to that. It was so fraternal, and that would be a great step towards peace. However, all the other animals were very offended with the Bear, and the Turkey fell into a perfect panic.

The discussion got so hot and angry, and all those animals began thinking so much about horns and teeth and hugging when they argued about the peaceful intentions that had brought them together that they began to look at one another in a very nasty way. Luckily the keepers were able to calm them down and persuade them to go back quietly to their cages, and they began to feel quite friendly with one another again.

I hope, however, I will not be asked to bring my parable into any relation with anything that has taken place or is taking place at the present time. . . .

THE BUDGET

April 15, 1929

House of Commons

It is appropriate at this stage to record the comment of The Annual Register *for 1929: "Mr. Churchill had proved himself the most able debater in the party, if not in the House, but as a financier his success had been questionable." Other comments were less charitable, and they have been subsequently endorsed by most historians. But his cooperation with Neville Chamberlain in social reforms–notably for Widows' Pensions–should not be forgotten. Fiascoes such as the Betting Tax–which was virtually abandoned in 1929–and errors such as the Silk Tax were of less importance than the absence of strategy behind Churchill's budgets, which resulted, as his official private secretary, P. J. (later Sir James) Grigg subsequently wrote, in the situation whereby "he was therefore reduced to all sorts of shifts and expedients." Not known at the time was his insistence on the formal establishment of the principle that the Service Estimates should be framed on the supposition that the Empire would not be involved in a major war for ten years. The "ten-year rule" was to have unfortunate–indeed tragic–results, and was to compromise Churchill's own position when he began to call for rearmament in the 1930s.*

[Extract] The financial year which has just closed resembles its predecessor in various ways. Again, the failure of beer was repaired by the harvest of death. Again, substantial supplementary charges were more than made good by savings from the current Estimates and, once again, the realised surplus exceeded both Estimates and expectations.

It is usual, in opening the Budget, to compare the current year with the last, but on this occasion, in presenting a fifth Budget, at the close of a Parliament, I feel entitled to look back over the whole period for which we have been responsible. It has been a chequered story. The difficulties have been more prominent than the good fortune. The immense industrial disaster of 1926 has cut a deep gash across the statistical record of our national life. I thought at one time, and I so informed the House of Commons three years ago, that the finances of the Parliament would have been completely ruined by a loss to the Exchequer, which, including the coal subsidy of 1925, was certainly not less than £80,000,000. However, on a review of the past five years, I must admit that matters have worked out a good deal better than I hoped or expected. [An Hon. Member: "Or deserved."] No one has more interest in things going well than the Government of the day and the Minister responsible for the finances of the country. In spite of the injury to every form of national life by the follies of 1926 we have realised a respectable and, as I shall show, a solid surplus in the year that has closed. The material prosperity of this country, whether judged by the condition of its finances, by the volume of its trade or by the saving and consuming power of its people, has maintained a steady advance. For more than two years now we have enjoyed a lucid interval without a general strike or a period of general elections, or a general war. That is the longest lucid interval that I can remember since 1914. Two years' recuperation is quite a long time for this country to allow itself between its ordeals, and, naturally, after two years of peace and quiet there must be a sensible improvement in the general situation. . . .

Tea Duty (Abolition)

I have never had much fiscal sympathy with the consumer of luxuries, and particularly of foreign luxuries. It is to the primary comforts and to some extent virtual necessities of the mass of the population that we should now turn our attention. I have already spoken of the immense boon of at least £160,000,000 a year conferred upon the wage-earners by the reduction in the cost of living. Compared with that universal easement, anything the present surplus can bestow must necessarily be small. We reduced last year the tax on sugar at a cost of £3,000,000 of revenue, and it is to tea that I now turn with feelings of good will. The Committee know, from the annual Debates in this House, that I have long desired to effect some reduction in the Tea Duty. There is no other comfort which enters so largely into the budget of the cottage home, or the still humbler budgets of the old, the weak, and the poor. The reduction or the removal of the tax on tea has been asked for in a long succession of Parliaments. Its mitigation would always have been regarded by social reformers of every party as an auspicious milestone in the history of the Customs House. There has been a tax on tea ever since the reign of Queen Elizabeth, and I am glad to think that the reign of His Majesty King George the Fifth will witness the total, immediate, and, I believe, final abolition:

"And while the bubbling and loud-hissing urn
Throws up a steamy column, and the cups

That cheer but not inebriate wait on each,
So let us welcome peaceful evening in."

I said that the remission would be total and I have said so advisedly, and, although over three-quarters of the tea drunk in these islands is produced within the British Empire, Javanese tea enters to a great extent into the cheapest blends used by the poorest people. To maintain for preferential reasons a tax on this foreign tea would therefore exclude from the benefits of remission the very class for whose sake, most of all, this serious sacrifice of revenue is being made. . . .

General Summary

In this very lengthy statement, during which the House has shown me such exceptional consideration and indulgence, I have thought it right to lay forth fully the financial situation, but I have not attempted to deal with the wider issue of Imperial and social development which will naturally constitute the main portion of the programme upon which His Majesty's Government intend to submit themselves to the country. I have confined myself to that considerable range of business which directly affects the finance of the present year. The main policy which we should pursue in the new Parliament will be set forth by my right hon. Friend the Prime Minister, at what may be called an early and a suitable occasion. I should like, therefore, in presenting my fifth Budget to add a very few words of general summary. Anyone can see that the coal disasters of 1925 and 1926 created a situation very different from that with which I hoped to deal. If I could have foreseen the lamentable course of events, I should certainly not have remitted 6d. from the Income Tax in 1925, but once the standard rate has been reduced to a clear cut figure like 4s. in the £, it would have been very injurious and very vexatious to raise it again. Neither did I wish in any way to detract from the great remissions of indirect taxation which had made the Budget of my predecessor in 1924 memorable. The last three years have been a struggle on my part to avoid reimposing either oppressive direct taxation or trenching upon the relief of the taxation of the comforts of the people which he had given. In this, I claim to have been successful. I have maintained, upon the average of the five Budgets, payments to the Sinking Fund and upon the accumulated interest of Savings Certificates substantially greater than those which were made in former days.

The successful re-establishment of the Gold Standard will still be regarded as a memorable event long after the exertions and sacrifices it has entailed have been forgotten. The preferences upon Empire products, notably upon wine, sugar and tobacco, have been carried to the furthest point that they have yet attained with a remarkable accompanying growth of inter-Imperial trade. I have spoken already of the remissions of taxation which it has been possible to effect. As far as expenditure is concerned, the upward trend has been stopped. It has proved beyond my power to reduce it as much as I had hoped. At any rate, it has been controlled, and it is £6,000,000 less, on a strictly comparable basis, than it was five years ago. Notwithstanding all this, the means have been found to inaugurate and to finance for periods extending far beyond the lifetime of the present Parliament the two most considerable

Measures of domestic reform with which I am acquainted, namely, the immense extension of the Pensions and Insurance scheme in 1925, and the relief of productive industry and the rating reform scheme of my right hon. Friend the Minister of Health, in 1928.

I feel that the corner in our economic fortunes may well now have been turned. There are no causes, apart from fresh causes of our own making, which should prevent the next four or five years being easier and more fruitful than those through which we have made our way. The future lies freely in our hands. Reviving trade, lower unemployment, expanding revenues, cheaper money, more favourable conditions for debt conversion, lie before us at this moment as reasonable and tangible probabilities. We can by wisdom and public spirit bring them nearer and realise these long sought for advantages. We can by faction, violence, and folly drive them far away again. The future is inscrutable, and it is equally vain to prophesy or boast, but for my part I have faith in the fair play and august common sense of the British nation, and to their judgment now, and in later years, I submit with confidence the financial record of a Conservative Administration.

THE GENERAL ELECTION

April 30, 1929

Broadcast, London

The General Election of May 1929 was a three-party contest, with each party putting up more than five hundred candidates. The Conservatives fought on the theme of "Safety First"; the Labour campaign concentrated essentially on the persistence of unemployment; the Liberals produced the most articulate programme, authored by John Maynard Keynes and Hubert Henderson. The weakness of the Liberal position lay in the continued divisions within the party, and by the fact that their programme was both ahead of its time and beyond the comprehension of most electors. In the event, Labour won 288 seats, the Conservatives 26 and Liberals 59. Baldwin resigned immediately and James Ramsay MacDonald became Prime Minister on June 5.

[Extract] . . . There is, in fact (apart from the miners), no standing army of over 1,000,000 unemployed. There are, on the contrary, a much larger number of people who are from time to time unemployed and who then draw the benefits to which they are entitled. If the trade of the country were to improve, hundreds of thousands of people would still lose time moving from one job to another. They would still be thrown out by hard weather and what are called seasonal and cyclical depressions in particular trades. But they would lose less time as trade improved in moving from job to job, and the 11 weeks which is the average benefit drawn by the course of a year now would be steadily shortened. If it were reduced to five weeks then we should be in as good a position, indeed rather a better position, than before the War.

If you understand that system you can easily see how very unsuitable and indeed, vicious is the remedy which Mr. Lloyd George has proposed of gathering larger numbers of unemployed persons to gather into gangs and setting them to make roads for motorcars. In many cases work on the roads would spoil men's hands for their own trades. It would not be suitable work for the older men, who form the largest proportion of those who are longest unemployed. It would interrupt the whole natural recovery of industry, and when the money for the relief work had been spent they might, it is true, have a good many more fine roads for motorists to go forty or fifty miles an hour upon, but the people who had made them would be thrown back upon the labour market, they would return to empty homes and the country would be saddled for several generations with the interest upon the money that had been borrowed and spent.

Mr. Lloyd George said that the election was to be fought on unemployment; but Mr. Ramsay MacDonald said, "I object strongly to the woes and troubles of the unemployed being exploited for election purposes." I hope Mr. MacDonald will live up to that statement during the next few weeks. It is a great temptation to irresponsible people who are looking for votes to say at election times that they have a sure remedy. It is easy to say, "I can cure it; only take my patent medicine and you will be well." The Socialists say, "If only you will nationalize everything and manage everybody's affairs by officials, and fill in plenty of paper forms, you will be cured." The inflationists–the people who think that everything can be put right by manipulating the currency–tell us that they have only to pretend that every 10d. in their pocket is really worth a shilling, and that that will cure unemployment. Lastly, there is Mr. Lloyd George, who said in short, I am not quoting him, "Borrow money freely and splash it about well, and all will come right–as long as I do the splashing." The question to ask yourselves about all these quack remedies is not whether they can make things better–they will certainly not do that–but whether they will not make them positively worse.

The only way in which things can be made better is by a general improvement in British trade. There has in the last four or five years been a considerable improvement. The balance of trade is less unfavourable and 600,000 more people have found employment. The amount of credit available for starting new British enterprises has greatly increased. Many of our industries under the pinch of hard times have adopted the latest machinery and better methods.

Although a third of our capital was spent in the war we are wealthier. There is no reason whatever for being downhearted. On the contrary, our prospects are bright if we do not spoil them.

I find it very difficult to believe that there is any short cut to prosperity. We have to march forward steadfastly along the high road. It may be dusty, it may be stony, it may be dull, it is certainly uphill all the way. But to leave it is only to flounder in the quagmires of delusion and have your coat torn off you by the brambles of waste. It is a good and plainly-marked road; the signposts are all well-known; they were set up by the wisdom and experience of those who have gone before us. Here are some of them:–Peace abroad; steady, stable government at home; clean, honest, impartial administration; good will in industry and cooperation between masters and men; public and private thrift. Lighten the burdens of galling rates and so forth upon productive industry and agriculture. Modernize factories and businesses; modernize particularly the railways, which are much behind the times, far more behind the times than your roads. Multiply and strengthen the hold upon markets abroad, especially those priceless new markets which are offered in the Empire. Cheapen the cost of living to the mass of the people as much as possible. That will not only promote contentment, but it will give industries in the long run a greater competitive power in the world market. Avoid chops and changes of policy; avoid thimble-riggers and three-card trick men; avoid all needless borrowings; and, above all, avoid as you would avoid the smallpox class warfare and violent political strife.

The issue at the election is much larger than unemployment. It is the well-being of the whole British people and the position of Britain and her Empire in the modern world. That and nothing less is what is at stake. Powerful, mighty countries are towering up as rivals–peaceful rivals it might be–but rivals none the less; competitors with us in every form of human activity. What are these other countries doing? Is there one that is not trying to make the most of itself? Are they not all engaged in setting up firm and steady systems of government and trying to assert their national rights and interests in the strongest manner? On the Continent of Europe we see many people actually casting down their Parliaments, abandoning the liberties they gained in the 19th century, setting up authoritarian forms of government in order, as they think, the better to take part in the intensified economic and political struggles. Look at the United States. The vast American democracy does not throw many chances away. It had pursued since the War a far more steady and purposeful policy than we have. The American democracy has no doubt many problems which we should not like to have here; but it adds, by every national vote it gives, to the solidity of its institutions, to the security of its capitalist system, and to the advancement of American interests and American power in every quarter of the globe.

These are critical years for the British Empire. Will it with its many communities and widespread races draw more closely together or drift apart and fall to pieces? If we can come through this critical period and draw ever closer together, then, indeed, we should be the equal of any organization yet founded among men, and the British Empire and the United States could walk forward side by side, leading mankind in majesty and peace.

EGYPT (LORD LLOYD'S RESIGNATION)

July 26, 1929

House of Commons

The Labour Government was anxious to achieve a new arrangement with the Egyptian Government. The ambition proved impossible because of Egyptian insistence upon the restoration of their joint control over the Sudan, ended in 1924 after the assassination of the British Governor-General, and the refusal of the British to concede this point. The British High Commissioner for Egypt and the Sudan, Lord Lloyd, did not approve of the initiative of the Government, and was in effect dismissed by the Foreign Secretary, Arthur Henderson. In the subsequent debate, Henderson revealed that the relationship between Lloyd and Austen Chamberlain had not always been harmonious.

[Extract] . . . Governments may change their agents, and may choose their agents. Why have the present Government been so very anxious to change Lord Lloyd? It is because, undoubtedly, Lord Lloyd has stood for firmness in defence of British rights in Egypt. That is why he has been singled out and selected for early change.

The fact that a man who, undoubtedly, was identified with the successful assertion of lawful British rights in Egypt, has had to resign, will not be confined in effect only to Egypt. It will raise great difficulties and embarrassments there and elsewhere. This quick and sudden change will cause difficulties all over the British Empire. Administrators, great and small, will have an example before their eyes of the fate which overtakes, under the present Government, public officials and public servants if they stand up with some firmness and stiffness for British rights and interest, and refuse to lend themselves to sloppy surrender and retreat. That is why he was obnoxious, and that is why he has been removed, and I say that it is a very curious action for a minority Government to have taken, at the very time when the Prime Minister has been appealing for national co-operation and goodwill in the treatment of external affairs. It would have been much more prudent and wise to have continued to discuss these matters with Lord Lloyd, and when you had some fault to find with him yourselves, and when you had some grievance with him or some difference had arisen with him in your administration, then you would have had a perfectly good ground for choosing whatever agent you thought would carry out your policy, and it would not have been necessary to go back into the past and to put a completely wrong gloss upon the inevitable discussions, sometimes very keen, which take place behind the closed door of Cabinets and Administrations. . . .

DOMESTIC AND IMPERIAL AFFAIRS

December 16, 1929

Essex Conservative Association Luncheon,
Hotel Cecil, London

Churchill was by now extremely concerned with developments in India and Egypt—particularly in India. His attitudes were already sharper and more definite than those of Baldwin, and a rift was opening even at this early stage.

[Extract] . . . The decision with regard to Egypt is the most urgent and the most fatal of all the decisions likely to be taken in the coming year. The Government are going to take the British troops away from Cairo and make them dig in along the Suez Canal. British troops have been for 50 years in Cairo. They have never been used against the Egyptian people. They have been used only to help the Egyptian people. The Egyptian people have been guided and helped from bankruptcy to great wealth, from anarchy to civilization, by the aid of British administrators, who had behind them the silent strength of the British troops in Cairo. Cairo is not only the Egyptian capital; it is a cosmopolitan city and we have undertaken before all the world the obligation of securing its order and its welfare. So far we have fulfilled that obligation. Now we are to cast it down, and with it all the fruits of 50 years of splendid achievement. Our soldiers are to leave the scene of their patient, peaceful duties and drink distilled water in desert fortifications east of Line 32. I wish to direct the attention of the country to this grave impending event. I am sure it will mean disaster not only for the people of Egypt and of Britain, but for the whole civilized communities of the world. I am sure also that it is a step that will ultimately, and perhaps at no great distance of time, lead to a serious effusion of blood.

But Egypt is only a preliminary. Behind Egypt stands not only the Middle East, with all its problems and perils, but mighty India itself. The very same processes that are thrusting, coaxing, or cajoling us out of Egypt, processes sometimes subtle, sometimes violent, sometimes secret, sometimes open, but never-ceasing, are at work in India. They are at work in India on a far larger scale. Our position in India is wholly different from our position in Egypt. We have rights in India which we do not claim in Egypt. When our interests in Egypt have been surrendered and our duties repudiated there, we must still define our interests and duties in India. But you may be sure that on the day when the British troops evacuate Cairo every enemy of the British Empire in every quarter of the globe will rejoice, and every subversive faction in India will be encouraged by the vision of another day when the last British battalion will be embarking from Indian shores, leaving behind them what Lord Morley, that great Liberal statesman, called "the dull roar and scream of carnage and confusion," coming back to us across the dark distances. The same spirit of pusillanimity, which the

Socialists embody, the same lack of conviction in our mission in the East which is liquidating the work of two generations in Egypt, will, if it is not dominated and exorcized, destroy the healing work of 10 generations in India. I urge you to get together, to rally all the forces on whom Britain can rely. I hope and believe we will succeed. We must repel no elements in this country that will fight steadily on our side. At any rate, we will have done our best, and no part of the shame, no unendurable self-reproach will rest on a resolute and united Conservative Party. (Cheers.)

EGYPT

December 23, 1929

House of Commons

[Extract] . . . I have tried to place before the House and the country the dangers now about to be created [by the proposed withdrawal of British troops from Cairo over the next five years]. I think causes of dispute will grow from year to year. The power of mitigating them in their early stages will be gone. To Egyptian eyes we shall still be the bugbear, we shall still be the interfering Power, the intruding Power, the trespassing Power, the threatening Power, and even, as it will seem to them, the bullying Power. The other European Governments and the American Government will profit from our exertions without suffering our odium. They will have the advantage without the labour. Once again Great Britain will be chained to the labouring oar without ever being allowed to lay a finger on the helm. At the same time, the Egyptians will be placed in a position to retaliate for every interference, however justified, however obligatory, however in accordance with the opinion of the world or the sanction of the League of Nations for every necessary advice that we have to tender by an increase of their military forces, by building up a numerous army under compulsory service and equipping it with deadly instruments of war, and thus forcing us to reinforce our garrison in the canal zone in an atmosphere of ever-increasing tension.

I cannot think that this is a good conclusion to all our work in Egypt. I think that we have deserved better than that. I cannot think that it is a safe course to take if we wish to avoid bloodshed. On the contrary, it seems to me the exact manner in which a catastrophe of violent deeds would be deliberately and almost mechanically prepared. Would it not be far better to leave the British troops in Cairo? Would it not be far better to make it clear that it is our unchanging policy that they shall remain there, and then to concede to Egyptian sentiment and to Egyptian susceptibilities every form of considerate usage and every possible latitude of self-guidance and self-development. That is my counsel. That is the way I shall give my vote at all stages in these discussions. The departure of the British troops from Cairo will be a momentous event. If and when it occurs, it will resound through all Asia. It will be noted by history like the recall of the legions many centuries ago. It will mark the point where great organisms slowly built up, exercising an immense pacifying and unifying influence upon the world, have reached their culmination and have begun the course of decline. I urge the House to resist the departure, but, if it should be within the power of the Government, which I am not sure it is, to carry through this dangerous and fateful step, I ask at least that the departure should be accompanied by a simultaneous restriction in the numbers of the Egyptian Army and the abolition of conscription throughout the valley of the Nile. Surely, that is not an improper demand to make, when it is the aim of the whole world to abolish armed violence from human affairs. Then, at least, if any trouble should arise at any future date, it will be a small and not a large fight to which you will have condemned our soldiers. . . .

Long before the five years are up events will occur which will afford evidence of the need of the British troops in Cairo. I do not know how long will be the life of His Majesty's Government, but I believe that they will live long enough to reap some at least of the wrath and evil and folly that they have sown.

There is a sombre philosophy nowadays which I hear in some quarters about Egypt and India. It is said:

> Give them all they ask for! Clear out and let things go to smash, and then there will be a case for us to come back again.

The action of His Majesty's Government would bear that construction, and it is, in my opinion, not the worst construction to be put upon it. Such a doctrine is no foundation for the continuance of British fame and power. Once we lose confidence in our mission in the East, once we repudiate our responsibilities to foreigners and to minorities, once we feel ourselves unable calmly and fearlessly to discharge our duties to vast helpless populations, then our presence in those countries will be stripped of every moral sanction, and, resting only upon selfish interests or military requirements, it will be a presence which cannot long endure.

NAVAL DISARMAMENT TREATY

June 2, 1930

House of Commons

The London Agreement between Britain, the United States, and Japan on naval construction seemed at the time to be a major achievement of the Labour Government. Churchill's opposition to it was not widely echoed.

[Extract] . . . We should make careful and searching examination into the details and the consequential reactions of the Treaty before we commit ourselves to it. It is, indeed, a grave matter, and may well occupy the attention of the House. It is not a treaty of parity; it is a treaty of inferiority. As I hold, it is a treaty of inferiority in form and on paper, and it is still more a treaty of inferiority in reality. When one applies what is written on paper to the actual problems of keeping the life and soul of the Empire together, it is undoubtedly a treaty of inferiority. I do not believe that this statement is seriously disputed. If it is all I can say is that we shall have very full opportunities of threshing it out in closest detail upon the Navy Estimates.

I was surprised at the First Lord's suggestion that any naval authority, official or unofficial, would have guaranteed that the British Fleet at the end of this five-year period, having regard to its practical obligations, would be the equal of the United States Fleet. I should have thought that it was not possible to find any authority to support that view. Therefore, I start from the basis that the Treaty is a declaration that the British Empire accepts the position of a second Power at sea. That is a very grave and formidable position from whatever point of view it is examined. Moreover, it is made certain that this position of inferiority shall be established before the Treaty can be reviewed in 1935. That is the point from which I start. We shall have inferiority in fact and in form, and it is beyond dispute that the measures now taken will place use in that position before we have an opportunity of reviewing our position. . . .

It seems to me that now we are abandoning our naval supremacy and all claim to it, and that it is merely the question of parity we are debating with another great Power. Never since the reign of Charles II has this country been so defenceless as this Treaty will make it, and never in the reign of Charles II was it so vulnerable. It is said that this does not matter because we have signed the Kellogg Pact, which pledges all nations to the abolition of war, and because war is unthinkable between us and the United States. This Treaty rests upon a self-destructive argument. We are told that war with the United States is unthinkable; we have ruled it out; the Kellogg Pact has abolished it; we do not mind if they have a stronger Navy than we have, or if they have the power, as they certainly would under this arrangement, to interrupt all our supplies of food and raw material. We have such confidence in them that we place ourselves unreservedly in the hands of our English-speaking kith and kin across the ocean.

That is the premise. What is the conclusion which the Government draw? The conclusion from this premise is that we must bring the United States to our council table, and measure swords round the table with the utmost nicety for weeks and months–how long they are to be, how heavy they are to be, how sharp they are to be, what kind of hilts they should have, and so forth. That is a strange conclusion to draw from the premise I have recited. The premise is no war–[*Interruption*.] Surely, we may be allowed to put our case without mockery. You have your majority; you will carry your policy over our heads; but, surely, we may be allowed without mockery to put our case. The premise, as I say; is that we omit the United States from all our calculations. The conclusion is a so-called parity, calculated to an inch, to an ounce, haggled over point by point in every category of ships, we, I think, getting somewhat the worse of it on each of the points. The premise is no competition; the conclusion, the worst form of competition; namely, parity, a neck-and-neck rivalry. The premise is entire detachment from each other's affairs; the conclusion, intense detailed concentration on most unhealthy and, as I consider, altogether unnecessary attention by each country to the other's naval establishment. . . .

I propound to the right hon. Gentleman the following exhaustive dilemma: If the idea of a hostile United States is not ruled out, this Treaty is impossible; if it is ruled out, it is quite unnecessary. If war between Great Britain and the United States is unthinkable–and that is certainly our heartfelt wish–what is the true conclusion to draw? Surely, it is to forget and to ignore the United States Navy altogether, and to reserve full freedom to study our own unique problems in our own way. That is the natural conclusion; that is the sensible conclusion; that is the safe conclusion. We have ruled the United States out of our calculations. Why, then, should we calculate about them to a decimal point? Let us address ourselves to our actual dangers. Let us have full freedom to build the Navy we require to shield us from European and Asiatic dangers, and no more than those dangers. Then, having done that, having settled what that standard is, let us by all means invite the United States to build to parity, and to set their own interpretation upon what they require to bring them to that point.

Let me examine the question of the battle fleets. All these conferences have had a tendency adverse to our interests. The Washington Treaty regulated the battle fleets, but it is not the battle fleets that really matter now. That is why agreement has been easy about battleships. It was easy at Washington, and it is easy now. All parties have agreed not to build the battleships that they were not going to build in any case. The right hon. Gentleman, with great success, has forced an open door; a lot of ships that would not have been built will now never be built at all. There are only three Powers in the world that have battle fleets, and they have them at opposite corners of the globe, separated from each other by thousands of miles of ocean. Whichever of those powers crosses the ocean to get at another will suffer the greatest naval disadvantages. Our danger is not that a battle fleet will be defeated in action; our danger is that our food will be cut off in far distant seas and oceans.

The hon. and learned Member for South Nottingham (Mr. Knight), who spoke just now, asked me to define the purpose of the British Navy, and how it differs from those of other Powers. Our purpose is not aggression; it is not blockade. It is clear that, with the naval forces now in the world, we could never enforce a blockade which was not in accordance with the wishes of the United States. That was so in the Great War, but it has been overwhelmingly more so since the War ended. The purpose of our Navy is to secure the arrival of our daily bread. We cannot and we ought not to let ourselves get into a position in which any Power, even the most friendly, has undoubted means of putting irresistible pressure upon us by threatening to starve us out. Such a power, once it existed, would not need even to be exercised to be effective; we should be forced to compliance once it was clear that the supplies of this country could be interrupted.

If trouble comes–I do not believe that trouble will come; I believe that wars are over for our day–it is indispensable that we should be able to survive for two years, and to feed ourselves for two years, so that we could rebuild, as we could in these Islands, with our unequalled resources, the naval power necessary to secure victorious escape from that trouble. By restricting the general battleship programme–which restriction I am not opposing–it must be recognised that we have turned the whole naval effort of other Powers into the building of commerce destroyers. What are these eight-inch gun, 10,000-ton cruisers which the right hon. Gentleman built–the five

"Kents"? They are commerce destroyers; and the ones that are going to be built in such great numbers in the United States are commerce destroyers, and the destroyers of the protecting vessels. While the whole naval argument to-day turns upon the attack and defence of trade, we alone being committed to the prodigious task of defending vital supplies–while the whole naval argument turns upon that, the drift of all these conferences and treaties has been increasingly to make it impossible for us to have any security for our food supplies.

I do not wish to plunge into the technical aspect to-night; when we come to the Votes, if the opportunity occurs, I will to into more detail; but I must say this, that our food and other supplies, in a war with a great naval Power, cannot be ensured only by cruisers. We can never have enough cruisers to clear the seas. Even if we had 70, we could not clear the seas in order to bring in our vital supplies. We must rely upon convoy.

Where are the ships to guard the convoys? In the late War we had great numbers of old battleships and armoured cruisers laid up in reserve, with nucleus crews, costing little or nothing. Now there are none. They have all been scrapped by international agreement. There is no material reserve for the British Fleet. That is a loss which falls only on us, because we alone have to bring in our food, and we alone have a reserve of seafaring manhood which would enable us to produce crews for a much larger Fleet than we keep in commission. That is a terrible weakening of our vital defence. Look at the five capital ships which are to be scrapped under this Agreement–the four Iron Dukes and the Tiger. Fine ships! We have spent, I suppose £15,000,000 upon them. The cost of keeping them in reserve would be negligible. They are the very ships to protect our convoys. These heavy ships, with enormous cannon, would each form the centre of a convoy in which 40 or 50 merchant ships laden with provisions might come with safety through areas infested with hostile cruisers to these islands. . . .

I want to know what we gain. We have this Paper here–"An International Treaty for the Limitation and Reduction of Naval Armaments." Is not this the most glaring misnomer that has ever stared at us from an official document? Let me suggest to the right hon. Gentleman the true title of this Treaty. "An international treaty for the limitation and reduction of British naval armaments and for the expansion, actual or relative, of the naval armaments of the United States, Japan, Italy and France." Let me give the right hon. Gentleman another title for this Treaty. "An international treaty for the limitation of the power and the right of Great Britain to safeguard its food supply and for the multiplication and improvement of all means possessed by other nations for interrupting the said food supply." Let me give a third alternative. "An international treaty for stereotyping naval armaments at a very high level to the special detriment of Great Britain." Let the right hon. Gentleman put these three definitions to his Naval Lords and ask whether they are not a more truthful account of this document than the misnomer that appears on its face.

You call it a Treaty of Disarmament. Do not delude yourselves with that. Nothing is going to happen under this Treaty which will give any satisfaction to the Germans in respect of the Clauses of the Treaty of Versailles. On the contrary, they are going to watch a vast process of re-armament going on over the greater part of the world. For the next five years after this Treaty, for which we are making such sacrifices and under which we are losing so much, all the arsenals of the world will be clanging with hammers and riveting machines building new formidable instruments of war. Even our own dockyards will not be idle. We shall soon have the First Lord making the most of all our own dockyards and large increases will be required in naval expenditure. In this Treaty of Disarmament our own dockyards will not be idle. What will they be doing? At great expense they will be fashioning a key which will not unlock the door of our own particular problem. At enormous expense they will be making a ten-foot plank to cross a 12-foot stream and, for that we shall have to pay in Navy Estimates greatly in excess of £50,000,000 and yet we shall not get the security that we require. [*Interruption.*] You may as well consider the facts patiently. It seems to me that from the point of view of the party opposite this is the most unfortunate and sterile ending of their hopes in regard to disarmament.

If it was a treaty of peace and good will among great nations, we might make great sacrifies for that, but there is the crowning disappointment. Since the War the only quarrels and causes of ill feeling among the nations had arisen through these Conferences over disarmament. Every conference except perhaps Washington, which dealt only with battle fleets, which were passing out of the area of seriously controversial discussion, has inflamed the fears and passions of the nations that have taken part in them. A set back has been caused by these Conferences through the well meant attempts of nations not themselves in danger to regulate and cut down the defences of those that are. These conferences have given an enormous advertisement to naval and military men and topics. They have focussed the attention of millions of people upon war topics. They have spread the war mind. They have forced Governments and statesmen to come back from policies of social reconstruction to concentrate upon ships and cannon and strategic problems. The right hon. Gentleman has been so busy that he has not been able even to look at the outlines of unemployment. They have raised the whole basis of debate on national power, prestige and existence. It would have been far better to have trusted the growing confidence that is in the world, and far better to have trusted to the enormous economic pressure of the wasteful expenditure upon armaments, and to have allowed the navies and armies to fall back gradually into the background, as they would have done in the progress of a long peace, shrunk and shrivelled, as they did after the Napoleonic wars, perhaps leaving our country, because of its unique naval needs, with mild primacy, or perhaps not. . . .

BRITAIN AND INDIA

November 5, 1930

Loughton

Churchill had been viewing the Indian policy of the Government–supported by the official Opposition–with unease since its declaration of October 31, 1929, that the granting of Dominion Status, wholly ignored by the Simon Commission, was implicit in the Montagu-Chelmsford declaration of 1917. Churchill, in an article in the Daily

Mail *on November 16, 1929, had described the proposal as "not practicable," "fantastic," and "criminally mischievous." By the end of 1930 the gulf between his views and Baldwin's had widened considerably.*

[Extract] . . . The gravest question of all is our position in India, our relations with the Indian people, and our Oriental possessions generally. This great Indian problem is marching steadily towards us and will soon occupy the minds of men and women almost to the exclusion of all other topics. Do not let it be thought that the connexion of Great Britain with India is purely a sentimental connexion. India and Great Britain have immense mutual services to render to each other and blessings to bestow upon each other. For over 150 years we have been economically associated and united. India has been raised from barbarism and anarchy, her population increased by 100 million, her wealth multiplied, and a measure, at any rate, of sanitation, health, and science bestowed upon her people. Peace has been preserved throughout this vast region—almost a continent in herself—and Britain by that association has also gained trade facilities and great influence and prestige which her connexion with India implies.

Sever that partnership, destroy that union, let the relations of Great Britain and India sink to the level of those between Great Britain and China, let the condition of India fall to the anarchy and horror of China, and you will see in this island another million unemployed and a bona fide million unemployed. (Cheers.) We have felt it our mission to sustain India, to help her population in their march forward, and there would be an economic loss of life to this country if we severed our connexion with India that could hardly be computed.

I hope that we are going to take a firm and resolute view about India. In my opinion the British Government have been too far occupied with dealing with the aspirations of a comparatively small number of highly educated Hindus. But they have not concentrated sufficiently upon the well-being of the masses of the population, which it was their duty to do. There has been a loss of confidence in our mission in the East and a lack of the strong assertion of our duty, which is to guide, to govern, and to control.

Unless we are going to do that we had better give up our task altogether. Unless we are prepared to use our knowledge and our science faithfully in the interests of the masses of the Indian peoples and insist upon them receiving good government and some at least of the benefits of expanding scientific civilization, we have no right to preserve our connexion with the Indian Empire.

I hope myself that we shall not fail. There has been too much of that lack of confidence. We have seen it in Egypt, a country which we brought out from the worst forms of tyranny and oppression and which we have now allowed to fall away and decline because we are afraid to give the guidance and the help to the population which we ought to give.

INDIA (THE ROUND TABLE CONFERENCE)

December 11, 1930

Cannon Street Hotel, London

This was the first meeting organised by the Indian Empire Society. The Round Table Conference had ceased its open sittings, and was divided into Committees engaged in examining a Federal constitution. Churchill's rift with the Conservative leadership was now acute and evident on this issue.

[Extract] We have thought it our duty to hold this meeting in order, so far as we can, to draw the attention of the country to the altogether unwarrantable change in the estimation of the facts and values of the Indian problem which has marked the last disastrous twelve months. From many quarters we hear statements that opinion in India has advanced with violent speed. Full Dominion status with the right to secede from the British Empire and responsible control of the executive Government are clamoured for by even the moderates represented at the Round Table Conference. The extremists who are, and will remain, the dominant force among the Indian political classes have in their turn moved their goal forward to absolute independence, and picture to themselves an early date when they will obtain complete control of the whole of Hindustan, when the British will be no more to them than any other European nation, when white people will be in India only upon sufference, when debts and obligations of all kinds will be repudiated and when an army of white janissaries, officered if necessary from Germany, will be hired to secure the armed ascendancy of the Hindu. All these absurd and dangerous pretensions have so far been met in speech with nothing but soft deprecatory and placatory words by the British Government in India, or at home. Vague high-sounding phrases about 'full Dominion status'; 'India a great world power' have filled the air. British-owned newspapers in India—of which there are still some—have been forced to the conclusion that Parliament will agree to anything that Indians can agree upon among themselves, provided that India remains nominally at least a part of the King's dominions. The effect of the speeches delivered during the five days' open session of the Conference has certainly been to give the impression that a vast extension of self-government is immediately contemplated and that all that remains is to settle the detail and method of the transference of powers, and to make some provision for the protection of minorities. . . .

We are told that the opinion of India has changed. But the facts of India have not changed. They are immemorial. The political classes of India are a mere handful compared to the population. The Western ideas they have gathered and reproduced have no relation whatever to the life and thought of India. The vast majority can neither read nor write. There are at least seventy different races and even more numerous religions and sects in India, many of them in a state of antagonism.

> Our rule in India [said Lord Randolph Churchill] is as it were a sheet of oil spread out over and keeping free from storms a vast and profound ocean of humanity.

The withdrawal or suspension of British control means either a Hindu despotism supported by an army of European mercenaries or a renewal of those ferocious internal wars which tortured the Indian masses for thousands of years before the British flag was hoisted in Calcutta. Left to herself, India would rapidly degenerate to the condition of China at the cost of measureless suffering among three hundred and fifty million people. I do not believe there is any responsible and independent man among the thousands in this country who are well acquainted with India, who will dispute these facts.

Yet we are told Indian opinion has changed so rapidly. India has found her soul at last. Classes, races, creeds, opposed for centuries, are now uniting in a common desire to terminate the British connection. What is the cause of this change? We certainly should not blame our Indian fellow-subjects for it. It is the weak-minded and defeatist tendency of our present politics which must bear the main responsibility. In one way or another in the last few years the impression has been spread far and wide throughout India that the British regime is coming to an end and that a new regime and authority are soon going to be erected. On the one hand, you have had the ever-mounting demands; on the other, the ever more apologetic responses.

Our defeatists eagerly point to the changed attitude of the princes, so long our faithful allies–not feudatories, but allies–joined to us by Treaties. The princes, we are told, are all now in favour of a vast change. But surely the explanation is simple! Once it is believed that British authority is about to be replaced by something new, that the Great Power which has hitherto ruled with irresistible force all over India and kept it quiet and safe from harm is about to wind up its affairs and depart, naturally, even its most loyal adherents must address themselves to a new situation, must prepare themselves for a new system. If the British Raj is to be replaced by the Gandhi Raj, the rulers of the native states must prepare themselves for a relationship with the new power at least as intimate as that which they have had with the old. The same is true of the Moslems. Why, even the representative of the depressed classes at the Round Table Conference, the representative of sixty million persons denied by the Hindu religion even the semblance of human rights, has spoken in favour of a responsible self-governing constitution. Naturally, all have to consider what will happen when we are gone or have ceased to function. Once the signal of retreat and departure has been given, all who are left behind must make terms with the new power. The next to be affected will be the Indian officials of the Civil Service, hitherto so skilful and loyal. After them will be affected that admirable police, who, amid every discouragement and in the face of every menace or temptation, have done their duty and kept order with hardly any loss of life except their own. And lastly, there will be the native army, who, when their allegiance is disowned by Great Britain, will be forced to transfer it to another centre, with consequences so horrible that we hardly care to dwell on them to-day.

The cause of all this change in Indian opinion is not a change of facts in the problem of India. It is the apparent lack of will-power and self-confidence exhibited by the representatives of Great Britain. I warn our Indian fellow-subjects and honoured friends not to be deceived by these superficial appearances. Underneath the smooth platitudes and euphemisms of Western democratic politics and all this airy Round Table talk, the actual process of governing India has been tardily but rigorously carried on. Twenty-four thousand Indian politicians or their dupes are in gaol. Everywhere disorder has been repressed. The Gandhi Movement, which measured its strength with the Government of India, has been for the moment, to a large extent, mastered, even by the most long-suffering of administrations—I thank God, with hardly any bloodshed and almost without the employment, except on the frontier, of any British troops! I invite the British nation to realise their own undoubted power of giving wise and good government to India. That power is overwhelming, until it is cast away. The shame is that our moral and intellectual guidance should not have been exerted as firmly as our material power. It is the contrast between the vague and soothing political sentiments on the one hand, and the rough, practical measures which have to be taken, and have been taken, in emergencies, on the other, which has produced a volume of avoidable punishment and suffering.

If the British Government and its servant and projection, the Government of India, had maintained a true contact with realities, three-quarters of the distress caused to the politically-minded classes in India could have been avoided. If, instead of raising alluring hopes of speedy Dominion status, we had concentrated upon practical steps to advance the material condition of the Indian masses; if the Congress at Lahore which burnt the Union Jack had been broken up forthwith and its leaders deported; if Gandhi had been arrested and tried as soon as he broke the law; if the will to rule had been firmly asserted, there would have been no necessity for the immense series of penal measures which have, in fact, been taken. Again, I appeal for confirmation to all those in England who really know India. Even now, at any time, the plain assertion of the resolve of Parliament to govern and to guide the destinies of the Indian people in faithful loyalty to Indian interests would in a few years—it might even be in a few months—bring this period of tantalised turmoil to an end.

Where, then, do we stand? The word of the King-Emperor is inviolable. We are pledged not only to labour for the welfare of India, but perseveringly to associate Indians of every race and creed with the processes of their own development. The Act of 1919 is a rock which cannot be removed. By that Act we conferred great and new constitutional powers upon the Indian political classes and we pledged ourselves to extend those constitutional powers honourably and perseveringly. We have assigned no theoretical limit to the extension of Indian constitutional development within the Empire. But by that same Act we reserved to ourselves an equal right to restrict, delay, or, if need be, for a spell to reverse that process. So far as there exists any contract between a people conquered by force in former times, and the modern Parliament of a benevolent nation vowed to promote their welfare, that is the contract, and there is no other.

Let us examine the problem upon this basis and in the light of practical events. The far-reaching extensions of self-government with which Mr. Montagu's name is associated were a bold experiment. They have not succeeded. The ten years which have passed have been years of failure. Every service which has been handed over to Indian administration has deteriorated; in particular, Indian agriculture, the sole prop of the life of hundreds of millions, has certainly not advanced in accordance with the ever-growing science and organisation of the modern world. The Indian political classes have not accepted the Montagu constitution. Even those for whose especial benefit and pleasure that constitution was devised have derived no satisfaction from it. Either they have refused to co-operate, or they have used the liberties which it conferred not for the purpose of improving the well-being of India, but merely as convenient tools and processes for political agitation and even sedition. There has resulted unrest, improverishment and discontent, drawing with them repressive measures and curtailments of civil liberties, which did not exist before the political liberties were widened.

In these circumstances, a new Parliament will have to decide what is now to be done. Our right and our power to restrict Indian constitutional liberties are unchallengeable. Our obligation to persevere in associating the peoples of India with their own government is undoubted. We are free to call a halt. We are free, for the time being, to retrace our steps, to retire in order to advance again. So long as the continuous purpose is sincerely and unswervingly pursued, Parliament has entire discretion. It is evident that our first efforts to create an all-India constitution have been ill-conceived. It may well be that our duty and our course now lie in curtailing the functions of an all-India body and in building up in each province more real, more intimate, more representative organisms of self-government. It may well be that these organisms, when developed and established, will form a surer foundation for an all-India Government than the present crude and unduly Westernised conception.

But here I must draw attention to a very grave danger. The Indian gentlemen and notabilities who are attending the Round Table Conference are in no way representative of the real forces which challenge British rule in India. It is true that, drifting with the tide, many of them have become the mouthpiece of extreme demands, but they have no power to pledge the Indian Congress Party to sincere acceptance of any agreement that may be outlined. The danger is that in an unwise endeavour to reach an agreement here in London, the Socialist Government will commit itself to concessions and extensions of self-government which will weaken our hands in the future, without in any way procuring the assent of the ruthless forces of sedition and outrage. Our concessions will, therefore, only be used as the starting-point for new demands by revolutionaries, while the loyal elements and the masses of the people will be the more unsettled by further evidences of British weakness. The truth is that Gandhi-ism and all it stands for will, sooner or later, have to be grappled with and finally crushed. It is no use trying to satisfy a tiger by feeding him with cat's-meat. The sooner this is realised, the less trouble and misfortune will there be for all concerned.

Above all, it must be made plain that the British nation has no intention of relinquishing its mission in India, or of failing in its duty to the Indian masses, or of parting with its supreme control in any of the essentials of peace, order and good government. We have no intention of casting away that most truly bright and precious jewel in the crown of the King, which more than all our other Dominions and Dependencies constitutes the glory and strength of the British Empire. The loss of

India would mark and consummate the downfall of the British Empire. That great organism would pass at a stroke out of life into history. From such a catastrophe there could be no recovery. But we have yet to learn that the race and nation which have achieved so many prodigies and have faithfully discharged so many difficult tasks, and come safely and invincibly through all the perils of the centuries, will now fall a victim to their own lack of self-confidence and moral strength.

INDIA–"A FRIGHTFUL PROSPECT"

January 26, 1931

House of Commons

On January 25 Lord Irwin released Gandhi and his chief colleagues from detention and removed the proscription on the Congress Working Committee. When Baldwin supported this action, as Churchill later wrote, "I reached my breaking-point in my relations with Mr. Baldwin." In reply to this speech Baldwin pledged himself and the Conservative Party to "try to implement" the Constitution outlined by the Round Table Conference.

[Extract] . . . I hold that the handling of Indian affairs during the last eighteen months has been most unfortunate and has led already to results which will be long lamented. I will make the briefest review which is necessary. Lord Birkenhead, with foresight and with wisdom, antedated by two years the setting up of the Commission laid down in the Act of 1919 for the reviewing of the Montagu-Chelmsford reforms. The Commission was set up by Act of Parliament, all the three parties co-operated in its setting up, and all three were represented on the Commission. The Commission, after immense labours, journeys, and studies, presented a report which was unanimous, and it presented that report to the Houses of Parliament which had called it into being. What has happened to that report of our Commission? Why has it been thrust altogether—though compliments have been paid to it—out of the sequence of events?

One would have thought that that report would have been debated by Parliament, probably on a series of Resolutions; that we should have heard, not for the first time, as we have done to-day, but repeatedly, the advice of the distinguished men of all parties who contributed to that report; and that the Government would then, guided by the Resolutions of the House and by the advice of those whom the House had charged, and whom the Act of 1919 indicates should be charged, with the duty of advising Parliament, have framed a Bill. It was also contemplated and generally agreed that this Bill, after being presented to Parliament and read a Second time, should be the subject of a Joint Committee of both Houses, to which Indian representatives of every shade of opinion should be invited to have recourse; and, finally, the Bill would have been passed through its stages and presented for the Royal Assent.

Such was the procedure marked out, coolly, calmly, and far in advance, and marked out by general assent. Why is it that we have departed from it? It is, I suppose, because the Viceroy, moved or influenced by His Majesty's Government–I do not know, I cannot tell–determined to make a pronouncement in the winter of 1929, opening up in general, guarded, but still spacious terms the idea of Dominion status. I hold that this pronouncement–I am afraid I must ask the House to permit me to state, with the candour which we have been invited to adopt my point of view–was uncalled for, that it was an interruption of the procedure prescribed by law, and that it was an intervention between Parliament and their Commission. Everyone had agreed to await the Report of the Commission, and it is most regrettable that Parliament and Indian opinion also were not permitted to receive that Report unprejudiced by prior declarations. For this, the accountable responsibility rests with the Government of the day; but as the result, see what happened.

The Report was profoundly prejudiced before its publication, and when it was seen that the Commissioners had deliberately and unanimously excluded the expression 'Dominion status' from their Report, a very painful difference was disclosed between the Viceroy and the Government of India on the one hand and our Statutory Commission on the other. At the same time, there was an enormous leap forward in the demands of the Indian political classes. What had been accepted before was now brushed aside. Moderate men adopted opinions which hitherto had been considered extreme. Outbreaks of disorder and lawlessness occurred in many parts of India, culminating in the Nationalist Congress at Lahore, at which the British flag was insulted with every circumstance of formality and publicity and, I may add, insulted with impunity. . . .

Could there be a worse way of dealing with so grave a problem? Here for weeks all the foundations of British power in India have been laid bare, and every principle has been treated as an open question. The orb of power has been dangled before the gleaming eyes of excitable millions and before the powerful forces of implacable hostility with whom we have, as is well known, to cope in India, while at the same time in the background, treated as if they were matters of machinery, are a whole series of formidable reservations and conditions. Thus, on the one hand the claims and expectancy of those in India have been raised to the highest pitch by sweeping concessions on general questions of principle, while on the other the rugged facts which have emerged in the speech of my right hon. and learned Friend (Sir John Simon) who preceded me, have all been kept in the shade by clouds of ceremonious and benevolent generalities. Meanwhile, the rapid landslide in British opinion and policy at home has been accompanied in India by a steady development of unrest, disorder, disloyalty and assassination. The well-meaning and high-minded Viceroy has had to couple with his kindly speeches and sentiments a succession of repressive measures and of restrictions on civil liberty without precedent in India since the Mutiny, except in some days of the Great War. Many of thousands of Indians are in prison in connection with political agitation. The world depression which has reached India is accentuated by the prolonged uncertainty, by the growing disaffection, by the widespread feeling that all the things which they have known for generations are about to be thrown into the melting pot, by the feeling that some enormous change is impending and that violent times are ahead. The result has been suffering and misfortune on a very large scale and as a prelude, as I fear, to even greater troubles, because this uncertainty about all the foundations of social and political life is not over. It is going to be prolonged indefinitely. This constitution, this Blue Book is now going to be paraded round India and discussed there. All the promises and concessions will be set at their maximum; all the safeguards narrowly canvassed with a view to demanding their diminution. All this uncertainty and agitation is going to continue not for months only, but possibly for years.

I have now completed my recital of the catalogue of errors and disasters which have brought us to our present position. Here I must make it perfectly clear that I accept not only the preamble of the Act of 1919, but also Section 41 of that Act. The preamble shows the ultimate goal to which we declare that India may aspire, and Section 41 shows precisely the full and uncompromised right of Parliament to advance or to divert or, if necessary, to restrict this forward movement in the development of constitutional government. Let us take the two together. I am quite willing fully to accept the implications of both. Of course, we assign no limits to the future potential development of our Indian fellow-subjects. We enlist their co-operation—have we not been doing so continuously?—in every branch of Indian administration and of Indian life. It all depends on time and on facts. My submission to the House to-night is that the time for this extension is premature, and that the facts are adverse. . . .

The clash and agitation in India will continue, but they will no longer be confined to rioting in the streets or demonstrations in the Legislature. They will invade the heart and the brain of the Government of India. There, at the summit of this wonderful creation, an instrument which, with all its shortcomings, has given peace and progress to nations more varied than the nations of Europe and populations in the aggregate almost as large as China—there, at the summit, by constitutional and Parliamentary weapons now, the process of gnawing and cutting down the safeguards will proceed, stimulated, perhaps, from outside by a continuance of lawlessness and rioting and of worse crimes, for the prevention of which you will no longer have the primary responsibility. What, may I ask, will be your line of moral and logical resistance then? You have declared that the safeguards are only transitory, they are temporary expedients, apologetically adopted pending what to anyone who reads this Blue Book, and notes the emphasis assigned to its various parts, can only mean the rapid and speedy realisation of full Dominion status. The struggle will go on; it will only be aggravated; it will proceed under conditions in which British rule will be shorn of all its argument and of half its apparatus. It will proceed steadily towards the goal which those who are driving this policy forward, both here in this country and in India, no longer hesitate to avow, namely, the goal of complete severance between Great Britain and India of every tie except tradition, which in India is adverse, and sentiment, which in India is hostile. Sir, I say that is a frightful prospect to have opened up so wantonly, so recklessly, so incontinently and in so short a time.

How will the British nation feel about all this? I am told that they do not care. I am told that from one quarter or another. They are all worried by unemployment or taxation or absorbed in sport and crime news. The great liner is sinking in a calm sea.

One bulkhead after another gives way; one compartment after another is bilged; the list increases; she is sinking; but the captain and the officers and the crew are all in the saloon dancing to the jazz band. But wait till the passengers find out what is their position! For thirty years I have watched from a central position the manifestations of the will power of Great Britain, and I do not believe our people will consent to be edged, pushed, talked and cozened out of India. No nation of which I am aware, great or small, has ever voluntarily or tamely suffered such an overwhelming injury to its interests or such a harsh abrogation of its rights. After all, there are British rights and interests in India. Two centuries of effort and achievement, lives given on a hundred fields, far more lives given and consumed in faithful and devoted service to the Indian people themselves! All this has earned us rights of our own in India. When the nation finds that our whole position is in jeopardy, that her whole work and duty in India is being brought to a standstill, when the nation sees our individual fellow-countrymen scattered about, with their women and children, throughout this enormous land, in hourly peril amidst the Indian multitudes, when, at any moment, this may produce shocking scenes, then I think there will be a sharp awakening, then, I am sure, that a reaction of the most vehement character will sweep this country and its unmeasured strength will once more be used. That, Sir, is an ending which I trust and pray we may avoid, but it is an ending to which step by step and day by day, we are being remorselessly and fatuously conducted.

"THE BONELESS WONDER"– TRADE DISPUTES AND TRADE UNIONS (AMENDMENT) BILL

January 28, 1931

House of Commons

This bitter attack upon MacDonald, uncharacteristically violent for Churchill speaking in the House of Commons, was long remembered and not easily forgiven.

[Extract] . . . The introduction of trade unionism into the very centre of party politics has certainly produced a very great change in the relations between our Parliamentary institutions taken as a whole and trade unionism. So far as trade unionism is concerned, the results, I think, have been, very largely, unfortunate. So far as the State is concerned, it obviously requires a complete review of the position of trade unions and of the privileges–not the rights, but the privileges–accorded to them. Their privileged position under the law, which was accorded to them for the sake of the industrial functions which they discharged, obviously required to be re-examined in the light of their immense political activity. It was gravely injurious to the State and to the nation that party politics–not general politics, but party politics, and the special partisanship and prejudice which they necessarily entail–should be intermingled with industrial matters. It was bad for politics, it was worse for industry. That was the change which had taken place, and of which we were bound to take notice....

No one can pretend—let me make this point clear at the outset of this passage in my remarks—no one can pretend that the Labour party have any grievance under the Constitution. On the contrary, they are the pampered pets, the spoiled darlings of the Constitution. The representatives of the most extreme opinions come into this Parliament with fewer votes behind them than any other class of Members who sit in this House. The Liberals might have a grievance, but the Labour party has no grievance under the Constitution. When they come into Parliament, they are treated with an indulgence and a consideration that no other party receives. They are enabled to form Governments one after another although they are in a minority. They are enabled to retain power in spite of mismanagement and incapacity—[*Interruption*]—which would have shattered half-a-dozen Administrations of the Liberal or the Conservative parties. What, I should like to know, would happen to a Conservative or Liberal Government if we had seen unemployment rise by 1,500,000 in a year—[*Interruption*]—while the Government of the day sat helpless without bringing forward one single illuminating or constructive idea?

So far from having a grievance, this new party, founded on the trade unions, have, under the Constitution of this country, been treated with exceptional indulgence and consideration. Do they bear their advantages with modesty? Listen to the Secretary of State for War, speaking in the debate last week. His attitude was an example, if I may say so, of very unseemly arrogance. [*Interruption*.]

> Our party—

he said, and I thoroughly agree with him here—

> Our party has got beyond the point when it is to be patronised.

Then why are they claiming these privileges?

> It has got to the point where it demands—not asks, but demands—the right to work through its organisation in the way it wishes.

Their wish is to be our law.

> If you want to prevent revolution—

language so suited to the position he occupies as the head of a great disciplined force—[*Interruption*.] That again is language which I do not think ought to be used on his behalf in this or in any other connection.

> If you desire to have discontent, if you desire that the country should be upset, then try to stop us from doing our own work in our own way.—[Official Report, 22nd January, 1931; col. 498, Vol. 247.]

That is the whole claim that we who oppose this Measure make. You are asking to set up a power within a power, a separate force within the State claiming to be immune from the ordinary restraints of law which the Constitution imposes on all other citizens. It has been said, "It is an assured sign of a noble and worthy spirit whom power amends." I do not think there is a very general feeling in the House that power has greatly amended the Secretary of State for War. The quotation which seems much more accurately to apply to him is taken from the Bible "But Jeshurun waxed fat, and kicked." . . .

What are the Government and the Labour party going to do about it, and what is the Prime Minister going to do? I spoke the other day, after he had been defeated in an important Division, about his wonderful skill in falling without hurting himself. He falls, but up he comes again, smiling, a little dishevelled, but still smiling. But this is a juncture, a situation, which will try to the very fullest the peculiar arts in which he excels. I remember, when I was a child, being taken to the celebrated Barnum's circus, which contained an exhibition of freaks and monstrosities, but the exhibit on the programme which I most desired to see was the one described as "The Boneless Wonder." My parents judged that that spectacle would be too revolting and demoralising for my youthful eyes, and I have waited 50 years to see the boneless wonder sitting on the Treasury Bench.

We have made our protest against this Bill. We have made our protest also against a procedure for which the Liberal party bear a keen responsibility, but it seems to me that the real grievance lies with the trade unions. They seem to me, after all has been said and done, the parties who are being deceived in this matter. I was not invited to the conference that took place last week in Downing Street between the Prime Minister and the leader of the Liberal party, but "my hon. friend the Member for Treorchy" gave me a very shrewd account of the interview between the two party leaders. After the usual compliments, the Prime Minister said, "We have never been colleagues, we have never been friends–at least, not what you would call holiday friends–but we have both been Prime Minister, and dog don't eat dog. Just look at the monstrous Bill the trade unions and our wild fellows have foisted on me. Do me a service, and I will never forget it. Take it upstairs and cut its dirty throat."

INDIA AND GANDHI

January 30, 1931

Free Trade Hall, Manchester

On January 28 Churchill resigned from the Opposition Business Committee and ceased to be a member of the Front Opposition Bench. Until September 1939 he spoke from the back benches as an independent Conservative.

This speech was made at the second meeting held under the auspices of the Indian Empire Society. Its vehemence was an augury of many others on this subject.

We have come here to Manchester to utter our solemn warning against the policy which the Socialist Government has pursued in India. It is our conviction that unless this policy is arrested it will bring a fatal disaster upon the British Empire and entail endless misery to hundreds of millions of harmless Indian subjects of the King. I feel obliged to claim complete party independence upon the Indian crisis, and I come here, where so much of my political work has been done, to ask for your earnest attention upon matters which are the deep concern of the nation. . . .

A draft federal Constitution for India with Dyarchy and responsible Government at the centre has been framed. In the words of the Socialist Lord Chancellor, "the responsibility for the Federal Government in India will in future"–mark the words "in future"–"rest on Indians themselves." This Constitution was very loosely put together. Not one of the thorny problems of Indian life or the real difficulties of machinery was settled. The gaps and faults in the structure were covered up with clouds of perorations and pious platitudes, and the result, embodied in a small Blue Book, is now to be hawked around India, already in a dangerously excited condition, in the hopes of winning more acceptance. It is this scheme which we are told the Conservative party will have to implement when it comes back into office. Of course, we are assured there are all kinds of safeguards. What is given in the word is taken back in the fact; what is given with one hand is taken away with the other. Sir Samuel Hoare, speaking with great ability in the House of Commons, laid down a list of safeguards and reservations which if they were made effective would reduce responsible government of India by Indians and early Dominion status for all India to very small dimensions. We are told to rely upon these safeguards, and that we shall all fight solidly together for them. I hope it may be so, but the Prime Minister is already apologising to the Indian newspapers for the safeguards, and the Secretary of State for India (Mr. Wedgwood Benn) says that we shall be 'compelled' to give full self-government to India.

It is also argued that we cannot afford to have party divisions in this country about India, because then the Socialist party will when in Opposition make the government of India impossible. This is a very grave argument, and everyone should give full weight to it. Nevertheless, I do not think we can accept it, because it means that the Socialist party in practice will be the final deciding factor in the whole of our policy towards India, and the Conservative party will be simply tied to its tail. I think upon this supreme question of India, which is no ordinary question of politics but involves the life of the British Empire, we ought to stand up for what we believe and face the consequences, whatever they may be. If the worst comes upon England and her Empire, let us make sure, above all things, that it does not come through us. Moreover, experience shows that the only safe plan for human action is to act with great simplicity, and give judgment on the merits of questions at each particular stage. I fear very greatly, if we continue to drift and jog along with the Socialists in their Indian policy, that when the time comes and we can go no further, our resisting power will be gone, and they will drag us all over the precipice with them.

But now let us see what has been happening in India. The Viceroy, a well-meaning man of the highest personal character, has had to cope with steadily increasing disorder. He put off arresting Mr. Gandhi as long as possible. Eight months ago, however, Gandhi's lawlessness became so flagrant that Lord Irwin was forced to lock him up. Instead of bringing him to trial and punishing him according to law, he locked him up as a State prisoner, and then tried to negotiate with him while he was in gaol. Gandhi, who is a fanatic and an ascetic of the fakir type well known in the East, rejected these overtures with contempt. But you can imagine how his prestige throughout to India "on approval," Gandhi and thirty of his leading fellow-conspirators and martyr in the eyes of his fellows, and then, while he was actually their captive, solicited his aid. Now that the Round Table Constitution has been drafted and sent out to India 'on approval,' Gandhi and thirty of his leading fellow-conspirators and revolutionaries have been set at liberty, unconditionally, in the hopes that they will at any rate say some kind words about the scheme.

As might have been expected, Gandhi was received rapturously by his followers. He has been made a martyr under very comfortable conditions, and a national hero without running any risk, and he now emerges on the scene a triumphant victor. It did not take him long to launch his new defiance at the Government of India. Nearly 25,000 of his followers had already been imprisoned under the Socialist policy of conciliation. Gandhi, of course, demands that they shall be released. He insists that the picketing of British shops and factories, the breaking of the law about salt, the boycotting of foreign cloth–you in Lancashire have something to do with that, I believe–and civil disobedience generally must continue. If the Government of India accept this and withdraw all the ordinances they have had to pass to keep the peace, then he will, perhaps, be graciously pleased to examine how far the new Constitution falls short of his declared aim of absolute and speedy independence for India. We have yet to learn what the answer of his Majesty's Government and the Government of India will be to these demands and to this situation. Surely the situation ought to have been expected. In fact, if the Viceroy and the Socialist Government had wished to manufacture and foment disorder instead of hoping to quiet it, they could hardly have acted otherwise than they have done.

The reason why, in my judgment, Lord Irwin, for all his virtue and courage, has not succeeded in India as he deserved to, is that he has been proceeding upon a wrong mental theme. His attitude towards India has throughout been an apology. He has not shown sufficient confidence in the indispensable work which our country has done, and is doing, for India, or in British resolution that it shall not be interrupted or destroyed. That is the sole foundation upon which the peaceful and successful administration of India can be based. It is never possible to make concessions to Orientals when they think you are weak or are afraid of them. If they once think they have got you at a disadvantage all their moods become violent, concessions are treated as valueless, and necessary acts of civil repression often only add fuel to the flames. This Viceroy, who meant so well and tried so hard, and has always been perfectly fearless where he himself was concerned, has had to enact more repressive measures and inflict more punishments and make greater curtailments of liberty and imprison more thousands of people than has ever happened before in India. And yet all these severities have been no more effective than his concessions and kindly words. Things have gone from bad to worse, and they are now all to be aggravated again.

What is wanted at this moment in India is not more repression or more concession. It is a fundamental change in the intellectual and moral attitude of Great

Britain and of the Government of India, which is a reflection of Great Britain. Instead of proclaiming, as this unwise Constitutional Blue Book does, that our object is to wind up our affairs and hand over the government of India to the tiny oligarchy of Indian politicians who have raised this agitation, we ought to begin now by making it perfectly clear that we intend to remain the effective rulers of India in every essential for a very long and indefinite period, and that though we welcome co-operation in every branch of government from loyal and faithful Indians, we will have no truck with lawlessness or treason, and will, if necessary, suspend even the most moderate Constitutional changes while there is a bad spirit abroad.

Now you will rightly say to me, "Is this not contrary to all our experience of the self-governing Dominions of the British Empire, and is it not contrary to what you did yourself in South Africa and in Ireland?" I answer, "Yes, it is contrary." The problem of Indian government is entirely different from any of the problems we have hitherto faced in any part of the world. India is a continent nearly as large as Europe, and, like Europe, it has now between three and four hundred millions of people. There are scores of nations and races in India and hundreds of religions and sects. Out of the three hundred and fifty millions of Indians only a very few millions can read or write, and of these only a fraction are interested in politics and Western ideas. The rest are primitive people absorbed in the hard struggle for life. They are dependent for their livelihood and for the happiness and peace of their humble homes upon the rule of a very small number of white officials who have no personal interests of their own to serve, who are quite impartial between race and race, and who have built up in 150 years an organisation which has given these enormous masses peace, justice, and a substantial increase in material well-being, which would have been even greater except for the vast increase in their numbers. This organisation and the great services by which it operates depends for its efficiency, and indeed for its existence, upon its authority. If that authority is weakened, or discredited, or loses confidence in itself, or is hampered and broken up, measureless disasters will descend upon these three hundred and fifty million perfectly helpless poor folk. They will soon be reduced to the miserable condition of the people of China, where anarchy has now reigned for many years and tyranny for ages.

We have, therefore, a supreme moral duty to discharge to the Indian people. We have no right whatever to hand them over to a comparatively small and utterly unrepresentative political faction, to be the prey of misgovernment, of deterioration in every public service, of religious bigotry of a kind not dreamed of for generations in the West, and finally of civil war. While we have strength we must discharge our duty. Neither taunts nor blandishments should move us from it. When we can no longer discharge our duty, then our reign in India is done, and many other great things in the history of the British Empire will come to their close at the same time.

But I shall be asked, "Have we the strength to carry out our task? Will not great numbers of soldiers be required and terrible events take place?" I reply it is not a case for warlike force. Do not allow yourselves to be frightened from your duty by language of that kind. In all the disasters that have occurred in the last eighteen months hardly a single British battalion has been used in India and not a shot has been fired, except on the frontier, by British troops. The admirable Indian police, for whose fidelity and restraint no praise is too great, has been quite sufficient to cope with every disorder, and hardly any life has been lost or blood shed in the almost ceaseless mob tumult which has occurred in so many places. Confidence in ourselves and in our mission, and firm support of our faithful agents and officials, patience and perseverance, have only to be displayed—and displayed upon the theme that Britain intends to govern India for many years to come—to save reinforcements of troops or serious bloodshed. In fact, this will be the only way by which such evils can be averted.

If, however, you continue to spread far and wide throughout the vast plains and cities of India the doctrine that the British are handing over their power to some new regime as a preliminary to clearing out of the country, and as part of the decline and fall of the British Empire, then, indeed, you may have upon your hands a situation of the most terrible kind. Then, indeed, you may find your police, hitherto so loyal and trustworthy, and your native Army thrown into a profound state of perturbation, asking one another what their future is to be, and how their new masters will view their actions, and then at any moment you may find yourself in a catastrophe of a character more horrible than anything we have experienced even in the awful times through which we have lived.

Finally, you will ask me what, then, are we to make of our promises of Dominion status and responsible government. Surely we cannot break our word! There I agree. The formal, plighted word of the King-Emperor is inviolable. It does not follow, however, that every Socialist jack-in-office can commit this great country by his perorations. In the very Act of Parliament in 1919 where responsible government is mentioned in the preamble there is also a special clause, Clause 41, which makes it plain that all progress towards responsible government must only be at the discretion of the British Parliament, and that Parliament can, if it chooses, stop the progress, or slow it down, or turn it into another channel, or even retrace our path if that were necessary. Therefore, until another Act of Parliament receives the Royal assent, there is no ground whatever on which we are committed to any particular step at any particular time.

As for this expression "Dominion Status," about which there has been so much misunderstanding: the abstraction called India, composed of so many different nations and States, is in a ceremonial sense a Dominion already. Indian representatives sit on the Imperial Conferences; they participated in the Imperial War Cabinet, and are represented in the British delegation of the League of Nations. With every mark of honour and dignity we have welcomed the aid and co-operation of eminent men among our Indian fellow-subjects. But except as an ultimate visionary goal, Dominion status like that of Canada or Australia is not going to happen in India in any period which we can even remotely foresee. It certainly could never happen until the mass of the Indian people were as well able to look after their own interests as are the Australians and Canadians of today. It is most dangerous and improvident of British political leaders of any party to try to smooth difficulties over in India by making believe that full Dominion status can possibly come to India in our time.

On the contrary, it is their duty now, while time remains, to make it clear that these ideas play no part in the important practical steps which should now be taken in constitutional reform. We should immediately proceed to build up in the provinces of India organisations of local government which will be truly related to the populations they represent and seek to serve. That is the task which, if it should succeed, will perhaps at a later stage enable another step to be taken with sureness and safety. And if it fails, if any disorders and collapses occur, the Central Government, having preserved its authority intact, will be able to come to the rescue and tow the ship off the shoals again. We should be wrong to complicate this hopeful task by trying at the same time to set up a make-believe responsible Government at the centre and summit of Indian affairs, and still more by using loose and vague language in this critical year about Dominion Status. Lord Birkenhead said: "Tell the truth to India." Yes, indeed, tell her no more than the truth.

The loss of India, however arising, would be final and fatal to us. It could not fail to be part of a process which would reduce us to the scale of a minor Power. Holland, once our equal, was outmatched in the world in spite of all her sturdy domestic strength, and became a small continental state. But Holland suffered this eclipse without having acquired the population of a modern first-class State. We have forty-five millions in this island, a very large proportion of whom are in existence because of our world position, economic, political, imperial. If, guided by counsels of madness and cowardice disguised as false benevolence, you troop home from India, you will leave behind you what John Morley called 'a bloody chaos,' and you will find Famine to greet you on the horizon on your return.

"A SEDITIOUS MIDDLE TEMPLE LAWYER"

February 23, 1931

Winchester House, Epping

The Council of the West Essex Conservative Association was called together to receive the explanation of their representative on his attitude towards Indian matters and on his resignation from the Front Bench. This speech was the most violent and memorable delivered by Churchill on the Indian question to date. In particular, the passage on Gandhi made an immense impression on opinion–not least in India. The Council of the West Essex Conservative Association unanimously carried a motion in support of Churchill's attack.

You have been called together at my desire in order that I may lay before you the reasons why I have felt it my duty to take an independent line about India and to withdraw from the Business Committee of the Conservative party of which I had the honour to be a member. The Business Committee is a very sensible name for the small group of those members of both Houses with whom Mr. Baldwin is accustomed to consult on the general policy of the party and its conduct in Parliament. I valued highly the privilege of being included in it, and also it gave an opportunity of continuing in close, confidential touch with several of my principal colleagues and personal friends in the late Conservative Government. I was therefore very sorry to have to cut myself off from this interesting and agreeable work, and I can assure you I should not have done so without due cause. I still propose, if that is desired, to remain Chairman of the Conservative Finance Committee and to conduct the criticism of the Budget and other financial measures of the Socialist Government. I need scarcely say that I intend to do my utmost to assist our leader in the opposition to the Government in the House of Commons. I shall do my utmost to turn them out at the earliest opportunity, and procure their condign punishment and defeat at the general election, and to bring about by every means in my power a decisive victory for a united Conservative party. I found, however, that while I remained a member of this small inner circle I could not give full effect to my convictions about India. Naturally when men sit round a table and discuss political matters in intimate confidence they are largely bound by the decisions which are taken, and although there is more latitude out of office than in a Cabinet, nevertheless it is most undesirable that differences should appear among those who are thus associated.

Now let us see what these differences are. I agreed to our Conservative delegates taking part in the Round Table Conference, as I thought they would keep the Socialist Government from committing us to any dangerous or unwise departure. This our delegates tell us they have done, and I agree with them that they may justly claim that we are not committed by any action of theirs to the scheme of a new constitution for India which emerged from the Round Table Conference. I was however surprised and alarmed at the sudden landslide of opinion which took place upon that Conference and at the impression which was created throughout this country and in India that all the three parties were in agreement in principle to set up a federal constitution under Indian ministers responsible to an all-India Assembly. Still more was I alarmed when this enormous departure was itself presented as only a temporary and transitory arrangement soon to give place to what is called 'full Dominion status' for India carrying with it the control not only of law and order and of finance, but of the Army, and the right to secede from the British Empire. I do not think it is wise to hold out any hopes of any such position being reached for many generations to come. At any rate, I hold it of the utmost importance that we should make it clear that there is no chance of such a goal being reached in our lifetime, or in any period which it is profitable for us to consider. Secondly, I much regret to have to state that I disapprove altogether of the policy pursued by the present Viceroy of India, which as I shall show you presently has been attended by results already disastrous and threatening greater evils in the future.

These difficulties came to a head when Mr. Baldwin expressed his complete disagreement with the speech I made in the House of Commons at the end of last month, and when he said that it would be the duty of the Conservative party if returned to power to try to 'implement' the scheme put forward by the Round Table Conference. It was quite evident to everyone after that speech that the differences between us upon India were not merely matters of emphasis or procedure, but that they were profound and practical differences covering the whole field of Indian Policy and affecting the whole mood and spirit in which we discharge our duty to India. In the words which Lord Hartington, afterwards Duke of Devonshire, used to Mr. Gladstone in 1886 about Ireland, I can only say that upon India Mr. Baldwin and I 'do not mean the same thing.' I am sure you will agree that in these circumstances I had no choice but to separate myself upon this single question in the most friendly manner from a leader for whom I entertain both high respect and regard.

Having taken up this position in public about India I must inform you that it is my intention to go through with it. I shall endeavour to marshal British opinion against a course of action which would bring in my judgment the greatest evils upon the people of India, upon the people of Great Britain, and upon the structure of the British Empire itself. It follows therefore of course that I should not be able to serve in any Administration about whose Indian policy I was not reassured. I would far rather be a loyal private member of the Conservative party than bear official responsibility for actions and events which might well involve a mortal injury to the greatness and cohesion of our Empire. I invite you to endorse this attitude on my part, and I hope you will find yourselves able to give me your full approval and even encouragement in acting in this matter in accordance with my convictions.

The Indian problem at the present time divides itself into two parts. There is the question of a new constitution for India, and there is the question of the day-to-day administration of that country and the proper maintenance of British authority. If you will permit me, I will say a few words on both these matters. In dealing with Oriental races for whose well-being you are responsible it is a mistake to try to gloss over grave differences, to try to dress up proposals in an unwarrantably favourable guise, to ignore or conceal or put in the background rugged but unpleasant facts. The right course on the contrary is to state soberly and firmly what the British position is, and not be afraid to say "this would not suit us," "that would not be good for you," "there is no chance of this coming to pass," "we shall not agree to that being done." All these firm negatives ought to be stated frankly and plainly so that false hopes are not excited unduly and lead to disappointment and reproaches. We should always try to be better than our word and let any concessions we make be real and true. The Socialist Government on the other hand has been trying to deal with the Indian Nationalist politicians by the same sort of blarney and palaver which sometimes passes muster in Parliament or on British political platforms. I do not want to see the Conservative party, which is the main instrument by which the British Empire can be defended, dragged any further in their wake. I do not want to see the Indian politicans misled as to what our real intentions are.

Now you will observe that statements have been made within the last few days upon Mr. Baldwin's authority that we are not committed to anything except to give fair consideration to any proposals that may be made. I was very glad to hear those statements. After all, it is everybody's duty to give fair consideration to any proposals on any subject which are sincerely advanced. But that is very different from the impression which the country has sustained, and it is very different from the impression conveyed to the Indian politicians. Our leader's phrase about "implementing" the constitution prepared by the Round Table Conference and the whole purport of his speech were cabled to the Indian delegates on the ship by which they were returning to India. We are told that they were overjoyed at what they read, and naturally they assumed that the great Conservative party was in agreement with the Socialist and Liberal parties and was prepared to implement a federal constitution with responsible government at the centre. On the strength of this they proceeded to draft a manifesto to the Indian Congress, and have ever since been labouring to persuade the more extreme elements to come and join them in a further conference to be held in India. They ought to be told, as we are told, that the Conservative party is wholly uncommitted, and that they have been unintentionally misled. But Mr. Ramsay MacDonald, the Prime Minister, is also evidently under a misapprehension; because he said in answer to a question which I put to him in the House of Commons last week that on the subject of India the Government considered that they "had got their marching orders from the House": meaning thereby that all parties were agreed. It seems to me important that these misapprehensions, if such they be, about the official attitude of the Conservative party, should be corrected both here and in India on the highest authority and with the least delay.

The proper constitutional course for Parliament to adopt is to proceed to consider the Simon Report which was signed by the representatives of all parties. There are no doubt many things in that report which would have to be very carefully examined, some of which are no longer applicable; nevertheless it forms the only proper constitutional basis upon which discussion of the reform of Indian government should proceed by the joint action of all parties. The Round Table Conference may have thrown some new and interesting light upon Indian affairs of which of course full notice should be taken. But the whole foundation for the joint treatment of the Indian problem by the three British parties is the Simon Report, and once that report has been put on one side, as it has been almost contemptuously by the Socialist Government, it is imperative that the Conservative party should recover the fullest possible liberty of judgment. So much for the constitutional aspect.

Now I come to the administration of India. In my opinion we ought to dissociate ourselves in the most public and formal manner from any complicity in the weak, wrong-headed and most unfortunate administration of India by the Socialists and by the Viceroy acting upon their responsibility. It is alarming and also nauseating to see Mr. Gandhi, a seditious Middle Temple lawyer, now posing as a fakir of a type well-known in the East, striding half-naked up the steps of the Vice-regal palace, while he is still organising and conducting a defiant campaign of civil disobedience, to parley on equal terms with the representative of the King-Emperor. Such a spectacle can only increase the unrest in India and the danger to which white people there are exposed. It can only encourage all the forces which are hostile to British authority. What good can possibly come of such extraordinary negotiations? Gandhi has said within the last few weeks that he demands the substance of independence, though he kindly adds that the British may keep the shadow. He declares that the boycott of foreign cloth must be continued until either prohibition or a prohibitive tariff can be put up against it by an Indian national Parliament. This, if accepted, would entail the final ruin of Lancashire. He has also pressed for the repudiation of the Indian loans, and has laid claim to the control of the Army and foreign affairs. These are his well-known aims. Surely they form a strange basis for heart-to-heart discussions—"sweet" we are told they were—between this malignant subversive fanatic and the Viceroy of India.

All this is intended by the Socialists to be the preliminary to another Round Table Conference in India to which it is hoped to persuade the extremists to come. At this new gathering the far-reaching and half-baked recommendations of the Round Table Conference will be taken only as a starting-point. From this starting-point will begin the attack upon the safeguards which have hitherto been kept apologetically in the background. I think it vital that the Conservative party should without delay get itself into a strong position of resistance, and should begin to arouse public opinion throughout the country against these most unwise and dangerous proceedings. I intend at any rate to do my best, and I shall be much strengthened if you put your whole weight behind me. India is no ordinary question of party politics. It is one of those supreme issues which come upon us from time to time. When they arise the men and women who faithfully guard the life of Britain and her Empire in every rank and employment, in every part of the country, feel the same vibration. They felt it on August 4, 1914. They felt it in the General Strike. They feel it now.

Our responsibility in India has grown up over the last 150 years. It is a responsibility for giving the best possible chance for peaceful existence and progress to about three hundred and fifty millions of helpless primitive people who are separated by an almost measureless gulf from the ideas and institutions of the Western world. We now look after them by means of British Officials on fixed salaries who have no axe to grind, who make no profit out of their duties, who are incorruptible, who are impartial between races, creeds and classes, and who are directed by a central Government which in its turn is controlled by the British Parliament based on twenty-nine million electors. It is now proposed to transfer these British responsbilities to an electorate comparatively small and almost entirely illiterate. The Indian Congress and other elements in this agitation represent neither the numbers, the strength nor the virtue of the Indian people. They merely represent those Indians who have acquired a veneer of Western civilisation, and have read all those books about democracy which Europe is now beginning increasingly to discard. There are among them many estimable and clever people, and it has always been and always must be our policy to associate them as much as we possibly can with the machinery of Indian Government. But it would be altogether wrong to entrust the welfare of the great masses to the Indian political classes. That would not be "India for the Indians"; that would only be India for some Indians, and would only be India for a very few Indians. Undoubtedly any such abrogation on our part of our duty would mean that the Indian peoples would be exploited, oppressed and cast down in the scale of the world's affairs as the proletariat of China is cast down in misery to-day. At present the Government of India is responsible to the British Parliament, which is the oldest, the least unwise and the most democratic parliament in the world. To transfer that responsibility to this highly artificial and restricted oligarchy of Indian politicians would be a retrograde act. It would be a shameful act. It would bring grave material evils, both upon India and Great Britain; but it would bring upon Great Britain a moral shame which would challenge for ever the reputation of the British Empire as a valiant and benignant force in the history of mankind.

The faithful discharge of our duty in India is not only a cause, but a symbol. It is the touchstone of our fortunes in the present difficult time. If we cannot do our duty in India, be sure we shall have shown ourselves unworthy to preserve the vast Empire which still centres upon this small island. The same spirit of unimaginative incompetence and weak compromise and supine drift will paralyse trade and business and prevent either financial reorganisation or economic resurgence. What we require to do now is to stand erect and look the world in the face, and do our duty without fear or favour. A decisive opportunity may soon be at hand. Victory may once again reward the Conservative party. Let it be a victory with a real meaning behind it. Let it be a victory which proclaims to all the world that the heart of the Empire is true and that its hand is just–and strong.

OUR DUTY IN INDIA

March 18, 1931

Albert Hall, London

At this moment of crisis for Baldwin, a by-election was taking place in St. George's, Westminster. At one point Baldwin considered resigning his seat and standing as a candidate, but in the event the pro-Baldwin banner was carried by Duff Cooper against an anti-Baldwin candidate vigorously supported by Beaverbrook and Rothermere. The impact of this meeting at the Albert Hall–just outside the constituency–was overshadowed by Baldwin's attack the same evening on the "Press Lords," whom he condemned as seeking "power without responsibility–the prerogative of the harlot throughout the ages." The phrase came from Baldwin's cousin, Rudyard Kipling. It was devastating. Duff Cooper won easily and Baldwin's leadership was preserved.

[Extract] I think it hard that the burden of holding and organising this immense meeting should be thrown upon the Indian Empire Society. One would have thought that if there was one cause in the world which the Conservative party would have hastened to defend, it would be the cause of the British Empire in India. One would have expected that the whole force of the Conservative party machine would have been employed for months past in building up a robust, educated opinion throughout the country, and in rallying all its strongest forces to guard our vital interests. Unhappily all that influence, and it is an enormous influence, has been cast the other way. The Conservative leaders have decided that we are to work with the Socialists, and that we must make our action conform with theirs. We therefore have against us at the present time the official machinery of all the three great parties in the State. We meet under a ban. Every Member of Parliament or Peer who comes here must face the displeasure of the party Whips. Mr. Baldwin has declared that the three-party collusion must continue, and in support of that decision he has appealed to all those sentiments of personal loyalty and partisan feeling which a leader can command. Is it not wonderful in these circumstances, with all this against us, that a few of us should manage to get together here in this hall to-night?

Our fight is hard. It will also be long. We must not expect early success. The forces marshalled against us are too strong. But win or lose, we must do our duty. If the British people are to lose their Indian Empire, they shall do so with their eyes open, and not be led blindfold into a trap. Already in our campaign we have had a measure of success. The movement and awakening of opinion in the Conservative party have already caused concern to our leaders. They feel they have to reckon with resolute forces in the party and far beyond it, who will not be easily quelled. Already they have rejected the plan of sending a three-party delegation out to India for which Lord Irwin pleaded so earnestly. For the moment, therefore, we have a breathing space. The Socialist and subversive enemy have been thrown into disarray by the breakdown of their scheme to entice the Conservatives out to India. They are arranging their forces for a renewed attack. Mr. Gandhi, their supreme hope, is to come to London, as soon as they can persuade him to come, and here in the centre of the Empire he will discuss with British ministers and politicians the best means for breaking it up. But by that time we shall be ready too. We shall not be taken by surprise, as the country was during the Round Table Conference. We are not entirely defenceless or without means of expression. We have behind us the growing strength of Conservative opinion. We have the prospect at no great distance of a Conservative victory. Nothing will turn us from our path, or discourage us from our efforts; and by the time Mr. Gandhi has arrived here to receive the surrender of our Indian Empire, the Conservative party will not be so ready to have its name taken in vain.

What spectacle could be more sorrowful than that of this powerful country casting away with both hands, and up till now almost by general acquiescence, the great inheritance which centuries have gathered? What spectacle could be more strange, more monstrous in its perversity, than to see the Viceroy and the high officials and agents of the Crown in India labouring with all their influence and authority to unite and weave together into a confederacy all the forces adverse and hostile to our rule in India? One after another our friends and the elements on which we ought to rely in India are chilled, baffled and dismissed, and finally even encouraged to band themselves together with those who wish to drive us out of the country. It is a hideous act of self-mutiliation, astounding to every nation in the world. The princes, the Europeans, the Moslems, the Depressed classes, the Anglo-Indians–none of them know what to do nor where to turn in the face of their apparent desertion by Great Britain. Can you wonder that they try in desperation to make what terms are possible with the triumphant Brahmin oligarchy?

I am against this surrender to Gandhi. I am against these conversations and agreements between Lord Irwin and Mr. Gandhi. Gandhi stands for the expulsion of Britain from India. Gandhi stands for the permanent exclusion of British trade from India. Gandhi stands for the substitution of Brahmin domination for British rule in India. You will never be able to come to terms with Gandhi. You have only to read his latest declarations, and compare them with the safeguards for which we are assured the official Conservatives will fight to the end, to see how utterly impossible agreement is. But let me tell you this. If at the sacrifice of every British interest and of all the necessary safeguards and means of preserving peace and progress in India, you come to terms with Gandhi, Gandhi would at that self-same moment cease to count any more in the Indian situation. Already Nehru, his young rival in the Indian Congress, is preparing to supersede him the moment that he has squeezed his last drop from the British lemon. In running after Gandhi and trying to build on Gandhi, in imagining that Mr. Ramsay MacDonald and Mr. Gandhi and Lord Irwin are going to bestow peace and progress upon India, we should be committing ourselves to a crazy dream, with a terrible awakening.

No! Come back from these perilous paths while time and strength remain. Study the report of your own statutory commission headed by Sir John Simon and signed unanimously by the representatives of all the three parties in the State. Let us take that as our starting-point for any extensions we may make of self-government in India. It is very wrong that the vast majority of Conservative electors throughout the country, and the vast majority of all those who are acquainted with and have practical experience of India, and of that enormous mass of patriotic people not attached to any party, should have these vital questions settled over their heads by an agreement or an understanding between the two front benches in the House of Commons, and have their future settled as if they were a lot of sheep. We are told that three-party unity must be preserved at all costs. What does that mean? Up to the present it has only meant one thing, namely, that the Conservative party has had to toe the Socialist line, and has been dragged at the Socialist tail. Here are these Socialists, maintained in office only on sufferance or by intrigue, expecting all other parties to serve them, and to dance to their tune. We are here to-night to say 'No, that shall not be.' We have a right to our own convictions; we are entitled to act in accordance with them. We will certainly make our faith apparent by every means in our power, and in every quarter of the land.

I repudiate the calumny which our opponents level at us that we have no policy for India but repression and force. Do not be deceived by these untruths. Do not be disquieted by exaggerations of the difficulty of maintaining order in India which are spread about for interested motives by the Socialist ministers and their allies. In the whole of the disturbances of the last year–except on the frontier–scarcely a British soldier has been required. Very few people have been killed or severely wounded in the rioting. But how did the most of them get hurt? They got hurt not by the Indian police, but in religious fights between Moslems and Hindus. The great body of expert opinion which is represented upon the Indian Empire Society will support me when I say that a calm, capable, determined Viceroy properly supported from home could maintain peace and tranquillity in India year after year with a tenth of the repressive measures which Lord Irwin in his misguided benevolence has been compelled to employ.

Neither is it true that we have no constructive policy. We take our stand upon views almost universally accepted until a few months ago. We believe that the next forward step is the development of Indian responsibility in the provincial governments of India. Efforts should be made to make them more truly representative of the real needs of the people. Indians should be given ample opportunities to try their hand at giving capable government in the provinces; and meanwhile the central Imperial executive, which is the sole guarantee of impartiality between races, creeds and classes, should preserve its sovereign power intact, and allow no derogation from its responsibility to Parliament. Is that Diehardism? That is the message of the Simon report, unanimously signed by the representatives of the three parties. That is the purport of the alternative scheme submitted a few months ago by the Viceroy himself. . . .

Why is it that the principles of Government and lessons of history which we have learnt in our experience with the great self-governing dominions, which we have learnt in Canada, in South Africa and in Ireland, apply only in a limited degree to India? It is because the problem of Indian government is primarily a technical one. In India far more than in any other community in the world moral, political and economic considerations are outweighed by the importance of technical and administrative apparatus. Here you have nearly three hundred and fifty millions of people, lifted to a civilisation and to a level of peace, order, sanitation and progress far above anything they could possibly have achieved themselves or could maintain. This wonderful fact is due to the guidance and authority of a few thousands of British officials responsible to Parliament who have for generations presided over the development of India. If that authority is injured or destroyed, the whole efficiency of the services, defensive, administrative, medical, hygienic, judicial; railway, irrigation, public works and famine prevention, upon which the Indian masses depend for their culture and progress, will perish with it. India will fall back quite rapidly through the centuries into the barbarism and privations of the Middle Ages. The question at stake is not therefore the gratification of the political aspirations towards self-government of a small number of intellectuals. It is, on the contrary, the practical, technical task of maintaining the peace and life of India by artificial means upon a much higher standard than would otherwise be possible. To let the Indian people fall, as they would, to the level of China, would be a desertion of duty on the part of Great Britain.

But that is not all. To abandon India to the rule of the Brahmins would be an act of cruel and wicked negligence. It would shame for ever those who bore its guilt. These Brahmins who mouth and patter the principles of Western Liberalism, and pose as philosophic and democratic politicians, are the same Brahmins who deny the primary rights of existence to nearly sixty millions of their own fellow countrymen whom they call 'untouchable,' and whom they have by thousands of years of oppression actually taught to accept this sad position. They will not eat with these sixty millions, nor drink with them, nor treat them as human beings. They consider themselves contaminated even by their approach. And then in a moment they turn round and begin chopping logic with John Stuart Mill, or pleading the rights of man with Jean Jacques Rousseau.

While any community, social or religious, endorses such practices and asserts itself resolved to keep sixty millions of fellow countrymen perpetually and eternally in a state of sub-human bondage, we cannot recognise their claim to the title-deeds of democracy. Still less can we hand over to their unfettered sway those helpless millions they despise. Side by side with this Brahmin theocracy and the immense Hindu population–angelic and untouchable castes alike–there dwell in India seventy millions of Moslems, a race of far greater physical vigour and fierceness, armed with a religion which lends itself only too readily to war and conquest. While the Hindu elaborates his argument, the Moslem sharpens his sword. Between these two races and creeds, containing as they do so many gifted and charming beings in all the glory of youth, there is no intermarriage. The gulf is impassable. If you took the antagonisms of

France and Germany, and the antagonisms of Catholics and Protestants, and compounded them and multiplied them ten-fold, you would not equal the division which separates these two races intermingled by scores of millions in the cities and plains of India. But over both of them the impartial rule of Britain has hitherto lifted its appeasing sceptre. Until the Montagu-Chelmsford reforms began to raise the question of local sovereignty and domination, they had got used to dwelling side by side in comparative toleration. But step by step, as it is believed we are going to clear out or be thrust out of India, so this tremendous rivalry and hatred of races springs into life again. It is becoming more acute every day. Were we to wash our hands of all responsibility and divest ourselves of all our powers, as our sentimentalists desire, ferocious civil wars would speedily break out between the Moslems and the Hindus. No one who knows India will dispute this.

But that is not the end. The Brahmins know well that they cannot defend themselves against the Moslems. The Hindus do not possess among their many virtues that of being a fighting race. The whole south of India is peopled with races deserving all earnest solicitude and regard, but incapable of self-defence. It is in the north alone that the fighting races dwell. Bengal, for instance, does not send from her forty-five million inhabitants any soldiers to the native army. The Punjab is [a place where fighting races dwell], on the other hand, and the Pathans, together with the Ghurkas and the Sikhs, who are entirely exceptional sects of Hindus, all dwelling in the north, furnish three-quarters of the entire army in the time of peace, and furnished more than three-quarters of it in time of war. There can be no doubt therefore that the departure of the British from India, which Mr. Gandhi advocates, and which Mr. Nehru demands, would be followed first by a struggle in the North and thereafter by a reconquest of the South by the North, and of the Hindus by the Moslems. This danger has not escaped the crafty foresight of the Brahmins. It is for that reason that they wish to have the control of a British army, or failing that, a white army of janissaries officered, as Mr. Gandhi has suggested, by Germans or other Europeans. They wish to have an effective foreign army, or foreign-organised army, in order to preserve their dominance over the Moslems and their tyranny over their own untouchables. There, is the open plot of which we are in danger of becoming the dupes, and the luckless millions of Indians the victims.

It is our duty to guard those millions from that fate. . . .

There is a more squalid aspect. Hitherto for generations it has been the British policy that no white official should have any interest or profit other than his salary and pension out of Indian administration. All concession-hunters and European adventurers, company-promoters and profit-seekers have been rigorously barred and banned. But now that there is spread through India the belief that we are a broken, bankrupt, played-out power, and that our rule is going to pass away and be transferred in the name of the majority to the Brahmin sect, all sorts of greedy appetites have been excited, and many itching fingers are stretching and scratching at the vast pillage of a derelict Empire. I read in the *Times* newspaper, in the *Times* mind you, only last week of the crowd of rich Bombay merchants and millionaire millowners, millionaires on sweated labour, who surround Mr. Gandhi, the saint, the lawyer, Lord Irwin's dear colleague and companion. What are they doing there, these men, and what is he doing in their houses? They are making arrangements that the greatest bluff, the greatest humbug and the greatest betrayal shall be followed by the greatest ramp. Nepotism, back-scratching, graft and corruption in every form will be the handmaidens of a Brahmin domination. Far rather would I see every Englishman quit the country, every soldier, every civil servant embark at Bombay, than that we should remain clutching on to the control of foreign relations and begging for trading facilities, while all the time we were the mere cloak of dishonour and oppression.

If you were to put these facts, hard, solid indigestible facts, before Mr. Ramsay MacDonald or Mr. Wedgwood Benn, or Sir Herbert Samuel, they would probably reply by pointing to the follies of Lord North in the American revolution, to the achievements of Lord Durham in Canada, or to what has happened in South Africa or in Ireland. All the Socialists and some of the Liberals, together with, I am sorry to say, the official Conservatives, have got these arguments on the tip of their tongue. They represent all of us and the millions who think with us, and the instructed Anglo-Indian administrators on whose advice we rely, as being mere dullards and reactionaries who have never been able to move with the age, or understand modern ideas. *We* are a sort of inferior race mentally deficient, composed principally of colonels and other undesirables who have fought for Britain. *They* are the sole possessors and monopolists of the spirit and of the message of our generation. But we do not depend on colonels—though why Conservatives should sneer at an honoured rank in the British army I cannot tell—we depend on facts. We depend on the private soldiers of the British democracy. We place our trust in the loyal heart of Britain. Our faith is founded upon the rock of the wage-earning population of this island which has never yet been appealed to, by duty and chivalry, in vain.

These great issues which arise from time to time in our history are never decided by the party caucuses. They are decided by the conscience and the spirit of the mass of the British people. It is upon the simple faith and profound unerring instinct of the British people, never yet found wanting in a crisis, that we must put our trust. We are deliberately trying to tell our story to the British masses, to the plain and simple folk to whom the fame of the British Empire is ever dear. In assailing the moral duty of Great Britain in India, the Socialist Government and all who aid and abet Mr. Ramsay Macdonald and his Socialist Government, or make their path smooth, will find they have stumbled upon a sleeping giant who, when he arises, will tread with dauntless steps the path of justice and of honour.

"THE MARCH OF EVENTS"

March 26, 1931

Constitutional Club, London

Following his crushing defeat at St. George's, Westminster, Beaverbrook called off his anti-Baldwin campaign. In India, Gandhi stopped the civil disobedience campaign and entered into serious negotiations with Irwin. Meanwhile, the Labour Government was at the beginning of the "economic blizzard" which eventually brought it down.

[Extract] Things are not going well. We have had two shameful and disastrous years. They have been years in which we have not merely been standing still; we have been galloping down the slope. They have been years in which even deeper anxieties have entered our hearts than we felt in the darkest days of the Great War. No great country is maltreating itself as we are and doing less justice to itself. Look where you will, on the continent of Europe or across the Atlantic, you will see our competitors, some ready to be our successors, in many of the great fields in which we have shone, concentrated upon the problems of marshalling their strength and defending with vigour their national interests. Here a sort of moral palsy seems to have descended upon us. We seem to be afraid to call our souls our own. The Socialist minority Government is only kept in being by all kinds of weaknesses and divergences among the strong forces which have hitherto maintained the life of the country.

But, wherever you may look, the worst scene of Socialist mismanagement and depredation is in their conduct and administration of our Indian Empire. There is the great target which Conservatives all over the country should steadily and remorselessly fire upon. I cannot accept the suggestion that we ought to keep India out of party politics, if it only means we are going to lose India with decorum and dignity. To lose India would be far worse than to bring it into party politics. How else are those who do not agree with what has been done by the Socialist Government in India to make their point of view effective except by public speech and action? I do not intend to mince my words. I wish to make it perfectly clear I am going to attack the Socialist record and policy in India. Nothing will turn me from it, and I have cheerfully and gladly put out of my mind all idea of public office. I intend to fight this question during the next two or three years, in which it will be the culminating issue in British politics, without regard to any aspect but the merits.

I am told I am alone among men who have held high public office in this country in the view I take about the Indian policy. If that were so it would be a great honour for me, because I should be left alone to plead a majestic cause, and I should be left alone to represent the opinions of many millions of British men and women in every party who are deeply concerned at the trend of events in the East. If I am alone I am going to receive shortly an ally–a very powerful ally–an ally whom I dread–an ally with a sombre title–his title is *THE MARCH OF EVENTS*. The march of events in India will be grim and may possibly be rapid. You have only to read your papers to-day to see how the situation there is steadily darkening. . . .

Gandhi has resolved, and those who work behind him and through him are still more resolved, to bring practically all British importations, certainly all Lancashire importations, to an absolute end. That spells the doom of Lancashire. The coastwise trade, the great enterprises and business institutions which we have founded in India, are all in succession to be swept away. As for the hundreds of millions of loans which we have advanced to create the railways and irrigation services and public works of India, in consequence of which the Indian population has increased by 30,000,000 in the last twenty years, all this is in jeopardy. Unless you are prepared to defend your rights and interests in India, you will be stripped of every vestige you possess and expelled with ignominy from its shores.

Wednesday's massacres at Cawnpore, a name of evil import, are a portent.

Because it is believed that we are about to leave the country, the struggle for power is now beginning between the Moslems and Hindus. A bloody riot broke out in which more than two hundred people lost their lives with many hundreds wounded, in which women and children were butchered in circumstances of bestial barbarity, their mutilated violated bodies strewing the streets for days. The British troops are now pacifying and calming the terrified and infuriated populace. But the feud is only at its beginning.

Let the Conservative party regain its freedom. Let there be no more co-operation with the Socialists. First of all I am asking that we should regain our full discretionary power. We must be free to rouse the people of our country to the approaching peril and to get our own forces into line.

You are in favour of tariffs. They are necessary on economic and financial grounds. But still more are they necessary as a part of a reassertion of our will to live and reign in the modern world. They are only a part. There is no use in uniting the Empire by trade preferences and losing India. The loss of India would destroy all that we have built up. Surely our generation which sent its brothers and sons and watched its fathers march to France and Flanders should be the last to be guilty of such a failure. We must weave together the strong forces in our island which have carried us through the tribulations of the past and which united are invincible.

A venerable member of the Conservative Party, one of my father's friends–in fact at one dramatic moment his only friend, Mr. Arthur Baumann–penned the other day some sentences with which I will now end. 'Surely,' he wrote, 'an effort should be made to save his kingdom for the Emperor of India. Let us set up a standard around which the brave and the loyal can rally. More than that we cannot do. The rest is in the hands of God.'

DISARMAMENT AND EUROPE

June 29, 1931

House of Commons

This prophetic speech attracted little attention at the time it was delivered, but stated a theme which was to be repeated often in the next eight years.

[Extract] . . . There has been one result of this great and beneficent movement for Disarmament. One nation has disarmed. One nation has disarmed to such an extent–it is admitted on both sides–that she has become extremely and dangerously vulnerable. We alone have disarmed. The figures which the Prime Minister recited to-day–an enormous structure of figures–show not only the passing of British sea power, but they show the descent of this country into a condition of unpreparedness, and but for political considerations of insecurity, such as we have never previously experienced. We have abandoned our naval supremacy. We have abandoned parity with the next strongest Power. We are, as I shall try very briefly to indicate to the Committee, incapable of maintaining our food supply and our oil supply in certain contingencies. Our Air Force is vastly inferior to that of our nearest neighbour—luckily a good friend of ours. Our Army was never measured against the armies of the Continent. Our Army was never more than a glorified police force to aid in preserving the tranquility of one-fifth of the human race, and as such it has been cut to the bone. . . .

These are the circumstances in which the Disarmament Conference of 1932 is to be held. The Foreign Secretary will be there, no doubt, a very competent chairman, unless any local troubles should rob Europe of his services in the interval, but his task will indeed be attended, as my hon. Friend who spoke from these benches has said, by difficulty and delicacy. All that line of small new States from the Baltic to the Black Sea are in lively apprehension of Russia. Finland, Estonia, Lithuania, Latvia, Poland and Rumania—every one is in great fear and anxiety about its neighbour. All of them have been carved in whole or in part out of the Russia of the Tsars. They have won their independence at the conclusion of the War, or they have won territory at the conclusion of the War. All are in fear of Russian propaganda or of Russian military force. All are strongly anti-Communist. They have gone through great internal stress and tension, and they have built themselves up on a Radical, democratic antithesis to Communism. As such, they are specially obnoxious to the ideals and interests of the mighty Power which lies to the eastward. All these States have universal military service; they are all heavily armed, so far as they can afford to pay for it. They all look to each other for mutual aid. They all look to France for guidance, and they all consider—I am bound to state these facts to the Committee, and I have many years of thought and study behind me—the French Army their ultimate guarantee. You may say, in fact, that the French Army to all these small States and their independence and liberty, plays the same sort of part that the British Navy in the days of its power did to the small countries and liberties of Europe. Sermons addressed to these States at the conference will no doubt be received with politeness when they come from people whom one knows to be entirely well-meaning.

But Communism and Russia are not to these countries the kind of topics they are to us, where they can be made a matter of mockery. The whole structure of these States is rent with a conflict that is proceeding, persecution of Communism and counter-attacks on all these Governments, and beyond the frontier there is always the sense of this enormous mass which may at any time be set against them. [An Hon. Member: "What about the White Army?"] That is not, I think, a very fertile contribution. Sermons and exhortations are all very well, but I was very glad to hear from various speakers this afternoon that it is realised this kind of advice and moral lecture may be pushed too far when it comes from countries not in anything like the same danger as those to whom the exhortation is addressed. Coming from England, we at least can say—as has been proved to-day—that we are setting an example, that we have exposed ourselves to real danger, that we are in a position of insecurity, and that we have done that in our desire to set an example. But, still, our dangers are very far off. Coming from the United States, such lectures would not, I think, be well received, because she is not only protected by two great oceans, but, since the War, has increased her armaments more than any other country. I am very glad the gist and tone of the Prime Minister's speech were such as to indicate we were not going to press our views unduly upon this very delicate combination of countries with which we shall be brought in contact next year.

I was, indeed, delighted to hear the Prime Minister making an appeal, addressed to his own party, to be fair to France. The Prime Minister, naturally, has to veil everything he says, but the significance of the few words he dropped during the latter part of his speech in regard to recognising the anxieties and position of France were, I venture to think, much more important than all those well-turned phrases which expressed sentiments which will never miss their proper reception of cheers in this Island. That is the most important part in the concluding portion of the Prime Minister's speech. It is not in the immediate interest of European peace that the French army should be seriously weakened. It is certainly not in British interests to antagonise France, or all these small States associated with France, by pressing unreasonably for its reduction. We may well think France is over-insured, but it is certain that if we press at this conference too heavily in that direction, we shall not succeed in improving the relations between the countries. I must say that the French Army at the present moment is a stabilising factor, and one of the strongest, apart from the general hatred and fear of war. We should beware of deranging the situation which exists. It is not satisfactory, but it is one that might easily be replaced by a worse situation. The sudden disappearance or weakening of that factor of stability, the unquestioned superiority of French military power, might open floodgates of measureless consequence in Europe at the present time, might break the dyke and

"Let the boundless deep
Down upon far-off cities while they dance–
Or dream."

Apart from that, it would be the highest imprudence for our Government to cast reflections or disturb the good relations which prevail between us and the French. . . .

I venture to submit to the Committee that in my judgment, whatever these dangers may be, whether you rate them high or low, they will be seriously aggravated if at any time there should be any approximation of military strength between Germany and France. In this connection we must not forget that the man-power of Germany, the contingent of youth arriving at the military age each year, is at the present moment double that of France. I am quite certain that the whole situation would become infinitely more critical if there were at any time an approximation of military power between those two countries. Thirdly, there is our own influence that we have to consider. We must use of our influence to modify the age-long antagonisms, as we have done, between Germany and France. We may have to use our authority in the discharge of our obligations under the Locarno Treaty, and our power to play our part will be deeply, and perhaps fatally, affected if we have not a sense of safety and security in regard to our naval defence and in regard to the supplies on which we live and which must come in through the narrow seas.

Those are the . . . considerations which I would venture to put before the Committee. I would not wish it to be supposed that I am an alarmist, or foresee another great war in our lifetime. I am as anxious as any Member in this House to work my utmost to keep us out of war, and, even if the peace should be broken by others, to prevent our being involved in the struggle, and I do not believe that, if we act with wisdom and prudence, we need be drawn into another war. But, believe me, much more is required than good will and fine sentiments to put us in a satisfactory position. We must be safe, as we are not safe now. England's hour of weakness is Europe's hour of danger. It was so in 1914, and it may be so again. Therefore, I recommend to the Committee, first of all, that we regain at the earliest moment our naval freedom to secure our food supplies in the narrow seas, and, consequently, regain our independence from European entanglements and our free judgment in regard to any issue which may arise and which may be inseparable from the secure position of our vital food supplies. Secondly, I greatly welcome the statement of the Prime Minister that we shall not seek to weaken unduly the power of France on land, and thus expose ourselves to a dangerous rebuff. Lastly, we must, simultaneously with these other two processes, ceaselessly endeavour to bring France and Germany together for a settlement of outstanding disputes and grievances. If all of these three policies—not any one of them will suffice, but, if all of these three policies are pursued at the same time, soberly, sincerely and skilfully, then we shall have done our best to contribute towards the maintenance of the peace of the world, and there is as yet no reason why we should not succeed.

THE FINANCIAL SITUATION

September 29, 1931

Liverpool

In August 1931 the Labour Government, in complex circumstances which have been often described but which still remain confused, broke asunder on the issue of the resolution of the urgent economic crisis. Ramsay MacDonald formed a National Government with Baldwin. Churchill was excluded from the Administration. It was curious that it was Churchill (in the House of Commons, September 8) who made the first public appeal for a General Election to strengthen the National Government and introduce Protection—but it was a curious period.

Snowden's emergency Budget increased income tax to five shillings on the pound, and made economies in government expenditure of £70 million. All state employees had their salaries reduced, including the armed services.

On September 15 there occurred the so-called "Invergordon Mutiny," when the sailors of the Atlantic fleet, based at Invergordon, refused duty in protest against the loss of pay, which was one feature of Snowden's emergency Budget. The matter was resolved, but on September 21 the Gold Standard was suspended.

[Extract] . . . No Government can exist without a purpose and a plan. When the present Government was formed it had a purpose—to preserve the gold standard—and it had a plan—to balance the Budget; but the gold standard has gone and the balancing of the Budget will be finished next week. After that the Government have neither purpose nor plan, and a Government without purpose or plan is a dead thing.

The question of the moment is whether this Parliament and Government can find a new purpose and a new plan to give it a new lease of life, or must it die and must we out of new birth throes find new agencies to serve our bitter, grave, and urgent needs. There is no escape from this question, however unwelcome it may be. No vain regrets, no shrinking from the ordeal, no loud trumpeting will avail. This Parliament must act or go. Is there, then, any new purpose or plan upon which this Parliament can act unitedly, with sincerity and vigour?

There is assuredly a purpose, a policy, a plan which is in all your minds. If pursued soberly and earnestly, without personal prejudice or party bias, it would give an honourable span of life to the present House of Commons. I mean, of course, a measure of protection for British industry and agriculture.

A tariff is not a quick or quack remedy for all our ills. It is only one part of a national policy; but presented as a necessary step in national self-regeneration, as a practical business measure, as a measure of Imperial reconstruction, it may become a bond of union for all the strongest forces in the country.

There is a need to find new revenue to mitigate the effect of the Budget. There is a need to balance healthily our exports and imports. There is a need to stimulate our flagging industries. Most of all, there is a need to rouse the spirit of Britain, to restore her self-confidence and resolution, to assert her authority and rights among the nations, to regather around the Mother Island the power and resources of the Empire. If this Parliament is incapable of giving any satisfaction to these needs, the sooner it is gone the better. (Loud cheers.)

I was brought up in the days of Queen Victoria. I saw our country at the head of the world; leader in so many spheres of social, industrial, and Imperial progress, sedate, serene, envied and honoured by all. I cannot bear now to see those standards dimmed. When I think of what we did in the Great War I ask myself, with millions of English folk: what have we done to lose our glories, and what can we do to bring them back? (Cheers.)

The greatness and prosperity of Britain has depended on three great glories and breadwinners—the Navy and Mercantile Marine, the Empire of India and the East, and the City of London. Without those it would have been impossible to maintain those superior standards of life and labour which have so long raised this country above all others in the world. The Socialist movement, which has grown so powerful in this century, attacked all three policies. It menaces our sea power, it undermines our Indian Empire, it has sapped the confidence of the world in the City of London.

If an election should come upon us, the duty of every loyal-hearted man and woman is plain—namely, to root out from Parliament all those subversive forces which have worn down the strength of Britain. . . .

We must rebuild, consolidate. We must join hands with one another in comradeship and effort to improve our position and even to hold what is left. We must be strong and self-reliant, and we must have a stronger system of government.

We must have a Parliament containing a large majority of members united in a resolve to lift our country from the ruts and quagmires into which it has fallen. I have asked myself, as you may have done no doubt, whether the present Parliament can achieve such a task, and whether the present National Government would be strong enough to take the necessary measures.

THE NEW PARLIAMENT

October 30, 1931

Constituency Meeting, Chingford

Churchill's arguments for an immediate General Election were shared by the leading Conservatives. Parliament was dissolved on October 7, and MacDonald and Baldwin appealed for "a doctor's mandate." With Labour in chaos and the Liberals in shambles, the result was not difficult to foresee.

The General Election was a landslide for the Conservatives and their Labour and Liberal allies, winning 521 seats. Labour was reduced to 52; the Liberals to 33. Lloyd George's "party" now consisted of 4. Of the former Labour Cabinet only Lansbury retained his seat.

[Extract] . . . The election result is a marvellous expression of the love which the British people have for their country, and for its fame and power. The condemnation of the foreign-made doctrines of Socialism is overwhelming. Foreign nations who thought our day was done have now their answer.

Universal suffrage has sent the largest majority of Tory members to Parliament which has ever been dreamed of. It is our national well-being and our ancient power which the nation wishes to see restored, and the electors have called into being a free Parliament to do it. The new Parliament is free as no Parliament for generations has been free. The members have appealed to their constituents for a free hand. They have been granted it in overflowing measure.

I hope that the new Parliament will be a true Council of State and that it will take broad and long views of the public interest. Opinion must be freely and fearlessly expressed, and the conclusions of the majority of the House, at every stage, must rule the policy of the State. The responsibilities which weigh upon the Government are even more intense than those which rest upon the House of Commons. They must be a Government of action and of clear-cut policies. They must pronounce without hesitation upon the fiscal problem, the currency problem, the Indian problem, and the Imperial problem. Upon the true solution of these high matters the future of Great Britain depends.

This is no time for weak compromises or ambiguous formulas designed to promote a semblance of unity among individual politicians. An integrity of thought and policy should inspire the Government and sustain the new House of Commons if we are to be worthy of your trust. If this is not forthcoming and a mere amalgam of irreconcilable opinions is produced, the House will have to take charge of the situation itself and produce harmonious and effective combinations.

The Conservative Party has made great sacrifices. It would be well advised at this juncture to encourage its allies to set their feet firmly on the path of national and Imperial regeneration. It would be far better if the measures which we all know are requisite to revive our national strength could be taken upon an authority greater than that of any single party. If they are not taken, then the inalienable responsibilities of the majority of the new Parliament will have to be asserted, and that Parliament will continue to enjoy its plenary powers.

DISARMAMENT

May 13, 1932

House of Commons

Ministers were still eagerly pursuing comprehensive disarmament agreements with limited success but strong public support. Churchill struck a more skeptical and less popular note.

[Extract] I could not bring myself altogether to disagree with the Leader of the Opposition when he said that he considered that the speech of my right hon. Friend the Foreign Secretary [Sir John Simon] was depressing and disappointing, certainly to those who have attached high hopes to Disarmament Conferences, and to the Conferences which are now proceeding. But when I listened to the speech of the Leader of the Opposition, to his admirable sentiments and his humane expressions, I could not see that, if he were at Geneva himself in the next few weeks, when, as the Foreign Secretary has said, these serious practical issues are going to arise, he would add any real forward impulse to the decisions on these issues. It is just because there is this very great difference—I am sorry that there should be—between the public professions, the warm sentiments which are expressed on all sides by political leaders on the one hand, and the actual forces which influence the decisions of Governments on the other—it is just because of this great gulf and division that the Conference on Disarmament has now got into a condition which I must regard as not only disappointing, but, from many points of view, discreditable. . . .

I come now to the proposals of qualitative disarmament about which my right hon. Friend was so very insistent. He told us that it was difficult to divide weapons into offensive and defensive categories. It certainly is, because almost every conceivable weapon may be used either in defence or offence; it all depends upon the circumstances; and every weapon, whether offensive or defensive, may be used either by an aggressor or by the innocent victim of his assault. My right hon. Friend said that he wished to make it more difficult for the invader, and for that reason, I gather, heavy guns, tanks and poison gas are to be relegated to the evil category of offensive weapons. The invasion of France by Germany in 1914 reached its climax without the employment of any of these weapons at all. The heavy gun is to be described as an offensive weapon. It is all right in a fortress; there it is virtuous and pacific in its character; but bring it out into the field–and, of course, if it were needed it would be brought out into the field–and it immediately becomes naughty, peccant, militaristic, and has to be placed under the ban of civilisation. Take the tank. The Germans, having invaded France, entrenched themselves; and in a couple of years they shot down 1,500,000 French and British soldiers who were trying to free the soil of France. The tank was invented to overcome the fire of machine guns with which the Germans were maintaining themselves in France, and it did save a lot of life in the process of eventually clearing the soil of the invader. Now, apparently, the machine gun, which was the German weapon for holding on to 13 provinces of France, is to be the virtuous, defensive machine gun, and the tank, which was the means by which these lives were saved, is to be placed again under the censure and obloquy of all just and righteous men.

There is also the question of gas. Nothing could be more repugnant to our feelings than the use of poison gas, but there is no logic at all behind the argument that suggests that it is quite proper in war to lay a man low with high explosive shell, fragments of which inflict poisonous and festering wounds, and altogether immoral to give him a burn with corrosive gas or make him cough and sneeze or otherwise suffer through his respiratory organs. There is no logical distinction between the two. A great many of our friends are here to-day because they were fired at by German gas shells, which inflicted minor injuries upon them. Had it been high explosive shell, they would in all human probability have been killed. The whole subject of war is, beyond all words, horrible, and the nations are filled with the deepest loathing of it, but, if wars are going to take place, it is by no means certain that the introduction of chemical warfare is going to make them more horrible than they have been. The attitude of the British Government has always been to abhor the employment of poison gas. As I understand it, our only procedure is to keep alive such means of steadying this subject as shall not put us at a hopeless disadvantage if, by any chance, it were used against us by other people.

Then there is the question of submarines, which I wish had never been discovered or invented. Everyone who has been connected with the Royal Navy or the Admiralty would take that view. But a small country, with seaport towns within range of bombardment from the sea, feels very differently about having two or three submarines to keep the bombarding squadrons at a respectful distance.

I have only gone into these details in order to try to show the House how very absurd is this attempt to distinguish between offensive and defensive weapons and how little prospect there is of any fruitful agreement being reached upon it. These illustrations that I have given will be multiplied a hundredfold when the naval, military and air experts on the committees to whom this subject is to be remitted get to work. I have not the slightest doubt that nothing will emerge from their deliberations, which no doubt will be prolonged, except agreements to differ in one form or another. I think a much truer line of classification might have been drawn if the Conference of all these nations at Geneva set itself to ban the use of weapons which tend to be indiscriminate in their action and whose use entails death and wounds, not merely to the combatants in the fighting zones but to the civil population, men, women and children, far removed from those areas. There, indeed, it seems to me would be a direction in which the united nations assembled at Geneva might advance with hope.

It may be said that in war no such conventions would be respected, and very few were respected in the Great War. We hope there will be no other wars, but, even if there are wars in the future, we need not assume that they will be world wars involving all the Powers of the world, with no external Powers to impose a restraint upon the passions of the belligerents or to judge of the merits of their cause. I do not at all despair of building up strong conventions and conceptions held by the great nations of the world against the use of weapons which fall upon enormous masses of non-combatant persons. Still more should I like to raise my voice in abhorrence of the idea, now almost accepted among so many leading authorities in different countries, that the bombing of open towns and the wholesale destruction of civilian life is compatible with any civilised decency. We are all allowing ourselves to be led step by step into contemplating such hideous episodes as part of the ordinary give and take of a war, should a war ever come.

I submit to the House that this attempt to employ the energies of Geneva upon discriminating between offensive and defensive weapons will only lead to rigmarole and delay and is in itself a silly expedient and that a much truer method would be to endeavour to focus and marshal opinion upon the lines of preventing the indiscriminate use of weapons upon non-combatant and civilian populations. I think the adoption of such topics for discussion really casts a certain air of insincerity over the proceedings at Geneva. I do not believe any of the naval or military experts who meet to discuss these matters will have any doubt whatever that no practical advantage can be gained. As for the French scheme of security, that certainly is a logical proposition, and I do not know whether, in a quite different world from that in which we live, the relegation of the air arm to a central police force might not conceivably be a means of providing a higher organisation of society than anything that we can achieve, but, of course, in the present circumstances it is obviously impossible that such a development should take place. Here, again, is another one of these very complicated propositions which have been put forward, the only purpose of which it would seem is to afford for those 53 nations who have arrived together to discuss Disarmament some provender upon which they could sustain themselves.

If you wish for Disarmament, it will be necessary to go to the political and economic causes which lie behind the maintenance of armies and navies. There are very serious political and economic dangers at the present time, and antagonisms which are by no means assuaged. I should very much regret to see any approximation in military strength between Germany and France. Those who speak of that as though it were right, or even a mere question of fair dealing, altogether underrate the gravity of the European situation. I would say to those who would like to see Germany and France on an equal footing in armaments: "Do you wish for war?" For my part, I earnestly hope that no such approximation will take place during my lifetime or in that of my children. To say that is not in the least to imply any want of regard or admiration for the great qualities of the German people, but I am sure that the thesis that they should be placed in an equal military position to France is one which, if it ever emerged in practice, would bring us to within practical distance of almost measureless calamity. . . .

Although I should like to see the foundation of European peace raised upon a more moral basis, I am very anxious that the present foundation should not be deranged until at any rate we have built up something satisfactory in its place. I hope and trust that the right hon. Gentleman the Foreign Secretary will continue his pious labours at Geneva, and that he will be able at some future date to give us a more favourable account of them. For my part, I shall continue to trust to the strong and ceaseless economic pressure of expense which is weighing upon all countries, to the growth of a greater confidence which a long peace must ensure, and to the patient and skilful removal of the political causes of antagonism which a wise foreign policy should eventually achieve.

REPARATIONS ABANDONED

July 11, 1932

House of Commons

The Lausanne Conference in effect ended the payment of German reparations. In this speech Churchill made reference, for the first time, to the dramatic rise of Adolph Hitler in Germany.

[Extract] I cannot associate myself with the Socialist Opposition in applauding the settlement of Lausanne or joining in the apparent jubilation which that event has caused. Of course, anything which removes friction between Germany and France is to the good, and I congratulate the Prime Minister [Mr. J. Ramsay MacDonald] on that. But it seems to me that it is Germany which is most to be felicitated upon what has taken place. Within less than fifteen years of the Great War Germany has been virtually freed from all burden of repairing the awful injuries which she wrought upon her neighbors. True, there are 3,000,000,000 marks which are to be payable by Germany, but I notice that Herr Hitler, who is the moving impulse behind the German Government and may be more than that very soon, took occasion to state yesterday that within a few months that amount would not be worth three marks. That is an appalling statement to be made while the ink is yet damp upon the parchment of the Treaty. Therefore I say that Germany has been virtually freed from all reparations.

What, then, has become of the Carthaginian peace of which we used to hear so much? That has gone. Some of it may have been written down in the Versailles Treaty, but its clauses have never been put into operation. There has been no Carthaginian peace. Neither has there been any bleeding of Germany white by the conquerors. The exact opposite has taken place. The loans which Britain and the United States particularly, and also other countries, have poured into the lap of Germany since the firing stopped, far exceed the sum of reparations which she had paid; indeed, they have been nearly double. If the plight of Germany is hard—and the plight of every country is hard at the present time—it is not because there has been any drain of her life's blood or of valuable commodities from Germany to the victors. On the contrary, the tide has flowed the other way. It is Germany that has received an infusion of blood from the nations with whom she went to war and by whom she was decisively defeated. Even these loans, which are almost double the payments Germany has made in reparations, are now in jeopardy. They are subject to a moratorium.

Let me give one striking instance which came to my notice when I was crossing the Atlantic Ocean. We and America took under the Peace Treaty three great liners from Germany. The Germans surrendered them at a valuation and then borrowed the money to build two very much better ones. They immediately captured the Blue Riband of the Atlantic, and they have it still. Now the loans with which the Germans built these ships are subject to a moratorium, while we are unable to go on with our new Cunarder because of our financial crisis. That is typical of what I mean when I say that Germany has not nearly so much reason to complain as some people suppose.

Absolved from all the burden of reparations, with a moratorium upon all commercial debts, with her factories equipped to the very latest point of science by British and American money, freed from internal debt, mortgages, fixed charges, debentures and so forth, by the original flight from the mark, Germany only awaits trade revival to gain an immense mercantile ascendancy throughout the world. I think that we are entitled to felicitate Germany on what has taken place, and I am sorry to see, as far as any information has reached us, that her only reaction is to ask for more. . . .

EUROPEAN DANGERS

November 23, 1932

House of Commons

As the European scene darkened, Churchill turned his attention away from India to deliver this, the first of a series of warnings which went unheeded.

[Extract] . . . Everything which has happened since July last shows how unwise it was to bring the Lausanne Conference to a conclusion, and to trumpet its results all round the globe. If we look back on those July days, when the Prime Minister [Mr. Ramsay MacDonald] was welcomed in triumph on his return, with all the Cabinet and Under-Secretaries drawn up like a row of Grenadiers of varying sizes at the railway-station, we can see how absurd were the claims which were then advanced that Lausanne had "saved Europe," and that a "new era" had opened for the world. There is quite a lot still to be done in Europe, and for many people it is very much the same old era in the world.

There is no doubt whatever that harm was done to the prospect of the settlement of the War debts by what happened at Lausanne. I ventured to warn the Government before this happened, in May or June of last year, of the extreme unwisdom of making the Debt Settlement an issue at the American elections. The consequences of Lausanne have been to force all the candidates for Congress and the Senate, on both sides of politics, to give specific pledges and to make definite declarations upon this subject. We all know what happens at elections.

If the House will be persuaded by me they will now embark upon a short voyage over a placid lake and come from Lausanne to Geneva. What a scene awaits them there! They will walk through streets guarded by machine-guns, whose pavements are newly stained with blood—I presume because of the conscientious scruples which prevented the use of the perfectly harmless tear gas—and they will enter those halls of debate where, with a persistency which rivals in duration the siege of Troy, the nations are pursuing the question of disarmament. [Editor's Note: On November 9, 1932, Swiss troops fired on Communist rioters in Geneva. Thirteen people were killed and seventy wounded.] It is a melancholy scene. I have sympathy with, and respect for, the well-meaning, loyal-hearted people who make up the League of Nations Union in this country, but what impresses me most about them is their long-suffering and inexhaustible gullibility. Any scheme of any kind for disarmament put forward by any country, so long as it is surrounded by suitable phraseology, is hailed by them, and the speeches are cheered, and those who speak gain the meed of their applause. Why do they not look down beneath the surface of European affairs to the iron realities which lie beneath? They would then see that France does not stand alone in Europe. France does not speak for herself alone when she speaks at Geneva. France is the head of a system of states, some large, others minor, including Belgium, Poland, Rumania, Czechoslovakia and Yugoslavia, comprising many millions of human beings, all of whom depend for their frontiers upon the existence of the present Peace Treaties, good or bad, all of whom are armed and organized to defend themselves and to defend their rights, and all of whom look to France and the French Army in very much the same sort of way as small nations before the War used to look to the British Navy in the days of its power. That is one side of the picture.

On the other side there is Germany, the same mighty Germany which so recently withstood almost the world in arms; Germany which resisted with such formidable capacity that it took between two and three Allied lives to take one German life in the four years of the Great War; Germany which has also allies, friends and associates in her train, powerful nations, who consider their politics as associated to some extent with hers; Germany whose annual quota of youth reaching the military age is already nearly double the youth of France; Germany where the Parliamentary system and the safeguards of the Parliamentary system which we used to be taught to rely upon after the Great War are in abeyance. I do not know where Germany's Parliamentary system stands today, but certainly military men are in control of the essentials.

Germany has paid since the War an indemnity of about one thousand millions sterling, but she has borrowed in the same time about two thousand millions sterling with which to pay that indemnity and to equip her factories. Her territories have been evacuated long before the stipulated time–I rejoice in it–and now she has been by Lausanne virtually freed from all those reparations which had been claimed from her by the nations whose territories have been devastated in the War, or whose prosperity, like ours, has been gravely undermined by the War. At the same time, her commercial debts may well prove ultimately to be irrecoverable. I am making no indictment of Germany. I have respect and admiration for the Germans, and desire that we should live on terms of good feeling and fruitful relations with them; but we must look at the fact that every concession which has been made–many concessions have been made, and many more will be made and ought to be made–has been followed immediately by a fresh demand.

Now the demand is that Germany should be allowed to rearm. Do not delude yourselves. Do not let His Majesty's Government believe–I am sure they do not believe–that all that Germany is asking for is equal status. I believe the refined term now is equal qualitative status, or, as an alternative, equal quantitative status by indefinitely deferred stages. That is not what Germany is seeking. All these bands of sturdy Teutonic youths, marching through the streets and roads of Germany, with the light of desire in their eyes to suffer for their Fatherland, are not looking for status. They are looking for weapons, and, when they have the weapons, believe me they will then ask for the return of lost territories and lost colonies, and when that demand is made it cannot fail to shake and possibly shatter to their foundations every one of the countries I have mentioned, and some other countries I have not mentioned.

Besides Germany, there is Russia. Russia has made herself an Ishmael among the nations, but she is one of the most titanic factors in the economy and in the diplomacy of the world. Russia, with her enormous, rapidly increasing armaments, with her tremendous development of poison gas, aeroplanes, tanks and every kind of forbidden fruit; Russia, with her limitless man-power and her corrosive hatreds, weighs heavily upon a whole line of countries, some small, others considerable, from the Baltic to the Black Sea, all situated adjacent to Russian territory. These countries have newly gained their independence. Their independence and nationhood are sacred to them, and we must never forget that most of them have been carved, in whole or in part, out of the old Russian Empire, the Russian Empire of Peter the Great and Catherine the Great. In some cases these countries are also in deep anxiety about Germany.

I am sure that I have not overdrawn the picture. I have marshalled the facts, but I have not overdrawn the picture. Can we wonder, can any reasonable, fair-minded, peace-loving person wonder, in the circumstances, that there is fear in Europe, and, behind the fear, the precautions, perhaps in some cases exaggerated precautions, which fear excites? We in these islands, with our heavy burdens and with our wide Imperial responsibilities, ought to be very careful not to meddle improvidently or beyond our station, beyond our proportionate stake, in this tremendous European structure. If we were to derange the existing foundations, based on force though they may be, we might easily bring about the very catastrophe that most of all we desire to avert. What would happen to us then? No one can predict. But if by the part we had played in European affairs we had precipitated such a catastrophe, then I think our honour might be engaged beyond the limitations which our treaties and agreements prescribe.

We must not forget, and Europe and the United States must not forget, that we have disarmed. Alone among the nations we have disarmed while others have rearmed, and we must not be expected to undertake a part larger than it is in our capacity to make good. . . .

Coming more closely to Geneva, I should like to say that I have watched the Disarmament Conferences which have now been going on for many years, and I have formed certain opinions about them. Disarmament divides itself into disarmament by scale and disarmament by ratio. Disarmament by scale is not so important, but disarmament by ratio, the altering of the relative positions of nations, is the part of the problem which excites the most intense anxiety and even passion. I have formed the opinion that none of the nations concerned in the Disarmament Conferences except Great Britain has been prepared willingly to alter to its own disadvantage its ratio of armed strength. I agree that there have been diminutions of armaments, but they have largely been produced, as they always will be produced, by the pressure of economic and political facts in a time when there is peace; and I do not think that any of these nations have intended to do anything which would destroy the status quo; and certainly they are not willing to impair their factor of safety. I prefer the expression "factor of safety" to another expression which has been used–insurance. Insurance is not a good word, because it does nothing to ward off a danger, and it only compensates, or attempts to compensate, after the evil or misfortune has occurred. "Factor of safety" is the expression which I prefer, and I do not think that any nation has been willing to impair that factor. Therefore, the first phase of the Disarmament Conferences, going on for four or five years, the Preparatory Commission and so on, consisted in every one of these nations trying to disarm some other nation, and a whole array of ingenious technical schemes were put forward by military experts, each of which was perfectly fair and reasonable until it was examined by the other side. Only in one case has this first phase of altering the ratio produced a success–when the United States wished to secure complete naval equality with Great Britain, and we complied with their request. For the rest, I do not think that anything so far has been achieved by the discussions.

But for some time a second phase has supervened at Geneva. The expectation of general disarmament upon a great scale has failed; the hope of one nation being able to disarm its rival has been frustrated by the very stout and stubborn resistance which every nation makes to that process. Now I am afraid that a large part of the object of every country is to throw the blame for an impending failure upon some other country while willing, if possible, to win the Nobel Peace Prize for itself. Again, we have had an elaborate series of technical maneuvers by military experts and by Governments and their advisers. I am not going to particularize, I am not going to put too sharp a point to my remarks, because I do not like to say anything which might be offensive to great nations who have put forward schemes for disarmament which place them in such a satisfactory light and cost them so very little in convenience. But every time one of these plans is launched the poor good people of the League of Nations Union clap their hands with joy, and every time they are disappointed–nay, I must say deceived. But their hope is unfailing. The process is apparently endless, and so is the pathetic belief with which it is invariably greeted. I repeat that we alone have been found willing to alter continually our ratio of armed strength to our disadvantage. We have done it on land, on sea, and in the air. Now His Majesty's Government have said that we have reached the limit, and I think we shall all agree with them in that statement.

I am sorry to be so pessimistic, but it is absolutely a duty to put the rugged facts as I conceive them before the House. I have constantly predicted, as the Prime Minister and the Lord President will bear me out, publicly and privately, that these Disarmament Conferences would not succeed in removing the danger of war, and I doubt if they will succeed in substantially reducing the burden of armaments. Indeed, I have held the view that the holding of all these conferences over the last seven or eight or nine years has had the opposite effect, and has actually prevented the burden from being lightened as it would have been if we has trusted to the normal and powerful working of economic and financial pressures. But these conferences have focused the attention of the leading men in all nations upon the competitive aspects of armaments, and upon technical questions which they never would have heard of. This process has intensified the suspicions and the anxieties of the nations, and has brought the possibilities of war nearer to us than they were some years ago. That, I fear, startling and unpleasant as it is, cannot be disputed by anyone who looks at the facts of the European situation today.

We have steadily marched backward since Locarno. I am sorry that Sir Austen Chamberlain is not in his place. Many criticisms have been applied to him. Since the War Locarno was the high-water mark of Europe. Look what a distance we have fallen since then. Compare the state of Europe on the morrow of Locarno with its condition today. Fears are greater, rivalries are sharper, military plans are more closely concerted, military organizations are more carefully and efficiently developed, Britain is weaker: and Britain's hour of weakness is Europe's hour of danger. The war mentality is springing up again in certain countries. All over Europe, except here, there is hardly a factory which is not prepared for its alternative war service; every detail worked out for its immediate transformation upon a signal. And all this has been taking place under Governments whose statesmen and diplomatists have never ceased to utter the most noble sentiments of peace amid the cheers of the simple and the good. . . .

There is a certain amount of exaggerated talk of what is called French ascendancy. I do not like the present situation; no one does. But there is this to be said about French ascendancy, the French system in Europe, or whatever you like to call it–it gives stability. As Lord Grey has recently reminded us, France, though armed to the teeth, is pacifist to the core. All the countries associated with France have no wish to do anything except to maintain the status quo. They only wish to keep what they have got, and no initiative in making trouble would come from them. At the present time, and until or unless Germany is rearmed, France and her associates are, I believe, quite capable of maintaining themselves, and are in no immediate danger of being challenged by countries which are dissatisfied with the status quo. There is nothing wrong in that. I am not saying that it is the last word. It could be improved, but there is nothing wrong in it from a legal or public point of view. The case of France and her associates stands on exactly the same treaty foundations as the League of Nations itself. Not only have they ample military force, as I believe, at present, but they have the public law of Europe behind them until it is changed.

I think we ought to feel assurance that there is something equally solid with which we can replace the French system before we press them unduly to weaken the military factors of safety upon which their security depends. Europe might easily go farther and fare worse. I am not saying that I am pleased with the situation as it is. I am pointing out how easily we might, in trying to improve it too rapidly or injudiciously, bring about what of all things in the world we wish to avoid. I say quite frankly, though I may shock the House, that I would rather see another ten or twenty years of one-sided armed peace than see a war between equally well-matched Powers or combinations of Powers—and that may be the choice.

That I am a realist in these matters I cannot deny, but I am not an alarmist. I do not believe in the imminence of war in Europe. I believe that with wisdom and with skill we may never see it in our time. To hold any other view would indeed be to despair. I put my confidence, first of all, upon the strength of the French Army; secondly, upon the preoccupation of Russia in the Far East, on account of the enormous increase in the armaments of Japan; and, thirdly, I put it, in the general way, upon the loathing of war which prevails among the nationals of all the countries not dissatisfied with the late peace. I believe that we have a considerable breathing-space in which to revive again those lights of goodwill and reconciliation in Europe which shone, so brightly but so briefly, on the morrow of Locarno. We shall never do that merely by haggling about cannons, tanks, aeroplanes and submarines, or measuring swords with one another, among nations already eying each other with so much vigilance.

Are there no other paths by which we may recover the spirit of Locarno? I would follow any real path, not a sham or a blind alley, which led to lasting reconciliation between Germany and her neighbors. Here at this moment, if the House will permit me, I would venture to propound a general principle which I humbly submit to the Government and the House, and which I earnestly trust they will follow. Here is my general principle. The removal of the just grievances of the vanquished ought to precede the disarmament of the victors. To bring about anything like equality of armaments [between the vanquished and the victor nations] if it were in our power to do so, which it happily is not, while those grievances remain unredressed, would be almost to appoint the day for another European war—to fix it as if it were a prize-fight. It would be far safer to reopen questions like those of the Dantzig Corridor and Transylvania, with all their delicacy and difficulty, in cold blood and in a calm atmosphere and while the victor nations still have ample superiority, than to wait and drift on, inch by inch and stage by stage, until once again vast combinations, equally matched, confront each other face to face.

There is another reason why I commend this to the House. It must be remembered that Great Britain will have more power and will run far less risk in pressing for the redress of grievances than in pressing for disarmament. We can only promote disarmament by giving further guarantees of aid. We can press for the redress of grievances by merely threatening, if our counsels are not attended to, to withdraw ourselves at the proper time from our present close entanglement in European affairs. The first road of pressing for disarmament and offering more aid only leads us deeper and deeper into the European situation. The second either removes the cause of danger or leads us out of the danger zone.

Just look to where our present policy is leading us. Look at the situation into which we are apparently marching blindly and with a sort of helpless chorus of approval. When we say to France and to Poland, "Why do you not disarm and set an example, and respond to our gesture, and so on?" they reply, "Will you then help us to defend ourselves, supposing that you are wrong in your view of what our factor of safety ought to be?" Nobody keeps armaments going for fun. They keep them going for fear. "We would gladly reduce," they say, "provided we get you in line with us for certain. If you will take some of our burden off our shoulders there will be no hesitation on our part in transferring that burden." And what they say to us they say still more to the United States—or if they do not say it, they think it. But surely this is very dangerous ground for us. We are to persuade our friends to weaken themselves as much as possible, and then we are to make it up to them by our own exertions and at our own expense.

It is as if one said, "I will go tiger-hunting with you, my friend, on the one condition that you leave your rifle at home." That is not the kind of excursion on which our old men ought to send our young men. We have, of course, serious obligations, which we have no intention of discarding, under Locarno. But under Locarno we remain the sole and free judge of the occasion and of the interpretation put upon these obligations. Without our own vote on the Council of the League of Nations, which must be unanimous, we cannot be involved in war. But see now what the French propose in this latest scheme. They propose, quite logically and naturally, in responding to the pressure of Britain and the United States on disarmament, that the decision of the Council should be by a majority. That would mean that our fate would be decided over our head. We might find ourselves pledged in honour and in law to enter a war against our will, and against our better judgment, in order to preserve those very injustices and grievances which sunder Europe today, which are the cause of present armaments and which, if not arrested, will cause another war.

These are not the days when you can order the British nation or the British Empire about as if it were a pawn on the chessboard of Europe. You cannot do it. Of course, if the United States were willing to come into the European scene as a prime factor, if they were willing to guarantee to those countries who take their advice that they would not suffer for it, then an incomparably wider and happier prospect would open to the whole world. If they were willing not only to sign, but to ratify, treaties of that kind, it would be an enormous advantage. It is quite safe for the British Empire to go as far in any guarantee in Europe as the United States is willing to go, and hardly any difficulty in the world could not be solved by the faithful co-operation of the English-speaking peoples. But that is not going to happen tomorrow. It is not in our power to anticipate our destiny. Meanwhile we ought not to take any further or closer engagements In Europe beyond those which the United States may be found willing to take.

I hope that the League of Nations is not going to be asked now to do the impossible. Those who believe, as I do sincerely, that the League of Nations is a priceless instrument of international comity, which may play as great a part as the most daring, hopeful founders ever forecast for it, should be especially careful not to put upon the League strains which in its present stage it is utterly incapable of bearing. I deprecate altogether the kind of thought that, unless the League can force a general disarmament, unless it can compel powerful nations in remote regions to comply with its decisions, it is dead—away with it. All that is as foolish as it is to grudge the small sums necessary to keep this precious international machinery in being. He is a bad friend to the League of Nations who would set its tasks beyond its compass.

There is only one thing more to say before I sit down, and it is suggested to me by the speech which the Lord President of the Council [Mr. Baldwin] delivered recently [November 10, 1932]. I did not hear it, but from all accounts it was one which profoundly impressed the House, and revealed the latent and often carefully concealed powers which reside in my right hon. Friend. But that speech, while it deeply impressed the House, I have no doubt—and I have read it with great attention—led to no practical conclusion. It created anxiety, and it created also perplexity. There was a sense of, what shall I say, fatalism, and even perhaps helplessness about it, and I take this opportunity of saying that, as far as this island is concerned, the responsibility of Ministers to guarantee the safety of the country from day to day and from hour to hour is direct and inalienable. It has always been so, and I am sure they will not differ from their predecessors in accepting that responsibility. Their duty is not only to try, within the restricted limits which, I fear, are all that is open to them, to prevent war, but to make sure that we ourselves are not involved in one, and, above all, to make sure that, if war should break out among other Powers, our country and the King's Dominions can be effectively defended, and will be able to preserve, if they desire to do so, that strong and unassailable neutrality from which we must never be drawn except by the heart and conscience of the nation.

AIR ESTIMATES

March 14, 1933

House of Commons

In this prescient speech Churchill dealt with the speech made by Baldwin in November. The speech included the phrase "the bomber will always get through."

[Extract] If our discussion this afternoon were confined solely to the topics upon which the Under-Secretary of State [Sir Philip Sassoon] thought it prudent to dwell, if, for instance, we were to go away, as we might easily go, with the idea that the Air Force exists to fight locusts and that it never drops anything but blankets, we should undoubtedly entertain incomplete impressions of some of the issues which are brought before the House when the Air Estimates for the year are introduced. I do not consider that the present state of Europe is comparable with the state of Europe in 1914. Although there is great unrest, and hatreds are as rife as ever, yet I feel that there is not the same explosive and catastrophic atmosphere as existed in 1914; and therefore we may discuss in cool blood and with calm hearts, or at any rate in tranquil circumstances, some of the technical issues which are raised by this Vote.

I must turn especially to the memorable speech which was delivered by the Lord President a few months ago. I agree with what I imagine were his feelings when he wished that neither aeroplanes nor submarines had ever been invented. I am sure they have both been deeply detrimental to the special interests and security of this island; and I agree also with his general theme that the air power may either end war or end civilization. But we are bound to examine carefully the speech of the Lord President because of the feeling that he aroused alarm without giving guidance. My right hon. Friend swept away many important things in that half-hour. He did not believe there was never to be another great war; he thought wars would come again some day, but he hoped, as we all hope, they would not come in our time. He had apparently no real faith in the sanctity of agreements, such as the Kellogg Pact; neither had he any faith in the means of defense which are open to civilized communities when confronted with dangers which they cannot avoid. He led us up to a conclusion which was no conclusion. We are greatly concerned, and yet we were afforded no solace, no solution. So far as he made an appeal to youth, it was very difficult to see what was the moral which he inculcated, and as far as I can understand, reading in the current publications, his appeal to youth has been widely misinterpreted in some of our leading universities. [Editor's Note: A reference to the Oxford Union's resolution "that this House will in no circumstances fight for its King and country."]

There is a certain helplessness and hopelessness which was spread about by his speech from which I hope the House will endeavor to shake itself free. There is the same kind of helplessness and hopelessness about dealing with this air problem as there is about dealing with the unemployment problem, or the currency question, or the question of economy. All the evils are vividly portrayed, and the most admirable sentiments are expressed, but as for a practical course of action, solid footholds on which we can tread step by step, there is in this great sphere, as in other spheres of Government activity, a gap, a hiatus, a sense that there is no message from the lips of the prophet. There is no use gaping vacuously on the problems of the air. Still less is there any use in indulging in pretense in any form. . . .

We ought not to deal in humbug. There are good people in this country who care about disarmament. In many ways I think they are wrong, but I do not see why they should be tricked. I think they should have the plain truth told them, and if they disagree they have their constitutional remedy. It is no kindness to this country to stir up and pay all this lipservice in the region of unrealities, and get a cheap cheer because you have said something which has not ruffled anyone, and then meanwhile do the opposite, meanwhile proceed on entirely pre-War lines, as all the nations of Europe are proceeding today in all the practical arrangements which they are making.

Another reason why these proposals had no chance of being accepted is their effect upon France. In the present temper of Europe can you ever expect that France would halve her air force and then reduce the residue by one-third? Would you advise her to do so? If she took your advice and did it, and then trouble occurred, would you commit this country to stand by her side and make good the injury? If we proceed to argue on lines which have no connection with reality, we shall get into trouble. You talk of secret diplomacy, but let me tell you that there is a worse kind of secret diplomacy, and it is the diplomacy which spreads out hope and soothing-syrup for the good, while all the time winks are exchanged between the people who know actually what is going on. That is a far worse situation. I am as a fact a member of the League of Nations Union. If I were one of their leading authorities I should be far more irritated with people who deceived me than with persons who, supposed to be lost souls, stated the blunt truth; because, unless the people know the truth, one day they are going to have a very surprising awakening.

These proposals which have been made by the Government at Geneva are not likely to be accepted, and I do not think there is a single man in any part of the House who thinks, or who has ever thought, that they had the slightest chance of being accepted. You are not going to get an international agreement which will obviate the necessity of having your own defenses or which will remove the appalling dangers which have been so freely stated. I am most anxious that in anything that is said to France at Geneva upon air armaments or upon military armaments we should do nothing which exposes us to the French retort, "Very well; then you are involved with us." I would far rather have larger Estimates and be absolutely free and independent to choose our own course than become involved in this Continental scene by a well-meant desire to persuade them all to give up arms. There is terrible danger there.

I read in the newspapers today that the Prime Minister has been giving an ultimatum or making a strong appeal to France to disarm. Whether you deal with the Army or the Air, you are taking an altogether undue responsibliity at a time like this in tendering such advice to a friendly nation. No; I hope and trust that the French will look after their own safety., and that we shall be permitted to live our life in our island without being again drawn into the perils of the continent of Europe. But if we wish to detach ourselves and lead a life of independence from European entanglements, we have to be strong enough to defend our neutrality. We are not going to preserve neutrality if we have no technical equipment. That reason might again be urged if we are discussing Navy Votes. I am strongly of opinion that we require to strengthen our armaments in the air and upon the seas in order to make sure that we are still judges of our own fortunes, our own destinies and our own action.

I now come to the technical issue which was raised by Mr. Baldwin's speech—a famous speech, I must say, because how many speeches we make in this House and how few are remembered a week after! But here months ago my right hon. Friend made his speech and in this Air Debate it is the dominant theme. He was dealing with the bombing of open towns and the murdering of women and children as an orthodox and legitimate means of civilized war. I cannot follow him in two respects. First, he assumes that it would certainly be done. Secondly, he assumes that there is no remedy. Neither of these impressions should guide public thought upon these matters. He said, with very great truth, that the only defense is offense. That is the soundest of all military maxims. But, as can be seen from the context of the phrase, my right hon. Friend had been led to believe that the only method of offense by which you could defend your own civil population from being murdered was to murder some of the civil population on the other side. But that is nonsense. The true defense would be entirely different.

In a war between two States with equal air forces it would not pay–I put it no higher; leave out morality, humanity and the public law of Europe–it would not pay, from the military self-preservation standpoint of any Power engaged in an equal fight to waste its strength upon non-combattants and open towns. To use an expression which I have heard, they could not afford to waste their bombs on mere women and children. Essentially a struggle of this kind–which I pray as much as any man we shall never live to see, and which I am resolved to do my utmost to avert–any struggle of this kind would resolve itself into a combat between the two air forces. If all of a sudden two Powers with equal forces went to war, and one threw its bombs upon cities so as to kill as many women and children as possible, and the other threw its bombs on the aerodromes and air bases and factories and arsenals and dockyards and railway local points of the other side, can anyone doubt that next morning the one who had committed the greatest crime would not be the one who had reaped the greatest advantage?

Mr. McLean: What do you mean by that?

Mr. Churchill: What I mean is that this horrible, senseless, brutal method of warfare, which we are told is the first military step that would be taken, the killing of women and children, would not be comparable, as a military measure, to an attack upon the technical centres and air bases of an enemy Power.

Mr. Godfrey Nicholson: What about the moral effect on the people?

Mr. Churchill: The moral effect would be far greater if it were found the next day that the hostile air forces were incapable of flying at all. That would have not only a moral effect, but a physical effect of very remarkable strength. But I must say this: while in the first instance in any conflict the air forces would fight and would not be able, if equally matched, to look elsewhere, yet once one side was decidedly beaten, this process of torturing the civil population by killing the women and children might well be used in order to extort abject surrender and submission from the Power whose air defense had been broken down. Anyone can see how that might be applied. If there were any Power in the world to which it would not be applied, perhaps it would be our island, because so much easier methods would be open for reducing us to submission. If we were completely defenseless in the air, if we were reduced to a condition where we could not deal with this form of warfare, I doubt very much whether even then the victorious Power would be well advised to come and kill the women and children. By intercepting all the trade passing through the narrow seas and on the approaches to this island, they could employ the weapon of starvation which would probably lead to a peace on terms which they thought were desirable.

Therefore, it seems to me that the possession of an adequate air force is almost a complete protection for the civilian population, not indeed against injury and annoyance, but against destruction such as was portrayed by the Lord President; and that, after all, is what we have to think of first. I cannot understand why His Majesty's

Government and the representatives of the Air Ministry do not inculcate these truths, for truths they are, as widely as they possibly can. The only defense is an adequate air force, and the possession of an adequate air force will relieve the civil population from this danger until that air force is victorious or is beaten. If it is victorious then the danger is removed for a long period. Therefore, I do not think that we should be led by the Lord President into supposing that no means of safety are open to a vigourous, valiant race. There is a means of safety open. While I would not abandon hope of international agreement, I would not base the life of this country upon it in their present stage, but to cut us off from that, on the one hand, and to suggest on the other that no remedy is in our hands in the region of force, is indeed to expose us to a gloomy vision.

Not to have an adequate air force in the present state of the world is to compromise the foundations of national freedom and independence. It is all very well to suppose that we are masters of our own actions in this country and that this House can assemble and vote as to whether it wishes to go to war or not. If you desire to keep that privilege, which I trust we shall never lose, it is indispensable that you should have armaments in this island which will enable you to carry on your life without regard to external pressure. I regretted very much to hear the Under-Secretary state that we were only the fifth air Power. I regretted very much to hear him say that the ten-year program was suspended for another year. I was sorry to hear him boast that they had not laid down a single new unit this year. All these ideas are being increasingly stultified by the march of events, and we should be well advised to concentrate upon our air defenses with greater vigour. Certainly it looks curious that while our Army and Navy have been increased in expenditure this year—no doubt absolutely necessarily, because we had disarmed far below what is reasonable—the Air Force, which is the most vital of all, should be the one subjected not to an increase but to an actual reduction.

Above all, we must not be led by the Lord President into this helpless, hopeless mood. Our island is surrounded by the sea. It always has been, and, although the House may not realize it, the sea was in early times a great disadvantage because an invader could come across the sea and no one knew where he would land; very often he did not know himself. On the Continent the lines of advance are fixed by the mountain passes, the roads, and the fertile plains and rivers. We were under a great disadvantage a thousand years ago in being surrounded by the sea, and we suffered terribly from it. But we did not give up; we did not evacuate the island and say that we must live on the mainland. Not at all. We conquered the sea; we became the mistress of the sea, and the very element which had given the invader access to the heart of our country, to our hearths and homes, became its greatest protection—became, indeed, the bridge which united us to the most distant parts of our Empire throughout the world. Now there is the air. The sea perhaps is no longer complete security for our island development; it must be the air too.

Why should we fear the air? We have as good technical knowledge as any country. There is no reason to suppose that we cannot make machines as good as any country. We have—though it may be thought conceited to say so—a particular vein of talent in air piloting which is in advance of that possessed by other countries. There is not the slightest reason to suppose that we are not capable of producing as good results for money put into aviation as any other country. That being so, I ask the Government to consider profoundly and urgently the whole position of our air defense. I am not going to commit myself, without an opportunity of examining all the technical and financial details, to any particular standard, but this I say—that, in view of the significance which this subject has at the present time, in view of the state of the world, and in view of the speech of the Lord President of the Council, it is absolutely indispensable that the necessary programme of air development should be carried out, and that our defenses in this matter should be adequate to our needs.

FOREIGN POLICY AND GERMAN REARMAMENT

April 13, 1933

House of Commons

Hitler had now achieved power in Germany, and the first indications could be seen of what that would mean for Germany—and possibly for Europe.

[Extract] I have heard, as everyone has of late years, a great deal of condemnation of the treaties of peace, of the Treaties of Versailles and of Trianon. I believe that that denunciation has been very much exaggerated, and in its effect harmful. These treaties, at any rate, were founded upon the strongest principle alive in the world today, the principle of nationalism, or, as President Wilson called it, self-determination. The principle of self-determination or of nationalism was applied to all the defeated Powers over the whole area of Middle and Eastern Europe. Europe today corresponds to its ethnological groupings as it has never corresponded before. You may think that nationalism has been excessively manifested in modern times. That may well be so. It may well be that it has a dangerous side, but we must not fail to recognize that it is the strongest force now at work. . . .

I recognize the anomalies and I recognize the injustices, but they are only a tiny proportion of the great work of consolidation and appeasement which has been achieved and is represented by the Treaties that ended the War. The nationalities and races of which Europe is composed have never rested so securely in their beds in accordance with their heart's desire. It would be a blessed thing if we could mitigate these anomalies and grievances, but we can only do that if and when there has been established a strong confidence that the Treaties themselves are not going to be deranged. So long as the Treaties are in any way challenged as a whole it will be impossible to procure a patient consideration for the redress of the anomalies. The more you wish to remove the anomalies and grievances the more you should emphasize respect for the Treaties. It should be the first rule of British foreign policy to emphasize respect for these great Treaties, and to make those nations whose national existence depends upon and arises from the Treaties feel that no challenge is leveled at their security. Instead of that, for a good many years a lot of vague and general abuse has been leveled at the Treaties with the result that these powerful States, comprising enormous numbers of citizens–the Little Entente and Poland together represent 80,000,000 strongly armed–have felt that their position has been challenged and endangered by the movement to alter the Treaties. In consequence, you do not get the consideration which in other circumstances you might get for the undoubted improvements which are required in various directions. . . .

New discord has arisen in Europe of late years from the fact that Germany is not satisfied with the result of the late War. I have indicated several times that Germany got off lightly after the Great War. I know that that is not always a fashionable opinion, but the facts repudiate the idea that a Carthaginian peace was in fact imposed upon Germany. No division was made of the great masses of the German people. No portion of Germany inhabited by Germans was detached, except where there was the difficulty of disentangling the population of the Silesian border. No attempt was made to divide Germany as between the northern and southern portions, which might well have tempted the conquerors at that time. No State was carved out of Germany. She underwent no serious territorial loss, except the loss of Alsace and Lorraine, which she herself had seized only fifty years before. The great mass of the Germans remained united after all that Europe had passed through, and they are more vehemently united today than ever before. We know what has happened to the War indemnity. They have lost their colonies, it is true; but these were not of great value to them, and it is not at all true for them to say that these colonies could ever have afforded any appreciable outlet for their working-class population. They are not suited for white colonization.

On the other hand, when we think of what would have happened to us, to France or to Belgium, if the Germans had won; when we think of the terms which they exacted from Rumania, or of the terms of the Treaty of Brest-Litovsk; when we remember that up to a few months from the end of the War German authorities refused to consider that Belgium could ever be liberated, but said that she should be kept in thrall for military purposes forever, I do not think that we need break our hearts in deploring the treatment that Germany is receiving now. Germany is not satisfied; but no concession which has been made has produced any very marked appearance of gratitude. Once it has been conceded it has seemed less valuable than when it was demanded. Many people would like to see, or would have liked to see a little while ago–I was one of them–the question of the Polish Corridor adjusted. For my part, I should certainly have considered that to be one of the greatest practical objectives of European peace-seeking diplomacy. There again, however, we must think of the rights of Poland. The Polish Corridor is inhabited almost entirely by Poles, and it was Polish territory before the Partition of 1772. This is a matter which in quiet times, with increasing goodwill, Europe should have set itself–and might well some day set itself–to solve.

The question of the Germans regaining their colonies is being pressed by them, and the question of their rearmament–which, personally, I consider more grave than any other question–is being brought to the front. They demand equality in weapons and equality in the organization of armies and fleets, and we have been told, "You cannot keep so great a nation in an inferior position. What others have they must have." I have never agreed. I think it is a most dangerous demand to make. Nothing in life is eternal, of course, but as surely as Germany acquires full military equality with her neighbours while her own grievances are still unredressed and while she is in the temper which we have unhappily seen, so surely should we see ourselves within a measurable distance of the renewal of general European war. If this process of rearmament or of equalization were actually to take place while the present conditions prevail, undoubtedly the nations who are neighbors of Germany and who fear Germany would ask themselves whether they would be well advised to postpone coming to a conclusion until the process of German rearmament has been completed. It is extremely dangerous for people to talk lightly about German rearmament and say that, if the Germans choose to do it, no one can stop them. I am very doubtful if Germany would rearm in defiance of the Treaty if there were a solidarity of European and world opinion that the Treaty could only be altered by discussion, and could not be altered by a violent one-sided breach. I, therefore, do not subscribe to the doctrine that we should throw up our hands and recognize the fact that Germany is going to be armed up to an equality with the neighbouring States in any period which we can immediately foresee. There may be other periods, but certainly we ought not to admit it at the moment.

I am not going to use harsh words about Germany and about the conditions there. I am addressing myself to the problem in a severely practical manner. Nevertheless, one of the things which we were told after the Great War would be a security for us was that Germany would be a democracy with Parliamentary institutions. All that has been swept away. You have dictatorship—most grim dictatorship. You have militarism and appeals to every form of fighting spirit, from the reintroduction of duelling in the colleges to the Minister of Education advising the plentiful use of the cane in the elementary schools. You have these martial or pugnacious manifestations, and also this persecution of the Jews, of which so many Members have spoken and which distresses everyone who feels that men and women have a right to live in the world where they are born, and have a right to pursue a livelihood which has hitherto been guaranteed them under the public laws of the land of their birth.

When I read of what is going on in Germany—I feel in complete agreement in this matter with hon. Gentlemen opposite—when I see the temper displayed there and read the speeches of the leading Ministers, I cannot help rejoicing that the Germans have not got the heavy cannon, the thousands of military aeroplanes and the tanks of various sizes for which they have been pressing in order that their status may be equal to that of other countries. . . .

We should be very careful not to mix ourselves up too deeply in this European scene. Our desire to promote peace must not lead us to press our views beyond a point where those views are no longer compatible with the actual facts of the situation. It may be very virtuous and high-minded to press disarmament upon nations situated as these nations are, but if not done in the right way and in due season, and in moderation, with regard for other people's points of view as well as our own sentiments, it may bring war nearer rather than peace, and may lead us to be suspected and hated instead of being honoured and thanked as we should wish to be. Even more vain is it for the United States to press indiscriminate disarmament upon the European States, unless, of course the United States is prepared to say that those nations which take her advice will receive her aid if trouble should arise, and is prepared to envisage the prospect of sending millions of soldiers again across the ocean.

Our country has a very important part to play in Europe, but it is not so large a part as we have been attempting to play, and I advocate for us in future a more modest role than many of our peace-preservers and peace-lovers have sought to impose upon us. I remember when I was very young, before I came into this House, a denunciation by Dr. Spence Watson of what he called "the filthy Tory rag of a spirited foreign policy." In those days the feelings of the forerunners of those who sit opposite were directed against jingo policies of bombast and Palmerstonian vigour. But you may have another kind of spirited foreign policy which may also lead you into danger, and that is a policy in which, without duly considering the circumstances in which others are placed, you endeavour to press upon them disarmament or to weaken their security, perhaps with a view to gaining a measure of approbation from good people here who are not aware of the dangerous state of affairs in Europe. There you could have a peace policy which may be too spirited.

It is easy to talk about the moral leadership of Europe. That great prize still stands before the statesmen of all countries, but it is not to be achieved merely by making speeches of unexceptionable sentiments. If it is to be won by any nation it will only be by an immense amount of wise restraint and timely, discreet action which, over a period of years, has created a situation where speeches are not merely fine exhortations but record the unity and conciliation which have been achieved. There is the moral leadership of Europe. It is not to be won by such easy methods as merely making speeches which will arouse the applause of every good-hearted person in this country. . . .

"EUROPE'S HOUR OF DANGER"

August 12, 1933

Theydon Bois

Churchill's speeches in 1933 were principally devoted to India, but the ever-worsening situation in Europe was becoming one of his dominant concerns.

[Extract] Our country is at peace. We enjoy a greater measure of freedom and security than any other nation in the world—perhaps the greatest measure of personal freedom and security combined that has ever been achieved by any community in all history. We are suffering less than most countries from the great depression of trade. You will not expect me to tell you that all this is due to the Government headed by Mr. Ramsay MacDonald. It is due to the genius of the British people and to the vitality and strength of their institutions. It is due to the traditions which are still so widely respected in our island life. Still, we must not underrate the advantage we have of a solid, stable Government, composed of honourable and upright men, respecting the ancient Constitution of the land and obeying the laws they themselves administer.

We know we have a Government capable of maintaining law and order and of respecting and guarding our individual liberties and civic rights, which our forefathers gained for us in many a hard-fought field. We know that in all this we can rely on a House of Commons elected upon an impulse of patriotism and still only in its Parliamentary prime. When we look out upon the tragic confusion of the world and see how many countries, great and small, have fallen a prey to anarchy or tyranny or are devoured by ferocious hatreds of race, class, or faction, we should be grateful to the Providence that has thus far preserved and protected us.

I see that Mr. MacDonald told a Dutch newspaper the other day that the National Government had three more years to run and would certainly last longer. Many of us would be quite content that that should be so. There are, however, three evil and dangerous storm clouds which either overhang us or lie on the horizon.

The first is the state of Europe. Nobody can watch the events which are taking place in Germany without increasing anxiety about what their outcome will be. At present Germany is only partly armed and most of her fury is turned upon herself. But already her smaller neighbours, Austria, Switzerland, Belgium, and Denmark, feel a deep disquietude. There is grave reason to believe that Germany is arming herself, or seeking to arm herself, contrary to the solemn treaties exacted from her in her hour of defeat.

I have always opposed the rearmament of Germany and have criticized in the House of Commons all this foolish talk of placing her upon some kind of equality with France. I denounced and derided the perilous policy to which we seemed inclined to lend ourselves of putting pressure upon the French to weaken their splendid army. The same people and the same perverse school of thought in England and the United States that have already weakened the British Navy sought to weaken the French army. But the French most prudently refused to hearken to this hazardous advice, and the fact that they refused is the main foundation of the peace of Europe to-day.

I hope our National Government, and especially the Cabinet Ministers in charge of the Navy and Army and the Air Force, will realize how grave is their responsibility. They are responsible, like the Ministers before the War, for our essential safety.

I trust they will make sure that the forces of the Crown are kept in a proper state of efficiency, with the supplies and munition factories which they require, and that they will be strong enough to enable us to count for something when we work for peace, and strong enough if war should come in Europe to maintain our effective neutrality, unless we should decide of our own free will to the contrary. Always remember that Britain's hour of weakness is Europe's hour of danger. I look to the League of Nations to rally the forces which make for the peace of the civilized world and not in any way to weaken them. . . .

GERMANY AND THE LEAGUE

November 7, 1933

House of Commons

On October 14 Germany walked out of the Disarmament Conference; a week later she left the League of Nations. On October 26 Labour won the East Fulham by-election on a blatantly pacifist platform. It is doubtful whether this element was the dominant one in this historic election, but it made a deep impression on all politicians, and particularly on Baldwin.

[Extract] . . . My right hon. Friend [Mr. Lloyd George] made tonight a deeply interesting speech, to which I listened, like everyone else, with admiration of the persuasive charm and skill with which he pressed his point. There is nothing that he can do so well as to draw one side of a picture in the most glowing manner and then reduce the other side to small and pitiable proportions. He gave an account of the state of Europe. He represented that Germany might have a few thousand more rifles than was allowed by the Treaty, a few more Boy Scouts, and then he pictured the enormous armies of Czechoslovakia and Poland and France, with their thousands of cannon, and so forth. If I could believe that picture I should feel much comforted, but I cannot. I find it difficult to believe it in view of the obvious fear which holds all the nations who are neighbours of Germany and the obvious lack of fear which appears in the behavior of the German Government and a large proportion of the German people. The great dominant fact is that Germany has already begun to rearm. We read of importations quite out of the ordinary of scrap iron and nickel and war metals. We read of the military spirit which is rife throughout the country; we see that the philosophy of blood lust is being inculcated into their youth in a manner unparalleled since the days of barbarism. . . .

I know that it is natural for Ministers, for the Prime Minister, to wish to play a great part on the European stage, to bestride Europe in the cause of peace, and to be as it were its saviours. You cannot be the saviours of Europe on a limited liability. I agree with the statement of the late Mr. Bonar Law, who said that we cannot be the policemen of the whole world. We have to discharge our obligations, but we cannot take upon ourselves undue obligations into which we shall certainly come if we are the leaders in compelling and pressing for a great diminution in the strength of France and other Powers which are neighbours of Germany. How lucky it is that the French did not take the advice that we have been tendering them in the last few years, or the advice which the United States has given them—advice tendered from a safe position 3000 miles across the ocean! If they had accepted it the war would be much nearer, and our obligation to come to their aid would be much more strictly interpreted. There should be recognition of the fact that we ought not to place ourselves continually in the most prominent position and endeavour to produce spectacular effects of disarmament in

Europe, because as surely as we do a great deal of our discretionary power will be gradually whittled away.

There is a fairly general measure of agreement as to the course which we should now pursue. We should adhere to the League of Nations. I did not agree with the Member for Carnarvon when he mocked and scolded the League in a speech in the country. Nor do I agree with those poor friends of the League who say that, just because the League was incapable of dealing with the situation in the Far East, on the other side of the world, it will have no efficacy in dealing with the European situation. What could you expect of the League in far-off Asia? China and Japan–what do they care for the League of Nations? Russia and the United States–neither of them members of the League. Those four countries comprise half the population of the globe. They form another world, a world in itself, and you should not judge of the success or power of a great international institution like this by the fact that it has not been able to make its will effective at the other side of the globe. Very different is the case in Europe. In Europe you have at least erected it upon the basis of the Treaties of Peace. That is a foundation on which you can build, and not only is it erected on that foundation, but powerful nations stand fully armed to defend those Treaties and, if necessary, to make themselves the agents and authorities of the League of Nations.

I believe that we shall find our greatest safety in co-operating with the other Powers of Europe, not taking a leading part but coming in with all the neutral States and the smaller States of Europe which will gather together anxiously in the near future at Geneva. We shall make a great mistake to separate ourselves entirely from them at this juncture. Whatever way we turn there is risk. But the least risk and the greatest help will be found in re-creating the Concert of Europe through the League of Nations, not for the purpose of fiercely quarreling and haggling about the details of disarmament, but in an attempt to address Germany collectively, so that there may be some redress of the grievances of the German nation and that that may be effected before this peril of [German] rearmament reaches a point which may endanger the peace of the world . . .

In these circumstances, proved as it is that we have disarmed to the verge of risk–nay, well into the gulf of risk–a very great responsibility rests upon the Ministers for the Defence Departments to assure us that adequate provision is made for our safety, and for having the power and the time, if necessary, to realize the whole latent strength of our country.

"WHITHER BRITAIN?"

January 16, 1934

Broadcast, London

We had never been–certainly not for hundreds of years–so defenceless as we are now. The hideous curse of war from the air has fallen on the world. We used to say that we would have a Navy stronger than that of any two Powers. Surely the least we ought now to do is to have an air force as strong as that of the nearest Power that can get at us.

If we have that, I do not believe we shall be attacked. Or, if we are, I do not think it would last long, or do us a mortal injury. I am all for diplomacy and good intentions, but first of all we ought to make the island safe. We ought also to have a clear, honest, foreign policy which anybody can explain and everybody can understand.

I do not agree with those who say the League of Nations is no use, and can never prevent another European war. It might be the only chance of preventing one; or, if it could not prevent it, of making sure that the guilty disturber of the peace has the worst of it. If the League of Nations is not broken up by wrangles and intrigues about disarmament, it might still remain an august tribunal to which not only Great Powers but small peoples might look, if not for protection, at any rate for a declaration of where right and justice lay. We must take our place there, and bear our share in building up a confederation of nations so strong and sincere that in Europe at least no aggressor would dare to challenge them.

The cause of the world depression is not famine or scarcity. It is our very power to supply our wants more abundantly that have upset the old arrangements. Man is conquering Nature, and the problem now is to spread the plenty which science can bestow. We have got to find out the answer to that; and I believe we should find a way. If it is so easy to produce surplus food, surely it ought not to be too hard to bring it to those who need it. We do not want a revolution to arrange that. All we want is a little more common sense and a better organization.

Many powerful forces threaten our Parliamentary system. The House of Lords should be reformed and made into a strong and effective Second Chamber. It should be different in character from the House of Commons, and its task should be to keep the main structure of our national life beyond the danger of sudden and violent change.

The House of Commons should also be strengthened and brought more effectively in touch with the active life of the people. Its present state is most unhealthy. All views should be represented there, and both sides should be heard on every question. The franchise ought to be strengthened, and what is called "weighted." There is no need to take away votes from anybody. We should give extra votes to the millions of men and women, the heads of households and fathers of families, who are really bearing the burden and responsibility of our fortunes on their shoulders.

I hope that before this Parliament breaks up it will reform the House of Lords and put it in its proper place in relation to the House of Commons. I also hope that it will reform the franchise of the House of Commons itself and make it a more true and permanent expression of the real forces that are alive in the nation.

We must be a strong, successful, scientific, commercial Empire or starve. There is no half-way house for Britain between greatness and ruin. That is why I feel so anxious and so angry when I hear all these high-brow sentimentalists and chop-logic feeble minds talking in their airy philosophical detachment about letting India go, or throwing away the Colonies, or losing touch with Canada, Australia, New Zealand, or South Africa, these young nations who stretch their hands to us across the oceans. Little do these clever chatterboxes know and little do they dream of the miseries to which they would condemn the faithful patriotic wage-earners of Britain.

DEFENCE

February 7, 1934

House of Commons

This speech was the first–and among the most dramatic–of Churchill's speeches on the perils of neglecting British air defence. The phrase "We are vulnerable as we have never been before" was not factually accurate, but this speech may be regarded as the opening barrage of a long campaign which, although initially unsuccessful, was to have momentous consequences for Britain and for Churchill.

[Extract] . . . We have an entirely different situation [in Europe] from that which we would all like to see. We have an entirely different situation, or a very greatly changed situation, from the one which existed only a very few years ago. I remember in the days of the late Conservative Administration, when I had the honour of serving under my right hon. Friend the Lord President of the Council, who is I believe, going to reply on the Debate to-night that we thought it right to take as a rule of guidance that there would be no major war within 10 years in which we should be engaged. Of course, such a rule can only be a very crude guidance to the military and naval chiefs who have to make their plans, and it had to be reconsidered prospectively at the beginning of each year. I believe that it was right in all the circumstances. With Locarno and the more mellow light which shone on the world at that time, with the hopes that were then very high, I think it was probably right to take that principle as a guide from day to day, and from year to year. No one could take that principle as a guide to-day. I am quite certain that any Cabinet, however pacific–and no one can impugn the peaceful desires of His Majesty's Government, except those who are divorced from the slightest desire for contact with truth–there is no Government, however pacific and peace-loving that could possibly arrange the basis of their naval and military organisation upon such an assumption as that. A new situation has been created, largely in the last few years, partly in the last three or four years, largely, I fear, by rubbing this sore of the Disarmament Conference until it has become a cancer, and also by the sudden uprush of Nazi-ism in Germany, with the tremendous covert armaments which are proceeding there to-day, to which the hon. Member for Broxtowe (Mr. Cocks), in a most interesting speech yesterday, drew our attention. He quoted figures, which may or may not be strictly accurate, but which now bear a very close relation to the grave underlying facts. That has changed the position very much indeed, and everyone sitting on the Government Bench knows how gravely the position has been changed. . . .

Wars come very suddenly. I have lived through a period when one looked forward, as we do now, with great anxiety and great uncertainty to what would happen in the future. Suddenly something did happen–tremendous, swift, overpowering, irresistible. Let me remind the House of the sort of thing that happened in 1914. There was absolutely no quarrel between Germany and France. One July afternoon the German Ambassador drove down to the Quai d'Orsay and said to, I think, M. Viviani, the French Prime Minister: "We have been forced to mobilise against Russia, and war will be declared. What is to be the position of France?" The French Prime Minister made the answer, which his Cabinet had agreed upon, that France would act in accordance with what she considered to be her own interests. The Ambassador said, "You have an alliance with Russia, have you not?" "Quite so," said the French Prime Minister. And that was the process by which, in a few minutes, the area of the struggle, already serious in the East, was enormously widened and multiplied by the throwing in of the two great nations of the West on either side. But sometimes even a declaration of neutrality does not suffice. On this very occasion, as we now know, the German Ambassador was authorised by his Government, in case the French did not do their duty by their Russian ally, in case they showed any disposition to back out of the conflict which had been resolved on by the German nation, to demand that the fortresses of Toul and Verdun should be handed over to German troops as a guarantee that the French, having declared neutrality, would not change their mind at a subsequent moment.

That is how the great thing happened in our own lifetime, and I am bound to say that I cannot see in the present administration of Germany any assurance that they would be more nice-minded in dealing with a vital and supreme situation than was the Imperial Government of Germany, which was responsible for this procedure being adopted towards France. No, Sir, and we may, within a measurable period of time, in the lifetime of those who are here, if we are not in a proper state of security, be confronted on some occasion with a visit from an ambassador, and may have to give an answer in a very few hours; and if that answer is not satisfactory, within the next few hours the crash of bombs exploding in London and the cataracts of masonry and fire and smoke will warn us of any inadequacy which has been permitted in our aerial defences. We are vulnerable as we have never been before. I have often heard criticisms of the Liberal Government before the War. It is said that its diplomacy was not sufficiently clear and precise, that it wrapped things up in verbiage, that it ought to have said downright and plain what it would do, and there were criticisms about its lack of preparation, and so forth. All I can say is that a far graver case rests upon those who now hold power if, by any chance, against our wishes and against our hopes, trouble should come—a far graver case.

Not one of the lessons of the past has been learned, not one of them has been applied, and the situation is incomparably more dangerous. Then we had the Navy, and no air menace worth speaking of. Then the Navy was the "sure shield" of Britain. As long as it was ready in time and at its stations we could say to any foreign Government: "Well, what are you going to do about it? We will not declare ourselves. We will take our own line, we will work out our own course. We have no wish or desire to hurt anyone, but we shall not be pressed or forced into any hasty action unless we think fit or well." We cannot say that now. This cursed, hellish invention and development of war from the air has revolutionised our position. We are not the same kind of country we used to be when we were an island, only 20 years ago. That is the thing that is borne in upon me more than anything else. It is not merely a question of what we like and what we do not like, of ambitions and desires, of rights and interests, but it is a question of safety and independence. That is what is involved now as never before.

I am going to mention only this, because I am not going to stand between the House and my right hon. Friend for more than a few minutes longer, but it does seem to me that there are three definite decisions which we should now take at once, and without any delay. The first affects the Army. We ought to begin the reorganisation of our civil factories so that they can be turned over rapidly to war purposes. All over Europe that is being done, and to an extraordinary extent—to an amazing extent. They are incomparably more efficient than anything that existed in the days of Prussian Imperialism before the War. Every factory in those countries is prepared to turn over to the production of some material for the deplorable and melancholy business of slaughter. What have we done? There is not an hour to lose. Those things cannot be done in a moment. The process should be started, and the very maximum of money that can be usefully spent should be spent from to-day on—if we act with wisdom.

Then there is the question of the Navy. For the Navy, at any rate, we should regain freedom of design. We should get rid of this London Treaty which has crippled us in building the kind of ships we want, and has stopped the United States from building a great battleship which she probably needed and to which we should have not had the slightest reason to object. It has forced us to spend some of our hard-earned, poor money—the little there is for these purposes—unwisely. It has forced us to take great ships which would have been of enormous utility in convoying vessels bearing food to these islands and to sink them in the ocean, when they had 10 to 15 years of useful life in them. We must regain our freedom at the earliest possible moment, and we shall be helped in doing so by the fact that another of the parties to that Treaty is resolved to regain her freedom, too. Then there is the air. I cannot conceive how, in the present state of Europe and of our position in Europe we can delay in establishing the principle of having an Air Force at least as strong as that of any Power that can get at us. I think that is a perfectly reasonable thing to do. It would only begin to put us back to the position in which we were brought up. We have lived under the shield of the Navy. To have an Air Force as strong as the air force of France or Germany, whichever is the stronger, ought to be the decision which Parliament should take, and which the National Government should proclaim. . . .

I think that the responsibility of His Majesty's Government is very grave indeed, and there is this which makes it all the graver: It is a responsibility which they have no difficulty in discharging if they choose. We are told they have to wait for public opinion, that they must bring that along and must be able to assure the good people here that everything is being done with the most pacific intentions—they must make a case. But they do not need to do anything like that, and nothing like that can stand between them and their responsibility to the Crown and Parliament for the safety and security of the country. The Government command overwhelming majorities in both branches of the Legislature. Nothing will be denied to them that they ask. They have only to make their proposals, and they will be supported in them. Let them not suppose that if they make proposals, with confidence and conviction, for the safety of the country that their countrymen will not support them as they have always done at every moment. Why take so poor a view of the great patriotic support which this nation gives to those who, it feels, are doing their duty by it? I cannot feel that at the present time the Government are doing their duty in these matters of defence, and particularly in respect of the air. It seems to me that while we are becoming ever more entangled in the European situation, and while we are constantly endeavouring to weaken, relatively, our friends upon the Continent of Europe, we nevertheless are left exposed to a mortal thrust, and are deprived of that sense of security and independence upon which the civilisation of our island has been built.

THE NEED FOR AIR PARITY

March 8, 1934

House of Commons

The introduction of the term "parity" with regard to air defence caused a very considerable amount of confusion over the next two years. In reply to Churchill's speech, Baldwin assured the House of Commons that the Government would "see to it that in air strength and air power this country shall no longer be in a position inferior to any country within striking distance of our shores."

[Extract] It is certain that the endeavours which have been made by the Government to procure a measure of disarmament from Europe similar to that which we have practiced ourselves as an example have failed. I have never thought that these efforts would succeed, and I have said so. Perhaps it was uncharitable to say it. I exceedingly regret that they have failed. The Government have admitted for more than a year past that in their desire to procure disarmament they have gone to the very edge of risk. Yes, Sir, and many of us think that they have gone beyond that edge. I have not been able to convince myself that the policy which the Government have pursued has been in sufficiently direct contact with the harsh realities of the European situation, but, of course, I admit most fully that they have made it clear before all the world, not only by words, which are so easy, but by actions, which are so hard, and by inaction, which is so questionable, how sincere has been, and still is, our desire to bring about a general measure of disarmament, especially in the air. That has failed, and nobody can deny it. You could not have chosen in this country anyone more qualified to bring success to his mission than the Lord Privy Seal [Mr. Eden]. It is not his fault that he has not met with success. No one could have stated our sincere case in a more agreeable manner, more simply and effectively, to the different countries which he has visited, but he has failed. In view of that failure we must now, from this moment, look to our own safety. That is the feeling which I believe is in the minds of all—that we must now betimes take measures to put ourselves in a state of reasonable security.

What are the measures that we can take? First of all, of course, there is the preservation of the peace of Europe. We should do everything that we can do to that end. I am astounded that this Government, which has laboured far beyond the bounds of practical expectation in the cause of disarmament and peace, should be abused and insulted as if it were an administration that was anxious to plunge this country into another war. But, putting the preservation of peace in the first place, what is the next great object that we must have in view? It is to secure our national freedom of choice to remain outside a European war, if one should break out. That I put as the more direct and more practical issue, subordinate to, but not less important than, the preservation of peace.

This is not the time, in this Debate, for us to argue about the duties and obligations which this country may have contracted or her interpretation of those obligations in regard to any Continental struggle that may arise. We all hope it will never take place, and I am not at all prepared, standing here, to assume that it will inevitably take place. On the contrary, I still grasp the larger hope and believe that we may wear our way through these difficulties and leave this grim period behind. But there can be no assurance upon that, and we must have the effective right and power to choose our own path, in accordance with the wishes and resolves of the nation, in any contingency or emergency which may arise upon the continent of Europe; and for this purpose we must be safe from undue foreign pressure.

We cannot afford to confide the safety of our country to the passions or to the panic of any foreign nation which may be facing some desperate crisis. We must be independent. We must be free. We must preserve our full latitude and discretion of choice. In the past we have always had this freedom and independence. I have heard reproaches about the Liberal Government before the War, that they did not make enough preparations or look far enough ahead. But we were in a position where, at any rate, we had a complete freedom of choice; much might be lost by delay, but, as far as the safety of this country was concerned, we were not in any danger. We could hold our own here and take what time we chose to make up our minds, and what time we required to raise the whole vast might of the British Empire, month after month and year after year, from a peace to a war footing.

Nothing of that sort exists today, and unless we regain that freedom of choice, this is no longer integrally or characteristically the same kind of country in which we have always dwelt, and for hundreds of years have built up our own special, insular character and culture. We have never lived at anybody's mercy. We have never lived upon the good pleasure of any Continental nation in regard to our fundamental requirements. We have never entrusted the home defense of this country to any foreign Power. We have never asked for any help from anyone. We have given help to many, but to make good the security of our own island we have asked for help from none. I recognize the strong ties of interest, of sentiment, and of modern sympathy which unite the two great still-remaining Parliamentary democracies of Western Europe. The French and British populations are profoundly bent on peace, and their Governments have nothing to gain by war, but everything to lose. There are great ties which we have in common with the French Republic, but, in spite of all that, we ought not to be dependent upon the French air force for the safety of our island home. [Editor's Note: At this time the French air force ranked first in Europe in numbers.] Although there may be no engagement, the mere fact that you cannot defend yourselves and that your friend across the Channel has additional power makes a whole series of implications which very nearly involve the condition of dependence upon overseas protection. All history has proved the peril of being dependent upon a foreign State for home defense instead of upon one's own right arm. This is not a party question, not a question between pacifists and militarists, but one of the essential independence of character of our island life and its preservation from intrusion or distortion of any kind.

Let us see what we mean by safety. It is a word easy to use, but somewhat difficult to explain. Now that the hideous air war has cast the shadow of its wings over harassed civilization, no one can pretend that by any measures which we could take it would be possible to give absolute protection against an aggressor dropping bombs in this island and killing a great many unarmed men, women and children. No Government can be asked to guarantee absolute immunity to the nation if we were attacked in this way by this new arm. It is certainly in our power, however, if we act in time, to guard ourselves, first of all, from a mortal blow which would compel us to capitulate; and, secondly, it is in our power, I firmly believe, to make it extremely unlikely that we should be attacked, or that we should be attacked by this particular method of terrorizing the civil population by the slaughter of non-combatants, which, to the shame of the twentieth century, we are now forced to discuss as a practical issue.

For this purpose we ought to use every method which is available. We cannot afford to neglect any. I am going to mention what I consider are the four simultaneous lines of defense which we should develop. The first, of course, is a peaceful foreign policy. We must continue to strive, as we are striving, by every means, by every action, by every restraint and suppression of harsh feelings and expressions, to preserve the peace and harmony of Europe. No one, unless blinded by malice or confused by ignorance, would doubt that that has been the main desire of His Majesty's present Administration, just as it was of the Administration which preceded it.

What is the second line? We ought not to neglect any security which we can derive from international conventions. We must get all we can from them. I do not agree with those who say that these international conventions are not worth the paper on which they are written. It may well be that vague, general pious affirmations like the Kellogg Pact do not carry much practical conviction to people's minds, because everyone can see that, the right of self-defense being conceded, every country which plunges into war will allege that it is fighting in self-defense, and will probably convince its own people that it is doing so. It may be an extremely good thing in itself to make this wide, general affirmation that there will be no more war, but it undoubtedly has not carried conviction, and thus it has weakened the virtue of these international instruments. A greater measure of confidence can be reposed in more definite, limited and precise arrangements. At any rate, we should be very foolish to neglect them. Whatever may happen to the discussions now going on about regulating the size of air fleets, we should strive to secure an international convention or a series of treaties confirming air warfare to military and naval objectives and to the zones of field armies.

Such schemes would have to be drawn up in full detail, but I do not believe that this would be impracticable, and I hope the House is not going to be led by very easy arguments to suppose there is no validity or virtue in such arrangements. All the experience of the world shows that they have played their parts even in the most hideous quarrels of nations, and any nation that refused to enter into discussions of a convention to regulate air warfare would consequently be left in a position of grisly isolation, proclaiming its intention deliberately to make war as a scientific and technical operation upon women and children for the terrorization of the civil population. It would be a wise thing for us to get as many nations as possible to join in a convention which would exclude, on paper at any rate, this method from the arena of recognized warfare. I deprecate anything that is said to assume that such a method is compatible at all with any form of decent civilization. His Majesty's Government have been perfectly right to make it clear that no question of the convenience of using air warfare for police purposes in savage countries and barbarous regions should stand in the way of such an agreement of convention if that police measure becomes the sole obstacle to the conclusion of an arrangement otherwise generally satisfactory. We must not balance convenience against safety. Even if we were faced with the old difficulty of expense in maintaining order in the mountain valleys of India without the facilities of an air arm, provided there was a world consensus of opinion against the use of bombing undefended areas, it would be to our advantage to make the sacrifice in order to secure a much greater gain. Even taking the lowest view of human nature, nations in war do not usually do things which give them no special advantage, and which grievously complicate their own position.

No convention of the kind of which I have been speaking would be of the slightest use between the Great Powers unless it were based on parity [*i.e.* upon our having an Air Force equal to any other country within striking distance of our shores]. That is the key to any convention which may be negotiated. If one side had an all-powerful air force and the other only a very weak defense, the temptation to use the weapons of terror upon the civil population might far outweigh any detrimental effects on neutral opinion. If, however, the two sides were in an equality and in the position to do equal and simultaneous harm to each other, then the uselessness of the crime would reinforce its guilt and horror, and the effects upon the action of neutrals. I hold that we should make conventions to limit and regulate the use of the air arm, and these conventions should be made, and can only be made, on the basis of parity. If both sides feel that they would suffer equally from a breach of an international convention and neither side can see how it can gain an advantage over the other, it seems likely that these conventions will be respected. Not only would the danger of our being attacked be greatly diminished, but the character of the attack would be confined within the limits of the convention by breaking which neither side would have anything to gain.

That is the argument for parity, and for immediate parity. I believe that conventions based on parity are the best only means of shielding the crowded populations of our great cities, and particularly of this enormous London, by making it certain that there will be no advantage to either side in departing from what has been agreed. I do not see how the most sincere lover of peace or the most inveterate hater of war in this House can dispute the good sense and reason of the argument for parity.

There is, of course, one other and ultimate method of defense which we must also develop by every conceivable means. I mean the effective punishment and destruction, by an active and efficient home defense, of any invaders who may come to our shores. I do not pretend to deal with technical matters this afternoon. This is not the time for us to deal with them, nor do I think the House of Commons is the best place in which they can be ventilated, but I must express this opinion. It ought to be possible, by making good arrangements both on the ground and in the air, to secure very real advantages for the force of aeroplanes which is defending its own air and which can rise lightly laden from its own soil. I cannot believe that that advantage, properly organized, would not give an additional and important measure of protection. We should be able by these means to impose deterrents upon an invader, and even upon a potential declaration of war, and gradually to bring attacks upon us, by attrition, to smaller dimensions and finally to an end altogether. In these matters we have, of course, to trust our experts. I hope that they are busy, that they are tirelessly working out methods of defense; and we trust the Government and the Ministers concerned to guide the experts, and to make sure that the necessary funds and authority are supplied to carry out a complete scheme of home defense.

Therefore, there seem to me to be four lines of protection by which we can secure the best chance, and a good chance, of immunity for our people from the perils of air war—a peaceful foreign policy; the convention regulating air warfare; the parity in air power to invest that convention with validity; and, arising out of that parity, a sound system of home defense—in addition to all these other arrangements if they all fail. We must not despair, we must not for a moment pretend that we cannot face these things. Dangers come upon the world; other nations face them. When, in old days, the sea gave access to this island, it was a danger to this island. It made it liable to invasion at any point; but by taking proper measures our ancestors gained the command of the sea, and consequently, what had been a means of inroad upon us became our sure protection; and there is not the slightest reason why, with our ability and our resources, and our peaceful intentions, our desire only to live quietly here in our island, we should not raise up for ourselves a security in the air above us which will make us as free from serious molestation as did our control of blue water in bygone centuries. . . .

Germany is ruled by a handful of autocrats who are the absolute masters of that gifted nation. They are men who have neither the long interests of a dynasty to consider, nor those very important restraints which a democratic Parliament and constitutional system impose upon any executive Government. Nor have they the restraint of public opinion, which public opinion, indeed, they control by every means which modern apparatus renders possible. They are men who owe their power to, and are, indeed, the expression of, the bitterness of defeat, and of the resolved and giant strength of that mighty German Empire. I am not going to speak about their personalities, because there is no one in the House who is not thoroughly aware of them and cannot form his own opinion after having read the accounts of what has been happening there, of the spirit which is alive there and of the language, methods and outlook of the leading men of that tremendous community, much the most powerful in the whole world. The German power is in their hands, and they can direct it this way or that by a stroke of the pen, by a single gesture.

I dread the day when the means of threatening the heart of the British Empire should pass into the hands of the present rulers of Germany. I think we should be in a position which would be odious to very man who values freedom of action and independence, and also in a position of the utmost peril for our crowded, peaceful population, engaged in their daily toil. I dread that day, but it is not, perhaps, far distant. It is, perhaps, only a year, or perhaps eighteen months, distant. Not come yet—at least, so I believe, or I hope and pray. But it is not far distant. There is still time for us to take the necessary measures, but it is the measures we want. Not this paragraph in this White Paper; we want the measures. It is no good writing that first paragraph and then producing £130,000. We want the measures to achieve parity. The hon. Gentleman opposite who spoke so many words of wisdom seemed to me to mar the significance and point of his argument when he interposed in it the statement that he was not committing himself to any increase.

Mr. Mander: At this stage.

Mr. Churchill: But this *is* the stage. I do not say today, but within the next week or so. The turning-point has been reached, and the new steps must be taken. There are very special dangers to be feared if any Great Power possessing Dominions and connections all over the world falls into a peculiarly vulnerable condition. How many wars have we seen break out because of the inherent weakness of some great empire, such as the Hapsburg Empire or the Turkish Empire, when they fell into decay? Then all the dangerous forces become excited. No nation playing the part we play in the world, and aspire to play, has a right to be in a position where it can be blackmailed. . . .

But the scene has changed. This terrible new fact has occurred. Germany is arming—she is rapidly arming—and no one will stop her. None of the grievances between the victors and the vanquished have been redressed. The spirit of aggressive nationalism was never more rife in Europe and in the world. Far away are the days of Locarno, when we nourished bright hopes of the reunion of the European family and the laying in the tomb of that age-long quarrel between Teuton and Gaul of which we have been the victims in our lifetime.

That hope is gone, and we must act in accordance with the new situation. Here I address myself particularly to the Lord President. I say nothing in derogation of the high responsibility of the Prime Minister, but I address myself particularly to the Lord President as he is in his place in the House. He alone has the power. He has the power not only because of the confidence which is placed by large numbers of people of the country in the sobriety of his judgment and in his peaceful intentions, but also because, as leader of the Conservative party, he possesses the control of overwhelming majorities of determined men in both Houses of the Legislature. My right hon. Friend has only to make up his mind and Parliament will vote all the supplies and all the sanctions which are necessary, if need be within forty-eight hours. There need be no talk of working up public opinion. You need not go and ask the public what they think about this. Parliament and the Cabinet have to decide, and the nation has to judge whether they have acted rightly as trustees. The Lord President has the power, and if he has the power he has also what always goes with power—he has the responsibility. Perhaps it is a more grievous and direct personal responsibility than has for many years fallen upon a single servant of the Crown. He may not have sought it, but he is tonight the captain of the gate. The nation looks to him to advise it and lead it, to guide it wisely and safely in this dangerous question, and I hope and believe that we shall not look in vain.

DELUSION OF DISARMAMENT

March 14, 1934

House of Commons

[Extract] . . . False ideas have been spread about the country that disarmament means peace. The Disarmament Conference has brought us steadily nearer–I will not say to war because I share the repulsion from using that word, but nearer to a pronounced state of ill-will than anything that could be imagined. First of all, you were met with a competition among the different countries to disarm the other fellow, to take away the peculiar weapons of this or that other country, while safeguarding their own special military or naval interests. Then, in the second place, at Disarmament Conferences which were persisted in again and again year after year in spite of every failure, the desire was to throw the blame of the inevitable breakdown on some one country or another. "It was not me but that other country."

So in the end what have we got? We have not got disarmament. We have the rearmament of Germany. That is the monstrous offspring of this immense labour–the rearmament of Germany. Why, it is only a little while ago that I heard Ministers say and read diplomatic documents which said that rearmament was unthinkable–"Whatever happens, we cannot have that. Rearmament is unthinkable." Now all our hope is to regulate the unthinkable. Regulated unthinkability–that is the proposal now; and very soon it will be a question of making up our minds to unregulated unthinkability.

It is always an error in diplomacy to press a matter when it is quite clear that no further progress is to be made. It is also a great error if you ever give the impression abroad that you are using language which is more concerned with your domestic politics than with the actual fortunes and merits of the various great countries upon the Continent to whom you offer advice. Even suppose that the hon. Gentleman's mission shall be judged eventually to have failed, I am not so sure that we shall be so much worse off than if he had succeeded. Suppose France had taken the advice which we have tendered during the last four or five years, and had yielded to the pressure of the two great English-speaking nations to set an example of disarmament: suppose she had taken the advice of the Liberal newspapers! Only three or four years ago we noted the derision with which they wrote about the French barrier of fortresses which had been put up. Suppose the French had followed our example. Suppose they had made this gesture which is so much talked of today and had reduced themselves to allowing their defenses to fall into the kind of disarray to which we, out of the highest motives, for which we do not always get credit abroad, have reduced ours–what would be the position today? Where should we be?

I honour the French for their resolute determination to preserve the freedom and security of their country from invasion of any kind; I earnestly hope that we, in arranging our forces, shall not fall below their example. The awful danger, nothing less, of our present foreign policy is that we go on perpetually asking the French to weaken themselves. And what do we urge as the inducement? We say, "Weaken yourselves," and we always hold out the hope that if they do it and get into trouble, we shall then in some way or other go to their aid, although we have nothing with which to go to their aid. I cannot imagine a more dangerous policy. There is something to be said for isolation; there is something to be said for alliances. But there is nothing to be said for weakening the Power on the Continent with whom you would be in alliance, and then involving yourself further in Continental tangles in order to make it up to them. In that way you have neither one thing nor the other; you have the worst of both worlds.

The Romans had a maxim, "Shorten your weapons and lengthen your frontiers." But our maxim seems to be, "Diminish your weapons and increase your obligations." Aye, and diminish the weapons of your friends. That has been the extraordinary policy of late years. Great hopes were set on the Disarmament Conference when it began, and after Locarno there were great hopes. I am not going to pretend or suggest that the nagging and harping on disarmament have been the sole cause of the degeneration of European affairs. That would be unfair. Hideous new factors have rushed up at us from the gulf. Hideous new events have taken place which no one could have foreseen. Surely now we have reached a point where we ought to make an end of this effort to force disarmament upon countries which feel themselves in danger, and to put ourselves in a reasonable position of security. That will be better for peace, and much better for our own safety if peace should fail. . . .

AIR DEFENCE

July 7, 1934

Constituency Meeting, Wanstead

During the night of June 30, Hitler successfully purged the S.A. and its leaders. The brutality of the act and the mass of executions established Hitler's position, but sent shock-waves throughout Europe.

[Extract] . . . I want to ask where Mr. Baldwin stands. The Prime Minister has gone for a long holiday and all the power is now in the hands of Mr. Baldwin. Where the power lies there also lies the responsibility. Mr. Baldwin promised in the House of Commons last March that if the Disarmament Conference failed we should have an Air Force which would be equal to that of any other Power which could get at us. Lord Londonderry, the Air Minister, and Mr. Eden have told us in unmistakable terms that the Disarmament Conference has failed. How can it help failing when the Germans are arming night and day? Why, then, is Mr. Baldwin's promise not fulfilled?

We were told that plans were being made and that paper work was proceeding. All that ought to have been done long ago. We ought to have had a large vote of credit to double our Air Force–we ought to have it now, and a larger vote of credit as soon as possible to redouble the Air Force. We ought to concert plans for mutual protection with the French and with other peace-loving Powers which are in danger from what is happening and what might happen in Germany.

I have previously stated that minds are oppressed by the grisly events which occurred in Germany a week ago. It seems difficult to realize that a great and highly educated and scientific nation, with all its treasures of literature, learning, and music behind it, should present itself to the world in such an awful guise. We are in the presence of a tyranny maintained by Press and broadcast propaganda and the ruthless murder of political opponents. Where a band of ferocious men rise from depths to dictatorships there is no guarantee for life, or for law, or for liberty. Far greater assurances are given to society by a limited hereditary monarchy such as that under which we have the blessing to dwell.

It is likely that even more violent convulsions will occur in Germany before the German people regain coherent self-expression and make assurances of civil and religious freedom which alone make life worth living to civilized men and women. We must all hope that that day will come before Europe is dragged again into a catastrophe which might well be final for our civilization.

GERMANY APPROACHING AIR PARITY

July 30, 1934

House of Commons

This speech should be read with care. Virtually all the "facts" which it contains were inaccurate, but it made a considerable impression, not erased by Baldwin's unwise assurance that "parity" would be retained until the end of 1936. Baldwin's figures were also wrong.

[Extract] The position which has been unfolded to us today and the state of the world leave us in no doubt that Europe is moving ever more rapidly into a tightly drawn condition. Hatreds are rampant, disorder is rife, almost all the nations are arming, and everyone feels, as the Lord President of the Council has admitted, that the danger which we dread most of all and which we seek most of all to avert is drawing nearer to us. If this be the state of Europe, what is our position in relation to Europe? We are deeply involved in Europe. We are more deeply involved, much more precisely and formally involved, in Europe than we were twenty years ago. I think that is indisputable. We have signed the Treaty of Locarno. There is no doubt that we are at the present moment under obligations in regard to acts of aggression by Germany which are far more precise than any which bound us twenty years ago.

Ministers, with the full assent of Parliament, have repeatedly affirmed the sanctity, reality and modernity of these obligations. There is the Eastern Pact, which the Houses approved so generally and warmly, which does not add to our obligations but which certainly increases the contingencies in which existing obligations might become effective. Only last week we had a declaration from the Foreign Secretary reaffirming our interest in maintaining the neutrality of Belgium, in terms even stronger than before the Great War. Then there have been declarations, made, as far as I can gather, with the assent of Parliament, both sides as far as there are two sides, which have associated us with other great and friendly Powers in earnestly desiring to maintain the independence of Austria. We are to hear more about that tomorrow. Lord Halifax [Editor's Note: At that time President of the Board of Education.] on Saturday, in a public speech which no doubt will be studied with great care abroad, made it clear that we were not to be excluded as a factor in a possible European conflict, and, finally, the Lord President of the Council uses a phrase which I am sure by now has travelled from one end of the world to the other when he said, with his customary directness, that our frontier is the Rhine. If the Socialist Opposition had their way I gather that we should now have added the cold, unforgetting, unforgiving hostility of Japan to all these other serious preoccupations, and that the acting Leader of the Opposition would be reminding us that our frontier was the Yangtse.

What are the measures which the Government propose? We have a general scheme to spend an extra £20,000,000 in five years upon increasing our Air Force, of which we should spend £4,000,000 or £5,000,000 before the end of this Parliament. That probably means an addition to our fighting aeroplanes of perhaps fifty machines in the lifetime of the present Parliament. Instead of five hundred and fifty, which is our present home defense air strength, we shall have about six hundred by the end of the financial year 1935-6. At the present time we are the fifth or sixth air Power in all the world. [Editor's Note: It had recently become known that Soviet Russia had constructed a large air force, second only to that of France. Britain consequently declined from fifth to sixth position in the list.] But every State is rapidly expanding its air force. They are all expanding, but much more rapidly than we. It is certain, therefore, that when the Government, this National Government and this National House of Commons, go in 1936 to the country and give an account of their stewardship, we shall have fallen farther behind other countries in air defense than we are now.

If we extend our view over the five year's programme, I believe it is also true that, having regard to the increases which are being made and projected by other countries, we shall, at the end of the period, if there is continuity of policy between the two Parliaments, be worse off in 1939 relatively than we are now–and it is relativity that counts. By that time France, Soviet Russia, Japan, the United States, and Italy, if they carry out their present intentions, will be farther ahead of us than they are now. There is no dispute about this, just in the same way as there is no dispute about the gravity of the European situation or the manner in which we are involved in it. Yet even for this tiny, timid, tentative, tardy increase of the Air Force, to which the Government have at length made up their mind, they are to be censured by the whole united forces of the Socialist and Liberal parties here and throughout the country.

One would have thought that the character of His Majesty's Government and the record of its principal Ministers would have induced the Opposition to view the request for an increase in the national defense with some confidence and some consideration. I do not suppose there has ever been such a pacifist-minded Government. There is the Prime Minister who in the War proved in the most extreme manner and with very great courage his convictions and the sacrifices he would make for what he believed was the cause of pacifism. The Lord President of the Council is chiefly associated in the public mind with the repetition of the prayer, "Give peace in our time." One would have supposed that when Ministers like these come forward and say that they feel it their duty to ask for some small increase in the means they have of guaranteeing the public safety, it would weigh with the Opposition and would be considered as a proof of the reality of the danger from which they seek to protect us.

Then look at the apologies which the Government have made. No one could have put forward a proposal in such extremely inoffensive terms. Meekness has characterized every word which they have spoken since this subject was first mooted. We are assured that we can see for ourselves how small is the proposal. We are assured that it can be topped at any minute if Geneva succeeds—on which, of course, we all have expectations; I beg pardon, official expectations. We are assured of that. And we are also assured that the steps we are taking, although they may to some lower minds have associated with them some idea of national self-defense, are really only associated with the great principle of collective security.

But all these apologies and soothing procedures are most curtly repulsed by the Opposition. Their only answer to these efforts to conciliate them is a Vote of Censure, which is to be decided tonight. It seems to me that we have got very nearly to the end of the period when it is worth while endeavouring to conciliate some classes of opinion upon this subject. We are in the presence of an attempt to establish a kind of tyranny of opinion, and if its reign could be perpetuated the effect might be profoundly injurious to the stability and security of this country. We are a rich and easy prey. No country is so vulnerable and no country would better repay pillage than our own. With our enormous Metropolis here, the greatest target in the world, a kind of tremendous, fat, valuable cow tied up to attract the beast of prey, we are in a position in which we have never been before, and in which no other country in the world is at the present time.

Let us remember this: Our weakness does not only involve ourselves; our weakness involves also the stability of Europe. I was very glad to hear some admission from the Lord President of the Council of how he had found himself hampered, or his representatives had found themselves hampered at Geneva, by our weakness. If it is thought that there is nothing behind your words, when you are in fact in a position of great danger yourself, not much attention is paid to what you say; the march of events takes place regardless of it. That march has been set in motion. Who can say that we shall not ourselves be dragged into it? There is also a European duty and talk about our being good Europeans. The best way in which a British Member of Parliament or statesman can be a good European is to make sure that our country is safe and strong in the first instance. The rest may be added to you afterwards, but without that you are no kind of European. All you are is a source of embarrassment and weakness to the whole of the rest of the world. . . .

The need and the interest which the Government have in doing their duty turn upon whether the measures which they propose are really a contribution to our security or not. If they are not, then the Government run the risk of falling between two stools. Their duty is to provide adequate measures of defense before it is too late. Whatever they propose, they are going to be assailed by the pacifists throughout the country with all that interested and unscrupulous vituperation which we saw in the squalid election at Fulham some time ago and which finds an echo in these Votes of Censure this afternoon. Whatever the Government do, they are going to have that thrown at them, and it is vital therefore that they should so shape their course as to gather around them and behind them all the forces upon which they would naturally rely and to which they would look for support upon a question of this character. To encounter all this storm for something which is insufficient to meet the need is to have the worst of both worlds. The Government will get their abuse, but we shall not get our defense.

We must assume, of course, that Ministers have considered this aspect of the matter and that they see where their duty and their interest lie, but I must point out that there are no grounds whatever for suggesting that it is not possible to increase the Air Force more rapidly than is now proposed. I conceive that there are many ways of rapidly augmenting our Air Force which the Government have not adopted at present. The decision which they have just taken is a deliberate decision, and I confess I find it difficult to believe that it makes adequate provision against the dangers which we have to face and which are admitted. . . .

My question to the Government is this: What is their view about the German military air force? The Lord President used some sentences upon this point which I think were not cast by him with the intention of achieving any special degree of clarity. I understand, of course, that officially Germany has no air force at all. She is prohibited by the solemn treaties which she signed after the War from having any military aviation. But the right hon. Gentleman said that the worst crime is not to tell the truth to the public, and I think we must ask the Government to assure us that Germany has observed and is observing her treaty obligations in respect of military aviation. If so, I shall be greatly relieved, and I think the House will be greatly relieved. But if that assurance cannot be given–and, of course, it cannot be given–then I say we are bound to probe and examine what is taking place as far as we are in a position to do so. It was different when we were talking about Dreadnoughts. You could not build Dreadnoughts in boat-houses on the Elbe, and what Admiral von Tirpitz said before the War was found to be true–that nothing outside the regular program was being embarked upon. It is a different matter with regard to aeroplanes which can be so easily constructed and their component parts assembled. Military aviation shades into civil aviation by such indefinable graduations that I dare say the Government are right in not making statements which would in fact be charges and no doubt would be capable of being rebutted or denied.

I will venture, however, to assert some broad facts. I shall be delighted if the

Government are able to contradict them. I first assert that Germany has already, in violation of the Treaty, created a military air force which is now nearly two-thirds as strong as our present home defense air force. That is the first statement which I put before the Government for their consideration. The second is that Germany is rapidly increasing this air force, not only by large sums of money which figure in her estimates, but also by public subscriptions–very often almost forced subscriptions–which are in progress and have been in progress for some time all over Germany. By the end of 1935 the German air force will be nearly equal in numbers and efficiency–and after all no one must underrate German efficiency, because there could be no more deadly mistake than that–it will be nearly equal, as I say, to our home defense air force at that date even if the Government's present proposals are carried out.

The third statement is that if Germany continues this expansion and if we continue to carry out our scheme, then some time in 1936 Germany will be definitely and substantially stronger in the air than Great Britain. Fourthly, and this is the point which is causing anxiety, once they have got that lead we may never be able to overtake them. If these assertions cannot be contradicted, then there is cause for the anxiety which exists in all parts of the House, not only because of the physical strength of the German air force, but I am bound to say also because of the character of the present German dictatorship. If the Government have to admit at any time in the next few years that the German air forces are stronger than our own, then they will be held, and I think rightly held, to have failed in their prime duty to the country.

I ask, therefore, for a solemn, specific assurance from the Government that at no moment for which they will have responsibility will they fail to have a substantially superior military air force at home to that which they have reason to believe has been set on foot in Germany. Can that assurance be given? Will it be given? I think it will make a great difference to the judgment which must be passed upon these proposals if the Government are in a position to say that that is their resolve. . . .

If, therefore, you have to add to the regular increase in German military aeroplanes, which we have to expect and which, I imagine, the Government are well informed about, and which alone will bring the forces almost to equality by the end of 1935–if you have to add to that an enormous and indefinite transference of pilots and machines from civil to military aviation, it would seem that there is a very obvious danger that before the end of next year we shall be definitely weaker than the German aviation. I have tried to state these facts with moderation, and, as I say, nothing would give me greater pleasure than to learn that I have discovered another mare's nest. I shall rejoice at my own discomfort if these facts are able to be overturned or superseded by other more reassuring facts. But unless these facts can be contradicted, precisely and categorically, it seems to me that our position is a very serious one, and that not only should we brush aside a Vote of Censure on this small increase, but that we should urge a much greater degree of action, both in scale and speed, upon the responsible Ministers. . . .

The hon. Gentlemen opposite are very free-spoken, as most of us are in this country, on the conduct of the German Nazi Government. No one has been more severe in criticism than the Labour party or that section of the Liberal party which I see opposite. And their great newspapers, now united in the common cause, have been the most forward in the severity of the strictures. But these criticisms are fiercely resented by the powerful men who have Germany in their hands. So that we are to disarm our friends, we are to have no allies, we are to affront powerful nations, and we are to neglect our own defenses entirely. That is a miserable and perilous situation. Indeed, the position to which they seek to reduce us by the course which they have pursued and by the vote which they ask us to take is one of terrible jeopardy, and in voting against them tonight we shall hope that a better path for national safety will be found than that along which they would conduct us.

"THE CAUSES OF WAR"

November 16, 1934

Broadcast, London

[Extract] As we go to and fro in this peaceful country, with its decent orderly people going about their business under free institutions, and with so much tolerance and fair play in their laws and customs, it is startling and fearful to realise that we are no longer safe in our island home. For nearly a thousand years England has never seen the camp fires of an invader. The stormy seas and our Royal Navy have been our sure defence. Not only have we preserved our life and freedom through the centuries, but gradually we have come to be the heart and centre of an Empire which surrounds the globe. It is indeed with a pang of stabbing pain that we see all this in mortal danger.

A thousand years scarce serve to form a State,
An hour may lay it in the dust.

What shall we do?

Many people think that the best way to escape war is to dwell upon its horrors, and to imprint them vividly upon the minds of the younger generation. They flaunt the grisly photographs before their eyes. They fill their ears with tales of carnage. They dilate upon the ineptitude of generals and admirals. They denounce the crime and insensate folly of human strife.

All this teaching ought to be very useful in preventing us from attacking or invading any other country, if anyone outside a madhouse wished to do so. But how would it help us if we were attacked or invaded ourselves? That is the question we have to ask. Would the invaders consent to visit Lord Beaverbrook's exhibition, or listen to the impassioned appeals of Mr. Lloyd George? Would they agree to meet that famous South African, General Smuts, and have their inferiority complex removed in friendly reasonable debate? I doubt it. I gravely doubt it.

But even if they did, I am not sure we should convince them, and persuade them to go back quietly home. They might say 'You are rich, we are poor. You seem well fed, we are hungry. You have been victorious, we have been defeated. You have valuable colonies, we have none. You have your Navy, where is ours? You have had the past, let us have the future.' Above all, I fear, they would say 'You are weak and we are strong.'

After all, only a few hours away by air there dwells a nation of nearly seventy millions of the most educated, industrious, scientific, disciplined people in the world, who are being taught from childhood to think of war and conquest as a glorious exercise, and death in battle as the noblest fate for man. There is a nation which has abandoned all its liberties in order to augment its collective might. There is a nation which with all its strength and virtues is in the grip of a group of ruthless men preaching a gospel of intolerance and racial pride, unrestrained by law, by Parliament or by public opinion. In that country all pacifist speeches, all morbid war books, are forbidden or suppressed and their authors rigorously imprisoned. From their new table of commandments they have omitted 'Thou shalt not kill.' It is but twenty years since these neighbours of ours fought almost the whole world, and almost defeated them. Now they are rearming with the utmost speed, and ready to their hands is this new lamentable weapon of the air, against which our Navy is no defence, before which women and children, the weak and frail, the pacifist and the jingo, the warrior and the civilian, the front line trenches and the cottage home, lie in equal and impartial peril.

Nay worse still, for with the new weapon has come a new method, or rather has come back the most brutish methods of ancient barbarism, namely the possibility of compelling the submission of races by terrorising and torturing their civil population. And worst of all—the more civilised a country is, the larger and more splendid its cities, the more intricate the structure of its social and economic life; the more is it vulnerable, the more it is at the mercy of those who may make it their prey.

Now these are facts—hard, grim indisputable facts—and in face of these facts I ask again, what are we to do?

There are those who say 'Let us ignore the continent of Europe. Let us leave it with its hatreds and its armaments to stew in its own juice, to fight out its own quarrels, and cause its own doom. Let us turn our backs upon this melancholy and alarming scene. Let us fix our gaze across the oceans and lead our own life in the midst of our peace-loving dominions and Empire.'

Now there would be much to be said for this plan, if only we could unfasten the British islands from their rock foundations and could tow them three thousand miles across the Atlantic Ocean, and anchor them safely upon the smiling coasts of Canada. I have not yet heard of any way in which this could be done. No engineer has come forward with any scheme. Even our best scientists are dumb. It would certainly take a long time. Have we got a long time? At present we lie within a few minutes' striking distance of the French, Dutch, and Belgian coasts, and within a few hours of the great aerodromes of Central Europe. We are even within cannon-shot of the Continent. So close as that! Is it prudent, is it possible, however we might desire it, to turn our backs upon Europe and ignore whatever may happen there? Everyone can judge this question for himself, and everyone ought to make up his mind about it without delay. It lies at the heart of our problem. For my part I have come to the conclusion—reluctantly I admit—that we cannot get away. Here we are and we must make the best of it. But do not underrate the risks—the grievous risks—we have to run.

I hope, I pray, and on the whole, grasping the larger hope, I believe, that no war will fall upon us. But if in the near future the Great War of 1914 is resumed again in Europe after the Armistice—for that is what it may come to—under different conditions no doubt—no one can tell where and how it would end, or whether sooner or later we should not be dragged into it, as the United States were dragged in against their will in 1917. Whatever happened and whatever we did, it would be a time of frightful danger for us. And when the war was over, or perhaps while it still raged, we should be left face to face with the victors whoever they might be. Indeed, we should, with our wealth and vast possessions, be the only prize sufficient to reward their exertions and compensate them for their losses. Then certainly those who had tried to forget Europe would have to turn round very quickly indeed. And then it would be too late. Therefore it seems to me that we cannot detach ourselves from Europe, and that for our own safety and self-preservation we are bound to make exertions and run risks for the sake of keeping peace.

There are some who say—indeed it has been the shrill cry of the hour—that we should run the risk of disarming ourselves in order to set an example to others. We have done that already for the last five years; but our example has not been followed. On the contrary, it has produced the opposite result. All the other countries have armed only the more heavily; and the quarrels and intrigues about disarmament have only bred more ill-will between the nations.

Everyone would be glad to see the burden of armaments reduced in every country. But history shows on many a page that armaments are not necessarily a cause of war and that the want of them is no guarantee of peace. If, for instance, all the explosives all over the globe could by the wave of a magic wand be robbed of their power and made harmless, so that not a cannon or a rifle could fire, and not a shell or a bomb detonate, that would be a measure of world disarmament far beyond the brightest dreams of Geneva. But would it ensure peace? On the contrary, war would begin almost the next day when enormous masses of fierce men, armed with picks and spades or soon with clubs and spears, would pour over the frontiers into the lands they covet, and would be furiously resisted by the local populations and those who went to their aid. This truth may be unfashionable, unpalatable, unpopular. But it is the truth. The story of mankind shows that war was universal and unceasing for millions of years before armaments were invented or armies organised. Indeed the lucid intervals of peace and order only occur in human history after armaments in the hands of strong governments have come into being. And civilisation has been nursed only in cradles guarded by superior weapons and discipline. To remove the causes of war we must go deeper than armaments, we must remove grievances and injustice, we must raise human thought to a higher plane and give a new inspiration to the world. Let moral disarmament come and physical disarmament will soon follow. But what sign of this is there now?

When we look out upon the state of Europe and of the world and of the position of our own country, as they are now, it seems to me that the next year or the next two years will be a fateful turning point in our history. I am afraid that if you look intently at what is moving towards Great Britain, you will see that the only choice open is the old grim choice our forbears had to face, namely, whether we shall submit to the will of a stronger nation or whether we shall prepare to defend our rights, our liberties and indeed our lives. If we submit, our submission should be timely. If we prepare, our preparation should not be too late. Submission will entail at the very least the passing and distribution of the British Empire and the acceptance by our people of whatever future may be in store for small countries like Norway, Sweden, Denmark, Holland, Belgium and Switzerland, within and under a Teutonic domination of Europe.

The difficulty about submission—I state it calmly—is that we have already in this island the population of a first-class Power. And on our new scale of life as a smaller state we could not feed more than perhaps half those who now live here. Great stresses will arise in deciding which half should survive. You have perhaps read the story of 'The Raft of the *Medusa*.' I will not dwell on that repulsive scene. These are the disadvantages of submission and of Britain definitely relinquishing her great situation in the world.

Preparation on the other hand involves statesmanship, expense and exertion, and neither submission nor preparation are free from suffering and danger. . . .

THE GERMAN AIR MENACE

November 28, 1934

House of Commons

In response to this alarming speech delivered to a packed House, Baldwin denied that "Germany is rapidly approaching equality [in the air] with us," and said that her air strength was fifty per cent less than that of Britain.

[Extract] I beg to move, at the end of the Question, to add the words:

> But humbly represent to Your Majesty that, in the present circumstances of the world, the strength of our national defences, and especially of our air defences, is no longer adequate to secure the peace, safety, and freedom of Your Majesty's faithful subjects.

To urge the preparation of defence is not to assert the imminence of war. On the contrary, if war were imminent preparations for defence would be too late. I do not believe that war is imminent or that war is inevitable, but it seems very difficult to resist the conclusion that, if we do not begin forthwith to put ourselves in a position of security, it will soon be beyond our power to do so. What is the great new fact which has broken in upon us during the last 18 months? Germany is rearming. That is the great new fact which rivets the attention of every country in Europe, indeed in all the world, and which throws almost all other issues into the background. Germany is rearming, that mighty Power which only a few years ago, within our own experience, fought almost the whole world, and almost conquered. That mighty Power is now equipping itself once again, 70,000,000 of people, with the technical apparatus of modern war, and at the same time is instilling into the hearts of its youth and manhood the most extreme patriotic nationalist and militarist conceptions. According to what we hear, according to what we are told and what comes in from every quarter, though little is said about it in public, Germany has already a powerful well-equipped army, with an excellent artillery, and an immense reserve of armed trained men. The German munition factories are working practically under war conditions, and war material is flowing out from them, and has been for the last 12 months certainly, in an ever broadening flow. Much of this is undoubtedly in violation of the treaties which were signed. Germany is rearming on land; she is rearming also to some extent at sea; but what concerns us most of all is the rearmament of Germany in the air.

In my Amendment other aspects of defence besides the air are comprised, but I shall confine myself absolutely to the danger from the air. I shall be specially careful not to exaggerate. Indeed, I hope that every statement that I make will be admitted to be an understatement. I shall try my utmost to keep within the limits of what is really known and proved. Let us, first of all, look at the dimensions of the danger as it affects this country at the present time. However calmly surveyed, the danger of an attack from the air must appear most formidable. I do not accept the sweeping claim of the extreme votaries of the air. I think that a great many statements which are made are calculated to frustrate the purpose of reasonable precautions by presenting the problem as if it were one which was insoluble. But without accepting these claims no one can doubt that a week or 10 days' intensive bombing attack upon London would be a very serious matter indeed. One could hardly expect that less than 30,000 or 40,000 people would be killed or maimed. I see that General Seely, now known as Lord Mottistone, in the other House made some calculations on this subject. They were said to be of a reassuring character. But even those reassuring figures and calculations, I think, at least justify the statement I have just made, that a week or 10 days of this kind of intensive attack would result in 30,000 or 40,000 being killed or maimed.

The most dangerous form of air attack is the attack by incendiary bombs. Such an attack was planned by the Germans for the summer of 1918, I think for the time of the harvest moon. The argument in favour of such an attack was that if in any great city there are, we will say, 50 fire brigades, and you start simultaneously 100 fires or 80 fires and the wind is high, an almost incalculable conflagration may result. The reason why the Germans did not carry out that attack in 1918 must be stated. It was not at all, as Lord Mottistone suggested in another place, that our air defence had become so excellent that we were protected against it. It was because the advance of the Allied Armies, with the British Army in the van, already confronted the heads of the German State, the Imperial Government of Germany, with the prospect of impending defeat, and they did not wish to incur the fury of retribution which would follow from such a dreadful act of power and terror as that which would have been involved in such a raid. Since those days the incendiary thermite bomb has become far more powerful than any that was used in the late War. It will in fact, I am assured by persons who are acquainted with the science, go through a series of floors in any building, igniting each one simultaneously.

Not less formidable than these material effects are the reactions which will be produced upon the mind of the civil population. We must expect that under the pressure of continuous air attack upon London at least 3,000,000 or 4,000,000 people would be driven out into the open country around the Metropolis. This vast mass of human beings, numerically far larger than any armies which have been fed and moved in war, without shelter and without food, without sanitation and without special provision for the maintenance of order, would confront the Government of the day with an administrative problem of the first magnitude, and would certainly absorb the energies of our small Army and of our Territorial Force. Problems of this kind have never been faced before, and although there is no need to exaggerate them, neither on the other hand is there any need to shrink from facing the immense, unprecedented difficulties which they involve.

Then there are the questions of the docks of London and the estuary of the Thames. Everyone knows the dependence of this immense community, the most prosperous in the whole world, upon the Eastern approaches by water. I need say no more about that. We studied it very carefully in the War, and I have not the slightest doubt that it has weighed very much on the minds of His Majesty's Government. It ought not to be supposed that the danger of an air attack, assuming that such a thing occurred—I am only making an assumption and not by any means saying it will come to pass—would necessarily be confined to London or the area around it. Birmingham and Sheffield and the great manufacturing towns might all be made the subject of special study, and every part of the country is equally interested in whatever measures of security can be taken to provide against such a peril. Not less dangerous than the attack upon the cities and the great working-class areas and upon the manufacturing centres, would be that directed upon the dockyards and the oil fuel storage which, unless proper precautions are taken, as I trust they have been or are being taken, might actually paralyse the Fleet, with consequences which no one can fail to perceive.

Therefore, I suggest to the House in this first part of the argument, that the danger which might confront us, however moderately put, would expose us not only to hideous suffering, but even to mortal peril, by which I mean peril of actual conquest and subjugation. It is just as well to confront those facts while time remains to take proper measures to cope with them. I may say that all these possibilities are perfectly well known abroad, and no doubt every one of them has been made the subject of technical study. I, therefore, have stated to the House as briefly as possible—and I trust I have not overstated the case—the kind of danger which reasonably ought to be taken into consideration should, unhappily, a breakdown in European peace occur. . . .

The fact remains that when all is said and done as regards defensive methods—and all that you can say now has been said already—pending some new discovery, the only direct measure of defence upon a great scale is the certainty of being able to inflict simultaneously upon the enemy as great damage as he can inflict upon ourselves. Do not let us under-value the efficacy of this procedure. It may well prove in practice—I admit you cannot prove it in theory—capable of giving complete immunity. If two Powers show themselves equally capable of inflicting damage upon each other by some particular process of war, so that neither gains an advantage from its adoption and both suffer the most hideous reciprocal injuries, it is not only possible but it seems to be probable that neither will employ that means. What would they gain by it? Certainly a Continental country like the one of which I have been speaking, with large foreign armies on its frontiers, would be most unwise to run the risk of exposing itself to intensive bombing attacks from this island upon its military centres, its munition establishments and its lines of communication at a time when it was engaged or liable to be engaged by the armies of another first-class Power.

We all speak under the uncertainty of the future which has so often baffled human foresight, but I believe that if we maintain at all times in the future an air power sufficient to enable us to inflict as much damage upon the most probable assailant, upon the most likely potential aggressor, as he can inflict upon us, we may shield our people effectually in our own time from all those horrors which I have ventured to describe. If that be so, what are £50,000,000 or a £100,000,000 raised by tax or by loan compared with an immunity like that? Never has so fertile and so blessed an insurance been procurable so cheaply.

Observe the reverse of the picture. Assume that one country has a powerful air force and that the other has none, or that the other country has been so decisively beaten in the air that it has hardly any air force left. Then not only war machines but almost any flying machine that can be fitted to carry bombs will be employed to go over and to torture every part of the State and the community in that other country until it surrenders all that is asked from it. Absolute subjugation could in the end be enforced by such air attack, once a country had lost all power to fight in the air. Once complete ascendancy in the air had been secured, the victor Power might almost at leisure pick out any aircraft factory and make a special study of it, an intensive attack upon it, and thus there could be no recovery. It is almost the only form of war that we have seen in the world in which complete predominance gives no opportunity of recovery. That is the odious new factor which has been forced upon our life in this twentieth century of Christian civilisation.

For all these reasons, it seems to me, and I submit to the House, that we ought to decide now to maintain, at all costs, in the next 10 years an Air Force substantially stronger than that of Germany, and that it should be considered a high crime against the State, whatever Government is in power, if that force is allowed to fall substantially below, even for a month, the potential force which may be possessed by that country abroad. That is the object with which I have put this Amendment on the Paper. I am not going into other questions than those with which I am specially concerned to-day, but I must just mention that if, to this provision which I have suggested, you add those measures towards collective security by what I would call placing special constables upon the dangerous beasts in Europe and perhaps later on elsewhere, under the aegis and authority of the League of Nations, I firmly believe that we may have it in our power to avert from this generation the supreme catastrophe of another war. The idea that we can intervene usefully in sustaining the peace of Europe while we ourselves are the most vulnerable of all, are the beggars in fact, is one which cannot be held firmly by any man who looks at this in the faithful discharge of his duty.

I have now spoken of the danger, and I have indicated, as far as I can see, what is the only remedy or mitigation which is in our power, and I have suggested that it is a good and effective mitigation and a very reasonable security. I now come to compare the actual strengths, present and prospective, of Great Britain and Germany, as far as I have been able to form an opinion about them. Here again there is no reason to assume that Germany will attack. In fact, the German people have very friendly feelings in many ways towards us, and there is no reason at all why we should expect that they would attack us; but it is not pleasant for us—I will put it to the right hon. Gentleman the Leader of the Opposition—to feel that it may soon be in the power of the German Government to do so unless we act.

I will not dwell this afternoon on the character of the present German Government, because the House knows it all, and there is no need to repeat all that. I will content myself by saying that the decision of a handful of men, men of the 30th June, is all that is required to launch an attack upon us, if such an attack were possible, and that only the shortest notice or no notice at all could be counted upon. Never in our history have we been in a position where we could be liable to be blackmailed, or forced to surrender our possessions, or take some action which the wisdom of the country or its conscience would not allow it to do. Never have we been in a position where we could be subjected to that or, alternatively, have to face the horrible ordeal I have tried, very briefly, to place before the House. It is a danger to all Europe that we should be in that position, and I do not think His Majesty's Government ought to put us or leave us in such a plight, where we, with our wealth and Empire, exist on the good behaviour and good faith, which may not be lacking, but which may not be present, of the present rulers of Germany. I am sure our people are not willing to run such risks, and yet, as I am going to show, I think indisputably, this is the kind of danger which is coming upon us in a very short time unless we act upon a great scale and act immediately. . . .

The time has come when the mystery surrounding the German rearmament must be cleared up. We must know where we are. The House naturally in these matters leaves the main responsibility to the Executive, and that is quite right, but at the same time it cannot divest itself of responsibility for the safety of the country, and it must satisfy itself that proper measures are being taken. I will therefore this afternoon assume the duty of stating what, to the best of my belief, are the strengths and programmes of the German military air force which is being built up in contravention of the Treaty, and I invite my right hon. Friend the Lord President to confirm, correct, or contradict me when he speaks, as I believe he is going to do immediately after I sit down. If he does not contradict me or correct me, the House should assume that the statements which I make are true or at any rate that they are understatements; that is to say, I have not revealed the real state of things. In order that my right hon. Friend might be able to deal effectively with these issues and might not be confronted with them abruptly in the House, I sent him in the last week a précis of the exact points which I propose to put to him, and I understand that he has had an opportunity of consulting with the high expert authorities upon this matter.

I therefore assert, first, that Germany already, at this moment, has a military air force—that is to say, military squadrons, with the necessary ground services, with the necessary reserves of trained personnel, and material—which only await an order to assemble in full open combination—and that this illegal air force is rapidly approaching equality with our own. That is my first submission to the Government and to the House. Secondly, by this time next year, if Germany executes her existing programme without acceleration, and if we execute our existing programme on the basis which now lies before us without slowing down, and carry out the increases announced to Parliament in August last, the German military air force will this time next year be in fact at least as strong as our own, and it may be even stronger. Thirdly, on the same basis, that is to say, both sides continuing with their existing programme as at present arranged, by the end of 1936—that is, one year further on, and two years from now—the German military air force will be nearly 50 per cent. stronger, and in 1937 nearly double. All this is on the assumption, as I say, that there is no acceleration on the part of Germany, and no slowing down on our part. So much for the comparison of what may be called the first line air forces of the two countries. . . .

I assert and I invite the Government to contradict the statement if they can, that by this time next year, taking both the military and the convertible civil aircraft into consideration, Germany will have a substantially stronger Air Force than we. Frankly, I do not think that the country has prepared itself to realise this fact. The conditions in 1936 and 1937 if the German convertible machines are added to the military machines, will be that the German Air Force will, of course, be far more adverse to this country than the purely military figures, which are bad enough, that I gave a few moments ago. . . .

I have now completed my review of the two countries and I invite my right hon. Friend the Lord President to state, if I am wrong, where I am wrong, and to what extent I am wrong. But I cannot leave this subject without also referring to another cause of anxiety. So far, I have dealt with what, I believe, is the known, but beyond the known there is also the unknown. We hear from all sides of an air development in Germany far in excess of anything which I have stated to-day. As to that, all I would say is: Beware. Germany is a country fertile in military surprises. The great Napoleon, in the years after Jena, was completely taken by surprise by the strength of the German army which fought the war of liberation. Although he had officers all over Germany the strength of the army which fought him in the Leipzig campaign was three or four times as strong as he expected. Similarly, when the Great War broke out, the French general staff had no idea of the reserve divisions which would be brought against them. They expected to be confronted by 25 army corps; actually more than 40 came against them.

It is never worth while to underrate the military qualities of this most remarkable and gifted people, nor to underrate the dangers that may be brought against us. I only say it does not follow that, in stating the figures I have to-day, I am not erring grievously on the side of under-statement. It sounds absurd to talk about 10,000 aeroplanes, and so on, but, after all, the resources of mass production are very great, and I remember when the War came to an end the organisation over which I presided at the Ministry of Munitions was actually making aeroplanes at the rate of 24,000 a year, and planning a very much larger programme for 1919. Of course, such numbers of aeroplanes could never be placed in the air at any one moment, nor a tenth of them, but the figures give one an idea of the scale to which manufacture might easily assume if long preparations have been made beforehand, and a great programme of production is launched.

The danger I have dealt with. I have mentioned the remedy so far as it can be described, and I have compared the two air forces. But what have we done in the last year? This is the last aspect with which I wish to deal. We had a Debate last March, and there was a good deal of anxiety expressed. My right hon. Friend the Lord President made a very weighty declaration, and he broke the back of the Debate. But in the evening the Debate revived, and a great deal of anxiety was expressed for a more explicit statement, and my right hon. Friend showed a little less than his usual imperturbable urbanity and patience, and said, "If you are not satisfied, you can go to a Division." What was the use of going to a Division? You might walk a majority round and round the Lobbies for a year, and not alter the facts by which we are confronted. What happened after the March Debate? Very little–so far as I can see, nothing happened for five months. Then we came to July. In July, the right hon. Gentleman came down to the House with the full authority of the Government and announced the programme of the 42 new squadrons to be added to the Air Force in five years. I pointed out there and then that this scheme did not propose to strengthen the Air Force even by one additional squadron before 31st March next, and only by 50 machines–that is to say, 50 machines in their proper squadrons with all their reserves, and so on–by 31st March, 1936. Another five months have passed, and we now know that nothing has been done, and that nothing will be done before 31st March which will involve a Supplementary Estimate. I am well aware of all that has been rightly said of the complication of this service and the necessity of preliminary preparation, and so forth. I will deal with that not now, but when an opportunity occurs upon the Air Estimates. I submit to the House that to continue this dilatory process in the present situation, even for a few more months, and certainly for another year, will deprive us of the power ever to overtake the German air effort. I therefore invite His Majesty's Government to tell us, firstly, what are the facts; and, secondly, if the facts are admitted, what will be their action?

I have only one more thing to say, and I address myself to the Liberal and Labour Oppositions. We read almost every day–certainly every week–in their great popular newspapers the most searching and severe criticism of the existing German regime. Nowhere is that criticism put with greater force and ability and from no quarter is it, I believe, more resented by the present rulers in Germany because it is in the main true. Things are said which are capable of raising the deepest antagonism, not in the breasts of the German people, because they have nothing to say as to their own destiny, but in the breasts of those powerful men who control the people. How can hon. Members opposite reconcile that criticism with the other parts of their policy, which is to cover with contumely and mockery and odium every attempt to secure a modest and reasonable defence to maintain the safety of the country? I have not always found myself in full agreement with this House of Commons, but I have never lost all hope that it will prove itself to be what its creators hoped for it, a great House of Commons in the history of the country. The election which brought this House into power was one in which the greatest number of voters ever called upon to record the franchise in this country voted, above all things, for the maintenance of the strength and the security of their native land. That was the emotion which brought us into power, and I would venture to say: Do not, whatever be the torrent of abuse which may obstruct the necessary action, think too poorly of the greatness of our fellow countrymen. Let the House do its duty. Let the Government give the lead, and the nation will not fail in the hour of need.

AIR PARITY LOST

May 2, 1935

House of Commons

In response to a formidable speech by Churchill on March 19, the Government gave assurances that Britain had not lost her air superiority. As we now know, this was correct, but on March 25 Hitler announced German "parity" in air power. For the first time serious Conservative uneasiness was apparent.

[Extract] If only Great Britain, France and Italy had pledged themselves two or three years ago to work in association for maintaining peace and collective security, how different might have been our position. Indeed, it is possible that the dangers into which we are steadily advancing would never have arisen. But the world and the Parliaments and public opinion would have none of that in those days. When the situation was manageable it was neglected, and now that it is thoroughly out of hand we apply too late the remedies which then might have effected a cure. There is nothing new in the story. It is as old as the Sibylline Books. It falls into that long, dismal catalogue of the fruitlessness of experience and the confirmed unteachability of mankind. Want of foresight, unwillingness to act when action would be simple and effective, lack of clear thinking, confusion of counsel until the emergency comes, until self-preservation strikes its jarring gong–these are the features which constitute the endless repetition of history.

All this leads me to the principal matter–namely, the state of our national defenses and their reactions upon foreign policy. Things have got much worse, but they have also got much clearer. It used to be said that armaments depend on policy. It is not always true, but I think that at this juncture it is true to say that policy depends, to a large extent, upon armaments. It is true to say that we have reached a position where the choice of policy is dictated by considerations of defense. During the last three years, under the Government of Herr Hitler, and before him under that of Chancellor Bruning, Germany worked unceasingly upon a vast design of rearmament on a scale which would give the Germans such a predominance in Europe as would enable them, if they chose–and why should they not choose?–to reverse the results of the Great War. The method should be noted. The method has been to acquire mastery in the air, and, under the protection of that mastery, to develop–and it is fortunately a much longer process–land and sea forces which, when completed, would dominate all Europe. This design is being completed as fast as possible, and the first part of it–German ascendancy in the air–is already a fact. The military part is far advanced, and the naval part is now coming into view. . . .

I have stated the position in general terms, and I have tried to state it not only moderately but quite frigidly. Here I pause to ask the Committee to consider what these facts mean and what their consequences impose. I confess that words fail me. In the year 1708 Mr. Secretary St. John, by a calculated Ministerial indiscretion, revealed to the House the fact the battle of Almanza had been lost in the previous summer because only 8,000 British troops were actually in Spain out of the 29,000 that had been voted by the House of Commons for this service. When a month later this revelation was confirmed by the Government, it is recorded that the House sat in silence for half an hour, no Member caring to speak or wishing to make a comment upon so staggering an announcement. And yet how incomparably small that event was to what we have now to face. That was merely a frustration of policy. Nothing that could happen to Spain in that war could possibly have contained in it any form of danger which was potentially mortal.

But what is our position today? For many months, perhaps for several years, most critical for the peace of Europe, we are inexorably condemned to be in a position of frightful weakness. If Germany were the only Power with which we were concerned, if we stood alone compared with Germany, and if there were no other great countries in Europe who shared our anxieties and dangers and our point of view, and if air warfare were the only kind of warfare by which the destinies of nations was decided, we should then have to recognize that this country, which seemed so safe and strong a few years ago, which bore with unconquerable strength all the strains and shocks of the Great War, which has guarded its homeland and its independence for so many centuries, would lie at the discretion of men now governing a foreign country. There are, however, friendly nations with whom we may concert our measures of air defense, and there are other factors, military and naval, of which in combination we can dispose. Under the grim panoply which Germany has so rapidly assumed there may be all kinds of stresses and weaknesses, economic, political and social, which are not apparent–but upon these we should not rest ourselves.

It seems undoubted that there is an effective policy open to us at the present time by which we may preserve both our safety and our freedom. Never must we despair, never must we give in, but we must face facts and draw true conclusions from them. The policy of detachment or isolation, about which we have heard so much and which in many ways is so attractive, is no longer open. If we were to turn our backs upon Europe, thereby alienating every friend, we should by disinteresting ourselves in their fate invite them to disinterest themselves in ours. Is it then expected that we could go off with a wallet full of German Colonies gathered in the last war and a world-wide collection of territories and trade interests gathered in the past, when the greatness of our country was being built up, while all the time we should in this vital matter of air defense be condemned to protracted, indefinite and agonizing inferiority? Such a plan has only to be stated to be rejected.

There is a wide measure of agreement in the House tonight upon our foreign policy. We are bound to act in concert with France and Italy and other Powers, great and small, who are anxious to preserve peace. I would not refuse the co-operation of any Government which plainly conformed to that test as long as it was willing to work under the authority and sanction of the League of Nations. Such a policy does not close the door upon a revision of the Treaties, but it procures a sense of stability, and an adequate gathering together of all reasonable Powers for self-defense, before any inquiry of that character can be entered upon. In this august association for collective security we must build up defense forces of all kinds and combine our action with that of friendly Powers, so that we may be allowed to live in quiet ourselves and retrieve the woeful miscalculations of which we are at present the dupes, and of which, unless we take warning in time, we may some day be the victims.

"DEEPENING AND DARKENING DANGER"

May 31, 1935

House of Commons

[Extract] . . . One would imagine, sitting in this House today, that the dangers were in process of abating. I believe that the exact contrary is the truth–that they are steadily advancing upon us, and that no one can be certain that a time may not be reached, or when it will be reached, when events may have passed altogether our of control. We must look at the facts. Nourish your hopes, but do not overlook realities.

The Secretary of State for Foreign Affairs [Sir John Simon] dropped out a phrase today which really is in keeping with what I call the illusion basis on which much of this discussion has proceeded. It was one of those casual phrases which nevertheless reveal an altogether unsound conception of the facts. He referred to countries with whom you feel it your absolute duty to remain on terms of air equality. Look at that. A "duty to remain on terms of air equality." We have not got equality. Speeches are made in the country by leading Ministers saying that we have decided that we must have air equality, that we cannot accept anything less. We have not got it. We are already decidedly inferior to Germany, and, it must be said, of course to France. All that lies before us for many months is that this inferiority becomes more and more pronounced. In the autumn of this year, in November, when we are supposed to be 50 per cent. stronger, I hazard the melancholy prediction that we shall not be a third, possibly not a quarter, of the German air strength. What is the use of saying "the countries with whom we consider it our absolute duty to remain on terms of air equality"? This is one of the terrible facts which lie before us and which will not be swept away merely by following the very natural inclination which we all have to say that they do not exist.

The German Army, already developed to twenty-one or twenty-two divisions, is working up to thirty-six as fast as it can, a division a month or something like that coming into full mobilizable capacity, tanks and the whole business. There is the Navy, and submarines have been made. Some are actually, I believe, practicing, training their crews in that difficult art. Let me tell the House that submarines can be manufactured very quickly. I remember in November 1914 arranging for Mr. Schwab, of Bethlehem, to make twenty submarines in what was then considered the incredibly short period of six months. Although these vessels had to be shifted from the United States to a Canadian dockyard for reasons of neutrality, it was possible to put sections on the railway-trucks and to deliver them in time. How do you know what progress has been made in constructing such sections? The arms production has the first claim on the entire industry of Germany. The materials required for the production of armaments are the first charge on the German exchange. The whole of their industry is woven into an immediate readiness for war. You have a state of preparedness in Germany industry which was not attained by our industry until after the late War had gone on probably for two years.

Besides this, there is tremendous propaganda, beginning with the schools and going right through every grade of youth to manhood, enforced by the most vigorous and harsh sanctions at every stage. All this is taking place. It is a very nice comfortable world that we look out on here in this country. It has found an apt reflection in this Debate today, but it has no relation whatever to what is going forward, and going forward steadily. Mark you, in time of peace, in peace politics, in ordinary matters of domestic affairs and class struggles, things blow over, but in these great matters of defense, and still more in the field of actual hostilities, the clouds do not roll by. If the necessary measures are not taken, they turn into thunderbolts and fall on your heads. The whole of this great process of psychological, moral, material and technical mobilization of German war power is proceeding ceaselessly and with ever-increasing momentum.

It is the growth of German armaments which has fascinated and petrified nation after nation throughout Europe. Just look at what has happened in the last few weeks since we were last engaged in a serious discussion on foreign affairs. We know perfectly well that Poland continues in the German system. The Czechoslovakian elections have created a new Nazi party in Czechoslovakia, which is, I believe, the second party in the State. [May 19.] That is a very remarkable fact, having regard to the energy which the German people, when inspired by the Nazi spirit, are able to exercise. The Austrian tension increases. Many people talk about guaranteeing the independence of Austria, but guaranteeing that Austria will be kept separate from Germany is a different thing. You may at any time be faced with the position that the will of the Austrian people will be turned in the reverse direction from that which our policy has hitherto proclaimed. There is the Danubian tour of General Goering. He has been to Yugoslavia, Bulgaria and to Hungary. He has, in Hungary and Bulgaria, been renewing those old ties of comradeship and confidence which existed between them and Germany in the days of the War. In Yugoslavia undoubtedly his presence has exercised a very important influence there as a counter-influence to others that may be brought to bear. Everywhere these countries are being made to look to Germany in a special way, and let me say that I read in the *Times* on the 30th of May a significant telegram from Vienna dealing with this tour of General Goering, which finished up with these words: "In the circumstances the strength and clarity of German policy gains by contrast"— that is, to the Allied policy—"and the waverers among the smaller States are closely watching events."

There is the question of the relations between Germany and Japan. It seems to me that that is a matter which must be in the thoughts of everyone who attempts to make an appreciation of the foreign situation. There are the difficulties of Italy's preoccupation with Abyssinia. There are the obvious stresses through which France is passing, not, indeed, in the matter of national defense, but in almost every other aspect of the life of that people. There is our own weakness in the air which is to become worse and worse month after month. All this is going forward.

It is easy, then, for Herr Hitler and the German Government to pursue a policy which I have heard described as "power diplomacy." What a transformation has taken place in the last two or three years! Two or three years ago it was considered sentimental, intellectual, liberally minded, to speak words of encouragement and compassion, and even to speak patronizingly of the German people, and to seek opportunities of making gestures to raise them up to more and greater equality with other countries. Now we see them with their grievances unredressed, with all their ambitions unsatisfied, continuing from strength to strength, and the whole world waits from week to week to hear what are the words which will fall from the heads of the German nation. It is a woeful transformation which has taken place.

It would be folly for us to act as if we were swimming in a halcyon sea, as if nothing but balmy breezes and calm weather were to be expected and everything were working in the most agreeable fashion. By all means follow your lines of hope and your paths of peace, but do not close your eyes to the fact that we are entering a corridor of deepening and darkening danger, and that we shall have to move along it for many months and possibly for years to come. While we are in this position, not only have we our own safety to consider, but we have to consider also whether the Parliamentary Governments of Western Europe, of which there are not many that function in the real sense of the word, are going to be able to afford to their subjects the same measure of physical security, to say nothing of national satisfaction, as is being afforded to the people of Germany by the dictatorship which has been established there. It is not only the supreme question of self-preservation that is involved in the realization of these dangers, but also the human and the world cause of the preservation of free Governments and of Western civilization against the ever-advancing forces of authority and despotism.

GOVERNMENT OF INDIA BILL
June 5, 1935

House of Commons

This speech marked the end of Churchill's long battle over India–described by Hoare as "Churchill's Seven Years' War." He was immediately followed in the debate by Leo Amery, who opened his remarks with the words "Here endeth the last chapter of the Book of Jeremiah."

[Extract] . . . We are now at the end of these prolonged debates. It has been a very prolonged fight, and a very uneven fight. We have had a great deal against us: all the forces of the National Government, and all the machinery, prestige, and loyalties of the Conservative party, used contrary to its instincts and traditions. We have had the Socialist and Liberal parties supporting the Bill, except that it does not go far enough for them. All the weight of their opinion, if they would like me to assign due weight to it, has been added to the current against us. All the social influence and political patronage, and power of the Government here and in India, the whole of the vast majority in this House, collected in 1931 on the impulse of a great emergency, on a wave of patriotism and a great desire expressed by the people that Britain should be honourable and strong; all this has been thrown against us. Even now, when I have hardly finished dealing with the hon. Member for Bodmin I understand that the right hon. Member for Sparkbrook (Mr. Amery) is sharpening up his Birmingham pencil for his rejoinder with his approved vigour.

I am ready to admit that these forces have proved too strong for us. Our consolation is that we have tried our best, that we have not left undone anything we could have done to place the resistance to this policy before the people of the country. The hon. and gallant Member for Bournemouth (Sir H. Croft) and I have worked together for five long years and have been ready to sacrifice our time and labour, and, I am sorry to say, in some cases personal friendships, in order that we might do what we consider, and still consider, to be no more than our duty. I am glad that these long debates in this House are now coming to an end and that they have not been inflamed or complicated by any conflict about procedure. We came to an arrangement about procedure and the minority have no reason to complain of the time allotted or that they have not been able to state their case with the fullest freedom of debate that could be desired. And I think we may all join in congratulating the Chairman of Committees–if it is not presumptuous to speak in that way of an officer of the House who has assisted us so much–and to congratulate also, I must add, the Chief Whip, who has played a great part in devising this plan for regulating our procedure. We may join in congratulating them on what may well be an invaluable revival of old English Parliamentary customs.

But there my compliments and tributes come to an abrupt conclusion. Speaking for the Conservative minority which voted 80 against the Second Reading and which represents, even under the hardest test that could be applied, at least one-third of the Conservative party in the country, I am bound to state that our views have not received the slightest consideration from His Majesty's Government. I suppose that if we had been a handful, a baker's dozen of Socialist refugees, great attention would have been paid to our opinions. I remember the great attention that was paid to the opinions of even one single Socialist Member of the Government–Mr. Snowden as he was then, and Viscount Snowden as he now is–when the land taxes were actually kept on for two whole years against the wishes of the great majority of the House simply in order not to hurt the feelings of so eminent a recruit from the Socialist ranks. But being what you are pleased to call Tory Die-hards our feelings and wishes can be safely brushed aside. However, the fact remains that our differences of principle and method upon this Bill are in no way diminished.

Our opposition is not in the slightest way mitigated by anything that has occurred. We must say that we remain quite unreconciled, except to the fact that you are carrying this Measure over our heads. Indeed, in all my Parliamentary experience I never knew a Measure where the gulf between Members of the same party and between men who have so much in common in the work they have to do in the future, as well as in their sentiments and relationship, has remained so profound and so unbridged. The processes of argument which usually lead to some understanding and which if not developed effectively upon the Floor of the House at any rate make it easy for people to talk over these matters outside—these processes of argument, though employed with so much patience and elaboration, only led many of us to the feeling that on this subject we no longer talked the same language. In our view not one of the main arguments against this Bill—some of which we have set forth in the Amendment on the Order Paper—has been met or even attempted to be met. Ministers have made speeches denying the validity of the arguments or traversing them by counter-assertions, and in every division they have brought in almost 200 gentlemen who have definitely made up their minds, not that this Bill is a good one, but that it would be a good thing to put it through and get it out of the way. I said I would pay no more tributes, but I must pay one more to the Chief Whip. He certainly deserves congratulations, not only for his part in evolving this procedure but on other counts as well. The Secretary of State has had the support of several able colleagues on the Front Bench—and particularly the Under-Secretary, who has distinguished himself greatly and has established a Parliamentary reputation of a high order. He has had many able colleagues to assist him on that Bench, but there was one colleague whose powers of dialectic, whose forcible eloquence, whose power to raise in people's minds the most weighty considerations, at any rate must not be overlooked. I do not know whether you could say of the Chief Whip that he was a flower to blush unseen, but certainly he has not wasted his fragrance upon the desert air. . . .

Surely, then, we are entitled to examine the question from this point of view: Is this really for the good of Indians? Is what you are offering India now for India's good? If there never had been any question of winning assent; if there never had been any chance of a settlement with the geographical abstraction called India, is it conceivable that we should be confronted with these proposals? No. These proposals are the rejected addresses of the Government, and in my opinion they bear no relation to the kind of proposal which would have been put forward if the merits and the merits alone had animated the Imperial Parliament in making this plan. Either a scheme must make for better government or it must command the agreement of those for whom it is devised. Either we must have a good system or we must have acceptance. Our case is that His Majesty's Government now have neither. They have reconciled themselves to a vast degeneration in the quality and character of British administration in India, but they have not attained the peace and harmony which come from the active consent and co-operation of those for whom their gifts are designed.

Everyone has the worst of both worlds. The Indian politicians and the Indian people have the worst of both worlds, because they get a poorer administrative service in forms which they dislike—and say they dislike—even more than they do the present system. The Government have the worst of both worlds, because, in their argument, they can neither claim to provide good government nor government by consent. All, then, that we have is an inferior form of government, federal and provincial, which encounters almost universal reprobation. In the name of liberty you have done what liberty disowns. In the name of theoretical progress, you have opened the door to practical retrogression. In the name of appeasement and the popular will, you have prescribed a course of endless irritation. In response to Indian public opinion, you have supplied what all Indians–all shades of Indian Public opinion–repudiate. Whatever may be said about the Constitution being fixed and unalterable, as you declare it to be, it is certainly not final and not enduring. In so far as so vast an instrument of government is worked at all–and I agree with the hon. Gentleman opposite that it will be worked–in so far as it is worked, it will be worked only that it may be changed. You have unsettled everything. You have settled nothing. Those whom you have sought to conciliate are those whom you have most offended. Those to whom your mission is most necessary are those whom you have most entirely abandoned. Those on whom you have to count most are those whom you are teaching least of all to count on you.

We must ask one final question–the greatest of all these questions. Does this Bill mean a broadening of Indian life, a widening and elevation of Indian thought? Does it mean that the Indian toiler when he rises to his daily task will have a better chance of, in the words of the American Constitution, "life, liberty and the pursuit of happiness"? India is a country, almost a continent, which responded to the influence of British peace, order and justice and all the applications of modern science, only by an increase of population. There has been a tremendous increase of population there. New wealth, new food, new facilities for locomotion, new hygiene, new canals, improvements in forestry and agriculture have not made the Indian masses better off. They have only brought into being in the last 50 years 100,000,000 more souls in India. A gigantic population has remained, upon the whole, at a very low level of human subsistence, but has become much more numerous.

Such a vast helpless mass requires extra British guidance, higher efficiency of government, more British civil servants and a stricter and more vigorous administration in all technical matters. All you offer them are liberal formulas, administrative relaxation and decline. The huge machine of Indian government is to be allowed to slow down, just at the time when the inhabitants of India have multiplied far beyond the limit of their basic food supply, just at the time when they require, above all things, a far higher measure of disinterested and enlightened autocracy. Just at that very time you offer this bouquet of faded flowers of Victorian Liberalism which, however admirable in themselves, have nothing to do with Asia and are being universally derided and discarded throughout the continent of Europe.

Mr. Isaac Foot: So much the worse for Europe.

Mr. Churchill: For this bouquet they have to pay a heavy price. Money raised by taxes in India which, like the salt tax, draw exactions from the poorest of the poor, from people whose poverty is inconceivable even to the poorest of the poor in this country–this money is needed and its extraction is only justified if it is used for hospitals, for plague prevention, for technical education, for improved irrigation and other modern apparatus. Only in this way can a population which is one-sixth of the human race be kept at its present artificial level of numbers. In the standard of life they have nothing to spare. The slightest fall from the present standard of life in India means slow starvation, and the actual squeezing out of life, not only of millions but of scores of millions of people who have come into the world at your invocation and under the shield and protection of the British power.

Of course you may say that India is a long way off, and that it will not happen all at once–that the process will be gradual. It is difficult for us to imagine the consequences of the long degeneration which will take place in the processes by which this vast population is maintained at its present artificial number in India. I came out of the House one day last week full of the news of the frightful earthquake which had taken place at Quetta with a death roll of 30,000. I thought to myself of how in a previous century when the news of the Lisbon earthquake arrived here, it was said that London was like a city of the dead for a week, so consternated were the people at the contemplation of so awful a catastrophe. As I went out into the streets that evening I found, indeed, some mention of the earthquake on the posters, but the bulk of the papers were concerned with a local murder case. That shows how very ineffectual is the popular imagination in realising catastrophes which are distant–as is still more the case when those catastrophes come insensibly and gradually upon us.

These harassed, helpless, utterly dumb scores of millions in India have now to pay a sum of money to the Indian Budget, quite an appreciable, indeed a substantial sum annually, and a much larger sum when an election is to be arranged and 5,000 candidates are to carry through their electoral duties. They are to be asked to pay this sum from their scanty means for a political excursion in a western char-a-banc. You are going to wring from some of the poorest people in the world a subscription for a worse form of government at a higher price. They have not asked for it. It arises out of your wish to gratify the political classes, the articulate classes–the landlords, the mill-owners, the lawyers and the politicians. You have taught yourselves that these classes represent that wonderful mystic conception of India–"India, She."

You have decided and you have the power. You have shown you have the power to force this through, and no doubt you have the power to force it upon the people of India. But is now appears that even these political classes are not satisfied with the government which you are going to give to them, with the constitution which you offer, or with the sacrifice which the Indian masses are to be asked to give. By every organ through which they can express their views, they reject your government and they spit upon your ill-conceived generosity, if generosity it be. Even the very classes of wealthy, small, unrepresentative minorities for whom you have set out to cater, have rejected the dish which your proffer to them.

This, then, is your plan for the better Government of India. We thank God that we have neither part nor lot in it. You have done what you like. You have now a harder thing before you, and that is to like what you have done. Only the years can make their proof of whether you will be successful in that or not. What has astounded me is that the Government should have pressed forward so obstinately with this Indian policy, which causes so much distress to many important elements in the Conservative party, at a time when the domestic political situation is so uncertain, when the Continent of Europe is drifting steadily nearer to the brink of catastrophe, when we have before us for so many months to come that awful hiatus in our air strength and in the vital defences of Great Britain. I should have thought that common prudence alone would have led them to make some modification of their plans which are admittedly makeshift, which conform to no logic or symmetry, which are not fixed by any agreement or treaty with any elements in Indian public life. It has astonished me that that has not occurred to them. . . .

Here we are at the end of the Bill, but we are not, unhappily, at the end of the controversy. When this Bill is on the Statute Book it is true that a memorable chapter in British history will be closed. A great and melancholy event will have occurred of which everyone, even the most ardent partisan against the Measure, must take account. It may also be true that even more serious events will supervene in Europe. We have neither the intention nor the power to obstruct the setting up of provincial government under this Bill. But the Bill is not instantaneous in its action. There is no day on which it can be said that it will come into operation. It may be a year, or it may be two years before the Provinces can be handed over. It may be five years or it may be more before the assent of the Princes is procured, or before other conditions, precedent to the inauguration of Federal Home Rule, such as conditions of financial solvency, have been effectively established. The interpretation which will be placed upon those conditions will, obviously, be most important. That is why it is necessary for those who feel that all these steps should be watched with the greatest vigilance, should remain in company, and should endeavour to limit and mitigate, as far as they can, the evils which we feel are now being let loose upon the State. In this House of Commons we are in a minority so small, and your majority is so large, that we can be sullenly or superciliously voted down. It is possible that in the new Parliament we may be a larger proportion of your forces than we are now and that consequently you may be more inclined to pay attention to our views. The Secretary of State for India has reached his day of triumph. Let me pronounce a valediction, or as near a valediction as it is in my power to pronounce.

Mr. Isaac Foot: Why not a benediction?

Mr. Churchill: No, though I wish him well in his future. He marches on from strength to strength. All his abilities, his industry, all the trouble he has put upon himself and upon so many others during the three or four years this Bill has been shaping, have, in my judgment, added nothing of use or value to the conclusions pronounced five years ago by the Statutory Commission, or the Simon Commission as it was then called, and have added nothing to the acceptance which the Bill received in India. But still the right hon. Gentleman has carried through the Joint Select Committee, by a mental effort of very remarkable merit, and through the Committee and the House, this monumental Bill, and as such it will always remain a very great event for which he is responsible. But responsibility, accountability, will remain upon the right hon. Gentleman, and when, a decade hence, any younger men now in the House survey the state of India, what they will see there will be in the main the handiwork of the Secretary of State. I can remember the conversation between the Wedding Guest and the Ancient Mariner:

"God save thee, ancient Mariner!
From the fiends, that plague thee thus!–

Why Look'st thou so?"–"With my crossbow
I shot the Albatross."

He has won his victory; he has won the victory for which he has fought hard, and long, and adroitly; but it is not a victory, in our opinion, for the interests of this country, nor a victory for the welfare of the peoples of India, and in the crashing cheers which no doubt will hail his majority to-night, we pray there may not mingle the knell of the British Empire in the East.

CONSEQUENCES IN FOREIGN POLICY

July 11, 1935

House of Commons

At the beginning of June Ramsay MacDonald became Lord President of the Council, and Baldwin succeeded him as Prime Minister. Sir Samuel Hoare replaced Sir John Simon as Foreign Secretary, and Lord Swinton (formerly Sir Philip Cunliffe-Lister) became Secretary of State for Air.

One of Swinton's first–and most momentous–decisions was to create the Air Defence Research Committee, to which he appointed Churchill. Churchill accepted on the condition that his friend and scientific adviser, Professor F. A. Lindemann, be appointed as well. In fact, Lindemann was appointed to the scientific committee chaired by Sir Henry Tizard, the Aeronautical Research Committee.

In April Britain, France and Italy agreed to establish the "Stresa front" against breaches of international order. The Anglo-German Naval Treaty in June limited the German Navy to thirty-five per cent of the Royal Navy, with submarines at forty-five per cent. This was a blatant repudiation of the Versailles Treaty. Meanwhile, it was evident that Italian ambitions toward Abyssinia were serious.

[Extract] When we last discussed foreign affairs I thought there was very general agreement. We were agreed, or we seemed to be agreed, on the declaration of comradeship between the three Great Powers that met at Stresa. We were agreed in supporting the resolution of the League of Nations condemning treaty-breaking by Germany in the matter of armaments. We were agreed to work in combination through the League of Nations for those principles of collective security–real collective security–which mean that the contributions to that security shall be adequate to give a sense of relief and assurance to all. I thought we were all agreed on that. I found myself in closer relation to His Majesty's Government on foreign affairs than I had been in the whole of this Parliament. Curiously enough, it seemed to me that the last act of the former Prime Minister [Mr. Ramsay MacDonald]–who is now Lord President–on foreign affairs, in the Stresa negotiations, made him more truly the mouthpiece of British feeling and British interest than ever before. We have now heard a speech from the new Foreign

Secretary [Sir Samuel Hoare] which in no way conflicts with the general principles established when we last discussed foreign affairs.

Meanwhile, however, a number of things have happened which do conflict most markedly with those general principles which the Foreign Secretary has recited to us today. The scene is gravely changed. We have condoned, and even praised, the German treaty-breaking in fleet-building. I see that Lord Beatty, speaking somewhere else, said that we ought to be grateful to Germany for not having demanded 50 per cent. On that basis we ought to be still more grateful that they did not demand 100 per cent. We have condoned this unilateral violation of the Treaty, and we have become a party to it without agreement with any of the other countries concerned. We have, however unintentionally, nullified and stultified the League of Nations' condemnation of treaty-breaking in respect of armaments, in which we were ourselves concerned, in which, indeed, we took a leading part. We have, it seems to me, revealed, again quite unintentionally, a very considerable measure of indifference to the interests of other Powers, particularly Powers in the Baltic, who were encouraged by our example to join with us in the League of Nations in condemning treaty-breaking. In the name of what is called practical realism we have seemed to depart very notably from the principle of collective security.

We have seemed to depart from–although I hope we may return again to–the comradeship agreed upon at Stresa, and from the League of Nations' resolution against treaty-breaking, and we have done it in order to make a side deal with Germany which we thought to be in our interest and not contrary to other interests in Europe. We cannot have done this without affecting prejudicially–although, again, I hope only for the time being–the confidence which exists between us and France, which is so vitally necessary for us at all times, but never more vitally necessary than during these years upon which we are now entering, when our air defense will be so woefully inferior to that of Germany. Thus it is not a very good tale which I have had to tell of what has happened since we last had a full-dress Debate on foreign affairs. But it is only one part of the story. At the same time that we have been diverging from the League of Nations in one direction for our particular and legitimate national interest, real or supposed, Italy has made it plain that she means to invade and conquer Abyssinia.

What is reported every day about the movement of troops and the declarations of the head of the Italian State leaves us very little room to doubt that as soon as the season of the year is suitable the only hope of the Abyssinians retaining their territory and the lands on which they have lived for so many thousands of years will be in the fighting qualities of their men. I greatly deplore that. Here is this defiance of the League, and it has happened at the very moment when 11,000,000 people in this island have attested their own fidelity to it. In this short space we have made a separate arrangement for ourselves, of a perfectly innocent character, but still separate, and at the same time the League is confronted with this grave embarrassment through the ambitions of Italy in Abyssinia. By the course we have taken we have made it very difficult for us to remonstrate too strongly with Italy without being exposed to the somewhat severe reply that when we think our particular interests are involved we show but little consideration for the decision against treaty-breaking which we have just urged the League of Nations. I have thought it right to place before the

Committee these two aspects of what has happened since we last discussed these matters.

There is, however, a third aspect. Simultaneously with all I have recited we have nevertheless seemed to allow–I say "seemed to allow" because I do not attribute it to the policy of the Government at all–the impression to be created that we were ourselves coming forward as a sort of bell-wether or fugleman to gather and lead opinion in Europe against Italy's Abyssinian designs. It was even suggested that we would act individually and independently. I am glad to hear from the Foreign Secretary that there is no foundation for that. We must do our duty, but we must do it only in conjunction with other nations and in accordance with obligations which others recognize as well. We are not strong enough–I say it advisedly–to be the lawgiver and the spokesman of the world. We will do our part, but we cannot be asked, and we ought not to put ourselves in a position of being supposed, to do more than our part in these matters. I rejoice, indeed, that my right hon. Friend corrected that, but still the fact remains that throughout Italy we have been regarded with great resentment, which has been fed by altogether false and absurd rumors.

As we stand today there is no doubt that a cloud has come over the old friendship between Great Britain and Italy, a cloud which may very easily not pass away, although undoubtedly it is everyone's desire that it should. It is an old friendship, and we must not forget, what is a little-known fact, that at the time Italy entered into the Triple Alliance in the last century she stipulated particularly that in no circumstances should her obligations under the Alliance bring her into armed conflict with Great Britain.

Lastly, not only have we as it seems got into a position in which we are thought to be working against Italy, but we have made this proposal of handing over a portion of British protected territory in the hope of procuring a relinquishment of Italian ambitions. No explanation has been offered by the Foreign Secretary in his excellent speech of the very unfortunate manner in which this project was put forward. The policy of ceding British protected territory and British protected subjects in order to get round some diplomatic difficulty, or to assuage the disputes of foreign countries, or even to pay our own way from year to year in the modern world, is a very dangerous one for this country to open. When we are considering our vast, innumerable possessions and the reduced state of our means of defense, and at the same time the obvious hunger which is exhibited in so many quarters on the continent of Europe, it seems to me that any steps that might tend to direct appetites upon ourselves should be viewed with the utmost caution and scrutinized with the greatest strictness by Parliament.

Still, supposing that in these years so critical for the peace of Europe the Minister for League of Nations Affairs [Mr. Eden] had returned from Italy with an agreement that she would abandon her dubious and alarming venture, I believe that the gain would have outweighed the loss; but what I do not see, and what I hope we shall be told by my right hon. Friend, is how it ever came to be supposed that this particular proposal would attract the Italian Government. Why should Signor Mussolini want to prolong the standstill on the borders of Abyssinia while Abyssinia enjoyed a corridor to the sea through which a transit of arms could take place year after year? However you look at it, it was a forlorn hope. It was an honest, well-meant proposal, but it was a forlorn hope. We have been told that it was an informal, tentative suggestion, and so forth. Why could not that have gone through ordinary diplomatic channels?

I must say one word to the Minister for League of Nations Affairs. Some two years ago I ventured to recite to him those words of Dr. Johnson:

> Ye who listen with credulity to the whispers of fancy, and pursue with eagerness the phantoms of hope, who expect that age will perform the promises of youth, . . . attend to the history of Rasselas, Prince of Abyssinia.

I am afraid my right hon. Friend has been taking my counsel too literally. Everyone has the greatest hopes of his career, and the whole House, irrespective of party, welcome the appearance of this new figure, but we hope he will choose his occasions with rather stricter discrimination and make quite sure before he undertakes these various journeys that he will not be asked to run risks which injure himself, without sufficient hope of a satisfactory result.

To recapitulate. During the last six weeks the League of Nations has been weakened by our action, the principle of collective security has been impaired, German treaty-making has been condoned and even extolled, the Stresa Front has been shaken, if not, indeed dissolved. Although I cannot believe that any nation in contact with the British Government can doubt our sincere desire for peace, British influence has to some extent been dissipated, and our moral position, or at any rate our logical position, has been to some extent obscured. You could not have had a more complete and perfect example of how not to do it than has been presented by the events which have taken place since we last discussed foreign affairs. Frankly, I cannot understand how it was done. Nothing that has been said shows us how or why it was done. It seems to me as if there were four or five different policies at work inside the Cabinet, and that now one and now the other gains the ascendancy according as the incidents of the hour or the events of the day bring these or those considerations to its attention. . . .

The Foreign Secretary dwelt upon the advantages which the Naval Agreement confers upon us. Those advantages are very doubtful. Of course, it is quite wrong to pretend that the apparition of Germany as a formidable naval Power, equipped with submarines and all the other apparatus of war, is the result of the Naval Agreement. That would have happened anyhow. The deep purposes of great nations are not, I am afraid, governed by the ebb and flow of political discussions or by temporary agreements which are made. It has for some time been evident that Germany intends to embark upon a gigantic process of rearming by land, sea and air, which will make her the most formidable military Power in the whole world. I am not blaming upon this Agreement these events and the misfortunes which will follow from them, but when the Prime Minister says, as he did the other day, that he hoped this would be a great measure of disarmament, let me tell him that I am afraid it will not. I hazard the prediction that this will inaugurate an outburst of shipbuilding in almost every country in the world the like of which has never been seen.

Let us suppose that some distinguished and powerful person who has played a great part in life dies, and his posts, offices, appointments and possessions are distributed, and then he suddenly comes back from the dead. A great deal of inconvenience would be caused. That is what has happened in the resuscitation of German naval power. The equilibrium–such equilibrium as we have been able to establish–in naval matters is entirely ruptured and deranged, and we shall find in every country, in the present temper of the world, that great new construction, replacing old ships or increasing the total tonnage, will be begun without the slightest delay. And let me say that if the first German program, which has already been announced, and which is really last year's program, the program of 1934, is followed by similar programs in the next few years, the German 35 per cent. limit will have been laid down, if not completed, by 1938 or 1939, and in the same period, if we are not to endanger our naval security, it will be necessary for us to rebuild and lay down in new construction practically half the tonnage of our existing Fleet. I cannot feel that this German Naval Agreement is at all a matter for rejoicing. I remain still under this impression, that the one great fear of Europe is the power and might of the rearmed strength of Germany, and that the one great hope is the gathering together of Powers who are conscious of that fear, but have no aggressive intentions of any kind, in a system of collective security under the League of Nations, in order that this tremendous process of the rearmament of Germany may not be attended by some lamentable breakdown of peace.

FOREIGN POLICY AND REARMAMENT

September 26, 1935

City Carlton Club Luncheon, London

Italian threats to Abyssinia became more menacing in the summer of 1935, placing the British Government–and the vaunted "Stresa Front"–in an acute predicament. On September 11, at Geneva, Hoare made a ringing speech to the League in favour of collective security. This left the Labour Party in a highly uncomfortable position between the pacifist wing and those demanding restraints on Italy, even to the point of war. This division had not been resolved when the General Election came in October, and led to the downfall of Labour Party leader George Lansbury, after a brutal attack by Ernest Bevin at the annual conference. He was succeeded by Clement Attlee, one of the few front-bench survivors of the 1931 holocaust.

[Extract] Germany is rearming on a gigantic scale and at an unexampled speed. The whole force and power of Nazidom are being concentrated on warlike preparations by land, sea, and air. The German nation, under Herr Hitler's dictatorship, is spending this year at least six times as much as we are on the Army, the Navy, and the Air Force put together. German finance is a perpetuated war budget. I admire the great German people, but the rearmament of Germany, organized and led as she is now, must appear to everyone with any sense of proportion as the greatest and most grim fact in the world to-day. . . .

[Editor's Note: Referring to the dispute between Italy and Abyssinia he said]: The whole country, indeed the whole Empire, is ready to support the Government in making their contribution to the authority of the League of Nations in accordance with our obligations. If the League is now found capable of preventing a Colonial war in Africa without broadening it out into a general European war that will be an immeasurable gain to the safety of all countries.

I trust that France will realize how vital to her own security in the future it is for the League to emerge successful from this decisive test. (Cheers.) Nothing can be more important to European peace than the close co-operation of Great Britain and France in maintaining the reality and the authority of the League of Nations. They all, I suppose, also support the Government in making it quite clear that there is no question of isolated action by Great Britain. I welcome the particularly explicit statements which Sir Samuel Hoare and other Ministers have made upon that point. Not only France, but many other countries, must do their part as well as we.

The Government has also been absolutely right, in my opinion, in strengthening our naval power in the Mediterranean and in making sure that every precaution has been taken by the British Fleet. We have held our position in the Mediterranean for more than 200 years; and I know of no reason why we should not be fully capable of maintaining it now. But these precautions which the Admiralty are bound to take in no way differentiate the position of Great Britain from that of other members of the League of Nations.

The issue does not lie between Italy and Great Britain, but between Italy and the League. I am surprised that so great a man, so wise a ruler, as Signor Mussolini should be willing, and even eager, to put his gallant nation in such an uncomfortable military and financial position. To cast an army of nearly a quarter of a million men, embodying the flower of Italian manhood, upon a barren shore 2,000 miles from home against the good will of the whole world and without command of the sea, and then, in that position, to embark on what might well be a series of campaigns against a people and in regions which no conqueror in 4,000 years ever thought it worth while to subdue—to do that is to give hostages to fortune unparalleled in all history. These conditions of entanglement and vulnerability are not risks to be run for only a few short weeks. Unless Italy accepts the good advice of the League of Nations and defers to its decisions such a condition might continue even for years. My experience of war is that it takes much longer and costs much more than one expects. Italy might one day be grateful to old friends like Great Britain for helping to keep her out of what might be a deadly trap. Some Powers in Europe would be very glad to see Italy get into a thoroughly compromised and dependent position. Britain is not one of them. We deplore a course which threatens—although I have by no means abandoned hope to remove our Italian comrades and old Allies from the group of great Powers striving to rebuild the harmony of the European family, in which the greatness of the revivified Italian nation must play a noble part. (Cheers.)

One obvious duty is to provide for our national safety by putting our defences in order. We must rearm. Our inadequate armaments have already brought us into contempt in some parts of Europe. I rejoice that, very late in the day, the Government are prepared to act. The private factories and industry of our country must without delay be thoroughly organized for conversion to defensive purposes. The second task is to fulfill Mr. Baldwin's pledge that we should not be inferior in air power to any country that can reach our shores. (Cheers.) An effort is now being made to overtake German construction and to fulfil Mr. Baldwin's pledge, but what is being done now is utterly inadequate to fulfil within any effective period the solemn undertakings which have been given.

I regard the Navy as being fully competent to discharge any duty which might be required of it in the present year and perhaps next year. But there I stop. Many new great ships are being built now, or are about to be built, elsewhere; and unless we replace our veterans while time remains we shall lose not only our position in the Mediterranean, with all that follows from that, but also our power to feed our crowded population in this island and to preserve the coherence of the Empire. Our third task, therefore, is to rebuild the British Fleet. (Cheers.)

INTERNATIONAL SITUATION

October 24, 1935

House of Commons

On October 3, Italy invaded Abyssinia. The League of Nations proclaimed Italy an aggressor, and imposed economic sanctions, except on oil. The Conservative Party was uneasy, and Churchill's obsession with Germany's ambitions made his condemnation of Italy something less than full-hearted. He was, furthermore, anxious to return to the Government, and had been chagrined by his exclusion after the end of the Government of India Act battle.

[Extract] When we separated in August, the House was concerned about the scale and rapidity of German rearmament. What has happened in the interval? The process has continued remorselessly. The incredible figure of more than £800,000,000 sterling is being spent in the currency of the present year on direct and indirect military preparations by Germany. The whole of Germany is an armed camp. Any Member of the House who has travelled there can add his corroboration of that statement. The industries of Germany are mobilised for war to an extent to which ours were not mobilised even a year after the Great War had begun. The whole population is being trained from childhood up to war. A mighty army is coming into being. Many submarines are already exercising in the Baltics. Great cannon, tanks, machine guns and poison gas are fast accumulating. The Germans are even able to be great exporters of munitions as well as to develop their own enormous magazines. The German air force is developing at a great speed, and in spite of ruthless loss of life. We have no speedy prospect of equalling the German air force or of overtaking Germany in the air, whatever we do in the near future.

We had a speech yesterday–it was a very welcome episode–from the right hon. Gentleman the Member for Carnarvon Boroughs (Mr. Lloyd George). He gave us some advice. But I must remind the House that he was very slow to recognise these tremendous developments in Germany. When I pointed out two or three years ago what was then beginning, getting on the move, he derided the idea; and he was not the only one. But neither he nor His Majesty's Government will, I imagine, disagree to-day with the statement that Germany is already well on her way to become, and must become incomparably, the most heavily armed nation in the world and the nation most completely ready for war. There is the dominant factor; there is the factor which dwarfs all others, the factor which we find affecting the movements of politics and diplomacy in every country throughout Europe; and it is a melancholy reflection that in the last hours of this Parliament we have been the helpless, perhaps even the supine, spectators of this vast transformation in Europe to the acute distress of Europe, and to our own grievous disadvantage.

I do not, of course, suggest that German re-armament is directed against us. It may well be that we are the last people the Germans would wish to attack. Certainly it would be in their interest to have our goodwill while they decided their deep differences with other countries. There is even a theory that the Germans are re-arming only out of national self-respect and that they do not mean to hurt anyone at all. Whatever you believe, whatever you think, however it may be, I venture to submit to the House that we cannot have any anxieties comparable to the anxiety caused by German re-armament. The House will pardon me if I continue to press that anxiety upon it. I bear no grudge, I have no prejudice against the German people. I have many German friends, and I have a lively admiration for their splendid qualities of intellect and valour, and for their achievements in science and art. The re-entry into the European circle of a Germany at peace within itself, with a heart devoid of hate, would be the most precious benefit for which we could strive, and a supreme advantage which alone would liberate Europe from its peril and its fear, and I believe that the British and French democracies, the ex-service men, would go a long way in extending the hand of friendship to realise such a hope.

But that is not the position which exists to-day. A very different position exists to-day. We cannot afford to see Nazidom in its present phase of cruelty and intolerance, with all its hatreds and all its gleaming weapons, paramount in Europe at the present time. In the shadow of German re-armament other dangers have taken shape on the Continent. We have, for instance, this war between Italy and Abyssinia, of which the newspapers are so full and which has occupied a good deal of our attention during this Debate. It is a very small matter compared with the dangers I have just described. I do not believe that Signor Mussolini would have embarked upon his Abyssinian venture but for the profound pre-occupation of France in German re-armament, and, I must add, but for the real or supposed military and naval weakness of Great Britain. It was the fear of a re-armed Germany that led France to settle her differences with Italy at the beginning of this year, and very likely when these matters were being settled what is called a free hand in Abyssinia was thrown in. We may regret it, but we must first see and consider the forces operative upon France before we presume to utter reproaches. At that time, in January of this year, neither France nor Italy knew the length to which Great Britain was prepared to go in support of the League of Nations. They knew our views but they did not know with what vigour we should press those views. The whole world has been astonished at the energy and vehemence displayed by His Majesty's Government, and I think we have been astonished ourselves. . . .

It is upon this basis of German rearmament and French apprehension that the Italian-Abyssinian war and the dispute between Italy and the League of Nations can alone be properly considered. We are all agreed that we should walk soberly and warily and discreetly and peacefully, and even humbly, through this dangerous world. Most of us have abstained from truculent or provocative language, though there were, I think, a few relapses at Margate. But we are all agreed as to the peaceful demeanour to adopt and the abstention from violent speech which we should observe. Then there is a division. Some people say: "Put your trust in the League of Nations." Others say: "Put your trust in British re-armament." I say we want both. I put my trust in both. We have to run risks for both, and we have got to make exertions for both. I see no antagonism between the two. Neither is there any antagonism between those who would defend the Covenant of the League of Nations with their lives and those who would defend the British Empire. I believe these two ideas are at present the only practical counterparts of one another.

It is quite certain that the British Empire will never fight another war contrary to the League of Nations. Any attempt to embark upon a war of aggrandisement, or pride or ambition would break the British Empire into fragments and any Government that was even suspected of such a motive would be chased from power long before its machinations could become effective. Therefore, if ever the British Empire is called upon to defend itself, its cause and the cause of the League of Nations will be one. Where, then, is the difference? The fortunes of the British Empire and its glory are inseparably interwoven with the fortunes of the world. We rise or we fall together. Indeed, if we survive to-day the extraordinary situation it is because even in bygone times our ancestors so managed that in the main the special interests of Britain conformed to the general interests of the world. [*Interruption.*] Read history and find there anything which can contradict what I have said. I, therefore, make no secret of the fact that personally I regard the British Navy and its sister services and all that is implied in the Covenant of the League of Nations as allied insurances for our peace and safety, and I am sure we need them both, and we need, besides, all our wit and wisdom, and all our patience and common sense in order to escape ourselves and to help the modern world out of the dangers which encompass us.

What is the great new fact about the League of Nations? What is the change that has taken place since we separated last August? It is this. The League of Nations is alive. It is alive and in action. It is fighting for its life. Probably it is fighting for all our lives. But it is fighting. No one can ever pretend that without the United States the League of Nations could be a supreme authority, but the question has been for a long time whether it was not dead and a sham. People were despairing of the League of Nations. They pointed, and my right hon. Friend the Member for Sparkbrook (Mr.

Amery) still points, with accusing and wounding finger to its powerlessness in the Far East and to its indifference in the Chaco War. When we separated in August the League of Nations was becoming a byword. Look at what has happened since. Here are 50 sovereign States solemnly sitting down together to devise and concert hostile economic action against a great Power, prohibiting the export of arms to Italy, encouraging such export to Italy's enemy, taking concerted measures to destroy Italian credit and financial strength in every quarter of the globe, laying an embargo on many kinds of exports to Italy and even attempting a complete boycott of Italian imports into each country. When we are told that there are leakages and loopholes, that difficulties will arise and disputes will break out between the boycotters and so forth, that may all be true, but these are, to anyone who views things in their due proportion, only the exceptions which are proving a most impressive rule. Such a system of pains and penalties has never been proclaimed against a single State, as far as I am aware, in the whole history of the world. If we could get away a little further from the scene and take a more general view than is possible to us living through events from day to day, I am sure we should see that we are already in the presence of a memorable event.

Still more remarkable is the Italian acceptance of these sanctions. When we separated in August, the story was, when these matters were viewed in an academic light, that economic sanctions meant war, and certainly the original attitude of Italy was that any attempt to apply sanctions would be treated as an unfriendly act and an affront. But what has happened? All this has proved to be untrue. Signor Mussolini—I think it is a sign of his commanding mind; to my mind it is one of the strongest things he has done—has submitted to these invidious sanctions and still preserved his contact with the League of Nations. Instead of saying "Italy will meet them with war," he says "Italy will meet them with discipline, with frugality and with sacrifice." That is a great saying in the setting, in the difficulties, in which he stands. So I say that we are not only in the presence of an assertion of the public law of Europe but of its recognition by the State affected and by the historic figure at the head of that State. That is also a truly remarkable fact, and one that is full of hope. . . .

I am not going to detain the House more than a very few minutes because we all feel, with a sense of approaching Dissolution, that we must not put too great a strain upon the fortitude of Members who are, no doubt, bracing themselves for the supreme ordeal, but I must make some remarks, or my arguments would lack completeness, about Abyssinia. I share the feeling common throughout the country of sympathy for this primitive, feudal people who are fighting for their hearths and homes and for the ancient freedom of their mountains against a scientific invader. The native independence of Abyssinia cannot be made a matter for compromise or barter. But no one, least of all the Liberal party, can justify the conditions that prevail in that country. The Abyssinian Government themselves do not pretend to do so. Whether they have the power to correct them is another matter, but they cannot justify them. No one can keep up the pretence that Abyssinia is a fit, worthy and equal member of a league of civilised nations. The wisdom of the British policy was shown in our opposing their admission and the unwisdom of Continental countries, who now bitterly regret what they did, was shown in its admission. It was a mistake. Steps must certainly be taken to make sure that the oppression by the dominant race in Abyssinia of the tribes which they have recently conquered is not perpetuated as the result of League of Nations action. Even in their own home and centre, now that they have appealed to the League of Nations, now that the searchlights of the world are bearing their glare upon the history and conditions of this region, the Abyssinians must be made to put their house in order. . . .

Then we must consider those economic sanctions. It was said yesterday that the economic sanctions will not really embarrass the Italian dictator, and he knows they will not embarrass him or else he would never have bowed to them. That all depends upon the length of time they are maintained. We live in such a febrile and sensational age that even a month or two is enough to make people not merely change their views, but forget the views and feelings they entertained before. I agree with the Chancellor of the Exchequer that this matter will be one involving a long strain which will require a cool and phlegmatic temperament.

Sir Herbert Samuel: From the Abyssinians?

Mr. Churchill: They are fighting for their lives. But the limitations of the action which can be taken by the League of Nations are defined and well known to the right hon. Gentleman, and no one has suggested that we could do more than we have done, or that we should take isolated action. As far as we are concerned, one of the causes and circumstances which make the strain painful to us is the prolongation of the spectacle we shall have to witness in Abyssinia—the painful spectacle of the desperate resistance of these people barely armed against all the resources of science. [Hon. Members: "Hear, hear!"] Certainly. But still do not let us suppose that the measures which are being taken are not most formidable. We must not only look a month or two ahead. Where will the Italian dictator be at this time next year? He may be far into Abyssinia with an army of a quarter of a million men, wasting rapidly by guerilla warfare and disease, and all the time Italy, under the boycott and censure of practically the whole world, will be bleeding at every pore, her gold reserve melting away, her prices rising, her credit gone. Do not let us under-value the extreme importance of the long, slow pressures which are being applied, and do not let us under-estimate the dangers which necessarily they excite in increasing the tension which prevails throughout all Europe.

I listened, like others in the House, with the very greatest attention and respect to the speech of my right hon. Friend the Member for Sparkbrook yesterday. No one who heard him will ignore the strength of the case he unfolded, and we are indebted to him for placing it so clearly before us. But it is quite plain that his view is not the view of this House of Commons, nor will it, I believe, be the view which the country will express in the forthcoming election. My right hon. Friend rendered a service in showing us so clearly where we used to stand, and where the League of Nations used to stand until a few months ago. But we have now moved on. Anyone can see that. We have moved on and we are not going to move back. The League of Nations has passed from shadow into substance, from theory into practice, from rhetoric into reality. We see a structure always majestic, but hitherto shadowy, which is now being clothed with life and power, and endowed with coherent thought and concerted action. We begin to feel the beatings of a pulse which may, we hope, and we pray, some day—and the sooner for our efforts—restore a greater measure of health and strength to the whole world. My right hon. Friend the Member for Sparkbrook dwelt upon the dangers of our acts, and the right hon. Member for Carnarvon Boroughs (Mr. Lloyd George) dwelt, unduly I thought, upon their difficulties. We can see these difficulties and dangers for ourselves, but if we confront them, and when we confront them, with a steady eye, I believe the House and the country will reach the conclusion that the case for perseverance holds the field.

ELECTION ADDRESS

October 28, 1935

Epping

Parliament was dissolved on October 25.

In the General Election the National Government won easily, but Labour took 154 seats, and the Liberals were further reduced to twenty seats.

Immediately after the election Churchill went on an extended holiday: "I set out with my paintbox for more genial climes without waiting for the meeting of Parliament." He was in Spain until the death of King George V in January 1936. During his absence the British and French Foreign Ministers, Samuel Hoare and Pierre Laval, concocted their famous Pact proposing to concede some two-thirds of Abyssinia to Italy in return for recognition of the right of Emperor Haile Selassie to rule the remaining third and a corridor to the sea. The storm of protest which instantly followed was so violent that Hoare had to be sacrificed; he resigned, and Anthony Eden replaced him at the Foreign Office. Although Churchill was urged to return by friends convinced that Baldwin was about to fall, he remained in Spain.

[Extract] As the result of the last election, there have been four years of steady and stable government, and every class and almost every district in the country has benefited thereby. If in the crisis of 1931 the new Government had promised to reduce unemployment by a million; to increase employment by a million and a half; to build a million new houses; to make our credit the best in the world, and our country the most envied, no one would have believed them. To-day these are obvious undisputed facts which all can see. The question which has now to be settled by the British people is whether the good work should go on for another four or five years, or whether we are to have a fresh dose of Socialist incapacity and misrule. Last time the people voted for national solvency. Now it is national safety which is at stake. This affects not only ourselves but the peace of the world.

The National Government pursued a policy about India which, in my judgment, was unwise. The India question has now passed from debate into experiment. It is our duty to give that experiment a fair chance. Also the national defences have been allowed to decline to what the Government themselves admit is 'the edge of risk.' We have fallen grievously behind in the air, and we now have to make an intense effort to have as strong and good an Air Force as that of any country which can get at us. We must rebuild our Fleet and fit it with all the appliances which modern science can devise. In this–and not in this only–we must keep in the closest touch with the United States of America, whose Navy is as important to the peace of the world as our own. These measures will not throw an undue burden upon us in view of the fine condition to which the Chancellor of the Exchequer has raised our credit.

The national effort will not prevent or delay the march to social betterment. On the contrary, the serving of great causes of peace and freedom will spur and stir progress at home. Men's wits will be sharpened and their spirits braced for renewed mental strife against the evils of poverty and the curse of worklessness.

FOREIGN POLICY

March 26, 1936

House of Commons

On March 7, 1936 German troops reoccupied the Rhineland. This complete violation of the Treaty of Versailles and the Locarno agreement was accepted by France and Britain. Churchill realised the grim implications, but at this point he was anxious to secure the position of Minister of Defence, under active discussion in the Cabinet. But on March 12 Baldwin announced the creation of a new post–the Minister for the Co-ordination of Defence. This was a very different concept, and the announcement included the name of the new Minister–Sir Thomas Inskip, at the time the Attorney-General.

[Extract] . . . What is, after all, the first great fact with which we are confronted? It is this. An enormous triumph has been gained by the Nazi regime. The German Chancellor, perhaps advised against the course he took by his military experts, nevertheless decided on ordering the violation of the Rhineland and the destruction of the Locarno Treaty. He has succeeded–it is no good blinding ourselves to it–his troops are there, and who is to say that they will be removed? He has accomplished this fact, and although the world has been alarmed and shocked, and many protests have been made, the event has occurred. And what an event. Under the brazen surface of the totalitarian State there stir and seethe all the emotions of a great, cultured, educated and once free community. The Protestant, the Catholic, the Jew, the Monarchist, the Communist, the Liberal–all these forces are there, held in suspense, held in a certain grip and vice as it were, but they are there.

Let us suppose that any one of us were a German and living there, and perhaps entirely discontented with many things that we saw around us, but thinking that here is the Fuehrer, the great leader of the country, who has raised his country so high–and I honour him for that–able to bring home once again a trophy. One year it is the Saar, another month the right of Germany to conscription, another month to gain from Britain the right to build submarines, another month the Rhineland. Where will it be next? Austria, Memel, other territories and disturbed areas are already in view. If we were Germans, and discontented with the present regime, nevertheless on patriotic grounds there is many a man who would say "While the Government is bringing home these trophies, I cannot indulge my personal, sectional or party feelings against this regime." This country is in the presence of facts which, apart from the technical consequences of the military occupation of the Rhineland, constitute an immense blow at the League of Nations and the principle of the reign of law, and constitute an immense gain in prestige to the Nazi Government in Germany. I think that a very serious fact at the present time.

There is another reason why I feel that the Foreign Secretary was bound to make the speech that he did. We had something to do with the events which made the conditions under which the Germans acted. From the highest and most benevolent motives—and I do not dissociate myself from the general course which the Government took—we have pressed a policy of sanctions against Italy upon France that is estranging France and Italy. When I was invited to give my opinion on the matter last August, I said that we must do our duty under the Covenant of the League, but that we should not press France unduly, and that we should not go beyond the point where we could carry France. I think we went much further than that in sanctions. As I tried to point out to the House, the friendship between France and Italy was vital to the defence and security of every home in France, and France, out of regard for Britain and out of loyalty for the principles of the League of Nations, went very far; not so far as some enthusiasts would have wished her to go, not so far as those who did not understand how fast she was moving expected her to move; but very far did she move, and considerable injury was inevitable in the relations of France and Italy. That produced a situation in which, it seems to me, all the elements were present which led to the recent outrage upon international law and the Treaties which regulate the peace of Europe.

When we think of the great power and influence which this country exercises we cannot look back with much pleasure on our foreign policy in the last five years. They certainly have been very disastrous years. God forbid that I should lay on the Government of my own country the charge of sole responsibility for the evils which have come upon the world in that period. I would not do such a thing, but certainly in that period we have seen the most depressing and alarming change in the outlook of mankind which has ever taken place in so short a period. Five years ago all felt safe, five years ago all were looking forward to peace, to a period in which mankind would rejoice in the treasures which science can spread to all classes if the conditions of peace and justice prevail. Five years ago to talk of war would have been regarded not only as a folly and a crime but almost as a sign of lunacy. The difference in our position now! We find ourselves compelled once again to face the hateful problems and ordeals which those of us who worked and toiled in the last great struggle hoped were gone for ever. . . .

The violation of the Rhineland is serious from the point of view of the menace to which it exposes Holland, Belgium and France. It is also serious from the fact that when it is fortified—and I listened with apprehension to what the Secretary of State said about the Germans declining even to refrain from entrenching themselves during the period of negotiations; I listened with sorrow to that—when there is there a line of fortifications, as I suppose there will be in a very short time, it will produce great reactions on the European situation. It will be a barrier across Germany's front-door, which will leave her free to sally out eastward and southward by the back door.

In spite of the seriousness which I attach to this reoccupation of the Rhineland, I must say that it seems to me the smallest part of the whole problem. What is the real problem, the real peril? It is not the reoccupation of the Rhineland, but this enormous process of the rearmament of Germany. There is the peril. My right hon. Friend opposite says that in the election I seemed to be haunted by this idea. I confess that I have been occupied with this idea of the great wheels revolving and the great hammers descending day and night in Germany, making the whole industry of that country an arsenal, making the whole of that gifted and valiant population into one great disciplined war machine. There is the problem that lies before you. There is what is bringing the war. This Rhineland business is but a step, is but a stage, is but an incident in this process. I agree very much with the spokesman of the official Labour Opposition when he said there was fear. There is fear, in every country, all round. Even here, in this country, with some protection from distance, there is fear, deep fear. It takes a deep fear to make the hon. Member for West Fife (Mr. Gallacher) speak in terms which commend themselves to almost every one who was in the House. What is the fear and what is the question which arises from that fear? It is, "How are we going to stop this war which seems to be moving towards us in so many ways?"

There are, of course, two practical foreign policies for our country. The first is an alliance between Great Britain and France, the two surviving liberal democracies of the West, who, strongly armed, rich, powerful, with the seas at their disposal, with great air forces and great armies, would stand with their backs to the ocean and allow the explosion which may come in Europe to blast its way eastward or southward. There is a practical foreign policy, but I do hope that we shall not resign ourselves to that, without first an earnest effort to persevere in the other policy, namely, the establishment of real collective security under the League of Nations and of the reign of law and respect for international law throughout Europe. I venture to make a suggestion which I feel will not be entirely repugnant to those who sit opposite, namely, that, apart from this particular emergency and apart from the measures which the Foreign Secretary has taken, we should endeavour now with great resolution to establish effective collective security. In my view, all the nations and States that are alarmed at the growth of German armaments ought to combine for mutual aid, in pacts of mutual assistance, approved by the League of Nations and in accordance with the Covenant of the League. . . .

I am looking for peace. I am looking for a way to stop war, but you will not stop it by pious sentiments and appeals. You will only stop it by making practical arrangements. When you have these two conditions established firmly, when you have linked up the forces at the disposal of the League for defence, and when you have given that guarantee to Germany, then is the first moment, when you should address Germany collectively, not only upon the minor question of the Rhine but upon the supreme question of German rearmament in relation to other countries—and they must not shirk presenting themselves to that test also. Further, at that moment you must invite Germany to state her grievances, to lay them on the council board and to let us have it out. But do not let us have it out as if we were a rabble flying before forces we dare not resist. Let us have it out on the basis that we are negotiating from strength and not from weakness; that we are negotiating from unity and not from division and isolation; that we are seeking to do justice, because we have power.

The whole history of the world is summed up in the fact that when nations are strong they are not always just, and when they wish to be just they are often no longer strong. I desire to see the collective forces of the world invested with overwhelming power. If you are going to run this thing on a narrow margin and to depend on a very slight margin, one way or the other, you are going to have war. But if you get five or ten to one on one side, all bound rigorously by the Covenant and the conventions which they own, then, in my opinion, you have an opportunity of making a settlement which will heal the wounds of the world. Let us have this blessed union of power and of justice:

> Agree with thine adversary quickly while thou art in the way with him.

Let us free the world from the approach of a catastrophe, carrying with it calamity and tribulation, beyond the tongue of man to tell.

THE ABYSSINIAN CRISIS

May 8, 1936

Chingford

On May 1 Emperor Haile Selassie left Abyssinia, accepting the Italian victory. At the end of the debate in the Commons on May 6, Churchill intervened briefly to denounce Baldwin for not speaking out; his words were warmly cheered by the Labour Party, and angrily received by the Conservatives.

Churchill's impatience with the Government, and Baldwin in particular, was evident in many of his speeches during the summer of 1936. This is one example.

[Extract] . . . Signor Mussolini has triumphed over the most ancient state in the world, Abyssinia, and also over its most modern institution, the League of Nations. I regard this as a lamentable event. I also feel concerned at the position of our own country. I hope that before we are led into another adventure of this kind our leaders will count the cost, measure their resources, and test the quality of their own resolves. Without any special call to do so, we placed ourselves at the head of 50 nations and summoned the Dominions of the Empire to share our efforts. The result has been a fiasco, ludicrous if it was not so tragical. I warned the Government three years ago against dabbling in Europe upon the limited liability principle. It is not only foolish and unfair but horribly dangerous.

No one is compelled to serve great causes unless he feels fit for it, but nothing is more certain than that they can not take the lead in great causes as a half-timer. Mr. Baldwin said two years ago that sanctions meant war: then he led us into sanctions with a thoroughly virtuous resolve against war. What was the result? The economic sanctions had to be confined within limits which would not lead to war. If oil sanctions had been imposed at the outset or even in November it might have produced a fatal effect upon the operations of the Italian armies. But that might have led to war. If our leaders had definitely decided that they would not go into war to stop Mussolini conquering Abyssinia they ought to have sung a very much smaller tune.

I have tried to support the Government and Mr. Baldwin–after all he has something to do with the Government, I believe–in their policy upon the League of Nations and about Abyssinia, but I must tell you, and perhaps you have had the same experience, that I have found it very difficult to keep in step with all their zigzags. Everyone can see now that the Hoare-Laval agreement was a very shrewd, far-seeing agreement which would have saved the Negus of Abyssinia from ruin before his army was destroyed. The serious thing against it was that it should never have been made by the same Sir Samuel Hoare who had sounded his wonderful trumpet call to the League of Nations scarcely three months before.

It was this violent revolution of policy, however sagacious in itself, which threw Parliament into such confusion before Christmas. But no one did it throw into more confusion than Mr. Baldwin. He and his Cabinet agreed with Sir Samuel Hoare, but then such a storm arose and he felt the force of such a great tide of public opinion that he had to turn round and sacrifice Sir Samuel Hoare, and tear up the Hoare-Laval agreement and then start off again on his old policy of "Sanctions which mean war," coupled with the proviso that there was to be no war. It has been very difficult to keep pace with all these chops and changes. What does the Government think about it all now? They say in effect that if the limited economic sanctions to which Signor Mussolini is prepared to submit had gone on long enough the Italian campaign in Abyssinia would have been defeated. However, it did not work out that way. It is not the Italians that collapsed but the Abyssinians.

Last Wednesday all these matters were debated in the House of Commons, and I thought we ought to have had from the Prime Minister his full explanation for the course upon which he has steered our country and his advice about what we ought now to do. I made my protest against his silence in a way which I thought would bring the point to the notice of almost every one in this island, but I do not underrate at all the difficulties of his position, not the good intentions by which he has throughout been governed. But something more is needed in the conduct of a great State in critical times than good intentions leading to disaster. It would be unfair to saddle any single man or any single Government with the responsibility for what has happened. Nevertheless, we expect from the Prime Minister true leadership upon the vital questions of our time.

I am not prepared to support sanctions against Italy merely for the purpose of injuring or weakening the Italian people. Unless we are convinced that what we do will be of real practical help to the tribesmen of Abyssinia, we have no right to go farther along that path. In the present state of Europe, which has gravely deteriorated even since the autumn, the continuance or aggravation of sanctions might bring about a hideous war without benching in the slightest degree the population of Abyssinia. Moreover, Abyssinia is now in the hands of Italy. Italy has by violence made herself responsible for the welfare of the Abyssinian people. In trying further to impoverish and weaken the Italian nation we may only weaken the resources out of which the Abyssinians can be nourished and sustained, and embitter and worsen their fate.

Many voices have been raised for breaking up and casting aside the League of Nations. That is a very reckless and short-sighted view. Although the League has failed to prevent aggression, war, and conquest in Abyssinia, no one could doubt that it is stronger and more alive to-day than it was a year ago. The task before us is not to abandon or abolish the League of Nations, but to strengthen it for the new and graver trials which might be before it in the future. I trust that our new Foreign Secretary, whose courage and ability have won so much admiration, will devote his influence and energies to this urgent and all important task.

REFORMING THE LEAGUE OF NATIONS

July 4, 1936

Chancellor's Address, Degree Conferment Ceremony,
Bristol University

[Extract] . . . If the idea of force–force in the extreme–is excluded from the procedure of a League of Nations, it is nought but an idle sham. There is no hope for the prevention of war except in the banding together of many nations, great and small, against an aggressor, whoever he might be. This has hitherto failed because those who sought to restrain the aggressor were not prepared to suffer and die for their convictions, because they were not united into a strong enough confederacy, and because, in a particular instance, the occasion was not one which united the vital interests of powerful States.

Though this cause has met with a single failure it is more urgent than ever to create in Europe a League of Nations which will confront a potential aggressor with overwhelming force, organized for use, capable of being used in support of a covenant entered into between all nations on the basis that he who strikes at one strikes at all. It is vain to suppose that any real progress towards world peace and law can be made unless they have the will and are willing and ready and prepared to make the same sacrifices and efforts that might be made by the aggressor.

"ADAMANT FOR DRIFT"

November 12, 1936

House of Commons

Throughout the summer and autumn of 1936, in Parliament and out, Churchill made speech after speech on the question of defence, and reiterated his arguments in many newspaper articles.

This must be regarded as among the most brilliant and most devastating of all Churchill's speeches. In reply, Baldwin said that he would speak "with appalling frankness" and referred to the 1933 East Fulham by-election and British hostility to rearmament at that stage. This passage has often been quoted out of context–notably by Churchill–to imply that Baldwin had "put party before country" in the 1935 General Election. At the time, Churchill's assault and Baldwin's reply were a severe blow to the Government's authority after a year of almost unrelieved misfortune.

[Extract] . . . What would have been said, I wonder, if I could two years ago have forecast to the House the actual course of events? Suppose we had then been told that Germany would spend for two years £800,000,000 a year upon warlike preparations; that her industries would be organized for war, as the industries of no country have ever been; that by breaking all Treaty engagements she would create a gigantic air force and an army based on universal compulsory service, which by the present time, in 1936, amounts to upwards of thirty-nine divisions of highly equipped troops, including mechanized divisions of almost unmeasured strength, and that behind all this there lay millions of armed and trained men, for whom the formations and equipment are rapidly being prepared to form another eighty divisions in addition to those already perfected. Suppose we had then known that by now two years of compulsory military service would be the rule, with a preliminary year of training in labor camps; that the Rhineland would be occupied by powerful forces and fortified with great skill, and that Germany would be building with our approval, signified by treaty, a large submarine fleet.

Suppose we had also been able to foresee the degeneration of the foreign situation, our quarrel with Italy, the Italo-German association, the Belgian declaration about neutrality–which, if the worst interpretation of it proves to be true, so greatly affects the security of this country–and the disarray of the smaller Powers of Central Europe. Suppose all that had been forecast–why, no one would have believed in the truth of such a nightmare tale. Yet just two years have gone by and we see it all in broad daylight. Where shall we be this time two years? I hesitate now to predict. . . .

No doubt as a whole His Majesty's Government were very slow in accepting the unwelcome fact of German rearmament. They still clung to the policy of one-sided disarmament. It was one of those experiments, we are told, which had to be, to use a vulgarism, "tried out," just as the experiments of non-military sanctions against Italy had to be tried out. Both experiments have now been tried out, and Ministers are accustomed to plume themselves upon the very clear results of those experiments. They are held to prove conclusively that the policies subjected to the experiments were all wrong, utterly foolish, and should never be used again, and the very same men who were foremost in urging those experiments are now foremost in proclaiming and denouncing the fallacies upon which they were based. They have bought their knowledge, they have bought it dear, they have bought it at our expense, but at any rate let us be duly thankful that they now at last possess it.

In July 1935, before the General Election, there was a very strong movement in this House in favor of the appointment of a Minister to concert the action of the three fighting Services. Moreover, at that time the Departments of State were all engaged in drawing up the large schemes of rearmament in all branches which have been laid before us in the White Paper and upon which we are now engaged. One would have thought that that was the time when this new Minister or Co-ordinator was most necessary. He was not, however, in fact appointed until nearly nine months later, in March 1936. No explanation has yet been given to us why these nine months were wasted before the taking of what is now an admittedly necessary measure. The Prime Minister dilated the other night, no doubt very properly, on the great advantages which had flowed from the appointment of the Minister for the Co-ordination of Defence. Every argument used to show how useful has been the work which he has done accuses the failure to appoint him nine months earlier, when inestimable benefits would have accrued to us by the saving of this long period.

When at last, in March, after all the delays, the Prime Minister eventually made the appointment, the arrangement of duties was so ill-conceived that no man could possibly discharge them with efficiency or even make a speech about them without embarrassment. I have repeatedly pointed out the obvious mistake in organization of jumbling together—and practically everyone in the House is agreed upon this—the functions of defence with those of a Minister of Supply. The proper organization, let me repeat, is four Departments—the Navy, the Army, the Air and the Ministry of Supply, with the Minister for the Co-ordination of Defence over the four, exercising a general supervision, concerting their actions, and assigning the high priorities of manufacture in relation to some comprehensive strategic conception. The House is familiar with the many requests and arguments which have been made to the Government to create a Ministry of Supply. These arguments have received powerful reinforcement from another angle in the report of the Royal Commission on Arms Manufacture.

The first work of this new Parliament, and the first work of the Minister for the Co-ordination of Defence if he had known as much about the subject when he was appointed as he does now, would have been to set up a Ministry of Supply which should, step by step, have taken over the whole business of the design and manufacture of all the supplies needed by the Air Force and the Army, and everything needed for the Navy, except warships, heavy ordnance, torpedoes and one or two ancillaries. All the rest of the industries of Britain should have been surveyed from a general integral standpoint, and all existing resources utilized so far as was necessary to execute the program.

The Minister for the Co-ordination of Defence has argued as usual against a Ministry of Supply. The arguments which he used were weighty, and even ponderous—it would disturb and delay existing programs; it would do more harm than good; it would upset the life and industry of the country; it would destroy the export trade and demoralize finance at the moment when it was most needed; it would turn this country into one vast munitions camp. Certainly these are massive arguments, if they are true. One would have thought that they would carry conviction to any man who accepted them. But then my right hon. Friend went on somewhat surprisingly to say, "The decision is not final." It would be reviewed again in a few weeks. What will you know in a few weeks about this matter that you do not know now, that you ought not to have known a year ago, and have not been told any time in the last six months? What is going to happen in the next few weeks which will invalidate all these magnificent arguments by which you have been overwhelmed, and suddenly make it worth your while to paralyze the export trade, to destroy the finances, and to turn the country into a great munitions camp?

The First Lord of the Admiralty [Sir Samuel Hoare] in his speech the other night went even farther. He said, "We are always reviewing the position." Everything, he assured us, is entirely fluid. I am sure that that is true. Anyone can see what the position is. The Government simply cannot make up their minds, or they cannot get the Prime Minister to make up his mind. So they go on in strange paradox, decided only to be undecided, resolved to be irresolute, adamant for drift, solid for fluidity, all-powerful to be impotent. So we go on preparing more months and years—precious, perhaps vital to the greatness of Britain—for the locusts to eat. They will say to me, "A Minister of Supply is not necessary, for all is going well." I deny it. "The position is satisfactory." It is not true. "All is proceeding according to plan." We know what that means.

Let me come to the Territorial Army. In March of this year I stigmatized a sentence in the War Office Memorandum about the Territorial Army, in which it was said the equipment of the Territorials could not be undertaken until that of the Regular Army had been completed. What has been done about all that? It is certain the evils are not yet removed. I agree wholeheartedly with all that was said by Lord Winterton the other day about the Army and the Territorial Force. When I think how these young men who join the Territorials come forward, almost alone in the population, and take on a liability to serve anywhere in any part of the world, not even with a guarantee to serve in their own units; come forward in spite of every conceivable deterrent; come forward—140,000 of them, although they are still not up to strength—and then find that the Government does not take their effort seriously enough even to equip and arm them properly, I marvel at their patriotism. It is a marvel, it is also a glory, but a glory we have no right to profit by unless we can secure proper and efficient equipment for them.

A friend of mine the other day saw a number of persons engaged in peculiar evolutions, genuflections and gestures in the neighborhood of London. His curiosity was excited. He wondered whether it was some novel form of gymnastics, or a new religion—there are new religions which are very popular in some countries nowadays—or whether they were a party of lunatics out for an airing. On approaching closer he learned that they were a Searchlight Company of London Territorials who were doing their exercises as well as they could without having the searchlights. Yet we are told there is no need for a Ministry of Supply.

In the manoeuvers of the Regular Army many of the most important new weapons have to be represented by flags and discs. When we remember how small our land forces are—altogether only a few hundred thousand men—it seems incredible that the very flexible industry of Britain, if properly handled, could not supply them with their modest requirements. In Italy, whose industry is so much smaller, whose wealth and credit are a small fraction of this country's, a Dictator is able to boast that he has bayonets and equipment for 8,000,000 men. Halve the figure, if you like, and the moral remains equally cogent.

The Army lacks almost every weapon which is required for the latest form of modern war. Where are the anti-tank guns, where are the short-distance wireless sets, where the field anti-aircraft guns against low-flying armored aeroplanes? We want to know how it is that this country, with its enormous motoring and motor-bicycling public, is not able to have strong mechanized divisions, both Regular and Territorial. Surely, when so much of the interest and the taste of our youth is moving in those mechanical channels, and when the horse is receding with the days of chivalry into the past, it ought to be possible to create an army of the size we want fully up to strength and mechanized to the highest degree.

Look at the Tank Corps. The tank was a British invention. This idea, which has revolutionized the conditions of modern war, was a British idea forced on the War Office by outsiders. Let me say they would have just as hard work today to force a new idea on it. I speak from what I know. During the War we had almost a monopoly, let alone the leadership, in tank warfare, and for several years afterwards we held the foremost place. To England all eyes were turned. All that has gone now. Nothing has been done in "the years that the locust hath eaten" to equip the Tank Corps with new machines. The medium tank which they possess, which in its day was the best in the world, is now long obsolete. Not only in numbers—for there we have never tried to compete with other countries—but in quality these British weapons are now surpassed by those of Germany, Russia, Italy and the United States. All the shell plants and gun plants in the Army, apart from the very small peace-time services, are in an elementary stage. A very long period must intervene before any effectual flow of munitions can be expected, even for the small forces of which we dispose. Still we are told there is no necessity for a Ministry of Supply, no emergency which should induce us to impinge on the normal course of trade. If we go on like this, and I do not see what power can prevent us from going on like this, some day there may be a terrible reckoning, and those who take the responsibility so entirely upon themselves are either of a hardy disposition or they are incapable of foreseeing the possibilities which may arise.

Now I come to the greatest matter of all, the air. We received on Tuesday night, from the First Lord of the Admiralty [Sir Samuel Hoare], the assurance that there is no foundation whatever for the statement that we are "vastly behindhand" with our Air Force program. It is clear from his words that we are behindhand. The only question is, what meaning does the First Lord attach to the word "vastly"? He also used the expression, about the progress of air expansion, that it was "not unsatisfactory." One does not know what his standard is. His standards change from time to time. In that speech of the 11th of September about the League of Nations there was one standard, and in the Hoare-Laval Pact there was clearly another. . . .

Parliament was promised a total of seventy-one new squadrons, making a total of 124 squadrons in the home defence force, by 31st March, 1937. This was thought to be the minimum compatible with our safety. At the end of the last financial year our strength was fifty-three squadrons, including auxiliary squadrons. Therefore, in the thirty-two weeks which have passed since the financial year began we have added twenty-eight squadrons–that is to say, less than one new squadron each week. In order to make the progress which Parliament was promised, in order to maintain the program which was put forward as the minimum, we shall have to add forty-three squadrons in the remaining twenty weeks, or over two squadrons a week. The rate at which new squadrons will have to be formed from now till the end of March will have to be nearly three times as fast as hitherto. I do not propose to analyze the composition of the eighty squadrons we now have, but the Minister, in his speech, used a suggestive expression, "skeleton squadrons"–applying at least to a portion of them–but even if every one of the eighty squadrons had an average strength of twelve aeroplanes, each fitted with war equipment, and the reserves upon which my right hon. Friend dwelt, we should only have a total of 960 first-line home-defence aircraft.

What is the comparable German strength? I am not going to give an estimate and say that the Germans have not got more than a certain number, but I will take it upon myself to say that they most certainly at this moment have not got less than a certain number. Most certainly they have not got less than 1500 first-line aeroplanes, comprised in not less than 130 or 140 squadrons, including auxiliary squadrons. It must also be remembered that Germany has not got in its squadrons any machine the design and construction of which is more than three years old. It must also be remembered that Germany has specialized in long-distance bombing aeroplanes and that her preponderance in that respect is far greater than any of these figures would suggest.

We were promised most solemnly by the Government that air parity with Germany would be maintained by the home defence forces. At the present time, putting everything at the very best, we are, upon the figures given by the Minister for the Co-ordination of Defence, only about two-thirds as strong as the German air force, assuming that I am not very much understating their present strength. How then does the First Lord of the Admiralty [Sir Samuel Hoare] think it right to say:

> On the whole, our forecast of the strength of other Air Forces proves to be accurate; on the other hand, our own estimates have also proved to be accurate.
>
> I am authorized to say that the position is satisfactory.

I simply cannot understand it. Perhaps the Prime Minister will explain the position. I should like to remind the House that I have made no revelation affecting this country and that I have introduced no new fact in our air defence which does not arise from the figures given by the Minister and from the official estimates that have been published. . . .

Owing to past neglect, in the face of the plainest warnings, we have now entered upon a period of danger greater than has befallen Britain since the U-boat campaign was crushed; perhaps, indeed, it is a more grievous period than that, because at that time at least we were possessed of the means of securing ourselves and of defeating that campaign. Now we have no such assurance. The era of procrastination, of half-measures, of soothing and baffling expedients, of delays, is coming to its close. In its place we are entering a period of consequences. We have entered a period in which for more than a year, or a year and a half, the considerable preparations which are now on foot in Britain will not, as the Minister clearly showed, yield results which can be effective in actual fighting strength; while during this very period Germany may well reach the culminating point of her gigantic military preparations, and be forced by financial and economic stringency to contemplate a sharp decline, or perhaps some other exit from her difficulties. It is this lamentable conjunction of events which seems to present the danger of Europe in its most disquieting form. We cannot avoid this period; we are in it now. Surely, if we can abridge it by even a few months, if we can shorten this period when the German Army will begin to be so much larger than the French Army, and before the British Air Force has come to play its complementary part, we may be the architects who build the peace of the world on sure foundations.

Two things, I confess, have staggered me, after a long Parliamentary experience, in these Debates. The first has been the dangers that have so swiftly come upon us in a few years, and have been transforming our position and the whole outlook of the world. Secondly, I have been staggered by the failure of the House of Commons to react effectively against those dangers. That, I am bound to say, I never expected. I never would have believed that we should have been allowed to go on getting into this plight, month by month and year by year, and that even the Government's own confessions of error would have produced no concentration of Parliamentary opinion and force capable of lifting our efforts to the level of emergency. I say that unless the House resolves to find out the truth for itself it will have committed an act of abdication of duty without parallel in its long history.

ARMS AND THE COVENANT

December 3, 1936

Albert Hall, London

The first intimation of the Abdication Crisis which the British public received was on December 3. On that evening the "Arms and the Covenant" movement had its first major public meeting at the Albert Hall. (Churchill, in The Gathering Storm, *217, gives the impression that it was the culminating meeting of the campaign, whereas it was in fact the first.)*

Before going to the meeting Churchill had seen the draft of a broadcast which the King wanted to deliver, and his mind was concentrated upon the Royal crisis when he *reached the Albert Hall. He told Walter Citrine, the General Secretary of the Trades Union Congress who was chairing the meeting, that he wanted to make a statement on the situation. Citrine, supported by Lord Lytton and Lady Violet Bonham-Carter, strongly resisted the suggestion and threatened to walk out if Churchill did so. Churchill later stated that he did make the statement (*The Gathering Storm, *217-18) but the recollections of Lady Asquith (*Daily Telegraph, *March 11, 1965) and Lord Citrine (*Men and Work, *357) contradict this, and their accounts are confirmed by various contemporary reports. The account of the speech which appeared in the* Times *on December 4, 1936, makes no reference to any statement by Churchill on the Royal crisis.*

Lady Asquith's account of this speech may be included: "At last came Winston's turn. He got a tremendous reception, and of course he made a good speech (he could not make a bad one). But many of us felt that he was not at the zenith of his form, and of course we knew why. His heart and mind were engaged elsewhere. At the end of the meeting he commented on the enthusiasm with which the audience had sung the National Anthem, which he interpreted as an endorsement of his attitude on the Royal marriage issue."

In this estimation he was to prove disastrously wrong. The evidence suggests strongly that Churchill came to the Albert Hall intent on making the statement quoted in his memoirs, but, in view of the hostility of the other members of the platform to the suggestion, he never did so.

We are gathered together on this platform with one object. We want to stop this war of which we have heard so much talk. We would like to stop it while time remains, for we have had enough of the last war not to want another. The seriousness and urgency of the danger is exemplified by the divergency of political opinion represented on the platform. We have reached a fateful milestone in human history.

Apostles of various kinds of error present themselves. There are those like Sir Oswald Mosley who are fascinated by the spectacle of brutal power. They would like to use it themselves. They grovel to Nazi dictatorship in order that they can make people in their turn grovel to them. They offer to the Nazi domination the Colonies for which Britain holds mandates under the League of Nations irrespective of the will of the natives. Sir Oswald Mosley hastens to pay his tribute to his spiritual lords and masters. At the other end of the political scale there are Trostsky-ite Communists, furious fanatics whose sole aim is to throw the world into one supreme convulsion. Then there is Sir Stafford Cripps, who is in a class by himself. He wishes British people to be conquered by the Nazis in order to urge them into becoming Bolsheviks. It seems a long way round. (Laughter.) And not much enlightenment when they get to the end of their journey.

Lastly, there are the absolute non-resisters like Canon Sheppard and Mr. Lansbury. They are pious men, but they will lead the country to ruin, even more surely than all the others.

Unhappily, it can be seen only too well how this most dangerous division is opening up all over the world. The agreement between Germany and Japan is only one of those most unmistakable manifestations. It is one of the rifts which exist in the world to-day. It is the war between the Nazis and the Communists: the war of the non-God religions, waged with the weapons of the twentieth century. The most striking fact about the new religions is their similarity. They substitute the devil for God and hatred for love. They are at each other's throats wherever they exist all over the world, and have even appeared in the East End of London.

If present dangers are to be averted there must be loyal aid from the whole masses of the people; there must be voluntary and spontaneous comradeship; and there must even be a measure of self-imposed discipline. But they must not blind their eyes to the power which these new religions exercise in the modern world. They are equipped with powerful agencies of destruction, and they do not lack their champions, their devotees, and even their martyrs.

It is not the duty of Britain to interfere in those countries. It has its own world. Let it look after that. But is it not time that the free nations, great or small, here or across the Atlantic Ocean, should take the measures necessary to place themselves in a state of security and in a state of adequate defence, not only for their own safety but also that they might hold aloft the beacon-lights of freedom which will carry their rays of encouragement to the thinker and toiler in every land?

In Spain a fratricidal war is being waged. What are the great nations of Europe doing? Some are pumping petrol on their flames and lashing the Spaniards into new frenzy one against the other. I wish the liberal, free nations of the world had the power and the strength to separate the combatants and procure a parley. Unhappily they are too weak and cast down, and it is largely their own fault. They have not kept their lamps burning for the cause and are behind with their preparations. But other calls might come. It will take all their efforts night and day to prevent the kind of abominations which broke out in Spain from reappearing perhaps at no great distant time over Europe.

I believe that the League of Nations was never so necessary for the peace of the world as it is now; that it has never had so fine a chance of such solid backing as it now has. They must not be disheartened by the failure and humiliation that has befallen the previous efforts of the League in circumstances unsuitable for the realization of its power. I believe its great days are still to come and that it would be madness in the present years of peril if they discarded the medium's potential for salvation which it can offer to the soldiers and servants of peace and freedom.

If we wish to stop this coming war–if coming it is–we must in the year that lies before us–nay, in the next six months–gather together the great nations, all as well armed as possible and united under the Covenant of the League in accordance with the principles of the League, and in this way we may reach a position where we can invite the German people to join this organization of world security; where we can invite them to take their place freely in the circle of nations to preserve peace, and where we shall be able to assure them that we seek no security for ourselves, which we do not extend most freely to them.

We should rally and invite under the League of Nations the greatest number of strongly armed nations that we can marshal. Let us invite Germany to take her part among us. Then we should, I believe, sincerely have done not only our best but have succeeded in warding off from the world calamities and horrors the end of which no man can forsee.

THE ABDICATION OF KING EDWARD VIII

December 10, 1936

House of Commons

It is not possible here to give an account of the crisis of October-November 1936 which ended with the abdication of King Edward VIII as a result of his insistence upon marrying Mrs. Wallis Simpson. The British public had no knowledge of the matter until December 3. Churchill was deeply sympathetic towards the King. In a public statement on December 5 he appealed for "time and patience," and by implication accused the Government of acting improperly. When he rose in the House of Commons on December 7 he was virtually denied a hearing, and eventually walked out of the chamber. One Member described the incident as "one of the angriest manifestations I have ever heard directed against any man in the House of Commons" (Lord Winterton, Orders of the Day, *223). Churchill's reputation was grievously damaged to the point that many thought he could not recover.*

Nothing is more certain or more obvious than that recrimination or controversy at this time would be not only useless but harmful and wrong. What is done is done. What has been done or left undone belongs to history, and to history, so far as I am concerned, it shall be left. I will, therefore, make two observations only. The first is this: It is clear from what we have been told this afternoon that there was at no time any constitutional issue between the King and his Ministers or between the King and Parliament. The supremacy of Parliament over the Crown: the duty of the Sovereign to act in accordance with the advice of his Ministers: neither of those was ever at any moment in question. Supporting my right hon. Friend the Leader of the Liberal party, I venture to say that no Sovereign has ever conformed more strictly or more faithfully to the letter and spirit of the Constitution than his present Majesty. In fact, he has voluntarily made a sacrifice for the peace and strength of his Realm which goes far beyond the bounds required by the law and the Constitution. That is my first observation.

My second is this: I have, throughout, pleaded for time; anyone can see how grave would have been the evils of protracted controversy. On the other hand, it was, in my view, our duty to endure these evils even at serious inconvenience, if there was any hope that time would bring a solution. Whether there was any hope or not is a mystery which, at the present time, it is impossible to resolve. Time was also important from another point of view. It was essential that there should be no room for aspersions, after the event, that the King had been hurried in his decision. I believe that, if this decision had been taken last week, it could not have been declared that it was an unhurried decision, so far as the King himself was concerned, but now I accept wholeheartedly what the Prime Minister has proved, namely, that the decision taken this week has been taken by His Majesty freely, voluntarily and spontaneously, in his own time and in his own way. As I have been looking at this matter, as is well known, from an angle different from that of most hon. Members, I thought it my duty to place this fact also upon record.

That is all I have to say upon the disputable part of this matter, but I hope the House will bear with me for a minute or two, because it was my duty as Home Secretary, more than a quarter of a century ago, to stand beside his present Majesty and proclaim his style and titles at his investiture as Prince of Wales amid the sunlit battlements of Carnarvon Castle, and ever since then he has honoured me here, and also in war-time, with his personal kindness and, I may even say, friendship. I should have been ashamed if, in my independent and unofficial position, I had not cast about for every lawful means, even the most forlorn, to keep him on the Throne of his fathers, to which he only recently succeeded amid the hopes and prayers of all. In this Prince there were discerned qualities of courage, of simplicity, of sympathy, and, above all, of sincerity, qualities rare and precious which might have made his reign glorious in the annals of this ancient monarchy. It is the acme of tragedy that these very virtues should, in the private sphere, have led only to this melancholy and bitter conclusion. But, although our hopes to-day are withered, still I will assert that his personality will not go down uncherished to future ages, that it will be particularly remembered in the homes of his poorer subjects, and that they will ever wish from the bottom of their hearts for his private peace and happiness and for the happiness of those who are dear to him.

I must say one word more, and I say it specially to those here and out of doors—and do not underrate their numbers—who are most poignantly afflicted by what has occurred. Danger gathers upon our path. We cannot afford—we have no right—to look back. We must look forward; we must obey the exhortation of the Prime Minister to look forward. The stronger the advocate of monarchical principle a man may be, the more zealously must he now endeavour to fortify the Throne and to give to His Majesty's successor that strength which can only come from the love of a united nation and Empire.

THE SPANISH CIVIL WAR

April 14, 1937

House of Commons

The Spanish Civil War—which began in July 1936—aroused intense emotions in Britain, particularly in favour of the Republicans. Churchill, while urging non-intervention, was more sympathetic to what he called "the Anti-Red Movement." He maintained this position, which alienated a substantial number of people sympathetic to his hostility to Nazi Germany, until late 1938. Yet he consistently reiterated his loathing for all forms of totalitarian government.

I have tried very sincerely to adopt a neutral attitude of mind in the Spanish quarrel; I refuse to become the partisan of either side. I will not pretend that, if I had to choose between Communism and Nazi-ism, I would choose Communism. I hope not to be called upon to survive in the world under a Government of either of those dispensations.

Mr. Maxton: You would not.

Mr. Churchill: It is not a question of opposing Nazi-ism or Communism, but of opposing tyranny in whatever form it presents itself; and, as I do not find in either of these two Spanish factions which are at war any satisfactory guarantee that the ideas which I care about would be preserved, I am not able to throw myself in this headlong fashion into the risk of having to fire cannon immediately on the one side or the other of this trouble. I have found it easier to maintain this feeling of detachment from both sides because, before we give any help to either side we ought to know what the victory of that side would mean to those who are beaten. I can understand a British subject espousing the cause of General Franco or Señor Caballero, but what would be that man's remorse if he found that, after contributing to the victory of either side, a horrible vengeance was wreaked, perhaps for years, upon the vanquished? Certainly I do not feel that the House of Commons ought to take any decisive action either way without knowing what the consequences would be to those who were conquered as the result of any intervention in which we engaged. I cannot feel any enthusiasm for these rival creeds. I feel unbounded sorrow and sympathy for the victims, but to give a decisive punch either way, without making sure that the result of it would not be to make ourselves responsible for a subsequent catalogue of foul atrocities, would be a responsibility which no one in the House ought willingly to accept. . . .

I am going to give my vote on this occasion to the Foreign Secretary. I think he has done very well not only as regards our defensive alliance with France, which is our only means of safety in these years of tardy preparation, but in the Non-Intervention Committee. I expect that the Non-Intervention Committee is full of swindles and cheats; anyhow it falls far short of strict interpretation and good faith, but it is a precious thing in these times of peril that five great nations should be slanging each other round a table instead of blasting and bombing each other in horrible war. Is it not an encouraging fact that German, French, Russian, Italian, and British naval officers are officially acting together, however crankily, in something which represents, albeit feebly, the concert of Europe, and affords, if it is only a pale, misshapen shadow, some idea of those conceptions of the reign of law and of collective authority which many of us regard as of vital importance? The man who mocks at the existence of the Non-Intervention Committee I put on the same level as the man who mocks at the hopes of Geneva and the League of Nations. Even if you tell me that it is vitiated by humbug, we should not be daunted. Hypocrisy, it is said, is the tribute which vice pays to virtue. I am not sure that virtue can afford to do without any tributes which are going about. I say frankly that I would rather have a peace-keeping hypocrisy than straightforward, brazen vice, taking the form of unlimited war.

I should not like to sit down without indulging for a few minutes in a day-dream. Alas, it is only a day-dream! Still, as an independent member whose utterances are sometimes noticed abroad, I should like to unfold this day-dream to the House. We have been talking about non-intervention, which is a policy to which we should adhere. But suppose all the great Powers were willing to abandon the policy of non-intervention in favor of a policy of combined intervention in Spain. Suppose some of them stopped pouring petrol on Spanish flames and poured cold water and good sense instead. Suppose a voice went out from Britian—and whose better than that of the Prime Minister?—which said, "Comrade Stalin"—or "Mr. Stalin"; I do not know what is the exact term—"we understand that you are not seeking the establishment of a militant Communist Government in Spain. All you want now is that there shall not be a Nazi or a Fascist Spain. Is that so?" Suppose he said, as I expect he would say, "That is so." Then suppose the voice said to Hitler, "You have rescued the German people from despair and defeat. Now will you not be the Hitler of peace? We understand that the Russian Government is not insisting upon the setting up of a Communist Government in Spain. Will you not also say that if the German people were sure that this would not happen, they would not insist upon the Spaniards adopting a Nazi regime?" Might not Signor Mussolini also hearken to these words of good sense and good faith? Might he not say, "I will not tolerate a Red Bolshevik State in Spain, but I am quite content to see the Spanish Peninsula settle down upon some Spanish basis which is neither one thing nor the other." Then might not the Liberal democracies of the West, France and Britain, and the British Empire, too, come along and say, "Well, if that is so, cannot the people of the middle view, the live-and-let-live people, have a chance? Cannot something be arranged which represents a purely Spanish solution and does not spell the triumph of any highly colored ideology?"

I make bold to say that that is what nineteen-twentieths of the Spanish people want. They do not want to go on killing each other for the entertainment of foreigners. War is very cruel. It goes on for so long. What about some such meeting as Lord Rosebery once suggested, at "a wayside inn," which would give Spain the chance at least of peace, of law, of bread, and of oblivion? I trespass upon the indulgence of the House in uttering such day-dreams, but if they will bear with me, I should like to carry them one step farther and try to cast sentiment into a mold. Of course, neither of the two Spanish sides can afford to say that it would tolerate the idea of a settlement. They are fighting for life; they are desperate men, and all their lives are at stake: They dare not show the slightest sign of weakness, but they have their seconds, they have their friends in these Great Powers who are in close touch with them. Is it not the time when this horrible duel might for the moment be considered by the seconds and not necessarily only by the principal parties, and when the seconds could decide, as they often did in private duels, that honor is satisfied, or, if you like to put it more truthfully, that dishonor is gorged?

Suppose those five Great Powers, whose fleets are now acting nominally on a common policy, after agreeing secretly among themselves, were to propose to the Spaniards a solution on the following lines—a period of six years, in three stages. The first stage would give little more than peace, order, and time to cool down, with no vengeance, no executions except for common murderers on either side. The second stage would be a kind of compromise, a hybrid Government of elements in Spain that have not been involved in the ferocity of this struggle. Let hon. Members opposite not throw away this idea without considering it. If you wish for a truce to this cruel war, you must be bold enough to consider novel and even fanciful propositions. The third stage would see the revival of those Parliamentary institutions which, in one form or another, it is my firm belief that nineteen out of twenty Spaniards never dreamed of losing or meant to see destroyed. Proud as they are, it might well be that the Spaniards, in their distress and agony, would not refuse outside help in putting the locomotive back upon the rails or pulling their wagon out of the ditch.

When millions of people are lacerated and inflamed against each other by reciprocal injuries, some element of outside aid and even of outside pressure is indispensable, and if these five Great Powers were agreed upon a plan, they might say, "If both of your factions refuse our proposals, well, then, go on with your war, and much good may it do you. But if one accepts and the other refuses, then we will all of us unite to give our favor and support, and that would be decisive, to the side which accepts the means of peace." If that course were adopted, it would show that we at any rate possess a leverage, a great leverage, in these matters, and it might well be that a result would come which would be acceptable to the mass of the Spanish people. There is fear in all Spanish hearts, even in districts which are apparently quite tranquil. They know that the turn of the wheel may send a new force into that area by which all their actions will be regarded as guilty; and it is the same on both sides. I cannot conceive that it is not a supreme object of endeavor to give them reassurance. If we try and fail, what is the loss? It is nothing worse than what all suffer anyhow. If we try and succeed, then what is the prize? The prize is far greater than any issue now at stake in Spain. It may be that the peace and glory of Europe would reward the valiant, faithful effort of the Great Powers.

We seem to be moving, drifting, steadily, against our will, against the will of every race and every people and every class, towards some hideous catastrophe. Everybody wishes to stop it, but they do not know how. We have talks of Eastern and Western Pacts, but they make no greater security. Armaments and counter-armaments proceed apace, and we must find something new. Worry has been defined by some nerve-specialists as "a spasm of the imagination." The mind, it is said, seizes hold of something and simply cannot let it go. Reason, argument, threats, are useless. The grip becomes all the more convulsive. But if you could introduce some new theme, in this case the practical effect of a common purpose and of co-operation for a common end, then indeed it might be that these clenched fists would relax into open hands, that the reign of peace and freedom might begin, and that science, instead of being a shameful prisoner in the galleys of slaughter, might pour her wealth abounding into the cottage homes of every land.

JAPANESE CAMPAIGN IN CHINA

October 26, 1937

Constituency Meetings, Loughton and Waltham Abbey

Stanley Baldwin retired as Prime Minister on May 28, and was succeeded by Neville Chamberlain. Ramsay MacDonald also retired, and died later the same year. Sir John Simon became Chancellor of the Exchequer, and there were some other minor changes, including Sir Samuel Hoare's move to the Home Office, with Duff Cooper taking his place as First Lord of the Admiralty. The new Secretary of State for War was Leslie Hore-Belisha.

Throughout 1937 the international scene in Europe was remarkably calm, and hopes began to grow that Churchill's alarmist warnings had been unjustified. His own speeches and articles reflected this new optimism. But, in reality, the international situation was becoming more sombre. German, Italian and Russian "volunteers" were active in Spain; there was tension and sporadic fighting in Palestine; and, at this time, Japan renewed her assault on China.

[Extract] . . . Japan has fallen into the grip of a military society before whom the wishes of the people and of the elder statesmen count for nothing. They have plunged out in an attack on China with a view to tearing off provinces from that vast weak State and adding them to their dominions. But what particularly strikes me is the method by which they are attacking China. They have been found willing to use the new air power in the most ruthless manner as a means of terrorizing China by the indiscriminate bombing of large civilian areas and of poor quarters in Shanghai and other cities.

To some extent there appears to be a relinquishing of that evil weapon, but surely to us here the feeling that this air power may be used to inflict an act of mass terror on vast non-combatant populations and compel the rulers to surrender the title deeds of the nation–surely that kind of policy against civilization and humanity ought to stir us to safeguard ourselves by every means in our power.

We must do that first of all in the general sense by associating ourselves with other countries who feel as we do, and within the circle of the League of Nations gather together as many strongly armed nations as possible, all of whom are pledged to act against the aggressor with what strength they can muster. But it is on our own resources that our first foundation-stone must be laid. We are to have a Bill in Parliament this year about air raid precautions, a matter which will come very much in the area of the local authorities. Every one must aid the Government in this matter.

I do not believe that passive defence is of itself going to be of any real protection. The only method of protecting our country from being ill-used from the air is by having a much more powerful Air Force. I do not consider a major war in Europe imminent. I think there is very clear evidence that among the populations of almost every country in Europe there is a great desire to avoid war; and, although I see many tendencies which are bad, I still feel that we may get through into a clear situation in which this horrible self-destruction of mankind will be avoided.

[Editor's Note: Later in a speech at Waltham Abbey Mr. Churchill referred to the question of imposing sanctions on Japan.] In this matter there is one single rule. We must act in support of the United States. If they are prepared to act you are quite safe in working with that great branch of the English-speaking people. If our two countries go together in this matter, I doubt whether any harm could come to either of us. Alone we cannot intervene effectively. It is too far off and we are not strong enough. Our rule must be to give more support to the United States. As far as they will go we will go.

ANTHONY EDEN'S RESIGNATION
February 22, 1938

House of Commons

Relations between Chamberlain and Eden deteriorated after the former became Prime Minister. A significant episode occurred when Eden was abroad on holiday in January 1938. Chamberlain replied to a letter from President Roosevelt proposing a world conference in a discouraging tone. Eden resented this action being taken without consultation with him, and exaggerated, then and later, the significance of the American suggestion. The final breach occurred shortly afterwards on their attitudes towards Italy. The difference was less over substance than over presentation, but it was clear that Chamberlain desired Eden's resignation. On February 20 Eden resigned. The Conservatives were dismayed, and in the Division which took place at the end of the debate twenty-five abstained. Eden's speech was so moderate that most M.P.s were confused as to what exactly had happened. The portrayal of a gallant young man standing up against drift and appeasement–which Churchill himself favoured–is no longer endorsed by historians. Churchill's account of his reaction to the news can be found in The Gathering Storm, *257-58.*

[Extract] It is with sorrow that I rise today to take part in this Debate. Since my right hon. Friend [Neville Chamberlain] became Prime Minister, I have tried my best to give him disinterested and independent support. I know what his difficulties are, and we all know the dangers by which we are encompassed; yet I could not sit silent here this afternoon without expressing in good faith and in sincerity my disagreement with the course which he has taken, and my increasing concern for the consequences attendant upon it. There is one thing, however, that I will not do; I will not say one word willingly to exacerbate the differences which have arisen between the late Foreign Secretary and his former colleagues. No man, with the best will and sense of detachment in the world, can resign from a Government without wounds given and taken. My hope is that those wounds will not rankle or fester into personal differences, however serious the political issues upon which the men are divided.

This is a moment to celebrate the achievements of the former Foreign Secretary. They ought not to be overlooked at this time. They have been remarkable. For a year and a half we have followed his policy of non-intervention in Spain, and even those who have been most irritated by many of its aspects must have admired the extraordinary tenacity of purpose and steadiness of aim with which he has maintained a central course, without undue bias on either side. And at the end of all this, with all the shifting scenes of the Spanish war, we are found to be the country most trusted by both sides, and the only country, perhaps, which still possesses some eventual power of merciful mediation. . . .

I thought I might recite these incidents to the House because it is only right that we should recognize that his tenure of the Foreign Office has been not only distinguished, but memorable. We had yesterday the conventional and official account by both sides of the differences that led to this series of misfortunes. For the first time we can form a clear picture of what happened. Evidently there were divergences, marked no doubt by goodwill and all the courtesies of Cabinet association, between the Foreign Secretary and the new Prime Minister. These divergences extended principally, first, to their conception of the present condition of the League of Nations and its Covenant; and, secondly, to the attitude which we should adopt towards the dictator Powers. . . .

The Prime Minister yesterday, speaking of the future, said that we must look forward, and not unduly look back. The Prime Minister has assumed the whole responsibility. He has taken control of foreign affairs, and of this decisive sphere of those affairs, into his own hands. The House, by a large majority, is, I am convinced, willing that he should do so. Whatever my views may be as to the wisdom or unwisdom of a particular course, I am not going to fail in the wish and hope that he may be rightly guided, and his efforts crowned with success. I will not attempt to predict the course of the negotiations with Italy to which we are now committed, but I must say that their initiation appears untimely and their outlook bleak. We shall certainly be asked to give a lot, and there is very little we can receive in return, except the discontinuance by Italy of wrong and unneighborly action in which she has long indulged.

There is, however, one consideration which I fully admit would throw a different light on this scene. Even at the risk of being accused of some illogicality in my argument, I would say that if it were possible for Italy to discharge her duty in aiding Great Britain and France in defending the integrity and independence of Austria, for the sake of that I would go as far as any man in making concessions. It would not be possible without some new service rendered by Italy to the general cause of European peace and appeasement. But here I was disappointed to read last week that my noble Friend Lord Halifax had said in another place that there could be no question of our trying to have the Rome-Berlin axis altered in any way. Then it does seem to me that this is very disconcerting. It is difficult to see what serious advantage can inure to Great Britain in the Mediterranean, beyond expressions of goodwill and temporary relief from wrongful annoyances to which we have been subjected.

This last week has been a good week for dictators—one of the best they ever had. The German Dictator has laid his heavy hand upon a small but historic country, and the Italian Dictator has carried his vendetta to a victorious conclusion against Mr. Eden. The conflict between the Italian Dictator and my right hon. Friend has been a long one. There can be no doubt whatever who has won. Signor Mussolini has won. All the might, majesty, power and dominion of the British Empire have not been able to secure the success of the causes which were entrusted to the late Foreign Secretary by the general will of Parliament and of the country. So that is the end of this part of the story—namely, the complete defeat and departure from power of the Englishman whom the British nation and the British Parliament, reinforced by the mandate of a General Election, entrusted with a certain task; and the complete triumph of the Italian Dictator at a moment when success was desperately needed by him for domestic reasons.

What has happened since the resignation was announced? All over the world, in every land, under every sky and every system of government, wherever they may be, the friends of England are dismayed, and the foes of England are exultant. Can anybody who reads the reports which come in hour by hour deny that? We have a heavy price to pay for all this. No one can compute it. Small countries in Europe balancing which way to turn, to which system to adhere, liberal or authoritarian—those countries are more inclined to move to the side of power and resolution. It will be universally believed that it is Signor Mussolini's superior power which has procured the overthrow of the British Foreign Secretary. I cannot myself contemplate the arrival of the British envoy at Rome to make a pact which, if it is successful, will involve the recognition of the conquest of Abyssinia without a pang of bitter humiliation, which I am sure will be felt in millions of cottage homes throughout this country.

But what has happened in the United States of America? There havoc has resulted from this event. I do not say that it cannot be repaired, but millions of people there who are our enemies have been armed with a means to mock the sincerity of British idealism, and to make out that we are all Continental people tarred with the same brush. That is the propaganda which has been given an enormous impetus, while our friends, those who are steadily working for the closer co-operation of the two countries on parallel lines, are downcast, baffled and bewildered.

The resignation of the late Foreign Secretary may well be a milestone in history. Great quarrels, it has been remarked, arise from small occasions, but seldom from small causes. That there was a complete divergence between the former Foreign Secretary and the Prime Minister is too plainly apparent. The former Foreign Secretary adhered to the old policy which we have all followed for so long. The Prime Minister and his colleagues have entered upon another and a new policy.

The old policy was an effort to establish the rule of law in Europe and build up through the League of Nations, or by regional pacts under the League of Nations, effective deterrents against the aggressor. That is the policy which we have followed. Is the new policy to come to terms with the totalitarian Powers in the hope that by great and far-reaching acts of submission, not merely in sentiment and pride, but in material factors, peace may be preserved? I earnestly hope that I may be reassured, and that

Ministers will take occasion to explain their policy more fully. It may be that when the new directors of our foreign policy study the grim face of Europe and the world at this moment, when they have studied it with direct responsibility and with full information from day to day, they will come back to the old conclusions. But then it may be too late. The situation may have vitally changed. Many forces now favorable may have disappeared. Many friends in Europe may have entered into new combinations. Many sources of strength, moral and physical, upon which we might now rely, may be gone.

I was glad to hear the Prime Minister say that our association with France was unchanged and unbroken, but let there be no mistake about it. Our own safety is bound up with that of France. We have our Navy, but that is no protection against the air. The peace of Europe rests today upon the French Army. That army at the present time is the finest in Europe, but with every month that passes its strength is being outmatched by the ceaseless development of the new formations into which the vastly superior manhood of Germany is being cast. Almost any foreign policy is better than duality or continual chops and changes. It is strange that the British people, who have such a reputation for stability in other matters, should have been in the last few years pursuing a foreign policy so baffling by its shifts and twists that foreign countries have been unable to keep step with us, while the little nations who are indirectly affected by our changes are thrown into the utmost bewilderment and confusion.

The other day Lord Halifax said that Europe was confused. The part of Europe that is confused is that part ruled by Parliamentary Governments. I know of no confusion on the side of the great Dictators. They pursue their path towards somber and impressive objectives with ruthless consistency and purpose. They know what they want, and no one can deny that up to the present at every step they are getting what they want. When I look back upon the last five or six years I discern many lost chances when we could have made a stand, a united stand, against the dangers, and when by an act of generosity and magnanimity following upon the marshaling of material strength we could have perhaps prevented the evils which are now upon us.

The grave and perhaps irreparable injury to world security took place in the years 1932 to 1935 in the tenure of the Foreign Office of the present Chancellor of the Exchequer [Sir John Simon]. In those days I ventured repeatedly to submit to the House the maxim that the grievances of the vanquished should be redressed before the disarmament of the victors was begun. But the reverse was done. Then was the time to make concessions to the German people and to the German rulers. Then was the time when they would have had their real value. But no such attempt was made. All that was done was to neglect our own defenses and endeavor to encourage the French to follow a course equally imprudent. The next opportunity when these Sibylline Books were presented to us was when the reoccupation of the Rhineland took place at the beginning of 1936. Now we know that a firm stand by France and Britain with the other Powers associated with them at that time, and with the authority of the League of Nations, would have been followed by the immediate evacuation of the Rhineland without the shedding of a drop of blood, and the effects of that might have been blessed beyond all compare, because it would have enabled the more prudent elements in the German Army to regain their proper position, and would not have given to the political head of Germany that enormous ascendancy which has enabled him to move forward. On the morrow of such a success we could have made a large and generous settlement.

Now we are in a moment when a third move is made, but when that opportunity does not present itself in the same favorable manner. Austria has been laid in thrall, and we do not know whether Czechoslovakia will not suffer a similar attack. Let me remind hon. Members when they talk about Germany's desire for peace that this small country has declared that it will resist, and if it resists that may well light up the flames of war, the limits of which no man can predict. It is because we have lost these opportunities of standing firm, of having strong, united forces, a good heart, and a resolute desire to defend the right and afterwards to do generously as the result of strength, that, when our resources are less and the dangers greater, we have been brought to this pass. I predict that the day will come when at some point or other, on some issue or other, you will have to make a stand, and I pray God that when that day comes we may not find that through an unwise policy we are left to make that stand alone.

THE ANNEXATION OF AUSTRIA

March 14, 1938

House of Commons

The deceptive calm of 1937 was now abruptly ended. On March 11 Germany annexed Austria swiftly and easily. This was the first of the succession of shocks which fell upon Europe in the terrible year 1938. Churchill's warning that Hitler had "a programme of aggression, nicely calculated and timed, unfolding stage by stage," began to be widely accepted, although the available evidence points to a general rather than a precise strategy by Hitler.

[Extract] . . . The gravity of the event of the 11th of March cannot be exaggerated. Europe is confronted with a program of aggression, nicely calculated and timed, unfolding stage by stage, and there is only one choice open, not only to us, but to other countries who are unfortunately concerned—either to submit, like Austria, or else to take effective measures while time remains to ward off the danger and, if it cannot be warded off, to cope with it. Resistance will be hard, yet I am persuaded—and the Prime Minister's speech confirms me—that it is to this conclusion of resistance to overweening encroachment that His Majesty's Government will come, and the House of Commons will certainly sustain them in playing a great part in the effort to preserve the peace of Europe, and, if it cannot be preserved, to preserve the freedom of the nations of Europe. If we were to delay, if we were to go on waiting upon events for a considerable period, how much should we throw away of resources which are now available for our security and for the maintenance of peace? How many friends would be alienated, how many potential allies should we see go, one by one, down the grisly gulf, how many times would bluff succeed, until behind bluff ever-gathering forces had accumulated reality? Where shall we be two years hence, for instance, when the German Army will certainly be much larger than the French Army, and when all the small nations will have fled from Geneva to pay homage to the ever-waxing power of the Nazi system, and to make the best terms they can for themselves?

We cannot leave the Austrian question where it is. We await the further statement of the Government, but it is quite clear that we cannot accept as a final solution of the problem of Central Europe the event which occurred on March 11. The public mind has been concentrated upon the moral and sentimental aspects of the Nazi conquest of Austria—a small country brutally struck down, its Government scattered to the winds, the oppression of the Nazi party doctrine imposed upon a Catholic population and upon the working-classes of Austria and of Vienna, the hard ill-usage of persecution which indeed will ensue—which is probably in progress at the moment—of those who, this time last week, were exercising their undoubted political rights, discharging their duties faithfully to their own country. All this we see very clearly, but there are some things which I have not seen brought out in the public Press and which do not seem to be present in the public mind, and they are practical considerations of the utmost significance.

Vienna is the center of all the communications of all the countries which formed the old Austro-Hungarian Empire, and of all the countries lying to the south-east of Europe. A long stretch of the Danube is now in German hands. This mastery of Vienna gives to Nazi Germany military and economic control of the whole of the communications of south-eastern Europe, by road, by river, and by rail. What is the effect of it upon what is called the balance of power, such as it is, and upon what is called the Little Entente? I must say a word about this group of Powers called the Little Entente. Taken singly, the three countries of the Little Entente may be called Powers of the second rank, but they are very vigorous States, and united they are a Great Power. They have hitherto been, and are still, united by the closest military agreement. Together they make the complement of a Great Power and of the military machinery of a Great Power. Rumania has the oil; Yugoslavia has the minerals and raw materials. Both have large armies; both are mainly supplied with munitions from Czechoslovakia. To English ears, the name of Czechoslovakia sounds outlandish. No doubt they are only a small democratic State, no doubt they have an army only two or three times as large as ours, no doubt they have a munitions supply only three times as great as that of Italy, but still they are a virile people; they have their treaty rights, they have a line of fortresses, and they have a strongly manifested will to live freely.

Czechoslovakia is at this moment isolated, both in the economic and in the military sense. Her trade outlet through Hamburg, which is based upon the Peace Treaty, can, of course, be closed at any moment. Now her communications by rail and river to the south, and after the south to the south-east, are liable to be severed at any moment. Her trade may be subjected to tolls of an absolutely strangling character. Here is a country which was once the greatest manufacturing area in the old Austro-Hungarian Empire. It is now cut off, or may be cut off at once unless, out of these discussions which must follow, arrangements are made securing the communications of Czechoslovakia. You may be cut off at once from the sources of her raw material in

Yugoslavia and from the natural markets which she has established there. The economic life of this small State may be practically destroyed as a result of the act of violence which was perpetrated last Friday night. A wedge has been driven into the heart of what is called the Little Entente, this group of countries which have as much right to live in Europe unmolested as any of us have the right to live unmolested in our native land. . . .

The serious nature of our affairs is realized and apprehended in all parts of the House. I have often been called an alarmist in the past, yet I affirm tonight that there is still, in my belief, an honorable path to safety and, I hope, to peace. What ought we to do? The Prime Minister today has made a declaration upon the subject of defense. There is to be a new effort of national rearmament and national service. We shall have to lay aside our easy habits and methods. We shall have to concentrate on securing our safety with something like the intensity that has been practiced in other countries whose excesses we may desire to restrain. I think the House will be grateful to the Prime Minister for that declaration, and I am certain that he may rely upon all those strong forces in every party throughout the country to second the efforts of the Government to place us in a position where we shall not feel ourselves liable to be blackmailed out of our duties, out of our interests and out of our rights.

It seems to me quite clear that we cannot possibly confine ourselves only to a renewed effort at rearmament. I know that some of my hon. Friends on this side of the House will laugh when I offer them this advice. I say, "Laugh, but listen." I affirm that the Government should express in the strongest terms our adherence to the Covenant of the League of Nations and our resolve to procure by international action the reign of law in Europe. I agree entirely with what has been said by the Leaders of the two Opposition parties upon that subject; and I was extremely glad to notice that at the beginning and in the very forefront of his speech the Prime Minister referred to the League of Nations and made that one of the bases of our right to intervene and to be consulted upon affairs in Central Europe. The matter has an importance in this country. There must be a moral basis for British rearmament and British foreign policy. We must have that basis if we are to unite and inspire our people and procure their wholehearted action, and if we are to stir the English-speaking people throughout the world.

Our affairs have come to such a pass that there is no escape without running risks. On every ground of prudence as well as of duty I urge His Majesty's Government to proclaim a renewed, revivified, unflinching adherence to the Covenant of the League of Nations. What is there ridiculous about collective security? The only thing that is ridiculous about it is that we have not got it. Let us see whether we cannot do something to procure a strong element of collective security for ourselves and for others. We have been urged to make common cause in self-defense with the French Republic. What is that but the beginning of collective security? I agree with that. Not so lightly will the two great liberal democracies of the West be challenged, and not so easily, if challenged, will they be subjugated. That is the beginning of collective security. But why stop there? Why be edged and pushed farther down the slope in a disorderly expostulating crowd of embarrassed States. Why not make a stand while there is still a good company of united, very powerful countries that share our dangers and aspirations? Why should we delay until we are confronted with a general landslide of those small countries passing over, because they have no other choice, to the overwhelming power of the Nazi regime?

If a number of States were assembled around Great Britain and France in a solemn treaty for mutual defense against aggression; if they had their forces marshaled in what you may call a Grand Alliance; if they had their Staff arrangements concerted; if all this rested, as it can honorably rest, upon the Covenant of the League of Nations, in pursuance of all the purposes and ideals of the League of Nations; if that were sustained, as it would be, by the moral sense of the world; and if it were done in the year 1938—and, believe me, it may be the last chance there will be for doing it—then I say that you might even now arrest this approaching war. Then perhaps the curse which overhangs Europe would pass away. Then perhaps the ferocious passions which now grip a great people would turn inwards and not outwards in an internal rather than an external explosion, and mankind would be spared the deadly ordeal towards which we have been sagging and sliding month by month. I have ventured to indicate a positive conception, a practical and realistic conception, and one which I am convinced will unite all the forces of this country without whose help your armies cannot be filled or your munitions made. Before we cast away this hope, this cause and this plan, which I do not at all disguise has an element of risk, let those who wish to reject it ponder well and earnestly upon what will happen to us if, when all else has been thrown to the wolves, we are left to face our fate alone.

THE THREAT TO CZECHOSLOVAKIA

March 24, 1938

House of Commons

For an admirable account of this historic and tragically prophetic speech and its impact upon the House of Commons, see Virginia Cowles, Winston Churchill: The Era and the Man, *308-09.*

[Extract] The Prime Minister [Neville Chamberlain], in what I think it is not presumptuous for me to describe as a very fine speech, set before us the object which is in all our minds—namely, how to prevent war. A country like ours, possessed of immense territory and wealth, whose defences have been neglected, cannot avoid war by dilating upon its horrors, or even by a continuous display of pacific qualities, or by ignoring the fate of the victims of aggression elsewhere. War will be avoided, in present circumstances, only by the accumulation of deterrents against the aggressor. If our defences are weak, we must seek allies; and, of course, if we seek allies, alliances involve commitments. But the increase of commitments may be justified if it is followed by a still greater increase of deterrents against aggression. . . .

Then we come to the case of Czechoslovakia. There has been a lot of talk about giving a guarantee, but I should be sorry if the grave issue now open in Europe were to turn solely on that point, cardinal though it be. Far wider decisions are called for; far larger interests are at stake. I listened with the utmost attention to all that the Prime Minister said about our relations to Czechoslovakia, and it seems to me that he has gone a long way in making a commitment. First, I was very glad to hear him reaffirm his adherence and that of the Government to the obligations of the Covenant of the League. Under the Covenant of the League we are not obliged to go to war for Czechoslovakia. But we are obliged not to be neutral, in the sense of being indifferent, if Czechoslovakia is the victim of unprovoked aggression. The Prime Minister seemed to me to go farther than those mere obligations of the League, and to indicate how very real was the interest which we took in affairs in that part of the world. Lord Halifax, speaking in another place, used language which is particularly important coming from the head of the Foreign Office. He said he had asked Field-Marshal Goering to repeat to him the assurances which he had given to the Prime Minister of Czechoslovakia, and that this had been done by the German Government; and then Lord Halifax said:

> By those assurances, solemnly given and more than once repeated, we naturally expect the German Government to abide, and if indeed they desire to see European peace maintained, as I earnestly hope they do, there is no quarter in Europe in which it is more vital that undertakings should be scrupulously respected.

We not only have, therefore, the general obligations of the Covenant of the League, but we have this particular reference to special assurances given and received and noted. There is a third aspect. We have our agreement, which I have described, and of which the Prime Minister has reminded us, with France, and if France is attacked by Germany for going to the rescue of Czechoslovakia, no one can say that we shall not be involved–not legally, not as a matter of bond, but by the force of events. The Prime Minister used language which undoubtedly had the effect of making it perfectly plain that the course of war once started could not be limited, that no one could tell what would happen, that other countries would be drawn in, and he mentioned especially France and Great Britain as two countries which might be involved.

Taking all these points together, I cannot doubt that we have considerable commitments, and personally, I am very thankful for any words that have been used which sustain that point of view. But this seems to be another case, if I may say so, of making very considerable commitments without gaining the full proportion of deterrent value. We are not taking the fullest steps in our power to stop the event occurring, and yet we are liable to suffer from it if it occurs. We are liable not only to be drawn in, but to be drawn in, perhaps, late in the day, and very likely in unfavorable circumstances. It is really for consideration whether, having gone so far, the bolder course might not be the safer. All attempts to bridge a twelve-foot stream by an eight-foot plank are doomed to failure, and the plank is lost. It is a concession, no doubt, to bring forward a nine-foot plank, but again that may be lost. The great point in view is to achieve the object, and to produce the effect of an adequate deterrent.

The question does not turn upon an automatic permanent pledge. What I should be inclined to ask if these matters could be at any time reconsidered is not that a permanent or automatic pledge should be given, but that now, on this present occasion, in the circumstances which surround us at the moment, with the rape of Austria before our eyes, Great Britain should say, "If the Germans march in upon this State of Czechoslovakia without even waiting for an impartial examination, perhaps by a commission of the League of Nations, or some other body, into the position of the Sudeten Deutsch and the remedies offered for their grievances–if in those circumstances an act of violent aggression were committed upon that country, then we should feel, on this occasion, and in this emergency, bound to act with France in resisting it." Such a declaration, although limited to this particular emergency, although limited until a tribunal has examined the position and until the negotiations now proceeding have reached their conclusion–such an assurance would, I believe, do a great deal to stabilize the position in Europe, and I cannot see that it would very seriously add to our risks.

I must say that I myself have not felt during this crisis that there is an immediate danger of a major land war breaking out over Czechoslovakia. I know it is very rash to make such a statement, but when there is so much natural, but misdirected, alarm in the country, now on one point and now on another, one must run some risks in stating one's honest opinion. At any rate, that is the assumption on which I base my argument this afternoon, and I will give my reasons to the House. The first reason is that, in the opinion of many good judges, Germany is not ready this year for such an ordeal as a major land war. The second reason carries more conviction to me, because obviously the first is based upon facts which one cannot measure and secrets which one cannot probe. It is that I cannot see that it would be to the interest of the rulers of Germany to provoke such a war.

Are they not getting all they want without it? Are they not achieving a long succession of most important objectives without firing a single shot? Is there any limit to the economic and political pressure which, without actually using military force, Germany will be able to bring to bear upon this unhappy State? She can be convulsed politically, she can be strangled economically, she is practically surrounded by superior forces, and unless something is done to mitigate the pressure of circumstances, she will be forced to make continuous surrenders, far beyond the bounds of what any impartial tribunal would consider just or right, until finally her sovereignty, her independence, her integrity, have been destroyed. Why, then, should the rulers of Germany strike a military blow? Why should they incur the risk of a major war? . . .

But the story of this year is not ended at Czechoslovakia. It is not ended this month. The might behind the German Dictator increases daily. His appetite may grow with eating. The forces of law and freedom have for a long time known nothing but rebuffs, failures and humiliations. Their influence would be immensely increased by any signs of concerted action and initiative and combination. The fact that Britain and France combined together at such a moment in such a cause would give them the strength and authority that they need in order to convince wavering States that they might find a good company of determined people to whom they might join themselves upon the basis of the Covenant and in accordance with its principles. On the morrow of such a proof of unity as could be given between Great Britain and France we might be able to make such an arrangement, or begin to make it, for the effective fulfillment of the Covenant. We might have a group of Powers, as it were Mandatories of the League, who would be the guardians of civilization, and once this was set up strong and real it would liberate us, at least over a long period, from the torments of uncertainty and anxiety which we now have to endure. Joint action on this occasion would make easier and safer the problem of dealing with the next occasion. If successful, it would certainly pave the way to more effective joint action in the enforcement of the non-intervention policy in Spain. Nations that have joined together to meet one particular emergency may well find, when they look around, that they have assembled forces sufficient to deal with other emergencies not yet before us, and thus we may gather an ever-growing company, ranged under standards of law and justice, submitting themselves to principles that they are ready to enforce: and thus, by military and moral means combined, we may once more regain the ascendant and the initiative for the free peoples of the world and throughout the Empire.

I have set the issue before the House in terms which do not shirk realities. It has been said by almost all speakers that, if we do not stand up to the Dictators now, we shall only prepare the day when we shall have to stand up to them under far more adverse conditions. Two years ago it was safe, three years ago it was easy, and four years ago a mere dispatch might have rectified the position. But where shall we be a year hence? Where shall we be in 1940? . . .

CZECHOSLOVAKIA

May 23, 1938

Chingford

As Churchill had warned–and continued to warn–the shadows were now gathering over Czechoslovakia. Behind a facade of determination to protect her integrity, Britain and France were beginning to apply pressure upon President Benes to make major concessions to the Sudeten Germans.

Churchill was not the only person to be interested in the plans of Herr Henlein, the Nazi leader in the Sudetenland, who visited London in May. Churchill's calculation that "Germany is not ready for a major land war" in 1938 was correct, but was not generally believed.

[Extract] . . . We have had an anxious week-end and I do not think it will be the last we shall experience in the near future. I remain hopeful of a peaceful solution on this occasion, because I have good reason to believe that the kind of plans which Herr Henlein described when he was over here would not be unacceptable to the Government of Czechoslovakia.

It would be a great responsibility for any outside Power to prevent a settlement being reached which would save the Sudeten Deutsche from being the first victims of war, and would give them an opportunity of playing an honourable part in the life of Czechoslovakia. If the present crisis passes and war is averted—as I believe it will be—that would be due to a rudimentary and emergency form of collective security; the firm attitude of France, supported to a very considerable extent by Great Britain, and to an extent we could not tell by Russia and Poland, and above all, the determination of the Czechs to fight in defence of their country might prevent violence and the bloody seizure of Czechoslovakia.

High authorities consider that Germany is not ready for a major land war. There is a shortage of food and of raw materials. The German Army is not fully officered. In these circumstances, unless the rulers of Germany go mad, we should have a further breathing space. But what is going to happen next year and in 1940? The German Army will be much stronger relatively than that of France, and the British Air Force is not catching up. Indeed, at the present time we are falling farther behind. Unless, therefore, we can gain other Powers to the side of peace, disaster may occur. We shall require a much stronger team in the future. More peace-seeking nations will have to act as special constables on the threatened beats of Europe.

Why should we not gain other Powers? Why should we not band together all the States of the Danube and Balkans into a stronger confederacy for peace? In order to do this it will be necessary for Britain and France to make common cause with them if any one of them is attacked. Why should we run more risk in doing this than we do at present? It would be far better to have firm arrangements with a large body of well-armed nations all obliged to defend one another against an aggressor than to drift from one crisis to another. This would be real collective security and not a sham. It is, in my belief, the safest and perhaps the only road to a lasting European peace.

I ask the country to support the Covenant, and deny it is an encirclement only of an aggressor. To form a war combination against a single State would be a crime, but to form a combination of mutual defence against a potential aggressor, is not only not a crime but a moral duty and a virtue. We ask no security for ourselves that we are not prepared freely to extend to Germany. If Germany nourishes no aggressive designs let her join the club and share freely and equally in all its privileges and safeguards. If Germany were the victim of unprovoked aggression from the East she would, according to the Covenant of the League, be entitled to receive the fullest aid from all its members. Even if Germany does not rejoin the League, I see no reason why assurances of the most decisive character should not be offered by France and Britain to help Germany in every possible way if she were the victim of an outrage. The aim of real collective security is a foreign policy which involves the country in no commitments more entangling or onerous than those which the country has undertaken, and it gives it the only possibility of reasonable security.

Parliament is to discuss air armaments again this week, and there ought to be better explanations than have been offered so far as to the condition of the Air Force, and why the solemn pledge given by Lord Baldwin that we should maintain our parity with any nation that could get at us should be broken. This is not a case for the Opposition to make party capital against the Government, nor for the Government to shield incompetence and misdirection—all ought to put country before party. There should be a fearless resolve to lay aside every impediment and sweep away every obstacle that stands in the path of our regaining our national security. At present this country is shielded by the strength of the French Army—a strength that the Germans are overtaking month by month. This country still has its Navy, never, happily, more supreme in European waters. The British Air Force, which ought to be overhauling them by leaps and bounds, is not in that position at present. If we are to place ourselves in security from these anxieties we must throw ourselves into the business of national defence with something of the vigour, and concentration which the dictator countries show.

"VOLCANIC FORCES ARE MOVING IN EUROPE"

June 2, 1938

League of Nations Union, Birmingham

By this time, Churchill's earlier support of Franco was fading rapidly, as this excerpt demonstrates.

[Extract] ... The idea that dictators can be appeased by kind words and minor concessions is doomed to disappointment.

Volcanic forces are moving in Europe, and sombre figures are at the head of the most powerful races. The dictator countries are prepared night and day to advance their ambition, if possible by peace, if necessary by war. I am under the impression that we and other countries stand in great danger. For four years Germany has been arming with might and main. There has never been seen such an outpouring of the munitions of war. At the present time we are sheltered to some extent by the strength of the French Army, but the German numbers are overtaking it, and in the next few years they will be much more numerous. We have our own Navy, happily still supreme in the European Mediterranean, but our air forces, on which so much depends, so far from overtaking Germany, are actually falling farther and farther behind. Britain must rearm at the earliest possible moment: we must stand by the League Covenant, which alone justifies a great rearmament; and on the basis of the Covenant we must unite with other countries desiring freedom and peace.

In this country we could be content to remain entirely neutral so far as Spain is concerned had it been only a Spanish quarrel. It is difficult to understand the rights and wrongs of a quarrel in a foreign country, but it excites my indignation when I see shameful interference disguised under the mocking terms "non-intervention" by two European Dictator States. General Franco, advancing with the aid of those foreign troops, proclaims that he will only accept the unconditional surrender of what was only half of his country. I find it very difficult to maintain the attitude of impartial neutrality.

The Anglo-Italian agreement is not operative until the Italian troops are withdrawn from Spain. If they waited until the Republican resistance is over that might be a very long time. Any attempt to give financial aid to Italy, direct or indirect, while those Italian troops are actively intervening in the Spanish quarrel should receive and deserve the strenuous resistance of the British people.

THE THREAT TO CZECHOSLOVAKIA

August 27, 1938

Constituency Meeting, Theydon Bois

The German threat to Czechoslovakia became more evident and dangerous in August. The British Government, anxious to secure concessions for the German minority in Czechoslovakia before Hitler intervened, despatched Lord Runciman as a mediator.

[Extract] It is difficult for us in this ancient Forest at Theydon Bois, the very name of which carries us back to Norman days–here, in the heart of peaceful, law-abiding England–to realize the ferocious passions which are rife in Europe. During this anxious month you have no doubt seen reports in the newspapers, one week good, another week bad; one week better, another week worse. But I must tell you that the whole state of Europe and of the world is moving steadily towards a climax which cannot be long delayed.

War is certainly not inevitable. But the danger to peace will not be removed until the vast German armies which have been called from their homes into the ranks have been dispersed. For a country which is itself not menaced by anyone, in no fear of anyone, to place over fifteen hundred thousand soldiers upon a war footing is a very grave step. The expense cannot be less than five or six hundred thousand pounds a day, which amounts to more than thirty millions in two months, all to be exacted from a country whose finances are already under severe strain, and whose people have long been living under what the rest of the world would call war conditions.

It seems to me, and I must tell it to you plainly, that these great forces have not been placed upon a war footing without an intention to reach a conclusion within a very limited space of time. The fabricated stories which are spread of a Marxist plot in Czechoslovakia, and the orders to the Sudeten Deutsch to arm and defend themselves, are disquieting signs, similar to those which preceded the seizure of Austria.

We are all in full agreement with the course our Government have taken in sending Lord Runciman to Prague. We hope–indeed, we pray, that his mission of conciliation will be successful, and certainly it looks as if the Government of Czechoslovakia were doing their utmost to put their house in order, and to meet every demand which is not designed to compass their ruin as a State. I have little doubt that Lord Runciman, if given a fair chance, would be able to bring about a friendly settlement on the spot. But it may be that outside forces, that larger and fiercer ambitions, may prevent this settlement, and then Europe and the civilized world will have to face the demands of Nazi Germany, or perhaps be confronted–and this is a possibility which you must not exclude–with some sudden violent action on the part of the German Nazi Party, carrying with it the invasion of a small country with a view to its subjugation. Such an episode would not be simply an attack upon Czechoslovakia; it would be an outrage against the civilization and freedom of the whole world. Every country would ask itself, "Whose turn will it be next?" . . .

"THROWING A SMALL STATE TO THE WOLVES"

September 21, 1938

Statement to Press Association, London

The Czechoslovakia crisis broke in September. On September 15 Chamberlain flew to Berchtesgaden to see Hitler, and proposed the partition of Czechoslovakia. The Cabinet was deeply unhappy, and public disquiet grew rapidly. War seemed very close. The Anglo-French pressure on President Benes to accept their "solution" became intense.

It is necessary that the nation should realize the magnitude of the disaster into which we are being led. The partition of Czechoslovakia under Anglo-French pressure amounts to a complete surrender by the Western Democracies to the Nazi threat of force. Such a collapse will not bring peace or safety to Great Britain and France. On the contrary, it will bring both countries into a position of ever-increasing weakness and danger.

The neutralization of Czechoslovakia alone means the liberation of 25 German divisions to threaten the Western Front. The path to the Black Sea will be laid wide open to triumphant Nazism.

Acceptance of Herr Hitler's terms involves the prostration of Europe before the Nazi power, of which the fullest advantage will certainly be taken. The menace, therefore, is not to Czechoslovakia, but to the cause of freedom and democracy in every country.

The idea that safety can be purchased by throwing a small State to the wolves is a fatal delusion. The German war power will grow faster than the French and British can complete their preparations for defence.

If peace is to be preserved on a lasting basis it can only be by combination of all the Powers whose convictions and whose vital interests are opposed to Nazi domination. A month ago this would have been possible. But all was cast away.

Parliament should be called together without further delay and duly informed upon these grievous matters which affect the whole life and future of our country.

ONE LAST PEACE EFFORT

September 26, 1938

London

On September 22 Chamberlain flew to Godesberg to see Hitler, only to find that Hitler had increased his demands to include the immediate military occupation of the Sudeten areas. The Cabinet was appalled, and preparation for war accelerated.

There is still one good chance of preserving peace. A solemn warning should be presented to the German Government in joint or simultaneous Notes by Great Britain, France, and Russia that the invasion of Czechoslovakia at the present juncture would be taken as an act of war against these Powers. The terms of this Note should be communicated to all neutral countries, some of whom may be balancing their actions, and most particularly to the Government of the U.S.A.

If such steps had been taken a month ago it is improbable matters would have reached their present pass. Even at the last moment clear and resolute action may avert the catastrophe into which we are drifting. Not only the German Government but the German people have a right to know where we all stand.

If the Government and people of the U.S.A. have a word to speak for the salvation of the world, now is the time and now is the last time when words will be of any use. Afterwards, through years of struggle and torment, deeds alone will serve and deeds will be forthcoming. It will indeed be a tragedy if this last effort is not made in the only way in which it may be effective to save mankind from martyrdom.

" A TOTAL AND UNMITIGATED DEFEAT"

October 5, 1938

House of Commons

On September 29 Chamberlain flew to Munich to see Hitler. The military occupation of the Sudentenland was accepted. Chamberlain returned to London on October 1 with an Anglo-German Agreement pledging that the two nations would never go to war again, and claiming "peace with honour." The public reaction was one of relief and joy; for a brief moment Chamberlain was an international hero. Amid this chorus of adulation, Churchill and Duff Cooper–who resigned from the Admiralty–struck a different note. In this debate on the Agreement, thirty Conservatives abstained, including Churchill, Eden, Duff Cooper, Amery, Macmillan, and Sandys. But they were in a very small majority–in the country as well as in the House of Commons.

Churchill's speech, one of the fiercest he ever made, was heard with ill-disguised anger by the majority of the Conservative Party.

[Extract] If I do not begin this afternoon by paying the usual, and indeed almost invariable, tributes to the Prime Minister for his handling of this crisis, it is certainly not from any lack of personal regard. We have always, over a great many years, had very pleasant relations, and I have deeply understood from personal experiences of my own in a similar crisis the stress and strain he has had to bear; but I am sure it is much better to say exactly what we think about public affairs, and this is certainly not the time when it is worth anyone's while to court political popularity. We had a shining example of firmness of character from the late First Lord of the Admiralty two days ago. He showed that firmness of character which is utterly unmoved by currents of opinion, however swift and violent they may be. My hon. Friend the Member for South-West Hull (Mr. Law), to whose compulsive speech the House listened on Monday—which I had not the good fortune to hear, but which I read, and which I am assured by all who heard it revived the memory of his famous father, so cherished in this House, and made us feel that his gifts did not die with him—was quite right in reminding us that the Prime Minister has himself throughout his conduct of these matters shown a robust indifference to cheers or boos and to the alternations of criticism and applause. If that be so, such qualities and elevation of mind should make it possible for the most severe expressions of honest opinion to be interchanged in this House without rupturing personal relations, and for all points of view to receive the fullest possible expression.

Having thus fortified myself by the example of others, I will proceed to emulate them. I will, therefore, begin by saying the most unpopular and most unwelcome thing. I will begin by saying what everybody would like to ignore or forget but which must nevertheless be stated, namely, that we have sustained a total and unmitigated defeat, and that France has suffered even more than we have.

Viscountess Astor: Nonsense.

Mr. Churchill: When the Noble Lady cries "Nonsense," she could not have heard the Chancellor of the Exchequer [Sir John Simon] admit in his illuminating and comprehensive speech just now that Herr Hitler had gained in this particular leap forward in substance all he set out to gain. The utmost my right hon. Friend the Prime Minister has been able to secure by all his immense exertions, by all the great efforts and mobilisation which took place in this country, and by all the anguish and strain through which we have passed in this country, the utmost he has been able to gain—[Hon. Members: "Is peace."] I thought I might be allowed to make that point in its due place, and I propose to deal with it. The utmost he has been able to gain for Czechoslovakia and in the matters which were in dispute has been that the German dictator, instead of snatching his victuals from the table, has been content to have them served to him course by course.

The Chancellor of the Exchequer said it was the first time Herr Hitler had been made to retract—I think that was the word—in any degree. We really must not waste time, after all this long Debate, upon the difference between the positions reached at Berchtesgaden, at Godesberg and at Munich. They can be very simply epitomised, if the House will permit me to vary the metaphor. £1 was demanded at the pistol's point. When it was given, £2 were demanded at the pistol's point. Finally, the dictator consented to take £1 17s. 6d. and the rest in promises of good will for the future.

Now I come to the point, which was mentioned to me just now from some quarters of the House, about the saving of peace. No one has been a more resolute and uncompromising struggler for peace than the Prime Minister. Everyone knows that. Never has there been such intense and undaunted determination to maintain and to secure peace. That is quite true. Nevertheless, I am not quite clear why there was so much danger of Great Britain or France being involved in a war with Germany at this juncture if, in fact, they were ready all along to sacrifice Czechoslovakia. The terms which the Prime Minister brought back with him–I quite agree at the last moment; everything had got off the rails and nothing but his intervention could have saved the peace, but I am talking of the events of the summer–could easily have been agreed, I believe, through the ordinary diplomatic channels at any time during the summer. And I will say this, that I believe the Czechs, left to themselves and told they were going to get no help from the Western Powers, would have been able to make better terms than they have got–they could hardly have worse–after all this tremendous perturbation.

There never can be any absolute certainty that there will be a fight if one side is determined that it will give way completely. When one reads the Munich terms, when one sees what is happening in Czechoslovakia from hour to hour, when one is sure, I will not say of Parliamentary approval but of Parliamentary acquiescence, when the Chancellor of the Exchequer makes a speech which at any rate tries to put in a very powerful and persuasive manner the fact that, after all, it was inevitable and indeed righteous–right–when we saw all this, and everyone on this side of the House, including many Members of the Conservative Party who are supposed to be vigilant and careful guardians of the national interest, it is quite clear that nothing vitally affecting us was at stake, it seems to me that one must ask, What was all the trouble and fuss about?

The resolve was taken by the British and the French Governments. Let me say that it is very important to realise that it is by no means a question which the British Government only have had to decide. I very much admire the manner in which, in the House, all references of a recriminatory nature have been repressed, but it must be realised that this resolve did not emanate particularly from one or other of the Governments but was a resolve for which both must share in common the responsibility. When this resolve was taken and the course was followed–you may say it was wise or unwise, prudent or short-sighted–once it had been decided not to make the defence of Czechoslovakia a matter of war, then there was really no reason, if the matter had been handled during the summer in the ordinary way, to call into being all this formidable apparatus of crisis. I think that point should be considered.

We are asked to vote for this Motion ["That this House approves the policy of His Majesty's Government by which war was averted in the recent crisis and supports their efforts to secure a lasting peace"] which has been put upon the Paper, and it is certainly a Motion couched in very uncontroversial terms, as, indeed, is the Amendment moved from the Opposition side. I cannot myself express my agreement with the steps which have been taken, and as the Chancellor of the Exchequer has put his side of the case with so much ability I will attempt, if I may be permitted, to put the case from a different angle. I have always held the view that the maintenance of peace depends upon the accumulation of deterrents against the aggressor, coupled with a sincere effort to redress grievances. Herr Hitler's victory, like so many of the famous struggles that have governed the fate of the world, was won upon the narrowest of margins. After the seizure of Austria in March we faced this problem in our Debates. I ventured to appeal to the Government to go a little further than the Prime Minister went, and to give a pledge that in conjunction with France and other Powers they would guarantee the security of Czechoslovakia while the Sudeten-Deutsch question was being examined either by a League of Nations Commission or some other impartial body, and I still believe that if that course had been followed events would not have fallen into this disastrous state. I agree very much with my right hon. Friend the Member for Sparkbrook (Mr. Amery) when he said on that occasion–I cannot remember his actual words–"Do one thing or the other: either say you will disinterest yourself in the matter altogether or take the step of giving a guarantee which will have the greatest chance of securing protection for that country."

France and Great Britain together, especially if they had maintained a close contact with Russia, which certainly was not done, would have been able in those days in the summer, when they had the prestige, to influence many of the smaller States of Europe, and I believe they could have determined the attitude of Poland. Such a combination, prepared at a time when the German dictator was not deeply and irrevocably committed to his new adventure, would, I believe, have given strength to all those forces in Germany which resisted this departure, this new design. They were varying forces, those of a military character which declared that Germany was not ready to undertake a world war, and all that mass of moderate opinion and popular opinion which dreaded war, and some elements of which still have some influence upon the German Government. Such action would have given strength to all that intense desire for peace which the helpless German masses share with their British and French fellow men, and which, as we have been reminded, found a passionate and rarely permitted vent in the joyous manifestations with which the Prime Minister was acclaimed in Munich.

All these forces, added to the other deterrents which combinations of Powers, great and small, ready to stand firm upon the front of law and for the ordered remedy of grievances, would have formed, might well have been effective. Of course you cannot say for certain that they would. [*Interruption.*] I try to argue fairly with the House. At the same time I do not think it is fair to charge those who wished to see this course followed, and followed consistently and resolutely, with having wished for an immediate war. Between submission and immediate war there was this third alternative, which gave a hope not only of peace but of justice. It is quite true that such a policy in order to succeed demanded that Britain should declare straight out and a long time beforehand that she would, with others, join to defend Czechoslovakia against an unprovoked aggression. His Majesty's Government refused to give that guarantee when it would have saved the situation, yet in the end they gave it when it was too late, and now, for the future, they renew it when they have not the slightest power to make it good.

All is over. Silent, mournful, abandoned, broken, Czechoslovakia recedes into the darkness. She has suffered in every respect by her association with the Western democracies and with the League of Nations, of which she has always been an obedient servant. She has suffered in particular from her association with France, under whose guidance and policy she has been actuated for so long. The very measures taken by His Majesty's Government in the Anglo-French Agreement to give her the best chance possible, namely, the 50 per cent. clean cut in certain districts instead of a plebiscite, have turned to her detriment, because there is to be a plebiscite too in wide areas, and those other Powers who had claims have also come down upon the helpless victim. Those municipal elections upon whose voting the basis is taken for the 50 per cent. cut were held on issues which had nothing to do with joining Germany. When I saw Herr Henlein over here he assured me that was not the desire of his people. Positive statements were made that it was only a question of home rule, of having a position of their own in the Czechoslovakian State. No one has a right to say that the plebiscite which is to be taken in areas under Saar conditions, and the clean-cut of the 50 per cent. areas–that those two operations together amount in the slightest degree to a verdict of self-determination. It is a fraud and a farce to invoke that name.

We in this country, as in other Liberal and democratic countries, have a perfect right to exalt the principle of self-determination, but it comes ill out of the mouths of those in totalitarian States who deny even the smallest element of toleration to every section and creed within their bounds. But, however you put it, this particular block of land, this mass of human beings to be handed over, has never expressed the desire to go into the Nazi rule. I do not believe that even now–if their opinion could be asked, they would exercise such an option.

What is the remaining position of Czechoslovakia? Not only are they politically mutilated, but, economically and financially, they are in complete confusion. Their banking, their railway arrangements, are severed and broken, their industries are curtailed, and the movement of their population is most cruel. The Sudeten miners, who are all Czechs and whose families have lived in that area for centuries, must now flee into an area where there are hardly any mines left for them to work. It is a tragedy which has occurred. I did not like to hear the Minister of Transport yesterday talking about Humpty Dumpty. It was the Minister of Transport who was saying that it was a case of Humpty Dumpty that could never be put together again. There must always be the most profound regret and a sense of vexation in British hearts at the treatment and the misfortunes which have overcome the Czechoslovakian Republic. They have not ended here. At any moment there may be a hitch in the programme. At any moment there may be an order for Herr Goebbels to start again his propaganda of calumny and lies; at any moment an incident may be provoked, and now that the fortress line is given away what is there to stop the will of the conqueror? [*Interruption.*] It is too serious a subject to treat lightly. Obviously, we are not in a position to give them the slightest help at the present time, except what everyone is glad to know has been done, the financial aid which the Government have promptly produced.

I venture to think that in future the Czechoslovak State cannot be maintained as an independent entity. You will find that in a period of time which may be measured by years, but may be measured only by months, Czechoslovakia will be engulfed in the Nazi régime. Perhaps they may join it in despair or in revenge. At any rate, that story is over and told. But we cannot consider the abandonment and ruin of Czechoslovakia in the light only of what happened only last month. It is the most grievous consequence which we have yet experienced of what we have done and of what we have left undone in the last five years—five years of futile good intention, five years of eager search started for the line of least resistance, five years of uninterrupted retreat of British power, five years of neglect of our air defences. Those are the features which I stand here to declare and which marked an improvident stewardship for which Great Britain and France have dearly to pay. We have been reduced in those five years from a position of security so overwhelming and so unchallengeable that we never cared to think about it. We have been reduced from a position where the very word "war" was considered one which would be used only by persons qualifying for a lunatic asylum. We have been reduced from a Position of safety and power—power to do good, power to be generous to a beaten foe, power to make terms with Germany, power to give her proper redress for her grievances, power to stop her arming if we chose, power to take any step in strength or mercy or justice which we thought right—reduced in five years from a position safe and unchallenged to where we stand now.

When I think of the fair hopes of a long peace which still lay before Europe at the beginning of 1933 when Herr Hitler first obtained power, and of all the opportunities of arresting the growth of the Nazi power which have been thrown away, when I think of the immense combinations and resources which have been neglected or squandered, I cannot believe that a parallel exists in the whole course of history. So far as this country is concerned the responsibility must rest with those who have the undisputed control of our political affairs. They neither prevented Germany from rearming, nor did they rearm ourselves in time. They quarralled with Italy without saving Ethiopia. They exploited and discredited the vast institution of the League of Nations and they neglected to make alliances and combinations which might have repaired previous errors, and thus they left us in the hour of trial without adequate national defence or effective international security.

In my holiday I thought it was a chance to study the reign of King Ethelred the Unready. The House will remember that that was a period of great misfortune, in which, from the strong position which we had gained under the descendants of King Alfred, we fell very swiftly into chaos. It was the period of Danegeld and of foreign pressure. I must say that the rugged words of the Anglo-Saxon Chronicle, written 1 ,000 years ago, seem to me apposite, at least as apposite as those quotations from Shakespeare with which we have been regaled by the last speaker from the Opposition Bench. Here is what the Anglo-Saxon Chronicle said, and I think the words apply very much to our treatment of Germany and our relations with her:

> All these calamities fell upon us because of evil counsel, because tribute was not offered to them at the right time nor yet were they resisted; but when they had done the most evil, then was peace made with them.

That is the wisdom of the past, for all wisdom is not new wisdom.

I have ventured to express those views in justifying myself for not being able to support the Motion which is moved to-night, but I recognise that this great matter of

Czechoslovakia, and of British and French duty there, has passed into history. New developments may come along, but we are not here to decide whether any of those steps should be taken or not. They have been taken. They have been taken by those who had a right to take them because they bore the highest executive responsibility under the Crown. Whatever we may think of it, we must regard those steps as belonging to the category of affairs which are settled beyond recall. The past is no more, and one can only draw comfort if one feels that one has done one's best to advise rightly and wisely and in good time. I therefore, turn to the future, and to our situation as it is to-day. Here, again, I am sure I shall have to say something which will not be at all welcome.

We are in the presence of a disaster of the first magnitude which has befallen Great Britain and France. Do not let us blind ourselves to that. It must now be accepted that all the countries of Central and Eastern Europe will make the best terms they can with the triumphant Nazi Power. The system of alliances in Central Europe upon which France has relied for her safety has been swept away, and I can see no means by which it can be reconstituted. The road down the Danube Valley to the Black Sea, the resources of corn and oil, the road which leads as far as Turkey, has been opened. In fact, if not in form, it seems to me that all those countries of Middle Europe, all those Danubian countries, will, one after another, be drawn into this vast system of power politics–not only power military politics but power economic politics–radiating from Berlin, and I believe this can be achieved quite smoothly and swiftly and will not necessarily entail the firing of a single shot. If you wish to survey the havoc of the foreign policy of Britain and France, look at what is happening and is recorded each day in the columns of the "Times." Why, I read this morning about Yugoslavia–and I know something about the details of that country–

> The effects of the crisis for Yugoslavia can immediately be traced. Since the elections of 1935, which followed soon after the murder of King Alexander, the Serb and Croat Opposition to the Government of Dr. Stoyadinovitch have been conducting their entire campaign for the next elections under the slogan: "Back to France, England, and the Little Entente; back to democracy." The events of the past fortnight have so triumphantly vindicated Dr. Stoyadinovitch's policy. . . .

–his is a policy of close association with Germany–

> that the Opposition has collapsed practically overnight; the new elections, the date of which was in doubt, are now likely to be held very soon and can result only in an overwhelming victory for Dr. Stoyadinovitch's Government.

Here was a country which, three months ago, would have stood in line with other countries to arrest what has occurred.

Again, what happened in Warsaw? The British and French Ambassadors visited Colonel Beck, or sought to visit him, the Foreign Minister, in order to ask for some mitigation in the harsh measures being pursued against Czechoslovakia about Teschen.

The door was shut in their faces. The French Ambassador was not even granted an audience and the British Ambassador was given a most curt reply by a political director. The whole matter is described in the Polish Press as a political indiscretion committed by those two Powers, and we are to-day reading of the success of Colonel Beck's blow. I am not forgetting, I must say, that it is less than 20 years ago since British and French bayonets rescued Poland from the bondage of a century and a half. I think it is indeed a sorry episode in the history of that country, for whose freedom and rights so many of us have had warm and long sympathy.

These illustrations are typical. You will see, day after day, week after week, entire alienation of those regions. Many of those countries, in fear of the rise of the Nazi Power, have already got politicians, Ministers, Governments, who were pro-German, but there was always an enormous popular movement in Poland, Rumania, Bulgaria and Yugoslavia which looked to the Western democracies and loathed the idea of having this arbitrary rule of the totalitarian system thrust upon them, and hoped that a stand would be made. All that has gone by the board. We are talking about countries which are a long way off and of which, as the Prime Minister might say, we know nothing. [*Interruption.*] The noble Lady says that that very harmless allusion is—

Viscountess Astor: Rude.

Mr. Churchill. She must very recently have been receiving her finishing course in manners. What will be the position, I want to know, of France and England this year and the year afterwards? What will be the position of that Western front of which we are in full authority the guarantors? The German army at the present time is more numerous than that of France, though not nearly so matured or perfected. Next year it will grow much larger, and its maturity will be more complete. Relieved from all anxiety in the East, and having secured resources which will greatly diminish, if not entirely remove, the deterrent of a naval blockade, the rulers of Nazi Germany will have a free choice open to them in what direction they will turn their eyes. If the Nazi dictator should choose to look westward, as he may, bitterly will France and England regret the loss of that fine army of ancient Bohemia which was estimated last week to require not fewer than 30 German divisions for its destruction.

Can we blind ourselves to the great change which has taken place in the military situation, and to the dangers we have to meet? We are in process, I believe, of adding, in four years, four battalions to the British Army. No fewer than two have already been completed. Here are at least 30 divisions which must now be taken into consideration upon the French front, besides the 12 that were captured when Austria was engulfed. Many people, no doubt, honestly believe that they are only giving away the interests of Czechoslovakia, whereas I fear we shall find that we have deeply compromised, and perhaps fatally endangered, the safety and even the independence of Great Britain and France. This is not merely a question of giving up the German colonies, as I am sure we shall be asked to do. Nor is it a question only of losing influence in Europe. It goes far deeper than that. You have to consider the character of the Nazi movement and the rule which it implies. The Prime Minister desires to see cordial relations between this country and Germany. There is no difficulty at all in having cordial relations with the German people. Our hearts go out to them. But they have no national and racial ambitious and animosities which have already inflicted such power. You must have diplomatic and correct relations, but there can never be friendship between the British democracy and the Nazi Power, that Power which spurns Christian ethics, which cheers its onward course by a barbarous paganism, which vaunts the spirit of aggression and conquest, which derives strength and perverted pleasure from persecution, and uses, as we have seen, with pitiless brutality the threat of murderous force. That Power cannot ever be the trusted friend of the British democracy.

What I find unendurable is the sense of our country falling into the power, into the orbit and influence of Nazi Germany, and of our existence becoming dependent upon their good will or pleasure. It is to prevent that that I have tried my best to urge the maintenance of every bulwark of defence–first the timely creation of an Air Force superior to anything within striking distance of our shores; secondly, the gathering together of the collective strength of many nations; and thirdly, the making of alliances and military conventions, all within the Covenant, in order to gather together forces at any rate to restrain the onward movement of this Power. It has all been in vain. Every position has been successively undermined and abandoned on specious and plausible excuses. We do not want to be led upon the high road to becoming a satellite of the German Nazi system of European domination. In a very few years, perhaps in a very few months, we shall be confronted with demands with which we shall no doubt be invited to comply. Those demands may affect the surrender of territory or the surrender of liberty. I foresee and foretell that the policy of submission will carry with it restrictions upon the freedom of speech and debate in Parliament, on public platforms, and discussions in the Press, for it will be said–indeed, I hear it said sometimes now–that we cannot allow the Nazi system of dictatorship to be criticised by ordinary, common English politicians. Then, with a Press under control, in part direct but more potently indirect, with every organ of public opinion doped and chloroformed into acquiescence, we shall be conducted along further stages of our journey.

It is a small matter to introduce into such a Debate as this, but during the week I heard something of the talk of Tadpole and Taper. They were very keen upon having a general election, a sort of, if I may say so, inverted khaki election. I wish the Prime Minister had heard the speech of my hon. and gallant Friend the Member for the Abbey Division of Westminster (Sir Sidney Herbert) last night. I know that no one is more patient and regular in his attendance than the Prime Minister, and it is marvellous how he is able to sit through so much of our Debates, but it happened that by bad luck he was not here at that moment. I am sure, however, that if he had heard my hon. and gallant Friend's speech he would have felt very much annoyed that such a rumour could even have been circulated. I cannot believe that the Prime Minister, or any Prime Minister possessed of a large working majority, would be capable of such an act of historic, constitutional indecency. I think too highly of him. Of course, if I have misjudged him on the right side, and there is a dissolution on the Munich Agreement, on Anglo-Nazi friendship, on the state of our defences and so forth, everyone will have to fight according to his convictions, and only a prophet could forecast the ultimate result; but, whatever the result, few things could be more fatal to our remaining chances of survival as a great Power than that this country should be torn in twain upon this deadly issue of foreign policy at a moment when, whoever the Ministers may be, united effort can alone make us safe.

I have been casting about to see how measures can be taken to protect us from this advance of the Nazi Power, and to secure those forms of life which are so dear to us. What is the sole method that is open? The sole method that is open is for us to regain our old island independence by acquiring that supremacy in the air which we were promised, that security in our air defences which we were assured we had, and thus to make ourselves an island once again. That, in all this grim outlook, shines out as the overwhelming fact. An effort at rearmament the like of which has not been seen ought to be made forthwith, and all the resources of this country and all its united strength should be bent to that task. I was very glad to see that Lord Baldwin yesterday in the House of Lords said that he would mobilise industry to-morrow. But I think it would have been much better if Lord Baldwin had said that 2-1/2 years ago, when everyone demanded a Ministry of Supply. I will venture to say to hon. Gentlemen sitting here behind the Government Bench, hon. Friends of mine, whom I thank for the patience with which they have listened to what I have to say, that they have some responsibility for all this too, because, if they had given one tithe of the cheers they have lavished upon this transaction of Czechoslovakia to the small band of Members who were endeavouring to get timely rearmament set in motion, we should not now be in the position in which we are. Hon. Gentlemen opposite, and hon. Members on the Liberal benches, are not entitled to throw these stones. I remember for two years having to face, not only the Government's deprecation, but their stern disapproval. Lord Baldwin has now given the signal, tardy though it may be; let us at least obey it. . . .

THE INTERNATIONAL SITUATION
November 25, 1938

Harlow

[Extract] . . . The time is serious and dire. Either Britain will rise again in her strength as a might, valiant nation, champion of lawful right, defender of human freedom, or she will collapse and be despoiled, plundered, mutilated, and reduced not merely to the rank of a second-rate country but to a dependent condition, a vassal status that I once heard Sir Edward Grey call "the conscript appendage to a stronger power." There is no choice at the moment except between an Empire valiantly maintained, or subjugation, servilely and irrevocably accepted.

One chapter of foreign policy is now closed. Czechoslovakia has been devoured, and is now being digested. All those States of Middle Europe–Poland, Yugoslavia, Hungary, and possibly Rumania–will fall very swiftly into Nazi control. They will be made to trade with the Germans to the exclusion of our trade. They will be made to promise, by binding treaties, to secure the Germans all the supplies of corn and oil they need. Some of them will actually join the Nazi forces in the further advances which are almost certain to take place towards the East.

We have to-day an entirely new situation—a very dark and difficult situation, full of danger, and full of disadvantages to Britain and France. What of the future? I see only one swift step—namely, to rearm, and, above all, to obtain effective defence and at least equal air power. I had nothing to do with all that process, extending over four or five years, which led us from a position of complete safety and power to our present dismal plight. I repudiate altogether responsibility either for having brought us to the verge of war or for the manner in which we escaped at the last moment from the perils into which we drifted.

"A YEAR OF DISASTER AND HUMILIATION"

December 11, 1938

League of Nations Union Meeting,
Chingford

Churchill's opposition to the Munich agreement was not widely appreciated in Epping, and for a time it appeared possible that he would be disowned by his Constituency Association. He survived by a vote of three to two.

[Extract] ... While the Mediterranean is being thrown into increasing disturbance by Italy's demands which are preoccupying France, the Nazi dictator is on the verge of a further movement in the East of Europe.

We do not know which direction it will take. Since Munich and the destruction of Czechoslovakia he has had so many choices open that his trouble is which to take first: whether it should be Memel or Danzig: whether he will stir up Polish Ukrainians against Poland or the Transylvanian population against Rumania. No one can tell, but everything points to an early resumption of Nazi aggression and no concerted resistance being made against it.

Signor Mussolini, so far from being appeased by British and French recognition of his so-called conquest of Abyssinia, has set on foot an agitation for Nice, Corsica, and Tunis. On the very morrow of the signing of the Anglo-Italian Agreement, while the ink was scarcely dry on the signatures, new demands were put forward and our Prime Minister thought it necessary to go to Rome to see what further appeasements were possible.

I have never seen such a division on foreign policy in this country. It is hampering the whole process of national defence. The Government do not dare to propose the measures which are necessary for fear of having to invite the cooperation of the Opposition parties.

Many people ask why should we rearm and make all kinds of exceptional exertions if it is only to grovel to the dictators and aid them in their domination of democracy. I cannot agree to that. However much we might deplore the leadership or want of leadership it is our duty to do our utmost for our country and the cause of freedom. We must try night and day, all parties, to put this country in a position where it can no longer be blackmailed by the threat of air bombing. Public opinion is far ahead of the Government in all matters of defence. We have to goad them on to take the measures which one would have thought their honour, their duty, their traditions, would have prompted them long ago to demand from us.

The foreign policy that will unite the country is to gather together all the forces of resistance to the aggression of dictators and to make a common cause, so far as is still possible, with other like-minded nations. So far from abandoning what is left of the League of Nations or whittling down its power till it becomes little more than a debate assembly, we must proclaim our resolve to clothe it with even greater powers and by our exertions to furnish it with the armed force which will make its judgments respected. Then we will find that much that now seems difficult will become easy and that the action of the democracies will be strengthened by the common comprehension of an exalted aim.

This has been a year of disaster and humiliation the like of which Great Britain has not known for many generations. An even more unpromising phase lies before us. We are told our policy was appeasement. If that is true it is obviously failing.

A Time of Triumph
1939–1963

A Time of Triumph 1939–1963

Churchill's view of life, history, and himself was essentially romantic and dramatic. Certainly no life could have had a more dramatic conclusion.

By the end of 1938, Churchill's career appeared to be in total eclipse. His opposition to the Chamberlain Government's policy of appeasement was so unpopular that an attempt was made in his constituency to disown him. He survived, as has been related, but only narrowly. It was a near thing and a significant indication; it was, as Churchill wrote, "a gloomy winter."

Churchill's isolation was increased by the fact that the growing number of Conservatives who were critical of the Government allied themselves with Anthony Eden, and took good care not to be associated with Churchill. The Eden group—derided by orthodox Conservatives as "the glamour boys"—believed that the most effective results would flow from reasoned and careful pressure on the Conservative Government. One of them, Harold Nicolson, wrote after a meeting with Eden on September 19 that "he doesn't want to lead a revolt or to secure any resignations from the Cabinet." Churchill, whose House of Commons allies consisted only of Brendan Bracken and Duncan Sandys, did not share this approach. Yet the position of even the Edenites was precarious. "The tide was, at present, too strong and it was flowing against us," as Harold Macmillan later wrote.

The situation changed abruptly and totally on March 14, 1939, when the Germans invaded and easily overran what remained of Czechoslovakia. The Government made—or appeared to make—a major policy change. A British guarantee to Poland was hastily prepared and published on March 31, and military conscription was introduced in April. But the essential corollary to the Polish Guarantee, the establishment of close links with Russia, was feebly pursued.

Although some Ministers still clung to the hope of a rapprochement with Germany, and the Labour and Liberal parties strongly opposed the introduction of conscription, a new mood was now abroad in the land. One indication of this was a strong campaign advocating Churchill's return to the Government. It was initiated by the Conservative *Daily Telegraph*, taken up by the Liberal *Manchester Guardian*, and endorsed by the Labour *Daily Mirror*. Neville Chamberlain vigorously resisted this pressure. "The more . . . the Press clamoured for Churchill's inclusion," wrote Sir Samuel Hoare, "the less likely [Chamberlain] was to take any action." Chamberlain himself wrote in his diary at this time that "Churchill's chances improve as war becomes more possible, and *vice versa.*" This situation existed until September, when, after the triumphant announcement of the German-Soviet Agreement, Poland was invaded, and the Chamberlain Government was dragged unhappily into war.

On September 1 Chamberlain invited Churchill to join the Cabinet, but no definite offer was made until the afternoon of September 3, when he was asked to return to the Admiralty. Thus, the wheel turned full circle. The man who had been dismissed from the Admiralty in May 1915 and whose career had seemed ruined, now returned to the same office at the outset of another world war.

This remarkable shift in Churchill's fortunes was a direct reflection of the dramatic change in British opinion concerning the realities of the European situation. But it was also a belated recognition of the essential validity of Churchill's long personal campaign for rearmament. The *Daily Mirror* perhaps exaggerated when it described Churchill as "the most trusted statesman in Britain," but it reflected a very real and very swift change in public attitudes. The mood of the House of Commons also underwent a substantial change.

Nonetheless, old bitternesses could not be easily eradicated. The bulk of the Conservative Party viewed Churchill's return with distaste and suspicion. The Labour Party, having long endured his vehement condemnations, was uneasy. In spite of all that had happened, there was great national and party confidence in, and affection for, Neville Chamberlain.

This situation was altered by a series of dramatic events. In the winter of 1939-1940, after the swift and merciless destruction of Poland, an eerie calm fell on the Western Front. What Chamberlain called the "Twilight War" and one disgruntled American journalist named the "Phoney War" puzzled the British public. The Russian invasion of Finland–which led to Russia's expulsion from the League of Nations–aroused considerable resentment, and the initial Russian reverses were warmly applauded. In this atmosphere, Churchill was one of those Ministers who supported the lunatic proposal of Allied assistance to Finland. Perhaps fortunately, Finland surrendered before the Allies had gratuitously acquired another enemy, but the diversion of attention to the Baltic was ominous, and paved the way for the abortive British intervention in Norway in April.

But the war at sea had been more spirited and aggressive. Immediately on reaching the Admiralty, Churchill ordered the re-introduction of the convoy system, but it was some time before this could be effectively instituted. Many British merchant ships were at sea on September 3, and one of them, the S.S. *Athenia*, was torpedoed and sunk by a German submarine within a few hours of the declaration of war. The old aircraft-carrier *Courageous* met a similar fate on September 18, with heavy loss of life, and the new carrier *Ark Royal* had narrowly avoided a U-boat attack three days before. In the first week of the war British shipping losses were 65,000 tons. On October 17 the battleship *Royal Oak* was torpedoed and sunk in Scapa Flow, and there were German air raids on the Navy at both Scapa Flow and Rosyth. In November the German battlecruisers *Scharnhorst* and *Gneisenau* entered the North Atlantic–fortunately, only briefly–while the pocket battleship *Graf Spee* caused havoc in the South Atlantic. Fortunately, the secrets of the magnetic mine were discovered and counter-measures put into effect before this additional threat did serious damage.

Churchill's public response to these misfortunes was highly effective. He frankly admitted the losses, and went out of his way to express admiration for the commander of the submarine which sank the *Royal Oak*. At the same time he gave the House of Commons, and a wider national audience through radio, a heartening impression of confidence and robust competence. His estimates of German submarine losses were deliberately exaggerated. This fact may disturb purists, but a surfeit of bad news needed counter-action. In December 1939 there came some genuine good news. The *Graf Spee* was brought to action off the River Plate, and forced to retreat to Montevideo. Unable to remain there, the battleship was scuttled. Churchill made the most of this famous victory.

These events, although most of them were reverses, placed Churchill in a forward position in the public's attention. Other Ministers had very little to report about the war, but Churchill appeared again and again. His voice was heard often over the radio, and the Press eagerly recorded his frequent visits to the Fleet, to naval dockyards, and to other installations. He gave an impression of immense vigour and determination, making his colleagues look pallid and uncertain in contrast. Furthermore, the fact that he had only just taken office removed him from public censure for British unpreparedness and the naval reverses–in marked contrast with 1914. Churchill saw to it that the public and Parliament were well informed of his presence and his activity.

Historians have taken an increasingly critical view of Churchill's responsibility for the fiasco of the Norwegian campaign in April 1940, which brought down the Chamberlain Government. But at the time the burden of criticism fell upon Chamberlain, not upon Churchill. It was somewhat ironic that Churchill, who had so often been unfairly cast as the scapegoat for others' errors, should on this occasion be the direct beneficiary of a situation for which he had a real responsibility. But, as he once wrote, "Life is a whole, and luck is a whole, and no part of them can be separated from the rest."

On May 7-8, 1940, there occurred one of the most dramatic debates in the history of the House of Commons. Discontent with the conduct of the war reached its climax. The immediate subject was the Norwegian campaign, but the debate swiftly became a widespread discussion of the competence of the Chamberlain Government. The most effective attacks came from Sir Roger Keyes, wearing his uniform as Admiral of the Fleet, Duff Cooper, Leo Amery, who, for the only time in his long Parliamentary career, scaled the heights of oratory, and Lloyd George. Chamberlain's response was ineffective, asking for a virtual vote of confidence. Churchill wound up the debate for the Government, fully aware that for once the main assault was upon somebody else. His attacks on Chamberlain since 1937 were well known to the House, and his loyalty to his leader was respected. In the ensuing Division, the nominal Government majority crumbled. Forty-one Conservatives voted against it, and some sixty abstained. A National Government was clearly called for, but the Labour leaders adamantly refused to serve under Chamberlain. The decision was essentially against Chamberlain, not for Churchill, but the consequence was Churchill's elevation.

It is a popular myth that there was a great national call for Churchill in May 1940. The first choice of the King and the Conservative Party (and the official staff at No. 10 Downing Street) for Chamberlain's successor was Lord Halifax, and it is clear that the Labour leadership would have accepted him. The matter was resolved when Halifax himself pointed out the extreme difficulties which having a Prime Minister in the House of Lords at such a time would cause. Churchill was the only possible alternative, and thus on May 10, 1940, he became Prime Minister. He was in his sixty-sixth year. The torrent of the German assault on the Western Front had already begun with the invasion of the Netherlands and Belgium. In these circumstances he created, within a very short time, an all-party Coalition which brought Britain through five years of desperate crisis, peril, and disappointment to complete victory. If this was Britain's "finest hour," it was also Churchill's.

I

At this moment of crisis Churchill's oratorical skills reached their glorious apogee. The printed word cannot fully convey the extraordinary impact of these speeches, particularly those of 1940. The voice itself, growling defiance and contempt for the enemy—"the Narzees"—was itself stirring. Above all, it was "the character breathing through the sentences" which moved his fellow-countrymen. His approach to the war was simple, direct, and no-nonsense. There would be no parley with, and no mercy for, the enemy. He would be fought to the death everywhere. No quarter would be given, and none asked. Nazi Germany was a hideous monstrosity, to be eliminated utterly. The British people had not merely the duty, but the privilege, of being the sole defenders of civilisation against the dark hordes of evil which were spreading rampantly across Western Europe.

Yet there was something more, which remains indefinable. "When men describe their love of their country," Attlee wrote, "I find it rather embarrassing. But when Churchill spoke of Britain, he always struck a chord in me." Speeches do not win wars, and there are those in Britain who still deeply resent the argument that Churchill single-handedly saved Britain in 1940. Defenders of Lord Swinton—Secretary of State for Air in the vital years between 1935 and 1938—and others point out that the aircraft, pilots and radar operators that won the Battle of Britain were created long before Churchill became Prime Minister. Only his most fervent admirers claim that Churchill's political and military judgements were infallible. But his speeches gave both the people of his country and the enormous public which now heard him around the world a confidence and a spirit which was unique. They persuaded the President of the United States and his closest advisers that Churchill meant every word he said, that the policy of the British nation was indeed Victory. They inspired the people of Britain to an extraordinary extent. They established his position in Parliament. And they convinced all listeners that the real war had only just begun.

Churchill subsequently wrote that "there was a white glow, overpowering, sublime, which ran through our island from end to end." So there was, but it had not been very evident before Churchill became Prime Minister. "So hypnotic was the force of his word," Sir Isaiah Berlin has written,

> so strong his faith, that by the sheer intensity of his eloquence he bound his spell upon [the British people] until it seemed to them that he was indeed speaking what was in their hearts and minds. Doubtless it was

> there, but largely dormant until he had awakened it within them. . . . They went forward into battle transformed by his words.

This may be an overstatement, and does not take account of the innate bloody-mindedness and cynicism of the British—qualities which should not be underestimated by friends or foes. Berlin better captured the mood of the British in 1940 when he described it as "not indeed, at any time, one of craven panic or bewilderment or apathy, but somewhat confused; stouthearted but unorganised." Churchill clarified the issues, clothing them in words and phrases which at once raised the struggle to a heroic level.

But—and this is a crucial factor—there were other audiences. Churchill's speeches had a profound impact in the United States, and greatly assisted Roosevelt's resolve to give Britain every help short of formal intervention. They gave a flicker of hope to Occupied Europe. And they were heard with pride and excitement throughout the Empire.

Most importantly, the words were accompanied by deeds. The destruction of the French fleet at Oran was a brutal act, however necessary. But it was a clear signal that Churchill and Britain were in deadly earnest. The Battle of Britain was a clear defeat for the supposedly invincible Germans. A courageous dispatch of scarce arms to North Africa led to the rout of the Italians. Words of encouragement to Occupied Europe were joined with practical assistance to the slowly burgeoning resistance movements. It was this combination of fine words and determined acts which gave Churchill's speeches their full power.

It is difficult to recall how desperate a situation the new Government faced in 1940. Within a month the French collapsed, and although the bulk of the British Expeditionary Force escaped, virtually all its equipment was abandoned. Italy entered the war and barred the Mediterranean. Only the Royal Navy and the Royal Air Force stood between Hitler and the invasion of Britain. It was a crucial moment, and it was only by a narrow margin that Britain survived. It is not to exaggerate the power of words to claim that this narrow margin might not have been secured without the national leadership which Churchill provided.

Churchill left it to Attlee and others to conduct the day-to-day business of Parliament, and came down only on major occasions. But he did not neglect Parliament. As he has written, he did not grudge ten or twelve hours' preparation on a major speech, and frequently spent more. Every speech was his own composition, and bore his stamp and personality. His technique has been described well by one of his private secretaries, J. R. Colville.

> The composition of a speech was not a task Churchill was prepared to skimp or to hurry; nor, except on some convivial occasion, was he willing to speak impromptu. He might improvise briefly, but only to elaborate or clarify, and he stuck closely to the text he had prepared. Quick as was his wit and unfailing his gift of repartee, he was not a man to depart in the heat of the moment from the theme or indeed the very words that he had laboriously conceived in set-speech form. To the last he retained a sense of apprehension in addressing the House of Commons or, for that matter, any

large assembly. . . . he never, to my knowledge, spoke words that were not his own. . . .

At times Churchill's relationship with the House of Commons—as with his colleagues and the Press—turned sour. He did not relish criticism, and he particularly resented the claim that he was dictatorial and overbearing—a charge which was by no means always unmerited. But these moods did not last long. The House of Commons, which had reviled and ignored him, which had howled him down in December 1936, became his most fervent supporter. Mindful of world opinion, Churchill often emphasized the fact that a free Parliament sat at Westminster, to which he and his colleagues had to render account. Although he was not always openly enthusiastic about this situation, as "a child of the House of Commons," he willingly accepted it.

II

It would be inappropriate to attempt a detailed assessment of Churchill's war leadership here. During the summer of 1940 and the dark winter of 1940-1941 the dominant priority was national survival. The key to this was support from the United States and the Dominions; it is very difficult to see how Britain could have remained in the war without Lend-Lease, American assistance to the Atlantic convoys, and the help which came from the Dominions. In North Africa the Australian, New Zealand, and Indian troops played a major part in the initial successes against the Italians and in the desperate battles against the Germans.

Churchill's personal relations with Roosevelt held the key. The lengthy correspondence between the "Former Naval Person" and the President is evidence of a remarkable alliance between two remarkable men. Roosevelt's confidence in Churchill and Churchill's understanding of the limitations on the President in the American political context of 1940 and 1941 were essential links in the tacit Anglo-American alliance.

The second turning-point was the German assault on Russia in June 1941, and Churchill's immediate declaration of solidarity with Russia. For the implacable anti-Communist to take such a step caused some surprise, but as Churchill himself remarked to his private secretary, "If Hitler invaded Hell, I would make at least a favourable reference to the Devil in the House of Commons." The new alliance had many moments of acute strain and even bitterness. Stalin's insistence on a Second Front and his lack of appreciation for British military assistance—given at great and terrible cost—must be seen in the context of the near-desperate Russian position and the appalling Russian losses.

Then, at the end of 1941, came the Japanese intervention. For the British, it caused a series of devastating defeats in Malaya and Burma, the surrender of Singapore, the virtual elimination of the Far East Fleet, and, we can now see, the end of the Far East Empire. But Churchill's reaction was one of immense relief, particularly when—in an act of gratuitous and fatal folly—Hitler declared war on the United States. Indeed, he was elated. "So we had won after all!" he later wrote, recalling his emotions of December 7, 1941.

The succession of disasters which fell upon the Americans and the British in the

Far East was matched for a time by the deteriorating situations in North Africa and Russia. The Russians had held the Germans outside Leningrad and Moscow, but their position remained grave. The 1941 British intervention in Greece proved fruitless, and the loss of Crete was a particularly heavy blow. Meanwhile, the key to Britain's survival, the Battle of the Atlantic, hung on a knife-edge.

As some speeches demonstrate, there were occasions when Churchill's position was seriously challenged in the House of Commons. But the loyalty of his colleagues–particularly the Labour members–was total, and his brilliance in counter-attack fought off all threats. After El Alamein, the tide began to turn in North Africa. The Japanese advance petered out at the frontiers of India. The Russians began to roll back the Germans in a series of massive campaigns. In North Africa, in Britain, and above all in the Far East, the American intervention began to turn the balance against the Axis. In Occupied Europe, the flames of Resistance were glowing.

From this point, Churchill's position as the dominant leader of the Free World necessarily declined; of the "Big Three," Roosevelt and Stalin were the more powerful figures. But Churchill's fame and spirit gave him–and through him, the British people–a stature which was perhaps greater than his actual power, but which their sacrifices certainly deserved. But the realities were too strong for Churchill, and his dismay at the changes in war objectives was understandable.

Churchill found his true fulfillment as a war leader. He was certainly very difficult to work for, and was often inconsiderate to his colleagues and military advisers. He had many ideas about how the war should be conducted, some of them wholly impracticable and others downright foolish. He made many mistakes, and his obsession with the war effort was responsible for some errors of omission. But he had learned a vital lesson from the First World War. At no time was there anything approaching the bitterness and rivalry between political and military leaders which had so bedevilled the conduct of that conflict. The quality of Churchill's principal advisers–notably Gen. Sir Alan Brooke, Gen. Sir John Dill, and Major-Gen. Sir Hastings Ismay–was very high indeed, and the calibre of the British commanding officers in all Services was exceptional. For the achievements of Montgomery, Alexander, Slessor, Slim, Mountbatten, and Cunningham, Churchill must receive much of the credit. Perhaps he was unfair to Wavell and Auchinleck, but this is debatable. The important thing was to win.

Churchill's personal courage and bearing were elements which, although intangible, played major parts. There were moments of deep anxiety and apprehension, but his confidence in ultimate victory never seriously wavered. It was this quality above all others which brought him and the British people through many dark and bitter hours.

In 1944 the Allied invasion of Europe and the relentless Russian advance brought the end of the European war into sight. In the East, the British and Dominion forces were on the offensive in Burma, and the American superiority on sea, air, and land was forcing the Japanese back. There remained some unexpected shocks–principally the German V-bomb assaults on London, and the vigorous German counter-attack in the Ardennes in December 1944. But the mass of men and metal was too great for the Germans. The last scenes in shattered Berlin marked the awful end of the "Thousand Year Reich." Thus it was on V-E (Victory in Europe) Day that Churchill stood before the exultant crowds in Whitehall and cried, "This is *your* victory," to which there came the massive roar in reply, "No, it is *yours*." Both were right. It was the supreme moment of Churchill's life.

III

At the height of Churchill's achievement and fame, his Government disintegrated when the Labour Party resigned from the Coalition after the defeat of Germany. In the General Election, the results of which were declared in July 1945, the Labour Party won overwhelmingly. Churchill was astounded and, for a time, deeply chagrined. Some of this bitterness emerged in his war memoirs.

Many who most admired and loved him lamented that he did not choose this moment to retire from political life. They feared the effect his zestful involvement in domestic politics would have on his reputation. Some doubted his ability to adjust to the postwar situation, to the social revolution in Britain, to the demise of the Empire, and to the greatly reduced status of Britain in the world. Some still regret Churchill's decision to fight on.

Judgements vary as to his ability as Leader of the Opposition between 1945 and 1951. His enjoyment of the asperities and exhilarations of rough-and-tumble debate distressed some admirers, and his general attitudes were not always congenial to the new and younger Conservatives who wished to see the Party become socially progressive and adventurous. But, for all these criticisms, he remained *the* dominant figure in Western politics. His 1946 speech at Fulton, Missouri, in which he dramatically called attention to the "Iron Curtain" in Europe, deeply affected American and European opinion. His advocacy of the United Europe movement gave it a momentum which was not, unhappily, maintained, but which left its mark.

Still, old charges rumbled on. He was castigated on Labour platforms and some Labour leaders–to their shame–still excoriated him as a warmonger. This evil calumny was particularly evident in the 1951 General Election, which the Conservatives narrowly won.

But the second and last Churchill Administration (1951-1955) must be accounted successful. The economic situation improved sharply, and the elimination of "austerity"–notably rationing–was warmly welcomed. A massive house-building programme was initiated. The international scene became less bleak. The Government was an able one, and partly through good luck and partly through good sense it weathered all storms. In the House of Commons the asperity of Churchill's opponents notably waned. His health and energy were failing, and he suffered a second stroke in 1953 (the first had been in 1948) which was serious enough to cause concern for his life. Yet, despite many controversies, he enjoyed a wonderful Indian Summer. Perhaps he stayed too long, but he was obsessed by the need for a summit conference and a new relationship between the Western nations and the Soviet Union. He failed, but it was a noble objective. His eightieth birthday, in November 1954, was a major national event. Parliament paid him a unique personal tribute at a great meeting in Westminster Hall. He departed from public office for the last time in April 1955 in a blaze of public affection and gratitude.

IV

Although Churchill remained a Member of Parliament for another nine years, he never addressed the House of Commons again, apart from a very brief expression of thanks for congratulations on his eighty-fifth birthday. He rarely spoke in public, and his last major address was a message read by his son in response to the American Congress's unique honor of bestowing upon him an Honorary Citizenship of the United States. The burdens of old age now relentlessly fell upon him. When he entered the House of Commons he had to be helped to his place, and although he appeared to be taking notice of events, one wondered how much interest and excitement rippling through the House and the public galleries.

In 1964, it was announced that he would not stand for Woodford in the forthcoming General Election. He made his last visit to the House of Commons in July. It was a warm, soporific day, and the House was only half-full. An uninspiring debate on the Family Doctor Service was in progress. At length, Churchill slowly rose from his place, and was helped to the Bar of the House.

It so happened that I was standing at the Door of the House, alone. I opened it for the aged statesman. His chair was waiting for him, and he was wheeled away from the Palace of Westminster for the last time. It was a curious chance that the latest biographer of Lord Randolph Churchill should assist the earliest on his final departure from the scene of his many triumphs and failures for nearly sixty years. I was reminded of the words which Churchill himself had written in 1905 about Gladstone in his biography of Lord Randolph: "So long as his light lasted the House of Commons lived, and amid the fiercest passions and even scenes of violence preserved its hold upon the sympathies and the imagination of the whole world. And at his death it sank at once, perhaps for ever, in public esteem."

He died peacefully in London on January 24, 1965, exactly seventy years to the day after the death of Lord Randolph Churchill. He was buried at Bladon, close to his birthplace, Blenheim Palace, beside the father whom he had hardly known, whose biography he had written, and whose memory he had cherished throughout his life.

In his only work of fiction, *Savrola*, Churchill anticipated much of his career and life. Its concluding words may be recalled.

> Those who care to further follow the annals of the Republic of Laurania may read how, after the tumults had subsided, the hearts of the people turned again to the illustrious exile who had won them freedom and whom they had deserted in the hour of victory. They may, scoffing at the fickleness of men, read of the return of Savrola and his beautiful escort to the city he had loved so well.

And perhaps his most appropriate epitaph may be found in the words which he used as the theme of his Second World War memoirs.

In War: Resolution.
In Defeat: Defiance.
In Victory: Magnanimity.
In Peace: Good Will.

THE FRUITS OF MUNICH

March 14, 1939

Waltham Abbey

On this day the Germans, with contemptuous disregard for the Munich Agreement, occupied Czechoslovakia. It was from this time that popular support for the policies of the Chamberlain Government faded rapidly.

Complaint has been made in some of the outlying parts of the Constituency of my speech on the Munich Agreement. In this I pointed out that a disaster of the first magnitude had befallen France and England. Is that not so? Why do you suppose we are making all these preparations? Why do you suppose that the French military service has been lengthened, and we have promised to send nineteen divisions to the Continent? It is because in the destruction of Czechoslovakia the entire balance of Europe was changed.

The great and growing German Army is now free to turn in any direction: we do not know in what direction it will turn. The whole structure of international co-operation to protect the small country from lawless offence—all that has been broken down and cast away. I pointed out that Munich sealed the ruin of Czechoslovakia. You remember the tales we were told, how they would have a better life after they were freed from the burdens of the unwilling Sudeten Germans in their midst. Besides that, they were to have a German guarantee of their reduced frontier, and there was to be a British and French guarantee of their frontier. I held the view that these guarantees were hardly worth the paper they were written on, or the breath that uttered them. What is the position now? The Czechoslovakian Republic is being broken up before our eyes. Their gold is to be stolen by the Nazis. The Nazi system is to blot out every form of internal freedom. Their army is to be reduced to negligible proportions, or incorporated in the Nazi power. They are about to lose all symbols of an independent democratic state. Does anybody deny it?

I said that once the Czechs had given up their fortified line, a pretext could be found to take everything from them. We have seen exactly the same methods used as were used in September. Disturbances have been fomented in Slovakia which, I have no doubt, are at the instigation of the German Nazi Party. And then the German Press has set to work to vilify the Czechs, and to accuse them of violent aggression against the Germans. The next thing is to order them to reduce their army, and take into their Government whatever Ministers the Germans choose. They are being completely absorbed; and not until the Nazi shadow has been finally lifted from Europe—as lifted I am sure it will eventually be—not until then will Czechoslovakia and ancient Bohemia march once again into freedom. Why should I not have said all these things? It was the truth. It was my duty to say them. Can anybody dispute them?

I saw in one of our papers today that we were not involved in this new Czechoslovakian crisis. It seems to me quite certain that we are not going to intervene. It is too late to intervene. The Czechs have surrendered their fortress line. Its cannon are now moving to the Western Front. They are defenseless. Their railways are interrupted. They are gripped about on every side. Instead of being able to resist thirty German divisions for a considerable time, they now have no power of resistance left at all. They have to obey all orders, however cruel, that they are given. It is no use going to their aid when they are defenseless, if we would not go to their aid when they were strong. Therefore I agree entirely with those who think we should not intervene at the present time. We cannot. That is the end of it.

But to suppose that we are not involved in what is happening is a profound illusion. Although we can do nothing to stop it, we shall be sufferers on a very great scale. We shall have to make all kinds of sacrifices for our own defense that would have been unnecessary if a firm resolve had been taken at an earlier stage. We shall have to make sacrifices not only of money, but of personal service in order to make up for what we have lost. This is even more true of the French than of ourselves.

Many people at the time of the September crisis thought they were only giving away the interests of Czechoslovakia, but with every month that passes you will see that they were also giving away the interests of Britain, and the interests of peace and justice. Now I have defended this speech which has been attacked, and I say never did I make a truer statement to Parliament. Practically everything that I said has already proved true. And who are these people who go about saying that even if it were true, why state the facts? I reply, why mislead the nation? What is the use of Parliament if it is not the place where true statements can be brought before the people? What is the use of sending Members to the House of Commons who say just the popular things of the moment, and merely endeavor to give satisfaction to the Government Whips by cheering loudly every Ministerial platitude, and by walking through the Lobbies oblivious of the criticisms they hear? People talk about our Parliamentary institutions and Parliamentary democracy; but if these are to survive, it will not be because the Constituencies return tame, docile, subservient Members, and try to stamp out every form of independent judgment.

"DO NOT YIELD ANOTHER YARD"

April 3, 1939

House of Commons

Following the invasion and occupation of Czechoslovakia, there was a remarkable change in the attitude of the British Government. Speaking in Birmingham on March 17, Chamberlain launched a startlingly strong attack on Hitler's perfidy. On March 31 he announced the British guarantee to Poland; two days earlier he had informed Parliament that the size of the Territorial Army was to be doubled.

[Extract] . . . I find myself in the most complete agreement with the Prime Minister. I hope it will not do him any harm if I say so. I listened to his speech with the greatest attention, and both in its assertions and its reservations, in its scope, in its emphasis, and in its balance, I find myself entirely in accord with what he said. I am sure he will believe that, if I did not do so, I should not hesitate to criticise and attack him, but, being in agreement with the Prime Minister on the speech he has made, I naturally am going to give him my support in such a way as will be a help, as I conceive it, and not a hindrance. Therefore, I shall not follow my right hon. Friend, who, as the Leader of an Opposition party, was perfectly entitled to do as he did in weighing up what has happened in the past. In all these extremely grave and baffling matters of public policy, where the terrible accidents and chances of peace and war hang in the balance, human judgment may easily go astray; and anyone can put himself in the position of the man upon whose decision the awful consequences turn. It is very easy to see clearly what should be done, and to advocate it in cogent terms, but even the most resolute of us would, I am inclined to think, have a note of soberness, of anguish, struck into his nature if he thought and felt that now, at the last, it had come to him, and he had to say the word. Therefore, I am going to give my full support to the policy which the Prime Minister has now declared. . . .

What my right hon. Friend the Member for St. George's (Mr. Duff Cooper) said in his resignation speech is now generally accepted. He said it was useless for us to try to play a more prominent part in Europe unless we are prepared, when all else fails, to resist a wrongdoer, to go to the last extreme. It is indeed wonderful that our country has been led by the Prime Minister to declare, in the clearest terms and with almost unanimity, that the defence of European freedom and the reign of law constitute causes in which this country will dare all and do all. This is the surprising transformation of the last few weeks. We have got to the position where we can no longer endure to be pushed from pillar to post, to expostulate and withdraw, and to utter what Lord Halifax called "warlike noises" with a mental reservation not to persist beyond a certain point.

What has happened in the last few weeks is not only the effect produced on the

Government by the perfidy with which they were treated by those to whom they offered a very great effort of conciliation, but a revival of the national spirit, with a united force which I think has surprised ourselves as much as it has surprised foreign countries. There is behind this revival a high cause, but there are also practical reasons. The nation has asked itself, and the Prime Minister in part of his speech seemed to indicate, "How can we go on like this?" Life is intolerable under present conditions. We wait from fortnight to fortnight for the various dictatorial speeches. No one can plan ahead. Business is stifled, employment is deranged, insecurity and anxiety overcloud our happy land, and lie still more darkly over Europe. A united stand must be made—and must be made now. Everyone knows the Prime Minister's love for peace, and that he has faced taunts and unpopularity without hesitation in that cause. The German and Italian peoples know that there is no English statesman whom they can trust more fully not to menace their lawful interests and prosperity. All parties know it, and know that he would not lightly or wantonly involve us in a terrible war.

When, at last, after so much has happened, he feels impelled to take the momentous steps that he has done, it seems to me that all will feel able—even the most pacific-minded, even the most isolationist-minded—to follow the course indicated by the Government, with a good conscience and without the slightest feeling that anything which could have been done to avert the dangers of the conflict has been left undone. When it is known that a powerful confederation of States will infallibly fight—I think it is wise to put it in blunt terms—if certain things are done, there are still great hopes and chances that these deeds will not be done. If the disease has got worse in the year that has passed, and if the remedy lacks some of the ingredients which it formerly possessed, nevertheless it is still potent. He would be a bold dictator who, apart from other enterprises at this moment, and taking into consideration all the facts of the world, would deliberately set himself to destroy the French Republic and the British Empire acting together in complete unity. But that is the task which would confront an aggressor in Europe once he had committed acts which had forced Great Britain and France into war; for these two ancient and powerful States, once committed by some outrage to the dire event, would persevere, whatever their sufferings, until they were either victorious or had ceased to be. It is in the fact of this supreme issue, this awful stake, that I myself draw the most solid reassurances of peace.

Having begun this new policy there can be no turning back. There is no halting-place. The arrangement is strictly limited at present to three Powers, but others are being consulted, and others have dangers and also have resources, and undoubtedly we must measure each case, so far as we can, because our own resources are not unlimited. But undoubtedly the process of building up mutual security on the basis of mutual exertion and effort, large, strong armed strength maintained in all quarters—that process must continue. To stop here with a guarantee to Poland would be to halt in No-man's Land under fire of both trench lines and without the shelter of either. That is why it seems to me that the announcement of the Prime Minister on Friday, which is explained and emphasised by his statement to-day, constitutes a milestone in our history. We must go forward now until a conclusion is reached. Having begun to create a Grand Alliance against aggression, we cannot afford to fail. We shall be in mortal danger if we fail. We shall be marked down and isolated if we fail. It has become a matter of life or death. The policy now proclaimed must be carried to success—to lasting success—if war is to be averted, and if British safety is to be secured. . . .

I have been expressing my agreement with all that has been said by the Prime Minister, but do not let us forget for a moment the marked and singular period of tension, perhaps to be prolonged, through which we are now passing. For the first time Great Britain has taken the initiative against the Nazi aggression. For nearly a fortnight the Nazi leaders at Berlin have known that we are in process of constructing a defensive bloc to resist another outrage. For the first time they see themselves confronted with the possibilities of war on two fronts. The men at the head of Germany are not restrained by any scruples. They have risen to their power by violence, cruelty and murder. Herr Hitler plumes himself particularly upon the lightning character of the blows which he strikes. These are men in the path of whose ambition it is very dangerous to stand, and we have taken up our stand right in their path.

I pause to pay my tribute to the calm resolve of the British nation. We read how, when Napoleon's army lay at Boulogne 140 years ago, the threat of invasion hung over this country from day to day, dependent upon the shift of the wind, our ancestors showed qualities of doggedness and phlegm deemed remarkable by all who observed it. But that is nothing to the ordeal which the British nation is to-day facing with complete composure. Nothing with which Napoleon threatened England is half as intimate or direct as the destruction and ordeal which would fall upon this country should we be involved in a modern war. I think it very remarkable that this House of Commons, elected by universal suffrage under conditions of free democracy, is ready quite calmly and resolutely, and not in any mood of excitement—far from it—to accept the perils with which we may be confronted, with a feeling that, God helping, we can do no other.

Personally, I believe that the weapon of air terror cuts both ways, and I believe also, that it cannot in any case be decisive against the life of a brave and free people. Nevertheless, the ordeal to which we should be subjected is one which we should not underrate. Do not let us neglect anything. Let us take every step to diminish this dangerous period and to abridge its duration. But precautions taken now are not only safeguards; they may be preventatives. I shall venture to mention only some of the measures which are required so that they may be considered and discussed on later occasions. First of all, everything should be done to remove the temptation of a surprise attack from desperate or perhaps abnormal minds. I have no doubt that the Fleet is in the highest state of readiness, short of actual mobilisation of the Royal Fleet Reserve, which is by no means indispensable to the immediate assertion of naval power. I have no doubt that steps have also been taken to secure a state of vigilance and preparedness in anti-aircraft defences. I trust that the Government will go farther and take other steps necessary to the instant and constant readiness of our air defences. Surely there is a state of emergency as far as purely defensive precautions are concerned. . . .

I have only a few more words to say, and they are on the same note that I struck when I began my speech. Last week at Doullens, was celebrated the twenty-first anniversary of the appointment of Marshal Foch to the supreme command of the

Allied Armies in the height of that terrible battle, the greatest battle of the War, which began on the 21st March, at a moment when the battle seemed a stricken field, and when it seemed that the union between the French and the British Armies would be lost. General Weygand, in celebrating the anniversary, used the following words about Marshal Foch:

> If Foch had been with us to-day he would not have spent his time deploring what had been lost. He would have said, "Do not yield another yard."

Those, it seems to me, are great words which may well be our guide not only in France but in Britain, at this stage in our journey which, though encompassed by unmeasured perils, is sustained by solid confidence and not uncheered by hope.

NATIONAL SERVICE (CONSCRIPTION)

April 24, 1939

Mansion House, London

On April 27, to the violent opposition of the Labour and Liberal Parties, the Government announced the introduction of military conscription. Three days earlier Churchill had advocated this course of action in the following appeal on behalf of territorial recruiting.

[Extract] . . . The first and highest form of national service is service in arms and with the fighting units. Nothing can compare with that in value or in honour, and until the ranks are full up to the limit thought necessary nothing can be put in the way of that service being rendered. Our weakness is that with national approval we have guaranteed to many countries in Europe that we will make common cause with them against further aggression, and that we have not so far taken any adequate steps, or attempted steps, to provide ourselves with a sufficient army with which to back our words.

That is a position morally indefensible; moreover, it is a position which lessens the chances of peace. It lessens those chances in two ways. First of all, military weakness in this country encourages potential enemies, and military weakness in this country discourages our allies, or possible allies, and prevents, or at any rate retards, the weaving together of that great association of peace-loving countries whose collective armed strength is the greatest guarantee of the maintenance of peace. All parties have agreed to join in the giving of those guarantees to other countries, and all parties are bound to make sure that we can honourably and faithfully execute them.

It is a splendid quality in the British national character that the more severe and more onerous the duty, the more near and grievous the danger, the more our men would come forward to volunteer in the face of that danger.

I do not want it to be thought that those volunteers are going to be left to bear the whole burden themselves. That would not be right. That would not be fair. Moreover, there would be far too few for the task. Anyone can see public opinion is growing in favour of compulsory national service in all its forms, and especially in the highest form. It is increasingly probable that we shall have compulsory national service before long. (Cheers.)

It is certain that we should have compulsory national service should war unhappily break out. Therefore those who now come forward voluntarily to bear the brunt, and sustain, if necessary, the first shock, may be sure their countrymen will be inspired by their example to go to their aid and insist that this burden of national defence and self-preservation shall be equally and justly shared without respect to class or fortune. Those, therefore, who volunteer to-day must not think of themselves as the lonely champions of British strength and honour but as a devoted vanguard of the British nation now arming reluctantly but resolvingly in the defence of the freedom and progress of mankind.

RUSSIA AND POLAND

May 19, 1939

House of Commons

*On April 15, with evident reluctance, the Chamberlain Government took the first, belated steps towards an agreement with Russia. A Soviet proposal for a Three-Power Alliance with France and Britain was treated with keen suspicion and uneasiness. On May 4 Litvinov was replaced by Molotov as Foreign Minister; since Litvinov had been for a long time an object of German criticism, this was an ominous development. In Churchill's words "the [Anglo] Russian negotiations proceeded languidly, and on May 19 the whole issue was raised in the House of Commons" (*The Gathering Storm, *371).*

Lloyd George opened the debate with a realistic and sombre interpretation of the German activity, which he asserted could clearly have no defensive purpose. "His speech," Churchill has related, "cast a chill on the Assembly."

Chamberlain's speech revealed his lack of enthusiasm for the Russian proposal—a fact subsequently confirmed in his diaries and letters, and in the Cabinet Minutes, made available to historians in 1971. Churchill expressed his support for a Soviet-British-French alliance against Germany and his concern at the "slow" progress of the negotiations.

[Extract] . . . There is a great identity of interests between Great Britain and the associated Powers in the South. Is there not a similar identity of interests in the North? Take the countries of the Baltic, Lithuania, Latvia and Estonia, which were once the occasion of the wars of Peter the Great. It is a vital major interest of Russia that these Powers should not fall into the hands of Nazi Germany. That is a vital interest in the North. I need not elaborate the arguments about the Ukraine which means an invasion of Russian territory. All along the whole of this eastern front you can see that the major interests of Russia are definitely engaged, and, therefore, it seems that you could fairly judge that they would pool their interests with other countries similarly affected.

I should have thought that this plan of a triple alliance is a preliminary step, and an invitation to other countries in danger on this front to come under its protection, was the most straightforward and practical manner of approaching the subject. I do not know whether I can commend it to my right hon. Friend by adopting a simile selected as a special compliment to him. It is like setting up an armoured umbrella, under which other countries will be invited to take shelter as and when they seek to do so. But we cannot exclude from our minds the fact that we are in a deadlock at the moment. What are the differences? We have already given guarantees to Poland and Rumania, and the Government tell us that they would be glad if Russia would give similar guarantees. Consequently, if Poland and Rumania are attacked we shall be in the war, and so will Russia. It is almost axiomatic that those who are allies of the same Power are allies of one another. It is almost axiomatic.

If you are ready to be an ally of Russia in time of war, which is the supreme test, the great occasion of all, if you are ready to join hands with Russia in the defence of Poland, which you have guaranteed, and of Rumania, why should you shrink from becoming the ally of Russia now, when you may by that very fact prevent the breaking out of war? I cannot understand all these refinements of diplomacy and delay. If the worst comes to the worst you are in the midst of it with them, and you have to make the best of it with them. If the difficulties do not arise, well, you will have had the security in the preliminary stages. . . .

There is only one more point I want to make, and I must make it if the House will bear with me. It is what I may call the technical military aspect of the defence of Poland. His Majesty's Government have given a guarantee to Poland. I was astounded when I heard them give this guarantee. I support it, but I was astounded by it, because nothing that had happened before led one to suppose that such a step would be taken. I want to draw the attention of the Committee to the fact that the question posed by the right hon. Gentleman the Member for Carnarvon Boroughs ten days ago, and repeated to-day has not been answered. The question was whether the General Staff was consulted before this guarantee was given as to whether it was safe and practical to give it, and whether there were any means of implementing it. The whole country knows that the question has been asked, and it has not been answered. That is disconcerting and disquieting, because obviously if it could have been answered it would have been, as promptly as the point was answered about giving £5,000,000 of Czech money back to Germany. I had hoped that it would be answered, but it was not, because it could not be answered in any satisfactory form.

If there had been a careful military examination of this problem, I think it would have been seen at the very outset that no great influx of Russian troops into Poland for the purposes of the defence of Poland is practically possible. The roads and the railroads, of which the gauges change at the Russo-Polish frontier, would not enable any large Russian army to come into action on the Western borders of Poland. Moreover, it is not necessary, for the Poles have a very large army; they do not lack brave men to defend their native land and their regained independence. What they need is not men: they need munitions. That is what I want to impress upon the Committee. That is what we shall all need should a war come—not only Poland and Great Britain, but all the countries engaged in it. In the last War, the fighting was very intense for two months or more, and then suddenly it stopped, not only because of the winter, but because both sides had fired their ammunition. There had to be a breathing-space. There will not be any breathing-space in the next war. Once the German bombardment is begun, it will continue for many months without the slightest slackening. This country and its allies must be equally able to maintain themselves, and that is where the aid of Russia to Poland is going to be absolutely vital, in aeroplanes, tanks, artillery, ammunition and equipment. This ought to be studied and thought out. It is not a question of bringing in great masses of Russian troops, but of giving aid in the form in which it is needed and in the form in which I have every reason to believe Russia would give it in practice, provided that, on these broad lines, a triple alliance were set up. That is why M. Potemkin's conversations were satisfactory.

Clearly, Russia is not going to enter into agreements unless she is treated as an equal, and not only treated as an equal, but has confidence that the methods employed by the allies—by the peace front—are such as would be likely to lead to success. No one wants to associate themselves with indeterminate leadership and uncertain policies. The Government must realise that none of these States in Eastern Europe can maintain themselves for, say, a year's war unless they have behind them the massive, solid backing of a friendly Russia, joined to the combination of the Western Powers. I do not agree altogether with the very dark colours with which my right hon. Friend invested his picture in order to bring out his points, but, in the main, I agree with him that if there is to be an effective Eastern front—an Eastern peace front, or a war front as it might become—it can be set up only with the effective support of a friendly Soviet Russia lying behind all those countries.

Unless there is an Eastern front set up, what is going to happen to the West? What is going to happen to those countries on the Western front to whom, if we had not given guarantees, it is admitted we are bound—countries like Belgium, Holland, Denmark and Switzerland? What is going to happen to those countries? How are they to be defended if there is no Eastern front in activity? Let us look back to the experiences we had in 1917. In 1917, the Russian front was broken and demoralised. Revolution and mutiny had sapped the courage of that great disciplined army, and the conditions at the front were indescribable; and yet, until the Treaty was made closing the front down, more than 1,500,000 Germans were held upon that front, even in its most ineffectual and unhappy condition. Once that front was closed down, 1,000,000 Germans and 5,000 cannon were brought to the West, and almost at the last moment turned the course of the War and forced upon us a disastrous peace.

It is a tremendous thing this question of the Eastern front. I am astonished that there is not more anxiety about it. Certainly, I do not ask favours of Soviet Russia. This is no time to ask favours of countries. But here is an offer, a fair offer, and a better offer, in my opinion, than the terms which the Government seek to get for themselves; a more simple, a more direct and a more effective offer. Let it not be put aside and come to nothing. I beg His Majesty's Government to get some of these brutal truths into their heads. Without any effective Eastern front, there can be no satisfactory defence of our interests in the West, and without Russia there can be no effective Eastern front. If His Majesty's Government, having neglected our defences for a long time, having thrown away Czecho-Slovakia with all that Czecho-Slovakia meant in military power, having committed us without examination of the technical aspects to the defence of Poland and Rumania, now reject and cast away the indispensable aid of Russia, and so lead us in the worst of all ways into the worst of all wars, they will have ill-deserved the confidence and, I will add, the generosity with which they have been treated by their fellow-countrymen.

PALESTINE

May 23, 1939

House of Commons

The Government White Paper on Palestine prompted one of the last major prewar controversies unconnected with the European situation. Churchill had been concerned in the campaign for a Jewish homeland in Palestine for many years, and was joined in this by a few Conservatives—of whom the most notable was the young M.P., Victor Cazalet. All their representations to the Government to honour the Balfour Declaration had proved fruitless, and a fierce debate ensued. The key provision in the White Paper was the proposal that Jewish immigration could be stopped at the end of a five-year period by a majority decision of the population; as the majority was heavily Arab, the outcome of such a decision was not difficult to anticipate. Churchill voted against the Government in the Division, and was joined by a number of other Conservatives.

[Extract] . . . I say quite frankly that I find this a melancholy occasion. Like my right hon. Friend the Member for Sparkbrook (Mr. Amery), I feel bound to vote against the proposals of His Majesty's Government. As one intimately and responsibly concerned in the earlier stages of our Palestine policy, I could not stand by and see solemn engagements into which Britain has entered before the world set aside for reasons of administrative convenience or—and it will be a vain hope—for the sake of a quiet life. Like my right hon. Friend, I should feel personally embarrassed in the most acute manner if I lent myself, by silence or inaction, to what I must regard as an act of repudiation. I can understand that others take a different view. There are many views which may be taken. Some may consider themselves less involved in the declarations of former Governments. Some may feel that the burden of keeping faith weighs upon them rather oppressively. Some may be pro-Arab and some may be anti-Semite. None of these motives offers me any means of escape because I was from the beginning a sincere advocate of the Balfour Declaration, and I have made repeated public statements to that effect.

It is often supposed that the Balfour Declaration was an ill-considered, sentimental act largely concerned with the right hon. Member for Carnarvon Boroughs (Mr. Lloyd George), for which the Conservative party had no real responsibility, and that, as the Secretary of State said yesterday, it was a thing done in the tumult of the War. But hardly any step was taken with greater deliberation and responsibility. I was glad to hear the account which my right hon. Friend the Member for Sparkbrook gave, derived from the days when he was working in the Secretariat of the War Cabinet, of the care and pains with which the whole field was explored at that time. Not only did the War Cabinet of those days take the decision, but all Cabinets of every party after the War, after examining it in the varying circumstances which have arisen, have endorsed the decision and taken the fullest responsibility for it. It was also endorsed in the most cordial and enthusiastic terms by many of the ablest Conservative Private Members who came into the House when a great Conservative majority arrived after the General Election at the end of 1918. It was endorsed from the very beginning by my right hon. Friend the Prime Minister. . . .

Now I come to the gravamen of the case. I regret very much that the pledge of the Balfour Declaration, endorsed as it has been by successive Governments, and the conditions under which we obtained the Mandate, have both been violated by the Government's proposals. There is much in this White Paper which is alien to the spirit of the Balfour Declaration, but I will not trouble about that. I select the one point upon which there is plainly a breach and repudiation of the Balfour Declaration—the provision that Jewish immigration can be stopped in five years' time by the decision of an Arab majority. That is a plain breach of a solemn obligation. I am astonished that my right hon. Friend the Prime Minister, of all others, and at this moment above all others, should have lent himself to this new and sudden default.

To whom was the pledge of the Balfour Declaration made? It was not made to the Jews of Palestine, it was not made to those who were actually living in Palestine. It was made to world Jewry and in particular to the Zionist associations. It was in consequence of and on the basis of this pledge that we received important help in the War, and that after the War we received from the Allied and Associated Powers the Mandate for Palestine. This pledge of a home of refuge, of an asylum, was not made to the Jews in Palestine but to the Jews outside Palestine, to that vast, unhappy mass of scattered, persecuted, wandering Jews whose intense, unchanging, unconquerable desire has been for a National Home—to quote the words to which my right hon. Friend the Prime Minister subscribed in the Memorial which he and others sent to us:

> the Jewish people who have through centuries of dispersion and persecution patiently awaited the hour of its restoration to its ancestral home.

Those are the words. They were the people outside, not the people in. It is not with the Jews in Palestine that we have now or at any future time to deal, but with world Jewry, with Jews all over the world. That is the pledge which was given, and that is the pledge which we are now asked to break, for how can this pledge be kept, I want to know, if in five years' time the National Home is to be barred and no more Jews are to be allowed in without the permission of the Arabs? . . .

I cannot understand what are the credentials of the Government in this matter of Palestine. It is less than two years–about 18 months if I remember aright–since they came forward and on their faith and reputation, with all their knowledge and concerted action, urged us to adopt a wholly different solution from that which they now place before us. The House persuaded them then not to force us into an incontinent acceptance of their partition plan, and within a few months, though they did not thank us for it, they had themselves abandoned and discarded it as precipitately as they had adopted it. Why, now, should they thrust this far more questionable bundle of expedients upon us? Surely it would only be prudent and decent for the Government, following the advice given by the Chancellor of the Exchequer when he was a private Member in 1930, following the opinion of the jurists of those days, to ascertain the view taken by the Mandates Commission of the League of Nations, before whom these proposals are to go, before claiming a Parliamentary decision in their favour.

I cannot understand why this course has been taken. I search around for the answer. The first question one would ask oneself is foreshadowed in a reference made in the speech of my hon. Friend, and is this: Is our condition so parlous and our state so poor that we must, in our weakness, make this sacrifice of our declared purpose? Although I have been very anxious that we should strengthen our armaments and spread our alliances and so increase the force of our position, I must say that I have not taken such a low view of the strength of the British Empire or of the very many powerful countries who desire to walk in association with us; but if the Government, with their superior knowledge of the deficiencies in our armaments which have arisen during their stewardship, really feel that we are too weak to carry out our obligations and wish to file a petition in moral and physical bankruptcy, that is an argument which, however ignominious, should certainly weigh with the House in these dangerous times. But is it true? I do not believe it is true. I cannot believe that the task to which we set our hand 20 years ago in Palestine is beyond our strength, or that faithful perseverance will not, in the end, bring that task through to a glorious success. I am sure of this, that to cast the plan aside and show yourselves infirm of will and unable to pursue a long, clear and considered purpose, bending and twisting under the crush and pressure of events–I am sure that that is going to do us a most serious and grave injury at a time like this.

We must ask ourselves another question, which arises out of this: Can we–and this is the question–strengthen ourselves by this repudiation? Shall we relieve ourselves by this repudiation? I should have thought that the plan put forward by the Colonial Secretary in his White Paper, with its arid constitutional ideas and safety catches at every point, and with vagueness overlaying it and through all of it, combines, so far as one can understand it at present, the disadvantages of all courses without the advantages of any. The triumphant Arabs have rejected it. The despairing Jews will resist it. What will the world think about it? What will our friends say? What will be the opinion of the United States of America? Shall we not lose more–and this is a question to be considered maturely–in the growing support and sympathy of the United States than we shall gain in local administrative convenience, if gain at all indeed we do?

What will our potential enemies think? What will those who have been stirring up these Arab agitators think? Will they not be encouraged by our confession of recoil? Will they not be tempted to say: "They're on the run again. This is another Munich," and be the more stimulated in their aggression by these very unpleasant reflections which they may make? After all, we were asked by the Secretary of State to approach this question in a spirit of realism and to face the real facts, and I ask seriously of the Government: Shall we not undo by this very act of abjection some of the good which we have gained by our guarantees to Poland and to Rumania, by our admirable Turkish Alliance and by what we hope and expect will be our Russian Alliance? You must consider these matters. May not this be a contributory factor–and every factor is a contributory factor now–by which our potential enemies may be emboldened to take some irrevocable action and then find out, only after it is all too late, that it is not this Government, with their tired Ministers and flagging purpose, that they have to face, but the might of Britain and all that Britain means? . . .

It is hoped to obtain five years of easement in Palestine by this proposal; surely the consequences will be entirely the opposite. A sense of moral weakness in the mandatory Power, whose many years of vacillation and uncertainty have, as the right hon. Gentleman admitted yesterday, largely provoked the evils from which we suffer, will rouse all the violent elements in Palestine to the utmost degree. In order to avoid the reproach, the bitter reproach, of shutting out refugees during this time of brutal persecution, the quota of immigration may be raised, as we were told by the Secretary of State, and may be continued at an even higher level in the next five years. Thus, irritation will continue and the incentive to resist will be aggravated. What about these five years? Who shall say where we are going to be five years from now? Europe is more than two-thirds mobilised to-night. The ruinous race of armaments now carries whole populations into the military machine. That cannot possibly continue for five years, nor for four, nor for three years. It may be that it will not continue beyond the present year. Long before those five years are past, either there will be a Britain which knows how to keep its word on the Balfour Declaration and is not afraid to do so, or, believe me, we shall find ourselves relieved of many oversea responsibilities other than those comprised within the Palestine Mandate.

Some of us hold that our safety at this juncture resides in being bold and strong. We urge that the reputation for fidelity of execution, strict execution, of public contracts, is a shield and buckler which the British Empire, however it may arm, cannot dispense with and cannot desire to dispense with. Never was the need for fidelity and firmness more urgent than now. You are not going to found and forge the fabric of a grand alliance to resist aggression, except by showing continued examples of your firmness in carrying out, even under difficulties, and in the teeth of difficulties, the obligations into which you have entered. I warn the Conservative party–and some of my warnings have not, alas, been ill-founded–that by committing themselves to this lamentable act of default, they will cast our country, and all that it stands for, one more step downward in its fortunes, which step will later on have to be retrieved, as it will be retrieved, by additional hard exertions. That is why I say that upon the large aspect of this matter the policy which you think is a relief and an easement you will find afterwards you will have to retrieve, in suffering and greater exertions than those we are making.

I end upon the land of Palestine. It is strange indeed that we should turn away from our task in Palestine at the moment when, as the Secretary of State told us yesterday, the local disorders have been largely mastered. It is stranger still that we should turn away when the great experiment and bright dream, the historic dream, has proved its power to succeed. Yesterday the Minister responsible descanted eloquently in glowing passages upon the magnificent work which the Jewish colonists have done. They have made the desert bloom. They have started a score of thriving industries, he said. They have founded a great city on the barren shore. They have harnessed the Jordan and spread its electricity throughout the land. So far from being persecuted, the Arabs have crowded into the country and multiplied till their population has increased more than even all world Jewry could lift up the Jewish population. Now we are asked to decree that all this is to stop and all this is to come to an end. We are now asked to submit—and this is what rankles most with me—to an agitation which is fed with foreign money and ceaselessly inflamed by Nazi and by Fascist propaganda.

It is 20 years ago since my right hon. Friend used these stirring words:

> A great responsibility will rest upon the Zionists, who, before long, will be proceeding, with joy in their hearts, to the ancient seat of their people. Theirs will be the task to build up a new prosperity and a new civilisation in old Palestine, so long neglected and mis-ruled.

Well, they have answered his call. They have fulfilled his hopes. How can he find it in his heart to strike them this mortal blow?

"A HUSH OVER EUROPE"

August 8, 1939

Broadcast to the United States from London

A most remarkable change occurred in Churchill's fortunes at this time. A widespread call for his return to the Government from the extremes of The Daily Telegraph *to* The Daily Mirror*—but not in* The Times*—was echoed on the Conservative benches. Chamberlain, still clinging to the possibility of a* rapprochement *with Germany, took the view that such an event would be regarded as provocative.*

The world situation continued to darken, and the mood of the House of Commons changed dramatically. On May 22 the "Pact of Steel" was signed between Germany and Italy. Meanwhile, secret Soviet-German negotiations were developing more swiftly. The dispatch of a Foreign Office official as a special envoy to Moscow was interpreted as yet another indication of the British reluctance to deal seriously with the Russians. Although the Soviet-German Non-Aggression Pact was not signed until August 23, the international situation was so tense that there was strong opposition to the Government's proposal on July 27 to adjourn Parliament from August 2 until October 3. A particularly memorable speech was made by Ronald Cartland who, like Victor Cazalet, was later killed in the war. German threats over Danzig, portending a casus belli *with Poland, were now a subject of widespread comment and concern. Belgium had announced its neutrality and its refusal to enter into staff talks with Britain and France. The pressures to bring Churchill and Eden back into the Government became stronger, but were still strongly resisted.*

Holiday time, ladies and gentlemen! Holiday time, my friends across the Atlantic! Holiday time, when the summer calls the toilers of all countries for an all too brief spell from the offices and mills and stiff routine of daily life and breadwinning, and sends them to seek if not rest at least change in new surroundings, to return refreshed and keep the myriad wheels of civilized society on the move.

Let me look back–let me see. How did we spend our summer holidays twenty-five years ago? Why, those were the very days when the German advance guards were breaking into Belgium and trampling down its people on their march towards Paris! Those were the days when Prussian militarism was–to quote its own phrase–"hacking its way through the small, weak, neighbor country" whose neutrality and independence they had sworn not merely to respect but to defend.

But perhaps we are wrong. Perhaps our memory deceives us. Dr. Goebbels and his Propaganda Machine have their own version of what happened twenty-five years ago. To hear them talk, you would suppose that it was Belgium that invaded Germany! There they were, these peaceful Prussians, gathering in their harvests, when this wicked Belgium–set on by England and the Jews–fell upon them; and would no doubt have taken Berlin, if Corporal Adolf Hitler had not come to the rescue and turned the tables. Indeed, the tale goes further. After four years of war by land and sea, when Germany was about to win an overwhelming victory, the Jews got at them again, this time from the rear. Armed with President Wilson's Fourteen Points they stabbed, we are told, the German armies in the back, and induced them to ask for an armistice, and even persuaded them, in an unguarded moment, to sign a paper saying that it was they and not the Belgians who had been the ones to begin the War. Such is history as it is taught in topsy-turvydom.

And now it is holiday again, and where are we now? Or, as you sometimes ask in the United States–where do we go from here? There is a hush over all Europe, nay, over all the world, broken only by the dull thud of Japanese bombs falling on Chinese cities, on Chinese Universities or near British and American ships. But then, China is a long way off, so why worry? The Chinese are fighting for what the founders of the American Constitution in their stately language called: "Life, liberty and the pursuit of happiness." And they seem to be fighting very well. Many good judges think they are going to win. Anyhow, let's wish them luck! Let's give them a wave of encouragement–as your President did last week, when he gave notice about ending the commercial treaty. After all, the suffering Chinese are fighting our battle–the battle of democracy. They are defending the soil, the good earth, that has been theirs since the dawn of time against cruel and unprovoked aggression. Give them a cheer across the ocean–no one knows whose turn it may be next. If this habit of military dictatorships' breaking into other people's lands with bomb and shell and bullet, stealing the property and killing the proprietors, spreads too widely, we may none of us be able to think of summer holidays for quite a while.

But to come back to the hush I said was hanging over Europe. What kind of a hush is it? Alas! it is the hush of suspense, and in many lands it is the hush of fear. Listen! No, listen carefully; I think I hear something—yes, there it was quite clear. Don't you hear it? It is the tramp of armies crunching the gravel of the parade-grounds, splashing through rain-soaked fields, the tramp of two million German soldiers and more than a million Italians—"going on maneuvers"—yes, only on maneuvers! Of course it's only maneuvers—just like last year. After all, the Dictators must train their soldiers. They could scarcely do less in common prudence, when the Danes, the Dutch, the Swiss, the Albanians—and of course the Jews—may leap out upon them at any moment and rob them of their living-space, and make them sign another paper to say who began it. Besides, these German and Italian armies may have another work of Liberation to perform. It was only last year they liberated Austria from the horrors of self-government. It was only in March they freed the Czechoslovak Republic from the misery of independent existence. It is only two years ago that Signor Mussolini gave the ancient kingdom of Abyssinia its Magna Charta. It is only two months ago that little Albania got its writ of Habeas Corpus, and Mussolini sent in his Bill of Rights for King Zog to pay. Why, even at this moment, the mountaineers of the Tyrol, a German-speaking population who have dwelt in their beautiful valleys for a thousand years, are being *liberated,* that is to say, uprooted, from the land they love, from the soil which Andreas Hofer died to defend. No wonder the armies are tramping on when there is so much liberation to be done, and no wonder there is a hush among all the neighbors of Germany and Italy while they are wondering which one is going to be "liberated" next.

The Nazis say that they are being encircled. They have encircled themselves with a ring of neighbors who have to keep on guessing who will be struck down next. This kind of guesswork is a very tiring game. Countries, especially small countries, have long ceased to find it amusing. Can you wonder that the neighbors of Germany, both great and small, have begun to think of stopping the game, by simply saying to the Nazis on the principle of the Covenant of the League of Nations: "He who attacks any, attacks all. He who attacks the weakest will find he has attacked the strongest"? That is how we are spending our holiday over here, in poor weather, in a lot of clouds. We hope it is better with you.

One thing has struck me as very strange, and that is the resurgence of the one-man power after all these centuries of experience and progress. It is curious how the English-speaking peoples have always had this horror of one-man power. They are quite ready to follow a leader for a time, as long as he is serviceable to them; but the idea of handing themselves over, lock, stock and barrel, body and soul, to one man, and worshiping him as if he were an idol—that has always been odious to the whole theme and nature of our civilization. The architects of the American Constitution were as careful as those who shaped the British Constitution to guard against the whole life and fortunes, and all the laws and freedom of the nation, being placed in the hands of a tyrant. Checks and counter-checks in the body politic, large devolutions of State government, instruments and processes of free debate, frequent recurrence to first principles, the right of opposition to the most powerful governments, and above all ceaseless vigilance, have preserved, and will preserve, the broad characteristics of British and American institutions. But in Germany, on a mountain peak, there sits one man who in a single day can release the world from the fear which now oppresses it; or in a single day can plunge all that we have and are into a volcano of smoke and flame.

If Herr Hitler does not make war, there will be no war. No one else is going to make war. Britain and France are determined to shed no blood except in self-defense or in defense of their Allies. No one has ever dreamed of attacking Germany. If Germany desires to be reassured against attack by her neighbors, she has only to say the word and we will give her the fullest guarantees in accordance with the principles of the Covenant of the League. We have said repeatedly we ask nothing for ourselves in the way of security that we are not willing freely to share with the German people. Therefore, if war should come there can be no doubt upon whose head the blood-guiltiness will fall. Thus lies the great issue at this moment, and none can tell how it will be settled.

It is not, believe me, my American friends, from any ignoble shrinking from pain and death that the British and French peoples pray for peace. It is not because we have any doubts how a struggle between Nazi Germany and the civilized world would ultimately end that we pray tonight and every night for peace. But whether it be peace or war—peace with its broadening and brightening prosperity, now within our reach, or war with its measureless carnage and destruction—we must strive to frame some system of human relations in the future which will bring to an end this prolonged hideous uncertainty, which will let the working and creative forces of the world get on with their job, and which will no longer leave the whole life of mankind dependent upon the virtues, the caprice, or the wickedness of a single man.

WAR

September 3, 1939

House of Commons

The German-Soviet Pact, permitting the cynical dismemberment of Poland, was now accompanied by an assurance of Italian non-intervention by Mussolini. Poland was attacked by Germany at dawn on September 1. That afternoon Chamberlain invited Churchill to join the War Cabinet, but Churchill heard no more of the matter for two days. When Parliament met on September 2, the British declaration of war under the Polish Guarantee had not been issued, and the House of Commons was in a ferment. Chamberlain's statement, which gave indications of the Government's continuing efforts to stay out of the conflict, was angrily received. As Mr. Arthur Greenwood rose from the Opposition front bench, Amery called out "Speak for England." That evening, in the midst of a violent thunderstorm, the Cabinet decided war was inevitable. September 3 dawned bright and clear. At 11:15 a.m. Chamberlain announced over the radio, in a melancholy voice, that Britain and Germany were at *war. After a false air-raid warning, the House of Commons met in the early afternoon. Churchill–still not informed as to whether he was in the Government or not–made his last speech from the back-benches. After the debate, Chamberlain invited Churchill to become First Lord of the Admiralty. Churchill accepted. He arrived at the Admiralty at six o'clock that evening. "So it was that I came again to the room I had quitted in pain and sorrow almost a quarter of a century before. . . . Once again we must fight for life and honour against all the might and fury of the valiant, disciplined, and ruthless German race. Once again! So be it" (*The Gathering Storm, *410). The Board of Admiralty signalled to the Fleet: "Winston is back."*

In this solemn hour it is a consolation to recall and to dwell upon our repeated efforts for peace. All have been ill-starred, but all have been faithful and sincere. This is of the highest moral value–and not only moral value, but practical value–at the present time, because the wholehearted concurrence of scores of millions of men and women, whose co-operation is indispensable and whose comradeship and brotherhood are indispensable, is the only foundation upon which the trial and tribulation of modern war can be endured and surmounted. This moral conviction alone affords that ever-fresh resilience which renews the strength and energy of people in long, doubtful and dark days. Outside, the storms of war may blow and the lands may be lashed with the fury of its gales, but in our own hearts this Sunday morning there is peace. Our hands may be active, but our consciences are at rest.

We must not underrate the gravity of the task which lies before us or the temerity of the ordeal, to which we shall not be found unequal. We must expect many disappointments, and many unpleasant surprises, but we may be sure that the task which we have freely accepted is one not beyond the compass and the strength of the British Empire and the French Republic. The Prime Minister said it was a sad day, and that is indeed true, but at the present time there is another note which may be present, and that is a feeling of thankfulness that, if these great trials were to come upon our Island, there is a generation of Britons here now ready to prove itself not unworthy of the days of yore and not unworthy of those great men, the fathers of our land, who laid the foundations of our laws and shaped the greatness of our country.

This is not a question of fighting for Danzig or fighting for Poland. We are fighting to save the whole world from the pestilence of Nazi tyranny and in defense of all that is most sacred to man. This is no war of domination or imperial aggrandizement or material gain; no war to shut any country out of its sunlight and means of progress. It is a war, viewed in its inherent quality, to establish, on impregnable rocks, the rights of the individual, and it is a war to establish and revive the stature of man. Perhaps it might seem a paradox that a war undertaken in the name of liberty and right should require, as a necessary part of its processes, the surrender for the time being of so many of the dearly valued liberties and rights. In these last few days the House of Commons has been voting dozens of Bills which hand over to the executive our most dearly valued traditional liberties. We are sure that these liberties will be in hands which will not abuse them, which will use them for no class or party interests, which will cherish and guard them, and we look forward to the day, surely and confidently we look forward to the day, when our liberties and rights will be restored to us, and when we shall be able to share them with the peoples to whom such blessings are unknown.

THE FIRST MONTH OF WAR

October 1, 1939

Broadcast, London

Within a few hours of the declaration of war the Athenia *was sunk in the North Atlantic. The old aircraft carrier* Courageous *was torpedoed and sunk in the Bristol Channel on September 18. Out of her crew of 1,260 over 500 were lost. On September 15, the new carrier* Ark Royal *was attacked by a submarine, but managed to avoid the torpedoes. These incidents emphasised the dangers to the Fleet in attempting to protect the unarmed and unorganised convoys. Churchill's speech on September 26 made a deep impression on the House, and Attlee complimented him on his "robust, vigorous statement."*

Churchill's broadcasts during the winter of 1939-1940 were in such marked contrast with those of his colleagues that he attracted, for the first time, a large national and international audience, which played a considerable part in his rising reputation.

[Extract] The British Empire and the French Republic have been at war with Nazi Germany for a month tonight. We have not yet come at all to the severity of fighting which is to be expected; but three important things have happened.

First, Poland, has been again overrun by two of the great Powers which held her in bondage for 150 years, but were unable to quench the spirit of the Polish nation. The heroic defense of Warsaw shows that the soul of Poland is indestructible, and that she will rise again like a rock, which may for a spell be submerged by a tidal wave, but which remains a rock.

What is the second event of this first month? It is, of course, the assertion of the power of Russia. Russia has pursued a cold policy of self-interest. We could have wished that the Russian armies should be standing on their present line as the friends and allies of Poland instead of as invaders. But that the Russian armies should stand on this line was clearly necessary for the safety of Russia against the Nazi menace. At any rate, the line is there, and an Eastern Front has been created which Nazi Germany does not dare assail. When Herr von Ribbentrop was summoned to Moscow last week, it was to learn the fact, and to accept the fact, that the Nazi designs upon the Baltic States and upon the Ukraine must come to a dead stop.

I cannot forecast to you the action of Russia. It is a riddle wrapped in a mystery inside an enigma; but perhaps there is a key. That key is Russian national interest. It cannot be in accordance with the interest or the safety of Russia that Germany should plant itself upon the shores of the Black Sea, or that it should overrun the Balkan States and subjugate the Slavonic peoples of southeastern Europe. That would be contrary to the historic life-interests of Russia.

But in this quarter of the world—the southeast of Europe—these interests of

Russia fall into the same channel as the interests of Britain and France. None of these three Powers can afford to see Rumania, Yugoslavia, Bulgaria, and above all Turkey, put under the German heel. Through the fog of confusion and uncertainty we may discern quite plainly the community of interests which exists between England, France and Russia–a community of interests to prevent the Nazis' carrying the flames of war into the Balkans and Turkey. Thus, my friends, at some risk of being proved wrong by events, I will proclaim tonight my conviction that the second great fact of the first month of the war is that Hitler, and all that Hitler stands for, have been and are being warned off the east and the southeast of Europe.

What is the third event? Here I speak as First Lord of the Admiralty, with especial caution. It would seem that the U-boat attack upon the life of the British Isles has not so far proved successful. It is true that when they sprang out upon us and we were going about our ordinary business, with two thousand ships in constant movement every day upon the seas, they managed to do some serious damage. But the Royal Navy has immediately attacked the U-boats, and is hunting them night and day–I will not say without mercy, because God forbid we should ever part company with that–but at any rate with zeal and not altogether without relish. And it looks tonight very much as if it is the U-boats who are feeling the weather, and not the Royal Navy or the world-wide commerce of Britain. A week has passed since a British ship, alone or in convoy, has been sunk or even molested by a U-boat on the high seas; and during the first month of the war we have captured by our efficient contraband control 150,000 tons more German merchandise–food, oil, minerals and other commodities–for our own benefit than we have lost by all the U-boat sinkings put together. In fact, up to date–please observe I make no promises (we must deal in performance and not in promises)–up to date we have actually got 150,000 tons of very desirable supplies into this Island more than we should have got if war had not been declared, and if no U-boat had ever cast sailormen to their fate upon the stormy seas. This seems to be a very solid, tangible fact which has emerged from the first month of the war against Nazidom.

Of course, we are told that all the U-boats have gone home just to tell their master about their exploits and their experiences. But that is not true, because every day we are attacking them upon the approaches to the British Isles. Some undoubtedly have preferred to go off and sink the unprotected neutral ships of Norway and Sweden. I hope the day will come when the Admiralty will be able to invite the ships of all nations to join the British convoys, and to insure them on their voyages at a reasonable rate. We must, of course, expect that the U-boat attack upon the sea-borne commerce of the world will be renewed presently on a greater scale. We hope, however, that by the end of October we shall have three times as many hunting-craft at work as we had at the beginning of the war; and we hope that by the measures we have taken, our means of putting down this pest will grow continually. I can assure you we are taking great care about all that.

Therefore, to sum up the results of the first month, let us say that Poland has been overrun, but will rise again; that Russia has warned Hitler off his Eastern dreams; and that U-boats may be safely left to the care and constant attention of the British Navy.

Now I wish to speak about what is happening in our own Island. When a peaceful democracy is suddenly made to fight for its life, there must be a lot of trouble and hardship in the process of turning over from peace to war. I feel very keenly for those thousands–scores of thousands of them–who wish to throw themselves into the fight at once, but for whom we cannot find full scope at the present time. All this will clear as we get into our stride. His Majesty's Government is unitedly resolved to make the maximum effort of which the British nation is capable, and to persevere, whatever may happen, until decisive victory is gained. Meanwhile patriotic men and women, especially those who understand the high causes in human fortunes which are now at stake, must not only rise above fear; they must also rise above inconvenience and, perhaps most difficult of all, above boredom. Parliament will be kept in session, and all grievances or muddles or scandals, if such there be, can be freely ventilated or exposed there. In past times the House of Commons has proved itself an instrument of national will power capable of waging stern wars. Parliament is the shield and expression of democracy, and Ministers of the Crown base themselves upon the Parliamentary system. You have seen the power of Parliament manifested in the last week, when a Budget, gigantic in its burdens–a Budget which would have infuriated everybody a year ago–has been accepted with prompt and stolid resolve.

In other fields our work goes forward. A large army has already gone to France. British armies upon the scale of the effort of the Great War are in preparation. The British people are determined to stand in the line with the splendid Army of the French Republic, and share with them, as fast and as early as we can, whatever may be coming towards us both. It may be that great ordeals are coming to us in this Island from the air. We shall do our best to give a good account of ourselves; and we must always remember that the command of the seas will enable us to bring the immense resources of Canada and the New World into play as a decisive ultimate air factor, a factor beyond the reach of what we have to give and take over here.

Directions have been given by the Government to prepare for a war of at least three years. That does not mean that victory may not be gained in a shorter time. How soon it will be gained depends upon how long Herr Hitler and his group of wicked men, whose hands are stained with blood and soiled with corruption, can keep their grip upon the docile, unhappy German people. It was for Hitler to say when the war would begin; but it is not for him or for his successors to say when it will end. It began when he wanted it, and it will end only when we are convinced that he has had enough.

The Prime Minister has stated our war aims in terms which cannot be bettered, and which cannot be too often repeated. These are his words:

> To redeem Europe from the perpetual and recurring fear of German aggression, and enable the peoples of Europe to preserve their independence and their liberties.

That is what the British and French nations are fighting for. How often have we been told that we are the effete democracies whose day is done, and who must now be replaced by various forms of virile dictatorships and totalitarian despotism? No doubt at the beginning we shall have to suffer, because of having too long wished to lead a peaceful life. Our reluctance to fight was mocked at as cowardice. Our desire to see an unarmed world was proclaimed as the proof of our decay. Now we have begun. Now we are going on. Now, with the help of God, and with the conviction that we are the defenders of civilization and freedom, we are going to persevere to the end. . . .

I do not underrate what lies before us, but I must say this: I cannot doubt we have the strength to carry a good cause forward, and to break down the barriers which stand between the wage-earning masses of every land and that free and more abundant daily life which science is ready to afford. That is my conviction, and I look back upon the history of the past to find many sources of encouragement. Of all the wars that men have fought in their hard pilgrimage, none was more noble than the great Civil War in America nearly eighty years ago. Both sides fought with high conviction, and the war was long and hard. All the heroism of the South could not redeem their cause from the stain of slavery, just as all the courage and skill which the Germans always show in war will not free them from the reproach of Nazism, with its intolerance and its brutality. We may take good heart from what happened in America in those famous days of the nineteenth century. We may be sure that the world will roll forward into broader destinies. We may remember the words of old John Bright after the American Civil War was over, when he said to an audience of English working folk:

> At last after the smoke of the battlefield had cleared away, the horrid shape which had cast its shadow over the whole continent had vanished and was gone for ever.

THE WAR SITUATION: "A HOUSE OF MANY MANSIONS"

January 20, 1940

Broadcast, London

After the first flurry of the war, a sinister calm fell upon Europe. There was little activity on the Western Front. Only in Finland, where the Russian invasion–bitterly resisted–aroused violent reaction in Britain and France, and at sea, did any significant action occur.

In addition to the menace of the submarines, the German surface raiders were now causing justifiable alarm. On November 23 the battle cruiser Scharnhorst *sank the armed merchant cruiser* Rawalpindi *near Iceland after brave resistance by the latter.* Scharnhorst *and* Gneisnau *decided to return to the Baltic. The fact that the Fleet was unable to bring them to battle aroused public criticism. Another danger was the magnetic mine, which had serious potentialities. One was recovered and its secrets discovered; all British ships were demagnetised. In the meanwhile the cruiser* Belfast *and the battleship* Nelson *were damaged by mines, and two destroyers sunk. Churchill became a strong proponent of mining the Rhine, but this could not be done until the following spring. At this moment of general depression, there occurred a famous event. The pocket battleship* Admiral Graf Spee *had sailed to the South Atlantic, and swiftly caused havoc to British merchantmen. Nine "hunting groups" were organised to discover and bring into battle the German warship, and on December 13 she was engaged by the cruisers* Exeter, Ajax *and* Achilles *and forced to withdraw to Montevideo. Unable to remain, and with the British ships eagerly awaiting her at the entrance of the River Plate,* Graf Spee *was scuttled. Her captain, Langsdorf, committed suicide.*

[Extract] Everyone wonders what is happening about the war. For several months past the Nazis have been uttering ferocious threats of what they are going to do to the Western Democracies–to the British and French Empires–when once they set about them. But so far it is the small neutral States that are bearing the brunt of German malice and cruelty. Neutral ships are sunk without law or mercy–not only by the blind and wanton mine, but by the coldly considered, deliberately aimed, torpedo. The Dutch, the Belgians, the Danes, the Swedes, and, above all, the Norwegians, have their ships destroyed whenever they can be caught upon the high seas. It is only in the British and French convoys that safety is to be found. There, in those convoys, it is five-hundred-to-one against being sunk. There, controlling forces are at work which are steadily keeping the seas open, steadily keeping the traffic going, and establishing order and freedom of movement amid the waves of anarchy and sea-murder.

We, the aggrieved and belligerent Powers who are waging war against Germany, have no need to ask for respite. Every week our commerce grows; every month our organization is improved and reinforced. We feel ourselves more confident day by day of our ability to police the seas and oceans and to keep open and active the salt-water highways by which we live, and along which we shall draw the means of victory. It seems pretty certain that half the U-boats with which Germany began the war have been sunk, and that their new building has fallen far behind what we expected. Our faithful Asdic detector smells them out in the depths of the sea and, with the potent aid of the Royal Air Force, I do not doubt that we shall break their strength and break their purpose.

The magnetic mine, and all the other mines with which the narrow waters, the approaches to this Island, are strewn, do not present us with any problem which we deem insoluble. It must be remembered that in the last war we suffered very grievous losses from mines, and that at the climax more than six hundred British vessels were engaged solely upon the task of mine-sweeping. We must remember that. We must always be expecting some bad thing from Germany, but I will venture to say that it is with growing confidence that we await the further developments or variants of their attack. . . .

Very different is the lot of the unfortunate neutrals. Whether on sea or on land, they are the victims upon whom Hitler's hate and spite descend. Look at the group of small but ancient and historic States which lie in the North; or look again at that other group of anxious peoples in the Balkans or in the Danube basin behind whom stands the resolute Turk. Every one of them is wondering which will be the next victim on whom the criminal adventurers of Berlin will cast their rending stroke. A German major makes a forced landing in Belgium with plans for the invasion of that country whose neutrality Germany has so recently promised to respect. In Rumania there is deep fear lest by some deal between Moscow and Berlin they may become the next object of aggression. German intrigues are seeking to undermine the newly strengthened solidarity of the southern Slavs. The hardy Swiss arm and man their mountain passes. The Dutch—whose services to European freedom will be remembered long after the smear of Hitler has been wiped from the human path—stand along their dykes, as they did against the tyrants of bygone days. All Scandinavia dwells brooding under Nazi and Bolshevik threats.

Only Finland—superb, nay, sublime—in the jaws of peril—Finland shows what free men can do. The service rendered by Finland to mankind is magnificent. They have exposed, for all the world to see, the military incapacity of the Red Army and of the Red Air Force. Many illusions about Soviet Russia have been dispelled in these few fierce weeks of fighting in the Arctic Circle. Everyone can see how Communism rots the soul of a nation; how it makes it abject and hungry in peace, and proves it base and abominable in war. We cannot tell what the fate of Finland may be, but no more mournful spectacle could be presented to what is left to civilized mankind than that this splendid Northern race should be at last worn down and reduced to servitude worse than death by the dull brutish force of overwhelming numbers. If the light of freedom which still burns so brightly in the frozen North should be finally quenched, it might well herald a return to the Dark Ages, when every vestige of human progress during two thousand years would be engulfed.

But what would happen if all these neutral nations I have mentioned—and some others I have not mentioned—were with one spontaneous impulse to do their duty in accordance with the Covenant of the League, and were to stand together with tne British and French Empires against aggression and wrong? At present their plight is lamentable; and it will become much worse. They bow humbly and in fear to German threats of violence, comforting themselves meanwhile with the thought that the Allies will win, that Britain and France will strictly observe all the laws and conventions, and that breaches of these laws are only to be expected from the German side. Each one hopes that if he feeds the crocodile enough, the crocodile will eat him last. All of them hope that the storm will pass before their turn comes to be devoured. But I fear—I fear greatly—the storm will not pass. It will rage and it will roar, ever more loudly, ever more widely. It will spread to the South; it will spread to the North. There is no chance of a speedy end except through united action; and if at any time Britain and France, wearying of the struggle, were to make a shameful peace, nothing would remain for the smaller States of Europe, with their shipping and their possessions, but to be divided between the opposite, though similar, barbarisms of Nazidom and Bolshevism.

The one thing that will be most helpful in determining the action of neutrals is their increasing sense of the power and resolution of the Western Allies. These small States are alarmed by the fact that the German armies are more numerous, and that their Air Force is still more numerous, and also that both are nearer to them than the forces of Great Britain and France. Certainly it is true that we are facing numerical odds; but that is no new thing in our history. Very few wars have been won by mere numbers alone. Quality, will power, geographical advantages, natural and financial resources, the command of the sea, and, above all, a cause which rouses the spontaneous surgings of the human spirit in millions of hearts—these have proved to be the decisive factors in the human story. If it were otherwise, how would the race of men have risen above the apes; how otherwise would they have conquered and extirpated dragons and monsters; how would they have ever evolved the moral theme; how would they have marched forward across the centuries to broad conceptions of compassion, of freedom, and of right? How would they ever have discerned those beacon lights which summon and guide us across the rough dark waters, and presently will guide us across the flaming lines of battle towards better days which lie beyond?

Numbers do not daunt us. But judged even by the test of numbers we have no reason to doubt that once the latent, and now rapidly growing, power of the British nation and Empire are brought, as they must be, and as they will be, fully into line with the magnificent efforts of the French Republic, then, even in mass and in weight, we shall not be found wanting. When we look behind the brazen fronts of Nazidom—as we have various means of doing—we see many remarkable signs of psychological and physical disintegration. We see the shortages of raw materials which already begin to hamper both the quality and the volume of their war industry. We feel the hesitancy of divided counsels, and the pursuing doubts which assail and undermine those who count on force and force alone.

In the bitter and increasingly exacting conflict which lies before us we are resolved to keep nothing back, and not to be outstripped by any in service to the common cause. Let the great cities of Warsaw, of Prague, of Vienna banish despair even in the midst of their agony. Their liberation is sure. The day will come when the joybells will ring again throughout Europe, and when victorious nations, masters not only of their foes but of themselves, will plan and build in justice, in tradition, and in freedom a house of many mansions where there will be room for all.

"LET US TO THE TASK"

January 27, 1940

Free Trade Hall, Manchester

[Extract] We have been five months at war against the world's greatest military power and the world's greatest air power. When the war began in September most of us expected that very soon our cities would be torn and charred by explosion and fire, and few would have dared to plan for the end of January a splendid gathering such as I see before me here this afternoon. I know of nothing more remarkable in our long history than the willingness to encounter the unknown, and to face and endure whatever might be coming to us, which was shown in September by the whole mass of the people of this Island in the discharge of what they felt sure was their duty. There never was a war which seemed so likely to carry its terrors at once into every home, and there never was a war into which the whole people entered with the same united conviction that, God helping, they could do no other.

This was no war planned and entered upon by a Government, or a class, or a Party. On the contrary, the Government labored for peace to the very end; and during those last days the only fear in Britain was lest, weighted down by their awful responsibilities, they should fail to rise up to the height of the occasion. They did not fail, and the Prime Minister led us forward in one great body into a struggle against aggression and oppression, against wrong-doing, faithlessness and cruelty, from which there can be no turning back. We cannot tell what the course of that struggle will be, into what regions it will carry us, how long it will last, or who will fall by the way. But we are sure that in the end right will win, that freedom will not be trampled down, that a truer progress will open, and a broader justice will reign. And we are determined to play our part worthily, faithfully, and to the end. . . .

Come then: let us to the task, to the battle, to the toil—each to our part, each to our station. Fill the armies, rule the air, pour out the munitions, strangle the U-boats, sweep the mines, plow the land, build the ships, guard the streets, succor the wounded, uplift the downcast, and honor the brave. Let us go forward together in all parts of the Empire, in all parts of the Island. There is not a week, nor a day, nor an hour to lose.

"A HIDEOUS STATE OF ALARM AND MENACE"

March 30, 1940

Broadcast, London

[Extract] It seems rather hard when spring is caressing the land, and when, after the rigors of winter, our fields and woodlands are reviving, that all our thoughts must be turned and bent upon sterner war. When I spoke to you six months ago, I said that if we reached the spring without any great event occurring, we should in fact have gained an important success. I still feel that this additional period of preparation has been an invaluable help to the Allies. Peaceful Parliamentary nations have more difficulty in transforming themselves into vast war-making organisms than Dictator States who glorify war and feed their youth on dreams of conquest. The British Empire and the French Republic are now joined together in indissoluble union so that their full purposes may be accomplished, and immense progress has been made in almost every direction—in strengthening our forces, in improving our defenses, and adapting our whole economy and way of life to the service of the common cause.

Up to the present, time has been on our side; but time is a changeable ally. He may be with you in one period and against you in another, and then if you come through that other, he may return again more faithful than before. It seems to me, taking a general view, that an intensification of the struggle is to be expected, and we are certainly by no means inclined to shrink from it. We must not boast, or speak in terms of vain conceit and overconfidence. We have never underrated the terrible nature of what we undertook when, after striving so long for peace, we set ourselves to the task of dealing with the Nazi and German menace and of dealing with it in such a fashion as would clear the path of human progress and enable all countries, great and small, old and new, to breathe freely for a long time to come. We do not minimize our task. But we can now measure it in its enormous magnitude more exactly than we could before we came into contact with our adversary on the sea and in the air.

People often ask me, Will the war be long or short? It might have been a very short war—perhaps indeed there might have been no war—if all the neutral States who share our convictions upon fundamental matters, and who openly or secretly sympathize with us, had stood together at one signal and in one line. We did not count on this, we did not expect it, and therefore we are not disappointed or dismayed. We trust in God and in our own arm uplifted in a cause which we devoutly feel carries with it the larger hopes and harmonies of mankind. But the fact that many of the smaller States of Europe are terrorized by Nazi violence and brutality into supplying Germany with the materials of modern war—this fact may condemn the whole world to a prolonged ordeal with grievous unmeasured consequences in many lands. Therefore I cannot assure you that the war will be short, and still less that it will be easy. . . .

All these outrages upon the sea, which are so clearly visible, pale before the villainous deeds which are wrought upon the helpless Czechs and Austrians, and they sink almost into insignificance before the hideous agony of Poland. What a frightful fate has overtaken Poland! Here was a community of nearly thirty-five millions of people, with all the organization of a modern government, and all the traditions of an ancient State, which in a few weeks was dashed out of civilized existence to become an incoherent multitude of tortured and starving men, women and children, ground beneath the heel of two rival forms of withering and blasting tyranny. The other day in a well-known British harbor I inspected the crew of a Polish destroyer. I have rarely seen a finer body of men. I was stirred by their discipline and bearing. Yet how tragic was their plight! Their ship was afloat, but their country had foundered. But as I looked around upon all the great ships of war which lay at their anchors, and at all the preparations which were being made on every side to carry this war forward at all costs as long as may be necessary, I comforted myself with the thought that when these Polish sailors have finished their work with the British Navy, we will take particular care that they once more have a home to go to. Although the fate of Poland stares them in the face, there are thoughtless dilettanti or purblind worldlings who sometimes ask us: "What is it that Britain and France are fighting for?" To this I answer: "If we left off fighting you would soon find out."

We shall follow this war wherever it leads us; but we have no wish to broaden the area of conflict. At the outbreak, seven months ago, we did not know that Italy would not be our enemy. We were not sure that Japan would not be our enemy. Many people, on the other hand, had hoped that Russia would re-enter the comity of nations and help to shield working folk all over the world from Nazi aggression. But none of these things, bad or good, has happened. We have no quarrel with the Italian or Japanese peoples. We have tried, and we shall try, our best to live on good terms with them.

All's quiet upon the Western Front; and today, this Saturday, so far, nothing has happened on the sea or in the air. But more than a million German soldiers, including all their active divisions and armored divisions, are drawn up ready to attack, at a few hours' notice, all along the frontiers of Luxembourg, of Belgium and of Holland. At any moment these neutral countries may be subjected to an avalanche of steel and fire; and the decision rests in the hands of a haunted, morbid being, who, to their eternal shame, the German peoples in their bewilderment have worshipped as a god. That is the situation of Europe tonight. And can anyone wonder that we are determined to bring such a hideous state of alarm and menace to an end, and to bring it to an end as soon as may be, and to bring it to an end once and for all? Few there are tonight who, looking back on these last seven months, would doubt that the British and French peoples were right to draw the sword of justice and of retribution. Fewer still there are who would wish to sheathe it till its somber, righteous work is done.

"BLOOD, TOIL, TEARS AND SWEAT"

May 13, 1940

House of Commons

The tangled history of the hapless Norwegian campaign of April 1940 cannot be briefly related. On April 8, the Royal Navy laid a minefield at the entrance of the fjord leading to Narvik. The German invasion of Denmark and Norway followed immed. ately, and the British action was too late even to save Narvik. Within two days the Germans controlled all the major ports. There followed a naval battle which inflicted heavy damage on the German Navy and which was of considerable importance in the summer, but it could not affect the situation in Norway. Churchill's attempt to portray Hitler's swift annexation of Denmark and Norway as "a grave strategic error" (April 11) may be viewed with scepticism. It was soon evident that the Allies had suffered a severe setback, and the position of the Chamberlain Government became critical.

On May 7-8 mounting criticism of the Government culminated in a historic debate, ostensibly on the Norwegian campaign, but in fact a debate on the entire record and competence of the Chamberlain Government. It included many memorable speeches, of which the most remembered were by Lloyd George–the last flash from that fading dynamo–and Leo Amery, who invoked Cromwell's words "In the name of God–Go!" Churchill wound up the debate in a tense and difficult situation.

In the division following his speech, the Government's majority fell to 81. It was evident that a National Government was essential, but it was also evident that Chamberlain was unacceptable to the Labour Party. The alternatives were Lord Halifax–preferred by the King and much of the Conservative Party–and Churchill. Halifax decided that the Prime Minister must be in the House of Commons, and Churchill became Prime Minister on May 10, on the eve of the gravest crisis which any British Government has ever faced.

The formation of the new Cabinet was achieved quickly. The principal difficulty arose with the Labour Party over Churchill's wish to make Chamberlain the Leader of the

House of Commons; in view of the objections of Attlee, Churchill became Leader himself, with Attlee as his deputy. The War Cabinet was announced on May 11, and its composition was as follows: Prime Minister and Minister of Defence, Winston Churchill; Lord President of the Council, Neville Chamberlain; Lord Privy Seal, Clement Attlee; Foreign Secretary, Lord Halifax; Minister Without Portfolio, Arthur Greenwood.

Among other key Cabinet appointees (although not members of the War Cabinet) were Anthony Eden (Secretary of State for War), Sir Archibald Sinclair (Secretary of State for Air), A. V. Alexander (First Lord of the Admiralty), Sir Kingsley Wood (Chancellor of the Exchequer), Sir John Anderson (Home Secretary), Herbert Morrison (Minister of Supply), Ernest Bevin (Minister of Labour), Lord Woolton (Minister of Food), and Lord Beaverbrook (Minister of Aircraft Production). By May 15 all senior posts had been filled, and the Great Coalition had been formed.

On May 13 Churchill invited the House of Commons to affirm its confidence in the new Administration. This was a crucial occasion. Many Conservatives were deeply distressed by Chamberlain's downfall, and viewed Churchill with dislike and distrust. No one could tell how the Labour Party would adapt itself to Office and to the strains of working with their political opponents. The news from Europe was bad, and was getting worse. The public, although not yet frightened, was confused and alarmed, and the House of Commons was tense.

On this crucial occasion, the words which Churchill had written in Bangalore, in 1897, can be recalled: "Of all the talents bestowed upon men, none is so precious as the gift of oratory." With this single speech Churchill electrified the House of Commons and the nation. The message was broadcast throughout the world. From this moment it was clear that Britain would fight to the death, and that it had a leader who could express the feelings of the nation in simple, clear, and truthful terms.

When the speech ended, the House of Commons, after a brief stunned silence, erupted into a rare and moving ovation. "I understood then," one of his listeners later wrote, "why the men of the Tenth Legion had loved Caesar." Churchill himself was deeply moved. As he walked out of the chamber, past the Speaker's Chair, he was almost in tears. He looked up, and caught the eye of his old friend and now personal aide, Desmond Morton. "That got the sods, didn't it?" he said to Morton.

I beg to move,

> That this House welcomes the formation of a Government representing the united and inflexible resolve of the nation to prosecute the war with Germany to a victorious conclusion.

On Friday evening last I received His Majesty's Commission to form a new Administration. It was the evident wish and will of Parliament and the nation that this should be conceived on the broadest possible basis and that it should include all parties, both those who supported the late Government and also the parties of the Opposition. I have completed the most important part of this task. A War Cabinet has been formed of five Members, representing, with the Opposition Liberals, the unity of the nation. The three party Leaders have agreed to serve, either in the War Cabinet or in high executive office. The three Fighting Services have been filled. It was necessary that this should be done in one single day, on account of the extreme urgency and rigour of events. A number of other positions, key positions, were filled yesterday, and I am submitting a further list to His Majesty to-night. I hope to complete the appointment of the principal Ministers during to-morrow. The appointment of the other Ministers usually takes a little longer, but I trust that, when Parliament meets again, this part of my task will be completed, and that the administration will be complete in all respects.

I considered it in the public interest to suggest that the House should be summoned to meet to-day. Mr. Speaker agreed, and took the necessary steps, in accordance with the powers conferred upon him by the Resolution of the House. At the end of the proceedings to-day, the Adjournment of the House will be proposed until Tuesday, 21st May, with, of course, provision for earlier meeting, if need be. The business to be considered during that week will be notified to Members at the earliest opportunity. I now invite the House, by the Motion which stands in my name, to record its approval of the steps taken and to declare its confidence in the new Government.

To form an Administration of this scale and complexity is a serious undertaking in itself, but it must be remembered that we are in the preliminary stage of one of the greatest battles in history, that we are in action at many other points in Norway and in Holland, that we have to be prepared in the Mediterranean, that the air battle is continuous and that many preparations, such as have been indicated by my hon. Friend below the Gangway, have to be made here at home. In this crisis I hope I may be pardoned if I do not address the House at any length to-day. I hope that any of my friends and colleagues, or former colleagues, who are affected by the political reconstruction, will make allowance, all allowance, for any lack of ceremony with which it has been necessary to act. I would say to the House, as I said to those who have joined this Government: "I have nothing to offer but blood, toil, tears and sweat."

We have before us an ordeal of the most grievous kind. We have before us many, many long months of struggle and of suffering. You ask, what is our policy? I can say: It is to wage war, by sea, land and air, with all our might and with all the strength that God can give us; to wage war against a monstrous tyranny, never surpassed in the dark, lamentable catalogue of human crime. That is our policy. You ask, what is our aim? I can answer in one word: It is victory, victory at all costs, victory in spite of all terror, victory, however long and hard the road may be; for without victory, there is no survival. Let that be realised; no survival for the British Empire, no survival for all that the British Empire has stood for, no survival for the urge and impulse of the ages, that mankind will move forward towards its goal. But I take up my task with buoyancy and hope. I feel sure that our cause will not be suffered to fail among men. At this time I feel entitled to claim the aid of all, and I say, "Come then, let us go forward together with our united strength."

"ARM YOURSELVES AND BE YE MEN OF VALOUR"

May 19, 1940

Broadcast, London

*By May 14 the news from the front was uniformly bad. The Germans had broken through the French defences at Sedan, and everywhere the French forces were reeling under a devastating barrage from land and air. "At almost all points where the armies had come in contact," Churchill later wrote, "the weight and fury of the German attack was overwhelming" (*Their Finest Hour, *40). Holland fell on May 15, and Churchill flew to Paris on the same day to confer with the French leaders. It was evident that the military situation was near to catastrophic, and that the military commanders and political leaders were resigned to overwhelming defeat. Churchill agreed to send ten fighter squadrons to France, thereby imperilling the situation in England, as a desperate attempt to restore the spirits of his Ally. On May 19, the Cabinet was informed that Lord Gort was "examining a possible withdrawal towards Dunkirk." In these sombre circumstances, Churchill made this, his first broadcast as Prime Minister to the British people.*

I speak to you for the first time as Prime Minister in a solemn hour for the life of our country, of our Empire, of our Allies, and, above all, of the cause of Freedom. A tremendous battle is raging in France and Flanders. The Germans, by a remarkable combination of air bombing and heavily armored tanks, have broken through the French defenses north of the Maginot Line, and strong columns of their armored vehicles are ravaging the open country, which for the first day or two was without defenders. They have penetrated deeply and spread alarm and confusion in their track. Behind them there are now appearing infantry in lorries, and behind them, again, the large masses are moving forward. The re-groupment of the French armies to make head against, and also to strike at, this intruding wedge has been proceeding for several days, largely assisted by the magnificent efforts of the Royal Air Force.

We must not allow ourselves to be intimidated by the presence of these armored vehicles in unexpected places behind our lines. If they are behind our Front, the French are also at many points fighting actively behind theirs. Both sides are therefore in an extremely dangerous position. And if the French Army, and our own Army, are well handled, as I believe they will be; if the French retain that genius for recovery and counter-attack for which they have so long been famous; and if the British Army shows the dogged endurance and solid fighting power of which there have been so many examples in the past—then a sudden transformation of the scene might spring into being.

It would be foolish, however, to disguise the gravity of the hour. It would be still more foolish to lose heart and courage or to suppose that well-trained, well-equipped armies numbering three or four millions of men can be overcome in the space of a few weeks, or even months, by a scoop, or raid of mechanized vehicles, however formidable. We may look with confidence to the stabilization of the Front in France, and to the general engagement of the masses, which will enable the qualities of the French and British soldiers to be matched squarely against those of their adversaries. For myself, I have invincible confidence in the French Army and its leaders. Only a very small part of that splendid Army has yet been heavily engaged; and only a very small part of France has yet been invaded. There is good evidence to show that practically the whole of the specialized and mechanized forces of the enemy have been already thrown into the battle; and we know that very heavy losses have been inflicted upon them. No officer or man, no brigade or division, which grapples at close quarters with the enemy, wherever encountered, can fail to make a worthy contribution to the general result. The Armies must cast away the idea of resisting behind concrete lines or natural obstacles, and must realize that mastery can only be regained by furious and unrelenting assault. And this spirit must not only animate the High Command, but must inspire every fighting man.

In the air—often at serious odds, often at odds hitherto thought overwhelming—we have been clawing down three or four to one of our enemies; and the relative balance of the British and German Air Forces is now considerably more favorable to us than at the beginning of the battle. In cutting down the German bombers, we are fighting our own battle as well as that of France. My confidence in our ability to fight it out to the finish with the German Air Force has been strengthened by the fierce encounters which have taken place and are taking place. At the same time, our heavy bombers are striking nightly at the tap-root of German mechanized power, and have already inflicted serious damage upon the oil refineries on which the Nazi effort to dominate the world directly depends.

We must expect that as soon as stability is reached on the Western Front, the bulk of that hideous apparatus of aggression which gashed Holland into ruin and slavery in a few days will be turned upon us. I am sure I speak for all when I say we are ready to face it; to ensure it; and to retaliate against it—to any extent that the unwritten laws of war permit. There will be many men and many women in this Island who when the ordeal comes upon them, as come it will, will feel comfort, and even a pride, that they are sharing the perils of our lads at the Front—soldiers, sailors and airmen, God bless them—and are drawing away from them a part at least of the onslaught they have to bear. Is not this the appointed time for all to make the utmost exertions in their power? If the battle is to be won, we must provide our men with ever-increasing quantities of the weapons and ammunition they need. We must have, and have quickly, more aeroplanes, more tanks, more shells, more guns. There is imperious need for these vital munitions. They increase our strength against the powerfully armed enemy. They replace the wastage of the obstinate struggle; and the knowledge that wastage will speedily be replaced enables us to draw more readily upon our reserves and throw them in now that everything counts so much.

Our task is not only to win the battle—but to win the war. After this battle in France abates its force, there will come the battle for our Island—for all that Britain is, and all that Britain means. That will be the struggle. In that supreme emergency we shall not hesitate to take every step, even the most drastic, to call forth from our people the last ounce and the last inch of effort of which they are capable. The interests of property, the hours of labor, are nothing compared with the struggle of life and honor, for right and freedom, to which we have vowed ourselves.

I have received from the Chiefs of the French Republic, and in particular from its indomitable Prime Minister, M. Reynaud, the most sacred pledges that whatever happens they will fight to the end, be it bitter or be it glorious. Nay, if we fight to the end, it can only be glorious.

Having received His Majesty's commission, I have formed an Administration of men and women of every Party and of almost every point of view. We have differed and quarreled in the past; but now one bond unites us all–to wage war until victory is won, and never to surrender ourselves to servitude and shame, whatever the cost and the agony may be. This is one of the most awe-striking periods in the long history of France and Britain. It is also beyond doubt the most sublime. Side by side, unaided except by their kith and kin in the great Dominions and by the wide Empires which rest beneath their shield–side by side, the British and French peoples have advanced to rescue not only Europe but mankind from the foulest and most soul-destroying tyranny which has ever darkened and stained the pages of history. Behind them–behind us–behind the Armies and Fleets of Britain and France–gather a group of shattered States and bludgeoned races: the Czechs, the Poles, the Norwegians, the Danes, the Dutch, the Belgians–upon all of whom the long night of barbarism will descend, unbroken even by a star of hope, unless we conquer, as conquer we must; as conquer we shall.

Today is Trinity Sunday. Centuries ago words were written to be a call and a spur to the faithful servants of Truth and Justice: "Arm yourselves, and be ye men of valor, and be in readiness for the conflict; for it is better for us to perish in battle than to look upon the outrage of our nation and our altar. As the Will of God is in Heaven, even so let it be."

"WE SHALL NEVER SURRENDER"

June 4, 1940

House of Commons

*Churchill visited Paris on May 22. The situation appeared slightly more hopeful, and the French more aggressive. Meanwhile, after severe fighting, the British Expeditionary Force had been forced to withdraw from Arras. The Belgian Front was broken, and it was becoming grimly evident that the only chance for the B.E.F. was to fight its way to Dunkirk. On May 26 Churchill insisted that Calais must be defended to the last man: "One has to eat and drink in war," Churchill later wrote, "but I could not help feeling physically sick as we afterwards sat silent at the table" (*Their Finest Hour, *82).*

The situation for the Belgians was now hopeless, and on May 27, King Leopold informed Admiral Roger Keyes that he was asking the Germans for a cessation of hostilities–thus placing the retreating B.E.F. in an even more critical situation.

A "general injunction" issued by Churchill on the following day should be noted: "In these dark days the Prime Minister would be grateful if all his colleagues in the Government, as well as important officials, would maintain a high morale in their circles; not minimising the gravity of events, but showing confidence in our ability and inflexible resolve to continue the war till we have broken the will of the enemy to bring all Europe under his domination. No tolerance should be given to the idea that France will make a separate peace; but whatever may happen on the Continent, we cannot doubt our duty, and we shall certainly use all our power to defend the Island, the Empire, and our Cause."

The position of the B.E.F. had now become critical; Churchill had warned the House on May 28 to prepare for "hard and heavy tidings." As a result of a most skillfully conducted retreat and German errors, the bulk of the British Forces reached the Dunkirk bridgehead. The peril facing the British nation was now suddenly and universally perceived. On May 26, "Operation Dynamo"–the evacuation from Dunkirk–began. The seas remained absolutely calm. The Royal Air Force–bitterly maligned at the time by the Army–fought vehemently to deny the enemy the total air supremacy which would have wrecked the operation. At the outset, it was hoped that 45,000 men might be evacuated; in the event, over 338,000 Allied troops reached England, including 26,000 French soldiers. On June 4, Churchill reported to the House of Commons, seeking to check the mood of national euphoria and relief at the unexpected deliverance, and to make a clear appeal to the United States.

[Extract] . . . When, a week ago today, I asked the House to fix this afternoon as the occasion for a statement, I feared it would be my hard lot to announce the greatest military disaster in our long history. I thought–and some good judges agreed with me–that perhaps 20,000 or 30,000 men might be re-embarked. But it certainly seemed that the whole of the French First Army and the whole of the British Expeditionary Force north of the Amiens-Abbeville gap would be broken up in the open field or else would have to capitulate for lack of food and ammunition. These were the hard and heavy tidings for which I called upon the House and the nation to prepare themselves a week ago. The whole root and core and brain of the British Army, on which and around which we were to build, and are to build, the great British Armies in the later years of the war, seemed about to perish upon the field or to be led into an ignominious and starving captivity.

That was the prospect a week ago. But another blow which might well have proved final was yet to fall upon us. The King of the Belgians had called upon us to come to his aid. Had not this Ruler and his Government severed themselves from the Allies, who rescued their country from extinction in the late war, and had they not sought refuge in what was proved to be a fatal neutrality, the French and British Armies might well at the outset have saved not only Belgium but perhaps even Poland. Yet at the last moment, when Belgium was already invaded, King Leopold called upon us to come to his aid, and even at the last moment we came. He and his brave, efficient Army, nearly half a million strong, guarded our left flank and thus kept open our only line of retreat to the sea. Suddenly, without prior consultation, with the least possible notice, without the advice of his Ministers and upon his own personal act, he sent a plenipotentiary to the German Command, surrendered his Army, and exposed our whole flank and means of retreat.

I asked the House a week ago to suspend its judgment because the facts were not clear, but I do not feel that any reason now exists why we should not form our own opinions upon this pitiful episode. The surrender of the Belgian Army compelled the British at the shortest notice to cover a flank to the sea more than 30 miles in length. Otherwise all would have been cut off, and all would have shared the fate to which King Leopold had condemned the finest Army his country had ever formed. So in doing this and in exposing this flank, as anyone who followed the operations on the map will see, contact was lost between the British and two out of the three corps forming the First French Army, who were still farther from the coast than we were, and it seemed impossible that any large number of Allied troops could reach the coast.

The enemy attacked on all sides with great strength and fierceness, and their main power, the power of their far more numerous Air Force, was thrown into the battle or else concentrated upon Dunkirk and the beaches. Pressing in upon the narrow exit, both from the east and from the west, the enemy began to fire with cannon upon the beaches by which alone the shipping could approach or depart. They sowed magnetic mines in the channels and seas; they sent repeated waves of hostile aircraft, sometimes more than a hundred strong in one formation, to cast their bombs upon the single pier that remained, and upon the sand dunes upon which the troops had their eyes for shelter. Their U-boats, one of which was sunk, and their motor launches took their toll of the vast traffic which now began. For four or five days an intense struggle reigned. All their armored divisions—or what was left of them—together with great masses of infantry and artillery, hurled themselves in vain upon the ever-narrowing, ever-contracting appendix within which the British and French Armies fought.

Meanwhile, the Royal Navy, with the willing help of countless merchant seamen, strained every nerve to embark the British and Allied troops; 220 light warships and 650 other vessels were engaged. They had to operate upon the difficult coast, often in adverse weather, under an almost ceaseless hail of bombs and an increasing concentration of artillery fire. Nor were the seas, as I have said, themselves free from mines and torpedoes. It was in conditions such as these that our men carried on, with little or no rest, for days and nights on end, making trip after trip across the dangerous waters, bringing with them always men whom they had rescued. The numbers they have brought back are the measure of their devotion and their courage. The hospital ships, which brought off many thousands of British and French wounded, being so plainly marked were a special target for Nazi bombs; but the men and women on board them never faltered in their duty.

Meanwhile, the Royal Air Force, which had already been intervening in the battle, so far as its range would allow, from home bases, now used part of its main metropolitan fighter strength, and struck at the German bombers and at the fighters which in large numbers protected them. This struggle was protracted and fierce. Suddenly the scene has cleared, the crash and thunder has for the moment—but only for the moment—died away. A miracle of deliverance, achieved by valor, by perseverance, by perfect discipline, by faultless service, by resource, by skill, by unconquerable fidelity, is manifest to us all. The enemy was hurled back by the retreating British and French troops. He was so roughly handled that he did not hurry their departure seriously. The Royal Air Force engaged the main strength of the German Air Force, and inflicted upon them losses of at least four to one; and the Navy, using nearly 1,000 ships of all kinds, carried over 335,000 men, French and British, out of the jaws of death and shame, to their native land and to the tasks which lie immediately ahead. We must be very careful not to assign to this deliverance the attributes of a victory. Wars are not won by evacuations. But there was a victory inside this deliverance, which should be noted. It was gained by the Air Force. Many of our soldiers coming back have not seen the Air Force at work; they saw only the bombers which escaped its protective attack. They underrate its achievements. I have heard much talk of this; that is why I go out of my way to say this. I will tell you about it.

This was a great trial of strength between the British and German Air Forces. Can you conceive a greater objective for the Germans in the air than to make evacuation from these beaches impossible, and to sink all these ships which were displayed, almost to the extent of thousands? Could there have been an objective of greater military importance and significance for the whole purpose of the war than this? They tried hard, and they were beaten back; they were frustrated in their task. We got the Army away; and they have paid fourfold for any losses which they have inflicted. Very large formations of German aeroplanes—and we know that they are a very brave race—have turned on several occasions from the attack of one-quarter of their number of the Royal Air Force, and have dispersed in different directions. Twelve aeroplanes have been hunted by two. One aeroplane was driven into the water and cast away by the mere charge of a British aeroplane, which had no more ammunition. All of our types—the Hurricane, the Spitfire and the new Defiant—and all our pilots have been vindicated as superior to what they have at present to face.

When we consider how much greater would be our advantage in defending the air above this Island against an overseas attack, I must say that I find in these facts a sure basis upon which practical and reassuring thoughts may rest. I will pay my tribute to these young airmen. The great French Army was very largely, for the time being, cast back and disturbed by the onrush of a few thousands of armored vehicles. May it not also be that the cause of civilization itself will be defended by the skill and devotion of a few thousand airmen? There never has been, I suppose, in all the world, in all the history of war, such an opportunity for youth. The Knights of the Round Table, the Crusaders, all fall back into the past—not only distant but prosaic; these young men, going forth every morn to guard their native land and all that we stand for, holding in their hands these instruments of colossal and shattering power, of whom it may be said that

> Every morn brought forth a noble chance
> And every chance brought forth a noble knight,

deserve our gratitude, as do all the brave men who, in so many ways and on so many occasions, are ready, and continue ready to give life and all for their native land.

I return to the Army. In the long series of very fierce battles, now on this front, now on that, fighting on three fronts at once, battles fought by two or three divisions against an equal or somewhat larger number of the enemy, and fought fiercely on some of the old grounds that so many of us knew so well—in these battles our losses in men have exceeded 30,000 killed, wounded and missing. I take occasion to express the sympathy of the House to all who have suffered bereavement or who are still anxious. The President of the Board of Trade [Sir Andrew Duncan] is not here today. His son has been killed, and many in the House have felt the pangs of affliction in the sharpest form. But I will say this about the missing: We have had a large number of wounded come home safely to this country, but I would say about the missing that there may be very many reported missing who will come back home, some day, in one way or another. In the confusion of this fight it is inevitable that many have been left in positions where honor required no further resistance from them.

Against this loss of over 30,000 men, we can set a far heavier loss certainly inflicted upon the enemy. But our losses in material are enormous. We have perhaps lost one-third of the men we lost in the opening days of the battle of 21st March, 1918, but we have lost nearly as many guns—nearly one thousand—and all our transport, all the armored vehicles that were with the Army in the north. This loss will impose a further delay on the expansion of our military strength. That expansion had not been proceeding as far as we had hoped. The best of all we had to give had gone to the British Expeditionary Force, and although they had not the numbers of tanks and some articles of equipment which were desirable, they were a very well and finely equipped Army. They had the first-fruits of all that our industry had to give, and that is gone. And now here is this further delay. How long it will be, how long it will last, depends upon the exertions which we make in this Island. An effort the like of which has never been seen in our records is now being made. Work is proceeding everywhere, night and day, Sundays and week days. Capital and Labor have cast aside their interests, rights, and customs and put them into the common stock. Already the flow of munitions has leaped forward. There is no reason why we should not in a few months overtake the sudden and serious loss that has come upon us, without retarding the development of our general program.

Nevertheless, our thankfulness at the escape of our Army and so many men, whose loved ones have passed through an agonizing week, must not blind us to the fact that what has happened in France and Belgium is a colossal military disaster. The French Army has been weakened, the Belgian Army has been lost, a large part of those fortified lines upon which so much faith had been reposed is gone, many valuable mining districts and factories have passed into the enemy's possession, the whole of the Channel ports are in his hands, with all the tragic consequences that follow from that, and we must expect another blow to be struck almost immediately at us or at France. We are told that Herr Hitler has a plan for invading the British Isles. This has often been thought of before. When Napoleon lay at Boulogne for a year with his flat-bottomed boats and his Grand Army, he was told by someone, "There are bitter weeds in England." There are certainly a great many more of them since the British Expeditionary Force returned.

The whole question of home defense against invasion is, of course, powerfully affected by the fact that we have for the time being in this Island incomparably more powerful military forces than we have ever had at any moment in this war or the last.

But this will not continue. We shall not be content with a defensive war. We have our duty to our Ally. We have to reconstitute and build up the British Expeditionary Force once again, under its gallant Commander-in-Chief, Lord Gort. All this is in train; but in the interval we must put our defenses in this Island into such a high state of organization that the fewest possible numbers will be required to give effective security and that the largest possible potential of offensive effort may be realized. . . .

Turning once again, and this time more generally, to the question of invasion, I would observe that there has never been a period in all these long centuries of which we boast when an absolute guarantee against invasion, still less against serious raids, could have been given to our people. In the days of Napoleon the same wind which would have carried his transports across the Channel might have driven away the blockading fleet. There was always the chance, and it is that chance which has excited and befooled the imaginations of many Continental tyrants. Many are the tales that are told. We are assured that novel methods will be adopted, and when we see the originality of malice, the ingenuity of aggression, which our enemy displays, we may certainly prepare ourselves for every kind of novel stratagem and every kind of brutal and treacherous maneuver. I think that no idea is so outlandish that it should not be considered and viewed with a searching, but at the same time, I hope, with a steady eye. We must never forget the solid assurances of sea power and those which belong to air power if it can be locally exercised.

I have, myself, full confidence that if all do their duty, if nothing is neglected, and if the best arrangements are made, as they are being made, we shall prove ourselves once again able to defend our Island home, to ride out the storm of war, and to outlive the menace of tyranny, if necessary for years, if necessary alone. At any rate, that is what we are going to try to do. That is the resolve of His Majesty's Government—every man of them. That is the will of Parliament and the nation. The British Empire and the French Republic, linked together in their cause and in their need, will defend to the death their native soil, aiding each other like good comrades to the utmost of their strength. Even though large tracts of Europe and many old and famous States have fallen or may fall into the grip of the Gestapo and all the odious apparatus of Nazi rule, we shall not flag or fail. We shall go on to the end. We shall fight in France, we shall fight on the seas and oceans, we shall fight with growing confidence and growing strength in the air, we shall defend our Island, whatever the cost may be, we shall fight on the beaches, we shall fight on the landing grounds, we shall fight in the fields and in the streets, we shall fight in the hills; we shall never surrender. And even if, which I do not for a moment believe, this Island or a large part of it were subjugated and starving, then our Empire beyond the seas, armed and guarded by the British Fleet, would carry on the struggle, until, in God's good time, the New World, with all its power and might, steps forth to the rescue and the liberation of the Old.

"THEIR FINEST HOUR"

June 18, 1940

House of Commons

Despite all Churchill's efforts to maintain French involvement in the war, Marshal Pétain formed a new Government on June 16, and on the next day, sued for an Armistice. The British forces were compelled to make a second evacuation, principally from Cherbourg and Brest.

This immortal speech, delivered to the House of Commons and then broadcast, was deliberately prepared to discount the widely considered possibility abroad that Britain would follow France's example, particularly in view of Italy's entry into the war.

[Extract] I spoke the other day of the colossal military disaster which occurred when the French High Command failed to withdraw the northern Armies from Belgium at the moment when they knew that the French front was decisively broken at Sedan and on the Meuse. This delay entailed the loss of fifteen or sixteen French divisions and threw out of action for the critical period the whole of the British Expeditionary Force. Our Army and 120,000 French troops were indeed rescued by the British Navy from Dunkirk but only with the loss of their cannon, vehicles and modern equipment. This loss inevitably took some weeks to repair, and in the first two of those weeks the battle in France has been lost. When we consider the heroic resistance made by the French Army against heavy odds in this battle, the enormous losses inflicted upon the enemy and the evident exhaustion of the enemy, it may well be the thought that these 25 divisions of the best-trained and best-equipped troops might have turned the scale. However, General Weygand had to fight without them. Only three British divisions or their equivalent were able to stand in the line with their French comrades. They have suffered severely, but they have fought well. We sent every man we could to France as fast as we could re-equip and transport their formations.

I am not reciting these facts for the purpose of recrimination. That I judge to be utterly futile and even harmful. We cannot afford it. I recite them in order to explain why it was we did not have, as we could have had, between twelve and fourteen British divisions fighting in the line in this great battle instead of only three. Now I put all this aside. I put it on the shelf, from which the historians, when they have time, will select their documents to tell their stories. We have to think of the future and not of the past. This also applies in a small way to our own affairs at home. There are many who would hold an inquest in the House of Commons on the conduct of the Governments—and of Parliaments, for they are in it, too—during the years which led up to this catastrophe. They seek to indict those who were responsible for the guidance of our affairs. This also would be a foolish and pernicious process. There are too many in it. Let each man search his conscience and search his speeches. I frequently search mine.

Of this I am quite sure, that if we open a quarrel between the past and the present, we shall find that we have lost the future. Therefore, I cannot accept the drawing of any distinctions between Members of the present Government. It was formed at a moment of crisis in order to unite all the Parties and all sections of opinion. It has received the almost unanimous support of both Houses of Parliament. Its Members are going to stand together, and, subject to the authority of the House of Commons, we are going to govern the country and fight the war. It is absolutely necessary at a time like this that every Minister who tries each day to do his duty shall be respected; and their subordinates must know that their chiefs are not threatened men, men who are here today and gone tomorrow, but that their directions must be punctually and faithfully obeyed. Without this concentrated power we cannot face what lies before us. I should not think it would be very advantageous for the House to prolong this Debate this afternoon under conditions of public stress. Many facts are not clear that will be clear in a short time. We are to have a secret Session on Thursday, and I should think that would be a better opportunity for the many earnest expressions of opinion which Members will desire to make and for the House to discuss vital matters without having everything read the next morning by our dangerous foes.

The disastrous military events which have happened during the past fortnight have not come to me with any sense of surprise. Indeed, I indicated a fortnight ago as clearly as I could to the House that the worst possibilities were open; and I made it perfectly clear then that whatever happened in France would make no difference to the resolve of Britain and the British Empire to fight on, "if necessary for years, if necessary alone." During the last few days we have successfully brought off the great majority of the troops we had on the line of communication in France; and seven-eighths of the troops we have sent to France since the beginning of the war–that is to say, about 350,000 out of 400,000 men–are safely back in this country. Others are still fighting with the French, and fighting with considerable success in their local encounters against the enemy. We have also brought back a great mass of stores, rifles and munitions of all kinds which had been accumulated in France during the last nine months.

We have, therefore, in this Island today a very large and powerful military force. This force comprises all our best-trained and our finest troops, including scores of thousands of those who have already measured their quality against the Germans and found themselves at no disadvantage. We have under arms at the present time in this Island over a million and a quarter men. Behind these we have the Local Defense Volunteers, numbering half a million, only a portion of whom, however, are yet armed with rifles or other firearms. We have incorporated into our Defense Forces every man for whom we have a weapon. We expect very large additions to our weapons in the near future, and in preparation for this we intend forthwith to call up, drill and train further large numbers. Those who are not called up, or else are employed during the vast business of munitions production in all its branches–and their ramifications are innumerable–will serve their country best by remaining at their ordinary work until they receive their summons. We have also over here Dominions armies. The Canadians had actually landed in France, but have now been safely withdrawn, much disappointed, but in perfect order, with all their artillery and equipment. And these very high-class forces from the Dominions will now take part in the defense of the Mother Country. . . .

Here is where we come to the Navy—and after all, we have a Navy. Some people seem to forget that we have a Navy. We must remind them. For the last thirty years I have been concerned in discussions about the possibilities of oversea invasion, and I took the responsibility on behalf of the Admiralty, at the beginning of the last war, of allowing all regular troops to be sent out of the country. That was a very serious step to take, because our Territorials had only just been called up and were quite untrained. Therefore, this Island was for several months particularly denuded of fighting troops. The Admiralty had confidence at that time in their ability to prevent a mass invasion even though at that time the Germans had a magnificent battle fleet in the proportion of 10 to 16, even though they were capable of fighting a general engagement every day and any day, whereas now they have only a couple of heavy ships worth speaking of—the *Scharnhorst* and the *Gneisenau.* We are also told that the Italian Navy is to come out and gain sea superiority in these waters. If they seriously intend it, I shall only say that we shall be delighted to offer Signor Mussolini a free and safeguarded passage through the Strait of Gibraltar in order that he may play the part to which he aspires. There is a general curiosity in the British Fleet to find out whether the Italians are up to the level they were at in the last war or whether they have fallen off at all.

Therefore, it seems to me that as far as sea-borne invasion on a great scale is concerned, we are far more capable of meeting it today than we were at many periods in the last war and during the early months of this war, before our other troops were trained, and while the B.E.F. had proceeded abroad. Now, the Navy have never pretended to be able to prevent raids by bodies of 5,000 or 10,000 men flung suddenly across and thrown ashore at several points on the coast some dark night or foggy morning. The efficacy of sea power, especially under modern conditions, depends upon the invading force being of large size. It has to be of large size, in view of our military strength, to be of any use. If it is of large size, then the Navy have something they can find and meet and, as it were, bite on. Now, we must remember that even five divisions, however lightly equipped, would require 200 to 250 ships, and with modern air reconnaissance and photography it would not be easy to collect such an armada, marshal it, and conduct it across the sea without any powerful naval forces to escort it; and there would be very great possibilities, to put it mildly, that this armada would be intercepted long before it reached the coast, and all the men drowned in the sea or, at the worst blown to pieces with their equipment while they were trying to land. We also have a great system of minefields, recently strongly reinforced, through which we alone know the channels. If the enemy tries to sweep passages through these minefields, it will be the task of the Navy to destroy the mine-sweepers and any other forces employed to protect them. There should be no difficulty in this, owing to our great superiority at sea.

Those are the regular, well-tested, well-proved arguments on which we have relied during many years in peace and war. But the question is whether there are any new methods by which those solid assurances can be circumvented. Odd as it may seem, some attention has been given to this by the Admiralty, whose prime duty and responsibility is to destroy any large sea-borne expedition before it reaches, or at the moment when it reaches, these shores. It would not be a good thing for me to go into details of this. It might suggest ideas to other people which they have not thought of, and they would not be likely to give us any of their ideas in exchange. All I will say is that untiring viligance and mind-searching must be devoted to the subject, because the enemy is crafty and cunning and full of novel treacheries and stratagems. The House may be assured that the utmost ingenuity is being displayed and imagination is being evoked from large numbers of competent officers, well-trained in tactics and thoroughly up to date, to measure and counterwork novel possibilities. Untiring vigilance and untiring searching of the mind is being, and must be, devoted to the subject, because, remember, the enemy is crafty and there is no dirty trick he will not do.

Some people will ask why, then, was it that the British Navy was not able to prevent the movement of a large army from Germany into Norway across the Skagerrak? But the conditions in the Channel and in the North Sea are in no way like those which prevail in the Skagerrak. In the Skagerrak, because of the distance, we could give no air support to our surface ships, and consequently, lying as we did close to the enemy's main air power, we were compelled to use only our submarines. We could not enforce the decisive blockade or interruption which is possible from surface vessels. Our submarines took a heavy toll but could not, by themselves, prevent the invasion of Norway. In the Channel and in the North Sea, on the other hand, our superior naval surface forces, aided by our submarines, will operate with close and effective air assistance.

This brings me, naturally, to the great question of invasion from the air, and of the impending struggle between the British and German Air Forces. It seems quite clear that no invasion on a scale beyond the capacity of our land forces to crush speedily is likely to take place from the air until our Air Force has been definitely overpowered. In the meantime, there may be raids by parachute troops and attempted descents of airborne soldiers. We should be able to give those gentry a warm reception both in the air and on the ground, if they reach it in any condition to continue the dispute. But the great question is: Can we break Hitler's air weapon? Now, of course, it is a very great pity that we have not got an Air Force at least equal to that of the most powerful enemy within striking distance of these shores. But we have a very powerful Air Force which has proved itself far superior in quality, both in men and in many types of machine, to what we have met so far in the numerous and fierce air battles which have been fought with the Germans. In France, where we were at a considerable disadvantage and lost many machines on the ground when they were standing round the aerodromes, we were accustomed to inflict in the air losses of as much as two and two-and-a-half to one. In the fighting over Dunkirk, which was a sort of no-man's-land, we undoubtedly beat the German Air Force, and gained the mastery of the local air, inflicting here a loss of three or four to one day after day. Anyone who looks at the photographs which were published a week or so ago of the re-embarkation, showing the masses of troops assembled on the beach and forming an ideal target for hours at a time, must realize that this re-embarkation would not have been possible unless the enemy had resigned all hope of recovering air superiority at that time and at that place.

In the defense of this Island the advantages to the defenders will be much greater than they were in the fighting around Dunkirk. We hope to improve on the rate of three or four to one which was realized at Dunkirk; and in addition all our injured machines and their crews which get down safely–and, surprisingly, a very great many injured machines and men do get down safely in modern air fighting–all of these will fall, in an attack upon these Islands, on friendly soil and live to fight another day; whereas all the injured enemy machines and their complements will be total losses as far as the war is concerned.

During the great battle in France, we gave very powerful and continuous aid to the French Army, both by fighters and bombers; but in spite of every kind of pressure we never would allow the entire metropolitan fighter strength of the Air Force to be consumed. This decision was painful, but it was also right, because the fortunes of the battle in France could not have been decisively affected even if we had thrown in our entire fighter force. That battle was lost by the unfortunate strategical opening, by the extraordinary and unforseen power of the armored columns, and by the great preponderance of the German Army in numbers. Our fighter Air Force might easily have been exhausted as a mere accident in that great struggle, and then we should have found ourselves at the present time in a very serious plight. But as it is, I am happy to inform the House that our fighter strength is stronger at the present time relatively to the Germans, who have suffered terrible losses, than it has ever been; and consequently we believe ourselves possessed of the capacity to continue the war in the air under better conditions than we have ever experienced before. I look forward confidently to the exploits of our fighter pilots–these splendid men, this brilliant youth–who will have the glory of saving their native land, their island home, and all they love, from the most deadly of all attacks.

There remains, of course, the danger of bombing attacks, which will certainly be made very soon upon us by the bomber forces of the enemy. It is true that the German bomber force is superior in numbers to ours; but we have a very large bomber force also, which we shall use to strike at military targets in Germany without intermission. I do not at all underrate the severity of the ordeal which lies before us; but I believe our countrymen will show themselves capable of standing up to it, like the brave men of Barcelona, and will be able to stand up to it, and carry on in spite of it, at least as well as any other people in the world. Much will depend upon this; every man and every woman will have the chance to show the finest qualities of their race, and render the highest service to their cause. For all of us, at this time, whatever our sphere, our station, our occupation or our duties, it will be a help to remember the famous lines:

He nothing common did or mean,
Upon that memorable scene.

I have thought it right upon this occasion to give the House and the country some indication of the solid, practical grounds upon which we base our inflexible resolve to continue the war. There are a good many people who say, "Never mind. Win or lose, sink or swim, better die than submit to tyranny–and such a tyranny." And I do not dissociate myself from them. But I can assure them that our professional advisers of the three Services unitedly advise that we should carry on the war, and that there are good and reasonable hopes of final victory. We have fully informed and consulted all the self-governing Dominions, these great communities far beyond the oceans who have been built up on our laws and on our civilization, and who are absolutely free to choose their course, but are absolutely devoted to the ancient Motherland, and who feel themselves inspired by the same emotions which lead me to stake our all upon duty and honor. We have fully consulted them, and I have received from their Prime Ministers, Mr. Mackenzie King of Canada, Mr. Menzies of Australia, Mr. Fraser of New Zealand, and General Smuts of South Africa—that wonderful man, with his immense profound mind, and his eye watching from a distance the whole panorama of European affairs—I have received from all these eminent men, who all have Governments behind them elected on wide franchises, who are all there because they represent the will of their people, messages couched in the most moving terms in which they endorse our decision to fight on, and declare themselves ready to share our fortunes and to presevere to the end. That is what we are going to do.

We may now ask ourselves: In what way has our position worsened since the beginning of the war? It has worsened by the fact that the Germans have conquered a large part of the coast line of Western Europe, and many small countries have been overrun by them. This aggravates the possibilities of air attack and adds to our naval preoccupations. It in no way diminishes, but on the contrary definitely increases, the power of our long-distance blockade. Similarly, the entrance of Italy into the war increases the power of our long-distance blockade. We have stopped the worst leak by that. We do not know whether military resistance will come to an end in France or not, but should it do so, then of course the Germans will be able to concentrate their forces, both military and industrial, upon us. But for the reasons I have given to the House these will not be found so easy to apply. If invasion has become more imminent, as no doubt it has, we, being relieved from the task of maintaining a large army in France, have far larger and more efficient forces to meet it.

If Hitler can bring under his despotic control the industries of the countries he has conquered, this will add greatly to his already vast armament output. On the other hand, this will not happen immediately, and we are now assured of immense, continuous and increasing support in supplies and munitions of all kinds from the United States; and especially of aeroplanes and pilots from the Dominions and across the oceans coming from regions which are beyond the reach of enemy bombers.

I do not see how any of these factors can operate to our detriment on balance before the winter comes; and the winter will impose a strain upon the Nazi regime, with almost all Europe writhing and starving under its cruel heel, which, for all their ruthlessness, will run them very hard. We must not forget that from the moment when we declared war on the 3rd September it was always possible for Germany to turn all her Air Force upon this country, together with any other devices of invasion she might conceive, and that France could have done little or nothing to prevent her doing so. We have, therefore, lived under this danger, in principle and in a slightly modified form, during all these months. In the meanwhile, however, we have enormously improved our methods of defense, and we have learned what we had no right to assume at the beginning, namely, that the individual aircraft and the individual British pilot have a sure and definite superiority. Therefore, in casting up this dread balance-sheet and contemplating our dangers with a disillusioned eye, I see great reason for intense vigilance and exertion, but none whatever for panic or despair.

During the first four years of the last war the Allies experienced nothing but disaster and disappointment. That was our constant fear: one blow after another, terrible losses, frightful dangers. Everything miscarried. And yet at the end of those four years the morale of the Allies was higher than that of the Germans, who had moved from one aggressive triumph to another, and who stood everywhere triumphant invaders of the lands into which they had broken. During that war we repeatedly asked ourselves the question: How are we going to win? and no one was able ever to answer it with much precision, until at the end, quite suddenly, quite unexpectedly, our terrible foe collapsed before us, and we were so glutted with victory that in our folly we threw it away.

We do not yet know what will happen in France or whether the French resistance will be prolonged, both in France and in the French Empire overseas. The French Government will be throwing away great opportunities and casting adrift their future if they do not continue the war in accordance with their Treaty obligations, from which we have not felt able to release them. The House will have read the historic declaration in which, at the desire of many Frenchmen–and of our own hearts–we have proclaimed our willingness at the darkest hour in French history to conclude a union of common citizenship in this struggle. However matters may go in France or with the French Government, or other French Governments, we in this Island and in the British Empire will never lose our sense of comradeship with the French people. If we are now called upon to endure what they have been suffering, we shall emulate their courage, and if final victory rewards our toils they shall share the gains, aye, and freedom shall be restored to all. We abate nothing of our just demands; not one jot or tittle do we recede. Czechs, Poles, Norwegians, Dutch, Belgians have joined their causes to our own. All these shall be restored.

What General Weygand called the Battle of France is over. I expect that the Battle of Britain is about to begin. Upon this battle depends the survival of Christian civilization. Upon it depends our own British life, and the long continuity of our institutions and our Empire. The whole fury and might of the enemy must very soon be turned on us. Hitler knows that he will have to break us in this Island or lose the war. If we can stand up to him, all Europe may be free and the life of the world may move forward into broad, sunlit uplands. But if we fail, then the whole world, including the United States, including all that we have known and cared for, will sink into the abyss of a new Dark Age made more sinister, and perhaps more protracted, by the lights of perverted science. Let us therefore brace ourselves to our duties, and so bear ourselves that, if the British Empire and its Commonwealth last for a thousand years, men will still say, "This was their finest hour."

DESTRUCTION OF THE FRENCH FLEET

July 4, 1940

House of Commons

Churchill decided, with full War Cabinet approval, that the loss of the French fleet at Oran to the Germans would be a major–perhaps fatal–event. When attempts to persuade the French commander to join the British had failed, "Force H"–the British Naval force at Gibraltar–destroyed the French fleet at Oran on July 3, with heavy loss of life. French ships in British harbours were commandeered–not without bloodshed. "This was a hateful decision, the most unnatural and painful in which I have ever been concerned," Churchill later wrote (Their Finest Hour, 232). *It provoked violent reactions in France–of which the echoes are still heard today–but the ruthlessness of the action made a profound impression abroad, particularly in the United States. At the end of Churchill's statement, he received a comprehensive ovation, "unique in [his] own experience." This was another turning-point in his mastery of the House of Commons.*

[Extract] It is with sincere sorrow that I must now announce to the House the measures which we have felt bound to take in order to prevent the French Fleet from falling into German hands. When two nations are fighting together under long and solemn alliance against a common foe, one of them may be stricken down and overwhelmed, and may be forced to ask its ally to release it from its obligations. But the least that could be expected was that the French Government, in abandoning the conflict and leaving its whole weight to fall upon Great Britain and the British Empire, would have been careful not to inflict needless injury upon their faithful comrade, in whose final victory the sole chance of French freedom lay, and lies.

As the House will remember, we offered to give full release to the French from their treaty obligations, although these were designed for precisely the case which arose, on one condition, namely, that the French Fleet should be sailed for British harbors before the separate armistice negotiations with the enemy were completed. This was not done, but on the contrary, in spite of every kind of private and personal promise and assurance given by Admiral Darlan to the First Lord and to his Naval colleague, the First Sea Lord of the British Admiralty, an armistice was signed which was bound to place the French Fleet as effectively in the power of Germany and its Italian following as that portion of the French Fleet was placed in our power when many of them, being unable to reach African ports, came into the harbors of Portsmouth and Plymouth about ten days ago. Thus I must place on record that what might have been a mortal injury was done to us by the Bordeaux Government with full knowledge of the consequences and of our dangers, and after rejecting all our appeals at the moment when they were abandoning the Alliance, and breaking the engagements which fortified it. . . .

I said last week that we must now look with particular attention to our own salvation. I have never in my experience seen discussed in a Cabinet so grim and somber a question as what we were to do about the French Fleet. It shows how strong were the reasons for the course which we thought it our duty to take, that every Member of the Cabinet had the same conviction about what should be done and there was not the slightest hesitation or divergence among them, and that the three Service Ministers, as well as men like the Minister of Information [Mr. Duff Cooper] and the Secretary of State for the Colonies, particularly noted for their long friendship with France, when they were consulted were equally convinced that no other decision than that which we took was possible. We took that decision, and it was a decision to which, with aching hearts but with clear vision, we unitedly came. Accordingly, early yesterday morning, 3rd July, after all preparations had been made, we took the greater part of the French Fleet under our control, or else called upon them, with adequate force, to comply with our requirements. Two battleships, two light cruisers, some submarines, including a very large one, the *Surcouf,* eight destroyers and approximately 200 smaller but extremely useful mine-sweeping and anti-submarine craft which lay for the most part at Portsmouth and Plymouth, though there were some at Sheerness, were boarded by superior forces, after brief notice had been given wherever possible to their captains. . . .

I need hardly say that the French ships were fought, albeit in this unnatural cause, with the characteristic courage of the French Navy, and every allowance must be made for Admiral Gensoul and his officers, who felt themselves obliged to obey the orders they received from their Government and could not look behind that Government to see the German dictation. I fear the loss of life among the French and in the harbor must have been very heavy, as we were compelled to use a severe measure of force and several immense explosions were heard. None of the British ships taking part in the action was in any way affected in gun-power or mobility by the heavy fire directed upon them. I have not yet received any reports of our casualties, but Admiral Somerville's Fleet is, in all military respects, intact and ready for further action. The Italian Navy, for whose reception we had also made arrangements and which is, of course, considerably stronger numerically than the Fleet we used at Oran, kept prudently out of the way. However, we trust that their turn will come during the operations which we shall pursue to secure the effectual command of the Mediterranean.

A large proportion of the French Fleet has, therefore, passed into our hands or has been put out of action or otherwise withheld from Germany by yesterday's events. The House will not expect me to say anything about other French ships which are at large except that it is our inflexible resolve to do everything that is possible in order to prevent them falling into the German grip. I leave the judgment of our action, with confidence, to Parliament. I leave it to the nation, and I leave it to the United States. I leave it to the world and history.

Now I turn to the immediate future. We must, of course, expect to be attacked, or even invaded, if that proves to be possible—it has not been proved yet—in our own Island before very long. We are making every preparation in our power to repel the assaults of the enemy, whether they be directed upon Great Britain, or upon Ireland, which all Irishmen, without distinction of creed or party, should realize is in imminent danger. These again are matters upon which we have clear views. These preparations are constantly occupying our toil from morn till night, and far into the night. But, although we have clear views, it would not, I think, be profitable for us to discuss them in public, or even, so far as the Government are concerned, except under very considerable reserve in a private Session. I call upon all subjects of His Majesty, and upon our Allies, and well-wishers—and they are not a few—all over the world, on both sides of the Atlantic, to give us their utmost aid. In the fullest harmony with our Dominions, we are moving through a period of extreme danger and of splendid hope, when every virtue of our race will be tested, and all that we have and are will be freely staked. This is no time for doubt or weakness. It is the supreme hour to which we have been called.

I will venture to read to the House a message which I have caused to be sent to all who are serving in positions of importance under the Crown, and if the House should view it with sympathy, I should be very glad to send a copy of it to every Member for his own use—not that such exhortations are needed. This is the message:

> On what may be the eve of an attempted invasion or battle for our native land, the Prime Minister desires to impress upon all persons holding responsible positions in the Government, in the fighting Services, or in the Civil Departments, their duty to maintain a spirit of alert and confident energy. While every precaution must be taken that time and means afford, there are no grounds for supposing that more German troops can be landed in this country, either from the air or across the sea, than can be destroyed or captured by the strong forces at present under arms. The Royal Air Force is in excellent order and at the highest strength it has yet attained. The German Navy was never so weak, nor the British Army at home so strong as now. The Prime Minister expects all His Majesty's servants in high places to set an example of steadiness and resolution. They should check and rebuke expressions of loose and ill-digested opinion in their circle, or by their subordinates. They should not hesitate to report, or if necessary remove, any officers or officials who are found to be consciously exercising a disturbing or depressing influence, and whose talk is calculated to spread alarm and despondency. Thus alone will they be worthy of the fighting men, who, in the air, on the sea, and on land, have already met the enemy without any sense of being outmatched in martial qualities.

In conclusion, I feel that we are entitled to the confidence of the House and that we shall not fail in our duty, however painful. The action we have already taken should be, in itself, sufficient to dispose once and for all of the lies and rumors which have been so industriously spread by German propaganda and through Fifth Column activities that we have the slightest intention of entering into negotiations in any form and through any channel with the German and Italian Governments. We shall, on the contrary, prosecute the war with the utmost vigor by all the means that are open to us until the righteous purposes for which we entered upon it have been fulfilled.

"THE FEW"

August 20, 1940

House of Commons

The Battle of Britain opened on July 10 and reached its crisis in August. All the resources of Fighter Command in the South were used. The most difficult and dangerous period of the battle was between August 24 and September 6, when the German attack was directed against the R.A.F. airfields in the South of England with considerable success. In this speech Churchill coined the phrase "The Few"–in emulation, conscious or otherwise, of Shakespeare's speech of Henry V before Agincourt ("We few, we happy few")–to describe the R.A.F. fighter-pilots. The phrase stuck. The final sentence of this speech, including the use of the word "benignant," is a good example of Churchill's choice of unexpected and assertive adjectives to make a phrase memorable.

[Extract] Hitler is now sprawled over Europe. Our offensive springs are being slowly compressed, and we must resolutely and methodically prepare ourselves for the campaigns of 1941 and 1942. Two or three years are not a long time, even in our short, precarious lives. They are nothing in the history of the nation, and when we are doing the finest thing in the world, and have the honor to be the sole champion of the liberties of all Europe, we must not grudge these years or weary as we toil and struggle through them. It does not follow that our energies in future years will be exclusively confined to defending ourselves and our possessions. Many opportunities may lie open to amphibious power, and we must be ready to take advantage of them. One of the ways to bring this war to a speedy end is to convince the enemy, not by words, but by deeds, that we have both the will and the means, not only to go on indefinitely, but to strike heavy and unexpected blows. The road to victory may not be so long as we expect. But we have no right to count upon this. Be it long or short, rough or smooth, we mean to reach our journey's end. . . .

Rather more than a quarter of a year has passed since the new Government came into power in this country. What a cataract of disaster has poured out upon us since then! The trustful Dutch overwhelmed; their beloved and respected Sovereign driven into exile; the peaceful city of Rotterdam the scene of a massacre as hideous and brutal as anything in the Thirty Years' War; Belgium invaded and beaten down; our own fine Expeditionary Force, which King Leopold called to his rescue, cut off and almost captured, escaping as it seemed only by a miracle and with the loss of all its equipment; our Ally, France, out; Italy in against us; all France in the power of the enemy, all its arsenals and vast masses of military material converted or convertible to the enemy's use; a puppet Government set up at Vichy which may at any moment be forced to become our foe; the whole western seaboard of Europe from the North Cape to the Spanish frontier in German hands; all the ports, all the airfields on this immense front employed against us as potential springboards of invasion. Moreover, the German air power, numerically so far outstripping ours, has been brought so close to our Island that what we used to dread greatly has come to pass and the hostile bombers not only reach our shores in a few minutes and from many directions, but can be escorted by their fighting aircraft. Why, Sir, if we had been confronted at the beginning of May with such a prospect, it would have seemed incredible that at the end of a period of horror and disaster, or at this point in a period of horror and disaster, we should stand erect, sure of ourselves, masters of our fate and with the conviction of final victory burning unquenchable in our hearts. Few would have believed we could survive; none would have believed that we should today not only feel stronger but should actually be stronger than we have ever been before.

Let us see what has happened on the other side of the scales. The British nation and the British Empire, finding themselves alone, stood undismayed against disaster. No one flinched or wavered; nay, some who formerly thought of peace, now think only of war. Our people are united and resolved, as they have never been before. Death and ruin have become small things compared with the shame of defeat or failure in duty. We cannot tell what lies ahead. It may be that even greater ordeals lie before us. We shall face whatever is coming to us. We are sure of ourselves and of our cause, and that is the supreme fact which has emerged in these months of trial.

Meanwhile, we have not only fortified our hearts but our Island. We have rearmed and rebuilt our armies in a degree which would have been deemed impossible a few months ago. We have ferried across the Atlantic, in the month of July, thanks to our friends over there, an immense mass of munitions of all kinds: cannon, rifles, machine guns, cartridges and shell, all safely landed without the loss of a gun or a round. The output of our own factories, working as they have never worked before, has poured forth to the troops. The whole British Army is at home. More than 2,000,000 determined men have rifles and bayonets in their hands tonight, and three-quarters of them are in regular military formations. We have never had armies like this in our Island in time of war. The whole Island bristles against invaders, from the sea or from the air. As I explained to the House in the middle of June, the stronger our Army at home, the larger must the invading expedition be, and the larger the invading expedition, the less difficult will be the task of the Navy in detecting its assembly and in intercepting and destroying it in passage; and the greater also would be the difficulty of feeding and supplying the invaders if ever they landed, in the teeth of continuous naval and air attack on their communications. All this is classical and venerable doctrine. As in Nelson's day, the maxim holds, "Our first line of defense is the enemy's ports." Now air reconnaissance and photography have brought to an old principle a new and potent aid.

Our Navy is far stronger than it was at the beginning of the war. The great flow of new construction set on foot at the outbreak is now beginning to come in. We hope our friends across the ocean will send us a timely reinforcement to bridge the gap between the peace flotillas of 1939 and the war flotillas of 1941. There is no difficulty in sending such aid. The seas and oceans are open. The U-boats are contained. The magnetic mine is, up to the present time, effectively mastered. The merchant tonnage under the British flag, after a year of unlimited U-boat war, after eight months of intensive mining attack, is larger than when we began. We have, in addition, under our control at least 4,000,000 tons of shipping from the captive countries which has taken refuge here or in the harbors of the Empire. Our stocks of food of all kinds are far more abundant than in the days of peace, and a large and growing program of food production is on foot.

Why do I say all this? Not, assuredly, to boast; not, assuredly, to give the slightest countenance to complacency. The dangers we face are still enormous, but so are our advantages and resources. I recount them because the people have a right to know that there are solid grounds for the confidence which we feel, and that we have good reason to believe ourselves capable, as I said in a very dark hour two months ago, of continuing the war "if necessary alone, if necessary for years." I say it also because the fact that the British Empire stands invincible, and that Nazidom is still being resisted, will kindle again the spark of hope in the breasts of hundreds of millions of down-trodden or despairing men and women throughout Europe, and far beyond its bounds, and that from these sparks there will presently come cleansing and devouring flame.

The great air battle which has been in progress over this Island for the last few weeks has recently attained a high intensity. It is too soon to attempt to assign limits either to its scale or to its duration. We must certainly expect that greater efforts will be made by the enemy than any he has so far put forth. Hostile air fields are still being developed in France and the Low Countries, and the movement of squadrons and material for attacking us is still proceeding. It is quite plain that Herr Hitler could not admit defeat in his air attack on Great Britain without sustaining most serious injury. If after all his boastings and blood-curdling threats and lurid accounts trumpeted round the world of the damage he has inflicted, of the vast numbers of our Air Force he has shot down, so he says, with so little loss to himself; if after tales of the panic-stricken British crushed in their holes cursing the plutocratic Parliament which has led them to such a plight—if after all this his whole air onslaught were forced after a while tamely to peter out, the Führer's reputation for veracity of statement might be seriously impugned. We may be sure, therefore, that he will continue as long as he has the strength to do so, and as long as any preoccupations he may have in respect of the Russian Air Force allow him to do so.

On the other hand, the conditions and course of the fighting have so far been favorable to us. I told the House two months ago that, whereas in France our fighter aircraft were wont to inflict a loss of two or three to one upon the Germans, and in the fighting at Dunkirk, which was a kind of no-man's-land, a loss of about three or four to one, we expected that in an attack on this Island we should achieve a larger ratio. This has certainly come true. It must also be remembered that all the enemy machines and pilots which are shot down over our Island, or over the seas which surround it, are either destroyed or captured; whereas a considerable proportion of our machines, and also of our pilots, are saved, and soon again in many cases come into action.

A vast and admirable system of salvage, directed by the Ministry of Aircraft

Production, ensures the speediest return to the fighting line of damaged machines, and the most provident and speedy use of all the spare parts and material. At the same time the splendid—nay, astounding—increase in the output and repair of British aircraft and engines which Lord Beaverbrook has achieved by a genius of organization and drive, which looks like magic, has given us overflowing reserves of every type of aircraft, and an ever-mounting stream of production both in quantity and quality. The enemy is, of course, far more numerous than we are. But our new production already, as I am advised, largely exceeds his, and the American production is only just beginning to flow in. It is a fact, as I see from my daily returns, that our bomber and fighter strength now, after all this fighting, are larger than they have ever been. We believe that we shall be able to continue the air struggle indefinitely and as long as the enemy pleases, and the longer it continues the more rapid will be our approach, first towards that parity, and then into that superiority, in the air upon which in a large measure the decision of the war depends.

The gratitude of every home in our Island, in our Empire, and indeed throughout the world, except in the abodes of the guilty, goes out to the British airmen who, undaunted by odds, unwearied in their constant challenge and mortal danger, are turning the tide of the World War by their prowess and by their devotion. Never in the field of human conflict was so much owed by so many to so few. All hearts go out to the fighter pilots, whose brilliant actions we see with our own eyes day after day; but we must never forget that all the time, night after night, month after month, our bomber squadrons travel far into Germany, find their targets in the darkness by the highest navigational skill, aim their attacks, often under the heaviest fire, often with serious loss, with deliberate careful discrimination, and inflict shattering blows upon the whole of the technical and war-making structure of the Nazi power. On no part of the Royal Air Force does the weight of the war fall more heavily than on the daylight bombers, who will play an invaluable part in the case of invasion and whose unflinching zeal it has been necessary in the meanwhile on numerous occasions to restrain. . . .

A good many people have written to me to ask me to make on this occasion a fuller statement of our war aims, and of the kind of peace we wish to make after the war, than is contained in the very considerable declaration which was made early in the autumn. Since then we have made common cause with Norway, Holland and Belgium. We have recognized the Czech Government of Dr. Benes, and we have told General de Gaulle that our success will carry with it the restoration of France. I do not think it would be wise at this moment, while the battle rages and the war is still perhaps only in its earlier stage, to embark upon elaborate speculations about the future shape which should be given to Europe or the new securities which must be arranged to spare mankind the miseries of a third World War. The ground is not new, it has been frequently traversed and explored, and many ideas are held about it in common by all good men, and all free men. But before we can undertake the task of rebuilding we have not only to be convinced ourselves, but we have to convince all other countries that the Nazi tyranny is going to be finally broken. The right to guide the course of world history is the noblest prize of victory. We are still toiling up the hill; we have not yet reached the crest-line of it; we cannot survey the landscape or even imagine what its condition will be when that longed-for morning comes. The task which lies before us immediately is at once more practical, more simple and more stern. I hope—indeed, I pray—that we shall not be found unworthy of our victory if after toil and tribulation it is granted to us. For the rest, we have to gain the victory. That is our task.

There is, however, one direction in which we can see a little more clearly ahead. We have to think not only for ourselves but for the lasting security of the cause and principles for which we are fighting and of the long future of the British Commonwealth of Nations. Some months ago we came to the conclusion that the interests of the United States and of the British Empire both required that the United States should have facilities for the naval and air defense of the Western Hemisphere against the attack of a Nazi power which might have acquired temporary but lengthy control of a large part of Western Europe and its formidable resources. We had therefore decided spontaneously, and without being asked or offered any inducement, to inform the Government of the United States that we would be glad to place such defense facilities at their disposal by leasing suitable sites in our Transatlantic possessions for their greater security against the unmeasured dangers of the future. The principle of association of interests for common purposes between Great Britain and the United States had developed even before the war. Various agreements had been reached about certain small islands in the Pacific Ocean which had become important as air fueling points. In all this line of thought we found ourselves in very close harmony with the Government of Canada.

Presently we learned that anxiety was also felt in the United States about the air and naval defense of their Atlantic seaboard, and President Roosevelt has recently made it clear that he would like to discuss with us, and with the Dominion of Canada and with Newfoundland, the development of American naval and air facilities in Newfoundland and in the West Indies. There is, of course, no question of any transference of sovereignty—that has never been suggested—or of any action being taken without the consent or against the wishes of the various Colonies concerned; but for our part, His Majesty's Government are entirely willing to accord defense facilities to the United States on a 99 years' leasehold basis, and we feel sure that our interests no less than theirs, and the interests of the Colonies themselves and of Canada and Newfoundland, will be served thereby. These are important steps. Undoubtedly this process means that these two great organizations of the English-speaking democracies, the British Empire and the United States, will have to be somewhat mixed up together in some of their affairs for mutual and general benefit. For my own part, looking out upon the future, I do not view the process with any misgivings. I could not stop it if I wished; no one can stop it. Like the Mississippi, it just keeps rolling alone. Let it roll. Let it roll on full flood, inexorable, irresistible, benignant, to broader lands and better days.

NIGHT BOMBING OF LONDON: "EVERY MAN TO HIS POST"

September 11, 1940

Broadcast, London

On September 15 the Battle of Britain was won. "The odds were great; our margins small; the stakes infinite," Churchill later wrote. The Germans lost 56 aircraft; although British estimates at the time were greatly exaggerated, the defeat was evident. On September 17, Hitler's invasion plan, "Operation Sea Lion," was postponed indefinitely.

When I said in the House of Commons the other day that I thought it improbable that the enemy's air attack in September could be more than three times as great as it was in August, I was not, of course, referring to barbarous attacks upon the civil population, but to the great air battle which is being fought out between our fighters and the German Air Force.

You will understand that whenever the weather is favorable, waves of German bombers, protected by fighters, often three or four hundred at a time, surge over this Island, especially the promontory of Kent, in the hope of attacking military and other objectives by daylight. However, they are met by our fighter squadrons and nearly always broken up; and their losses average three to one in machines and six to one in pilots.

This effort of the Germans to secure daylight mastery of the air over England is, of course, the crux of the whole war. So far it has failed conspicuously. It has cost them very dear, and we have felt stronger, and actually are relatively a good deal stronger, than when the hard fighting began in July. There is no doubt that Herr Hitler is using up his fighter force at a very high rate, and that if he goes on for many more weeks he will wear down and ruin this vital part of his Air Force. That will give us a very great advantage.

On the other hand, for him to try to invade this country without having secured mastery in the air would be a very hazardous undertaking. Nevertheless, all his preparations for invasion on a great scale are steadily going forward. Several hundreds of self-propelled barges are moving down the coasts of Europe, from the German and Dutch harbors to the ports of northern France; from Dunkirk to Brest; and beyond Brest to the French harbors in the Bay of Biscay.

Besides this, convoys of merchant ships in tens of dozens are being moved through the Straits of Dover into the Channel, dodging along from port to port under the protection of the new batteries which the Germans have built on the French shore. There are now considerable gatherings of shipping in the German, Dutch, Belgian and French harbors–all the way from Hamburg to Brest. Finally, there are some preparations made of ships to carry an invading force from the Norwegian harbors.

Behind these clusters of ships or barges, there stand very large numbers of German troops, awaiting the order to go on board and set out on their very dangerous and uncertain voyage across the seas. We cannot tell when they will try to come; we cannot be sure that in fact they will try at all; but no one should blind himself to the fact that a heavy, full-scale invasion of this Island is being prepared with all the usual German thoroughness and method, and that it may be launched now—upon England, upon Scotland, or upon Ireland, or upon all three.

If this invasion is going to be tried at all, it does not seem that it can be long delayed. The weather may break at any time. Besides this, it is difficult for the enemy to keep these gatherings of ships waiting about indefinitely, while they are bombed every night by our bombers, and very often shelled by our warships which are waiting for them outside.

Therefore, we must regard the next week or so as a very important period in our history. It ranks with the days when the Spanish Armada was approaching the Channel, and Drake was finishing his game of bowls; or when Nelson stood between us and Napoleon's Grand Army at Boulogne. We have read all about this in the history books; but what is happening now is on a far greater scale and of far more consequence to the life and future of the world and its civilization than these brave old days of the past.

Every man and woman will therefore prepare himself to do his duty, whatever it may be, with special pride and care. Our fleets and flotillas are very powerful and numerous; our Air Force is at the highest strength it has ever reached, and it is conscious of its proved superiority, not indeed in numbers, but in men and machines. Our shores are well fortified and strongly manned, and behind them, ready to attack the invaders, we have a far larger and better equipped mobile Army than we have ever had before.

Besides this, we have more than a million and a half men of the Home Guard, who are just as much soldiers of the Regular Army as the Grenadier Guards, and who are determined to fight for every inch of the ground in every village and in every street.

It is with devout but sure confidence that I say: Let God defend the Right.

These cruel, wanton, indiscriminate bombings of London are, of course, a part of Hitler's invasion plans. He hopes, by killing large numbers of civilians, and women and children, that he will terrorize and cow the people of this mighty imperial city, and make them a burden and an anxiety to the Government and thus distract our attention unduly from the ferocious onslaught he is preparing. Little does he know the spirit of the British nation, or the tough fiber of the Londoners, whose forebears played a leading part in the establishment of Parliamentary institutions and who have been bred to value freedom far above their lives. This wicked man, the repository and embodiment of many forms of soul-destroying hatred, this monstrous product of former wrongs and shame, has now resolved to try to break our famous Island race by a process of indiscriminate slaughter and destruction. What he has done is to kindle a fire in British hearts, here and all over the world, which will glow long after all traces of the conflagration he has caused in London have been removed. He has lighted a fire which will burn with a steady and consuming flame until the last vestiges of Nazi tyranny have been burnt out of Europe, and until the Old World–and the New–can join hands to rebuild the temples of man's freedom and man's honor, upon foundations which will not soon or easily be overthrown.

This is a time for everyone to stand together, and hold firm, as they are doing. I express my admiration for the exemplary manner in which all the Air Raid Precautions services of London are being discharged, especially the Fire Brigade, whose work has been so heavy and also dangerous. All the world that is still free marvels at the composure and fortitude with which the citizens of London are facing and surmounting the great ordeal to which they are subjected, the end of which or the severity of which cannot yet be foreseen.

It is a message of good cheer to our fighting Forces on the seas, in the air, and in our waiting Armies in all their posts and stations, that we send them from this capital city. They know that they have behind them a people who will not flinch or weary of the struggle–hard and protracted though it will be; but that we shall rather draw from the heart of suffering itself the means of inspiration and survival, and of a victory won not only for ourselves but for all–a victory won not only for our own time, but for the long and better days that are to come.

THE WAR SITUATION

October 8, 1940

House of Commons

Defeated in its attempt to destroy Fighter Command, the Luftwaffe's main assault was transferred to the bombing of London; the "Blitz" had begun in earnest.

By this stage the hitherto unknown General Charles de Gaulle had become the embodiment of French resistance to Germany. A plan had been evolved for a landing at Dakar as the first step to rally French support in West and North Africa to the Free French side. The British involvement steadily increased, but on September 11, three Vichy French carriers and three destroyers passed through the Strait of Gibraltar and sailed down the African coast. As a result of a number of errors and delays, they were not intercepted. By September 16 they were at Dakar. The Cabinet agreed with Churchill that the Anglo-Free French operation should be aborted, but de Gaulle and the British commander protested so vigorously that the Cabinet reversed its decision. The operation was a total fiasco.

[Extract] . . . Because we feel easier in ourselves and see our way more clearly through our difficulties and dangers than we did some months ago, because foreign countries, friends or foes, recognise the giant, enduring, resilient strength of Britain and the British Empire, do not let us dull for one moment the sense of the awful hazards in which we stand. Do not let us lose the conviction that it is only by supreme and superb exertions, unwearying and indomitable, that we shall save our souls alive. No one can predict, no one can even imagine, how this terrible war against German and Nazi aggression will run its course or how far it will spread or how long it will last. Long, dark months of trials and tribulations lie before us. Not only great dangers, but many more misfortunes, many shortcomings, many mistakes, many disappointments will surely be our lot. Death and sorrow will be the companions of our journey; hardship our garment; constancy and valour our only shield. We must be united, we must be undaunted, we must be inflexible. Our qualities and deeds must burn and glow through the gloom of Europe until they become the veritable beacon of its salvation.

"LE DIEU PROTÉGE LA FRANCE"
October 21, 1940

Broadcast, London

Frenchmen! For more than thirty years in peace and war I have marched with you, and I am marching still along the same road. Tonight I speak to you at your firesides wherever you may be, or whatever your fortunes are: I repeat the prayer around the *louis d'or, "Dieu protége la France."* Here at home in England, under the fire of the Boche, we do not forget the ties and links that unite us to France, and we are persevering steadfastly and in good heart in the cause of European freedom and fair dealing for the common people of all countries, for which, with you, we drew the sword. When good people get into trouble because they are attacked and heavily smitten by the vile and wicked, they must be very careful not to get at loggerheads with one another. The common enemy is always trying to bring this about, and, of course, in bad luck a lot of things happen which play into the enemy's hands. We must just make the best of things as they come along.

Here in London, which Herr Hitler says he will reduce to ashes, and which his aeroplanes are now bombarding, our people are bearing up unflinchingly. Our Air Force has more than held its own. We are waiting for the long-promised invasion. So are the fishes. But, of course, this for us is only the beginning. Now in 1940, in spite of occasional losses, we have, as ever, command of the seas. In 1941 we shall have the command of the air. Remember what that means. Herr Hitler with his tanks and other mechanical weapons, and also by Fifth Column intrigue with traitors, has managed to subjugate for the time being most of the finest races in Europe, and his little Italian accomplice is trotting along hopefully and hungrily, but rather wearily and very timidly, at his side. They both wish to carve up France and her Empire as if it were a fowl; to one a leg, to another a wing or perhaps part of the breast. Not only the French Empire will be devoured by these two ugly customers, but Alsace-Lorraine will go once again under the German yoke, and Nice, Savoy and Corsica–Napoleon's Corsica–will be torn from the fair realm of France. But Herr Hitler is not thinking only of stealing other people's territories, or flinging gobbets of them to his little confederate. I tell you truly what you must believe when I say this evil man, this monstrous abortion of hatred and defeat, is resolved on nothing less than the complete wiping out of the French nation, and the disintegration of its whole life and future. By all kinds of sly and savage means, he is plotting and working to quench for ever the fountain of characteristic French culture and of French inspiration to the world. All Europe, if he has his way, will be reduced to one uniform Boche-land, to be exploited, pillaged, and bullied by his Nazi gangsters. You will excuse my speaking frankly because this is not a time to mince words. It is not defeat that France will now be made to suffer at German hands, but the doom of complete obliteration. Army, Navy, Air Force, religion, law, language, culture, institutions, literature, history, tradition—all are to be effaced by the brute strength of a triumphant Army and the scientific low cunning of a ruthless Police Force.

Frenchmen—rearm your spirits before it is too late. Remember how Napoleon said before one of his battles: "These same Prussians who are so boastful today were three to one at Jena, and six to one at Montmirail." Never will I believe that the soul of France is dead. Never will I believe that her place amongst the greatest nations of the world has been lost for ever! All these schemes and crimes of Herr Hitler's are bringing upon him and upon all who belong to his system a retribution which many of us will live to see. The story is not yet finished, but it will not be so long. We are on his track, and so are our friends across the Atlantic Ocean, and your friends across the Atlantic Ocean. If he cannot destroy us, we will surely destroy him and all his gang, and all their works. Therefore, have hope and faith, for all will come right.

Now, what is it we British ask of you in this present hard and bitter time? What we ask at this moment in our struggle to win the victory which we will share with you, is that if you cannot help us, at least you will not hinder us. Presently you will be able to weight the arm that strikes for you, and you ought to do so. But even now we believe that Frenchmen, wherever they may be, feel their hearts warm and a proud blood tingle in their veins when we have some success in the air or on the sea, or presently—for that will come—upon the land.

Remember we shall never stop, never weary, and never give in, and that our whole people and Empire have vowed themselves to the task of cleansing Europe from the Nazi pestilence and saving the world from the new Dark Ages. Do not imagine, as the German-controlled wireless tells you, that we English seek to take your ships and colonies. We seek to beat the life and soul out of Hitler and Hitlerism. That alone, that all the time, that to the end. We do not covet anything from any nation except their respect. Those French who are in the French Empire, and those who are in so-called unoccupied France, may see their way from time to time to useful action. I will not go into details. Hostile ears are listening. As for those to whom English hearts go out in full, because they see them under the sharp discipline, oppression, and spying of the Hun—as to those Frenchmen in the occupied regions—to them I say, when they think of the future let them remember the words which Thiers, that great Frenchman, uttered after 1870 about the future of France and what was to come: "Think of it always: speak of it never."

Good night, then: sleep to gather strength for the morning. For the morning will come. Brightly will it shine on the brave and true, kindly upon all who suffer for the cause, glorious upon the tombs of heroes. Thus will shine the dawn. *Vive la France!* Long live also the forward march of the common people in all the lands towards their just and true inheritance, and towards the broader and fuller age.

NEVILLE CHAMBERLAIN

November 12, 1940

House of Commons

After his resignation as Prime Minister, Chamberlain's health deteriorated, and it was discovered that he was suffering from cancer. He resigned from the Government on October 3, and also from the leadership of the Conservative Party. Mindful of Lloyd George's experience in the 1916-1922 Coalition, Churchill willingly accepted the suggestion that he succeed Chamberlain. Lord Halifax proposed the motion, which was unanimously approved. Churchill's tribute to Chamberlain in the House of Commons was one of his most moving and precisely phrased speeches.

Since we last met, the House has suffered a very grievous loss in the death of one of its most distinguished Members, and of a statesman and public servant who, during the best part of three memorable years, was first Minister of the Crown.

The fierce and bitter controversies which hung around him in recent times were hushed by the news of his illness and are silenced by his death. In paying a tribute of respect and of regard to an eminent man who has been taken from us, no one is obliged to alter the opinions which he has formed or expressed upon issues which have become a part of history; but at the Lychgate we may all pass our own conduct and our own judgments under a searching review. It is not given to human beings, happily for them, for otherwise life would be intolerable, to foresee or to predict to any large extent the unfolding course of events. In one phase men seem to have been right, in another they seem to have been wrong. Then again, a few years later, when the perspective of time has lengthened, all stands in a different setting. There is a new proportion. There is another scale of values. History with its flickering lamp stumbles along the trail of the past, trying to reconstruct its scenes, to revive its echoes, and kindle with pale gleams the passion of former days. What is the worth of all this? The only guide to a man is his conscience; the only shield to his memory is the rectitude and sincerity of his actions. It is very imprudent to walk through life without this shield, because we are so often mocked by the failure of our hopes and the upsetting of our calculations; but with this shield, however the fates may play, we march always in the ranks of honour.

It fell to Neville Chamberlain in one of the supreme crises of the world to be contradicted by events, to be disappointed in his hopes, and to be deceived and cheated by a wicked man. But what were these hopes in which he was disappointed? What were these wishes in which he was frustrated? What was that faith that was abused? They were surely among the most noble and benevolent instincts of the human heart—the love of peace, the toil for peace, the strife for peace, the pursuit of peace, even at great peril, and certainly to the utter disdain of popularity or clamour. Whatever else history may or may not say about these terrible, tremendous years, we can be sure that Neville Chamberlain acted with perfect sincerity according to his lights and strove to the utmost of his capacity and authority, which were powerful, to save the world from the awful, devastating struggle in which we are now engaged. This alone will stand him in good stead as far as what is called the verdict of history is concerned.

But it is also a help to our country and to our whole Empire, and to our decent faithful way of living that, however long the struggle may last, or however dark may be the clouds which overhang our path, no future generation of English-speaking folks—for that is the tribunal to which we appeal—will doubt that, even at a great cost to ourselves in technical preparation, we were guiltless of the bloodshed, terror and misery which have engulfed so many lands and peoples, and yet seek new victims still. Herr Hitler protests with frantic words and gestures that he has only desired peace. What do these ravings and outpourings count before the silence of Neville Chamberlain's tomb? Long, hard, and hazardous years lie before us, but at least we entered upon them united and with clean hearts.

I do not propose to give an appreciation of Neville Chamberlain's life and character, but there were certain qualities always admired in these Islands which he possessed in an altogether exceptional degree. He had a physical and moral toughness of fibre which enabled him all through his varied career to endure misfortune and disappointment without being unduly discouraged or wearied. He had a precision of mind and an aptitude for business which raised him far above the ordinary levels of our generation. He had a firmness of spirit which was not often elated by success, seldom downcast by failure, and never swayed by panic. When, contrary to all his hopes, beliefs and exertions, the war came upon him, and when, as he himself said, all that he had worked for was shattered, there was no man more resolved to pursue the unsought quarrel to the death. The same qualities which made him one of the last to enter the war, made him one of the last who would quit it before the full victory of a righteous cause was won.

I had the singular experience of passing in a day from being one of his most prominent opponents and critics to being one of his principal lieutenants, and on another day of passing from serving under him to become the head of a Government of which, with perfect loyalty, he was content to be a member. Such relationships are unusual in our public life. I have before told the House how on the morrow of the Debate which in the early days of May challenged his position, he declared to me and a few other friends that only a National Government could face the storm about to break upon us, and that if he were an obstacle to the formation of such a Government, he would instantly retire. Thereafter, he acted with that singleness of purpose and simplicity of conduct which at all times, and especially in great times, ought to be the ideal of us all.

When he returned to duty a few weeks after a most severe operation, the bombardment of London and of the seat of Government had begun. I was a witness during that fortnight of his fortitude under the most grievous and painful bodily afflictions, and I can testify that, although physically only the wreck of a man, his nerve was unshaken and his remarkable mental faculties unimpaired.

After he left the Government he refused all honours. He would die like his father, plain Mr. Chamberlain. I sought permission of the King, however, to have him supplied with the Cabinet papers, and until a few days of his death he followed our affairs with keenness, interest and tenacity. He met the approach of death with a steady eye. If he grieved at all, it was that he could not be a spectator of our victory; but I think he died with the comfort of knowing that his country had, at least, turned the corner.

At this time our thoughts must pass to the gracious and charming lady who shared his days of triumph and adversity with a courage and quality the equal of his own. He was, like his father and his brother Austen before him, a famous Member of the House of Commons, and we here assembled this morning, Members of all parties, without a single exception, feel that we do ourselves and our country honour in saluting the memory of one whom Disraeli would have called an "English worthy."

"A DARK AND DEADLY VALLEY"
(THE WAR SITUATION)

January 22, 1941

House of Commons

[Extract] To try to carry on a war, a tremendous war, without the aid and guidance of the House of Commons, would be a superhuman task. I have never taken the view that the Debates and criticisms of this House are a drag and a burden. Far from it. I may not agree with all the criticism–I may be stirred by it, and I may resent it; I may even retort–but at any rate, Debates on these large issues are of the very greatest value to the life-thrust of the nation, and they are of great assistance to His Majesty's Government. . . .

Criticism is easy; achievement is more difficult. I do not pretend that there is no room for improvement and for acceleration, even apart from the methodical expansion which is going on. It is certain that the peak of our war effort has not yet been reached. It cannot be reached until the plants are all working, but my mind goes back, not to what has been said here, but to what I read outside a few weeks ago, when our critics were crying out about our inaction against Italy and wondering whose was the hidden hand that was shielding Mussolini from British wrath. At that time I endured the taunts in silence because I knew that the large and daring measures had already been taken which have since rendered possible the splendid victories in Libya–Sidi Barrani, Bardia, and it may well be that while I am speaking Tobruk and all it contains are in our hands. Apart from the Libyan victories, extremely important developments are taking place on both frontiers of Abyssinia and in Eritrea which may themselves be productive and fruitful of pregnant results.

Far be it from me to paint a rosy picture of the future. Indeed, I do not think we should be justified in using any but the more sombre tones and colours while our people, our Empire and indeed the whole English-speaking world are passing through a dark and deadly valley. But I should be failing in my duty if, on the other side, I were not to convey the true impression, namely, that this great nation is getting into its war stride. It is accomplishing the transition from the days of peace and comfort to those of supreme, organized, indomitable exertion. Still more should I fail in my duty were I to suggest that the future, with all its horrors, contains any element which justifies lassitude, despondency or despair. His Majesty's Government welcome the stimulus that the House of Commons and the Press and the public of this island give to us in driving forward our war effort, and in trying to gain an earlier inch or a more fruitful hour, wherever it may be possible; but I have no doubt that the House, in its overwhelming majority, nay almost unanimously, will wish also to give its tribute of encouragement as well as its dose of correction, and will lend the heave of its own loyal strength to the forward surges which have now begun.

"GIVE US THE TOOLS"

February 9, 1941

Broadcast, London

When Wendell Willkie, the defeated Republican candidate in the 1940 United States presidential election, visited Britain at the end of January, he carried a letter of introduction from President Roosevelt containing the celebrated lines from Longfellow, which moved Churchill greatly. He quoted from them at the end of a long broadcast, from which these extracts have been taken.

[Extract] Five months have passed since I spoke to the British nation and the Empire on the broadcast. In wartime there is a lot to be said for the motto: "Deeds, not words." All the same, it is a good thing to look around from time to time and take stock, and certainly our affairs have prospered in several directions during these last four or five months, far better than most of us would have ventured to hope.

We stood our ground and faced the two Dictators in the hour of what seemed their overwhelming triumph, and we have shown ourselves capable, so far, of standing up against them alone. After the heavy defeats of the German air force by our fighters in August and September, Herr Hitler did not dare attempt the invasion of this Island, although he had every need to do so and although he had made vast preparations. Baffled in this mighty project, he sought to break the spirit of the British nation by the bombing, first of London, and afterwards of our great cities. It has now been proved, to the admiration of the world, and of our friends in the United States, that this form of blackmail by murder and terrorism, so far from weakening the spirit of the British nation, has only roused it to a more intense and universal flame than was ever seen before in any modern community.

The whole British Empire has been proud of the Mother Country, and they long to be with us over here in even larger numbers. We have been deeply conscious of the love for us which has flowed from the Dominions of the Crown across the broad ocean spaces. *There* is the first of our war aims: to be worthy of that love, and to preserve it.

All through these dark winter months the enemy has had the power to drop three or four tons of bombs upon us for every ton we could send to Germany in return. We are arranging so that presently this will be rather the other way round; but, meanwhile, London and our big cities have had to stand their pounding. They remind me of the British squares at Waterloo. They are not squares of soldiers; they do not wear scarlet coats. They are just ordinary English, Scottish and Welsh folk–men, women and children–standing steadfastly together. But their spirit is the same, their glory is the same; and, in the end, their victory will be greater than far-famed Waterloo.

All honor to the Civil Defense Services of all kinds–emergency and regular, volunteer and professional–who have helped our people through this formidable ordeal, the like of which no civilized community has ever been called upon to undergo. If I mention only one of these services here, namely the Police, it is because many tributes have been paid already to the others. But the Police have been in it everywhere, all the time, and as a working woman wrote to me: "What gentlemen they are!". . .

Here then, in Libya, is the third considerable event upon which we may dwell with some satisfaction. It is just exactly two months ago, to a day, that I was waiting anxiously, but also eagerly, for the news of the great counter-stroke which had been planned against the Italian invaders of Egypt. The secret had been well kept. The preparations had been well made. But to leap across those seventy miles of desert, and attack an army of ten or eleven divisions, equipped with all the appliances of modern war, who had been fortifying themselves for three months–that was a most hazardous adventure.

When the brilliant decisive victory at Sidi Barrani, with its tens of thousands of prisoners, proved that we had quality, maneuvering power and weapons superior to the enemy, who had boasted so much of his virility and his military virtues, it was evident that all the other Italian forces in eastern Libya were in great danger. They could not easily beat a retreat along the coastal road without running the risk of being caught in the open of our armored divisions and brigades ranging far out into the desert in tremendous swoops and scoops. They had to expose themselves to being attacked piecemeal.

General Wavell–nay, all our leaders, and all their lithe, active, ardent men, British, Australian, Indian, in the Imperial Army–saw their opportunity. At that time I ventured to draw General Wavell's attention to the seventh chapter of the Gospel of St. Matthew, at the seventh verse, where, as you all know–or ought to know–it is written: "Ask, and it shall be given; seek, and ye shall find; knock, and it shall be opened unto you." The Army of the Nile has asked, and it was given; they sought, and they have found; they knocked, and it has been opened unto them. In barely eight weeks, by a campaign which will long be studied as a model of the military art, an advance of over 400 miles has been made. The whole Italian Army in the east of

Libya, which was reputed to exceed 150,000 men, has been captured or destroyed. The entire province of Cyrenaica–nearly as big as England and Wales–has been conquered. The unhappy Arab tribes, who have for thirty years suffered from the cruelty of Italian rule, carried in some cases to the point of methodical extermination, these Bedouin survivors have at last seen their oppressors in disorderly flight, or led off in endless droves as prisoners of war.

Egypt and the Suez Canal are safe, and the port, the base and the airfields of Benghazi constitute a strategic point of high consequence to the whole of the war in the Eastern Mediterranean. . . .

While these auspicious events have been carrying us stride by stride from what many people thought a forlorn position, and was certainly a very grave position in May and June, to one which permits us to speak with sober confidence of our power to discharge our duty, heavy though it be in the future–while this has been happening, a mighty tide of sympathy, of good will and of effective aid, has begun to flow across the Atlantic in support of the world cause which is at stake. Distinguished Americans have come over to see things here at the front, and to find out how the United States can help us best and soonest. In Mr. Hopkins, who has been my frequent companion during the last three weeks, we have the Envoy of the President, a President who has been newly re-elected to his august office. In Mr. Wendell Willkie we have welcomed the champion of the great Republican Party. We may be sure that they will both tell the truth about what they have seen over here, and more than that we do not ask. The rest we leave with good confidence to the judgment of the President, the Congress and the people of the United States.

I have been so very careful, since I have been Prime Minister, not to encourage false hopes or prophesy smooth and easy things, and yet the tale that I have to tell today is one which must justly and rightly give us cause for deep thankfulness, and also, I think, for strong comfort and even rejoicing. But now I must dwell upon the more serious, darker and more dangerous aspects of the vast scene of the war. We must all of us have been asking ourselves: What has that wicked man whose crime-stained regime and system are at bay and in the toils–what has he been preparing during these winter months? What new devilry is he planning? What new small country will he overrun or strike down? What fresh form of assault will he make upon our Island home and fortress; which–let there be no mistake about it–is all that stands between him and the dominion of the world?

We may be sure that the war is soon going to enter upon a phase of greater violence. Hitler's confederate, Mussolini, has reeled back in Albania, but the Nazis–having absorbed Hungary and driven Rumania into a frightful internal convulsion–are now already upon the Black Sea. A considerable Nazi German army and air force is being built up in Rumania, and its forward tentacles have already penetrated Bulgaria. With–we must suppose–the acquiescence of the Bulgarian Government, airfields are being occupied by German ground personnel numbering thousands, so as to enable the German air force to come into action from Bulgaria. Many preparations have been made for the movement of German troops into or through Bulgaria, and perhaps this southward movement has already begun.

We saw what happened last May in the Low Countries, how they hoped for the best; how they clung to their neutrality; how woefully they were deceived, overwhelmed, plundered, enslaved and since starved. We know how we and the French suffered when, at the last moment, at the urgent belated appeal of the King of the Belgians, we went to his aid. Of course, if all the Balkan people stood together and acted together, aided by Britain and Turkey, it would be many months before a German army and air force of sufficient strength to overcome them could be assembled in the southeast of Europe. And in those months much might happen. Much will certainly happen as American aid becomes effective, as our air power grows, as we become a well-armed nation, and as our armies in the East increase in strength. But nothing is more certain than that, if the countries of southeastern Europe allow themselves to be pulled to pieces one by one, they will share the fate of Denmark, Holland and Belgium. And none can tell how long it will be before the hour of their deliverance strikes. . . .

But after all, the fate of this war is going to be settled by what happens on the oceans, in the air, and–above all–in this Island. It seems now to be certain that the Government and people of the United States intend to supply us with all that is necessary for victory. In the last war the United States sent two million men across the Atlantic. But this is not a war of vast armies, firing immense masses of shells at one another. We do not need the gallant armies which are forming throughout the American Union. We do not need them this year, nor next year; nor any year that I can foresee. But we do need most urgently an immense and continuous supply of war materials and technical apparatus of all kinds. We need them here and we need to bring them here. We shall need a great mass of shipping in 1942, far more than we can build ourselves, if we are to maintain and augment our war effort in the West and in the East.

These facts are, of course, all well known to the enemy, and we must therefore expect that Herr Hitler will do his utmost to prey upon our shipping and to reduce the volume of American supplies entering these Islands. Having conquered France and Norway, his clutching fingers reach out on both sides of us into the ocean. I have never underrated this danger, and you know I have never concealed it from you. Therefore, I hope you will believe me when I say that I have complete confidence in the Royal Navy, aided by the Air Force of the Coastal Command, and that in one way or another I am sure they will be able to meet every changing phase of this truly mortal struggle, and that sustained by the courage of our merchant seamen, and of the dockers and workmen of all our ports, we shall outwit, outmaneuver, outfight and outlast the worst that the enemy's malice and ingenuity can contrive. . . .

I must again emphasize what General Dill has said, and what I pointed out myself last year. In order to win the war Hitler must destroy Great Britain. He may carry havoc into the Balkan States; he may tear great provinces out of Russia; he may march to the Caspian; he may march to the gates of India. All this will avail him nothing. It may spend his curse more widely throughout Europe and Asia, but it will not avert his doom. With every month that passes the many proud and once happy countries he is now holding down by brute force and vile intrigue are learning to hate the Prussian yoke and the Nazi name as nothing has ever been hated so fiercely and so widely among men before. And all the time, masters of the sea and air, the British Empire–nay, in a certain sense, the whole English-speaking world–will be on his track, bearing with them the swords of justice.

The other day, President Roosevelt gave his opponent in the late Presidential Election [Mr. Wendell Willkie] a letter of introduction to me, and in it he wrote out a verse, in his own handwriting, from Longfellow, which he said, "applies to you people as it does to us." Here is the verse:

. . . Sail on, O Ship of State!
Sail on, O Union, strong and great!
Humanity with all its fears,
With all the hopes of future years,
Is hanging breathless on thy fate!

What is the answer that I shall give, in your name, to this great man, the thrice-chosen head of a nation of a hundred and thirty millions? Here is the answer which I will give to President Roosevelt: Put your confidence in us. Give us your faith and your blessing, and, under Providence, all will be well.

We shall not fail or falter; we shall not weaken or tire. Neither the sudden shock of battle, nor the long-drawn trials of vigilance and exertion will wear us down. Give us the tools, and we will finish the job.

"A NEW MAGNA CARTA" (LEND-LEASE)
March 12, 1941

House of Commons

By the end of 1940 the dollar situation was acute; it was evident that cash purchases of vital American supplies could not continue. Churchill laid this problem before President Roosevelt in a long and carefully prepared letter on December 8, 1940, and what he subsequently called "the glorious concept of Lend-Lease" was initiated. It transformed the entire situation. The Act was not passed until March 1941, and in the meanwhile, desperate devices were used to raise dollars for essential purchases in the United States. But from this moment the British were able to order all they required without the necessity for immediate payment, and it may be judged a major turning point of the war, as important as any military victory.

The Lease-Lend Bill became law yesterday, when it received the signature of the President. I am sure the House would wish me to express on their behalf, and on behalf of the nation, our deep and respectful appreciation of this monument of generous and far-seeing statesmanship.

The most powerful democracy has, in effect, declared in solemn Statute that it will devote its overwhelming industrial and financial strength to ensuring the defeat of Nazism in order that nations, great and small, may live in security, tolerance and freedom. By so doing, the Government and people of the United States have in fact written a new Magna Carta, which not only has regard to the rights and laws upon which a healthy and advancing civilisation can alone be erected, but also proclaims by precept and example the duty of free men and free nations, wherever they may be, to share the responsibility and burden of enforcing them.

In the name of His Majesty's Government and speaking, I am sure, for Parliament and for the whole country, and indeed, in the name of all freedom-loving peoples, I offer to the United States our gratitude for her inspiring act of faith.

WELCOME TO MR. WINANT

March 18, 1941

Pilgrims' Society Luncheon, London

As a further indication of his determination to give all possible assistance to Britain, President Roosevelt replaced the defeatist Joseph P. Kennedy and appointed Mr. John G. Winant as Ambassador to Britain.

We are met here to-day under the strong impression and impact of the historic declaration made on Saturday last by the President of the United States, and where could there be a more fitting opportunity than at this gathering of the Pilgrims to greet the new American Ambassador for me to express on behalf of the British nation and Empire the sense of encouragement and fortification in our resolve which has come to us from across the ocean in those stirring, august, and fateful presidential words? You have come here, Mr. Winant, to a community which is being tried and proved before mankind and history, and tried and proved to a degree and on a scale and under conditions which have not previously been known to human experience.

We have here a free society, governed through a Parliament which rests upon universal suffrage and upon the public opinion of the whole nation. We are being subjected to daily assaults which, if not effectively resisted and repelled, would soon prove mortal. We have to call upon our whole people—men, women, and children alike—to stand up with composure and fortitude to the fire of the enemy, and to accept increasing privations while making increasing efforts. Nothing like this has ever been seen before.

We have our faults, and our social system has its faults, but we hope that, with God's help, we shall be able to prove for all time, or at any rate, for a long time, that a State or Commonwealth of Nations, founded on long-enjoyed freedom and steadily-evolved democracy, possesses amid the sharpest shocks the faculty of survival in a high and honourable and, indeed, in a glorious degree. At such a moment, and under such an ordeal, the words and the acts of the President and people of the United States come to us like a draught of life, and they tell us by an ocean-borne trumpet call that we are no longer alone.

We know that other hearts in millions and scores of millions beat with ours; that other voices proclaim the cause for which we strive; other strong hands wield the hammers and shape the weapons we need; other clear and gleaming eyes are fixed in hard conviction upon the tyrannies that must and shall be destroyed. We welcome you here, Mr. Winant, at the moment when a great battle in which your Government and nation are deeply interested is developing its full scope and severity. The Battle of the Atlantic must be won in a decisive manner. It must be won beyond all doubt if the declared policies of the Government and people of the United States are not to be forcibly frustrated. Not only German U-boats, but German battle cruisers have crossed to the American side of the Atlantic and have already sunk some of our independently-routed ships not sailing in convoy. They have sunk these ships as far west as the 42nd meridian of longitude.

Over here upon the approaches to our island an intense and unrelenting struggle is being waged to bring in the endless stream of munitions and food without which our war effort here and in the Middle East—for that shall not be relaxed—cannot be maintained. Our losses have risen for the time being, and we are applying our fullest strength and resource, and all the skill and science we can command, in order to meet this potentially mortal challenge. And not only, I must remind you, does our shipping suffer by the attacks of the enemy, but also the fertility of its importing power is reduced by many of the precautions and measures which we must take to master and dominate the attacks which are made upon us.

But our strength is growing every week. The American destroyers which reached us in the autumn and winter are increasingly coming into action. Our flotillas are growing in number. Our air power over the island and over the seas is growing fast. We are striking back with increasing effect. Only yesterday I received the news of the certain destruction of three German U-boats. Not since October 13, 1939, had I been cheered by such delectable tidings of a triple event.

It is my rule, as you know, not to conceal the gravity of the danger from our people, and therefore I have a right to be believed when I also proclaim our confidence that we shall overcome them. But anyone can see how bitter is the need of Hitler and his gang to cut the sea roads between Great Britain and the United States, and, having divided these mighty Powers, to destroy them one by one. Therefore we must regard this Battle of the Atlantic as one of the most momentous ever fought in all the annals of war. Therefore, Mr. Winant, you come to us at a grand turning-point in the world's history. We rejoice to have you with us in these days of storm and trial, because we know we have a friend and a faithful comrade who will "report us and our cause aright." But no one who has met you can doubt that you hold, and embody in a strong and intense degree, the convictions and ideals which in the name of American democracy President Roosevelt has proclaimed.

In the last few months we have had a succession of eminent American citizens visiting these storm-beaten shores and finding them unconquered and unconquerable—Mr. Hopkins, Mr. Willkie, Colonel Donovan, and now to-day we have here Mr. Harriman and yourself. I have dwelt with all these men in mind and spirit, and there is one thing I have discerned in them all—they would be ready to give their lives, nay, be proud to give their lives, rather than that the good cause should be trampled down and the darkness of barbarism again engulf mankind. Mr. Ambassador, you share our purpose, you will share our dangers, you will share our anxieties, you shall share our secrets, and the day will come when the British Empire and the United States will share together the solemn but splendid duties which are the crown of victory.

THE WAR SITUATION

April 9, 1941

House of Commons

On April 6 the German storm fell on Yugoslavia, and the balance of attention swung to the Balkans. It was necessary that the bulk of the German forces pass through Hungary; the German demand to do so was accepted despite the protests of the Premier, Count Teleki, who committed suicide on April 3 when he learned the Germans had crossed the Hungarian frontier.

The invasion opened with a devastating air attack on Belgrade; when it ended two days later, the greater part of the city had been destroyed.

Also on April 6, German armies attacked Greece, to which British forces had been despatched. On April 24, Greece surrendered.

Meanwhile, the British had won a signal victory over the Italian fleet off Cape Matapan in southern Greece on March 28. Three cruisers and two destroyers were sunk, and the battleship Vittorio Veneto *was crippled. The British suffered no losses and no casualties.*

In his speech to the House of Commons on April 9, Churchill also dealt with the situation in the North Atlantic, where the U-boat offensive caused deep concern in London. To this constant menace were added those of long-range aircraft and German surface raiders–notably the Scheer, Hipper, Scharnhorst *and* Gneisenau. *What Churchill called the "Battle of the Atlantic" had been joined, and at this stage the issue was very much in doubt. In the three months ending in May 1941 the British lost 99 ships from U-boats alone.*

[Extract] I beg to move,

> That this House on the occasion of the recent victories by sea, land and air in North Africa, Greece and the Mediterranean, records with gratitude its high appreciation of the services of all ranks of His Majesty's Forces in these brilliant operations, and also of those who by their labours and fortitude at home have furnished the means which have made these successes possible.

. . . Although we were most anxious to promote such a defensive front by which alone the peace of the Balkans could be maintained, we were determined not to urge the Greeks, already at grips with the Italians, upon any course contrary to their desires or judgment. The support which we can give to the peoples who are fighting, or are ready to fight, for freedom in the Balkans and in Turkey, is necessarily limited at the present time, and we did not wish to take the responsibility of pressing the Greeks to engage in a conflict with the new and terrible foe gathering upon their frontiers. However, on the first occasion when the Foreign Secretary and the Chief of the Imperial General Staff met the Greek King and Prime Minister, the Prime Minister declared spontaneously on behalf of the Government that Greece was resolved, at all costs, to defend her freedom and her native soil against any aggressor, and that even if they were left wholly unsupported by Great Britain, or by their neighbours Turkey and Yugoslavia, they would, nevertheless, remain faithful to their alliance with Great Britain, which came into play at the opening of the Italian invasion, and that they would fight to the death against both Italy and Germany.

This being so, it seemed that our duty was clear. We were bound in honour to give them all the aid in our power. If they were resolved to face the might and fury of the Huns, we had no doubts but that we should share their ordeal and that the soldiers of the British Empire must stand in the line with them. We were advised by our generals on the spot, the Chief of the Imperial General Staff, and Generals Wavell and Papagos, both victorious commanders-in-chief, that a sound military plan, giving good prospects of success, could be made. Of course, in all these matters there is hazard and in this case, as any one can see, without particularizing unduly, there was for us a double hazard. It remains to be seen how well those opposing risks and duties have been judged, but of this I am sure, that there is no less likely way of winning a war than to adhere pedantically to the maxim of "Safety first." Therefore, in the first weeks of March we entered into a military agreement with the Greeks, and the considerable movement of British and Imperial troops and supplies which has since developed began to take place. The House would very rightly reprove me if I entered into any details, or if while this widespread battle is going on I attempted in any way to discuss either the situation or its prospects.

I therefore turn to the story of Yugoslavia. This valiant, steadfast people whose history for centuries has been a struggle for life, and who owe their survival to their mountains and to their fighting qualities, made every endeavour to placate the Nazi monster. If they had made common cause with the Greeks when the Greeks, having been attacked by Italy, hurled back the invaders, the complete destruction of the Italian armies in Albania could certainly and swiftly have been achieved long before the German forces could have reached the theatre of war. And even in January and February of this year, this extraordinary military opportunity was still open. But the Government of Prince Paul, untaught by the fate of so many of the smaller countries of Europe, not only observed the strictest neutrality and refused even to enter into effective Staff conversations with Greece or with Turkey or with us, but hugged the delusion that they could preserve their independence by patching up some sort of pact or compromise with Hitler. Once again we saw the odious German poisoning technique employed. In this case, however, it was to the Government rather than to the nation that the doses and the inoculations were administered. The process was not hurried. Why should it have been? All the time the German armies and air force were massing in Bulgaria. From a few handfuls of tourists, admiring the beauty of the Bulgarian landscape in the wintry weather, the German forces grew to 7, 12, 20, and finally to 25 divisions. Presently, the weak and unfortunate Prince and afterwards his Ministers, were summoned, like others before them, to Herr Hitler's footstool, and a pact was signed which would have given Germany complete control not only over the body but over the soul of the Slav nation. Then at last the people of Yugoslavia saw their peril, and with a universal spasm of revolt and national resurgence very similar to that which in 1808 convulsed and glorified the people of Spain, they swept from power those who were leading them into a shameful tutelage, and resolved at the eleventh hour to guard their freedom and their honour with their lives. All this happened only a fortnight ago.

A boa constrictor who had already covered his prey with his foul saliva and then had it suddenly wrested from his coils, would be in an amiable mood compared with Hitler, Goering, Ribbentrop and the rest of the Nazi gang when they experienced this bitter disappointment. A frightful vengeance was vowed against the Southern Slavs. Rapid, perhaps hurried, redispositions were made of the German forces and German diplomacy. Hungary was offered large territorial gains to become the accomplice in the assault upon a friendly neighbour with whom she had just signed a solemn pact of friendship and non-aggression. Count Teleki preferred to take his own life rather than join in such a deed of shame. A heavy forward movement of the German armies already gathered in and dominating Austria was set in motion through Hungary to the northern frontier of Yugoslavia. A ferocious howl of hatred from the supreme miscreant was the signal for the actual invasion. The open city of Belgrade was laid in ashes, and at the same time a tremendous drive by the German armoured forces which had been so improvidently allowed to gather in Bulgaria was launched westward into Southern Serbia. And as it was no longer worth while to keep up the farce of love for Greece, other powerful forces rolled forward into Greece, where they were at once unflinchingly encountered, and have already sustained more than one bloody repulse at the hands of that heroic Army. The British and Imperial troops have not up to the present been engaged. Further than this I cannot, at the moment. go. Further than this I cannot attempt to carry the tale. . . .

But, after all, everything turns upon the Battle of the Atlantic, which is proceeding with growing intensity on both sides. Our losses in ships and tonnage are very heavy, and vast as are the shipping resources which we control, these losses could not continue indefinitely without seriously affecting our war effort and our means of subsistence. It is no answer to say that we have inflicted upon the Germans and Italians a far higher proportion of loss compared with the scale of their merchant tonnage and the fleeting opportunities they offer us, than they have upon us, with our world-wide traffic continually maintained. We have in fact sunk, captured or seen scuttled over 2,300,000 tons of German and Italian shipping. But we have lost ourselves since the beginning of the war nearly 4,000,000 tons of British tonnage. As against that, we have gained under the British flag over 3,000,000 of foreign or newly-constructed tonnage, not counting the considerable foreign tonnage which has also come under our control. Therefore, at the moment our enormous fleets sail the seas without any serious or obvious diminution, as far as the number of ships is concerned.

But what is to happen in the future if these losses continue at the present rate? Where are we to find another three or four million tons to fill the gap which is being created and carry us on through 1942? We are building merchant ships upon a very considerable scale and to the utmost of our ability, having regard to other calls upon our labour. We are also making a most strenuous effort to make ready for sea the large number of vessels which have been damaged by the enemy and the still larger number which have been damaged by the winter gales. We are doing our utmost to accelerate the turn-round of our ships, remembering—this is a striking figure—that even ten days' saving on turn-round in our immense fleets is equal to a reinforcement of 5,000,000 tons of imports in a single year. I can assure the House that all the energy and contrivance of which we are capable have been and will continue to be devoted to these purposes, and that we are already conscious of substantial results. But, when all is said and done, the only way in which we can get through the year 1942 without a very sensible contraction of our war effort is by another gigantic building of merchant ships in the United States similar to that prodigy of output accomplished by the Americans in 1918. All this has been in train in the United States for many months past. There has now been a very large extension of the programmes, and we have the assurance that several millions of tons of new-built American shipping will be available for the common struggle during the course of the next year. Here, then, is the assurance upon which we may count for the staying power without which it will not be possible to save the world from the criminals who assail its future.

The Battle of the Atlantic must, however, be won, not only in the factories and shipyards, but upon the blue water. I am confident that we shall succeed in coping with the air attacks which are made upon the shipping in the Western and North-Western approaches. I hope that eventually the inhabitants of the sister Island may realise that it is as much in their interest as in ours that their ports and airfields should be available for the naval and air forces which must operate ever farther into the Atlantic. But, while I am hopeful that we shall gain mastery over the air attack upon our shipping, the U-boats and the surface raiders, ranging ever farther to the Westward, ever nearer to the shores of the United States, constitute a menace which must be overcome if the life of Britain is not to be endangered, and if the purposes to which the Government and the people of the United States have devoted themselves are not to be frustrated. We shall, of course, make every effort in our power. The defeat of the U-boats and of the surface raiders has been proven to be entirely a question of adequate escorts for our convoys. It would be indeed disastrous if the great masses of weapons, munitions and instruments of war of all kinds, made with the toil and skill of American hands, at the cost of the United States, and loaned to us under the Aid to Britain Act, were to sink into the depths of the ocean and never reach the hard-pressed fighting line. That would be a result lamentable to us over here, and I cannot believe that it would be found acceptable to the proud and resolute people in the United States. Indeed, I am now authorized to state that ten United States Revenue cutters, fast vessels of about 2,000 tons displacement, with a fine armament and a very wide range of endurance, have already been placed at our disposal by the United States Government and will soon be in action. These vessels, originally designed to enforce prohibition, will now serve an even higher purpose.

It is, of course, very hazardous to try to forecast in what direction or directions

Hitler will employ his military machine in the present year. He may at any time attempt the invasion of this Island. That is an ordeal from which we shall not shrink. At the present time he is driving south and south-east through the Balkans, and at any moment he may turn upon Turkey. But there are many signs which point to a Nazi attempt to secure the granary of the Ukraine, and the oilfields of the Caucasus and thus to gain the resources wherewith to wear down the English-speaking world. All this is speculation. I will say only one thing more. Once we have gained the Battle of the Atlantic and are certain of the constant flow of American supplies which is being prepared for us, then, however far Hitler may go, or whatever new millions and scores of millions he may lap in misery, he may be sure that, armed with the sword of retributive justice, we shall be on his track.

"WESTWARD, LOOK"

April 27, 1941

Broadcast, London

The situation in Greece at this time was hopeless, and the only chance of resistance in Yugoslavia rested with guerrilla bands who had escaped into the mountains from the triumphant German forces. The British fought a determined rearguard action, and the evacuation of over 50,000 British and Dominion troops began on April 24. London was under attack from the air; the Battle of the Atlantic was going badly. At this dark moment, Churchill broadcast to the nation.

[Extract] I was asked last week whether I was aware of some uneasiness which it was said existed in the country on account of the gravity, as it was described, of the war situation. So I thought it would be a good thing to go and see for myself what this "uneasiness" amounted to, and I went to some of our great cities and seaports which had been most heavily bombed, and to some of the places where the poorest people had got it worst. I have come back not only reassured, but refreshed. To leave the offices in Whitehall with their ceaseless hum of activity and stress, and to go out to the front, by which I mean the streets and wharves of London or Liverpool, Manchester, Cardiff, Swansea or Bristol, is like going out of a hothouse on to the bridge of a fighting ship. It is a tonic which I should recommend any who are suffering from fretfulness to take in strong doses when they have need of it.

It is quite true that I have seen many painful scenes of havoc, and of fine buildings and acres of cottage homes blasted into rubble-heaps of ruin But it is just in those very places where the malice of the savage enemy has done its worst, and where the ordeal of the men, women and children has been most severe, that I found their morale most high and splendid. Indeed, I felt encompassed by an exaltation of spirit in the people which seemed to lift mankind and its troubles above the level of material facts into that joyous serenity we think belongs to a better world than this.

Of their kindness to me I cannot speak, because I have never sought it or dreamed of it, and can never deserve it. I can only assure you that I and my colleagues, or comrades rather—for that is what they are—will toil with every scrap of life and strength, according to the lights that are granted to us, not to fail these people or be wholly unworthy of their faithful and generous regard. The British nation is stirred and moved as it has never been at any time in its long, eventful, famous history, and it is no hackneyed trope of speech to say that they mean to conquer or to die.

What a triumph the life of these battered cities is, over the worst that fire and bomb can do. What a vindication of the civilized and decent way of living we have been trying to work for and work towards in our Island. What a proof of the virtues of free institutions. What a test of the quality of our local authorities, and of institutions and customs and societies so steadily built. This ordeal by fire has even in a certain sense exhilarated the manhood and womanhood of Britain. The sublime but also terrible and sombre experiences and emotions of the battlefield which for centuries had been reserved for the soldiers and sailors, are now shared, for good or ill, by the entire population. All are proud to be under the fire of the enemy. Old men, little children, the crippled veterans of former wars, aged women, the ordinary hard-pressed citizen or subject of the King, as he likes to call himself, the sturdy workmen who swing the hammers or load the ships; skilful craftsmen; the members of every kind of A. R. P. service, are proud to feel that they stand in the line together with our fighting men, when one of the greatest of causes is being fought out, as fought out it will be, to the end. This is indeed the grand heroic period of our history, and the light of glory shines on all.

You may imagine how deeply I feel my own responsibility to all these people; my responsibility to bear my part in bringing them safely out of this long, stern, scowling valley through which we are marching, and not to demand from them their sacrifices and exertions in vain. . . .

During the last year we have gained by our bearing and conduct a potent hold upon the sentiments of the people of the United States. Never, never in our history, have we been held in such admiration and regard across the Atlantic Ocean. In that great Republic, now in much travail and stress of soul, it is customary to use all the many valid, solid arguments about American interests and American safety, which depend upon the destruction of Hitler and his foul gang and even fouler doctrines. But in the long run—believe me, for I know—the action of the United States will be dictated, not by methodical calculations of profit and loss, but by moral sentiment, and by that gleaming flash of resolve which lifts the hearts of men and nations, and springs from the spiritual foundations of human life itself. . . .

I turn aside from the stony path we have to tread, to indulge a moment of lighter relief. I daresay you have read in the newspapers that, by a special proclamation, the Italian Dictator has congratulated the Italian army in Albania on the glorious laurels they have gained by their victory over the Greeks. Here surely is the world's record in the domain of the ridiculous and the contemptible. This whipped jackal, Mussolini, who to save his own skin has made all Italy a vassal state of Hitler's Empire, comes frisking up at the side of the German tiger with yelpings not only of appetite—that can be understood—but even of triumph. Different things strike different people in different ways. But I am sure there are a great many millions in the British Empire and in the United States, who will find a new object in life in making sure that when we come to the final reckoning this absurd impostor will be abandoned to public justice and universal scorn.

While these grievous events were taking place in the Balkan Peninsula and in Greece, our forces in Libya have sustained a vexatious and damaging defeat. The Germans advanced sooner and in greater strength than we or our Generals expected. The bulk of our armoured troops, which had played such a decisive part in beating the Italians, had to be refitted, and the single armoured brigade which had been judged sufficient to hold the frontier till about the middle of May was worsted and its vehicles largely destroyed by a somewhat stronger German armoured force. Our Infantry, which had not exceeded one division, had to fall back upon the very large Imperial armies that have been assembled and can be nourished and maintained in the fertile delta of the Nile.

Tobruk—the fortress of Tobruk—which flanks any German advance on Egypt, we hold strongly. There we have repulsed many attacks, causing the enemy heavy losses and taking many prisoners. That is how the matter stands in Egypt and on the Libyan front.

We must now expect the war in the Mediterranean on the sea, in the desert, and above all in the air, to become very fierce, varied and widespread. We had cleaned the Italians out of Cyrenaica, and it now lies with us to purge that province of the Germans. That will be a harder task, and we cannot expect to do it at once. You know I never try to make out that defeats are victories. I have never underrated the German as a warrior. Indeed I told you a month ago that the swift, unbroken course of victories which we had gained over the Italians could not possibly continue, and that misfortunes must be expected. There is only one thing certain about war, that it is full of disappointments and also full of mistakes. It remains to be seen, however, whether it is the Germans who have made the mistake in trampling down the Balkan States and in making a river of blood and hate between themselves and the Greek and Yugoslav peoples. It remains also to be seen whether they have made a mistake in their attempt to invade Egypt with the forces and means of supply which they have now got. Taught by experience, I make it a rule not to prophesy about battles which have yet to be fought out. This, however, I will venture to say, that I should be very sorry to see the tasks of the combatants in the Middle East exchanged, and that General Wavell's armies should be in the position of the German invaders. That is only a personal opinion, and I can well understand you may take a different view. It is certain that fresh dangers besides those which threaten Egypt may come upon us in the Mediterranean. The war may spread to Spain and Morocco. It may spread eastward to Turkey and Russia. The Huns may lay their hands for a time upon the granaries of the Ukraine and the oil-wells of the Caucasus. They may dominate the Black Sea. They may dominate the Caspian. Who can tell? We shall do our best to meet them and fight them wherever they go. But there is one thing which is certain. There is one thing which rises out of the vast welter which is sure and solid, and which no one in his senses can mistake. Hitler cannot find safety from avenging justice in the East, in the Middle East, or in the Far East. In order to win this war, he must either conquer this Island by invasion, or he must cut the ocean life-line which joins us to the United States.

Let us look into these alternatives, if you will bear with me for a few minutes longer. When I spoke to you last, early in February, many people believed the Nazi boastings that the invasion of Britain was about to begin. It has not begun yet, and with every week that passes we grow stronger on the sea, in the air, and in the numbers, quality, training and equipment of the great Armies that now guard our Island. When I compare the position at home as it is to-day with what it was in the summer of last year, even after making allowance for a much more elaborate mechanical preparation on the part of the enemy, I feel that we have very much to be thankful for, and I believe that provided our exertions and our vigilance are not relaxed even for a moment, we may be confident that we shall give a very good account of ourselves. More than that it would be boastful to say. Less than that it would be foolish to believe.

But how about our life-line across the Atlantic? What is to happen if so many of our merchant ships are sunk that we cannot bring in the food we need to nourish our brave people? What if the supplies of war materials and war weapons which the United States are seeking to send us in such enormous quantities should in large part be sunk on the way? What is to happen then? In February, as you may remember, that bad man in one of his raving outbursts threatened us with a terrifying increase in the numbers and activities of his U-boats and in his air attack—not only on our Island but, thanks to his use of French and Norwegian harbours, and thanks to the denial to us of the Irish bases—upon our shipping far out into the Atlantic. We have taken and are taking all possible measures to meet this deadly attack, and we are now fighting against it with might and main. That is what is called the Battle of the Atlantic, which in order to survive we have got to win on salt water just as decisively as we had to win the Battle of Britain last August and September in the air.

Wonderful exertions have been made by our Navy and Air Force; by the hundreds of mine-sweeping vessels which with their marvellous appliances keep our ports clear in spite of all the enemy can do; by the men who build and repair our immense fleets of merchant ships; by the men who load and unload them; and need I say by the officers and men of the Merchant Navy who go out in all weathers and in the teeth of all dangers to fight for the life of their native land and for a cause they comprehend and serve. Still, when you think how easy it is to sink ships at sea and how hard it is to build them and protect them, and when you remember that we have never less than two thousand ships afloat and three or four hundred in the danger zone; when you think of the great armies we are maintaining and reinforcing in the East, and of the world-wide traffic we have to carry on—when you remember all this, can you wonder that it is the Battle of the Atlantic which holds the first place in the thoughts of those upon whom rests the responsibility for procuring the victory?

It was therefore with indescribable relief that I learned of the tremendous decisions lately taken by the President and people of the United States. The American Fleet and flying boats have been ordered to patrol the wide waters of the Western Hemisphere, and to warn the peaceful shipping of all nations outside the combat zone of the presence of lurking U-boats or raiding cruisers belonging to the two aggressor nations. We British shall therefore be able to concentrate our protecting forces far more upon the routes nearer home, and to take a far heavier toll of the U-boats there. I have felt for some time that something like this was bound to happen. The President and Congress of the United States, having newly fortified themselves by contact with their electors, have solemnly pledged their aid to Britain in this war because they deem our cause just, and because they know their own interests and safety would be endangered if we were destroyed. They are taxing themselves heavily. They have passed great legislation. They have turned a large part of their gigantic industry to making the munitions which we need. They have even given us or lent us valuable weapons of their own. I could not believe that they would allow the high purposes to which they have set themselves to be frustrated and the products of their skill and labour sunk to the bottom of the sea. U-boat warfare as conducted by Germany is entirely contrary to international agreements freely subscribed to by Germany only a few years ago. There is no effective blockade, but only a merciless murder and marauding over wide, indiscriminate areas utterly beyond the control of the German seapower. When I said ten weeks ago: "Give us the tools and we will finish the job," I meant, *give* them to us: put them within our reach—and that is what it now seems the Americans are going to do. And that is why I feel a very strong conviction that though the Battle of the Atlantic will be long and hard, and its issue is by no means yet determined, it has entered upon a more grim but at the same time a far more favourable phase. When you come to think of it, the United States are very closely bound up with us now, and have engaged themselves deeply in giving us moral, material, and, within the limits I have mentioned, naval support.

It is worth while therefore to take a look on both sides of the ocean at the forces which are facing each other in this awful struggle, from which there can be no drawing back. No prudent and far-seeing man can doubt that the eventual and total defeat of Hitler and Mussolini is certain, in view of the respective declared resolves of the British and American democracies. There are less than seventy million malignant Huns—some of whom are curable and others killable—many of whom are already engaged in holding down Austrians, Czechs, Poles, French, and the many other ancient races they now bully and pillage. The peoples of the British Empire and of the United States number nearly two hundred millions in their homelands and in the British Dominions alone. They possess the unchallengeable command of the oceans, and will soon obtain decisive superiority in the air. They have more wealth, more technical resources, and they make more steel, than the whole of the rest of the world put together. They are determined that the cause of freedom shall not be trampled down, nor the tide of world progress turned backwards, by the criminal Dictators.

While therefore we naturally view with sorrow and anxiety much that is happening in Europe and in Africa, and may happen in Asia, we must not lose our sense of proportion and thus become discouraged or alarmed. When we face with a steady eye the difficulties which lie before us, we may derive new confidence from remembering those we have already overcome. Nothing that is happening now is comparable in gravity with the dangers through which we passed last year. Nothing that can happen in the East is comparable with what is happening in the West.

Last time I spoke to you I quoted the lines of Longfellow which President Roosevelt had written out for me in his own hand. I have some other lines which are less well known but which seem apt and appropriate to our fortunes to-night, and I believe they will be so judged wherever the English language is spoken or the flag of freedom flies:

For while the tired waves, vainly breaking,
Seem here no painful inch to gain,
Far back, through creeks and inlets making,
Comes silent, flooding in, the main.
And not by eastern windows only,
When daylight comes, comes in the light;
In front the sun climbs slow, how slowly!
But westward, look, the land is bright.

THE WAR SITUATION

May 7, 1941

House of Commons

New German forces in North Africa under Field Marshal Erwin Rommel completely changed the balance of a situation which had been steadily improving. Rommel arrived on February 12, and launched his first attack on March 31. On April 3 British troops evacuated Benghazi in retreat. Tobruk was invested, and Churchill realized that "evidently there was a severe defeat." The weakening of the British forces by the Greek expedition now proved decisive. On April 21 Tripoli was heavily bombarded, but the fact that the British armour had been severely defeated, and the news of the imminent arrival of another German armoured division, emphasised the peril of the British position. Churchill decided that the huge risk must be taken of sending tanks to General Wavell through the Mediterranean, rather than suffering the long delays of the Cape route. Operation "Tiger," heavily protected, was successful–only two transports being lost. Churchill was eager to repeat the operation, but was dissuaded. The next convoy did not reach Suez until July 15.

In the debate on May 7 Lloyd George criticised the character of the Government and accused Churchill of being surrounded by "yes-men." Churchill's comparison of Lloyd George to Pétain was deeply resented.

[Extract] . . . I must, however, say that I did not think Mr. Lloyd George's speech was particularly helpful at a period of what he himself called discouragement and disheartenment. It was not the sort of speech which one would have expected from the great war leader of former days, who was accustomed to brush aside despondency and alarm, and push on irresistibly towards the final goal. It was the sort of speech with which, I imagine, the illustrious and venerable Marshal Pétain might well have enlivened the closing days of M. Reynaud's Cabinet. But in one respect I am grateful to my right hon. Friend for the note which he struck, because if anything could make it clearer that we ought to close our Debate by a Vote of Confidence, it is the kind of speech which he delivered, and the kind of speeches we have heard from some of the ablest and most eminent Members of the House. I think the Government were right to put down a Motion of Confidence, because after our reverses and disappointments in the field, His Majesty's Government have a right to know where they stand with the House of Commons, and where the House of Commons stands with the country. Still more is this knowledge important for the sake of foreign nations, especially nations which are balancing their policy at the present time, and who ought to be left in no doubt about the stability or otherwise of this resolved and obstinate war Government. Questions are asked, conversations take place in the Lobbies, paragraphs are written in the political columns of the newspapers, and before you know where you are, you hear in all the Embassies with which we are in relation queries, "Will the Government last?–Are they going to break up?–Will there be a change of administration and a change of policy?"

I think it is essential, considering the tremendous issues which are at stake, and, not to exaggerate, the frightful risks we are all going to run, and are running, that we should have certitude on these matters. In enemy countries they take a lively interest in our proceedings, and I flatter myself that high hopes are entertained that all will not go well with His Majesty's present advisers. The only way in which these doubts can be removed and these expectations disappointed is by a full Debate followed by a Division, and the Government are entitled to ask that such a Vote shall express itself in unmistakable terms. I see that one of the newspapers, which is described as a supporter of the Government, and which supports us by being the most active in keeping us up to the mark–like the Noble Lord the Member for Horsham (Earl Winterton), now relieved from all necessity of keeping himself up to the mark–has deplored the fact of this Motion of Confidence being proposed, because such a procedure might lead some Members to make speeches in favour of the Government, whereas it would be much more useful if the Debate consisted entirely of informative criticism. I am not one, and I should be the last, unduly to resent unfair criticism, or even fair criticism, which is so much more searching. I have been a critic myself–I cannot at all see how I should have stood the test of being a mere spectator in the drama which is now passing. But there is a kind of criticism which is a little irritating. It is like that of a bystander who, when he sees a team of horses dragging a heavy wagon painfully up a hill, cuts a switch from the fence, and there are many switches, and belabours them lustily. He may well be animated by a benevolent purpose, and who shall say the horses may not benefit from his efforts, and the wagon get quicker to the top of the hill?

I think that it would be a pity if this important and critical Debate at this moment which my right hon. Friend describes as disheartening and discouraging, consisted solely of critical and condemnatory speeches, because, apart from the inartistic monotony, it would tend to give a distorted impression to many important and interested foreign observers who are not very well acquainted with our Parliamentary or political affairs. Therefore I ask the House for a Vote of Confidence. I hope that those, if such there be, who sincerely in their hearts believe that we are not doing our best and that they could do much better, I hope that they will carry their opinion to its logical and ultimate conclusion in the Lobby. Here I must point out, only for the benefit of foreign countries, that they would run no risk in doing so. They are answerable only to their consciences and to their constituents. It is a free Parliament in a free country. We have succeeded in maintaining, under difficulties which are unprecedented, and in dangers which, in some cases, might well be mortal, the whole process and reality of Parliamentary institutions. I am proud of this. It is one of the things for which we are fighting. Moreover, I cannot imagine that any man would want to bear, or consent to bear, the kind of burden which falls upon the principal Ministers in the Government, or upon the head of the Government in this terrible war, unless he were sustained, and continually sustained, by strong convinced support, not only of the House of Commons, but of the nation to which the House of Commons is itself responsible.

It is very natural that the House should not be entirely satisfied with the recent turn of events in the Middle East, and that some Members should be acutely disappointed that we have not been able to defend Greece successfully against the Italian or German armies, and that we should have been unable to keep or extend our conquests in Libya. This sudden darkening of the landscape, after we had been cheered by a long succession of victories over the Italians, is particularly painful. For myself, I must confess that I watched the fate of Greece, after her repulse of the Italian invader, with agony. The only relief I feel is that everything in human power was done by us and that our honour as a nation is clear. If anything could add a pang to this emotion, it would be the knowledge we had of the approaching and impending outrage, with so little power to avert from this heroic and famous people a fate so hideous and so undeserved. . . .

My right hon. Friend the Member for Carnarvon Boroughs (Mr. Lloyd George) made his usual criticisms about the composition and character of the Government, of the war control and of the War Cabinet, and the House is entitled to know, has a right to know, who are responsible for the conduct of the war. The War Cabinet consists of eight members, five of whom have no regular Department, and three of whom represent the main organisms of the State, to wit, Foreign Affairs, Finance and Labour, which in their different ways come into every great question that has to be settled. That is the body which gives its broad sanction to the main policy and conduct of the war. Under their authority, the Chiefs of Staff of the three Services sit each day together, and I, as Prime Minister and Minister of Defence, convene them and preside over them when I think it necessary, inviting, when business requires it, the three Service Ministers. All large issues of military policy are brought before the Defence Committee, which has for several months consisted of the three Chiefs of Staff the three Service Ministers, and four members of the War Cabinet, namely, myself, the Lord Privy Seal, who has no Department, the Foreign Secretary, and Lord Beaverbrook. This is the body, this is the machine; it works easily and flexibly at the present time, and I do not propose to make any changes in it until further advised.

My right hon. Friend spoke of the great importance of my being surrounded by people who would stand up to me and say, "No, No, No." Why, good gracious, has he no idea how strong the negative principle is in the constitution and working of the British war-making machine? The difficulty is not, I assure him, to have more brakes put on the wheels; the difficulty is to get more impetus and speed behind it. At one moment we are asked to emulate the Germans in their audacity and vigour, and the next moment the Prime Minister is to be assisted by being surrounded by a number of "No-men" to resist me at every point and prevent me from making anything in the nature of a speedy, rapid and, above all, positive constructive decision. . . .

I ask you to witness, Mr. Speaker, that I have never promised anything or offered anything but blood, tears, toil and sweat, to which I will now add our fair share of mistakes, shortcomings and disappointments, and also that this may go on for a very long time, at the end of which I firmly believe–though it is not a promise or a guarantee, only a profession of faith–that there will be complete, absolute and final victory.

Now–I think there is just time for it–we come to the Battle of the Atlantic. It is a mistake to say that the Battle of the Atlantic is won. First of all, how is it won? It would be quite easy to reduce our losses at sea to vanishing point by the simple expedient of keeping our ships in harbour, or to reduce them markedly by overloading our ships with precautions. The Admiralty, on whom the first burden rests, naturally measure their struggle by the ships which they bring safely into port; but that is not the test by which those responsible for the highest direction of the country have to be guided. Our test is the number of tons of imports brought into this island in a given quarter or a given year. At present we are maintaining great traffics, although with heavy losses. We try to meet these losses by building new ships, repairing damaged ships, by repairing them more speedily, and by acceleration of the turn-round of our ships in our ports and in foreign ports. We have made great progress in these spheres since the beginning of the year, but there is much more to do in that field.

With the continued flow of assistance which has already been given to us by the United States, and promised to us, we can probably maintain our minimum essential traffic during 1941. As for 1942, we must look for an immense construction of merchant ships by the United States. This is already in full swing, and since I last mentioned this subject to the House a month ago, I have received assurances that the construction of merchant vessels by the United States, added to our own large programme of new building and repair, should see us through the year of 1942. It may be that 1943, if ever we have to endure it as a year of war, will present easier problems. The United States patrol, announced by President Roosevelt, on which the American Navy and Air Force are already engaged, takes a very considerable part of the Atlantic Ocean, in a certain degree, off our hands; but we need a good deal more help, and I expect we shall get a good deal more help in a great many ways. In fact, it has been declared that we are to have all the help that is necessary; but here I speak with very great caution, for it is not for a British Minister to forecast, still less to appear to prescribe, the policy of the United States. So far in our relations with that great Republic, which began so well under the auspices of Lord Lothian, I do not think we have made any serious mistakes. Neither by boasting nor by begging have we offended them. When a mighty democracy of 130,000,000 gets on the move one can only await the full deployment of these vast psychological manifestations and their translation into the physical field. Anyone can see Hitler's fear of the United States from the fact that he has not long ago declared war upon them.

In some quarters of the House, or at any rate among some Members, there is a very acute realization of the gravity of our problems and of our dangers. I have never underrated them. I feel we are fighting for life and survival from day to day and from hour to hour. But, believe me, Herr Hitler has his problems, too, and if we only remain united and strive our utmost to increase our exertions, and work like one great family, standing together and helping each other, as 5,000,000 families in Britain are doing to-day under the fire of the enemy, I cannot conceive how anyone can doubt that victory will crown the good cause we serve. Government and Parliament alike have to be worthy of the undaunted and unconquerable people who give us their trust and who give their country their all.

It is a year almost to a day since, in the crash of the disastrous Battle of France, His Majesty's present Administration was formed. Men of all parties, duly authorized by their parties, joined hands together to fight this business to the end. That was a dark hour, and little did we know what storms and perils lay before us, and little did Herr Hitler know, when in June, 1940, he received the total capitulation of France and when he expected to be master of all Europe in a few weeks and the world in a few years, that ten months later, in May, 1941, he would be appealing to the much-tried German people to prepare themselves for the war of 1942. When I look back on the perils which have been overcome, upon the great mountain waves through which the gallant ship has driven, when I remember all that has gone wrong, and remember also all that has gone right, I feel sure we have no need to fear the tempest. Let it roar, and let it rage. We shall come through.

[Editor's Note: The vote of confidence in the Government was then carried by 447 to 3. This was Churchill's last speech in the old House of Commons, which was totally destroyed in an air raid three days later.]

"OUR SOLID, STUBBORN STRENGTH"

June 12, 1941

Dominion High Commissioners and Allied Countries' Ministers Conference, London

On the night of May 10 London suffered the worst attack of the winter Blitz. Although not realized until later, this was in fact the last blow of the aerial attack on London until 1944 because the bulk of the Luftwaffe was being moved to the East for the forthcoming invasion of Russia. The Chamber of the House of Commons was gutted in the raid. After a brief interlude in Church House, Westminster, the House of Commons met in the Lords; the Lords took over the Robing Room in the Palace of Westminster. These arrangements lasted until the rebuilt House of Commons was opened in 1951.

Britain's defeat in Greece was followed by an equally grave development in Crete. Much controversy still flows over the British decision to defend the island, and the manner in which the defence was undertaken.

The battle opened on the morning of May 20, with a large German parachute landing at Maleme airfield. Other parachute landings followed.

Churchill's second statement on May 20 contained the allegation that German soldiers had landed in New Zealand uniforms; this was incorrect, as Churchill made clear in a June 10 statement.

Heavy fighting followed the German landings in Crete, and German possession of the vital aerodrome at Maleme enabled reinforcements to be landed by transport aircraft. British warships, although subjected to incessant air attack, inflicted heavy losses on German troop transports.

*The battle for Crete continued to be fiercely contested as the Germans steadily pursued their advantage. Their dominance of the air proved decisive, and by the evening of May 26 it was clear to the local British commanders that evacuation was inevitable. "We had to face once again the bitter and dismal task of an evacuation and the certainty of heavy losses" (*The Grand Alliance, *297).*

At this gloomy moment public attention was dramatically diverted by the hunt for the battleship Bismarck. *This magnificent ship, accompanied by the cruiser* Prinz Eugen, *had sailed from Bergen in southwest Norway and sunk the battle cruiser* Hood *in the Denmark Strait between Iceland and Greenland on May 24. The fastest capital ship in the world, the* Hood *had a glamour which fully merited Churchill's description of her as "one of our most cherished possessions."*

The full resources of the Home Fleet were extended to meet this peril. The ensuing pursuit was recounted by Churchill on May 27 to the House of Commons, still meeting in Church House, Westminster. Just after he sat down, he received notice that the Bismarck, *crippled by a gallant attack by aircraft from the carrier* Ark Royal, *had been sunk. Of the reaction of the House to this news, Churchill subsequently wrote: "They seemed content."*

In the twenty-second month of the war against Nazism we meet here in this old Palace of St. James's, itself not unscarred by the fire of the enemy, in order to proclaim the high purposes and resolves of the lawful constitutional Governments of Europe whose countries have been overrun; and we meet here also to cheer the hopes of free men and free peoples throughout the world. Here before us on the table lie the title-deeds of ten nations or States whose soil has been invaded and polluted, and whose men, women, and children lie prostrate or writhing under the Hitler yoke. But here also, duly authorized by the Parliament and democracy of Britain, are gathered the servants of the ancient British Monarchy and the accredited representatives of the British Dominions beyond the seas, of Canada, Australia, New Zealand, and South Africa, of the Empire of India, of Burma, and of our Colonies in every quarter of the globe. They have drawn their swords in this cause. They will never let them fall till life is gone or victory is won. Here we meet, while from across the Atlantic Ocean the hammers and lathes of the United States signal in a rising hum their message of encouragement and their promise of swift and ever-growing aid.

What tragedies, what horrors, what crimes have Hitler and all that Hitler stands for brought upon Europe and the world! The ruins of Warsaw, of Rotterdam, of Belgrade are monuments which will long recall to future generations the outrage of the unopposed air-bombing applied with calculated scientific cruelty to helpless populations. Here in London and throughout the cities of our Island, and in Ireland, there may also be seen the marks of devastation. They are being repaid, and presently they will be more than repaid.

But far worse than these visible injuries is the misery of the conquered peoples. We see them hounded, terrorized, exploited. Their manhood by the million is forced to work under conditions indistinguishable in many cases from actual slavery. Their goods and chattels are pillaged, or filched for worthless money. Their homes, their daily life are pried into and spied upon by the all-pervading system of secret political police which, having reduced the Germans themselves to abject docility, now stalk the streets and byways of a dozen lands. Their religious faiths are affronted, persecuted, or oppressed in the interests of a fantastic paganism devised to perpetuate the worship and sustain the tyranny of one abominable creature. Their traditions, their culture, their laws, their institutions, social and political alike, are suppressed by force or undermined by subtle, coldly-planned intrigue.

The prisons of the Continent no longer suffice. The concentration camps are overcrowded. Every dawn the German volleys crack. Czechs, Poles, Dutchmen, Norwegians, Yugoslavs and Greeks, Frenchmen, Belgians, Luxembourgers, make the great sacrifice for faith and country. A vile race of quislings—to use the new word which will carry the scorn of mankind down the centuries—is hired to fawn upon the conqueror, to collaborate in his designs, and to enforce his rule upon their fellow-countrymen, while grovelling low themselves. Such is the plight of once glorious Europe, and such are the atrocities against which we are in arms.

It is upon this foundation that Hitler, with his tattered lackey Mussolini at his tail and Admiral Darlan frisking by his side, pretends to build out of hatred, appetite, and racial assertion a new order for Europe. Never did so mocking a fantasy obsess the mind of mortal man. We cannot tell what the course of this fell war will be as it spreads remorselessly through ever-wider regions. We know it will be hard, we expect it will be long; we cannot predict or measure its episodes or its tribulations. But one thing is certain, one thing is sure, one thing stands out stark and undeniable, massive and unassailable, for all the world to see.

It will not be by German hands that the structure of Europe will be rebuilt or the union of the European family achieved. In every country into which the German armies and the Nazi police have broken there has sprung up from the soil a hatred of the German name and a contempt for the Nazi creed which the passage of hundreds of years will not efface from human memory. We cannot yet see how deliverance will come, or when it will come, but nothing is more certain than that every trace of Hitler's footsteps, every stain of his infected and corroding fingers will be sponged and purged and, if need be, blasted from the surface of the earth.

We are here to affirm and fortify our union in that ceaseless and unwearying effort which must be made if the captive peoples are to be set free. A year ago His Majesty's Government was left alone to face the storm, and to many of our friends and enemies alike it may have seemed that our days too were numbered, and that Britain and its institutions would sink for ever beneath the verge. But I may with some pride remind your Excellencies that, even in that dark hour when our Army was disorganized and almost weaponless, when scarcely a gun or a tank remained in Britain, when almost all our stores and ammunition had been lost in France, never for one moment did the British people dream of making peace with the conqueror, and never for a moment did they despair of the common cause. On the contrary, we proclaimed at that very time to all men, not only to ourselves, our determination not to make peace until every one of the ravaged and enslaved countries was liberated and until the Nazi domination was broken and destroyed.

See how far we have travelled since those breathless days of June a year ago. Our solid, stubborn strength has stood the awful test. We are masters of our own air, and now reach out in ever-growing retribution upon the enemy. The Royal Navy holds the seas. The Italian fleet cowers diminished in harbour, the German Navy is largely crippled or sunk. The murderous raids upon our ports, cities, and factories have been powerless to quench the spirit of the British nation, to stop our national life, or check the immense expansion of our war industry. The food and arms from across the oceans are coming safely in. Full provision to replace all sunken tonnage is being made here, and still more by our friends in the United States. We are becoming an armed community. Our land forces are being perfected in equipment and training.

Hitler may turn and trample this way and that through tortured Europe. He may spread his course far and wide, and carry his curse with him: he may break into Africa or into Asia. But it is here, in this island fortress, that he will have to reckon in the end. We shall strive to resist by land and sea. We shall be on his track wherever he goes. Our air power will continue to teach the German homeland that war is not all loot and triumph.

We shall aid and stir the people of every conquered country to resistance and revolt. We shall break up and derange every effort which Hitler makes to systematize and consolidate his subjugation. He will find no peace, no rest, no halting-place, no parley. And if, driven to desperate hazards, he attempts the invasion of the British Isles, as well he may, we shall not flinch from the supreme trial. With the help of God, of which we must all feel daily conscious, we shall continue steadfast in faith and duty till our task is done.

This, then, is the message which we send forth to-day to all the States and nations, bond or free, to all the men in all the lands who care for freedom's cause, to our allies and well-wishers in Europe, to our American friends and helpers drawing ever closer in their might across the ocean: this is the message–Lift up your hearts. All will come right. Out of the depths of sorrow and sacrifice will be born again the glory of mankind.

THE GERMAN INVASION OF RUSSIA

June 22, 1941

Broadcast, London

*Following the defeats in Greece and Crete, General Wavell's attack in the Western Desert ("Operation Battleaxe") ended in a British reverse, and failed to relieve Tobruk. It was, as Churchill related, "a most bitter blow" (*The Grand Alliance, *343). This prompted Churchill to relieve Wavell of his command of the armies of the Middle East and appoint General Auchinleck, Commander-in-Chief in India, in his stead. Mr. Oliver Lyttelton was appointed "War Cabinet Minister resident in the Middle East," and Wavell succeeded Auchinleck in India.*

Meanwhile, more dramatic events were unfolding. British Intelligence had clear advance warning of the German invasion of Russia, although Stalin appeared to ignore the implications of the massive German build-up on his frontiers. Early on the morning of June 22 the German onslaught began. The Russians were overwhelmed.

Churchill worked on this broadcast at Chequers (the Prime Minister's official country residence, in Buckinghamshire) throughout the day, completing it only twenty minutes before it was delivered. When his private secretary, J. R. Colville, remarked on the irony of this devoted enemy of Communism speaking in warm support of the Soviet Union, Churchill retorted, "If Hitler invaded Hell I would make at least a favourable reference to the Devil in the House of Commons."

At the time, this broadcast made a profound impression. Read coldly, over thirty years later, it may seem excessively emotional and rhetorical, and its references to "the Nazi war machine, with its clanking, heel-clicking, dandified Prussian officers" almost comical. The reality, of course, was far from comical. The lack of hesitation with which Churchill allied the British with the Russians marked another major turning-point of the war.

I have taken occasion to speak to you to-night because we have reached one of the climacterics of the war. The first of these intense turning-points was a year ago when France fell prostrate under the German hammer, and when we had to face the storm alone. The second was when the Royal Air Force beat the Hun raiders out of the daylight air, and thus warded off the Nazi invasion of our island while we were still ill-armed and ill-prepared. The third turning-point was when the President and Congress of the United States passed the Lease-and-Lend enactment, devoting nearly 2,000 millions sterling of the wealth of the New World to help us to defend our liberties and their own. Those were the three climacterics. The fourth is now upon us.

At four o'clock this morning Hitler attacked and invaded Russia. All his usual formalities of perfidy were observed with scrupulous technique. A non-aggression treaty had been solemnly signed and was in force between the two countries. No complaint had been made by Germany of its non-fulfilment. Under its cloak of false confidence, the German armies drew up in immense strength along a line which stretches from the White Sea to the Black Sea; and their air fleets and armoured divisions slowly and methodically took their stations. Then, suddenly without declaration of war, without even an ultimatum, German bombs rained down from the air upon the Russian cities, the German troops violated the frontiers; and an hour later the German Ambassador, who till the night before was lavishing his assurances of friendship, almost of alliance, upon the Russians, called upon the Russian Foreign Minister to tell him that a state of war existed between Germany and Russia.

Thus was repeated on a far larger scale the same kind of outrage against every form of signed compact and international faith which we have witnessed in Norway, Denmark, Holland and Belgium, and which Hitler's accomplice and jackal Mussolini so faithfully imitated in the case of Greece.

All this was no surprise to me. In fact I gave clear and precise warnings to Stalin of what was coming. I gave him warning as I have given warning to others before. I can only hope that this warning did not fall unheeded. All we know at present is that the Russian people are defending their native soil and that their leaders have called upon them to resist to the utmost.

Hitler is a monster of wickedness, insatiable in his lust for blood and plunder. Not content with having all Europe under his heel, or else terrorized into various forms of abject submission, he must now carry his work of butchery and desolation among the vast multitudes of Russia and of Asia. The terrible military machine, which we and the rest of the civilized world so foolishly, so supinely, so insensately allowed the Nazi gangsters to build up year by year from almost nothing, cannot stand idle lest it rust or fall to pieces. It must be in continual motion, grinding up human lives and trampling down the homes and the rights of hundreds of millions of men. Moreover it must be fed, not only with flesh but with oil.

So now this bloodthirsty guttersnipe must launch his mechanized armies upon new fields of slaughter, pillage and devastation. Poor as are the Russian peasants, workmen and soldiers, he must steal from them their daily bread; he must devour their harvests; he must rob them of the oil which drives their ploughs; and thus produce a famine without example in human history. And even the carnage and ruin which his victory, should he gain it—he has not gained it yet—will bring upon the Russian people, will itself be only a stepping-stone to the attempt to plunge the four or five hundred millions who live in China, and the three hundred and fifty millions who live in India, into that bottomless pit of human degradation over which the diabolic emblem of the Swastika flaunts itself. It is not too much to say here this summer evening that the lives and happiness of a thousand million additional people are now menaced with brutal Nazi violence. That is enough to make us hold our breath. But presently I shall show you something else that lies behind, and something that touches very nearly the life of Britain and of the United States.

The Nazi régime is indistinguishable from the worst features of Communism. It is devoid of all theme and principle except appetite and racial domination. It excels all forms of human wickedness in the efficiency of its cruelty and ferocious aggression. No one has been a more consistent opponent of Communism than I have for the last twenty-five years. I will unsay no word that I have spoken about it. But all this fades away before the spectacle which is now unfolding. The past with its crimes, its follies and its tragedies, flashes away. I see the Russian soldiers standing on the threshold of their native land, guarding the fields which their fathers have tilled from time immemorial. I see them guarding their homes where mothers and wives pray—ah yes, for there are times when all pray—for the safety of their loved ones, the return of the breadwinner, of their champion, of their protector. I see the ten thousand villages of Russia, where the means of existence was wrung so hardly from the soil, but where there are still primordial human joys, where maidens laugh and children play. I see advancing upon all this in hideous onslaught the Nazi war machine, with its clanking, heel-clicking, dandified Prussian officers, its crafty expert agents fresh from the cowing and tying-down of a dozen countries. I see also the dull, drilled, docile, brutish masses of the Hun soldiery plodding on like a swarm of crawling locusts. I see the German bombers and fighters in the sky, still smarting from many a British whipping, delighted to find what they believe is an easier and a safer prey.

Behind all this glare, behind all this storm, I see that small group of villainous men who plan, organize and launch this cataract of horrors upon mankind. And then my mind goes back across the years to the days when the Russian armies were our allies against the same deadly foe; when they fought with so much valour and constancy, and helped to gain a victory from all share in which, alas, they were—through no fault of ours—utterly cut off. I have lived through all this, and you will pardon me if I express my feelings and the stir of old memories.

But now I have to declare the decision of His Majesty's Government—and I feel sure it is a decision in which the great Dominions will, in due course, concur—for we must speak out now at once, without a day's delay. I have to make the declaration, but can you doubt what our policy will be? We have but one aim and one single, irrevocable purpose. We are resolved to destroy Hitler and every vestige of the Nazi régime. From this nothing will turn us—nothing. We will never parley, we will never negotiate with Hitler or any of his gang. We shall fight him by land, we shall fight him by sea, we shall fight him in the air, until with God's help we have rid the earth of his shadow and liberated its peoples from his yoke. Any man or state who fights on against Nazidom will have our aid. Any man or state who marches with Hitler is our foe. This applies not only to organized states but to all representatives of that vile race of quislings who make themselves the tools and agents of the Nazi régime against their fellow-countrymen and the lands of their birth. They—these quislings—like the Nazi leaders themselves, if not disposed of by their fellow-countrymen, which would save trouble, will be delivered by us on the morrow of victory to the justice of the Allied tribunals. That is our policy and that is our declaration. It follows, therefore, that we shall give whatever help we can to Russia and the Russian people. We shall appeal to all our friends and allies in every part of the world to take the same course and pursue it, as we shall, faithfully and steadfastly to the end.

We have offered the Government of Soviet Russia any technical or economic assistance which is in our power, and which is likely to be of service to them. We shall bomb Germany by day as well as by night in ever-increasing measure, casting upon them month by month a heavier discharge of bombs, and making the German people taste and gulp each month a sharper dose of the miseries they have showered upon mankind. It is noteworthy that only yesterday the Royal Air Force, fighting inland over French territory, cut down with very small loss to themselves 28 of the Hun fighting machines in the air above the French soil they have invaded, defiled and profess to hold. But this is only a beginning. From now forward the main expansion of our Air Force proceeds with gathering speed. In another six months the weight of the help we are receiving from the United States in war materials of all kinds, and especially in heavy bombers, will begin to tell.

This is no class war, but a war in which the whole British Empire and Commonwealth of Nations is engaged without distinction of race, creed or party. It is not for me to speak of the action of the United States, but this I will say: if Hitler imagines that his attack on Soviet Russia will cause the slightest division of aims or slackening of effort in the great Democracies who are resolved upon his doom, he is woefully mistaken. On the contrary, we shall be fortified and encouraged in our efforts to rescue mankind from his tyranny. We shall be strengthened and not weakened in determination and in resources.

This is no time to moralize on the follies of countries and governments which have allowed themselves to be struck down one by one, when by united action they could have saved themselves and saved the world from this catastrophe. But when I spoke a few minutes ago of Hitler's blood-lust and the hateful appetites which have impelled or lured him on his Russian adventure, I said there was one deeper motive behind his outrage. He wishes to destroy the Russian power because he hopes that if he succeeds in this, he will be able to bring back the main strength of his army and air force from the East and hurl it upon this Island, which he knows he must conquer or suffer the penalty of his crimes. His invasion of Russia is no more than a prelude to an attempted invasion of the British Isles. He hopes, no doubt, that all this may be accomplished before the winter comes, and that he can overwhelm Great Britain before the fleet and air power of the United States may intervene. He hopes that he may once again repeat, upon a greater scale than ever before, that process of destroying his enemies one by one, by which he has so long thrived and prospered, and that then the scene will be clear for the final act, without which all his conquests would be in vain—namely, the subjugation of the Western Hemisphere to his will and to his system.

The Russian danger is therefore our danger, and the danger of the United States, just as the cause of any Russian fighting for his hearth and home is the cause of free men and free peoples in every quarter of the globe. Let us learn the lessons already taught by such cruel experience. Let us redouble our exertions, and strike with united strength while life and power remain.

THE ATLANTIC CHARTER

August 24, 1941

Broadcast, London

Churchill and President Roosevelt agreed they should meet "in some lonely bay or other." Despite the voluminous correspondence between the "Former Naval Person" and the President, this was their first meeting since 1917, and of which Churchill had had no recollection.

The site chosen was Placentia Bay, Newfoundland, and Churchill travelled to the "lonely bay" on the new battleship Prince of Wales.

The principal public result of this historic meeting was the Atlantic Charter–in all but a few details, Churchill's own production. Other–unpublicised–results were discussions on the deteriorating relations with Japan, and the American assumption of responsibility for protecting convoys between Iceland and the United States. On the return journey to Britain, Prince of Wales *made a stop at Iceland, and Churchill visited members of the Icelandic Cabinet and inspected British and American forces. Churchill and his party reached London on August 19.*

[Extract] I thought you would like me to tell you something about the voyage which I made across the ocean to meet our great friend, the President of the United States. Exactly where we met is a secret, but I don't think I shall be indiscreet if I go so far as to say that it was "somewhere in the Atlantic."

In a spacious, landlocked bay which reminded me of the West Coast of Scotland, powerful American warships protected by strong flotillas and far-ranging aircraft awaited our arrival, and, as it were, stretched out a hand to help us in. Our party arrived in the newest, or almost the newest, British battleship, the *Prince of Wales,* with a modern escort of British and Canadian destroyers, and there for three days I spent my time in company, and I think I may say in comradeship, with Mr. Roosevelt; while all the time the chiefs of the staff and the naval and military commanders both of the British Empire and of the United States sat together in continual council.

President Roosevelt is the thrice-chosen head of the most powerful state and community in the world. I am the servant of King and Parliament at present charged with the principal direction of our affairs in these fateful times, and it is my duty also to make sure, as I have made sure, that anything I say or do in the exercise of my office is approved and sustained by the whole British Commonwealth of Nations. Therefore this meeting was bound to be important, because of the enormous forces at present only partially mobilized but steadily mobilizing which are at the disposal of these two major groupings of the human family: the British Empire and the United States, who, fortunately for the progress of mankind, happen to speak the same language, and very largely think the same thoughts, or anyhow think a lot of the same thoughts.

The meeting was therefore symbolic. That is its prime importance. It symbolizes, in a form and manner which everyone can understand in every land and in every clime, the deep underlying unities which stir and at decisive moments rule the English-speaking peoples throughout the world. Would it be presumptuous for me to say that it symbolizes something even more majestic—namely; the marshalling of the good forces of the world against the evil forces which are now so formidable and triumphant and which have cast their cruel spell over the whole of Europe and a large part of Asia?

This was a meeting which marks for ever in the pages of history the taking-up by the English-speaking nations, amid all this peril, tumult and confusion, of the guidance of the fortunes of the broad toiling masses in all the continents; and our loyal effort without any clog of selfish interest to lead them forward out of the miseries into which they have been plunged back to the broad highroad of freedom and justice. This is the highest honour and the most glorious opportunity which could ever have come to any branch of the human race. . . .

But Europe is not the only continent to be tormented and devastated by aggressions. For five long years the Japanese military factions, seeking to emulate the style of Hitler and Mussolini, taking all their posturing as if it were a new European revelation, have been invading and harrying the 500,000,000 inhabitants of China. Japanese armies have been wandering about that vast land in futile excursions, carrying with them carnage, ruin and corruption and calling it the 'Chinese Incident.' Now they stretch a grasping hand into the southern seas of China; they snatch Indo-China from the wretched Vichy French; they menace by their movements Siam; menace Singapore, the British link with Australia; and menace the Philippine Islands under the protection of the United States. It is certain that this has got to stop. Every effort will be made to secure a peaceful settlement. The United States are labouring with infinite patience to arrive at a fair and amicable settlement which will give Japan the utmost reassurance for her legitimate interests. We earnestly hope these negotiations will succeed. But this I must say: that if these hopes should fail we shall of course range ourselves unhesitatingly at the side of the United States.

And thus we come back to the quiet bay somewhere in the Atlantic where misty sunshine plays on great ships which carry the White Ensign, or the Stars and Stripes. We had the idea, when we met there—the President and I—that without attempting to draw up final and formal peace aims, or war aims, it was necessary to give all peoples, especially the oppressed and conquered peoples, a simple, rough-and-ready wartime statement of the goal towards which the British Commonwealth and the United States mean to make their way, and thus make a way for others to march with them upon a road which will certainly be painful, and may be long!

There are, however, two distinct and marked differences in this joint declaration from the attitude adopted by the Allies during the latter part of the last war; and no one should overlook them. The United States and Great Britain do not now assume that there will never be any more war again. On the contrary, we intend to take ample precautions to prevent its renewal in any period we can foresee by effectively disarming the guilty nations while remaining suitably protected ourselves.

The second difference is this: that instead of trying to ruin German trade by all kinds of additional trade barriers and hindrances as was the mood of 1917, we have definitely adopted the view that it is not in the interests of the world and of our two countries that any large nation should be unprosperous or shut out from the means of making a decent living for itself and its people by its industry and enterprise. These are far-reaching changes of principle upon which all countries should ponder. Above all, it was necessary to give hope and the assurance of final victory to those many scores of millions of men and women who are battling for life and freedom, or who are already bent down under the Nazi yoke. . . .

The ordeals, therefore, of the conquered peoples will be hard. We must give them hope; we must give them the conviction that their sufferings and their resistances will not be in vain. The tunnel may be dark and long, but at the end there is light. That is the symbolism and that is the message of the Atlantic meeting. Do not despair, brave Norwegians: your land shall be cleansed not only from the invader but from the filthy quislings who are his tools. Be sure of yourselves, Czechs: your independence shall be restored. Poles, the heroism of your people standing up to cruel oppressors, the courage of your soldiers, sailors and airmen, shall not be forgotten: your country shall live again and resume its rightful part in the new organization of Europe. Lift up your heads, gallant Frenchmen: not all the infamies of Darlan and of Laval shall stand between you and the restoration of your birthright. Tough, stout-hearted Dutch, Belgians, Luxembourgers, tormented, mishandled, shamefully castaway peoples of Yugoslavia, glorious Greece, now subjected to the crowning insult of the rule of the Italian jackanapes; yield not an inch! Keep your souls clean from all contact with the Nazis; make them feel even in their fleeting hour of brutish triumph that they are the moral outcasts of mankind. Help is coming; mighty forces are arming in your behalf. Have faith. Have hope. Deliverance is sure.

There is the signal which we have flashed across the water; and if it reaches the hearts of those to whom it is sent, they will endure with fortitude and tenacity their present misfortunes in the sure faith that they, too, are still serving the common cause, and that their efforts will not be in vain.

You will perhaps have noticed that the President of the United States and the British representative, in what is aptly called the 'Atlantic Charter,' have jointly pledged their countries to the final destruction of the Nazi tyranny. That is a solemn and grave undertaking. It must be made good; it will be made good. And, of course, many practical arrangements to fulfil that purpose have been and are being organized and set in motion.

The question has been asked: how near is the United States to war? There is certainly one man who knows the answer to that question. If Hitler has not yet declared war upon the United States, it is surely not out of his love for American institutions; it is certainly not because he could not find a pretext. He has murdered half a dozen countries for far less. Fear of immediately redoubling the tremendous energies now being employed against him is no doubt a restraining influence. But the real reason is, I am sure, to be found in the method to which he has so faithfully adhered and by which he has gained so much.

What is that method? It is a very simple method. One by one: that is his plan; that is his guiding rule; that is the trick by which he has enslaved so large a portion of the world. Three and a half years ago I appealed to my fellow countrymen to take the lead in weaving together a strong defensive union within the principles of the League of Nations, a union of all the countries who felt themselves in ever-growing danger. But none would listen; all stood idle while Germany rearmed. Czechoslovakia was subjugated; a French Government deserted their faithful ally and broke a plighted word in that ally's hour of need. Russia was cajoled and deceived into a kind of neutrality or partnership, while the French Army was being annihilated. The Low Countries and the Scandinavian countries, acting with France and Great Britain in good time, even after the war had begun, might have altered its course, and would have had, at any rate, a fighting chance. The Balkan States had only to stand together to save themselves from the ruin by which they are now engulfed. But one by one they were undermined and overwhelmed. Never was the career of crime made more smooth.

Now Hitler is striking at Russia with all his might, well knowing the difficulties of geography which stand between Russia and the aid which the Western Democracies are trying to bring. We shall strive our utmost to overcome all obstacles and to bring this aid. We have arranged for a conference in Moscow between the United States, British and Russian authorities to settle the whole plan. No barrier must stand in the way. But why is Hitler striking at Russia, and inflicting and suffering himself or, rather, making his soldiers suffer, this frightful slaughter? It is with the declared object of turning his whole force upon the British Islands, and if he could succeed in beating the life and the strength out of us, which is not so easy, then is the moment when he will settle his account, and it is already a long one, with the people of the United States and generally with the Western Hemisphere. One by one, there is the process; there is the simple, dismal plan which has served Hitler so well. It needs but one final successful application to make him the master of the world. I am devoutly thankful that some eyes at least are fully opened to it while time remains. I rejoiced to find that the President saw in their true light and proportion the extreme dangers by which the American people as well as the British people are now beset. It was indeed by the mercy of God that he began eight years ago that revival of the strength of the American Navy without which the New World today would have to take its orders from the European dictators, but with which the United States still retains the power to marshal her gigantic strength, and in saving herself to render an incomparable service to mankind.

We had a church parade on the Sunday in our Atlantic bay. The President came on to the quarter-deck of the *Prince of Wales,* where there were mingled together many hundreds of American and British sailors and marines. The sun shone bright and warm while we all sang the old hymns which are our common inheritance and which we learned as children in our homes. We sang the hymn founded on the psalm which John Hampden's soldiers sang when they bore his body to the grave, and in which the brief, precarious span of human life is contrasted with the immutability of Him to Whom a thousand ages are but as yesterday, and as a watch in the night. We sang the sailors' hymn 'For those in peril'—and there are very many—'on the sea.' We sang 'Onward Christian Soldiers.' And indeed I felt that this was no vain presumption, but that we had the right to feel that we were serving a cause for the sake of which a trumpet has sounded from on high.

When I looked upon that densely-packed congregation of fighting men of the same language, of the same faith, of the same fundamental laws and the same ideals, and now to a large extent of the same interests, and certainly in different degrees facing the same dangers, it swept across me that here was the only hope, but also the sure hope, of saving the world from measureless degradation.

And so we came back across the ocean waves, uplifted in spirit, fortified in resolve. Some American destroyers which were carrying mails to the United States marines in Iceland happened to be going the same way, too, so we made a goodly company at sea together.

And when we were right out in mid-passage one afternoon a noble sight broke on the view. We overtook one of the convoys which carry the munitions and supplies of the New World to sustain the champions of freedom in the Old. The whole broad horizon seemed filled with ships; seventy or eighty ships of all kinds and sizes, arrayed in fourteen lines, each of which could have been drawn with a ruler, hardly a wisp of smoke, not a straggler, but all bristling with cannons and other precautions on which I will not dwell, and all surrounded by their British escorting vessels, while overhead the far-ranging Catalina air-boats soared–vigilant, protecting eagles in the sky. Then I felt that–hard and terrible and long drawn-out as this struggle may be–we shall not be denied the strength to do our duty to the end.

THE WAR SITUATION

September 9, 1941

House of Commons

[Extract] . . . Thus far then we have travelled along the terrible road we chose at the call of duty. The mood of Britain is wisely and rightly averse from every form of shallow or premature exultation. This is no time for boasts or glowing prophecies, but there is this–a year ago our position looked forlorn and well nigh desperate to all eyes but our own. To-day we may say aloud before an awe-struck world, "We are still masters of our fate. We are still captain of our souls."

THE WAR SITUATION

September 30, 1941

House of Commons

[Extract] . . . I hope, indeed, that some of our ardent critics out of doors–I have nothing to complain of here–will reflect a little on their own records in the past, and by searching their hearts and memories will realize the fate which awaits nations and individuals who take an easy and popular course or who are guided in defence matters by the shifting winds of well-meaning public opinion. Nothing is more dangerous in wartime than to live in the temperamental atmosphere of a Gallup Poll, always feeling one's pulse and taking one's temperature. I see that a speaker at the week-end said that this was a time when leaders should keep their ears to the ground. All I can say is that the British nation will find it very hard to look up to leaders who are detected in that somewhat ungainly posture. If to-day I am very kindly treated by the mass of the people of this country, it is certainly not because I have followed public opinion in recent years. There is only one duty, only one safe course, and that is to try to be right and not to fear to do or say what you believe to be right. That is the only way to deserve and to win the confidence of our great people in these days of trouble.

Our hearts go out to our British Army, not only to those who in the Mediterranean and in the East may soon have to bear the brunt of German fury and organization, but also to that splendid, but not too large, band of men here at home whose task is monotonous and unspectacular, whose duty is a long and faithful vigil, but who must be ready at any hour of any day to leap at the throat of the invader. It may well be the occasion will never come. If that should be the final story, then we may be sure that the existence of the kind of army we have created would be one of the reasons why once again in a war which has ravaged the world our land will be undevastated and our homes inviolate.

Of course we strive to profit from well-informed criticism, whether friendly or spiteful, but there is one charge sometimes put forward which is, I think, a little unfair. I mean the insinuation that we are a weak, timid, lethargic Government, usually asleep, and in our waking hours always held back by excessive scruples and inhibitions, and unable to act with the vehemence and severity which these violent times require.

. . . Let me once again repeat to the House that I cannot give them any flattering hopes, still less any guarantee, that the future will be bright or easy. On the contrary, even the coming winter affords no assurance, as the Russian Ambassador has candidly and shrewdly pointed out, that the German pressure upon Russia will be relaxed; nor, I may add, does the winter give any assurance that the danger of invasion will be entirely lifted from this island. Winter fog has dangers of its own, and, unlike last year, the enemy has now had ample time for technical preparation. We must certainly expect that in the spring, whatever happens in the meanwhile, very heavy fighting, heavier than any we have yet experienced in this war, will develop in the East, and also that the menace to this island of invasion will present itself in a very grave and sharp form. Only the most strenuous exertions, a perfect unity of purpose, added to our traditional unrelenting tenacity, will enable us to act our part worthily in the prodigious world drama in which we are now plunged. Let us make sure these virtues are forthcoming.

"THESE ARE GREAT DAYS"

October 29, 1941

Harrow School

When Churchill visited Harrow on October 29 to hear the traditional songs again, he discovered that an additional verse had been added to one of them. It ran:

"Not less we praise in darker days
The leader of our nation,
And Churchill's name shall win acclaim
From each new generation.
For you have power in danger's hour
Our freedom to defend, Sir!
Though long the fight we know that right
Will triumph in the end, Sir!"

Almost a year has passed since I came down here at your Head Master's kind invitation in order to cheer myself and cheer the hearts of a few of my friends by singing some of our own songs. The ten months that have passed have seen very terrible catastrophic events in the world–ups and downs, misfortunes–but can anyone sitting here this afternoon, this October afternoon, not feel deeply thankful for what has happened in the time that has passed and for the very great improvement in the position of our country and of our home? Why, when I was here last time we were quite alone, desperately alone, and we had been so for five or six months. We were poorly armed. We are not so poorly armed to-day; but then we were very poorly armed. We had the unmeasured menace of the enemy and their air attack still beating upon us, and you yourselves had had experience of this attack; and I expect you are beginning to feel impatient that there has been this long lull with nothing particular turning up!

But we must learn to be equally good at what is short and sharp and what is long and tough. It is generally said that the British are often better at the last. They do not expect to move from crisis to crisis; they do not always expect that each day will bring up some noble chance of war; but when they very slowly make up their minds that the thing has to be done and the job put through and finished, then, even if it takes months–if it takes years–they do it.

Another lesson I think we may take, just throwing our minds back to our meeting here ten months ago and now, is that appearances are often very deceptive, and as Kipling well says, we must

"...meet with Triumph and Disaster
And treat those two impostors just the same."

You cannot tell from appearances how things will go. Sometimes imagination makes things out far worse than they are; yet without imagination not much can be done. Those people who are imaginative see many more dangers than perhaps exist. certainly many more than will happen; but then they must also pray to be given that extra courage to carry this far-reaching imagination. But for everyone, surely, what we have gone through in this period–I am addressing myself to the School–surely from this period of ten months this is the lesson: never give in, never give in, *never, never, never, never*–in nothing, great or small, large or petty–never give in except to convictions of honour and good sense. Never yield to force; never yield to the apparently overwhelming might of the enemy. We stood all alone a year ago, and to many countries it seemed that our account was closed, we were finished. All this tradition of ours, our songs, our School history, this part of the history of this country, were gone and finished and liquidated.

Very different is the mood to-day. Britain, other nations thought, had drawn a sponge across her slate. But instead our country stood in the gap. There was no flinching and no thought of giving in; and by what seemed almost a miracle to those outside these Islands, though we ourselves never doubted it, we now find ourselves in a position where I say that we can be sure that we have only to persevere to conquer.

You sang here a verse of a School Song; you sang that extra verse written in my honour, which I was very greatly complimented by and which you have repeated to-day. [Editor's Note: The boys had previously sung the school song, "Stet Fortuna Domus," and this verse had been added in Churchill's honour.] But there is one word in it I want to alter–I wanted to do so last year, but I did not venture to. It is the line–

"Not less we praise in darker days."

I have obtained the Head Master's permission to alter "*darker*" to "*sterner*":

"Not less we praise in sterner days."

Do not let us speak of darker days; let us speak rather of sterner days. These are not dark days: these are great days–the greatest days our country has ever lived; and we must all thank God that we have been allowed, each of us according to our stations, to play a part in making these days memorable in the history of our race.

THE GOLDEN WEDDING OF MR. SPEAKER FITZROY

November 19, 1941

House of Commons

This brief speech, delivered at the height of the war, is included as an example of Churchill's wonderful felicity of phrasing and human warmth.

I rise to commit an irregularity, and I will venture to ask the indulgence of the House. The intervention which I make is without precedent, and the reason for that intervention is also without precedent, and the fact that the reason for my intervention is without precedent is the reason why I must ask for a precedent for my intervention.

We have searched the records of Parliament back, generation after generation, century after century, at any rate until we have reached the time of Mr. Speaker Rous in 1653, before which time the occupants of the Chair held their tenure for shorter and more precarious periods; and in all this long range of Parliamentary history, there has been no occasion when a Speaker of the House of Commons has celebrated his golden wedding while occupying the Chair.

This unique event demands a procedure of its own, and I would like to assure you, Sir, that you are generally beloved throughout the House of Commons, and that this affection extends to your home and your family. I would like to assure you that we have in thirteen years gained complete confidence in your impartiality, in the firmness with which you vindicate and champion the rights of the House of Commons, in the fairness with which you protect minorities and their interventions in discussion, and in the kindliness and courtesy with which you treat all Members when they have access to you.

I know I shall be expressing the feeling of the whole House–all of them, every one–when I say that we wish to share with you in this joyous event; and we desire that our expression shall be borne upon the records of the House and shall stand as a precedent for future times, should any such extraordinary but happy occurrence arise in the cycles of the future.

I must add that it has been arranged to make a presentation to you later to-day, and that my right hon. Friend the Member for Carnarvon Boroughs (Mr. Lloyd George), the Father of the House, will bring a considerable delegation to meet you. For the convenience of Members, it would be a good thing if our Debate could end a little earlier than usual so as to enable this ceremony to take place. I thank the House for having indulged me in this manner. I trust that my action may be condoned on account of the general unanimity in the sentiments which I have expressed.

WAR WITH JAPAN

December 8, 1941

House of Commons

The purpose of "Operation Crusader" in Libya was to recapture Cyrenaica and relieve Tobruk. On November 17 a daring but unsuccessful attempt to murder Field Marshal Rommel at his headquarters was made by thirty men of the Scottish Commando. In the fighting Lieutenant Colonel Keyes, the son of Sir Roger Keyes, died. He was posthumously awarded the Victoria Cross.

The main attack opened on November 18, and on November 24 Rommel launched one of the most daring attacks in modern military history by sweeping his tanks across the desert past the main British forces. The strike failed, but it created so much consternation that only Auchinleck's personal intervention prevented withdrawal, and a major defeat. Auchinleck relieved General Cunningham of his command of the newly named

Eighth Army and appointed in his stead General Ritchie. The British victory was assured at a cost of over 17,000 casualties.

At this time, the naval situation in the Mediterranean was disastrously reversed. Ark Royal *and the battleship* Barham *were both torpedoed and sunk. The battleships* Queen Elizabeth *and* Valiant *were crippled in a heroic attack by the Italian frog-men in Alexandria; the cruiser* Neptune *struck a mine and was sunk, while two other cruisers and a destroyer were severely damaged. The Eastern Mediterranean fleet was reduced to three cruisers and a few destroyers. The air attack on Malta increased and the Germans had full air dominance in the Eastern Mediterranean.*

At this moment there occurred another major turning point in the war.

Although the eventuality of a Japanese attack had gradually hardened into a strong probability, the blow fell with unexpected skill and ferocity.

Churchill was at Chequers on December 7 with the American Ambassador, Mr. John Winant, and the Lend-Lease Coordinator, Mr. Averell Harriman, when they heard the news of the Japanese attack on Pearl Harbor on the radio. Churchill telephoned Roosevelt for confirmation of the report. The War Cabinet authorized the immediate declaration of war on Japan. The House of Commons met at 3 p.m. on the afternoon of December 8.

On December 11 Germany declared war on the United States.

[Extract] As soon as I heard, last night, that Japan had attacked the United States, I felt it necessary that Parliament should be immediately summoned. It is indispensable to our system of government that Parliament should play its full part in all the important acts of State and at all the crucial moments of the war; and I am glad to see that so many Members have been able to be in their places, despite the shortness of the notice. With the full approval of the nation, and of the Empire, I pledged the word of Great Britain, about a month ago, that should the United States be involved in war with Japan, a British declaration of war would follow within the hour. I therefore spoke to President Roosevelt on the Atlantic telephone last night, with a view to arranging the timing of our respective declarations. The President told me that he would this morning send a Message to Congress, which, of course, as is well known, can alone make a declaration of war on behalf of the United States, and I then assured him that we would follow immediately.

However, it soon appeared that British territory in Malaya had also been the object of Japanese attack, and later on it was announced from Tokyo that the Japanese High Command—a curious form; not the Imperial Japanese Government—had declared that a state of war existed with Great Britain and the United States. That being so, there was no need to wait for the declaration by Congress. American time is very nearly six hours behind ours. The Cabinet, therefore, which met at 12.30 to-day, authorized an immediate declaration of war upon Japan. . . .

Now that the issue is joined in the most direct manner, it only remains for the two great democracies to face their task with whatever strength God may give them. We must hold ourselves very fortunate, and I think we may rate our affairs not wholly ill-guided, that we were not attacked alone by Japan in our period of weakness after Dunkirk, or at any time in 1940, before the United States had fully realized the dangers which threatened the whole world and had made much advance in its military preparation. So precarious and narrow was the margin upon which we then lived that we did not dare to express the sympathy which we have all along felt for the heroic people of China. We were even forced for a short time, in the summer of 1940, to agree to closing the Burma Road. But later on, at the beginning of this year, as soon as we could regather our strength, we reversed that policy, and the House will remember that both I and the Foreign Secretary have felt able to make increasingly outspoken declarations of friendship for the Chinese people and their great leader, General Chiang-Kai-Shek.

We have always been friends. Last night I cabled to the Generalissimo assuring him that henceforward we would face the common foe together. Although the imperative demands of the war in Europe and in Africa have strained our resources, vast and growing though they are, the House and the Empire will notice that some of the finest ships in the Royal Navy have reached their stations in the Far East at a very convenient moment. Every preparation in our power has been made, and I do not doubt that we shall give a good account of ourselves. The closest accord has been established with the powerful American forces, both naval and air, and also with the strong, efficient forces belonging to the Royal Netherlands Government in the Netherlands East Indies. We shall all do our best. When we think of the insane ambition and insatiable appetite which have caused this vast and melancholy extension of the war, we can only feel that Hitler's madness has infected the Japanese mind, and that the root of the evil and its branch must be extirpated together.

It is of the highest importance that there should be no underrating of the gravity of the new dangers we have to meet, either here or in the United States. The enemy has attacked with an audacity which may spring from recklessness, but which may also spring from a conviction of strength. The ordeal to which the English-speaking world and our heroic Russian Allies are being exposed will certainly be hard, especially at the outset, and will probably be long, yet when we look around us over the sombre panorama of the world, we have no reason to doubt the justice of our cause or that our strength and will-power will be sufficient to sustain it. We have at least four-fifths of the population of the globe upon our side.

We are responsible for their safety and for their future. In the past we have had a light which flickered, in the present we have a light which flames, and in the future there will be a light which shines over all the land and sea.

THE WAR SITUATION

December 11, 1941

House of Commons

In October the decision had been made to reinforce the British Far East Fleet at Singapore with the battleships Prince of Wales *and* Repulse. *The War Cabinet was considering Churchill's proposal that the warships join the American fleet when the news was received that they were sunk by Japanese aircraft on December 10. "In all the war," Churchill later wrote, "I never received a more direct shock. . . . As I turned over and twisted in bed the full horror of the news sank in upon me. There were no British or American capital ships in the Indian Ocean or the Pacific. . . . Over all this vast expanse of water Japan was supreme, and we were everywhere weak and naked" (*The Grand Alliance, *620).*

On December 12 Churchill sailed to America on the Duke of York *to confer with Roosevelt. He later wrote, "All our problems travelled with us" (*The Grand Alliance, *627).*

[Extract] A great many things of far-reaching and fundamental importance have happened in the last few weeks. Most of them have happened in the last few days, and I think it opportune to give the House the best account I can of where we stand and how we are. . . .

At the beginning of the offensive I told the House that we should for the first time be fighting the Germans on equal terms in modern weapons. This was quite true. Naturally there have been some unpleasant surprises, and also some awkward things have happened, as might be expected beforehand. Those who fight the Germans fight a stubborn and resourceful foe, a foe in every way worthy of the doom prepared for him. Some of the German tanks carried, as we knew, a six-pounder gun which, though it of course carries many fewer shots, is sometimes more effective than the gun with which our tanks are mainly armed. Our losses in tanks were a good deal heavier than we expected, and it may be that at the outset, before it was disorganized, the enemy's recovery process for damaged vehicles worked better than ours. I am not so sure of it, but it may be so. It is very good at that. However, we had a good superiority in numbers of armoured vehicles, and in the long rough and tumble we gradually obtained mastery so far as the first phase of the battle is concerned.

Our Air Force was undoubtedly superior throughout in numbers and quality to the enemy, and although the Germans have drawn in the most extravagant manner upon reinforcements from many quarters, including the Russian front, that superiority has been more than maintained. The greatest satisfaction is expressed by the troops and by the Military Authorities with the way in which they have been helped and protected by the action of the Royal Air Force. None of the complaints in the previous enterprises have reached us here upon that score. Like other people concerned, I had hoped for a quick decision, but it may well be that this wearing-down battle will be found in the end to have inflicted a deeper injury upon the enemy than if it had all been settled by manœuvre and in a few days. In no other way could a second front have been brought into action under conditions more costly to the enemy and more favourable to ourselves than by this Libyan attack. This will be realized when it is remembered that about a half, and sometimes more than a half, of everything, men, munitions and fuel, which the enemy sends to Africa is sunk before it gets there, by our submarines, cruisers and destroyers, and by the activities of our Air Force, acting both from Libya and from Malta. In this way, the prolongation of the battle may not be without its compensations to us. From the point of view of drawing weight from the vast Russian front, the continuance of the fighting in its severity is not to be regarded as an evil.

The first stage of the battle is now over. The enemy has been driven out of all the positions which barred our westward advance, positions which he had most laboriously fortified. Everything has been swept away except certain pockets at Bardia and Halfaya, which are hopelessly cut off, and will be mopped up, or starved out, in due course. It may be definitely said that Tobruk has been relieved–or, as I prefer to state it, has been disengaged. The enemy, still strong but severely mauled and largely stripped of his armour, is retreating to a defensive line to the west of the Tobruk forts, and the clearance of the approaches to Tobruk, and the establishment of our air power thus far forward to the west in new airfields, enables the great supply depots of Tobruk, which have been carefully built up, to furnish support for the second phase of our offensive, with great economy in our lines of communication. Substantial reinforcements and fresh troops are available close at hand. Many of the units which were most heavily engaged have been relieved and their places taken by others, although we have to keep the numbers down strictly to the level which our vast transportation facilities permit. The enemy, who has fought with the utmost stubbornness and enterprise, has paid the price of his valour, and it may well be that the second phase will gather more easily the fruits of the first than has been our experience in the fighting which has taken place so far. As the House knows, I make it a rule never to prophesy, or to promise, or to guarantee future results, but I will go so far on this occasion as to say that all danger of the Army of the Nile not being able to celebrate Christmas and the New Year in Cairo has been decisively removed. . . .

A week ago the three great spheres, Libya, the Atlantic and Russia, would almost have covered the scene of war with which we were concerned. Since then it has taken an enormous and very grave expansion. The Japanese Government, or ruling elements in Japan, have made a cold-blooded, calculated, violent, treacherous attack upon the United States and ourselves. The United States have declared war upon their assailants, and we and the Royal Netherlands Government have done the same. A large part of the Western hemisphere, State after State, Parliament after Parliament, is following the United States. It is a great tribute to the respect for international law and for the independence of less powerful countries which the United States has shown for many years, particularly under the Presidency of Mr. Roosevelt, that so many other States in Central and South America and in the West Indies, powerful, wealthy, populous communities, are in the process of throwing in their lot with the great Republic of North America.

It will not stop here. It seems to me quite certain that Japan, when she struck her treacherous and dastardly blow at the United States, counted on the active support of the German Nazis and of the Italian Fascists. It is, therefore, very likely that the United States will be faced with the open hostility of Germany, Italy and Japan. We are in all this too. Our foes are bound by the consequences of their ambitions and of their crimes to seek implacably the destruction of the English-speaking world and all it stands for, which is the supreme barrier against their designs. If this should be their resolve, if they should declare themselves determined to compass the destruction of the English-speaking world, I know that I speak for the United States as well as for the British Empire when I say that we would all rather perish than be conquered. And on this basis, putting it at its worst, there are quite a lot of us to be killed. The Chinese Generalissimo, Chiang-Kai-Shek, has sent me a message announcing his decision to declare war against Japan and also against Japan's partners in guilt, Germany and Italy. He has further assured me that the whole of the resources of China are at the disposal of Great Britain and the United States. China's cause is henceforth our cause. The country which has faced the Japanese assault for over four years with undaunted courage is indeed a worthy Ally, and it is as Allies that from now on we shall go forward together to victory, not only over Japan alone, but over the Axis and all its works.

The Japanese onslaught has brought upon the United States and Great Britain very serious injuries to our naval power. In my whole experience I do not remember any naval blow so heavy or so painful as the sinking of the *Prince of Wales* and the *Repulse* on Monday last. These two vast, powerful ships constituted an essential feature in our plans for meeting the new Japanese danger as it loomed against us in the last few months. These ships had reached the right point at the right moment, and were in every respect suited to the task assigned to them. In moving to attack the Japanese transports and landing-craft which were disembarking the invaders of Siam and Malaya at the Kra Isthmus or thereabouts, Admiral Phillips was undertaking a thoroughly sound, well-considered offensive operation, not indeed free from risk, but not different in principle from many similar operations we have repeatedly carried out in the North Sea and in the Mediterranean. Both ships were sunk in repeated air attacks by bombers and by torpedo-aircraft. These attacks were delivered with skill and determination. There were two high-level attacks, both of which scored hits, and three waves of torpedo-aircraft of nine in each wave which struck each of our ships with several torpedoes. There is no reason to suppose that any new weapons or explosives were employed, or any bombs or torpedoes of exceptional size. The continued waves of attack achieved their purpose, and both ships capsized and sank, having destroyed seven of the attacking aircraft. . . .

Naturally, I should not be prepared to discuss the resulting situation in the Far East and in the Pacific or the measures which must be taken to restore it. It may well be that we shall have to suffer considerable punishment, but we shall defend ourselves everywhere with the utmost vigour in close co-operation with the United States and the Netherlands. The naval power of Great Britain and the United States was very greatly superior—and is still largely superior—to the combined forces of the three Axis Powers. But no one must underrate the gravity of the loss which has been inflicted in

Malaya and Hawaii, or the power of the new antagonist who has fallen upon us, or the length of time it will take to create, marshal and mount the great force in the Far East which will be necessary to achieve absolute victory.

We have a very hard period to go through, and a new surge of impulse will be required, and will be forthcoming, from everybody. We must, as I have said, faithfully keep our engagements to Russia in supplies, and at the same time we must expect, at any rate for the next few months, that the volume of American supplies reaching Britain and the degree of help given by the United States Navy will be reduced. The gap must be filled, and only our own efforts will fill it. I cannot doubt, however, now that the 130,000,000 people in the United States have bound themselves to this war, that once they have settled down to it and have bent themselves to it—as they will—as their main purpose in life, then the flow of munitions and aid of every kind will vastly exceed anything that could have been expected on the peacetime basis that has ruled up to the present. Not only the British Empire now but the United States are fighting for life; Russia is fighting for life, and China is fighting for life. Behind these four great combatant communities are ranged all the spirit and hopes of all the conquered countries in Europe, prostrate under the cruel domination of the foe. I said the other day that four-fifths of the human race were on our side. It may well be an understatement. Just these gangs and cliques of wicked men and their military or party organizations have been able to bring these hideous evils upon mankind. It would indeed bring shame upon our generation if we did not teach them a lesson which will not be forgotten in the records of a thousand years.

"A STRANGE CHRISTMAS EVE"

December 24, 1941

Broadcast, Washington, D.C.

Churchill reached Washington on December 22. In the meanwhile, the situation in Hong Kong became hopeless, despite a valiant resistance (the British forces surrendered on December 25). The Japanese landed in Malaya and were advancing rapidly; the Dutch East Indies were under successful assault. In Libya, the fighting was inconclusive, but the increase in German domination of the air was an ominous portent for 1942.

I spend this anniversary and festival far from my country, far from my family, yet I cannot truthfully say that I feel far from home. Whether it be the ties of blood on my mother's side, or the friendships I have developed here over many years of active life, or the commanding sentiment of comradeship in the common cause of great peoples who speak the same language, who kneel at the same altars and, to a very large extent, pursue the same ideals, I cannot feel myself a stranger here in the centre and at the summit of the United States. I feel a sense of unity and fraternal association which, added to the kindliness of your welcome, convinces me that I have a right to sit at your fireside and share your Christmas joys.

This is a strange Christmas Eve. Almost the whole world is locked in deadly struggle, and, with the most terrible weapons which science can devise, the nations advance upon each other. Ill would it be for us this Christmastide if we were not sure that no greed for the land or wealth of any other people, no vulgar ambition, no morbid lust for material gain at the expense of others, had led us to the field. Here, in the midst of war, raging and roaring over all the lands and seas, creeping nearer to our hearts and homes, here, amid all the tumult, we have tonight the peace of the spirit in each cottage home and in every generous heart. Therefore we may cast aside for this night at least the cares and dangers which beset us, and make for the children an evening of happiness in a world of storm. Here, then, for one night only, each home throughout the English-speaking world should be a brightly-lighted island of happiness and peace.

Let the children have their night of fun and laughter. Let the gifts of Father Christmas delight their play. Let us grown-ups share to the full in their unstinted pleasures before we turn again to the stern task and the formidable years that lie before us, resolved that, by our sacrifice and daring, these same children shall not be robbed of their inheritance or denied their right to live in a free and decent world.

And so, in God's mercy, a happy Christmas to you all.

"A LONG AND HARD WAR"

December 26, 1941

Joint Session of Congress,
Washington, D.C.

The Churchill-Roosevelt discussions opened with a draft declaration to be affirmed by all the anti-Axis nations–proposed by Roosevelt and at once accepted by the British. The principal discussions concerned the deteriorating situation in the East, and the need to establish a Supreme Allied Command in Southeast Asia. The United Nations Pact was important, but of more practical value was the establishment of the Combined Chiefs of Staff Committee.

On December 26 Churchill addressed a Joint Session of the United States Congress. This speech was also broadcast.

I feel greatly honoured that you should have invited me to enter the United States Senate Chamber and address the representatives of both branches of Congress. The fact that my American forebears have for so many generations played their part in the life of the United States, and that here I am, an Englishman, welcomed in your midst, makes this experience one of the most moving and thrilling in my life, which is already long and has not been entirely uneventful. I wish indeed that my mother, whose memory I cherish across the vale of years, could have been here to see. By the way, I cannot help reflecting that if my father had been American and my mother British, instead of the other way round, I might have got here on my own. In that case, this would not have been the first time you would have heard my voice. In that case I should not have needed any invitation, but if I had, it is hardly likely it would have been unanimous. So perhaps things are better as they are. I may confess, however, that I do not feel quite like a fish out of water in a legislative assembly where English is spoken.

I am a child of the House of Commons. I was brought up in my father's house to believe in democracy. "Trust the people"—that was his message. I used to see him cheered at meetings and in the streets by crowds of working men way back in those aristocratic Victorian days when, as Disraeli said, the world was for the few, and for the very few. Therefore I have been in full harmony all my life with the tides which have flowed on both sides of the Atlantic against privilege and monopoly, and I have steered confidently towards the Gettysburg ideal of "government of the people by the people for the people." I owe my advancement entirely to the House of Commons, whose servant I am. In my country, as in yours, public men are proud to be the servants of the State and would be ashamed to be its masters. On any day, if they thought the people wanted it, the House of Commons could by a simple vote remove me from my office. But I am not worrying about it at all. As a matter of fact, I am sure they will approve very highly of my journey here, for which I obtained the King's permission in order to meet the President of the United States and to arrange with him all that mapping-out of our military plans, and for all those intimate meetings of the high officers of the armed services of both countries, which are indispensable to the successful prosecution of the war.

I should like to say first of all how much I have been impressed and encouraged by the breadth of view and sense of proportion which I have found in all quarters over here to which I have had access. Anyone who did not understand the size and solidarity of the foundations of the United States might easily have expected to find an excited, disturbed, self-centred atmosphere, with all minds fixed upon the novel, startling, and painful episodes of sudden war as they hit America. After all, the United States have been attacked and set upon by three most powerfully-armed dictator States. The greatest military power in Europe, the greatest military power in Asia, Germany and Japan, Italy, too, have all declared, and are making, war upon you, and a quarrel is opened, which can only end in their overthrow or yours. But here in Washington, in these memorable days, I have found an Olympian fortitude which, far from being based upon complacency, is only the mask of an inflexible purpose and the proof of a sure and well-grounded confidence in the final outcome. We in Britain had the same feeling in our darkest days. We, too, were sure in the end all would be well. You do not, I am certain, underrate the severity of the ordeal to which you and we have still to be subjected. The forces ranged against us are enormous. They are bitter, they are ruthless. The wicked men and their factions who have launched their peoples on the path of war and conquest know that they will be called to terrible account if they cannot beat down by force of arms the peoples they have assailed. They will stop at nothing. They have a vast accumulation of war weapons of all kinds. They have highly-trained, disciplined armies, navies, and air services. They have plans and designs which have long been tried and matured. They will stop at nothing that violence or treachery can suggest.

It is quite true that, on our side, our resources in man-power and materials are far greater than theirs. But only a portion of your resources is as yet mobilized and developed, and we both of us have much to learn in the cruel art of war. We have therefore, without doubt, a time of tribulation before us. In this time some ground will be lost which it will be hard and costly to regain. Many disappointments and unpleasant surprises await us. Many of them will afflict us before the full marshalling of our latent and total power can be accomplished. For the best part of twenty years the youth of Britain and America have been taught that war is evil, which is true, and that it would never come again, which has been proved false. For the best part of twenty years the youth of Germany, Japan and Italy have been taught that aggressive war is the noblest duty of the citizen, and that it should be begun as soon as the necessary weapons and organization had been made. We have performed the duties and tasks of peace. They have plotted and planned for war. This, naturally, has placed us in Britain and now places you in the United States at a disadvantage which only time, courage, and strenuous, untiring exertions can correct.

We have indeed to be thankful that so much time has been granted to us. If Germany had tried to invade the British Isles after the French collapse in June, 1940, and if Japan had declared war on the British Empire and the United States at about the same date, no one could say what disasters and agonies might not have been our lot. But now at the end of December, 1941, our transformation from easy-going peace to total war efficiency has made very great progress. The broad flow of munitions in Great Britain has already begun. Immense strides have been made in the conversion of American industry to military purposes, and now that the United States are at war it is possible for orders to be given every day which a year or eighteen months hence will produce results in war power beyond anything that has yet been seen or foreseen in the dictator States. Provided that every effort is made, that nothing is kept back, that the whole man-power, brain-power, virility, valour, and civic virtue of the English-speaking world with all its galaxy of loyal, friendly, associated communities and States—provided all that is bent unremittingly to the simple and supreme task, I think it would be reasonable to hope that the end of 1942 will see us quite definitely in a better position than we are now, and that the year 1943 will enable us to assume the initiative upon an ample scale.

Some people may be startled or momentarily depressed when, like your President, I speak of a long and hard war. But our peoples would rather know the truth, sombre though it be. And after all, when we are doing the noblest work in the world, not only defending our hearths and homes but the cause of freedom in other lands, the question of whether deliverance comes in 1942, 1943, or 1944 falls into its proper place in the grand proportions of human history. Sure I am that this day—now—we are the masters of our fate; that the task which has been set us is not above our strength; that its pangs and toils are not beyond our endurance. As long as we have faith in our cause and an unconquerable will-power, salvation will not be denied us. In the words of the Psalmist, "He shall not be afraid of evil tidings; his heart is fixed, trusting in the Lord." Not all the tidings will be evil.

On the contrary, mighty strokes of war have already been dealt against the enemy; the glorious defence of their native soil by the Russian armies and people have inflicted wounds upon the Nazi tyranny and system which have bitten deep, and will fester and inflame not only in the Nazi body but in the Nazi mind. The boastful Mussolini has crumbled already. He is now but a lackey and serf, the merest utensil of his master's will. He has inflicted great suffering and wrong upon his own industrious people. He has been stripped of his African empire, Abyssinia has been liberated. Our armies in the East, which were so weak and ill-equipped at the moment of French desertion, now control all the regions from Teheran to Benghazi, and from Aleppo and Cyprus to the sources of the Nile.

For many months we devoted ourselves to preparing to take the offensive in Libya. The very considerable battle, which has been proceeding for the last six weeks in the desert, has been most fiercely fought on both sides. Owing to the difficulties of supply on the desert flanks, we were never able to bring numerically equal forces to bear upon the enemy. Therefore we had to rely upon a superiority in the numbers and quality of tanks and aircraft, British and American. Aided by these, for the first time, we have fought the enemy with equal weapons. For the first time we have made the Hun feel the sharp edge of those tools with which he has enslaved Europe. The armed forces of the enemy in Cyrenaica amounted to about 150,000, of whom about one-third were Germans. General Auchinleck set out to destroy totally that armed force. I have every reason to believe that his aim will be fully accomplished. I am glad to be able to place before you, members of the Senate and of the House of Representatives, at this moment when you are entering the war, proof that with proper weapons and proper organization we are able to beat the life out of the savage Nazi. What Hitler is suffering in Libya is only a sample and foretaste of what we must give him and his accomplices, wherever this war shall lead us, in every quarter of the globe.

There are good tidings also from blue water. The life-line of supplies which joins our two nations across the ocean, without which all might fail, is flowing steadily and freely in spite of all the enemy can do. It is a fact that the British Empire, which many thought eighteen months ago was broken and ruined, is now incomparably stronger, and is growing stronger with every month. Lastly, if you will forgive me for saying it, to me the best tidings of all is that the United States, united as never before, have drawn the sword for freedom and cast away the scabbard.

All these tremendous facts have led the subjugated peoples of Europe to lift up their heads again in hope. They have put aside for ever the shameful temptation of resigning themselves to the conqueror's will. Hope has returned to the hearts of scores of millions of men and women, and with that hope there burns the flame of anger against the brutal, corrupt invader, and still more fiercely burn the fires of hatred and contempt for the squalid quislings whom he has suborned. In a dozen famous ancient States now prostrate under the Nazi yoke, the masses of the people of all classes and creeds await the hour of liberation, when they too will be able once again to play their part and strike their blows like men. That hour will strike, and its solemn peal will proclaim that the night is past and that the dawn has come.

The onslaught upon us so long and so secretly planned by Japan has presented both our countries with grievous problems for which we could not be fully prepared.

If people ask me—as they have a right to ask me in England—why is it that you have not got ample equipment of modern aircraft and Army weapons of all kinds in Malaya and in the East Indies, I can only point to the victories General Auchinleck has gained in the Libyan campaign. Had we diverted and dispersed our gradually growing resources between Libya and Malaya, we should have been found wanting in both theatres. If the United States have been found at a disadvantage at various points in the Pacific Ocean, we know well that it is to no small extent because of the aid you have been giving us in munitions for the defence of the British Isles and for the Libyan campaign, and, above all, because of your help in the battle of the Atlantic, upon which all depends, and which has in consequence been successfully and prosperously maintained. Of course it would have been much better, I freely admit, if we had had enough resources of all kinds to be at full strength at all threatened points; but considering how slowly and reluctantly we brought ourselves to large-scale preparations, and how long such prepartions take, we had no right to expect to be in such a fortunate position.

The choice of how to dispose of our hitherto limited resources had to be made by Britain in time of war and by the United States in time of peace; and I believe that history will pronounce that upon the whole—and it is upon the whole that these matters must be judged—the choice made was right. Now that we are together, now that we are linked in a righteous comradeship of arms, now that our two considerable nations, each in perfect unity, have joined all their life energies in a common resolve, a new scene opens upon which a steady light will glow and brighten.

Many people have been astonished that Japan should in a single day have plunged into war against the United States and the British Empire. We all wonder why, if this dark design, with all its laborious and intricate preparations, had been so long filling their secret minds, they did not choose our moment of weakness eighteen months ago. Viewed quite dispassionately, in spite of the losses we have suffered and the further punishment we shall have to take, it certainly appears to be an irrational act. It is, of course, only prudent to assume that they have made very careful calculations and think they see their way through. Nevertheless, there may be another explanation. We know that for many years past the policy of Japan has been dominated by secret societies of subalterns and junior officers of the Army and Navy, who have enforced their will upon successive Japanese Cabinets and Parliaments by the assassination of any Japanese statesman who opposed, or who did not sufficiently further, their aggressive policy. It may be that these societies, dazzled and dizzy with their own schemes of aggression and the prospect of early victories, have forced their country against its better judgment into war. They have certainly embarked upon a very considerable undertaking. For after the outrages they have committed upon us at Pearl Harbour, in the Pacific Islands, in the Philippines, in Malaya, and in the Dutch East Indies, they must now know that the stakes for which they have decided to play are mortal.

When we consider the resources of the United States and the British Empire compared to those of Japan, when we remember those of China, which has so long and valiantly withstood invasion and when also we observe the Russian menace which hangs over Japan, it becomes still more difficult to reconcile Japanese action with prudence or even with sanity. What kind of a people do they think we are? Is it possible they do not realize that we shall never cease to persevere against them until they have been taught a lesson which they and the world will never forget?

Members of the Senate and members of the House of Representatives, I turn for one moment more from the turmoil and convulsions of the present to the broader basis of the future. Here we are together facing a group of mighty foes who seek our ruin; here we are together defending all that to free men is dear. Twice in a single generation the catastrophe of world war has fallen upon us; twice in our lifetime has the long arm of fate reached across the ocean to bring the United States into the forefront of the battle. If we had kept together after the last War, if we had taken common measures for our safety, this renewal of the curse need never have fallen upon us.

Do we not owe it to ourselves, to our children, to mankind tormented, to make sure that these catastrophes shall not engulf us for the third time? It has been proved that pestilences may break out in the Old World, which carry their destructive ravages into the New World, from which, once they are afoot, the New World cannot by any means escape. Duty and prudence alike command first that the germ-centres of hatred and revenge should be constantly and vigilantly surveyed and treated in good time, and, secondly, that an adequate organization should be set up to make sure that the pestilence can be controlled at its earliest beginnings before it spreads and rages throughout the entire earth.

Five or six years ago it would have been easy, without shedding a drop of blood, for the United States and Great Britain to have insisted on fulfilment of the disarmament clauses of the treaties which Germany signed after the Great War; that also would have been the opportunity for assuring to Germany those raw materials which we declared in the Atlantic Charter should not be denied to any nation, victor or vanquished. That chance has passed. It is gone. Prodigious hammer-strokes have been needed to bring us together again, or if you will allow me to use other language, I will say that he must indeed have a blind soul who cannot see that some great purpose and design is being worked out here below, of which we have the honour to be the faithful servants. It is not given to us to peer into the mysteries of the future. Still, I avow my hope and faith, sure and inviolate, that in the days to come the British and American peoples will for their own safety and for the good of all walk together side by side in majesty, in justice, and in peace.

"SOME CHICKEN! SOME NECK!"

December 30, 1941

Joint Session of the Canadian Parliament,
Ottawa

Churchill travelled from Washington D.C. to Canada by train on December 28, and attended a meeting of the Canadian War Cabinet on the following day. On December 30 he addressed the Canadian Parliament. This speech was also broadcast.

After his visit to Canada, Churchill returned to Washington for the signature of the United Nations Pact. It was agreed that American troops should be sent to Northern Ireland. Churchill had a brief holiday in Florida before returning to Washington again on January 11, 1942.

[Extract] It is with feelings of pride and encouragement that I find myself here in the House of Commons of Canada, invited to address the Parliament of the senior Dominion of the Crown. I am very glad to see again my old friend Mr. Mackenzie King, for fifteen years out of twenty your Prime Minister, and I thank him for the too complimentary terms in which he has referred to myself. I bring you the assurance of good will and affection from every one in the Motherland. We are most grateful for all you have done in the common cause, and we know that you are resolved to do whatever more is possible as the need arises and as opportunity serves. Canada occupies a unique position in the British Empire because of its unbreakable ties with Britain and its ever-growing friendship and intimate association with the United States. Canada is a potent magnet, drawing together those in the new world and in the old whose fortunes are now united in a deadly struggle for life and honour against the common foe. The contribution of Canada to the Imperial war effort in troops, in ships, in aircraft, in food, and in finance has been magnificent. . . .

We did not make this war, we did not seek it. We did all we could to avoid it. We did too much to avoid it. We went so far at times in trying to avoid it as to be almost destroyed by it when it broke upon us. But that dangerous corner has been turned, and with every month and every year that passes we shall confront the evil-doers with weapons as plentiful, as sharp, and as destructive as those with which they have sought to establish their hateful domination.

I should like to point out to you that we have not at any time asked for any mitigation in the fury or malice of the enemy. The peoples of the British Empire may love peace. They do not seek the lands or wealth of any country, but they are a tough and hardy lot. We have not journeyed all this way across the centuries, across the oceans, across the mountains, across the prairies, because we are made of sugar candy.

Look at the Londoners, the Cockneys; look at what they have stood up to. Grim and gay with their cry "We can take it," and their war-time mood of "What is good enough for anybody is good enough for us." We have not asked that the rules of the game should be modified. We shall never descend to the German and Japanese level, but if anybody likes to play rough we can play rough too. Hitler and his Nazi gang have sown the wind; let them reap the whirlwind. Neither the length of the struggle nor any form of severity which it may assume shall make us weary or shall make us quit.

I have been all this week with the President of the United States, that great man whom destiny has marked for this climax of human fortune. We have been concerting the united pacts and resolves of more than thirty States and nations to fight on in unity together and in fidelity one to another, without any thought except the total and final extirpation of the Hitler tyranny, the Japanese frenzy, and the Mussolini flop.

There shall be no halting, or half measures, there shall be no compromise, or parley. These gangs of bandits have sought to darken the light of the world; have sought to stand between the common people of all the lands and their march forward into their inheritance. They shall themselves be cast into the pit of death and shame, and only when the earth has been cleansed and purged of their crimes and their villainy shall we turn from the task which they have forced upon us, a task which we were reluctant to undertake, but which we shall now most faithfully and punctiliously discharge. According to my sense of proportion, this is no time to speak of the hopes of the future, or the broader world which lies beyond our struggles and our victory. We have to win that world for our children. We have to win it by our sacrifices. We have not won it yet. The crisis is upon us. The power of the enemy is immense. If we were in any way to underrate the strength, the resources or the ruthless savagery of that enemy, we should jeopardize, not only our lives, for they will be offered freely, but the cause of human freedom and progress to which we have vowed ourselves and all we have. We cannot for a moment afford to relax. On the contrary we must drive ourselves forward with unrelenting zeal. In this strange, terrible world war there is a place for everyone, man and woman, old and young, hale and halt; service in a thousand forms is open. There is no room now for the dilettante, the weakling, for the shirker, or the sluggard. The mine, the factory, the dockyard, the salt sea waves, the fields to till, the home, the hospital, the chair of the scientist, the pulpit of the preacher—from the highest to the humblest tasks, all are of equal honour; all have their part to play. The enemies ranged against us, coalesced and combined against us, have asked for total war. Let us make sure they get it.

That grand old minstrel, Harry Lauder—Sir Harry Lauder, I should say, and no honour was better deserved—had a song in the last War which began, "If we all look back on the history of the past, we can just tell where we are." Let us then look back. We plunged into this war all unprepared because we had pledged our word to stand by the side of Poland, which Hitler had feloniously invaded, and in spite of a gallant resistance had soon struck down. There followed those astonishing seven months which were called on this side of the Atlantic the "phoney" war. Suddenly the explosion of pent-up German strength and preparation burst upon Norway, Denmark, Holland, and Belgium. All these absolutely blameless neutrals, to most of whom Germany up to the last moment was giving every kind of guarantee and assurance, were overrun and trampled down. The hideous massacre of Rotterdam, where 30,000 people perished, showed the ferocious barbarism in which the German Air Force revels when, as in Warsaw and later Belgrade, it is able to bomb practically undefended cities.

On top of all this came the great French catastrophe. The French Army collapsed, and the French nation was dashed into utter and, as it has so far proved, irretrievable confusion. The French Government had at their own suggestion solemnly bound themselves with us not to make a separate peace. It was their duty and it was also their interest to go to North Africa, where they would have been at the head of the French Empire. In Africa, with our aid, they would have had overwhelming sea power. They would have had the recognition of the United States, and the use of all the gold they had lodged beyond the seas. If they had done this Italy might have been driven out of the war before the end of 1940, and France would have held her place as a nation in the counsels of the Allies and at the conference table of the victors. But their generals misled them. When I warned them that Britain would fight on alone whatever they did, their generals told their Prime Minister and his divided Cabinet, "In three weeks England will have her neck wrung like a chicken." Some chicken! Some neck!

What a contrast has been the behaviour of the valient, stout-hearted Dutch, who still stand forth as a strong living partner in the struggle! Their venerated Queen and their Government are in England, their Princess and her children have found asylum and protection here in your midst. But the Dutch nation are defending their Empire with dogged courage and tenacity by land and sea and in the air. Their submarines are inflicting a heavy daily toll upon the Japanese robbers who have come across the seas to steal the wealth of the East Indies, and to ravage and exploit its fertility and its civilization. The British Empire and the United States are going to the aid of the Dutch. We are going to fight out this new war against Japan together. We have suffered together and we shall conquer together.

But the men of Bordeaux, the men of Vichy, they would do nothing like this. They lay prostrate at the foot of the conqueror. They fawned upon him. What have they got out of it? The fragment of France which was left to them is just as powerless, just as hungry as, and even more miserable, because more divided, than the occupied regions themselves. Hitler plays from day to day a cat-and-mouse game with these tormented men. One day he will charge them a little less for holding their countrymen down. Another day he will let out a few thousand broken prisoners of war from the one-and-a-half or one-and-three-quarter millions he has collected. Or again he will shoot a hundred French hostages to give them a taste of the lash. On these blows and favours the Vichy Government have been content to live from day to day. But even this will not go on indefinitely. At any moment it may suit Hitler's plans to brush them away. Their only guarantee is Hitler's good faith, which, as everyone knows, biteth like the adder and stingeth like the asp.

But some Frenchmen there were who would not bow their knees and who under General de Gaulle have continued the fight on the side of the Allies. They have been condemned to death by the men of Vichy, but their names will be held and are being held in increasing respect by nine Frenchmen out of every ten throughout the once happy, smiling land of France. But now strong forces are at hand. The tide has turned against the Hun. Britain, which the men of Bordeaux thought and then hoped would soon be finished, Britain with her Empire around her carried the weight of the war alone for a whole long year through the darkest part of the valley. She is growing stronger every day. You can see it here in Canada. Anyone who has the slightest knowledge of our affairs is aware that very soon we shall be superior in every form of equipment to those who have taken us at the disadvantage of being but half armed.

The Russian armies, under their warrior leader, Josef Stalin, are waging furious war with increasing success along the thousand-mile front of their invaded country. General Auchinleck, at the head of a British, South African, New Zealand and Indian army, is striking down and mopping up the German and Italian forces which had attempted the invasion of Egypt. Not only are they being mopped up in the desert, but great numbers of them have been drowned on the way there by British submarines and the R. A. F. in which Australian squadrons played their part.

As I speak this afternoon an important battle is being fought around Jedabia. We must not attempt to prophesy its result, but I have good confidence. All this fighting in Libya proves that when our men have equal weapons in their hands and proper support from the air they are more than a match for the Nazi hordes. In Libya, as in Russia, events of great importance and of most hopeful import have taken place. But greatest of all, the mighty Republic of the United States has entered the conflict, and entered it in a manner which shows that for her there can be no withdrawal except by death or victory.

[Editor's Note: Churchill then spoke in French as follows] : Et partout dans la France occupée et inoccupée (car leur sort est égal), ces honnêtes gens, ce grand peuple, la nation française, se redresse. L'espoir se rallume dans les cœurs d'une race guerrière, même désarmée, berceau de la liberté révolutionnaire et terrible aux vainqueurs esclaves. Et partout, on voit le point du jour, et la lumière grandit, rougeâtre, mais claire. Nous ne perdrons jamais la confiance que la France jouera le rôle des hommes libres et qu'elle reprendra par des voies dures sa place dans la grande compagnie des nations libératrices et victorieuses.

Ici, au Canada, où la langue française est honorée et parlée, nous nous tenons prêts et armés pour aider et pour saluer cette résurrection nationale.

[Translation: And everywhere in France, occupied and unoccupied, for their fate is identical, these honest folk, this great people, the French nation, are rising again. Hope is springing up again in the hearts of a warrior race, even though disarmed, cradle of revolutionary liberty and terrible to slavish conquerors. And everywhere dawn is breaking and light spreading, reddish yet, but clear. We shall never lose confidence that France will play the role of free men again and, by hard paths, will once again attain her place in the great company of freedom-bringing and victorious nations.

Here in Canada, where the French language is honoured and spoken, we are armed and ready to help and to hail this national resurrection.]

Now that the whole of the North American continent is becoming one gigantic arsenal, and armed camp; now that the immense reserve power of Russia is gradually becoming apparent; now that long-suffering, unconquerable China sees help approaching; now that the outraged and subjugated nations can see daylight ahead, it is permissible to take a broad forward view of the war.

We may observe three main periods or phases of the struggle that lies before us. First there is the period of consolidation, of combination, and of final preparation. In this period, which will certainly be marked by much heavy fighting. we shall still be gathering our strength, resisting the assaults of the enemy, and acquiring the necessary overwhelming air superiority and shipping tonnage to give our armies the power to traverse, in whatever numbers may be necessary, the seas and oceans which, except in the case of Russia, separate us from our foes. It is only when the vast shipbuilding programme on which the United States has already made so much progress, and which you are powerfully aiding, comes into full flood, that we shall be able to bring the whole force of our manhood and of our modern scientific equipment to bear upon the enemy. How long this period will take depends upon the vehemence of the effort put into production in all our war industries and shipyards.

The second phase which will then open may be called the phase of liberation. During this phase we must look to the recovery of the territories which have been lost or which may yet be lost, and also we must look to the revolt of the conquered peoples from the moment that the rescuing and liberating armies and air forces appear in strength within their bounds. For this purpose it is imperative that no nation or region overrun, that no Government or State which has been conquered, should relax its moral and physical efforts and preparation for the day of deliverance. The invaders, be they German or Japanese, must everywhere be regarded as infected persons to be shunned and isolated as far as possible. Where active resistance is impossible, passive resistance must be maintained. The invaders and tyrants must be made to feel that their fleeting triumphs will have a terrible reckoning, and that they are hunted men and that their cause is doomed. Particular punishment will be reserved for the quislings and traitors who make themselves the tools of the enemy. They will be handed over to the judgment of their fellow-countrymen.

There is a third phase which must also be contemplated, namely, the assault upon the citadels and the home-lands of the guilty Powers both in Europe and in Asia. Thus I endeavour in a few words to cast some forward light upon the dark, inscrutable mysteries of the future. But in thus forecasting the course along which we should seek to advance, we must never forget that the power of the enemy and the action of the enemy may at every stage affect our fortunes. Moreover, you will notice that I have not attempted to assign any time-limits to the various phases. These time limits depend upon our exertions, upon our achievements, and on the hazardous and uncertain course of the war.

Nevertheless I feel it is right at this moment to make it clear that, while an ever-increasing bombing offensive against Germany will remain one of the principal methods by which we hope to bring the war to an end, it is by no means the only method which our growing strength now enables us to take into account. Evidently the most strenuous exertions must be made by all. As to the form which those exertions take, that is for each partner in the grand alliance to judge for himself in consultation with others and in harmony with the general scheme. Let us then address ourselves to our task, not in any way underrating its tremendous difficulties and perils, but in good heart and sober confidence, resolved that, whatever the cost, whatever the suffering, we shall stand by one another, true and faithful comrades, and do our duty God helping us, to the end.

THE WAR SITUATION

January 27, 1942

House of Commons

*To Churchill's dismay, the North African situation deteriorated further when General Rommel's counter-offensive in Libya seized the initiative from the British forces. This severe reverse was, however, overshadowed by the catastrophic news from Malaya. By January 27, the British forces had retired to Singapore. Churchill realized that "a vast, measureless array of disasters approached us in the onslaught of Japan." In these dark circumstances, Churchill "resolved to yield nothing to any quarter, to take the prime and direct personal responsibility upon myself, and to demand a Vote of Confidence from the House of Commons" (*The Hinge of Fate, *61). This speech was exceptionally long, even for Churchill's wartime speeches, and only excerpts are given.*

[Extract] From time to time in the life of any Government there come occasions which must be clarified. No one who has read the newspapers of the last few weeks about our affairs at home and abroad can doubt that such an occasion is at hand.

Since my return to this country, I have come to the conclusion that I must ask to be sustained by a Vote of Confidence from the House of Commons. This is a thoroughly normal, constitutional, democratic procedure. A Debate on the war has been asked for. I have arranged it in the fullest and freest manner for three whole days. Any Member will be free to say anything he thinks fit about or against the Administration or against the composition or personalities of the Government, to his heart's content, subject only to the reservation which the House is always so careful to observe about military secrets. Could you have anything freer than that? Could you have any higher expression of democracy than that? Very few other countries have institutions strong enough to sustain such a thing while they are fighting for their lives.

I owe it to the House to explain to them what has led me to ask for their exceptional support at this time. It has been suggested that we should have a three days' Debate of this kind in which the Government would no doubt be lustily belaboured by some of those who have lighter burdens to carry, and that at the end we should separate without a Division. In this case sections of the Press which are hostile—and there are some whose hostility is pronounced—could declare that the Government's credit was broken, and it might even be hinted, after all that has passed and all the discussion there has been, that it had been privately intimated to me that I should be very reckless if I asked for a Vote of Confidence from Parliament.

And the matter does not stop there. It must be remembered that these reports can then be flashed all over the world, and that they are repeated in enemy broadcasts night after night in order to show that the Prime Minister has no right to speak for the nation and that the Government in Britain is about to collapse. Anyone who listens to the fulminations which come from across the water knows that that is no exaggeration. Of course, these statements from foreign sources would not be true, but neither would it be helpful to anyone that there should be any doubt about our position.

There is another aspect. We in this Island for a long time were alone, holding aloft the torch. We are no longer alone now. We are now at the centre and among those at the summit of 26 United Nations, comprising more than three-quarters of the population of the globe. Whoever speaks for Britain at this moment must be known to speak, not only in the name of the people—and that I feel pretty sure I may—but in the name of Parliament and, above all, of the House of Commons. It is a genuine public interest that requires that these facts should be made manifest afresh in a formal way.

We have had a great deal of bad news lately from the Far East, and I think it highly probable, for reasons which I shall presently explain, that we shall have a great deal more. Wrapped up in this bad news will be many tales of blunders and shortcomings, both in foresight and action. No one will pretend for a moment that disasters like these occur without there having been faults and shortcomings. I see all this rolling towards us like the waves in a storm, and that is another reason why I require a formal, solemn Vote of Confidence from the House of Commons, which hitherto in this struggle has never flinched. The House would fail in its duty if it did not insist upon two things, first, freedom of debate, and, secondly, a clear, honest, blunt vote thereafter. Then we shall all know where we are, and all those with whom we have to deal, at home and abroad, friend or foe, will know where we are and where they are. It is because we are to have a free debate, in which perhaps 20 to 30 Members can take part, that I demand an expression of opinion from the 300 or 400 Members who will have to sit silent.

It is because things have gone badly and worse is to come that I demand a Vote of Confidence. This will be placed on the Paper to-day, to be moved at a later stage. I do not see why this should hamper anyone. If a Member has helpful criticisms to make, or even severe corrections to administer, that may be perfectly consistent with thinking that in respect of the Administration, such as it is, he might go farther and fare worse. But if an hon. Gentleman dislikes the Government very much and feels it in the public interest that it should be broken up, he ought to have the manhood to testify his convictions in the Lobby. There is no need to be mealy-mouthed in debate. There is no objection to anything being said, plain, or even plainer, and the Government will do their utmost to conform to any standard which may be set in the course of the debate. But no one need be mealy-mouthed in debate, and no one should be chicken-hearted in voting. I have voted against Governments I have been elected to support, and, looking back, I have sometimes felt very glad that I did so. Everyone in these rough times must do what he thinks is his duty.

The House of Commons, which is at present the most powerful representative Assembly in the world, must also—I am sure, will also—bear in mind the effect produced abroad by all its proceedings. We have also to remember how oddly foreigners view our country and its way of doing things. When Rudolf Hess flew over here some months ago he firmly believed that he had only to gain access to certain circles in this country for what he described as "the Churchill clique" to be thrown out of power and for a Government to be set up with which Hitler could negotiate a magnanimous peace. The only importance attaching to the opinions of Hess is the fact that he was fresh from the atmosphere of Hitler's intimate table. But, I can assure you that since I have been back in this country I have had anxious inquiries from a dozen countries, and reports of enemy propaganda in a score of countries, all turning upon the point whether His Majesty's present Government is to be dismissed from power or not. This may seem silly to us, but in those mouths abroad it is hurtful and mischievous to the common effort. I am not asking for any special, personal favours in these circumstances, but I am sure the House would wish to make its position clear; therefore I stand by the ancient, constitutional, Parliamentary doctrine of free debate and faithful voting. . . .

For this decision [to concentrate the bulk of the British forces in the Middle East] in its broad strategic aspects, and also for the diplomatic policy in regard to Russia, I take the fullest personal responsibility. If we have handled our resources wrongly, no one is so much to blame as me. If we have not got large modern air forces and tanks in Burma and Malaya to-night, no one is more accountable than I am. Why then should I be called upon to pick out scapegoats, to throw the blame on generals or airmen or sailors? Why then should I be called upon to drive away loyal and trusted colleagues and friends to appease the clamour of certain sections of the British and Australian Press, or in order to take the edge off our reverses in Malaya and the Far East, and the punishment which we have yet to take there? I should be ashamed to do such a thing at such a time, and if I were capable of doing it, believe me, I should be incapable of rendering this country or this House any further service.

I say that without in the slightest degree seeking to relieve myself from my duty and responsibility to endeavour to make continual improvements in Ministerial positions. It is the duty of every Prime Minister to the House, but we have to be quite sure that they are improvements in every case, and not only in every case but in the setting. I could not possibly descend to what the German radio repeatedly credits me with—an attempt to get out of difficulties in which I really bear the main load by offering up scapegoats to public displeasure. Many people, many very well-meaning people, begin their criticisms and articles by saying, "Of course, we are all in favour of the Prime Minister because he has the people behind him. But what about the muddles made by this or that Department; what about that general or this Minister?" But I am the man that Parliament and the nation have got to blame for the general way in which they are served, and I cannot serve them effectively unless, in spite of all that has gone wrong, and that is going to go wrong, I have their trust and faithful aid.

I must linger for a moment on our political affairs, because we are conducting the war on the basis of a full democracy and a free Press, and that is an attempt which has not been made before in such circumstances. A variety of attacks are made upon the composition of the Government. It is said that it is formed upon a party and political basis. But so is the House of Commons. It is silly to extol the Parliamentary system and then, in the next breath, to say, "Away with party and away with politics." From one quarter I am told that the leaders of the Labour party ought to be dismissed from the Cabinet. This would be a return to party Government pure and simple. From opposite quarters it is said that no one who approved of Munich should be allowed to hold office. To do that would be to cast a reflection upon the great majority of the nation at that time, and also to deny the strongest party in the House any proportionate share in the National Government, which again, in turn, might cause inconvenience. Even my right hon. Friend the leader of the Liberal party, the Secretary of State for Air [Sir Archibald Sinclair] whose help to-day I value so much and with whom, as a lifelong friend, it is a pleasure to work, even he has not escaped unscathed. If I were to show the slightest weakness in dealing with these opposite forms of criticism, not only should I deprive myself of loyal and experienced colleagues, but I should destroy the National Government and rupture the war-time unity of Parliament itself.

Other attacks are directed against individual Ministers. I have been urged to make an example of the Chancellor of the Duchy of Lancaster, who is now returning from his mission in the Far East. Thus, he would be made to bear the blame for our misfortunes. The position of the Chancellor of the Duchy of Lancaster at the head of the Council which he had been instructed to form at Singapore was rendered obsolete by the decision which I reached with the President of the United States to set up a Supreme Commander for the main fighting zone in the Far East. The whole conception of a Supreme Commander is that, under the direction of the Governments he serves, he is absolute master of all authorities in the region assigned to him. This would be destroyed if political functionaries representing the various nations—for it is not only this country which would be represented; others would have to be represented as well as ours—were clustered round him. The function of the Chancellor of the Duchy was therefore exhausted by the appointment of General Wavell to the Supreme Command. I may say that regret was expressed at his departure by the New Zealand and Australian Governments, and still more by the Council he formed at Singapore, which, in a localised and subordinate form, it has been found necessary to carry on. When I am invited, under threats of unpopularity to myself or the Government, to victimise the Chancellor of the Duchy, and throw him to the wolves, I say to those who make this amiable suggestion, I can only say to them, "I much regret that I am unable to gratify your wishes"—or words to that effect. [*Laughter*]

The outstanding question upon which the House should form its judgment for the purposes of the impending Division is whether His Majesty's Government were right in giving a marked priority in the distribution of the forces and equipment we could send overseas, to Russia, to Libya, and, to a lesser extent, to the Levant-Caspian danger front, and whether we were right in accepting, for the time being, a far lower standard of forces and equipment for the Far East than for these other theatres. . . .

I should like to express, in the name of the House, my admiration of the splendid courage and quality with which the small American Army, under General MacArthur, has resisted brilliantly for so long, at desperate odds, the hordes of Japanese who have been hurled against it by superior air power and superior sea power. Amid our own troubles, we send out to General MacArthur and his soldiers, and also to the Filipinos, who are defending their native soil with vigour and courage, our salute across the wide spaces which we and the United States will presently rule again together. Nor must I fail to pay a tribute, in the name of the House, to the Dutch, who, in the air and with their submarines, their surface craft, and their solid fighting troops, are playing one of the main parts in the struggle now going on in the Malaysian Archipelago. . . .

When I reached the United States, accompanied by our principal officers and large technical staffs, further important steps were taken by the President, with my cordial assent, and with the best technical advice we could obtain, to move from many directions everything that ships could carry and all air power that could be flown transported and serviced to suitable points. The House would be very ill-advised to suppose that the seven weeks which have passed since 7th December have been weeks of apathy and indecision for the English-speaking world. Odd as it may seem, quite a lot has been going on. But we must not nourish or indulge light and extravagant hopes or suppose that the advantages which the enemy has gained can soon or easily be taken from him. However, to sum up the bad and the good together, in spite of the many tragedies past and future, and with all pity for those who have suffered and will suffer, I must profess my profound thankfulness for what has happened throughout the whole world in the last two months.

I now turn for a short space—I hope I am not unduly wearying the House, but I feel that the war has become so wide that there are many aspects that must be regarded—to the question of the organisation, the international, inter-Allied or inter-United Nations organisation, which must be developed to meet the fact that we are a vast confederacy. To hear some people talk, however, one would think that the way to win the war is to make sure that every Power contributing armed forces and every branch of these armed forces is represented on all the councils and organisations which have to be set up, and that everybody is fully consulted before anything is done. That is in fact the most sure way to lose a war. You have to be aware of the well-known danger of having "more harness than horse," to quote a homely expression. Action to be successful must rest in the fewest number of hands possible. Nevertheless, now that we are working in the closest partnership with the United States and have also to consider our alliances with Russia and with China, as well as the bonds which unite us with the rest of the 26 United Nations and with our Dominions, it is evident that our system must become far more complex than heretofore.

I had many discussions with the President upon the Anglo-American war direction, especially as it affects this war against Japan, to which Russia is not yet a party. The physical and geographical difficulties of finding a common working centre for the leaders of nations and the great staffs of nations which cover the whole globe are insuperable. Whatever plan is made will be open to criticism and many wild objections. There is no solution that can be found by which the war can be discussed from day to day fully by all the leading military and political authorities concerned. I have, however, arranged with President Roosevelt that there should be a body in Washington called the Combined Chiefs of the Staff Committee, consisting of the three United States Chiefs of the Staff, men of the highest distinction, and three high officers representing and acting under the general instructions of the British Chiefs of the Staff Committee in London. This body will advise the President, and in the event of divergence of view between the British and American Chiefs of the Staff or their representatives, the difference must be adjusted by personal agreement between him and me as representing our respective countries. We must also concert together the closest association with Premier Stalin and Generalissimo Chiang Kai-shek as well as with the rest of the Allied and Associated Powers. We shall, of course, also remain in the closest touch with one another on all important questions of policy. . . .

During those three weeks which I spent in Mr. Roosevelt's home and family, I established with him relations not only of comradeship, but, I think I may say, of friendship. We can say anything to each other, however painful. When we parted he wrung my hand, saying, "We will fight this through to the bitter end, whatever the cost may be." Behind him rises the gigantic and hitherto unmobilised power of the people of the United States, carrying with them in their life and death struggle the entire, or almost the entire, Western hemisphere. . . .

Although I feel the broadening swell of victory and liberation bearing us and all the tortured peoples onwards safely to the final goal, I must confess to feeling the weight of the war upon me even more than in the tremendous summer days of 1940. There are so many fronts which are open, so many vulnerable points to defend, so many inevitable misfortunes, so many shrill voices raised to take advantage, now that we can breathe more freely, of all the turns and twists of war. Therefore, I feel entitled to come to the House of Commons, whose servant I am, and ask them not to press me to act against my conscience and better judgment and make scapegoats in order to improve my own position, not to press me to do the things which may be clamoured for at the moment but which will not help in our war effort, but, on the contrary, to give me their encouragement and to give me their aid. I have never ventured to predict the future. I stand by my original programme, blood, toil, tears and sweat, which is all I have ever offered, to which I added, five months later, "many shortcomings, mistakes and disappointments." But it is because I see the light gleaming behind the clouds and broadening on our path, that I make so bold now as to demand a declaration of confidence of the House of Commons as an additional weapon in the armoury of the United Nations.

THE WAR SITUATION

January 29, 1942

House of Commons

*The Vote of Confidence debate continued for three days. "The tone was to me unexpectedly friendly" Churchill later wrote. He was anxious to force his critics into voting against the Government. In the event, the Government triumphed by 464 votes to 1. Churchill's final speech was designed, in his words, "to urge our critics into the lobby against us without at the same time offending the now thoroughly reconciled assembly" (*The Hinge of Fate, *70).*

[Extract] No one can say that this has not been a full and free Debate. No one can say that criticism has been hampered or stifled. No one can say that it has not been a necessary Debate. Many will think it has been a valuable Debate. But I think there will be very few who upon reflection will doubt that a Debate of this far-reaching character and memorable importance, in times of hard and anxious war, with the state of the world what it is, our relationships to other countries being what they are, and our own safety so deeply involved—very few people will doubt that it should not close without a solemn and formal expression of the opinion of the House in relation both to the Government and to the prosecution of the war.

In no country in the world at the present time could a Government conducting a war be exposed to such a stress. No dictator country fighting for its life would dare allow such a discussion. They do not even allow the free transmission of news to their peoples, or even the reception of foreign broadcasts, to which we are all now so hardily inured. Even in the great democracy of the United States the Executive does not stand in the same direct, immediate, day-to-day relation to the Legislative body as we do. The President, in many vital respects independent of the Legislature, Commander-in-Chief of all the Forces of the Republic, has a fixed term of office, during which his authority can scarcely be impugned. But here in this country the House of Commons is master all the time of the life of the Administration. Against its decisions there is only one appeal, the appeal to the nation, an appeal it is very difficult to make under the conditions of a war like this, with a register like this, with air raids and invasion always hanging over us.

Therefore, I say that the House of Commons has a great responsibility. It owes it to itself and it owes it to the people and the whole Empire, and to the world cause, either to produce an effective, alternative Administration by which the King's Government can be carried on, or to sustain that Government in the enormous tasks and trials which it has to endure. I feel myself very much in need of that help at the present time, and I am sure I shall be accorded it in a manner to give encouragement and comfort, as well as guidance and suggestion. I am sorry that I have not been able to be here throughout the whole Debate, but I have read every word of the Debate, except what has been spoken and has not yet been printed, and I can assure the House that I shall be ready to profit to the full from many constructive and helpful lines of thought which have been advanced, even when they come from the most hostile quarters. I shall not be like that saint to whom I have before referred in this House, but whose name I have unhappily forgotten, who refused to do right because the devil prompted him. Neither shall I be deterred from doing what I am convinced is right by the fact that I have thought differently about it in some distant, or even in some recent past. . . .

I have finished, and it only remains for us to act. I have tried to lay the whole position before the House as far as public interest will allow, and very fully have we gone into matters. On behalf of His Majesty's Government, I make no complaint of the Debate, I offer no apologies, I offer no excuses, I make no promises. In no way have I mitigated the sense of danger and impending misfortunes of a minor character and of a severe character which still hang over us, but at the same time I avow my confidence, never stronger than at this moment, that we shall bring this conflict to an end in a manner agreeable to the future welfare of the world. I have finished. Let every man act now in accordance with what he thinks is his duty in harmony with his heart and conscience.

THE FALL OF SINGAPORE

February 15, 1942

Broadcast, London

On February 15, General Percival, commanding the British and Dominion troops in Singapore, surrendered unconditionally to the Japanese. It was, as Churchill sombrely said, "a heavy and far-reaching military defeat"–one of the worst of the war–and was a profound shock to the British public. The fact that it occurred four days after the battle cruisers Scharnhorst, Gneisenau *and* Prinz Eugen *had sailed from Brest through the English Channel to their home ports in daylight further increased public, Press and Parliamentary clamour.*

[Extract] Nearly six months have passed since at the end of August I made a broadcast directly to my fellow-countrymen; it is therefore worthwhile looking back over this half-year of struggle for life, for that is what it has been, and what it is, to see what has happened to our fortunes and to our prospects. . . .

How do matters stand now? Taking it all in all, are our chances of survival better or are they worse than in August, 1941? How is it with the British Empire or Commonwealth of Nations? Are we up or down? What has happened to the principles of freedom and decent civilisation for which we are fighting? Are they making headway, or are they in greater peril? Let us take the rough with the smooth, let us put the good and bad side by side, and let us try to see exactly where we are. The first and greatest of events is that the United States is now unitedly and whole-heartedly in the war with us. The other day I crossed the Atlantic again to see President Roosevelt. This time we met not only as friends, but as comrades standing side by side and shoulder to shoulder in a battle for dear life and dearer honour in the common cause and against a common foe. When I survey and compute the power of the United States and its vast resources and feel that they are now in it with us, with the British Commonwealth of Nations all together, however long it lasts, till death or victory, I cannot believe there is any other fact in the whole world which can compare with that. That is what I have dreamed of, aimed at and worked for, and now it has come to pass.

But there is another fact, in some ways more immediately effective. The Russian armies have not been defeated, they have not been torn to pieces. The Russian people have not been conquered or destroyed. Leningrad and Moscow have not been taken. The Russian armies are in the field. They are not holding the line of the Urals or the line of the Volga. They are advancing victoriously, driving the foul invader from that native soil they have guarded so bravely and loved so well. More than that: for the first time they have broken the Hitler legend. Instead of the easy victories and abundant booty which he and his hordes had gathered in the West, he has found in Russia so far only disaster, failure, the shame of unspeakable crimes, the slaughter or loss of vast numbers of German soldiers, and the icy wind that blows across the Russian snow.

Here, then, are two tremendous fundamental facts which will in the end dominate the world situation and make victory possible in a form never possible before. But there is another heavy and terrible side to the account, and this must be set in the balance against these inestimable gains. Japan has plunged into the war, and is ravaging the beautiful, fertile, prosperous, and densely populated lands of the Far East. It would never have been in the power of Great Britain while fighting Germany and Italy—the nations long hardened and prepared for war—while fighting in the North Sea, in the Mediterranean and in the Atlantic—it would never have been in our power to defend the Pacific and the Far East single-handed against the onslaught of Japan. We have only just been able to keep our heads above water at home; only by a narrow margin have we brought in the food and the supplies; only by so little have we held our own in the Nile Valley and the Middle East. The Mediterranean is closed, and all our transports have to go round the Cape of Good Hope, each ship making only three voyages in the year. Not a ship, not an aeroplane, not a tank, not an anti-tank gun or an anti-aircraft gun has stood idle. Everything we have has been deployed either against the enemy or awaiting his attack. We are struggling hard in the Libyan Desert, where perhaps another serious battle will soon be fought. We have to provide for the safety and order of liberated Abyssinia, of conquered Eritrea, of Palestine, of liberated Syria, and redeemed Iraq, and of our new ally, Persia. A ceaseless stream of ships, men, and materials has flowed from this country for a year and a half, in order to build up and sustain our armies in the Middle East, which guard those vast regions on either side of the Nile Valley. We had to do our best to give substantial aid to Russia. We gave it her in her darkest hour, and we must not fail in our undertaking now. How then in this posture, gripped and held and battered as we were, could we have provided for the safety of the Far East against such an avalanche of fire and steel as has been hurled upon us by Japan? Always, my friends, this thought overhung our minds.

There was, however, one hope and one hope only—namely that if Japan entered the war with her allies, Germany and Italy, the United States would come in on our side, thus far more than repairing the balance. For this reason, I have been most careful, all these many months, not to give any provocation to Japan, and to put up with Japanese encroachments, dangerous though they were, so that if possible, whatever happened, we should not find ourselves forced to face this new enemy alone. I could not be sure that we should succeed in this policy, but it has come to pass. Japan has struck her felon blow, and a new, far greater champion has drawn the sword of implacable vengeance against her and on our side.

I shall frankly state to you that I did not believe it was in the interests of Japan to burst into war both upon the British Empire and the United States. I thought it would be a very irrational act. Indeed, when you remember that they did not attack us after Dunkirk when we were so much weaker, when our hopes of United States help were of the most slender character, and when we were all alone, I could hardly believe that they would commit what seemed to be a mad act. To-night the Japanese are triumphant. They shout their exultation round the world. We suffer. We are taken aback. We are hard pressed. But I am sure even in this dark hour that "criminal madness" will be the verdict which history will pronounce upon the authors of Japanese aggression, after the events of 1942 and 1943 have been inscribed upon its sombre pages.

The immediate deterrent which the United States exercised upon Japan—apart of course from the measureless resources of the American Union—was the dominant American battle fleet in the Pacific, which, with the naval forces we could spare, confronted Japanese aggression with the shield of superior sea-power. But, my friends, by an act of sudden violent surprise, long-calculated, balanced and prepared, and delivered under the crafty cloak of negotiation, the shield of sea-power which protected the fair lands and islands of the Pacific Ocean was for the time being, and only for the time being, dashed to the ground. Into the gap thus opened rushed the invading armies of Japan. We were exposed to the assault of a warrior race of nearly eighty millions, with a large outfit of modern weapons, whose war lords had been planning and scheming for this day, and looking forward to it perhaps for twenty years—while all the time our good people on both sides of the Atlantic were prating about perpetual peace, and cutting down each other's navies in order to set a good example. The overthrow, for a while, of British and United States sea-power in the Pacific was like the breaking of some mighty dam; the long-gathered pent-up waters rushed down the peaceful valley, carrying ruin and devastation forward on their foam, and spreading their inundations far and wide.

No one must underrate any more the gravity and efficiency of the Japanese war machine. Whether in the air or upon the sea, or man to man on land, they have already proved themselves to be formidable, deadly, and, I am sorry to say, barbarous antagonists. This proves a hundred times over that there never was the slightest chance, even though we had been much better prepared in many ways than we were, of our standing up to them alone while we had Nazi Germany at our throat and Fascist Italy at our belly. It proves something else. And this should be a comfort and a reassurance. We can now measure the wonderful strength of the Chinese people who under Generalissimo Chiang Kai-shek have single-handed fought this hideous Japanese aggressor for four and a half years and left him baffled and dismayed. This they have done, although they were a people whose whole philosophy for many ages was opposed to war and warlike arts, and who in their agony were caught ill-armed, ill-supplied with munitions, and hopelessly outmatched in the air. We must not underrate the power and malice of our latest foe, but neither must we undervalue the gigantic, overwhelming forces which now stand in the line with us in this world-struggle for freedom, and which, once they have developed their full natural inherent power, whatever has happened in the meanwhile, will be found fully capable of squaring all accounts and setting all things right for a good long time to come.

You know I have never prophesied to you or promised smooth and easy things, and now all I have to offer is hard adverse war for many months ahead. I must warn you, as I warned the House of Commons before they gave me their generous vote of confidence a fortnight ago, that many misfortunes, severe torturing losses, remorseless and gnawing anxieties lie before us. To our British folk these may seem even harder to bear when they are at a great distance than when the savage Hun was shattering our cities and we all felt in the midst of the battle ourselves. But the same qualities which brought us through the awful jeopardy of the summer of 1940 and its long autumn and winter bombardment from the air, will bring us through this other new ordeal, though it may be more costly and will certainly be longer. One fault, one crime, and one crime only, can rob the United Nations and the British people, upon whose constancy this grand alliance came into being, of the victory upon which their lives and honour depend. A weakening in our purpose and therefore in our unity—that is the mortal crime. Whoever is guilty of that crime, or of bringing it about in others, of him let it be said that it were better for him that a millstone were hanged about his neck and he were cast into the sea.

Last autumn, when Russia was in her most dire peril, when vast numbers of her soldiers had been killed or taken prisoner, when one-third of her whole munitions capacity lay, as it still lies, in Nazi German hands, when Kiev fell, and the foreign Ambassadors were ordered out of Moscow, the Russian people did not fall to bickering among themselves. They just stood together and worked and fought all the harder. They did not lose trust in their leaders; they did not try to break up their Government. Hitler had hoped to find quislings and fifth columnists in the wide regions he overran, and among the unhappy masses who fell into his power. He looked for them. He searched for them. But he found none.

The system upon which the Soviet Government is founded is very different from ours or from that of the United States. However that may be, the fact remains that Russia received blows which her friends feared and her foes believed were mortal, and through preserving national unity and persevering undaunted, Russia has had the marvellous come-back for which we thank God now. In the English-speaking world we rejoice in free institutions. We have free parliaments and a free press. This is the way of life we have been used to. This is the way of life we are fighting to defend. But it is the duty of all who take part in those free institutions to make sure, as the House of Commons and the House of Lords have done, and will I doubt not do, that the National Executive Government in time of war have a solid foundation on which to stand and on which to act; that the misfortunes and mistakes of war are not exploited against them; that while they are kept up to the mark by helpful and judicious criticism or advice, they are not deprived of the persisting power to run through a period of bad times and many cruel vexations and come out on the other side and get to the top of the hill.

To-night I speak to you at home; I speak to you in Australia and New Zealand, for whose safety we will strain every nerve; to our loyal friends in India and Burma; to our gallant Allies, the Dutch and Chinese; and to our kith and kin in the United States. I speak to you all under the shadow of a heavy and far-reaching military defeat. It is a British and Imperial defeat. Singapore has fallen. All the Malay Peninsula has been overrun. Other dangers gather about us out there, and none of the dangers which we have hitherto successfully withstood at home and in the East are in any way diminished. This, therefore, is one of those moments when the British race and nation can show their quality and their genius. This is one of those moments when it can draw from the heart of misfortune the vital impulses of victory. Here is the moment to display that calm and poise combined with grim determination which not so long ago brought us out of the very jaws of death. Here is another occasion to show—as so often in our long story—that we can meet reverses with dignity and with renewed accessions of strength. We must remember that we are no longer alone. We are in the midst of a great company. Three-quarters of the human race are now moving with us. The whole future of mankind may depend upon our action and upon our conduct. So far we have not failed. We shall not fail now. Let us move forward steadfastly together into the storm and through the storm.

THE CONDUCT OF THE WAR

July 2, 1942

House of Commons

*On June 17 Churchill flew to Washington, and thence to Hyde Park two days later to confer with Roosevelt. One of the key topics was that of "Tube Alloys," the code-word for the development of the atomic bomb, on which Churchill was convinced that there must be full Anglo-American cooperation. Such cooperation had been initiated in October 1941, and had produced results which raised the question of turning the research programme toward the development and production of a bomb. It was agreed that the main plant should be established in the United States. On June 21, in Washington, Roosevelt handed Churchill a telegram informing him of the fall of Tobruk. "This was one of the heaviest blows I can recall during the war" (*The Hinge of Fate, *383). It was, however, mitigated by the immediate practical assistance to the British forces offered by the Americans, and gratefully accepted.*

The long succession of British defeats, culminating in the fall of Tobruk, led to a Motion of Censure, moved by Sir John Wardlaw-Milne and seconded by Admiral Sir Roger Keyes, expressing "no confidence in the central direction of the war." The debate was arranged for July 1. Wardlaw-Milne offered to withdraw his motion in view of the critical situation in the Middle East, but the Cabinet refused.

In moving his Motion of Censure, Wardlaw-Milne destroyed a good speech by making the incredible proposal that the Duke of Gloucester should become Commander-in-Chief of the British Army. Although Wardlaw-Milne criticised Churchill for taking too much upon himself, Keyes, in seconding the motion, argued that Churchill had not interfered enough. Indeed, Keyes said that Churchill's resignation "would be a deplorable disaster."

Despite this unpromising start, the Government's critics attacked its record with vigour, and just before Churchill spoke there was a strong attack on him by Hore-Belisha: "In a hundred days we lost our Empire in the Far East. What will happen in the next hundred days?" Churchill's speech was very long and related the military situation in considerable detail.

After Churchill's speech, the motion was rejected 475 to 25.

[Extract] This long Debate has now reached its final stage. What a remarkable example it has been of the unbridled freedom of our Parliamentary institutions in time of war! Everything that could be thought of or raked up has been used to weaken confidence in the Government, has been used to prove that Ministers are incompetent and to weaken their confidence in themselves, to make the Army distrust the backing it is getting from the civil power, to make the workmen lose confidence in the weapons they are striving so hard to make, to represent the Government as a set of nonentities over whom the Prime Minister towers, and then to undermine him in his own heart and, if possible, before the eyes of the nation. All this poured out by cable and radio to all parts of the world, to the distress of all our friends and to the delight of all our foes. I am in favour of this freedom, which no other country would use, or dare to use, in times of mortal peril such as those through which we are passing. But the story must not end there, and I make now my appeal to the House of Commons to make sure that it does not end there.

Although I have done my best, my utmost, to prepare a full and considered statement for the House, I must confess that I have found it very difficult, even during the bitter animosity of the diatribe of the hon. Member for Ebbw Vale (Mr. Bevan), with all its carefully aimed and calculated hostility, to concentrate my thoughts upon this Debate and to withdraw them from the tremendous and most critical battle now raging in Egypt. At any moment we may receive news of grave importance. But the right hon. Gentleman the Member for Devonport (Mr. Hore-Belisha) has devoted a large part of his speech, not to this immediate campaign and struggle in Egypt, but to the offensive started in Libya nearly eight months ago, and he, as did the mover of the Motion of Censure, accused me of making misstatements in saying that, for the first time, our men met the Germans on equal terms in the matter of modern weapons. This offensive was not a failure. Our Armies took 40,000 prisoners. They drove the enemy back 400 miles. They took the great fortified positions on which he had rested so long. They drove him to the very edge of Cyrenaica, and it was only when his tanks had been reduced to 70 or perhaps 80 that, by a brilliant tactical resurgence, the German general set in motion a series of events which led to a retirement I think to a point 150 miles more to the West than that from which our offensive had started. Ten thousand Germans were taken prisoner among those in that fight. I am not at all prepared to regard it as anything but a highly creditable and highly profitable transaction for the Army of the Western Desert. I do not understand why this point should be made now, when, in all conscience, there are newer and far graver matters which fill our minds.

The military misfortunes of the last fortnight in Cyrenaica and Egypt have completely transformed the situation, not only in that theatre, but throughout the Mediterranean. We have lost upwards of 50,000 men, by far the larger proportion of whom are prisoners, a great mass of material, and, in spite of carefully-organised demolitions, large quantities of stores have fallen into the enemy's hands. Rommel has advanced nearly 400 miles through the desert, and is now approaching the fertile Delta of the Nile. The evil effects of these events, in Turkey, in Spain, in France and in French North Africa, cannot yet be measured. We are at this moment in the presence of a recession of our hopes and prospects in the Middle East and in the Mediterranean unequalled since the fall of France. If there are any would-be profiteers of disaster who feel able to paint the picture in darker colours, they are certainly at liberty to do so.

A painful feature of this melancholy scene was its suddenness. The fall of Tobruk, with its garrison of about 25,000 men, in a single day, was utterly unexpected. Not only was it unexpected by the House and the public at large, but by the

War Cabinet, by the Chiefs of the Staff, and by the General Staff of the Army. It was also unexpected by General Auchinleck and the High Command in the Middle East. On the night before its capture, we received a telegram from General Auchinleck that he had allotted what he believed to be an adequate garrison, that the defences were in good order, and that 90 days' supplies were available for the troops. It was hoped that we could hold the very strong frontier positions which had been built up by the Germans and improved by ourselves, from Sollum to Halfaya Pass, from Capuzzo to Fort Maddalena. From this position our newly-built railroad ran backwards at right angles, and we were no longer formed to a flank—as the expression goes—with our backs to the sea, as we had been in the earlier stages of the new Libyan battle. General Auchinleck expected to maintain these positions until the powerful reinforcements which were approaching, and have in part arrived, enabled him to make a much stronger bid to seize the initiative for a counter-offensive.

The question of whether Tobruk could have been held or not is difficult and disputable. It is one of those questions which are more easy to decide after the event than before it. It is one of those questions which could be decided only with full knowledge of the approaching reinforcements. The critics have a great advantage in these matters. As the racing saying goes, they "stand on velvet." If we had decided to evacuate the place, they could have gone into action on "the pusillanimous and cowardly scuttle from Tobruk," which would have made quite a promising line of advance. But those who are responsible for carrying on the war have no such easy options open. They have to decide beforehand. The decision to hold Tobruk and the dispositions made for that purpose were taken by General Auchinleck, but I should like to say that we, the War Cabinet and our professional advisers, thoroughly agreed with General Auchinleck beforehand, and, although in tactical matters the commander-in-chief in any war theatre is supreme and his decision is final, we consider that, if he was wrong, we were wrong too, and I am very ready on behalf of His Majesty's Government to take my full share of responsibility. The hon. Member for Kidderminster (Sir J. Wardlaw-Milne) asked where the order for the capitulation of Tobruk came from. Did it come from the battlefield, from Cairo, from London or from Washington? In what a strange world of thought he is living, if he imagines I sent from Washington an order for the capitulation of Tobruk! The decision was taken to the best of my knowledge by the Commander of the Forces, and certainly it was most unexpected to the Higher Command in the Middle East. . . .

Shortly after the present National Government was formed, in June, 1940, to be exact, I called a meeting of all the authorities to design and make a new tank, capable of speedy mass production and adapted to the war conditions to be foreseen in 1942. In 1942—that was the test. Of course I do not attempt to settle the technical details of tank design, any more than I interfere with the purely tactical decisions of generals in the field. All the highest expert authorities were brought together several times and made to hammer out a strong and heavy tank, adapted primarily for the defense of this Island against invasion, but capable of other employment in various theatres. This tank, the A.22, was ordered off the drawing-board, and large numbers went into production very quickly. As might be expected, it had many defects and teething troubles, and when these became apparent the tank was appropriately rechristened the

"Churchill." These defects have now been largely overcome. I am sure that this tank will prove, in the end, a powerful, massive and serviceable weapon of war....

To return to the main argument which is before the House, I willingly accept, indeed I am bound to accept, what the Noble Lord (Earl Winterton) has called the "constitutional responsibility" for everything that has happened, and I consider that I discharged that responsibility by not interfering with the technical handling of armies in contact with the enemy. But before the battle began I urged General Auchinleck to take the command himself, because I was sure nothing was going to happen in the vast area of the Middle East in the next month or two comparable in importance to the fighting of this battle in the Western Desert, and I thought he was the man to handle the business. He gave me various good reasons for not doing so, and General Ritchie fought the battle. As I told the House on Tuesday, General Auchinleck, on 25th June, superseded General Ritchie and assumed the command himself. We at once approved his decision, but I must frankly confess that the matter was not one on which we could form any final judgment, so far as the superseded officer is concerned. I cannot pretend to form a judgment upon what has happened in this battle. I like commanders on land and sea and in the air to feel that between them and all forms of public criticism the Government stands like a strong bulkhead. They ought to have a fair chance, and more than one chance. Men may make mistakes and learn from their mistakes. Men may have bad luck, and their luck may change. But anyhow you will not get generals to run risks unless they feel they have behind them a strong Government. They will not run risks unless they feel that they need not look over their shoulders or worry about what is happening at home, unless they feel they can concentrate their gaze upon the enemy. And you will not, I may add, get a Government to run risks unless they feel that they have got behind them a loyal, solid majority. Look at the things we are being asked to do now, and imagine the kind of attack which would be made on us if we tried to do them and failed. In war time if you desire service you must give loyalty....

I wish to speak a few words "of great truth and respect"—as they say in the diplomatic documents—and I hope I may be granted the fullest liberty of debate. This Parliament has a peculiar responsibility. It presided over the beginning of the evils which have come on the world. I owe much to the House, and it is my hope that it may see the end of them in triumph. This it can do only if, in the long period which may yet have to be travelled, the House affords a solid foundation to the responsible Executive Government, placed in power by its own choice. The House must be a steady, stabilising factor in the State, and not an instrument by which the disaffected sections of the Press can attempt to promote one crisis after another. If democracy and Parliamentary institutions are to triumph in this war, it is absolutely necessary that Governments resting upon them shall be able to act and dare, that the servants of the Crown shall not be harassed by nagging and snarling, that enemy propaganda shall not be fed needlessly out of our own hands, and our reputation disparaged and undermined throughout the world. On the contrary, the will of the whole House should be made manifest upon important occasions. It is important that not only those who speak, but those who watch and listen and judge, should also count as a factor in world affairs. After all, we are still fighting for our lives, and for causes dearer than life itself. We have no right to assume that victory is certain; it will be certain only if we do not fail in our duty. Sober and constructive criticism, or criticism in Secret Session, has its high virtue; but the duty of the House of Commons is to sustain the Government or to change the Government. If it cannot change it, it should sustain it. There is no working middle course in war-time. Much harm was done abroad by the two days' Debate in May. Only the hostile speeches are reported abroad, and much play is made with them by our enemy.

A Division, or the opportunity for a Division, should always follow a Debate on the war, and I trust, therefore, that the opinion of the overwhelming majority of the House will be made plain not only in the Division, but also in the days which follow, and that the weaker brethren, if I may so call them, will not be allowed to usurp and almost monopolise the privileges and proud authority of the House of Commons. The Majority of the House must do their duty. All I ask is a decision one way or another.

There is an agitation in the Press, which has found its echo in a number of hostile speeches, to deprive me of the function which I exercise in the general conduct and supervision of the war. I do not propose to argue this to-day at any length, because it was much discussed in a recent Debate. Under the present arrangement the three Chiefs of the Staff, sitting almost continuously together, carry on the war from day to day, assisted not only by the machinery of the great Departments which serve them, but by the Combined General Staff, in making their decisions effective through the Navy, Army and Air Forces over which they exercise direct operational control. I supervise their activities, whether as Prime Minister or Minister of Defence. I work myself under the supervision and control of the War Cabinet, to whom all important matters are referred, and whom I have to carry with me in all major decisions. Nearly all my work has been done in writing, and a complete record exists of all the directions I have given, the inquiries I have made, and the telegrams I have drafted. I shall be perfectly content to be judged by them.

I ask no favours either for myself or for His Majesty's Government. I undertook the office of Prime Minister and Minister of Defence, after defending my predecessor to the best of my ability, in times when the life of the Empire hung upon a thread. I am your servant, and you have the right to dismiss me when you please. What you have no right to do is to ask me to bear responsibilities without the power of effective action, to bear the responsibilities of Prime Minister but clamped on each side by strong men, as the hon. Member said. If to-day, or at any future time, the House were to exercise its undoubted right, I could walk out with a good conscience and the feeling that I have done my duty according to such light as has been granted to me. There is only one thing I would ask of you in that event. It would be to give my successor the modest powers which would have been denied to me.

But there is a larger issue than the personal issue. The mover of this Vote of Censure has proposed that I should be stripped of my responsibilities for Defence in order that some military figure or some other unnamed personage should assume the general conduct of the war, that he should have complete control of the Armed Forces of the Crown, that he should be the Chief of the Chiefs of the Staff, that he should nominate or dismiss the generals or the admirals, that he should always be ready to resign, that is to say, to match himself against his political colleagues, if colleagues they could be considered, if he did not get all he wanted, that he should have under him a Royal Duke as Commander-in-Chief of the Army, and finally, I presume, though this was not mentioned, that this unnamed personage should find an appendage in the Prime Minister to make the necessary explanations, excuses and apologies to Parliament when things go wrong, as they often do and often will. That is at any rate a policy. It is a system very different from the Parliamentary system under which we live. It might easily amount to or be converted into a dicatatorship. I wish to make it perfectly clear that as far as I am concerned I shall take no part in such a system. . . .

The setting down of this Vote of Censure by Members of all parties is a considerable event. Do not, I beg you, let the House underrate the gravity of what has been done. It has been trumpeted all round the world to our disparagement, and when every nation, friend and foe, is waiting to see what is the true resolve and conviction of the House of Commons, it must go forward to the end. All over the world, throughout the United States, as I can testify, in Russia, far away in China, and throughout every subjugated country, all our friends are waiting to know whether there is a strong, solid Government in Britain and whether its national leadership is to be challenged or not. Every vote counts. If those who have assailed us are reduced to contemptible proportions and their Vote of Censure on the National Government is converted to a vote of censure upon its authors, make no mistake, a cheer will go up from every friend of Britain and every faithful servant of our cause, and the knell of disappointment will ring in the ears of the tyrants we are striving to overthrow.

"WE CUT THE COAL"

October 31, 1942

Coal-Owners and Miners Conference,
Central Hall, Westminster

[Extract] War is made with steel, and steel is made with coal. This is the first and only industry I have addressed as an industry during the time of my responsibility. I am doing so because coal is the foundation and, to a very large extent, the measure of our whole war effort. I thought it would be a good thing if we met in private. The Press are our good friends, they play their part in the battle, a valuable part and an indispensable part, but the difficulty about making reported speeches is–look at all the ears that listen, look at the different audiences that have to be considered! So, if you will allow me to say so, I thought it would be a compliment to the coal industry if I, in my position, and the other Ministers who are here, came and had a talk in private with you about our great affairs. Of course, I cannot see the whole of the coal industry, but I have come here to give you first-hand guidance, and I am going to ask you to go back to your pits as the ambassadors of His Majesty's Government, to tell them the impressions you have formed and assist to the utmost in promoting the common cause. . . .

My Lords and Gentlemen, we have great Allies. We are no longer alone. Thirty nations march with us. Russia has come in, the United States have come in, there is another great ally on the way–supremacy in the air. We have got that supremacy in Egypt now. Presently we shall have it everywhere. Already we are blasting their war industries, already they are receiving what they gave, with interest–with compound interest. Soon they will get a bonus. Help us in all this. I know you will. All depends upon inflexible willpower based on the conviction shared by a whole people that the cause is good and righteous. Let it be the glory of our country to lead this world out of the dark valley into the broader and more genial sunshine. In the crisis of 1940, it is no more than the sober truth to say, we saved the freedom of mankind. We gave Russia time to arm, and the United States to organise; but now it is a long cold strain we have to bear, harder perhaps for the British to bear than the shocks which they know so well how to take. We must not cast away our great deliverance; we must carry our work to its final conclusion. We shall not fail, and then some day, when children ask "What did you do to win this inheritance for us, and to make our name so respected among men?" one will say: "I was a fighter pilot"; another will say: "I was in the Submarine Service"; another: "I marched with the Eighth Army"; a fourth will say: "None of you could have lived without the convoys and the Merchant Seamen"; and you in your turn will say, with equal pride and with equal right: "We cut the coal."

"THE END OF THE BEGINNING"

November 10, 1942

The Lord Mayor's Luncheon,
Mansion House, London

On July 31, in response to a cable from Churchill suggesting a meeting, Stalin invited him to Moscow for consultations. Churchill flew to Cairo on August 2, where he met Field-Marshal Smuts and the senior British commanders. Churchill was convinced that "a drastic and immediate change is needed in the High Command." During this crucial visit he decided to make Alexander Commander-in-Chief, Near East, and to appoint General Montgomery to command the Eighth Army. Auchinleck "received this stroke with soldierly dignity." On August 10 Churchill flew to Moscow, where Harriman had already established himself. Churchill's account of these often very difficult meetings may be found in pages 472-502 of The Hinge of Fate. *Churchill then returned to Cairo, and was briefed by Montgomery and Alexander on the preparations for the British counter-attack at El Alamein. Churchill returned to London, well satisfied with the results of his journey, on August 24.*

On August 19 British and Canadian troops attacked Dieppe. Heavy casualties were sustained, and the operation was bitterly criticised in Canada.

The Battle of El Alamein opened on October 23. By November 4 it was evident that the Germans had sustained an overwhelming defeat. On November 7, "Operation

Torch," the massive Anglo-American operation in French North Africa, opened. It was a brilliant success. Churchill was entitled to claim that "we have a new experience. We have victory." This speech is also memorable for its imagery–"the bright gleam [of victory] has caught the helmets of all our soldiers"; "the end of the beginning"; "I have not become the King's First Minister in order to preside over the liquidation of the British Empire." After the long, dark, difficult months of defeat and disappointment, Churchill's excitement was justified.

I notice, my Lord Mayor, by your speech that you had reached the conclusion that the news from the various fronts has been somewhat better lately. In our wars the episodes are largely adverse, but the final results have hitherto been satisfactory. Away we dash over the currents that may swirl around us, but the tide bears us forward on its broad, resistless flood. In the last war the way was uphill almost to the end. We met with continual disappointments, and with disasters far more bloody than anything we have experienced so far in this one. But in the end all the oppositions fell together, and all our foes submitted themselves to our will.

We have not so far in this war taken as many German prisoners as they have taken British, but these German prisoners will no doubt come in in droves at the end just as they did last time. I have never promised anything but blood, tears, toil, and sweat. Now, however, we have a new experience. We have victory–a remarkable and definite victory. The bright gleam has caught the helmets of our soldiers, and warmed and cheered all our hearts.

The late M. Venizelos observed that in all her wars England–he should have said Britain, of course–always wins one battle–the last. It would seem to have begun rather earlier this time. General Alexander, with his brilliant comrade and lieutenant, General Montgomery, has gained a glorious and decisive victory in what I think should be called the Battle of Egypt. Rommel's army has been defeated. It has been routed. It has been very largely destroyed as a fighting force.

This battle was not fought for the sake of gaining positions or so many square miles of desert territory. General Alexander and General Montgomery fought it with one single idea. They meant to destroy the armed force of the enemy, and to destroy it at the place where the disaster would be most far-reaching and irrecoverable.

All the various elements in our line of battle played their parts–Indian troops, Fighting French, the Greeks, the representatives of Czechoslovakia and the others who took part. The Americans rendered powerful and invaluable service in the air. But as it happened–as the course of the battle turned–it has been fought throughout almost entirely by men of British blood from home and from the Dominions on the one hand, and by Germans on the other. The Italians were left to perish in the waterless desert or surrender as they are doing.

The fight between the British and the Germans was intense and fierce in the extreme. It was a deadly grapple. The Germans have been outmatched and outfought with the very kind of weapons with which they had beaten down so many small peoples, and also large unprepared peoples. They have been beaten by the very technical apparatus on which they counted to gain them the domination of the world. Especially is this true of the air and of the tanks and of the artillery, which has come back into its own on the battlefield. The Germans have received back again that measure of fire and steel which they have so often meted out to others.

Now this is not the end. It is not even the beginning of the end. But it is, perhaps, the end of the beginning. Henceforth Hitler's Nazis will meet equally well armed, and perhaps better armed troops. Henceforth they will have to face in many theatres of war that superiority in the air which they have so often used without mercy against others, of which they boasted all round the world, and which they intended to use as an instrument for convincing all other peoples that all resistance to them was hopeless. When I read of the coastal road crammed with fleeing German vehicles under the blasting attacks of the Royal Air Force, I could not but remember those roads of France and Flanders, crowded, not with fighting men, but with helpless refugees—women and children—fleeing with their pitiful barrows and household goods, upon whom such merciless havoc was wreaked. I have, I trust, a humane disposition, but I must say I could not help feeling that what was happening, however grievous, was only justice grimly reclaiming her rights.

It will be my duty in the near future to give to Parliament a full and particular account of these operations. All I will say of them at present is that the victory which has already been gained gives good prospect of becoming decisive and final so far as the defence of Egypt is concerned.

But this Battle of Egypt, in itself so important, was designed and timed as a prelude and counterpart of the momentous enterprise undertaken by the United States at the western end of the Mediterranean—an enterprise under United States command in which our Army, Air Force, and, above all, our Navy, are bearing an honourable and important share. Very full accounts have been published of all that is happening in Morocco, Algeria, and Tunis. The President of the United States, who is Commander-in-Chief of the armed forces of America, is the author of this mighty undertaking, and in all of it I have been his active and ardent lieutenant. . . .

Let me, however, make this clear, in case there should be any mistake about it in any quarter. We mean to hold our own. I have not become the King's First Minister in order to preside over the liquidation of the British Empire. For that task, if ever it were prescribed, someone else would have to be found, and, under democracy, I suppose the nation would have to be consulted. I am proud to be a member of that vast Commonwealth and society of nations and communities gathered in and around the ancient British monarchy, without which the good cause might well have perished from the face of the earth. Here we are, and here we stand, a veritable rock of salvation in this drifting world.

There was a time, not long ago, when for a whole year we stood all alone. Those days, thank God, have gone. We now move forward in a great and gallant company. For our record we have nothing to fear, we have no need to make excuses or apologies. Our record pleads for us, and will gain gratitude in the breasts of free men and women in every part of the world.

As I have said, in this war we desire no territorial gains and no commercial favours; we wish to alter no sovereignty or frontier for our own benefit or profit. We have come into North Africa shoulder to shoulder with our American friends and Allies for one purpose, and one purpose only—namely, to gain a vantage ground from which to open a new front against Hitler and Hitlerism, to cleanse the shores of Africa from the stain of Nazi and Fascist tyranny, to open the Mediterranean to Allied sea power and air power, and thus effect the liberation of the peoples of Europe from the pit of misery into which they have been cast by their own improvidence and by the brutal violence of the enemy.

These two African undertakings, in the east and in the west, were part of a single strategic and political conception which we have laboured long to bring to fruition, and about which we are now justified in entertaining good and reasonable confidence. Thus, taken together, they were two aspects of a grand design, vast in its scope, honourable in its motive, noble in its aim. The British and American affairs continue to prosper in the Mediterranean, and the whole event will be a new bond between the English-speaking peoples and a new hope for the whole world.

I recall to you some lines of Byron, which seem to me to fit the event, the hour, and the theme:–

Millions of tongues record thee, and anew
Their children's lips shall echo them, and say–
"Here, where the sword united nations drew,
Our countrymen were warring on that day!"
And this is much, and all which will not pass away.

THE FALL OF MUSSOLINI

July 27, 1943

House of Commons

Following their complete triumph in North Africa, the Allies invaded Sicily on July 10. The Allied advance proceeded swiftly and successfully. On July 19 Rome was bombed for the first time. On July 21 it was announced that Mussolini had resigned and Marshal Badoglio was appointed Prime Minister on July 25; Italy was placed under martial law.

[Extract] The House will have heard with satisfaction of the downfall of one of the principal criminals of this desolating war. The end of Mussolini's long and severe reign over the Italian people undoubtedly marks the close of an epoch in the life of Italy. The keystone of the Fascist arch has crumbled, and, without attempting to prophesy, it does not seem unlikely that the entire Fascist edifice will fall to the ground in ruins, if it has not already so fallen. The totalitarian system of a single party, armed with secret police, engrossing to itself practically all the offices, even the humblest, under the Government, with magistrates and courts under the control of the executive, with its whole network of domestic spies and neighbourly informants–that system, when applied over a long period of time, leaves the broad masses without any independent figures apart from the official classes. That, I think is a defence for the people of Italy–one defence–although there can be no really valid defence for any country or any people which allows its freedom and inherent rights to pass out of its own hands.

The external shock of war has broken the spell which in Italy held all these masses for so long, in fact for more than twenty years, in physical and even more in moral subjection. We may, therefore, reasonably expect that very great changes will take place in Italy. What their form will be, or how they will impinge upon the forces of German occupation and control, it is too early to forecast. The guilt and folly of Mussolini have cost the Italian people dear. It looked so safe and easy in May, 1940, to stab falling France in the back and advance to appropriate the Mediterranean interests and possessions of what Mussolini no doubt sincerely believed was a decadent and ruined Britain. It looked so safe and easy to fall upon the much smaller State of Greece. However, there have been undeceptions. Events have taken a different course. By many hazardous turns of fortune and by the long marches of destiny, the British and United States Armies, having occupied the Italian African Empire, the North of Africa, and the bulk of Sicily, now stand at the portals of the Italian mainland armed with the powers of the sea and the air, and with a very large land and amphibious force equipped with every modern weapon and device.

What is it that these masterful forces bring to Italy? They bring, if the Italian people so decide, relief from the war, freedom from servitude, and, after an interval, a respectable place in the new and rescued Europe. When I learn of the scenes enacted in the streets of the fine city of Palermo on the entry of the United States Armies, and review a mass of detailed information with which I have been furnished, I cannot doubt that the main wish of the Italian people is to be quit of their German taskmasters, to be spared a further and perfectly futile ordeal of destruction, and to revive their former democratic and parliamentary institutions. These they can have. The choice is in their hands. As an alternative, the Germans naturally desire that Italy shall become a battle ground, a preliminary battle ground, and that by Italian sufferings the ravages of war shall be kept as far away as possible for as long as possible from the German Fatherland. If the Italian Government and people choose that the Germans shall have their way, no choice is left open to us. We shall continue to make war upon Italy from every quarter; from North and South, from the sea and from the air, and by amphibious descents, we shall endeavour to bring the utmost rigour of war increasingly upon her. Orders to this effect have been given to all the Allied commanders concerned....

Therefore, my advice to the House of Commons, and to the British nation, and to the Commonwealth and Empire, and to our Allies may, at this juncture be very simply stated. We should let the Italians, to use a homely phrase, stew in their own juice for a bit, and hot up the fire to the utmost in order to accelerate the process, until we obtain from their Government, or whoever possesses the necessary authority, all our indispensable requirements for carrying on the war against our prime and capital foe, which is not Italy but Germany. It is the interest of Italy, and also the interest of the Allies, that the unconditional surrender of Italy should be brought about wholesale and not piecemeal. Whether this can be accomplished or not, I cannot tell, but people in this country and elsewhere who cannot have the necessary knowledge of all the forces at work, or assign true valuations to the various facts and factors, should, I think, at this juncture be restrained in speech and writing, lest they should add to the tasks, the toils and the losses of our Armies, and prolong and darken the miseries which have descended upon the world. . . .

THE QUEBEC CONFERENCE

August 31, 1943

Broadcast, Quebec

On August 17 General Alexander telegraphed Churchill that "by 10 a.m. this morning, August 17, 1943, the last German soldier was flung out of Sicily, and the whole island is now in our hands." The total Allied casualties had been over 31,000. Churchill had decided early in July that another meeting with Roosevelt was desirable, and Quebec was suggested as the site by the President. Churchill, accompanied by his wife, daughter Mary, Brigadier Wingate–whom Churchill had just met for the first time, and who had impressed him greatly–and Wing-Commander Guy Gibson, the hero of the "dambusters" raid on the Möhne and Eder dams, sailed on the Queen Mary *on August 5. He took with him the preparatory plans for the invasion of Europe and for the "Mulberry" artificial harbour which would be needed for the landings. Churchill was anxious that all this should be explained to Roosevelt, as "at least it would convince the American authorities that we were not insincere about 'Overlord.' "*

Before the conference, Churchill visited Roosevelt at Hyde Park, and the conference itself opened on August 19. One of the major developments was Churchill's offer to the President that the Commander of "Overlord" should be American and not, as previously agreed, General Alan Brooke. The Americans agreed that Lord Louis Mountbatten should become Supreme Commander of the Southeast Asia Command (SEAC). "There is no doubt," Churchill cabled to Attlee on August 22, "of the need of a young and vigorous mind in this lethargic and stagnant Indian scene." The conference ended on August 24. After a few days' rest, Churchill delivered this broadcast, which had "hung overhead me like a vulture in the sky."

[Extract] At the beginning of July I began to feel the need for a new meeting with the President of the United States and also for another conference of our joint staffs. We were all delighted when, by a happy inspiration, President Roosevelt suggested that Quebec should be the scene, and when the Governor-General and the Government of Canada offered us their princely hospitalities. Certainly no more fitting and splendid setting could have been chosen for a meeting of those who guide the war policy of the two great Western democracies at this cardinal moment in the Second World War than we have here in the Plains of Abraham, the Château Frontenac, and the ramparts of the Citadel of Quebec, from the midst of which I speak to you now.

Here at the gateway of Canada, in mighty lands which have never known the totalitarian tyrannies of Hitler and Mussolini, the spirit of freedom has found a safe and abiding home. Here that spirit is no wandering phantom. It is enshrined in Parliamentary institutions based on universal suffrage and evolved through the centuries by the English-speaking peoples. It is inspired by the Magna Carta and the

Declaration of Independence. It is guarded by resolute and vigilant millions, never so strong or so well armed as to-day. . . .

We have heard a lot of talk in the last two years about establishing what is called a Second Front in Northern France against Germany. Anyone can see how desirable that immense operation of war would be. It is quite natural that the Russians, bearing the main weight of the German armies on their front, should urge us ceaselessly to undertake this task, and should in no way conceal their complaints and even reproaches that we have not done it before.

I do not blame them at all for what they say. They fight so well, and they have inflicted such enormous injury upon the military strength of Germany, that nothing they could say in honest criticism of our strategy, or the part we have so far been able to take in the war, would be taken amiss by us, or weaken our admiration for their own martial prowess and achievement.

We once had a fine front in France, but it was torn to pieces by the concentrated might of Hitler; and it is easier to have a front pulled down than it is to build it up again. I look forward to the day when British and American liberating armies will cross the Channel in full force and come to close quarters with the German invaders of France. You would certainly not wish me to tell you when that is likely to happen, or whether it be soon or late; but whenever the great blow is struck, you may be sure that it will be because we are satisfied that there is a good chance of continuing success, and that our soldiers' lives will be expended in accordance with sound military plans and not squandered for political considerations of any kind.

I submit to the judgment of the United Nations, and of history, that British and American strategy, as directed by our combined Chiefs of Staff, and as approved and to some extent inspired by the President and myself, has been the best that was open to us in a practical sense. It has been bold and daring, and has brought into play against the enemy the maximum effective forces that could have been deployed up to the present by Great Britain and the United States, having regard to the limitations of ocean transport, to the peculiar conditions of amphibious warfare, and to the character and training of the armies we possess, which have largely been called into being since the beginning of the war. . . .

It is not given to the cleverest and the most calculating of mortals to know with certainty what is their interest. Yet it is given to quite a lot of simple folk to know every day what is their duty. That is the path along which the British Commonwealth and Empire, the Great Republic of the United States, the vast Union of Soviet Socialist Republics, the indomitable and innumerable people of China—all the United Nations—that is the path along which we shall march till our work is done and we may rest from our labours, and the whole world may turn with hope, with science, with good sense, and dear-bought experience, from war to lasting peace.

ANGLO-AMERICAN UNITY

September 6, 1943

Harvard University, Boston

Churchill travelled to Washington on September 1 to discuss the developing situation in Italy, and in particular the secret discussions with the Badoglio Government concerning Italian surrender. On September 6 he received an honorary degree at Harvard University. "It was to be," Churchill later wrote, "an occasion for a public declaration to the world of Anglo-American unity and amity."

[Extract] The last time I attended a ceremony of this character was in the spring of 1941, when, as Chancellor of Bristol University, I conferred a degree upon the United States Ambassador, Mr. Winant, and *in absentia* upon President Conant, our President, who is here today and presiding over this ceremony. The blitz was running hard at that time, and the night before, the raid on Bristol had been heavy. Several hundreds had been killed and wounded. Many houses were destroyed. Buildings next to the University were still burning and many of the University authorities who conducted the ceremony had pulled on their robes over uniforms begrimed and drenched; but all was presented with faultless ritual and appropriate decorum, and I sustained a very strong and invigorating impression of the superiority of man over the forces that can destroy him.

Here now, today, I am once again in academic groves–groves is, I believe, the right word–where knowledge is garnered, where learning is stimulated, where virtues are inculcated and thought encouraged. Here, in the broad United States, with a respectable ocean on either side of us, we can look upon the world in all its wonder and in all its woe. But what is this that I discern as I pass through your streets, as I look around this great company.

I see uniforms on every side. I understand that nearly the whole energies of the University have been drawn into the preparation of American youth for the battlefield. For this purpose all classes and courses have been transformed, and even the most sacred vacations have been swept away in a round-the-year and almost round-the-clock drive to make warriors and technicians for the fighting fronts.

Twice in my lifetime the long arm of destiny has searched across the oceans and involved the entire life and manhood of the United States in a deadly struggle. There was no use in saying 'We don't want it; we won't have it; our forebears left Europe to avoid these quarrels; we have founded a new world which has no contact with the old.' There was no use in that. The long arm reaches out remorselessly, and everyone's existence, environment, and outlook undergo a swift and irresistible change. What is the explanation, Mr. President, of these strange facts, and what are the deep laws to which they respond? I will offer you one explanation–there are others, but one will suffice. The price of greatness is responsibility. If the people of the United States had continued in a mediocre station, struggling with the wilderness, absorbed in their own affairs, and a factor of no consequence in the movement of the world, they might have remained forgotten and undisturbed beyond their protecting oceans: but one cannot rise to be in many ways the leading community in the civilized world without being involved in its problems, without being convulsed by its agonies and inspired by its causes.

If this has been proved in the past, as it has been, it will become indisputable in the future. The people of the United States cannot escape world responsibility. Although we live in a period so tumultuous that little can be predicted we may be quite sure that this process will be intensified with every forward step the United States make in wealth and in power. Not only are the responsibilities of this great republic growing, but the world over which they range is itself contracting in relation to our powers of locomotion at a positively alarming rate.

We have learned to fly. What prodigious changes are involved in that new accomplishment. Man has parted company with his trusty friend the horse and has sailed into the azure with the eagles, eagles being represented by the infernal (*loud laughter*)–I mean internal–combustion engine. Where, then, are those broad oceans, those vast staring deserts? They are shrinking beneath our very eyes. Even elderly Parliamentarians like myself are forced to acquire a high degree of mobility.

But to the youth of America, as to the youth of Britain, I say 'You cannot stop.' There is no halting-place at this point. We have now reached a stage in the journey where there can be no pause. We must go on. It must be world anarchy or world order. Throughout all this ordeal and struggle which is characteristic of our age, you will find in the British Commonwealth and Empire good comrades to whom you are united by other ties besides those of State policy and public need. To a large extent, they are the ties of blood and history. Naturally, I a child of both worlds, am conscious of these.

Law, language, literature–these are considerable factors. Common conceptions of what is right and decent, a marked regard for fair play, especially to the weak and poor, a stern sentiment of impartial justice, and above all the love of personal freedom, or as Kipling put it; 'Leave to live by no man's leave underneath the law'–these are common conceptions on both sides of the ocean among the English-speaking peoples. We hold to these conceptions as strongly as you do.

We do not war primarily with races as such. Tyranny is our foe, whatever trappings or disguise it wears, whatever language it speaks, be it external or internal, we must for ever be on our guard, ever mobilized, ever vigilant, always ready to spring at its throat. In all this, we march together. Not only do we march and strive shoulder to shoulder at this moment under the fire of the enemy on the fields of war or in the air, but also in those realms of thought which are consecrated to the rights and the dignity of man. . . .

It would, of course, Mr. President, be lamentable if those who are charged with the duty of leading great nations forward in this grievous and obstinate war were to allow their minds and energies to be diverted from making the plans to achieve our righteous purposes without needless prolongation of slaughter and destruction.

Nevertheless, we are also bound, so far as life and strength allow, and without prejudice to our dominating military tasks, to look ahead to those days which will surely come when we shall have finally beaten down Satan under our feet and find ourselves with other great allies at once the masters and the servants of the future.

Various schemes of achieving world security while yet preserving national rights, tradition and customs are being studied and probed.

We have all the fine work that was done a quarter of a century ago by those who devised and tried to make effective the League of Nations after the last war. It is said that the League of Nations failed. If so, that is largely because it was abandoned, and later on betrayed: because those who were its best friends were till a very late period infected with a futile pacifism: because the United States, the originating impulse, fell out of the line: because, while France had been bled white and England was supine and bewildered, a monstrous growth of aggression sprang up in Germany, in Italy and Japan.

We have learned from hard experiences that stronger, more efficient, more rigorous world institutions must be created to preserve peace and to forestall the causes of future wars. In this task the strongest victorious nations must be combined, and also those who have borne the burden and heat of the day and suffered under the flail of adversity; and, in this task, this creative task, there are some who say: 'Let us have a world council and under it regional or continental councils,' and there are others who prefer a somewhat different organization.

All these matters weigh with us now in spite of the war, which none can say has reached its climax, which is perhaps entering for us, British and Americans, upon its most severe and costly phase. But I am here to tell you that, whatever form your system of world security may take, however the nations are grouped and ranged, whatever derogations are made from national sovereignty for the sake of the large synthesis, nothing will work soundly or for long without the united effort of the British and American peoples.

If we are together nothing is impossible. If we are divided all will fail. I therefore preach continually the doctrine of the fraternal association of our two peoples, not for any purpose of gaining invidious material advantages for either of them, not for territorial aggrandisement or the vain pomp of earthly domination, but for the sake of service to mankind and for the honour that comes to those who faithfully serve great causes.

Here let me say how proud we ought to be, young and old alike, to live in this tremendous, thrilling, formative epoch in the human story, and how fortunate it was for the world that when these great trials came upon it there was a generation that terror could not conquer and brutal violence could not enslave. Let all who are here remember, as the words of the hymn we have just sung suggest, let all of us who are here remember that we are on the stage of history, and that whatever our station may be, and whatever part we have to play, great or small, our conduct is liable to be scrutinized not only by history but by our own descendants.

Let us rise to the full level of our duty and of our opportunity, and let us thank God for the spiritual rewards he has granted for all forms of valiant and faithful service.

THE WAR SITUATION

September 21, 1943

House of Commons

On September 3 the Allied invasion of Italy began. Five days later General Eisenhower announced the unconditional surrender of Italy although German forces occupied Rome and other key centres. On September 18 Mussolini proclaimed his liberation by the Germans, and the establishment of the Republican Fascist Party. Allied landings were made on September 8-9 at Salerno, and were bitterly resisted. As Churchill related in this speech, the situation was for some time critical. The speech lasted over two and a half hours, and at Churchill's suggestion there was an adjournment of an hour midway. Here is a very brief extract from this major address.

[Extract] . . . In order to have the correct perspective and proportion of events, it is necessary to survey the whole chain of causation, the massive links of which have been forged by the diligence and burnished with the devotion and skill of our combined Forces and their commanders until they shine in the sunshine of to-day, and will long shine in the history of war.

This same year of victory on land has been accompanied by an ever-increasing mastery of the air by the British, Americans and Russians over the enemy in Europe. Speaking particularly of our own air power, the weight of bombs discharged by the Royal Air Force on Germany in the last twelve months is three times that of the preceding twelve months. The weight of bombs discharged in the last three months is half as great again as that of the preceding three months. There has also been a great improvement in accuracy, owing to technical devices. The percentage of loss for the first eight months of 1943 is less than in the same period last year, and the morale and ardour of our bombing crews are very high. The almost total systematic destruction of many of the centres of German war effort continues on a greater scale and at a greater pace. The havoc wrought is indescribable, and the effects upon the German war production in all its forms and upon U-boat building are matched by those wrought upon the life and economy of the whole of the guilty organisation. There has been an enormous diversion of German energy from the war fronts to internal defence against air attack, and the offensive power of the enemy has been notably crippled thereby. The German Air Force has been driven increasingly on to the defensive. The attacks we have had in this island, though marked by occasional distressing incidents, are at present negligible compared with the vast scale of the war. The enemy is increasingly compelled to concentrate on building fighter aircraft and night fighter aircraft for home defence at the expense of bomber production. He is also forced to save his strength as far as possible on all the fighting fronts, and is, therefore, restricted to a far lower rate of activity than we and our Allies maintain. This throws the burden increasingly upon his fully occupied ground forces. The Royal Air Force is at present maintaining in action throughout the war scene in all the theatres nearly 50 per cent. more first line aircraft than Germany. That is the Royal Air Force alone, apart from Russia. . . .

I call this front we have opened, first in Africa, next in Sicily, and now in Italy, the Third Front. The Second Front, which already exists potentially and which is rapidly gathering weight, has not yet been engaged, but it is here, holding forces on its line. No one can tell—and certainly I am not going to hint at—the moment when it will be engaged. But the Second Front exists, and is a main preoccupation already of the enemy. It has not yet opened, or been thrown into play, but the time will come. At what we and our American Allies judge to be the right time, this front will be thrown open, and the mass invasion from the West, in combination with the invasion from the South, will begin.

It is quite impossible for those who do not know the facts and figures of the American assembly in Britain, or of our own powerful expeditionary Armies now preparing here, who do not know the dispositions of the enemy on the various fronts, who cannot measure his reserves and resources and his power to transfer large forces from one front to another over the vast railway system of Europe, who do not know the state and dimensions of our fleet and landing-craft of all kinds—and this must be proportionate to the work they have to do—who do not know how the actual processes of a landing take place, or what are the necessary steps to build it up, or what has to be thought out beforehand in relation to what the enemy can do in days or weeks—it is impossible for those who do not know these facts, which are the study of hundreds of skilful officers day after day and month after month, to pronounce a useful opinion upon this operation.

Mr. Gallacher: Does that apply to Marshal Stalin?

Mr. Churchill: We should not in a matter of this kind take advice from British Communists, because we know that they stood aside and cared nothing for our fortunes in our time of mortal peril. Any advice that we take will be from friends and Allies who are all joined together in the common cause of winning the victory. The House may be absolutely certain that His Majesty's present Government will never be swayed or overborne by any uninstructed agitation, however natural, or any pressure, however well-meant, in matters of this kind. We shall not be forced or cajoled into undertaking vast operations of war against our better judgment in order to gain political unanimity or a cheer from any quarter. The bloodiest portion—make no mistake about it—of this war for Great Britain and the United States lies ahead of us. Neither the House nor the Government will shrink from that ordeal. We shall not grudge any sacrifice for the common cause. I myself regard it as a matter of personal honour to act only with the conviction of success founded upon the highest professional advice at our disposal in operations of the first magnitude. I decline, therefore, to discuss at all the questions when, where, how and on what scale the main assault from the West will be launched, and I am confident that the House will support the Government in this attitude. . . .

I have now finished my survey, and have but one word more to say. The political atmosphere in the United States is not the same as it is over here. The Constitution decrees elections at fixed intervals, and parties are forced to assert and defend their special interests at the elections in a manner which we have under our more flexible system been able to lay aside for the time being. Nevertheless, I was made conscious of the resolve and desire of all parties to drive forward the war on all fronts and against all foes with the utmost determination. I was also conscious of a feeling of friendliness towards Great Britain and the British Commonwealth and Empire such as I have never known before, and a respect for the war effort of the 46,000,000 in this small Island and for the conduct of our troops who are the comrades of the Americans in the hard-fought fields of this war. All this was very dear and refreshing to my heart. I found also the feeling everywhere that the war was being well managed, that the central direction made good plans, and that highly competent and resolute officers were entrusted with their execution in every part of the globe. It is my hope that this conviction is generally shared at home, and that the House of Commons will feel no need to reproach itself for the unwavering confidence it has given to His Majesty's servants in their discharge of the exceptional burdens which have been thrust upon them. . . .

"A SENSE OF CROWD AND URGENCY"

October 28, 1943

House of Commons

Although historians might question Churchill's assertion that the shape of the House of Commons–which originated when the Commons took over St. Stephen's Chapel in the 16th century–played a major part in the evolution of the two-party system, this speech is probably the best description of the particular characteristics of the House of Commons that has ever been made.

I beg to move,

> That a Select Committee be appointed to consider and report upon plans for the rebuilding of the House of Commons, and upon such alterations as may be considered desirable while preserving all its essential features.

On the night of 10th May, 1941, with one of the last bombs of the last serious raid, our House of Commons was destroyed by the violence of the enemy, and we have now to consider whether we should build it up again, and how, and when. We shape our buildings, and afterwards our buildings shape us. Having dwelt and served for more than forty years in the late Chamber, and having derived very great pleasure and advantage therefrom, I, naturally, should like to see it restored in all essentials to its old form, convenience, and dignity. I believe that will be the opinion of the great majority of its Members. It is certainly the opinion of His Majesty's Government, and we propose to support this Resolution to the best of our ability.

There are two main characteristics of the House of Commons which will command the approval and the support of reflective and experienced Members. They will, I have no doubt, sound odd to foreign ears. The first is that its shape should be oblong and not semi-circular. Here is a very potent factor in our political life. The semi-circular assembly, which appeals to political theorists, enables every individual or every group to move round the centre, adopting various shades of pink according as the weather changes. I am a convinced supporter of the party system in preference to the group system. I have seen many earnest and ardent Parliaments destroyed by the group system. The party system is much favoured by the oblong form of Chamber. It is easy for an individual to move through those insensible gradations from Left to Right, but the act of crossing the Floor is one which requires serious consideration. I am well informed on this matter, for I have accomplished that difficult process, not only once but twice. Logic is a poor guide compared with custom. Logic, which has created in so many countries semi-circular assemblies with buildings that give to every Member, not only a seat to sit in, but often a desk to write at, with a lid to bang, has proved fatal to Parliamentary Government as we know it here in its home and in the land of its birth.

The second characteristic of a Chamber formed on the lines of the House of Commons is that it should not be big enough to contain all its Members at once without over-crowding, and that there should be no question of every Member having a separate seat reserved for him. The reason for this has long been a puzzle to uninstructed outsiders, and has frequently excited the curiosity and even the criticism of new Members. Yet is not so difficult to understand if you look at it from a practical point of view. If the House is big enough to contain all its Members, nine-tenths of its Debates will be conducted in the depressing atmosphere of an almost empty or half-empty Chamber. The essence of good House of Commons speaking is the conversational style, the facility for quick, informal interruptions and interchanges. Harangues from a rostrum would be a bad substitute for the conversational style in which so much of our business is done. But the conversational style requires a fairly small space, and there should be on great occasions a sense of crowd and urgency. There should be a sense of the importance of much that is said, and a sense that great matters are being decided, there and then, by the House.

We attach immense importance to the survival of Parliamentary democracy. In this country this is one of our war aims. We wish to see our Parliament a strong, easy, flexible instrument of free Debate. For this purpose a small Chamber and a sense of intimacy are indispensable. It is notable that the Parliaments of the British Commonwealth have to a very large extent reproduced our Parliamentary institutions in their form as well as in their spirit, even to the Chair in which the Speakers of the different Assemblies sit. We do not seek to impose our ideas on others; we make no invidious criticisms of other nations. All the same we hold none the less tenaciously to them ourselves. The vitality and the authority of the House of Commons, and its hold upon an electorate based upon universal suffrage, depend to no small extent upon its episodes and great moments, even upon its scenes and rows, which, as everyone will agree, are better conducted at close quarters. Destroy that hold which Parliament has upon the public mind and has preserved through all these changing, turbulent times, and the living organism of the House of Commons would be greatly impaired. You may have a machine, but the House of Commons is much more than a machine; it has earned and captured and held through long generations the imagination and respect of the British nation. It is not free from shortcomings; they mark all human institutions. Nevertheless, I submit to what is probably not an unfriendly audience on that subject that our House has proved itself capable of adapting itself to every change which the swift pace of modern life has brought upon us. It has a collective personality which enjoys the regard of the public, and which imposes itself upon the conduct not only of individual Members but of parties. It has a code of its own which everyone knows, and it has means of its own of enforcing those manners and habits which have grown up and have been found to be an essential part of our Parliamentary life.

The House of Commons has lifted our affairs above the mechanical sphere into the human sphere. It thrives on criticism, it is perfectly impervious to newspaper abuse or taunts from any quarter, and it is capable of digesting almost anything or almost any body of gentlemen, whatever be the views with which they arrive. There is no situation to which it cannot address itself with vigour and ingenuity. It is the citadel of British liberty; it is the foundation of our laws; its traditions and its privileges are as lively to-day as when it broke the arbitrary power of the Crown and substituted that Constitutional Monarchy under which we have enjoyed so many blessings. In this war the House of Commons has proved itself to be a rock upon which an Administration, without losing the confidence of the House, has been able to confront the most terrible emergencies. The House has shown itself able to face the possibility of national destruction with classical composure. It can change Governments, and has changed them by heat of passion. It can sustain Governments in long, adverse, disappointing struggles through many dark, grey months and even years until the sun comes out again. I do not know how else this country can be governed than by the House of Commons playing its part in all its broad freedom in British public life. We have learned–with these so recently confirmed facts around us and before us–not to alter improvidently the physical structures which have enabled so remarkable an organism to carry on its work of banning dictatorships within this Island, and pursuing and beating into ruins all dictators who have molested us from outside.

His Majesty's Government are most anxious, and are indeed resolved, to ask the House to adhere firmly in principle to the structure and characteristics of the House of Commons we have known, and I do not doubt that that is the wish of the great majority of the Members in this the second longest Parliament of our history. If challenged, we must take issue upon that by the customary Parliamentary method of debate followed by a Division. The question of Divisions again relates very directly to the structure of the House of Commons. We must look forward to periods when Divisions will be much more frequent than they are now. Many of us have seen twenty or thirty in a single Parliamentary Sitting, and in the lobbies of the Chamber which Hitler shattered we had facilities and conveniences far exceeding those which we are able to enjoy in this lordly abode. I am, therefore, proposing in the name of His Majesty's Government that we decide to rebuild the House of Commons on its old foundations, which are intact, and in principle within its old dimensions, and that we utilise so far as possible its shattered walls. That is also the most cheap and expeditious method we could pursue to provide ourselves with a habitation.

I now come to some of the more practical issues which are involved. It is said that we should wait until the end of the war, and I think perhaps that was the point my hon. Friend opposite wished to put. Certainly we must do nothing which appreciably detracts from the war effort, but what we have to do in the first instance is to make up our minds and have a plan and have the preliminary work and survey effectively done, so that at the end of the war, if not earlier, we can start without delay and build ourselves a House again. All this will be a matter for the Committee, which will certainly have more than fifteen Members of the House, representative of the different parties and different points of view. I am, however, not entirely convinced that it may not be found possible to make definite progress with this work even during the course of the war. The First Commissioner of Works has submitted a scheme which would enable the old House of Commons to be reconstructed, with certain desirable improvements and modernisations, accommodation for the Press, the Ladies' Gallery and other prominent features. This scheme would take only 18 months, but it would be prudent—and those concerned with building houses would, I think, feel that it would be prudent—to count on double that period, because everything must be fitted in with war needs, and also because it is the habit of architects and builders to be more sanguine when putting forward their plans than is subsequently found to be justified by the actual facts. The last House of Commons, the one which was set up after the fire in 1834, was promised in six years and actually took 27 years, and so, when I speak of rebuilding the House of Commons in 18 months, it is, of course, without panelling or carving, which can be added as the years pass by. It is simply a Chamber for us to dwell in and conduct our Business as we require to do. The timber must be set aside now if it is to be properly seasoned. The Clipsham Quarry, from which the stone was produced for the maintenance and replacement of the Houses of Parliament is temporarily closed. It would have to be reopened. We must then consider very carefully the strain upon our labour resources. The First Commissioner informs me that for the first six months after the plan has been started, after the word "Go" has been given, only 46 quarrymen and demolition men would be required, of whom half would be over 40 years of age and the other half over 50 years of age. In the second six months 185 men would be required over 40 and an equal number over 50. But of those over 50 years of age 60 would be masons, whose trade has so little work at the present time. In the third six months—and we shall be getting on by then—we shall require 170 men, not additional, over 40 and an equal number over 50. All the 170 over 50 would come from the building trade; the 170 over 40 and under 50 would come from the engineering trade. This last is a much more serious consideration. But there is no need for us, even when the whole scheme is approved and the work has begun, to commit ourselves to the rate of reconstruction. We can fit it in as a stand-by job. It might well be that in a year's time, when we require men from the engineering trade, our affairs might be in such a posture that we shall be looking for jobs rather than men.

However, the House is not asked to commit itself to any decisions of this kind. On the contrary, the Committee has first of all to make its decisions of principle, and then the execution of those decisions must be a matter for the Government to carry out as and when the public interest requires, and strictly within the limits of the war effort. All the same, I must tell you, Mr. Speaker, that it would be a real danger if at the end of the war we found ourselves separated by a long period from the possibility of obtaining a restored and suitable House of Commons Chamber. We are building warships that will not be finished for many years ahead, and various works of construction are going forward for war purposes. But I am bound to say that I rank the House of Commons–the most powerful Assembly in the whole world–at least as important as a fortification or a battleship, even in time of war. Politics may be very fierce and violent in the after-war days. We may have all the changes in personnel following upon a General Election. We shall certainly have an immense press of business and, very likely, of stormy controversy. We must have a good, well-tried and convenient place in which to do our work. The House owes it to itself, it owes it to the nation, to make sure that there is no gap, no awkward, injurious hiätus in the continuity of our Parliamentary life. I am to-day only expressing the views of the Government, but if the House sets up the Committee and in a few months' time the Committee gives us their Report, we shall be able to take decisions together on the whole matter, and not be caught at a disadvantage in what must inevitably be a time of particular stress and crisis at the end of the war, from a Parliamentary point of view. Therefore, I ask that the Committee should be set up, and I feel sure that it will be able to make a good plan of action, leaving the necessary latitude to the Government as to the time when this action can be taken and the speed at which it can be carried into effect, having regard to the prime exigencies of the war. We owe a great debt to the House of Lords for having placed at our disposal this spacious, splendid hall. We have already expressed in formal Resolution our thanks to them. We do not wish to outstay our welcome. We have been greatly convenienced by our sojourn on these red benches and under this gilded, ornamented, statue-bedecked roof. I express my gratitude, and my appreciation of what we have received and enjoyed, but

Mid pleasures and palaces though we may roam,
Be it ever so humble, there's no place like home.

THE INVASION OF FRANCE

June 6, 1944

House of Commons

On September 28 Marshal Badoglio formally signed the Italian surrender aboard H.M.S. Nelson *at Malta. The situation in Italy was, to put it mildly, extremely confusing in the midst of virtual civil war and fierce German reprisals. The Allied forces, however, met more determined and skillful resistance from the Germans, and a situation approaching deadlock was reached.*

Strains were developing again with the Russians, particularly over their insistence upon the resumption of the Arctic convoys. On October 18 Eden arrived in Moscow for three-power discussions, and on the same day Churchill refused to receive a highly

offensive message from Stalin relating to the conditions of British servicemen in Northern Russia. The convoys were resumed in November. The Foreign Ministers' Conference ended on November 2. "There had been a smoothing of many points of friction, practical steps for cooperation had been taken, the way had been prepared for an early meeting of the heads of the three major Allied Governments, and the mounting deadlock in our working with the Soviet Union had in part been removed" (Closing the Ring, *299).*

At Stalin's insistence, the meeting of the Big Three was held in Teheran, despite Roosevelt's reluctance to travel so far while Congress was in session.

On November 12 Churchill left Britain on board H.M.S. Renown, *reaching Alexandria nine days later. There were discussions with Chiang Kai-shek and Roosevelt in Cairo from November 23 on. The Teheran Conference opened on November 28, and the principal topic was "Overlord."*

On November 29 Churchill presented the Sword which the King had ordered to commemorate the defence of Stalingrad. Churchill relates: "When, after a few sentences of explanation, I handed the splendid weapon to Marshal Stalin, he raised it in a most impressive gesture to his lips and kissed the blade. He then handed it to [General] Voroshilov, who dropped it. It was carried from the room in great solemnity, escorted by a Russian guard of honour" (Closing the Ring, *364)*

The Teheran Conference, after several moments of tension and misunderstanding, ended on December 1 with a wide measure of agreement. "Surveying the whole military scene, as we separated in an atmosphere of friendship and unity of immediate purpose, I personally was well content" (Closing the Ring, *405). On December 2 Churchill returned to Cairo for further discussions with Roosevelt about operations in Burma and the possibility of bringing Turkey into the war. Roosevelt, with reluctance, reduced the proposed scale of operations in the Bay of Bengal in order to concentrate landing-craft for the invasion of Europe. It was during this meeting that Roosevelt informed Churchill of his decision to appoint General Eisenhower commander of "Overlord."*

Throughout this arduous series of meetings Churchill was unwell and below his normal high energy level. In Carthage, on December 12, Churchill realised, he was seriously ill; on the following day pneumonia was diagnosed. Thanks to "this admirable M and B . . . the intruders were repulsed." Churchill convalesced at Marrakesh, and returned to England aboard H.M.S. King George V, *January 17, 1944.*

On June 4, British and American troops entered Rome. On June 6 the long-awaited Allied invasion of Europe began, the principal landings being in Normandy. Churchill's statement that fighting was taking place in Caen was, however, incorrect.

[Extract] The House should, I think, take formal cognisance of the liberation of Rome by the Allied Armies under the Command of General Alexander, with General Clark of the United States Service and General Oliver Leese in command of the Fifth and Eighth Armies respectively. This is a memorable and glorious event, which rewards the intense fighting of the last five months in Italy. . . .

I have also to announce to the House that during the night and the early hours of this morning the first of the series of landings in force upon the European Continent has taken place. In this case the liberating assault fell upon the coast of France. An immense armada of upwards of 4,000 ships, together with several thousand smaller craft, crossed the Channel. Massed airborne landings have been successfully effected behind the enemy lines, and landings on the beaches are proceeding at various points at the present time. The fire of the shore batteries has been largely quelled. The obstacles that were constructed in the sea have not proved so difficult as was apprehended. The Anglo-American Allies are sustained by about 11,000 first-line aircraft, which can be drawn upon as may be needed for the purposes of the battle. I cannot, of course, commit myself to any particular details. Reports are coming in in rapid succession. So far the Commanders who are engaged report that everything is proceeding according to plan. And what a plan! This vast operation is undoubtedly the most complicated and difficult that has ever taken place. It involves tides, wind, waves, visibility, both from the air and the sea standpoint, and the combined employment of land, air and sea forces in the highest degree of intimacy and in contact with conditions which could not and cannot be fully foreseen.

There are already hopes that actual tactical surprise has been attained, and we hope to furnish the enemy with a succession of surprises during the course of the fighting. The battle that has now begun will grow constantly in scale and in intensity for many weeks to come, and I shall not attempt to speculate upon its course. This I may say, however. Complete unity prevails throughout the Allied Armies. There is a brotherhood in arms between us and our friends of the United States. There is complete confidence in the supreme commander, General Eisenhower, and his lieutenants, and also in the commander of the Expeditionary Force, General Montgomery. The ardour and spirit of the troops, as I saw myself, embarking in these last few days was splendid to witness. Nothing that equipment, science or forethought could do has been neglected, and the whole process of opening this great new front will be pursued with the utmost resolution both by the commanders and by the United States and British Governments whom they serve. [Editor's Note: Mr. Churchill added the following statement later in the day] : I have been at the centres where the latest information is received, and I can state to the House that this operation is proceeding in a thoroughly satisfactory manner. Many dangers and difficulties which at this time last night appeared extremely formidable are behind us. The passage of the sea has been made with far less loss than we apprehended. The resistance of the batteries has been greatly weakened by the bombing of the Air Force, and the superior bombardment of our ships quickly reduced their fire to dimensions which did not affect the problem. The landings of the troops on a broad front, both British and American—Allied troops, I will not give lists of all the different nationalities they represent—but the landings along the whole front have been effective, and our troops have penetrated, in some cases, several miles inland. Lodgments exist on a broad front.

The outstanding feature has been the landings of the airborne troops, which were on a scale far larger than anything that has been seen so far in the world. These landings took place with extremely little loss and with great accuracy. Particular anxiety attached to them, because the conditions of light prevailing in the very limited period of the dawn—just before the dawn—the conditions of visibility made all the difference. Indeed, there might have been something happening at the last minute which would have prevented airborne troops from playing their part. A very great degree of risk had to be taken in respect of the weather.

But General Eisenhower's courage is equal to all the necessary decisions that have to be taken in these extremely difficult and uncontrollable matters. The airborne troops are well established, and the landings and the follow-ups are all proceeding with much less loss—very much less—than we expected. Fighting is in progress at various points. We captured various bridges which were of importance, and which were not blown up. There is even fighting proceeding in the town of Caen, inland. But all this, although a very valuable first step—a vital and essential first step—gives no indication of what may be the course of the battle in the next days and weeks, because the enemy will now probably endeavour to concentrate on this area, and in that event heavy fighting will soon begin and will continue without end, as we can push troops in and he can bring other troops up. It is, therefore, a most serious time that we enter upon. Thank God, we enter upon it with our great Allies all in good heart and all in good friendship.

THE FLYING BOMB

July 6, 1944

House of Commons

British concern over the relatively slow progress being made in Normandy was aggravated by the wave of attacks on Southern England by the V1 jet-propelled flying bombs. Meanwhile, in Italy, Allied troops were advancing—but the cost of the Italian campaign remained heavy, as the Germans maintained their gradual but brilliantly conducted retreat.

[Extract] . . . This form of attack is, no doubt, of a trying character, a worrisome character, because of its being spread out throughout the whole of the 24 hours, but people have just got to get used to that. Everyone must go about his duty and his business, whatever it may be—every man or woman—and then, when the long day is done, they should seek the safest shelter that they can find and forget their cares in well-earned sleep. We must neither underrate nor exaggerate. In all up to six a.m. to-day, about 2,750 flying bombs have been discharged from the launching-stations along the French coast. A very large proportion of these have either failed to cross the Channel or have been shot down and destroyed by various methods, including the great deployment of batteries, aircraft and balloons which has been very rapidly placed in position. Batteries move to any position in which they are required and take up their positions rapidly, but once on the site great improvements can be made in the electrical connections and so forth; and the Air Force, confronted with the somewhat novel problem of chasing a projectile, has found new methods every day. . . .

As to evacuation, as I have said, everyone must remain at his post and discharge his daily duty. This House would be affronted if any suggestion were made to it that it should change its location from London. Here we began the war, and here we will see it ended. We are not, however, discouraging people who have no essential work to do from leaving London at their own expense if they feel inclined to do so by the arrangements they make. In fact, they assist our affairs by taking such action at their own expense. We do not need more people in London than are required for business purposes of peace and war. For people of small means, who are not engaged in war work and wish to leave, registers have been opened and arrangements will be made for their transfer as speedily as possible to safer areas. Children are already being sent at their parents' wish out of the danger areas, which are by no means exclusively confined to the Metropolis. There is, of course, the bomb highway over which the robots all pass before reaching that point of Southern England which I have ventured to particularize this morning. Children are being sent if their parents wish out of the danger areas, and in all cases mothers with small children, or pregnant women, will be given full facilities by the State. And we do not propose to separate the mother from the child except by her wish, but a terrible thing happened last time. Mothers were separated from children of two or three years of age, and, after a period, when they had saved up money and got time to go down and see them, the children hardly knew them. I hope now with our growing strength, reserves and facilities for removal, we shall be able to say to a mother with three or four children, "If you wish to leave, it is perfectly possible. Arrangements will be made to take you into the country with your children. If you wish them to go by themselves and you wish to stay here with your husband, or because of your job, then arrangements can be made that way too." We do not consider that the scale of attack under which we lie at present justifies Governmental compulsion in any case. . . .

The House will ask, What of the future? Is this attack going to get worse, or is it going to be beat like the magnetic mine, or beat like the attempted destruction of Britain by the aeroplane, or beat has the U-boat campaign was beat? Will new developments, on the other hand, of a far more formidable character, come upon us? Will the rocket bomb come? Will improved explosives come? Will greater ranges, faster speeds, and larger war-heads come upon us? I can give no guarantee that any of these evils will be entirely prevented before the time comes, as come it will, when the soil from which these attacks are launched has been finally liberated from the enemy's grip. In the meantime I can only say that when I visited various scenes of bomb explosions on Saturday, only one man of many hundreds whom I saw asked a question. The question was, "What are you going to do about it?" I replied, "Everything in human power, and we have never failed yet." He seemed contented with the reply. That is the only promise I can make.

I must, however, make it perfectly plain—I do not want there to be any misunderstanding on this point—that we shall not allow the battle operations in Normandy or the attacks we are making against special targets in Germany to suffer. They come first, and we must fit our own domestic arrangements into the general scheme of war operations. There can be no question of allowing the slightest weakening of the battle in order to diminish in scale injuries which, though they may inflict grievous suffering on many people and change to some extent the normal, regular life and industry of London, will never stand between the British nation and their duty in the van of a victorious and avenging world. It may be a comfort to some to feel that they are sharing in no small degree the perils of our soldiers overseas, and that the blows which fall on them diminish those which in other forms would have smitten our fighting men and their Allies. But I am sure of one thing, that London will never be conquered and will never fail, and that her renown, triumphing over every ordeal, will long shine among men. . . .

THE WAR SITUATION

August 2, 1944

House of Commons

On all fronts the Allies were advancing. In Normandy the Germans suffered an overwhelming defeat; in Burma the British and Imperial Powers had turned the tide; in the Pacific Americans were brilliantly in the ascendent; and the Russians continued to move forward.

[Extract] I have, upon the whole, a good report to make to the House. On every battle front all over the world the arms of Germany and Japan are recoiling. They are recoiling before the armed forces of the many nations which in various groupings form the Grand Alliance. In the air, on the sea and under the sea, our well-established supremacy increases with steady strides. The losses by U-boats since the beginning of 1944, compared to former years, are almost negligible. The vast fleets of the allies have sailed the seas and oceans from January to June with less than half the losses we have inflicted upon the small, dwindling, and largely immobile naval resources of the enemy, both in the East and in the West. It is always possible that there may be a return of the U-boat war. There is talk of Germany trying to make U-boats faster under the water: there are various tales, and it is never well to discount these matters. It is always possible that the Germans may gain some temporary relative advantage in their aircraft. For these reasons we must be very careful not to relax unduly either our precautions or our exertions in order to turn our strength to other channels. Naturally, we wish to turn our strength increasingly to other channels: when one danger is removed a new opportunity presents itself; but we must be very careful, in view of the possibility of unexpected and usually unpleasant things turning up in future. But at this moment, throughout the world there is no theatre in which Allied mastery has not become pronounced. . . .

The ordeal of the House is very nearly at an end, and I hesitate to inflict myself on it any further; but there are so many important things to say that if you start to give an account of what is going on in this war and leave out anything important, great complaints are made.

At the present time, no speech by a prominent politician in any of the victorious countries would be deemed complete without a full exposition of the future organization of the world. I was severely reproached last time for not having dealt methodically with this considerable topic. One of my difficulties is that it does not rest with me to lay down the law for all our Allies. If it were the general wish, I could certainly make one or two suggestions; but, odd as it may seem, countries like the United States and Soviet Russia might wish to have their say in the matter, and might not look on it from exactly the same angle or express it in exactly the same terms as would gain the loudest applause in this House. I am sorry about this, because nothing would have given me greater pleasure than to devote a couple of hours to giving my personal ideas about the general layout; but it would be very troublesome to all of us here if I made a great pronouncement on this subject and found myself contradicted and even repudiated by our most powerful Allies. From time to time a great many very eloquent statements are made on the future organization of the world by the most eminent people. In spite of all demands that we should take the lead in laying down the law, I personally should prefer to hear the opinions of other powerful nations before committing our country to too many details.

Can we not be content with the broad declaration upon which we are all agreed, that there is to be a World Council to preserve peace which will, in the first instance, be formed and guided by the major Powers who have gained the war, and that thereafter other Powers, and eventually all Powers, will be offered their part in this world organization? Can we not be content with that, and concentrate our efforts on winning a victory, bearing ourselves so prominently in the conflict that our words will receive honoured consideration when we come to the organization of the peace?

In the meanwhile, as the House will be aware, important discussions on the official level are shortly to begin in Washington, and when those are completed we shall have a very much better idea where we stand. As I have said, it is vain and idle for any one country to try to lay down the law on this subject or to trace frontiers or describe the intricate instruments by which those frontiers will be maintained without further bloodshed; it is vain, and it is even unwise. The man who sold the hyena's skin while the beast lived was killed in hunting it–if I might venture to make a slight emendation of the poet's words.

Not only are those once proud German armies being beaten back on every front and by every one of the many nations who are in fighting contact with them, every single one, but, in their homeland in Germany, tremendous events have occurred which must shake to their foundations the confidence of the people and the loyalty of the troops. The highest personalities in the German Reich are murdering one another, or trying to, while the avenging Armies of the Allies close upon the doomed and ever-narrowing circle of their power. We have never based ourselves on the weakness of our enemy, but only on the righteousness of our cause. Therefore, potent as may be these manifestations of internal disease, decisive as they may be one of these days, it is not in them that we should put our trust, but in our own strong arms and the justice of our cause.

Let us go on, then, to battle on every front. Thrust forward every man who can be found. Arm and equip the Forces in bountiful supply. Listen to no parley from the enemy. Vie with our valiant Allies to intensify the conflict. Bear with unflinching fortitude whatever evils and blows we may receive. Drive on through the storm, now that it reaches its fury, with the same singleness of purpose and inflexibility of resolve as we showed to the world when we were all alone.

THE WAR SITUATION

September 28, 1944

House of Commons

The end of the drawn out Battle of Normandy caused the German collapse in France, and the Allies advanced with virtually no opposition. At this point the British and Americans made an airborne landing at Arnheim, Holland, which after initial success, could not be consolidated. Despite this reverse, the end seemed near. On July 20 an assassination attempt upon Hitler narrowly failed. Meanwhile, serious difficulties were arising between the British and the Russians over the future of Poland. Feelings on the subject were running high in the House of Commons.

Little more than seven weeks have passed since we rose for the summer vacation, but this short period has completely changed the face of the war in Europe. When we separated, the Anglo-American Armies were still penned in the narrow bridgehead and strip of coast from the base of the Cherbourg Peninsula to the approaches to Caen, which they had wrested from the enemy several weeks before. The Brest Peninsula was untaken, the German Army in the West was still hopeful of preventing us from striking out into the fields of France, the Battle of Normandy, which had been raging bloodily from the date of the landing, had not reached any decisive conclusion. What a transformation now meets our eyes! Not only Paris, but practically the whole of France, has been liberated as if by enchantment. Belgium has been rescued, part of Holland is already free, and the foul enemy, who for four years inflicted his cruelties and oppression upon these countries, has fled, losing perhaps 400,000 in killed and wounded, and leaving in our hands nearly half a million prisoners. Besides this, there may well be 200,000 cut off in the coastal fortresses or in Holland, whose destruction or capture may now be deemed highly probable. The Allied Armies have reached and in some places crossed the German frontier and the Siegfried Line.

All these operations have been conducted under the supreme command of General Eisenhower, and were the fruit of the world-famous battle of Normandy, the greatest and most decisive single battle of the entire war. Never has the exploitation of victory been carried to a higher perfection. The chaos and destruction wrought by the Allied Air Forces behind the battle front have been indescribable in narrative, and a factor of the utmost potency in the actual struggle. They have far surpassed, and reduce to petty dimensions, all that our Army had to suffer from the German Air Force in 1940. Nevertheless, when we reflect upon the tremendous fire-power of modern weapons and the opportunity which they give for defensive and delaying action, we must feel astounded at the extraordinary speed with which the Allied Armies have advanced. The vast and brilliant encircling movement of the American Armies will ever be a model of military art, and an example of the propriety of running risks not only in the fighting–because most of the armies are ready to do that–but even more on the Q. side, or, as the American put it, the logistical side. It was with great pleasure that all of us saw the British and Canadian Armies, who had so long fought against heavy resistance by the enemy along the hinge of the Allied movement, show themselves also capable of lightning advances which have certainly not been surpassed anywhere.

Finally, by the largest airborne operation ever conceived or executed, a further all-important forward bound in the North has been achieved. Here I must pay a tribute, which the House will consider due, to the superb feat of arms performed by our First Airborne Division. Full and deeply-moving accounts have already been given to the country and to the world of this glorious and fruitful operation, which will take a lasting place in our military annals, and will, in succeeding generations, inspire our youth with the highest ideals of duty and of daring. The cost has been heavy; the casualties in a single division have been grievous; but for those who mourn there is at least the consolation that the sacrifice was not needlessly demanded nor given without results. The delay caused to the enemy's advance upon Nijmegen enabled their British and American comrades in the other two airborne divisions, and the British Second Army, to secure intact the vitally important bridges and to form a strong bridgehead over the main stream of the Rhine at Nijmegen. "Not in vain" may be the pride of those who have survived and the epitaph of those who fell. . . .

In thus trying to do justice to the British and American achievements, we must never forget, as I reminded the House before we separated, the measureless services which Russia has rendered to the common cause, through long years of suffering, by tearing out the life of the German military monster. The terms in which Marshal Stalin recently, in conversation, has referred to our efforts in the West have been of such a generous and admiring character that I feel, in my turn, bound to point out that Russia is holding and beating far larger hostile forces than those which face the Allies in the West, and has through long years, at enormous loss, borne the brunt of the struggle on land. There is honour for all. It is a matter of rejoicing that we, for our part and in our turn, have struck resounding blows, and it is right that they should be recorded among the other feats of arms so loyally performed throughout the Grand Alliance.

I must again refer to the subject of the campaign in Burma, on which I touched in my last statement to the House. I was somewhat concerned to observe from my reading of the American Press, in which I indulged during my stay on the other side, that widespread misconception exists in the public mind, so far as that is reflected by the newspapers, about the scale of our effort in Burma and the results to date of Admiral Mountbatten's campaign. Many important organs of United States opinion seem to give the impression that the British campaign of 1944 in Burma had been a failure, or at least a stalemate, that nothing much had been done, and that the campaign was redeemed by the brilliant capture of Myitkyina–which I may say is spelt

"Myitkyina" but pronounced "Michynaw"–by General Stilwell at the head of an American Regiment of very high-class commando troops and with the assistance of the Chinese. That is the picture, but I must present these matters in their true light. It is well known that the United States have been increasingly engaged in establishing an air route to China capable of carrying immense supplies, and, by astounding efforts and at vast cost, they are now sending over the terrible Himalayas, or the Hump as it is called in the Army, I will not say how many times as much as the Burma Road has ever carried in its palmiest days, or will carry for several years to come; an incredible feat of transportation–over mountains 20,000 or 22,000 feet high in the air, over ground where an engine failure means certain death to the pilot–has been performed by a main effort which the United States have been made in their passionate desire to aid the resistance of China. Certainly no more prodigious example of strength, science and organization in this class of work has ever been seen or dreamed of. . . .

I regret to say the fighting on the Burma Front throughout the year has been most severe and continuous, and there were times when the issue in particular localities appeared to hang in doubt. However, the ten Japanese Divisions which were launched against us with the object of invading India and cutting the air line have been repulsed and largely shattered, as the result of a bloody and very costly campaign which is still being continued in spite of the monsoon conditions. How costly this campaign has been in disease may be judged from the fact that in the first six months only of this present year the 14th British Imperial Army sustained no fewer than 237,000 cases of sickness, which had to be evacuated to the rear over the long, difficult communications and tended in hospital. More than 90 per cent. of these cases returned within six months, but the ceaseless drain upon the Army and the much larger numbers required to maintain a fighting strength, in spite of this drain, in the neighbourhood of a quarter of a million may well be imagined. When you have a loss and drain like that going on, much larger numbers are needed to maintain your limited fighting strength. In addition, there were over 40,000 battle casualties in the first six months, that is to say, to the end of June, and the number has certainly increased by now.

I think these facts ought to be known; I think they ought to be given wide publicity, as I am sure they will now that I have stated them, because the campaign of Admiral Mountbatten on the Burma Frontier constitutes–and this is the startling fact–the largest and most important ground fighting that has yet taken place against the armies of Japan. Far from being an insignificant or disappointing stalemate, it constitutes the greatest collision which has yet taken place on land with Japan, and has resulted in the slaughter of between 50,000 and 60,000 Japanese and the capture of several hundred prisoners. The Japanese Army has recoiled before our troops in deep depression and heavily mauled. We have often, too, found circles of their corpses in the jungle where each one had committed suicide in succession, the officer, who had supervised the proceedings, blowing out his own brains last of all. We did not ask them to come there, and it is entirely their own choice that they find themselves in this difficult position. . . .

When Herr Hitler escaped his bomb on July 20th he described his survival as providential; I think that from a purely military point of view we can all agree with him, for certainly it would be most unfortunate if the Allies were to be deprived, in the closing phases of the struggle, of that form of warlike genius by which Corporal Schickelgruber has so notably contributed to our victory. . . .

I shall certainly not hazard a guess–it could be no more–as to when the end will come. Many persons of the highest technical attainments, knowledge and responsibility have good hopes that all will be over by the end of 1944. On the other hand, no one, and certainly not I, can guarantee that several months of 1945 may not be required. . . .

It is my duty to impress upon the House the embarassment to our affairs and the possible injury to Polish fortunes which might be caused by intemperate language about Polish and Russian relations in the course of this Debate. It is my firm hope, and also my belief, that a good arrangement will be achieved and that a united Polish Government will be brought into being, which will command the confidence of the three great Powers concerned and will assure for Poland those conditions of strength, sovereignty and independence which we have all three proclaimed as our aim and our resolve. Nothing is easier than to create by violent words a prospect far less hopeful than that which now opens before us. Hon. Members will take upon themselves a very grave responsibility if they embroil themselves precipitately in these controversies and thus mar the hopes we cherish of an honourable and satisfactory solution and settlement. We recognize our special responsibilities towards Poland, and I am confident that I can trust the House not to engage in language which would make our task harder.

We must never lose sight of our prime and overwhelming duty, namely, to bring about the speediest possible destruction of the Nazi power. We owe this to the soldiers who are shedding their blood and giving their lives in the cause at this moment. They are shedding their blood in the effort to bring this fearful struggle in Europe to a close; and that must be our paramount task. Every problem--and there are many; they are as legion; they crop up in vast array–which now faces the nations of the world will present itself in a far easier and more adaptable form once the cannons have ceased to thunder in Europe, and once the victorious Allies gather round the table of armistice or peace. I have every hope that wise and harmonious settlements will be made, in confidence and amity, between the great Powers, thus affording the foundations upon which to raise a lasting structure of European and world peace. I say these words on the Polish situation; and I am sure that our friends on both sides will realize how long and anxious has been the study which the Cabinet have given to this matter, how constantly we see representatives of the Poles, how frequent and intimate our correspondence is with Russia on this subject.

I cannot conceive that it is not possible to make a good solution whereby Russia gets the security which she is entitled to have, and which I have resolved that we will do our utmost to secure for her, on her Western Frontier, and, at the same time, the Polish Nation have restored to them that national sovereignty and independence for which, across centuries of oppression and struggle, they have never ceased to strive. . . .

To shorten the war by a year, if that can be done, would in itself be a boon greater than many important acts of legislation. To shorten this war, to bring it to an end, to bring the soldiers home, to give them a roof over their heads, to re-establish the free life of our country, to enable the wheels of commerce to revolve, to get the nations out of their terrible frenzy of hate, to build up something like a human world and a humane world–it is that makes it so indispensable for us to struggle to shorten, be it even by a day, the course of this terrible war.

It is right to make surveys and preparations beforehand, and many have been made and are being made; but the great decisions cannot be taken finally, even for the transition period, without far closer, calmer, and more searching discussions than can be held amid the clash of arms. Moreover, we cannot be blind to the fact that there are many factors, at present unknowable, which will make themselves manifest on the morrow of the destruction of the Nazi regime. I am sure this is no time for taking hard and fast momentous decisions on incomplete data and at breakneck speed. Hasty work and premature decisions may lead to penalties out of all proportion to the issues immediately involved. That is my counsel to the House, which I hope they will consider. I hope that the House will notice that, in making my statement to-day, I have spoken with exceptional caution about Foreign Affairs, and, I hope, without any undue regard for popular applause. I have sedulously avoided the appearance of any one country having to lay down the law to its powerful Allies or to the many other States involved. I hope, however, that I have given the House some impression of the heavy and critical work that is going forward and will lie before us even after the downfall of our principal enemy has been effected. I trust that what I have said may be weighed with care and goodwill not only in this House and in this country but also in the far wider circles involved.

FRENCH UNITY

November 12, 1944

Paris Liberation Committee Reception,
Hôtel de Ville, Paris

This speech was delivered in French on Churchill's visit to liberated Paris.

It is with the most vivid sensations that I find myself here this afternoon. I am going to give you a warning: be on your guard, because I am going to speak, or try to speak, in French, a formidable undertaking and one which will put great demands on your friendship for Great Britain.

To be here in Paris is an extraordinary realization for me. I have never lost my faith in the citizens of Paris. In the hard years when you were beneath the yoke of the Huns and we were suffering the blitz (which was in comparison a minor ill), during all those years I always had a feeling of unity with the people of Paris, this immortal city whence great movements for the liberation of the world have sprung, and which, at every point in its long history, has proved its faculty for guiding the world's progress. But, ladies and gentlemen, I have never lost my faith in the French Army–never. It may well be that there are mechanical devices which the enemy can use and which do not give people a chance of showing their courage, their devotion, and their skill in military affairs. Things like this have happened, and we too, if it had not been for the Channel, should have been put to a hard test had we been attacked by 2,000 tanks without our having the means to destroy them or tanks to oppose them. I am sure that if there had been an opportunity of fighting on equal terms, the French Army would have shown, and was going to show, qualities which have made its fame imperishable in the pages of history, under the leadership of the great men of the past, Clemenceau, Foch and Napoleon, by whose tomb I stood yesterday. Have no fears for the power of the French Army. I am not speaking only to you, but I am also expressing the feelings of England and the policy of her Government in saying that the French Army, a strong army, and a strong army as quickly as possible, is absolutely necessary to re-establish a balance in Europe and to provide those elements of strength and stability which are so greatly desired by this world which has suffered so horribly.

When I spoke to you in French from London four years ago, four years almost to a week, I said I had always known for certain that France would again take her place with the greatest nations and exercise her power and her influence on the whole development, cultural, political and military, of the future world.

Then came a great event. I was thrilled when, at the front in Italy, I heard the news that Paris had risen, and I rejoiced with you that Paris had been freed, freed from the Huns by the strong, bold and vigorous effort of her people guided by many of the men and women whom I see here at this moment. It was a great affair, and the Leclerc Division, for the dispatching of which to France I had done my utmost, was there. I could not prophesy what was going to happen, but I did everything in my power to have arrangements made for the transport of that Division by sea and for its equipment with heavy arms. And what a stroke of fortune that they should have been brought here to Paris at the very moment when they could assist the powerful and vigorous effort of the citizens themselves to liberate this great and historic city!

Now most of France is free. Great battles are being joined. I well understand that you wish to take as great a part as possible in the line of battle, and it is essential that you should be helped as far as possible by the Allies. In Italy your soldiers have already given proof of their skill and have struck heavy blows against the Germans. But it is here in France that you wish to be represented by the most powerful force which can be raised and equipped. I assure you that the war cannot be prolonged; it may be that in six months' time the desperate enemy will be beaten on the field, and that part of the need for a line of modern divisions will have disappeared. Well, we will do our best to enable everything possible to be done so that the forces of France may be actively engaged against the enemy in the months that remain to us in this frightful war.

But there are other battles to win. There are other works to accomplish, and if in your courtesy you will allow me, at this moment when you have arranged in my honour a demonstration which I shall remember to the last moment of my life, I will say these words to you: Unity, unity, stability and solidarity!

This is the moment when the whole might of the nation should be directed to the foundation, on an unshakable basis, of the grandeur and authority of the great French people. Happily, you have at your head an incontestable leader, General de Gaulle. From time to time I have had lively arguments with him about matters relating to this difficult war, but I am absolutely sure that you ought to rally round your leader and do your utmost to make France united and indivisible. This is the moment to forget many things, to remember great things, and it is the moment when France should take her place with the other great Powers and march with them, not only to sweep the Prussians from her territory, not only to tear their name from the book of honour, not only to arrange matters as they must be arranged if we are to be saved from a repetition of the horror which we have twice suffered in my lifetime; but also in order that France and the genius of France, eminent in so many spheres, may make a united contribution to the great movement of progress which is budding in the hearts of men and women of goodwill in all the countries of the world.

"THE TASKS WHICH LIE BEFORE US"

November 29, 1944

House of Commons

[Extract] . . . I must admit, as an aged Member of this House, and as one who has done some forty-two years of service here—unhappily for me there was a break of two years, two Parliaments which lasted for a year apiece—that after all this long experience and service in the House, I find it very unpleasant to have the Debate on the Adjournment one day, and the Debate on the new Session the next. In the high and far-off times when I first entered this building, there was usually a six months' or five months' Recess, between the grouse on the 12th August and the latter part of January or the beginning of February, when the House reassembled. I do not consider those days were without their wisdom. Do not—and this has a bearing on some of the remarks which have recently been made—ever suppose that you can strengthen Parliament by wearying it, and by keeping it in almost continuous session. If you want to reduce the power of Parliament, let it sit every day in the year, one-fifth part filled, and then you will find it will be the laughing-stock of the nation, instead of being, as it continues to be, in spite of all the strains of modern life, the citadel as well as the cradle of Parliamentary institutions throughout the world; almost the only successful instance of a legislative body with plenary powers, elected on universal suffrage, which is capable of discharging, with restraint and with resolution, all the functions of peace and of war.

This digression on general topics will, perhaps, be excused by another digression which I find it my duty to make, and this is a more sober and more sombre digression. All our affairs, down to the smallest detail, continue to be dominated by the war. Parliamentary business is no exception. I must warn the House and the country against any indulgence in the feeling that the war will soon be over. It may be; but do not indulge that feeling, and think that we should now all be turning our thoughts to the new phase in world history which will open at the close of this war. The truth is that no one knows when the German war will be finished, and still less how long the interval will be between the defeat of the Germans and the defeat of the Japanese. I took occasion, some months ago, to damp down premature hopes by speaking of the German war running into January and February. I could see disappointment in several quarters as I looked around the House, and I followed this up quickly by indicating the late Spring or the early Summer as periods which we must take into account as possibilities. My present inclination is not at all to mitigate these forecasts, or guesses. "Guesses" is the right word, for they can be little more. Indeed, if I were to make any change in the duration of the unfolding of events it would be to leave out the word "early" before the word "summer." . . .

I am not giving a review of the war situation, I have no intention of doing so; later on, perhaps when we meet after Christmas, it will be right to review it, and it may be very much easier then than it is now. There may be hard facts and cheering facts to put before the House. The House knows that I have never hesitated to put hard facts before it. I know the British people and I know this House, and there is one thing they will not stand, and that is not being told how bad things are. If it is humanly possible to do it without endangering affairs, one is always well-advised to tell people how bad things are. I remember occasions when I have greatly revived the energy and ardour of the House by giving them an account of the shocking position we occupied in various quarters, and how very likely things were to get worse before they would get better.

My motive in doing so was to strengthen the position of the Government. I say that I am not giving a review of the war situation to-day, but I mention these outstanding, these commanding facts in order to dissipate lightly-founded impressions that we can avert our eyes from the war and turn to the tasks of transition and of reconstruction, or still more that we can turn to the political controversies and other diversions of peace, which are dear to all our hearts, and rightly dear to the democracies in action, because without controversy democracies cannot achieve their health-giving processes. But I do not think we can look on any of these matters with a sense of detachment from the war issue, which is right over us, which weighs intensely and preponderantly upon us and upon every form of our national life. All else must be still subordinated to this supreme task. It is on the foe that our eyes must be fixed, and to break down his resistance demands and will receive the most intense exertions of Great Britain, of the United States, and of all the United Nations and converted satellites—all forces that can be brought to bear.

This is just the moment not to slacken. All the races which the calendar holds, or nearly all of them, are won in the last lap; and it is then, when it is most hard, when one is most tired, when the sense of boredom seems to weigh upon one, when even the most glittering events, exciting, thrilling events, are, as it were, smothered by satiation, when headlines in the newspaper, though perfectly true, succeed one another in their growing emphasis, and yet the end seems to recede before us, like climbing a hill when there is another peak beyond—it is at that very moment that we in this Island have to give that extra sense of exertion, of boundless, inexhaustible, dynamic energy that we have shown, as the records now made public have emphasized in detail. Tirelessness is what we have to show now. Here I must observe that it is one thing to feel these tremendous drives of energy at the beginning of a war, when your country is likely to be invaded and you do not know whether you will not all have to die honourably but soon; it is one thing to exhibit these qualities, which certainly the House has never been estranged from, at such a moment, and quite another thing to show them in the sixth year of a war. On the other hand we must remember that the enemy whose country is invaded has also those supreme stimuli to which we ourselves responded in the very dark days of 1940 and 1941. . . .

Remember we have a missing generation, we must never forget that—the flower of the past, lost in the great battles of the last war. There ought to be another generation in between these young men and us older figures who are soon, haply, to pass from the scene. There ought to be another generation of men, with their flashing lights and leading figures. We must do all we can to try to fill the gap, and, as I say, there is no safer thing to do than to run risks in youth. It is very difficult to live your life in this world and not to get set in old ways, rather looking back with pleasure to the days of your youth. That is quite right, and tradition is quite right. A love of tradition has never weakened a nation, indeed it has strengthened nations in their hour of peril; but the new view must come, the world must roll forward.

Let the great world spin for ever down the ringing grooves of change. . .

as Tennyson said many years ago. Let us have no fear of the future. We are a decent lot, all of us, the whole nation. Wherever you go you need have no fear. I was brought up never to fear the English democracy, to trust the people. We need have no fear in these matters, and those speeches made by those two young Members give one the feeling that there must be rich reserves in the Army, in the industries and in the workshops, of men of assured quality and capacity who, whatever their differing views on political affairs, are none the less absolutely united in maintaining the historic greatness of Britain and of the British Commonwealth of Nations throughout the world. . . .

REVIEW OF THE WAR

January 18, 1945

House of Commons

On December 16, to the surprise of the Allies, the Germans launched a major counteroffensive in the Ardennes, the brunt of the assault falling upon the Americans. Fierce fighting ensued, and heavy casualties were sustained, but by mid-January the Germans had been halted. The Russian advance in Prussia continued and the Anglo-Indian forces in Burma maintained their progress. In Greece, however, Communist forces (E.L.A.S.) precipitated a serious crisis, to which Churchill devoted a considerable portion of this speech—one of his longest during the entire war. The British action against the E.L.A.S. aroused strong criticism in Britain and the United States.

[Extract] . . . How necessary it is for Britain and the United States, who bear the chief responsibilities, to maintain the closest and most intimate contact in the solution of all these new problems! Let me say once and for all that we have no political combinations, in Europe or elsewhere, in respect of which we need Italy as a party. We need Italy no more than we need Spain, because we have no designs which require the support of such Powers. We must take care that all the blame of things going wrong is not thrown on us. This, I have no doubt, can be provided against, and to some extent I am providing against it now.

We have one principle about the liberated countries or the repentant satellite countries which we strive for according to the best of our ability and resources. Here is the principle. I will state it in the broadest and most familiar terms: Government of the people, by the people, for the people, set up on a basis of election by free and universal suffrage, with secrecy of the ballot and no intimidation. That is and has always been the policy of this Government in all countries. That is our only aim, our only interest, and our only care. It is to that goal that we try to make our way across all the difficulties, obstacles and perils of the long road. Trust the people, make sure they have a fair chance to decide their destiny without being terrorized from either quarter or regimented. There is our policy for Italy, for Yugoslavia and for Greece. What other interest have we than that? For that we shall strive, and for that alone.

The general principle which I have enunciated guides us in our relations with Yugoslavia. We have no special interest in the political régime which prevails in Yugoslavia. Few people in Britain, I imagine, are going to be more cheerful or more downcast because of the future Constitution of Yugoslavia. However, because the King and the Royal Yugoslav Government took refuge with us at the time of the German invasion, we have acquired a certain duty towards the Government and peoples on the other side of the Adriatic which can only be discharged in a correct and formal manner such as, for instance, would be provided by a plebiscite. I am the earliest outside supporter of Marshal Tito. It is more than a year since in this House I extolled his guerrilla virtues to the world. Some of my best friends and the hon. and gallant Member for Preston [his son, Major Randolph Churchill] are there with him or his Forces now. I earnestly hope he may prove to be the saviour and the unifier of his country, as he is undoubtedly at this time its undisputed master. . . .

From the troubles of Italy and Yugoslavia, we come naturally to those of Greece. Once again, we are guided by our simple policy: Victory against the Germans; the establishment of and aid to the most coherent and substantial government machine that can be found; the delivery of such food as we and our Allies can spare and our combined shipping afford; the maintenance of tolerable conditions of law and order; and the holding of plebiscites or general elections fairly and squarely—then, exit at the earliest practicable moment. We toil through a mighty maze, but I can assure you it is not without plan. The story of events in Greece has been told so fully in the newspapers that I shall not attempt a chronological or descriptive account, but there is no case in my experience, certainly not in my war-time experience, where a British Government has been so maligned and its motives so traduced in our own country by important organs of the Press or among our own people. That this should be done amid the perils of this war, now at its climax, has filled me with surprise and sorrow. It bodes ill for the future in which the life and strength of Britain compared to other Powers will be tested to the full, not only in the war but in the aftermath of war. How can we wonder at, still more how can we complain of, the attitude of hostile or indifferent newspapers in the United States, when we have, in this country, witnessed such a melancholy exhibition as that provided by some of our most time-honoured and responsible journals—and others to which such epithets would hardly apply? Only the solid and purposeful strength of the National Coalition Government could have enabled us to pursue, unflinching and unyielding, the course of policy and principle on which we were and are resolved.

But our task, hard as it was, has been and is still being rendered vastly more difficult by a spirit of gay, reckless, unbridled partisanship which has been let loose on the Greek question and has fallen upon those who have to bear the burden of Government in times like these. I have never been connected with any large enterprise of policy about which I was more sure in mind and conscience of the rectitude of our motives, of the clarity of our principles, and of the vigour, precision and success of our action, than what we have done in Greece. . . .

I must speak a little about these Greek Communists, among whom Macedonian and Bulgarian elements are also found, possibly with territorial ideas of their own. They are a very formidable people. They have a theme and a policy which they have pursued by merciless methods while all sorts of other people in these regions have only been trying to keep body and soul together. I have been told that I made a mistake in under-rating the power of the Communist-directed E.L.A.S. I must admit that I judged them on their form against the Germans. I do not wish to do them any military injustice. Of course, it was not against the Germans they were trying to fight to any great extent. They were simply taking our arms, lying low and awaiting the moment when they could seize power in the capital by force or intrigue, and make Greece a Communist State with the totalitarian liquidation of all opponents. I was misled by the little use they were against the Germans, especially once the general victory of the Allies became probable, in spite of the arms we gave to them. I certainly under-rated them as a fighting force. If I am accused of this mistake, I can only say with M. Clemenceau on a celebrated occasion: "Perhaps I have made a number of other mistakes of which you have not heard." . . .

When men have wished very much to kill each other, and have feared very much that they would be killed quite soon, it is not possible for them next day to work together as friends with colleagues against whom they have nursed such intentions or from whom they have derived such fears. We must recognize the difference between our affairs and those which prevailed in Athens, especially while the firing was continuous all round us. That cannot possibly be overlooked. We should have been very glad to have seen a united Government set up. We left them to it, with a strong urge and appeal to unite and save their country, no exception being made of Communists or any one at that moment. All next day they struggled. On several occasions, the entire Liberal Party left the room and were with difficulty shepherded back into their places. It was absolutely certain that no agreement to form a united front could be reached, and, since then, far worse things have happened than had happened before.

The days passed. Our reinforcements rapidly and steadily arrived. They were found, without altering the operations on the Italian front, by putting, I am sorry to say, an extra effort on divisions which were resting and which would otherwise have gone to rest camps. But the troops accepted these duties in the most loyal and hearty spirit, and have frequently expressed the opinion that the people they were fighting were even dirtier than the Germans. Street by street, Athens was cleared. Progress was very slow, because of the care taken to disentangle the women and children and innocent civilians who were all intermingled with people in plain clothes who were firing.

The assailants have fled; Attica is free; a truce has been signed, giving a much larger area of peace and order around Athens and the Piraeus, which are the heart of Greece and which have always been the dominant centre of the life of Greece. More than one quarter of the entire population lives there and in the region now liberated. I have not the slightest doubt that, in the opinions they express and in the views they take, they represent at least four-fifths of the whole Greek nation, if it could express its view in conditions of peace and normal tranquillity. Fighting has ceased now, except for skirmishes with parties of E.L.A.S. troops, who probably have not yet heard the news in this primitive country. Now the Greek people can talk things over as they choose under the guidance of Archbishop Damaskinos, who is also ready to receive, and has invited, the representatives of E.A.M., or what is left of E.A.M., in the political structure, and E.L.A.S., to come and meet him.

What do we seek in Greece? Do we want anything from Greece? What part do they play in our so-called power politics? How much does it matter to us, from a national point of view, what form their Government takes? I repeat: we want nothing from Greece but her friendship, and, to earn that and deserve that, we have to do our duty. We cannot disentangle ourselves from Greece immediately after what has happened. We cannot do so until there can be either a free vote, or a guarantee of a free vote, under the most stringent and impartial supervision, a vote of all the Greek people as to what they want in the future. Whatever they decide, Monarchy or Republic, Left or Right, that shall be their law, as far as we are concerned. When I see all the fury expended on this subject, and when we are abused, without one shadow of truth, as if we wanted some islands or bases from Greece, as if we needed their aid to keep ourselves alive, I feel added anxiety for the future, which with all its sombre and infinitely complicated problems is closing rapidly upon us. . . .

Now I turn to a very different theme and story. I turn from the pink and ochre panorama of Athens and the Piraeus, scintillating with delicious life and plumed by the classic glories and endless miseries and triumphs of its history. This must give way to the main battlefront of the war. In this, my chief contribution will be the recital of a number of facts and figures which may or may not be agreeable in different quarters. I have seen it suggested that the terrific battle which has been proceeding since 16th December on the American front is an Anglo-American battle. In fact, however, the United States troops have done almost all the fighting and have suffered almost all the losses. They have suffered losses almost equal to those on both sides in the battle of Gettysburg. Only one British Army Corps has been engaged in this action. All the rest of the 30 or more divisions, which have been fighting continuously for the last month, are United States troops. The Americans have engaged 30 or 40 men for every one we have engaged, and they have lost 60 to 80 men for every one of ours. That is a point I wish to make. Care must be taken in telling our proud tale not to claim for the British Army an undue share of what is undoubtedly the greatest American battle of the war, and will, I believe, be regarded as an ever famous American victory.

I never hesitate, as the Committee, I think, will bear me witness, to stand up for our own soldiers when their achievements have been cold-shouldered or neglected or overshadowed as they sometimes are; but we must not forget that it is to American homes that the telegrams of personal losses and anxiety have been going during the past month, and that there has been a hard and severe ordeal during these weeks for our brave and cherished Ally. This implies no disparagement of our own exertions, for we ourselves, a month or two earlier, lost 40,000 men in opening the Scheldt. The bulk of our Army on this occasion, when von Rundstedt attacked, was separated by scores of miles from the impact of the new offensive. They could not possibly have been moved into battle in large numbers without criss-crossing the lines of communication and creating utter confusion. The British Army stood, and stands, in its Northern position between the enemy and Antwerp in a strategic attitude, capable of averting all possibility of a major disaster. Our Armies are under the supreme command of General Eisenhower, and we march with discipline wherever we are told to go.

According to the professional advice which I have at my disposal, what was done to meet von Rundstedt's counter-stroke was resolute, wise, and militarily correct. A gap was torn open, as a gap can always be torn open in a line hundreds of miles long. General Eisenhower at once gave the command to the North of the gap to Field-Marshal Montgomery and to the South of it to General Omar Bradley. Many other consequential movements were made, and rightly made, and in the result both these highly skilled commanders handled the very large forces at their disposal in a manner which, I think I may say without exaggeration, may become the model for military students in the future. . . .

In short, as I see it, the Germans have made a violent and costly sortie which has been repulsed with heavy slaughter, and have expended in the endeavour forces which they cannot replace, against an enemy who has already more than replaced every loss he has sustained. These German forces are needed now, not only to support the German front in the West, but even more to fill the awful rents, only now emerging upon our consciousness as the telegrams come in, which have been torn in their Eastern line by the magnificent onslaught of the main Russian Armies along the entire front from the Baltic to Budapest. Marshal Stalin is very punctual. He would rather be before his time than late in the combinations of the Allies. I cannot attempt to set limits to the superb and titanic events which we are now witnessing in the East, or to their reactions in every theatre. I can only say it is certain that the whole of the Eastern and Western fronts, and the long front in Italy, where 27 German divisions are still held by no more than their own numbers, will henceforward be kept in constant flame until the final climax is reached. The advance of the enormous Forces of Soviet Russia across Poland and elsewhere into Germany and German-held territory must produce consequences of a character and degree about which the wisest strategists and the most far-sighted prophets will reserve their opinion until the results are known. . . .

We have reached the 65th month of the war, and its weight hangs heavy upon us. No one knows what stresses are wrought in these times by this long persistence of strain, quite above the ordinary normal life of human society. Let us be of good cheer. Both in the West and in the East overwhelming forces are ranged on our side. Military victory may be distant, it will certainly be costly, but it is no longer in doubt. The physical and scientific force which our foes hurled upon us in the early years has changed sides, and the British Commonwealth, the United States and the Soviet Union undoubtedly possess the power to beat down to the ground in dust and ashes the prodigious might of the war-making nations and the conspiracies which assailed us. But, as the sense of moral peril has passed from our side to that of our cruel foes, they gain the stimulus of despair, and we tend to lose the bond of combined self-preservation, or are in danger of losing it.

There is therefore demanded of us a moral and intellectual impulse to unity and a clear conception and definition of joint purpose sufficient to overbear the fleeting reinforcement which our enemies will derive from the realization of their forlorn condition. Can we produce that complete unity and that new impulse in time to achieve decisive military victory with the least possible prolongation of the world's misery, or must we fall into jabber, babel and discord while victory is still unattained? It seems to me to be the supreme question alike of the hour and of the age. This is no new problem in the history of mankind. Very often have great combinations almost attained success and then, at the last moment, cast it away. Very often have the triumphs and sacrifices of armies come to naught at the conference table. Very often the eagles have been squalled down by the parrots. Very often, in particular, the people of this Island, indomitable in adversity, have tasted the hard-won cup of success only to cast it away.

I therefore consider that this is a most grave moment to address the House, and it is one which affects the Members of every party—and all parties have the credit of our war effort; it is no monopoly to be flung from side to side in some future party dispute—we are all in this for good or ill. We all come through it together. Very often, I say, these troubles have arisen at a moment of success, at a period when no one can doubt what the ultimate result will be; and it is the duty of all parties to rouse themselves to the highest sense of their obligations and of the services which this House has already rendered to the cause of freedom.

At a time like this it is necessary to concentrate with clarity and command and mental perseverance upon the main practical issues with which we are confronted, and upon which we hope and believe we are in accord with our principal Allies. What, for instance, should be our attitude towards the terrible foes with whom we are grappling? Should it be unconditional surrender, or should we make some accommodation with them through a negotiated peace, leaving them free to regather their strength for a renewal of the struggle after a few uneasy years? The principle of unconditional surrender was proclaimed by the President of the United States at Casablanca, and I endorsed it there and then on behalf of this country. I am sure it was right at the time it was used, when many things hung in the balance against us which are all decided in our favour now. Should we then modify this declaration which was made in days of comparative weakness and lack of success, now that we have reached a period of mastery and power?

I am clear that nothing should induce us to abandon the principle of unconditional surrender, or to enter into any form of negotiation with Germany or Japan, under whatever guise such suggestions may present themselves, until the act of unconditional surrender has been formally executed. But the President of the United States, and I in your name, have repeatedly declared that the enforcement of unconditional surrender upon the enemy in no way relieves the victorious Powers of their obligations to humanity, or of their duties as civilized and Christian nations. I read somewhere that when the ancient Athenians, on one occasion, overpowered a tribe in the Peloponnesus which had wrought them great injury by base, treacherous means, and when they had the hostile army herded on a beach naked for slaughter, they forgave them and set them free, and they said:

> This was not because they were men; it was done because of the nature of Man.

Similarly, in this temper, we may now say to our foes, "We demand unconditional surrender, but you well know how strict are the moral limits within which our action is confined. We are no extirpators of nations, or butchers of peoples. We make no bargain with you. We accord you nothing as a right. Abandon your resistance unconditionally. We remain bound by our customs and our nature."

There is another reason why any abrogation of the principle of unconditional surrender would be most improvident at the present time, and it is a reason by no means inconsistent with, or contradictory to, that which I have just given. We should have to discuss with the enemy, while they still remained with arms in their hands, all the painful details of the settlement which their indescribable crimes have made necessary for the future safety of Europe and of the world; and these, when recited in detail, might well become a greater obstacle to the end of the struggle than the broad generalization which the term "unconditional surrender" implies.

The Germans know perfectly well how these matters stand in general. Several countries have already surrendered unconditionally to the victorious Allies, to Russia, to Britain and to the United States. Already there is a tolerable life appointed for their peoples. Take Finland, take Italy: these peoples have not all been massacred and enslaved. On the contrary, so far as Italy is concerned, there are moments when one has almost wondered whether it was they who had unconditionally surrendered to us, or whether we were about to surrender unconditionally to them. This, at least, I can say on behalf of the United Nations to Germany: "If you surrender now, nothing that you will have to endure after the war will be comparable to what you are otherwise going to suffer during the year 1945."

Peace, though based on unconditional surrender, will bring to Germany and Japan an immense, immediate amelioration of the suffering and agony which now lie before them. We, the Allies, are no monsters, but faithful men trying to carry forward the light of the world, trying to raise, from the bloody welter and confusion in which mankind is now plunged, a structure of peace, of freedom, of justice and of law, which system shall be an abiding and lasting shelter for all. That is how I venture to set before the Committee to-day the grave issue called "unconditional surrender." . . .

The expression "power politics" has lately been used in criticism against us in some quarters. I have anxiously asked the question, "What are power politics?" I know some of our friends across the water so well that I am sure I can always speak frankly without causing offence. Is having a Navy twice as big as any other Navy in the world power politics? Is having the largest Air Force in the world with bases in every part of the world power politics? Is having all the gold in the world power politics? If so, we are certainly not guilty of these offences, I am sorry to say. They are luxuries that have passed away from us.

I am, therefore, greatly indebted to my friend, the illustrious President of the United States, four times summoned by the popular vote to the headship of the most powerful community in the world, for his definition of "power politics." With that marvellous gift which he has of bringing troublesome issues down to earth and reducing them to the calm level of ordinary life, the President declared, in his recent Message to Congress, that power politics were "the misuse of power." I am sure I can say, on behalf of all parties in the House, that we are absolutely in agreement with the President. We go farther; we define our position with even more precision. We have sacrificed everything in this war. We shall emerge from it, for the time being, more stricken and impoverished than any other victorious country. The United Kingdom and the British Commonwealth are the only unbroken force which declared war on Germany of its own free will. We declared war not for any ambition or material advantage, but for the sake of our obligation to do our best for Poland against German aggression, in which aggression, there or elsewhere, it must also in fairness be stated, our own self-preservation was involved.

After the defeat of France in June, 1940, for more than a year we were alone. We stood alone; we kept nothing back in blood, effort or treasure from what has now become the common cause of more than thirty nations. We seek no territory; we covet no oilfields; we demand no bases for the forces of the air or of the seas. We are an ancient Commonwealth dwelling, and wishing to dwell, at peace within our own habitations. We do not set ourselves up in rivalry of bigness or might with any other community in the world. We stand on our own rights.

We are prepared to defend them, but we do not intrude for our own advantage upon the rights of any friendly country in the world, great or small. We have given, and shall continue to give, everything we have. We ask nothing in return except that consideration and respect which is our due, and even if that were denied us, we should still have a good conscience. Let none, therefore, in our own country and Commonwealth or in the outside world, misname us or traduce our motives. Our actions are no doubt subject to human error, but our motives in small things as in great are disinterested, lofty and true. I repulse those calumnies, wherever they come from, that Britain and the British Empire is a selfish, power-greedy, land-greedy, designing nation obsessed by dark schemes of European intrigue or Colonial expansion. I repulse these aspersions, whether they come from our best friends or our worst foes. Let us all march forward against the enemy, and, for the rest, let all men here and in all countries search their hearts devoutly, as we shall certainly continue to do. . . .

THE YALTA CONFERENCE

February 27, 1945

House of Commons

Under conditions of great secrecy, Stalin, Roosevelt and Churchill met at Yalta early in February. The most bitterly controversial item of their conference concerned the new frontiers and the political future of Poland. Later, many M.P.s felt the Western Allies had betrayed their trust to the Free Poles in London in favour of the Russian-dominated Lublin Government.

[Extract] The recent Conference of the three Powers in the Crimea faced realities and difficulties in so exceptional a manner that the result constituted an act of State, on which Parliament should formally express their opinion. His Majesty's Government feel they have the right to know where they stand with the House of Commons. A strong expression of support by the House will strengthen our position among our Allies. The intimate and sensitive connections between the Executive Government and the House of Commons will thereby also be made plain, thus showing the liveliness of our democratic institutions, and the subordination of Ministers to Parliamentary authority. The House will not shrink from its duty of pronouncing. We live in a time when equality of decision is required from all who take part in our public affairs. In this way also, the firm and tenacious character of the present Parliament, and, generally, of our Parliamentary institutions, emerging as they do fortified from the storms of the war, will be made manifest. We have therefore thought it right and necessary to place a positive Motion on the Paper, in support of which I should like to submit some facts and arguments to the House at the opening of this three days' Debate. . . .

On world organization, there is little that I can say beyond what is contained in the Report of the Conference, and, of course, in the earlier reports which emanated from Dumbarton Oaks. In the Crimea, the three Great Powers agreed on a solution of the difficult question of voting procedure, to which no answer had been found at Dumbarton Oaks. Agreement on this vital matter has enabled us to take the next step forward in the setting-up of the new world organization, and the arrangements are in hand for the issue of invitations to the United Nations Conference which, as I have said, will meet in a couple of months at San Francisco. I wish I could give to the House full particulars of the solution of this question of the voting procedure, to which representatives of the three Great Powers, formerly in disagreement, have now whole-heartedly agreed. We thought it right, however, that we should consult both France and China, and should endeavour to secure their acceptance before the formula was published. For the moment, therefore, I can only deal with the matter in general terms.

Here is the difficulty which has to be faced. It is on the Great Powers that the chief burden of maintaining peace and security will fall. The new world organization must take into account this special responsibility of the Great Powers, and must be so framed as not to compromise their unity, or their capacity for effective action if it is called for at short notice. At the same time, the world organization cannot be based upon a dictatorship of the Great Powers. It is their duty to serve the world and not to rule it. We trust the voting procedure on which we agreed at Yalta meets these two essential points, and provides a system which is fair and acceptable, having regard to the evident difficulties, which will meet anyone who gives prolonged thought to the subject. . . .

The former League of Nations, so hardly used and found to be inadequate for the tasks it attempted, will be replaced by a far stronger body in which the United States will play a vitally important part. It will embody much of the structure and characteristics of its predecessor. All the work that was done in the past, all the experience that has been gathered by the working of the League of Nations, will not be cast away; but the new body will differ from it in the essential point that it will not shrink from establishing its will against the evil-doer, or evil-planner, in good time and by force of arms. This organization, which is capable of continuous progress and development, is at any rate appropriate to the phase upon which the world will enter after our present enemies have been beaten down, and we may have good hopes, and, more than hopes, a resolute determination that it shall shield humanity from a third renewal of its agonies. We have all been made aware in the interval between the two world wars of the weaknesses of international bodies, whose work is seriously complicated by the misfortune which occurred in the building of the Tower of Babel. Taught by bitter experience, we hope now to make the world conscious of the strength of the new instrument, and of the protection which it will be able to afford to all who wish to dwell in peace within their habitations.

This new world structure will, from the outset and in all parts of its work, be aided to the utmost by the ordinary channels of friendly diplomatic intercourse, which it in no way supersedes. For our part, we are determined to do all in our power to ensure the success of the Conference. On such an occasion it is clearly right that the two leading parties in His Majesty's Government and in the British nation should be represented, and all parties bound for the future in these decisions. I am glad to inform the House that His Majesty's chief representatives at this Conference will be my right hon. Friend the Secretary of State for Foreign Affairs (Mr. Eden), and the Lord President of the Council, the leader of the Labour Party (Mr. Attlee). I am most anxious that this principle should be established, even in what are perhaps the closing stages of this memorable coalition. I am anxious that all parties should be united in this new instrument, so that these supreme affairs shall be, in Mr. Gladstone's words, "high and dry above the ebb and flow of party politics." I confess that I have not verified that quotation, and I ask for all indulgence if I should be proved to have made any slip. . . .

I now come to the most difficult and agitating part of the statement which I have to make to the House—the question of Poland. For more than a year past, and since the tide of war has turned so strongly against Germany, the Polish problem has been divided into two main issues—the frontiers of Poland and the freedom of Poland.

The House is well aware from the speeches I have made to them that the freedom, independence, integrity and sovereignty of Poland have always seemed to His Majesty's Government more important than the actual frontiers. To establish a free Polish nation with a good home to live in has always far outweighed, in my mind, the actual tracing of the frontier line, or whether these boundaries should be shifted on both sides of Poland farther to the West. The Russian claim, first advanced at Teheran in November, 1943, has always been unchanged for the Curzon Line in the East, and the Russian offer has always been that ample compensation should be gained for Poland at the expense of Germany in the North and in the West. All these matters are tolerably well known now. The Foreign Secretary explained in detail last December the story of the Curzon Line. I have never concealed from the House that, personally, I think the Russian claim is just and right. If I champion this frontier for Russia, it is not because I bow to force. It is because I believe it is the fairest division of territory that can, in all the circumstances, be made between the two countries whose history has been so chequered and intermingled. . . .

In supporting the Russian claim to the Curzon Line, I repudiate and repulse any suggestion that we are making a questionable compromise or yielding to force or fear, and I assert with the utmost conviction the broad justice of the policy upon which, for the first time, all the three great Allies have now taken their stand. Moreover, the three Powers have now agreed that Poland shall receive substantial accessions of territory both in the North and in the West. In the North she will certainly receive, in the place of a precarious Corridor, the great city of Danzig, the greater part of East Prussia west and south of Koenigsberg, and a long, wide sea front on the Baltic. In the West she will receive the important industrial province of Upper Silesia and, in addition, such other territories to the east of the Oder as it may be decided at the peace settlement to detach from Germany after the views of a broadly based Polish Government have been ascertained.

Thus, it seems to me that this talk of cutting half of Poland off is very misleading. In fact, the part which is to be east of the Curzon Line cannot in any case be measured by its size. It includes the enormous, dismal region of the Pripet Marshes, which Poland held between the two wars, and it exchanges for that the far more fruitful and developed land in the West, from which a very large portion of the German population has already departed. We need not fear that the task of holding these new lines will be too heavy for Poland, or that it will bring about another German revenge, or that it will, to use a conventional phrase, sow the seeds of future wars. We intend to take steps far more drastic and effective than those which followed the last war, because we know much more about this business, so as to render all offensive action by Germany utterly impossible for generations to come.

Finally, under the world organization of nations great and small, victors and vanquished will be secured against aggression by indisputable law and by overwhelming international force. The published Crimea Agreement is not a ready-made plan, imposed by the great Powers on the Polish people. It sets out the agreed views of the three major Allies on the means whereby their common desire to see established a strong, free, independent Poland may be fulfilled in cooperation with the Poles themselves, and whereby a Polish Government which all the United Nations can recognize may be set up in Poland. This has become for the first time a possibility now that practically the whole country has been liberated by the Soviet Army. The fulfilment of the plan will depend upon the willingness of all sections of democratic Polish opinion in Poland or abroad to work together in giving it effect. The plan should be studied as a whole, and with the main common objective always in view. The three Powers are agreed that acceptance by the Poles of the provisions on the Eastern Frontiers and, so far as they can now be ascertained, on the Western Frontiers, is an essential condition of the establishment and future welfare and security of a strong, independent, homogeneous Polish State. . . .

But even more important than the frontiers of Poland, within the limits now disclosed, is the freedom of Poland. The home of the Poles is settled. Are they to be masters in their own house? Are they to be free, as we in Britain and the United States or France are free? Is their sovereignty and their independence to be untrammelled, or are they to become a mere projection of the Soviet State, forced against their will, by an armed minority, to adopt a Communist or totalitarian system? Well, I am putting the case in all its bluntness. It is a touchstone far more sensitive and vital than the drawing of frontier lines. Where does Poland stand? Where do we all stand on this?

Most solemn declarations have been made by Marshal Stalin and the Soviet Union that the sovereign independence of Poland is to be maintained, and this decision is now joined-in both by Great Britain and the United States. Here also, the world organization will in due course assume a measure of responsibility. The Poles will have their future in their own hands, with the single limitation that they must honestly follow, in harmony with their Allies, a policy friendly to Russia. That is surely reasonable.

The procedure which the three Great Powers have unitedly adopted to achieve this vital aim is set forth in unmistakable terms in the Crimea declaration. The agreement provides for consultations, with a view to the establishment in Poland of a new Polish Provisional Government of National Unity, with which the three major Powers can all enter into diplomatic relations, instead of some recognizing one Polish Government and the rest another, a situation which, if it had survived the Yalta Conference, would have proclaimed to the world disunity and confusion. We had to settle it, and we settled it there. No binding restrictions have been imposed upon the scope and method of those consultations. His Majesty's Government intend to do all in their power to ensure that they shall be as wide as possible, and that representative Poles of all democratic parties are given full freedom to come and make their views known. Arrangements for this are now being made in Moscow by the Commission of three, comprising M. Molotov, and Mr. Harriman and Sir Archibald Clark Kerr, representing the United States and Great Britain respectively. It will be for the Poles themselves, with such assistance as the Allies are able to give them, to agree upon the composition and constitution of the new Polish Government of National Unity. Thereafter, His Majesty's Government, through their representative in Poland, will use all their influence to ensure that the free elections to which the new Polish Government will be pledged shall be fairly carried out under all proper democratic safeguards.

Our two guiding principles in dealing with all these problems of the Continent and of liberated countries, have been clear: While the war is on, we give help to anyone who can kill a Hun; when the war is over, we look to the solution of a free, unfettered, democratic election. Those are the two principles which this Coalition Government have applied, to the best of their ability, to the circumstances and situations in this entangled and infinitely varied development.

The agreement does not affect the continued recognition by His Majesty's Government of the Polish Government in London. This will be maintained until such time as His Majesty's Government consider that a new Provisional Government has been properly formed in Poland in accordance with the agreed provisions; nor does it involve the previous or immediate recognition by His Majesty's Government of the present Provisional Government which is now functioning in Poland. Let me remind the House, and those who have undertaken what I regard as the honourable duty of being very careful that our affairs in Poland are regulated in accordance with the dignity and honour of this country, that there would have been no Lublin Committee or Lublin Provisional Government in Poland if the Polish Government in London had accepted our faithful counsel given to them a year ago. They would have entered into Poland as its active Government, with the liberating Armies of Russia. Even in October, when the Foreign Secretary and I toiled night and day in Moscow, M. Mikolajczyk could have gone from Moscow to Lublin with every assurance of Marshal Stalin's friendship, and become the Prime Minister of a more broadly constructed Government, which would now be seated at Warsaw, or wherever, in view of the ruin of Warsaw, the centre of Government is placed.

But these opportunities were cast aside. Meanwhile, the expulsion of the Germans from Poland has taken place, and of course the new Government, the Lublin Government, advanced with the victorious Russian Armies, who were received with great joy in very great areas in Poland, many great cities changing hands without a shot fired, and with none of that terrible business of underground armies being shot by both sides, and so forth, which we feared so much, having actually taken place during the great forward advance. The Russians, who are executing and preparing military operations on the largest scale against the heart of Germany, have the right to have the communications of their armies protected by an orderly countryside, under a government acting in accordance with their needs. It was not therefore possible, so far as recognition was concerned, to procure the dissolution of the Lublin Government as well as of the London Government simultaneously, and start from a swept table. To do that would be to endanger the success of the Russian offensive, and consequently to prolong the war, with increased loss of Russian, British and American blood.

The House should read carefully again and again—those Members who have doubts—the words and the terms of the Declaration, every word of which was the subject of the most profound and searching attention by the Heads of the three Governments, and by the Foreign Secretaries and all their experts. How will this Declaration be carried out? How will phrases like "Free and unfettered elections on the basis of universal suffrage and secret ballot" be interpreted? Will the "new" Government be "properly" constituted, with a fair representation of the Polish people, as far as can be made practicable at the moment, and as soon as possible? Will the elections be free and unfettered? Will the candidates of all democratic parties be able to present themselves to the electors, and to conduct their campaigns? What are democratic parties? People always take different views. Even in our own country there has been from time to time an effort by one party or the other to claim that they are the true democratic party, and the rest are either Bolsheviks or Tory landlords. What are democratic parties? Obviously, this is capable of being settled. Will the election be what we should say was fair and free in this country, making some allowance for the great confusion and disorder which prevails? There are a great number of parties in Poland. We have agreed that all those that are democratic parties—not Nazi or Fascist parties or parties of collaborators with the enemy—all these will be able to take their part.

These are questions upon which we have the clearest views, in accordance with the principles of the Declaration on liberated Europe, to which all three Governments have duly subscribed. It is on that basis that the Moscow Commission of three was intended to work, and on that basis it has already begun to work.

The impression I brought back from the Crimea, and from all my other contacts, is that Marshal Stalin and the Soviet leaders wish to live in honourable friendship and equality with the Western democracies. I feel also that their word is their bond. I know of no Government which stands to its obligations, even in its own despite, more solidly than the Russian Soviet Government. I decline absolutely to embark here on a discussion about Russian good faith. It is quite evident that these matters touch the whole future of the world. Sombre indeed would be the fortunes of mankind if some awful schism arose between the Western democracies and the Russian Soviet Union, if the future world organization were rent asunder, and if new cataclysms of inconceivable violence destroyed all that is left of the treasures and liberties of mankind. . . .

Here is the moment when the House should pay its tribute to the work of my right hon. Friend the Foreign Secretary. I cannot describe to the House the aid and comfort he has been to me in all our difficulties. His hard life when quite young in the infantry in the last war, his constant self-preparation for the tasks which have fallen to him, his unequalled experience as a Minister at the Foreign Office, his knowledge of foreign affairs and their past history, his experience of conferences of all kinds, his breadth of view, his powers of exposition, his moral courage, have gained for him a position second to none among the Foreign Secretaries of the Grand Alliance. It is not only my own personal debt, but even more that of the House to him, which I now acknowledge.

I suppose that during these last three winter months the human race all the world over has undergone more physical agony and misery than at any other period through which this planet has passed. In the Stone Age the numbers were fewer, and the primitive creatures, little removed from their animal origin, knew no better. We suffer more, and we feel more. I must admit that in all this war I never felt so grave a sense of responsibility as I did at Yalta. In 1940 and 1941, when we in this Island were all alone, and invasion was so near, the actual steps one ought to take and our attitude towards them seemed plain and simple. If a man is coming across the sea to kill you, you do everything in your power to make sure he dies before finishing his journey. That may be difficult, it may be painful, but at least it is simple. Now we are entering a world of imponderables, and at every stage occasions for self-questioning arise. It is a mistake to look too far ahead. Only one link in the chain of destiny can be handled at a time.

I trust the House will feel that hope has been powerfully strengthened by our meeting in the Crimea. The ties that bind the three great Powers together, and their mutual comprehension of each other, have grown. The United States has entered deeply and constructively into the life and salvation of Europe. We have all three set our hands to far-reaching engagements at once practical and solemn. United, we have the unchallengeable power to lead the world to prosperity, freedom and happiness. The Great Powers must seek to serve and not to rule. Joined with other States, both large and small, we may found a world organization which, armed with ample power, will guard the rights of all States, great or small, from aggression, or from the gathering of the means of aggression. I am sure that a fairer choice is open to mankind than they have known in recorded ages. The lights burn brighter and shine more broadly than before. Let us walk forward together.

THE DEATH OF LLOYD GEORGE

March 28, 1945

House of Commons

Shortly after David Lloyd George first took Cabinet office as President of the Board of Trade, the Liberals, who had been in eclipse for twenty years, obtained in January, 1906, an overwhelming majority over all other parties. They were independent of the Irish; the Labour Party was in its infancy; the Conservatives were reduced to little more than 100. But this moment of political triumph occurred in a period when the aspirations of 19th century Liberalism had been largely achieved. Most of the great movements and principles of Liberalism had become the common property of enlightened men all over the civilized world. The chains had been struck from the slave; a free career was open to talent; the extension of the franchise was moving irresistibly forward; the advance in education was rapid and continuous, not only in this Island but in many lands. Thus at the moment when the Liberal Party became supreme, the great and beneficent impulses which had urged them forward were largely assuaged by success. Some new and potent conception had to be found by those who were called into power.

It was Lloyd George who launched the Liberal and Radical forces of this country effectively into the broad stream of social betterment and social security along which all modern parties now steer. There was no man so gifted, so eloquent, so forceful, who knew the life of the people so well. His warm heart was stirred by the many perils which beset the cottage homes: the health of the bread-winner, the fate of his widow, the nourishment and upbringing of his children, the meagre and haphazard provision of medical treatment and sanatoria, and the lack of any organized accessible medical service of a kind worthy of the age, from which the mass of the wage earners and the poor suffered. All this excited his wrath. Pity and compassion lent their powerful wings. He knew the terror with which old age threatened the toiler–that after a life of exertion he could be no more than a burden at the fireside and in the family of a struggling son. When I first became Lloyd George's friend and active associate, now more than forty years ago, this deep love of the people, the profound knowledge of their lives and of the undue and needless pressures under which they lived, impressed itself indelibly upon my mind.

Then there was his dauntless courage, his untiring energy, his oratory, persuasive, provocative, now grave, now gay. His swift, penetrating, comprehensive mind was always grasping at the root, or what he thought to be the root, of every question. His eye ranged ahead of the obvious. He was always hunting in the field beyond. I have often heard people come to him with a plan, and he would say "That is all right, but what happens when we get over the bridge? What do we do then?"

In his prime, his power, his influence, his initiative, were unequalled in the land. He was the champion of the weak and the poor. Those were great days. Nearly two generations have passed. Most people are unconscious of how much their lives have been shaped by the laws for which Lloyd George was responsible. Health Insurance and Old Age Pensions were the first large-scale State-conscious efforts to set a balustrade along the crowded causeway of the people's life, and, without pulling down the structures of society, to fasten a lid over the abyss into which vast numbers used to fall, generation after generation, uncared-for and indeed unnoticed. Now we move forward confidently into larger and more far-reaching applications of these ideas. I was his lieutenant in those bygone days, and shared in a minor way in the work. I have lived to see long strides taken, and being taken, and going to be taken, on this path of insurance by which the vultures of utter ruin are driven from the dwellings of the nation. The stamps we lick, the roads we travel, the system of progressive taxation, the principal remedies that have so far been used against unemployment—all these to a very great extent were part not only of the mission but of the actual achievement of Lloyd George; and I am sure that as time passes his name will not only live but shine on account of the great, laborious, constructive work he did for the social and domestic life of our country.

When the calm, complacent, self-satisfied tranquillities of the Victorian era had exploded into the world convulsions and wars of the terrible Twentieth Century, Lloyd George had another part to play on which his fame will stand with equal or even greater firmness. Although unacquainted with the military arts, although by public repute a pugnacious pacifist, when the life of our country was in peril he rallied to the war effort and cast aside all other thoughts and aims. He was the first to discern the fearful shortages of ammunition and artillery and all the other appliances of war which would so soon affect, and in the case of Imperial Russia mortally affect, the warring nations on both sides. He saw it before anyone. Here I must say that my hon. and gallant Friend the Member for Wycombe [Sir A. Knox] was a truthful and vigilant prophet and guide in all that information which we received. He was our military representative in Russia. But it was Mr. Lloyd George who fixed on these papers, brought them forth before the eyes of the Cabinet, and induced action to be taken with the utmost vigour possible at that late hour.

Lloyd George left the Exchequer, when the Coalition Government was formed, for the Ministry of Munitions. Here he hurled himself into the mobilization of British industry. In 1915 he was building great war factories that could not come into operation for two years. There was the usual talk about the war being over in a few months, but he did not hesitate to plan on a vast scale for two years ahead. It was my fortune to inherit the output of those factories in 1917–the vast, overflowing output which came from them. Presently Lloyd George seized the main power in the State and the leadership of the Government. [Hon. Members: "Seized?"] Seized. I think it was Carlyle who said of Oliver Cromwell:

"He coveted the place; perhaps the place was his."

He imparted immediately a new surge of strength, of impulse, far stronger than anything that had been known up to that time, and extending over the whole field of war-time Government, every part of which was of equal interest to him.

I have already written about him at this time, when I watched him so closely and enjoyed his confidence and admired him so much, and I have recorded two characteristics of his which seemed to me invaluable in those days: first, his power to live in the present yet without taking short views; and secondly, his power of drawing from misfortune itself the means of future success. All this was illustrated by the successful development of the war; by the adoption of the convoy system, which he enforced upon the Admiralty and by which the U-boats were defeated; by the unified command on the Western Front which gave Marshal Foch the power to lead us all to victory; and in many other matters which form a part of the story of those sombre and tremendous years, the memory of which for ever abides with me, and to which I have often recurred in thought during our present second heavy struggle against German aggression, now drawing towards its victorious close.

Thus the statesman and guide whose gentle passing in the fullness of his years we mourn to-day served our country, our Island and our age, both faithfully and well in peace and in war. His long life was, from almost the beginning to almost the end, spent in political strife and controversy. He aroused intense and sometimes needless antagonisms. He had fierce and bitter quarrels at various times with all the parties. He faced undismayed the storms of criticism and hostility. In spite of all obstacles, including those he raised himself, he achieved his main purposes. As a man of action, resource and creative energy he stood, when at his zenith, without a rival. His name is a household word throughout our Commonwealth of Nations. He was the greatest Welshman which that unconquerable race has produced since the age of the Tudors. Much of his work abides, some of it will grow greatly in the future, and those who come after us will find the pillars of his life's toil upstanding, massive and indestructible; and we ourselves, gathered here to-day, may indeed be thankful that he voyaged with us through storm and tumult with so much help and guidance to bestow.

THE DEATH OF PRESIDENT ROOSEVELT

April 17, 1945

House of Commons

President Roosevelt died suddenly at Warm Springs, Georgia, on April 12; on receiving the news, Churchill later recorded that he felt "as if I had been struck a physical blow." Churchill's first intention was to go to Washington to attend the funeral and meet the new President, Harry S. Truman, but he was persuaded by his colleagues not to leave London at such a critical time.

I beg to move:

> That an humble Address be presented to His Majesty to convey to His Majesty the deep sorrow with which this House has learned of the death of the President of the United States of America, and to pray His Majesty that in communicating his own sentiments of grief to the United States Government, he will also be generously pleased to express on the part of this House their sense of the loss which the British Commonwealth and Empire and the cause of the Allied nations have sustained, and their profound sympathy with Mrs. Roosevelt and the late President's family, and with the Government and people of the United States of America.

My friendship with the great man to whose work and fame we pay our tribute today began and ripened during this war. I had met him, but only for a few minutes, after the close of the last war, and as soon as I went to the Admiralty in September 1939, he telegraphed inviting me to correspond with him direct on naval or other matters if at any time I felt inclined. Having obtained the permission of the Prime Minister, I did so. Knowing President Roosevelt's keen interest in sea warfare, I furnished him with a stream of information about our naval affairs, and about the various actions, including especially the action of the Plate River, which lighted the first gloomy winter of the war.

When I became Prime Minister, and the war broke out in all its hideous fury, when our own life and survival hung in the balance, I was already in a position to telegraph to the President on terms of an association which had become most intimate and, to me, most agreeable. This continued through all the ups and downs of the world struggle until Thursday last, when I received my last messages from him. These messages showed no falling off in his accustomed clear vision and vigour upon perplexing and complicated matters. I may mention that this correspondence which, of course, was greatly increased after the United States entry into the war, comprises to and fro between us, over 1,700 messages. Many of these were lengthy messages, and the majority dealt with those more difficult points which come to be discussed upon the level of heads of Governments only after official solutions have not been reached at other stages. To this correspondence there must be added our nine meetings—at

Argentia, three in Washington, at Casablanca, at Teheran, two at Quebec and, last of all, at Yalta, comprising in all about 120 days of close personal contact, during a great part of which I stayed with him at the White House or at his home at Hyde Park or in his retreat in the Blue Mountains, which he called Shangri-la.

I conceived an admiration for him as a statesman, a man of affairs, and a war leader. I felt the utmost confidence in his upright, inspiring character and outlook, and a personal regard—affection I must say—for him beyond my power to express today. His love of his own country, his respect for its constitution, his power of gauging the tides and currents of its mobile public opinion, were always evident, but added to these were the beatings of that generous heart which was always stirred to anger and to action by spectacles of aggression and oppression by the strong against the weak. It is, indeed, a loss, a bitter loss to humanity that those heart-beats are stilled for ever.

President Roosevelt's physical affliction lay heavily upon him. It was a marvel that he bore up against it through all the many years of tumult and storm. Not one man in ten millions, stricken and crippled as he was, would have attempted to plunge into a life of physical and mental exertion and of hard, ceaseless political controversy. Not one in ten millions would have tried, not one in a generation would have succeeded, not only in entering this sphere, not only in acting vehemently in it, but in becoming indisputable master of the scene. In this extraordinary effort of the spirit over the flesh, of will-power over physical infirmity, he was inspired and sustained by that noble woman his devoted wife, whose high ideals marched with his own, and to whom the deep and respectful sympathy of the House of Commons flows out today in all fullness.

There is no doubt that the President foresaw the great dangers closing in upon the pre-war world with far more prescience than most well-informed people on either side of the Atlantic, and that he urged forward with all his power such precautionary military preparations as peacetime opinion in the United States could be brought to accept. There never was a moment's doubt, as the quarrel opened, upon which side his sympathies lay. The fall of France, and what seemed to most people outside this island, the impending destruction of Great Britain, were to him an agony, although he never lost faith in us. They were an agony to him not only on account of Europe, but because of the serious perils to which the United States herself would have been exposed had we been overwhelmed or the survivors cast down under the German yoke. The bearing of the British nation at that time of stress, when we were all alone, filled him and vast numbers of his countrymen with the warmest sentiments towards our people. He and they felt the blitz of the stern winter of 1940-41, when Hitler set himself to rub out the cities of our country, as much as any of us did, and perhaps more indeed, for imagination is often more torturing than reality. There is no doubt that the bearing of the British and, above all, of the Londoners, kindled fires in American bosoms far harder to quench than the conflagrations from which we were suffering. There was also at that time, in spite of General Wavell's victories—all the more, indeed, because of the reinforcements which were sent from this country to him—the apprehension widespread in the United States that we should be invaded by Germany after the fullest preparation in the spring of 1941. It was in February that the President sent to England the late Mr. Wendell Willkie, who, although a political rival and an opposing candidate, felt as he did on many important points. Mr. Willkie brought a letter from Mr. Roosevelt, which the President had written in his own hand, and this letter contained the famous lines of Longfellow:

> . . . Sail on, O ship of State!
> Sail on, O Union, strong and great!
> Humanity with all its fears,
> With all the hopes of future years,
> Is hanging breathless on thy fate!

At about that same time he devised the extraordinary measure of assistance called Lend-Lease, which will stand forth as the most unselfish and unsordid financial act of any country in all history. The effect of this was greatly to increase British fighting power, and for all the purpose of the war effort to make us, as it were, a much more numerous community. In that autumn I met the President for the first time during the war at Argentia in Newfoundland, and together we drew up the declaration which has since been called the Atlantic Charter, and which will, I trust, long remain a guide for both our peoples and for other people of the world.

All this time in deep and dark and deadly secrecy, the Japanese were preparing their act of treachery and greed. When next we met in Washington, Japan, Germany and Italy had declared war upon the United States, and both our countries were in arms, shoulder to shoulder. Since then we have advanced over the land and over the sea through many difficulties and disappointments, but always with a broadening measure of success. I need not dwell upon the series of great operations which have taken place in the Western Hemisphere, to say nothing of that other immense war proceeding on the other side of the world. Nor need I speak of the plans which we made with our great ally, Russia, at Teheran, for these have now been carried out for all the world to see.

But at Yalta I noticed that the President was ailing. His captivating smile, his gay and charming manner, had not deserted him, but his face had a transparency, an air of purification, and often there was a faraway look in his eyes. When I took my leave of him in Alexandria harbour I must confess that I had an indefinable sense of fear that his health and his strength were on the ebb. But nothing altered his inflexible sense of duty. To the end he faced his innumerable tasks unflinching. One of the tasks of the President is to sign maybe a hundred or two State papers with his own hand every day, commissions and so forth. All this he continued to carry out with the utmost strictness. When death came suddenly upon him 'he had finished his mail.' That portion of his day's work was done. As the saying goes, he died in harness, and we may well say in battle harness, like his soldiers, sailors, and airmen, who side by side with ours are carrying on their task to the end all over the world. What an enviable death was his! He had brought his country through the worst of its perils and the heaviest of its toils. Victory had cast its sure and steady beam upon him.

In the days of peace he had broadened and stabilized the foundations of American life and union. In war he had raised the strength, might and glory of the great Republic to a height never attained by any nation in history. With her left hand she was leading the advance of the conquering Allied armies into the heart of Germany, and with her right, on the other side of the globe, she was irresistibly and swiftly breaking up the power of Japan. And all the time ships, munitions, supplies, and food of every kind were aiding on a gigantic scale her allies, great and small, in the course of the long struggle.

But all this was no more than worldly power and grandeur, had it not been that the causes of human freedom and of social justice, to which so much of his life had been given, added a lustre to this power and pomp and warlike might, a lustre which will long be discernible among men. He has left behind him a band of resolute and able men handling the numerous interrelated parts of the vast American war machine. He has left a successor who comes forward with firm step and sure conviction to carry on the task to its appointed end. For us, it remains only to say that in Franklin Roosevelt there died the greatest American friend we have ever known, and the greatest champion of freedom who has ever brought help and comfort from the new world to the old.

THE END OF THE WAR IN EUROPE

May 8, 1945

Broadcast, London, and House of Commons

The final assault on Berlin began on April 18 with the Allied forces advancing rapidly. On April 25 Russian and American forces met at the River Elbe. Three days later Mussolini was captured and executed by Italian partisans. On May 1 the death of Hitler was announced; all German troops in Italy surrendered unconditionally to General Alexander the next day.

German armed forces surrendered unconditionally on May 7. Hostilities in Europe ended officially at midnight, May 8, 1945.

Yesterday morning at 2.41 a.m. at Headquarters, General Jodl, the representative of the German High Command, and Grand Admiral Doenitz, the designated head of the German State, signed the act of unconditional surrender of all German land, sea, and air forces in Europe to the Allied Expeditionary Force, and simultaneously to the Soviet High Command.

General Bedell Smith, Chief of Staff of the Allied Expeditionary Force, and General François Sevez signed the document on behalf of the Supreme Commander of the Allied Expeditionary Force, and General Susloparov signed on behalf of the Russian High Command.

To-day this agreement will be ratified and confirmed at Berlin, where Air Chief Marshal Tedder, Deputy Supreme Commander of the Allied Expeditionary Force, and General de Lattre de Tassigny will sign on behalf of General Eisenhower. Marshal

Zhukov will sign on behalf of the Soviet High Command. The German representatives will be Field-Marshal Keitel, Chief of the High Command, and the Commanders-in-Chief of the German Army, Navy, and Air Forces.

Hostilities will end officially at one minute after midnight to-night (Tuesday, May 8), but in the interests of saving lives the "Cease fire" began yesterday to be sounded all along the front, and our dear Channel Islands are also to be freed to-day.

The Germans are still in places resisting the Russian troops, but should they continue to do so after midnight they will, of course, deprive themselves of the protection of the laws of war, and will be attacked from all quarters by the Allied troops. It is not surprising that on such long fronts and in the existing disorder of the enemy the orders of the German High Command should not in every case be obeyed immediately. This does not, in our opinion, with the best military advice at our disposal, constitute any reason for withholding from the nation the facts communicated to us by General Eisenhower of the unconditional surrender already signed at Rheims, nor should it prevent us from celebrating to-day and to-morrow (Wednesday) as Victory in Europe days.

To-day, perhaps, we shall think mostly of ourselves. To-morrow we shall pay a particular tribute to our Russian comrades, whose prowess in the field has been one of the grand contributions to the general victory.

The German war is therefore at an end. After years of intense preparation, Germany hurled herself on Poland at the beginning of September, 1939; and, in pursuance of our guarantee to Poland and in agreement with the French Republic, Great Britain, the British Empire and Commonwealth of Nations, declared war upon this foul aggression. After gallant France had been struck down we, from this Island and from our united Empire, maintained the struggle single-handed for a whole year until we were joined by the military might of Soviet Russia, and later by the overwhelming power and resources of the United States of America.

Finally almost the whole world was combined against the evil-doers, who are now prostrate before us. Our gratitude to our splendid Allies goes forth from all our hearts in this Island and throughout the British Empire.

We may allow ourselves a brief period of rejoicing; but let us not forget for a moment the toil and efforts that lie ahead. Japan, with all her treachery and greed, remains unsubdued. The injury she has inflicted on Great Britain, the United States, and other countries, and her detestable cruelties, call for justice and retribution. We must now devote all our strength and resources to the completion of our task, both at home and abroad. Advance, Britannia! Long live the cause of freedom! God save the King!

[Editor's Note: After making his broadcast announcement of Germany's unconditional surrender, Churchill read the same statement to the House of Commons shortly afterwards and added] : That is the message which I have been instructed to deliver to the British Nation and Commonwealth. I have only two or three sentences to add. They will convey to the House my deep gratitude to this House of Commons, which has proved itself the strongest foundation for waging war that has ever been seen in the whole of our long history. We have all of us made our mistakes, but the strength of the Parliamentary institution has been shown to enable it at the same moment to preserve all the title-deeds of democracy while waging war in the most stern and protracted form. I wish to give my hearty thanks to men of all Parties, to everyone in every part of the House where they sit, for the way in which the liveliness of Parliamentary institutions has been maintained under the fire of the enemy, and for the way in which we have been able to persevere—and we could have persevered much longer if need had been—till all the objectives which we set before us for the procuring of the unlimited and unconditional surrender of the enemy had been achieved. I recollect well at the end of the last war, more than a quarter of a century ago, that the House, when it heard the long list of the surrender terms, the armistice terms, which had been imposed upon the Germans, did not feel inclined for debate or business, but desired to offer thanks to Almighty God, to the Great Power which seems to shape and design the fortunes of nations and the destiny of man; and I therefore beg, Sir, with your permission to move:

> That this House do now attend at the Church of St. Margaret, Westminster, to give humble and reverent thanks to Almighty God for our deliverance from the threat of German domination.

This is the identical Motion which was moved in former times.

"THIS IS YOUR VICTORY"

May 8, 1945

Ministry of Health, London

During the celebrations that followed the announcement of the end of the war in Europe, Churchill and his principal colleagues appeared on the balcony of the Ministry of Health in Whitehall, and made two brief speeches to the vast crowd. After the words "This is your *victory" the crowd roared back, "No–it* is *yours." It was an unforgettable moment of love and gratitude.*

God bless you all. This is your victory! It is the victory of the cause of freedom in every land. In all our long history we have never seen a greater day than this. Everyone, man or woman, has done their best. Everyone has tried. Neither the long years, nor the dangers, nor the fierce attacks of the enemy, have in any way weakened the independent resolve of the British nation. God bless you all.

TO V-E DAY CROWDS

May 8, 1945

London

My dear friends, this is your hour. This is not victory of a party or of any class. It's a victory of the great British nation as a whole. We were the first, in this ancient island, to draw the sword against tyranny. After a while we were left all alone against the most tremendous military power that has been seen. We were all alone for a whole year.

There we stood, alone. Did anyone want to give in? [The crowd shouted "No."] Were we down-hearted? ["No!"] The lights went out and the bombs came down. But every man, woman and child in the country had no thought of quitting the struggle. London can take it. So we came back after long months from the jaws of death, out of the mouth of hell, while all the world wondered. When shall the reputation and faith of this generation of English men and women fail? I say that in the long years to come not only will the people of this island but of the world, wherever the bird of freedom chirps in human hearts, look back to what we've done and they will say "do not despair, do not yield to violence and tyranny, march straight forward and die if need be—unconquered." Now we have emerged from one deadly struggle—a terrible foe has been cast on the ground and awaits our judgment and our mercy.

But there is another foe who occupies large portions of the British Empire, a foe stained with cruelty and greed—the Japanese. I rejoice we can all take a night off today and another day tomorrow. Tomorrow our great Russian allies will also be celebrating victory and after that we must begin the task of rebuilding our heath and homes, doing our utmost to make this country a land in which all have a chance, in which all have a duty, and we must turn ourselves to fulfill our duty to our own countrymen, and to our gallant allies of the United States who were so foully and treacherously attacked by Japan. We will go hand and hand with them. Even if it is a hard struggle we will not be the ones who will fail.

TO THE PEOPLES OF THE BRITISH EMPIRE IN THE FAR EAST

May 8, 1945

Broadcast, London

In the name of His Majesty's Government I bring you great news. The war in Europe is over. It is finished in the complete and overwhelming triumph of the Allies, and has today been officially declared at an end by Britain, United States and Russia, speaking with one voice.

Germany, the ally of Japan, is utterly and finally defeated and has been forced to unconditional surrender. All her armies, fleets and aircraft have been destroyed or captured. All resistance has ceased and Germany is occupied from end to end by the armies of the Allied Nations.

After a gigantic struggle of nearly six years war has ceased in Europe, and all the millions of her people who were enslaved have been liberated from the foul Nazi domination.

This means that the time for your liberation also is at hand, and it is of you that we are thinking on this day. The armed might of the British Commonwealth and America with their Allies against Japan is now free to strike with tremendous and undivided power. You know how much has been accomplished already. There is no slackening in our effort, for we know full well that the war is not over until the same freedom has been brought to you.

Be of good cheer and rejoice with us on this day. Let my words and my message penetrate to the remotest villages of your lands. Lift up your hearts, for we are coming.

"GOOD OLD LONDON!"

May 9, 1945

Ministry of Health, London

My dear friends, I hope you have had two happy days. Happy days are what we have worked for, but happy days are not easily worked for. By discipline, by morale, by industry, by good laws, by fair institutions–by those ways we have won through to happy days for millions and millions of people.

You have been attacked by a monstrous enemy–but you never flinched or wavered.

Your soldiers were everywhere in the field, your airmen in the skies–and never let us forget our grand Navy. They dared and they did all those feats of adventure and audacity which have ever enabled brave men to wrest victory from obstinate and bestial circumstances. And you people at home have taken all you had to take–which was enough, when all is said and done. You never let the men at the front down. No one ever asked for peace because London was suffering.

London, like a great rhinoceros, a great hippopotamus, saying: "Let them do their worst. London can take it." London could take anything.

My heart goes out to the Cockneys. Any visitors we may happen to have here to-day–and many great nations are represented here, by all those who have borne arms with us in the struggle–they echo what I say when I say "Good Old London!"

In every capital of the victorious world there are rejoicings to-night, but in none is there any lack of respect for the part which London has played.

I return my hearty thanks to you for never having failed in the long, monotonous days and in the long nights black as hell.

God bless you all. May you long remain as citizens of a great and splendid city. May you long remain as the heart of the British Empire.

PARTY POLITICS AGAIN– THE SOCIALIST "GESTAPO"

June 4, 1945

Broadcast, London

The end of the war in Europe also brought the end of the great wartime Coalition. Churchill formed a Conservative Government until elections could be held in July, and the Parliament which had lasted for ten years dissolved into the almost forgotten cries of electioneering. This broadcast by Churchill may or may not have had any influence on the result, but it appalled his friends, and gave Mr. Attlee the opportunity for a devastatingly quiet reply on the following evening. The Conservative campaign never fully recovered from this disastrous start.

[Extract] I am sorry to have lost so many good friends who served with me in the five years' Coalition. It was impossible to go on in a state of "electionitis" all through the summer and autumn. This election will last quite long enough for all who are concerned in it, and I expect many of the general public will be sick and tired of it before we get to polling day.

My sincere hope was that we could have held together until the war against Japan was finished. On the other hand, there was a high duty to consult the people after all these years. I could only be relieved of that duty by the full agreement of the three parties, further fortified, perhaps, by a kind of official Gallup Poll, which I am sure would have resulted in an overwhelming request that we should go on to the end and finish the job. That would have enabled me to say at once, "There will be no election for a year," or words to that effect.

I know that many of my Labour colleagues would have been glad to carry on. On the other hand, the Socialist Party as a whole had been for some time eager to set out upon the political warpath, and when large numbers of people feel like that it is not good for their health to deny them the fight they want. We will therefore give it to them to the best of our ability.

Party, my friends, has always played a great part in our affairs. Party ties have been considered honourable bonds, and no one could doubt that when the German war was over and the immediate danger to this country, which had led to the Coalition, had ceased, conflicting loyalties would arise. Our Socialist and Liberal friends felt themselves forced, therefore, to put party before country. They have departed, and we have been left to carry the nation's burden.

I have therefore formed, exactly as I said I would two years ago, another form of National Government, resting no longer on the agreement of the three official party machines, but on the Conservative Party, together with all the men of good will of any party or no party who have been ready to give their services. I claim the support of all throughout the country who sincerely put the nation first in their thoughts. This is a National Government. I shall stand myself as a Conservative and National candidate. Others may choose to call themselves National or National Liberal, and those who give us their support should vote National rather than Party on polling day.

Why do I claim the right to call this Government National? First of all, because those who have left us have left us on party grounds alone. Secondly, because the Conservative Party, which has for many years been the strongest party in this country, has been willing to abandon party feeling to such an extent that more than one-third of the members of Cabinet rank in this new Government are not members of the Conservative Party. Many of these very able men, without whose aid we could not have got through the war, would prefer not to call themselves Conservative in a party sense. They prefer to call themselves National. And many Conservatives who might have looked forward to high office have accepted cheerfully the interruption of their political careers in order to aid the nation in its time of trouble.

Particularly do I regret the conduct of the Liberal Party. Between us and the orthodox Socialists there is a great doctrinal gulf, which yawns and gapes. Of this continental conception of human society called Socialism, or in its more violent form Communism, I shall say more later. There is no such gulf between the Conservative and National Government I have formed and the Liberals. There is scarcely a Liberal sentiment which animated the great Liberal leaders of the past which we do not inherit and defend. Above all, there is our championship of freedom at home and abroad. All the guiding principles of the British Constitution are proclaimed and enforced by us in their highest degree. . . .

But I appeal to Liberals in all parts of the land, and I call upon them to search their hearts as to whether their differences with a British Government which will put through the Four Years' Plan, a Government which is animated by the love of freedom, which is vowed to that harmonious medium of justice and generosity so befitting to the conqueror, has not more claim on their ancestral loyalties than has a Socialist Party administration, whose principles are the absolute denial of traditional Liberalism. Let them think it out carefully in the light of the speeches of the famous Liberal leaders of the past. Let them think it out carefully in the warmth which may come to the weary Liberal combatant when he sees his ideas increasingly accepted by enlightened peoples and victorious nations.

My friends, I must tell you that a Socialist policy is abhorrent to the British ideas of freedom. Although it is now put forward in the main by people who have a good grounding in the Liberalism and Radicalism of the early part of this century, there can be no doubt that Socialism is inseparably interwoven with Totalitarianism and the abject worship of the State. It is not alone that property, in all its forms, is struck at, but that liberty, in all its forms, is challenged by the fundamental conceptions of Socialism.

Look how even to-day they hunger for controls of every kind, as if these were delectable foods instead of war-time inflictions and monstrosities. There is to be one State to which all are to be obedient in every act of their lives. This State is to be the arch-employer, the arch-planner, the arch-administrator and ruler, and the arch-caucus-boss.

How is an ordinary citizen or subject of the King to stand up against this formidable machine, which, once it is in power, will prescribe for every one of them where they are to work; what they are to work at; where they may go and what they may say; what views they are to hold and within what limits they may express them; where their wives are to go to queue-up for the State ration; and what education their children are to receive to mould their views of human liberty and conduct in the future?

A Socialist State once thoroughly completed in all its details and its aspects–and that is what I am speaking of–could not afford to suffer opposition. Here in old England, in Great Britain, of which old England forms no inconspicuous part, in this glorious Island, the cradle and citadel of free democracy throughout the world, we do not like to be regimented and ordered about and have every action of our lives prescribed for us. In fact we punish criminals by sending them to Wormwood Scrubs and Dartmoor, where they get full employment, and whatever board and lodging is appointed by the Home Secretary.

Socialism is, in its essence, an attack not only upon British enterprise, but upon the right of the ordinary man or woman to breathe freely without having a harsh, clumsy, tyrannical hand clapped across their mouths and nostrils. A Free Parliament–look at that–a Free Parliament is odious to the Socialist doctrinaire. Have we not heard Mr. Herbert Morrison descant upon his plans to curtail Parliamentary procedure and pass laws simply by resolutions of broad principle in the House of Commons, afterwards to be left by Parliament to the executive and to the bureaucrats to elaborate and enforce by departmental regulations? As for Sir Stafford Cripps on "Parliament in the Socialist State," I have not time to read you what he said, but perhaps it will meet the public eye during the election campaign.

But I will go farther. I declare to you, from the bottom of my heart, that no Socialist system can be established without a political police. Many of those who are advocating Socialism or voting Socialist to-day will be horrified at this idea. That is because they are short-sighted, that is because they do not see where their theories are leading them.

No Socialist Government conducting the entire life and industry of the country could afford to allow free, sharp, or violently-worded expressions of public discontent. They would have to fall back on some form of *Gestapo,* no doubt very humanely directed in the first instance. And this would nip opinion in the bud; it would stop criticism as it reared its head, and it would gather all the power to the supreme party and the party leaders, rising like stately pinnacles above their vast bureaucracies of Civil servants, no longer servants and no longer civil. And where would the ordinary simple folk–the common people, as they like to call them in America–where would they be, once this mighty organism had got them in its grip?

I stand for the sovereign freedom of the individual within the laws which freely elected Parliaments have freely passed. I stand for the rights of the ordinary man to say what he thinks of the Government of the day, however powerful, and to turn them out, neck and crop, if he thinks he can better his temper or his home thereby, and if he can persuade enough others to vote with him.

But, you will say, look at what has been done in the war. Have not many of those evils which you have depicted been the constant companions of our daily life? It is quite true that the horrors of war do not end with the fighting-line. They spread far away to the base and the homeland, and everywhere people give up their rights and liberties for the common cause. But this is because the life of their country is in mortal peril, or for the sake of the cause of freedom in some other land. They give them freely as a sacrifice. It is quite true that the conditions of Socialism play a great part in war-time. We all submit to being ordered about to save our country. But when the war is over and the imminent danger to our existence is removed, we cast off these shackles and burdens which we imposed upon ourselves in times of dire and mortal peril, and quit the gloomy caverns of war and march out into the breezy fields, where the sun is shining and where all may walk joyfully in its warm and golden rays.

Our present opponents or assailants would be, I am sure, knowing many of them, shocked to see where they are going, and where they are trying to lead us. So they adopt temporary expedients. They say, let us just nationalize anything we can get hold of according to the size of our majority and get the Bank of England into the hands of trustworthy Socialist politicians, and we will go ahead and see what happens next. Indeed you would see what happens next.

But let me tell you that, once a Socialist Government begins monkeying with the credit of Britain and trying, without regard to facts, figures, or confidence, to manipulate it to Socialist requirements, there is no man or woman in this country who has, by thrift or toil, accumulated a nest-egg, however small, who will not run the risk of seeing it shrivel before their eyes. . . .

What a mad thing it would be to slash across this whole great business of resettlement and reorganization with these inflaming controversies of Socialistic agitation! How foolish to plunge us into the bitter political and party fighting which must accompany the attempt to impose a vast revolutionary change on the whole daily life and structure of Britain! Surely at least we can wait till another Election? The world is not coming to an end in the next few weeks or years. The progress of free discussion can show whose fears or whose hopes are well founded. Can we not get Europe settled up, and Britain settled down? Before we plunge out on this hateful internal struggle, let us concentrate on practical and immediate action, and make sure that in gazing at the stars we do not fail in our duty to our fellow-mortals.

On with the forward march! Leave these Socialist dreamers to their Utopias or their nightmares. Let us be content to do the heavy job that is right on top of us. And let us make sure that the cottage home to which the warrior will return is blessed with modest but solid prosperity, well fenced and guarded against misfortune, and that Britons remain free to plan their lives for themselves and for those they love.

A THREAT TO FREEDOM

June 21, 1945

Political Broadcast, London

Professor Harold Laski, chairman of the Labour Party's National Executive Committee, had made some claims of the power of the Party over its leaders–notably in Foreign Policy–which were seized upon by the Conservatives as evidence of a sinister resolve to remove decision-making from the Parliament and entrust it to an unelected Party caucus.

Many voices sound to you amid the clatter and hum of this election, and you have got to decide as well as you can which are right and true, and which will bring our country into happier and better times.

We have been through a cruel ordeal lasting for nearly six years. We have yet another struggle against Japan before us, which must be wound up and finished off before peace returns to this tortured world. The Americans have stood by us, and we must stand by them. Quite apart from this, we have our own possessions, conquered and ravaged by the Japanese, from which there comes an additional call of honour for their clearance and redemption.

The Socialists tell us very loudly that the only way to save Great Britain and the future is to put them in power, with a mandate to transform our island life as fast as possible into that of a Socialist community under their authority. From many sides we hear their war-cries, and from many sides we hear the promises that all the evils and miseries of mankind will be cured by the plans they will make for us and by the rules they will make us obey.

In order to prove that their policies are right and will lead us out of our troubles, they pour out their abuse and condemnation of the world in which we have hitherto lived, and they assert that none of the evils that happened after the last war or before it, or even now in the few weeks since they left the Government, would have befallen us if only their system had been in force.

Sir Stafford Cripps addressed you last night about how we had suffered between the two wars. There certainly was great distress between those two shattering and terrific earthquakes, and we know much more now than we did then; but on the other hand there was much less suffering in Great Britain in this period than in any other war-stricken State in Europe, and great advances were made even in those circumstances of difficulty. The British nation that entered the new war on September 3, 1939, was a far stronger, healthier, better bred, better fed, better housed, and better educated race than the bygone heroes who drew the sword on August the 4th, 1914.

But now we are told that the existing structure must be swept away. There is to be made as a result of this Election a Socialist world, a Socialist Britain where all the means of production, distribution, and exchange are to be owned by the State, and worked by the State through public departments with their officials in Whitehall, or wherever convenient. Moreover the central Government is to plan for all our lives and tell us exactly where we are to go and what we are to do, and any resistance to their commands will be punished. This is of course their ultimate goal, and how long they take to reach it must assuredly depend on you.

Sir Stafford Cripps has made it clear that he and his kind must give the orders to us all, and that if Parliament says no, or even asks awkward questions, it will be controlled or swept out of the way and its rights of debate curtailed. On the very first day, according to him, an Emergency Powers Bill must be passed, leaving the majority leaders the power to act without restraint by the courts of law.

He and some of the Socialist leaders, though others repudiate them I am glad to see, talk of violence to be used upon us, if necessary, to make us conform sharply and promptly to the benevolent ideas of these autocratic philanthropists who aspire to change the human heart as if by magic and make themselves our rulers at the same time.

I have given you my warnings in the past, and they were not listened to. I do sincerely believe that I can help you, in this critical future which is rushing towards us, in as good a way as anyone else, and as long as my faculties and your confidence last I will strive to do so.

But do not let it be put about, as I have heard it is in some quarters, that I would ever associate myself with plans to impose the yoke of Socialism upon the necks of the free British people. Such an attempt would lead us into a period of disorder and party strife and of Parliamentary eclipse such as has never been seen in the long, steady, developing history of our country.

This they will do, if you give them power, at a moment when the whole of our strength should be concentrated upon solving practical problems, those practical problems which present themselves grimly every morning on the doorstep, demanding attention and demanding reply—to bring the armies home; to build the houses which could not be built in the war or were blasted by the enemy; to make up the new armies and fleets and air forces which must advance against Japan; to get our trade working both at home and abroad; to carry through Parliament and put into operation the enormous social programme comprised in the Four Years Plan, upon which so large a measure of agreement exists. Why cannot we concentrate on these realities without being at the same time forced to argue about the acceptance of an entirely new system of society?

These piercing discussions into the roots of human society are new to many who will cast what may be a decisive vote at this election. When they make their cross on the corner of the ballot paper, they may not, because of the hard times and the hard service which we have endured, realize the perils which may spring from a wrong decision.

I told you the other day that the violent imposition of the socialistic system, such as has now emerged as a demand from the extreme and potentially dominant forces of the Socialist Party, would involve the restriction of Parliamentary Government as we have known it, and the denial of the rights of effectual opposition as hitherto practised in this country.

But how would it affect the ordinary wage-earner? Let me tell you that it would rob him of his personal freedom to an extent unknown. I will go so far as to say a rather odd thing, about which no doubt there will be several opinions. It might well be in the interest of the factory workers, or indeed of the wage-earners generally, not to have too strong an employer over them. I should like to feel that he would be strong in the sense of being capable and efficient as a producer or competitor in the world markets. But it is abhorrent to our idea of freedom that the employer should have undue power over his employees.

Now under our present democratic system the wage-earner can of course appeal to his trade union, and also the sacred right of collective bargaining, largely promoted in bygone days by the Conservative Party, comes into play. Then there is Parliament, while it is free, in which the behaviour of all employers of labour, either generally or in individual cases, can be brought out and discussed in the full light of day.

But none of this would be possible in a Socialist State, where the central executive authority could not allow itself to be challenged or defeated at any time in any form of Parliament they might allow to exist. And I declare to you that the freedom of the wage-earner to choose or change his employment, or to use collective bargaining by all means, including the right to strike, runs absolutely counter to the Socialist doctrine and theory of the State.

I have read great complaints about our calling ourselves a National Government, and I gave you, in my first broadcast, several reasons why we had a right to do so.

But what about the Socialist Party calling themselves the Labour Party? Of course, every one can call himself anything he likes in a free country, but what about the Labour Party as a title? Are they the only people who labour in this country? Are they the only people who have fought in the war? Are they the only people who have hearts pure from all selfish interest? Are they the only ones who join the trade unions and take effective action with them?

Why, my friends, millions of trade unionists are Conservatives, and several other millions are going to vote for the National Government for patriotic reasons, they are going to give their vote for the National Government on account of the dangers amid which we stand at the present time. The Socialist Party have far less right to call themselves the Labour Party than Mr. Attlee has to call himself their leader.

Look what has happened in the last week, and ponder gravely upon where we are and what you ought to do.

When I proposed to my Socialist and Liberal colleagues in the late Coalition that we should march on in good comradeship and loyal co-operation until the Japanese war was victoriously concluded, one of the matters which weighed most heavily and anxiously upon my mind was the need to maintain our direction of foreign affairs upon a steady course through the careful and intimate negotiations which must take place between the defeat of Nazi Germany and the defeat of Japan.

My hopes that the coalition of all parties would continue were disappointed. I tried hard to get the next best thing. I recalled the fruitful and cordial meeting of minds which had existed on all the main issues of foreign policy between the Socialist

Ministers of the coalition and all the other Ministers of that Government. It appeared to me, therefore, as the best solution in the changed circumstances, to invite Mr. Attlee, the titular Socialist leader, to accompany Mr. Eden and myself to the forthcoming Conference with President Truman and Marshal Stalin.

It was my conception that I should enjoy Mr. Attlee's counsel at every stage of the discussions, and that what he said and agreed to he would naturally stand by. And from what I knew of him and his views over these last five years I did not expect there would arise in foreign affairs a single issue which could not be reconciled in an agreeable manner. In accepting my invitation Mr. Attlee showed that he shared this hopeful opinion.

However, a new figure has leaped into notoriety. The situation has now been complicated and darkened by the repeated intervention by Professor Laski, chairman of the Socialist Party Executive. He has reminded all of us, including Mr. Attlee, that the final determination on all questions of foreign policy rests, so far as the Socialist Party is concerned, with this dominating Socialist Executive.

Professor Laski has declared on several occasions, three at least, that there is no identity of purpose between the coalition foreign policy of the last five years, as continued by the present National Government, and the foreign policy of the powerful backroom organizations, over one of which he presides.

My friends, the British people have always hitherto wanted to have their affairs conducted by men they know, and that the men should work under the scrutiny and with the approval of the House of Commons. Now it seems we must refer to an obscure committee and be governed by unrepresentative persons, and that they will share the secrets and give the orders to the so-called responsible Ministers of the Crown, who will appear on the front Socialist bench of Parliament if they are returned and deliver orations upon which they have been instructed not from their own heart and conscience, not even from their constituencies, but from these dim conclaves below.

I confidently believe that the British democracy, with their long-trained common sense and innate love of independence, even while they are still struggling forward out of the exhaustion and sacrifices inseparable from hard-won victory, will ward off these dangers and make their way steadfastly towards something that can justly be called "hearth and home" in the land of hope and glory.

RESIGNATION STATEMENT
July 26, 1945

No. 10 Downing Street

The Potsdam Conference of the "Big Three" opened on July 15. Churchill had invited Attlee to join the British delegation as an observer–which he did in spite of Professor Laski. The most important single event was the British approval given to the United

States to use the atomic bomb against Japan. On July 25 Churchill, Attlee and Eden returned to London for the election results.

To the amazement of victors and vanquished alike, the Labour Party won an overwhelming victory in the General Election. Labour won 393 seats, the Conservatives and supporters 212, and the Liberals 12. It was a landslide disaster for the Conservatives. In Churchill's own constituency he was unopposed by Labour, but an unknown and somewhat eccentric independent won over 10,000 votes. Churchill was deeply shocked and distressed, but his resignation statement was a model of dignity.

The decision of the British people has been recorded in the votes counted to-day. I have therefore laid down the charge which was placed upon me in darker times. I regret that I have not been permitted to finish the work against Japan. For this, however, all plans and preparations have been made, and the results may come much quicker than we have hitherto been entitled to expect. Immense responsibilities abroad and at home fall upon the new Government, and we must all hope that they will be successful in bearing them.

It only remains for me to express to the British people, for whom I have acted in these perilous years, my profound gratitude for the unflinching, unswerving support which they have given me during my task, and for the many expressions of kindness which they have shown towards their servant.

"THE TRUE GLORY" THE SURRENDER OF JAPAN

August 15, 1945

House of Commons

On August 6 the first atomic bomb devastated Hiroshima, and on the ninth the second was dropped on Nagasaki. The following day the Japanese Government offered to surrender. Agreement was reached on August 14, thus ending the Second World War.

This crowning deliverance from the long and anxious years of danger and carnage should rightly be celebrated by Parliament in accordance with custom and tradition. The King is the embodiment of the national will, and his public acts involve all the might and power not only of the people of this famous Island but of the whole British Commonwealth and Empire. The good cause for which His Majesty has contended commanded the ardent fidelity of all his subjects spread over one-fifth of the surface of the habitable globe. That cause has now been carried to complete success. Total war has ended in absolute victory.

Once again the British Commonwealth and Empire emerges safe, undiminished and united from a mortal struggle. Monstrous tyrannies which menaced our life have been beaten to the ground in ruin, and a brighter radiance illumines the Imperial

Crown than any which our annals record. The light is brighter because it comes not only from the fierce but fading glare of military achievement such as an endless succession of conquerors have known, but because there mingle with it in mellow splendour the hopes, joys, and blessings of almost all mankind. This is the true glory, and long will it gleam upon our forward path.

THE IRON CURTAIN BEGINS TO FALL

August 16, 1945

House of Commons

In this remarkable speech, Churchill's first major statement since the General Election, he drew attention to the dark shadows gathering again over Europe and referred for the first time to the "iron curtain." The speech was not generally well received in the euphoria of the hour.

[Extract] . . . The [atomic] bomb brought peace, but men alone can keep that peace, and henceforward they will keep it under penalties which threaten the survival, not only of civilization but of humanity itself. I may say that I am in entire agreement with the President that the secrets of the atomic bomb should so far as possible not be imparted at the present time to any other country in the world. This is in no design or wish for arbitrary power, but for the common safety of the world. Nothing can stop the progress of research and experiment in every country, but although research will no doubt proceed in many places, the construction of the immense plants necessary to transform theory into action cannot be improvised in any country.

For this and many other reasons the United States stand at this moment at the summit of the world. I rejoice that this should be so. Let them act up to the level of their power and their responsibility, not for themselves but for others, for all men in all lands, and then a brighter day may dawn upon human history. So far as we know, there are at least three and perhaps four years before the concrete progress made in the United States can be overtaken. In these three years we must remould the relationships of all men, wherever they dwell, in all the nations. We must remould them in such a way that these men do not wish or dare to fall upon each other for the sake of vulgar and out-dated ambitions or for passionate differences in ideology, and that international bodies of supreme authority may give peace on earth and decree justice among men. Our pilgrimage has brought us to a sublime moment in the history of the world. From the least to the greatest, all must strive to be worthy of these supreme opportunities. There is not an hour to be wasted; there is not a day to be lost. . . .

It would be at once wrong and impossible to conceal the divergences of view which exist inevitably between the victors about the state of affairs in Eastern and Middle Europe. I do not at all blame the Prime Minister or the new Foreign Secretary, whose task it was to finish up the discussions which we had begun. I am sure they did their best. We have to realize that no one of the three leading Powers can impose its solutions upon others, and that the only solutions possible are those which are in the nature of compromise. We British have had very early and increasingly to recognize the limitations of our own power and influence, great though it be, in the gaunt world arising from the ruins of this hideous war. It is not in the power of any British Government to bring home solutions which would be regarded as perfect by the great majority of Members of this House, wherever they may sit. I must put on record my own opinion that the provisional Western Frontier agreed upon for Poland, running from Stettin on the Baltic, along the Oder and its tributary, the Western Neisse, comprising as it does one quarter of the arable land of all Germany, is not a good augury for the future map of Europe. We always had in the Coalition Government a desire that Poland should receive ample compensation in the West for the territory ceded to Russia East of the Curzon Line. But here I think a mistake has been made, in which the Provisional Government of Poland have been an ardent partner, by going far beyond what necessity or equity required. There are few virtues that the Poles do not possess—and there are few mistakes they have ever avoided.

I am particularly concerned, at this moment, with the reports reaching us of the conditions under which the expulsion and exodus of Germans from the new Poland are being carried out. Between eight and nine million persons dwelt in those regions before the war. The Polish Government say that there are still 1,500,000 of these, not yet expelled, within their new frontiers. Other millions must have taken refuge behind the British and American lines, thus increasing the food stringency in our sector. But enormous numbers are utterly unaccounted for. Where are they gone, and what has been their fate? The same conditions may reproduce themselves in a modified form in the expulsion of great numbers of Sudeten and other Germans from Czechoslovakia. Sparse and guarded accounts of what has happened and is happening have filtered through, but it is not impossible that tragedy on a prodigious scale is unfolding itself behind the iron curtain which at the moment divides Europe in twain. . . .

At the present time—I trust a very fleeting time—"police governments" rule over a great number of countries. It is a case of the odious 18B, carried to a horrible excess. The family is gathered round the fireside to enjoy the scanty fruits of their toil and to recruit their exhausted strength by the little food that they have been able to gather. There they sit. Suddenly there is a knock at the door, and a heavily armed policeman appears. He is not, of course, one who resembles in any way those functionaries whom we honour and obey in the London streets. It may be that the father or son, or a friend sitting in the cottage, is called out and taken off into the dark, and no one knows whether he will ever come back again, or what his fate has been. All they know is that they had better not inquire. There are millions of humble homes in Europe at the moment, in Poland, in Czechoslovakia, in Austria, in Hungary, in Yugoslavia, in Rumania, in Bulgaria—where this fear is the main preoccupation of the family life. President Roosevelt laid down the four freedoms, and these are expressed in the Atlantic Charter which we agreed together. "Freedom from fear"—but this has been interpreted as if it were only freedom from fear of invasion from a foreign country. That is the least of the fears of the common man. His patriotism arms him to withstand invasion or go down fighting; but that is not the fear of the ordinary family in Europe to-night. Their fear is of the policeman's knock. It is not fear for the country, for all men can unite in comradeship for the defence of their native soil. It is for the life and liberty of the individual, for the fundamental rights of man, now menaced and precarious in so many lands, that peoples tremble.

Surely we can agree in this new Parliament, or the great majority of us, wherever we sit–there are naturally and rightly differences and cleavages of thought–but surely we can agree in this new Parliament, which will either fail the world or once again play a part in saving it, that it is the will of the people freely expressed by secret ballot, in universal suffrage elections, as to the form of their government and as to the laws which shall prevail, which is the first solution and safeguard. Let us then march steadily along that plain and simple line. I avow my faith in Democracy, whatever course or view it may take with individuals and parties. They may make their mistakes, and they may profit from their mistakes. Democracy is now on trial as it never was before, and in these Islands we must uphold it, as we upheld it in the dark days of 1940 and 1941, with all our hearts, with all our viligance, and with all our enduring and inexhaustible strength. While the war was on and all the Allies were fighting for victory, the word "Democracy," like many people, had to work overtime, but now that peace has come we must search for more precise definitions. Elections have been proposed in some of these Balkan countries where only one set of candidates is allowed to appear, and where, if other parties are to express their opinion, it has to be arranged beforehand that the governing party, armed with its political police and all its propaganda, is the only one which has the slightest chance. Chance, did I say? It is a certainty.

Now is the time for Britons to speak out. It is odious to us that governments should seek to maintain their rule otherwise than by free unfettered elections by the mass of the people. Governments derive their just powers from the consent of the governed, says the Constitution of the United States. This must not evaporate in swindles and lies propped up by servitude and murder. In our foreign policy let us strike continually the notes of freedom and fair play as we understand them in these Islands. Then you will find there will be an overwhelming measure of agreement between us, and we shall in this House march forward on an honourable theme having within it all that invests human life with dignity and happiness. In saying all this, I have been trying to gather together and present in a direct form the things which, I believe, are dear to the great majority of us. I rejoiced to read them expressed in golden words by the President of the United States when he said:

"Our victory in Europe was more than a victory of arms. It was a victory of one way of life over another. It was a victory of an ideal founded on the right of the common man, on the dignity of the human being, and on the conception of the State as the servant, not the master, of its people."

I think there is not such great disagreement between us. Emphasis may be cast this way and that in particular incidents, but surely this is what the new Parliament on the whole means. This is what in our heart and conscience, in foreign affairs and world issues, we desire. Just as in the baleful glare of 1940, so now, when calmer lights shine, let us be united upon these resurgent principles and impulses of the good and generous hearts of men. Thus to all the material strength we possess and the honoured position we have acquired, we shall add those moral forces which glorify mankind and make even the weakest equals of the strong. . . .

I have offered these comments to the House, and I do not wish to end on a sombre or even slightly controversial note. As to the situation which exists to-day, it is evident that not only are the two Parties in the House agreed in the main essentials of foreign policy and in our moral outlook on world affairs, but we also have an immense programme, prepared by our joint exertions during the Coalition, which requires to be brought into law and made an inherent part of the life of the people. Here and there there may be differences of emphasis and view, but in the main no Parliament ever assembled with such a mass of agreed legislation as lies before us this afternoon. I have great hopes of this Parliament, and I shall do my utmost to make its work fruitful. It may heal the wounds of war, and turn to good account the new conceptions and powers which we have gathered amid the storm. I do not underrate the difficult and intricate complications of the task which lies before us; I know too much about it to cherish vain illusions; but the morrow of such a victory as we have gained is a splendid moment both in our small lives and in our great history. It is a time not only of rejoicing but even more of resolve. When we look back on all the perils through which we have passed and at the mighty foes we have laid low and all the dark and deadly designs we have frustrated, why should we fear for our future? We have come safely through the worst.

Home is the sailor, home from sea,
And the hunter home from the hill.

THE SINEWS OF PEACE

March 5, 1946

Westminster College,
Fulton, Missouri

Churchill decided to take a respite from Parliamentary affairs and, leaving the Opposition in the capable hands of Anthony Eden, he sailed to the United States on the Queen Elizabeth *on January 9, 1946. He stayed in Miami as the guest of Colonel Frank Clarke, received an Honorary Degree from the University of Miami, and visited Cuba as the guest of the Cuban Government.*

The principal event of Churchill's visit to other parts of the United States was his speech at Westminister College in Fulton, Missouri–President Truman's home state. The President travelled with Churchill from Washington and introduced him to his audience.

This speech may be regarded as the most important Churchill delivered as Leader of the Opposition (1945-1951). It contains certain phrases–"the special relationship," "the sinews of peace"–which at once entered into general use, and which have survived. But it is the passage on the "iron curtain" which, although used before, attracted immediate international attention, and had incalculable impact upon public opinion in the United States and in Western Europe. In its phraseology, in its intricate drawing together of several themes to an electrifying climax, this speech is a technical classic.

I am glad to come to Westminster College this afternoon, and am complimented that you should give me a degree. The name "Westminster" is somehow familiar to me. I seem to have heard of it before. Indeed, it was at Westminster that I received a very large part of my education in politics, dialectic, rhetoric, and one or two other things. In fact we have both been educated at the same, or similar, or, at any rate, kindred establishments.

It is also an honour, perhaps almost unique, for a private visitor to be introduced to an academic audience by the President of the United States. Amid his heavy burdens, duties, and responsibilities—unsought but not recoiled from—the President has travelled a thousand miles to dignify and magnify our meeting here to-day and to give me an opportunity of addressing this kindred nation, as well as my own countrymen across the ocean, and perhaps some other countries too. The President has told you that it is his wish, as I am sure it is yours, that I should have full liberty to give my true and faithful counsel in these anxious and baffling times. I shall certainly avail myself of this freedom, and feel the more right to do so because any private ambitions I may have cherished in my younger days have been satisfied beyond my wildest dreams. Let me, however, make it clear that I have no official mission or status of any kind, and that I speak only for myself. There is nothing here but what you see.

I can therefore allow my mind, with the experience of a lifetime, to play over the problems which beset us on the morrow of our absolute victory in arms, and to try to make sure with what strength I have that what has been gained with so much sacrifice and suffering shall be preserved for the future glory and safety of mankind.

The United States stands at this time at the pinnacle of world power. It is a solemn moment for the American Democracy. For with primacy in power is also joined an awe-inspiring accountability to the future. If you look around you, you must feel not only the sense of duty done but also you must feel anxiety lest you fall below the level of achievement. Opportunity is here now, clear and shining for both our countries. To reject it or ignore it or fritter it away will bring upon us all the long reproaches of the after-time. It is necessary that constancy of mind, persistency of purpose, and the grand simplicity of decision shall guide and rule the conduct of the English-speaking peoples in peace as they did in war. We must, and I believe we shall, prove ourselves equal to this severe requirement.

When American military men approach some serious situation they are wont to write at the head of their directive the words "over-all strategic concept." There is wisdom in this, as it leads to clarity of thought. What then is the over-all strategic concept which we should inscribe today? It is nothing less than the safety and welfare, the freedom and progress, of all the homes and families of all the men and women in all the lands. And here I speak particularly of the myriad cottage or apartment homes where the wage-earner strives amid the accidents and difficulties of life to guard his wife and children from privation and bring the family up in the fear of the Lord, or upon ethical conceptions which often play their potent part.

To give security to these countless homes, they must be shielded from the two giant marauders, war and tyranny. We all know the frightful disturbances in which the ordinary family is plunged when the curse of war swoops down upon the bread-winner and those for whom he works and contrives. The awful ruin of Europe, with all its vanished glories, and of large parts of Asia glares us in the eyes. When the designs of wicked men or the aggressive urge of mighty States dissolve over large areas the frame of civilised society, humble folk are confronted with difficulties with which they cannot cope. For them all is distorted, all is broken, even ground to pulp.

When I stand here this quiet afternoon I shudder to visualise what is actually happening to millions now and what is going to happen in this period when famine stalks the earth. None can compute what has been called "the unestimated sum of human pain." Our supreme task and duty is to guard the homes of the common people from the horrors and miseries of another war. We are all agreed on that.

Our American military colleagues, after having proclaimed their "over-all strategic concept" and computed available resources, always proceed to the next step—namely, the method. Here again there is widespread agreement. A world organisation has already been erected for the prime purpose of preventing war, UNO, the successor of the League of Nations, with the decisive addition of the United States and all that that means, is already at work. We must make sure that its work is fruitful, that it is a reality and not a sham, that it is a force for action, and not merely a frothing of words, that it is a true temple of peace in which the shields of many nations can some day be hung up, and not merely a cockpit in a Tower of Babel. Before we cast away the solid assurances of national armaments for self-preservation we must be certain that our temple is built, not upon shifting sands or quagmires, but upon the rock. Anyone can see with his eyes open that our path will be difficult and also long, but if we persevere together as we did in the two world wars—though not, alas, in the interval between them—I cannot doubt that we shall achieve our common purpose in the end.

I have, however, a definite and practical proposal to make for action. Courts and magistrates may be set up but they cannot function without sheriffs and constables. The United Nations Organisation must immediately begin to be equipped with an international armed force. In such a matter we can only go step by step, but we must begin now. I propose that each of the Powers and States should be invited to delegate a certain number of air squadrons to the service of the world organisation. These squadrons would be trained and prepared in their own countries, but would move around in rotation from one country to another. They would wear the uniform of their own countries but with different badges. They would not be required to act against their own nation, but in other respects they would be directed by the world organisation. This might be started on a modest scale and would grow as confidence grew. I wished to see this done after the first world war, and I devoutly trust it may be done forthwith.

It would nevertheless be wrong and imprudent to entrust the secret knowledge or experience of the atomic bomb, which the United States, Great Britain, and Canada now share, to the world organisation, while it is still in its infancy. It would be criminal madness to cast it adrift in this still agitated and un-united world. No one in any country has slept less well in their beds because this knowledge and the method and the raw materials to apply it, are at present largely retained in American hands. I do not believe we should all have slept so soundly had the positions been reversed and if some Communist or neo-Fascist State monopolised for the time being these dread agencies. The fear of them alone might easily have been used to enforce totalitarian systems upon the free democratic world, with consequences appalling to human imagination. God has willed that this shall not be and we have at least a breathing space to set our house in order before this peril has to be encountered: and even then, if no effort is spared, we should still possess so formidable a superiority as to impose effective deterrents upon its employment, or threat of employment, by others. Ultimately, when the essential brotherhood of man is truly embodied and expressed in a world organisation with all the necessary practical safeguards to make it effective, these powers would naturally be confided to that world organisation.

Now I come to the second danger of these two marauders which threatens the cottage, the home, and the ordinary people—namely, tyranny. We cannot be blind to the fact that the liberties enjoyed by individual citizens throughout the British Empire are not valid in a considerable number of countries, some of which are very powerful. In these States control is enforced upon the common people by various kinds of all-embracing police governments. The power of the State is exercised without restraint, either by dictators or by compact oligarchies operating through a privileged party and a political police. It is not our duty at this time when difficulties are so numerous to interfere forcibly in the internal affairs of countries which we have not conquered in war. But we must never cease to proclaim in fearless tones the great principles of freedom and the rights of man which are the joint inheritance of the English-speaking world and which through Magna Carta, the Bill of Rights, the Habeas Corpus, trial by jury, and the English common law find their most famous expression in the American Declaration of Independence.

All this means that the people of any country have the right, and should have the power by constitutional action, by free unfettered elections, with secret ballot, to choose or change the character or form of government under which they dwell; that freedom of speech and thought should reign; that courts of justice, independent of the executive, unbiased by any party, should administer laws which have received the broad assent of large majorities or are consecrated by time and custom. Here are the title deeds of freedom which should lie in every cottage home. Here is the message of the British and American peoples to mankind. Let us preach what we practise—let us practise what we preach.

I have now stated the two great dangers which menace the homes of the people; War and Tyranny. I have not yet spoken of poverty and privation which are in many cases the prevailing anxiety. But if the dangers of war and tyranny are removed, there is no doubt that science and co-operation can bring in the next few years to the world, certainly in the next few decades newly taught in the sharpening school of war, an expansion of material well-being beyond anything that has yet occurred in human experience. Now, at this sad and breathless moment, we are plunged in the hunger and distress which are the aftermath of our stupendous struggle; but this will pass and may pass quickly, and there is no reason except human folly or sub-human crime which should deny to all the nations the inauguration and enjoyment of an age of plenty. I have often used words which I learned fifty years ago from a great Irish-American orator, a friend of mine, Mr. Bourke Cockran. "There is enough for all. The earth is a generous mother; she will provide in plentiful abundance food for all her children if they will but cultivate her soil in justice and in peace." So far I feel that we are in full agreement.

Now, while still pursuing the method of realising our overall strategic concept, I come to the crux of what I have travelled here to say. Neither the sure prevention of war, nor the continuous rise of world organisation will be gained without what I have called the fraternal association of the English-speaking peoples. This means a special relationship between the British Commonwealth and Empire and the United States. This is no time for generalities, and I will venture to be precise. Fraternal association requires not only the growing friendship and mutual understanding between our two vast but kindred systems of society, but the continuance of the intimate relationship between our military advisers, leading to common study of potential dangers, the similarity of weapons and manuals of instructions, and to the interchange of officers and cadets at technical colleges. It should carry with it the continuance of the present facilities for mutual security by the joint use of all Naval and Air Force bases in the possession of either country all over the world. This would perhaps double the mobility of the American Navy and Air Force. It would greatly expand that of the British Empire Forces and it might well lead, if and as the world calms down, to important financial savings. Already we use together a large number of islands; more may well be entrusted to our joint care in the near future.

The United States has already a Permanent Defence Agreement with the Dominion of Canada, which is so devotedly attached to the British Commonwealth and Empire. This Agreement is more effective than many of those which have often been made under formal alliances. This principle should be extended to all British Commonwealths with full reciprocity. Thus, whatever happens, and thus only, shall we be secure ourselves and able to work together for the high and simple causes that are dear to us and bode no ill to any. Eventually there may come—I feel eventually there will come—the principle of common citizenship, but that we may be content to leave to destiny, whose outstretched arm many of us can already clearly see.

There is however an important question we must ask ourselves. Would a special relationship between the United States and the British Commonwealth be inconsistent with our over-riding loyalties to the World Organisation? I reply that, on the contrary, it is probably the only means by which that organisation will achieve its full stature and strength. There are already the special United States relations with Canada which I have just mentioned, and there are the special relations between the United States and the South American Republics. We British have our twenty years Treaty of Collaboration and Mutual Assistance with Soviet Russia. I agree with Mr. Bevin, the Foreign Secretary of Great Britain, that it might well be a fifty years Treaty so far as we are concerned. We aim at nothing but mutual assistance and collaboration. The British have an alliance with Portugal unbroken since 1384, and which produced fruitful results at critical moments in the late war. None of these clash with the general interest of a world agreement, or a world organisation; on the contrary they help it. "In my father's house are many mansions." Special associations between members of the United Nations which have no aggressive point against any other country, which harbour no design incompatible with the Charter of the United Nations, far from being harmful, are beneficial and, as I believe, indispensable.

I spoke earlier of the Temple of Peace. Workmen from all countries must build that temple. If two of the workmen know each other particularly well and are old friends, if their families are inter-mingled, and if they have "faith in each other's purpose, hope in each other's future and charity towards each other's shortcomings"—to quote some good words I read here the other day—why cannot they work together at the common task as friends and partners? Why cannot they share their tools and thus increase each other's working powers? Indeed they must do so or else the temple may not be built, or, being built, it may collapse, and we shall all be proved again unteachable and have to go and try to learn again for a third time in a school of war, incomparably more rigorous than that from which we have just been released. The dark ages may return, the Stone Age may return on the gleaming wings of science, and what might now shower immeasurable material blessings upon mankind, may even bring about its total destruction. Beware, I say; time may be short. Do not let us take the course of allowing events to drift along until it is too late. If there is to be a fraternal association of the kind I have described, with all the extra strength and security which both our countries can derive from it, let us make sure that that great fact is known to the world, and that it plays its part in steadying and stabilising the foundations of peace. There is the path of wisdom. Prevention is better than cure.

A shadow has fallen upon the scenes so lately lighted by the Allied victory. Nobody knows what Soviet Russia and its Communist international organisation intends to do in the immediate future, or what are the limits, if any, to their expansive and proselytising tendencies. I have a strong admiration and regard for the valiant Russian people and for my wartime comrade, Marshal Stalin. There is deep sympathy and goodwill in Britain—and I doubt not here also—towards the peoples of all the Russias and a resolve to persevere through many differences and rebuffs in establishing lasting friendships. We understand the Russian need to be secure on her western frontiers by the removal of all possibility of German aggression. We welcome Russia to her rightful place among the leading nations of the world. We welcome her flag upon the seas. Above all, we welcome constant, frequent and growing contacts between the Russian people and our own people on both sides of the Atlantic. It is my duty however, for I am sure you would wish me to state the facts as I see them to you, to place before you certain facts about the present position in Europe.

From Stettin in the Baltic to Trieste in the Adriatic, an iron curtain has descended across the Continent. Behind that line lie all the capitals of the ancient states of Central and Eastern Europe. Warsaw, Berlin, Prague, Vienna, Budapest, Belgrade, Bucharest and Sofia, all these famous cities and the populations around them lie in what I must call the Soviet sphere, and all are subject in one form or another, not only to Soviet influence but to a very high and, in many cases, increasing measure of control from Moscow. Athens alone—Greece with its immortal glories—is free to decide its future at an election under British, American and French observation. The Russian-dominated Polish Government has been encouraged to make enormous and wrongful inroads upon Germany, and mass expulsions of millions of Germans on a scale grievous and undreamed-of are now taking place. The Communist parties, which were very small in all these Eastern States of Europe, have been raised to pre-eminence and power far beyond their numbers and are seeking everywhere to obtain totalitarian control. Police governments are prevailing in nearly every case, and so far, except in Czechoslovakia, there is no true democracy.

Turkey and Persia are both profoundly alarmed and disturbed at the claims which are being made upon them and at the pressure being exerted by the Moscow Government. An attempt is being made by the Russians in Berlin to build up a quasi-Communist party in their zone of Occupied Germany by showing special favours to groups of left-wing German leaders. At the end of the fighting last June, the American and British Armies withdrew westwards, in accordance with an earlier agreement, to a depth at some points of 150 miles upon a front of nearly four hundred miles, in order to allow our Russian allies to occupy this vast expanse of territory which the Western Democracies had conquered.

If now the Soviet Government tries, by separate action, to build up a pro-Communist Germany in their areas, this will cause new serious difficulties in the British and American zones, and will give the defeated Germans the power of putting themselves up to auction between the Soviets and the Western Democracies. Whatever conclusions may be drawn from these facts—and facts they are—this is certainly not the Liberated Europe we fought to build up. Nor is it one which contains the essentials of permanent peace.

The safety of the world requires a new unity in Europe, from which no nation should be permanently outcast. It is from the quarrels of the strong parent races in Europe that the world wars we have witnessed, or which occurred in former times, have sprung. Twice in our own lifetime we have seen the United States, against their wishes and their traditions, against arguments, the force of which it is impossible not to comprehend, drawn by irresistible forces, into these wars in time to secure the victory of the good cause, but only after frightful slaughter and devastation had occurred. Twice the United States has had to send several millions of its young men across the Atlantic to find the war; but now war can find any nation, wherever it may dwell between dusk and dawn. Surely we should work with conscious purpose for a grand pacification of Europe, within the structure of the United Nations and in accordance with its Charter. That I feel is an open cause of policy of very great importance.

In front of the iron curtain which lies across Europe are other causes for anxiety. In Italy the Communist Party is seriously hampered by having to support the Communist-trained Marshal Tito's claims to former Italian territory at the head of the Adriatic. Nevertheless the future of Italy hangs in the balance. Again one cannot imagine a regenerated Europe without a strong France. All my public life I have worked for a strong France and I never lost faith in her destiny, even in the darkest hours. I will not lose faith now. However, in a great number of countries, far from the Russian frontiers and throughout the world, Communist fifth columns are established and work in complete unity and absolute obedience to the directions they receive from the Communist centre. Except in the British Commonwealth and in the United

States where Communism is in its infancy, the Communist parties or fifth columns constitute a growing challenge and peril to Christian civilisation. These are sombre facts for anyone to have to recite on the morrow of a victory gained by so much splendid comradeship in arms and in the cause of freedom and democracy; but we should be most unwise not to face them squarely while time remains.

The outlook is also anxious in the Far East and especially in Manchuria. The Agreement which was made at Yalta, to which I was a party, was extremely favourable to Soviet Russia, but it was made at a time when no one could say that the German war might not extend all through the summer and autumn of 1945 and when the Japanese war was expected to last for a further 18 months from the end of the German war. In this country you are all so well-informed about the Far East, and such devoted friends of China, that I do not need to expatiate on the situation there.

I have felt bound to portray the shadow which, alike in the west and in the east, falls upon the world. I was a high minister at the time of the Versailles Treaty and a close friend of Mr. Lloyd George, who was the head of the British delegation at Versailles. I did not myself agree with many things that were done, but I have a very strong impression in my mind of that situation, and I find it painful to contrast it with that which prevails now. In those days there were high hopes and unbounded confidence that the wars were over, and that the League of Nations would become all-powerful. I do not see or feel that same confidence or even the same hopes in the haggard world at the present time.

On the other hand I repulse the idea that a new war is inevitable; still more that it is imminent. It is because I am sure that our fortunes are still in our own hands and that we hold the power to save the future, that I feel the duty to speak out now that I have the occasion and the opportunity to do so. I do not believe that Soviet Russia desires war. What they desire is the fruits of war and the indefinite expansion of their power and doctrines. But what we have to consider here to-day while time remains, is the permanent prevention of war and the establishment of conditions of freedom and democracy as rapidly as possible in all countries. Our difficulties and dangers will not be removed by closing our eyes to them. They will not be removed by mere waiting to see what happens; nor will they be removed by a policy of appeasement. What is needed is a settlement, and the longer this is delayed, the more difficult it will be and the greater our dangers will become.

From what I have seen of our Russian friends and Allies during the war, I am convinced that there is nothing they admire so much as strength, and there is nothing for which they have less respect than for weakness, especially military weakness. For that reason the old doctrine of a balance of power is unsound. We cannot afford, if we can help it, to work on narrow margins, offering temptations to a trial of strength. If the Western Democracies stand together in strict adherence to the principles of the United Nations Charter, their influence for furthering those principles will be immense and no one is likely to molest them. If however they become divided or falter in their duty and if these all-important years are allowed to slip away then indeed catastrophe may overwhelm us all.

Last time I saw it all coming and cried aloud to my own fellow-countrymen and to the world, but no one paid any attention. Up till the year 1933 or even 1935,

Germany might have been saved from the awful fate which has overtaken her and we might all have been spared the miseries Hitler let loose upon mankind. There never was a war in all history easier to prevent by timely action than the one which has just desolated such great areas of the globe. It could have been prevented in my belief without the firing of a single shot, and Germany might be powerful, prosperous and honoured to-day; but no one would listen and one by one we were all sucked into the awful whirlpool. We surely must not let that happen again. This can only be achieved by reaching now, in 1946, a good understanding on all points with Russia under the general authority of the United Nations Organisation and by the maintenance of that good understanding through many peaceful years, by the world instrument, supported by the whole strength of the English-speaking world and all its connections. There is the solution which I respectfully offer to you in this Address to which I have given the title "The Sinews of Peace."

Let no man underrate the abiding power of the British Empire and Commonwealth. Because you see the 46 millions in our island harassed about their food supply, of which they only grow one half, even in war-time, or because we have difficulty in restarting our industries and export trade after six years of passionate war effort, do not suppose that we shall not come through these dark years of privation as we have come through the glorious years of agony, or that half a century from now, you will not see 70 or 80 millions of Britons spread about the world and united in defence of our traditions, our way of life, and of the world causes which you and we espouse. If the population of the English-speaking Commonwealths be added to that of the United States with all that such co-operation implies in the air, on the sea, all over the globe and in science and in industry, and in moral force, there will be no quivering, precarious balance of power to offer its temptation to ambition or adventure. On the contrary, there will be an overwhelming assurance of security. If we adhere faithfully to the Charter of the United Nations and walk forward in sedate and sober strength seeking no one's land or treasure, seeking to lay no arbitrary control upon the thoughts of men; if all British moral and material forces and convictions are joined with your own in fraternal association, the high-roads of the future will be clear, not only for us but for all, not only for our time, but for a century to come.

THE DARKENING INTERNATIONAL SCENE

March 15, 1946

Waldorf Astoria Hotel, New York

Churchill's Fulton speech had aroused a storm. Pravda *denounced it and accused him of trying to destroy the United Nations; Stalin declared that Churchill had called for war against the Soviet Union. There were harsh criticisms voiced in the U.S. Congress, and in the House of Commons Attlee pointedly declined comment on "a speech delivered in another country by a private individual." President Truman, however, appeared not to be greatly distressed. Churchill was unrepentant, and in this speech he set out to clarify his position.*

[Extract] When I spoke at Fulton ten days ago I felt it was necessary for someone in an unofficial position to speak in arresting terms about the present plight of the world. I do not wish to withdraw or modify a single word. I was invited to give my counsel freely in this free country and I am sure that the hope which I expressed for the increasing association of our two countries will come to pass, not because of any speech which may be made, but because of the tides that flow in human affairs and in the course of the unfolding destiny of the world. The only question which in my opinion is open is whether the necessary harmony of thought and action between the American and British peoples will be reached in a sufficiently plain and clear manner and in good time to prevent a new world struggle or whether it will come about, as it has done before, only in the course of that struggle.

I remain convinced that this question will win a favourable answer. I do not believe that war is inevitable or imminent. I do not believe that the rulers of Russia wish for war at the present time. I am sure that if we stand together calmly and resolutely in defence of those ideals and principles embodied in the Charter of the United Nations, we shall find ourselves sustained by the overwhelming assent of the peoples of the world, and that, fortified by this ever-growing moral authority, the cause of peace and freedom will come safely through and we shall be able to go on with the noble work–in which the United States has a glorious primacy–of averting famine, of healing the awful wounds of Hitler's war and rebuilding the scarred and shattered structure of human civilisation. Let me declare, however, that the progress and freedom of all the peoples of the world under a reign of law enforced by a World Organisation, will not come to pass, nor will the age of plenty begin, without the persistent, faithful, and above all fearless exertions of the British and American systems of society.

In the last ten days the situation has greatly changed as the result of decisions which must have been taken some time ago. Instead of a calm discussion of broad and long-term tendencies we now find ourselves in the presence of swiftly moving events which no one can measure at the moment. I may be called upon to speak about the new situation when I get back home.

There are however a few things I am bound to say to-night lest a good cause should suffer by default. If any words that I have spoken have commanded attention, that is only because they find an echo in the breasts of those of every land and race who love freedom and are the foes of tyranny. I certainly will not allow anything said by others to weaken by regard and admiration for the Russian people or my earnest desire that Russia should be safe and prosperous and should take an honoured place in the van of the World Organisation. Whether she will do so or not depends only on the decisions taken by the handful of able men who, under their renowned chief, hold all the 180 million Russians, and many more millions outside Russia, in their grip. We all remember what frightful losses Russia suffered in the Hitlerite invasion and how she survived and emerged triumphant from injuries greater than have ever been inflicted on any other community. There is deep and widespread sympathy throughout the English-speaking world for the people of Russia and an absolute readiness to work with them on fair and even terms to repair the ruin of the war in every country. If the Soviet Government does not take advantage of this sentiment, if on the contrary they discourage it, the responsibility will be entirely theirs. . . .

It has been frequently observed in the last few days that there is a great measure of misunderstanding. I entirely agree with that. Could you have a greater example of misunderstanding than when we are told that the present British Government is not a free democratic government because it consists only of the representatives of a single party, whereas Poland, Rumania, Bulgaria and other countries have the representatives of several parties in their governments. But this also applies to the United States, where one party is in office and wields the executive power. All this argument overlooks the fact that democratic governments are based on free elections. The people choose freely and fairly the party they wish to have in office. They have every right to criticise that party, or the government based upon it and can change it by constitutional processes at any time they like or at frequent intervals. It can hardly be called a democratic election where the candidates of only one party are allowed to appear and where the voter has not even the secrecy of the ballot to protect him. These misunderstandings will be swept away if we get through the present difficult period safely and if the British, American and Russian peoples are allowed to mingle freely with one another and see how things are done in their respective countries. No doubt we all have much to learn from one another. I rejoice to read in the newspapers that there never were more Russian ships in New York harbour than there are to-night. I am sure you will give the Russian sailors a hearty welcome to the land of the free and the home of the brave.

Now I turn to the other part of my message—the relations between Great Britain and the United States. On these the life and freedom of the world depend. Unless they work together, in full loyalty to the Charter, the organisation of the United Nations will cease to have any reality. No one will be able to put his trust in it and the world will be left to the clash of nationalisms which have led us to two frightful wars. I have never asked for an Anglo-American military alliance or a treaty. I asked for something different and in a sense I asked for something more. I asked for fraternal association, free, voluntary, fraternal association. I have no doubt that it will come to pass, as surely as the sun will rise to-morrow. But you do not need a treaty to express the natural affinities and friendships which arise in a fraternal association. On the other hand, it would be wrong that the fact should be concealed or ignored. Nothing can prevent our nations drawing ever closer to one another and nothing can obscure the fact that, in their harmonious companionship, lies the main hope of the world instrument for maintaining peace on earth and goodwill to all men.

I thank you all profoundly for all your gracious kindness and hospitality to me during this visit I have paid to your shores. Mine is not the first voice raised within your spacious bounds in the cause of freedom and of peace. Nor will it be the last that will be encouraged by the broad tolerance of the American people. I come to you at a time when the United States stands at the highest point of majesty and power ever attained by any community since the fall of the Roman Empire. This imposes upon the American people a duty which cannot be rejected. With opportunities comes responsibility. Strength is granted to us all when we are needed to serve great causes. We in the British Commonwealth will stand at your side in powerful and faithful friendship, and in accordance with the World Charter, and together I am sure we shall succeed in lifting from the face of man the curse of war and the darker curse of tyranny. Thus will be opened even more broadly to the anxious toiling millions the gateways of happiness and freedom.

FOREIGN AFFAIRS

June 5, 1946

House of Commons

By this stage the actions and attitudes of the Soviet Government were arousing resentment and concern in the West, and Churchill's warnings were finally being heeded. Although the phrase had not yet been coined, the "cold war" had already begun.

[Extract]. . .The House could not but be impressed by the measured and formidable complaint which the Foreign Secretary unfolded yesterday, step by step and theatre by theatre, about the treatment which the Western Allies have been receiving from the Soviet Government. Deep and widespread sorrow has been caused in Britain by the decline of contact and goodwill between our country and Russia. There was, and there still is, an earnest desire to dwell in friendly co-operation with the Soviet Government and the Russian people. On the other hand, the Foreign Secretary received the approval of the vast majority of the people when he protested against the prolonged, systematic campaign of vilification which has been, and is being daily pumped out upon us by the Soviet propaganda machine. Apart from the Communists and the "cryptos"–that is to say, the Communists without the pluck to call themselves by their proper name–very few people were shocked by the homely language he chose to employ at the London Conference in January, nor indeed, do the vast majority of the House of Commons dissent from the argument he unfolded in the speech with which he opened this Debate.

Nevertheless, I am sure that it is the general wish of the British and Russian peoples that they should have warm and friendly feelings towards each other. We seek nothing from them except their goodwill, and we could play our part, with other nations, in coming to their aid with such resources as we may have if their just rights or safety were assailed. We were all glad to hear the Foreign Secretary say that he was still in favour of the 50-years treaty or 20-years treaty with Russia. Personally, I attach great importance to the existing Treaty. I have never made a speech on European questions without referring to it. It may go through bad times–lots of treaties do–but it would be a great misfortune if it were incontinently discarded. But surely, talking of treaties, this Four Power 25 year treaty between America, Britain, Russia and France, which the United States have proposed to deal with Germany, is a tremendous project. The Foreign Secretary was right to say how much more valuable such a guarantee of the United States to be in the forefront of European affairs for 25 years would be to Soviet Russia for her own security, than the harnessing–"harnessing" was the word–of a number of reluctant or rebellious border or satellite States. I am very glad to know that we are to support the United States proposal, and I thought the words which the Foreign Secretary used about it were singularly well chosen.

However, there is no use in concealing the fact that the Soviet propaganda and their general attitude have made a profound impression upon this country since the war, and all kinds of people in great numbers are wondering very much whether the Soviet Government really wish to be friends with Britain or to work wholeheartedly for the speedy re-establishment of peace, freedom and plenty throughout the world. Across the ocean, in Canada and the United States, the unfriendly Soviet propaganda has also been very effective in the reverse direction to what was intended. The handful of very able men who hold 180 million Soviet citizens in their grasp ought to be able to get better advice about the Western democracies. For instance, it cannot be in the interest of Russia to go on irritating the United States. There are no people in the world who are so slow to develop hostile feelings against a foreign country as the Americans, and there are no people who, once estranged, are more difficult to win back. The American eagle sits on his perch, a large, strong bird with formidable beak and claws. There he sits motionless, and M. Gromyko is sent day after day to prod him with a sharp pointed stick–now his neck, now under his wings, now his tail feathers. All the time the eagle keeps quite still. But it would be a great mistake to suppose that nothing is going on inside the breast of the eagle. I venture to give this friendly hint to my old wartime comrade, Marshal Stalin. Even here, in our patient community, Soviet propaganda has been steadily making headway backwards. I would not have believed it possible that in a year, the Soviets would have been able to do themselves so much harm, and chill so many friendships in the English-speaking world.

Let us also remember that the Soviet Government is greatly hampered in its relations with many foreign countries by the existence of Communist fifth columns. There are some States which hang in the balance, where these Communist organisms are aspiring, or conspiring, to seize the control of the Governments, although they are in a small majority in the population. Of course, if they succeed, the State is overturned and becomes harnessed as a satellite, but everywhere else the activities of Communist fifth columns only do Russia harm. In fact, they are an active process in bringing about the very thing which the Soviets most dislike, namely, a general consensus of opinion against them and their ways. I earnestly hope that when this present technique and these methods have been fully tried and found not helpful to the interests and the greatness of Soviet Russia, they will be discarded, and that a more reasonable and neighbourly spirit will prevail, in which case I am sure we would all be very ready, so far as words are concerned, to let bygones be bygones. . . .

Far more serious than anything in the sphere of propaganda or espionage are the facts of the European situation. I have been censured for wrongly championing the Russian claims to the Curzon Line. So far as the Curzon Line is concerned, I hold strongly that this was a rightful Russian frontier, and that a free Poland should receive compensation at the expense of Germany both in the Baltic and in the West, going even to the line of the Oder and the Eastern Neisse. If I and my colleagues erred in these decisions we must be judged in relation to the circumstances of the awful conflict in which we were engaged. We are not now in the presence of the Curzon Line as the Western frontier of Soviet authority. It is no longer a question of the line of the Oder. So long as Poland is held in control the Soviet domination in one form or another, runs from Stettin in the Baltic to the outskirts of Trieste in the Adriatic, and far South of that. The Russified frontier in the North is not the Curzon Line; it is not on the Oder; it is on the Elbe. That is a tremendous fact in European history, and one which it would be the height of unwisdom to ignore. Not only has a curtain descended, from the Baltic to the Adriatic, but behind that, is a broad band of territory containing all the capitals of Eastern and Central Europe and many ancient States and nations, in which dwell nearly one-third of the population of Europe, apart from Russia. At the present moment all this is ruled or actively directed by that same group of very able men, the Commissars in the Kremlin, which already disposes with despotic power of the fortunes of their own mighty Empire. It is here in this great band or belt, if anywhere, that the seeds of a new world war are being sown.

We may be absolutely sure that the Sovietising and, in many cases, the Communising of this gigantic slice of Europe, against the wishes of the overwhelming majority of the people of many of these regions, will not be achieved in any permanent manner without giving rise to evils and conflicts which are horrible to contemplate. Meanwhile, it was clear from the speech of the Foreign Secretary that the policy of the Soviet Government seems, up to the present, to be to delay all final settlements of peace and to prevent the peoples of Western and Eastern Europe from getting together in friendly, social and economic association, as many of them would like to do. On a short-term view, time is on the side of the Soviets, because the longer a free and peaceful settlement of Europe is delayed, the more time the Russian forces and Communist organisations have at their disposal in order to liquidate whatever elements obnoxious to their ambitions venture to show themselves in these wide lands. The populations of the Baltic States are no longer recognisable as those which existed before the war. They have suffered a double liquidation, both at German hands and Russian hands. The population of Pomerania is said to be but a third of what it was before the war. There was a very interesting article in the *Manchester Guardian* on that point the other day. Every effort is being made to Communise and Russify the whole of the Soviet-occupied zone of Germany.

Poland is denied all free expression of her national will. Her worst appetities of expansion are encouraged. At the same time, she is held in strict control by a Soviet-dominated government who do not dare have a free election under the observation of representatives of the three or four Great Powers. The fate of Poland seems to be an unending tragedy, and we, who went to war, all ill-prepared, on her behalf, watch with sorrow the strange outcome of our endeavours. I deeply regret that none of the Polish troops—and I must say this—who fought with us on a score of battlefields, who poured out their blood in the common cause, are to be allowed to march in the Victory Parade. They will be in our thoughts on that day. We shall never forget their bravery and martial skill, associated with our own glories at Tobruk, at Cassino and at Arnhem. Austria and Hungary are stifled, starved and weighed down by masses of Russian troops. We agree with the Foreign Secretary in all he said on this point yesterday. I do not speak of Czechoslovakia, which is a special case. For the time being I accept President Benes's statement that it is the duty of Czechoslovakia to interpret Russia to Western Europe and Western Europe to Russia. But for the rest—I do not want to go into more detail—the position is gravely and woefully disquieting. . . .

There are obvious limits to our powers, but so far as we have power, and in agreement with the United States great power may be exercised, we must do our best for the German people, and after the guilty have been punished for their horrible crimes we must banish revenge against an entire race from our minds. We must make sure they do not rearm, and that their industries are not capable of rapid transition to war production, but the danger to European peace and to the future of free democratic civilisation is not, at this moment, Germany—that menace belongs to the first and second acts of the world tragedy. The danger is the confusion and degeneration into which all Europe, or a very large part of it, is rapidly sinking. Moreover, we need not fear that our position will be worsened, or that its dangers will be brought more near, by the adoption of clear and firm policies. . . .

It is in this world organisation that we must put our final hopes. If we are to be told that such a procedure as this would rend the world organisation, and that a line of division, and even of separation, might grow up between Soviet Russia and the countries she controls on the one hand, and the rest of the world on the other, then I say—and I say it with much regret, but without any hesitancy—that it would be better to face that, when all has been tried and tried in vain, than tamely to accept a continued degeneration of the whole world position. It is better to have a world united than a world divided; but it is also better to have a world divided, than a world destroyed. Nor does it follow that even in a world divided there should not be equilibrium from which a further advance to unity might be attempted as the years pass by. Anything is better than this ceaseless degeneration of the heart of Europe. Europe will die of that. . . .

Europe is far worse off in every respect than she was at the end of the last war. Her miseries, confusion and hatreds far exceed anything that was known in those bygone days. More than once the formidable truth has been stated that great nations are indestructible. Let us beware of delay and further degeneration. With all their virtues, democracies are changeable. After the hot fit, comes the cold. Are we to see again, as we saw the last time, the utmost severities inflicted upon the vanquished, to be followed by a period in which we let them arm anew, and in which we then seek to appease their wrath? We cannot impose our will on our Allies, but we can, at least, proclaim our own convictions. Let us proclaim them fearlessly. Let Germany live. Let Austria and Hungary be freed. Let Italy resume her place in the European system. Let Europe arise again in glory, and by her strength and unity ensure the peace of the world.

"THE TRAGEDY OF EUROPE"

September 19, 1946

Zurich University

In a series of speeches during 1946-1951 Churchill elaborated on the theme of European Unity. In this speech he advocated a new partnership between France and Germany–at that stage regarded as unthinkable and impossible.

[Extract] I wish to speak to you to-day about the tragedy of Europe. This noble continent, comprising on the whole the fairest and the most cultivated regions of the earth, enjoying a temperate and equable climate, is the home of all the great parent races of the western world. It is the fountain of Christian faith and Christian ethics. It is the origin of most of the culture, arts, philosophy and science both of ancient and modern times. If Europe were once united in the sharing of its common inheritance, there would be no limit to the happiness, to the prosperity and glory which its three or four hundred million people would enjoy. Yet it is from Europe that have sprung that series of frightful nationalistic quarrels, originated by the Teutonic nations, which we have seen even in this twentieth century and in our own lifetime, wreck the peace and mar the prospects of all mankind.

And what is the plight to which Europe has been reduced? Some of the smaller States have indeed made a good recovery, but over wide areas a vast quivering mass of tormented, hungry, care-worn and bewildered human beings gape at the ruins of their cities and homes, and scan the dark horizons for the approach of some new peril, tyranny or terror. Among the victors there is a babel of jarring voices; among the vanquished the sullen silence of despair. That is all that Europeans, grouped in so many ancient States and nations, that is all that the Germanic Powers have got by tearing each other to pieces and spreading havoc far and wide. Indeed, but for the fact that the great Republic across the Atlantic Ocean has at length realised that the ruin or enslavement of Europe would involve their own fate as well, and has stretched out hands of succour and guidance, the Dark Ages would have returned in all their cruelty and squalor. They may still return.

Yet all the while there is a remedy which, if it were generally and spontaneously adopted, would as if by a miracle transform the whole scene, and would in a few years make all Europe, or the greater part of it, as free and as happy as Switzerland is to-day. What is this sovereign remedy? It is to re-create the European Family, or as much of it as we can, and provide it with a structure under which it can dwell in peace, in safety and in freedom. We must build a kind of United States of Europe. In this way only will hundreds of millions of toilers be able to regain the simple joys and hopes which make life worth living. The process is simple. All that is needed is the resolve of hundreds of millions of men and women to do right instead of wrong and gain as their reward blessing instead of cursing. . . .

We all know that the two world wars through which we have passed arose out of the vain passion of a newly-united Germany to play the dominating part in the world. In this last struggle crimes and massacres have been committed for which there is no parallel since the invasions of the Mongols in the fourteenth century and no equal at any time in human history. The guilty must be punished. Germany must be deprived of the power to rearm and make another aggressive war. But when all this has been done, as it will be done, as it is being done, there must be an end to retribution. There must be what Mr. Gladstone many years ago called "a blessed act of oblivion." We must all turn our backs upon the horrors of the past. We must look to the future. We cannot afford to drag forward across the years that are to come the hatreds and revenges which have sprung from the injuries of the past. If Europe is to be saved from infinite misery, and indeed from final doom, there must be an act of faith in the European family and an act of oblivion against all the crimes and follies of the past.

Can the free peoples of Europe rise to the height of these resolves of the soul and instincts of the spirit of man? If they can, the wrongs and injuries which have been inflicted will have been washed away on all sides by the miseries which have been endured. Is there any need for further floods of agony? Is it the only lesson of history that mankind is unteachable? Let there be justice, mercy and freedom. The peoples have only to will it, and all will achieve their hearts' desire.

I am now going to say something that will astonish you. The first step in the re-creation of the European family must be a partnership between France and Germany. In this way only can France recover the moral leadership of Europe. There can be no revival of Europe without a spiritually great France and a spiritually great Germany. The structure of the United States of Europe, if well and truly built, will be such as to make the material strength of a single state less important. Small nations will count as much as large ones and gain their honour by their contribution to the common cause. The ancient states and principalities of Germany, freely joined together for mutual convenience in a federal system, might each take their individual place among the United States of Europe. I shall not try to make a detailed programme for hundreds of millions of people who want to be happy and free, prosperous and safe, who wish to enjoy the four freedoms of which the great President Roosevelt spoke, and live in accordance with the principles embodied in the Atlantic Charter. If this is their wish, they have only to say so, and means can certainly be found, and machinery erected, to carry that wish into full fruition.

But I must give you a warning. Time may be short. At present there is a breathing-space. The cannon have ceased firing. The fighting has stopped; but the dangers have not stopped. If we are to form the United States of Europe or whatever name or form it may take, we must begin now.

In these present days we dwell strangely and precariously under the shield and protection of the atomic bomb. The atomic bomb is still only in the hands of a State and nation which we know will never use it except in the cause of right and freedom. But it may well be that in a few years this awful agency of destruction will be widespread and the catastrophe following from its use by several warring nations will not only bring to an end all that we call civilisation, but may possibly disintegrate the globe itself.

I must now sum up the propositions which are before you. Our constant aim must be to build and fortify the strength of U.N.O. Under and within that world concept we must re-create the European family in a regional structure called, it may be, the United States of Europe. The first step is to form a Council of Europe. If at first all the States of Europe are not willing or able to join the Union, we must nevertheless proceed to assemble and combine those who will and those who can. The salvation of the common people of every race and of every land from war or servitude must be established on solid foundations and must be guarded by the readiness of all men and women to die rather than submit to tyranny. In all this urgent work, France and Germany must take the lead together. Great Britain, the British Commonwealth of Nations, mighty America, and I trust Soviet Russia–for then indeed all would be well–must be the friends and sponsors of the new Europe and must champion its right to live and shine.

"EVERY DOG HIS DAY"

October 5, 1946

Conservative Party Conference,
Blackpool

The Conservatives were beginning to recover from the shock of their defeat by capitalising on the difficulties of the Labour Government and developing their own revised programmes and philosophy, of which "a property-owning democracy" was to be among the most popular.

[Extract] We have certainly had a depressing year since the General Election. I do not blame the Socialist Government–for the weather. We must also make allowances for all the difficulties which mark the aftermath of war. These difficulties would have taxed to the utmost the whole moral and physical resources of a united nation, marshalled and guided by a National Government. The Socialists broke up the national unity for the sake of their political interests, and the nation decided at the polls for a Socialist Party Government. This was their right under our well-tried Constitution. The electors, based on universal suffrage, may do what they like. And afterwards they have to like what they do. There is a saying in England, "Experience bought is better than taught." We have bought the experience. I do not complain at all of the workings of our constitutional democratic system. If the majority of the people of Britain on the morrow of our survival and victory, felt as they did, it was right that they should have their way. In consequence a Party Government has come into office which has shown itself markedly unequal to holding our place in the world or making the best of Britain on the morrow of its prolonged, intense exertions and immortal services to mankind.

The Socialist Party have only done their duty in accepting the responsibility so unexpectedly cast upon them by the electors. If they cannot do the job, that is our misfortune, but it was their duty to try. Also it was the duty of everyone to help them to overcome the national and world problems with which they are confronted. That still remains the settled policy of His Majesty's Opposition. . . .

But after all we are entitled to be treated with respect. We embody many of the strongest elements in the nation. We stand for high causes. Even under the confused conditions of the General Election ten and a half million people voted for us. To-day we are half, or more than half, the country.

The Socialist Government itself did not represent a majority of the nation. Under our present electoral system they have a majority of two to one in Parliment, and as on every occasion they seem to set Party before country, they can certainly vote us down in the House of Commons and carry through their fads and fancies and, regardless of the national interests, wreak their Party spite upon the other half of their fellow-countrymen. In little more than a year they have diminished British influence abroad and very largely paralysed our revival at home. Surely after all we have gone through we have enough to bear and dangers enough to face without the obtrusion upon us of this aggressive partianship. One would have hoped that victors of the election would rise to the level of their task, that they would have due regard for our common inheritance, that they would think for the country as a whole, and do their best for their native land. But, alas, they feel differently. They have to ram Socialist dogmas, which only a small minority of them even comprehend, down the throats of the British people in order to show what good Party men they are, no matter what it costs the ordinary working-class family in common everyday prosperity, convenience and freedom of life.

To all this they add quite exceptional ineptitude and inefficiency and many silly blunders in the conduct of our affairs. Do you seek for proofs? Look around you. Look at the taxes. Look at the unbridled expenditure which is leading us daily into inflation, with all its bitter consequences. Look at the queues as you walk about our streets. Look at the restrictions and repressions on every form of enterprise and recovery. Look at the ever-growing bureaucracy of officials quartered permanently on the public. Let us look at Food. The German U-boats in their worst endeavour never made bread-rationing necessary in war. It took a Socialist Government and Socialist planners to fasten it on us in time of peace when the seas are open and the world harvests good. At no time in the two world wars have our people had so little bread, meat, butter, cheese and fruit to eat.

Look at the housing of the people. At the end of 13 months of his housing performance, Mr. Aneurin Bevan points proudly to 22,000 new permanent houses completed. Before the war between 25,000 and 30,000 permanent houses were erected in Great Britain every *month.* But now, in August, only 4,566 permanent houses were completed, that is to say only about one-sixth of the number built mainly by private enterprise without any fuss or bother every month before the war.

How shall we stigmatise the incompetence which left large numbers of buildings, camps and habitations vacant under Government control while hundreds of thousands of families yearn for any kind of roof over their heads and privacy at their hearths till something better can be provided? I have before expressed my astonishment that any man responsible for housing, like Mr. Aneurin Bevan, should not have tried to deal with his problem on the merits and make as many homes as possible in the shortest time by every means available, even if he had to lay aside during these years of emergency some of his doctrinaire malice. The amount of needless suffering, vexation and frustration his prejudices have caused cannot be measured. There is however a poetic justice in the fact that the most mischievous political mouth in wartime has also become, in peace, the most remarkable administrative failure. . . .

I have on other occasions set before you the immense injury which has been done to our process of recovery by the ill-considered schemes and threats of nationalisation which have cast their shadows over so many of our leading industries. The attempts to nationalise the steel industry, which was so effective in war and so buoyant in its plans for the future, is the most foolish of all the experiments in Socialism from which we have yet suffered. The wanton destruction by Sir Stafford Cripps of the Liverpool Cotton Exchange has inflicted a deep lasting injury upon the Lancashire cotton trade and upon the City of Liverpool. The nationalisation of Cables and Wireless, although agreeable to Australian Socialist conceptions, has been a dead loss to this Island, not only in foreign exchange but in facilities of communication which private enterprise had patiently built up to the national advantage. The shortage of all necessary articles for ordinary domestic consumption persists. We are complacently assured that the number of people employed on manufacture for home consumption is getting back to pre-war level, but what of the maldistribution of effort? In June we had 515,000 more people working in the metal and chemical industries than pre-war, but 456,000 less in the textile and clothing industries. Again, we had nearly 300,000 more non-industrial civil servants, but 677,000 less workers in the distributive trades. And now the British housewife, as she stands in the queue to buy her bread ration, will fumble in her pocket in vain for a silver sixpence. Under the Socialist Government *nickel* will have to be good enough for her. In future we shall still be able to say "Every cloud has a *nickel* lining."

Look where you will, we are suffering a needless decline and contraction at a time when we had the right to brighter days. I have visited many of the smaller countries on the Continent. All are making much more of themselves and of their chances than we are. Nowhere is there the drab disheartenment and frustration which the Socialist Party have fastened on Britain.

But now I turn abroad. I wish to speak of India. I am very glad you passed the Resolution about India at the Conference yesterday. You all know my views about India and how we have desired to give full Dominion Status to India, including the right embodied in the Statute of Westminster for the Indian peoples, like other Dominions, to quit the British Commonwealth of Nations altogether. The way in which the Socialist Government have handled this problem has been such as to give the vast masses of the people of India hardly any choice but to become separated from the British Crown which has so long shielded them from internal convulsions or foreign invasion. The Government of India has been placed—or I should rather say thrust—into the hands of men who have good reason to be bitterly hostile to the British connection, but who in no way represent the enormous mass of nearly 400 millions of all the races, States, and peoples of India who have dwelt so long in peace with one another. I fear that calamity impends upon this sub-Continent, which is almost as big as Europe, more populous, and even more harshly divided. It seems that in quite a short time India will become a separate, a foreign and a none too friendly country to the British Commonwealth of Nations. Indian unity created by British rule will swiftly perish, and no one can measure the misery and bloodshed which will overtake these enormous masses of humble helpless millions, or under what new power their future and destiny will lie. All this is happening every day, every hour. The great ship is sinking in the calm sea. Those who should have devoted their utmost efforts to keep her afloat have instead opened the sea-cocks. The event will long leave its mark in history. It may well be that Burma will soon suffer the same fate. I am grieved to have to state these sombre tidings to you. Most of you will certainly live to see whether I am right or wrong. Sometimes in the past I have not been wrong. I pray that I may be wrong now.

What has been the effect of our immense act of surrender in India? On the morrow of our victory and of our services, without which human freedom would not have survived, we are divesting ourselves of the mighty and wonderful empire which had been built up in India by two hundred years of effort and sacrifice, and the number of the King's subjects is being reduced to barely a quarter of what it has been for generations. Yet at this very moment and in the presence of this unparalleled act of voluntary abdication, we are still ceaselessly abused by the Soviet wireless and by certain unfriendly elements in the United States for being a land-grabbing Imperialist power seeking expansion and aggrandisement. While Soviet Russia is expanding or seeking to expand in every direction, and has already brought many extra scores of millions of people directly or indirectly under the despotic control of the Kremlin and the rigours of Communist discipline, we, who sought nothing from this war but to do our duty and are in fact reducing ourselves to a fraction of our former size and population, are successfully held up to world censure. It is astonishing that no effective reply should be made by His Majesty's Government and that it should be left to Field Marshal Smuts, the great South African, our former valiant enemy of Boer War days, to raise his voice in vindication of British magnanimity, tolerance and good faith.

What are we to say of the handling of the Palestine problem by the Socialist Government? At the election they made lavish promises to the Zionists and their success at the polls excited passionate expectations throughout the Jewish world. These promises were no sooner made than they were discarded, and now all through this year the Government stand vacillating without any plan or policy, holding on to a mandate in which we have no vital interest, gaining the distrust and hostility both of Arab and Jew, and exposing us to worldwide reprobation for their manifest incapacity. Thus both at home and abroad the British nation and Empire have been deprived of the rewards their conduct deserves.

I have naturally considered very carefully what is my own duty in these times. It would be easy for me to retire gracefully in an odour of civic freedoms, and this plan crossed my mind frequently some months ago. I feel now however that the situation is so serious and what may have to come so grave, that I am resolved to go forward carrying the flag as long as I have the necessary strength and energy, and have your confidence. It is of the highest importance to our name and endurance as a great power and to the cohesion of our national and imperial life that there should be re-established at the earliest moment some poise and balance between the political forces in our island, and that those who were so unexpectedly clad with overwhelming Parliamentary power should be made to realise that they are the servants, and not the masters, of the British nation. When I think of what has already happened, what is happening, and what is going to happen in the next year or two, I feel, as you feel, profoundly stirred. Our reaction must not be despair, because that is an emotion which we do not allow. It must be wrath–not despair but wrath– and wrath must translate itself not in vain expletives but in earnest action and well-conceived measures and organisation. . . .

I do not believe in looking about for some panacea or cure-all on which we should stake our credit and fortunes trying to sell it like a patent medicine to all and sundry. It is easy to win applause by talking in an airy way about great new departures in policy, especially if all detailed proposals are avoided. We ought not to seek after some rigid, symmetrical form of doctrine, such as delights the minds of Socialists and Communists. Our own feelings and the British temperament are quite different. So are our aims. We seek a free and varied society, where there is room for many kinds of men and women to lead happy, honourable and useful lives. We are fundamentally opposed to all systems of rigid uniformity in our national life and we have grown great as a nation by indulging tolerance, rather than logic.

It certainly would be an error of the first order for us to plunge out into a programme of promises and bribes in the hopes of winning the public favour. But if you say to me: "What account are we to give of the policy of the Conservative Party? What are we to say of our theme and our cause and of the faith that is in us?" That is a question to which immediate answer can always be given.

Our main objectives are: To uphold the Christian religion and resist all attacks upon it. To defend our Monarchical and Parliamentary Constitution. To provide adequate security against external aggression and safety to our seaborne trade. To uphold law and order, and impartial justice administered by Courts free from interference or pressure on the part of the executive. To regain a sound finance and strict supervision of national income and expenditure. To defend and develop our Empire trade, without which Great Britain would perish. To promote all measures to improve the health and social conditions of the people. To support as a general rule free enterprise and initiative against State trading and nationalisation of industries.

To this I will add some further conceptions. We oppose the establishment of a Socialist State, controlling the means of production, distribution and exchange. We are asked, "What is your alternative?" Our Conservative aim is to build a property-owning democracy, both independent and interdependent. In this I include profit-sharing schemes in suitable industries and intimate consultation between employers and wage-earners. In fact we seek so far as possible to make the status of the wage-earner that of a partner rather than of an irresponsible employee. It is in the interest of the wage-earner to have many other alternatives open to him than service under one all-powerful employer called the State. He will be in a better position to bargain collectively and production will be more abundant; there will be more for all and more freedom for all when the wage-earner is able, in the large majority of cases, to choose and change his work, and to deal with a private employer who, like himself, is subject to the ordinary pressures of life and, like himself, is dependent upon his personal thrift, ingenuity and good-housekeeping. In this way alone can the traditional virtues of the British character be preserved. We do not wish the people of this ancient island reduced to a mass of State-directed proletarians, thrown hither and thither, housed here and there, by an aristocracy of privileged officials or privileged Party, sectarian or Trade Union bosses. We are opposed to the tyranny and victimisation of the closed shop. Our ideal is the consenting union of millions of free, independent families and homes to gain their livelihood and to serve true British glory and world peace. . . .

How then do we draw the lines of political battle? The British race is not actuated mainly by the hope of material gain. Otherwise we should long ago have sunk in the ocean of the past. It is stirred on almost all occasions by sentiment and instinct, rather than by programmes or worldly calculation. When this new Parliament first met, all the Socialist Members stood up and sang "The Red Flag" in their triumph. Peering ahead through the mists and mysteries of the future so far as I can, I see the division at the next election will be between those who wholeheartedly sing "The Red Flag" and those who rejoice to sing "Land of Hope and Glory." There is the noble hymn which will rally the wise, the soberminded and the good to the salvation of our native land.

FOREIGN AFFAIRS

October 23, 1946

House of Commons

A situation of great seriousness now existed in Palestine, where British forces unavailingly–and at ever-increasing losses–endeavoured to continue the United Nations mandate. Churchill, an avowed supporter of the Jewish National Home, consistently urged the return of the mandate to the U.N.–the course which was eventually followed. Meanwhile, Western fears of Soviet actions and intentions mounted.

[Extract] . . . I must comment first this afternoon upon two or three special questions which are likely to cause trouble and are, indeed, already causes of disquiet. I have nothing to add to-day to the statements which I have made on previous occasions about Egypt and Palestine. No one can say that His Majesty's Government have not done their best to meet Egyptian wishes. Indeed, many of us thought that they had gone too far and had adopted the wrong methods in stating, at the outset of their negotiations, that they were willing to evacuate the Canal zone, which zone is secured to us for the next few critical years to come by the Anglo-Egyptian treaty of 1936. The result has been what was then predicted, namely, that their maximum offer was taken as the starting point for new discussions, and these discussions now even involve the whole sovereignty and future of the Sudan. I remind the right hon. Gentleman the Prime Minister of his statement on 7 May, when he said that, obviously, if negotiations break down the original treaty still stands. I hope that His Majesty's Government will act in this sense.

Before we separated for the Autumn Recess, I spoke about Palestine. I must refer to that subject, linked as it is with all other questions of the Middle East. If we are not able to fulfil our pledge to the Jews to create a national home for the Jewish people in Palestine–which is our undoubted pledge–we are entitled and, indeed, bound in my view–because it is our duty, to lay our Mandate at the feet of the United Nations Organisation. The burden may yet be too heavy for one single country to bear. It is not right that the United States, who are so very keen on Jewish immigration into Palestine, should take no share in the task, and should reproach us for our obvious incapacity to cope with the difficulties of the problem.

At present, we have no policy as far as I can make out, nor have we had one for more than a year. The amount of suffering which this indecision in regard to a question which, I admit, may well be called the "riddle of the Sphinx," is causing to all concerned, simply cannot be measured. From the moment when we declare that we will give up the Mandate–giving proper notice, of course–all our difficulties will be considerably lessened, and if other interested Powers wish us to continue, it is for them to make proposals and help us in our work. We have at this moment a large proportion of our overseas Army in Palestine engaged in a horrible, squalid conflict with the Zionist community there. This is a disproportionate exertion for us, a wrong distribution of our limited forces, and the most thankless task ever undertaken by any country. If we stand on the treaty with Egypt about the Canal zone, we have no need to seek a new strategic base of very doubtful usefulness in Palestine, and we can present ourselves to the world organisation as a totally disinterested party. Superior solutions may then, for the first time, become open. I strongly commend this course of action to His Majesty's Government and to the House. . . .

Eight months ago, I made a speech at Fulton in the United States. It had a mixed reception on both sides of the Atlantic, and quite a number of hon. Members of this House put their names to a Motion condemning me for having made it. As events have moved, what I said at Fulton has been outpaced and overpassed by this movement of events, and by the movement of American opinion. If I were to make that speech at the present time and in the same place, it would attract no particular attention. At that time, I said that I did not believe the Soviet Government wanted war. I said that what they wanted were the fruits of war. I fervently hope and pray that the view which I then expressed is still correct, and on the whole I believe it is still correct. However, we are dealing with the unknowable. Like everyone else, I welcome the recent declarations of Marshal Stalin, and I always welcome any signs of affability which M. Molotov may display. I know him quite well, and, as the right hon. Gentleman the Foreign Secretary will corroborate, he is not nearly so spiky in private relationship as he appears in his public declarations. In these matters, it is not words that count, it is deeds and facts.

This afternoon I am not going to examine the likelihood of another war, which would, of course, be total war. In the Foreign Secretary's calm, assured and measured review of the world situation yesterday, it was evident that various differences of policy exist between the Soviet Government and what are called, for want of a better name—and it is not a bad name—the Western democracies. There are differences in the Far East; there are disputes about Persia; there are various grave and serious questions connected with the Dardanelles; above all, there is the situation at Trieste, there is Poland and its elections, and there are others. The right hon. Gentleman found it necessary—and he was quite right—to survey the whole far from cheering panorama, and touch upon all those points of view; and though his language was diplomatically correct in every respect, one could not help seeing those points of direct difference emerging as between the great Powers which are involved. It would be most unwise to ignore those differences, and every effort should be made to adjust them. I am sure every effort will be made by patient, friendly and, I hope, occasionally secret discussions between the principal Powers and personalities involved.

It was easier in Hitler's day to feel and forecast the general movement of events than it is now. Now we have to deal not with Hitler and his crude Nazi gang, with anti-Semitism as its principal theme; we are in the presence of something very much more difficult to measure than what was set out so plainly in the pages of *Mein Kampf*. We are in the presence of the collective mind, whose springs of action we cannot define. There are 13 or 14 very able men in the Kremlin who hold all Russia and more than a third of Europe in their control. Many stresses and pressures, internal as well as external, are working upon them, as upon all human beings. I cannot presume to forecast what decisions they will take, or to observe what decisions they may have already have taken; still less can I attempt to foresee the time factor in their affairs. One of our main difficulties in judging all these matters is that real intercourse and intimacy between our peoples are, to all intents and purposes, very much discouraged and prevented by the Soviet Government. There is none of that free comradely life and mixing which very soon would bring immense changes in the relationships of these vast communities, and might sweep away suspicion, without relaxing vigilance. . . .

INDIA

December 12, 1946

House of Commons

Churchill viewed the approach of independence to India and Burma with keen regret, but recognized its inevitability. His speeches on the subject were in very marked contrast to those of 1929-1935.

[Extract] . . . It is several months since we have even discussed the Indian drama which is unfolding itself remorselessly. So far, in this Parliament, we have never voted in a Division on these issues, momentous though they be to Britain, to the British Commonwealth of Nations, to the world at large and, even more, to the 400 million who dwell in the Indian Continent. Words are almost inadequate to describe their vastness. But memorable as these issues may be, we have never divided the House on them, nor shall we do so on this occasion. We must still indulge the hope that agreement will be reached between the two great Indian religions and between the political parties which give modern expression to their age-long antagonisms. We should, however, be failing in our duty if we in this House gave the impression to India that we were inattentive, or even indifferent, to what is happening, and what is going to happen out there. For many generations, Parliament has been responsible for the government of India, and we can only relieve ourselves, or be relieved, from that burden by the passing of a solemn Act. While we are responsible, it would, in my opinion, be disastrous and be discreditable to the House if the whole Session passed away, with nothing but a casual reference being made to these tremendous and immeasurable events which are taking place.

There is another aspect. If we remained silent after all these months, it might be thought that we were in agreement with His Majesty's Government, and that the policy which they were pursuing was a national policy and not a party policy of the forces which they represent. It might be thought that this was a policy of Britain as a whole, and that the execution of it was endorsed by the British people as a whole, whereas, for good or ill, the responsibility rests with His Majesty's Government. On their heads lies the responsibility, not only for the execution of the policy, but for the powerful impulse they have given to a great many tendencies which are dominant in this matter to-day. I say nothing to derogate from any utterances or statements which have been made by the Members of other parties. They are all excellent, but I should be very sorry indeed, to feel that, as matters unfold in India, there is any question of our being held accountable at the present moment, for the course of events. Therefore, we are bound to take an opportunity to challenge the Government on this matter by bringing the affair to the light of day. . . .

There are three main new features to which I would direct the attention of the House this afternoon. There was, and there still is, a general measure of consent here and throughout the island to the final transference of power from the House of Commons to Indian hands, but also it is agreed that that transference, if it is to take place, must be based upon the agreement and the co-operation of the principal masses and forces among the inhabitants of India. Only in this way could that transference take place without measureless bloodshed out there, and lasting discredit to our name in the world. Those who are content with the general movement of our relations with India over the last 20 years have hoped that the desire of many Indians to be rid for ever of British rule and guidance would have brought about a melting of hearts among the vast populations inhabiting the Indian continent, and that they would have joined together to maintain the peace and the unity of India, and stride forth boldly into their independent future, on which we impose no bar.

Those are not my views; they are the views of a very great number of people. But it is necessary to place on record the undoubted fact that no such melting of hearts has, so far, occurred. I think that that would be considered in harmony with the habit of understatement which has often received acceptance in this House. On the contrary, all the facts and all the omens point to a revival, in an acute and violent form, of the internal hatreds and quarrels which have long lain dormant under the mild incompetence of liberal-minded British control. This is the dominating fact which stares us in the face to-day. The House will probably be of the opinion that it is too soon for us to accent this melancholy conclusion, or to regulate our conduct by it. To me, however, it would be no surprise if there were a complete failure to agree. I warned the House as long ago as 1931, when I said that if we were to wash our hands of all responsibility, ferocious civil war would speedily break out between the Muslims and Hindus. But this, like other warnings, fell upon deaf and unregarding ears. . . .

The second point to which I would like to draw the attention of the House is the cardinal error of His Majesty's Government when, on 12 August, they invited one single Indian party, the Congress Party, having made other efforts, to nominate all the members of the Viceroy's Council. Thereby they precipitated a series of massacres over wide regions, unparalleled in India since the Indian Mutiny of 1857. Indeed, it is certain that more people have lost their lives or have been wounded in India by violence since the interim Government under Mr. Nehru was installed in office four months ago by the Viceroy, than in the previous 90 years, of four generations of men, covering a large part of the reigns of five Sovereigns. This is only a foretaste of what may come. It may be only the first few heavy drops before the thunderstorm breaks upon us. These frightful slaughters over wide regions and in obscure uncounted villages have, in the main, fallen upon Muslim minorities. I have received from high and credible witnesses, accounts of what has taken place, for instance, in Bihar. The right hon. and learned Gentleman gave us his report. What happened in Bihar casts into the shade the Armenian atrocities with which Mr. Gladstone once stirred the moral sense of Liberal Britain. We are, of course, cauterised by all that we ourselves have passed through. Our faculty for wonder is ruptured, our faculty for horror is numbed; the world is full of misery and hatred. What Mr. Gollancz, in a remarkable book–which, I may say, shows an evident lack of peace of mind–has called "our threatened values," do not stir us as they would have done our fathers or our predecessors in this House; nor, perhaps, after all our exertions and in our present eclipse, have we the physical and psychic strength to react against these shocking tidings, as former generations and earlier Parliaments, who have not suffered like us, would certainly have done.

The official figure of the lives lost since the Government of India was handed over to the Interim Administration of Mr. Nehru is stated at 10,000. I doubt very much whether that figure represents half the total racial and religious murders which have occurred up to date. An outbreak of animal fury had ravaged many large districts, and may at any time resume or spread its devastation through teeming cities and Provinces as big as England or the main British island. It is some comfort to recall, and I was glad the right hon. and learned Gentleman reminded us of it, that both Muslim and Hindu leaders have joined together to arrest, or at least mitigate this appalling degeneration. I have been informed that it was Mr. Nehru himself who gave the order which the Provincial Government of Bihar had been afraid to give, for the police and troops to fire upon Hindu mobs who were exterminating the Muslim minorities within their midst. That was certainly to his credit and may be taken, so far as it goes, as an encouraging sign.

Nevertheless, I must record my own belief, which I have long held and often expressed, that any attempt to establish the reign of a Hindu numerical majority in India will never be achieved without a civil war, proceeding, not perhaps at first on the fronts of armies or organised forces, but in thousands of separate and isolated places. This war will, before it is decided, lead through unaccountable agonies to an awful abridgement of the Indian population. Besides and in addition to this, I am sure that any attempt by the Congress Party to establish a Hindu Raj on the basis of majorities measured by the standards of Western civilisation—or what is left of it—and proceeding by the forms and formulas of governments with which we are familiar over here, will, at a very early stage, be fatal to any conception of the unity of India. . . .

I am grateful to the House for listening to me after we have had so full an account from the responsible Minister of the Crown. I feel bound, however, to end upon a positive conclusion, although I will express it rather in terms of negation. In all this confusion, uncertainty and gathering storm, which those who have studies the Indian problem over long years might well have foreseen, there appear at the present time to be three choices—the proverbial three choices—before the British Parliament. The first is to proceed with ruthless logic to quit India regardless of what may happen there. This we can certainly do. Nothing can prevent us, if it be the will of Parliament, from gathering together our women and children and unarmed civilians, and marching under strong rearguards to the sea. That is one choice. The second is to assert the principle, so often proclaimed, that the King needs no unwilling subjects and that the British Commonwealth of Nations contemplates no compulsory partnership, that, in default of real agreement, the partition of India between the two different races and religions, widely differing entities, must be faced; that those who wish to make their own lives in their own way may do so, and the gods be with them; and that those who desire to find, in a variety of systems, a means of association with our great free Commonwealth may also be permitted to take the course which, ultimately, they may show themselves ready to take.

It follows, of course, from this second alternative, that anarchy and massacre must be prevented and that, failing a measure of agreement not now in sight, an impartial Administration responsible to Parliament, shall be set up to maintain the fundamental guarantees of "life, liberty and the pursuit of happiness" to the millions, nay, the hundreds of millions, of humble folk who now stand in jeopardy, bewilderment and fear. Whether that can be achieved or not by any apparatus of British controlled government that we can form from our dissipated resources, is, again, a matter upon which it is now impossible to form a final judgment.

One thing there is, however, that, whatever happens, we must not do. We must not allow British troops or British officers in the Indian Army to become the agencies and instruments of enforcing caste Hindu domination upon the 90 million Muslims and the 60 million Untouchables; nor must the prestige or authority of the British power in India, even in its sunset, be used in partisanship on either side of these profound and awful cleavages. Such a course, to enforce religious and party victory upon minorities of scores of millions, would seem to combine the disadvantages of all policies and lead us ever deeper into tragedy, without giving us relief from our burdens, or liberation, however sadly purchased, from moral and factual responsibility. It is because we feel that these issues should be placed bluntly and plainly before the British and Indian peoples, even amid their present distresses and perplexities, that we thought it our bounden duty to ask for this Debate.

BURMA

December 20, 1946

House of Commons

[Extract] . . . It is less than a year since the Japanese were expelled or destroyed. There have been no adequate elections, no representative assembly formed, and nothing that could be said to be a representative or settled view of the people there. Those people are only now returning, with great difficulty, as the Government have pointed out, and as was pointed out in the White Paper issued last year, to their ruined homes in many parts of that country, which were ravaged by the Japanese. Yet we are told that we must accelerate the process of our departure as much as possible, that special measures must be taken, and these gentlemen invited from Burma to come over here and discuss with the Government the peaceful transference of power and the rapid departure of the British. Before they come, before they would even condescend to come, a declaration has to be made in terms which place this matter in the same state as what is happening now in India.

This must be realised. We have held Burma since 1885. We have followed its affairs with attention. My father was the Minister responsible for the annexation of Burma. During that time, great progress has been made in that small country. There are 17 million people, mostly, or a very large proportion of them, primitive people. Good progress has been made. We defended them as well as we could against the Japanese invasion, but we were not successful. It was only after the tremendous campaign of three years of heavy fighting that the Japanese were driven out, and the country was liberated from the invaders' hands. In those circumstances it would have been reasonable to allow law and order to be established, and the people to settle down on their farms and in their habitations. Then we could have resumed consideration of the question of self-government, to which we had definitely pledged ourselves, but all in due course, and in due time. Again, by the unfortunate form of the Prime Minister's declaration to which the right hon. Gentleman has now given vent, and which has taken its place as an operative declaration, the intermediate stage of Dominion status is, to all intents and purposes, eliminated, just as it was in India. In eliminating that interim stage in India it was said: "This makes no difference, because Dominion status implies the right to contract out of the British Empire."

The proper stages are of the utmost consequence. If, in India, we had proceeded under Dominion status, and had established a Government based upon Dominion status, that Government could then have addressed itself to the question whether to use what I call the escalator Clause or not. A very different situation would then have arisen. There would have been an opportunity for the friends of this country who desire that we should stay, and who appreciate the blessings which British rule has conferred upon these regions, to rally. They would have had a chance to decide whether, upon a basis of full Dominion status, they would be partners in the British Commonwealth of Nations or not. The elimination of that stage, the short circuiting of that process, has the effect, and could only have the effect, of repulsing all loyalties, the abandoning of friends, and compelling everyone in India to face the fact that the British were going. The result is that no fair chance has been given to the people of India to express themselves, in a calm atmosphere and under proper conditions, upon the question whether, having obtained full self-government, they would wish to leave the British Commonwealth of Nations or not.

This evil process, which has been attended by disasters of which at present we are only on the threshold, and which will to a large extent occupy or dominate the mind and attention of the present Parliament in the months and years to come, is now quite needlessly extended to Burma. I cannot see why this should be done, unless it is to try to induce the Burmese representatives to come over here and discuss this matter with us. This haste is appalling. "Scuttle" is the only word that can be applied. What, spread over a number of years, would be a healthy and constitutional process and might easily have given the Burmese people an opportunity of continuing their association with our congregation of nations, has been cast aside. We are seeing in home affairs the unseemly rush of legislation, disorganising our national life and impeding our recovery, legislation thrust upon Parliament at break-neck speed, hon. Members debarred from taking part in Debates by matters being transferred from the Floor of this House to other parts of the building. We see the same haste which, I suppose, will be paraded as vigour. "Labour gets things done!"

As regards divesting ourselves of these great possessions of the British Crown, and freeing ourselves from all responsibility for the populations–primitive and often divided–who have hitherto looked to British justice and administration for the means of lending their ordinary lives in peace, I thought it necessary at the earliest moment to dissociate myself and those who sit on this side from the course of action which the Government are taking. I said the other day about India that we take no responsibility for the course the Government take; they must bear the responsibility. I see it was said in another place that I was suggesting that should the Conservative Party be returned to power, we would reverse this process. I think it would be utterly impossible to reverse it. The words that have come from the lips of the right hon. Gentleman today, supported as they are by the overwhelming majority of this House–unrepresentative of the balance of forces in the country–are irrevocable. He has in fact shorn Burma away from the British Crown by what is being done. That, at least, is a matter of which notice should be taken, if it be only passing notice, even in this period when we are getting so accustomed and indurated to the process of the decline and fall of the British Empire.

INDIA

March 6, 1947

House of Commons

As the spectre of civil war in India became more likely to become a reality as independence drew nearer, Conservative support for the Government's policies disappeared. The dismissal of the Viceroy, Lord Wavell, and his replacement by Lord Louis Mountbatten aroused fears of a precipitate "scuttle"–which in fact occurred.

[Extract] When great parties in this country have for many years pursued a combined and united policy on some large issue, and when for what seemed to them to be good reasons, they decide to separate, not only in Debate but by Division, it is desirable and even necessary, that the causes of such separation and the limitations of the differences which exist, should be placed on record. This afternoon we begin a new chapter in our relations across the Floor of the House in regard to the Indian problem. We on this side of the House have, for some time, made it clear that the sole responsibility for the control of India's affairs rests, of course, with His Majesty's Government. We have criticised their action in various ways but this is the first time we have felt it our duty as the official Opposition to express our dissent and difference by a formal vote. . . .

First there was the attempt to formulate a Constitution and press it upon the Indians, instead of leaving the Indians, as had been promised, the duty of framing their own proposals. That action, however well intended, has proved to be devoid of advantage, and must be rated as a mistake. Secondly, there was the summoning of a so-called Constituent Assembly upon the altogether inadequate and unrepresentative franchise, an Assembly which was called into being, but which had absolutely no claim or right to decide the fate of India, or any claim to express the opinion of the great masses of the Indians. That is the second mistake. The third mistake was the dismissal of the eminent Indians composing the Viceroy's Council, and the handing over of the government of India to Mr. Nehru.

This government of Mr. Nehru has been a complete disaster, and a great degeneration and demoralisation in the already weakened departmental machinery of the Government of India has followed from it. Thirty or forty thousand people have been slaughtered in the warfare between the two principal religions. Corruption is growing apace. They talk of giving India freedom. But freedom has been restricted since this interim Nehru Government has come to power. Communism is growing so fast that it has been found necessary to raid and suppress Communist establishments and centres which, in our broad British tolerance we do not do here, and have never done in India. [*Interruption.*] I am illustrating the steps to freedom which, so far, have been marked by every degree in which British control is relaxed, by the restriction of the ordinary individual, whatever his political view. It was a cardinal mistake to entrust the government of India to the caste Hindu, Mr. Nehru. He has good reason to be the most bitter enemy of any connection between India and the British Commonwealth.

I consider that that must be regarded as the third practical administrative mistake, apart from those large departures in principle which may be charged against the present British Government in this Indian sphere. Such was the situation before the latest plunge which the Government have taken, was made, and it is this plunge which, added to all that has gone before, makes it our duty to sever ourselves altogether from the Indian policy of His Majesty's Government, and to disclaim all responsibility for the consequences which will darken–aye, and redden the coming years. . . .

India is to be subjected not merely to partition, but to fragmentation, and to haphazard fragmentation. A time limit is imposed–a kind of guillotine–which will certainly prevent the full, fair and reasonable discussion of the great complicated issues that are involved. These 14 months will not be used for the melting of hearts and the union of Muslim and Hindu all over India. They will be used in preparation for civil war; and they will be marked continually by disorders and disturbances such as are now going on in the great city of Lahore. In spite of the great efforts which have been made by the leaders on both sides to allay them, out of sheer alarm and fear of what would happen, still these troubles break out, and they are sinking profoundly into India, in the heart of the Indian problem–[*Laughter.*]–the right hon. and learned Gentleman [Sir Stafford Cripps] ought not to laugh. Although of fanatical disposition, he has a tender heart. I am sure that the horrors that have been going on since he put the Nehru Government in power, the spectacle we have seen in viewing these horrors, with the corpses of men, women and children littering the ground in thousands, have wrung his heart. I wonder that even his imagination does not guide him to review these matters searchingly in his own conscience.

Let the House remember this. The Indian political parties and political classes do not represent the Indian masses. It is a delusion to believe that they do. I wish they did. They are not as representative of them as the movements in Britain represent the surges and impulses of the British nation. This has been proved in the war, and I can show the House how it was proved. The Congress Party declared non-co-operation with Great Britain and the Allies. The other great political party, to whom all main power is to be given, the Muslim League, sought to make a bargain about it, but no bargain was made. So both great political parties in India, the only forces that have been dealt with so far, stood aside. Nevertheless, the only great volunteer army in the world that fought on either side in that struggle was formed in India. More than three and a half million men came forward to support the King Emperor and the cause of Britain; they came forward not by conscription or compulsion, but out of their loyalty to Britain and to all that Britain stood for in their lives. In handing over the Government of India to these so-called political classes we are handing over to men of straw, of whom, in a few years, no trace will remain. . . .

I thank the House for listening so long and so attentively to what I have said. I have spoken with a lifetime of thought and contact with these topics. It is with deep grief I watch the clattering down of the British Empire with all its glories, and all the services it has rendered to mankind. I am sure that in the hour of our victory now not so long ago, we had the power to make a solution of our difficulties which would have been honourable and lasting. Many have defended Britain against her foes. None can defend her against herself. We must face the evils that are coming upon us and that we are powerless to avert. We must do our best in all these circumstances and not exclude any expedient that may help to mitigate the ruin and disaster that will follow the disappearance of Britain from the East. But, at least, let us not add—by shameful flight, by a premature hurried scuttle—at least, let us not add to the pangs of sorrow so many of us feel, the taint and smear of shame.

NATIONAL SERVICE

May 7, 1947

House of Commons

The National Service Bill provided for eighteen months' compulsory service in the armed forces for all males between 18 and 26, with certain exceptions, including underground coalminers (exempt from call-up for five years). It was supported by the Conservatives, but violently opposed by the Left Wing of the Labour Party. As a result of this opposition, the Government subsequently reduced the period of service to twelve months, to the fury of the Opposition. It was restored to eighteen months in November 1948.

[Extract] I have been looking around for something upon which to congratulate the right hon. Gentleman [Mr. A. V. Alexander, Defence Minister]. After some difficulty, I have found at least one point on which I can offer him my compliments, and that is the control of his facial expression, which enabled him to deliver the ridiculous and deplorable harangue to which we have listened, and yet keep an unsmiling face. Indeed, there were moments when I was not quite sure whether he was not taking his revenge on the forces which compelled him to his present course of action, by showing them how ridiculous their case was, and how absurd their position would be when it was presented to the House of Commons. I spoke yesterday of the care and thought given to the social and industrial side of the Bill as explained by the Minister of Labour, and I am willing to believe that equal attention was given to the military side. That is the foundation of the complaint which we make. . . .

The party on this side of the House have suffered a great deal from the taunt of "guilty men," which was made great use of at the Election, and which hon. Gentlemen think they can jeer about to-day. But nothing I have seen in my Parliamentary experience, and I have a right to speak on this matter, has been equal, in abjectness, in failure of duty to the country, and in failure to stand up for convictions and belief, to this sudden *volte-face,* change and scuttle of which the Prime Minister and his Minister of Defence were guilty. They may never be called to account in the future for what they are doing now, but it is perfectly certain that, henceforward, we have no foundation to rest upon in respect of defence. The title of the Minister of Defence should be changed. He should be called the "Minister of Defence unless Attacked."

What a lamentable exhibition he has made of himself—one which must be deeply injurious to the reputation which he built up for himself during the war, when he had different leadership. . . .

UNITED EUROPE

May 14, 1947

Albert Hall, London

[Extract] All the greatest things are simple, and many can be expressed in a single word: Freedom; Justice; Honour; Duty; Mercy; Hope. We who have come together here to-night, representing almost all the political parties in our British national life and nearly all the creeds and churches of the Western world—this large audience filling a famous hall—*we also* can express our purposes in a single word—"Europe." At school we learned from the maps hung on the walls, and the advice of our teachers that there is a continent called Europe. I remember quite well being taught this as a child, and after living a long time, I still believe it is true. However, professional geographers now tell us that the Continent of Europe is really only the peninsula of the Asiatic land mass. I must tell you in all faith that I feel that this would be an arid and uninspiring conclusion, and for myself, I distinctly prefer what I was taught when I was a boy. . . .

In our task of reviving the glories and happiness of Europe, and her prosperity, it can certainly be said that we start at the bottom of her fortunes. Here is the fairest, most temperate, most fertile area of the globe. The influence and the power of Europe and of Christendom have for centuries shaped and dominated the course of history. The sons and daughters of Europe have gone forth and carried their message to every part of the world. Religion, law, learning, art, science, industry, throughout the world all bear, in so many lands, under every sky and in every clime, the stamp of European origin, or the trace of European influence.

But what is Europe now? It is a rubble-heap, a charnel-house, a breeding-ground of pestilence and hate. Ancient nationalistic feuds and modern ideological factions distract and infuriate the unhappy, hungry populations. Evil teachers urge the paying-off old scores with mathematical precision, and false guides point to unsparing retribution as the pathway to prosperity. Is there then to be no respite? Has Europe's mission come to an end? Has she nothing to give to the world but the contagion of the Black Death? Are her peoples to go on harrying and tormenting one another by war and vengeance until all that invests human life with dignity and comfort has been obliterated? Are the States of Europe to continue for ever to squander the first fruits of their toil upon the erection of new barriers, military fortifications and tariff walls and passport networks against one another? Are we Europeans to become incapable, with all our tropical and colonial dependencies, with all our long-created trading connections, with all that modern production and transportation can do, of even averting famine from the mass of our peoples? Are we all, through our poverty and our quarrels, for ever to be a burden and a danger to the rest of the world? Do we imagine that we can be carried forward indefinitely upon the shoulders—broad though they be—of the United States of America?

The time has come when these questions must be answered. This is the hour of choice and surely the choice is plain. If the people of Europe resolve to come together and work together for mutual advantage, to exchange blessings instead of curses, they still have it in their power to sweep away the horrors and miseries which surround them, and to allow the streams of freedom, happiness and abundance to begin again their healing flow. This is the supreme opportunity, and if it be cast away, no one can predict that it will ever return or what the resulting catastrophe will be.

In my experience of large enterprises, I have found it is often a mistake to try to settle everything at once. Far off, on the skyline, we can see the peaks of the Delectable Mountains. But we cannot tell what lies between us and them. We know where we want to go; but we cannot foresee all the stages of the journey, nor can we plan our marches as in a military operation. We are not acting in the field of force, but in the domain of opinion. We cannot give orders. We can only persuade. We must go forward, step by step, and I will therefore explain in general terms where we are and what are the first things we have to do. We have now at once to set on foot an organisation in Great Britain to promote the cause of United Europe, and to give this idea the prominence and vitality necessary for it to lay hold of the minds of our fellow countrymen, to such an extent that it will affect their actions and influence the course of national policy.

We accept without question the world supremacy of the United Nations Organisation. In the Constitution agreed at San Francisco direct provision was made for regional organisations to be formed. United Europe will form one major Regional entity. There is the United States with all its dependencies; there is the Soviet Union; there is the British Empire and Commonwealth; and there is Europe, with which Great Britain is profoundly blended. Here are the four main pillars of the world Temple of Peace. Let us make sure that they will all bear the weight which will be imposed and reposed upon them.

There are several important bodies which are working directly for the federation of the European States and for the creation of a Federal Constitution for Europe. I hope that may eventually be achieved. There is also the movement associated with Mr. Van Zeeland for the economic integration of Europe. With all these movements we have the most friendly relations. We shall all help each other all we can because we all go the same way home. It is not for us at this stage to attempt to define or prescribe the structure of constitutions. We ourselves are content, in the first instance, to present the idea of United Europe, in which our country will play a decisive part, as a moral, cultural and spiritual conception to which all can rally without being disturbed by divergencies about structure. It is for the responsible statesmen, who have the conduct of affairs in their hands and the power of executive action, to shape and fashion the structure. It is for us to lay the foundation, to create the atmosphere and give the driving impulsion.

First I turn to France. For 40 years I have marched with France. I have shared her joys and sufferings. I rejoice in her reviving national strength. I will never abandon this long comradeship. But we have a proposal to make to France which will give all Frenchmen a cause for serious thought and valiant decision. If European unity is to be made an effective reality before it is too late, the wholehearted efforts both of France and Britain will be needed from the outset. They must go forward hand in hand. They must in fact be founder-partners in this movement.

The central and almost the most serious problem which glares upon the Europe of to-day is the future of Germany. Without a solution of this problem, there can be no United Europe. Except within the framework and against the background of a United Europe this problem is incapable of solution. In a continent of divided national States, Germany and her hard-working people will not find the means or scope to employ their energies. Economic suffocation will inevitably turn their thoughts to revolt and to revenge. Germany will once again become a menace to her neighbours and to the whole world; and the fruits of victory and liberation will once more be cast away. But on the wider stage of a United Europe German industry and German genius would be able to find constructive and peaceful outlets. Instead of being a centre of poverty and a source of danger, the German people would be enabled to bring back prosperity in no small measure, not only to themselves, but to the whole continent.

Germany to-day lies prostrate, famishing among ruins. Obviously no initiative can be expected from her. It is for France and Britain to take the lead. Together they must, in a friendly manner, bring the German people back into the European circle. No one can say, and we need not attempt to forecast, the future constitution of Germany. Various individual German States are at present being recreated. There are the old States and Principalities of the Germany of former days to which the culture of the world owed much. But without prejudice to any future question of German federation, these individual States might well be invited to take their place in the Council of Europe. Thus, in looking back to happier days we should hope to mark the end of that long trail of hatred and retaliation which has already led us all, victors and vanquished alike, into the pit of squalor, slaughter and ruin. . . .

It will of course be asked: "What are the political and physical boundaries of the United Europe you are trying to create? Which countries will be in and which out?" It is not our task or wish to draw frontier lines, but rather to smoothe them away. Our aim is to bring about the unity of all nations of all Europe. We seek to exclude no State whose territory lies in Europe and which assures to its people those fundamental personal rights and liberties on which our democratic European civilisation has been created. Some countries will feel able to come into our circle sooner, and others later, according to the circumstances in which they are placed. But they can all be sure that whenever they are able to join, a place and a welcome will be waiting for them at the European Council table.

When I first began writing about the United States of Europe some 15 years ago, I wondered whether the U.S.A. would regard such a development as antagonistic to their interest, or even contrary to their safety. But all that has passed away. The whole movement of American opinion is favourable to the revival and re-creation of Europe. This is surely not unnatural when we remember how the manhood of the United States has twice in a lifetime been forced to re-cross the Atlantic Ocean and give their lives and shed their blood and pour out their treasure as the result of wars originating from ancient European feuds. One cannot be surprised that they would like to see a peaceful and united Europe taking its place among the foundations of the World Organisation to which they are devoted. I have no doubt that, far from encountering any opposition or prejudice from the Great Republic of the New World, our Movement will have their blessing and their aid.

We here in Great Britain have always to think of the British self-governing Dominions–Canada, Australia, New Zealand, South Africa. We are joined together by ties of free will and affection which have stood unyielding against all the ups and downs of fortune. We are the centre and summit of a world-wide commonwealth of nations. It is necessary that any policy this island may adopt towards Europe and in Europe should enjoy the full sympathy and approval of the peoples of the Dominions. But why should we suppose that they will not be with us in this cause? They feel with us that Britain is geographically and historically a part of Europe, and that they also have their inheritance in Europe. If Europe united is to be a living force, Britain will have to play her full part as a member of the European family. The Dominions also know that their youth, like that of the United States, has twice in living memory traversed the immense ocean spaces to fight and die in wars brought about by European discord in the prevention of which they have been powerless. We may be sure that the cause of United Europe, in which the mother country must be a prime mover, will in no way be contrary to the sentiments which join us all together with our Dominions in the august circle of the British Crown.

It is of course alleged that all advocacy of the ideal of United Europe is nothing but a manœuvre in the game of power politics, and that it is a sinister plot against Soviet Russia. There is no truth in this. The whole purpose of a united democratic Europe is to give decisive guarantees against aggression. Looking out from the ruins of some of their most famous cities and from amid the cruel devastation of their fairest lands, the Russian people should surely realise how much they stand to gain by the elimination of the causes of war and the fear of war on the European Continent. The creation of a healthy and contented Europe is the first and truest interest of the Soviet Union. We had therefore hoped that all sincere efforts to promote European agreement and stability would receive, as they deserve, the sympathy and support of Russia. Instead, alas, all this beneficent design has been denounced and viewed with suspicion by the propaganda of the Soviet Press and radio. We have made no retort and I do not propose to do so to-night. But neither could we accept the claim that the veto of a single power, however respected, should bar and prevent a movement necessary to the peace, amity and well-being of so many hundreds of millions of toiling and striving men and women.

And here I will invoke the interest of the broad, proletarian masses. We see before our eyes hundreds of millions of humble homes in Europe and in lands outside which have been affected by war. Are they never to have a chance to thrive and flourish? Is the honest, faithful, breadwinner never to be able to reap the fruits of his labour? Can he never bring up his children in health and joy and with the hopes of better days? Can he never be free from the fear of foreign invasion, the crash of the bomb or the shell, the tramp of the hostile patrol, or what is even worse, the knock upon his door of the political police to take the loved one far from the protection of law and justice, when all the time by one spontaneous effort of his will he could wake from all these nightmare horrors and stand forth in his manhood, free in the broad light of day? The conception of European unity already commands strong sympathy among the leading statesmen in almost all countries. "Europe must federate or perish," said the present Prime Minister, Mr. Attlee, before the late terrible war. He said that, and I have no reason to suppose that he will abandon that prescient declaration at a time when the vindication of his words is at hand. Of course we understand that until public opinion expresses itself more definitely, Governments hesitate to take positive action. It is for us to provide the proof of solid popular support, both here and abroad, which will give the Governments of Europe confidence to go forward and give practical effect to their beliefs. We cannot say how long it will be before this stage is reached. We ask, however, that in the meantime His Majesty's Government, together with other Governments, should approach the various pressing Continental problems from a European rather than from a restricted national angle. In the discussions on the German and Austrian peace settlements, and indeed throughout the whole diplomatic field the ultimate ideal should be held in view. Every new arrangement that is made should be designed in such a manner as to be capable of later being fitted into the pattern of a United Europe.

We do not of course pretend that United Europe provides the final and complete solution to all the problems of international relationships. The creation of an authoritative, all-powerful world order is the ultimate aim towards which we must strive. Unless some effective World Super-Government can be set up and brought quickly into action, the prospects for peace and human progress are dark and doubtful.

But let there be no mistake upon the main issue. Without a United Europe there is no sure prospect of world government. It is the urgent and indispensable step towards the realisation of that ideal. After the First Great War the League of Nations tried to build, without the aid of the U.S.A., an international order upon a weak, divided Europe. Its failure cost us dear.

To-day, after the Second World War, Europe is far weaker and still more distracted. One of the four main pillars of the Temple of Peace lies before us in shattered fragments. It must be assembled and reconstructed before there can be any real progress in building a spacious superstructure of our desires. If, during the next five years, it is found possible to build a world organisation of irresistible force and inviolable authority for the purpose of securing peace, there are no limits to the blessings which all men may enjoy and share. Nothing will help forward the building of that world organisation so much as unity and stability in a Europe that is conscious of her collective personality and resolved to assume her rightful part in guiding the unfolding destinies of man.

In the ordinary day-to-day affairs of life, men and women expect rewards for successful exertion, and this is often right and reasonable. But those who serve causes as majestic and high as ours need no reward; nor are our aims limited by the span of human life. If success come to us soon, we shall be happy. If our purpose is delayed, if we are confronted by obstacles and inertia, we may still be of good cheer, because in a cause, the righteousness of which will be proclaimed by the march of future events and the judgment of happier ages, we shall have done our duty, we shall have done our best.

BURMA INDEPENDENCE BILL
November 5, 1947

House of Commons

[Extract] . . . We on this side of the House have no power to prevent what the Government intend to do, but we have to consider what our own attitude must be on an occasion of his kind. I say that we can accept no responsibility for this Bill, and I do not think it should be settled merely on questions of oil companies or vested interests. It raises whole issues affecting the British Commonwealth of Nations and our actions must be based on Imperial and moral grounds. We accept no responsibility for this Bill. We wish to dissociate ourselves from the policy and the methods pursued by the Government. They must bear the burden and it falls with peculiar weight upon the Prime Minister himself. I interrupted him the other night and said that I did not mean to charge him with personal blood guilt. There is a difference. He individually is a humane man, but he is in the position of the signalman who has made a fatal mistake rather than that of the murderer who has placed an obstruction on the line. The responsibility rests upon him in a broad political manner, and I am bound to say I would be very sorry to go down to history bearing upon me the name and the burden which will rest on him. The Government must bear the burden.

Burma is a pendant of India and is likely to reproduce, though, of course, on a far smaller scale, the horrors and disasters which have overspread her great neighbour and which should ever haunt the consciences of the principal actors in this tragedy. All loyalties have been discarded and rebuffed; all faithful service has been forgotten and brushed aside. There is no assurance that the power of the new Government will be sufficient to maintain internal order, or, I might add, national independence against far larger and far more powerful neighbours. We stand on the threshold of another scene of misery and ruin, marking and illustrating the fearful retrogression of civilisation which the abandonment by Great Britain of her responsibilities in the East have brought and are bringing upon Asia and the world. I say this to the Government: You shall bear that burden. By your fruits you will be judged. We shall have no part or lot in it. We have not obstructed your policies or measures and they must now take their own course. We, at least, will not be compromised or disgraced by taking part in them, or denied the opportunity of pointing the moral to the British nation as and when occasion may occur. On those grounds we shall, at the close of the Debate, move the rejection of the Bill.

THE THREE CIRCLES–BRITISH FOREIGN POLICY

October 9, 1948

Annual Conservative Conference,
Llandudno, Wales

In the grim summer of 1948, with the cynical absorption of Czechoslovakia into the Soviet sphere of influence and the brazen threat to West Berlin, war seemed very close. In this major speech Churchill pledged full Conservative support to the Government and also intimated the philosophy of the "three circles"–the Atlantic Alliance, Western Europe, and the Commonwealth–which was to have a baleful impact on British attitudes toward Europe.

[Extract] . . . When I come to wider spheres, then the position of our country in the world has sunk to levels which no one could have predicted. Our minds are oppressed by the accounts of our relations with Soviet Russia, which we read every day in our restricted newspapers and in the speeches of one kind or another of Cabinet Ministers of one kind or another. We are confronted with the deadly enmity and continued aggression of the Russian Communist Government and its imprisoned satellites. No words which I could use could surpass the declarations of the Foreign Secretary, Mr. Bevin, or of Mr. McNeil, the Minister of State, and their words are only on a par with what is said by the leading responsible statesmen of America, of France, of our Dominions, and of all the smaller States of Europe who have spoken with great eloquence and are still free outside the Iron Curtain. In fact, what should be the majestic centre of world security and later on of world co-operation and finally of world government has been reduced to a mere cockpit in which the representatives of mighty nations and ancient States hurl reproaches, taunts and recrimination at one another, to marshal public opinion and inflame the passions of their peoples in order to arouse and prepare them for what seems to be a remorselessly approaching third world war. That is a sad disappointment to us. Bolshevik Russia is already heavily armed and her forces in Europe far exceed those of all the western countries put together. . . .

Whatever I may think of the unskilful manner in which our foreign affairs have been handled, I do not reproach the British Socialist Government with creating the abyss which now yawns across Europe and the world. This was inevitable once the Russian Communist leaders gave full rein to their instincts of Imperialism and expansion. Indeed I only wondered that it took the British and American peoples, in spite of all the lessons of the past, so long to realize the challenge to their life and freedom which was being opened upon them from the East.

I will not encourage you this afternoon with false hopes of a speedy friendly settlement with Soviet Russia. It may be that some formula will be found or some artificial compromise effected which will be hailed as a solution and deliverance. But the fundamental danger and antagonisms will still remain. The 14 men in the Kremlin, who rule nearly 300 million human beings with an arbitrary authority never possessed by any Czar since Ivan the Terrible, and who are now holding down nearly half Europe by Communist methods, these men dread the friendship of the free, civilized world as much as they would its hostility. If the Iron Curtain were lifted, if free intercourse, commercial and cultural, were allowed between the hundreds of millions of good-hearted human beings who dwell on either side, the power of this wicked oligarchy in Moscow would soon be undermined and the spell of their Communist doctrines broken. Therefore, for the sake of their own interests and for their skins, they cannot allow any intercourse or intermingling. Above all they fear and hate the genial influences of free and easy democratic life, such as we have gradually evolved for ourselves in varying forms throughout the Western World. These they know would be fatal, not only to their ideological theories and to their imperialistic appetite for domination but even more to their own dictorial power. Therefore, while patience should be practised to the utmost limits which our safety allows, we should not delude ourselves with the vain expectation of a change of heart in the ruling forces of Communist Russia.

Neither should we be under any delusion about the foundations of peace. It is my belief, and I say it with deep sorrow, that at the present time the only sure foundation of peace and of the prevention of actual war rests upon strength. If it were not for the stocks of atomic bombs now in the trusteeship of the United States there would be no means of stopping the subjugation of Western Europe by Communist machinations backed by Russian armies and enforced by political police. We have the example of Czechoslovakia before our eyes, where Stalin has perpetrated exactly the same act of aggression in 1948 as Hitler did when he marched into Prague in 1939 nine years ago. There seems to be no end to the sufferings of the Czechs. They are now writhing under a new degraded bondage as ruthless as and more subtle than any they have previously known. It is part of the established technique of the "cold war" the Soviets have begun against us all, that in any country which has fallen into their power, people of character and men of heart and personality outstanding in any walk of life, from the manual worker to the university professor, shall be what is called in their savage jargon "liquidated." All men, whatever their occupation, are to be reduced to a uniform and mediocre level so as to make it easy to govern them by commissars and masses of officials and police, all well-trained in the Communist colleges and dependent for their very existence upon the satisfaction they give their superiors in the party hierarchy. This is all set forth before our eyes as plainly as Hitler told us about his plans in his book *Mein Kampf.* I hope that the Western nations, and particularly our own country and the United States will not fall into the same kind of deadly trap twice over. Of one thing I am quite sure, that if the United States were to consent in reliance upon any paper agreement to destroy the stocks of atomic bombs which they have accumulated, they would be guilty of murdering human freedom and of committing suicide themselves.

I hope you will give full consideration to my words. I have not always been wrong. Nothing stands between Europe today and complete subjugation to Communist tyranny but the atomic bomb in American possession. If the Soviet Government wish to see atomic energy internationalized and its military use outlawed, it is not only by verbal or written agreements that they must reassure the world but by actions, which speak louder than words. Let them release their grip upon the satellite States of Europe. Let them retire to their own country, which is one-sixth of the land surface of the globe. Let them liberate by their departure the eleven ancient capitals of Eastern Europe which they now hold in their clutches. Let them go back to the Curzon Line as was agreed upon in the days when we were fighting as comrades together. Let them set free the million or more German and Japanese prisoners they now hold as slaves. Let them cease to oppress, torment, and exploit the immense part of Germany and Austria which is now in their hands. We read continually of the blockage of Berlin. The lifting of the blockade at Berlin would be merely the stopping of blackmail. There should be no reward for that. Let them cease to distract Malaya and Indonesia. Let them liberate the Communist-held portion of Korea. Let them cease to foment the hideous protracted civil war in China.

Above all, let them throw open their vast regions on equal terms to the ordinary travel and traffic of mankind. Let them give others the chance to breathe freely, and let them breathe freely themselves. No one wants to take anything they have got and that belongs to them away from them. After all, we are asking them to do no more than what the other victorious States have done of their own free will. None of the other allies has tried to add large territories and populations to its domain. Britain indeed has gone to the opposite extreme and cast away her Empire in the East with both her hands. Let the Russians be content to live on their own and cease to darken the world and prevent its recovery by these endless threats, intrigues and propaganda. When they have done this or even some of it and given these proofs of good faith, and given up what they had no right to take, which is all they are being asked, then indeed it will be time to raise the question of putting away the one vast, and I believe sure and overwhelming means of security which remains in the hands of the United States and which guards the progress of mankind.

It was my dream during the war years, when we were all united against the Hitler onslaught that after the war Russia, whatever her ideology, should become one of the three of four supreme factors in preserving peace; that she would receive all the honour which the valour, fortitude and patriotism of her armies had won; that she would help to bring about that Golden Age on which all our hearts are set, which would be possible but for the follies of men, and which President Roosevelt heralded with his declaration of the Four Freedoms. I hoped that Russia after the war would have access to unfrozen waters into every ocean, guaranteed by the world organization of which she would be a leading member; that she would have the freest access–which indeed she has at the present time–to raw materials of every kind, and that the Russians would be everywhere received as brothers in the human family. That still remains our aim and ideal. If it has not been attained, if on the contrary enormous barriers have been erected against it, it is the Soviet Government that has set them up and is fortifying them every day over even-larger areas. . . .

As I look out upon the future of our country in the changing scene of human destiny I feel the existence of three great circles among the free nations and democracies. I almost wish I had a blackboard. I would make a picture for you. I don't suppose it would get hung in the Royal Academy, but it would illustrate the point I am anxious for you to hold in your minds. The first circle for us is naturally the British Commonwealth and Empire, with all that that comprises. Then there is also the English-speaking world in which we, Canada, and the other British Dominions and the United States play so important a part. And finally there is United Europe. These three majestic circles are co-existent and if they are linked together there is no force or combination which could overthrow them or even challenge them. Now if you think of the three inter-linked circles you will see that we are the only country which has a great part in every one of them. We stand, in fact, at the very point of junction, and here in this Island at the centre of the seaways and perhaps of the airways also, we have the opportunity of joining them all together. If we rise to the occasion in the years that are to come it may be found that once again we hold the key to opening a safe and happy future to humanity, and will gain for ourselves gratitude and fame. . . .

THE NORTH ATLANTIC TREATY

May 12, 1949

House of Commons

The Russians ended the Berlin Blockade on May 5, 1949, but that experience played a major part in the creation of the North Atlantic Treaty Organization (N.A.T.O.).

[Extract] . . . The prime agent is the United States. I agree with what the Foreign Secretary said, that if the United States had acted in this way at an earlier period in their history they might well have averted the first world war, and could certainly, by sustaining the League of Nations from its birth, have warded off the second. The hope of mankind is that by their present valiant and self-sacrificing policy they will be the means of preventing a third world war. The future is, however, shrouded in obscurity.

As I have said on former occasions, we are dealing with absolutely incalculable factors in dealing with the present rulers of Russia. No one knows what action they will take, or to what internal pressures they will respond. He would be a bold, and, I think, an imprudent man who embarked upon detailed prophecies about what will be the future course of events. But it is absolutely certain that the strengthening by every means in our power of the growing ties which unite the signatories of the Atlantic Pact, of the Brussels Treaty, and the signatories of the Statute of the Council of Europe—on all of which there is overwhelming agreement in this House—is our surest guarantee of peace and safety. Now we must persevere faithfully and resolutely along these courses.

While I like the strong note which was struck by the Foreign Secretary in his speech this afternoon, we must persevere along these courses. It has been said that democracy suffers from the weakness of chopping and changing, that it can never pursue any course for any length of time, especially Parliamentary democracy. But I think that may prove to be a phase from which we are shaking ourselves free. At any rate, persistence at this time and a perseverance which is emphasized in the speech of the Foreign Secretary is, we on this side are quite certain, the safest course for us to follow and also the most right and honourable course for us to follow. It has been said that the Atlantic Pact and the European Union are purely defensive conceptions. The Foreign Secretary has claimed that they are not aggressive in any way. How could they be? When we consider the great disparity of military strength on the continent of Europe, no one can doubt that these measures are of a defensive and non-aggressive character. The military forces of the Soviet Union are at least three or four times as great as those which can be set against them on land. Besides this, they have their fifth column in many countries, waiting eagerly for the moment when they can play the quisling and pay off old scores against the rest of their fellow countrymen. Nothing that can be provided in the Atlantic Pact or the Western Union Agreement on land can make our position and policy other than purely defensive. It remains the first duty of all the signatory Powers to do their utmost to make Europe, and for us here to make Britain, self-supporting and independently secure. For this we must all labour. . . .

THE COUNCIL OF EUROPE

August 12, 1949

Open-Air Meeting,
Place Kleber,
Strasbourg

Take heed! I am going to speak in French.

In this ancient town, still marked by the wounds of war, we have gathered together to form an Assembly which, we hope, will be one day the Parliament of Europe. We have taken the first step and it is the first step which counts. This magnificent assemblage of the citizens of Strasbourg has been convened by the European Movement to show the world what force there is in the idea of United Europe, what power, not only in the minds of political thinkers, but in the hearts of the great common masses in all European countries where the people are free to express their opinion.

I feel encouraged, but I am astonished also, to see what remarkable results we have obtained in such a short time. It is not much more than a year since, at our Congress of The Hague, we demanded the creation of a European Assembly. We had to mobilize public opinion to persuade powerful governments to transform our requests into realities. We had to overcome serious misgivings.

But we had also, on our side, with us, many friends of this great cause of United Europe, and among them some friends who held ministerial power. None of these friends has done more for the European Movement than Mr. Spaak, who has been the longtime champion of a European Parliament and who, yesterday here in this city, was unanimously elected its first President.

We are reunited here, in this new Assembly, not as representatives of our several countries or various political parties, but as Europeans forging ahead, hand in hand, and if necessary elbow to elbow, to restore the former glories of Europe and to permit this illustrious continent to take its place once more, in a world organization, as an independent member sufficient unto itself.

That primary and sacred loyalty that one owes to one's own country is not difficult to reconcile with this larger feeling of European fellowship. On the contrary, we will establish that all legitimate interests are in harmony and that each one of us will best serve the real interests and security of his country if we enlarge at the same time both our sentiment of citizenship and of common sovereignty–if we include in this sentiment the entire continent of States and of nations who have the same way of life.

These principles which govern us are defined in the Constitution of the United Nations, of which Europe should be a vigorous and guiding element; these principles are also, in general terms, formulated in the Declaration of the Rights of Man proclaimed by the United Nations. Thus, not only will we find the road to the rebirth and to the prosperity of Europe, but at the same time we will protect ourselves against all risk of being trampled, of being crushed by whatever form of totalitarian tyranny, whether it be the hated domination of the Nazis, which we have swept away, or any and all other forms of despotism.

For my part, I am not the enemy of any race or any nation in the world. It is not against any race, it is not against any nation whatever that we are gathered. It is against tyranny in all its forms, ancient or modern, that we resolutely rise. Tyranny remains always the same, whatever its false promises, whatever name it adopts, whatever the disguises with which it clothes its servants.

But if we wish to win our supreme reward, we must cast aside all our obstacles and become masters of ourselves. We must elevate ourselves above those passions which have ravaged Europe and put her in ruins. We must have done with our old quarrels; we must renounce territorial ambitions; national rivalries must become a creative rivalry in all spheres where we can give the most genuine service to our common cause.

In addition, we should take all the steps and all the precautions necessary to be very sure that we will have the power and that we will have the time to realize this transformation of Europe in which the European Assembly (now in actual fact assembled at Strasbourg) has such a great role to play. It will only be able to play this role if it shows those qualities of good sense, of tolerance, of independence, and above all of courage, without which nothing great is done in this world.

And to finish, I ask the help of this vast gathering of the citizens of Strasbourg; you belong to the tremendous masses of men that we affirm to represent and whose rights and interests we have the duty to defend. There are, in Europe, on both sides of the iron curtain, millions of simple hearths where all hearts are with us. Will we never give them a chance to prosper and to thrive? Will they never live with security? Will they never be able to delight in the simple joys and freedoms that God and Nature have given them? Will the man who works honestly for his bread never be able to reap the fruits of his labour? Will he never be able to raise children in good health, happy, with the hope of better days?

Will he never be free of fear–fear of foreign invasion, fear of the bursting of bombs and shells, fear of the heavy step of the enemy patrol, and above all, and it is this that is the worst, fear of knocks pounded on the door by the political police, who come to abduct a father or a brother outside the normal protection of the Law and of Justice–whereas each day, by a single spontaneous effort of his will, this man, this European could awaken from this nightmare and rise free and virile in the great light of day?

In our long history we have triumphed over the dangers of religious wars and of dynastic wars; after thirty years of strife I am confident that we have come to the end of nationalist wars. After all our victories and all our sufferings, are we now going to sink into a final chaos, into ideological wars launched among us by barbaric and criminal oligarchies, prepared by the agitators of the fifth column who infiltrate and conspire in so many countries?

No, I am certain that it is in our power to pass through the dangers that are still ahead of us, if we so wish. Our hopes and our work are leading to a time of peace, of prosperity, of plenitude, where the inexhaustible richness and genius of Europe will make her once more the very source and inspiration of the life of the world. In all of this we are advancing with the support of the powerful Republic beyond the Atlantic and the sovereign states who are members of the Empire and the Commonwealth of British nations.

The dangers which threaten us are great, but great also is our strength and there is no reason to not succeed in realizing the goal and in establishing the structure of this United Europe whose moral concepts will be able to reap the respect and recognition of humanity, and whose physical strength will be such that no one will dare molest her on her tranquil march to the future.

[Translation by Ingrid Russell.]

"THE SHORT WORDS ARE THE BEST"

November 2, 1949

Receiving the London Times *Literary Award, Grosvenor House, London*

[Extract] . . . As an author, I can speak about the difficulties and dangers of writing a book. I have written a great many, and when I was 25 years old, I had, I believe, written as many books as Moses. I have almost kept up that pace since. Writing a book is an adventure. To begin with it is a toy, an amusement; then it becomes a mistress, and then a master, and then a tyrant; and then the last phase is that, just as one is about to be reconciled to one's servitude, one kills the monster.

It is of the utmost importance that every one should strive to devote some portion of every week to reading. We must refresh our minds. My advice to English people is to make sure they read the great books of the English language, and my advice to the young is not to begin to read them too soon. It is a great pity to read works of classical value hurriedly or at an immature period in one's development. Above all, schoolmasters should be careful not to set the reading of famous books as holiday tasks for their pupils. But everyone reaching manhood ought to master the great literature of his own country and, if possible, of another country too. It is a great advantage to be able to read in two languages. But some school curricula tries to teach four or five languages at once, which means that one gets a smattering of all and profit from none. The object of learning another language is to gain access to another literature.

English literature is a glorious inheritance which is open to all—there are no barriers, no coupons, and no restrictions. In the English language and in its great writers there are great riches and treasures, of which, of course, the Bible and Shakespeare stand alone on the highest platform. English literature is one of our greatest sources of inspiration and strength. The English language is the language of the English-speaking people, and no country, or combination or power so fertile and so vivid exists anywhere else on the surface of the globe. We must see that it is not damaged by modern slang, adaptations, or intrusions. We must endeavour to popularize and strengthen our language in every way. Broadly speaking, short words are best, and the old words, when short, are the best of all. Thus, being lovers of English, we will not only improve and preserve our literature, but also make ourselves a more intimate and effective member of the great English-speaking world, on which, if wisely guided, the future of mankind will largely rest.

THE MOMENT OF DECISION

February 17, 1950

Political Broadcast, London

Parliament had been dissolved in January 1950. In the course of the campaign Churchill had urged a summit conference with the Russians, a suggestion which was dismissed by Ministers as a "stunt."

[Extract] Nearly three weeks have passed, my friends, since I last spoke to you all, and we now approach the end of this momentous election which all the world has watched with anxious eyes. The moment of decision draws near, and all can vote freely. They can vote with the certainty that the ballot is secret, and that if they live in council houses, or are on the long waiting-lists to get a house, or even if they are State employees, they cannot be called to account for the way in which they use their vote any more than they can by the landlord or private employer. This we owe to the respect still shown to our slowly built up British constitution and British way of life. Long may it be preserved.

All the same, everyone is accountable to his or her conscience, and everyone has an honourable responsibility to give their vote according to what they believe will be best for our country at this difficult moment in its history. We are in fact at a turning point in our fortunes, and the result of your action on Thursday may well shape the whole structure of our island life for long years to come. As Mr. Gladstone said on a famous occasion: 'Think well, think wisely, think not for the moment, but for the years that are to come, before you make your choice.' Above all, do not abstain; do not stand out of the fight through indolence or hesitation or throw your votes away on candidates who have no chance of becoming Members of Parliament.

Since the election fight began, the issues at stake have become more serious. This is due to the statements about ultimate aims in Socialism by the Prime Minister and the Chancellor of the Exchequer, with all their high authority. Mr. Attlee has made it clear that he does not regard the Socialist election manifesto—except, I presume, in the coming Parliament—as setting any limit to his aims. 'Socialism does not stop,' he said. 'It goes on. Nothing can stand between a nation and its goal—no one.' Here then is the proclamation by the Prime Minister of his resolve to create the complete Socialist State as soon as he can, by the nationalization of all the means of production, distribution and exchange—that is to say, the creation of a monster State monopoly, owning everything and employing everybody. Here is the goal towards which Mr. Attlee seeks to lead the British nation. In fact, however, I doubt very much whether even a fifth part of our people are convinced Socialists, or that they realize the sacrifice of personal liberty, both economic and political, which must inexorably follow from the concentration of all industry and the direction of labour in the hands of the State.

The Chancellor of the Exchequer has not lagged behind his chief; for at Bristol on Saturday last he used words which reveal his mind and purpose. This is what he said, and when challenged he has not withdrawn, about sharing out the national resources: 'We have not shared them out equally yet. It takes a bit of time to do these things.' That is what he said. These are indeed grave words. They imply a levelling down of British society to a degree not hitherto presented by any responsible person. There would of course be the governmental and political and official class lifted, as in Soviet Russia, into a privileged position above the mass of the people whose lives they direct and plan. But on the basis of 'equal shares for all' there would it seems to me be little consideration for what Mr. Arthur Deakin, the General Secretary of our largest trade union, has aptly called the 'differentials' in industry, and for all the infinite variations in the human contribution. This confession of the Chancellor of the Exchequer's inner purpose spells the death-blow, so long as he remains at the Treasury, to the great savings movement which at his request we have all supported. He is of course angry with me for giving world-wide publicity to his own imprudent and baleful words. His rival, Mr. Aneurin Bevan, during this election has at least given us this reassurance: 'It is not part of our programme,' he said, 'this time that all private enterprise should be destroyed.' Thank you so much. . . .

Now you will have to say on Thursday whether we are to plunge deeper into the thickets and briars of Socialist regulations and controls, or whether, by a resolute effort, we shall rejoin our friends and comrade nations on the high-road of ordered freedom and progress. By one heave of her shoulders Britain can shake herself free. Do not miss this opportunity. It may not return. I am reminded of the tale of the prisoner in the Spanish dungeon. For years he longed to escape from his bondage. He tried this, he tried that–all in vain. One day he pushed the door of his cell–it was open. It had always been open. He walked out free into the broad light of day. You can do that now on this very Thursday, and what a throng there will be to welcome us back in the forefront of the nations who now regard us with bewilderment and pity, but for whom only a few years ago we kept the flag of freedom flying amid all the winds that blew....

I have now dealt with the great choice we have to make in our domestic affairs. I have once again contradicted the falsehoods by which we are assailed. But I cannot end my message and appeal to you (as you sit in your homes searching your hearts and minds, I hope, and wondering who is telling you the truth, I daresay, and what it is best to do for our dear land)–I cannot end my message without looking beyond our island coasts to the terrible and tremendous world that has grown up around us in this twentieth century of shock and strife. At Edinburgh the other night I said: 'I cannot help coming back to this idea of another talk with Soviet Russia upon the highest level. The idea appeals to me of a supreme effort to bridge the gulf between the two worlds so that each can live their lives, if not in friendship at least without the hatreds of the cold war. At least I feel,' I said, 'that Christian men and women should not close the door upon any hope of finding a new foundation for the life of the self-tormented human race.'

Mr. Bevin, the Secretary of State for Foreign Affairs, dismissed all this by the scornful word 'stunt.' By this he only showed how far his mind dwells below the true level of events. Why should it be wrong for the British nation to think about these supreme questions of life and death, perhaps for the whole world, at a time when there is a general election? Is not that the one time of all others when they should think about them? What a reflection it would be upon our national dignity and moral elevation, and indeed upon the whole status of British democracy, if at this time of choice, this turning point in world history, we found nothing to talk about but material issues and nice calculations about personal gain or loss! What a humiliation it would be if proud Britain, in this fateful hour, were found completely absorbed in party and domestic strife! I am glad I put a stop to all that.

Even on the material basis a continuance of the present arms race can only cause increasing danger, increasing military expense and diminishing supplies to the homes. The only time when the people really have a chance to influence and in fact decide events is at a general election. Why should they be restricted to the vote-catching or vote-snatching game? Why should they be told that it is a 'stunt' or 'soapbox diplomacy' to speak to them of the great world issues upon which our survival and salvation may well depend?

Mr. Bevin says that everything must be reserved to the United Nations. We all support the great ideal of world government; but the United Nations cannot function while it is rent asunder by the conflicting forces of the two worlds which are ranged against each other. It is only by the agreement of the greatest Powers that security can be given to ordinary folk against an annihilating war with atomic or hydrogen bombs or bacteriological horrors. I cannot find it in my heart and conscience to close the door upon that hope. By its fruition alone can the United Nations discharge their supreme function.

My friends, I ask for a strong majority, for one capable of giving both guidance and design and securing the necessary time to make great purposes effective. We do not seek the power to enable one party to ride rough-shod over the other, we do not seek the power in order that special interests or classes should have privileges or unearned increment and profit. This will be the supreme opportunity for the Conservative and National Liberal Parties to prove that they stand high above the level of mere sectional appetites. Should we become responsible we shall govern on behalf of the entire British people no matter to what party or class or part of the country they belong. We shall respect the sentiments of minorities in what is just and fair no matter whether they vote for or against us. This is the true essence of democracy. It is only by inspiring the nation with unity and common purpose and by taking without fear or favour the necessary measures to restore our solvency and independence that we shall overcome the dangers and solve the problems that confront us.

Of course, I am—as I am reminded—an old man. It is true that all the day-dreams of my youth have been accomplished. I have no personal advantage to gain by undertaking once more the hard and grim duty of leading Britain and her Empire through and out of her new and formidable crisis. But while God gives me the strength, and the people show me their good will, it is my duty to try, and try I will. I do not know tonight the full extent of the harm which has been done to our finances, to our defences and to our standing in the world. I am grieved at what I see and hear but it may well be there are worse facts, not made public, and perhaps not even understood by our present rulers. Therefore we are not going to promise you smooth and easy times. What we promise is, that, laying aside every impediment, we will faithfully and resolutely carry forward the policy we have proclaimed, we will do our best for all, and build on a sure foundation the structures of British greatness and world peace. Goodnight to you all. Think—and act!

DEBATE ON THE ADDRESS

March 7, 1950

House of Commons

The 1950 General Election was virtually a tie, Labour receiving a 19-seat majority over the Conservatives, but an overall majority of only 7. Labour held 315 seats, the Conservatives 296, Liberals 10, and others 2.

This was a bitter disappointment for the Conservatives, who had confidently expected a Parliamentary majority—however small—over Labour. The fact that the overwhelming Labour majority of 1945 had been almost eliminated was small consolation, and there was strong–although carefully hidden–criticism of Churchill for his deficiencies as a Leader of the Opposition and as party leader in the election. Churchill was not unaware of these sentiments.

[Extract] I must frankly confess, as I look around, that I like the appearance of these Benches better than what we had to look at during the last 4½ years. It is certainly refreshing to feel, at any rate, that this is a Parliament where half the nation will not be able to ride rough-shod over the other half, or to sweep away in a Session what has been carefully and skilfully constructed by generations of thought, toil and thrift. I do not see the Attorney-General [Sir Hartley Shawcross] in his place, but no one will be able to boast 'We are the masters now.' On the contrary, if it be not presumptuous for me to say so, we are equals. So far as the Conservative and Socialist parties are concerned, we seem to have reached in the electoral field that position–if I may listen to the echoes of the election–of equal shares for both. I will not say equal shares for all, for we certainly have not achieved even fair shares for all. . . .

The two sides of the House face each other deeply divided by ideological differences. I have lived through many of the fierce quarrels of the past, about Irish Home Rule, about church or chapel, about free trade and protection, which all seemed to be very important at the time. They were, however, none of them, fundamental to our whole system of life and society. Those who believe in the creation of a Socialist State controlling all the means of production, distribution and exchange, and are working towards such a goal, are separated from those who seek to exalt the individual and allow freedom of enterprise under well-known laws and safeguards–they are separated by a wider and deeper gulf than I have ever seen before in our island.

This was, in my view, the moral and intellectual issue which was at stake in the election, and which a substantial Socialist majority, if obtained, would in four or five years have carried, in all probability, to irrevocable depths. It is a significant and serious fact which should not escape the attention of thoughtful men that the differences which separate us have become more pronounced by the voting, because each of the main parties has very often increased its strength in those very parts of the country where it was already the stronger. We shall certainly not survive by splitting into two nations. Yet that is the road we are travelling now, and there is no sign of our reaching or even approaching our journey's end.

The basic fact before us is that the electors by a majority of 1,750,000 have voted against the advance to a Socialist State, and, in particular, against the nationalization of steel and other industries which were threatened. The Government, therefore, have no mandate, as is recognized in the Gracious Speech, to proceed in this Parliament with their main policy. The Prime Minister is the only Socialist Prime Minister in the English-speaking world–the only one; and he has behind him a majority of only seven–or it soon may be only six. Nevertheless, he continues not only to persevere upon his path, but to state the differences which separate him and his followers from the rest of us all over the world in the most extreme terms.

The right hon gentleman complained during the election that I quoted his interview with an American journalist, which he had not disavowed for some time after it was published and which was much commented on. In fact I saw only the comments and then searched for the actual text. I will meet the right hon Gentleman. I promise him that I will quote that interview no more. I do not need to quote it any more because in his letter to his candidate at Moss Side he has proclaimed his faith and policy beyond the slightest doubt and in the most sweeping terms. He wrote on 2 March:

> Labour stands for the policy of equal shares, and for the ordered and progressive realization of a society based on social justice.

The last part covers both sides of the House. But this 'equal shares' declaration goes even further than the speeches of the Chancellor of the Exchequer in his election campaign at Bristol, when he spoke of 'fair shares for all' being only a preliminary step to 'equal shares for all.' It is at least an advantage that the differences between us should be stated so plainly, because there can be no excuse for anyone making a mistake about them afterwards.

The *Tribune,* which is believed to express the views of the Minister of Health, fully supports the Prime Minister's pronouncement. I quote from its latest issue of 3 March:

> It is the faith of Socialism carried across this land with a new crusading zeal which can win the second election in 1950. And once that fact is securely grasped, how futile becomes the talk of compromise and manoeuvre in the House of Commons, which must continue until the new appeal to the country takes place.

The Prime Minister has accepted the burden of government in virtue of his majority of seven; and no one doubts that it was his right and his duty to do so. But we on this side feel that he, and those whom he leads or with whom he goes, have inflicted deep injury upon our country in years when our task of recovery was heavy enough, and we are sure that the course he now proclaims has only to be followed far enough to lead to our economic ruin, and to our inability to maintain 50,000,000 people in this island, still less to maintain them on their present standards of living, such as they are. We are therefore bound to confront him and those who follow him with our united and resolute resistance, and we believe that this is the first duty which we owe to our country, to the British Commonwealth of Nations, to Western Europe and to the English-speaking world.

A CONSERVATIVE-LIBERAL ALLIANCE?

May 18, 1950

Usher Hall, Edinburgh

In this speech Churchill extended the offer of an alliance with the Liberals against Labour which was to result in a compact whereby either gave the other a clear run against Labour in certain constituencies. Churchill also dealt with the proposed Schuman Plan, which was to be the precursor of the European Economic Community (the "Common Market") from which Britain, tragically, remained aloof.

[Extract] I think I must regard this as a red-letter day. This afternoon I am victor in the Paradise Stakes. [Editor's Note: Churchill's racehorses were at this stage enjoying a certain success.] This evening I have the honour once again to address a great audience in the Usher Hall. When I was here last we had good hopes of bringing about an immediate and decisive change in the politics of our country and of establishing in effective power a Unionist and Conservative Government which would prove itself worthy of its trust and equal to these difficult and dangerous times. Now we see that in spite of the substantial advantages we gained, a second intense effort will be necessary. It is certain that another General Election must come soon. How soon we cannot tell. The initiative does not at present rest with us. It depends upon what the Socialist Government think will pay them best. Meanwhile we lie in the lull between two storms. The only Socialist Government in the English-speaking world and, apart from Scandinavia, the only Socialist Government in Europe outside the Iron Curtain, continues its control of our affairs, although in a minority of more than 1,500,000 votes in the country and with a majority of only seven in the House of Commons. . . .

While we put forth every scrap of strength we can command, we should also endeavour to gather the support of all men and women of goodwill outside our own party limits. We should endeavour to unite in the common front against Socialism, not only Liberals, but the large floating vote, which played such a hesitating part last time in the trial of strength. For this purpose I should like to see an honourable understanding reached with the Liberals as a party, or where that is not possible, with individuals. This is a moment when we have a right to appeal to all patriotic and broadminded men and women who are in agreement on the main issues to do their utmost to secure the establishment of a strong, broadly-based, and stable Government capable of dealing in a courageous and progressive spirit with the ever-darkening problems that confront us. You read in the newspapers about negotiations. There are no negotiations. You read about party deals in seats. There are no party deals in seats. The Conservative and Unionist Parties have not the power to override and do not seek the power to override the decided will of constituency associations. Still, I feel this is the time when those who agree on fundamental issues should stand together. Let me mention to you some of the great issues on which Unionists and

Liberals are agreed, and which constitute the elements of the common cause vital to our national welfare.

First, we proclaim that the State is the servant and not the master of the people. We reject altogether the Socialist conception of a division of society between officials and the common mass. We repudiate their policy of levelling down to a minimum uniformity, above which only politicians and their agents may rise. We stand for the increasingly higher expression of individual independence. We hold most strongly to the Declaration of Human Rights, as set forth by the United Nations at Geneva. It is worth noting that among all these United Nations we are the only great Power under Socialist rule. That is why Socialist policy has been in these past years increasingly out of step and out of harmony with, or lagging behind, the movement of thought among the democracies of the modern world.

Then we declare ourselves inveterately opposed to any further nationalization of industry, including, of course, and especially, the nationalization of steel. Further, we come to those large bodies of practical, domestic reforms set forth in *This is the Road,* and, from a very slightly different angle, and, with several interesting features, set forth in the Liberal manifesto. No doubt there are other points upon which Liberals and Unionists do not agree. But how small they are in scale and importance compared to the great body of fundamental principles and practical schemes of application on which both anti-Socialist Parties are in accord and which are supported by a large majority of electors all over the country.

There is a great overlap of agreement, both in doctrine and in action, between those who have hitherto been brought up to regard themselves as political opponents. But now the times are very grave, and it is the duty of every man and woman who agrees upon so large a proportion of the main principles and practical steps, to make sure that these are not overwhelmed by the ignorant and obsolete fallacy of Socialism, against which the British nation stands today in marked recoil. All I ask, and as your leader I have a right to ask, and it is a modest demand, is that those who agree upon the fundamentals shall, in our party conflicts, try to help each other as much as they can, and to harm each other as little as they must. Let that climate of opinion and theme of conduct prevail, and we shall have cleared the path of progress of many of its pitfalls and barriers, and perhaps gain the power to rescue our native land from some of the perils and forms of degeneration to which it is exposed.

There is no doubt that nationalization, so far as it has gone, has proved an utter failure financially, economically and morally. But there is now an argument against it which undoubtedly makes an impression upon the Socialist leaders—it is evidently politically unpopular. Therefore there is to be a conference this weekend at Dorking to see whether they can think of something else. They do not know whether to bury Socialism and nationalization, which they have been preaching for fifty years and practising for five, and look for some other method of carrying on the class war. In any case, we are confronted with a party which has lost its convictions and has no longer a theme and plan and which, instead of proclaiming an ideological design for the reconstruction of human society, is now hungrily looking around for a new election cry.

I see that some of the newspapers say the whole seventy of them at Dorking are to be *locked up* together. That I think would be going too far. After all we are still a free country. Besides Dorking is much too close to my home at Chartwell. I might have to go and feed them through the bars. If they ran short of coupons I might be put in among them. Then I should be told I was trying to form a coalition by backstage methods. It would never do. . . .

In all these five years we have supported the Government on the broad lines of foreign policy. It was, and still is, easy for us to do so, because that policy has followed, although tardily, the path we have pointed and prescribed. For more than forty years I have worked with France. At Zurich I appealed to her to regain the leadership of Europe by extending her hand to bring Germany back into the European family. We have now the proposal which M. Schuman, the French Foreign Minister, has made for the integration of French and German coal and steel industries. This would be an important and effective step in preventing another war between France and Germany and lay at last to rest that quarrel of 1,000 years between Gaul and Teuton. Now France has taken the initiative in a manner forward rather than back. For centuries France and England, and latterly Germany and France, have rent the world by their struggles. They have only to be united together to constitute the dominant force in the Old World and to become the centre of United Europe around which all other countries could rally. But added to this you have all the mighty approval of the great world power which has arisen across the Atlantic, and has shown itself in its hour of supremacy anxious only to make further sacrifices for the cause of freedom.

While therefore this Schuman proposal is right in principle we must consider with proper attention the way in which Great Britain can participate most effectively in such a larger grouping of European industry. We must be careful that it does not carry with it a lowering of British wages and standards of life and labour. We must I feel assert the principle of levelling up and not of levelling down. We are all surely proud of the British steel industry which plays so large a part in our export trade. The terms on which we could combine with Continental nations must be carefully and searchingly studied. If we were to destroy or even impair the efficiency of our steel industry by nationalization, we might find ourselves at a serious disadvantage compared to Continental countries which are free from Socialist abuses. We must be reassured on these and other points while welcoming cordially the whole principle and spirit of what is proposed. At present no detailed information has been published and the Government themselves were taken by surprise. I have therefore assented to Mr. Attlee's request that the debate upon this matter should be postponed until after the Whitsuntide holidays, by which time we should all know more than we do now. Great events are happening. They happen from day to day, and headlines are never lacking. But we must not allow the ceaseless clack and clatter which is the characteristic of our age to turn our minds from these great events. I still hope that the unities now being established among all the Western democracies and Atlantic Powers will ward off from us the terrors and unspeakable miseries of a third world war. I wish also that every effort should be made on the highest level to bring home to the Russian Soviet Government the gravity of the facts which confront us all. I do not give up the hope which I expressed to you here on this very spot three months ago, of 'a supreme effort to bridge the gulf between the two worlds, if not in friendship, at least without the hatreds and manoeuvres of the cold war.' I have not abandoned that hope. But of this I am sure: that the best hopes will be founded upon the strength of the Western democracies and upon their unwavering willpower to defend the causes for which they stand. To work from weakness and fear is ruin. To work from wisdom and power may be salvation. These simple but tremendous facts are I feel being understood by the free nations better than they have ever been before.

I believe that the faithful discharge of our national duty by everyone of us laying aside all impediments, all prejudices, all temptation, will give the Unionist Party a chance of rendering true service to Britain, its Empire and the world.

KOREA

July 5, 1950

House of Commons

Heavy fighting broke out on June 25 on the borders of North and South Korea. The United States came to the aid of South Korea on June 29, two days after the U.N. Security Council had authorized international assistance to the Republic. The British Government fully supported these actions and offered military aid.

[Extract] ... We consider that the Government were right to place a Motion on the Order Paper asking for approval in general terms of the course which they have adopted since the invasion of South Korea began. There are grave reasons, as we learned in the war, that false impressions may be created abroad by a Debate prominantly occupied by a handful of dissentients. It is better to have a Division so that everyone can know how the House of Commons stands and in what proportion. Should such a Division occur, we on this side will vote with the Government. I do not propose to embark upon a detailed argument about the merits of questions which have been raised by events in Korea, nor upon the decision reached by the Security Council and the United Nations. They have been ventilated in the Press and have just now been clearly explained to us by the Prime Minister. I do not believe that Soviet and Communist propaganda, with its perverted facts and inverted terminology, has made the slightest impression upon the well-tried common sense of the British people. No one outside the small Communist circles in this island or their fellow-travellers believes for an instant that it is South Korea which is the aggressor and North Korea which is the victim of a well and deliberately-planned and organized attack. On the contrary, the very unpreparedness and inefficiency of South Korea is the proof of their innocence, though not, perhaps of their wisdom. . . .

THE KOREAN WAR

July 15, 1950

Saltram Park, Plymouth

[Extract] . . . Armed conflict has broken out between the United Nations, comprising almost all the free peoples of the world, and the Russian organized and well-equipped Communists of Northern Korea. The United States are bearing with courage and resolution in a noble way the burden of this clash which is in all essentials a renewal of our fight for human freedom against Hitler. I do not say that what has happened and is happening in Korea has made the dangers of a third world war greater. They were already grave. It has brought them nearer, and they are more apparent and I trust indeed that it has made the great masses of peoples throughout the free world more aware, awake and alive to where they stand.

I have myself for some time past believed that the worst chance for the life of the free world was to continue a policy of drift. At least three precious years of the United Nations have been wasted in floating along from day to day hoping, in spite of ceaseless disappointments and warnings, that all would come out right if we hoped for the best and let things take their course. But meanwhile the Communist menace and aggression continues to spread throughout the world. The fourteen men in the Kremlin are not drifting with events. They work on calculation and design. They have a policy the aim of which we can see; but the execution and timing of their ambition for Communist world government we cannot predict. They infiltrate in all countries with adepts and agents. Their adherents have no loyalty to any home. They care nothing for their native lands. They owe allegiance solely to Moscow. Communism is a religion with all its discipline and some of its fervour—a religion not only without God, but anti-God. It is a philosophy of base materialism in the name of which the world is to be reduced to the Soviet-Socialist pattern just as Hitler wanted it reduced to the Nazi-Socialist pattern. They have condemned Christian ethics and civilization, as we have known them, to a formidable struggle.

But behind all this doctrinal and ideological movement of thought which might well be defeated, and is indeed being defeated by the free play of Parliamentary democracy in countries where this is allowed, lies the mighty Russian armed power. The Communists pay lip-service to the doctrine of peace, but by peace they mean submission to their will and system. They preach the reduction of armaments, but they have more men organized and trained under arms than all the rest of the world put together. They urge the banning of the atomic bomb which in the hands of the United States is at this moment the only physical shield and protection of the free world, while they themselves have rejected any bona fide international control and inspection, and are trying to make bombs as fast as they can. Meanwhile around all the vast frontiers of Soviet Russia and her satellite or conquered countries they maintain a policy of unending aggression or menace. Since the war nearly all China with its hundreds of millions of people has been incorporated in the Soviet system. They are massing troops against Tibet. They threaten Persia. They are seeking to overawe and quell Yugoslavia. They cause deep fear in Finland and Sweden.

President Truman, under the full sanction and authority of the United Nations, and with the overwhelming support of the American people, and of the British Empire, and of its Commonwealth, has confronted aggression in Korea. I have not the knowledge to enable me to predict how this Korean fighting will end. But let me here express our admiration for the daring and skill with which the handful of American soldiers, three or four battalions at most, who have as yet been brought into action in Korea have fought their delaying action against overwhelming odds. I rejoice to learn that so far they have suffered only a few hundred casualties. Now, however, a more serious collision impends, or has begun. But whatever happens in Korea is only a part, and a small part of the pressures under which our free civilization lies, and which it must face or perish. . . .

To work from weakness and fear is ruin. To work from wisdom and power may be salvation. These simple but tremendous facts are, I feel, being understood by the free nations better than they have ever been before. I believe, moreover, that the faithful discharge of our national duty by everyone of us laying aside all impediments will give the Conservative Party a chance of rendering true service to Britain, its Empire and the world. In this there lies before us an opportunity such as the centuries do not often bring.

HOUSING THE PEOPLE

October 14, 1950

Conservative Annual Conference,
Blackpool

At the Annual Conference a proposal to commit the Conservative Government to building 300,000 new houses a year was passed overwhelmingly, to the dismay of many Party notables. This goal was actually exceeded and was a major element in the subsequent political rise of Harold Macmillan.

[Extract] . . . I have been impressed and encouraged by what I was told of the gust of passion which swept through our body yesterday about the shameful failure of the Socialist housing policy. Without the struggles imposed by extreme need, without the spur of seeing bomb-shattered sites, the Tory Government before the war was building 350,000 houses a year. We were doing this mainly by private enterprise and with comparatively few subsidies. Moreover, under the slum clearance campaign begun in 1933, 1,500,000 slum dwellers have been rehoused in England and Wales. In the last year before the war slum dwellers were moving into better houses at a rate of 1,000 people a day. If the war had not brought the Conservatives' programme to a stop, England would today be free from slumdom. The Socialist Government have been us all 'vermin,' you can remember his name for yourself and the name he called you after five years of power in time of peace, can only build us 200,000 houses at triple the expense and with enormous subsidies. I do not wonder at your anger. We share it with you. I agree with you that housing comes first in the whole field of social progress.

Well was it said of old: 'The foxes have holes; the birds of the air have nests, but the Son of Man hath nowhere to lay his head.' It is strange that this task of housing should have been deemed and found insuperable by those who have the handling of our affairs. For there is no object except self-preservation which could enlist behind it a greater drive of British ingenuity and effort.

You have demanded that the target that we should put in our programme should be 300,000 a year. I accept it as our first priority in time of peace. I and the Government of which I was head are the authors of all that is real and effective in the Health Act. We took all the decisions and had the plans worked out in great detail, but it seems to me that houses and homes come even before the reform of the health system, etc. Houses and homes come before health, because overcrowding and slum dwellings are fatal to the family life and breed more illnesses than the doctors can cure. It may well be that hard times lie before us, and that the opportunities for making a better Britain, which these foolish Ministers have squandered for party purposes, will not be open to those who take their places when the nation records its final verdict. No one can tell how the rearmament burden may strike our industry and finances, but this I am sure, that homes for people to live in and rear their families in in decent independence come ever in front of wigs, spectacles and false teeth, however desirable all these may be and however urgent it is to press forward with meeting the public requirements in every respect. However, our fortunes may go and from whatever angle the pressures of life may come, the Tory Party puts homes for the people in the very forefront of all schemes of our development.

We are ready for an election whenever it may come. Thanks to Lord Woolton's energy and inspiration, we now have a national organization second to none. It has achieved results far above the expectations which any of us had when the National Union last met in conference at Blackpool four years ago. Also I have the aid of colleagues whose ability has been proved in war and peace. In Mr. Eden I have a friend and helper upon whom any office of the State, however great, could be devolved with the assurance that he has both given the proof and acquired the experience to do full justice to it.

In February's election we added nearly 3,000,000 to our poll, and 100 members to our Parliamentary representation. Now we need just one more heave. If all of us make the best use of whatever time and strength we may have, we may well fling this Socialist Government out of power and replace it by a broad, progressive and tolerant administration, the slave neither of class nor of dogma but putting national need first and determined to make Britain and the British Empire once again both great and free.

THE INTERNATIONAL SITUATION

December 14, 1950

House of Commons

Although the Korean War situation had dramatically changed after General MacArthur's counter-stroke at Inchon, Labour Party unease became so intense that Attlee, somewhat reluctantly, had flown to Washington to seek assurances that the United States would not use atomic weapons. Churchill consistently described the Korean War as a "diversion," and he was concerned by the possibility of United Nations involvement with China, as this speech demonstrates.

[Extract] . . . The Prime Minister's visit to Washington has done nothing but good. The question we all have to consider this afternoon in the House of Commons is, how much good. The Prime Minister spoke of the importance of renewing the series of meetings between the President and the Prime Minister which had taken place during the war and since the war. We all agree with that. We all agree with the advantages of direct discussion to which the Prime Minister has just referred. I must say it seems to me that five years is rather a long interval, and the decision when it came was very suddenly taken. My right hon. Friend the Member for Warwick and Leamington [Mr. Eden] spoke on 29 November and urged that we should have stronger representation at Washington at the highest level. I endorsed this when I spoke the next day. I did not wish to appear to reflect any more than he did in the slightest degree upon our excellent Ambassador in Washington, and I used the particular phrase 'Ministerial representation.' That very evening we were told that the Prime Minister was going. During the afternoon there was some excitement caused in the House by the accounts of Mr. Truman's interview with the Press which appeared on the tape. But I understand that this was not the reason that led to the Prime Minister's decision to go and that this was taken earlier in the day. Certainly the decision was very hastily arrived at after an interval of five years. . . .

The months slip quickly away all the time. Several years have already been wasted, frittered away. The overwhelming Russian military power towers up against us, committees are multiplied, papers are written, words are outpoured and one declaration succeeds another, but nothing in the slightest degree in proportion to the scale of events or to their urgency has been done. When we return after our anxious Recess we shall require a full and prolonged debate upon defence, and we shall demand that a portion of it shall be in secret. It was with the danger of Europe in my mind that I said some weeks ago that I hoped that we should not get entangled in China. In order to protect myself from the charge of being wise after the event, I venture to remind the House that on 16 November, before these recent reverses in Korea had taken place, I asked the Minister of Defence a supplementary question, which I do not think he resented in any way:

> . . . whether he and the Foreign Secretary will constantly bear in mind the great importance of our not becoming, and of our Allies so far as we can influence their actions not becoming, too much pinned down in China or in the approaches to China at a time when the danger in Europe is . . . occupying all our minds?

I need scarcely say that I hold to that conviction still.

In view, however, of what has happened since then in Korea, and in the United Nations Assembly, I feel it requires to be stated witn more precision and refinement. We must not at any time be drawn into urging a policy which would inflict dishonour or humiliation upon the United States or upon the United Nations. Such a course would be at least as full of danger as any other now open to us. We learn from the newspapers that the proposals for a truce or cease fire which were proposed by the thirteen Asiatic and Arab States, have been opposed by the Soviet delegation. They certainly seemed to be very far-reaching proposals from our point of view.

I will not say more about them, but, while the fullest priority should be given to the defence of Western Europe, it would be a great mistake to lose our sense of proportion and cast everything to the winds elsewhere. The only prudent course open to the United States and ourselves is to stabilize the local military position and, if the opportunity then occurs, to negotiate with the aggressors and at least make sure that we negotiate from strength and not from weakness. We shall no doubt hear from the Foreign Secretary tonight how the question of further conversations with Soviet Russia stands. There was, I think, fairly complete agreement in the House that no abrupt negative or merely dilatory action would be appropriate to the Russian request, and from what we have read in the newspapers it does not seem likely that there will be any serious disagreement between us upon the procedure eventually to be adopted.

I am strongly in favour of every effort being made by every means, to secure a fair and reasonable settlement with Russia. I should, however, be failing in frankness to the House, and to some of those who agree with me upon this matter, to whom I am much opposed in many ways, if I did not make it clear at this stage that we must not place undue hopes upon the success of any negotiations which may be undertaken. It is our duty—and a duty which we owe to the cause of peace and to our own consciences—to leave no effort unmade that wisdom and fair play can suggest, and that patience can bring forward. But on this side of the House we have never contemplated that if negotiations failed we should abandon any of the great causes for which we have stood in the past, and for which the United Nations Organization stands today.

The declaration of the Prime Minister that there will be no appeasement also commands almost universal support. It is a good slogan for the country. It seems to me, however, that in this House it requires to be more precisely defined. What we really mean, I think, is no appeasement through weakness or fear. Appeasement in itself may be good or bad according to the circumstances. Appeasement from weakness and fear is alike futile and fatal. Appeasement from strength is magnanimous and noble and might be the surest and perhaps the only path to world peace. When nations or individuals get strong they are often truculent and bullying, but when they are weak they become better mannered. But this is the reverse of what is healthy and wise. I have always been astonished, having seen the end of these two wars, how difficult it is to make people understand Roman wisdom, 'Spare the conquered and war down the proud.' I think I will go so far as to say it in the original: *Parcere subjectis, et debellare superbos.* The modern practice has too often been, punish the defeated and grovel to the strong. . . .

"OUR RACE AND DESTINY"

April 27, 1951

Grand Habitation of the Primrose League
Albert Hall, London

On April 21 Aneurin Bevan resigned from the Government on the grounds of the decision of the new Chancellor of the Exchequer, Hugh Gaitskell, to introduce charges for National Health facilities. In his speech of resignation he widened the area of disagreement with the Government to cover its defence policy and rearmament. Two days later Harold Wilson (President of the Board of Trade) also resigned, as did John Freeman (Parliamentary Secretary, Ministry of Supply) on April 24.

[Extract] We meet for our Annual Meeting this year in a grave hour for our country. I cannot recall any period in my long life when mismanagement and incompetence have brought us into greater danger. At home prices and taxes go up and up, abroad the influence of Britain goes down and down. In every quarter of the world we are regarded by our friends with anxiety, with wonder and pity; and by our enemies, including some of those countries we have helped most in the past, like Egypt and Persia, we are regarded or treated with hostility or even contempt. Not one of them is so weak that they cannot spare a kick or a taunt for Britain. It is hard to believe that we are the same nation that emerged from the last war respected and admired throughout the grand alliance for all the part we played, for a long time alone, in the defence of the cause of freedom. Six years of Socialist rule have brought us low.

Nevertheless we must not lose faith in our race and in our destiny. We are the same people, in the same islands, as we were in the great days we can all remember. Our spirit is unconquerable, our ingenuity and craftsmanship unsurpassed. Our latent resources are unmeasured. Our underlying unities are enduring. We have but to cast away by an effort of will the enfeebling tendencies and fallacies of Socialism and to free ourselves from restrictive Socialist rule to stand erect once more and take our place among the great Powers of the world. Never must we lose our faith and our courage, never must we fail in exertion and resolve.

We are all glad that the Prime Minister has left the hospital and can turn from the jigsaw-puzzles of Cabinet shuffling to the urgent tasks which confront him. It is hard on any country when no one is looking after it. Mr. Attlee combines a limited outlook with strong qualities of resistance. He now resumes the direction and leadership of that cluster of lion-hearted limpets–a new phenomenon in our natural history, almost a suggestion I could offer Mr. Herbert Morrison for his fun fair–who are united by their desire to hold on to office at all costs to their own reputations and their country's fortunes, and to put off by every means in their power to the last possible moment any contact with our democratic electorate. This they do in the name not of principle or policy but of party loyalty enforced by party discipline carried to lengths not previously witnessed in our system of representative and Parliamentary Government. . . .

"WHOSE FINGER ON THE TRIGGER?"

October 6, 1951

Loughton County High School

Mr. Attlee announced on September 19 that a General Election would be held on October 25. On September 27, the British oil refinery at Abadan came completely under Persian control, and most of the staff of the Anglo-Iranian Oil Company returned to England. Much heat was aroused by this question and by Labour's allegations of Churchill's "war-mongering."

[Extract] . . . Mr. Bartholomew's newspaper, the *Daily Mirror*, coined a phrase the other day which is being used by the Socialist Party whom he supports. 'Whose finger,' they asked, 'do you want on the trigger, Attlee's or Churchill's?' I am sure we do not want any fingers upon any trigger. Least of all do we want a fumbling finger. I do not believe that a Third World War is inevitable. I even think that the danger of it is less than it was before the immense rearmament of the United States. But I must now tell you that in any case it will not be a British finger that will pull the trigger of a Third World War. It may be a Russian finger, or an American finger, or a United Nations Organization finger, but it cannot be a British finger. Although we should certainly be involved in a struggle between the Soviet Empire and the free world, the control and decision and the timing of that terrible event would not rest with us. Our influence in the world is not what it was in bygone days. I could wish indeed that it was greater because I am sure it would be used as it always has been used to the utmost to prevent a life-and-death struggle between the great nations.

OUR POLITICAL FUTURE

October 8, 1951

Broadcast, London

[Extract] We have reached a moment when it is the duty of the British people to make a decision one way or the other about our political future. Nothing could be worse than no decision at all. We have lost a lot in the last two years by the party strife which belongs to electioneering times. We cannot go on like this with two party machines baying at each other in Parliament and grinding away all over the country in order to gain votes for one side or the other. We could not afford it for long even if the world were calm and quiet and if we were a self-supporting nation safer and more independent than we ever were before.

The uncertainty has got to come to an end at home if we are to play our part in the world and receive due consideration for our British point of view and, still more, if we are to keep a decent standard of life for our people and even keep them all alive. Remember, we have brought into being through the progress of Victorian times fifty million people in an island which only grows the food for thirty million and that all the rest has to be provided for by the goods and services we can render to other countries. There never was a community of fifty million people, standing at our high level of civilization, on such an insecure foundation. We have maintained ourselves there by the qualities of our race, by the soundness of our institutions, by the peaceful progress of our democracy, and by the very great lead which we had gained in former generations.

Thus we have been able to withstand and surmount all the shocks and strains of this terrible twentieth century with its two awful wars. We shall endanger our very existence if we go on consuming our strength in bitter party or class conflicts. We need a period of several years of solid stable administration by a Government not seeking to rub party dogmas into everybody else. It will take us all we can do to keep going at home and play our part, which is a great one, in maintaining the freedom and peace of the world. . . .

The difference between our outlook and the Socialist outlook on life is the difference between the ladder and the queue. We are for the ladder. Let all try their best to climb. They are for the queue. Let each wait in his place till his turn comes. But, we ask: 'What happens if anyone slips out of his place in the queue?' 'Ah!' say the Socialists, 'our officials–and we have plenty of them–come and put him back in it, or perhaps put him lower down to teach the others.' And when they come back to us and say: 'We have told you what happens if anyone slips out of the queue, but what is your answer to what happens if anyone slips off the ladder?' Our reply is: 'We shall have a good net and the finest social ambulance service in the world.' This is of course only a snapshot of a large controversy.

But now, since the General Election of 1950, an additional heavy burden has come upon us. The Soviet aggression in Korea led to a fierce war on a considerable scale. This has started an immense additional process of rearmament against Communist Russia by all the free democracies of the world, with the United States doing and paying the bulk. We have supported the Socialist Government's proposals. At first we were told they amounted to £3,600 million, but later on, when they added the bill up again, they told us that it is nearly £5,000 million military expenditure spread over three years. This is a very heavy load for our island to bear. A Conservative Government would have the full right to examine in severe detail the way in which the money is being spent and what is the fighting-power and defensive security resulting from it. If anything like the groundnuts and Gambia egg muddles are being repeated in this vast field heavy sacrifices will be exacted from our hard-pressed people without enabling them to take their proper share in the world defence of freedom.

What are we rearming for? It is to prevent Communist Russia, its reluctant satellites and its ardent votaries spread about in many countries–some of them even here–from beating us all down to their dead level as they have done as much as they can to the people of every country they have occupied during and since the war. But rearmament is only half a policy. Unless you are armed and strong you cannot expect any mercy from the Communists; but if you are armed and strong you may make a bargain with them which might rid the world of the terror in which it now lies and relieve us all from much of the impoverishment and privations into which we shall otherwise certainly sink.

The Conservative and Liberal Parties and part of the Socialist Party support the policy of rearmament and the effective binding together of all the nations all over the world outside the Iron Curtain, not because we are seeking war, but because we believe it is the only method by which a reasonable and lasting settlement might be reached. I believe that if the British Empire and Commonwealth joined together in fraternal association with the United States and the growing power of Western Europe–including a reconciled France and Germany–worked together steadfastly, then the time will come, and may come sooner than is now expected, when a settlement may be reached which will give us peace for a long time. That is our hearts' desire.

I do not hold that we should rearm in order to fight. I hold that we should rearm in order to parley. I hope and believe that there may be a parley. You will remember how, at Edinburgh in the 1950 election, I said that there should be a meeting with Soviet Russia, not of subordinates but of heads of Governments in order to enable us at least to live peacefully together. You will remember, also, that this gesture, which I did not make without some knowledge of the personalities and forces involved, was curtly dismissed by the Socialist Government as an electioneering stunt. It might be that if such a meeting as I urged had taken place at that time the violent dangers of the Korean War and all that might spring out of it would not have come upon us.

But now we have a different situation. In a way it is more tense. We are actually at war. Blood is being shed and cannons fire. The murder on Saturday of our High Commissioner in Malaya, Sir Henry Gurney, reminds us how fiercely the struggle there burns on. On the other hand, the gigantic rearmament of the United States, their development of the atom bomb, the growth of British and of European defence and the unities which have sprung into being among the free democracies, including our old enemies in the war, give a foundation, ever growing in strength and solidity, upon which a fruitful and durable peace settlement might be made.

Britain has a great part to play in this if only she can regain the influence and the power she wielded during the war. She injures and weakens herself by her Parliamentary stalemate. She strikes herself cruel blows when she accepts humiliations such as we have suffered in the Persian Gulf. We have to face a great lowering of our reputation. The Persian outrage, in disregard of the decision of The Hague Court, has weakened the cause of peace all over the world. It is a grievous injury to the whole of the Western Allies in Europe or in the Atlantic Pact when Britain falls flat on her face as if she were a booby and a coward. But this is not the real Britain, it is only the grimace of an exhausted and divided administration, upon whose conduct the nation will soon be able to pronounce.

I have explained from time to time the Tory outlook upon our ever-changing British society. We feel that process of bringing larger numbers to an ever wider table ever more bountifully provided with the moral and material satisfactions of life is the true way to measure our national progress. Give everyone a better chance to rise and let the successful help to pick up and bring along those who do not succeed. We are resolved that this evolution shall be tireless and perennial.

If the electors choose to entrust to the Conservatives an effective measure of power for a considerable period I pledge my word that the party I have led so long through such historic years will not be the partisans of any hidebound doctrine but will try its best to make things good and continually improving for the nation as a whole. We stand for freedom and unceasing progress and this can only be achieved by valiant perseverance. On the other hand we make no promises of easier conditions in the immediate future. Too much harm has been done in these last six years for it to be repaired in a few months. Too much money has been spent for us to be able to avoid another financial crisis. It will take all our national strength to stop the downhill slide and get us back on the level, and after that we shall have to work up.

We ask to be judged by our performances and not by our promises. We do not promise to create a paradise—and certainly not a fool's paradise. We are seeking to build a lighthouse rather than to dress a shop window. All I will say is that we will do our best for all our fellow-countrymen without distinction of class or party. I cannot offer you any immediate relaxation of effort. On the contrary, we have not yet got through the danger zone at home or abroad. We must do our duty with courage and resolution. But there is a wise saying 'the trees do not grow up to the sky.'

If we can stave off a war for even five or ten years all sorts of things may happen. A new breeze may blow upon the troubled world. I repudiate the idea that a Third World War is inevitable. The main reason I remain in public life is my hope to ward it off and prevent it. The desire of mankind in this tragic twentieth century can be seen and felt. The human race is going through tormenting convulsions and there is a profound longing for some breathing space, for some pause in the frenzy. Why not make a change in this harassed island and get a steady stable Government, sure of its strength, fostering the expansion of our society, making sure of our defences, being faithful to our allies and to the common cause of law and freedom, but seeking as its final and supreme aim that all classes, all nations, friends and enemies alike, can dwell in peace within their habitations?

"ABADAN, SUDAN, AND BEVAN"

October 12, 1951

Constituency Meeting, Woodford

[Extract] Abadan, Sudan and Bevan are a trio of misfortune.

The Prime Minister has been enlivening his tour throughout our land by making many attacks on me. I have not wished to be in personal controversy with him, especially when he is having such a bad time, but there is one statement in his speech at Leicester which I cannot overlook, and which is so remarkable that the general panorama of this Election would not be complete without it. Mr. Attlee, speaking of the achievements of his Government, said that he was not satisfied with what had been done. Here are his words: 'How can we clear up in six years the mess of centuries?' 'The mess of centuries!' This is what the Prime Minister considers Britain and her Empire represented when in 1945 she emerged honoured and respected from one end of the world to the other by friend and foe alike after her most glorious victory for freedom. 'The mess of centuries'—that was all we were.

The remark is instructive because it reveals with painful clarity the Socialist point of view and sense of proportion. Nothing happened that was any good until they came into office. We may leave out the great struggles and achievements of the past—Magna Charta, the Bill of Rights, Parliamentary institutions, Constitutional Monarchy, the building of our Empire—all these were part of 'the mess of centuries.' Coming to more modern times, Gladstone and Disraeli must have been pygmies. Adam Smith, John Stuart Mill, Bright and Shaftesbury, and in our lifetime, Balfour, Asquith and Morley, all these no doubt were 'small fry.' But at last a giant and Titan appeared to clear up 'the mess of centuries.' Alas, he cries, he has only had six years to do it in. Naturally he was not able to accomplish his full mission. We have endured these six years. They have marked the greatest fall in the rank and stature of Britain in the world, which has occurred since the loss of the American colonies nearly two hundred years ago. Our Oriental Empire has been liquidated, our resources have been squandered, the pound sterling is only worth three-quarters of what it was when Mr. Attlee took over from me, our influence among the nations is now less than it has ever been in any period since I remember. Now the Titan wants another term of office!

I have not replied to Mr. Attlee before, but it would hardly be respectful of me to ignore all that he says about me. He charges me with putting party before the nation. This is ungrateful considering that the Conservative Party has supported him in every important measure that he has taken for national defence and safety. Last year when he proposed the great scheme of spending £4,700 million in three years upon rearmament, we immediately gave him our full support, although if we had suggested that such steps were necessary he and his friends would no doubt have called us warmongers. We also supported him in increasing the cumpulsory military service from eighteen months to two years, although at the Election of 1950 his party had tried to gain votes by accusing the Tories of this very intention. But what was the return we received from the Prime Minister for our aid in his rearmament scheme? Within a week of our giving him our full support he announced the intention to complete the nationalization of steel. This was a harsh act of partisanship which was bound to make the gulf between the parties wider. Now that we know what forces the Prime Minister had to contend with in his own Cabinet and party, and how he was being continually harried from behind and from inside by Mr. Bevan and his crowd, we see the explanation of his conduct. In order to do what he knew was his duty to his country, he had to pay his way with these evil elements by creating fresh antagonism with the Tory Party, without whose support he would have fallen.

After all I suppose that it is a very complicated business to clear up 'the mess of centuries' and to have only six years to do it in. . . .

"A PERSONAL ISSUE"

October 23, 1951

Home Park Football Ground, Plymouth

[Extract] . . . I must now refer to a personal issue. The Socialists somewhat shamefacedly, and the Communists brazenly, make the charge that I am a 'warmonger.' This is a cruel and ungrateful accusation. It is the opposite of the truth. If I remain in public life at this juncture it is because, rightly or wrongly, but sincerely, I believe that I may be able to make an important contribution to the prevention of a Third World War and to bringing nearer that lasting peace settlement which the masses of the people of every race and in every land fervently desire. I pray indeed that I may have this opportunity. It is the last prize I seek to win. I have been blessed with so much good fortune throughout my long life, and I am treated with so much kindness by my fellow countrymen far outside the ranks of party, and indeed also in the United States and in Europe, that all the daydreams of my youth have been surpassed. It is therefore with a single purpose and a strong sense of duty that I remain at my post as Leader of the Conservative Party through these baffling and anxious years. I applied the word 'ungrateful' a moment ago to the slander by which some of our opponents hope to gain advantage. I think it is the right word to use. It is quite true that at a very dark moment in our history I was called upon to take the lead for more than five years of awful war and that I did my best until victory was won. But that that should be made the ground, as Mr. Shinwell suggests, for saying that I want to have a Third World War to show off my talents is mean and shabby. Trusting as I do to the sense of justice and fair play which inspires the British race, I am sure that these taunts and insults will recoil upon the heads of those who make them. We shall not have very much longer to wait before we shall see what the British answer is to all that. . . .

DEBATE ON THE ADDRESS

November 6, 1951

House of Commons

At the General Election on October 25, the Conservatives and their allies won 321 seats, Labour 295, the Liberals 6, and others 3. On the following day Mr. Attlee resigned, and Churchill kissed hands to become Prime Minister for the second and last time.

[Extract] . . . The right hon. Gentleman [Mr. Attlee] will excuse me if I say that he does not seem quite to have got clear of the General Election. A great deal of his speech was made up of very effective points and quips which have a great deal of satisfaction to those behind him. We all understand his position: 'I am their leader, I must follow them.' A hard task lies before His Majesty's Government and grave responsibilities weigh upon the new Parliament. For two whole years our island has been distracted by party strife and electioneering. I do not see how this could have been avoided. Our Parliamentary institutions express themselves through party government, at any rate in times of peace. The nation is deeply and painfully divided, and the opposing forces are more or less evenly balanced. Naturally, neither side approves of what the other has done or said in the course of the conflict. We think on this side that the 'Warmonger' campaign did us great harm, and is probably answerable for the slender majority upon which His Majesty's Government must rest, with all its many Parliamentary disadvantages and uncertainties. We are, however, now in a position to answer this cruel and ungrateful charge not merely by words but by deeds. It may well be, therefore, that in due course of time it will recoil with compound interest upon the heads of those who profited by it.

We meet together here with an apparent gulf between us as great as I have known in fifty years of House of Commons life. What the nation needs is several years of quiet, steady administration, if only to allow Socialist legislation to reach its full fruition. What the House needs is a period of tolerant and constructive debating on the merits of the questions before us without nearly every speech on either side being distorted by the passions of one Election or the preparations for another. Whether we shall get this or not is, to say the least, doubtful. We ask no favours in the conduct of Parliamentary business. We believe ourselves capable of coping with whatever may confront us. Still, it would not be good for our country if, for instance, events so shaped themselves that a third General Election came upon us in, say, a year or eighteen months. Still worse for our country if that conflict, in its turn, led only to a continuance of an evenly matched struggle in the House and out of doors.

We must all be conscious of the realities of our position. Fifty million people are now crowded in our small island which produces food for only three-fifths of them, and has to earn the rest from over the seas by exporting manufactures for which we must also first import the raw material. No community of such a size, and standing at so high a level of civilization, has ever been economically so precariously poised. An ever larger and more formidable world is growing up around us. Very soon severe competition from Germany and Japan must be expected in our export markets. The problem of earning our independent livelihood stares us in the face. All our united strength will be needed to maintain our standards at home and our rank among the nations. If in these circumstances the electioneering atmosphere is to continue indefinitely, with the nation split in half in class and ideological strife, it will present a spectacle which the world will watch with wonder, and I believe, on the whole, with dismay.

My hope is that the instinct of self-preservation may grow steadily during this Parliament. Controversy there must be on some of the issues before us, but this will be but a small part of the work and interests we have in common. Although, while present conditions last, we all live in the shadow of another General Election, the Government will not fear to do unpopular things where these are found, in our opinion, to be indispensable to the general welfare. I trust, however, that British good sense may avoid an era of annual elections, narrow majorities, and fierce, bitter, exciting class and party war. . . .

Now I come to the greatest matter that I have to bring before the House today—the financial and economic situation. The right hon. Gentleman spoke in a jocular manner about making bricks without straw, but I quote that only to emphasize by contrast the seriousness of the position. We were confronted on taking over with a Treasury report setting forth the position as it stood at that date, ten days ago. I sent a copy of this to the Leader of the Opposition in order that he might know our starting point. It was certainly scratch. In overseas payments we are in a deficit crisis worse than 1949, and in many ways worse than even 1947. Confidence in sterling is impaired. In the present half-year, we are running into an external deficit at the rate of £700 million a year compared with an annual rate of surplus of about £350 million in the same period a year ago. That means a deterioration of more than £1,000 million a year.

The latest estimates show that in 1952, on present trends and policies and without making any allowance for further speculative losses, the United Kingdom would have a deficit on its general balance of overseas payments of between £500 million and £600 million, and the loss to the central gold and dollar reserves in the transactions of the sterling areas as a whole with the rest of the world might be appreciably more. These figures mean, in short, that we are buying much more than we can afford to pay for from current earnings, and this can only in time lead to national bankruptcy. The position has been made worse by the loss of confidence in sterling and by the additional strain of the loss of Persian oil supplies, to which the Leader of the Opposition has made reference in some of his speeches. Such was the statement presented to us within a few hours of our taking office, and it has taken first place in our minds and discussions since. We are convinced that it is necessary to present the facts plainly to the nation in order that they may realize where we stand. We do not believe that a full and frank statement of our position will aggravate the loss of confidence abroad which has been taking place. On the contrary, many of the facts are known in foreign and financial circles and are, in some cases, exaggerated foreign speculation. We feel that a solemn resolve by Parliament and the British people to set their house in order without delay, and the measures necessary to give effect to that resolve, would act as a tonic to our credit all the world over. A full statement of the financial position and the remedial measures which, in the time we have had to consider these matters we consider imperative, will be made by my right hon Friend the Chancellor of the Exchequer at the opening of tomorrow's debate. I will not now elaborate the matter further. . . .

I do not propose to deal at any length this afternoon with the foreign situation. When the Foreign Secretary has returned from the conferences in Paris he will make his report to the House in a special debate. We cannot accept the ill-treatment we have received about Persian oil supplies. His Majesty's Government are always ready to negotiate a settlement on the basis of a fair partnership for the actual benefit of those who live in the country which provides the oil, and for those who have created the wonderful industry and have the technical experience to extract the oil and to market it. We have so far suffered a great injustice and disaster, and we shall strive patiently and resolutely to repair the position as far as that is now possible.

In Egypt and the Sudan we are pursuing the policy adopted by the late Government and by the right hon. Gentleman the Member for Lewisham, South [Mr. Herbert Morrison], who was Foreign Secretary. We are resolved to maintain our rightful position in the Canal Zone in spite of the illegal and one-sided Egyptian action over the 1936 Treaty. We shall do our utmost to safeguard the Canal as an international highway, using, of course, no more force than is necessary. Here again I think that time, within certain limits, and restraint and forbearance–not so strictly limited–may give the best chance of the crisis being successfully surmounted.

But our great hope in foreign affairs is, of course, to bring about an abatement of what is called 'the cold war' by negotiation at the highest level from strength and not from weakness. Perhaps I may read again to the House, as I have already read to them, what I wrote to Mr. Stalin and his colleagues in April 1945:

> There is not much comfort in looking into a future where you and the countries you dominate, plus the Communist parties in many other States are all drawn up on one side, and those who rally to the English-speaking nations and their associates, or Dominions are on the other. It is quite obvious that their quarrel would tear the world to pieces and that all of us leading men on either side who had anything to do with that would be shamed before history. Even embarking on a long period of suspicions, of abuse and counter-abuse and of opposing policies would be a disaster, hampering the great developments of world prosperity for the masses which are attainable only by our trinity.

That was written more than six years ago, and, alas, all came to pass with horrible exactitude. I must explain that in speaking of our trinity I was, of course, referring to a period when France had not fully resumed her rightful place in the international sphere.

At Edinburgh, in February 1950, I appealed for a conference between the heads of States or Governments, and I and my right hon. Friend the Foreign Secretary, who have acted in the closest, spontaneous accord in all these matters, still hold to the idea of a supreme effort to bridge the gulf between the two worlds, so that each can live its life, if not in friendship at least without the fear, the hatreds and the frightful waste of the 'cold war.' I must, however, today utter a word of caution. The realities which confront us are numerous, adverse and stubborn. We must be careful not to swing on a wave of emotion from despondency to over-confidence; but even if the differences between West and East are, for the time being, intractable, the creation of a new atmosphere and climate of thought, and of a revived relationship and sense of human comradeship, would, I believe, be an enormous gain to all the nations.

Never must we admit that a Third World War is inevitable. I heard some months ago of a foreign diplomatist who was asked: 'In which year do you think the danger of war will be the greatest?' He replied: 'Last year.' If that should prove true, as we pray it may, no one will deny their salute to the memory of Ernest Bevin, or their compliments to those who worked faithfully with him. Let us, in these supreme issues with party politics far beneath them, move forward together in our united fight as faithful servants of our common country, and as unwearying guardians of the peace and freedom of the world.

"THE PATH OF DUTY"

November 9, 1951

The Lord Mayor's Banquet,
The Guildhall, London

[Extract] . . . What is the world scene as presented to us today? Mighty forces armed with fearful weapons are baying at each other across a gulf which I have the feeling tonight neither wishes, and both fear to cross, but into which they may tumble or drag each other to their common ruin. On the one side stand all the armies and air forces of Soviet Russia and all their Communist satellites, agents and devotees in so many countries. On the other are what are called 'the Western Democracies' with their far superior resources, at present only partly organized, gathering themselves together around the United States with its mastery of the atomic bomb. Now there is no doubt on which side we stand. Britain and the Commonwealth and Empire still centering upon our island, are woven by ever-growing ties of strength and comprehension of common need and self-preservation to the great Republic across the Atlantic Ocean.

The sacrifices and exertions which the United States are making to deter, and if possible prevent, Communist aggression from making further inroads upon the free world are the main foundation of peace. A tithe of the efforts now being made by America would have prevented the Second World War and would have probably led to the downfall of Hitler with scarcely any blood being shed except perhaps his own. I feel a deep gratitude towards our great American Ally. They have risen to the leadership of the world without any other ambition but to serve its highest causes faithfully. I am anxious that Britain should also play her full part, and I hope to see a revival of her former influence and initiative among the Allied Powers, and indeed with all Powers.

It must not be forgotten that under the late Government we took peculiar risks in providing the principal atomic base for the United States in East Anglia, and that in consequence we placed ourselves in the very forefront of Soviet antagonism. We have therefore every need and every right to seek and to receive the fullest consideration from Americans for our point of view, and I feel sure this will not be denied us.

In order to regain our position we must do our utmost to re-establish as quickly as possible our economic and financial solvency and independence. We were shocked and surprised by the situation with which we were confronted after accepting responsibility a fortnight ago. This resulted partly from world causes, but also partly from the prolonged electioneering atmosphere in which we have dwelt for nearly two years, and especially for the past two months. We have certainly been left a tangled web of commitments and shortages, the like of which I have never seen before, and I hope and pray we may be granted the wisdom and the strength to cope with them effectively. If these conditions of furious political warfare between the two halves of our party-divided Britain are to continue indefinitely, and we are all to live under the shadow of a third General Election, it will not be at all good for the main life interests of the British nation, or for her influence in world affairs. Nevertheless, whatever way things may go, we shall not fail to do our duty however unpopular that may be. It is not cheers that we seek to win or votes we are playing to catch, but respect and confidence. This cannot come from words alone, but only from action which proves itself by results. Results cannot be achieved by the wave of a wand. Time is needed for a new Administration to grasp and measure the facts which surround us in baffling and menacing array. More time is needed for the remedies we propose and will propose to produce their curative effects. Nothing would be easier than for this country, politically rent asunder as it is, to shake and chatter itself into bankruptcy and ruin. But under grave pressures in the past we have proved ourselves to be a wise and unconquerable people, and I am sure that we shall succeed. No doubt His Majesty's Government will make mistakes. We shall not hesitate to admit them. I made many in the war. It is, however, always a comfort in times of crisis to feel that you are treading the path of duty according to the lights that are granted you. Then one need not fear whatever may happen. It was in this spirit that we all came through our worst perils eleven years ago; and I have a good and buoyant hope that the great mass of the nation will give us its ungrudging aid in all matters of truly national import. If this happens they may feel in two or three years' time that they have not been led on wrong courses and that Britain stands erect again, calm, resolute and independent, the faithful servant of peace, the valiant champion of freedom, and an honoured member of a united world instrument for preserving both.

ADDRESS TO THE UNITED STATES CONGRESS
January 17, 1952

Washington, D.C.

[Extract] This is the third time it has been my fortune to address the Congress of the United States upon our joint affairs. I am honoured indeed by these experiences which I believe are unique for one who is not an American citizen. It is also of great value to me, on again becoming the head of His Majesty's Government, to come over here and take counsel with many trusted friends and comrades of former anxious days. There is a lot for us to talk about together so that we can understand each other's difficulties, feelings and thoughts, and do our best for the common cause. Let us, therefore, survey the scene this afternoon with cool eyes undimmed by hate or passion, guided by righteous inspiration and not uncheered by hope.

I have not come here to ask you for money to make life more comfortable or easier for us in Britain. Our standards of life are our own business and we can only keep our self-respect and independence by looking after them ourselves. During the war we bore our share of the burden and fought from first to last, unconquered–and for a while alone–to the utmost limits of our resources. Your majestic obliteration of all you gave us under Lend-Lease will never be forgotten by this generation in Britain, or by history. . . .

There is a jocular saying: 'To improve is to change; to be perfect is to have changed often.' I had to use that once or twice in my long career. But if that were true everyone ought to be getting on very well. The changes that have happened since I last spoke to Congress are indeed astounding. It is hard to believe we are living in the same world. Former allies have become foes. Former foes have become allies. Conquered countries have been liberated. Liberated nations have been enslaved by Communism. Russia, eight years ago our brave ally, has cast away the admiration and goodwill her soldiers had gained for her by their valiant defence of their own country. It is not the fault of the Western Powers if an immense gulf has opened between us. It took a long succession of deliberate and unceasing works and acts of hostility to convince our peoples–as they are now convinced–that they have another tremendous danger to face and that they are now confronted with a new form of tyranny and aggression as dangerous and as hateful as that which we overthrew.

When I visited Washington during the war I used to be told that China would be one of the Big Four Powers among the nations, and most friendly to the United States. I was always a bit sceptical, and I think it is now generally admitted that this hopeful vision has not yet come true. But I am by no means sure that China will remain for generations in the Communist grip. The Chinese said of themselves several thousand years ago: 'China is a sea that salts all the waters that flow into it.' There's another Chinese saying about their country which is much more modern–it dates only from the fourth century. This is the saying: 'The tail of China is large and will not be wagged.' I like that one. The British democracy approves the principles of movable party heads and unwaggable national tails. It is due to the working of these important forces that I have the honour to be addressing you at this moment.

You have wisely been resolute, Members of the Congress, in confronting Chinese Communist aggression. We take our stand at your side. We are grateful to the United States for bearing nine-tenths, or more, of the burden in Korea which the United Nations have morally assumed. I am very glad that whatever diplomatic divergencies there may be from time to time about procedure you do not allow the Chinese anti-Communists on Formosa to be invaded and massacred from the mainland. We welcome your patience in the armistice negotiations and our two countries are agreed that if the truce we seek is reached, only to be broken, our response will be prompt, resolute and effective. What I have learnt over here convinces me that British and United States policy in the Far East will be marked by increasing harmony. . . .

We must not lose patience, and we must not lose hope. It may be that presently a new mood will reign behind the Iron Curtain. If so it will be easy for them to show it, but the democracies must be on their guard against being deceived by a false dawn. We seek or covet no one's territory; we plan no forestalling war; we trust and pray that all will come right. Even during these years of what is called the 'cold war,' material production in every land is continually improving through the use of new machinery and better organization and the advance of peaceful science. But the great bound forward in progress and prosperity for which mankind is longing cannot come till the shadow of war has passed away. There are, however, historic compensations for the stresses which we suffer in the 'cold war.' Under the pressure and menace of Communist aggression the fraternal association of the United States with Britain and the British Commonwealth, and the new unity growing up in Europe–nowhere more hopeful than between France and Germany–all these harmonies are being brought forward, perhaps by several generations in the destiny of the world. If this proves true–and it has certainly proved true up to date–the architects in the Kremlin may be found to have built a different and a far better world structure than what they planned.

Members of the Congress, I have dwelt today repeatedly upon many of the changes that have happened throughout the world since you last invited me to address you here and I am sure you will agree that it is hardly possible to recognize the scene or believe it can truly have come to pass. But there is one thing which is exactly the same as when I was here last. Britain and the United States are working together and working for the same high cause. Bismarck once said that the supreme fact of the nineteenth century was that Britain and the United States spoke the same language. Let us make sure that the supreme fact of the twentieth century is that they tread the same path.

KING GEORGE VI

February 7, 1952

Broadcast, London

King George VI died in his sleep at Sandringham on the night of February 5-6. On February 7, Churchill delivered a broadcast to the nation. The passage which begins ". . . the King walked with death, as if death were a companion . . . " may be regarded as one of the most moving of all Churchill's phrases, and struck a deep chord at the time.

My friends, when the death of the King was announced to us yesterday morning there struck a deep and solemn note in our lives which, as it resounded far and wide, stilled the clatter and traffic of twentieth-century life in many lands and made countless millions of human beings pause and look around them. A new sense of values took, for the time being, possession of human minds and mortal existence presented itself to so many at the same moment in its serenity and in its sorrow, in its splendour and in its pain, in its fortitude and in its suffering.

The King was greatly loved by all his peoples. He was respected as a man and as a prince far beyond the many realms over which he reigned. The simple dignity of his life, his manly virtues, his sense of duty alike as a ruler and a servant of the vast spheres and communities for which he bore responsibility—his gay charm and happy nature, his example as a husband and a father in his own family circle, his courage in peace or war—all these were aspects of his character which won the glint of admiration, now here, now there, from the innumerable eyes whose gaze falls upon the Throne.

We thought of him as a young naval lieutenant in the great Battle of Jutland. We thought of him, when calmly, without ambition, or want of self-confidence, he assumed the heavy burden of the Crown and succeeded his brother, whom he loved, and to whom he had rendered perfect loyalty. We thought of him so faithful in his study and discharge of State affairs, so strong in his devotion to the enduring honour of our country, so self-restrained in his judgments of men and affairs, so uplifted above the clash of party politics, yet so attentive to them; so wise and shrewd in judging between what matters and what does not. All this we saw and admired. His conduct on the Throne may well be a model and a guide to constitutional sovereigns throughout the world today, and also in future generations.

The last few months of King George's life, with all the pain and physical stresses that he endured—his life hanging by a thread from day to day—and he all the time cheerful and undaunted—stricken in body but quite undisturbed and even unaffected in spirit—these have made a profound and an enduring impression and should be a help to all. He was sustained not only by his natural buoyancy but by the sincerity of his Christian faith. During these last months the King walked with death, as if death were a companion, an acquaintance, whom he recognized and did not fear. In the end death came as a friend; and after a happy day of sunshine and sport, and after 'good night' to those who loved him best, he fell asleep as every man or woman who strives to fear God and nothing else in the world may hope to do.

The nearer one stood to him the more these facts were apparent. But the newspapers and photographs of modern times have made vast numbers of his subjects able to watch with emotion the last months of his pilgrimage. We all saw him approach his journey's end. In this period of mourning and meditation, amid our cares and toils, every home in all the realms joined together under the Crown, may draw comfort for tonight and strength for the future from his bearing and his fortitude.

There was another tie between King George and his people. It was not only sorrow and affliction that they shared. Dear to the hearts and the homes of the people is the joy and pride of a united family; with this all the troubles of the world can be borne and all its ordeals at least confronted. No family in these tumultuous years was happier, or loved one another more, than the Royal Family around the King.

My friends, I suppose no Minister saw so much of the King during the war as I did. I made certain he was kept informed of every secret matter; and the care and thoroughness with which he mastered the immense daily flow of State papers made a deep mark on my mind. Let me tell you another fact. On one of the days, when Buckingham palace was bombed, the King had just returned from Windsor. One side of the courtyard was struck, and if the windows opposite out of which he and the Queen were looking had not been, by the mercy of God, open, they would both have been blinded by the broken glass instead of being only hurled back by the explosion. Amid all that was then going on–although I saw the King so often–I never heard of this episode till a long time after. Their Majesties never mentioned it, or thought it of more significance than a soldier in their armies would of a shell bursting near him. This seems to me to be a revealing trait in the Royal character.

There is no doubt that of all the institutions which have grown up among us over the centuries, or sprung into being in our lifetime, the constitutional monarchy is the most deeply founded and dearly cherished by the whole association of our peoples. In the present generation it has acquired a meaning incomparably more powerful than anyone had dreamed possible in former times. The Crown has become the mysterious link–indeed, I may say, the magic link–which unites our loosely bound but strongly interwoven Commonwealth of nations, States and races. Peoples who would never tolerate the assertions of a written constitution which implied any diminution of their independence, are the foremost to be proud of their loyalty to the Crown.

We have been greatly blessed amid our many anxieties, and in the mighty world that has grown up all around our small island–we have been greatly blessed tnat this new intangible, inexpressible but for practical purposes apparently, an all-powerful element of union should have leapt into being among us. How vital it is, not only to the future of the British Commonwealth and Empire, but I believe also to the cause of world freedom and peace which we serve, that the occupant of the Throne should be equal to the august and indefinable responsibilities which this supreme office requires. For fifteen years King George VI was king; never at any moment in all the perplexities at home and abroad, in public or in private, did he fail in his duties; well does he deserve the farewell salute of all his governments and peoples.

My friends, it is at this time that our compassion and sympathy go out to his Consort and widow. Their marriage was a love match with no idea of regal pomp or splendour. Indeed, there seemed to lie before them the arduous life of royal personages denied so many of the activities of ordinary folk and having to give so much in ceremonial public service. May I say, speaking with all freedom, that our hearts go out tonight to that valiant woman with famous blood of Scotland in her veins who sustained King George through all his toils and problems and brought up, with their charm and beauty, the two daughters who mourn their father today. May she be granted strength to bear her sorrow. To Queen Mary, his mother, another of whose sons is dead—the Duke of Kent having been killed on active service—there belongs the consolation of seeing how well the King did his duty and fulfilled her hopes, and of always knowing how much he cared for her.

Now I must leave the treasures of the past and turn to the future. Famous have been the reigns of our Queens. Some of the greatest periods in our history have unfolded under their sceptres. Now that we have the Second Queen Elizabeth, also ascending the Throne in her twenty-sixth year, our thoughts are carried back nearly 400 years to the magnificent figure who presided over, and in many ways embodied and inspired, the grandeur and genius of the Elizabethan Age. Queen Elizabeth the Second, like her predecessor, did not pass her childhood in any certain expectation of the Crown. But already we know her well, and we understand why her gifts, and those of her husband, the Duke of Edinburgh, have stirred the only part of our Commonwealth she has yet been able to visit. She has already been acclaimed as Queen of Canada: we make our claim, too, and others will come forward also; and tomorrow the proclamation of her sovereignty will command the loyalty of her native land and of all other parts of the British Commonwealth and Empire.

I, whose youth was passed in the august, unchallenged and tranquil glories of the Victorian Era, may well feel a thrill in invoking, once more, the prayer and the Anthem, "God Save the Queen!"

SIR STAFFORD CRIPPS
April 23, 1952

House of Commons

In this noble tribute to his old opponent and wartime colleague particular note should be taken of the final paragraph and the reference to Lady Cripps's ordeal over many months.

[Extract] Since we met here yesterday we have learned of the death of a statesman of national pre-eminence who had long served with distinction in the House of Commons, and it is in accordance with recent precedents that I should attempt to pay some tribute, necessarily brief and inadequate, to his memory. Stafford Cripps was a man of force and fire. His intellectual and moral passions were so strong that they not only inspired but not seldom dominated his actions. They were strengthened and also governed by the working of a powerful, lucid intelligence and by a deep and lively Christian faith. He strode through life with a remarkable indifference to material satisfaction or worldly advantages. There are few members in any part of the House who have not differed violently from him at this time or that, and yet there is none who did not regard him with respect and with admiration, not only for his abilities but for his character.

His friends–and they were many, among whom I am proud to take my place–were conscious, in addition to his public gifts, of the charm of his personality and of the wit and gaiety with which he enlivened not only the mellow hours, but also the hard discharge of laborious business in anxious or perilous times. In all his complicated political career he was the soul of honour and his courage was proof against every test which the terrible years through which we have passed could bring.

Having sat with him in the wartime Cabinet, which he joined in 1942 and of which he was always a member–or, as we called it in those days, a constant attender–I can testify to the immense value of his contributions to our discussions. There was no topic I can remember–no doubt right hon Gentlemen opposite have longer experiences of their own–on which he did not throw a clarifying light and to which he did not often bring a convenient and apt solution. Most of us have in our memories the distinction with which he filled the great office of the Exchequer and how easily he explained and interpreted the problems of finance. We all could not always agree with his policy, but everyone was grateful for its exposition. . . .

It is not for me in these few words to attempt to epitomize the place which Stafford Cripps will bear in the history of our life and times, or of his contribution to their political philosophy; but that, as a man, he had few equals in ability or virtue will be generally affirmed by his contemporaries, and that he brought an unfailing flow of courage, honour and faith to bear upon our toils and torments will be attested by all who knew him and, most of all, by those who knew him best.

Our hearts go out to the noble woman, his devoted wife, who through these long months of agony, mocked by false dawns, has been his greatest comfort on earth. To her we express profound sympathy, and we trust that she may find some solace in the fact that Stafford's memory shines so brightly among us all.

"THE COMMON INTEREST OF THE WHOLE PEOPLE"

November 10, 1952

The Lord Mayor's Banquet,
The Guildhall, London

This speech was delivered immediately following the election of General Dwight D. Eisenhower to the American presidency.

[Extract] When I came to your Banquet a year ago our Government had only just been formed and we had to face with a slender, and it might well have been a precarious, majority not only the partisanship of our opponents, but a task, the full magnitude of which was becoming every day more plain. We were moving into bankruptcy at an alarming rate. Only prompt, vigorous and unpopular action could gain us the breathing space necessary to place our affairs upon a sound foundation. By severe exertions we have gained the breathing space, but it will require several years of sober and persevering government to restore our financial and economic strength, without which our nation cannot play an effectual part, during this twentieth century of storm and tumult and terrible wars, in the vast world which has grown up around us.

I should not wish tonight to exaggerate our achievements. I am content with the modest plea that we have tried our best with no other aim but the common interest of the whole people. We are still only at the beginning of our task, and it may well be that disappointments and set-backs will afflict us. They will not, however, conquer us. We are encouraged by the fact that both at home and abroad there is a feeling that our position has definitely improved; that we are recovering our strength; that danger of a Third World War seems to have receded, and that our national solvency has been freed from immediate peril. We are also cheered by a confident feeling that, no matter how much we are abused by our opponents, if we do our duty faithfully and without fear, we shall get fair play from the British people.

There has been an Election lately in the United States which we have all watched with unflagging attention. For me, I must admit it has been painful to see so many of my best friends over there and comrades in war and peace fighting one another with all the ardour which we associate with party politics and democracy. Nothing like that could have happened under the Soviets or their satellite states. There all is presented with glacial decorum. One party only is allowed, and majorities are presented of 98 per cent. What I always wonder at is how the remaining 2 per cent are persuaded to deny their votes to the mighty oligarchy who hold their lives and every detail of their daily life in its grasp. Are they rewarded, or are they punished, and if punished, does this take place beforehand or afterwards? After all, it would be a very serious thing if any of these elections produced a hundred per cent result. That might easily lead the capitalist world to doubt whether actually all had been fair and square. They might even suggest that the whole performance was humbug, enforced by iron discipline. Personally I prefer the kind of thing that happens at British and American Elections, even though I must admit there ought, in both countries, to be some lucid intervals between them.

At any rate there was one thing about the American Elections which gave us great comfort here and throughout the Commonwealths who together are partners in the English-speaking world. Both the candidates were the finest figures American public life could present. Both were worthy of the highest traditions of the Great Republic which is now so valiantly sustaining the freedom of the world. With full confidence I express, in your name here tonight, our salutations to General Eisenhower and our assurance that, to the utmost limit of our strength, we will work with him for those great causes which we have guarded and cherished in ever greater unity as the generations have rolled by. . . .

A year ago I said here, in this famous Guildhall, that Britain stood erect, calm, resolute, and independent. What report should I make tonight? Surely it is that we have gained both in strength and in purpose. Britain is loyal to her faith: to her belief in the principles of the United Nations and in the dignity of the individual: and to her determination to see, with all her Allies, a true and lasting settlement among the nations. With this faith, and in this high companionship, we shall march forward undaunted by danger, unwearied by toil.

WESTMINSTER ABBEY APPEAL

January 30, 1953

Jerusalem Chamber

The Parliamentary Session of 1952-1953 opened turbulently, but divisions within the Labour Party, particularly the emergence of a group of Labour M.P.s who were termed "Bevanites" and grouped themselves around Aneurin Bevan, made the task of Ministers less difficult. But the Government's position, with the continuing economic crisis and the Korean War still unended, remained precarious.

This speech is included as another example of Churchill's wonderful felicity of expression, even on non-political occasions.

We are met here to-day for a purpose for which we believe that at least a million people throughout the English-speaking world will be happy to give a pound and perhaps repeat the process; and others less wealthy will be proud to join with their friends in giving a pound. That is what we are asking for to-day–a million pounds from a million people. We have one gift already; the Queen is the first subscriber. The purpose is to save from decay and ruin Westminster Abbey, in the famous words of Macaulay: 'That temple of silence and reconciliation where the enmities of twenty generations lie buried.'

Westminster Abbey is not only an active centre of our religious faith, but the shrine of nearly a thousand years of our history. Founded by King Edward the Confessor it presents the pilgrimage of our race, and has been in many ways the focus of our island life. Here all may see the panorama of our various fortunes, from the triumph of a Norman conqueror through the long succession of sovereigns who, in good or evil days, in glory and tragedy, safety and peril, unity and strife, have formed the chain of our ancient monarchy, until now we are looking forward to the moment next June when the Crown of St. Edward will be set upon the head of our young and beautiful Queen Elizabeth the Second.

But the Abbey has not only been associated with the Coronation of all our sovereigns. The Chapter House across the way sheltered over a period of many generations the vigorous beginnings of that system of representative and Parliamentary government which has spread far and wide through so many lands. For us in the

British Empire and Commonwealth of Nations the Abbey must be considered not only as the embodiment and enshrinement of our long record, but as a living spring of hope, inspiration, and unfailing interest wherever the English language is spoken in any quarter of the globe. To-day we stand where, in the words of Kipling, 'The Abbey makes us one.' I speak in the Jerusalem Chamber, where, as Shakespeare tells us, Henry V tried on the Crown while his dying father slept, and where the Star Chamber achieved its variegated reputation. In the Abbey itself are the tombs and monuments of famous men, from Norman and Plantagenet kings to the Unknown Warrior of the First World War. In Macaulay's words: 'In no other cemetery do so many citizens lie within so narrow a space.'

We in our day have come through many perils but we have been helped and sustained by that sense of continuity which finds no other symbol more commanding than this historic edifice which links the past with the present and gives us confidence in the future. Shall we in this valiant generation allow the building to moulder under our eyes? Both the monuments and the stonework of the centuries are falling into decay. The soot of London must be cleaned away if we are to prevent the stones from crumbling. The structure must be restored. The Choir School, with its long tradition of musical excellence, must be given security and an assured income must be provided for the daily work of maintenance.

Our generation would indeed be held to shame by those who come after us if we failed to preserve this noble inheritance. I ask those whom my words may reach, in Great Britain, in the Commonwealth, and across the oceans, to join me in sending the Dean of Westminster their one pound contributions so that the glorious memories that have come down to us may be preserved as the treasures of generations yet to come. All the pounds should be sent to the Dean of Westminster, whose address, I may mention, is Westminster Abbey, London.

CONSERVATIVE PARTY CONFERENCE

October 10, 1953

Margate, Kent

The death of Joseph Stalin gave rise to hopes that the most bitter part of the cold war might be over and the time might be ripe for new overtures from the West. At home, however, Mr. Eden had been obliged to undergo a major operation. It was not wholly successful, and subsequent complications required a further operation. His health never fully recovered. In his absence, Churchill assumed responsibility for foreign affairs, assisted by Lord Salisbury, who became acting Foreign Secretary on June 30.

One of the principal actions of the last Churchill Government was the decision to relinquish the British bases on the Suez Canal. It was fiercely opposed by a group of Conservatives, but Churchill became convinced that the action was inevitable.

In the Coronation Honours at the beginning of June Churchill was created a Knight of the Garter. Shortly afterwards, on the evening of June 23, he suffered a stroke.

Although his recovery was surprisingly swift, the few who knew what had happened were very anxious about his ability to address the Annual Conference in Margate. However, the speech was, in the words of The Times, *"a personal triumph."*

[Extract] . . . It is now nearly two years since the Conservative Party became responsible for the government and guidance of Britain. Two years is not a long time in human affairs. But it is nearly half the span of a Parliament and I think it is our duty to take stock of our position and to present to our friends and supporters in the National Union the main features of what we have done and what we are trying to do. If I compare our work with that of our predecessors to their disadvantage, it is not because I wish to raise ill-feeling and faction but rather to gain encouragement and strength for the future—for our future and for the future of our country.

Certainly we have tried very hard to make our administration loyal, sober, flexible, and thrifty, and to do our best to be worthy of the anxious responsibilities confided to us. We have tried to be worthy of the confidence and energy of our Members of Parliament and of the great political organization which sustains them in the constituencies. Never in its long history has it been so lively and efficient and never more free from class interests or personal motives. . . .

Do you know that I think danger is farther away then when we went into harness? Certainly the sense of crisis in our world relations is less than it was two years ago, and we hope that if we persevere recovery from the convulsions of the past and barriers against their recurrence will grow surer and firmer as the clattering months roll by.

Take our finances. Surely they come first to our minds, for it is not much use being a famous race and nation with institutions which are the envy of the free world and the model of many states, if at the end of the week you cannot pay your housekeeping bills. I see the Chancellor of the Exchequer [Mr. R. A. Butler]. He deserves our admiration and the respect of our fellow-countrymen. No one has tried harder to handle and solve the intricate problems left by nearly six years of war and more than six years of Socialist Government.

We are not out of the wood yet, but we have the feeling of increasing strength, and certainly we have far larger reserves. Two years ago we were sliding into bankruptcy and now at least we may claim solvency. There is something more to aim at. Solvency must be the stepping-stone of independence. (Mr. Butler spoke of that on Thursday.) We are no longer living on loans or doles, not even from our best friends. I care above all for the brotherhood of the English-speaking world, but there could be no true brotherhood without independence, founded as it can only be on solvency.

We do not want to live upon others and be kept by them, but faithfully and resolutely to earn our own living without fear or favour by the sweat of our brow, by the skill of our craftsmanship and the use of our brains. And do not let us underrate the strength and quality of British industry and inventiveness. The task of maintaining 50,000,000 people in this small island at a level superior to the average European standards might indeed appal a bold man. But when the life and death of our country is at stake we have sometimes found ways and means of helping one another which no other society has been able to surpass, in peace or in war. Let us make sure that Tory democracy is a fountain of activity and hope to our race and age.

And what about 300,000 houses a year? I remember well at Blackpool three years ago how you clamoured for a tremendous effort and an audacious target and how a gust of passion swept the hall as we proclaimed the goal of 300,000 houses a year. I remember also how we were mocked by the Socialist Ministers and told we were promising the impossible.

One can quite understand how a politician who thinks more than half his fellow-countrymen are vermin cannot feel much enthusiasm for providing them with homes. 'Homes for vermin' can hardly seem an inspiring theme for the Socialist Party. 'Soak the Rich' and 'Jobs for the Boys,' they seem to have a much more cheerful smack about them. But we persevered and now this second year at least 300,000 houses to let or sell will actually be built. Moreover we are building more schools than ever before—and there is the man who did it [Mr. Harold Macmillan]. A fine piece of work for which his countrymen will always respect him and they will also respect the capable building industry and makers of building materials who have served the nation well. . . .

Well, what about meat? Even red meat! Lord Woolton cannot any longer be derided for what he said because it has been made good. But they tell us that if there is more meat in the shops it is only because the prices are so high and the people so poor that it cannot be bought.

Now I am always very chary about loading a speech with percentages. I like the simplest forms of statement. I have had this matter very carefully examined, and this is the fact which I have been furnished with by our Food Minister, Mr. Gwilym Lloyd-George. He is rapidly and skilfully reducing his Ministry and his officials. And also, we must all recognize, adding to his own stature thereby. But he found time to work me out this fact which I asked for because I knew it would be plain and simple and could be well understood even by collective ideologists (those professional intellectuals who revel in decimals and polysyllables).

Personally I like short words and vulgar fractions. Here is the plain vulgar fact. In the first two years of Tory Government the British nation has actually eaten 400,000 tons more meat, including red meat, than they did in the last two years of Socialist administration. That at any rate is something solid to set off against the tales we are told of the increasing misery of the people—and the shortage of television sets. . . .

Our Conservative principles are well known. Lord Salisbury in his very kindly speech opening our proceedings touched upon them broadly. We stand for the free and flexible working of the laws of supply and demand. We stand for compassion and aid for those who, whether through age, illness, or misfortune, cannot keep pace with the march of society. We stand for the restoration of buying and selling between individual importers and exporters in different countries instead of the clumsy bargainings of one state against another, biased by politics and national feelings as these must necessarily be.

We have made great advances in restoring this method of active, nimble, multiple private trading which should be allowed to flourish so long as the necessary laws against the abuses of monopoly are vigilantly enforced. We are for private enterprise with all its ingenuity, thrift, and contrivance, and we believe it can flourish best within a strict and well-understood system of prevention and correction of abuses. We are against state trading except in emergencies.

I am sure it is much better for the consumer to buy his food or raw materials from a private trade, who has to make a profit by good management and shrewd business or go into bankruptcy and out of business. That is much better than to use large numbers of salaried officials who, if they make a blunder and lose millions or hundreds of millions, have only to mark up the prices to the public or send in the bill to the House of Commons.

In a complex community like our own no absolute rigid uniformity of practice is possible. But we here speaking of Party causes and Party principles must make it clear, as Lord Salisbury did, that we are on the side of free enterprise with proper safeguards against state monopoly in the hands of officials.

Now I come to the vexed and formidable sphere of foreign affairs, and we all rejoice to see Mr. Eden recovered from his cruel six months of pain and danger, and able to bring his unrivalled experience and knowledge to bear upon the problem which haunts all our minds–namely, finding a secure foundation for world peace.

I too have thought a great deal about this overpowering problem which hangs so heavily on the daily lives of every one of us. My prime thought at this moment is to simplify. We have lived through half a century of the most terrible events which have ever ravaged the human race. The vast majority of all the peoples wherever they may dwell desire above all things to earn their daily bread in peace. To establish conditions under which they can do this and to provide deterrents against aggression are the duties confided by the heart's desire of mankind to the United Nations. Our first duty is to aid this world instrument loyally and faithfully in its task.

But the world also needs patience. It needs a period of calm rather than vehement attempts to produce clear-cut solutions. There have been many periods when prompt and violent action might have averted calamities. This is not one of them. Even if we entered on a phase only of easement for five or ten years that might lead to something still better when it ended. So long as the cause of freedom is sustained by strength, beware of that, never forget that, and guided by wisdom it might well be that after those five or ten years improvement would be continued on an even larger scale. Patience.

In Mr. Attlee's speech here a week ago there were several sensible statements on foreign policy. There was one that struck my attention particularly, when he said that in all international matters it was well to remember there was a limit to what could be done by one government. But I view with some concern the attitude which the Bevanite faction and some others of his Party are adopting not only against the United States but against the new Germany. Mr. Robens, a former Minister of Labour–the man who predicted that we should have a million unemployed by last Christmas (that shows you what his judgment is worth even on questions where he has a right to speak as an authority)–Mr. Robens argued at Strasbourg that there must be no German army as a part of the European Defence Community for five years.

There are no doubt some Socialist politicians who hope to win popularity both by carping and sneering at United States and by raising hostility to the new Germany. Of course, it is vital to maintain ever strengthening ties of friendship with the United

States. It would also be a great disaster if Germany were needlessly made an enemy of Britain and the free world against her will. It is nearly four years ago since I said that Western Europe could never be defended against Soviet Russia without German military aid. Mr. Attlee denounced that statement as irresponsible. But a year later he and his colleagues committed themselves and all of us to the arrangements for European defence which involved the creation of twelve German divisions.

We inherited these arrangements and pledges–which we supported at the time–which involve British good faith from our predecessors, the very men who, some of them because they are not in office, think they are entitled to cast aside the work that they have done and the position to which they have committed us all.

At the present time the Soviet Armies in Europe, even without their satellites, are four times as strong as all the Western allies put together. It would indeed be an act of unwisdom to weaken our efforts to build up a Western defence. It would be madness to make our heavily-burdened island take up an attitude which if not hostile was at any rate unsympathetic both to the United States and to the new Germany which Dr. Adenauer is building, and yet all the time for us to remain bound by the treaties which the Socialists have made to defend friendly European Powers who are incapable of maintaining themselves alone.

I am sure that the decisions taken by the Socialist Government, which were supported by us at the time and are now being carried forward steadfastly and soberly by Her Majesty's Government, constitute the best chance–and indeed I think it is a good chance–of getting through this awful period of anxiety without a world catastrophe.

We at any rate are going to adhere faithfully to them, and do our utmost to promote the formation of the European Army, with a strong contingent of Germans in it. We, like the Americans, shall maintain our forces in Europe, thus restoring the French balance of equality with our new German associates. If the European Defence Community should not be adopted by the French, we shall have no choice in prudence but to fall in with some new arrangement which will join the strength of Germany to the Western allies through some rearrangement of what is called N. A. T. O. You must not mind my putting these things plainly to you because I have had a life of experience in the matter and I am bound to say that I feel that every word that I am now saying gives us the best chance of securing the peaceful development of the world.

Five months ago, on 11 May, I made a speech in the House of Commons. I have not spoken since (the first time in my political life that I have kept quiet for so long). I asked for very little. I held out no glittering or exciting hopes about Russia. I thought that friendly, informal, personal talks between the leading figures in the countries mainly involved might do good and could not easily do much harm, and that one good thing must lead to another as I have just said.

This humble, modest plan announced as the policy of Her Majesty's Government raised a considerable stir all over the place and though we have not yet been able to persuade our trusted allies to adopt it in the form I suggested no one can say that it is dead.

I still think that the leading men of the various nations ought to be able to meet together without trying to cut attitudes before excitable publics or using regiments of experts to marshal all the difficulties and objections, and let us try to see whether there is not something better for us than tearing and blasting each other to pieces, which we can certainly do.

Her Majesty's Government (as Mr. Eden and Lord Salisbury told you on Thursday) still believe we should persevere in seeking such a meeting between the Heads of Governments.

The interest of Britain and of Europe and of the N. A. T. O. alliance is not to play Russia against Germany or Germany against Russia, but to make them both feel they can live in safety with each other in spite of their grievous problems and differences. For us who have a very definite part in all this, our duty is to use what I believe is our growing influence both with Germany and with Russia to relieve them of any anxiety they may feel about each other.

Personally I welcome Germany back among the great Powers of the world. If there were one message I could give to the German people as one, a large part of whose life has been spent in conducting war against them or preparing to do so, I would urge them to remember the famous maxim: 'The price of freedom is eternal vigilance.' We mustn't forget that either.

When in this same speech I spoke about the master thought of Locarno I meant of course the plan of everybody going against the aggressor, whoever he may be, and helping the victim large or small. That is no more than the United Nations was set up to do. We are told the Locarno Treaty failed and did not prevent the war. There was a very good reason for that. The United States was not in it. Had the United States taken before the First World War or between the wars the same interest and made the same exertions and sacrifices and run the same risks to preserve peace and uphold freedom which I thank God she is doing now, there might never have been a First War and there would certainly never have been a Second. With her mighty aid I have a sure hope there will not be a third.

One word personally about myself. If I stay on for the time being bearing the burden at my age it is not because of love for power or office.

I have had an ample share of both. If I stay it is because I have a feeling that I may through things that have happened have an influence on what I care about above all else, the building of a sure and lasting peace.

Let us then go forward together with courage and composure, with resolution and good faith to the end which all desire.

"A CALMER AND KINDLIER AGE"

November 9, 1954

The Lord Mayor's Banquet,
The Guildhall, London

[Extract] . . . This is now the fourth Guildhall speech I have made in my present tenure of office and I am very glad that I can once again report to you a definite improvement in our own affairs, and it seems to me also in the moods of and the fortunes of the ever-growing and quivering world around us. We live in an age where the mood decides the fortunes rather than the fortunes decide the mood. If the human race wishes to have a prolonged and indefinite period of material prosperity, they have only got to behave in a peaceful and helpful way towards one another, and science will do for them all that they wish and more than they can dream. If of course their wish is to be quarrelsome and think it fun to bite one another, there is no doubt that every day they can kill each other in a quicker and more wholesale manner than ever before. The choice is theirs. Man is becoming increasingly master of his own fate and increasingly uncertain about it, and I think he is beginning to understand this fact better than he has ever done before.

In our own island we are conscious of having more influence over other countries than we used to have in this present century and certainly since the war, in which we did the best we could. We have tried to show ourselves well-informed, sedate, preserving, and resolute. We have not shrunk either at home or abroad from doing things which we believed were necessary, even though anyone could see they might be unpopular, and we have found a strong measure of responsibility among many of the Leaders of the Opposition and among the strongest–I did not say the loudest–elements in their rank and file. This, and the sober, stable view of the great trade unions, have aided Her Majesty's Government in the conduct of foreign affairs, and given the feeling that a government in this ancient kingdom has a stature and substance considerably above the ordinary ins and outs and ups and downs of party politics. In fact, although we no longer play so dominating a role in the modern world as we used to, we are nevertheless a people whose opinion is very widely respected. Encircled by our sister Commonwealths, we are felt to deserve attention from enlightened men and women of varied outlook in many lands. . . .

I am one of those who believe that the powers of the West and of the East should try to live in a friendly and peaceful way with each other. It would certainly not be to anyone's disadvantage if they tried. We don't agree with Soviet Communism or with their system of one-party uniformity. We think there is a great deal to be said for nature and variety, and that governments are made for men, not men for governments. But if the Soviets really like being governed by officials in a sealed pattern, and so long as they do not endanger the safety or freedom of others, that is a matter for them to decide themselves for themselves. Nothing is final. Change is unceasing and it is likely that mankind has a lot more to learn before it comes to its journey's end.

One thing is certain: with the world divided as it is at present, the freedom of our vast international association of the free peoples can only be founded upon strength and strength can only be maintained by unity. The whole foundation of our existence stands on our alliance, friendship, and an increasing sense of brotherhood with the United States, and we are also developing increasingly intimate ties with France, Germany, Italy, and the Low Countries which are stronger and more practical than any that have yet been devised. From these solemn and important agreements we hope that we shall be able to create that peace through strength which will allow time to play its part and bring about an altogether easier relationship all over the world. We might even find ourselves in a few years moving along a smooth causeway of peace and plenty instead of roaming around on the rim of Hell. For myself I am an optimist–it does not seem to be much use being anything else–and I cannot believe that the human race will not find its way through the problems that confront it, although they are separated by a measureless gulf from any they have known before. I look forward to the time when, to use Sir Anthony Eden's words, having brought about a stability and a common purpose in the West, we shall have established the essential basis on which we can seek an understanding with the East. Thus we may by patience, courage, and in orderly progression reach the shelter of a calmer and kindlier age.

EIGHTIETH BIRTHDAY

November 30, 1954

Presentation from Both Houses of Parliament, Westminster Hall

On Churchill's eightieth birthday he received a unique tribute at a special meeting of both Houses of Parliament; he was presented with a portrait by Graham Sutherland (which Churchill abhorred) and an illuminated address. Attlee made the principal introductory speech and Churchill, deeply moved, responded. Some M.P.s refused to sign the address, and in his speech Churchill referred to this–glaring at the Sutherland portrait.

This is to me the most memorable public occasion of my life. No one has ever received a similar mark of honour before. There has not been anything like it in British history, and indeed I doubt whether any of the modern democracies has shown such a degree of kindness and generosity to a party politician who has not yet retired and may at any time be involved in controversy. It is indeed the most striking example I have ever known of that characteristic British Parliamentary principle cherished in both Lords and Commons–"Don't bring politics into private life." It is certainly a mark of the underlying unity of our national life which survives and even grows in spite of vehement party warfare and many grave differences of conviction and sentiment. This unity is, I believe, the child of freedom and fair play fostered in the cradle of our ancient island institutions, and nursed by tradition and custom.

I am most grateful to Mr. Attlee for the agreeable words he has used about me this morning, and for the magnanimous appraisal he has given of my variegated career. I must confess, however, that this ceremony and all its charm and splendour may well be found to have seriously affected my controversial value as a party politician. However, perhaps with suitable assistance I shall get over this reaction and come round after a bit.

The Leader of the Opposition and I have been the only two Prime Ministers of this country in the last fourteen years. There are no other Prime Ministers alive. Mr. Attlee was also Deputy Prime Minister with me in those decisive years of war. During our alternating tenure, tremendous events have happened abroad, and far-reaching changes have taken place at home. There have been three general elections on universal suffrage and the activity of our Parliamentary and party machinery has been absolutely free. Mr. Attlee's and my monopoly of the most powerful and disputatious office under the Crown all this time is surely the fact which the world outside may recognize as a symbol of the inherent stability of our British way of life. It is not, however, intended to make it a permanent feature of the Constitution.

I am sure this is the finest greeting any Member of the House of Commons has yet received and I express my heartfelt thanks to the representatives of both Houses for the gifts which you have bestowed in their name. The portrait is a remarkable example of modern art. It certainly combines force and candour. These are qualities which no active Member of either House can do without or should fear to meet. The book with which the Father of the House of Commons [Mr. David Grenfell] has presented me is a token of the goodwill and chivalrous regard of members of all parties. I have lived my life in the House of Commons, having served there for fifty-two of the fifty-four years of this tumultuous and convulsive century. I have indeed seen all the ups and downs of fate and fortune, but I have never ceased to love and honour the Mother of Parliaments, the model to the legislative assemblies of so many lands.

The care and thought which has been devoted to this beautiful volume and the fact that it bears the signatures of nearly all my fellow-Members deeply touches my heart. And may I say that I thoroughly understand the position of those who have felt it their duty to abstain. The value of such a tribute is that it should be free and spontaneous. I shall treasure it as long as I live and my family and descendants will regard it as a most precious possession. When I read the eulogy so gracefully and artistically inscribed on the title page, with its famous quotation from John Bunyan, I must confess to you that I was overpowered by two emotions—pride and humility. I have always hitherto regarded them as opposed and also corrective of one another; but on this occasion I am not able to tell you which is dominant in my mind. Indeed both seem to dwell together hand in hand. Who would not feel proud to have this happen to him and yet at the same time I never was more sure of how far it goes beyond what I deserve.

I was very glad that Mr. Attlee described my speeches in the war as expressing the will not only of Parliament but of the whole nation. Their will was resolute and remorseless and, as it proved, unconquerable. It fell to me to express it, and if I found the right words you must remember that I have always earned my living by my pen and by my tongue. It was a nation and race dwelling all round the globe that had the lion heart. I had the luck to be called upon to give the roar. I also hope that I sometimes suggested to the lion the right places to use his claws. I am now nearing the end of my journey. I hope I still have some services to render. However that may be and whatever may befall I am sure I shall never forget the emotions of this day or be able to express my gratitude to those colleagues and companions with whom I have lived my life for this superb honour they have done me.

THE DETERRENT–NUCLEAR WARFARE

March 1, 1955

House of Commons

This was the last great speech made by Churchill in the House of Commons. It was listened to with deep respect and almost total silence in a packed Chamber. It contains the last of the remembered Churchill phrases–". . . safety will be the sturdy child of terror, and survival the twin brother of annihilation." The two final sentences may be regarded as Churchill's farewell to the House of Commons and to the British people.

[Extract] We live in a period, happily unique in human history, when the whole world is divided intellectually and to a large extent geographically between the creeds of Communist discipline and individual freedom, and when, at the same time, this mental and psychological division is accompanied by the possession by both sides of the obliterating weapons of the nuclear age.

We have antagonisms now as deep as those of the Reformation and its reactions which led to the Thirty Years' War. But now they are spread over the whole world instead of only over a small part of Europe. We have, to some extent, the geographical division of the Mongol invasion in the thirteenth century, only more ruthless and more thorough. We have force and science, hitherto the servants of man, now threatening to become his master.

I am not pretending to have a solution for a permanent peace between the nations which could be unfolded this afternoon. We pray for it. Nor shall I try to discuss the cold war which we all detest, but have to endure. I shall only venture to offer to the House some observations mainly of a general character on which I have pondered long and which, I hope, may be tolerantly received, as they are intended by me. . . .

What is the present position? Only three countries possess, in varying degrees, the knowledge and the power to make nuclear weapons. Of these, the United States is overwhelmingly the chief. Owing to the breakdown in the exchange of information between us and the United States since 1946 we have had to start again independently on our own. Fortunately, executive action was taken promptly by the right hon. Gentleman the Leader of the Opposition to reduce as far as possible the delay in our nuclear development and production. By his initiative we have made our own atomic bombs.

Confronted with the hydrogen bomb, I have tried to live up to the right hon. Gentleman's standard. We have started to make that one, too. It is this grave decision which forms the core of the Defence Paper which we are discussing this afternoon. Although the Soviet stockpile of atomic bombs may be greater than that of Britain, British discoveries may well place us above them in fundamental science.

May I say that for the sake of simplicity and to avoid verbal confusion I use the expression 'atomic bombs' and also 'hydrogen bombs' instead of 'thermo-nuclear' and I keep 'nuclear' for the whole lot. There is an immense gulf between the atomic and the hydrogen bomb. The atomic bomb, with all its terrors, did not carry us outside the scope of human control or manageable events in thought or action, in peace or war. But when Mr. Sterling Cole, the Chairman of the United States Congressional Committee, gave out a year ago–17 February 1954–the first comprehensive review of the hydrogen bomb, the entire foundation of human affairs was revolutionized, and mankind placed in a situation both measureless and laden with doom.

It is now the fact that a quantity of plutonium, probably less than would fill the Box on the Table–it is quite a safe thing to store–would suffice to produce weapons which would give indisputable world domination to any great Power which was the only one to have it. There is no absolute defence against the hydrogen bomb, nor is any method in sight by which any nation, or any country, can be completely guaranteed against the devastating injury which even a score of them might inflict on wide regions.

What ought we to do? Which way shall we turn to save our lives and the future of the world? It does not matter so much to old people; they are going soon anyway; but I find it poignant to look at youth in all its activity and ardour and, most of all, to watch little children playing their merry games, and wonder what would lie before them if God wearied of mankind.

The best defence would of course be bona fide disarmament all round. This is in all our hearts. But sentiment must not cloud our vision. It is often said that 'facts are stubborn things.' A renewed session of a sub-committee of the Disarmament Commission is now sitting in London and is rightly attempting to conduct its debates in private. We must not conceal from ourselves the gulf between the Soviet Government and the N.A.T.O. Powers, which has hitherto, for so long, prevented an agreement. The long history and tradition of Russia makes it repugnant to the Soviet Government to accept any practical system of international inspection.

A second difficulty lies in the circumstance that, just as the United States, on the one hand, has, we believe, the overwhelming mastery in nuclear weapons, so the Soviets and their Communist satellites have immense superiority in what are called 'conventional' forces–the sort of arms and forces with which we fought the last war, but much improved. The problem is, therefore, to devise a balanced and phased system of disarmament which at no period enables any one of the participants to enjoy an advantage which might endanger the security of the others. A scheme on these lines was submitted last year by Her Majesty's Government and the French Government and was accepted by the late Mr. Vyshinsky as a basis of discussion. It is now being examined in London.

If the Soviet Government have not at any time since the war shown much nervousness about the American possession of nuclear superiority, that is because they are quite sure that it will not be used against them aggressively, even in spite of many forms of provocation. On the other hand, the N.A.T.O. Powers have been combined together by the continued aggression and advance of Communism in Asia and in Europe. That this should have eclipsed in a few years, and largely effaced, the fearful antagonism and memories that Hitlerism created for the German people is an event without parallel. But it has, to a large extent, happened. There is widespread belief throughout the free world that, but for American nuclear superiority, Europe would already have been reduced to satellite status and the Iron Curtain would have reached the Atlantic and the Channel.

Unless a trustworthy and universal agreement upon disarmament, conventional and nuclear alike, can be reached and an effective system of inspection is established and is actually working, there is only one sane policy for the free world in the next few years. That is what we call defence through deterrents. This we have already adopted and proclaimed. These deterrents may at any time become the parents of disarmament, provided that they deter. To make our contribution to the deterrent we must ourselves possess the most up-to-date nuclear weapons, and the means of delivering them.

That is the position which the Government occupy. We are to discuss this not only as a matter of principle; there are many practical reasons which should be given. Should war come, which God forbid, there are a large number of targets that we and the Americans must be able to strike at once. There are scores of airfields from which the Soviets could launch attacks with hydrogen bombs as soon as they have the bombers to carry them. It is essential to our deterrent policy and to our survival to have, with our American allies, the strength and numbers to be able to paralyse these potential Communist assaults in the first few hours of the war, should it come.

The House will perhaps note that I avoid using the word 'Russia' as much as possible in this discussion. I have a strong admiration for the Russian people–for their bravery, their many gifts, and their kindly nature. It is the Communist dictatorship and the declared ambition of the Communist Party and their proselytizing activities that we are bound to resist, and that is what makes this great world cleavage which I mentioned when I opened my remarks. . . .

I shall content myself with saying about the power of this weapon, the hydrogen bomb, that apart from all the statements about blast and heat effects over increasingly wide areas there are now to be considered the consequences of 'fall out,' as it is called, of wind-borne radio-active particles. There is both an immediate direct effect on human beings who are in the path of such a cloud and an indirect effect through animals, grass, and vegetables, which pass on these contagions to human beings through food.

This would confront many who escaped the direct effects of the explosion with poisoning, or starvation, or both. Imagination stands appalled. There are, of course, the palliatives and precautions of a courageous Civil Defence, and about that the Home Secretary will be speaking later on to-night. But our best protection lies, as I am sure the House will be convinced, in successful deterrents operating from a foundation of sober, calm, and tireless vigilance.

Moreover, a curious paradox has emerged. Let me put it simply. After a certain point has been passed it may be said, 'The worse things get, the better.'

The broad effect of the latest developments is to spread almost indefinitely and at least to a vast extent the area of mortal danger. This should certainly increase the deterrent upon Soviet Russia by putting her enormous spaces and scattered population on an equality or near-equality of vulnerability with our small densely populated island and with Western Europe.

I cannot regard this development as adding to our dangers. We have reached the maximum already. On the contrary, to this form of attack continents are vulnerable as well as islands. Hitherto, crowded countries, as I have said, like the United Kingdom and Western Europe, have had this outstanding vulnerability to carry. But the hydrogen bomb, with its vast range of destruction and the even wider area of contamination, would be effective also against nations whose population, hitherto, has been so widely dispersed over large land areas as to make them feel that they were not in any danger at all.

They, too, become highly vulnerable; not yet equally perhaps, but, still, highly and increasingly vulnerable. Here again we see the value of deterrents, immune against surprise and well understood by all persons on both sides—I repeat 'on both sides'—who have the power to control events. That is why I have hoped for a long time for a top level conference where these matters could be put plainly and bluntly from one friendly visitor to the conference to another.

Then it may well be that we shall by a process of sublime irony have reached a stage in this story where safety will be the sturdy child of terror, and survival the twin brother of annihilation. Although the Americans have developed weapons capable of producing all the effects I have mentioned, we believe that the Soviets so far have tested by explosion only a type of bomb of intermediate power.

There is no reason why, however, they should not develop some time within the next four, three, or even two years more advanced weapons and full means to deliver them on North American targets. Indeed, there is every reason to believe that within that period they will. In trying to look ahead like this we must be careful ourselves to avoid the error of comparing the present state of our preparations with the stage which the Soviets may reach in three or four years' time. It is a major error of thought to contrast the Soviet position three or four years hence with our own position to-day. It is a mistake to do this, either in the comparatively precise details of aircraft development or in the measureless sphere of nuclear weapons. . . .

I must make one admission, and any admission is formidable. The deterrent does not cover the case of lunatics or dictators in the mood of Hitler when he found himself in his final dug-out. That is a blank. Happily, we may find methods of protecting ourselves, if we were all agreed, against that.

All these considerations lead me to believe that, on a broad view, the Soviets would be ill-advised to embark on major aggression within the next three or four years. One must always consider the interests of other people when you are facing a particular situation. Their interests may be the only guide that is available. We may calculate, therefore, that world war will not break out within that time. If, at the end of that time, there should be a supreme conflict, the weapons which I have described this afternoon would be available to both sides, and it would be folly to suppose that they would not be used. Our precautionary dispositions and preparations must, therefore, be based on the assumption that, if war should come, these weapons would be used.

I repeat, therefore, that during the next three or four years the free world should, and will, retain an overwhelming superiority in hydrogen weapons. During that period it is most unlikely that the Russians would deliberately embark on major war or attempt a surprise attack, either of which would bring down upon them at once a crushing weight of nuclear retaliation. In three or four years' time, it may be even less, the scene will be changed. The Soviets will probably stand possessed of hydrogen bombs and the means of delivering them not only on the United Kingdom but also on North American targets. They may then have reached a stage, not indeed of parity with the United States and Britain but of what is called 'saturation.'

I must explain this term of art. 'Saturation' in this connexion means the point where, although one Power is stronger than the other, perhaps much stronger, both are capable of inflicting crippling or quasi-mortal injury on the other with what they have got. It does not follow, however, that the risk of war will then be greater. Indeed, it is arguable that it will be less, for both sides will then realize that global war would result in mutual annihilation.

Major war of the future will differ, therefore, from anything we have known in the past in this one significant respect, that each side, at the outset, will suffer what it dreads the most, the loss of everything that it has ever known of. The deterrents will grow continually in value. In the past, an aggressor has been tempted by the hope of snatching an early advantage. In future, he may be deterred by the knowledge that the other side has the certain power to inflict swift, inescapable, and crushing retaliation.

Of course, we should all agree that a world-wide international agreement on disarmament is the goal at which we should aim. The Western democracies disarmed themselves at the end of the war. The Soviet Government did not disarm, and the Western nations were forced to rearm, though only partially, after the Soviets and Communists had dominated all China and half Europe. That is the present position. It is easy, of course, for the Communists to say now, 'Let us ban all nuclear weapons.' Communist ascendancy in conventional weapons would then become overwhelming. That might bring peace, but only peace in the form of the subjugation of the Free World to the Communist system.

I shall not detain the House very much longer, and I am sorry to be so long. The topic is very intricate. I am anxious to repeat and to emphasize the one word which is the theme of my remarks, namely, 'Deterrent.' That is the main theme.

The hydrogen bomb has made an astounding incursion into the structure of our lives and thoughts. Its impact is prodigious and profound, but I do not agree with those who say, 'Let us sweep away forthwith all our existing defence services and concentrate our energy and resources on nuclear weapons and their immediate ancillaries.' The policy of the deterrent cannot rest on nuclear weapons alone. We must, together with our N.A.T.O. allies, maintain the defensive shield in Western Europe. . . .

The argument which I have been endeavouring to unfold and consolidate gives us in this island an interlude. Let us not waste it. Let us hope we shall use it to augment or at least to prolong our security and that of mankind. But how? There are those who believe, or at any rate say, 'If we have the protection of the overwhelmingly powerful United States, we need not make the hydrogen bomb for ourselves or build a fleet of bombers for its delivery. We can leave that to our friends across the ocean. Our contribution should be criticism of any unwise policy into which they may drift or plunge. We should throw our hearts and consciences into that.'

Personally, I cannot feel that we should have much influence over their policy or actions, wise or unwise, while we are largely dependent, as we are to-day, upon their protection. We, too, must possess substantial deterrent power of our own. We must also never allow, above all, I hold, the growing sense of unity and brotherhood between the United Kingdom and the United States and throughout the English-speaking world to be injured or retarded. Its maintenance, its stimulation, and its fortifying is one of the first duties of every person who wishes to see peace in the world and wishes to see the survival of this country.

To conclude: mercifully, there is time and hope if we combine patience and courage. All deterrents will improve and gain authority during the next ten years. By that time, the deterrent may well reach its acme and reap its final reward. The day may dawn when fair play, love for one's fellow-men, respect for justice and freedom, will enable tormented generations to march forth serene and triumphant from the hideous epoch in which we have to dwell. Meanwhile, never flinch, never weary, never despair.

TOAST TO THE QUEEN

April 4, 1955

No. 10 Downing Street

On April 4 Churchill gave a farewell dinner party at No. 10 Downing Street, to which were invited the Queen, the Duke of Edinburgh, and Churchill's closest colleagues and friends. At the conclusion he proposed the health of the Queen and she graciously responded.

I have the honour of proposing a toast which I used to enjoy drinking during the years when I was a cavalry subaltern in the reign of your Majesty's great-great-grandmother, Queen Victoria.

Having served in office or in Parliament under the four sovereigns who have reigned since those days, I felt, with these credentials, that in asking your Majesty's gracious permission to propose this toast I should not be leading to the creation of a precedent which would often cause inconvenience.

Madam, I should like to express the deep and lively sense of gratitude which we and all your peoples feel to you and to his Royal Highness the Duke of Edinburgh for all the help and inspiration we receive in our daily lives and which spreads with ever-growing strength throughout the British realm and the Commonwealth and Empire.

Never have we needed it more than in the anxious and darkling age through which we are passing and through which we hope to help the world to pass.

Never have the august duties which fall upon the British monarchy been discharged with more devotion than in the brilliant opening of your Majesty's reign.

We thank God for the gift he has bestowed upon us and vow ourselves anew to the sacred cause, and wise and kindly way of life of which your Majesty is the young, gleaming champion.

"The Queen."

ELECTION ADDRESS

May 16, 1955

Woodford

On April 5 Sir Winston Churchill submitted his resignation as Prime Minister to the Queen and Sir Anthony Eden kissed hands as his successor. On May 6 Parliament was dissolved, and the General Election was held on May 26. Sir Winston was the Conservative candidate for Woodford.

The General Election of May 26 gave the Conservatives a majority of over fifty seats in the new Parliament.

[Extract] . . . At this juncture, the British electors have the great opportunity of casting their votes in favour of the sincere effort for a friendly way of living between States great and small which has now to be made and nations all over the world are waiting on tenterhooks to see if Britain will rise to the occasion. In this terrible twentieth century, our country has played an honourable and famous part. Britain is regarded as being territorially unambitious, wise, and sober and, above all, morally and physically fearless and unconquerable. Let us make sure we do not cast away by casual or careless behaviour the reputation upon which both our influence in the world and our safety depend.

LIBERTY AND THE LAW

July 31, 1957

Law Society Dinner to the American Bar Association, The Guildhall, London

Churchill maintained a complete public silence about the events of 1956–including the unsuccessful Hungarian uprising and the combined Anglo-French-Israeli assault on Egypt, which ended in total failure. Sir Anthony Eden resigned the Premiership on January 9, 1957, and was succeeded by Harold Macmillan.

This was Churchill's first major comment on the role of the United Nations during the crisis.

I am very glad that it has fallen to me to propose the toast of the Legal Profession and at the same time to welcome the many illustrious American guests who have come from within and outside the ranks of the profession. Several thousand members of the American Bar Association have come to our island for part of their Annual Convention. That is a remarkable fact, and a compliment of which we are all deeply sensible.

It illuminates a great truth. In the main, Law and Equity stand in the forefront of the moral forces which our two countries have in common, and rank with our common language in that store of bonds of unity on which I firmly believe our life and destiny depend. You are 160 millions and we, with our Dominions gathered round us, are 70 or 80 millions, and if we work together there is no doubt that we shall together represent a factor in the development of the whole world which no one will have cause to regret. The alliances of former days were framed on physical strength, but the English-speaking unity can find its lasting coherence above all in those higher ties of intellect and spirit of which the law and language are a supreme expression.

Last week you visited Runnymede. There was the foundation, on which you have placed a monument. It has often been pointed out that the 5th and 14th Amendments of the American Constitution are an echo of the Magna Carta. No person shall under the 5th Amendment be deprived of life, liberty, or property without due process of law, and the 14th Amendment says that no State shall deprive any person of life, liberty, or property without due process of law, nor deny any person within its jurisdiction equal protection of the laws. National governments may indeed obtain sweeping emergency powers for the sake of protecting the community in times of war or other perils. These will temporarily curtail or suspend the freedom of ordinary men and women, but special powers must be granted by the elected representatives of those same people by Congress or by Parliament, as the case may be.

They do not belong to the State or Government as a right. Their exercise needs vigilant scrutiny, and their grant may be swiftly withdrawn. This terrible twentieth century has exposed both our communities to grim experiences, and both have emerged restored and guarded. They have come back to us safe and sure. I speak, of course, as a layman on legal topics, but I believe that our differences are more apparent than real, and are the result of geographical and other physical conditions rather than any true division of principle. An omnipotent Parliament and a small legal profession, tightly bound by precedent, are all very well in an island which has not been invaded for nearly 2,000 years. Forty-nine states, each with fundamental rights and a different situation, is a different proposition.

Between Magna Carta and the formulation of the American Constitution we in Britain can claim the authorship of the whole growth of the English Common Law. Our pioneers took it with them when they crossed the Atlantic. For many centuries in the Middle Ages English lawyers would not admit that the law could be changed, even by Parliament. It was something sacrosanct, inviolable, above human tampering, like right and wrong. And this seems to have been the view of the English Chief Justice, Coke, as late as the early sixteen hundreds. His dream of a Supreme Court above the legislature for Great Britain vanished in the Civil War. The Supreme Court survived and flourished in the United States. England was too compact and too uniform a community to have need of it. But the Supreme Court in America has often been the guardian and upholder of American liberty. Long may it continue to thrive.

There are wider aspects to these considerations. Justice knows no frontiers. Within our considerable communities we have sought to regulate our affairs with equity. We have now reached the point where nations must contrive a system and practice to resolve their disputes and settle them peacefully. We have not succeeded so far in this. Some have tried at one swoop in the hour of victory to draw up an all-comprehending scheme such as the Charter of the United Nations to meet most international possibilities. In a recent speech that most distinguished Australian statesman, Mr. Menzies, said that justice was not being achieved there. A serious charge, but it is true. I do not throw in my lot with those who say that Britain should leave the United Nations. But it is certain that if the Assembly continues to take its decisions on grounds of enmity, opportunism, or merely jealousy and petulance, the whole structure may be brought to nothing.

The shape of the United Nations has changed greatly from its original form and from the intention of its architects. The differences between the Great Powers have thrown responsibility increasingly on the Assembly. This has been vastly swollen by the addition of new nations. We wish these new nations well. Indeed, we created many of them, and have done our best since to ensure their integrity and prosperity. But it is anomalous that the vote or prejudice of any small country should affect events involving populations many times its own numbers and affect them as momentary self-advantage may direct. This should be changed. There are many cases where the United Nations have failed. [Editor's Note: The refusal of the Soviet Union to permit the U.N. Secretary-General to go to Hungary was often used by critics of the U.N. to refer to the fact that it had "double standards"–condemning Britain, Israel, and France for the Suez operation, and unable to intervene in Hungary.] Hungary is in my mind. Justice cannot be a hit-or-miss system. We cannot be content with an arrangement where our new system of international laws applies only to those who are willing to keep them.

I do not want to-night to suggest an elaborate new charter for the United Nations, but I think we can all agree that its present conception is imperfect, and must be improved.

The mere creation, however, of international organizations does not relieve us of our individual responsibility–at least not until the international systems are truly reliable and effective. It falls to the righteous man individually to do what he can and to form with his friends alliances that are manifestly crowned with justice and honour. Such are the North Atlantic Treaty and the other combinations of the Free World. Such, I trust and believe, is the union of the English-speaking peoples. The Legal Profession.

A FRIEND OF FRANCE

November 6, 1958

On Receiving the Croix de la Liberation from General de Gaulle, Paris

I am going to speak English to-day. I have often made speeches in French, but that was wartime, and I do not wish to subject you to the ordeals of darker days.

I am particularly happy that it should be my old friend and comrade, General de Gaulle, who should be paying me this honour. He will always be remembered as the symbol of the soul of France and of the unbreakable integrity of her spirit in adversity. I remember, when I saw him in the sombre days of 1940, I said, 'Here is the Constable of France.' How well he lived up to that title!

Now he is back again in a position of the greatest and gravest responsibility for his country. The problems which confront us are no less important than our struggle for survival eighteen years ago. Indeed, in some ways they may be more complicated, for there is no clear-cut objective of victory in our sight. It is harder to summon, even among friends and allies, the vital unity of purpose amidst the perplexities of a world situation which is neither peace nor war.

I trust that I may be permitted these observations of a very general character. I think that I can claim always to have been a friend of France. Certainly your great country and your valiant people have held a high place in my thoughts and affection in all the endeavours and great events with which we have been associated in the last half-century. Some of these events have been terrible: they have brought great suffering on the world and on our peoples. The future is uncertain, but we can be sure that if Britain and France, who for so long have been the vanguard of the Western civilization, stand together, with our Empires, our American friends, and our other allies and associates, then we have grounds for sober confidence and high hope.

I thank you all for the honour you have done me.

Vive la France!

ADOPTION MEETING

September 29, 1959

Hawkey Hall, Woodford

The Macmillan Government, which began its existence in apparently doomed circumstances in January 1957, had gradually gained confidence and public support. In September 1959 Mr. Macmillan advised the Queen to dissolve Parliament, and the new General Election was held on October 8. Churchill was a Parliamentary candidate for the last time.

[Extract] I am much touched by your action, Ladies and Gentlemen, in doing me the honour of adopting me as your candidate for the ninth time. We have had eight victories running, and I am sure that if everyone plays his part as you have always done we shall increase our score on 8 October.

Thirty-five years have now passed since you first adopted me, and it is a source of great satisfaction and pleasure to my wife, the President of your Association, and to me that we have been sustained over this long period by your unfailing confidence and goodwill. The Conservative campaign has opened in this election on a wave of optimism for a Conservative victory. I find a most solid basis of national prosperity on which we can build, and every class of society in this country has benefited demonstrably from eight years of Conservative rule. But do not let us allow ourselves to be lulled into a false sense of security.

You will, I am confident, spare some of your time and energy in neighbouring seats where the forces of Socialism are stronger and our own may be hard pressed. It is not merely that we require to gain a decided victory on our own ground. We seek with determination to participate in a general success. . . .

The country next month will be deciding two very important questions. The first, which concerns affairs at home, is this: Does the country wish to travel further along our Conservative road of freedom and opportunity; or does it wish to turn back and go down the Socialist road of controls and state interference of every kind?

Fortunately nowadays people can make their choice on the basis of fact, not just simple theory. They had six long years of the Socialist method. It brought us one crisis after another. It never succeeded in ending shortages, whether of houses, food, or fuel. In those days taxation was kept at penal levels. Rationing, often even harder than what was necessary during the war, was rigorously maintained. Prices rose remorselessly to the detriment especially of those living on fixed incomes, and those relying on pensions and other social service benefits.

Since then we have had eight years of the Conservative policy of freedom and incentive. The transformation has been remarkable. The houses have been built. Rationing has long since ended. The shortages have disappeared. Taxes have come down. Prices have been steady for the past year and more. Pension rates have been improved and the social services have been extended.

Mr. Macmillan is giving the country a good account of his stewardship. I was always confident that he would be able to do that. But could anybody seriously imagine that this happy state of affairs would continue under a Socialist administration? The past provides the best pointer to the future. Look, for instance, at the record of the three last Socialist Chancellors of the Exchequer. In each case taxes went up, and the value of money went down. And, of course, the same thing would happen again. The only difference next time would be that taxes would go up even higher and the value of money fall even lower. That would be the inevitable result of Socialist extravagance, combined with another round of experiments in nationalization, municipalization, public accountability, or whatever they choose to call it.

Their whole policy would inevitably undermine the very foundations of that considerable degree of prosperity which it has taken eight years of exertion to build up. To build may have to be the slow and laborious task of years. To destroy can be the thoughtless act of a single day. Let us pray that 8 October is not such a day. . . .

HONORARY UNITED STATES CITIZENSHIP

April 9, 1963

Washington, D.C.

In the 1959 General Election the Conservatives doubled their Parliamentary majority and Churchill was easily victorious in Woodford. But his age was now becoming painfully evident; his public appearances increasingly rare. In 1960 and 1962, he had serious falls, injuring his back. It was obvious that his long public career was drawing to a close. In 1963 he received the unique distinction of the bestowal of Honorary Citizenship of the United States from Congress.

This statement was read by Churchill's son, Randolph, during a ceremony at the White House in the presence of President Kennedy.

Mr. President, I have been informed by Mr. David Bruce that it is your intention to sign a Bill conferring upon me Honorary Citizenship of the United States.

I have received many kindnesses from the United States of America, but the honour which you now accord me is without parallel. I accept it with deep gratitude and affection.

I am also most sensible of the warm-hearted action of the individual States who accorded me the great compliment of their own honorary citizenships as a prelude to this Act of Congress.

It is a remarkable comment on our affairs that the former Prime Minister of a great sovereign state should thus be received as an honorary citizen of another. I say "great sovereign state" with design and emphasis, for I reject the view that Britain and the Commonwealth should now be relegated to a tame and minor role in the world. Our past is the key to our future, which I firmly trust and believe will be no less fertile and glorious. Let no man underrate our energies, our potentialities and our abiding power for good.

I am, as you know, half American by blood, and the story of my association with that mighty and benevolent nation goes back nearly ninety years to the day of my Father's marriage. In this century of storm and tragedy I contemplate with high satisfaction the constant factor of the interwoven and upward progress of our peoples.

Our comradeship and our brotherhood in war were unexampled. We stood together, and because of that fact the free world now stands. Nor has our partnership any exclusive nature: the Atlantic community is a dream that can well be fulfilled to the detriment of none and to the enduring benefit and honour of the great democracies.

Mr. President, your action illuminates the theme of unity of the English-speaking peoples, to which I have devoted a large part of my life. I would ask you to accept yourself, and to convey to both Houses of Congress, and through them to the American people, my solemn and heartfelt thanks for this unique distinction, which will always be proudly remembered by my descendants.

Index

A

Abadan refinery, 938
abdication of Edward VIII, 457, 458, 461, 629-30, 632-33
Abyssinia, 621-23
  and Italy, 607-9, 610-11, 612-17
aerial navigation. *See* aviation
aerial warfare, 457-58
  World War II, 680, 707, 718, 729, 738, 740, 763-64, 818
  see also, air raids; Royal Air Force
Africa. *See* British East Africa; North African Campaign; South Africa
air raids, 729, 737-38, 747
  anticipated (1916) 352, (1940) 718
  defence against, 680
  World War I, 352
Air Service, British
  naval, 328
  see also, Royal Air Force
Alexander, Albert V., 908-9
Alexander, Harold R.L.G., 825
Amery, Leo, 324, 450, 455, 461, 669
Anglo-Saxon Fellowship. *See* English-speaking people
Anson, Sir W., 199-200
Arabs, 686-88
Archangel, Soviet Union, 371, 378
Ardennes. *See* Battle of Ardennes
Argentia meeting (1941), 765-69
aristocracy defended, 181-83
armed forces, 937
arms race, 228-29
  naval, 218-21, 222-26, 243
army, British, 34-36, 371-72
  between-war crises
    in India, 526-28
    in Soviet Union (1919), 378
  and civil disturbances, 393-98
  expenditure, 35-44, 561-62
  organization
    efficiency questioned, 357-60, 736-37
  recruitment, 295-97, 300
  strength, 331, 357
  weapons and equipment, 626-27
  World War I, 331
  World War II, 725, 770
  see also, demobilization; National Service and conscription
art, 319
Asia. *See* Far Eastern Theatre
Asquith, Herbert Henry, 1st Earl of Oxford, 135
  and Churchill, 17, 318, 336
  and Irish problem, 399
  and party politics, 361, 391
Asquith, Lady Margot, 10, 11, 13, 461, 462
Astor, Nancy, Viscountess, 654, 660
Athenia, S.S., 668, 694
Atlantic Charter, 765, 767, 892
Atlantic Conference, 765-69
Atlantic Pact, 918-19
atom bomb, 802, 873, 932
  see also, nuclear weapons
Attlee, Clement, 671
  on Churchill, 457, 670
  defence policies, 908-9, 935
  foreign policy, 935, 960-61
  and party discipline, 870-71, 937-38
  postwar government, 942-44
  and United Europe, 913
Auchinleck, Claude J.E., 761, 773, 783, 804, 805
Austria, 642
aviation, 261-62

B

Baldwin, Stanley, 422, 533, 581, 621, 637
  foreign policy, 444-45
  and Indian problem, 528-30
  personality, 452-56, 477, 480-91
  policies praised, 444
  as Prime Minister, 325
Balfour, A.J., 25, 77-78
  and armed forces, 347-53 *passim*
  and Conservative party, 210, 422
  in (1906) election, 86
  and Parliament
    House of Commons, 80-81
    House of Lords, 101, 114-15
Balfour Declaration, 685-86
Balkans, the
  war with Turkey (1912), 249-50
  World War II, 740, 745
Baltic States, 383, 541, 682
Bank of England, nationalization of, 467-68
Bannerman, Henry Campbell, 63, 77-80, 135

Battenberg, Louis Alexander, 1st Marquess of Milford Haven, 292
Battle of Ardennes, 843
Battle of the Atlantic, 673, 742-44, 746-48, 751-52, 756, 784
Battle of Britain, 671, 707, 720, 724, 726, 729-31
Battle of Egypt, 809-11
Battle of France, 706-8
Battle of Normandy, 831
Battle of the River Plate, 698
Battle of Rome, 825
Battle of the Somme, 356
Beaconsfield, Lord. *See* Disraeli, Benjamin, 1st Earl of Beaconsfield
Beaverbrook, William M. Aitken, 1st Baron, 18, 19, 453, 461, 538
Beerbohm, Max, 4
Belgium
  World War I, 292
  World War II, 708-10
Benn, William Wedgwood, 538
Bennett, Arnold, 320
Beresford, Lord Charles, 329
Berlin, Sir Isaiah, 7, 462, 463, 670-71
Berlin
  crisis, 915-18
  division of, 882
Bevan, Aneurin, 894-95, 937
Bevin, Ernest, 899
Birkenhead, Lord. *See* Smith, Frederick E., 1st Earl of Birkenhead
Bismarck (German battleship), 758
Bismarck, Otto von, 950
Black and Tans. *See* Royal Irish Constabulary
Blunt, Wilfred, 6
Boers, 31-32, 99-100, 104-5, 213
Boer War, 27-29, 30-34
Bolshevism. *See* Communism; Russia; Soviet Union
Bonar Law. *See* Law, Andrew Bonar
Boothby, Robert, 399, 457, 461
Bordeaux Government, 432, 721
  see also, Vichy Government
Bracken, Brendan, 457, 667
Britain. *See* British people; Empire, British; United Kingdom
British East Africa, 124
British Empire. *See* Empire, British
British Gazette, 450, 483, 486-87
British people, 433, 771
  romanticized view of, 260, 462, 494
Brodrick, William St. John, 1st Earl of Middleton, 34, 35, 38-39
Brooke, Sir Alan, 673, 813
Brooke, Rupert, 464
Budgets
  (1909), 157-60, 162-66, 166-69, 171-79
  (1925), 464-69
  (1928), 496-98
  (1929), 499-502
  (1931-32), 543-45
Bulgaria, 739-40, 744-46
Burma
  Dominion status, 904-5
  independence of, 896, 914
  World War II and after, 832-33, 904-5
Burma Road Closing, 775

C

campaign speeches
  (1899) 24-27
  (1900) 27-29
  (1904) 60-63, 68-70
  (1905-6) 72-85
  (1908) 134-51
  (1910 [1st]) 178-84
  (1910 [2nd]) 193-98
  (1912) 244-49
  (1922) 422-24
  (1923) 427-28
  (1924) 428-30, 438-41
  (1929) 502-4
  (1931) 545-46
  (1935) 610-12, 617-18
  (1945) 864-67, 868-71
  (1946) 893-98
  (1948) 915-18
  (1950) 922-27, 928-31, 932-36
  (1951) 938-43
  (1955) 972
  (1959) 975-77
Campbell, J. R., 436-37, 438
Campbell-Bannerman, Henry. *See* Bannerman, Henry Campbell
Canada
  and Anglo-American relations, 786, 880

Dominion status of, 488-89
in World War II, 786
capitalism, 429, 923-24
and Conservative party, 46-47, 50-51
value of, 382, 959-60
Carden, Sackville Hamilton, 315-17
Carson, Sir Edward, 361, 395
and Irish problem, 210, 281-83, 284, 285, 290-91
Cartland, Ronald, 690
Cawnpore riots. *See* India, violence in
Cazalet, Victor, 685, 690
Cecil, Lord Hugh, 47, 48
Chamberlain, Austen, 422, 456
on domestic issues, 320-21
foreign policy of, 442
and Irish problem, 236, 286
on tariffs, 55, 57, 61, 102
on Ulster problem, 282
Chamberlain, Joseph, 102
and Chinese labour, 87-90, 92
colonial policy of, 103
and South Africa, 103
and tariffs, 44-47, 49-51, 426
Chamberlain, Neville, 449, 696, 734-36
foreign policies, 463, 686, 689
toward Hitler, 652-62, 678-80
toward Soviet Union, 682-83
as Prime Minister, 637, 667-68, 669
Chanak crisis, 321, 324, 422
Cherwell, Lord. *See* Lindemann, Frederick A.
Chiang Kai-shek, 775, 778, 800
Chiefs of Staff Committee. *See* World War II, administration of, Combined Chiefs of Staff Committee
Childers, Erskine, 420
China
communism in, 949-50
disturbances in, 513, 515
war with Japan, 690, 766, 775
World War II, 800
Churchill, Lord Randolph, 3-5, 14, 38, 431, 451, 781
Churchill, Sir Winston L. S.
biographical information, 3-20, 315-26, 449-63, 667-77
Commons seats and candidacies
Conservative from Oldham (1900-4), 27-59
Liberal from N.W. Manchester (1904-8), 60-142
Liberal from Dundee (1908-22), 142-424
Liberal from West Leicester (1923), 425-28
Anti-Socialist from Westminster (1924), 428-30
Conservative from Epping (1924-45), 438-872; resignation from Front Bench (1931), 528
Conservative from Epping (1945-64), 839-978; as leader of the opposition, 674; last appearance in Commons (1964), 675
personality, 460
social attitudes, 11-12
as war leader, 672-74
as warmonger, 462
posts
Under-secretary of State for Colonies (1905-8), 77-135
President of Board of Trade (1908-10), 135-89
Secretary of State for Home Department (1910-11), 189-207
First Lord of the Admiralty (1911-15), 208-336; resignation, 318-19, 343-49
Chancellor of the Duchy of Lancaster (1915), 317, 336-49
Secretary of State for Munitions (1917-19), 320, 360-70
Secretary of State for War (and Air) (1919-21), 371-403
Secretary of State for Colonies (1921-22), 403-22, 455
Chancellor of the Exchequer (1924-29), 442-504
First Lord of the Admiralty (1939-40), 668-69, 692-703
Prime Minister (1940-45), 669-74, 703-872; resignation, 871-72
Prime Minister and Secretary for Defence (1951-52), 944-53
Prime Minister (1952-55), 953-72
on Western Front (World War I), 350
Church of England, 112, 136
class structure, 385-86, 391-92

in India. *See* India, class structure
and Labour party, 411-12
and social justice, 174-75
Coalition Government (Lloyd George, World War I), 340-41, 369, 422
continuation of urged, 414-15, 417
defended, 378-83
formation of, 317, 320-25, 336
Coalition Government (1931). *See* National Government (1931)
Coalition Government (Churchill, World War II)
defended, 753-55, 757
extension of urged, 864, 870-71
formation of, 670, 674, 703-5
coal mining industry
strikes in, 470, 472-75, 485, 487-88, 491, 503-4
subsidies, 470-72
work conditions in, 151-52
in World War II, 807
see also, strikes
Cockran, Bourke, 880
Cold War, 876-87, 915-17, 940, 946-47
Colville, J. R., 671
Combined Chiefs of Staff Committee. *See* World War II, administration of, Combined Chiefs of Staff Committee
Committee of Imperial Defence, 244
Commonwealth, British
Dominion status, 488-89
for India. *See* India, Dominion status
communism, 384-87, 401-3, 882-83, 932-33
in Britain, 441, 819
and fascism, 634, 762-63
and Labour party, 401
nature of criticized, 372-73, 382, 395-96
in Russia, 390, 478
threatened spread of, post-World War I, 374, 384, 415, 541-43
in post-World War II Europe, 881-83, 887-90, 915-17
conferences. *See individual conferences*; Roosevelt, Franklin Delano, meetings with Churchill
Congress party, India. *See* India, political structure, Congress party
Congress, United States
speeches to, 780-85, 949-50
conscription. *See* National Service
Conservative party
Churchill's relation to, 325, 450, 451, 455-56, 457-58, 461, 668, 674
and Lloyd George, 320, 323-24
(1897-1904) (before Churchill's break with), 34, 44-47, 51-52, 61
(1904-13)
domestic policies, 136, 245-46
in elections, 87, 193-95
and Ireland, 400-01; Home Rule, 235-37, 247-48; Ulster opposition, 237-38, 263-73 *passim,* 281-91
and labour, 89
in Parliament
House of Lords, 101, 114-15, 157-58
and social services
old-age pensions, 163
and tariffs, 123
(1923-24) (Churchill's return to), 430-34
anti-Labour party campaigns, 430, 431-34, 435-36
and liberalism, 380-81, 416
(1925-29), 442-43, 452-53
opposed to socialism, 478-79
(1930-39)
and India, 524, 528-33, 533-35, 601-2
party conditions, 545-46, 667
(1945-51) (in opposition)
principles of, 897-98, 939-41
(1952-59), 975-77
Constitution, British, 522
Constitution, Irish. *See* Ireland, constitution
convoy system, 332, 668, 694
Cooper, Alfred Duff, 637, 653, 669, 678, 794
"Coupon" Election (1918), 321
Craig, James, 409
Crete campaign, 673, 758
criminal justice. *See* justice, criminal
Cripps, Sir Stafford, 866, 953-54
and economy, 895
and India, 907
political views of criticized, 630
Cunningham, Alan Gordon, 773
Curragh crisis, 263, 281-91
currency policies. *See* gold standard
Curzon, George Nathaniel Curzon, 1st Marquis, 321, 422

on House of Lords, 179-83
and India, 75
Curzon Line, 888-89, 917
see also, Poland
Cyrenaica
World War II, 739, 750, 773, 783, 803-4
Czechoslovakia, 916
and Nazi Germany, 643-62 *passim,* 667, 676-77

D

Dakar, French fleet at, 731
Dardanelles, 900
campaign in World War I, 315-20, 327, 336-39, 343-48
Dardanelles Commission, 318-19, 343, 361
Darlan, Jean Louis Xavier Francois, 721
Davidson, J. C. C., 453
D-Day, 825-26
Deakin, Alfred, 119-20
death penalty. *See* justice, criminal
defeat, attitude of, 384
defence
and British Empire, 244
World War I, 274-81
post-World War I, 387-88, 449, 458-59
pre-World War II Conservative Government, 618
demands for strengthening of, 457-61, 579-80, 583, 624-29
World War II, 715-16, 729-31, 806-7
air defence, 575-77, 580-81, 582-85
civil defence, 577, 730
post-World War II Labour Government and rearmament, 940
post-World War II Conservative Government, 970-71
see also, army, British; disarmament; National Service; Royal Air Force; Royal Navy
de Gaulle, Charles, 727, 731, 975
demobilization, 375
democracy
compared with totalitarianism, 691-92, 878-84 *passim,* 918-19
and Parliamentary system, 483-84, 696, 791
in wartime, 793-94, 875
Denikin, Anton Ivanovich, 373, 383
Denmark, 703
de Robeck, John Michael, 317, 336
dictatorships, *see* totalitarianism
Dilke, Charles, 7
Dill, John, 740
disarmament
dangers of, 558-60, 570-71, 573-74, 579-80, 588
in Europe, 540-43, 565, 785
and international conferences, 546, 550-54
Disraeli, Benjamin, 1st Earl of Beaconsfield, 452
Dominions, 342
naval defence of (1913), 253, 259
Dominion status
and India, 512-28 *passim,* 895-96
see also, Commonwealth, British
Dunkirk, evacuation of, 709-12
"Dunkirk Circus" (World War I), 299
duties
betting, 499
oil and petrol, 497-98
silk, 499
tea, 500-01
Dyer, Reginald Edward Harry, 393-98
Dyer Case (Irish uprising), 394-95

E

economy, British
during Conservative Government (1920's), 470-71
effects of coal stoppage on, 470
post-World War II, 944-45, 948
see also, budgets; gold standard
Eden, Anthony, 653
centre of Conservative party faction, 457, 461, 667
foreign policies, 608-9
as Prime Minister, 972
resignation as Foreign Secretary (1938), 461, 638-42
education, 130, 434-35
and Conservative party, 113
and religion, 113, 136-37
Edward VIII (King of England)
abdication of, 457, 458, 461
Egypt, 898-99

British policy toward, 505
British troops in, 506, 507-8
Egyptian Army, 507-8
politics in, 507-8
post-World War I, 397-98
and Suez Canal, 898-99, 946, 957, 972
World War II, 738-39, 808-11
see also, Battle of Egypt
Eisenhower, Dwight D., General, 843, 954-55
elections. *See* campaign speeches; politics
Elizabeth II (Queen of England), 971-72
Emmott, Alfred, 24-25
Empire, British, 672
changing conceptions of, 488-89
colonial conferences, 118-19
greatness of, 454-55
and India, 517-18, 523-38
and Ireland, 406-7
party policies on, 392
tariffs, 62, 119-21
unity of, 118-19
see also, Commonwealth; tariffs, Imperial Preference
employment. *See* unemployment
English language, 132-33, 434-35
English-speaking people, 815-17, 877, 880, 884, 917-18, 977-78
Ethiopia, 458
see also, Abyssinia
Europe
military strength of, 935-36
occupied, 671, 758-60
political situation, 229, 548-49, 566, 599-600, 642-45, 650-51, 662-63, 690-92, 701-2
in World War II, 881-83
and Soviet Union, 541-43, 889-90, 912
united, 891-93, 909-13, 918, 919-21
unity of, 891-92
and Labour party, 912-13
and United States, 911-12
post-World War II reconstruction, 890, 909-10
European Assembly (1948), 920
European Theatre of Operations, 831-33, 842-43
see also, individual battles and campaigns
evacuation (World War II), 828

F

Far Eastern Theatre
World War II, 778-79
(1942), 672-73, 792, 794-95, 798-800
(1944), 832-33
fascism, 489-90
see also, Germany, Nazi tyranny; Mussolini
fifth column activities, 723, 882-83, 888
Finland, 699
Fisher, John A. Fisher, 1st Baron
appointment to Admiralty, 292, 352-53
on Churchill's personality, 462
Dardanelles, 315-17, 336-37, 345-48
recall urged, 319, 350
Fisher, Warren, 459
Fitzroy, Edward Algemon, 772-73
flying bombs, 827-29
Foch, Ferdinand, 680-81
food supply, 894
foreign affairs, 396-98, 562-63, 575-76
bargaining from strength, 260, 280-81, 460
to avert war, 250-51, 681
Conservative party policies, 893-94
Far East policy, 793-95
Labour party policies, 392-93, 432, 887-89, 898-900
policy of intervention, 677-80, 767-69, 815-16
post-World War II, 883-84
Four Freedoms, 917
Four-Power Pact, 888
Four Years' Plan, 865
France
Anglo-French relations
friendship with, 611, 620, 641, 835-36
military cooperation with, 646-48
treaties and alliances: (1919-30), 498; mutual defence (1939), 720, 788; Treaty of Alliance (1946), 911
communism in, 882
disarmament of, 559
and Europe, 554-55, 596, 613-14
and Italy, 613-14, 619
and Germany, 542-43, 613, 892
military strength, 542, 574
romanticized view of, 835-37
and Soviet Union, 388

in World War I, 292
in World War II, 727
fall of, 706-8, 714-15
fleet, 721-22
see also, Bordeaux Government; Vichy Government
Franco, Francisco, 458
frog-men, Italian, 774
fuel. *See* oil
Fulton, Missouri speech. *See* "Sinews of Peace" speech

G

Gallipoli Campaign. *See* Dardanelles, the
Gandhi, Mohandas Karamchand, 455, 525
civil disobedience of, 524-25, 531
and Indian self-government, 515-18, 537-38
negotiations with Lord Irwin, 537, 538-39
Gardiner, A. G., 4, 7, 9, 12, 17, 450, 451
General Strike (1926). *See* strikes, General (1926)
Geneva Conference (1954), 547-49
see also, disarmament
Geneva Convention. *See* international laws of war
Gensoul, Marcel, 722
George V (King of England), 212
George VI (King of England), 951-53
Germany, 594-95
Anglo-German relations
between World Wars, 667, 678-80
post-World War II, 890, 891-92
and Europe
between World Wars, 476, 567, 631
post-World War II, 882-84, 888
and France
between World Wars, 542
post-World War II, 892
people of, characterized, 222, 252, 342, 711
socialism in, 108-9
and trade, 766-67
World War I, 570-71
arms race, prewar, 209-10, 218-21, 222-26, 240-42, 257-59
background of, 257-59, 296-97, 300-02
military strength: navy, 275-76, 278-79, 309-10, 332-33
propaganda about, 690
World War I, postwar conditions, 375-76
political instability, 373-74, 389
reparations, 370, 549-50
World War II
air force. *See* aerial warfare; air raids
background of
–aggressive acts, 630-31, 642, invasion of Rhineland, 618-20; occupation of Czechoslovakia, 676-77
–Anglo-German relations, 692-93
–"The German Menace," 456, 461, 563-64, 586-88, 620, 678, 690-92, 698-99
–military preparations, 550-53, 555-56, 561-62, 563-65, 567-68, 589-90, 592-96, 612, 620, 646-47, 649, 659-61; air force, 584-86, 589-91, 593-94, 596-98; navy, 606-10
–prewar politics, 577-78, 581
bombing of during, 727
in Europe, 653-61, 831-32; Balkans, 739-40, 744-46; Belgium, 708; France, 706-8, 718, 721-22; Italy, 689; Poland, 692-93, 848-49, 874; Soviet Union, 692-93, 694-95, 761-64, 768
fighting ability, 843
navy in, 698, 702
naziism, 570
Nazi tyranny and atrocities, 676-77, 702, 758-59, 766
in North Africa, 753, 773, 803-4
propaganda in, 690-92, 749-50, 791-92
surrender,859-61
see also, individual battles and campaigns; tanks and tank warfare
World War II, postwar conditions, 889-90
reconstruction of, 911
see also, Berlin; Cold War; Hitler, Adolf
Gibson, Guy, 813
gold standard, 449, 466-68
government administration
in Admiralty, 208-10
cabinet, 755
Churchill's titles and responsibilities (World War II), 793-94
see also, individual ministries; Parliament Act

governmental forms
  restoration of free choice of, granted (post-World War II), 849-51
  see also, individual ideologies
Government of Ireland Bill. *See* Ireland, Home Rule Bill
Graf Spee (German battleship), 668-69, 698
Greece
  British intervention in, 673, 755
  post-World War II stabilization of, 881
  relationship with Germany, 744-45
Grey, Sir Edward Grey, 1st Viscount, 320
Grigg, James, 449
Guedalla, Philip, 324
Gurney, Henry, 940

H

Haldane, Richard B. Haldane, 1st Viscount, 340
Halifax, Edward F. L. Wood, 1st Earl of, 454, 669-70, 703
Hamilton, Edward, 25
Hamilton, Sir Ian, 316-17, 336, 343
Hardie, James Keir, 108-9
Harington, Sir Charles H. (General), 324
Harmsworth, Alfred. *See* Northcliffe, Lord
Harrow School, 771-72
Harvard University, 815
Henderson, Arthur, 505
Henderson, Hubert, 449
Herbert, Alan, 461-62
Hess, Rudolph, 792-93
Hicks-Beach, Sir Michael, 1st Earl St. Aldwyn, 44
Hitler, Adolf, 580, 600, 653, 735, 793, 833-34
  evaluated, 459-60, 600, 618-19
  strategy of, 642
  and United States, 767-68
Hoare, Samuel, 455, 627-28, 637, 667
Hoare-Laval Pact, 458
Hood (British battle cruiser), 758
Hopkins, Harry, 739
Hore-Belisha, Leslie, 637, 802-3
House of Commons, 569
  censure and inquiry by, 281-91, 487-88
    on conduct of World War II, 791-93, 796-97, 802-7
  and Churchill, 672, 675
  constitutional role of, 186-88
  as democratic institution, 736, 821-22
  members and ministers of
    criticized, 678
    membership status, 235-37
  and H. Morrison, 866
  parliamentary privilege, 458
  physical arrangement of, 757, 820-24
  procedures of, 837
  in wartime, 689-90
  see also, Parliamentary system
House of Lords, 112-18, 122-23, 128, 199
  character of, 178-79
    hereditary, 179-81, 187
  and Conservative party, 157-60, 161, 195-98
  creation of peers, 199-200
  and education bill (1906), 158
  and House of Commons, 116-18
  and "People's Budget" (1909), 159, 169, 177-78, 181-82
  reform of, 200, 569
  veto power of, 177, 185-88, 195-98
  see also, Parliament Act
housing, 894-95, 933-34
Hozier, Clementine, 155
Hungary, 384, 744-46
Hyam, Ronald, 455
hydrogen bomb. *See* atom bomb; nuclear weapons

I

Iceland, 765
Imperial Conference (1926), 488-89
Imperial Preference. *See* tariffs
India
  British role in, 513, 602-5
  civil disobedience
    boycott of British cotton, 531, 539-40
  civil war, 902-3, 907
  class structure of, 336-37
    Hindus as rulers, 513, 514-15
    Muslims vs. Hindus, 536-37, 902-3, 907
  conditions in, 603-4
    famine, 156
  Conservative party policy on, 524

constitutional reforms for, criticized, 600-06
Dominion status, problem of, 512-13, 514-18, 518-20, 524-28, 895-96
finances, 603-4
independence, 900-03, 906-8
Labour party policy on, 539-40
Montagu-Chelmsford reforms, 518-20, 537
people of, 526
political structure of
Blue Book (constitution), 520, 524-26
Congress party, 517
Round Table Conference on, 514-18, 518-19, 534
self-government for, issue of, 453-57, 524, 528-33, 533-38
and tariffs, 57, 58
violence in, 906-7
Cawnpore massacre, 539-40
Punjab massacre, 393-98
as vital part of Empire, 517-18, 523-33
see also, Gandhi; Nehru
industry, 156-57, 521-22
taxation of, relief from, 496-97
World War II
war production, 736-37
see also, individual industries; labour; strikes
Inskip, Sir Thomas, 1st Viscount Caldecote, 618
insurance, 335
unemployment, National Insurance Act, 245-46
international laws of war, violations of, 334-35
invasion of Great Britain
defences against, 729-31
German preparation for, 729-30, 764
threat of (1916), 712-13, 715-16, 720, 722-23, 740-41, 750-51, 770
Iran, 938
see also, Persia
Ireland, 61, 234, 393, 398-99
British forces in, 353-55
Collins-de Valera compact, 420-21
conditions in, 407-9
constitution, 421
Home Rule, movement for, 13-17, 65-67, 210-18, 254-55, 263-73, 281-91, 398-99
Ireland as threat to Great Britain, 232-34, 246-48
and Ulster, 254-55, 263-73, 290-91
violence and rebellion in, 281-91
Home Rule Bill (third)
as political issue, 246-48
local government, 83-84
Nationalists, 87
relations with British Empire, 406-7, 414
tariffs, 52-59
and Treaty of 1921, 408-10
turmoil in, 400-01
see also, Irish Free State; Irish Republican Army; Northern Ireland; Royal Irish Constabulary (Black and Tans)
Ireland, Northern. *See* Northern Ireland
Ireland, Southern. *See* Ireland; Irish Free State
Irish Free State, 407-10, 412-14
British opposition to Republicanism, 421
and General Election (1922), 420
Provisional Government, 407, 416, 419
Republican insurrection, 323-24, 419-20
and Treaty of 1921, 404-7, 420-22
see also, Ireland
Irish Republican Army (IRA), 393
at Four Courts, 419, 421
Iron Curtain, 881-84, 916
"Iron Curtain" speech. *See* "Sinews of Peace" speech
Irwin Declaration on India, 453-54
Irwin of Kirkby Underdale, 1st Baron. *See* Halifax, Earl of
Isaacs, George, 461
Ismay, Hastings L., 673
Israel. *See* Jews; Palestine; zionism
Italy, 489-90
British sanctions against, 622-23
political situation (post-World War II), 811-12
and communism, 882
in World War II, 692, 736, 744-46
see also, Sicily campaign

J

Jackson, Henry, 315-16
Japan
Anglo-Japanese agreements, 511
war with China, 637-38, 690, 766
in World War II, 800

declarations of, 672-73, 774-75, 784
strategy, 784, 799
see also Far Eastern Theatre
Jellicoe, John R. Jellicoe, Earl, 291-92
Jews
National Home in Palestine, 685-89
Jones, Thomas, 452
journalism. *See* press, the
Joynson-Hicks, Sir William, 1st Viscount Brentford, 70-71, 139
justice, 973-74
Campbell case (1924), 436-38
criminal, 399-400

K

Kemal Atatürk (Mustapha), 422
Kennedy, Joseph P., 742
Kerensky, Alexander F., 441
Keyes, Roger, 669, 773, 802
Keynes, John Maynard Keynes, 1st Baron, 449, 450, 462
Kitchener, Horatio Herbert Kitchener, 1st Earl
and World War I, 316, 347
Kolchak, Aleksandr Vasilievich, 373, 376-78, 383
Korean War, 931-33, 939, 950
Kun, Bela, 384

L

labour, 232, 390
collective bargaining rights, 870
see also, industry; strikes; unemployment; working class
Labour Exchanges, 195
Labour party, 391-92, 669
and Churchill, 325, 457-58, 668, 673
and class politics, 391-93, 411-12, 491-92
and communism, 389-91, 478-79
criticized in campaign speeches
(1908), 149
(1922), 423
(1929), 502-4
(1959), 976-77
discipline in, 440, 871
domestic policies of, 392
and Empire, 391
Indian policy, 513, 533-40
and foreign affairs, 392, 610-11, 942-43
Governments
(1924-31), 427, 432-34, 436-38, 443, 543, 545-46
(1945-51), 937-38; levelling policies, 923, 926-27, 929
and labour, 487-88
trade unions, 491
nationalization policy, 391-93
and Parliament, 522
partisanship of, 894
political philosophy of, 411-12
likened to totalitarianism, 864-67
moderation doubted, 428
position in relation to Liberal and Conservative parties, 105-9, 435-36, 939
Russian influence on, 376-77, 401, 437-38
and socialism, 898
land, 166-69
land policies
taxation under, 167-69
Lansbury, George, 610
Lansdowne, Henry C. K. Petty-Fitzmaurice, 5th Marquis of, 158
Laski, Harold J., 320
Lauder, Harry, 787
Laurier, Wilfred, 44
Lausanne Conference, 549-52
Law, Andrew Bonar, 151-52, 245-46, 324-25, 422, 425, 567
and Churchill, 321, 382, 452
and Conservative party, 210
disagreements with Lloyd George coalition, 323-24
on Irish Home Rule, 254-55, 270-71
and tariffs, 53, 57
Lawrence, T. E., 461
League of Nations, 364, 387-88, 507, 614, 644-45
and Abyssinian War, 610-12, 615-16
failure of, 767-68, 817
and Germany, 374, 476
and Italy, 612, 614
mandates
in Palestine, 687
mutual defence agreements, 556-57, 620-21, 623, 630-31, 699
powers of, 568
and Soviet Union, 383, 668
value of, 389
Lend-Lease, 741-42

Leninism, 489-90
liberalism, 450
Liberalism and the Social Problem, 11-12
Liberal party, 55-56, 141-42
  and British Empire, 126, 159-60
  and Churchill, 450
  and Conservative party, 416, 431, 433-34, 435-36, 864-66
  domestic policies of, 87
  elections
    (1906), 85-86, 87
    (1912), 246-48
    (1950), 925
  and Irish Home Rule, 211-12
  political philosophy of, 478
  record defended, 173-74
  and social reform, 129-31
  support of Labour party, 105-9, 166, 432, 495
  theme of, 109-11
  weakening of, 74-75
    (1915) collapse, 317, 320, 443-44
Libyan campaign, 736, 738-39, 750, 773, 777, 782-84, 791, 809-11
  see also, Battle of Egypt
Lindemann, Frederick Alexander, 1st Viscount Cherwell, 458, 459, 460, 461, 606
Litvinov, Maxim, 682
Liverpool Cotton Exchange, 895
Lloyd, George Ambrose, Lord Lloyd of Dolobrane, 505
Lloyd George, David, 1st Earl Lloyd George, 315, 318-19, 382, 475, 483, 669, 853-55
  and Churchill, 322-23, 325, 753-56
  Coalition Government of, 320-25, 414
  and Conservative party, 414, 431
  economic views of, 171-72
  and election campaign, 503
  and foreign affairs, 422, 613, 682, 686
  and labour disputes, 201
  as Prime Minister, 371, 422
Lockhart, Robert Bruce, 322
London, 591, 863-64
Lyttelton, Alfred, 99, 100
Lyttelton, Oliver, 761

M

MacArthur, Douglas, 794
MacDonald, J. Ramsay, 452, 543, 606, 637
  criticized, 503
  and foreign affairs, 322, 432
    Soviet loan, 439-40
  Indian policy criticized, 535-38
  and labour disputes, 202-3
  as Prime Minister, 427
Macmillan, Harold, 452, 653, 667, 975
Malaya, 774, 784, 791, 794
Malta, 124, 774
Marx, Karl, 433, 479
Masterman, Charles, 7, 9-10
Mawdsley, James, 24-25
Mediterranean Theatre, 774
  see also Battle of Egypt; Mideastern Theatre; Royal Navy, Mediterranean fleet
Mein Kampf, 900
Middleton, Lord. *See* Brodrick, William St. John
Mideast
  See individual countries; Mideastern Theatre
Mideastern Theatre, 750, 753, 793, 803-4
  see also Battle of Egypt; Libyan campaign; Mediterranean Theatre
military strategy
  in World War I, 358-59
  in World War II, 683-85
  see also, second front
Milner, Alfred Milner, 1st Viscount, 92-98, 397
mines, 308, 316, 668, 698
mining industry. *See* coal mining industry
Minister of Supply
  See Ministry of Supply
Ministry of Supply, 625-27, 662
Molotov, Vyacheslav Mikhailovich, 682, 899
monarchy, 180
monopoly, 148, 166
  see also, land
Monro, Charles, 343
Montagu-Chelmsford reforms, 453
Morley, John Morley, 1st Viscount, 5
Morrison, Herbert S. Morrison, 1st Baron, 462, 866, 938
Morton, Desmond, 461
Mosley, Sir Oswald, 630
Mountbatten, Louis Mountbatten, 1st Earl,

813, 906
Munich Agreement, 463-64, 663-64, 676-77
Murmansk, Russia, 371
Mussolini, Benito, 458, 489, 608, 611, 615-16, 640, 749-50, 783, 811-12

N

National Government (1931), 456, 543
nationalization, 895
  of Bank of England, 467-68
  criticized, 110-11, 929
  and Labour party, 392
National Service and conscription
  in World War I, 341-42, 353-55, 359-60
  post-World War I, 375-76
  in World War II, 681-82
  post-World War II, 908
naval strategy, 223-24, 227-28, 351-52
nazism. *See* Germany
Nehru, Jawaharlal, 534-37. 902-3, 906
Netherlands, the, 787-88
Nicolson, Sir Harold, 450, 667
Normandy, Battle of. *See* Battle of Normandy
North, John, 319
North African campaign, 673
  see also, Libyan campaign
Northern Ireland, 408-10, 419-22
  see also, Ireland; Irish Free State; Ulster
Norway, 669, 703
nuclear weapons, 878-79, 892, 916-17, 935
  see also, atom bomb

O

oil, 327-28, 946
old age pensions, 129-31
Oliver, F. S., 318
one-power standard. *See* Royal Navy
"Operation Crusader." *See* Libyan campaign
"Operation Overlord," 813
"Operation Torch." *See* Battle of Egypt
Orange River Colony. *See* South Africa
oratory
  Churchill's style of, 451, 455-56, 670-72, 704
Oxford, Lord. *See* Asquith, Herbert Henry, 1st Earl of Oxford

P

Pacific Theatre. *See* Far Eastern Theatre
"Pact of Steel" (Italy and Germany, 1939), 689
Palestine
  and Arab-Jewish problem, 403-4, 896, 899
  Balfour Declaration on, 685-86, 688
  Jewish homeland in, 685-89, 898
  League of Nations mandate for, 898-99
  see also, Israel; zionism
Parliament. *See* House of Commons; House of Lords
Parliament Act (1911), 270
Parliamentary system, 483-84, 755, 793-94, 796-97, 802-3, 821-22, 973-74
Parnell, Charles Stuart, 96-97
Paul (Prince of Yugoslavia), 745-46
peace, 376, 389, 542-43, 876-84, 916
Pearl Harbor, 774-75, 784, 799-800
pensions. *See* old age pensions
Persia, 882
  see also, Iran
Pétain, Henri Philippe, 753
Phillips, Thomas, 778
Poland
  relations with Soviet Union, 834, 889-90
    boundary problem, 874
  in World War II, 683-84, 702
    guarantees to (1939), 667, 679, 683
    invaded by Germany, 668, 690, 692-93
"police governments," 874
politics, 430, 457, 846
  Liberal-Conservative Centre party urged, 431-34, 435-36
  party
    vs. Lloyd George Coalition Government, 379-83
    and Parliamentary institutions, 793-94
    post-World War II, 963
  stability urged, 440, 490
  and trade unions, 491-92, 521-22
Ponsonby, Arthur A. Ponsonby, 1st Baron, 450
postwar planning
  See Atlantic Charter; Four Years' Plan
press, the
  and Churchill, 461, 689
  and Conservative party, 173-74, 284
  on Irish problem, 216-18
  newspapers
    British Gazette, 483, 486-87

Tribune, 927
stoppage during General Strike (1926), 483
and World War I, 306-7, 338-39
and World War II, 806
see also, individual publications
Prime Minister, role of, 485
Prince of Wales (British battleship), 776, 778
public speaking. *See* oratory

Q

Quebec Conference, 813

R

racial prejudice, 455
radio, 451, 669
railways, 201-6, 504
rating relief, 497-98
rationing, 894
rearmament. *See* defence; disarmament
Redmond, John, 255, 354-55
religion, 113, 136-37, 891
Renan, Joseph Ernest, 181-82
reparations, 368-70, 549-50
Repulse (British battleship), 776, 778
resignations by Churchill
as First Lord of Admiralty (1915), 318-19, 343-49
as Prime Minister (1945), 871-72
Reynaud, Paul, 753
Ritchie, C. T., 45
Ritchie, Neil M., 774, 805
roads, construction of, 503
Rome, Battle of. *See* Battle of Rome
Rommell, Erwin, 753, 773
Roosevelt, Franklin Delano, 728, 795, 856-59, 917
correspondence with Churchill, 741
friendship with Churchill, 672, 796
meetings with Churchill
(Aug. 1941) Atlantic Charter Meeting Argentia, Newfoundland, 765-69
(Dec. 1941-Jan. 1942) Washington Conference, 776, 779-85, 798
(June 1942) in US, 802
(Aug. 1943) Quebec Conference, 813
(Feb. 1945) Yalta Conference, 847-53
re-election of, 737, 739, 741
Rosebery, Archibald P. Primrose, 5th Earl of, 4, 66, 185-86, 457
Rothermere, Harold S. Harmsworth, 1st Viscount, 453
Round Table Conference. *See* India
Royal Air Force
achievements of, World War II, 711, 727, 776
compared to German Air Force, 578, 581-86, 589-96 *passim*, 598, 612-13, 627-28
strength of
between World Wars, 560-62, 572, 574-75, 580-81, 582, 581-98 *passim*, 650
World War II, 717-18, 763-64
see also, Air Service, British
Royal Irish Constabulary (Black and Tans), 323, 393, 398, 424
Royal Navy, 13-14, 18-19, 464-65
Admiralty administration of, 343-49
affected by treaty arrangements, 508-12
reduced by Treaty of London (1930), 511-12
construction, 220-21, 223-26, 276, 295, 309-10
dissatisfaction with in World War I, 350-51
disposition of, 252-53, 259
expenditures for, 39, 41-42, 164, 219-20, 221-29, 255-60, 274-81, 561
fleet organization, 228
fuel oil, 330-31
Mediterranean fleet, 292
naval parity with United States, 509-10
personnel, 252, 294-95, 310, 327-28
preparedness (1913), 327-29
strength of
compared with Germany, 218-21, 259, 598-99, 606
and international standards, 224-26, 278-79
need to increase, 571-72
pre-World War I, 208-10, 259
World War I, 275-76, 337-38
training, 219
types of ships, 276-78
battleships, 276-78
submarines, 547, 606

in World War I, 303-11, 331-32
progress reports: (1914), 293-95, 299-300; (1915), 329-30, 332-34
in World War II, 716-17
see also, submarine warfare; U-boat warfare
Royal Oak (British battleship), 668-69
Rumania, 683, 886
Russia
British forces in (1919), 371, 373, 375-78
Northern campaign, 376-77
British policies toward, 383-84
fall of, 362-63, 365-66, 372-73
revolutions, 321-23
in World War I, 327
see also, communism; Soviet Union

S

Salvidge, Archibald, 431
Sandys, Duncan, 457, 458, 653, 667
Scharnhorst (German cruiser), 668, 697, 716
science, 484, 513
Scrymgeour, M. P., 422, 423
second front (World War II), 672, 814, 819, 826
Seely, John E. B., 263
Selassie, Haile, 617, 621
Selborne, William W. Palmer, 2d Earl, 299
Shinwell, Emanuel, 943
shipbuilding. *See* Royal Navy, construction
shipping industry
in World War II, 668, 743, 746-47
Sicily campaign, 813
Simon, Sir John Simon, 1st Viscount, 453, 637
see also, Simons Commission Report
Simon Commission Report (1931), 518-20, 533-36
Sinclair, Archibald, 1st Viscount Thurson, 794
"Sinews of Peace" speech (Fulton, Missouri), 674, 876-84, 899
Singapore, 798
Sinn Feiners, 393, 399
Smith, Frederick Edwin, 1st Earl of Birkenhead, 283, 319, 422
Smuts, Jan, 719, 896
Snowden, Philip Snowden, 1st Viscount, 190, 449, 466
on Budgets, 431, 543-45
socialism, 428-29
in Britain, 417-19, 432-33
and Labour party, 898
and Liberal party, 105-11, 116, 127-28, 417-18
as tyranny, 127, 494-95, 926
Socialist party, British. *See* Labour party
South Africa
Chinese labour in, 75-77, 84-85, 87-98, 104-5
compared with Ireland, 354-55
gold mining in, 89-90
race relations, 98, 101, 125-26
self-government, 99-100, 101-2, 105, 107, 112
see also, Boer War
Soviet Union
Anglo-Soviet relations
during Civil War (1919), 378, 388-89
under Labour Government (1924), 437-38; proposed loan, 440
in World War II, 672, 763-64
post-World War II, 881-84, 915-17; *see also,* "Sinews of Peace" speech
foreign affairs, between World Wars, 388-89, 541, 668
foreign affairs, post-World War II
Berlin crisis, 915, 918
Cold War, 887-90, 947, 949, 961
Korean War, 932-33
need for international talks, 936
war possibilities, 899-900, 912, 915-16
western fears, 888-89, 932-33, 940-41
internal conditions, 386-87, 389-91, 398, 418, 478, 955
military strength of
pre-World War II, 582
post-World War II, 967-70
in World War II
alliances, 682-85, 689, 694-95, 761
–pressure for second front, 814
and Czechoslovakia, 653, 656
German invasion of, 761-64, 768, 798, 801, 818, 832
and Poland, 683-84
see also, communism; Russia
Spaak, Paul-Henri, 919-20
Spain
Civil War in (1936-39), 633-36, 650-51

Stalin, Joseph
admired, 881
and Churchill
correspondence, 946
meetings, 847-53
in World War II, 672, 761
in post-World War II years, 888, 916
Stansgate, William Wedgwood Benn, 1st Viscount. *See* Benn, William Wedgwood
steel industry, 895
Storr, Anthony, 6
strikes, 22-23, 481
by coal miners
in South Wales mines (1910), 192-93, 198
General (1926), 450, 479-83, 495
effect of, on economy, 491-93
in Liverpool, 200-01, 205
railway, 200-01
strike-breaking, 203-06
during World War I, 365
submarine warfare, 277, 457, 308, 351-52
see also, U-boat warfare
Suez Canal. *see* Egypt, Suez Canal
sugar industry, 59
Swinton, Philip Cunliffe-Lister, 1st Viscount, 459, 670

T

tanks and tank warfare, 457, 546-47, 627, 776
Churchill tanks, 804-5
tariffs
and Austen Chamberlain, 102
and Joseph Chamberlain, 46, 61
Conservative party policy on, 46-47
effect of, on classes, 72-73
effect of, on industry, 57, 59
free trade *vs* protectionism controversy, 70-73, 425-26
Imperial Preference, 119-21, 454
relation of, to war, 426
retaliatory, 71-72, 135
and taxation, 119-21
and trusts, 56-57
see also, Asquith, Herbert Henry; Balfour, A.J.; duties; taxation
taxation and taxes
and food, 70, 72
local rates, 167-68, 176
policy, in specific Budgets
(1909), 175-76
revenue from, 500-01
and tariffs, 119-20
see also, duties; tariffs
Teleki, Count Paul, 744, 746
Times, The, 659
Tizard, Henry, 459
Tobruk, 750, 753, 761, 773, 777, 802-4
Tory Democracy, 5
totalitarianism, 691-92, 811, 879-84
trade, 245
free. *See* tariffs, free trade *vs* protectionism controversy; tariffs, Imperial Preference
with Germany, 308-9
Indian boycott, 534-35, 539
protection of, by Royal Navy, 510-11, 541
see also, tariffs
Trade Union Congress (TUC), 322, 483
trade unions, 461
and Bolsheviks, 376-77
politicalization of, 491-94
and socialism, 148-50
and working class, 108-9
see also, labour; unemployment; women; working class
tradition, role of, 813-14, 839
Parliamentary, 820-24, 837
threatened, 433, 771-72
transport
World War I, 330-31
Transvaal. *See* South Africa
Treaty of Locarno, 581
Treaty of London. *See* disarmament
Treaty of Versailles, 549, 593, 606, 883
Tribune, 927
Triple Alliance (France, Britain, Russia), 682-85
trusts. *See* tariffs and
Turkey, 748
Chanak affair, 321, 324, 422
peace policy toward, 389
and Soviet Union, 882
see also, Dardanelles
Tweedmouth, Edward Marjoribanks, Baron, 60

U

U-boat warfare (World War II)
(1939), 694-95
(1940), 725-26
(1941), 743, 747, 751-52
(1944), 829
see also, submarine warfare
Uganda, 125
Ulster, 14-16
and Home Rule Bill, 210-18 *passim,* 237-39, 247-48
Curragh crisis, 263, 281-91
exclusion from, 263-73, 285-86
see also, Northern Ireland
unemployment
under Conservative Governments, 502-4
insurance, 164-66
see also, Labour Exchanges
Unionists. *See* Conservative party
Union of South Africa. *See* South Africa
unions. *See* trade unions
United Kingdom, 915, 942
Constitution, 138
see also, Constitution, British
fiscal policies. *See* economy; gold standard
foreign relations, 153-55, 416, 556
world role, 280, 396-98, 565
see also, foreign affairs; *individual countries*; League of Nations; United Nations
ideologies in
see also, capitalism; democracy; *individual ideologies*; Parliamentary system
military strength of, 592-96
see also, armed forces; army, British; nuclear weapons; Royal Air Force; Royal Navy; weapons
romanticized view of. *See* British people, romanticized view of
social conditions in. *See* class structure; labour; working class
see also, Commonwealth, British; Dominions; Empire, British; *individual Dominions*; Northern Ireland
United Nations (UN), 780, 786, 878-81, 910, 974
as peacekeeper, 883-84, 885, 890
see also, world organizations
United States
Anglo-American relations, 42, 640, 935
adversely influenced by Irish question, 211-12, 234
bonds between, 365-66, 749, 760, 765-66, 816, 880, 886-87, 918, 973
Churchill and, 779-80
broadcasts to, 689-92
honorary citizenship of, 977-78
speeches in: Boston, 815-17; Fulton, Mo., 876-84; New York City, 884-86; Washington, D.C., 779-80, 780-85, 949-50
see also, Roosevelt, Franklin Delano, meetings with Churchill
Constitution, 138
defence policies of
naval, 509-10
–parity with Britain, 509-10
nuclear weapon strength, 916-17, 966-70
economy of, 155-56
fiscal policy of, 109
foreign affairs
Canada, 880
Europe, 918
–unity of, 911-12
Far East
–Korean War, 931
Soviet Union
–Cold War, 947, 949-50
military relations with Britain, 509-10
politics in
parties, 47, 51
presidential elections, 955
world standing, 504, 877
in World War I, 365-66, 962
war debts
–Anglo-American, 468
in World War II, 819-20, 871-72
aid, to Britain, 725, 740, 741-42, 747, 761
alliances, 816-17
Atlantic patrols, 751-52, 756
entry into, 672, 767-68, 774, 781-82, 796, 798
leasing of air bases, 728

V

V-E Day, 673-74, 859-64
Versailles, Treaty of. *See* Treaty of Versailles
Vichy Government, 788
 see also, Bordeaux Government
victory, 368, 872-73
 in Europe, 673-74, 859-64

W

wages
 of mine workers, 480
 see also, Labour Exchanges
war
 causes of, 250-51, 586-89
 dangers of, 239-40, 662-63
 deterrents to, 228-29, 967-68
 future
  how fought, 457-58
  possibility of, 883, 938, 947
 role of armed forces in
  air power, 571-72, 591-92, 637-38
  navy, 242-43
war crimes, 297, 368, 369
Wardlaw-Milne, John, 802
Washington Conference (1922). *See* disarmament
Wavell, Archibald Percival Wavell, 1st Earl, 738, 761, 906
weapons, 546-47
 secret, German (World War II), 828
 see also, army, British, weapons; nuclear weapons
Wedgwood Benn, William. *See* Benn, William Wedgwood
Western Union Agreement, 919
Westminster Abbey, 956-57
Westminster College, Missouri
 speech at, 876-84
Willkie, Wendell, 737, 739, 741
Wilson, Sir Henry Hughes, 322-23, 419-20
Wilson, Woodrow, 364, 690
Winant, John G., 742-44, 815
Wingate, Sir Francis Reginald, 813
women
 and suffrage, 80-83, 184, 189-91, 193, 195, 213, 457
 and trade unions, 190-91
working class, 51, 52, 106, 166-67, 176
 in mining, 151-52
 see also, coal mining industry
 and trade unions, 108-9
 see also, labour; strikes; trade unions
world organizations
 forecast, 817, 830
 world government (post-World War II), 913
 see also, League of Nations; United Nations
World War I, 356-58, 690
 Allied aims, 362, 363-64
 armistice, 367
 British entry into, 292
 causes of, 297-98, 300, 570-71
 peace settlement, 364-66
 see also, army, British; Dardanelles; *individual battles*; *individual theatres*; Royal Air Force; Royal Navy; submarine warfare
World War II, 692-93, 701-2
 administration of
  Allied, 795, 820; Combined Chiefs of Staff Committee, 780, 795, 806-7
 Allied aims, 696-97, 727-28
 avoidability of, 785, 883-84
 Churchill's leadership in, 672, 755-56, 806-7
 course of
  predicted, 782-83, 789-90, 837-38
  reviewed, 787-88
 morale, 723, 748-49
 moral responsibilities in, 700-01, 702-3, 714, 735
 see also, army, British; Germany; *individual battles*; *individual campaigns*; *individual theatres*; Italy; Royal Air Force; Royal Navy; second front; Soviet Union; U-boat warfare; United States
writing, 131-33

Y

Yalta Conference, 847-53, 883
young people
 speeches to. *See* Harrow School
Yugoslavia
 in World War II, 748
  and Nazi Germany, 659, 744, 745-46

Z

Zinoviev letter, the, 441
zionism, 689, 896, 899
see also, Palestine